Books For Inner Development

The
yes!
Guide

Cris Popenoe

Yes! Bookshop • 1035 31st Street, N.W., Washington, D.C. 20007

Distributed by Random House

COVER: Muslim poet-scholar sitting in a Kashmir garden. Miniature by
Muhammad Ali in the Mughal taste, Golkonda, ca. 1630.
Courtesy Museum of Fine Arts, Boston.

OVERLEAF: Rosace from the Mosque of Sulaiman I,
Constantinople, 16th Century.

ISBN: 0-394-73294-4

LCC: 76-16941

TABLE OF CONTENTS

HOW TO USE THE YES! GUIDE

Books in the **Guide** are arranged first into subjects, as listed in the Table of Contents, then alphabetically by author. However, within each section are numerous subsections in which books about a particular person, book, or concept are grouped. So we suggest that when you start into a major section, you skim over it quickly to see what the subsections are before you look for individual books. These subsections are easily identified because they are surrounded by double lines.

When there are several books by the same author, her or his name is listed only once. Subsequent listings begin with a short line. If you don't find a book you are looking for in the section you expect to find it in and you know the author, turn to the author index at the back. It lists all the pages on which books by that author appear, and you can see where else to try. Our ideas about classification and yours may not agree.

Following the author and title we list the price. If it begins with a *c*, it means the book is in cloth (hardcover); otherwise it is in paper. Our policy is to list the paper edition wherever possible. We sometimes list the cloth edition as well when it is markedly superior or there is a substantial demand for it. The prices are the prices at which we sell the book at this writing. Because many of the books are imported, prices at your local bookstore may be above or below ours from time to time.

Quotations within the reviews are set in italics. At the end of each review is a three letter code for the publisher and two numbers for the date of this edition. The names and addresses of the publishers are given in the list of Publishers' Codes and Addresses on page 367. The date we cite is not that of the most recent printing or the paperback edition, but generally represents when the book first came out with this exact text. The idea is to let you know how current the material is.

We have picked out a few books in each section that we particularly recommend and boxed them with a single line. These are usually introductory books or books suitable for the general reader.

You may wonder how we select books for the **Guide**. Our effort in the **Guide**, as in our bookshop, is to be as comprehensive as possible within the subjects we handle. This means we try to include all the books that we feel make a significant contribution to their subjects. On the other hand, we do not include books that we feel are essentially worthless (such as most mass-market astrology books), no matter how popular. And we do not include books that we feel do not make a positive contribution— such as many books on magic and the "occult."

We're in this business because we love it and we specialize in these fields because they interest us the most. The individual reviews represent our view and our view alone. They have not been influenced by authors or publishers. We appreciate the difficulty of sorting through the vast proliferation of books in many fields (such as forty-four translations of or books about the **Bhagavad Gita**). We have tried to make the reviews as useful as possible for those of you who don't have easy access to the actual books. We hope we have succeeded. If we have not, please let us hear from you.

Happy reading!

4

ALCHEMY

Alchemy ... was called an art—even the *royal art (ars regia)*—by its masters, and, with its image of the transmutation of base metals into the noble metals gold and silver, serves as a highly-evocative symbol of the inward process referred to. In fact alchemy may be called the art of the transmutation of the soul. In saying this I am not seeking to deny that alchemists also knew and practised metallurgical procedures such as the purification and alloying of metals; their real work, however, for which all these procedures were merely the outward supports or *operational* symbols, was the transmutation of the soul. The testimony of the alchemists on this point is unanimous. For example, in **The Book of Seven Chapters**, which has been attributed to Hermes Trismegistus, the father of Near-Eastern and Western alchemy, we read: *See, I have opened unto you what was hid: The [alchemical] work is with you and amongst you; in that it is to be found within you and is enduring; you will always have it present, wherever you are, on land or on sea ...* And in the famous dialogue between the Arab king Khalid and the sage Morienus (or Marianus) it is told how the king asked the sage where one could find the thing with which one could accomplish the Hermetic work. At this Morienus was silent, and it was only after much hesitation that he answered: *O King, I declare the truth to you, that God in His mercy has created this extraordinary thing in yourself; wherever you may be, it is always in you, and cannot be separated from you ...*

From all this it will be seen that the difference between alchemy and any other sacred art is that in alchemy mastery is attained, not visibly on the outward artisanal plane as in architecture and painting, but only inwardly; for the transmutation of lead into gold which constitutes the alchemical work far exceeds the possibilities of artisanal skill. The miraculousness of this process, effecting a *leap* which, according to the alchemists, nature by herself can only accomplish in an unforeseeably long time highlights the difference between corporeal possiblities and those of the soul. While a mineral substance, whose solutions, crystallizations, smelting, and burnings can reflect up to a point the changes within the soul, must remain confined within definite limits, the soul, for its part, can overcome the corresponding *psychic* limits, thanks to its meeting with the Spirit, which is bound by no form. Lead represents the chaotic, *heavy*, and sick condition of metal or of the inward man, while gold—*congealed light* and *earthly sun*—expresses the perfection of both metallic and human existence. According to the alchemists' way of looking at things, gold is the real goal of the metallic nature; all other metals are either preparatory steps or experiments to that end. Gold alone possesses in itself a harmonious equilibrium of all metallic properties, and therefore also possesses durability. *Copper is restless until it becomes gold* said Meister Eckhart, referring in reality to the soul, which longs for its own eternal being. Thus, in contradistinction from the usual reproach against them, the alchemists did not seek, by means of secretly conserved formulas in which only they believe, to make gold from ordinary metals. Whoever really wished to attempt this belonged to the so-called *charcoal burners* who, with-

out any connection with the living alchemical tradition, and purely on the basis of a study of the texts which they could only understand in a literal sense, sought to achieve the *great work*.

As a way which can lead man to a knowledge of his own eternal being, alchemy can be compared with mysticism. This is already indicated by the fact that alchemical expressions were adopted by Christian, and even more so by Islamic, mysticism. The alchemical symbols of perfection refer to the spiritual mastery of the human state, to the return to the centre or mean, to what the three monotheistic religions call the regaining of the earthly paradise. Nicolas Flamel (1330–1417), who as an alchemist had recourse to the language of his Christian faith, writes of the completion of the work, that it *makes man good by effacing from him the root of all sins, namely covetousness, so that he becomes generous, mild, pious, believing, and God-fearing, however bad he may have been previously; because from now on he is continually filled with the great grace and mercy which he has received from God, and with the depth of His wonderful works.*

The essence and aim of mysticism is union with God. Alchemy does not speak of this. What is related to the mystical way, however, is the alchemical aim to regain the original *nobility* of human nature and its symbolism; for its union with God is possible only by virtue of that which, in spite of the incommensurable gulf between the creature and God, unites the former to the latter—and this is the *theomorphism* of Adam, which was *displaced* or rendered ineffective by the Fall. The purity of the symbol man must be regained, before the human form can be reassumed into its infinite and divine Archetype. Spiritually understood, the transmutation of lead into gold is nothing other than the regaining of the original nobility of human nature. Just as the inimitable quality of gold cannot be produced by the outward summation of metallic properties such as mass, hardness, colour, etc., so *Adamic* perfection is no mere assemblage of virtues. It is as inimitable as gold, and the man who has *realized* this perfection cannot be compared with others. Everything in him is *original*, in the sense that his being is fully awakened and united with its origin. As the realization of this state necessarily belongs to the mystical way, alchemy can in fact be regarded as a branch of mysticism.

And yet, the *style* of alchemy is so different from that of mysticism, which is directly based on a religious faith, that some have been tempted to call it a *mysticism without God*. This expression, however, is perfectly inept, not to say completely false, for alchemy presupposes a belief in God, and almost all masters place great importance on the practice of prayer. The expression is true only to the extent that alchemy as such possesses no theological framework. Thus the theological perspective so characteristic of mysticism does not delimit the spiritual horizon of alchemy. Jewish, Christian, or Islamic mysticism is centred on the contemplation of a revealed truth, an aspect of God, or an *idea* in the deepest sense of the word; it is the spiritual realization of this idea. Alchemy, for its part, is primarily neither theological (or metaphysical) nor ethical; it looks on the play of the powers of the soul from a purely cosmological point of view, and treats the soul as a *substance* which has to be purified, dissolved, and crystallized anew. Alchemy acts like a science or art of nature, because for it all states of inward consciousness are but ways of the one and only *Nature*, which encompasses both the outward, visible and corporeal forms, and the inward and invisible forms of the soul.

For all that, alchemy is not without a contemplative aspect. It by no means consists of mere pragmatism void of spiritual insight. Its spiritual, and in a certain sense contemplative, nature resides directly in its concrete form, in the analogy between the mineral realm and that of the soul; for this similarity can only be perceived by a vision which can look on material things qualitatively—inwardly, in a certain sense—and which grasps the things of the soul *materially*—that is to say objectively and concretely. In other words, alchemical cosmology is essentially a doctrine of being, an ontology. The metallurgical symbol is not merely a makeshift, an approximate description of inward processes; like every true symbol, it is a kind of revelation.

With its *impersonal* way of looking at the world of the soul, alchemy stands in closer relation to the *way of knowledge* (gnosis) than to the *way of love*.

For it is the prerogative of gnosis—to regard the *I*-bound soul *objectively*, instead of merely experiencing it subjectively. This is why it was a mysticism founded on the *way of knowledge* that on occasion used alchemical modes of expression, if in fact it did not actually assimilate the forms of alchemy with the degrees and modes of its own *way*. The expression *mysticism* comes from *secret* and *to withdraw* (Greek *myein*); the essence of mysticism eludes a merely rational interpretation, and the same holds good in the case of alchemy.

Another reason why alchemical doctrine hides itself in riddles is because it is not meant for everyone. The *royal art* presupposes a more than ordinary understanding and also a certain cast of soul, failing which its practice may involve no small dangers for the soul. *Is it not recognized*, writes Artephius, a famous alchemist of the Middle Ages, *that ours is a cabbalistic art? By this I mean that it is passed on orally, and is full of secrets. But you, poor deluded fellow, are you so simple as to believe that we would clearly and openly teach the greatest and most important of all secrets, with the result that you would not take our words literally? I assure you in good faith (for I am not so jealous as other philosophers), that whoever would take literally what the other philosophers* (that is, the other alchemists) *have written, will lose himself in the recesses of a labyrinth from which he will never escape, for want of Ariadne's thread to keep him on the right path and bring him safely out.* And Synesios, who probably lived in the fourth century A.D., writes: *The [true alchemists] only express themselves in symbols, metaphors, and similes, so that they can only be understood by saints, sages, and souls endowed with understanding. For this reason they have observed in their works a certain way and a certain rule, of such a kind that the wise man may understand and, perhaps after some stumbling, attain to everything that is secretly described therein.* Finally Geber, who resumes the whole of medieval alchemical science in his **Summa**, declared: *One must not explain it so clearly that all may understand it. I therefore teach it in such a way that nothing will remain hidden to the wise man, even though it may strike mediocre minds as quite obscure; the foolish and the ignorant, for their part, will understand none of it at all.* One may well be surprised that, in spite of these warnings, of which many more examples could be furnished, many people—especially in the seventeenth and eighteenth centuries—believed that by diligent study of the alchemical texts they would be able to find the means of making gold. It is true that alchemist authors imply that they preserve the secret of alchemy only to prevent anyone unworthy acquiring a dangerous power. They thus made use of an unavoidable misunderstanding to keep unqualified persons at a distance. Yet they never spoke of the seemingly material aims of their art, without also mentioning the truth in the same breath. Whoever was motivated by worldly passion would automatically fail to grasp the essential in any explanation. Thus in the **Hermetic Triumph** it is written: *The philosophers' stone* (with which one can turn base metals into gold) *grants long life and freedom from disease to the one who possesses it, and its power brings more gold and silver than all the mightiest conquerors have between them. In addition, this treasure has an advantage above all others in this life, namely, that whoever enjoys it will be perfectly happy—the very sight of it making him happy—and will never be assailed by the fear of losing it.* The first sentence appears to confirm the outward interpretation of alchemy, whereas the second indicates as clearly as is deemed desirable, that the possession in question here is inward and spiritual. The same is to be found in the already mentioned **Book of Seven Chapters**: *With the help of Almighty God this [philosopher's] stone will free you and protect you from the severest illnesses; it will also guard you against sadness and trouble, and especially against whatever may be harmful to body and soul. It will lead you from darkness to light, from the desert to home, and from indigence to riches.* The double meaning which is to be perceived in all these quotations is in keeping with the often expressed intention to teach the *wise* and mislead the *foolish*.

Because the alchemical mode of expression, with its *hermetical* taciturnity, is no arbitrary invention, but something entirely authentic, Geber was able to say, in an appendix to his famous **Summa**: *Whenever I have seemed to speak most clearly and openly about our science, I have in reality expressed myself most obscurely and have hidden the object of my discourse most fully. And yet in spite of all that, I have never clothed the alchemical work in allegories or riddles, but have dealt with it in clear and intelligible words and have described it honestly, just as I know it to be and have myself learnt it by divine inspiration. . . . On the other hand, other alchemists have purposely composed their writings in such a way that the reading of them brings about the separation of the sheep from the goats.* The last mentioned work is an example of

this, for Geber says in the same appendix: *I hereby declare that in this* **Summa** *I have not taught our science systematically, but have spread it out here and there in various chapters; for if I had presented it coherently and in logical order, the evil-minded, who might have misused it, would be able to learn it just as easily as people of good will. . . .* If one studies closely the seemingly metallurgically-intended expositions of Geber, one will discover, in the midst of the more or less artisanal descriptions of chemical procedures, remarkable leaps of thought: for example, the author, who has not previously mentioned a *substance* (in connection with the *work*), will suddenly say: *Now, take this substance, which you know well enough, and put it into the vessel. . . .* Or suddenly, after stressing at length that metals are not transmuted by outward means, he speaks of a *medicine that heals all sick metals* by turning them into silver and gold. On each such occasion, mental understanding is rudely brought to a halt, and this indeed is the purpose of an exposition of this kind. The pupil is made to experience directly the limits of his reason (*ratio*), so that finally, as Geber says of himself, he may look within himself: *In turning back on myself and meditating on the way in which nature produces metals in the interior of the earth, I perceived that true substance which nature has prepared for us, so as to enable us to perfect them on earth.* Here one will note a certain similarity with the method of Zen Buddhism, which seeks to transcend the limits of the mental faculty by concentrated meditation on certain paradoxes enunciated by a master.

That is the spiritual threshold which the alchemist has to cross. The ethical threshold, as we have seen, is the temptation to pursue the alchemical art only on account of gold. Alchemists constantly insist that the greatest obstacle to their work is covetousness. This vice is for their art what pride is for the *way of love* and what self-deception is for the *way of knowledge*. Here covetousness is simply another name for egoism, for attachment to one's own limited ego in thrall to passion. On the other hand, the requirement that the pupil of Hermes must only seek to transmute elements in order to help the poor—or nature herself—in need, recalls the Buddhist vow to seek the highest enlightenment only with a view to the salvation of all creatures. Compassion alone delivers us from the artfulness of the ego, which in its every action seeks only to mirror itself.

It might be objected, that my attempt to explain the meaning of alchemy is an infringement of the alchemists' prime requirement, namely, the need for reserve in this domain. To this it may be answered that it is in any case impossible to exhaust by mere words the meaning of the symbols which contain the key to the innermost secret of alchemy. What can to a large extent be explained are the cosmological doctrines fundamental to the alchemical art, its view on man and nature, and also its general mode of procedure. And even if one were able to interpret the whole of the Hermetical work, there would always be something left over which no written word can convey and which is indispensable for the perfection of the work. Like every sacred art in the true sense of the term (that is, like every *method* which can lead to the realization of higher states of consciousness) alchemy depends on an initiation: the permission to undertake the work must normally be obtained from a master, and only in the rarest instances, when the chain from man to man has been broken, may it happen that the spiritual influence leaps miraculously over the gap. In the conversation between King Khalid and Morienus it is said concerning this: *The foundation of this art is that whoever wishes to pass it on must himself have received the teaching from a master. . . . It is also necessary that the master should often have practised it in front of his pupil. . . . For whoever knows well the order of the work and has experienced it himself cannot be compared with one who has only sought it in books. . . . And the*

Alchemists at work, from MUTUS LIBER, 1702

alchemist Denis Zachaire writes: *Above all I should like it to be understood—in case one has not yet learned it—that this divine philosophy far exceeds purely human power; still less can we acquire it from books, unless God has introduced it into our hearts by the power of His Holy Spirit, or has taught us through the mouth of a living man. . . .*

—from **ALCHEMY** by Titus Burckhardt

AGRIPPA, CORNELIUS. OCCULT PHILOSOPHY OR MAGIC, c$8.95. Contains the basic works of Agrippa, the fifteenth century German alchemist and philosopher. Influenced by the works of Albertus Magnus, he reflects the influence of Magnus combined with his own investigations into the elements, their divine correspondence, astrological correspondence, occult properties, and astrological symbolism. This edition also contains a critique of Agrippa by Henry Morley. This volume is one of the foundations of Western occultism. Illustrations, 288pp. Wei 1897

ALBERTUS, FRATER. THE ALCHEMIST'S HANDBOOK, c$7.95. Frater Albertus is a member of the Paracelsus Research Society of Salt Lake City, Utah—a group which attempts to present the ancient teachings in a practical, easily understood fashion. This volume gives detailed directions for setting up an inexpensive home alchemical laboratory and includes photographs of the necessary equipment. This information is followed by step-by-step instructions for the work of the Lesser Circulation: the alchemical transformation within the plant kingdom which is a prerequisite for work in the mineral kingdom. 124pp. Wei 74

ALLEN, PAUL, ed. A CHRISTIAN ROSENKREUTZ ANTHOLOGY, c$30.25/15.00. This massive 8½x11" anthology presents an excellent study of the life and work of Christian Rosenkreutz, a legendary figure. Included in this volume is *The Chemical Wedding of Christian Rosenkreutz* and *The Fame and Confession of the Rosy Cross*. These are amplified by writing by some of the most important figures in this field, among them Robert Fludd, Thomas Vaughn, Hinricus Madathanus, Daniel Stolcius, Heinrich Khunrath, and Rudolf Steiner. *The Secret Symbols of the Rosicrucians*, one of the most prized works, is reproduced here in its entirety. For us the highlight of the text is the incredible selection of illustrations, woodcuts, and emblems. The reproduction is fairly good and most of these cannot be found in any other book in print today. Extensive notes and an annotated bibliography accompany the text. This is an essential work for all interested seriously in the study of alchemy. 704pp. Mul 68

ASHMOLE, ELIAS. THEATRUM CHEMICUM BRITANNICUM, c$26.75. During the latter part of the fourteenth century in Europe a reaction developed among natural philosophers, as scientists were then called, against a dogmatic reliance on Aristotle. This reaction resulted in a new emphasis on neo-Platonic, Pythagorean, and Hermetic philosophies of late antiquity, philosophies that saw in nature mystical interrelationships of the great and small worlds. In England the greatest philosopher in the Hermetic tradition was John Dee. Ashmole perpetuated this tradition by gathering in the **Theatrum** the writings of early seventeenth century English Hermetic philosophers. It was an important collection read by Isaac Newton and Robert Boyle, founders of modern science. This is a facsimile reprint of the 1652 London edition, with a long, good introduction by Allen Debus, professor of the History of Science at the University of Chicago. 563pp. JRC 67

BACON, ROGER. MIRROR OF ALCHEMY, c$25.00. This is a beautifully produced new rendering of Bacon's classic work, bound quarter cloth over French marbled boards and in a limited edition of 250 copies. The seven short chapters discuss transmutation and the making of the elixir and the text also includes the Smaragdine Table of *Hermes, Trismegistus of Alchemy*. First published in 1597, 20pp. Glo 75

BARBAULT, ARMAND. GOLD OF A THOUSAND MORNINGS, c$8.40. Barbault was a practicing French alchemist who died recently. This volume is a detailed, step-by-step account of his discoveries which have affected the miraculous cure of disease and which he felt to be an alchemical elixir for long life. The preparation is a mixture of a few drops of potable gold, incinerated ash, powdered gold, and distilled dew combined at the right astrological moment. Barbault was known as a modern-day Paracelsus who could condense energies and use them to create new matter with properties unknown to science. The text includes clear information about alchemy and many illustrations. 147pp. Spe 75

BEST, MICHAEL and FRANK BRIGHTMAN, eds. BOOK OF SECRETS OF ALBERTUS MAGNUS, $2.50. This book was compiled in Latin toward the end of the thirteenth century and translated into all major European languages. The first English translation was published about 1550. It is one of the best known of all early works. An anthology, it is divided into the following sections: herbs, stones, beasts, and astrology. Extensive notes and illustrations accompany the text and the editors supply a long introduction. Index, 148pp. Oxf 73

BONNELLI, M.L. and WILLIAM SHEA, eds. REASON, EXPERIMENT AND MYSTICISM, c$21.50. A collection of recent essays which demonstrate that hermiticism and alchemy contributed positively to the development of the experimental method by stressing the importance of observation. Included are essays on Newton, Galileo, Robert Fludd, and other important seventeenth century figures, along with several essays on alchemy. Notes, 320pp. WAP 75

BURCKHARDT, TITUS. ALCHEMY, $3.25. An excellent alchemical survey by a noted Sufi scholar. In these pages, Burckhardt relates alchemy to some of the world's great psychospiritual teachings. Most especially, he discredits the false view of alchemists as primitive chemists who tried to change lead into gold. To the real alchemist, *man himself is the dull lead that by a refining process can become the Gold of the Sun*. Every aspect of alchemy is introduced and discussed at length here—and the text contains reproductions of many alchemical drawings. Highly recommended. 206pp. Pen 74

CHKASHIGE, MASUMI. ORIENTAL ALCHEMY, $1.95. *Here is one of the clearest outlines of the schools of Oriental alchemy. Long out of print, this volume presents eminent alchemists of both Chinese and Japanese traditions. There is a survey of alchemical elixirs, with their compositions and uses. Recipes are given for the making of gold, and there is detailed discussion of the chemical reactions occurring in the process. Many Chinese terms, but gives a good presentation of early metallurgy in eastern alchemy which was several centuries ahead of western methods. 102pp. Wei 36*

JOHN DEE

DEACON, RICHARD. JOHN DEE, c$7.50. The subtitle describes John Dee as scientist, geographer, astrologer and secret agent to Elizabeth I. The book makes the case that Dee (1527-1608), in addition to being one of the foremost mathematicians of his time, developer of navigational aids for the Royal Navy, maker of gold, and instructor to Elizabeth in telepathy, was also a secret agent who kept his observations in code. It also gives a description of Dee's involvement in angelic magic. This text provides an interesting view of the Elizabethan period. References, bibliography, index, 309pp. Mll 68

DEE, JOHN. THE HIEROGLYPHIC MONAD, c$8.50. *This book written in thirteen days in 1564 by the Elizabethan magus, Dr. John Dee, explains his discovery of the monad, or unity underlying the universe, as expressed in a hieroglyph, or symbol. The monad represents the alchemic process and the goal of the Magus, who in partaking of the Divine, achieves that gnostic regenerative experience of becoming God, and thus furthering the redemption and transmutation of worlds. This is a very difficult text by a person considered by many to be the Einstein of his time. A short but helpful introduction by Diane di Prima. 76pp. Wei 75*

_____. THE MATHEMATICAL PREFACE, c$9.65. This is generally considered one of Dee's most important scientific works. It was designed as a commentary to a translation of Euclid. In the preface Dee discusses the essential nature of mathematics—and, in fact, discusses mathematics so well that Dee's work became far better known than the translation. This is a photographic reprint of the first edition of 1570 and includes an excellent introduction by Allen Debus which covers Dee the man, his work, and his times. The reproduction of the text is more than adequate. About 100pp. WAP 75

FRENCH, PETER. JOHN DEE, c$15.00. John Dee was Renaissance England's first great Hermetic magus as well as a respected practical scientist. French's study of Dee shows that he was truly a universal man who investigated all areas of knowledge. Not only magic and science, but geography, antiquarianism, theology and the fine arts were the fields in which he was deeply involved, and the author demonstrates that Dee's varied interests were integrated into a single philosophy. Through his teaching, writing and friendships with many of the most important figures of the age, Dee had a profound influence on certain of the major developments in sixteenth century England. By examining his philosophy and placing this extraordinary individual within his proper historical context, Dr. French directs much new light on the intellectual life of the Elizabethan Age. Dr. French also examines in detail the black legend which grew up about Dee after his death and has influenced later thinking about him. He also looks at the court circles where astrology and magic were rife, and follows Dee's fortunes in changing political circumstances. This is the definitive book on Dee to date and includes a comprehensive bibliography and many notes. Index, 253pp. RKP 72

DE JONG, H.M.E. MICHAEL MAIER'S ATALANTA FUGIENS: SOURCES OF AN ALCHEMICAL BOOK OF EMBLEMS, c$42.65. A strict academic study of the sources used by Maier in the construction of **Atalanta Fugiens**, a book of alchemical emblems which is important not only to an understanding of Renaissance emblamotological alchemy, but also the basic theories of alchemy and the collective unconscious of Carl Jung. 77 engravings, 464pp. Bri 69

DOBBS, BETTY. **THE FOUNDATIONS OF NEWTON'S ALCHEMY**, c$22.50. This is a comprehensive, definitive volume which traces Newton's heretofore little studied alchemical work and integrates it with the English alchemical currents which influenced him deeply. Dr. Dobbs collates the chemical experiments Newton recorded in his notebooks with his alchemical manuscripts, establishing that Newton's chemical research can be interpreted only from an alchemical point of view. Included are Newton's own procedures for the preparation of *philosophical mercury*. Biographical material on Newton and his colleagues is also included along with extensive textual notes. The bibliography is the longest and the best we've ever seen. Index, 315pp. CUP 75

DOBERER, KURT. **THE GOLDMAKERS**, c$17.15. Subtitled *10,000 Years of Alchemy*, this is an account of the major figures of alchemy throughout the ages. Each of the biographical sketches is fairly short—however the main value of this book lies in the comprehensiveness of its coverage. Biographical material of any reputable scholarship (which this seems to be) is very hard to come by on alchemists since their trade was, by nature, secretive. The emphasis is on the facts of their lives rather than on their philosophies. Bibliography, 301pp. Gre 48

ELIADE, MIRCEA. **THE FORGE AND THE CRUCIBLE: THE ORIGINS AND STRUCTURES OF ALCHEMY**, $3.95. The alchemist, who is conscious of penetrating into the secrets of matter, aspires to transmute Nature and to control time. Eliade believes alchemy to be a sacred science, which concerns itself with the problems of the human soul. He is mainly concerned with Chinese and Indian alchemy. His treatment is quite philosophical, and well documented. A scholarly study, many notes. 230pp. H&R 56

FLAMEL, NICOLAS. **EXPOSITION OF HYEROGLYPHICAL FIGURES**, $2.50. Contains his account of the discovery of an ancient Jewish book on the transmutation of metals, his search to understand it, his eventual success, and his description of the inner meaning of the processes of alchemy. Written in 1413. This is a photo offset of the English translation of 1624. 45+pp. Alm 74

FRANZ, MARIÉ-LOUISE VON, ed. **AURORA CONSURGENS**, c$21.50. A translation of a rare medieval alchemical treatise, reputed to be the last work of St. Thomas Aquinas, which was discovered by Carl Jung in the course of his researches. It bears out Jung's view that the alchemical tradition, through its symbols, served to express unconscious psychic content. Edited, with a commentary by Marie-Louise von Franz; originally published as part of **Mysterium Conjunctionis** (without the commentary). The medieval Latin text is given. 555pp. PUP 66

FULCANELLI: MASTER ALCHEMIST, c$10.95. Rosicrucian and Masonic Legend asserts that Fulcanelli (whose real name, to this day, is unknown) is the only man in the West to have *made the Stone* in this century and that on the eve of completing the Magnum Opus he handed over to his student, Eugene Canseliet, what was in effect the literary counterpart of his own great work and then vanished—never to be seen again. This is his masterpiece **Le Mystere des Cathedrales** (translated here for the first time). It has long been believed that the Gothic cathedrals of Europe were secret textbooks of a hidden science, that behind the gargoyles and the glyphs a mighty secret lay—all but openly displayed. Fulcanelli's work is a masterly exposition of an incredible fact: that the Gothic cathedrals have, for 700 years, offered mankind instruction in the technique of its own evolution. *About one thing there is no possible doubt. Fulcanelli KNEW. There is no speculation.* Mary Sworder, tr. Many plates. 190pp. Spe 71

HOLZER, HANS. **THE ALCHEMIST**, c$7.95. The story of Rudolf von Hapsburg's retreat into the world of alchemy and magic while ruler of the Holy Roman Empire during the sixteenth century. The material in this volume is derived from diary entries discovered recently in the grave of Rudolf's Jesuit confessor and confidant. 192pp. S&D 74

HOPKINS, ARTHUR. **ALCHEMY, CHILD OF GREEK PHILOSOPHY**, c$12.75. This is a detailed academic study of alchemy, beginning with a survey of Greek and Egyptian influences and a study of the early literature and ending with a review of the Mohammedan revival. The information presented here is not readily available in any other volume. The account is historically-oriented, and Hopkins attempts to present complicated information in as clear a fashion as possible. Notes, bibliography, 272pp. AMS 67

JUNG, C.G. **PSYCHOLOGY AND ALCHEMY, VOL. 12 OF COLLECTED WORKS**, c$15.00. This work deals with a psychoanalytic interpretation of archetypical symbols that have existed for 1,700 years. These alchemical symbols are analyzed in depth as they appear in the dreams of a patient. The manifestation of these symbols in modern patients is Jung's basis for his hypothesis of the collective unconscious. The book contains 270 illustrations, mostly from old alchemical manuscripts, many notes, and an extensive bibliography. 571pp. PUP 68

_____. **ALCHEMICAL STUDIES, VOL. 13 OF COLLECTED WORKS**, c$15.00. Introductory work for Jung's alchemical volumes, this book consists of essays outlining and explaining the development of his basic alchemical constructs. Essays on Paracelsus, spirit mercurius, philosophical tree, etc. Many notes, extensive bibliography, 444pp. PUP 67

_____. **MYSTERIUM CONIUNCTIONIS, VOL. 14 OF COLLECTED WORKS**, c$15.00. One of Jung's last works, it represents his synthesis of alchemical symbolism and modern psychoanalytic thinking. Dealing with the relationship of esoteric development and psychoanalysis, Jung uses the archetypical symbolism found in ancient and modern man as the starting point and structure for the evolution of the whole and complete man. Many notes and an extensive bibliography. 697pp. PUP 70

KING, FRANCIS, ed. **ASTRAL PROJECTION, MAGIC AND ALCHEMY**, c$6.95. This book contains advanced inner teachings of the Golden Dawn, material that has not been published in Israel Regardie's **Golden Dawn**. It is a collection of manuscripts circulated among members with detailed instructions and illustrations concerning imagination and willpower, Astral Projection, Esoteric Psychology, Alchemy, Hermetic Wisdom, Higher Magic, Rosicrucian Adeptship. Contains explanatory notes for technical chapters. 253pp. Wei ND

MAGNUS, ALBERTUS. **BOOK OF MINERALS**, c$19.15. A document by the thirteenth century commentator on Aristotle that is a bridge between medieval alchemical theories about metals and the modern science of mineralogy. He wrote about the magical and astrological value of gems, theories of transmutation, and formulated chemical explanations of geologic processes. Extensive references and bibliography. For the specialist. Index, 309pp. Oxf 67

MICHEL, PAUL-HENRI. **THE COSMOLOGY OF GIORDANO BRUNO**, c$16.75. Bruno, a Dominican friar who was burned as a heretic in 1600, was a philosopher of remarkable originality. While not strictly an alchemist, his work was influential with both the leading alchemical figures and the early Rosicrucians. This is the only book that focuses fully on his philosophy. After a biographical and historical introduction, Michel examines Bruno's theory of the universe in all its aspects. Focusing on the poetry and dialogues, he interprets Bruno's cosmology in the light of concepts inherited from ancient times and demonstrates that Bruno's work embodies a systematic philosophy of nature that is compatible in many ways with twentieth century thought. This is an important work which should be welcomed by all Renaissance scholars and those with a deep interest in alchemy. Many notes accompany the text. Index, 306pp. Cor 73

NEEDHAM, JOSEPH. **SCIENCE AND CIVILISATION IN CHINA, VOL. 5, PART II**, c$35.00. One part of what must be the most exhaustive academic study in the West of Chinese alchemy and its relation to the rise of modern science. Dr. Needham traces Chinese alchemy from three roots: the pharmaceutical-botanical search for macrobiotic plants to produce immortality; the metallurgical-chemical practices for making artificial gold; and the medical-mineralogical use of inorganic substances in therapy. It has illustrations, photographs, bibliographies of Chinese and Japanese books both before and after 1800, and a bibliography of books and journal articles in Western languages. References, index, 510pp. CUP 74

PARACELSUS

One of the very greatest physicians, occultists, and alchemists of all time, Theophrastus Paracelsus of Hohenheim (1493-1541) is remembered as the discoverer of a wealth of esoteric secrets of the workings of nature, a profound mystic who investigated the occult law of the interrelationships between macrocosm and microcosm, and the author of a host of highly original, authoritative writings on many branches of the spiritual sciences, including esoteric aspects of medicine, secrets of healing plants and minerals, occult anatomy, astrology, character analysis, and the elemental beings.

HALL, MANLY P. **THE MYSTICAL AND MEDICAL PHILOSOPHY OF PARACELSUS**, $2.00. An excellent introduction to the life work and philosophy of Paracelsus. This is a developmental, historical tracing of his life and confrontations with medical men of his time. Deals with theory of disease, metaphysical healing, sympathetic forces, universal energy, etc. 78pp. PRS64

HARTMANN, FRANZ. **PARACELSUS: LIFE AND PROPHECIES**, $2.75. A reproduction of **The Prophecies of Paracelsus: Occult Symbols, and Magic Figures With Esoteric Explanations**, extensively illustrated, and one of the rarest of all his writing. This is supplemented by the often-cited, very readable and comprehensible survey of his life and teachings by Hartmann. Dr. Hartmann also supplies a long, detailed explanation of the terms used by Paracelsus, and a complete list of his writings. 220pp. Mul 73

JACOBI, JOLANDE. **PARACELSUS: SELECTED WRITINGS**, c$16.80. Dr. Jacobi emphasizes the moral aspect of Paracelsus. She lets the master speak for himself on crucial points so that the reader can gain first-hand information about this person so amply endowed with genius. An excellent feature is the glossary of Paracelsus' concepts, each with a succinct definition. The addition of over 148 original woodcut illustrations makes this a well-rounded book on Paracelsus. 283pp. PUP 69

PARACELSUS. **ARCHIDOXES OF MAGIC**, c$13.50. This is a verbatim reprinting (in the original style and type) of Robert Turner's 1655 translation. The text itself is a source work on medieval angelic magic which gives complete sets of zodiacal lamens, characters and planetary sigils, with full details of their manufacture and consecration. Paracelsus here is primarily concerned with the practical applications of this magic, especially with regard to healing. Other sections include details of the planetary spirits, the conjunction of the male and female principles and each step on the Path to the Tincture. The text includes many illustrations and is considered one of the most accurate descriptions in the whole Hermetic canon. 168pp. Wei 75

_____. **THE PROPHECIES OF PARACELSUS**, $2.50. The prophecies comprise 32 allegorical pictures each accompanied by a prognostication, a preface and an elucidation. Most of the events predicted are concerned with the church or state and the span of time involved seems to be 24 and 42, or multiples thereof. With introductory commentary. 115pp. Wei 74

WAITE, A.E., ed. **THE HERMETIC AND ALCHEMICAL WRITINGS OF PARACELSUS**, c$35.00/9.90. This is considered the definitive collection of Paracelsus' writings on hermetic chemistry, medicine, and philosophy. It is a massive work, in two volumes, including notes and a glossary. ShP 76

PERNETY, ANTOINE-JOSEPH. AN ALCHEMICAL TREATISE ON THE GREAT ART, c$12.50. Pernety lived in the eighteenth century and spent over 25 years researching the material ultimately incorporated in this volume. He carefully compared all the schools of Hermetism, and has here presented a synthesis of their doctrines as well as introductory material and a concise and complete system of The Great Art. The editors have preserved all his notes and added notes from several other sources. The volume also includes the *Dictionary of Hermetic Symbols* from Albert Poisson's **Theories et Symboles des Alchimistes.** Following the dictionary is a complete display of alchemical characters. 255pp. Wei 73

REDGROVE, STANLEY. ALCHEMY: ANCIENT AND MODERN, c$5.00. The author is both a scientist and mystic. In his book he gives a brief account of alchemical doctrines both in their relation to mysticism and to physical science. He also gives a history of alchemical methodology by following the lives of noted figures in alchemy. 144pp. UNB 69

REGARDIE, ISRAEL. THE PHILOSOPHER'S STONE, $3.95. *Alchemy is philosophy; it is the philosophy, the seeking out of Sophia in the mind.* This book is an analysis of three alchemical texts—**The Golden Tractate of Hermes, The Six Keys of Eudoxus,** and Basil Valentine's **Triumphant Chariot of Antimony**—interpreted with extensive commentary from the standpoint of psychological and mystical symbolism. A very clear presentation. LLP 38

ROLA, STANISLAS KLOSSOWSKI de. ALCHEMY: THE SECRET ART, $4.95. An oversized book, with 193 illustrations (33 in full color), which presents a picture of what alchemy was and is in the true spiritual sense. Each of the original plates are commented upon and de Rola provides a short, excellent introduction. Since alchemy in medieval times took the form of paintings and drawings, this book is a very good introduction to this esoteric science. 128pp. Avo 73

SILBERER, HERBERT. HIDDEN SYMBOLISM OF ALCHEMY AND THE OCCULT ARTS, $3.00. A thoughtful study, the first serious attempt (antedating the work of Jung) to correlate the methods of psychoanalysis with the literature of alchemy. Included is a wealth of material taken directly from alchemical and Rosicrucian sources. Passages from the work of Hermes Trismegistus, Flamel, Lacinius, Michael Maier, Paracelsus, and Boehme are cited. This is an unaltered republication of the first English edition originally entitled **Problems of Mysticism and its Symbolism.** Extensive notes and bibliography, 451pp. Dov 74

STILLMAN, JOHN MAXSON. THE STORY OF ALCHEMY AND EARLY CHEMISTRY, $4.00. The more scientific aspects of alchemy are dealt with in this volume. The author has constructed his text from many original sources and has quoted liberally from writers of all periods. 566pp. Dov 60

WAITE, ARTHUR E. THE ALCHEMICAL WRITING OF EDWARD KELLY, c$8.50. Kelly was a very controversial figure in his time. He worked at times with Dr. John Dee, and some consider his writings to contain keys to understanding the Stone. His knowledge is said to have been acquired from the Book of St. Dunstan. This edition contains the full text of his treatises on *The Philosopher's Stone* and *The Theatre of Terrestrial Astronomy*, along with a long biographical preface by Waite. 211pp. Wei 1893

_____ . **ALCHEMISTS THROUGH THE AGES,** $2.75. A compact presentation of the lives of all the great alchemists. Waite has outlined the principles and aims of alchemy in an introductory essay. 320pp. Mul 70

_____ . **THE HERMETIC MUSEUM—CONTAINING 22 MOST CELEBRATED CHEMICAL TRACTS, 2 VOLS.,** c$35.00. This book originally appeared in 1625, restored and enlarged it was published in Frankfurt in 1678. It was designed to supply in compact form a representative collection of the more brief and less ancient alchemical writers. It faithfully instructed all Disciples of the Sopho-Spagyric Art how the Philosopher's Stone could be found and held, and it urged its readers to study the contents most diligently. 2 volumes. Wei 74

_____ . **THE TURBA PHILOSOPHORUM,** c$8.50. A translation of the most ancient extant treatise on alchemy in Latin. 215pp. Wei 73

_____ . **THE WORKS OF THOMAS VAUGHAN, MYSTIC AND ALCHEMIST,** c$15.00. A complete presentation of the writings of perhaps the most authoritative and significant European alchemist. It includes a discourse as to the nature of man and his state after death. Many explanatory notes, 498pp. UnB 68

WALKER, D.P. SPIRITUAL AND DEMONIC MAGIC, $6.65. The change in attitude toward Renaissance thought which has taken place in recent years rests largely on a new understanding of Renaissance Neoplatonism. Rather than being merely a somewhat mystical and Christianized revival of Platonic idealism arising from the rediscovery of the works of Plato and his early followers, it included a deep interest in the magic and mystical writings attributed to ancient sages such as Zoroaster and Hermes. As Frances Yates has noted, it was Walker's book which first provided a firm basis for this major reinterpretation. In a precise, scholarly manner, Walker traces the history of a tradition of Neoplatonic magic, as exemplified by Ficino, and the spiritual magic which grew out of that

tradition. He demonstrates how demonic magic, combined with medieval planetary magic, led to the magic of Agrippa and Paracelsus, and how spiritual magic dissolved into something else: music and poetry and orthodox and unorthodox Christianity. At the end of the sixteenth century the two strands of the tradition came together again and thus entered into important movements of the seventeenth century. A chapter is devoted to each of the major individual figures. 244pp. UND 58

WARE, JAMES, tr. and ed. ALCHEMY, MEDICINE AND RELIGION IN THE CHINA OF A.D. 320: THE NEI P'IEN OF KO HUNG, c$20.00. See section on Chinese philosophy.

WILLIAMS, DAVID, tr. THE BOOK OF LAMBSPRING, c$13.00. *A system of initiation and an account of evolution describing the creation of the philosopher's stone or a path of self-realisation using the universal principle of transmutation.* Typescript accompanies large alchemical illustrations. 35pp. Rig 72

YATES, FRANCES A. THE ART OF MEMORY, $5.95. The study of memory in its lowest form was undertaken to produce better oratory skill; in its more advanced form it helped to transmit knowledge before the invention of movable type and the widespread reproduction of written records; in its highest form it was a meditational science that used as mandalas hierarchies of angels and cosmologies of the physical and superphysical worlds to remind a person of the First Principle behind the arts and the sciences. Memory study is followed through the Greek and Latin sources, the Middle Ages, and the works of Camillo, Lull, Bruno, and Fludd. Extensive references, illustrations, index, 400pp. UcH 66

_____ . **GIORDANO BRUNO AND THE HERMETIC TRADITION,** $2.45. This book looks at the sixteenth century cosmology of Bruno from its sources in the writings of Hermes Trismegistus, Ficino's natural magic, Pico della Mirandola and cabalist magic, Pseudo-Dionysus and the theology of a Christian magus, and the work of Cornelius Agrippa. Yates writes very well, and while her approach is fairly academic her scholarship is excellent and she makes the often dry material come alive. Extensive notes and illustrations accompany the text. Index, 478pp. RaH 64

The risen Christ as symbol of the filius philosophorum, from ROSARIUM PHILOSOPHORUM, 1550

_____ . **THE ROSICRUCIAN ENLIGHTENMENT,** c$15.00. This is a historical analysis of the *Rosicrucian manifestos*, mysterious documents published in Germany in the early seventeenth century. Dr. Yates reveals that the manifestos were connected with movements stirred up by John Dee in Bohemia during the reign of Queen Elizabeth, and with contemporary movements in South Germany which culminated in the short-lived reign of Frederick, the *Winter King* of Bohemia. The time period covered by this study is a phase in the history of European culture that was intermediate between the Renaissance and the so-called scientific revolution. Amongst the personages and themes discussed here are Johann Andrea, John Dee and Robert Fludd, Comenius and Hartlib, Boyle's *Invisible College*, the rise of the Royal Society and of Freemasonry. Major figures like Francis Bacon, Descartes, and Newton are seen in a new context. Rosicrucianism, as seen in this volume, represents a stage in which the Hermetic-Qabalist tradition received the influx of another Hermetic tradition, that of alchemy. Extensive textual notes, illustrations, index, 284pp. RKP 72

_____ . **SHAKESPEARE'S LAST PLAYS,** c$10.25. A detailed study based on Dr. Yates' extensive research. RKP 75

_____ . **A THEATRE OF THE WORLD: A STUDY OF JOHN DEE,** $3.45. In this volume Dr. Yates touches upon the Vitruvian influences in Tudor and Jacobean England in their relation to Renaissance philosophy and outlook. The book centers primarily on John Dee and Robert Fludd, with particular reference to evidence in their works of the influence of Vitruvius. She suggests that the London public theaters, including the Globe, were an adaptation of the ancient theater as described by Vitruvius; that is, a theater with cosmological proportions which expressed a Renaissance outlook on man and the universe. Notes, index, 243pp. UCh 69

AMERICAN INDIAN RELIGION

BOYD, DOUG. **ROLLING THUNDER**, $3.45. See Healing Section. RaH 74

BROWN, JOSEPH EPES, ed. **THE SACRED PIPE**, $1.45. This is a unique account of the ancient religion of the Sioux Indians. Black Elk was the only qualified priest still alive when he gave the material in this book to Brown. Beginning with White Buffalo Cow Woman's first visit to the Sioux to give them the sacred pipe, he tells of the seven rites which were disclosed to the Sioux through visions. The reader is led through the sun dance, the purification rite, the *keeping of the soul*, and the other ceremonies, learning how the Sioux have come to terms with God, nature, and their fellow men. Index, 164pp. Pen 53

BROWN, VINSON. **GREAT UPON THE MOUNTAIN**, c$5.95. This is a very personal study of Crazy Horse, based on fact, legend, and the author's personal vision. Crazy Horse was driven by visions in which he saw himself leading his braves through a hail of bullets. He had visions of impenetrable darkness and also had visions of a new and better age. He has been an inspiration to all the generations after him. *It is very possible this new spirit is in the world now and beginning to grow . . . and when the light comes . . . our spirit will come back again . . . our people will be in the forefront of the greatest of battles, the battle to unite the great circle of earth and sky and bring justice to all men.* This account reads as well as a novel. Introduction, glossary, 191pp. McM 71

COOKE, GRACE. **SUNMEN OF THE AMERICAS**, c$5.95. A presentation of White Eagle's teaching (see the Revealed Teaching section) on the American Indians: *Try to forget all you have read and heard about savage Indians . . . our Indian brethren were simple at heart, loving and gentle. They were men of character and strength of purpose, possessing great courage and endurance . . . . The civilisation of the Indian was one of the most beautiful and ancient civilisations there has ever been on earth.* 104pp. WET 75

DELORIA, VINE. **GOD IS RED**, $2.95. Deloria is generally recognized as today's leading Indian spokesman. Here he offers an alternative to Christianity through a return to Indian beliefs and concepts. He explains that Christianity, an imported religion, has failed the Indian both in terms of its theology and its application to social issues. He urges his fellow Indians to seek God in the North American landscape and think of the land and feel its richness. 376pp. Del 73

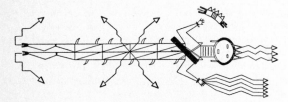

HUNGRY WOLF, ADOLF. **THE GOOD MEDICINE BOOK**, $2.50. A compilation of all eight of Hungry Wolf's **Good Medicine Books**, chronicling the legends, lore, and spirituality of the American Indians. Drawn from song fragments and stories, the ways of the Ancient Ones are described. The narrative includes portraits of tribal life and sacred ritual, instructions and patterns for making tipis, moccasins, beadwork and ceremonial dress. The book also reviews the Indians' cosmology. Many illustrations accompany the text. 473pp. War 73

LAME DEER, JOHN and RICHARD ERDOES. **LAME DEER—SEEKER OF VISIONS**, $2.95. Lame Deer is a Sioux medicine man who upholds the old religion and the ancient ways of his people. This is the story of his life today, of his visions, and of his problems living in the contemporary world. The reader can get a good idea of what it means to be an Indian from his account. This is one of the most popular books on the American Indian and is considered a classic. Illustrations, glossary, 288pp. S&S 72

McLUHAN, T.C., ed. **TOUCH THE EARTH**, c$3.98. Subtitled *A Self-Portrait of Indian Existence*, this is a moving compilation of statements and writings by North American Indians, chosen to illuminate the course of Indian history and the abiding values of Indian life. The selections are accompanied by a beautiful series of photographs taken by Edward Curtis in the early years of this century. We highly recommend this book to all who seek a better understanding of the American Indians and their way of life. Notes, 185pp. Prm 71

NEIHARDT, JOHN. **BLACK ELK SPEAKS**, $1.95. *My friend, I am going to tell you the story of my life . . . . It is the story of all life that is holy and is good to tell, and of us two-leggeds sharing in it with the four-leggeds and the wings of the air and all green things; for these are children of one mother and their father is one spirit. This, then, is not the tale of a great hunter or of a great warrior, or of a great traveler . . . it was the story of a mighty vision given to a man too weak to use it; of a holy tree that should have flourished in a people's heart with flowers and singing birds, and now is withered; and of a people's dream that died in the bloody snow.* This is universally considered one of the greatest of all books about the life of an American Indian. This edition includes a series of watercolors of Black Elk's visions. 238pp. S&S 32

NEWCOMB, FRANC and GLADYS REICHARD. **SAND PAINTING OF THE NAVAJO SHOOTING CHANT**, $5.95. A full color reproduction of the sand paintings, one of the most important healing ceremonies, together with a thorough description and explanation of the rites. The Navajo were not allowed to put the paintings down in permanent form, so Ms. Newcomb learned to memorize them as they were made, then produced exact copies from memory once the ceremony was over. Her drawings capture not only the prescribed

details but also the style and form of the originals. The accompanying text by Ms. Reichard describes the role of chant and chanter in Navajo culture, the details of the ceremony, and the many symbolic elements that go into the paintings. Oversize, 132pp. Dov 37

RADIN, PAUL. **THE TRICKSTER: A STUDY IN AMERICAN INDIAN MYTHOLOGY**, $2.95. See the Mythology section.

REICHARD, GLADYS. **NAVAHO RELIGION**, $6.95. *In writing* **Navaho Religion**, *Gladys Reichard undertook a stupendous task, at which she was eminently successful. She set out to expound all the manifold elements . . . that make up a complex and apparently disorderly ceremonial system, to classify and explain the symbolism, and, in her Concordances, to reduce most of the diverse elements at least tentatively to order . . . . An able writer, aesthetically sensitive, she has the quality that enable some students to penetrate to the full values and beauties of an alien belief and ceremonial, as many anthropologists never do, and to communicate her findings.—Oliver La Farge.* Illustrations, notes, bibliography, index, 852pp. PUP 63

SPENCE, LEWIS. **MYTHS AND LEGENDS OF THE NORTH AMERICAN INDIANS**, $5.50. This is a recent reprint of an early twentieth century text that is generally considered one of the finest collections of North American Indian mythology ever published. All the important traditions are included and the selections read well. Index, 397pp. Jul 75

STEIGER, BRAD. **MEDICINE TALK**, $2.95. Brad Steiger believes that the spirituality of the American Indian medicine man offers the single most effective kind of mystical experience for our hemisphere; it provides a means of transcending an automated and impersonal society through the spiritual heritage bequeathed to this continent by its native people. This volume includes the direct accounts of several medicine men. Twylah Nitsch, a Seneca, shares the account of the Seven Worlds and the meditative techniques called the Pathway of Peace. Dallas Chief Eagle, chief of the Teton Sioux and a descendant of the spiritual warrior Crazy Horse, translates the legend of the White Buffalo and defines *Indianism*. Sun Bear, a Chippewa Medicine man, explains how to survive off the land and how to prepare for the coming Great Purification. This is an illuminating account which explores the ancient techniques and gives practical instructions for living in today's world. 213pp. Dou 75

STORM, HYEMEYOHSTS. **SEVEN ARROWS**, $7.95. This is the first book about the ancient ways of the Plains Indians to be written entirely by an Indian. It is a moving novel about their proud but doomed struggle against the white tide and its *manifest destiny*. We learn about the symbolic meaning of the people's names and shields, of the medicines of the Four Great Directions and the Vision Quest, and about the brotherhood of all the earth's creatures and the Great Balancing Harmony of the Total Universe. Many old photographs and a series of beautiful full color mandalas accompany the narrative. Recommended. Oversize, 374pp. RaH 72

TEDLOCK, DENNIS and BARBARA, eds. **TEACHINGS FROM THE AMERICAN EARTH**, c$9.95. This is a collection of essays by a variety of American Indians on their religion and philosophy. The selections are often a bit academic, but fascinating nonetheless. Introduction, notes, index, 277pp. Nor 75

WATERS, FRANK. **BOOK OF THE HOPI**, $1.95. This is unquestionably the best book ever published about the history, mythology, and rituals of the Hopi Indians of the American Southwest. The thirty-two Hopi elders told their legends, the meaning of their religious rituals and annual ceremonies, and their deeply rooted view of the world to Waters for the first time. Waters himself writes beautifully and the result is a deeply moving book which brings to life a culture now almost completely destroyed. The volume also includes many drawings by Oswald White Bear Fredericks, who also helped transcribe the source material. There are also a number of photographs. Highly recommended. Glossary, 446pp. RaH 63

_____. **MASKED GODS**, $1.95. This is a profound exploration of the history, legends, and ceremonialism of the Navaho and Pueblo Indians of the Southwest. Waters himself is deeply immersed in these cultures and he brings his material to life. 477pp. RaH 50

ANCIENT CIVILIZATIONS

The existence of similar and highly developed cosmologies in such widely separated countries as Egypt, China and Mexico implies that all the great civilizations of our era derived from a common source, from some great tradition, of which each preserved certain relics. That there have been worlds and civilizations before our own there can be no reasonable doubt. The early philosophers knew that the earth's geography is ever fluid. Changes in the seas and continents occur in two ways, through erosion and sedimentation and through sudden disasters and cosmic upheavals. The researches of Horbiger, Bellamy, Velikovsky and Blanchard provide strong evidence that the latter process has been active on occasions within the last few thousand years. Certainly the existence of the frozen mammoths of Siberia allows no other explanation than that they were destroyed by a dramatically sudden change of climate. So numerous are these carcasses that mammoth ivory has provided almost all the material for Chinese craftsmen within historical times. No series of isolated accidents can account for their number nor for the natural positions in which the animals were found. Sometimes they were overwhelmed in the act of chewing their last mouthful of vegetation in country which is now barren waste. Evidently the fall of the ice took place in a flash, petrifying all life within its sphere. From the number of depressions in the earth's surface which, like that near Hudson Bay over a hundred miles in diameter, are now recognized as being of meteoric origin, there must undisputedly have been cataclysmic upheavals at intervals all through the history of the world. It is therefore not only probable but virtually certain that there have been occasions when whole areas of populated land have, like Plato's Atlantis, suddenly vanished beneath the waves.

Yet this conclusion merely lengthens the accepted span of human civilization without explaining its origin. There are those who believe that in former times men on earth were in contact with people from outside our galaxy and that it was from them that they first acquired knowledge of the universe and the arts of civilization. Obviously there is nothing particularly absurd or unlikely in this idea. Space travel may well have taken place in the past, and in some form, it almost certainly did. Yet, as the philosophers of the ancient world recognized, physical journeys through space are unnecessary and to a large extent meaningless. The clues to the nature of life and death, to the structure of the universe itself, are freely available to men on earth, for they lie within the range of the natural human sense.

The Great Pyramid . . . is a model of universal growth. Its measurements, springing from the invisible mote at its very tip, expand in stone through the human scale of perception and pass beyond to encompass the earth. Its height, a ten millionth part of the distance between the earth and the sun, demonstrates the unity of terrestrial and heavenly geometry. Certainly the whole edifice was built by men who knew something of the laws which govern the intergalactic flow of living energy and of their application to the development of life on earth. By acute observation of nature, leading to the detection of certain numerical patterns behind the process of growth, it is possible to gain complete knowledge of the universal system, verifiable both by reason and directly by the senses. The perfect geometric figures, to which imperfect natural forms relate, develop from the basic structure of the cell, and this structure is shaped by particular combinations of the elements. Thousands of years before Kepler explained the mechanics of the universe through the manipulation of the five perfect solids, a system of three dimensional geometry had been developed to illustrate every possible form of growth. The chief cosmic intervals and numbers, together with the ratios that determine the patterns of life, were related to each other by means of numerological combinations such as magic squares. Within the crystalline structures of these figures was stored the universal scheme.

The essential truth of the philosophical system, distilled from a synthesis of every natural science, did not in the earliest days rest upon the word of priests and leaders, but was to every one universally apparent. At a time before the violation of the earth, before the disturbances which involved loss of contact with the former spirit and the spread of confusion and superstition, men on earth must have exercised certain faculties which in us are now for the most part dormant. The heightened state of perception enjoyed by those who live close to the natural sources of life can amount practically to a fur-

ther dimension of vision. People whose livelihood depends entirely upon familiarity with their native country and its resources become aware of certain qualities in the landscape and in the atmosphere which are not apparent to strangers. The native inhabitants of countries still unravaged know both instinctively and by tradition those places where the currents of vital energy, transmitted through the earth's magnetic field, combine to the best advantage. The practice of magic by the direction of these currents must be almost as old as the human race itself, the dream of forming laws to explain their function stimulating the earliest scientific endeavour. . . .

To invoke the fertilizing influences of the ore buried within the mind is the aim of mystics, for it was once generally recognized that all true sciences, arts and religions are of divine origin. Inspiration is Mercury, the messenger of the gods. Centres of the mercurial influence, like the Great Pyramid, were places of initiation into the mysteries, for within their labyrinths could be found the spirit whom God had sent to speak directly with men. In the presence of Hermes nothing was concealed except the person of God himself. The mercurial is ever active although we have now forgotten the procedures by which it can be summoned. Yet the Pyramid was built as a meeting place for Mercury and for those who sought his instruction into the hidden secrets of creation.

The myths of human enlightenment refer everywhere to the same source. Mercury or the quicksilver serpent introduced the civilized arts. In Egypt he was Thoth, who taught men to read and write to the subsequent confusion of all true science. In Islam he was Idris, in Mexico Quetzalcoatl, the winged serpent. The Polynesians were inspired by a worm from the sea, the Japanese by a dragon. In China the first geomancer, Foo-he, saw a monster like a water horse coming out of a river, the curly hair on its back arranged in geometrical patterns and symbols illustrating the entire range of art and science, and the harmonious proportions of the universe. The Welsh Adam, Einigen, saw all the sciences, past and present, engraved on three colums of light. The original inspiration is renewed in every generation. Kepler received the key to the mechanics of the planetary system in a moment as he stood in front of a blackboard. From that time he learnt nothing new. . . .

Of the various human and superhuman races that have occupied the earth in the past we have only the dreamlike accounts of the earliest myths. The magical powers of the first men are now beyond conception. All we can suppose is that some overwhelming disaster, whether or not of natural origin, destroyed a system whose maintenance depended upon its control of certain natural forces across the entire earth. All attempts at reconstructing whatever it was that collapsed during the great upheaval have ever since been frustrated by schism and degeneration. Falling ever deeper into ignorance, increasingly at the mercy of rival idealists, the isolated groups of survivors all over the world forgot their former unity, and in the course of striving to recreate some local version of the old universal system, perverted the tradition and lost the secret of spiritual invocation.

The history of our era is one of continuous defeat for those groups and individuals who have attempted to reverse the flowing tide of ignorance, superstition and arbitrary violence. An endless series of enlightened men, disguised as priests, conquerors, evangelists, mathematicians, philosophers and in every other way, have looked for means of convincing the rest that our view of history is entirely wrong. The chief heretical assumption that has taken root since the collapse of the old world is that which supposes the inevitable and perpetual nature of the conflict of ideas. Secure in this faith, tyrants and opportunists have flourished and a huge vested interest has developed, to which we are to some extent unconsciously committed, in suppressing the truth about the past. Until recently this suppression was active and vicious: the violent, clerical persecution of mediaeval scientists represents its last organized manifestation. Now, however, that the old tradition is dormant, the reasons for its suppression have themselves been forgotten. Only the attitudes remain. These attitudes and the assumptions which go with them form the only barrier which prevents us from recognizing the nature of the fall. The transparent myth of the recent origin of true civilization is still perpetuated by those who accept at second hand the conditioned philosophies of experts in archaeological techniques and in other narrowly specialized sciences. This myth is, however, destroyed by the evidence for the survival into recent times of the same tradition as that which inspired the builders of the Pyramids at the very start of our era and which they preserved from the ruins of a stricken world.

—from **THE VIEW OVER ATLANTIS** by John Michell.

BAILEY, JAMES. THE GOD KINGS AND THE TITANS, c$9.95. A profusely illustrated account of trade and colonization between the Old World and the New, in the third and fourth centuries BC. Bailey offers evidence that voyagers from the Old World landed on both the Atlantic and Pacific shores of the Americas where they founded and developed sophisticated civilizations whose rulers ultimately became accepted as mythological deities. Taking advantage of the most advanced archaeological dating procedures, he examines Bronze Age civilizations in the Old World and the New, comparing their architecture, sculpture, theories of astronomy, mathematics and religion, cultivation of language and use of symbols, and their myths and legends. A fascinating work, recommended to all interested in past civilizations. Bibliography, 350pp. SMP 73

BELENITSKY, ALEKSANDR. CENTRAL ASIA, c$26.20. A part of the *Archaeologia Mundi* series, this book covers the area between the Caspian and Lake Balkash, in Turkmenistan, Uzbekistan and Kazakhstan, in which stretch the great barren foothills of the Himalayan range. These steppe lands have been the meeting-place of the civilizations of East and West. This cultural intermingling is followed through the artifacts left by the various peoples. The author is with the Institute of Archaeology of the Soviet Academy of Science. Many photographs, bibliography, index, 251pp. Nag 68

BERGIER, JACQUES. EXTRA-TERRESTRIAL VISITATIONS FROM PRE-HISTORIC TIMES TO THE PRESENT, $1.50. A comprehensive, documented account which identifies visitations and expands upon items that science has dismissed as nonsense or explained quickly by categorization. The author is a French scientist, and co-author of the popular book, **Morning of the Magicians.** 207pp. NAL 74

BERLITZ, CHARLES. MYSTERIES FROM FORGOTTEN WORLDS, $1.25. Presentation of facts and evidence pointing to the existence of previous great civilizations not generally recognized in orthodox history. Berlitz fits puzzle pieces together that indicate lost civilizations to have been located in America and on the continent of Atlantis, now sunk beneath waters of the Atlantic Ocean. Many archaeological discoveries and scientific explanations. Bibliography, 225pp. Del 73

_____. **THE MYSTERY OF ATLANTIS,** $1.75. One of the best modern books on this intriguing subject, containing the most recent evidence and discoveries. Numerous photographs of archaeological artifacts and geographical mysteries are included in this authoritative text. 201pp. Avo 76

BESANT, ANNIE AND C.W. LEADBEATER. MAN: WHENCE, HOW, AND WHITHER, c$7.50. This is an interesting, informative work done by two clairvoyants on the vast subject of human evolution. The gradual growth of humanity is traced through progressive Root Races and Civilizations including a look at the Atlantean culture and society. It closes with a view into the future and man's awesome destiny as he fulfills the Divine Plan. 523pp. TPH 13

BIBBY, GEOFFREY. FOUR THOUSAND YEARS AGO, c$8.95. A panoramic narrative of life in the second millennium BC. The style is novelistic and the emphasis is on quality of everyday life within the total picture of the times. The civilizations covered include those of Egypt, Crete, Asia Minor and Mesopotamia, northern Europe, Russia, and the sea-faring people. 411pp. RaH 73

BLACKER, CARMEN and MICHAEL LOEWE, eds. ANCIENT COSMOLOGIES, c$22.50. Nine eminent scholars, each a specialist in his or her own field, seek to answer the question: what was the shape of the universe imagined by the ancient people of Egypt, Babylonia, Israel, India, China, Arabia, Greece, and Scandinavia? A remarkable range of answers is presented in this study and in the process the cosmological conceptions of each of these early civilizations is examined at length. A fascinating study, recommended to those who are deeply interested in the subject. Illustrations, notes, bibliography, index. 270 pp. A&U 75

BLUMRICH, JOSEF. THE SPACESHIPS OF EZEKIEL, $1.95. Blumrich is chief of the systems layout branch of NASA. After reading **Chariots of the Gods** by Erich von Daniken he set out to prove the fallacy of von Daniken's allegations that there is a description of a spacecraft in the Book of Ezekiel. He carried the work out from the viewpoint of an engineer and came to the conclusion that historic technology was at least as advanced as our own in this area and he details his findings in the work. An illuminating study for the specialist and the general reader. 179pp. Ban 74

BRAMWELL, JAMES. LOST ATLANTIS, $3.45. An easy to read survey of the literature on Atlantis, written in 1936. Examines the writings and conclusions of authorities from Plato to Ignatius Donnelly and Lewis Spence, and includes the early twentieth century researches. 188pp. NPC 74

BRANDON, S.G.F., ed. ANCIENT EMPIRES, c$10.00. One way to know where the human tribe is headed is to look at where it came from. And the best way to see where it came from is with pictures. This book has pictures showing 3,000 years of the tribe's history—Egypt, the Aryan invasion of India, the Exodus of the Jews, Ramses III defeating the Sea People, the Great Wall of China, the Slaves' Revolt in Rome, the rise of Christian-

ity and the destruction of Zion. The pictures also have texts by specialists who have the ability to translate scholarly material into an informative essay. Charts, index, 160pp. Nsw73

CALDWELL, TAYLOR. ROMANCE OF ATLANTIS, $1.75. A novel written when Ms. Caldwell was twelve and prepared for publication by Jess Stearn. The Atlantis that is pictured is a high technology society that has harnessed both nuclear and solar energy but is in moral decay. It is a caste society with factions fighting each other and in its streets are foreigners proclaiming a new god. To the north the Althustrian king plots invasion. There is a cosmic climax. 285pp. Faw 75

CAMP, SPRAGUE DE. THE ANCIENT ENGINEERS, $1.95. A detailed study of the engineers who *learned to exploit the properties of matter and the sources of power for the benefit of mankind.* De Camp explores the accomplishments of the engineers in Egypt, Mesopotamia, Rome, the Orient, and Europe. His narrative illuminates our knowledge of the technology of these ancient civilizations. The text includes illustrations, notes, and a 31pp bibliography. Recommended for the serious student. 450pp. RaH 74

CAMP, SPRAGUE AND CATHERINE DE. CITADELS OF MYSTERY, $1.25. A fascinating exploration of the ruins of twelve ancient civilizations: Atlantis, Troy, the Pyramids, Tikal, Stonehenge, Zimbabwe, Tintagel Castle, Machu Picchu, Rapa Nui, Angkor Wat, and Nan Matol. In each case the authors describe the site, review its factual and legendary history, and evaluate comtemporary theories. Notes, an extensive bibliography, and illustrations. 292pp. RaH 73

_____. **LOST CONTINENTS,** $3.50. A book with scope as large as the subject it covers. Treating the theme of Atlantis as it appears continuously throughout history, literature, culture and science, this book offers a wide list of sources and indicates the universal interest in the subject of sunken continents and civilizations. 311pp. Dov 70

CAYCE, EDGAR EVANS. ATLANTIS: FACT OR FICTION, $1.25. Written by Edgar Cayce's son, this pamphlet looks at evidence for and against the Atlantis legend and goes over the information on Atlantis, from prior to 50,000 BC to its final destruction around 10,000 BC, as given in the Edgar Cayce readings. 36pp. ARE 62

_____. **EDGAR CAYCE ON ATLANTIS,** $1.25. An expanded version of **Atlantis: Fact or Fiction** with more readings and commentary. 170pp. 68

CERVE, W.S. LEMURIA: THE LOST CONTINENT OF THE PACIFIC, c$6.55. A Rosicrucian compilation of all the tabulated and recorded facts on Lemuria and its people, prepared for the general reader. 274pp. Amo 72

CHARROUX, ROBERT. THE GODS UNKNOWN, $1.25. The newest of Charroux's revelations and speculations on the unsolved enigmas of the ages. Illustrations, 271pp. Ber 74

_____. **LEGACY OF THE GODS,** $1.25. More of the same. 301pp. Ber 74

_____. **THE MYSTERIOUS UNKNOWN,** $1.95. Consists of a collection of amazing facts and stories dealing with relatively unknown yet fascinating aspects of history, civilization and its obscure phenomena; includes such topics as pyramid mysteries, ancient air travel and space craft, and the mystery of vanished continents. A fascinating narration. Many photographs, 288pp. CRg 73

_____. **100,000 YEARS OF MAN'S UNKNOWN HISTORY,** $1.50. A well-illustrated, documented account. 191pp. Ber 71

CHURCHWARD, JAMES. THE LOST CONTINENT OF MU, c$6.00. This series represents an attempt by the author to prove that a great civilization existed on Mu (Lemuria) in the central Pacific, stretching from the Hawaiian Islands to the Fijis and from Easter Island to the Marianas, and having a population in excess of sixty-four million. He believed that there was once a universal esoteric language of symbols which the ancients used in recording their secret wisdom, and that by staring at ancient symbols long enough an intuitively gifted person can conjure their meanings out of his inner consciousness and thus recover forgotten historical facts. Churchward said that he based his theory upon two sets of tablets, found in India and Mexico. Spe 34

_____. **COSMIC FORCES OF MU,** c$3.35. A detailed explanation of the sciences as they were taught in Mu, with chapters devoted to the following topics: origin of the great forces, the earth's forces, the atmosphere, rays, the life force, specialization, the sun and sundry phenomena. Many drawings illustrate the text. While the sources of Churchward's information have been questioned over the years, no one has ever denied the intriguing qualities of his exposition. 246pp. Spe 34

_____. **THE SECOND BOOK OF THE COSMIC FORCES OF MU,** c$4.00. An exploration of cosmic forces as they were taught in Mu relating to the earth. A great deal of information about the earth's history and geology is presented along with many illustrative drawings and maps. 269pp. Spe 70

COTTRELL, LEONARD. LOST CITIES, $2.95. An eminent British archaeologist and scholar narrates the story of cities and whole civilizations that have been lost for centuries. He writes in a novelistic style and recreates the life of each civilization he discusses. He also brings the discovery of each to life and includes many quotations from original sources. The cities include Nimrud, Ninevah, Ur, Nippur, Pompeii, Chichen-Itza, Vilcabamba, Harappa, and some Babylonian sites. Index, 251pp. G&D 57

DANIKEN, ERICH VON. CHARIOTS OF THE GODS, $1.25. This book and a television show based upon it created a nationwide stir of interest in the possiblity of extraterrestrial beings who have directly influenced human history. The author claims that visitors from space have frequently visited our planet and made contact with earthly humanity. He uses as evidence the numerous suggestive archaeological mysteries that exist in virtually all portions of the world, but especially in South America. 153pp. Ban 71

_____. **GODS FROM OUTER SPACE**, $1.25. This second book by the author of Chariots takes up where the first book left off. 166pp. Ban 72

_____. **THE GOLD OF THE GODS**, $1.75. More of the same with the addition of fascinating material on a system of caves and tunnels up to 200 miles long recently discovered in Ecuador—filled with gold and silver treasures as well as many inscribed gold plaques. Other interesting new findings are also explored in detail. The text is illustrated with over 100 photographs and color plates as well as numerous drawings and includes a fine bibliography. 216pp. Ban 74

_____. **IN SEARCH OF ANCIENT GODS**, $1.95. Von Daniken's newest. The subtitle is *My Pictorial Evidence for the Impossible* and this describes the book as well as anything we could say. 319 black and white and 57 color pictures present the story more clearly and credibly than anything else von Daniken has written. An interpretative text/commentary goes along with the photographs. Whatever the merits of von Daniken's thesis, this is an impressive collection of food for thought. Photographic credits included. 149pp. Ban 74

DONNELLY, IGNATIUS. **ATLANTIS: THE ANTEDILUVIAN WORLD**, c$2.49. When originally published in 1882, this book caused a stir of interest and was immediately popular. It remains so today and has been the modern keystone for all such books on the subject of Atlantis and lost continents. Donnelly has approached the subject with scientific accuracy and a precise, detailed inquiry into the mystery out of man's past. It has been said that of all writers on the subject of Atlantis, Donnelly ranks next to Plato in importance and influence. 326pp. Out ND

_____. **THE DESTRUCTION OF ATLANTIS: RAGNOROK: THE AGE OF FIRE AND GRAVEL**, $3.25. Second book by the author on the subject of Atlantis is concerned with the possible causes of the cataclysm that resulted in the continent's destruction. His pioneering theory was that a comet grazing the earth could have been the key to the deluge which obliterated that mysterious land. 441pp. Mul 71

DOWNING, BARRY. **THE BIBLE AND FLYING SAUCERS**, $.95. A detailed exploration of the role ancient astronauts played in Old Testament history. Notes, bibliography, 191pp. Avo 70

DRAKE, W. RAYMOND. **GODS AND SPACEMEN IN THE ANCIENT EAST**, $1.50. Was Earth once ruled by extra-terrestrial beings? This book is an attempt to answer this question affirmatively by presenting a barrage of evidence and data, both suggestive and conclusive, that has come to us from our racial past. The main emphasis is upon the rich heritage of the East that is laden with provocative hints of divinely intelligent beings from other planets. 289 item bibliography, 246pp. NAL 68

_____. **GODS AND SPACEMEN OF THE ANCIENT PAST**, $1.50. Considers the questions of whether the blood of ancient spacemen flows in our veins; if Sodom and Gomorrah were destroyed by nuclear attack; if the angel Gabriel, who foretold the birth of Jesus, could have been an extraterrestrial; and the possibility that Martians who had destroyed their own civilization came to Earth to teach humans war. 266pp. NAL 74

_____. **GODS AND SPACEMEN THROUGHOUT HISTORY**, c$9.95. This is hopefully the last book in this series. It is also by far the best. Here Drake assembles and analyzes the legends, folklore and scientific (or quasi-scientific) data that other writers have touched on to prove his thesis that extraterrestrial visitation was and is a practical reality. Drake writes very well and he reproduces a great number of fascinating tales. The book begins with a general discussion and then is divided into separate chapters on each geographical area. Index, bibliography, 264pp. Reg 75

HEYERDAHL, THOR. **THE ART OF EASTER ISLAND**, c$35.00. The full story of Heyerdahl's explorations on Easter Island, including his discovery of art treasures in secret caves. He devotes a great deal of space to exploring the mystery of the great stone men, with theories on why and how they were carved, transported and raised. The historical and religious meaning of the art is also analyzed and new findings on the ancient and later history of the Island and its people are explored. Oversize, 1163 photographs, index, bibliography. Dou 75

HIGGINS, GODFREY. **ANACALYPSIS**, $30.00/set. This is a massive two volume inquiry into the origin of languages, nations, and religions—the product of the author's life study. Virtually every aspect of ancient civilizations is discussed in some depth. Higgins believes that civilization came from the East and he quotes profusely from source material to prove his thesis. The only edition of this classic work that remains in print is a spiral bound 8½x11" book that probably will not hold together too well. However, it can easily be rebound, and since the last regular edition cost $75 it can be rebound for far less than a bound edition would cost today. The presentation is out-of-date, but it still remains a fascinating work and an excellent historical document of the time it was produced. Notes, illustrations, index, 1440pp. HeR 1836.

HUTIN, SERGE. **ALIEN RACES AND FANTASTIC CIVILIZATIONS**, $1.25. A mass-market overview of *prehistory* and ancient civilizations divided into the following topics: Mysteries in the Sky and on Earth; Gondwana, Lemuria, and Mu; Atlantis; Eldorado and the Amazons; In the Bowels of the Earth; and The Heritage of the Giants. The information shouldn't be taken as serious scholarship, however the casual reader does get a general feeling of the civilizations and their achievements. 150pp. Ber 70

IVIMY, JOHN. **THE SPHINX AND THE MEGALITHS**, c$8.95. An in-depth study of how the builders of the English megaliths acquired the knowledge and skills that they have thus been shown to have possessed and why those skills and knowledge were applied in the way they were. Ivimy examines the conflicting arguments, highlights the significant facts, and then advances an original solution of his own. Many illustrations (including geometric drawings) are included, as are notes and an index. 215pp. H&R 75

EYDOUX, HENRI-PAUL. **IN SEARCH OF LOST WORLDS**, c$9.98. A profusely illustrated pictorial account of the great archaeological discoveries from the finds of the early Egyptologists to the explorations at Masada in Israel in the early 1960's. The civilization and culture of each area is discussed and the individual archaeologists are mentioned. This is primarily a popular history rather than a scholarly account and while it goes into no depth in any area, it does provide a good overview of countless civilizations. Oversize, index, bibliography, 344 pp. Ham 71

FERRO, ROBERT and MICHAEL GRUMLEY. **ATLANTIS: AUTOBIOGRAPHY OF A SEARCH**, c$1.98. The story of the authors' 1968 quest for traces of the lost continent, which led them to Bimini in the Caribbean where they discovered unmistakable traces of an ancient civilization. Many photographs document the authors' findings. 168pp. Crn 70

FOX, HUGH. **GODS OF THE CATACLYSM**, c$10.95. This is a fairly scattered and aesthetically not very pleasant survey of ancient cultures from the Mediterranean area to the Americas. Fox traces the different cultures in the light of his thesis that there is an almost hundred percent correspondence in theological/mythical concepts of the various cultures. The Mesoamerican civilization is emphasized in the discussion. Fox also believes that there was a major cataclysm in which most of the world's population was destroyed and new cultures and new versions of the gods appeared. The second half of the book is devoted to an analysis of the post-cataclysmic world. A profusion of line drawings accompany the text. Some interesting points are raised, but it's hard to get a feeling of where the author is coming from. Notes, bibliography, index, 301pp. H&R 76

GALANOPOULOS, A.G. and EDWARD BACON. **ATLANTIS: THE TRUTH BEHIND THE LEGEND**, c$12.50. The most extensive scientific treatment of the Atlantis theme we've seen. The topics include the following: what Plato said and meant; where was Atlantis; geophysical theories and facts; and the case that Atlantis was in the Crete-Santorini area, proven. The text is illustrated with 24 full-page color photographs and well over 100 illustrations. An amazingly comprehensive, enlightening work. The proofs and the arguments are very well done. Oversize, 216pp. BoM 69

GARVIN, RICHARD. **THE CRYSTAL SKULL**, $1.25. *The story of the mystery, myth and magic of the Mitchell-Hedges crystal skull discovered in a lost Mayan city during a search for Atlantis.* Includes many illustrations of this 12,000 year old artifact. 128pp. S&S 74

GIMBUTAS, MARITA. **THE GODS AND GODDESSES OF OLD EUROPE, 7000-3500** c$20.00. An in-depth study of the naturalistic pantheon developed in Old Europe during the early Stone Age. These *gods and goddesses* are the familiars of the hunters and fishers, objects of worship evoked by the animal world and other natural phenomena. In support of her thesis, the author presents a unique body of illustrations depicting cult figures from the Balkan countries. She also has provided a comprehensive catalog of the objects illustrated as well as a detailed list of the principal sites where they were found. Long bibliography, 303pp. UCP 74

HANSEN, L. TAYLOR. **THE ANCIENT ATLANTIC**, $10.00. Hansen has attempted to present a pictorial biography of the Atlantic Ocean, including material on the civilizations in the coastal land areas and the physical, seismological, and legendary facts about the Atlantic. This is an unique study, replete with maps and relevant illustrations. Covers a multitude of topics. Indexed, 437 oversize pages. Amh 69

HAWKES, JULIA, ed. **ATLAS OF ANCIENT ARCHAEOLOGY**, c$19.50. This atlas traces the patterns of cultures and civilizations down to the beginning of the classical world. It is arranged according to global regions and each region is presented by a specialist in that area. Each regional map shows cultural areas and marks a large number of archaeological sites and is accompanied by a general introduction to the ancient history of the region, followed by detailed descriptions, plans, and reconstructions of the most interesting monuments. Over 170 sites are described and illustrated. Oversize, glossary, index, 272pp. MGH 74

HAWKES, JACQUETTA, ed. **THE WORLD OF THE PAST**, $5.95/each. This is a very noted anthology of the history of archaeology. Most of the accounts have been written by very well known archaeologists and Ms. Hawkes has also included reports of observant lay travelers like Herodotus. She also presents an introduction to each section together with a discussion of the pleasures and purposes of archaeology, some of its classic errors, and its modern techniques. Her introduction (long enough to be a book in itself) and the introductory notes together provide a consecutive history of archaeological discoveries and a vast spectacle of movement in time; of cultures and civilizations, each unique in form and style, each growing, flowering, and dying. Volume I presents a panorama of the Old Stone Age and the Evolution of Man, the New Stone Age and the Beginnings of Farming, Mesopotamia, Palestine, and Egypt. Volume II surveys the ancient civilizations of Asia Minor, Greece and Italy; of Indian, China and Easter Island; of Britain, Scandinavia and Eastern Europe; and of the entire Western Hemisphere from the Eskimos to South America. Each volume is indexed and the two volumes cover about 1350pp. S&S 63

Stonehenge (Dr. Charleton's perspective, 1663)

HAWKINS, GERALD S. **BEYOND STONEHENGE**, c$12.95. Explores many of the mysteries of ancient civilizations, using a computer as a base. His topics include the vast linear Nasca lines in the Peruvian desert which can only be appreciated from the air; Machu-Picchu and its temple; the Great Temple of Karnak and the temple of Amon-Ra where the Pharaoh made his sun observations, as well as other temples of the Nile; the Mayan ruins in Central America. He feels that anything which shows today as clearly astronomical was known in antiquity to the builders. Fascinating scholarly speculation, with over 100 plates. 308pp. H&R 73

KELLER, WERNER. **THE BIBLE AS HISTORY**, $1.95. A massive attempt to integrate all of the scientific and archaeological research on the history of the Biblical period: *In view of the overwhelming mass of authentic and well-attested evidence now available . . . there kept hammering in my brain this one sentence: 'The Bible is right after all!'*—Werner Keller. Includes an index of Bible references, a general index, and a long bibliography. 520pp. Ban 56

KOLOSIMO, PETER. **NOT OF THIS WORLD**, $1.25. A scientifically oriented study of possible extra-terrestrial visits in ancient and more recent times. The author's thesis is similar to von Daniken's in that he believes that men from space were responsible for many well-known and little-known archaeological mysteries. Includes more documentation than the von Daniken books. Photographs, 248pp. Ban 71

_____. **TIMELESS EARTH**, $1.50. The theme of this detailed, scholarly book is the development and real age of human civilization, and the possibility that it has been influenced by beings from outer space. Kolosimo believes that Atlantis may have been the cradle of a new type of man who penetrated the mysteries of nature and split the atom. He also analyzes a wealth of information about ancient civilizations. Many photographs. 264pp. Ban 68

LANDAY, JERRY. **DOME OF THE ROCK**, c$10.00. Jerusalem's ancient Temple Mount, now dominated by the Dome of the Rock, is sacred to Jews, Christians and Moslems. This is a study of the Holy City, focusing on its most famous monument. Manuscript illuminations, statuary, ancient maps, and modern diagrams complement the text—along with numerous photographs. 120 illustrations are included in all, one half in full color. There's also a section *Jerusalem in Literature*. This volume will be especially appreciated by those who are interested in Islamic architecture. 172pp. Nws 72

LAROUSSE **ENCYCLOPEDIA OF ANCIENT AND MEDIEVAL HISTORY**, $6.95. A comprehensive volume covering universal history from the origins to the late Middle Ages in Europe and to the rise of the Aztec and Incan empires in America. It is translated from the famous French original encyclopedia, **Histoire Universal**, and adapted for English speaking readers. The panorama depicted here is enormous and the text is illustrated with over 500 pictures and maps (32 in color). Comprehensive index, 413pp, oversize. Crn 64

LE PLONGEON, AUGUSTUS. **QUEEN MOO AND THE EGYPTIAN SPHINX**, $2.95. Le Plongeon, a well known researcher in this field, wrote this book and took the photographs presented here over eighty years ago in order to present to the world the true esoteric, occult, and historical significance of the ancient Mayans. He shows the connection between the Mayan temples and pyramids and the contemporary structures in Egypt, the Sphinx and the Great Pyramid. 384pp. RSP 73

LUCE, J.V. **THE END OF ATLANTIS**, $4.40. An erudite study which presents a picture of Santorini and its Bronze Age eruption based on the evidence accumulated by archaeologists as well as an equation, extensively documented, of Atlantis with Minoan Crete. Many full color plates and photographs supplement the text. Includes material on the recent excavations. 187pp. PaL 70

McNEILL, WILLIAM and JEAN SEDLAR, eds. **THE CLASSICAL MEDITERRANEAN WORLD**, $2.60. *The readings in this volume were chosen to emphasize the distinctive character of ancient Greek (or Hellenic) civilization and to show how it met and mingled with other cultural strands as it expanded eastward and westward . . . . The book opens with selections which illustrate the two central realities of Greek life: the polis or city-state as a basic institution . . . and the idea of natural law . . . . The readings in Section II illustrate how Greek ideas met and combined with diverse elements of Near Eastern culture in the period following the conquests of Alexander . . . . The readings in Section III present some Roman reactions to the Greek civilizations encountered after Rome became the overlord, first of Greece itself, then of the entire Mediterranean basin.* Each selection includes introductory material. 300pp. Oxf 69

MAVOR, JAMES. **VOYAGE TO ATLANTIS**, $2.65. Mavor led the scientific expeditions to Thera which verified (at least to his satisfaction) that it was the site of Atlantis. He uncovered, on land and under the sea, a great deal of archaeological and geological evidence—all of which is discussed here in great detail. An interesting, first hand account. Many illustrations and a long bibliography. 310pp. Fon 69

MELVILLE, LEINANI. **CHILDREN OF THE RAINBOW: THE RELIGION, LEGENDS AND GODS OF PRE-CHRISTIAN HAWAII**, $1.95. A fascinating effort to capture the remaining oral tradition and secrets of the Kahumas by a native Hawaiian. Many illustrations and explanations of their sacred symbols. For more details on the Kahunas see Max Freedom Long's volumes (Mysticism section). 183pp. TPH 69

MEREJKOWSKI, DMITRI. **ATLANTIS/EUROPE**, $3.50. Explores the occult practices and tradition of Atlantis in a novelistic way. The author feels that there is a comparison between the evil that overtook Atlantean civilization in its decline and contemporary Western civilization. 449pp. Mul 71

MERRY, ELEANOR. **THE ASCENT OF MAN**, c$12.60. This is a highly spiritual review of man's civilizations throughout the world from earliest times through the Middle Ages. Ms. Merry is an Anthroposophist (see the Steiner section) and is especially interested in the Celtic and early Nordic cultures. She insists that Christianity is the oldest religion and her review of other cultures must be viewed in the light of this bias. With this in mind **The Ascent of Man** is still a fascinating journey through the ancient Near East, Egypt, Greece, and India. The main characters come alive in a moving narrative; the spiritual teachings of each civilization are examined; and the text includes long quotes from sacred texts. The material is illustrated with 77 beautiful paintings and photographs, over half in color. Index, 480pp. NKB 63

MICHELL, JOHN. **CITY OF REVELATION**, c$1.49. Presents evidence for the view that earlier civilizations understood better than our own the natural laws controlling seasons, human behavior, and the most subtle relationships between the whole universe and its parts. These relationships, says Michell, are analogues of harmonic relationships in music and of the sacred geometry of the ancients. They are preserved, as he demonstrates, in the forms of the great temples of man—the cathedral at Chartres, Stonehenge, the Chapel at Glastonbury, the Great Pyramid, and others. An important work, highly recommended. Many illustrative diagrams. 205pp. ABD 72

_____. **THE EARTH SPIRIT: ITS WAYS, SHRINES AND MYSTERIES**, $5.95. From earliest times men have believed that the earth is a living creature, animated by a spirit that corresponds to the spirit in men. Science originated in the attempts of the first cultivators to adapt the roving ways of the earth spirit to the new settled way of life. This volume illustrates the natural shrines and channels of the earth spirit and the relics of the old, once universal, science by which its powers were concentrated for the benefit of all life on earth. 113 illustrations (22 in color)—part of the **Art and Cosmos** Series. 8x11, 96pp. Avo 75

MONTGOMERY, JOHN. **THE QUEST FOR NOAH'S ARK**, $1.75. A detailed, illustrated exploration of every *responsible* sighting of Noah's vessel on Mount Ararat from the first century to modern times. Also includes is a narration of the author's own ascent of Mount Ararat. Each of the accounts is presented quite fully, with references where available. Notes, bibliography, index, 384pp. Pyr 72

MOONEY, RICHARD. **COLONY: EARTH**, $1.50. The advertising blurb on the front of this book says *This book begins where von Daniken leaves off*—and this is as good an explanation of the content as any we can think of. Mooney's style is much the same as von Daniken's: topical chapters more or less held together by a central theme, and without notes or any *factual* backup. As the title suggests, Mooney believes that the earth was colonized by beings from another universe thousands of years ago—and that these people came equipped with weapons and technology superior to what we have today: came, colonized the planet, and stayed. Mooney devotes chapters to constant themes like Atlantis, the Great Pyramid, and Stonehenge—and he also has some ideas we have not seen elsewhere. Index, 310pp. Faw 74

_____. **GODS OF AIR AND DARKNESS**, c$8.95. In this sequel to **Colony: Earth** Mooney explores what happened to the colonizers. In the process he discusses the ancients' knowledge of atomic physics and suggests that a nuclear holocaust of global proportions in 5000 BC may not only have destroyed whole civilizations, but may also have changed the very climate of our planet. The writing style is similar to Mooney's earlier book. 191pp. S&D 75

MORRILL, SIBLEY, ed. **THE KAHUNAS**, $2.50. A collection of nine essays on the Kahunas including two long articles, *The Lesser Hawaiian Gods* by J.S. Emerson and *Kahunas and the Hawaiian Religion* by W.D. Alexander. 111pp. BrP 68

MYLONAS, GEORGE. **ELEUSIS AND THE ELEUSINIAN MYSTERIES**, $6.95. *Few archaeological sites have so much material, so much interest, so many problems, in such close concentration, as Eleusis. The tremendous value of this book is that it presents the whole picture, including most of the details, in a brief but solid treatment . . . . Professor Mylonas collects, assimilates, and interprets it all: the legends and history of the sanctuary and cult, the development architecturally from Mycenaean through Roman times, the evidence pertaining to the myth and rites from archaeology and literature . . . .* —**Classical Philology**. The author is Director of the Excavations at Mycenae and is the leading scholar today on the Eleusian Mysteries. Many photographs accompany the text. Notes, glossary, bibliography, index, 416pp. PUP 61

PAUWELS, LOUIS and JACQUES BERGIER. **THE ETERNAL MAN**, $1.50. An imaginative, popular account of the beginnings of man which greatly differs from generally accepted theories. The authors searched throughout the world and throughout recorded and unrecorded history for answers to universal questions. Includes photographs and a good bibliography. 254pp. Avo 72

PHELON, W.P. **OUR STORY OF ATLANTIS OR THE THREE STEPS**, c$6.95. A treatise on the esoteric truths discovered and practiced by the Atlanteans as well as on how those truths have come to America and especially to the rulers of America. Much of the narrative is devoted to the *true mission of America* as seen by the brotherhood of the Rosy Cross. The text also includes a history of the brotherhood of the Rosy Cross by George Lippard. 247pp. BHC 72

PHILLIP, BROTHER. **SECRET OF THE ANDES**, c$6.55. Covers the history and work of those at the Monastery of the Brotherhood of the Seven Rays, which is situated in the Andes. According to this first-person narrative, the secret knowledge which has been hidden away for thousands of years is stored at this Mystery School. It will be revealed *when the children of the earth have progressed enough spiritually to be allowed to use it again.* Half of the volume consists of inspirational transcripts of the hierarchy. 151pp. Spe 61

PHYLOS. **A DWELLER ON TWO PLANETS**, $2.95. Originally written down by an eighteen year old in 1884 by automatic writing. The author is a teacher who claims to be an occult adept. Much of the book is given to a revelation of the nature and activities of Atlantean civilization, their government, science and daily life. Predictions are given which have come to pass in the years since the book was written and many more prophetic statements deal with coming events. A popular and enduring occult classic. 442pp. Mul 69

__________. **AN EARTH DWELLER RETURNS**, c$8.50. A companion volume to **Dweller** which discusses many incarnations of the principal character, a former high priest of Lemuria. Topics include: the mystery teachings; forces beyond magnetism; astral records; karma; inventions and their development through psychic channels; and Atlantean records. 510pp. Bor 69

ROBERTSON, LYLE. **EDGAR CAYCE'S STORY OF THE ORIGIN AND DESTINY OF MAN**, $1.25. The first comprehensive organization and interpretation of the great psychic's vision of history from the dawn of creation to a revelation of the new millenium due to arrive in 1998. At the center of Cayce's theory of history is the secret of the lost civilization of Atlantis—the primal society from which, through holocaust and migration, reincarnation and the forces of karma, Western civilization sprang. 108pp. Ber 72

SCHUON, FRITHJOF. **LIGHT ON THE ANCIENT WORLDS**, c$4.70. This is a philosophical study of the ancient world. Schuon writes extremely well (although symbolically) and his work in comparative religion and philosophy is highly regarded. Chapters on the ancient Greeks and early Christians are included as well as a very interesting essay on the nature religion of the American Indians, along with several other topics. 144pp. Tom 65

SCHURE, EDWARD. **FROM SPHINX TO CHRIST: AN OCCULT HISTORY**, $2.50. See section on Steiner. Mul 70

SCHWARTZ, JEAN-MICHEL. **THE MYSTERIES OF EASTER ISLAND**, $1.75. This is one of the few in-depth studies of Easter Island which is approachable by the non-specialist. M. Schwartz has done an excellent job in conveying some of the enigmas of Easter Island. He describes what is known about the monumental statues that dot the landscape and the script which can be likened only to that found in China and the Indus Valley. He also goes into the religious beliefs of the early islanders and the reasons for the disappearance of most of the native population. And he offers his own explanations for these mysteries—along with a review of the explanations of others. The text is filled with line drawings and photographs and a great deal of space is devoted to translations and interpretations of early writings. 107pp. Avo 75

SCOTT-ELLIOT, W. **THE STORY OF ATLANTIS AND THE LOST LEMURIA**, c$6.95. Two classic, comprehensive studies. The information was obtained by astral clairvoyance. Includes large, fold-out maps. 119pp. TPH 04

SENDY, JEAN. **THE MOON: OUTPOST OF THE GODS**, $1.50. Sendy delves into the Qabala and contemporary astrophysics to advance his theory that extraterrestrials arrived in our solar system about 21,000 BC and set up an Earth-observation post on the Moon. Soon after they built a spaceport from which they hoped to colonize the earth. He cites the Biblical and Qabalistic accounts of the *Elohim* (the sons of the gods who had intercourse with the daughters of men) and explores the reasons why they gave up their efforts and returned to the Moon. And finally, he hypothesizes that our own Moon-explorers will find some startling things when the Moon is finally fully explored. Another interesting account—however, Sendy does try a little too hard to make his theories appear to be gospel for our taste, but one never knows. 158pp. Ber 75

__________. **THOSE GODS WHO MADE HEAVEN AND EARTH**, $1.25. Sendy's thesis stems from the Hebrew word *Elohim*, which is a plural (*the gods*) rather than *God* as it is usually translated: *Genesis appears as an account of the arrival of perfectly concrete Celestials, physically in our image, who behaved on earth as we can imagine our own astronauts behaving on another planet.* He treats Genesis as a historical narrative whose text, already ancient at the time of Christ, takes on coherence in the light of our present scientific knowledge. 191pp. Ber 72

SILVERBURG, ROBERT. **LOST CITIES AND VANISHED CIVILIZATIONS**, $.95. Presents a general picture of the following civilizations: Troy, Babylon, Angkor, Knossos, Chichen Itza, and Pompeii. This is an introductory, easy-to-read work, designed to give the general reader a taste of each civilization. 152pp. Ban 63

SINNETT, A.P. **THE PYRAMIDS AND STONEHENGE**, $.95. Two lectures delivered before the Theosophical Society, London, in 1892-3, mainly incorporating material garnered through psychic channels. 27pp. TPH 1893

SPENCE, LEWIS. **ATLANTIS DISCOVERED**, c$3.98. Spence was a noted Scottish anthropologist, and the author of nearly fifty books, many concerned with the Atlantis story. His greatest contribution was to assemble reliable evidences from many disciplines: archaeology, anthropology, geology, and folklore. In this volume he shows that a definite Atlantean culture-complex existed on both sides of the Atlantic. He discusses the myths and legends, traces images and inscriptions which link the iconography of the Americas with Egyptian and European themes, showing their derivation from a common cultural source. Spence writes well and his scholarship is good. 242pp. Can 74

__________. **THE HISTORY OF ATLANTIS**, $3.95. Written by this Atlantean scholar who has examined and studied deeply the available evidence. He has gathered a wide scope of material to include in this convincing text including the sources of Atlantean history down to the most recent realizations. 238pp. CiP 68

__________. **OCCULT SCIENCES IN ATLANTIS**, c$5.00. A scientific and reasonable account. Much is related concerning magical practice in ancient Atlantis and the various forms it took, some lofty and others debased. The influence of Atlantis on various cults in Britain is also discussed. 133pp. Wei 70

STACY-JUDD, ROBERT. **ATLANTIS: MOTHER OF EMPIRES**, c$20.00. Stacy-Judd wrote **Atlantis** in 1939, after years of study, research, and personal exploration of Mayan ruins in the jungles of the Yucatan. Through his studies he developed the theory that the Mayas and other South American and African people were descendants of the people of Atlantis. This monumental work covers every aspect of man's development and the development of his early civilizations. Stacy-Judd was an architect and the text is replete with analyses of building design and iconography as well as many illustrations. It has been out of print for years and was just recently reprinted in a limited edition. A fascinating, well-developed study. Index, oversize, 365pp. Dev 39

STEIGER, BRAD. **ATLANTIS RISING**, $1.25. A flamboyant journalistic account by a writer who specializes in *unexplained phenomena* and the *occult*. Many of the major theories are explored and Steiger offers some explanations of his own. Bibliography, 220pp. Del 73

STEINER, RUDOLF. **COSMIC MEMORY: ATLANTIS AND LEMURIA**, $2.50. Steiner's first written expression of a cosmology resulting from his spiritual perception. He includes essential elements of man's prehistory and early history when he forfeited divine direction for the attainment of his present self-dependent freedom. Steiner traces in detail each step that man took in arriving at his present situation. He also includes material on his belief in the insoluble link between man and cosmos. A rather difficult, though highly enlightening, philosophical work. 262pp. Mul 59

TOMAS, ANDREW. **THE HOME OF THE GODS**, $1.25. This seems to be the best inexpensive paperback treatment of the Atlantean theme, formerly titled **Atlantis: From Discovery to Legend.** The most modern findings are incorporated into a historical narrative and sources are cited. Illustrations, index, 155pp. Ber 72

__________. **WE ARE NOT THE FIRST**, $1.25. Tomas' aims may be summed up as follows: to show that in former eras people possessed many scientific notions that we have today; that they were more technically skilled than is generally believed; and certain advanced scientific and technical ideas of the ancients came from an unknown outside source. The narrative is illustrated, documented, and well written. Bibliography. 180pp. Ban 71

TRENCH, BRINSLEY. **FORGOTTEN HERITAGE**, $5.25. The author deals with the dramatic view of man as a microcosm within a greater macrocosm. He traces this world anthropocosmic conception back to ancient civilizations and cultures. The origins of humanity are traced and a theory is revealed as to the nature of the universe in which we live and of possible universes co-existing simultaneously with ours. 271pp. Spe 64

__________. **THE SKY PEOPLE**, $1.25. Much evidence is given to support the author's conclusions that visitors from other planets have come to earth often in man's past and always at moments of Earthian crisis as we have today. He says that Apollo, Hermes, Prometheus and other Greek gods, as well as Egyptian deities, Osriris, and Biblical angels were all numbered among our friendly alien companions and guides. 224pp. ASC 70

__________. **TEMPLE OF THE STARS**, $1.50. Formerly titled **Men Among Mankind**, Trench here again demonstrates his ability to link together ancient history and the more recent past. He shows that through all the megalithic ruins around the world there runs an identifiable pattern. He concludes that there is a link between mankind on earth and another breed of man believed to live among the stars. Notes, index, bibliography, 223pp. RaH62

URANTIA FOUNDATION. **URANTIA BOOK**, c$20.00. See section on Revealed Teachings. UrP 55

VEER, M.H.J. Th. VAN DER and P. MOERMAN. **HIDDEN WORLDS**, $1.50. This is a fairly serious study of prehistory, ancient civilizations, and the evolution of mankind.

Various artifacts and theories are examined in a scattered fashion. The authors seem to have delved deeply into the available *evidence* and they have produce an interesting account. Part of the text is devoted to an analysis of the discovery of America and of the origin of the maps used by the ancients. Index, 206pp. Ban 74

VELIKOVSKY, IMMANUEL. **AGES IN CHAOS**, c$8.95. A radical revision of ancient history. Taking for the starting point the simultaneity of physical catastrophes described in the book of Exodus and in Egyptian documents, Dr. Velikovsky reconstructs the political and cultural histories of the ancient world. His work greatly enriches the records of biblical history and changes the concepts of the cultural and historical progress of Egypt, Assyria, Babylonia, Greece, and other lands of the ancient East. *If Dr. Velikovsky is right, this volume is the greatest contribution to the investigation of ancient times ever written.* —Dr. Robert Pfeiffer, Harvard University. 340pp. Dou 52

_____. **OEDIPUS AND AKHNATON**, c$7.95. Unraveling myth, lore, and fact, Velikovsky identifies the scene and all the personages of the Greek Oedipus legend with the life patterns of the family of the Egyptian King Akhnaton, reputedly the first monotheist during the most famous period of Egyptian history. The material is well documented and the narrative is fascinating. 208pp. Dou 60

WACHSMUTH, GUENTHER. **THE EVOLUTION OF MANKIND**, c$10.20. This book *. . . strives to show the growth of the human race, mankind's own history in connection with the evolution of the earth as a whole and of the cosmos . . . . We must go back to the remotest times. In so doing, the study of random discoveries of ruins, documents, artifacts, and bones must more and more be replaced by spiritual-scientific research which can recognize and describe the single steps of evolution from its grasp of higher impulses, laws, and processes. The basis for this is found in the work of Rudolf Steiner . . . . The span of time handled here is much larger than anything familiar to modern history. To divide it into manageable fragments, we have adopted the phases of the Platonic world-year. We hope to show that these phases represents steps in the unfolding of man that coincide with cosmic rhythms and periodicities . . . .We have drawn deeply on modern research in paleontology, archaeology, and anthropology, trying to work it into our general plan and to show its relations to the periodicity of the entire process . . . . We have tried not to favor any particular peoples, cultures, or areas, but to show how each portrayed specific shades in the broad spectrum of spiritual history.* This is an excellent detailed presentation which needs to be read slowly and carefully. Once the material Wachsmuth presents is assimilated our entire consciousness of prehistory and ancient history is altered significantly. Many maps, photographs, and line drawings are included along with many notes. For more on Rudolf Steiner, see the section devoted to his work. Oversize, 108pp. PAV 61

WHITE, PETER. **THE PAST IS HUMAN**, c$8.50. An archaeologist responds to books like **Chariots of the Gods**, reviewing the relics that they claim were created by extra-terrestrials, and basing his response on the latest discoveries in archaeology. Dr. White's thesis is that these mysteries can be explained by man's own actions and his evolution. The author teaches Prehistory at the University of Sydney and he has aimed his presentation at the general reader. Illustrations, index. 163pp. Tap 74

WILLIAMSON, GEORGE. **OTHER TONGUES, OTHER FLESH**, c$7.55. An attempt to show scientifically, through many reports and other sources, that there exist human beings on other planets and in other solar systems. Includes many quotations from saucer communications and reports on UFO phenomena. Also includes prophecies of the New Age and of our transition into that age. 448pp. Spe 65

_____. **ROAD IN THE SKY**, $4.70. The road referred to in the title is the highway linking the stars together and moving out beyond the known universe into the infinite vastness of galactic space. Williamson presents evidence which links ancient civilizations and the mysteries of their temple rituals with the beginnings of humanity and visitations from outer space. 248pp. Spe 59

_____. **SECRET PLACES OF THE LION**, c$5.05. Williamson reveals answers to many ancient mysteries (his knowledge obtained from records of *the Most Ancient wisdom*). He also talks of places where this wisdom is stored and how it can be found. Topics are many and varied, and go into considerable detail. 230pp. Spe 58

THE WORLD OF ANCIENT CIVILIZATIONS SERIES, c$3.95/each. These are large format picture books which explore the culture and philosophies of each of the civilizations, basically through a simple text, illustrated profusely with photographs (many in full color) and line drawings. Each forms a good introduction for the general reader. Oversize, about 150pp.

Champollion, Jacques — **The World of the Egyptians**
Duruy, Victor — **The World of the Romans**
Gobineau, J.A. de — **The World of the Persians**
Grosier, J.B. — **The World of Ancient China**
LeBon, G. — **The World of Ancient India**
LeBon, G. — **The World of Islamic Civilization**
Massa, Aldo — **The World of the Etruscans**
Meilsheim, David — **The World of Ancient Israel**
Prescott, William — **The World of the Aztecs**
Prescott, William — **The World of the Incas**

WUNDERLICH, H.G. **THE SECRET OF CRETE**, c$8.95. Prof. Wunderlich is a geologist who has studied Sir Arthur Evans's celebrated reconstruction of the so-called Palace of King Minos at Knossos—the legendary labyrinth where Theseus once defeated the Minotaur. One contradiction struck him after another in the *established* interpretation of Minoan culture. This book is his attempt to resolve the paradoxes that have obsessed the archaeological world since Evans' spectacular finds at the beginning of this century. Wunderlich suggests that the finds at Knossos represent not an isolated lost civilization, but one of the greatest turning points in history: the moment when the earliest Greeks turned

from the ancient monumental form of the cult of the dead—such as persisted in Egypt—toward remembrance through drama, and the cult of the hero. This is an excellent study which immerses the reader in the culture of ancient Crete and its antecedents. Every aspect of the ancient Cretan civilization is examined in detail and like a good detective the author puts the clues together to form a fascinating account. Wunderlich's scholarship seems to be excellent and the account is illustrated throughout with line drawings. There's also an extensive bibliography and an index. 382pp. McM 74

ANCIENT AMERICAS

ADAMSON, DAVID. **THE RUINS OF TIME**, c$12.50. This volume traces the history of the Mayas from the time of the Conquest to their present day *rediscovery* by archaeologists and explorers. It is a tale told by a reporter, and this should be kept in mind. All the important facts and incidents are there, as is the flavor of the times and the people. While the book can by no means be considered a work of scholarship, all the standard works are cited. And many references are made to the culture of the earlier Mayas. As Adamson tells his story, it is an exciting tale—and he does seem to have done a good deal of research. Bibliography, index, and many beautiful plates (some in color), 272pp. Pra 75

ANDREWS, GEORGE. **MAYA CITIES**, c$20.00. In this volume an architect who is also an excellent photographer turns his trained eye on Mayan cities from the point of view of their physical form and spatial organization. The book is arranged in two parts. The first part discusses Maya architecture and settlements in general and shows how small ceremonial centers developed into large cities. Basic building groupings are examined in detail. The second part describes and analyzes twenty settlements from all parts of the Maya area. Emphasis is on physical form and spatial organization, and the basic differences between ceremonial centers and urban centers are clearly set forth. The discussion of each site is supplemented with maps, drawings, and photos. 9½x10½", bibliography, index, 486pp. UOk 75

ASHE, GEOFFREY. **LAND TO THE WEST**, c$6.75. It would be interesting to think that the Irish discovered America. This book makes no such positive claim, but it presents a wholly plausible case for knowledge of America in medieval Ireland and perhaps long before that. 352pp. Vik 62

AVENI, ANTHONY, ed. **ARCHAEOASTRONOMY IN PRE-COLUMBIAN AMERICA**, c$22.00. This volume contains selected papers from a symposium that was part of the first joint scientific meeting of the American Association for the Advancement of Science and the Consejo Nacional de Ciencia y Tecnologia held in Mexico City in 1973. Contributors include anthropologists, astronomers, a geographer, a psychologist, an architect, and a historian. Three broad interlocking topics are discussed: early American rock art in the Southwestern U.S., astronomical orientations of buildings, and native Americans. The papers are all carefully written and contain important and often controversial new insights. Illustrations often accompany the text along with notes and there is an excellent long bibliography and the volume is indexed, 451pp. UTx 75

BAUDEZ, CLAUDE. **CENTRAL AMERICA**, c$26.20. This is a fairly dry analysis of important archaeological information about the Central American region—an area that is often considered *peripheral* and is ignored by the specialists who concentrate on Mexico or South America. M. Baudez has based this comprehensive study on documentation assembled throughout Central America and he includes introductory material along with detailed studies of specific cites and analyses of theories, problems, and methods. There is also a chronological chart, detailed bibliography and notes, and 160 illustrations, 54 in color. All in all, it's a good survey, part of Nagel's **Archaeologia Mundi** series. Oversize, index, 254pp. Nag 70

BELLAMY, H.S. and P. ALLAN. **THE CALENDAR OF TIAHUANACO**, c$11.75. The Tiahuanaco Gateway is an immensely old stone monument standing in the high Andes, near the shores of Lake Titicaca. It carries an extraordinary sequence of intricate, obviously symbolical, carvings. Bellamy has made this monument his life's study and has written an earlier book about it. Here he incorporates new research and explicates in detail all of the symbolism to show that the Gateway is a calendar—the oldest calendar in the world and one that has come to us from *another* world. This is a very complete analysis, with many excellent illustrations and an immense amount of introductory and background information. 440pp. Fab 56

BERNAL, IGNACIO. **MEXICO BEFORE CORTES**, $2.50. A vivid cultural history of the origins and development of the civilizations in Mexico from the eighth century BC to the Spanish conquest in 1521. Ignacio Bernal is Director of the National Museum of Anthropology in Mexico City. The narrative is geared toward the general reader and often reads like a novel and yet the scholarship is impeccable. A chapter is devoted to each of the major civilizations and the text is well illustrated. There's also an extensive glossary which has pronunciation keys. 140pp. Dou 75

_____. **THE OLMEC WORLD**, c$16.50. The Olmecs developed the first great civilization in the Western hemisphere between the thirteenth and first centuries BC. They built ceremonial centers such as La Venta, with monumental pyramids, a spacious courtyard, a basalt-columned tomb, and offerings of stones, celts, and mosaics. At La Venta also are four of the twelve colossal carved Olmec heads that have thus far been discovered. The Olmecs were not only artists but engineers and scientists as well. They discovered the value of zero and achieved the most complete system of calculating time conceived in America. In an engrossing reconstruction, Bernal examines Olmec art, society, and religious beliefs. He traces the efflorescence and decline of the Olmecs and insists on the basic unity of all Mesoamerican civilizations. This is the first full-length study of the Olmecs in English and is illustrated with 150 maps, photos, and drawings. Oversize, index, 287pp. UCP 69

BRUCE, ROBERT D. **LACANDON DREAM SYMBOLISM**, $9.25. See Dreams section.

BRUNHOUSE, ROBERT. **IN SEARCH OF THE MAYA**, c$8.80. The remains of Maya civilization were first discovered during the eighteenth and nineteenth centuries by amateur archaeologists who came to Mexico, Guatemala, and Honduras to search for ruins. This book tells the story of the rediscovery of the Maya cities by describing the explorations of eight of these pioneering archaeologists. The emphasis is as much on personality as it is on contributions to knowledge and it makes an exciting story, using first-hand accounts to recreate the flavor of the initial discoveries. Bibliography, index, illustrations, 243pp. UNM 73

_____. **PURSUIT OF THE ANCIENT MAYA**, c$9.90. In this sequel to **In Search of the Maya**, Brunhouse tells the story of seven later Maya archaeologists and describes the coming of age of Maya studies. The subjects of this book are a great deal better known than the men in the earlier book. Again, a vivid picture is given of the discoveries and of the personalities of the individuals. Notes, bibliography, index, 252pp. UNM 75

Tlahuizcalpantechutli and Mixcoatl

BRUNDAGE, BURR. **EMPIRE OF THE INCA**, c$9.95. This is a well written history of the Inca which begins by tracing the legends and known facts about their initial settlements and goes from there to a discussion of the development of their civilization and empire. There are also sections on their religious beliefs and rituals and on their engineering prowess, as evidenced in the still-existing Royal Road. Extensive notes, index, 413pp. UOk 63

_____. **LORDS OF CUZCO**, c$10.95. An in depth description of the Incas at the peak of their power and in the period of their decline. In contrast to Brundage's earlier work which is essentially a political history, this volume probes into all aspects of the life of the people. Illustrations, extensive notes, index. 471pp. UOk 67

BURLAND, C.A. **PERU UNDER THE INCAS**, c$6.95. This is a nice account of Inca Peru, entertainingly written and replete with photographs and drawings. Burland is an ethnographer and he has written many books. In this account he begins by reviewing the land of the Incas and the characteristics of the people who lived there. The next chapter is devoted to an exposition of the tight governmental administration. From there Burland discusses their religious beliefs. The other chapters review their social life, their territorial expansion, and their artistic achievement. Oversize, index, bibliography, 144pp. Put 67

BURLAND, C.A. and WERNER FORMAN, **FEATHERED SERPENT AND SMOKING MIRROR: THE GODS AND CULTURES OF ANCIENT MEXICO**, c$12.95. This oversize book includes some of the most beautiful color photographs we have seen along with

an excellent text. The general reader with little background in the area can get a good feeling for the civilization and the cosmological and mythological beliefs of the people. The story of the two main gods is related in detail. While the early cultures in Mesoamerica are reviewed briefly, the bulk of the text is devoted to the Aztec culture. There's a chapter on each of the main gods, Quetzalcoatl and Tezcatlipoca; one on the daily life of the people; and another one on astrology and the priesthood. A final chapter, *The Earthly Confrontation*, reviews the Conquest and the early omens of its coming. There's also a glossary, chronology, bibliography, and index. 128pp. Put 75

BUSHNELL, G.H.S. **THE FIRST AMERICANS**, $3.95. A pictorial essay presenting the history of American civilizations from 5000 BC to the Hispanic conquests. Presents a brief review of each of the civilizations and also gives the sources of each of the illustrations for those who wish to do further study. Bibliography, 144pp. MGH 73

CARLSON, VADA. **THE GREAT MIGRATION**, $1.50. Subtitled *Emergence of the Americas as Indicated in the Readings of Edgar Cayce*, this pamphlet traces the rise of South and North American Indian cultures from Lemurian and Atlantian migrations. Bibliography, 58pp. ARE 70

CASO, ALFONSO. **THE AZTECS**, c$9.95. Here, translated into English for the first time, is Alfonso Caso's brilliant account of the Aztec people: their art, customs, religion, and practice of magic. Caso surveys the gods that appear in the codices and archaeological remains and the purposes they fulfilled with respect to nature and society, supporting his conclusions by reference to the accounts of the Spanish chroniclers. The gods who make up the pantheon of the Aztecs are explained, with examples which illuminate the whole religious system. Caso directed the explorations at Monte Alban and is director of archaeology in the National Museum in Mexico City. Miguel Covarrubias, who supplied the illustrations (in as many as six colors) is one of Mexico's best known illustrators. His drawings portray the divinities and objects related to Aztec religious life. Oversize, index, 140pp. UOk 58

COE, MICHAEL. **THE MAYA**, $5.75. *Dr. Coe . . . has written an excellent survey of the civilization of the ancient Maya, concentrating mainly on the achievements of the classic period. The rise, development, and fall of this amazing culture is explained factually and succinctly. Mayan life and thought are not neglected either. The maps and life figures are so well integrated into the text that a visual understanding of the Maya is obtained. The plates and a select bibliography of the most important major works enhance the value of this book.*—Library Journal. The material is organized in chronological order and is succinctly presented. Coe devotes chapters to Mayan life and thought and each of the 83 plates is described. Coe's work is generally considered the finest available from an academic point of view. Index, 252pp. Pra 66

_____. **MEXICO**, $6.00. Again Coe has produced an excellent volume which synthesizes Mesoamerican cultural history, tracing its development from earliest times in a chronological sequence. Fact and speculation are carefully distinguished and line drawings are well integrated into the text. A series of photos (all described) follow the main body of the text and there is a chapter-by-chapter bibliography and an index. The style is less dry than in Coe's more detailed books and this forms an admirable general introduction to the archaeology of the area. 245pp. Pra 62

DAVIES, NIGEL. **THE AZTECS**, c$10.00. Davies is an Englishman who has lived in Mexico since 1962 and has studied the history and culture of the ancient peoples of the country extensively. He holds advanced degrees from the National University and has had books published by the National Institute of Anthropology of Mexico. Most of the books on Meso-America give short shrift to the Aztecs and if they are discussed in any depth it is the Conquest and the horrors of their bloodthirsty wars that are concentrated on. This is an excellent presentation of the Aztec civilization, from its beginnings to the time of the Conquest. The mythological and religious underpinnings are discussed at some length. This is the best single account of the Aztecs for the general reader. It reads well and the scholarship seems to be excellent. Notes, illustration, bibliography, index, 380pp. Put 74

DIAZ DEL CASTILLO, BERNAL. **THE DISCOVERY AND CONQUEST OF MEXICO**, $4.95. Diaz served under Cortes throughout the entire Mexico campaign. This volume was written late in his life from memory and from his journal notes and it is considered the basic source book on the Conquest. All the following writers, including W.H. Prescott, have relied heavily on this account when writing their histories. Diaz is not always the most objective narrator—however he was definitely in on the action and his is a fascinating account not only of the Conquest, but also of the Mexican civilizations. This edition was edited by Genaro Garcia from an exact copy of the original manuscript and extracts from Garcia's long introduction are printed in this volume, together with the commentary and notes from the translator, A.P. Maudslay. Additional introductory material is also included along with an index. 509pp. FSG 56

DRAKE, RAYMOND. **GODS AND SPACEMEN IN THE ANCIENT WEST**, $1.50. Formerly titled **Ancient Secrets of Mysterious America**, this is a fascinating, well-researched look into America's past, beginning with the origin of man and continuing through the last of the pre-Columbian civilizations. This is the most complete narrative we've seen in this area. 281 item bibliography, 230pp. NAL 74

DURAN, DIEGO. **BOOK OF THE GODS AND RITES AND THE ANCIENT CALENDAR**, c$12.50/5.95. This is the first English translation of two classic works about Aztec ritual and calendar which, though written in the late 1500's by Fray Duran, a Dominican missionary, were not published until 1867. Since that time they have been among the most quoted works on ancient Mexico. Duran's stated purpose was to help the missionaries combat the religious beliefs of the Indians. But despite himself he became deeply absorbed in their rich culture. To assure the accuracy of his account, he searched out Indian survivors of pre-Conquest times and Spaniards who had accompanied Cortes to Mexico. He recorded descriptions of the gods and goddesses, the rituals attending their worship, the festivals and ceremonies, the calendrical system, and the Indians' occupations, games and social life. The translators based their work on the original manuscript, now in the National Library of Madrid. Accompanying the text are reproductions of the excellent illustrations from Ramirez' nineteenth century copy of the manuscript. The drawings vividly portay the rites and dress of the people. They were executed at Duran's request by an anonymous fellows missionary (or perhaps a mission-trained Indian) who copied them from ancient Aztec manuscripts. The text includes a glossary, bibliography, and an excellent index. 526pp. UOk 71

Figurines from the Early Preclassic

GALLENKAMP, CHARLES. **MAYA**, c$12.95. *It is of the rise and decline of the Maya that the author of this book speaks. This is a book intended primarily for the general reader . . . . Rather than detail in all their complexities the many sites and centers of Mayan life and ceremony, he has selected those sites and those elements which, when combined, give a readable and delightful account of the rise of Maya civilization and its inexorable march through pride and glory to extinction. . . . Though the author has visited and photographed virtually all of the important Maya sites on various occasions, this book is not presented as the result of his personal field work. Rather, he has examined the work of the scholars . . . and has presented a synthesis. . . . He has tried, in most cases, to begin with a specific problem and trace its solution as far as evidence permits. Where there are points of controversy . . . he has presented the several viewpoints.—from the preface. Many photographs and illustrations are included along with an index and bibliography.* 266pp. McK 76

GARCILASO DE LA VEGA, EL INCA. **THE INCAS**, $1.65. This classic narrative by one of the last Inca princes traces the legends surrounding the rise of his people, their wars, customs, and religion. It ends with the arrival of Pizarro and the beginning of Spanish hegemony. This is a complete edition translated by Maria Jolas from the annotated French edition, edited and introduction by Alain Gheerbrant. Illustrated and bibliography, 447pp. Avo 64

GENDROP, PAUL and DORIS HEYDEN. **PRE-COLUMBIAN ARCHITECTURE OF MESOAMERICA**, c$37.50. The awesome temples and cities of the Mayas, Toltecs, and Aztecs, and all the other highly developed cultures of Mexico and Mesoamerica are shown in hundreds of unusually fine photographs and discussed by two leading scholars. 363 illustrations, including 95 reconstructions, diagrams, and groundplans. 10x11", 340pp. Abr 76

GORENSTEIN, SHIRLEY. **NOT FOREVER ON EARTH**, $7.95. Subtitled *Prehistory of Mexico*, this is a well-written general account of the native civilizations in Mexico from their beginnings to the Spanish Conquest. Introductory chapters set the stage and discuss elements common to all the civilizations. This is followed by a chronological discussion of the major cultures, with accompanying photos and line drawings. The emphasis is on what archaeological findings have revealed about political organization, military systems, hunting and farming practices, social relationships, and religious beliefs and ideology. Ms. Gorenstein is an anthropology professor at Columbia University, and has directed several digs in Mexico. The book is neither technical nor is it a detailed account of the cultures. Bibliography, index, 169pp. Scr 75

HAGEN, VICTOR von. **THE AZTEC**, $1.25. This is the best general account available of the Aztec people and their civilization. Von Hagen was a scientist and writer and he devoted much of his life to analyzing and writing about the pre-Columbian American civilizations. Here he discusses the Aztecs, from the political and social structure of their city-state to their method of preparing human beings for religious sacrifice (and the reasons behind this sacrifice). He tells how the Aztec made war and conquest the basic pattern of their daily life; analyzes their advanced forms of art, writing. and sculpture; and describes their temples and palaces, particularly the lavish city of Tenochtitlan, built in the midst of a lake deep in the interior of Mexico. Every aspect of the Aztec culture is well-represented and the text is illustrated with photographs and 55 line drawings. Bibliography, index, 224pp. NAL 61

_____, ed. **THE INCAS OF PEDRO DE CIEZA DE LEON**, c$8.95. Cieza arrived in Cartagena in 1535, a boy of thirteen, and for the next seventeen years traveled through South America, observing and describing the country and its peoples, preserving for posterity the achievements of the Inca civilization even as it was being destroyed. The *Chronicler of the Indies* was not a scholar making a record of the Conquest, rather he *saw strange and wonderful things that exist in this New World . . . and there came over me a great desire to write certain of them*. And write them he did—so well that his contemporaries plagiarized from him freely and present day scholars regard his histories as *the cornerstone when writing of Inca achievements*. This translation is universally regarded as the finest and this edition is edited by Victor von Hagen, who also supplies an excellent introduction and many notes. Illustrations, bibliography, index. 479pp. UOk 59

_____ **THE ROYAL ROAD OF THE INCA**, c$29.95. A beautifully produced, fully illustrated account of von Hagen's discovery of the *Golden Roads of the Royal Inca*, with an account of the history and legends about the roads. Cre 76

_____. **WORLD OF THE MAYA**, $1.50. A vivid exploration of Maya civilization. Von Hagen, through his personal knowledge of the land, and through archaeology and ancient documents, restores the picture of Maya society as it was at its height. He explores the everyday life of the people (birth, marriage, sex, customs) which was regulated by complicated rituals. The author also details the amazing Maya astronomical calculations and their philosophy of time. Another section is devoted to the life of the ruling theocracy and the nobles and life in the Mayan cities. Von Hagen is writing for the general reader and his account is comprehensive, a work of good scholarship, and interesting reading as well. Many line drawings and photographs illustrate the text. Bibliography, notes, index, 224pp. NAL 60

HANSEN, L. TAYLOR. **HE WALKED THE AMERICAS**, c$6.95. A unique account of the various legends existing in North and South America telling of a mysterious and powerful saint, imbued with supernormal healing abilities who apparently came from Palestine at the time of Christ. The author researched for over twenty-five years in an attempt to ascertain the identity of this great healing prophet of three continents who was in some way associated with the Christ and whose message was similar. This edition has many line drawings and its appearance reminds us of a junior high school text. An excellent annotated bibliography is included. 255pp. Amh 63

HATT, CAROLYN. **THE MAYA**, $1.50. A collection of excerpts from the Edgar Cayce readings tied together with commentary from many of the most noted works on the ancient Maya. Ms. Hatt critiques both Cayce's comments and those of the scholars she cites and ties the whole together well. The material is topically arranged and there is an emphasis on Mayan concepts of time and Mayan predictions for the future and explanations of the past. Notes, 68pp. ARE 72

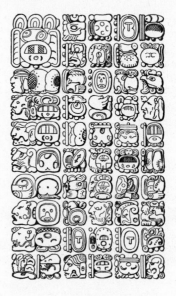

Mayan Tablet of Holy Days

HEMMING, JOHN. **THE CONQUEST OF THE INCAS**, $4.95. This book has been widely praised as the finest account of the annihilation of the Incan empire since W.H. Prescott's **History of the Conquest of Peru.** Hemming spent six years preparing the volume and during that time he consulted more than a thousand books and documents and traveled to Peru and Spain to investigate sources. It is an excellent, moving account distinguished by an extraordinary empathy. The reader is drawn into the minds of the sixteenth century Spaniards and Indians and he can sense their response as events move quickly around them. The narrative is comprehensive and over 100 pages are devoted to notes and references, a bibliography, and an index. Maps, line drawings, and photographs are also included. 641pp. HBJ 70

HOMET, MARCEL F. **ON THE TRAIL OF THE SUN GODS**, c$5.90. Prof. Homet is one of the world's leading archaeologists. In this follow-up to **Sons of the Sun**, he details further discoveries he made in the Amazon in his search for the lost cities of the sun worshippers. He has also attempted to link, by scientific hypotheses, the civilizations of the Old World with those of Brazil and Peru. A fascinating personal narrative, well-illustrated with photographs and line drawings. Good bibliography. 272pp. Spe 65

_____. **SONS OF THE SUN**, $4.70. The first-hand account of perious scientific journeys into the *green hell* of the Amazon jungles of Brazil and Peru and the discoveries made by Homet. It is a highly exciting and adventurous narrative that is informative and stimulating. Many photographs and drawings illustrate his findings. Includes a glossary of 30pp. and a bibliography. 239pp. Spe

HUNTER, C. BRUCE. **A GUIDE TO ANCIENT MAYA RUINS**, c$9.95. An illustrated guide to the Maya ceremonial areas of Mexico, Guatemala, and Honduras that can be visited. Following an introduction to the civilization and history of the Mayas, the author lists and discusses separate archaeological areas. Each is presented in the light of recent excavations and restorations and illuminated by photographs and site maps. Appended are a list of selected readings and suggestions for reaching the archaeological zones. Index, 349pp. UOk 74

IVANOFF, PIERRE. **MAYA,** c$19.95. A monumental work, 12x16", illustrated with over 150 color plates. In simple narrative and stunning photographs the complete survey of the Mayan world unfolds: its religious and ceremonial beliefs, agriculture and commerce, social, political and everyday life, its scientific achievements in astronomy and the development of a calendar, the language, literature, art and architecture. Selections from indigenous sacred and historical writings provide an insight into this civilization as seen by the Mayans themselves. 191pp. G&D 74

KEEN, BENJAMIN. **THE AZTEC IMAGE,** c$20.00. *This book studies reflections of the Aztec civilization of ancient Mexico in Western social science, literature, and art over a period of four and a half centuries. It attempts to trace the rise of divergent interpretations of that vanished culture and to show how the resulting clash of views periodically produced new syntheses that incorporated the most valuable data and insights of the rival schools of thought.... My basic method has been to outline the historical setting of each period, to describe the major schools of thought on Aztec culture in that period, and to analyze the ideas of leading exponents of each school, with a stress on the most original or distinctive facets of each man's thought.* Notes, index, 685pp. RUP 71

LAPINER, ALAN. **PRE-COLUMBIAN ART OF SOUTH AMERICA,** c$45.00. Emphasizes the art and artifacts of Peru. Cultural contexts are provided and works now in collections all over the world are compared. 911 illustrations, 226 in color, maps and charts, chronological tables, visual glossary. Considered the definitive work in the field. 10x13", 460pp. Abr 76

LEON-PORTILLA, MIGUEL. **AZTEC THOUGHT AND CULTURE,** c$6.95. The fundamental concepts of the Aztecs presented and examined in this study have been taken from more than ninety original Aztec documents. They concern the origin of the universe and of life, conjectures on the mystery of God, the possibility of comprehending things beyond the realm of experience, life after death, and the meaning of education, history, and art. The documents that these selections were taken from were generally written by natives after the Conquest. Adapting the Latin alphabet, which they had been taught by the missionary friars, to their native tongue, they recorded the poems, song, chronicles, and traditions that they or their fathers had learned by rote before Spanish domination. Leon-Portilla is a widely respected Mexican scholar. Bibliography, index, 260pp. UOk 63

__________,ed. **THE BROKEN SPEARS,** $2.95. Leon-Portilla, one of the leading scholars in the field of Nahuatl studies, has by editing the post-Conquest chronicles written by the remnants of the Aztec intellectual class, presented a coherent view of the Spanish Conquest as witnessed and experienced by the Aztecs themselves. The introduction gives details on the historical and cultural background of the Aztecs along with the origins and histories of the native text. The text is well illustrated and fully indexed. Bibliography, 200pp. Bea 59

__________. **PRE-COLUMBIAN LITERATURES OF MEXICO,** c$5.95. This volume presents a selection of myths and sacred hymns, lyric poetry, rituals, drama, and various forms of prose—together with critical commentary and background information. The selections come from the Aztecs, the Mayas, the Mixtecs and Zapotecs of Oaxaca, the Tarascans of Michoacan, the Otomis of central Mexico, and others. Many of them are translated into English for the first time. Bibliography, index, 199pp. UOk 69

LE PLONGEON, AUGUSTUS. **SACRED MYSTERIES AMONG THE MAYAS AND THE QUICHES,** c$7.95. Last century Le Pongeon discovered numerous ruins and ancient relics of the once mighty Mayans. His knowledge of esoteric lore enables him to reconstruct their sacred cosmology. This book communicates the extent of his discoveries and includes photographs of some Mayan relics. 153pp. Wiz 1886

LUCKERT, KARL. **OLMEC RELIGION,** c$9.95. This is a revolutionary interpretation of the oldest religion in Middle America. A historian of religion proposes that it was a serpent, not the commonly represented jaguar, that was the religious symbol of the ancient Olmecs. The author's primary objective in this study is an interpretation of Olmec religious symbolism. An engrossing presentation, illustrated with sixty-four photographs and drawings. Bibliography, index. 199pp. UOk 76

McKERN, SHARON. **EXPLORING THE UNKNOWN,** c$7.95. A pictorial, journalistic account of pre-Columbian archaeological mysteries. Each topic is dealt with at length. Indexed, bibliography, 124pp. Pra 72

MASON, J. ALDEN. **ANCIENT CIVILIZATIONS OF PERU,** $4.95. This is considered the definitive work on the subject. Topics discussed include environment; physique and language; history of Peruvian culture; Incan history, economic life, public works, social organization, political organization and government, religion, and intellectual life; and arts and crafts. The scholarship is excellent and the writing style is not overly ponderous. Many illustrations, fully indexed, 43pp bibliography. 350pp. Pen 57

MERCER, HENRY A. **THE HILL CAVES OF YUCATAN,** $4.50. This book, originally published in 1896, details Mercer's search through twenty-nine caves, thirteen of which he excavated. While he did find evidence of occupation, he found no trace of early man. This is a classic account which has been an extremely rare book. The Yucatan landscape, the caves, and the native population come alive in this account. Mercer speculates on the uses of the caves and cites the findings of his exploratory group. J. Eric Thompson has contributed an extensive introduction to this edition and the text is enhanced by 44 photographs and a number of line drawings. 227pp. UOk 75

MERTZ, HENRIETTE. **GODS FROM THE FAR EAST,** $1.50. As the subtitle *How the Chinese Discovered America* suggests, this narrative (based on written accounts from Chinese archives dates back as far as 2250 BC) discusses the Chinese exploration of North and Central America many aeons ago. The author supports her theory by examining similarities between Asian and American art and pottery, especially Mayan work. She believes, for example, that the Mayan calendar was a direct result of these visits, and she provides a possible explanation for the myth of Quetzalcoatl. The Chinese accounts are cited and referenced and many illustrations accompany the text. Bibliography, index, 280pp. RaH 72

METRAUX, ALFRED. **HISTORY OF THE INCAS,** $2.45. Generally, the material on pre-Columbian civilizations in the Americas has concentrated on the Mayas-Aztecs in what is now known as Mexico and on the Incas. By far the bulk of the published material discusses the Mexican early civilizations. While this book is by no means a definitive, comprehensive study, it is a readable work with fairly good scholarship and eminently suitable for the general reader. The Inca civilization is discussed in historical, sociological, and religious terms from its earliest stages through the Conquest up to the twentieth century (although the emphasis, of course, is on the Empire as it was at its height). M. Metraux was a French ethnologist and worked in South America for many years. He writes well and illustrates his account with 79 photos and line drawings. 205pp. ScB 69

MEYER, KARL. **TEOTIHUACAN,** c$10.00. In the high point of its culture and prestige—around 500 AD—Teotihuacan was the most important city in the Americas. For some two and a half centuries the city held sway. Then, for reasons we cannot yet fathom, it was suddenly, totally abandoned. This oversize volume examines the rise and fall of the city, and also examines the areas's other civilizations, notably the Olmec, Toltec, Mixtec, Maya, and Aztec. Supplementing the text are some 140 illustrations, over a third in full color. The pictures range from ritual objects to everyday ware, from whimsical creations to depiction of historical events by the peoples concerned. A special section, **Ancient Mexico in Literature**, contains accounts of the confrontation between European and Indian culture, as well as reports of explorations and of scholars. Index, 172pp. Nws 73

MORLEY, SYLVANUS. **THE ANCIENT MAYA,** $4.95. The most noted study of every aspect of the ancient Mayas, a delight to read and to look at. This is a revised edition which incorporates the most recent archaeological findings. Illustrated with hundreds of plates and line drawings and extensively documented. 507pp. SUP 46

__________. **IN SEARCH OF MAYA GLYPHS,** $3.45. Edited selections from Morley's field journals, gleaned from the 39 volumes Morley left at his death. Morley did pioneering research into the Mayas and their history and went to great pains to record every detail or observations about his findings that might be of any possible significance to other scholars. The editors (Robert and Florence Lister) selected material from five representative journals (1916, 1918, 1920, 1921, 1932) for this volume. Bibliography, glossary, photography, 171pp. MNM 70

NUTTALL, ZELIA, ed. **THE CODEX NUTTALL,** $7.50. Originating in what is now the State of Oaxaca, Mexico, the Codex Nuttall was painted by Mixtec artists at some time not too long before the Spanish Conquest. It is, in effect, a Book of Kings, one of a series of masterworks narrating in picture and hieroglyph the sacred history of the Mixtecs. Centering around the year 1000 AD, it shows the births of kings, their marriages, offspring, and major events in their lives. Over a dazzling white background swarm hundreds of figures painted in rich earth colors. Kings in elaborate costumes of textiles and skins, ornamented with feathers, wearing elaborate masks of the gods, carrying ceremonial objects, appear throughout. Warriors in battle dress advance, marriage ceremonies are celebrated, kings and their consorts face one another in solemn rites, a child is born, a naked priestess rips the heart out of a victim in a stark temple, rows of figures bear tribute or offer ceramics and decorated aprons, fantastic twin temples rise to the sky. This is a strange world of vision, awe-inspiring for its simple, powerful technique—at times baffling, but a realm of beauty and visual symbol without modern counterpart. This volume is the only pre-Columbian codex that is generally available and it is an essential work for all who seek to understand the culture of the early Americas which the Spaniards so ruthlessly wiped out. The 8½x11 text includes 88 plates in color and has an excellent long introduction. The reproductions are also excellent. Dov 75

PADGEN, A.R., tr. **THE MAYA: DIEGO DE LANDA'S ACCOUNT OF THE AFFAIRS OF THE YUCATAN,** c$15.00. De Landa, a sixteenth century Spanish missionary, dedicated many years to compiling a comprehensive survey of Maya beliefs, customs, and social organization. The translator also supplies an introduction. Includes illustrations and a reproduction of the Maya alphabet. 224pp. OHa 75

PRESCOTT, WILLIAM. **HISTORY OF THE CONQUEST OF MEXICO AND HISTORY OF THE CONQUEST OF PERU,** c$5.95. This is the only edition of these classic works in which the complete texts of both of Prescott's histories are published together in one volume. Prescott's delight in vivid narrative and his striking descriptions of all aspects of the native cultures are evident throughout these pages. Together with Bernal Diaz del Castillo's volume on Mexico, Prescott's work is considered the definitive account of the Conquests. And while he did not participate directly in the events he discusses so compellingly, he lived close enough to their time that many first-hand accounts have been integrated into the narratives. Prescott was an excellent historian, whose accounts range far beyond a mere military history and delve deeply into *weltanschaung* of the conquered civilizations. 1324pp. RaH

RANNEY, EDWARD. **STONEWORK OF THE MAYA**, $12.75. A beautiful study of Maya stonework seen not as documentation of a particular style, but rather as part of the natural setting in which they stand today. The sites chosen are not only the most important or best known. The study provides a good cross-section of all the sites. The photographs are quite well done and there is extensive commentary and background information covering each selection. Oversize, bibliography, index, 133pp. UNM 74

RECINOS, ADRIAN and DELIA GOETZ. **THE ANNALS OF THE CAKCHIQUELS AND THE TITLE OF THE LORDS OF TOTONICAPAN**, $2.95. Two recent translations of important Mayan native documents. **The Annals** was written at the end of the sixteenth century. The manuscript corroborates the theories of the creation of man advanced in the **Popul Vuh** (the Cakchiquels were originally part of the Quiche nation) and relates many tales of the heroic age, enveloped in the mists of legend. But its principal value is its important contribution to history, from the beginnings of the Indian culture through the Spanish Conquest and the first century of colonization. **The Title of the Lords**, written in 1554, contains a brief history of the Quiches from their legendary origins to the reign of their greatest king, Quikab. Signed by the kings and dignitaries of the Quiche court, it completes the source material provided by the **Popul Vuh** for the study of the life and thought of the Quiche Mayas before the coming of the Spaniards. Notes, index, bibliography, 232pp. UOk 53

_____. **POPUL VUH, THE SACRED BOOK OF THE ANCIENT QUICHE MAYA**, c$5.95. This is the only complete version in English of the **Book of the People** of the Quiche Maya, generally regarded as America's oldest book. The mythology, traditions, cosmogony, and history of the Quiche Maya, including the chronology of their kings down to 1550, are related in simple yet literary style by the Indian chronicler. Adrian Recinos has provided an illuminating 80 page introduction and many detailed footnotes as well as the Spanish translation from which this English edition was taken. Good bibliography and index, 267pp. UOk 50

REICHEL-DOLMATOFF, GERARDO. **AMAZONIAN COSMOS**, $5.25. Subtitled *The Sexual and Religious Symbolism of the Tukano Indians*, this is a detailed ethnographic study of an isolated Northwest Amazon tribe. The author worked with a single informant over a prolonged period, and later checked his findings extensively in the field. This is an in-depth investigation, written for the specialist but comprehendable by all interested readers. Much of the anthropological detail can be skipped over and the myths and symbols present a fascinating universe, so unlike our modern society. The ideas of man and the universe expressed by these people can help the reader understand some of the motivation and beliefs of the pre-Columbian native cultures. Index, bibliography, 313pp. UCh 71

ROYS, RALPH, tr. **THE BOOK OF CHILAM BALAM OF CHUMAYEL**, c$8.95. A translation of one of the **Books of the Prophet Balam**, native Maya documents written after the Conquest which contain much of what the Mayas remembered of their old culture. This volume contains comparatively little of the intrusive European material which predominates in the other **Books**. It is rich in Maya rituals, history, and traditions. Roys also provides extensive notes and there's an introduction by J. Eric Thompson. Illustrations, bibliography, index. 8½x12", 247pp. OUk 67

_____. **RITUAL OF THE BACABS**, c$6.95. This is the first English translation of a Maya colonial manuscript, never before published in any language, containing forty-two incantations which add materially to knowledge of the religion of the Mayas and their conception of the cosmos and ideas about the origin of life. The gods themselves are often cited but rarely, if ever, are they addressed in supplication. The role of the speaker is to give orders. The title comes from the four Bacabs, who hold up the sky, the deities most frequently mentioned. In addition to the translation, the book contains a transcription in the original Maya, a comprehensive introduction, glossaries of Maya terms, and an appendix of intrusive material in the manuscript. Index, notes, illustrations. 222pp. UOk 65

SAHAGUN, FRAY BERNARDINO DE. **A HISTORY OF ANCIENT MEXICO**, c$18.80. Fray Bernardino is without question the premier historian of the Aztec civilization. He came over to Mexico soon after the Conquest and learned the native language almost immediately. He had been trained as a historian and *he gathered about him native inform-*

ants, first writing down in the original language what these informants narrated. Yet, not content with this procedure, other informants were sought out to listen to these texts and comment upon their accuracy. Futher, natives were encouraged to sketch and write in their own symbols, and finally, with all these original materials in hand, the good Father sat himself down to write. His final history was divided into the following four sections, all of which are reproduced here in full in a translation into English from Bustamante's Spanish version: I: *The Gods Which Ancient Mexicans Adored*; II: *Calendar-Festivals*; III: *The Origin of the Mexican Gods*; and IV: *Astrology of the Ancient Mexicans*. The text reads very well and its accuracy has never been questioned. A fairly extensive biographical sketch is included along with a detailed study of Sahagun's writing and his work with the native population. Index, BIE 32

SAVOY, GENE. **ON THE TRAIL OF THE FEATHERED SERPENT**, c$10.00. Peruvian myth tells of a wise man who sailed away to the north after a period of persecution. And Mexican legend is filled with tales of Quetzalcoatl, a godlike figure who appeared by sea from the south, established law, and was famous as a just and wise man. There are many similarities in stone carvings and ornamental work between the two civilizations. Savoy felt that a cultural interchange had taken place between the two, and he theorized a sea link. To prove his assumption he set out to duplicate the mythological voyage of Viracocha/Quetzalcoatl from Peru to Mexico and he describes his adventure here, complete with photographs, maps and drawings. 217pp. BoM 74

SEJOURNE, LAURETTE. **BURNING WATER** $3.95. Subtitled *Thought and Religion in Ancient Mexico*, this is a vivid reconstruction by one of the leading contemporary archaeologists in the field. Ms. Sejourne relates the findings of her excavations at Teotihuacan and retells the fundamental myths of the Toltec religion to demonstrate that the doctrine of Quetzalcoatl marked the advent of the soul and spirituality in pre-Columbian life. She presents the Toltecs as unique and magnificent craftsmen and artists who bequeathed their religion to the conquering Aztecs. 104 drawings and photographs bring the ancient culture to life. 192pp. ShP 76

SILVERBERG, ROBERT. **THE MOUND BUILDERS**, $1.50. Large mounds appear in the area between the Southeast and Ohio and the Mississippi Valley which the American Indians claim predate their culture considerably. No one knows who built the mounds or what their function was. This is a very full exploration of all that is known about the mounds and the past research that has been undertaken. The text is a serious study and includes photographs and line drawings. Bibliography, index, 184pp. RaH 70

SPENCE, LEWIS. **ARCANE SECRETS AND OCCULT LORE OF MEXICO AND MAYAN CENTRAL AMERICA**, c$16.80. Subtitled *A Treasury of Magic, Astrology, Witchcraft, Demonology, and Symbolism*, the material here was gleaned from Spence's many years of detailed study of the area. He is not attempting to be sensational and the material presented is intended to be understandable to the non-specialist and sufficiently authoritative to be useful to the anthropologist. In any event it makes for fascinating reading and we do not know of another place where much of this material can be found. Spence was a prolific writer and researcher and all of his books are good. This is a limited edition reprint—which is the reason for its high price. Illustrations, index, 288pp. BIE 30

_____. **THE CIVILIZATION OF ANCIENT MEXICO.** $2.50. A comprehensive account derived totally from original sources covering the following topics: the Mexican peoples; their early history; the settlements; mythology and religion; and the calendar system. The life of the people and their civilization comes to life. Index, biblibography, 127pp. HeR 12

SPINDEN, HERBERT. **A STUDY OF MAYA ART**, $5.95. This book created a field of art history and interpretation. Before Spinden, Maya studies consisted of a few field reports of excavations, some architectural surveys, and the germs of paleography. It was Spinden's contribution to provide the first cartography of the ranges of Maya art, to offer the first understanding of its subject matter, and to supply the first appreciation of the aesthetics that underlie its manifestations. Every aspect of Maya art is considered in detail: from the basic religious and philosophical ideas to town planning and ceramics. While much work has obviously been done in the sixty-odd years since Spinden wrote, much of this simply expands certain areas in Spinden. J. Eric Thompson has supplied an introduction and a long bibliography for this edition. Oversize, index, many plates, 308pp. Dov 75

STEPHENS, JOHN. **INCIDENTS OF TRAVEL IN CENTRAL AMERICA, CHIAPAS, AND YUCATAN**, $8.00/set. Stephens' two expeditions to Mexico and Central America in 1839 and 1841 yielded the first solid information on the culture of the Mayas. In this book and its companion volume, **Incidents of Travel in Yucatan**, he tells the story of his travels to some fifty ruined Maya cities. This two volume set is an unabridged reproduction of the first edition and includes 111 illustrations—highly exact, realistic drawings which show overall views, ground plans of the cities, elevations of palaces and temples, sculpture, carved hieroglyphics, and much else. 898pp. Dov 1841

_____. **INCIDENTS OF TRAVEL IN YUCATAN**, $6.00/set. A companion volume to Stephens' other set. Two volumes, 127 illustrations plus one fold-out plate, maps, 671pp. Dov 1841

THOMPSON, J. ERIC. **MAYA ARCHAEOLOGIST**, $3.95. Dr. Thompson is one of the world's foremost Maya scholars and is a veteran of many archaeological field expeditions to southern Mexico and Central America. Here Thompson relates his experiences during expeditions to the Maya area at a time when the attitudes and patterns of daily life were very similiar to those of the time of the Conquest. Along with an account of the people and the most memorable field studies, the reader also gets some fine descriptions of the early archaeologists. Index, glossary, 295pp. UOk 63

_____. **MAYA HIEROGLYPHIC WRITINGS**, $9.95. The greatest development of Maya civilization was its philosophy of time. So far as it is known, the hieroglyphic texts deal largely with the passage of time and astronomical matters, and the gods and ceremonies associated therewith. In the absence of a Maya equivalent of a Rosetta stone and of an alphabet, progress has been slow in deciphering the glyphs. This is a new, greatly enlarged edition of this definitive work. The text covers the principles of Mayan glyphic writing; the cycle of 260 days; the year of 365 days; methods of recording numbers; the ritualistic and astronomical cycles; the moon; and aids to decipherment. There is a detailed introduction summarizing what is know of Mayan civilization and history, as well as a plethora of technical material. Many drawings of glyphs illustrate the text. Oversize, 400pp+. UOk 60

_____. MAYA HISTORY AND RELIGION, c$7.95. This is a scholarly study of Maya history and religion from the standpoint of ethno-history. Here Thompson seeks to correlate data from colonial writings and observations of the modern Indian with archaeological information in order to extend and clarify the panorama of Maya culture. Topics discussed include Putun Maya expansion in Yucatan and the Pasion drainage, the depopulation of the Maya central area at the time of the Conquest on account of newly introduced diseases, the location of the controversial eastern boundary of the Maya area, trade relations between the highlands and the lowlands, the use of hallucinatory drugs, lowlands Maya religion, and the creation myths of the Maya in relation to those of other Middle American cultures. Bibliography, index, 445pp. UOk 70

_____. THE RISE AND FALL OF MAYA CIVILIZATION, c$6.95. This is an absorbing account of Maya civilization. Dr. Thompson begins with a discussion of the emergence of the culture and goes from there to a description of Maya art and architecture as well as Maya achievements in the fields of astronomy, mathematics, and hieroglyphic writing. One chapter contains sketches of daily life based on careful archaeological and ethnological research. This is a revised version of the highly acclaimed first edition which is enlarged to include recent archaeological discoveries. It contains new and expanded material on the beginnings of Maya culture, political and social organization, settlement patterns, commerce, and their philosophy of time. Thompson writes well and his text is suitable both for the interested layman and the specialist. This is as good a place as we can think of to learn about Maya civilization. Illustrated, bibliography, 343pp. UOk 66

TOMPKINS, PETER. MYSTERIES OF THE MEXICAN PYRAMIDS, c$18.50. This magnificent volume by the author of the highly acclaimed Secrets of the Great Pyramid probes the history, origin, and purpose of the pyramids in the Valley of Mexico, the Yucatan and Central America. Tompkins recounts the history of these structures from their first sightings by the Spaniards in the sixteenth century to the present day. He shows what discoveries have been made and what conclusions can be drawn about how and why the Mayan and Mexican pyramids were built, and what links there might have been between their builders and other historic and prehistoric cultures such as the lost continent of Atlantis. Four hundred illustrations illuminate the text. An important work which we recommend highly. 8x10", index. 320pp. H&R 76

UMLAND, ERIC AND CRAIG. MYSTERY OF THE ANCIENTS, $1.50. This is an exploration of some of the mysteries of the Maya civilization. The Umlands analyze the latest findings of archaeology, lunar research, and geology of the polar ice caps to paint a picture of the Mayas as the remnants of space explorers whose attempts to colonize our planet went awry more than 40,000 years ago. Many of the most noted aspects of the Maya culture are analyzed in the light of this hypothesis and some startling theories are advanced. Interesting food for thought, although the scholarship can by no means be considered careful. Bibliography, index, 160pp. NAL 74

VAILLANT, GEORGE. AZTECS OF MEXICO, $3.95. Vaillant was considered the foremost authority of his day on the early civilization of Mexico and Central America. His field studies included numerous expeditions to the area. This monumental study was first published in 1950 and then totally revised and updated by Vaillant's wife Suzannah in 1962. In this definitive work Dr. Vaillant discusses the historical and cultural background of Aztec civilization, the basic beliefs of Aztec society in relation to government, education and law. At the same time he captures the spirit of the age, and in one fascinating chapter takes the reader on a conducted tour of the capital city of Tenochtitlan at the heyday of its power. Includes almost 100pp of notes, index and bibliography and 64 plates, 427pp. Pen 44

VLAHOS, OLIVIA. NEW WORLD BEGINNINGS—INDIAN CULTURES IN THE AMERICAS, $.95. A simply written anthropological/archaeological chronicle of the Indians who lived in the Americas before Columbus. The peoples discussed range in area from the north of Canada to Tierra del Fuego. Index, bibliography, illustration, 266pp. Faw 70

WATERS, FRANK. MEXICO MYSTIQUE, c$10.00. Ancient Mesoamerican civilization is an area that we have studied in depth and we have read most of the literature. This is far and away the most exciting study we've seen. Part I, The History, gives a brief summary of the primary cultures. The major section, Part II, The Myths, extends the limit of history into the immeasurable depths of mythology expressed in hermetic myths, religious symbols, astronomical cycles, and mathematical computations of time far beyond our comprehension. Two main exploratory approaches have been made into this realm: one into the hermetic myth of Quetzalcoatl, so concerned with the meaning of space; and the other with the Mayan concept of time. Here is offered an interpretation of the present world cycle whose beginning was projected to 3113 BC and whose end was predicted to be AD 2011. Waters also explores in depth the creation and destruction of the four previous world cycles and their suns and includes a good summary of the myth of Atlantis as it relates to Mesoamerica. An especially fascinating section, The Voyage of Venus Through Hell, details one of these creation myths and also explores the relation of Quetzalcoatl to Venus. Further along he delves deeply into the images and symbols of this civilization and their esoteric meanings. The final section on time is perhaps the most fascinating of all. The calendric and astrological systems are studied along with astronomical and cosmological ideas and the whole is fitted into an exploration of the present Great Cycle and the coming Sixth World—or Age of Aquarius. Most of Waters' examples and references are well documented and an excellent bibliography and notes are included, along with an index. Highly recommended. 326pp. Swa 75

WILKINS, HAROLD. MYSTERIES OF ANCIENT SOUTH AMERICA, $2.95. This is an interesting account which ranges over all the pre-Columbian civilizations in an informal

manner, relating some of the most interesting tales and legends, and discussing the most important theories and explorers. Nothing is analyzed in detail, and the reader can get a feeling for the culture without being overwhelmed by information. We would have liked a bit more depth to the narration and a great deal more organization though. Bibliography, index, 216pp. CiP 56

WOLF, ERIC. SONS OF THE SHAKING EARTH, $2.45. A study of the people of Mexico and Guatemala: their land, history, and culture. The narrative reads well as the text is illustrated throughout. This is the best book we know of to read to get an idea of the subject. Wolf is a noted anthropologist and he provides extensive references and a long index. Recommended. 314pp. UCh 59

ANCIENT BRITAIN

ALCOCK, LESLIE. ARTHUR'S BRITAIN, $5.95 This book assembles all that is known or can be deduced about life between the fourth and seventh centuries in Celtic Britain. Alcock is a noted archaeologist who directed the excavations at Cadbury Castle in Somerset, the site originally identified with Camelot. Extensive bibliography, illustrations. 415pp., Pen 73

ASHE, GEOFFREY. CAMELOT AND THE VISION OF ALBION, $4.10. Drawing on varied researches, and on the insight embodied in William Blake's symbol of the shadowy Giant Albion behind Arthur, the author goes into the deeper psychological basis that underlies the story of the enchanted King, his city Camelot, his mysterious departure to Avalon, his promised return. The inquiry starts from the facts discovered in the Cadbury/Camelot excavation and moves on to the world of gods and mortals. 233pp. Pan 71

_____. KING ARTHUR'S AVALON, $3.25. Subtitled The Story of Glastonbury, this is a very readable historical recreation of the Glastonbury area: its early years as a cultural site, its classical period and connections with Arthur and his court. A great deal of space is devoted to the quest for the Grail and the Grail legend. Ashe presents many of the most common speculations and formulates his own hypothesis. The book reads well and is more historical than archaeological. Illustrations, bibliography, index, 315pp. Fon 57

_____, ed. THE QUEST FOR ARTHUR'S BRITAIN, $5.30. A collection of essays by noted archaeologists and scholars which examines the historical foundations of the Arthurian tradition, and then, in five chapters, presents the results of excavations to date at Cadbury, Tintagel, Glastonbury and less-known places. This is the most complete account available of western Britain between AD 400 and 600. Many illustrations, 238pp. Pal 71

BAIN, GEORGE. CELTIC ART, $4.00. The construction principles of Celtic art were rediscovered in the middle of this century by Bain. Until then the intricate knots, interlacements and spirals used in illuminating Celtic literature and in decorating craftwork and jewelry seemed almost impossible. In this pioneering work he shows how simple principles, no more difficult than those used in needlepoint, were used to create some of the finest artistic works ever seen. Step-by-step procedures carefully introduce the rules and method of Celtic knot work and the well-known design from the great manuscripts and stone work. Altogether over 225 different patterns are presented, with modification suggestions, 110 artifacts, and a great number of letters. Explanatory material accompanies the illustrations. Oversize, 159pp. Dov 51

BORD, JANET AND COLIN. MYSTERIOUS BRITAIN, c$14.95. A fascinating, lavishly illustrated account of the archaeological remains in England, Wales, Scotland, and Ireland. The oversize full page photographs and commentary suggest many unsuspected properties in ancient sites. Bibliography, 262pp. Dou 73

BRANSTON, BRIAN. THE LOST GODS OF ENGLAND, c$10.00. The Old English gods still around each week from Sunday to Friday—Sun, Moon, Tiw, Woden, Thunor, and Frig—are described in this book illustrated with many fine photographs. The author points out the meaning the northern deities had for the early Anglo-Saxons, how Christianity did and did not accept the customs associated with these older gods, and how, to a certain degree, these early beliefs affect our outlook today. This is an excellent study. 216pp. Oxf 74

CHADWICK, NORA. THE CELTS, $3.25. Describes the rise and spread of the Celts and their arrival in the British Isles, and includes a good amount of material on their religion, art and literature. 301pp. Pen 70

COOKE, GRACE AND IVAN. THE LIGHT IN BRITAIN, c$5.00. Describes what was revealed when Grace Cooke, a highly developed clairvoyant, used her faculty to uncover some of the mysteries of such prehistoric centers as Stonehenge, Avebury and Silbury Hill. It reveals the spiritual development of the ancient British people. 118pp. WET 71

COX, R.H. THE GREEN ROADS OF ENGLAND, c$11.30. In this book, originally published in 1914, strong evidence is produced to show that earthworks and forts were arranged systematically along watersheds and were connected by a fully developed system of travel-ways throughout the country. All the important sites play their part in this book, which is lavishly illustrated with pictures, maps and diagrams. 220pp. GaP

HADINGHAM, EVAN. **ANCIENT CARVING IN BRITAIN**, c$16.00. Scattered all over the countryside of Britain are hundreds of mysterious prehistoric rock carvings—strange abstract circles, branching lines, hollows and zig-zags. The puzzle of the extraordinary carvings (who made them and why?) is explored in this profusely illustrated oversize book, which is the first to be published on the subject since 1865. This book is an attempt to introduce the subject to the general reader in an easily understood form, with full reference to where original technical papers and the carvings themselves can be found. It presents some of the abundant evidence that the meaning of these ancient signs and symbols cannot be resolved by a single theory or solution, despite the attempts of so many scholars and students to impose one. Hadingham has travelled extensively, making photographs and rubbings of the carvings at firsthand, and many illustrations are reproduced here. Notes, bibliography, index, 130pp. GaP 74

_____. **CIRCLES AND STANDING STONES**, $4.95. Here Hadingham explores the megalith mysteries of early Britain from every possible angle. He summarizes the recent archaeological studies of Gerald Hawkins, Alexander Thom, Colin Renfrew, and others, and he presents his own review of the work of hundreds of local archaeologists and antiquarians. Hadingham also offers his own observations based on extensive field studies, augmented by hundreds of his drawings, maps and photographs. This is a fascinating exploration of the most important sites and the culture of early Britain. The reader does not have to have any background in the field to enjoy the book. Oversize, bibliography, index, 247pp. Dou 75

HATT, JEAN-JACQUES. **CELTS AND GALLO-ROMANS**, c$26 20. A very detailed profusely illustrated study of Celtic and Gallic archaeology. Dr. Hatt has been deeply involved in recent research and he is very qualified to present this account which begins with a study of the history of archaeological research in France and goes from there to an exploration of the methods and techniques employed by archaeologists. The bulk of the volume is devoted to an in depth analysis of the civilizations in the area from the dawn of recorded time to the fifth century AD. In addition to analyses of the cultural achievements of the people, sections are also devoted to religion, gods, and mythology. The text includes a chronological table, notes, bibliography, index, and maps. 333pp. Nag 70

HAWKINS, GERALD. **STONEHENGE DECODED**, $2.45. Hawkins is an astronomer who has attempted to decode the monument at Stonehenge through the use of a computer. His thesis is that Stonehenge was actually a sophisticated astronomical observatory, rather than a Druid temple as is commonly believed. Tables, illustrations and photographs supplement the text and Hawkins provides a good bibliography. 202pp. Del 65

MARKALE, J. **WOMEN OF THE CELTS**, c$17.95. This is a very thorough review of the title subject. The major portion of the text is a detailed exploration of women in Celtic mythology. In addition there is a survey of women in Celtic societies including information on social life, marriage, sexual liberation, and love. Much of the mythology cited and liberally quoted here is not generally well known. The presentation is well written and should be of great interest to those seeking deeper insights into Celtic society and mythology and the role of women in that society. Notes, index, 315pp. Crc 75

MERRY, ELEANOR. **THE FLAMING DOOR**, c$12.25. Subtitled *A Preliminary Study of the Mission of the Celtic Folk-Soul by Means of Legends and Myths*, this is one of the few contemporary books to delve at length into the Celts. All of the important myths are traced at length and the main gods, goddesses, and saints are discussed. Special attention is devoted to the beautiful legends of the Cauldron of Ceridwen, of Odrun, of St. Columbia, and of the Rose and the Lily. The myths and legends are seen as archetypes of initiation; and other chapters are devoted to Druidic Science and the Bards. The material is divided into pre-Christian and Christian times and covers the period through the twelfth century. The text also includes 66 illustrations, some in color. Index, 426pp. NKB 62

MICHELL, JOHN. **THE VIEW OVER ATLANTIS**, $4.10. We all live within the ruins of an ancient structure, whose vast size has hitherto rendered it invisible. The entire surface of the earth is marked with traces of a gigantic work of prehistoric engineering, the remains of a once universal system of natural magic, involving the use of polar magnetism together with another positive force related to solar energy. This book contains evidence to support these conclusions. In particular, it describes a system of leys or lines laid out throughout the British Isles connecting religious and *power* sites. Numerous drawings and photographs illustrate the text. The physical evidence is pretty clear, and while Michell's hypothesis as to the meaning is speculative, it makes sense to us. We recommend this book to all who seek a greater understanding of the make-up of the cosmos. 211pp. SBL 72

NIEL, FERNAND. **THE MYSTERIES OF STONEHENGE**, $1.75. *There have been hundreds of works written on Stonehenge since the sixteenth century when the famous architect Inigo Jones became fascinated by Stonehenge and wrote the first know comprehensive study of it, illustrated with drawings that included an attempt to depict its original state. Many questions have been given satisfactory answers, precise plans have been drawn, intelligent and methodical excavations have been carried out, and a number of discoveries*

have been made, some of them sensational .... But important questions still remain unanswered, for one of the most bewildering aspects of that enigmatic structure is its uniqueness. Nowhere else in the world is there anything comparable to it....I have spent 30 entire days studying Stonehenge at the site itself. Among other things, I have verified its measurements and alignments. But although my own studies were one of the factors that prompted me to write this book, it is based to a large extent on the great works of British scientists....Most of the great works on Stonehenge contain many plans, diagrams, maps, and drawings to which the reader is often referred. This book ...follows that rule. —from the foreword. This is a well-written, fascinating account. Niel is thorough in his treatment and he introduces material not readily found in other sources. This is a serious study which should be appreciated by all who are fascinated by ancient archaeology. Niel sets the stage, reviews the findings of others, and then advances his own evidence and conclusions. 208pp. Avo 75

Tile from Chertsey Abbey

O'BRIEN, HENRY. **ATLANTIS IN IRELAND**, $6.95. Originally titled **The Round Towers of Ireland**, this volume should be of interest to those who seek a better understanding of the life and culture of the Druids, including their monuments and religious cults. The book has been long out of print and only recently reprinted. It does not read particularly well and many of the ideas advanced have been disputed by later scholars. Nevertheless, it remains an intriguing study that seems to be a work of fairly good scholarship. Illustrations, notes, 524pp. Mul 1834

PIGGOT, STUART. **THE DRUIDS**, $2.25. Druidism, according to traditional belief, was the religion of the Celts of pre-Roman Gaul and Britain, among whom the Druids were the priestly class. References to Druids by Greek and Roman writers provide much of the limited knowledge we have of their nature and characteristics, but this has been supplemented by archaeological evidence of early Celtic society. This is an interesting synoptic treatment of the source material in the area. Piggott's aim is to present the Druids to the general reader, and this he does in a good manner. Includes Notes on the text and the plates, illustrations, bibliography, index. 236pp. Pen 74

RIMMER, ALFRED. **ANCIENT STONE CROSSES OF ENGLAND**, c$8.50. The most complete description available of their sites and appearances, first published in 1875. 72 woodcuts, 176pp. GaP 73

ROSS, ANNE. **THE PAGAN CELTS**, c$7.55. By piecing together archaeological discoveries, classical references and the rural vernacular literature of Ireland, Ms. Ross recreates the life of the early Celts. She outlines the structure of the society and describes their appearance and their activities. She also reviews their complex religious beliefs and practices; their temples and shrines, festivals and rites, deities and cults, and their ideas about the afterlife. Examples of Celtic art are scattered throughout the book. The text is written in a conversational style and the reader does get a good feeling for the times from the author's presentation. Notes, index, bibliography, 224pp. Put 70

SCREETON, PAUL. **QUICKSILVER HERITAGE**, $11.75. Screeton is the editor and publisher of **The Ley Hunter**, an English publication devoted solely to ley lines throughout the world. Here he builds on the earlier work of Watkins and Michell in presenting a comprehensive study embracing leys, prehistoric monuments, terrestrial zodiacs, astronomy, astrology, alchemy, and spiritual physics. The ley system is a network of straight lines—age-old trackways and paths of a subtle energy—which run across Britain and other parts of the world. This is a fascinating study for all who are interested in understanding the magnetic and electric properties of the earth and learning how the ancients used these forces and how they can be applied today. Includes notes and references. Index, 304pp. Put 70

SHARKEY, JOHN. **CELTIC MYSTERIES**, $5.95. The last tribal culture in Europe was that of the Celtic lands, whose landscape and traditions hold echoes of the ancient religion of nature, with its emphasis on the fairy and the spirit world and its symbols of death and rebirth. The Mysteries begin in the frenzy of battle, where the hero is transfigured and the god appears; or a ghostly circle of stones left by an unknown people; or in the mystic center of the Celtic cross; or in the stone heads of Gaul and Ireland, which face both ways. The ancient oral tradition that perpetuated the laws, legends and tribal teachings through the trained memories of a group of poets and priests made the act of writing unnecessary.

And, much like the prohibitions laid on the Celtic warrior heroes, which predestined their lives and actions, the taboo on writing continued as long as the old religion lasted. Therefore it is in pictures of Celtic art, artifacts, and religious sites that the culture comes the clearest. And this volume, part of Avon's beautiful *Art and Cosmos* series, is made up of 117 illustrations, 24 in color. Each of the plates is fully described and the book begins with an excellent introduction summing up what is known of the Celtic mysteries and setting the stage for the art that follows. Oversize, 96pp. Avo

SPENCE, LEWIS. **THE HISTORY AND ORIGINS OF DRUIDISM**, c$7.95. An examination of the origins and practices of the Druids in past centuries. Druidic theology, ritual, places of worship and priesthood activities are discussed as well as their magical practices. Those occult practices definitely revealed to be of Druidic origin are described extensively. 178pp. Wei 49

THOM, A. **MEGALITHIC LUNAR OBSERVATORIES**, c$14.10. A technical study which shows that the methods used by Megalithic man for astronomical observations were more elaborate than was formerly believed. Descriptions are given of 35 lunar and solar sites in Britain from which accurate declinations can be obtained. Analysis of these declinations yields values of the Moon's orbital inclination, parallax, etc., that are in remarkable agreement with modern values. The way in which the Megalithic observers extrapolated the turning values of the declination, which could not in general be observed directly, is shown by the remains at several sites. The book includes details of the astronomical background necessary for an understanding of the Moon's movements. Thom is a very careful researcher and his work is highly thought of. Index, notes, and many detailed drawings, maps, and graphs. Oxf 73

_____. **MEGALITHIC SITES IN BRITAIN**, c$17.50. This book is the result of a study of 500 Megalithic sites in Britain. Thom establishes the megalithic yard and uses it to elucidate the geometry of the rings, ellipses and other compound shapes that the Megalithic erectors used. He shows astronomically that a sophisticated solar calendar was in use, and that extensive observations of the Moon were made in its four limiting positions. Typical surveys of many sites show the kind of material on which the author's conclusions are based, and several introductory chapters are devoted to such aspects of statistics, mathematics, and astronomy as are necessary to an understanding of the analysis. The material is highly technical and the text includes a profusion of line drawings, charts and diagrams. Index, 174pp. Oxf 67

THOMAS, CHARLES. **BRITAIN AND IRELAND IN EARLY CHRISTIAN TIMES, AD 400–800**, $3.95. The four centuries between the end of the Roman occupation and the first Viking raids are the most obscure in British history. Professor Thomas here recreates this era, based on his own research and personal insights. He discusses migration and settlement, the rise of Christianity, and the spread of spoken and written languages and covers development throughout the British Isles, including Ireland, with special stress on the Celtic areas. The text is supported by 110 plates, 19 in color, drawings and maps, and includes a topically organized bibliography and an index. 144pp. MGH 71

WILDMAN, S.G. **PICTURES ON THE HILLS**, c$11.30. A survey in words and photographs of those mysterious figures of man and animals carved onto hillsides, with possible explanations of their origins and meaning. Many illustrations. GaP 74

WRIGHT, DUDLEY. **DRUIDISM**, c$10.00. Druids were members of a pre-Christian religious order of the ancient Celts of Gaul, Ireland and Britain. The Romans massacred them in a wholesale slaughter during their conquest because they felt that the Druids were heathens performing human sacrificial ceremonies and they would interrupt the smooth running of the state. This book is a concise history of the Druids which describes their origins, their beliefs, their ceremonies, festivals, and customs, their magic and their affinity with other religions. Many legends about druidical temples have come down to us, some of which are described here. This is a photographic reprint of the 1924 edition. Illustrations, bibliography, index, 192pp. EPG 74

ANCIENT EGYPT

ALDRED, CYRIL. **AKHENATEN**, $4.10. The Pharaoh Akhenaten, who reigned in the fourteenth century BC, imposed a monotheistic cult of sun-worship and caused a convulsion in Egyptian society. This is the most complete study of the subject in English and is considered the standard work. Includes extensive plates (some in color), notes, bibliography, and index. 222pp. SBL 68

_____. **ART IN ANCIENT EGYPT—OLD KINGDOM**, $4.25. It was during the Old Kingdom, 3200–2300 BC, that the conventions that dominated Egyptian art for 2,000 years were established. In this concise study, Aldred, Keeper of Art and Archaeology in the Royal Scottish Museum, examines the motives behind Egyptian art and traces the development of statuary defining the changes that took place. Seventy-two illustrations, each fully annotated. 119pp. Tnt 49

_____. **ART IN ANCIENT EGYPT—MIDDLE KINGDOM**, $4.25. The art of the Middle Kingdom, 2300–1500 BC, is austere. Aldred analyzes the character of art during the period, relating the stylistic changes to developments in the social, religious and political background. Eighty-three illustrations, each with a detailed commentary. 147pp. Tnt 50

_____. **ART IN ANCIENT EGYPT—NEW KINGDOM**, $5.25. Same format as the earlier works—this time with 175 illustrations and detailed commentary. 268pp. Tnt 72

_____. **EGYPT TO THE END OF THE OLD KINGDOM**, $3.95. A study of the development of Egyptian civilization from its earliest beginnings to the end of the Old Kingdom. It includes over 130 plates (about one-third of which are in color) and covers every aspect of the culture of the period. The text is chronologically arranged. Bibliography, index, 143pp. MGH 65

_____. **TUTANKHAMUN'S EGYPT**, $3.95. When the boy Tut-ankh-amun came to the throne of his ancestors about the year 1362 BC, Egypt had already existed as a kingdom for over 1700 years with a characteristic culture which, however, had adapted itself to the changed conditions of the Late Bronze Age. The great stone pyramids of Giza, Sakkarah, and Dahshur had by then fallen into ruins, their mortuary cults had lapsed and they were visited only by sightseers looking at the past. Despite all this the Egyptians buried Tut-ankh-amun with a wealth of treasure which was still intact when the tomb was discovered in 1922. This volume is a profusely illustrated account of life in Tutankhamun's Egypt, based on a series of television programs developed for the BBC. Oversize, 80pp. BBC 72

ALLEN, THOMAS, tr. **THE BOOK OF THE DEAD**, c$26.90. This is a very exacting translation of the **Book of the Dead** based on Empire manuscripts, rather than later copies. The translation is in a form which does not make for easy perusal—however all scholars who wish to integrate the newest findings in Egyptology into their understanding of the **Book of the Dead** should be interested in this text. The spells are arranged in order and footnotes indicate the texts actually followed. Over 50pp of indices are included. Virtually no introductory or explanatory material is included. Oversize, 361pp. UCh 74

BAROCAS, CLAUDIO. **EGYPT**, c$19.95. A monumental work, 12x16". Illuminating the text are 115 full-color illustrations, as well as numerous extracts from ancient texts which describe all aspects of Egyptian life. Barocas is a noted Egyptologist and his commentary greatly adds to our understanding. 192pp. G&D 72

BENAVIDES, RODOLFO. **DRAMATIC PROPHECIES OF THE GREAT PYRAMID**, $6.00. A personal interpretation of the meaning, in terms of prophecy, of the symbols found in the Great Pyramid of Gizeh. The author spent years of intensive research and scientific investigation-calculation to make the predictions of dire circumstance that live in these pages. Benavides predicts that a transformation of humanity will take place after the destruction. 475pp. EMU 61

BLEEKER, C.J. **EGYPTIAN FESTIVALS**, c$31.75. General background information followed by a detailed study of each of the most important festivals of ancient Egypt. A very scholarly study with notes, bibliography, and index. 158pp. Bri 67

_____. **HATHOR AND THOTH**, c$22.00. Hathor and Thoth are typical exponents of the religion of ancient Egypt. Hathor represents creative life; Thoth is the wise god who gives laws to gods and mortals, who maintains the world order and restores harmony. This is a very detailed study of the two gods, based on ancient texts and on the most recent studies. The gods are discussed in each of their aspects and in the process the reader gets a good feeling for the religion and culture of the ancient Egyptians. A plethora of notes accompany the text. Index, 171pp. Bri 73

BREASTED, JAMES. **THE DAWN OF CONSCIENCE**, $2.98. A detailed philosophical look at the origins of the *moral sentiments of civilized society* by this pioneering Egyptologist. It begins with the emergence of moral ideas from nature worship and culminates in the tragic effort of the Pharaoh Ikhnaton to usher in a new age in 2000 BC. A scholarly historical study. Illustrations, 431pp. Scr 33

_____. **A HISTORY OF EGYPT: FROM THE EARLIEST TIMES TO THE PERSIAN CONQUEST**, c$20.25. This is accepted as the standard history of the ancient Egyptians. Every aspect of the civilization and the dynastic rulers is examined in great detail by Breasted, a noted Orientalist. The text is very readable and is illustrated with over 200 illustrations and maps. 636pp. Scr 09

BROMAGE, BERNARD. **OCCULT ARTS OF ANCIENT EGYPT**, c$6.95. The author reveals some of the esoteric practices of Egyptian priests and magicians, and explains how their magic really worked. 204pp. Wei 53

BRUNTON, PAUL. **A SEARCH IN SECRET EGYPT**, $3.50. The author reveals the wondrous events of his journey through Egypt. Included in the narrative are his mystical experience inside the Great Pyramid at night and meetings with seers, dervishes, fakirs and magicians of modern Egypt. There is a vivid portrayal of the secret mysteries and initiatory rites of the ancient Egyptians. 287pp. Wei 35

BUDGE, E.A. WALLIS. **THE EGYPTIAN BOOK OF THE DEAD**, c$9.95/4.95. This is a copy of the **Egyptian Book of the Dead**, written about 1500 B.C. for Ani, Royal Scribe of Thebes. The text embodies a ritual to be performed for the dead, with detailed instructions for the behavior of the disembodied spirit in the *Land of the Gods*. This work, like the **Tibetan Book of the Dead**, is considered a guidebook to initiatory practices rather than death and it served as the most important repository of religious authority for over 3000 years. Reproduced in full here are a clear copy of the Egyptian hieroglyphs, an inter-linear transliteration of their sounds, a word-for word translation, a more flowing trans-creation, and a detailed 150 page introduction. 527pp. Dov 67

_____. THE EGYPTIAN HEAVEN AND HELL, $3.45. A recently reprinted explanation of the Guides to the Other World: The Theban Book of the Dead, The Book of Two Ways, The Book of What is in the Underworld (The Am-Taut) and The Book of Gates. Budge includes explanatory material in addition to translations of the texts. Index, 212pp. OpC 74

_____. EGYPTIAN LANGUAGE, c$5.00. A detailed study. Dov

_____. EGYPTIAN MAGIC, $2.50. Covers the role of magic in Egyptian religion, the use of wax images and amulets, magical pictures and formulas. Combined with a study of the mythological role of magicians, this volume presents a comprehensive overview of the Egyptian hermetic system. 234pp. Dov 01

_____. EGYPTIAN RELIGION, c$5.95. A study of the fundamental religious ideas and beliefs, combined with serious speculation about its inception. Budge shows that the ideas of immortality and resurrection were the crux of Egyptian social and religious life for thousand of years. 198pp. UnB 1900

_____. THE GODS OF THE EGYPTIANS, $10.00/set. Information on the origins of the ancient religions, its peculiarly Egyptian aspects, evolution of cults, rites and gods, the cult of Osiris; the Book of the Dead; detailed descriptions of all the Gods and mythological figures, and much other wisdom that has been discovered in mummy cases or written on tomb walls. The text is profusely illustrated with many reproductions of tomb and mummy-case paintings, and includes some full texts with both hieroglyphs and translation. 2 volumes, 956pp. Dov 04

_____. A HISTORY OF EGYPT, c$51.75. *The narrative begins with an account of Egypt and her people in the latter part of the Neolithic Period and ends with the description of her conquest by the Romans under Caesar, BC 30 . . . . Each volume describes a certain period of Egyptian history, and is divided into chapters each of which treats of a dynasty, or group of dynasties, or contains a summary of the principal characteristics with which the volume is concerned. The reign of each king is described . . . , wherein will be found not only an enumeration of the bare facts of history, but also extracts from papyri and stela and other Egyptian documents, which serve to illustrate the condition of his rule. Besides such extracts there have been added a number of passages from the works of Herodotus, Diodorus, and other classical writers, which supplement the bald statements of the hieroglyphic inscriptions and supply interesting and often important information about Egypt and the Egyptians, not only whilst they were ruled by their native Pharaohs, but also whilst the country was under the domination of the Assyrians, Persians, Macedonians, and other conquerors.* —from the Preface. This is a rare work, in four volumes, by the pioneering Egyptologist and can be considered a definitive study. Notes, bibliography, index, 125 illustrations, 1072pp. Atp 68

_____. THE MUMMY, $3.95. Describes in detail the entire tradition of burial among the Egyptians, illuminating much of the ancient Egyptian culture in the process. The intricacies of mummifying are described and profusely illustrated with many examples of Egyptian hieroglyphics and accurate renderings of idols and god figures as well as a reproduction of the Rosetta Stone. 404pp. McM 72

_____. OSIRIS AND THE EGYPTIAN RESURRECTION, $10.00/set. Osiris, the king, was slain by his brother Seth, dismembered, scattered, then gathered up and reconstituted by his wife Isis and finally placed in the underworld as lord and judge of the dead (and thus of the initiates). He was worshipped in Egypt throughout the entire period of its civilization and elements of Osiris-worship still exist today. This is the most thorough explanation ever offered of Osirism. Budge goes directly to numerous Egyptian texts and makes use of the writings of classical authors. Includes many translations of Pyramid texts (often with the original hieroglyphs) and illustrations. 2 volumes, 873pp. Dov 11

BURGOYNE, THOMAS. THE LIGHT OF EGYPT, $10.00/set. For nearly twenty years the author was deeply engaged investigating the hidden realms of occult force. He was induced to place the general results of these researches into a series of lessons for private occult study. The whole, when completed, presents the dual aspects of occult lore as seen and realized in the soul and the stars, corresponding to the microcosm and the macrocosm of ancient Egypt and Chaldea, and thus giving a brief epitome of Hermetic philosophy as taught by the Hermetic Brotherhood of Luxor, Egypt. 2 volumes. 501pp. APP 63

CHAMPDOR, ALBERT. THE BOOK OF THE DEAD, $10.00. A very readable translation, based on the same texts as Budge's but done by a Frenchman who was considerably more learned in the esoteric aspects of the ancient text. Champdor also introduces new material, discovered since Budge's classic 1898 translation. Includes interpretive and descriptive material and over sixty pages of beautifully reproduced illustrations as well as many illustrations in the text itself. If you can afford it we recommend this text rather than Budge's. Translated from the French by Faubion Bowers. 180pp. G&P 66

CHAMPOLLION, JACQUES. THE WORLD OF THE EGYPTIANS, c$3.95. See the WORLD OF ANCIENT CIVILIZATIONS SERIES in Ancient Civilizations section.

CLAYSON, RODMAN R. EGYPT'S ANCIENT HERITAGE, c$6.50. Information is included in such areas as their religious life, arts and science, medicine and the Egyptian social and family life. 221pp. Amo 71

COTTRELL, LEONARD. THE LOST PHARAOHS, $2.25. An excellent, quite readable study of ancient Egypt, recreating the times vividly and discussing the origin of the civilization and the meaning of its monuments. The discoveries of archaeologists are also re-

viewed. All in all, this is as good an introduction to ancient Egypt as any book we know of. The book also includes many illustrations and selected translations. Bibliography, index, 250pp. G&D 61

DESROCHES-NOBLECOURT, CHRISTIANE. TUTANKHAMEN, $8.95. There is a plethora of books on Tutankhamen. This is the most comprehensive one—both in terms of the number of plates (75 color and 187 black-and-white) and the excellence of the textual material. The author and the photographer, F.L. Kennett, reconstruct the king's early life, the ceremony of his coronation and the years of his reign, and interpret the objects found in the burial treasure. Index, 312pp. NYG 63

DURDIN-ROBERTSON, LAWRENCE. THE GODDESSES OF CHALDEA, SYRIA, AND EGYPT, $5.00. A detailed account, arranged by area, but not alphabetically within the areas giving the following information: name, etymology, genealogy, offices and titles, associated places, and folklore and legends about the individual. An extensive index helps somewhat to relieve the confusion over the lack of alphabetical order among the entries (although the index itself is not always 100% accurate). 440pp. Des 75

EDWARDS, I.E.S. THE PYRAMIDS OF EGYPT, $3.50. Edwards is Keeper of Egyptian Antiquities at the British Museum. This is a description of some of the principal features of the most important pyramids. The final chapter discusses the construction methods used and the motives behind their construction. A very detailed account, revised and updated from the original 1947 edition. Many illustrations, bibliography, index, 319pp. Pen 72

_____. THE TREASURES OF TUTANKHAMUN, c$14.00. An annotated catalog of an exhibition of Tutankhamun treasures held at the British Museum in 1972. Includes color and black and white illustrations as well as extensive commentary on the personal and ritual possessions. Vik 72

ERMAN, ADOLF. THE ANCIENT EGYPTIANS: A SOURCEBOOK OF THEIR WRITING, $4.35. A superlative way of determining the temperament and psychological features of the early Egyptians is through the remains of their art and architecture. Now their literature gives us an even more intimate picture of their life and character. Hundreds of contributions covering a large area of subjects. 265pp. H&R 66

_____. LIFE IN ANCIENT EGYPT, $5.00. A profusely illustrated account, covering every aspect of the subject. This is the definitive work. Fascinating reading. 570pp. Dov 71

FAIRSERVIS, WALTER. ANCIENT KINGDOMS OF THE NILE, $1.50. The Nile flows through Northern Africa into the Mediterranean and all along its banks stand monuments. In this volume a noted archaeologist and anthropologist describes the stone records of many civilizations as he plots the historic course of the river from the empires of the Pharaohs in Egypt to the British Empire in the Sudan. The account reads well and is illustrated with diagrams, maps, and photographs. Notes, index, bibliography, 269pp. NAL 62

FAKHRY, AHMED. THE PYRAMIDS, $3.25. Fakhry was professor of ancient history at Cairo University. His account of the pyramids is both a good readable academic study combining the different viewpoints of the archaeologist, the religious historian, the engineer, the architect, the mathematical expert, and the ordinary individual. The sequence of the pyramids is treated historically, from the first essentially uncomplicated structures, through the grandeur of the finest examples, to the less lavish monuments at the end of the era. The dry, technical material is alleviated by excerpts from medieval historians or anecdotes about ancient personages and modern excavators. Many illustrations and diagrams are included. Index, 272pp. UCh 69

FORD, S.H. GREAT PYRAMID OF EGYPT, $4.00. A late nineteenth century interpretation of Piazzi Smyth's pioneering scientific work. Also includes quotes from and references to numerous other scientific and historical accounts. Illustrations. 208pp. HeR 73

GARDINER, SIR ALAN. EGYPT OF THE PHARAOHS, $3.95. An authoritative account which traces the social and economic history as well as the dynasties from the earliest times down to Alexander the Great. Includes plates and maps. 482pp. Oxf 61

_____. EGYPTIAN GRAMMAR, c$15.00. A scholarly introduction to the study of hieroglyphs. Includes vocabularies and exercises. Oversize, 482pp. Oxf 57

GHALIOUNGUI, PAUL. THE HOUSE OF LIFE: MAGIC AND MEDICAL SCIENCES IN ANCIENT EGYPT, c$28.00. A newly revised edition of the author's study of the medical history of Egypt—from gynecology and obstetrics to burial and embalming. The author is a former professor at the Faculty of Medicine of Ain Shams in Cairo. Over 50 illustrations. Wit 75

GRANT, JOAN. EYES OF HORUS, $2.25. Joan Grant became aware as a child of her uncanny gift of *far memory*—the ability to recall in detail previous incarnations, both male and female, in other centuries and other lands. Her books, published and reviewed as historical novels, have been highly praised for their extraordinary vividness and rich detail, and are in fact the author's memories of her earlier lives. Her books are very popular. See the Mysticism section for more of them and for her autobiography. This volume is the story of her life as a young prince devoted to restoring the rule of decency in Egypt's most corrupt age. 406pp. Crg 42

_____. LORD OF THE HORIZON, $1.95. A young prince and his wife raise the son of the Pharaoh according to the benevolent and progressive tenets of Ra during a time of violence and corruption. 255pp. Crg 44

_____. SO MOSES WAS BORN, $1.75. The story of the Pharaoh's court during the early years of Moses' life and of Moses' upbringing by the brother of the Pharaoh. 224pp. Crg 52

GRIFFITH, F. and HERBERT THOMPSON, eds. **THE LEYDEN PAPYRUS**, $2.50. This papyrus is an ancient Egyptian manuscript that dates from around the beginning of the Christian era. It was probably the textbook of a practicing sorcerer in Egypt and contains many spells, incantations, and other forms of magic. In addition to purely native elements involving the gods, the manuscript shows the influence of Gnostic beliefs, and Greek and other magical traditions. A transliteration of the script is printed on facing pages with a complete translation, which is copiously supplied with explanatory footnotes and there is also a long introduction. 212pp. Dov 74

HAICH, ELISABETH . **INITIATION**, $5.00. Ms. Haich is a European yoga teacher. **Initiation** is an autobiographical novel bringing together her present life story, with the events and experiences that contributed to her spiritual growth, and vivid recollections of her earlier life experiences as a young priestess in ancient Egypt. A story within a story emerges, describing in detail how she is prepared for initiation by the High Priest, who leads her, step by step, to an understanding of the ultimate mysteries. **Initiation** can be appreciated and enjoyed at many levels. It is a moving novel and is also the best presentation of the cosmic view of the Egyptians that we know of. The book is one of the favorites of many of the people who work here and has helped us to understand many difficult concepts. Excellent diagrams illustrate the work. Highly recommended. 366pp. Spe 65

HALL, MANLY P. **FREEMASONRY OF THE ANCIENT EGYPTIANS**, c$6.75. An effort to interpret the Freemasonry of the ancient Egyptians as set forth in the teachings of the State Mysteries, an exalted doctrine relating to the life, death, and resurrection of man. Among the subjects discussed are Egyptian magic, the Osirian Cycle, the secret doctrine of Egypt, and the initiation of Plato. See Mysticism section for more on M.P. Hall. 366pp. PRS 65

HARRIS, J.R., ed. **THE LEGACY OF EGYPT**, c$10.00. This is an excellent collection of scholarly essays covering the following topics: The Calendars and Chronology; Mathematics and Astronomy; The Canonical Tradition; Technology and Materials; Medicine; Mystery, Myth and Magic; The Hieroglyphic Tradition; Language and Writing; Literature; Egypt and Israel; The Concept of Law in Ancient Egypt; Graeco-Roman Egypt; The Greek Papyri; Christian and Coptic Egypt; The Legacy to Africa; and The Contribution to Islam. The essays read well, in general, and include notes and bibliography, and there is an index and plates. 534pp. Oxf 71

HARRIS, JAMES and KENT WEEKS. **X-RAYING THE PHARAOHS**, $4.95. An account of the University of Michigan School of Dentistry's examination and analysis of a collection of mummies housed in the Egyptian Museum in Cairo. Written in nontechnical terms and well illustrated, the work provides an understanding of the civilization of ancient Egypt which is not available by any other means. A great deal of background information on the pharaohs and their times is included. Notes, index. 194pp. Scr 73

HERMES

CHAMBERS, JOHN D., tr. **THE DIVINE PYMANDER AND OTHER WRITINGS OF HERMES TRISMEGISTUS**, $3.95. Hermes was considered to be the impersonation of the religion, art, learning, and sacerdotal discipline of the Egyptian priesthood. This is the translation from the original Greek of a number of discourses attributed to Hermes. 155pp. Wei 72

EVERARD, DR. **THE DIVINE PYMANDER OF HERMES**, c$6.95. Hermes is the Greek name for Thoth. Manetho says that Thoth exumed engraved tablets which he interpreted in several books that were later deposited in the sanctums of the temples. Plato, in his **Phaedrus** says that Thoth was the inventor of numbers and letters. Of the forty-two books mentioned by ancient historians, seventeen are translated in this volume. **The Secret Doctrine** by H.P. Blavatsky elucidates much that seems obscure here and singles out this translation. This is a photographic copy of the 1884 edition which was reset verbatim with that of 1650, plus introduction. 226pp. Wiz 73

RANDOLPH, P.B., ed. **DIVINE PYMANDER**, c$6.00. A reproduction of Dr. Everard's translation, with explanatory prefaces. 144pp. YPS 71

SHRINE OF WISDOM. **THE DIVINE PYMANDER OF HERMES TRISMEGISTUS**, c$2.95. *The Pymander is a book most choice for the elegance of its language, most weighty for the abundance of its information, full of grace and propriety, full of wisdom and mysteries. For it contains the profoundest mysteries of the most ancient theology, and the arcana of all philosophy.*—Cornelius Agrippa. This is an excellent edition which presents the fundamental truths in a systematic manner. 53pp. ShW nd

---

IONS, VERONICA. **EGYPTIAN MYTHOLOGY**, c$4.95. See Hamlyn Mythology Series in the Mythology section. Ham 65

JAMES, T.G.H. **THE ARCHAEOLOGY OF ANCIENT EGYPT**, $4.95. This history of Egypt began at least 5000 years ago, but the scientific study of its ancient remains, usually called Egyptology, was born only in 1822. In that year Jean-Francois Champollion presented the first results of his decipherment of Egyptian hieroglyphics. Over the years many different scholars have contributed to the study. This book shows how some of the great discoveries about Egypt's past have been made, and how they and others, not so spectacular, have contributed to a better understanding of obscure periods. The selections have been chosen to cover both the range of Egyptian history and the work of significant excavators. This oversize book includes over 55 black and white and color photographs, maps, and drawings. Index, 144pp. McK 72

KISCHKEWITZ, HANNELORE. **EGYPTIAN DRAWINGS**, c$9.98. This is a beautifully produced work, 9½x12", which includes sixty-one full page plates (most of them in color) from papyrus and from tomb paintings, all with commentary. An introductory section dis-

cusses Egyptian drawings and paintings and analyzes the working methods of the ancient Egyptians and their use of color. Bibliography, 155pp. Oco 72

LEHNER, MARK. **THE EGYPTIAN HERITAGE**, $2.95. The material in this book is based on the Edgar Cayce readings—1,159 of which contain references and information on the Ra Ta period in Egypt. The story presented in this volume has been culled from about 300 of these readings. Basically Lehner lets the readings speak for themselves, and there is little editorial comment. The bulk of the book is devoted to a description of life in the Egypt of 10,500 BC. Ra Ta, the high priest of those times, is the central character in the drama presented by the readings. All aspects of the culture are described in detail and, as Cayce saw it, all the later developments in science, technology, religion, and art had their foundations in this period. Notes, bibliography, 144pp. ARE 74

LEWIS, H.S. **THE SYMBOLIC PROPHECY OF THE GREAT PYRAMID**, c$6.00. A penetrating look into the mysteries surrounding the Great Pyramid, its purpose, meaning, symbolism, influence and prophecy. Includes evidence supporting beliefs of the mystery school and their ancient use of the Great Pyramid. 192pp. Amo 36

MACAULAY, DAVID. **PYRAMID**, c$7.95. Macaulay is a teacher and designer whose two previous books have won him overwhelming praise and international recognition. His books are geared toward children and the text and illustrations are so clearly presented that they are illuminating for people of all ages. Here he graphically explains the step-by-step construction process of an imaginary pyramid and through a concise text and detailed illustrations he explores the philosophy of life and death that led the ancient Egyptians to construct these massive structures. We don't always agree with his explanations of the construction and its reason for being, but it makes a good story and helps to bring history alive. 9½x12", 80pp. HMC 75

MASSEY, GERALD. **ANCIENT EGYPT: THE LIGHT OF THE WORLD**, c$45.00/set. A massive, scholarly tome written at the turn of the century and concerned with an inclusive range of Egyptological subjects. The author explores the mythology, symbolism, religion, astronomy, and primitive origins of the Egyptian cultural genius with its influence on the Judeo-Christian tradition. Penetration is made into the Egyptian mysteries with light thrown on the Book of the Dead and the wisdom of its ancient teachings. In the second book the author elaborates on the Great Flood and the Ark legend and proceeds to elucidate the Hebrew Exodus from Egypt. The Revelation of John the Divine is reviewed in terms of the Egyptian influence and wisdom contained therein. The final 200 pages are given to an historical investigation of the Jesus-legend as it is found in 10,000 years of Egyptian symbolism, religion and story. Two volumes, 905pp. Wei 74

_____. **A BOOK OF THE BEGINNINGS**, c$30.00/set. Subtitled *Containing an Attempt to Recover and Reconstitute the Lost Origins of the Myths and Mysteries, Types and Symbols, Religion and Language, with Egypt for the Mouthpiece and Africa as the Birthplace*, this is a voluminous account, with an incredible amount of detailed information as revealed through the author's research. The controversial material presented here has not been documented; however, Massey was a very serious scholar. Includes an Egyptian/English vocabulary listing and a new introduction to this edition. 2 volumes, notes, 1384pp. UnB 74

_____. **EGYPTIAN BOOK OF THE DEAD AND THE MYSTERIES OF AMENTA**, $3.00. A reprint of Book IV of **Ancient Egypt: The Light of the World**. Includes a long, interpretative introduction by Hilton Hotema. 125pp. HeR nd

_____. **GERALD MASSEY'S LECTURES**, c$12.50. A collection of lectures in which Massey contends that the gnosis of Christianity was primarily derived from Egypt on various lines of descent—Hebrew, Greek, Persian, Essenian, and Nazarene. These converged in Rome. As usual, Massey has to be read very carefully and it is often hard to follow his references. Introduction, 294pp. Wei 74

_____. **THE NATURAL GENESIS**, c$50.00. This two-volume set builds on the material Massey presented in **The Book of the Beginnings**. It is equally voluminous and equally hard to follow. However for those who can decipher his writings Massey is highly thought of. When reading Massey it's always good to have a good symbolical dictionary handy and also a reference book on mythology. Boxed, glossary, illustrations, index, 1103pp. Wei 1883

MENDELSSOHN, KURT. **THE RIDDLE OF THE PYRAMID**, c$8.95. Dr. Mendelssohn is a noted physicist who has devoted a great deal of time to pyramidology. The ruined state of the pyramid at Meidum led him through a series of deductions to a new theory about the purpose of the pyramids that he supports by his hypotheses of the parallel development of pyramids in Mesoamerica. The author's thesis is not as clear or as well-documented as the material in Tompkins' massive study, but does provide some interesting material and insights not available elsewhere, in addition to over 100 plates and line drawings, many in color. Oversize, 224pp. Pra 74

MORENZ, SIEGFRIED. **EGYPTIAN RELIGION**, c$26.00. Morenz is a noted Egyptologist and this is his most important work. After a general statement about religion as the center of Egyptian civilization, Morenz discusses the gods and treats the entire range of their relationship with man. He describes the complex structure of Egyptian cosmological systems and the Egyptian concept of time, and his thoughtful observations on determinism and freedom constitute in effect an essay on moral philosophy in the ancient world. The text includes almost 100 pages of notes and bibliography. Index, 395pp. Cor 73

MURRAY, MARGARET. **THE SPLENDOR THAT WAS EGYPT**, $4.95. A revised edition of this monumental work on Egyptian civilization. Profusely illustrated, excellent bibliography. A good introduction for the general reader. 280pp. Prg 64

NEUBERT, OTTO. **TUTANKHAMUN**, $2.25. Neubert is one of the few survivors of the *Opening of the Tomb* and writes a first-hand account of the splendors revealed within it and also tells a tale of the Egypt of Nefertiti and Tutankhamun at the height of that ancient civilization's cruelest and most excessive era. Illustrations, 235pp. May 57

PIANKOFF, ALEXANDRE, tr. **THE LITANY OF RE**, c$20.00. Contains the translations of the **Litany** text, the most important theological work of the New Kingdom (sixteenth to eleventh century BC), restored on the basis of the version on the shroud of Thutmosis III and those on the walls of royal tombs; translations and descriptions of papyri that also contain the names of Re; and a theological commentary. Piankoff understands the god Re as the cosmic principle of energy, who manifests himself in the gods of the Egyptian pantheon. PUP 64

_____. **MYTHOLOGICAL PAPYRI**, c$35.00. Texts and descriptions of thirty-one *mythological papyri* of the 21st Dynasty from museums all over the world. Prepared for the use of the priesthood in the afterworld, these documents contains many magical formulas and representations not found elsewhere in ancient Egyptian culture. 2 volumes, many plates. PUP

_____. **THE PYRAMID OF UNAS**, c$23.50. The earliest version of religious texts of ancient Egypt appeared first on the walls of the burial chambers of King Unas (third millenium BC) in his pyramid at Sakkara, near Cairo. These potent spells were inscribed in order to assist in the king's passage from his earthly body into the world of the beyond, and they imply the recognition of his human qualities that must undergo divine transformation after death. It is one of the oldest literary documents not only of Egypt but of mankind itself. Piankoff, who died in 1966 during the preparation of this volume, devoted years to the study of the hieroglyphic texts. This volume contains his annotated translation, his introduction, and a complete photographic record of the texts (over 70 plates). PUP

_____. **THE TOMB OF RAMESSES VI**, c$35.00. Texts of the most nearly complete versions of the four great sacred books of the New Empire, presenting in effect a liturgical description of the cycle of birth, life, and death. Texts illustrated with well over 350 plates. 2 volumes. PUP

RANDALL-STEVENS, H.C. **ATLANTIS TO THE LATTER DAYS**, c$5.00. In Part I the story of Atlantis and Ancient Egypt is given, linking both with the present. There is a detailed description of the Pyramid area of Gizeh, which is shown to be an *Ancient Masonic Center or University of Initiation*. The symbology of the Sphinx is also explained. Part II comprises five essays which review the trend of world events both from a temporal and a spiritual standpoint. 175pp. OKT 66

_____. **THE BOOK OF TRUTH OR THE VOICE OF OSIRIS**, c$5.00 Inspirational writings received through the author from a higher intelligence accompanied by pencil sketches, symbolically drawn, received in the same manner. The teaching is concerned with the theology of the ancient and prehistoric Egyptian civilizations. This is the first book in the series. 201pp. OKT 66

_____. **THE TEACHINGS OF OSIRIS**, c$5.00. Incorporates the original Teachings, inspirationally received by the author. The *Laws of Atlantis* and the *Commandments of Osi-ra-es* have been included. OKT 66

_____. **THE WISDOM OF THE SOUL**, c$3.50. A book of teachings, both theoretical and practical, that try to bridge the gap between the exoteric and the esoteric. The

intent is to quicken human consciousness by the cultivation of higher qualities of the human soul. Present earthly conditions are outlined and suggestions made for remedying the destructive trends in the light of certain prophecies. 126pp. OKT 66

ROCHE, RICHARD. **EGYPTIAN MYTHS AND THE RA TA STORY**, $1.75. This study is based on the Edgar Cayce readings. However, it is not a verbatim transcript of the readings as was Lehner's book. Roche does summarize the story of Ra Ta and he goes far beyond this and focuses on Egyptian mythology and parallels between some of the early gods and later ones. Countless references are cited on each page (which tends to make the text fairly hard to read, but gives the reader an excellent idea of where to go for more information on a specific topic). Bibliography, 56pp. ARE 75

RUTHERFORD, ADAM. **PYRAMIDOLOGY — BOOK I: ELEMENTS OF PYRAMIDOLOGY, REVEALING THE DIVINE PLAN FOR OUR PLANET**, c$14.10. This massive series is the product of the author's life-long research. It is the most complete work we could imagine. This volume elucidates, with many graphic diagrams and tables, the meaning of every passage and chamber and deals with the historical chronology of the world. For serious students only! 220pp. IPy 57

_____. **BOOK II: THE GLORY OF CHRIST AS REVEALED BY THE GREAT PYRAMID**, c$17.65. Covers in great detail, again with many tables and diagrams, the entire life of Jesus on Earth as portrayed and foretold in the Great Pyramid. 288pp. IPy 62

_____. **BOOK III: CO-ORDINATION OF THE GREAT PYRAMID'S CHRONOGRAPH, BIBLE CHRONOLOGY AND ARCHAEOLOGY**, c$17.65. A great mass of new material is contained in this volume. It deals with every nook and corner in the vast structure of the Great Pyramid and contains full-page photographs of every passage and chamber including parts prohibited to the public. A large section is devoted to Old Testament chronology, and the whole work is related to recent archaeological discoveries. 644pp. IPy 66

_____. **BOOK IV: THE HISTORY OF THE GREAT PYRAMID AND PYRAMIDOLOGY**, c$14.10. The most comprehensive history imaginable, including many diagrams and photographs. This is probably the most readable of any of the volumes for the interested student. 400pp. IPy 70

SCHWALLER DE LUBICZ, ISHA. **HER-BAK, VOL. I: THE LIVING FACE OF ANCIENT EGYPT**, $3.95. The author's many years of research made this story possible. She recreates the spiritual tapestry of this ancient land, whose life was permeated with Ancient Wisdom of Divine Law. The youthful life of an Egyptian lad is woven into a revealing tale of Egyptians religion and everyday life. The young boy learns the lessons of nature and becomes a student-apprentice to a master craftsman and sage. 385pp. Pen 72

Head of Nefertari, from her tomb at Thebes

SEISS, JOSEPH. **THE GREAT PYRAMID: A MIRACLE IN STONE**, $2.50. This is a classic, published almost 100 years ago, which has influenced all subsequent work on the subject. *The Great Pyramid . . . is a time capsule from another age. . . . [It] contains scientific information and clues to the knowledge that produced it. The information is contained in the measurements and proportions of the stone structure with its interior rooms and corridors, and in its orientation on the Earth and to the stars.* 250pp. Mul nd

SIMPSON, WILLIAM, ed. **THE LITERATURE OF ANCIENT EGYPT**, $3.95. An authoritative anthology of stories, instructions and poetry—newly revised. 354pp. YUP 72

SKINNER, RALSTON. **KEY TO THE HEBREW-EGYPTIAN MYSTERY IN THE SOURCE OF MEASURES**, c$17.50. A treatise using geometrical calculation and formula to show the esoteric intricacies of the Kaballah and the ancient foundation of the Bible while revealing the numerological and geometrical basis for the construction of the Great

Pyramid and the origins of the British inch and the ancient cubit. Recommended for those who are esoterically inclined and who possess more than superficial geometric knowledge and aptitude. 394pp. Wiz 1875

SPENCE, LEWIS. **MYSTERIES OF ANCIENT EGYPT**, $2.25. A very clearly written presentation of the esoteric traditions of Egypt. Spence spent forty years studying the Egyptian mysteries and especially the initiation rituals. A good starting place for the general reader. 260pp. Mul nd

STEINER, RUDOLF. **EGYPTIAN MYTHS AND MYSTERIES**, $2.25. Twelve lectures given by the influential modern day occultist on the subject of Egypt, its influence today, relation of past to present and future, cosmic events, initiation, evolution, and all other subjects. 151pp. API 71

STEWART, DESMOND. **THE PYRAMIDS AND SPHINX**, c$10.00. A beautifully produced oversize book tracing the course of Egyptian civilization. Supplementing the narrative are some 140 illustrations—nearly one-half in full color. Colossal statues, delicately colored wall paintings, elaborate funerary objects, payprus scrolls, and modern views of temples and ruins combine to recreate the spirit of a vanished civilization. Also includes a selection of the accounts of Egyptian explorers. An excellent historical/cultural account for the general reader. Index, 172pp. Nsw 71

STEWART, T.M. **SYMBOLISM OF THE GODS OF THE EGYPTIANS AND THE LIGHT THEY THROW ON FREEMASONRY**, c$6.95. The significance of each of the Egyptian gods and goddesses is treated in regard to symbolical designation and relating to nature, the world of spirit, and the human consciousness. The Egyptian deities are representations of divine principles or forces of nature and man. Included also are picture representations of each deity and a glossary. 126pp. Weh nd

TOMPKINS, PETER. **SECRETS OF THE GREAT PYRAMID**, c$17.50. This beautifully illustrated book presents the thousand-year drama which has centered on the mysteries of the Great Pyramid of Cheops. The author recreates the adventures and explorations of the archaeologists, treasure-hunters, soldiers, scientists, and eccentrics who have tunnelled into and studied the Pyramid over many centuries. He analyzes the various theories as to how and why the Pyramid was built; its relation to other structures of antiquity, including Stonehenge, the ziggurats of Babylon, and other pyramids; and its influence on the fields of astronomy, astrology and the occult, geodesy, and history. Recommended for all serious students. 416pp. H&R 71

THREE INITIATES. **THE KYBALION: HERMETIC PHILOSOPHY**, c$5.50. From Egypt have come the fundamental esoteric and occult teachings which have so strongly influenced the philosophies of all races, nations and people for several thousand years. This book is a study of that knowledge, the Hermetic philosophy of Ancient Egypt and Greece. It is one of our most popular books. 223pp. YPS 12

VALENTINE, TOM. **THE GREAT PYRAMID**, $1.50. This is a detailed exploration of the Great Pyramid written for the general reader and based on the author's explorations into history, archaeology, astronomy, geometry, and religion. Many older works are cited and quoted and the whole work is readable and well organized. 176pp. Pin 75

VANDENBERG, PHILIPP. **THE CURSE OF THE PHARAOHS**, c$8.95. More than thirty researchers and archaeologists who have excavated in Egypt since 1900 have died suddenly. Delving into the pyramids' secrets, Vandenberg discovered three principal causes for the deaths: fever with delusions, strokes accompanied by circulatory collapse, and sudden cancers that were quickly terminal. He links the deaths to several remarkable explanations while taking the reader on an excursion into ancient Egyptian history, customs, medicine, and science. Bibliography, notes, index, 252pp. Lip 75

WAINWRIGHT, G. A. **THE SKY-RELIGION IN EGYPT**, c$12.10. This is a detailed, scholarly study of a heretofore little understood aspect of ancient Egyptian religion complete with an extremely detailed index and many notes. 135pp. Gre 38

WAKE, C.S. **THE ORIGIN AND SIGNIFICANCE OF THE GREAT PYRAMID**, c$6.50. A recent reprint of an important rare esoteric volume from 1882, with new material and additional notes. 131pp. Wiz 75

WEEKS, JOHN. **THE PYRAMIDS**, $2.95. A profusely illustrated account for the general reader covering the following topics: Land of the Pyramids, Planning the Pyramids, The Stones; Transporting the Stone, The Building of the Pyramid, and The Workmen of the Pyramid. Oversize, 48pp. CUP 71

WHITE, J.E. **ANCIENT EGYPT**, $3.00. A well written historical view of Nile civilizations illustrated with numerous photographs. Includes material about the life of the pharaoh, the priest, the aristocrat, the architect, craftsman and commoner in the Egypt of antiquity. 206pp. Dov 70

WILSON, JOHN A. **THE CULTURE OF ANCIENT EGYPT**, $3.45. This is an interpretive work by a noted Egyptologist, based not on a stringing together of facts, but rather on his intuitive understanding of what the civilization was like: *What we have to do, then, is to learn our material as thoroughly as its vast bulk will permit; test it constantly against itself, against evidence known from other peoples and cultures, and against good common sense; then form certain tentative generalizations about ancient Egyptian culture; and, finally, apply those generalizations to the material as a broad interpretation of the specific.* Fully indexed, with many illustrations. 344pp. UCh 51

ZABKAR, LOUIS. **A STUDY OF THE BA CONCEPT IN ANCIENT EGYPTIAN TEXTS**, $10.50. The author believes that in ancient Egypt the Ba was considered to represent man himself, the totality of his physical and psychic capacities. This is a fully annotated scholarly study of everything anyone could possible want to know about the Ba Concept divided into the following sections: The Ba and the Gods, the King and the Ba, the Ba in the Coffin Texts, The Ba in Didactic Literature, and The Ba in the New Kingdom and Later Periods. Plates, 169pp. UCh 68

ANCIENT NEAR EAST

BOHLIG, ALEXANDER and FREDERIK WISSE. **THE GOSPEL OF THE EGYPTIANS**, c$34.65. This volume is part of the **Nag Hammadi Studies**. It contains an English translation, the full Coptic text, introductory material, commentary, notes, bibliography, and indices. The text translated here is also known as **The Holy Book of the Great Invisible Spirit** and it is one of the most important of all the texts. 245pp. Eer 75

BREASTED, JAMES. **THE CONQUEST OF CIVILIZATION**, c$16.80. Dr. Breasted, probably the foremost twentieth century Egyptologist, here presents the culmination of his lifetime study of the ancient world. Breasted, in addition to being a wonderful scholar and researcher, also writes well! And this volume is an excellent review of the ancient Near East. The book begins with a review of prehistory and then goes on to study the origins and early history of civilization in the ancient Near East. Next there's a detailed study of the Greeks followed by a chapter on the Mediterranean world in the Hellenistic Age and the Roman Republic and ending with a study of the Roman Empire. Many illustrations accompany the text. 679pp. H&R 38

BUDGE, E.A. WALLIS. **BABYLONIAN LIFE AND HISTORY**, c$13.20. This is a popular survey, based on the best available scholarship and covering the following topics: The Country of Babylonia and the Euphrates and Tigris, Babylonian Chronology and History, The City of Babylon, The Babylonian Story of the Creation, The Babylonian Story of the Flood as Told in the Gilgamesh Epic, Babylonian Religious Beliefs, The Code of Laws of Khammurabi, Babylonian Religious and Magical Literature and Legends, The King of Babylonia and His People and Their Lives, Babylonian Writing and Learning, British Museum Excavations in Babylonia, The Excavations at Kish. Budge writes well and defines all the terms he uses and the text is illustrated throughout. Index, bibliography, 312pp. Csq 25

_____. **A HISTORY OF ETHIOPIA: NUBIA AND ABYSSINIA**, c$42.00. Budge brings his excellent scholarship to this little studied (in comparison with Egypt) part of the ancient world. The material in the text is drawn from the Ethiopian Royal Chronicles and the hieroglyphic inscriptions of Egypt and Nubia; there are few inscribed buildings, obelisks, tombs, etc. to draw on. Budge has done an admirable job in compiling all the known history and his work has yet to be excelled in the fifty years since its original publication. Many plates, maps, and illustrations are included as well as a long bibliography and a detailed index. Two volumes, bound in one, 743pp. Atp 70

BURY, J. B., et al, eds. **THE PERSIAN EMPIRE AND THE WEST**, c$32.50. Volume IV of **The Cambridge Ancient History**. In addition to the Persian Empire, the Athenean civilization is traced in depth. Each of the chapters is written by a specialist and is accompanied by an extremely complete bibliography and extensive notes. There's also an excellent index and many charts and maps. 723pp. CUP 69

CERNY, JAROSLAV. **COPTIC ETYMOLOGICAL DICTIONARY**, c$47.50. 350pp. Can 75

CONTENAU, GEORGES. **EVERYDAY LIFE IN BABYLON AND ASSYRIA**, $3.95. A survey of Mesopotamian civilization between 700 and 530 BC. During these three hundred years the Near East was dominated first by the Assyrians and then by the Babylonians, who were to be subdued by the Persians. M. Contenau covers every conceivable aspect of Mesopotamian life. He also discusses Mesopotamian thought and religion, and covers the doctrine of names, literature and the sciences, and religious beliefs and practices. The information has been reconstructed from a wealth of evidence, both written records and the evidence of monuments. The book reads fairly well and seems to contain good scholarship. Notes, bibliography, index, illustrations, 339pp. Nor 66

DARMESTER, JAMES, tr. **THE ZEND-AVESTA**, c$36.00/set. **The Zend-Avesta** is the sacred book of the Parsis (the religion of the Parsis is known today as Zoroastrianism) which flourished in Persia between the fifth century BC and the seventh century AD. Very little is known today about the Parsis. When the Muslims conquered Persia in the seventh century most of the citizens converted and the few who remained loyal to the old religion fled to India, where a small Zoroastrian population exists to this day. The first part of the **Avesta** is a compilation of religious laws and of mythical tales; the second part is composed of short prayers which are recited not only by the priests, but by all the faithful, at certain moments of the day, month or year, and in the presence of the different elements. The **Avesta** itself does not profess to be a religious encyclopedia, but only a liturgical collection, and it bears more likeness to a prayer book than to the western Bible. Three volumes, extensive introductory material. 1186pp. MoB 1884

DORESSE, JEAN. **THE SECRET BOOKS OF THE EGYPTIAN GNOSTICS**, c$26.20. This is the clearest and best study of Gnosticism available. Doresse was one of the handful of people involved in the rediscovery of the Gnostic texts discussed here and he is probably the finest Gnostic scholar alive today. And, in addition, he writes very well! It is unfortunate that the trade edition of this book is out of print and the only edition available is this limited circulation, expensive volume. Doresse begins with an excellent general study of Gnosticism, including a review of early writings about the sect. A second section is devoted to a detailed study of some of the most important original texts and monuments. This is followed by the story of the recent discovery at Chenoboskion. The bulk of the book is a textual analysis of forty-four secret (and hitherto unknown) books, and an analysis of the Sethians according to their writings. Doresse also reviews the survival of Gnosticism from Manichaeism to the Islamic sects. An appendix contains an English translation and critical evaluation of **The Gospel According to Thomas**. There's also a 60pp index. 462pp. AMS 60

EDWARDS, I.E.S., et al, eds. **EARLY HISTORY OF THE MIDDLE EAST**, c$35.00. Volume I, Part 2 of **The Cambridge Ancient History**, dealing with the history of the Near East from about 3000 to 1750 BC. The material is chronologically arranged and the period covered includes the Egyptian Old Kingdom and the greatest flourishing of Babylonian civilization. Every aspect of the society of the period is covered in depth and the text includes many diagrams and maps. Each of the chapters is written by a noted authority. There's also an extremely complete chapter-by-chapter bibliography, extensive notes, and a long index. 1081pp. CUP 71

_________. **HISTORY OF THE MIDDLE EAST AND AEGEAN REGION**, c$32.50. Volume II, Part 1 of **The Cambridge Ancient History**, dealing with the history of the region from about 1800 to 1380 BC. This was the era of Hammurabi in Western Asia, the Hyksos and the warrior-kings of the Eighteenth Dynasty in Egypt, and the Minoan and early Mycenaean civilizations in Crete and mainland Greece. The format of each part of the **History** is the same. 891pp. CUP 73

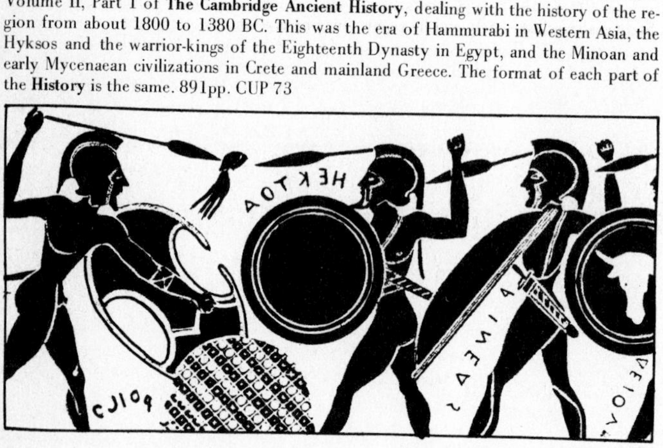

FERDOWSI. **THE EPIC OF KINGS**, c$16.75. The **Shah-nama** is the national epic poem of Persia. Written in the tenth century, it contains the country's myths, legends, and historical reminiscences. It deals with the reign of fifty kings and queens. The beginning is the creation of the world out of nothingness; the end is the Islamic conquest of Persia. Between that period, Ferdowsi devoted a separate section to each ruler. In the present edition, Prof. Reuben Levy has made a valuable prose translation, selecting the most representative parts of the original and has provided an informative prologue. Persian Heritage Series. 450pp. RKP 67

FOERSTER, WERNER, ed. **GNOSIS, VOL. I**, c$25.85. This is the first volume of a two-volume comprehensive selection of Gnostic texts. Included here are extracts from patristic sources, together with one Coptic document known before the Nag Hammadi discovery. The selection has been made, and the extracts introduced and annotated, by recognized German authorities, and R. McL. Wilson's translation has been prepared in close collaboration with these scholars. Bibliography, 367pp. Oxf 72

_________. **GNOSIS, VOL. 2**, c$32.00. This volume presents a selection of original Gnostic material, drawn partly from the Nag Hammadi Gnostic library and partly from the literature of Mandaism. Some of these texts have not hitherto been available in English, and no other single volume offers so extensive a coverage. Martin Krause has edited the section on Coptic sources, and Kurt Rudolph the one on Mandean. Indices of concepts, texts, and passages; bibliography. 360pp. Oxf 74

FRANKFORT, HENRI et al. **BEFORE PHILOSOPHY**, $2.25. Before philosophy, in t strict sense of abstract, critical, and methodical thought, came into being, man's specu tions, when they turned to the perennial problems of self and the universe, were express in myths. This book, subtitled *The Intellectual Adventure of Ancient Man* is a study the Egyptian and Mesopotamian points of view in matters of life and death, the functi of the State, and the nature of the phenomenal world as expressed in the myths that ha been preserved. There is also a discussion of the emergence of Greek philosophy and ho it differed from the Egyptian and Mesopotamian thought. Index, 275pp. Pen 46

FRYE, R.N., ed. **THE CAMBRIDGE HISTORY OF IRAN, VOLUME 4: FROM TH ARAB INVASION TO THE SALJUQS**, c$29.50. This is a survey of every aspect of th civilizations which flourished in the Iranian region from the Arab conquest to the Salju expansion. In particular, it studies the gradual transition of Iran from Zoroastrianism Islam, the uniting of all Iranians under one rule, the flowering into full magnificence c the Persian language, and the development of the culture which we associate today wi Persia. The text includes essays on Philosophy and Cosmology and on the Religious Sc ences by S.H. Nasr, and critical selections from literature along with many notes and illu trations. This is definitely a historical textbook, and yet most of the selections read wel and all of the contributors are tops in their fields. Index, bibliography, 733pp. CUP 7

GOBINEAU, J.A. DE. **THE WORLD OF THE PERSIANS**, c$3.95. See the description o the **World of Ancient Civilizations** Series in the Ancient Civilizations section. MnR 7

GRANT, R.M. **GNOSTICISM AND EARLY CHRISTIANITY**, c$11.00. Varying in deta from locality to locality, Gnosticism was a synthesis of elements from many religions an taught that salvation resulted from a special *gnosis* (knowledge) rather than from faith ritual, or good works. This is the most clearly written of the books on Gnosticism an covers the following topics: *The Nature of Gnosticism; The Heavenly World; Simon Magu and Helen, His Thought; The Unknown Father; Gnosticism and Early Christianity; Beyon Judaism and Christianity: The Gospels of Thomas, Philip, and Mary.* Dr. Grant is a profes sor at the University of Chicago Divinity School and the material presented here was or ginally put together as part of a series of lectures he gave at major universities in 1957–8 Notes, bibliography, index, 249pp. CUP 66

GREENLESS, DUNCAN. **THE GOSPEL OF THE PROPHET MANI**, c$3.75. This is ar edited version of the original Manichean texts, many translated here for the first time with a Life of the Prophet, an outline of Manichean history, and other introductory anc explanatory material—all fully annotated. Mani (216-74 AD) was a Persian prince whc converted members of the court to his faith. Finally he was opposed by the Magi (Zoro astrian priests) and died in chains. Mani claimed to fulfill the teachings of Zoroaster, Jesus and the Buddha. His distinctive belief was Dualism, in which he believed that the Father of Greatness is opposed by the Prince of Darkness, and the soul is imprisoned in matter. Release from evil would come by ascetic self-denial and by the Saviour of various names. This is one of the few modern works on Manicheanism available. Appendix includes translations of several coptic texts. Notes, bibliography, 567pp. TPH 56

HAARDT, ROBERT. **GNOSIS**, c$33.80. The most extensive anthology of Gnostic writings available, accompanied by extensive introductory and textual notes. Includes all the important well-known texts such as the **Gospel According to Thomas** and the **Gospel of Phillip** as well as many lesser-known writings. In all, fifty texts (or excerpts therefrom) are presented. Index, bibliography, 434pp. Bri 71

HOOKE, S.H. **BABYLONIAN ASSYRIAN RELIGON**, $2.95. This is one of the few full studies available of the ancient civilizations of the Tigris-Euphrates Valley. Apart from its intrinsic interest, the religion of the Babylonians and Assyrians has an added importance because of its great influence on Hebrew religion and life. Chapters discuss the cultural background of the religion, the pantheon, the rituals, mythology, religion and daily life, and divination techniques and astrology. An appendix offers a selection of ritual texts. Dr. Hooke is the author of many distinguished volumes on Semitic and comparative religions and is an authority on biblical archaeology. Index, bibliography, 143pp. UOk 63

HUOT, JEAN-LOUIS. **PERSIA I**, c$26.20. A detailed archaeological study of ancient Persia from its origins to the Achaemids. This volume is part of the **Archaeologia Mundi** series and it presents an analysis of virtually all the known material accompanied by 153 illustrations, 62 in color. Oversize, notes, bibliography, index, 219pp. Nag 65

JONAS, HANS. **THE GNOSTIC RELIGIONS**, $3.95. A full scale study of Gnosticism, its literature, symbolic language and main tenets, based on actual Gnostic documents and written by a noted authority in the field. Gnosticism is a little-understood pre-Christian religion that was vilified by the early Christians, forgotten for centuries, and finally resurrected in the nineteenth century. Opinions differ as to its origins. Some limit it to Hellenistic Greece, others trace it to the Orient. This investigation takes all the conflicting theories into account. A very serious study, many notes. 358pp. Bea 58

KAUS, MULLA FIRUZ BIN. **THE DESATIR**, c$7.00. A photographic reproduction of the original 1888 edition, which was itself a reprint of the first edition from 1818. **The Desatir** professes to be a collection of the writings of different Persian prophets from the time of Mahabad to the time of the fifth Sasan, of whom Zoroaster was the thirteenth. The writings of these fifteen prophets are in a tongue of which no other vestige appears to remain, and which would have been unintelligible without the assistance of an ancient Persian translation. The old Persian translation was made by the fifth Sasan, who has added a commentary. There is also an extensive discussion of the **Desatir** by Anthony Troyer following the text, and many notes. 192pp. Wiz 75

KERENYI, C. **THE RELIGION OF THE GREEKS AND ROMANS**, c$26.20. This is a very interesting study which is highlighted by a collection of 124 monochrome plates scattered through the text. The material is reviewed in a great deal of detail, but in a manner which should not overwhelm the general reader. It is rare to find a good study on this subject, so this volume is welcome in spite of its high price. Notes, index, 303pp. GRE 62

KING, CHARLES WILLIAM. **GNOSTICS AND THEIR REMAINS**, c$17.50. This is a very recent reprint of this important work, which first appeared in 1864 and was revised and enlarged for an 1887 edition (of which this is a photo-offset copy). The emphasis here is on the esoteric, oriental aspects of Gnosticism, and as King examines the ancient evidence, he makes many comparisons with hermetic philosophies. A very scholarly text, with illustrations and appendices. 500pp. Wiz 73

LAROCHE, LUCIENNE. **THE MIDDLE EAST**, c$19.95. This 10x13" text is lavishly illustrated with over 100 full color photographs and carefully reviews the main contributions of the early Middle Eastern civilizations centering around Mesopotamia. Altogether some 7,000 years are surveyed through the architecture, sculpture, literature, religious forms, and social structure of the religions that existed there. Augmenting the text and photographs are excerpts from ancient Middle Eastern tablets, inscriptions, and other records providing contemporaneous documentation of sites and personages depicted. Site plans, a chronology, and a glossary are included. Ms. Laroche is a noted French archaeologist, specializing in Mesopotamia. 190pp. G&D 74

LEGGE, FRANCIS. **FORERUNNERS AND RIVALS OF CHRISTIANITY FROM 330 BC TO 330 AD**, c$10.00. The first chapters of this monumental work form a historical narrative of the many religious movements of the time, with emphasis on the Gnostics, Mithraism, and the Manichean religion. Beyond this introduction the going becomes harder. There is a full, detailed description of the religious beliefs and practices of the time along with analyses of the major historical figures and documents. Includes a detailed index, many notes, and an extensive bibliography. 462pp. UnB 64

LLOYD, STETON. **THE ART OF THE ANCIENT NEAR EAST**, $4.50. Long before the beginnings of written history, the Near East gave birth to works of monumental sculpture and painting. By the time Athens was bursting into flower as a center of Western culture, Egypt, Mesopotamia, and their neighbors could look back on nearly twenty-five centuries of continuous artistic development. This volume has 249 plates, many in color and a great deal of commentary. Index, 302pp. Pra 61

MACDERMOT, VIOLET. **THE CULT OF THE SEER IN THE ANCIENT MIDDLE EAST**, c$24.00. Books on the ancient Near East seem to be weightier (literally) than most other sections. This is certainly a mammoth tome which is a multi-faceted study of the lives, ascetic practices, and visionary experiences of a group of seers of the early Christian period, accompanied by a medico-historical commentary which aims to clarify the practice of self-induced hallucinations. The material is drawn mainly from recently translated Coptic texts and a direct translation of many of the early writings is presented along with an analysis of the spiritual experience of the seers, distinguishing how these ancient religious experiences differ from contemporary psychedelic experiences. Notes, bibliography, indices. 841pp. UCa 71

McNEILL, W.H., ed. **THE ANCIENT NEAR EAST**, $4.00. The readings compiled in this volume all date from before 500 BC when the civilization of the Near East was still clearly the most advanced in the world. Section I illustrates the succession of empires and some facets of their political evolution. In Section II, selections from ancient law codes have been arranged under a number of more or less arbitrary rubrics. Section III reproduces documents from three religions unique in their concept of a single god: Atonism in Egypt, the worship of Yahweh in Palestine, and Zoroastrianism in Persia. The editors supply introductory material on each selection and there are textual notes throughout. 274pp. Oxf 68

McNEILL, WILLIAM and JEAN SEDLAR, eds. **THE ORIGINS OF CIVILIZATION**, $2.50. *This collection of readings concerns the origins of civilization in the ancient Orient. We begin with sample legends of creation that answered the naive and universal human question: How did the world begin? .... The main portion of the volume is organized around two themes: the nature of kingship and the relationship between men and gods. One group of readings presents Mesopotamian views on these two questions; the second does the same for ancient Egypt .... The editors have supplied numerous footnotes of their own in order to aid the non-specialist in comprehending these texts .... Technical discussions and scholarly references have been almost entirely omitted.* This is a useful compilation. Much of the material presented here is not easily available elsewhere. 213pp. Oxf 68

MEAD, G.R.S. **PISTIS SOPHIA**, c$10.00. This work is all that survives of the Gnostic bible called **The Books of the Savior**. The **Pistis Sophia** claims to present revelations of Jesus delivered after the resurrection. This secret doctrine of higher mysteries was said to have been taught by Jesus in the eleven years that followed the crucifixion. The surviving fragments present the story of Pistis Sophia, a female entity of the thirteenth Aeon of the world of light and matter, as told by Jesus to Mary and the disciples. Pistis Sophia was led astray from her work and trapped by a jealous power in the realms of Chaos, but finally rescued through the efforts of Gabriel and Michael. Mead, a noted Gnostic scholar and Theosophist, includes detailed background notes and introductory material. Bibliography, 402pp. UnB 74

__________. **FRAGMENTS OF A FAITH FORGOTTEN: THE GNOSTICS, A CONTRIBUTION TO THE ORIGINS OF CHRISTIANITY**, c$10.00. An anthology of Gnostic texts which survived in Coptic in Ethiopia and Egypt, together with Mead's explanations. Though this book was written over seventy years ago, it is still considered the most reliable guide to the corpus of Gnosticism that we have. It is an unbelievably complicated, ambiguous and difficult subject, and Mead's exposition is as lucid as could possibly be expected. The introduction by Kenneth Rexroth is correctly called *A Primer of Gnosticism*. Extensive bibliography, 633pp. UnB 60

MELLAART, JAMES. **EARLIEST CIVILIZATIONS OF THE NEAR EAST**, $3.95. A profusely illustrated anthropological study of the civilizations beginning with the tenth century BC. The author describes his own excavations as well as the discoveries of others. 108 plates, 30 in color. Bibliography, index. 143pp. MGH 65

ORT, L.J.R. **MANI**, c$26.50. Subtitled *A Religio-Historical Description of His Personality*. This seems to be a reprint of the author's dissertation—at least it reads like one! Ort begins with a survey of studies about Mani and his religion. This is followed by a survey of source works by Mani and his disciples including transcriptions, with translation, of books of the Manichaeans in a variety of languages. There are also transcriptions of writings about Mani and his religions, again in many languages. This is followed by a selection of texts detailing Mani's religious ideas, with translation and a great deal of commentary, all topically arranged. Ort also supplies biographical data. Notes, bibliography, indices. 296pp. Bri 67

RINGGREN, HELMER. **RELIGIONS OF THE ANCIENT NEAR EAST**, c$7.50. The majority of the material presented here is devoted to study of the Sumerian, Babylonian and Assyrian, and West Semitic religions. After outlining the literary and archaeological sources for these studies, Dr. Ringgren discusses the gods, mythology, cults and ideas of kingship, man, piety, ethics, and the afterlife. He has written a number of interpretative works on the Old Testament and here he emphasizes certain elements which are of special interest for the study of the Old Testament. This is an in-depth study, but it is written in an easily understood manner, without an over-abundance of details. Notes, bibliography, index, 198pp. Wes 73

Cult vase in the form of a stylized bull, East Balkan civilization, c.4000 BC

ROUX, GEORGE. **ANCIENT IRAQ**, $3.95. A political, cultural, and economic history which covers the whole of Mesopotamia from the prehistoric era to Christian times. Dr. Roux describes the empires, dynasties, and religions of each millennium. He also reviews what is known today about the art, science, and literature of the Sumerians, Akkadians, Babylonians, and Assyrians. The material is well-organized and well-presented and this seems to be an authoritative study. Many illustrations and maps are included along with notes, a bibliography, chronology, and index. 480pp. Pen 64

SHORE, A.F., ed. **JOSHUA I–VI AND OTHER PASSAGES IN COPTIC**, $9.00. A presentation of the Old Testament passages in the Sahidic dialect, followed by a translation of the material as well as introductory notes on the fourth century manuscript. Notes, index of Coptic words with translation and page references. Oversize, 76pp. HFC 63

STEPHENS, JOHN. **INCIDENTS OF TRAVEL IN EGYPT, ARABIA PETRAEA, AND THE HOLY LAND**, c$9.95. First published in 1837, this was the volume that made Stephens famous. It is a very detailed travelogue which is many cuts above the usual fare. Stephens travelled widely and he reports his observations and impressions vividly. Victor von Hagen supplied a long introduction. Maps and illustrations. 527pp. UOk 70

SZEKELY, EDMOND BORDEAUX. **THE ZEND AVESTA OF ZARATHUSTRA**, $4.80. Szekely's translation is from the original text. He sees the **Avesta** as not only a work of art, but also a universal encyclopedia, with chapters dealing with astronomy, organic gardening, health, psychology, philosophy, and religious thought. Szekeley also includes portions of the pictographs that made up the original manuscript. 100pp. Aca 73

THOMAS. **THE GOSPEL ACCORDING TO THOMAS**, c$5.00. This gospel was found with other early Christian manuscripts in 1945 preserved under layers of dry sand in northern Egypt. Scholars believe it may date back as far as 130 AD and contains personal records of Jesus not contained in the other traditional gospels. This edition, the tireless work of five recognized scholars, has the original Coptic as well as the faithful English translation next to it. 62pp. H&R 59

WEST, E.W., tr. **PAHLAVI TEXTS, VOL. I–V**, c$13.50/each. These volumes contain the only extant English translations of these texts. They are part of the **Sacred Books of the East** series. Each volume is over 400pp and each is separately indexed. MoB 65

WYNN-TYSON, ESME. **MITHRAS**, c$10.00. The cult of Mithras was an offshoot of Zoroastrianism and was based on the idea of the perpetual warfare between Light and Darkness and Good and Evil, in which Mithras was the chief warrior who inspired and aided the most worthy rulers of the world, ensuring them victory. This was the religion of the Roman legionnaires and Mithras was considered the special friend and protector of kings and soldiers, demanding in his worshippers the discipline, courage, and non-attachment necessary if the armies of the monarchs who worshipped him were to be victorious. This volume is one of the only full-scale studies available. The cult is described in full and its influence down the ages is revealed. Notes, bibliography, index, 250pp. Ctr 72

YAMAUCHI, EDWIN. **PRE-CHRISTIAN GNOSTICISM**, c$7.95. This is a very thorough study of Gnostic thought and its relation to Christianity. Dr. Yamauchi is an authority in the field of Mandaean studies. In compiling this study he draws on and analyzes what he terms *evidences* from the following areas: Patristic, Hermetic, Iranian, Syriac, Coptic, Mandaic, and Judaic. A profusion of notes accompany the text and there's an extensive bibliography and indices. 219pp. Eer 73

ZAEHNER, R.C. **THE TEACHINGS OF THE MAGI**, $2.95. Subtitled *A Compendium of Zoroastrian Beliefs*, this book provides a clear introduction to the main tenets of Zoroastrian dualism presented largely in the words of the Zoroastrian texts themselves. There are chapters on cosmology, the relation of man to God, the nature of religion, ethics, sacraments and sacrifice, the soul's fate at death, and eschatology. Dr. Zaehner provides minimal commentary and basically lets the texts speak for themselves. Index, bibliography. 156pp. Oxf 56

ASTRAL PROJECTION

BAKER, DOUGLAS. **THE TECHNIQUES OF ASTRAL PROJECTION**, $5.50. A detailed, comprehensive account with sections on the nature of astral projection; types and stages of astral projection; techniques for projecting; and the astral world itself. Baker writes from personal experience as well as a scientific study and he includes many historical examples. His techniques section is one of the clearest we've seen and the whole forms a well put together, helpful book. Many illustrations, 93pp. Bak 74

BATTERSBY, H.F.P. **MAN OUTSIDE HIMSELF**, c$4.95. A survey of the literature and description of the experiences of the pioneers of astral projection and the methods by which they achieve their results. Bibliography. 102pp. UnB 69

THE THOUGHT WHICH SEES by Rene Magritte   —detail

BLACK, DAVID. **EKSTASY: OUT OF BODY EXPERIENCES**, c$7.95. *An eminently sensible and comprehensive job on a difficult subject . . . . Ekstasy has more than literary merit. It provides a clear overview of the out-of-the-body experience . . . . Black's research has gone far. His account of the work done at major scientific centers around the country is quite good, and he laces it with engaging asides about the lives of various scientists and subjects . . . . A good springboard for your flight into an intriguing problem.* —John White. To our knowledge this is the only review of the recent scientific experiments with OOBs that is available. The text is well-written and the material reviewed makes fascinating reading. An excellent 21pp bibliography cites and relates papers and books. Index, 243pp. BoM 75

BORD, JANET. **ASTRAL PROJECTION**, $1.25. An overview, with material on what astral projection is, case histories, when projection happens and what it feels like. Bibliography, 64pp. Wei 73

CROOKALL, ROBERT. **CASEBOOK OF ASTRAL PROJECTION**, c$7.95. Dr. Crookall is a scientist who has spent more than thirty years in the study of astral projection. He has done pioneering research work and in this, his latest work, has brought the number of case studies up to 746. Over 200 cases are included in this volume together with detailed notes and critical discussion. Bibliography. 160pp. UnB 72

_____. **THE JUNG-JAFFE VIEW OF OUT-OF-THE-BODY EXPERIENCES**, $2.25. A detailed analysis of five cases of out-of-body experiences studied by Ms. Jaffe, Carl Jung's personal secretary. This is followed by some cases taken directly from Dr. Jung's writings and his own personal experiences, with Dr. Crookall's interpretations. Appendices provide interpretations of the psychedelic experience based on Timothy Leary et al's manual and a review of the experimental corroboration of astral projection. Glosary, notes, bibliography, index, 134pp. ChF 70

_____. **OUT-OF-THE-BODY EXPERIENCES: A FOURTH ANALYSIS**, c$6.00. Cases and discussion dealing almost exclusively with *doubles*. Topics are discussed and related bits from various cases are introduced. Extensive references, bibliography. 219pp. UnB

_____. **THE STUDY AND PRACTICE OF ASTRAL PROJECTION**, $3.95. A record of 160 out-of-the-body experiences, divided into various categories as well as about 100 pages of interpretative and theoretical material. 231pp. CiP 60

_____. **THE TECHNIQUES OF ASTRAL PROJECTION**, c$5.95. A practical manual, containing precise descriptions of various techniques. Extensive quotations and page references to the basic books in the field make the actual reading slow, but are extremely helpful to those desiring further research in specific areas. Extensive bibliography. 111pp. Wei 64

FOX, OLIVER. **ASTRAL PROJECTION—A RECORD OF OUT-OF-THE-BODY EXPERIENCES**, $2.95. Detailed, scientific and first-hand account of a series of conscious and voluntarily controlled projections. Considered one of the best accounts in the field. Includes much interpretative data. 160pp. Cit 62

GREEN, CELIA. **OUT-OF-THE-BODY EXPERIENCES**, $1.25. Celia Green is the Director of the Institute for Psychophysical Research at Oxford, England. A public appeal was made for subjects. Those replying filled out questionnaires and submitted written narratives. The factors were studied, punched into a computer, and then statistically analyzed. This collection includes the written reports as well as the statistical analyses of the various groupings that were obtained. The results are quite fascinating, both from a physical and psychological point of view. 165pp. RaH 73

GREENHOUSE, HERBERT. **THE ASTRAL JOURNEY**, c$8.95. This is the best account of the evidence for out-of-the body experiences that we know of. The text is very well written and the experiences discussed are more interesting than most. From the accounts of such historical figures as Aristotle, Goethe, Admiral Byrd, and Ernest Hemingway, through out-of-the-body travels by primitive shamans, to first-hand reports by contemporary Americans, Greenhouse describes in detail the *why* and *how* of astral projection. He also provides the most up-to-date and detailed accounts of the breakthroughs in four ESP laboratories in the last few years, where scientists are getting hard evidence that astral projection is indeed a reality. In addition, the author carefully examines the criteria for a valid astral projection experience and the physical and psychological conditions that make it possible to project. Greenhouse, a member of the American Society for Psychical Research, has participated in many of its experiments, and has personally experienced out-of-the-body travel. The book is fully indexed and there's an excellent bibliography. Recommended. 359pp. Dou 74

KING, FRANCIS, ed. **ASTRAL PROJECTION, MAGIC AND ALCHEMY**, c$6.95. Contains advanced inner teachings of the Golden Dawn. It is a collection of manuscripts circulated among members with detailed instructions and illustrations on imagination and willpower, astral projection, esoteric psychology, alchemy, hermetic wisdom, higher magic, and Rosicrucian adeptship. Also includes explanatory notes for some of the more technical material. 253pp. Wei 71

LEADBEATER, C.W. **THE ASTRAL PLANE**, c$2.75. A detailed investigation of the astral plane as a whole—covering every aspect in a clear, concise manner. Highly recommended. 183pp. TPH 33

Illustration by Susan Ida Smith

MONROE, ROBERT. **JOURNEYS OUT-OF-THE-BODY**, $3.50. In 1958, Monroe, a Virginia businessman, began to leave his body at night and travel to locales far removed from the physical and spiritual realities of life. He began taking systematic notes from the beginning—and his is a very rational account. With this book he hopes to pass his experiences to others so that they won't have to go through some of the confusion and terror he did learning on his own. He includes practical instructions on how to initiate the out-of-the-body experience. Many cases are cited and there is a great deal of explanatory material. We recommend this book for those with a general interest as well as for all who desire scientific presentation. It's also the most interesting of the lot, overall. 279pp. Dou 71

MOSER, ROBERT. **MENTAL AND ASTRAL PROJECTION**, $2.00. Gives detailed instructions on how to project and stresses the dangers involved in projection. Various techniques are outlined. Moser teaches these techniques in a school he runs in Arizona. 56pp. EsP 74

MULDOON, SYLVAN. **THE CASE FOR ASTRAL PROJECTION**, c$3.00. A casebook of projections, written down to strengthen the scientific case for astral projection. Muldoon has not included his own experiences in this volume. 173pp. ArP 36

MULDOON, SYLVAN and HEREWARD CARRINGTON. **THE PHENOMENA OF ASTRAL PROJECTION**, $3.75. A theoretical book, written twenty years after **Projection**, in which the authors discuss the scientific issues involved. A large portion of the book is devoted to case studies, grouped according to the cause of projection. Bibliography. 222pp. Wei 51

_____. **THE PROJECTION OF THE ASTRAL BODY**, $3.75. Dr. Carrington is a noted psychical researcher and Sylvan Muldoon has been having frequent out-of-the-body experiences since he was twelve. They have collaborated on this work and the results are fascinating as well as instructive. All aspects of the astral plane, sleep, dreams, voluntary and involuntary projection are discussed. The personal accounts are vivid and Muldoon's instructions on how to project and what the dangers are, are very clear. Carrington discusses the historical and scientific aspects. This is probably the basic book for those interested in astral projection. 316pp. Wei 70

OPHIEL. **THE ART AND PRACTICE OF ASTRAL PROJECTION**, $3.00. Gives the occultist all the necessary information about the art of astral projection as well as simple and concise directions on how to project in a safe manner. Four techniques are explained, each building on knowledge gained in the former one. A very clear presentation—though we don't recommend it to the scientifically inclined. 122pp. Wei 75

PANCHADASI, SWAMI. **THE ASTRAL WORLD: ITS SCENES, DWELLERS, AND PHENOMENA**, $1.00. Every aspect of the astral world and related phenomena seems to be touched on in this account. A good overview. 94pp. YPS nd

POWELL, ARTHUR E. **THE ASTRAL BODY AND OTHER ASTRAL PHENOMENA**, c$7.95. Another volume in Powell's series, this is a synthesis of the information concerning the astral body of man, together with a description and explanation of the astral world and its phenomena. Topics include colors, kundalini, thought forms, sleep-life and entities, rebirth, clairvoyance, and much else. An extremely complete treatment. 252pp. TPH 65

_____. **THE ETHERIC DOUBLE**, $1.45. This is the first volume in a series dealing with the inner structure of man. Powell has consolidated the information obtained from a large number of books, a list of which is given, arranging the material, which covers a vast field and is exceedingly complex, as methodically as possible. Much of the material came from the works of Leadbeater and Besant. The etheric double is a subtle body of fine matter which extends slightly beyond the physical body. It is said to be the transformer

of energy and is also known as the health aura. This volume contains material on prana, the body's centers, kundalini, birth, death, healing, mediumship, magnetism and much else. 24 related diagrams. 136pp. TPH

SMITH, SUSY. **THE ENIGMA OF OUT-OF-THE-BODY TRAVEL**, $1.25. A reporter's very well documented study of fifteen different types of projection, including case studies and background material for each area discussed and the most extensive chapter-by-chapter bibliography we've seen. 157pp. NAL 76

_____. **OUT-OF-THE-BODY EXPERIENCES**, $2.50. A more general, later treatment of the same material in **Enigma**, utilizing different case studies and less documentation. If you want to get one of these, we recommend **Enigma**. 160pp. She 68

STEIGER, BRAD and LORING WILLIAMS. **MINDS THROUGH SPACE AND TIME**, $.75. An examination and narration of astral trips that people have taken into the past and the future by two parapsychological investigators. 155pp. ASC 71

TURVEY, VINCENT. **THE BEGINNINGS OF SEERSHIP**, c$4.95. Turvey was one of the first men in modern times who claimed to have taught himself how to leave his body, astrally travel to places he had never been, and come back and report what he had seen. This is his personal story. It includes material on clairvoyance and prophecy as well as astral projection. Introduction by Leslie Shepard. 240pp. UnB 69

WALKER, BENJAMIN. **BEYOND THE BODY**, c$9.25. In examining the elements that lie _beyond the body_, Walker analyzes the traditional and contemporary data in the light of psychology, metaphysics, and science. He describes the various methods for inducing astral projection, and the circumstances in which spontaneous out-of-the-body experiences might occur, when the second body is separated from the physical. His account is supported by information from folklore, anthropology, occultism, psychic research, and from first-hand testimony. A well written, comprehensive account with an excellent bibliography and index. Recommended. 232pp. RKP 74

WHITEMAN, J.H.M. **THE MYSTICAL LIFE**, c$5.80. For over thirty years Dr. Whiteman has sought first-hand knowledge of various kinds of mystical experience: opening, separation from the body, and habitual spiritual consciousness. Here he gives a systematic account of the nature of such experience, drawing corroboration and clarification from a very wide field, including Christian and non-Christian religions, Plato and neo-Platonism, psychical research, philosophy, and modern science. A large portion of the text is devoted to new evidence on the _transforming union_ and the _spiritual body_. The book concludes with a summary of mystical cosmology correlated to the types of experience discussed. A very important work. 250pp. Fab 61

YRAM. **PRACTICAL ASTRAL PROJECTION**, $2.45. This is a practical technique book on astral projection, but is much more than a simple how-to book or a collection of experiences. It deals with all manner of existence on the astral plane as well as the material plane, as well as man's place in the universal order. It is recommended reading for anyone interested in a philosophical treatment of the psychic world. 253pp. Wei 67

THE REUNION OF THE SOUL AND THE BODY
by William Blake

ASTROLOGY

Astrology and Free Will

The study of planetary cosmic cycles and their relationship to life on earth has been a central interest to man since the beginnings. Some of the earliest known fragments of inscriptions remaining from ancient civilizations are records of planetary positions. Among the Egyptians, Babylonians, Chaldeans, Persians, Indians, and Chinese there were always members of the scholar-priest caste who specialized in investigations of cosmic phenomena and sought to relate their observations to the needs of community and individuals. It is only in very recent times that this branch of learning has atrophied so that the contemporary scientist-priest caste concerns itself exclusively with the precision of quantitative measurement of cosmic cycles (astronomy); while the study of the relationship of these cycles to biological and psychological processes on earth (astrology) is dismissed as *pseudo-science* and left indiscriminately to undisciplined fortune-tellers and only a few serious students.

Up to the times of Johannes Kepler and Isaac Newton, a mere three hundred years ago, this was not the case; and these two fathers of astronomy were interested in and proficient at astrology, and motivated in their researches in part by the attempt to understand its scientific basis. Kepler, in his **Terius Interveniens**, wrote that *it should not seem incredible that from the stupidities and blasphemies of the astrologers a new, healthy and useful learning may arise.* His laws of planetary motion were discovered as a result of persistent efforts on his part to verify the Pythagorean concept that the cycles of the planets were related to each other in the manner of the notes of a musical octave—the doctrine of *the music of the spheres.* It is an intriguing question in the history of science why Kepler's astronomical successors failed to share his interest in astrology.

The result of this split has been that astrological practice, with few exceptions, has not kept up with development in astronomical knowledge, and the symbol systems used by astrologers are largely based on obsolete information. As a consequence, there is much dispute among astrologers as to the best zodiac and the best house-system, and this disagreement is adduced as proof of astrology's unscientific nature by the skeptical orthodoxy. The fact that similar far-reaching disagreements exist among the cosmological theories of orthodox science does not seem to alter this evaluation. The reason for the discomfort of the rational, scientifically trained mind at the thought of astrology seems to be basically two-fold: astrology seems to eliminate free will or choice; and there is no presently known way to account for the supposed effects.

The notion that astrology does not allow for free will is one for which the commercialized fortune-tellers and their overcredulous clients are responsible. It is ever the path of least resistance to attribute our mishaps and difficulties to external causes, whether another person, or, more conveniently, since they won't talk back, the stars. Yet sophisticated astrologers have always pointed out they are dealing not with compelling influences, but with tendencies; not with forces, but with inclinations; with *probabilities* to behave, think, feel in certain ways, which the individual could follow or not as he chose.

Kepler himself was quite clear on this point: *There is no evil star in the heavens . . . for the following reasons: it is the nature of man as such, dwelling as it does here on earth, that lends to the planetary radiations their effect on itself; just as the sense of hearing, endowed with the faculty of discerning chords, lends to music such power that it incites him who hears it to dance.* Kepler is pointing here to what we might call the response factor, which is not often brought out by modern astrologers: namely, that astrological forces or influences are subject to great individual variability, just as is responsiveness to music. The same astrological configuration or aspect may be very influential in one person and not another, depending on response factors.

Albertus Magnus, the medieval churchman, alchemist, and astrologer, explained the free will question as follows: *There is in man a double spring of action, namely nature and will; and nature for its part is ruled by the stars, while the will is free; but unless it resists it is swept along by nature and becomes mechanical.* This is very similar to Gurdjieff's notion that the attempt

to develop consciousness and being means to exert will in a direction contrary to nature, to struggle against natural habits, if one is not to remain a machine.

The great modern clairvoyant and prophet Edgar Cayce formulated the effects of the planets also in just this way: *For will is the factor which affords the opportunity to choose what is for development or for retardation. . . . Each soul chooses its manifestations. . . . Use such directions* (from the planets) *as stepping-stones and do not let them become stumbling stones in thy experience.*

The idea that astrology precludes free will is a complete inversion of its original function, as developed by the Chaldean and Egyptian schools of adepts. These schools charted planetary cycles and observed their characteristic effects on the different human types, and then invented symbols to indicate what some of the influences and factors were, what a man had to deal with. In other words, astrological symbolism was designed to help man in his evolutionary development; help him to liberate his higher will by making clear what some of the factors opposing it are.

The problem of free will arises only if astrology is considered separately from the purpose of evolutionary growth and development. In the context of growth, planetary *aspects*, like hereditary or acquired characteristics or experiences encountered in life, become factors to work with, to assimilate and transmute for the goal of individuation. For this reason esoteric philosophy has taught that there are two kinds of astrology, or two kinds of horoscope: the astrology of man *on the wheel*, and the astrology of man *on the path*; or the horoscope of *personality*, and the horoscope of *individuality*. The latter could only be constructed by an astrologer who was also a teacher and who could accurately determine the level of development of being of the person.

Astrological Theories

The question of *how* astrological influences work is, of course, the other major stumbling block to academic acceptance. Science is notoriously resistant to accepting observations it cannot explain; and the highly indeterminate and probabilistic nature of astrologers' observations has not made this any easier. Early attempts to make systematic observations of supposed astrological effects were spectacularly unsuccessful; largely because they were based on naive assumptions about astrology. Through the use of modern statistical methods of analysis and high-speed computers, data are beginning to be collected which can provide a more empirical base for the new astrology.

Physical Theories. Two major research interests of present day biology are directly relevant to the perspectives of traditional astrology. *Ecology*, the science of the interrelations of life forms and environments, when extended beyond the planet to include the entire solar system, becomes the study of the reciprocally interacting field forces of sun and planets. This has been called *biocosmology* or *cosmo-ecology.* The study of *circadian rhythms* has gained increasing importance in recent years, and much research now exists demonstrating the susceptibility of plants and animals to the twenty-four hour cycle of the earth's rotation. Extended to sun, moon, and other planets, this branch of learning coincides with some facets of astrology.

Frank Brown, a biologist at Northwestern University, has carried out numerous experiments on behavior and physiological process in small animals, unicellular organisms, and plants showing not only that they are of a periodic nature, but that their rhythmic functioning is due to their sensitivity to subtle but pervasive physical stimuli. They have been shown to be responsive to very weak magnetic fields of the order of strength of the earth's own; to electrostatic fields; to ultrashort and very long electromagnetic waves; and to changes in the gravitational field of their environment. Sea animals show rhythms correlated to lunar phase, even when shielded from external stimuli; when moved to a different locality, still under constant conditions, they can reset their cycles to correspond to the new local lunar phase.

Brown postulated that organisms have a mechanism which acts as *a harmonic analyzer for solar and lunar geophysical rhythms and under some circumstan-*

ces becomes a variable frequency transformer. The capability of biological life forms, and especially man, to act as energy transformers is one of the key concepts of esoteric philosophy and is implicit in astrology.

The gross effects of solar and lunar cycles on the earth's oceans, on the atmosphere, and on climate has been observed and studied for some time. Michael Gauquelin, in his book **The Cosmic Clocks**, has summarized much of this work, showing the relationship of the eleven-year sun-spot cycle, as well as monthly and daily fluctuations in solar magnetic activity to processes as varied as physical and psychic epidemics, revolutions, accidents, heart and lung diseases, psychiatric diseases, blood counts, and even molecular chemical reactions.

Thus the influence of the sun on all manner of processes on earth is demonstrable. The influence of the moon, particularly on the fluids of the earth, namely tides and rainfall, has also been demonstrated. The combined influence of sun and moon on female fertility and sex of offspring has been the subject of intensive investigations by the Czechoslovakian gynecologist and psychiatrist Eugen Jonas. He has been able to show, in studies now covering thousands of cases, that a woman's fertile period recurs each month on her *lunation birthday*, when sun and moon repeat the same angular relationship they had when she was born; and that the sex of offspring conceived depends on the position of the moon at this time—if the moon was in one of the positive fields of the ecliptic, a male child will result and if in one of the alternating negative fields, a female. Jonas explains his findings by postulating that the ovum's receptivity to sperm with XX chromosomes (female) or XY chromosomes (male) varies with cyclic variations in the polarity of the lines of force of the sun's field.

Traditional astrology teaches that this field polarity alternates through the twelve divisions of the ecliptic, called the signs of the zodiac. Thus Aries is positive, Taurus negative, and so on. The sun passes through these fields in one year; the moon passes through them in a month. Recent satellite studies of the interplanetary magnetic field have confirmed the presence of periodic reversals of polarity in this field. When positive, solar energy is streaming from the sun; when negative, the flow is reversed.

Satellite observations of the interplanetary solar magnetic field have found it to lie close to the plane of the ecliptic, to have a spiral form, and to rotate with the sun in a twenty-seven day period. We see in these observations confirmation of some classical astrological assumptions: the so-called signs of the zodiac (not to be confused with the constellations bearing the same name) is a twelve-fold division of the ecliptic, a map of the earth's path around the sun. The rotation of the sun's field, plus the movement of the earth in its orbit, would generate an approximately twelve-fold variation in the interacting field relationships of earth and sun.

Evidence has been found that the sun's magnetic and gravitational fields are modulated by changes in planetary positions. In 1954, J.H. Nelson, who was employed by RCA to research factors interfering with the propagation of radio waves through the ionosphere, found that predictable disturbances occurred when three or more planets were either aligned with the sun (in *conjunction* or in *opposition*), or formed angles of 90 degrees (astrologically *square*). Angles of 30 degrees and 60 degrees and their multiples were also disturbing, and the more planets thus related the greater the effect. The planet Mercury (traditionally associated with communication) was involved in the greatest number of interferences. The angles though were heliocentric (sun-centered), not the geocentric (earth-centered) aspects of classical astrology. The planets' positions, through their effects on the sun's gravitational field, also influence solar flare activity. This in turn affects weather as well as biological and psychosocial processes on earth, as noted above.

Angular positions of the planets have been shown to effect indices of activity in the earth's magnetic field. In particular, inferior conjunctions of Venus (when Venus lies in a straight line between earth and sun) consistently and significantly reduce magnetic storm activity on the earth. Since such magnetic activity has been related to physical, psychic, and social disturbances, these data are an interesting confirmation of the traditionally *benign* effect of the planet Venus.

These findings are all suggestive of a model of solar-planetary interaction in which the planets, through their interacting gravitational and magnetic fields, modulate the basic radiation channeled by the sun. The entire solar system functions like a gigantic frequency transformer in which the energy generated by the sun, or received by it from outside cosmic sources, is transmitted to the planets, each modulating its intensity and frequency in characteristic ways according to the angular relationships between them.

On such a hypothesis, the different frequency rates channeled by the planets at different intensities are linked to various biological, psychological, and social processes on earth. In particular, man as a microcosm has a system of glands, each of which is assumed to be responsive to a particular frequency or type of energy. Intensity of activity of the various glandular systems in various combinations can certainly be related to personality and temperamental variations. Although several sets of correlations of planets and glands have been proposed, there is only little agreement among them. This is an area awaiting empirical research.

A somewhat different and intriguing kind of direct physical linkage has been proposed by the physicist H. Prescott Sleeper. He has pointed out that the resonant frequency of the ionosphere is eight cycles per second, which corresponds to the frequency of the alpha rhythm of the human brain. Thus, the pulsating ionosphere is thought of as *driving* the brain waves. Variations in the interplanetary magnetic field an other parameters could thus affect human thinking and behavior directly through their effects on the pulsing of the ionosphere.

Symbolic Theories. The majority of practicing astrologers adopt what is called a pragmatic point of view, which says: *I use it because it works*; and do not concern themselves further with questions of *how* or *why*. The more sophisticated ones see astrological planets and signs as symbols or metaphors for psychological functions; they analyze the patterns of relationships of the symbols in a chart and hence infer the pattern of relationships of the associated psychological functions.

Thus, Dane Rudhyar, in his **The Practice of Astrology**, writes that *Astrology, as I understand it, has no concern with whether a conjunction of planets causes some things to happen to a person or nation; it only* indicates *the possibility or probability of a certain type of event's occurring in a certain place at a certain time.* What Rudhyar and the majority of astrologers do is to regard the planets and signs as metaphors for psychological processes just as the alchemists took sulphur and salt as metaphors for internal energy processes. The metaphorical meaning is derived in part from the ancient sources, in part from their own experience and intuition, and in part from the astronomical facts. Thus, for example, the meaning of Mars and Venus in a chart is partly derived from the Greek myths of the gods Mars and Venus, partly from experience of seeing the role of Mars and Venus in many charts, and partly from the position of the planets Mars and Venus on the outward and sunward side of the earth respectively.

This approach undoubtedly will give some results as long as the empirical, factual basis is not ignored altogether. There are surely distortions and deviations in the traditional meaning-attributes of the astrological symbols, and these must be verified anew. In addition, since we are entering a new age in which the planetary and sidereal relationships are different, it must be assumed that the actual functional patterns of effects on earth are changing. They will have to be established on fresh empirical observations for the new astrology.

Astrology as an Evolutionary Way. The new astrology will be new because it will incorporate modern astronomical knowledge; it will also be very old because it will recover what has been lost, the significance of astrological factors as guidelines for individual growth and development. It is this which distinguishes astrology from other existing models of personality or typologies: it has an inherent growth factor enabling a person to determine not only what he is, but what he can become.

If for example we ask why the twelve zodiacal types have the symbolism they do, simplistic answers in terms of the visual appearance of the constellations will clearly not do. We could see anything we want to in a pattern of lights. Is it not rather, as Gurdjieff suggested, that the adepts in very ancient times who devised this typology, chose for each type a symbol that represents that person's *chief feature*? It is difficult to imagine an arbitrary symbol system having the extraordinary longevity and popularity that the zodiac signs have enjoyed. Something about them *fits*; and by seeking to discover how it *fits* one learns to observe oneself and becomes more aware.

According to the viewpoint of esoteric teachings the basic linkage between the psyche and the cosmic factors mapped out in the natal horoscope is not causal, or even synchronous, but *purposeful*. The Higher, Immortal Self chooses a particular life pattern for incarnation, for the purpose of learning and growth while in the particular personality and physical vehicle of that incarnation. Higher Self writes a script for itself, as it were; which personality ego then discovers, deciphers, and plays out in order to *re-member* its essential unity with the Immortal within.

This, it is taught, is the situation of one who is on the path of conscious evolution. He *has to become consciously aware of the planetary influences and begin to use them for the carrying out of soul purpose.* This is a statement from **Esoteric Astrology** by Alice Bailey, a work said to be the record of telepathically transmitted teachings of a Tibetan initiate. In this work it is also stated that for the average man, the man not consciously searching for purpose, man *on the wheel*, the planetary influences condition the major trends of personality and outer life circumstances. However, *the moment that a man becomes aware of his own soul and is endeavoring to control his own* path in life, *the influence of the planets, per se, definitely weakens and steadily becomes less and less.* He then becomes more receptive to the forces flowing *through* the planets, rather than the forces *of* the planets, and to the subtler and higher energies of the solar system.

What the precise nature of the linkage between cosmic cycles and human cycles is remains to be discovered in future investigations; whether it is by means of glandular activity rates, or by genetic synchronization, or by imprinted thoughtforms—or by means of the *centers* (*chakras*) and higher bodies. A full understanding of the nature of astrological forces can, I believe, only come after the actual design of man has been clarified and experienced in the context of the practice of methods of expanding awareness and extending perception.

In other words there is a zodiac within, and factors corresponding to the signs and the planets within, because man is a microcosm organized according to the same designs that operate in the macrocosmos. With extended perception one becomes increasingly aware of what the inner correspondences of planets and signs are; and only then can one correctly evaluate their influence.

—from **Maps of Consciousness** by Ralph Metzner.

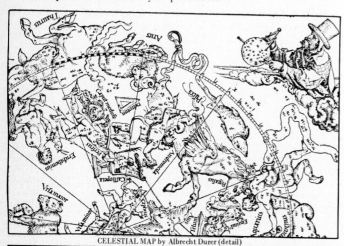

CELESTIAL MAP by Albrecht Durer (detail)

ADAMS, EVANGELINE. ASTROLOGY: YOUR PLACE AMONG THE STARS, c$6.95. This volume stresses at great length the effects of the sun, moon, and planets in their passage through the twelve signs of the zodiac, and gives numerous examples of well-known persons in different periods and walks of life to illustrate their operation. Tabulations give the position of the planets, Uranus, Saturn and Jupiter, from about 1850 and through the twentieth century, and the sign position of the planets from about 1880 on. 478pp. DMd 30

_____. **ASTROLOGY: YOUR PLACE IN THE SUN,** c$6.95. Includes an exhaustive description of the zodiac sign, the houses, and the planets. Also contains a table

which will make it possible to determine the exact position of the ascendant for every hour of the day. A good general text for the layman. 343pp. DMd 27

_____. **THE BOWL OF HEAVEN,** c$1.00. Ms. Adams is one of the twentieth century's most noted astrologers. This is her autobiography. She includes case histories of some of the people who came to her for guidance. 216pp. DMd 26

ADAMS, H. EUGENE. A PRACTICAL APPROACH IN ASTROLOGICAL ANALYSIS, $5.60. This is a very comprehensive study, recommended to astrologers beyond the beginning stage. Topics covered include judging planetary quality and quantity, the finality of the ascendant, the houses, planets and houses combined, and predictive astrology. The text is clearly written and illustrated with sample charts and detailed examples. There's also material on transits and solar and lunar returns. Oversize, 91pp. Ada 74

ADDEY, JOHN. THE DISCRIMINATION OF BIRTHTYPES IN RELATION TO DISEASE. $3.95. This is a technical monograph which analyzes and graphically illustrates the extensive research Addey has done in the area. 25 pp. CCL 75.

ALDRICH, ELIZABETH. DAILY USE OF THE EPHEMERIS, $4.50. A complete, instructive account for the beginning astrologer. 67pp. Hug 71

AMERICAN FEDERATION OF ASTROLOGERS. THE BASIC PRINCIPLES OF ASTROLOGY, $1.00. AFA propaganda with good general look at astrology past, present, and future. 64pp. AFA

ANRAIS, DAVID. MAN AND THE ZODIAC, $3.50. An esoteric study which provides methods of synchronizing the planets, houses, and their mutual aspects, giving solid definitions of the signs and their decanates. Signs are discussed in relation to conscious, unconscious, and superconscious minds. 211pp. Wei 70

ARCANA WORKSHOPS. FULL MOON MAGIC, $.75. The material in this pamphlet is designed to supplement Alice Bailey's **Esoteric Astrology.** Included are new and full moon charts for 1976 for many different time zones, information on the three and seven year cycles, and on the esoteric rays and rulerships. 16pp. ArW 75

_____. **FULL MOON MEDITATIONS,** $1.00. *These twelve meditations, one for each month, are designed for group use at the time of each full moon. The full moon marks the point in each month when energies not normally or usually contacted are available. At the time of the full moon it is as if a door opened wide, which at other times stands closed....In the symbology of astrology, the sun represents the soul. From one point of view (ours) each sign of the zodiac represents one station upon the path of expanding consciousness.* 16pp. ArW

ARROYO, STEPHEN. ASTROLOGY, PSYCHOLOGY, AND THE FOUR ELEMENTS, $5.95. This is a truly excellent presentation in every sense of the word. It is subtitled *An Energy Approach to Astrology and Its Use in the Counseling Arts.* Arroyo is a psychologist and part of this book was originally included in his Master's thesis in psychology. The book deals with the relation of astrology to modern psychology and with the use of astrology as a practical method of understanding one's attunement to universal forces. It clearly shows how to approach astrology with a real understanding of the energies involved, and it includes practical instruction in the interpretation of astrological factors in a great deal more depth than is commonly found in astrological textbooks. The approach Arroyo takes is practical application based on the actual energies involved (air, fire, water, and earth) in all life processes. The book is dedicated to Dane Rudhyar, and Rudhyar's influence is apparent throughout. Highly recommended. Notes, bibliography. 207pp. CRC 76

ASHMAND, J.M., tr. PTOLEMY'S TETRABIBLOS: FOUR BOOKS OF THE INFLUENCE OF THE STARS, $6.00. A comprehensive text on the elements of astrology written in the first century AD. This translation has been made from Procius' Greek paraphrase of Ptolemy's original text. Numerous references to the original text are included as are copious notes. 240pp. HeR 69

ASTRO-ANALYTICS. HOROSCOPES: MUSICIANS AND COMPOSERS, $7.00. 100 charts of famous composers and musicians of the past and present. The format is the same as the previous book. AsA 74

AYER, V.A.K. EVERYDAY ASTROLOGY, $2.40. This is the clearest presentation of Hindu Astrology that we have seen. The author has integrated parts of the Western system to make the computations clearer. The whole volume is oriented toward practical use and is the result of years of research and practical experience. Many illustrations. 169pp. Tar 58

BACHER, ELMAN. STUDIES IN ASTROLOGY - VOLS. I- IX, $1.50 ea. This series has been compiled from articles which first appeared in **Rays from the Rose Cross** over a period of many years. They present an excellent picture of the spiritual basis of astrology as it relates to many specific cases. Many of the essays cover material which is not found in any astrological literature. Each book is over 100pp. Ros

BAILEY, ALICE. ESOTERIC ASTROLOGY, c$9.50/5.00. Astrology is described here as *the science of relationships*—the relationship existing between all living organisms within the universe. This is an excellent comprehensive account for the advanced student. The main chapter headings provide the sequence in developing study: The Zodiac and the Rays; The Nature of Esoteric Astrology; The Science of Triangles; The Sacred and Non-Sacred Planets; Three Major Rays, Constellations and Planets. An appendix summarizes and tabulates many important factors. See our section on Alice Bailey. 742pp. LPC 51

_____. **LABOURS OF HERCULES,** $1.75. See the Theosophy section.

BAILEY, E.M. THE PRENATAL EPOCH, $6.95. The prenatal epoch can be used as a method of rectification of doubtful horoscopes and for determining the actual period of human conception. This is the only work on the subject. It includes practical step-by-step instructions on working out pre-natal charts and ascendant tables. 239pp. Wei 70

BAKER, DOUGLAS. ESOTERIC ASTROLOGY, $16.00. The format here is the same as the earlier volumes in Dr. Baker's series, *The Seven Pillars of Ancient Wisdom.* As the title suggests, this is a very thorough study of esoteric astrology, with the emphasis on esoteric, based on the pioneering work of Alice Bailey. He begins with a description of the nature of esoteric astrology and goes from there to an analysis of the twelve signs, the esoteric planetary rulers (which differ from the traditional ones), the twelve houses, and a final section on interpretation. As is usual with Baker's books, many interesting illustrations are included. Many of the illustrations are in full color and they add meaning to some obscure textual elements. There is a profusion of material here, but often we are not sure exactly what Baker is saying. There's also a lot of material relating the rays to astrology. Bak 75

BARTOLET, SAM. ECLIPSES AND LUNATIONS IN ASTROLOGY, $3.00. The contents of this book are valuable to those who require an introduction to the subject as well as instructions regarding procedure in the applications of lunations. Advanced students should find the various tables on eclipses and lunations useful and a good foundation for further study. 60pp. AFA

BENJAMINE, ELBERT. ASTRODYNE MANUAL, $2.95. The basic principles and rules for the calculations of the units of astrological power known as the astrodynes, harmodynes, and discordynes. This is the mathematical method of computing the number of astrodynes by each birth-chart aspect, planet, signs and house. Detailed explanations are given so that the whole matter of Stellar Dynamics can be easily understood and put into practice. Complete with a large Astrodyne Chart. 100pp. ChL 50

_____. ASTROLOGICAL LORE OF ALL AGES, c$3.00. Interesting collection of stories and theories gathered by the President of the Church of Light (who also wrote under the pseudonym C.C. Zain). Much of the material is derived from pre-Columbian American sources. 141pp. ArP

_____. BEGINNER'S HOROSCOPE MAKER AND READER, $7.25. Complete instructions for casting a chart and guidance toward elementary interpretation. 198pp. ChL 72

_____. HOW TO USE MODERN EPHEMERIDES, $1.00. Not as good an attempt as Jeff Mayo's book, but adequate if you don't want to pay the higher price. 63pp. ArP

_____. CHURCH OF LIGHT ASTROLOGICAL RESEARCH AND REFERENCE CYCLOPEDIA, VOL. I AND VOL. II, $6.95/each. These two volumes are a reprint of out-of-print reference books written by Elbert Benjamine, under the name of C.C. Zain. They are an excellent text for the advanced and serious student in the fields in which they cover. Not only do they explain the technical and statistical information of the factors involved, but also a great deal of information on the delineation of charts. Included in these two volumes are a very comprehensive and complete explanation of the Progressed Aspects of Standard Astrology, When and What Events Will Happen, with statistical analysis of 2,000 charts progressed to time of Events; Stellar Dietetics; How to Select a Vocation; also with statistical analysis of 3,000 birth charts and thirty vocations and Body Disease and its Stellar Treatment. Recommended. Vol. I, 350pp. Vol. II, 300pp. ChL 72

_____. THE INFLUENCE OF THE PLANET PLUTO, $1.00. A six page treatise (written in 1939), plus an Ephemeris of Pluto, 1840-1960. ArP

BILLS, REX. THE RULERSHIP BOOK, c$12.50. In the symbolic language of astrology, the planets, signs, and houses are said to *rule* over everything on earth and every facet of our lives. This book presents a practical list of these correspondences, conveniently arranged alphabetically as well as by signs, houses, and planets. Mac 71

BISHOP, GORDON. THE MOON BOOK, c$14.85. The origin of the moon, the moon in religion, personifications of the moon, the moon in the occult sciences, the lore of eclipses, moon rituals, and the latest scientific findings about the moon's influence on human behavior. Illustrated with over 100 pictures (some in color) and including interviews with many people whose life work is associated with the moon. Presents the moon in every aspect. GaP 75

BLACKMAN, EVERETT. ASTROLOGY: WORLDS VISIBLE AND INVISIBLE, $5.25. This is a detailed study of mundane astrology, focusing on three areas: the Presidency— and especially the charts of those Presidents who were assassinated or who succeeded to the Presidency due to the death of the previous President; Cycles and Progressions; and New Horizons—with a look at the U.S. Chart. The text is illustrated with numerous case studies and should be of interest to all who find astrological prediction fascinating. The material is quite recent. 94pp. AFA 74

_____. SO YOU WANT TO BE PRESIDENT, $2.00. This is a study of the U.S.'s Presidents and Presidential candidates between 1932 and 1972. It also includes material on what to keep in mind when choosing a President and a profile of what to expect in 1976. 81pp. AFA 72

BOYD, HELEN. THE TRUE HOROSCOPE OF THE UNITED STATES. $7.25. This is a very careful analysis, based on ten years of study. Ms Boyd feels that the true birth-time of the U.S. is July 6, 1775 at 11:00 AM. She presents the chart for this time along with many charts for other possible times and important events in U.S. history. The account includes documented historical data based on the Journals of the First and Second Continental Congresses. 100 charts are presented, including ones for each of the U.S. birth-times previously advanced by others. It's hard to know when the correct time is, however the author has built a good case for her choice and her background charts

and exposition are a welcome addition to the material on Mundane Astrology of the U.S. It is too bad that she did not cite her sources more exactly. Glossary, 174 pp. ASI 75

BRADLEY, DONALD. SOLAR AND LUNAR RETURNS, $3.95. Presents information for the beginning astrologer on casting and interpreting solar and lunar returns according to the sidereal zodiac of the constellations, an accurate system of predicting future events. The planetary positions are delineated fully, the meaning of planetary vibrations in daily life is discussed, and the text is illustrated with actual examples of *Solunar Returns.* 123pp. LIP

BRAM, JEAN, tr. ANCIENT ASTROLOGY, THEORY AND PRACTICE, c$18.90. This is the first English translation from the Latin of the Matheseos Libri VII of Firmicus Maternus, written in the fourth century AD. It is the most complete classical book on astrology. We have seen numerous references to it and we're delighted to have tracked down a source for it. The organization is sometimes a bit hard to follow, however, the material itself is excellent and the book makes fascinating reading. All of the basic information is included and the reader gets a wonderful feeling for the times and for the changes in astrology when s/he reads the various descriptions and analyses. We recommend this volume highly to all those who are interested in the development of astrology over the centuries and also to all who are serious students and practitioners and would like a new source of information and insight. Intro, notes, glossary, index, bibliography, 347 pp. Noy 75

BROWN, W. KENNETH, CHARLES and VIVIA JAYNE. FUNDAMENTALS OF ASTROLOGY, $3.00. Basic sun sign analyses, a good deal deeper than most, and detailed information on casting a horoscope, not as clearly presented as some of the other volumes on chart erection. Oversize, 31pp. AsB

BUTLER, HIRAM. SOLAR BIOLOGY, c$8.00. A revised edition of the oldest astrology text (1887) that we know of. Includes material on every aspect of astrology—with emphasis on personal interrelationships and tables giving daily positions of the planets for the years 1840–1974. Much of the language is archaic, but there is some interesting material presented. 325pp. EsF

CARELLI, ADRIANO. THE 360 DEGREES OF THE ZODIAC, $4.50. Illustrative meditations on each degree, with notes and historical references. 199pp. AFA 51

CARTER, C.E.O. ASTROLOGY OF ACCIDENTS, c$4.50. A useful astrological encyclopedia of character and observations on the astrological characteristics. Begins at A, with Ability, Abcesses, etc., and goes to Z. It gives the aspects, signs, planets, and houses for each subject, which may help one to understand potential in the chart, susceptibility to disease, etc. For the advanced student. 195pp. TPH

_____. THE ASTROLOGICAL ASPECTS, $2.45. A detailed treatise on the thirty-three possible combinations of the sun, the moon, and the seven known planets. A number of examples is given of each combination. Each is treated under three headings: harmonious aspects, the conjunction, and inharmonious aspects. All terms used are well-defined. Carter is a noted British astrologer of the Margaret Hone school. 160pp. Fow 30

_____. AN ENCYCLOPEDIA OF PSYCHOLOGICAL ASTROLOGY, c$7.25. *This work is an attempt to produce a useful astrological Encyclopedia of Character, and, as far as data permits, of Disease.* The approach is scientific and the examples are drawn from easily accessible and reliable sources such as the nativities of royalty. 199pp. TPH 63

_____. ESSAYS ON THE FOUNDATIONS OF ASTROLOGY, $5.95. A useful work with chapters on the sun, moon, and planets; aspects and exaltations; the positive-negative polarity; aspects in terms of the signs; the northern and southern signs; and the houses. 106pp. Hug 65

_____. INTRODUCTION TO POLITICAL ASTROLOGY, $1.70. *At the moment the horoscope of an individual . . . appears to be the principal field of astrological study. But actually the nativity cannot adequately be considered as isolated from the social environment, as represented astrologically by other horoscopes of great amplitude. Sooner or later, I believe, 'mundane' astrology will have to be replaced at the top of the astrological tree, and the more the state controls the individual, the truer this will be . . . . Our subject here is Political Astrology, or the study in the light of Astrology of politically organized and significant communities . . . . We shall find that this study embraces, in terms of itself, most other kinds of Astrology in greater or lesser degrees.* This is the most comprehensive study available; well written and illustrated with many sample charts. 103pp. Fow 51

_____. THE PRINCIPLES OF ASTROLOGY, $2.45. A revised edition of a popular introductory astrology textbook. It contains a concise statement of known astrological facts as well as explanations of how these facts affect human life. 188pp. TPH 63

_____. SOME PRINCIPLES OF HOROSCOPE DELINEATION, $5.95. An illustrative, instructive work, designed to follow The Principles of Astrology, and which may be read in conjunction with The Astrological Aspects and The Encyclopedia of Psychological Astrology. 76pp. Hug

_____. SEVEN GREAT PROBLEMS OF ASTROLOGY, $1.00. Includes explanations of the problems and suggestions as to the lines along which they might be successfully handled. 37pp. AsB 70

_____. THE ZODIAC AND THE SOUL, c$4.50. An inspiring philosophical work, covering many of the major aspects of astrology. 120pp. TPH 28

CARUS, PAUL. CHINESE ASTROLOGY, $2.95. See Chinese Philosophy section.

COLLIN, RODNEY. **THE THEORY OF CELESTIAL INFLUENCE: MAN, THE UNIVERSE AND COSMIC MYSTERY**, $5.00. See Gurdjieff Section. Wei 73

CORNELL, H.L., M.D. **ENCYCLOPEDIA OF MEDICAL ASTROLOGY**, c$16.50 A comprehensive, thoroughly indexed and cross-referenced text which covers: general medicine—planetary influences for every condition, natural or pathological; alphabetical listings for each sign, luminary, and planet, indicating the diseases ruled by them; non-medical information on everything that appeals to or affects our physical body and the senses. 958pp. Wei 72

COUNCEL, PAUL. **X MARKS MY PLACE.** $3.50. This recent reprint is the only text on geographical astrology that we know of. The first section gives the theoretical background and a second one tells how to make practical applications. Astro-geographic tables and location maps are included. Many astrologers feel that correct or incorrect location according to the birth chart and progressions has a great deal to do with an individual's health, happiness, and success. 78 pp. Dar 38

CROSSLEY, PATRICIA. **LET'S LEARN ASTROLOGY**, c$7.50. An excellent comprehensive workbook for beginning students, the clearest and best that we know of. Dr. Crossley shows how to prepare astrological charts; how to read and make use of a Table of Houses and an Ephemeris; how to understand many astrological concepts. She discusses the solar charts, aspects, rulerships and exaltations, lunations and eclipses, elements and qualitites, parallels of declination, and depositing the planets. Every possible option is discussed clearly and the text is illustrated with charts, diagrams, and special tables, including many work sheets. Highly recommended. Bibliography, oversize, 96pp. Exp 73

CROWLEY, ALEISTER. **ASTROLOGY**, c$7.95. Crowley explains astrology within the context of the mythology and mysteries of the West. For him, the signs and planets are not mere ciphers in a mathematical calculation, but living archetypes which have developed along with the men who conceived them. Crowley also analyzes other symbolic systems such as the tarot and alchemy. This is a reprint of the 1915 text. Stephen Skinner has edited and annotated it. 224pp. Wei 15

CULPEPER, NICHOLAS. **ASTROLOGICAL JUDGMENT OF DISEASE**, $4.55. Culpeper was a seventeenth century English physician, best known today for his Herbal. This is an offset reprint of his major work on disease as it relates to astrology. Many cases and specific instances are cited. The material is archaic, but some valuable insights are included. Oversize, 135pp. AFA nd

CUMONT, FRANZ. **ASTROLOGY AND RELIGION AMONG THE GREEKS AND ROMANS**, $2.00. Reconstructs the beginnings of astrology in eighth century BC Babylonia, giving a full discussion of both the state of Chaldean astronomy and the motives that impelled scientists to study the stars. Also gives the history and development of early astrology in Greece, Syria, Egypt, and the Roman Empire. 110pp. Dov 60

DALTON, LYNN. **WORLD TRANSITS, 1975-1976.** $2.25. A review of mundane astrology for these two years, with chapters on earth houses (based on the material in Rudhyar's **Astrological Timing**), which analyzes the transiting planets as they affect various parts of the globe; aspects of 1975 and 1976; the United States horoscope; and America's leadership. A number of sample charts are included. 41 pp. Vul 75

DARLING, HARRY and RUTH H. OLIVER. **ASTRO-PSYCHIATRY**, c$11.95. The definitive work to date on criminal and abnormal psychiatry and astrology. It discusses in detail, with case histories and a wealth of diagrams, how mental problems can be recognized in birth charts. Relates abstractions of James, Freud, Adler, and Jung to specific birth chart configurations. CSA 74

DARR, CLARA. **COMPARISON**, $5.00. A follow-up to Ms. Darr's **Keys**, which analyzes the effects of another's planets falling in your natal houses, and shows how you affect others. Also has some material on the transiting planets not included in her **Transits.** Her books are incredibly overpriced, but many of our professional customers say they are well worth having. 48pp. Dar 73

_____. **KEY TO INTER RELATIONS**, $3.15. Guidelines for comparing horoscopes which include aspects to nodes, part of fortune, ascendant, and mid-heaven. 25pp. Dar 61

_____. **NEPTUNE IN TRANSIT WITH ASPECTS**, $3.00. This is the first in a projected series taking each planet through the houses and analyzing each transiting aspect in detail. The material here expands greatly upon Ms. Darr's earlier work, **Transits.** Dar 75

_____. **TRANSITS**, $10.00. One of the most complete books on transits available. Guidelines for the six major aspects are given for each of the planets plus the sun and moon. This is Ms. Darr's most informative book. 126pp. Dar 71

_____. **URANUS IN TRANSIT WITH THE ASPECTS**, $3.00. 48pp. Dar 76

DAVIDSON, WILLIAM. **SET OF LECTURES ON MEDICAL ASTROLOGY**, $19.50/set. A transcript of nine lectures on medical astrology and health Dr. Davidson gave in 1958. They form the fullest treatment of the subject available anywhere by an authority in this field. 5 volumes, 266pp. AsB 73

DAVIS, GERALDINE. **HORARY ASTROLOGY**, $4.25. A practical and comprehensive guide to the use of horary astrology applied to the mundane affairs and problems of daily living, business, travel, relationships, legal matters, etc. The author tells when and under what aspects two conditions may arise and indicates many possible routes an individual may take in coping with two situations. (You need a basic knowledge of astrological principles to understand the technical terminology of this book.) Recommended. 270pp. Sym 42

DAVIS, T.P. **ASTROLOGER'S CONDENSED MANUAL**, $4.95. This manual was designed to give the beginning student a solid basis of condensed information on which to begin learning astrology and to be used as a reminder for the more advanced student. Every aspect of astrology seems to be touched on. A well organized introduction, including charts, illustrations and tables. Oversize, 53pp. Dav 72

_____. **ASTROLOGER'S ESSENTIAL TABLES AND FORMULAS**, $4.90. Includes 24 hour log table; declination degrees for sun; midheaven and ascendant; latitude correction table; quick planetary and moon motion calculator; midpoint calculator graph; planetary strength table and decanate ruler table; correction table for sidereal time; table for turning degrees into time and time into degrees. All the sheets are plasticized for durability. ArB

CELESTIAL SPHERE woodcut by E. Schon, Germany, 1515

DAVISON, RONALD. **ASTROLOGY**, c$.95. Complete instructions for erecting a birthchart, as well as brief definitions of major astrological concepts. This book is well-regarded by many astrologers, but we don't feel that the material is very clearly presented. 171pp. Arc 63

_____. **THE TECHNIQUE OF PREDICTION**, c$7.35. Discussion and illustration of a new method of prediction which combines new measures of prediction discovered by Davidson with the Arabian system of secondary directions. Numerous examples and special tables are included. 152pp. Fow 55

DELPHICA. **ASTROLOGICAL CHARACTERISTICS IN LITERATURE**, $1.75. Interpretative studies of the charts of Carl Jung, Picasso, and several writers whom we have never heard of. 86pp. TPH 68

DELSOL, PAULA. **CHINESE ASTROLOGY**, $2.95. A light hearted look into the *moon signs* of Oriental lunar astrology. 248pp. Hip 72

DOANE, DORIS CHASE. **ASTROLOGY**, $6.50. This book is the result of thirty years of research into the golden key of astrology based on the statistical studies of birth charts, paralleled with the case histories of people's lives. It statistically shows by tabulations of aspects, signs, planets, etc., certain predispositions to conditions, vocations, journeys, disease, etc. It also has a section on stellar dynamics, a brief outline of the mathematical calculation of astrodynes, harmodynes, and discordynes, and twenty-four historical events occurring at the time of twenty-four major progressions in the chart of the U.S.A. For the advanced student. 300pp. PAs 56

_____. **ASTROLOGY RULERSHIPS**, $2.95. Small dictionary of predictable objects and events and the astrological factors they involve. 62pp. FOS 70

_____. **HOROSCOPES OF U.S. PRESIDENTS**, $5.00. Precise birth data and natal charts (with declinations) for each of the U.S. presidents through Nixon. Includes comparative data to pinpoint astrological constants for events, vocations, and diseases in their lives as well as listings of important events. 195pp. PAs 71

_____. **HOW TO READ COSMODYNES**, $4.95. Cosmodynes is a new term for *stellar dynamics*, which is defined as follows: *Judging the relative power, harmony and discord of the four basic factors in the natal and progressed chart—planets, signs, houses and aspects—by employing astrodynes, harmodynes and discordynes. With cosmodynes the astrologer can determine the amount and kind of astral energy a native has at his disposal at any given time.* They eliminate much of the guess work that astrologers have had to deal with in the past and aid the astrologer in determining what trends to expect from each birthchart position or progressed aspect. This is a detailed, step-by-step description of how to use them and how to compute them, graphically illustrated with many case studies. Oversize, 49pp. PAs 74

_____. **HOW TO PREPARE AND PASS AN ASTROLOGER'S CERTIFICATE EXAM**, $4.00. A detailed compilation. Oversize, 56pp. PAs 73

DOBYNS, ZIPPORAH and NANCY ROOF. **THE ASTROLOGER'S CASEBOOK**, $4.00. *This small volume is designed for the serious students of astrology who are already working with charts and who seek a deeper psychological insight into the uses of the horoscope as a diagnostic tool. It is primarily a casebook, with the cases taken from people attending a series of workshops designed to teach the methods presented here.* The cases are interpreted and after the interpretation the subject was interviewed and more material was brought out; a final section consists of comments on the material brought out in the interview. Each chart discussed is also presented graphically. Highly recommended. 140pp. TIA 73

DOBYNS, ZIPPORAH. **DISTANCE VALUES 1971–1980**, $1.50. Percentages of distance based on smallest and largest distances of the sun, moon, and planets from earth for use in astrological research and chart interpretation. Includes introduction covering possible meanings and giving examples. Dr. Dobyns has a doctorate in clinical psychology and has spent over fifteen years working in the fields of humanistic psychology, parapsychology, and astrology, seeking to integrate their respective insights into the nature of man in order to facilitate self-actualization and growth through self-knowledge. 67pp. TIA 72

_____. **EVOLUTION THROUGH THE ZODIAC**, $1.50. Subtitled *The World-View of Astrology*, this book presents the essential meaning of the twelve signs as a symbolic portrayal of man's spiritual evolution. *The signs have been presented here primarily on a path of evolution, a spiral path of growth, but they are also the twelve sides of a complete life. In a real chart, everyone has the potential for all twelve, however limited may be the expression of some of them.* An appendix contains house-planet-sign combinations and key phrases. 33pp. TIA 72

_____. **FINDING THE PERSON IN THE HOROSCOPE**, $2.50. This is a humanistic analysis of selected topics in astrology: fixed stars, midpoints, nodes, the asteroids, aspects, elements and qualities, and Saturn. Each topic is briefly discussed and illustrated with examples. An appendix presents key phrases for house-planet-sign combinations. 63pp. TIA 73

_____. **THE NODE BOOK**, $3.50. Table of longitudes of the nodes of the planets from a geocentric point of view from 1971–1974, with a table of equivalent years to apply them to any year. Includes a discussion of the planetary nodes and the moon's nodes in the six zodiacal polarities, with illustrative examples. TIA 73

_____. **PROGRESSIONS, DIRECTIONS AND RECTIFICATION**, $4.00. This is a detailed study, taking the approach of humanistic astrology, including clear directions and defining at length all the technical terms. Over one half of the book is devoted to an in depth analysis of the chart (or, rather, charts) of Senator Edward Kennedy as an illustration of how progressions, directions, and rectifications are worked out. This section includes eighteen fold-out pages—most of which are the charts of Edward Kennedy, and including charts of both Robert and John. The book is an interesting presentation and the reader is given a good idea of how these techniques work and what they show. 100pp. TIA 75

_____. **THE ZODIAC AS A KEY TO HISTORY**, $1.50. A presentation of the historical astrological ages, splitting them into sub-ages and explaining the rationale behind this division. Dr. Dobyns feels that this division explains the contemporary confusion over the timing of the Aquarian Age as well as other historical incidents and helps in understanding present day trends. 23pp. TIA 68

DODSON, CAROLYN. **HOROSCOPES OF THE U.S. STATES & CITIES**, $8.00. This is the first book to give the charts on each of the 50 states and their major cities. The charts are done by a computer and are very clear. An invaluable tool for astrologers who want an aid in selecting the best location in which to live, and in forecasting upcoming state and city changes, growth, and economic trends. Oversize, biblio., 205pp. CaD 75

DONAT, EMMA. **ASTEROIDS IN THE BIRTH CHART**, $4.00. A discussion of the four main asteroids (which the author feels are the true rulers of Gemini) including keywords, chart examples, and a review of each of the asteroids in the signs and the houses. There's not much psychological depth here, but it certainly is good to have the meanings of the asteroids in a handy form. 63pp. GeW 76

DUZ, M. **A PRACTICAL TREATISE OF ASTRAL MEDICINE AND THERAPEUTICS**, $4.00. In this book Dr. Duz presents an in depth study of the relationship between medicine and astrology. Many diagrams, 252pp. HeR 12

EBERTIN, ELSBETH. **ASTROLOGY AND ROMANCE**, c$7.00. A recent reprint of a 1926 treatise which presents many ancient and modern astrological observations and rules of interpretation, together with over twenty male and female horoscopes. The writing style (or perhaps the translation) is quite dated but the content is often insightful. The theme is lovers and what makes them suited or not suited to one another and the whole is presented in an almost novelistic vein. The author's son, Reinhold, adds an afterword to this edition. 132pp. ASI 26

EBERTIN, REINHOLD. **THE ANNUAL DIAGRAM**, $5.50. A new system for setting up an annual diagram using the graphic 45° ephemeris which gives the astrologer a quick, easy and readable picture of an entire year and enables him to ascertain when positive or negative reaction points make their appearance. 152pp. EbV 73

_____. **APPLIED COSMOBIOLOGY**, $10.50. *The term cosmobiology designates those methods applied to the study of the relationship between the cosmic rhythms and life on earth. Experience has taught us that weather, climate, plant growth, natural catastrophes, and the individual's life as well are linked with the cosmic phenomena. . . . The particular aim of cosmobiological research is to honor the knowledge of the ancient world, but at the same time to survey with a critical eye the rules of traditional astrology and incorporate modern methods, such as statistics, to the investigation of cosmobiological concepts.* This is a very technical work which shows how to apply cosmobiology to daily life. Not recommended for the beginning student. 200pp. EbV 72

_____. **THE COMBINATION OF STELLAR INFLUENCES**, $10.50. The interpretations of certain planetary constellations presented in this book are intended to provide an insight into the disposition, capabilities, aspects of character, and possibilities of fate of the individual. The reader is shown how he can combine the various aspects of his chart into a meaningful picture of himself. This book points out the stellar relationships to the biological, organic, psychologic and sociological elements. The correlation between cosmic constellations and biological events has never been so convincingly and clearly shown through example as by this method. It is technical and the reader needs a knowledge of basic astrology principles to use this book. 256pp. Ebv 72

_____. **THE CONTACT COSMOGRAM**, $5.50. Ebertin's venture into chart comparison. As usual he has presented a method quite different from traditional astrology. His *contact cosmogram* is primarily concerned with the stellar positions at the time of birth and is brought into relation with current constellations or with a particular event. Here he shows how to set one up and gives many examples, graphically illustrated with the actual charts and discussed at length. 151pp. Ebv 74

_____. **THE COSMIC MARRIAGE**, $5.50. This is Ebertin's most extensive analysis of astrological compatability, or *synastry*. He includes many sample charts with accompanying discussion of them. A major portion of the book is devoted to an interpretation of the stellar positions in the signs with respect to marital disposition and fate. Other chapters discuss the midpoints, significant aspects, and celestial bodies in the *house of marriage*. There are also detailed directions for comparative analysis using the 90° workboard. 160pp. EbV 74

_____. **THE INFLUENCE OF PLUTO ON HUMAN LOVE LIFE**, $2.50. The aspects and influences of Pluto and its aspects to other planets, constellations, etc., according to the Ebertin method of cosmobiology. 28pp. Ebv 70

_____. **MAN IN THE UNIVERSE**, $4.00. This is intended as an introduction to cosmobiology. Following a short history of cosmobiological concepts, the reader is made familiar with various methods of working and interpretation which have proved their worth. This is by far the clearest presentation available, including step-by-step instructions and graphic illustrations. A very welcome addition to the Ebertin literature. 103pp. EbV 73

_____. **90° DIAL [Plastic] ASPECTARIAN** , $7.50. An aid in determining separate aspects and any angular relation according to the Ebertin method. Ebv

_____. **RAPID AND RELIABLE ANALYSIS**, $4.50. Attempts to show by a diagnostic delineation how to pick out the vital elements from a cosmogram and to draw from them certain conclusions as to when the tendencies shown therein may make their appearance. Includes many examples of charts or cosmograms of famous people as statistical evidence. 65pp. EbV 70

_____. **TRANSITS—WHAT DAY IS FAVORABLE FOR ME?** $2.50. Complete delineation of transit aspects, with real life examples and Ebertin philosophy. 136pp. EbV 71

EBERTIN, R. and GEORG HOFFMAN. **FIXED STARS AND THEIR INTERPRETATION**, $5.00. A working basis in which to incorporate fixed stars into natal charts and to have a review of a cosmic analogy to world events as well. In Ebertin's interpretation of fixed stars, he has tried to include many cases in order to clarify just how there are any *effects* resulting from fixed stars. The examples cited are meant to be ones relating to the radical position in the cosmogram. Very technical, not recommended for the beginning student. 95pp. EbV 71

ELENBAAS, VIRGINIA. **FOCUS ON PLUTO**, $4.00. The newest book on Pluto, examining Pluto in the signs, the houses, the planets, and in aspect. The analyses are related to the historical/national scene. Basic material, well presented. Bibliography and notes, 85pp. AFA 74

ELSNAU, MARY. **ASTROLOGER'S NOTEBOOK ON THE ASPECTS OF THE TRANSITING PLANETS**, $4.00. Basic details, often simplistically written. Includes blank space throughout for the student to add her/his own observations. The spiritual aspects of astrology are emphasized here. Oversize, 92+pp. HeR 62

ERLEWINE, MICHAEL and MARGARET, and DAVID WILSON. **INTERFACE: PLANETARY NODES**, $5.00. Tables of the interface points between the planetary nodes for the years between 1700 and 2000. The points are designed to be used in astrological work with the heliocentric coordinate system. Instructional and background material is also included. 25pp. Cir 73

ERLEWINE, STEPHEN. **THE CIRCLE BOOK OF CHARTS**, $5.50. Hundreds of charts of famous and not so famous people over the ages, the majority being noted twentieth century figures. A good reference tool. Oversize, 275pp. Cir 72

ESCOBAR, THYRZA. **144 DOORS OF THE ZODIAC: THE DWAD TECHNIQUE**, $8.00. The Dwads (Duodenary Divisions of the Zodiac) are widely used in Hindu astrology. A Dwad is the twelfth part of a sign (02°30'), and each sign contains 30°. There are, in all, 144 Duodenary Divisions. They are known as the *Doors of Consciousness* and are considered as very important *focal areas*. The Dwad is thought to work together with the Decan: the Decan shows a kind of coloring or modification, while the Dwad gives the *specifics and particulars*, and both are interpreted in light of the meaning of the sign itself. This is the only manual which describes how to find them and how to interpret them in the signs. Also included in this volume is J. Allen Jones' **Ephemerides for the True Nodes of the Moon and Planets (1900-80) and Lilith and Lulu (1900-2000).** GSR 74

_____. **SIDE LIGHTS OF ASTROLOGY,** $3.00. A basic interpretative booklet, emphasizing elements which are not considered in other books. Planetary patterns and unusual configurations are stressed. None of the material is discussed in depth, however the student can get a good idea of the over-all intuitive approach to chart analysis from the guidelines set forth here. A good supplement to more traditional interpretative texts, but hardly something that can be used alone. 51pp. GSR 60

EVANS, COLIN. **NEW WAITE'S COMPENDIUM OF NATAL ASTROLOGY,** c$6.95. The major portion of this text is devoted to a condensed ephemeris for the years 1880–1980, table of houses, latitudes and longitudes table, and time changes table. The written portion of the text presents introductory material along with a discussion of planets, aspects, houses, character delineation, rival systems of house division, and instructions for casting a chart (with examples). 252pp. Wei 17

FAGAN, CYRIL. **ASTROLOGICAL ORIGINS,** $2.95. Fagan, in the late 1940's and 1950's, rediscovered sidereal astrology, the type of astrology used by the ancients. This is an introductory historical treatment of its origins and development. 224pp. Llp 71

FAGAN, CYRIL and ROY FIREBRACE. **A PRIMER OF SIDEREAL ASTROLOGY,** $7.25. This is virtually the only instructional book on the sidereal system available. The authors developed the system as we think of it today and this is their basic book. Includes detailed instructions, sample charts, tables explaining sidereal techniques, and a dictionary of aspect meanings. LjP

FOELSCH, KUNO. **TRANSITS,** $4.95. A clearly presented, complete treatise on the transit system for astrological prognosis. Includes a review of the better known systems of astrological prediction as well as a review of the character and purpose of astrological prognosis. The technical, explanatory information contained herein was developed by the author out of twenty years of empirical research. 71pp. Hug nd

FURZE-MORRISH, L. **THE PARALLEL IN ASTROLOGY,** $5.00. Furze-Morrish is one of Australia's leading astrologers. This book discusses parallels to the Ascendant and progresses parallels. Vul 74

GADBURY, JOHN. **THE NATIVITY OF KING CHARLES,** $4.00. A verbatim offset reproduction of a 1659 text, for those interested in historical research. 128pp. Dar 74

GALLANT, ROY. **ASTROLOGY: SENSE OR NONSENSE?** c$5.95. This is an objective illustrated general account of astrology written by an astronomer. The bulk of the book is devoted to a fairly good historical survey of astrology and astrologers and early views about the zodiac. Only about one-fifth of the book discusses the meaning of the signs and planets. Many illustrations are included along with a glossary and index. 216pp. Dou 74

GAMMON, MARGARET. **ASTROLOGY AND THE EDGAR CAYCE READINGS,** $2.00. Beams of knowledge about signs, planets, transits, cusps, etc., from the Akashic Records in Mr. Cayce's superconscious. 85pp. ARE 74

GARRISON, OMAR. **MEDICAL ASTROLOGY,** $1.25. Presents astrology as an early warning system which enables one to prevent as well as prepare for illnesses. Medical astrology aims at preventing the occurrence of illness by identifying certain inherent physical weaknesses in the birth chart and determining the periods when one will be subject to discordant planetary influences. 269pp. War 71

GAUQUELIN, MICHEL. **THE COSMIC CLOCKS,** $3.95. One of the original, and undoubtedly still among the very best, scientific statistical researches into the Earth's connection to her solar system. The objectively produced rational conclusions are apt to startle skeptic and devotee both into more complete awareness of our true relation to the cosmic flow. Reg 67

_____. **SCIENTIFIC BASIS OF ASTROLOGY,** $2.95. A serious and comprehensive look at astrology. Includes discussions of Jung's differentiation between astrological and para-psychological conditions, and many scientific experiments connected with astrology as well as a complete history of astrology. Recommended for the skeptic. Index, bibliography, 255pp. S&D 69

GEORGE, LLEWELLYN. **A TO Z HOROSCOPE MAKER AND DELINEATOR,** c$12.00. One of the most popular astrology texts available (thought not one of our favorites). It contains all the information necessary to erect and interpret natal and progressed charts, with complete definitions of every term used. Graphically illustrated with charts, tables, and examples, and quite comprehensive. 813pp. LIP 10

_____. **IMPROVED PERPETUAL PLANETARY HOUR BOOK,** $5.00. *Each hour of the day is ruled by a planet and the nature of any hour corresponds to the nature of the planet ruling it. If you possess a Planetary Hour Book you may choose a fortunate hour to commence important undertakings.... It is the object of this edition to meet the needs...of students with a practical text and tables having range from 27 to 55 degrees latitude.* A great deal of explanatory material is also included. 217pp. LIP 06

_____. **POWERFUL PLANETS,** $1.00. An archaic text which presents a detailed discussion of horary astrology and covers a wide variety of astrological applications—including agriculture, medicine, and meteorology. Many references, 224pp. LIP 31

GETTINGS, FRED. **BOOK OF THE ZODIAC,** c$4.98. Meanings of the signs illustrated with well reproduced art and photographs. 143pp. Tri 72

_____. **THE HAND AND THE HOROSCOPE,** c$5.98. See Palmistry section. Tri 73

GLEADOW, RUPERT. **THE ORIGIN OF THE ZODIAC.** c$2.98. Gleadow begins with astrology today, especially the difference between tropical and sidereal astrology, and then he goes back and traces the nature, philosophy, and history of the zodiac in the ancient cultures of Tibet, China, India, Greece, and Egypt, quoting, in the process, many great philosophers. An excellent presentation, many notes. 238pp. BoS 68

_____. **THE ZODIAC REVEALED,** $2.00. Explains how horoscopes have been cast over the years, and sheds light on the different interpretations given to the twelve signs of the zodiac. Also contains a listing of the signs of many famous people. 186pp. Wil 68

GOODAVAGE, JOSEPH. **ASTROLOGY: THE SPACE AGE SCIENCE,** $.95. Shows the modern scientific case for the ancient wisdom of astrology. Relates astrology to the creation of the universe, astro twins, the lost continent of Atlantis, the meaning of the Great Flood myth, the mystical United States, predicting weather, earthquakes, disasters and more. 250pp. NAL 66

_____. **WRITE YOUR OWN HOROSCOPE,** $1.50. Offers charts and tables that enable you to determine easily the position of the sun, moon, and planets at the precise time of your birth. Also, the meaning of various conjunctions of heavenly bodies, the Vital Power points in the chart, and significance of signs and patterns in the personal horoscope are explained. 275pp. NAL

GOODMAN, DAVID. **PSYCHOLOGICAL ASTROLOGY,** $4.00. Dr. Goodman is a clinical psychologist who is co-director of the Astro-Psychological Consultation Center in New York, the first public professional collaboration between the two disciplines. The temperament of each sign is analyzed and a number of case studies (with charts) are given for each sign. 55pp. AFA 74

GOODMAN, LINDA. **SUN SIGNS,** $1.95. An introductory text for those whose image of astrology has been formed by the daily newspaper horoscope. Goes into the basics. 484pp. Ban 68

GOODMAN, MORRIS. **ASTROLOGY AND SEXUAL ANALYSIS,** $1.50. An illustrated account covering the male and female of each sign and including a compatibility key. 184pp. War 73

GORDON, HENRY. **RECTIFICATION OF UNCERTAIN BIRTH HOURS,** $5.95. Rectification is always an uncertain thing and there is great controversy as to what is the best method. Gordon makes the case that a true understanding of an individual's character will allow the astrologer to rectify a chart. His system is based on individual delineation of the rising degree and midheaven degree and the key word of each degree. A few application examples are also included. 212pp. JPA

GREBNER, BERNICE. **LUNAR NODES,** $4.50. There's almost nothing written on the nodes, so it's good to have a book length exposition of them. Ms. Grebner seems to be coming from a positive place and her discussion should be helpful to those who seek a deeper understanding of the nodes. The nodes are individually discussed through the houses and in aspect and the general meaning of the nodes is presented. There's also some material on transits and progressions and on the astronomical explanation of the nodes. Two other sections discuss nodal points in the charts of famous people and synastry. Oversize, 41pp. BGr 73

GREEN, LANDIS. **THE ASTROLOGERS MANUAL,** $11.95 This is a brand new text which came in just as we were putting this list together. The approach is very positive and the writing style is excellent. We looked up some of the planets and signs that interested us most (the ones that are most prominent in our chart!) and we thought the descriptions excellent. The author begins with a general discussion of the history of astrology and some of the main astrological concepts (complete with excellent long definitions). He goes from there to a detailed analysis of the signs, both individually and in terms of the four elements. Next comes an analysis of the houses, both individually and in terms of house patterns and after that the Sun, Moon, and Planets are discussed. Another long chapter is devoted to astrological categories and correlations. There's also an illuminating section on Astrology and Human Relationships. Highly recommended as a basic text for the beginning student and as an aid in interpretation for all astrologers. Index, 255pp. Arc 75

GREEN, H.S. **DIRECTIONS AND DIRECTING**, $2.00. *The heavenly bodies are all in constant motion, so that although at birth they indicate accurately the nature of the physical vehicle and personality, they do not maintain this relationship unchanged. Day by day the signs rise and set, and the planets continue their revolutions; thus any heavenly body changes its position not only with regard to the rest that are also moving, but also in relation to the positions it and they occupied at birth . . . . This movement constitutes a direction, and will coincide with an event in the life.* This small book includes chapters on calculating and interpreting directions; on the effects of directions; on solar and lunar revolutions on transits and eclipses; and on pre-natal directions. Many examples are also presented. 81pp. AFA 72

GRELL, PAUL R. **KEYWORDS**, $2.00. Listing of keywords associated with all the planets, signs, and houses. 31pp. AFA 70

HALL, MANLY PALMER. **ASTROLOGICAL KEYWORDS**, $2.95. The keyword system is the most efficient means by which the student can analyze the implications of a horoscope as well as the most convenient method for finding the meaning of various factors in astrological charts. This is an extremely useful and timesaving work. 229pp. L&A 68

_____. **ASTROLOGY AND REINCARNATION**, $1.50. A collection of three essays: *How to Read Your Past and Future Lives, Astrology and Reincarnation,* and *Astrology and Karma.* 45pp. PRS 36

_____. **THE PHILOSOPHY OF ASTROLOGY**, $3.00. An esoteric approach which traces the philosophy of astrology throughout history. Highly recommended. 91pp. PRS70

_____. **PLANETARY INFLUENCE AND THE HUMAN SOUL**, $1.50. Lecture on the spiritual approach to astrology and the spiritual benefits to be gained. 32pp. PRS57

_____. **PLUTO IN LIBRA**, $1.50. A general interpretation of Pluto, with emphasis on its meaning in the sign of Libra. The influences are discussed in relation to the individual and to the United States. 31pp. PRS 71

_____. **PSYCHOANALYZING THE TWELVE ZODIACAL TYPES**, $1.50. Individual analyses of each of the signs, from Manly Hall's insightful point of view. 64pp. PRS 37

_____. **THE STORY OF ASTROLOGY**, c$5.00 A general survey of astrology's development throughout time, with separate chapters devoted to the astrology of each of the following: the Orient, the Hindus, the Burmese, the Tibetans, the Greeks, the Romans, the Arabs, the Aztecs. There are also chapters on astrology as a religion and as a philosophy and on astrology and science and on astrology's place in the modern world. Much of the source material for this book was derived from rare books and manuscripts in Mr. Hall's library. 156pp. PRS 75

_____. **STUDENTS CALCULATION FORM**, $1.25. Briefly and clearly explains the procedure for erecting a natal chart. There isn't enough information given to allow an individual to learn solely from this pamphlet; however, it provides a good supplement to the material given in the general textbooks. Oversize, 11pp. PRS

HAND, ROBERT. **PLANETS IN COMPOSITE**, c$10.00. Subtitled *Analyzing Human Relationships,* this is a welcome addition to the scanty material in this area. Heretofore astrologers have relied on a complicated technique of chart comparison known as synasty. The composite technique was developed in Germany about 30 years ago, and has been researched and tested quite extensively—although it is much too soon to comment on how effective and accurate the method is. The technique combines two individual charts (using midpoints) and creates a composite third chart, a chart of the relationship itself. This book contains a clear explanation of the composite technique, chapters on casting and reading the composite horoscope, 5 case studies illustrating the use and validity of composite charts, plus twelve chapters of delineations. There are delineations for all the planets (including Sun and Moon) in each house and every major aspect (conjunction, sextile, square, trine, opposition). All together there are 374 interpretations, each about 300 words. And there are also 41 delineations of the Moon's nodes. Recommended. Index, 376pp. Par 75

_____. **PLANETS IN TRANSIT**, c$12.00. Descriptions of the typical effects associated with the transited of the planets over the factors of the natal horoscope. Transits of the sun, moon, and planets to the ascendant, M.C., planets, and houses of the chart are described in passages averaging 300 words. Transits by conjunction, sextile, trine, and opposition are delineated. In each case emphasis is on the feelings, psychological shifts, and inner energies of the transits. Events indicated by the transit are treated as consequences of these psychological patterns, rather than as fated inevitabilities. In addition, there are introductory chapters describing the use of transits in forecasting, factors that effect timing, and various other matters. There is also an extended case study illustrating the principles set forth. Recommended. 400pp. PaR 76

HARDING, ARTHUR, ed. **SYNASTRY**, $3.00. Synastry is the comparison of horoscopes for the purpose of judging the extent and character of their interaction. This is a collection of practically, graphically illustrated essays: *Synastry as Therapy* by Ingrid Lind; *Synastry, Its Principles and Practice* by Sheila Geddes; *The Synastry Problem* by Reinhold Ebertin; *A Key to Relationships* by Stephen Arroyo; and *Synastry in Depth* by Patrick Harding. Only those familiar with cosmobiology should consider this work. 79pp. AsA 72

HAYES, JAMES. **INTRODUCTION TO NATAL ASTROLOGY**, c$7.95. This is one of the newest over-all textbooks available. Hayes writes clearly and he covers a lot of material. He begins with an essay on what astrology is and is not and goes on to chapters on the planets, the signs, and the houses. His section on erecting a chart is more detailed than most of the general texts and he also includes instructions on calculating aspects along

with notes on what many of the aspects mean. A final section discusses delineation and explains how a beginning astrologer should organize her/his material in preparing a written delineation. Oversize, 238pp. UnB 74

HEINDEL, MAX. **ASTRO-DIAGNOSIS: A GUIDE TO HEALING**, $4.50. Astro-diagnosis is the science and art of obtaining scientific knowledge regarding disease and its causes as shown by the planets, as well as the means of overcoming it. A chapter is devoted to each of the different parts of the body, with actual examples of diagnosis from the horoscope. 482pp. Ros 29

_____. **THE MESSAGE OF THE STARS**, c$8.00/5.50. Heindel was one of the most noted twentieth century astrologers as well as a noted Rosicrucian. This is a basic book, though it's not recommended for the beginning student. Contains chapters on progression, medical astrology, complete information on each planet and sign, as well as a spiritual survey of astrological history. 728pp. Ros 73

_____. **SIMPLIFIED SCIENTIFIC ASTROLOGY—HOW TO CHART YOUR HOROSCOPE**, $2.00. A clear, complete textbook on the art of erecting a horoscope. Includes many tables. 198pp, Wil 28

HEINDEL, MAX. **YOUR CHILD'S HOROSCOPE, VOL. I & II**, $1.50 ea. Case studies of the horoscopes of many children, seemingly chosen at random to show how various planetary configurations and signs and houses relate to a child's life. About 100pp each. Ros 71,73

HELINE, CORINNE. **THE BIBLE AND THE STARS**, $3.50. A series of esoteric lecture-lessons on the sacred science of the stars. An inspiring presentation. See other Heline books in the Mysticism and Christianity sections. 128pp. NAP 71

_____. **THE TWELVE LABORS OF HERCULES IN THE ZODIACAL SCHOOL OF LIFE**, $1.50. 69pp. NAP 70

HICKEY, ISABEL. **ASTROLOGY: A COSMIC SCIENCE**, c$11.00. An excellent, inspiring basic textbook—one of our favorites. Especially recommended for students interested in the karmic and reincarnational aspects of astrology. The presentation is comprehensive and very clearly written. The basic material on learning how to erect a birth chart is quite skimpy, but the explanatory, interpretative material is generally very good. 280pp. Hic 70

_____. **PLUTO OR MINERVA—THE CHOICE IS YOURS**, $3.85. *Pluto, the most invisible of the planets, represents the energy in us which is unknown on the surface but which works ceaselessly in the depths of our being. It rules the underworld in us as well as the highest part of us.* This is a very nice analysis of Pluto— in the signs, the houses, natal aspects, transits, and its meaning. Also included are a number of letters to Isabel Hickey, with charts and responses. 83pp. Hic 74

HIROZ, ROBIE. **THE ASTROLOGICAL CHART**, $2.00. This is in the form of a portfolio with separate sheets devoted to outlining key concepts and phrases for the beginning student. The material is very clearly presented and forms an excellent review and learning tool. Each of the sheets is laminated and the emphasis is on astrology as a tool for understanding people and defining the dynamics of personal growth. Examples are drawn from the chart of Carl Jung. Recommended. Mag 72

_____. **PLANETARY ACTIVITY ON THE DEGREES OF THE ZODIAC: 1970—1979**, $4.75. Well organized tables for each degree of each sign trace the dynamic aspects of transiting Mars through Pluto; stations of Mercury and Venus; lunations and eclipses. The author hopes to facilitate the observation of dynamic aspects made to the Zodiacal degrees. Only the major active aspects (conjunction, opposition, and square) are included. This is a very well laid out book which should be of great assistance to all practicing astrologers. Mag 73

HODGSON, JOAN. **WISDOM IN THE STARS**, $2.50. This is a spiritual analysis of the sun signs which discusses each one as a stage of soul development. Many beautiful insights are revealed. 124pp. WEP 73

HOLLEY, GERMAINE. **PLUTO/NEPTUNE**, $3.95. Ms. Holley is a French astrologer who believes that the sign Pisces is ruled not by Jupiter, nor even by Jupiter and Neptune—but by Pluto and Neptune jointly. This is a detailed exposition of this theory along with a study of the role played by Pluto and Neptune in an individual's chart. There is also a very complete aspectarian for the two planets, an analysis of their tenancy in the signs and houses, and an analysis of Pisces on the house cusps. A final section explores the placement of Pluto and Neptune in the charts of the U. S., Egypt, and Israel. This is an interesting study which sheds some light on Pluto through a highly spiritual analysis. 150pp. Wei 74

THE HOLY ORDER OF MANS. **THE STARS OF HEAVEN.** $3.00. This book is a well written, very spiritual discussion of the basics of astrology. The author uses mythological references and material from the ancient mystery teachings in his presentation of the signs, planets, and houses. Color correspondences are provided for each sign and planet and there is an excellent review of astrological symbolism. The astrological ages are also discussed and there's a good deal of supplementary material. All in all, a nice book for those on the path who want to get a feel for astrology. Illustrations, 133 pp. HOM 75

HONE, MARGARET. **APPLIED ASTROLOGY**, c$6.50. Companion volume to the **Modern Textbook.** Gives examples of chart interpretation with marginal astrological references, and case histories which illustrate astro-analysis. Very clearly presented interpretative work, including many diagrams. 119pp. Fow 53

Natural Rulerships

Planet: Life Urge	Sign: Psychological Type	House: Sphere of Life
♂ Personal Will, Action	♈ Self-Assertive, Active	1 The Self, Personal Actions
♀ Feeling, Sense Experience	♉ Physically Sustaining	2 Possessions, The Senses
☿ Thought, Communication	♊ Aware, Communicative	3 Travels, Communications
☽ Nurturance, Motherhood	♋ Nurturing, Domestic	4 Foundations, The Home
☉ Creativity, Fatherhood	♌ Self-Expressive, Paternal	5 Creative Expression, Sex
☿ Mental Efficiency	♍ Discriminative, Efficient	6 Adjustments, work, Service
♀ Unity of Relationship	♎ Unifying, Interdependent	7 Other People, Partners
♇ Transformation	♏ Self-Transforming	8 Death and Rebirth
♃ Mental Expansion	♐ Exploratory, Philosophical	9 Distant Travel, Philosophy
♄ Discipline, Achievement	♑ Responsible, Ambitious	10 Authority, The Career
♅ Self-Liberation, Progress	♒ Independent, Progressive	11 New Ideas, Social Objectives
♆ Spiritual Union	♓ Transcendental, Surrendering	12 Self-Sacrifice, The Unknown

from **The Astrological Chart** by Robie Hiroz

_____. **MODERN TEXTBOOK OF ASTROLOGY**, c$9.35. One of the best all-around astrology general texts, designed as a complete self-study course for beginners—and also quite useful for experienced astrologers. Establishes a sound basis of knowledge. Well written. Ms. Hone was the founder of the Faculty of Astrological Studies of Great Britain and its Director for many years. 315pp. Fow 51

HOWELL, IRENE. **CYCLIC ASTROLOGY**, $3.50. Presents a new method for the rectification of a birth chart when the hour is not known, or only approximately known. Howell uses the Ascendant as the vital point of the chart and follows its course through the natal chart in the three cycles. She gives detailed specifics here which are the fruit of six years of research and application and includes many graphic examples. Accurate rectification is one of the most difficult things in astrology and the method presented here seems to be a good clear one. 68pp. Dar 74

HUGHES, DOROTHY. **THE BASIC ELEMENTS OF ASTROLOGY**, $2.50. Concise condensation of volumes of material. Aims at showing the beginner a wide view right from the start. 37pp. AFA 70

MOMENT OF BIRTH woodcut, 1587 (detail)

JACOBSON, IVY. **ALL OVER THE EARTH ASTROLOGICALLY**, c$6.50. Ms. Jacobson is a very respected astrologer who has been teaching for many years. Her books often overlap each other—but each presents exciting and enlightening new concepts not discussed in a previous work. They are written for the intermediate student who is well acquainted with the mechanics of astrology but who needs further guidance in *reading the scriptures.* The main emphasis in this volume is on reading the natal and progressed chart and understanding the various aspects presented. Astrology is seen as a key to self-growth and understanding. A section is devoted to transits and there is a good glossary. 215pp. Jac 63

_____. **THE DARK MOON LILITH IN ASTROLOGY**, c$6.00. A comprehensive account for those interested in the effects of this little understood, and little seen moon. Includes a complete ephemeris for Lilith. 55pp. Jac 61

_____. **FOUNDATION OF THE ASTROLOGICAL CHART** , c$6.50. *This work is designed for use as a textbook in setting up a chart for the exact location of the planets for any given date, hour and place on earth. It also goes further, to include progressing the chart to show the advanced positions at any desired future date.* The text is arranged to be learned entirely at home, without a teacher. The mathematics is very clearly presented and the text is graphically illustrated. Much of the material presented here is found in no other book we have seen. Includes questions and detailed answers to assist the student. 125pp. Jac 59

_____. **HERE AND THERE IN ASTROLOGY**, c$6.50. *The first part of this work is comprised of special sections designed to give the student . . . a new, different, and much simpler approach to his work with natal charts,* enlightening in many areas. The second part is devoted to a system the author derived through extended research for making and interpreting event charts. 215pp. Jac 61

_____. **IN THE BEGINNING ASTROLOGY**, c$10.00. This is Ivy's newest book. She reviews a number of little understood areas in depth including pre-natal astrology, rectification, delineation, vocational astrology, and mundane astrology. The delineation section expands upon the material she presented in her book on horary. Many sample charts illustrate her exposition and the technical instructions are excellent. We like Ivy's books a lot and we are delighted with this one. 237pp. Jac 75

_____. **SIMPLIFIED HORARY ASTROLOGY**, c$9.50. Horary *is the branch of Astrology in which we set up a chart for the time that a question takes shape, either seriously in the mind or put into words. The position of the planets at that moment will reveal the problem, its background, and also its final outcome or answer.* This is an excellent, detailed account of how to set up a horary chart and how to go about interpreting it. Includes an extensive section on planets and questions in each house. 278pp. Jac 60

_____. **THE TURN OF A LIFETIME ASTROLOGICALLY**, $7.50. Presents a simplified method for calculating primary arcs (important for pinpointing event dates in life), including all the necessary tables in larger print than usual. 115pp. Jac 64

_____. **THE WAY OF ASTROLOGY**, c$9.00. A fascinating account of the history of astrology; the natal chart and its development; reading the natal chart; progressions; the election chart; forecasting; special aspects; and a clear glossary. 233pp. Jac 67

JAIN, M.C. **ASTROLOGY AND THE LAW OF SEX**, $5.00. A treatise by one of India's leading astrologers. Lots of strange material combined with more traditional ideas. Includes chapters on sex abnormality and sex perversion, sex potentiality and sex drive, marriage, love, and much else. Final sections discuss chart comparison and present some case studies. 215pp. All 74

_____. **ASTROLOGY IN MARRIAGE COUNSELLING**, c$8.00. This is a primer of Indian ideas of romance and marriage. Pyt 74

_____. **MUNDANE ASTROLOGY**, c$4.00. A review of the general principles of mundane astrology, followed by studies of the planets, signs, houses and aspects as seen in mundane astrology. There's also material on mundane maps and how to erect them along with information on judging the maps and examples of maps. The bulk of the book is devoted to analyses of the individual houses and the planets therein. There are also chapters on eclipses, planetary conjunctions, earthquakes, and comets. 182pp. Sag 73

_____. **THE SIGNS AND YOUR FUTURE**, c$4.00. A study of the fixed stars in the signs, with interpretations of each degree in each sign according to the Hindu system of astrology. 194pp. Sag 73

JANSKY, ROBERT. **GETTING YOUR CORRECT BIRTH DATA**, $5.00. Tells where to write for birth data for each of the fifty states; the address, the cost, the time required, when birth times were recorded, and the pecularities of each state in recording births. Sample application forms from various states are included as an appendix and there are chapters on reading and interpreting Birth Certificate information and on obtaining information in cases of adoption. AsA 75

_____. **HOROSCOPES: HERE AND NOW**, $7.50. This is a collection of the horoscopes of contemporary figures. The charts are accurate, with cusps and planets shown to the nearest minute of a degree—major and all outstanding chart features are clearly shown. Time, place and date of birth are indicated, and all charts are classified by planetary pattern. The book was designed to provide astrologers with living examples of such things at T-crosses, singletons, retrograde rulers, and planetary patterns as they affect the everyday life of people in today's news. AsA 74

_____. **INTERPRETING THE ASPECTS**, $7.00. Most of the material on aspects and planetary structures simply contains definitions of what each particular aspect means without delving into the fundamental meaning of each type of aspect or structure. This excellent book studies the major aspects and their interpretations. Jansky is concerned with helping the student gain a basic understanding which s/he can later apply to specific situations. This is much more than a planetary aspect dictionary. Planetary structures (the grand trine, the crosses, the yod, and the kite) are examined in greater detail here than in any other book. The aspects and structures are presented in terms of assets and liabilities, and in light of present-day mid-point theory. The material is very clearly presented. Oversize, bibiography, 40pp. AsA 74

_____. **INTRODUCTION TO NUTRITIONAL ASTROLOGY**, $7.50. This is the only book devoted completely to nutrition and astrology. It reviews the essential body processes and how they are influenced astrologically, and covers such topics as obesity, how hormones affect your personality, low blood sugar, selection of foods most agreeable to one's body chemistry, and cell salts. AsA 75

_____. **MODERN MEDICAL ASTROLOGY**, $7.50. This text, the first of five planned by Jansky, a biochemist-astrologer, introduces you to the technique of delineating the astrological relationship to health and disease. It shows the relationship between the planets and signs and the various parts of the body and their proper function. Vitamins and minerals are related to the planets, cell salts to the signs. Illustrated by many careful case studies it covers such topics as birth control techniques, alcoholism, asthma, violence, conditions surrounding death, sexual preference, diabetes, and hypoglycemia. Rather than simply for diagnosis, these topics are used to illustrate the research techniques that can be used—both the classical and modern (midpoint) methods. This is the best overall book on medical astrology we've seen. Topically organized and graphically illustrated. AsA 74

_____. **PLANETARY PATTERNS**, $6.50. Nearly forty years ago Marc Edmund Jones (in **Guide to Horoscope Interpretation**) described seven basic planetary distribution patterns to each of which he ascribed certain general characteristics of self-expression or temperament. Since that time his system has received wide acceptance by professional astrologers with very little change made to the original system. Jones speaks of each pattern as a *Temperament Type* with each type having a characteristic set of general traits that can be objectively observed. In this book Jansky reviews Jones' pattern system, challenges certain of his ideas, and presents contemporary example charts. This is an excellent delineation tool. AsA 74

_____. **SELECTED TOPICS IN ASTROLOGY**, $7.00. Jansky put this book together as an aid to students who have a basic working knowledge of astrology and want to learn interpretation. It includes detailed instructions in how to use an ephemeris and discusses the meaning of retrograde planets, parallel aspects, focal determinators, the sign qualities, natural disposition, singleton planets, intercepted signs, planetary dignities, and many other not-easily-understood areas. The text is very clearly written and graphically illustrated. AsA 74

_____. SYNASTRY, $6.50. Synastry is the study of the way in which two persons will relate to each other by comparing the planetary positions in one chart with those in the other. This book teaches a technique for making this comparison, using your own chart as the primary one. Jansky shows you how to predict both compatibilities and potential problem areas and illustrates how to deal with them through increased understanding. Well written, with graphic illustrations and sample charts. AsA 74

JAYNE, CHARLES, ed. BEST IN ASTROLOGY FROM IN SEARCH, $4.00. In Search was the first international astrological periodical. It was published from 1958–1961. The best astrologers contributed to it. The articles in this reprint are by Marc Jones, William Davidson, W. Kenneth Brown, Dane Rudhyar, Charles Carter, Pauline Messina, Edouard Symours, Ludwig Rudolph, and W.O. Sucher. Many pioneering concepts were introduced in its pages. Oversize, 60pp. AsB 74

_____. HOROSCOPE INTERPRETATION OUTLINED, $4.25. Tries to correct the widespread fallacy of examining the horoscope in a piecemeal manner. Chart is interpreted first as a whole and then gradually to the chart-in-particular. It presupposes knowledge of the fundamentals. Included are explanations of the major components of the horoscope (i.e., the major configurations), the lights and angles and their relationships, the pivotal and singular factors, and a section on declination parallels. 53pp. AsB 70

_____. PROGRESSIONS AND DIRECTIONS, $5.00. First part briefly describes progressions, secondary or major, minor, and tertiary; the second part, new directions in astrology, deals with the solar arcs; the third part deals with primary directions; and a fourth, very brief section is concerned with symbolic directions. The appendix is an explanation of how to do a double interpolation. Very technical. 53pp. AsB

_____. THE TECHNIQUE OF RECTIFICATION, $5.00. Techniques of rectification using mainly solar, ascendant arc directions and vertical arcs. Very technical. 60pp. AsB 72

_____. THE UNKNOWN PLANETS, $5.00. This is a detailed discussion of the *unknown* planets, including their effects and ephemerides for them. Oversize, 29pp. AsB 74

JAYNE, VIVIA. ASPECTS TO HOROSCOPE ANGLES, $4.25. Vivia Jayne has spent twenty of her twenty-five years as an astrologer in rectification of the horoscope angles. She discusses aspects to the ascendant, midheaven, and vertex angles and illustrates her exposition with many examples. The material presented here is not available in the texts on aspects. 53pp. AsB 74

JENKYN, RICHARD. ASTROLOGY AND DIET, $1.75. Shows tendencies in each different sign of the zodiac toward certain deficiencies in body chemistry and gives an analysis of foods and cell salts which are valuable remedies for each individual sign and its afflictions. 62pp. HSP 67

JINNI and JOANNE. DIGESTED ASTROLOGER, VOLUME I, $3.00. A very clearly written introductory survey of the basics of chart interpretation. All aspects of the natal chart are simply and fully discussed. 59pp. ANW 72

_____. WHEN YOUR SUN RETURNS, $3.50. Vol. II of the Digested Astrologer. The only book based on tropical astrology that teaches the math and interpretation of the solar return charts. ANW 73

_____. YOUR COSMIC MIRROR, $1.50. *This workbook is for the purpose of helping you find greater self-awareness through your own personal astrological birth chart. The techniques we use are based on concepts fully developed in* The Spiral of Life. *In the following pages, you will find sets of key phrases for aspects, signs and houses. The last section contains a form for analyzing the structure and activity of your personality through the planets that rule your natal houses and signs. There are spaces for you to write in your analysis, using the key phrases as indicated.* This is a very useful tool in humanistically understanding a natal chart. The key phrases are well chosen and the material is clearly organized. Oversize, 18pp. ANW 73

_____. THE SPIRAL OF LIFE, $6.95. This is a very full explanation of all aspects of interpretation in the form of an exploration of the relationship between the signs and their corresponding natural houses which reveals a dynamic growth process constantly operating in the natal chart which can be seen without the use of progressions and transits. Signs and houses are described at the level of psychological functioning and their planetary rulerships are integrated. Major and minor aspects are explained and every planet is related to every other planet, whether in aspect or not. The lunation phases are also discussed and there is a complete listing of every type of phase-aspect. In addition, Pluto and the Nodes are analyzed and one section describes the effects of Solar and Lunar Eclipses in the natal chart. The book covers a lot of ground—but it does so well and in a unique way that seems very suited to today's astrologers. 160pp. ANW 74

JOCELYN, JOHN. MEDITATIONS ON THE SIGNS OF THE ZODIAC, $2.50. This book presents the spiritual nature of the zodiac for meditation and relates it to self-knowledge. The right use of these meditations enables one to achieve wholeness within oneself and in one's environment. 277pp. Mul 70

JOHNDRO, EDWARD. THE ASTROLOGICAL DICTIONARY, $2.00. The major part of this book consists of a listing of keywords for each planet. There's also material on aspects. Oversize, 41pp. AFA nd

_____. THE EARTH IN THE HEAVENS—RULING DEGREES OF CITIES, c$6.50. A very technical book which starts with a detailed discussion of the precession and its equinoctial and ecliptic rectifications, and then shows how to adjust the midheavens and ascendants of locations. Coordinates are given for over 400 cities, along with a workable table. 151pp. Wei 70

_____. A NEW CONCEPTION OF SUN RULERSHIP, $2.00. This is a companion volume to Astrological Dictionary. The material presented here is not available in any other book and it has been influential among astrologers seeking to show the relation between the native and his environment and the reactions between the individual and his society. Oversize, 30pp. AFA 71

_____. THE STARS: HOW AND WHERE THEY INFLUENCE, c$6.50. A graphic explanation of how the latitudinal positions of the fixed stars are related to people, places and events, as well as periodic states such as prosperity and depression. 120pp. Wei 73

JONES, MARC EDMUND. ASTROLOGY: HOW AND WHY IT WORKS, $2.95. A technical introduction to the basics of astrology, not recommended as a beginning text. Opens by showing how astrology arose from primitive man's confrontation with a world of chance and risk, and goes from there to show how the fundamentals have been developed and how they can be applied to daily life. The houses, signs, planets, and each horoscopic element is discussed at great length. Includes a large amount of interpretative material. 364pp. Pen 71

_____. THE ESSENTIALS OF ASTROLOGICAL ANALYSIS, c$16.50. A complete exposition of the horoscope, and an explanation of how its total view becomes an approach to better understanding the human potential. Not recommended for the beginning student. 455pp. Sab 60

_____. THE GUIDE TO HOROSCOPE INTERPRETATION, $2.75. Presents a technique of interpretation which divides all horoscopes into seven simple types, which the experienced astrologer can identify at a glance, and then explains how to interpret each type. Twenty-eight horoscopes are given full preliminary delineation, to illustrate the technique, and the basis for a similar interpretation of forty-four others is provided. 195pp. TPH 72

_____. HORARY ASTROLOGY, $4.95. A complete horary manual which explains the mechanisms, and tells how to use them. It is an extensive philosophical work, but the techniques outlined are not as clear as some of the more modern texts, such as Ivy Jacobson's or Barbara Watters'. 464pp. ShP 43

_____. HOW TO LEARN ASTROLOGY. $1.95. Presents a simplified method for looking at a horoscope, defining each of the elements and giving a basic approach to interpretation; and also explains chart erection in great detail. Includes a detailed glossary. 190pp. Dou 43

_____. MUNDANE PERSPECTIVES IN ASTROLOGY, c$22.50. This is a major work in which we are given an intimate, sometimes tedious study of the techniques Jones has developed for studying the astrological nature of a corporate entity as well as an autobiographical study of certain years during his early career. In this latter part Jones demonstrates how the positions of the Arabian Parts and the geocentric nodes in his horoscope signalled certain events in his life. The Parts (with the exception of the Part of Fortune) belong to a technique not very widely used today––they demonstrate the significance of the relationship that exists between two planets. He goes on to discuss the use of and importance of the Parts and the geocentric nodes. The bulk of the book is taken up with discussion of *astrological surrogation*, Jones' term for the symbolic mantle of power given to and assumed by the central figure of any given field. The idea originates in the historic fact that until fairly recently only the rulers of nations had their horoscopes calculated, since the destiny of the citizens depended on that of their ruler. In a lengthy and important section Jones delineates several hundred progressions and transits of Presidents Lincoln through Franklin Roosevelt according to the parallel events and decisions that took place during their terms in office. Then he introduces his version of the U.S. national horoscope, exploring it at length to demonstrate his particular techniques for mundane analysis. This is a mammoth study, often unclearly written, but containing many gems for the experienced astrologer nonetheless. Index, 463pp. Sab 75

_____. THE SABIAN BOOK, c$12.00. A collection of letters selected from about 1200 weekly messages written by Dr. Jones to students of the Sabian Assembly, often re-edited by the author. They consist of page-long inspirational messages on everyday issues and on problems of individual aspiration. Jones feels that they present the best possible introduction to the Sabian materials. 389pp. Sab 73

_____. THE SABIAN MANUAL: A RITUAL FOR LIVING. c$10.50. A method of personal development and self-discipline through knowledge of the complete rituals of the Sabian Assembly, and an introduction to the esoteric tradition. Includes a healing ritual and a full moon ceremony. 287pp. Sab 57

_____. THE SABIAN SYMBOLS IN ASTROLOGY, c$12.00. A comprehensive analysis of the Sabian degrees, giving the symbolical picture and interpretation for each of the 360 fundamental divisions of the zodiac. The origin and use of the symbols is explained in clear language. 437pp. Sab 53

_____. SCOPE OF ASTROLOGICAL PREDICTION, c$15.00. A discussion of the primary, secondary, and tertiary directions as projected by the horoscope. Other information includes solar and lunar returns, the problem of rectification when the precise moment of birth is unknown, and a primer of calculation. 461pp. Sab 69

KAYHLE, ALEXANDRA. ASTROLOGY GUIDE TO GOOD HEALTH. $2.00. A comprehensive philosophical treatise, including many practical examples. 139pp. Wil 56

KEANE, JERRYL L. PRACTICAL ASTROLOGY: HOW TO MAKE IT WORK FOR YOU, $2.95. A basic, quite well presented astrology text which contains the usual instructions for casting a chart as well as some unusual features, such as an abbreviated ephemeris for the years 1900–1970 and readings on each sign of the zodiac. 240pp. PrH 67

KEMP, CHESTER. PROGRESSIONS, $1.25. A detailed, clear exposition of the technique of progression. Kemp empirically studied most of the works on the subject and experimented until he came up with this precise treatise. The basis of his technique is tertiary progressions. 24pp. AAs 72

KENTON, WARREN. ASTROLOGY, $4.95. An excellent new pictorial study of astrology, part of Avon's new **Art and Cosmos** series, with 146 illustrations (30 in full color) and an excellent 32 page historical survey. Each of the illustrations is well analyzed. This is the best book of this type we have seen and the illustrations are incomparable. Oversize. Avo74

KEYES, KING. MASTER GUIDE TO PREPARING YOUR NATAL HOROSCOPE, c$7.95. This is an excellent new step-by-step guide, including test questions which follow each chapter and detailed, graphically illustrated answers. It shows the beginning student how to use all of the astrological tools (with sample pages from ephemerides, tables of houses, etc.). All the necessary calculations are well explained and every possible option seems to have been covered. Includes many tables, charts, and graphs, with ample explanations. Highly recommended for the beginning student. Bibliography, index, 214pp. PrH 74

_____. **PARALLELS TO MIDHEAVEN AND ASCENDANT,** $1.25. A parallel aspect is formed when a planet, the midheaven, or the ascendant occupy the same degree of declination. This is an eight page overpriced treatise on calculation and interpretation with *E-Z Tables*. ChL 68

_____. **PROGRESSION FORMULAS,** $1.60. *It is difficult to find clear rules with examples of problems that come up in progressions. For this reason, I have written this little booklet in hopes it may solve some of these problems. I have concentrated on ten examples only, using a Raphael's Ephemeris for noon and Dalton's Tables of Houses. This is a very clear presentation.* 12pp. PAs 75

KIMBALL, ROBERT. CELESTIAL HORIZONS, $3.50. Full, clear instructions for calculating ascendants to within 1½° for births occurring within latitude 36° to 44° North. This seems to be the best *instant aspect finder* that we've seen. Additionally, there is an excellent section on the decanates of each sign (the ten degree divisions) with planetary rulerships and examples. Oversize, 44pp. Mag 74

KIMMEL, ELEONORA and MANFRED. FUNDAMENTALS OF COSMOBIOLOGY, $7.65. As the title suggests, this is a detailed instructional manual. Ebertin's works, even his more basic ones, have been hard for students to grasp. The Kimmels run the Cosmobiology Center in Denver and they devised this book as a correspondence course for students. The difficult material is presented in as clear a manner as seems possible and the text is profusely illustrated with tables, charts, graphs, and examples of the special cosmobiological tools—all well analyzed. Each chapter is summarized and includes an assignment for further study. If you want to learn this method without a teacher, this is the book for you. Oversize, 84pp. CBC 72

KLOCKLER, H. BARON von. ASTROLOGY AND VOCATIONAL APTITUDE, $5.00. First published in 1928, this book presents a system and structure for interpretation within the individual personality based on the author's research. Many vocations are analyzed and examples of individual charts of people in the vocation are illustrated and discussed. 94pp. AFA 74

KNAPP, ELSIE. HORARY ART AND ITS SYNTHESIS, $5.00. Ms. Knapp has been specializing in horary charts for over twenty years and in this volume she illustrates and interprets about thirty of her charts. The first section of the book reviews the technique she uses in some detail. The author was a student of Ellen McCaffery, and the latter's spiritual inclinations seem to be shared by Ms. Knapp. There's a good deal of variety in the cases presented which should help the student understand horary astrology. We do not recommend this as a basic book, but it is useful as a supplement to a more detailed text. Snd nd

KOPARKAR, MOHAN. DEGREES OF THE ZODIAC MAGNIFIED, $10.00. Most of the degree books we've seen don't seem to fit the charts of the people around Yes! very well. This one fits better than most. That's not necessarily to say that it is any better than the others, it's just an observation and it's hard to judge astrology books on other than a personal basis. The analysis is basically positive and psychologically oriented. 199pp. Moh 76

_____. **MATHEMATICAL ASTROLOGY,** $4.25. An interpretative presentation of the techniques of Hindu astrology. Instruction is presented in all the basic techniques and appropriate charts and diagrams are included. Special features include chapters on planetary period, chart magnification, planetary transits, planetary power, fixed stars, and marriage compatibility. The material is adequately presented, although it is hard for someone immersed in tropical (or Western) astrology to understand this system. 105pp. AFA 74

_____. **MOON MANSIONS,** $4.50. *Influence of MOON on human beings was was more prominently observed by ancient Indian Astrologers than the influence of any celestial objects. Since the motion of MOON relative to Earth is faster than any other planet, its effects in a natal chart are to be considered very important. As the Moon takes about twenty-seven days to complete one revolution around the Earth, it seemed most logical, in those days, to divide the constellation into twenty-seven equal parts. Thus, the distance of space traveled by Moon in one day is considered as a MOON MANSION. The 360°... when divided by twenty-seven lunar mansions, brings each MOON MANSION as 13°20'.*—from the Introduction. This is step-by-step handbook on reading a natal chart using the Moon Mansions. Oversize, 92pp. ArB 74

KOZMINSKY, ISIDORE. ZODIACAL SYMBOLOGY AND ITS PLANETARY POWER, $5.00. A comprehensive study of the planetary influence for each degree of the zodiac in each of the signs. 194pp. AFA nd

KRIYANANDA, SWAMI. YOUR SUN SIGN AS A SPIRITUAL GUIDE, $3.50. A beautifully written work which discusses the sun signs as they relate to human nature and soul maturity. 132pp. AnP 71

LANDSCHEIDT, THEODOR. COSMIC CYBERNETICS, $4.00. A summary of concepts the author has presented in previous articles. Central themes which are explored are: the theoretical foundations of cosmobiology and their correlations with structural elements of mathematics, theoretical physics, cybernetics, music, etc.; mathematical statistics as instruments of cosmobiological research; the forecasting of solar eruptions and natural catastrophes on Earth; and the significance of the galactic center for the interpretation of a personal cosmogram. Very technical. 80pp. EbV 73

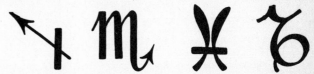

LAURENCE, THEODOR. THE FOUNDATION BOOK OF ASTROLOGY, c$10.00. A general text with basic material on the signs, the planets in the signs and in the houses, plus some introductory material. A section is devoted to instructional material on casting an approximate chart, with the appropriate tables, and another to *Astrology and Human Life*. The interpretations are scanty but if one wants to get a general idea of what astrology is about without being overwhelmed by details then this would be a useful text. 316pp. UnB 73

LEE, DAL. DICTIONARY OF ASTROLOGY, $.95. This is the most modern astrological dictionary available. It is geared to the non-professional and the definitions are not always very precise. Includes general background material. 250pp. War 68

LEINBACH, ESTHER. DEGREES OF THE ZODIAC, $5.00. A new book which gives the guidelines of the influence that the degrees have shown from the behavior of individuals. The material has been gathered from the author's practical experience as an astrologer as well as from the leading authorities. Analysis of the degrees is an important part of seeing a person's chart as a whole, and this is the most complete work we've seen. 206pp. Mac72

_____. **PLANETS AND ASTEROIDS—RELATIONSHIPS IN CONJUNCTIONS,** $7.00. The strongest expression of any two planets occurs when they are conjunct. Every planet has some kind of relationship to every other planet in the chart. This is the most detailed study we have seen, exploring in a spiritual sense the relationship of each planet and asteroid to each other. This book can be an invaluable guide to interpretation for the professional astrologer. Oversize, 90pp. Vul 74

_____. **SUN-ASCENDANT RULERSHIPS: THEIR INFLUENCE IN THE HOROSCOPE,** $3.45. A detailed analysis. Vul 72

LEO, ALAN. ART OF SYNTHESIS, c$9.35. Leo was one of the best known astrologers of the early twentieth century. His work still includes some of the most valuable insights available to the intermediate and advanced astrologer. His books synthesize his first hand experience. Leo was a Theosophist and he stresses the philosophical and intuitional aspects of astrology along with the esoteric and the psychological. The original version of this book was known as **How to Judge A Nativity, Part II.** Later it was revised and retitled. It still forms a companion volume to **How to Judge A Nativity.** This work is a detailed study of the planets as they relate to consciousness. Each of the individual planets (with the exception of Pluto) is studied, as are the sun and moon. There's also a section of sample horoscopes, including an analysis of the chart of Rudolf Steiner. Oversize, 284pp. Fow 68

_____. **ASTROLOGY FOR ALL,** c$9.35. This is Leo's most general text, designed for the beginning student. It includes a bit of background material; an analysis of the characteristics of each of the signs; a description of the sun and the moon together through the signs; and the planets in the signs. There's also a brief description of each of the degrees of each sign and tables for the place of the moon, 1850–1909. Leo is not at his best when analyzing the various signs. He often tends to negativity and excessive Victorian morality. Oversize, 336pp. Fow 69

_____. **CASTING THE HOROSCOPE,** c$10.50. This is a guide to all the intricacies involved in chart erection—not recommended to the beginning student. The coverage is comprehensive, and includes areas not detailed in other similar works, but the format and the writing style are not as clear as some other works. Includes material on rectification, directions, methods of house division, lessons in astronomy, and sample tables. Oversize, 353pp. Fow 69

_____. **THE DEGREES OF THE ZODIAC SYMBOLISED,** $3.00. This is a reprint of Leo's **Astrological Manual No. 8,** credited to Charubel, to which is added Sepharial's translation of a similar series. Each degree is named, and the interpretations are especially recommended to esoteric astrologers. 136pp. ArP

_____. **ESOTERIC ASTROLOGY,** c$9.35 An excellent presentation which examines all aspects of esoteric astrology. Covers chart interpretation in terms of reincarnation and the working out of karma in great detail. Recommended. 294pp. Fow 67

_____. **HOW TO JUDGE A NATIVITY,** c$9.35 This is a comprehensive analysis of the individual houses as they relate to chart interpretation. Also includes material on the aspects. Leo shows how to synthesize the individual elements. Oversize, 336pp. Fow 69

_____. **JUPITER, THE PRESERVER**, $2.00. An entire book devoted to the planet Jupiter. The planet is presented as the preserver, remarkable for its own symbolism and its relation to other symbols. It is regarded as the great life wave and is often compared to the trinity. 88pp. Wei 73

_____. **THE KEY TO YOUR OWN NATIVITY**, c$9.35 This is an attempt to show how to break up the constituent parts of a natal chart and understand the significance of each detail. Leo has written this volume from the point of view of the practical astrologer with the aim of teaching the beginning student how to write out a delineation of a chart. He analyzes the sign and planet rulerships and the aspects and then considers the material under such headings as health, occupation, finance, marriage, friends, personal characteristics. Oversize, 303pp. Fow 69

_____. **MARS, THE WAR LORD**, $2.50. Leo presents the horoscopes of ten famous people to illustrate the significant part Mars played in their lives. The illusion that Mars is utterly warlike and vindictive is corrected. 99pp. Wei 73

_____. **PRACTICAL ASTROLOGY**, $3.00. A small comprehensive astrological text, emphasizing the esoteric side of astrology. Extensive charts and text. Not recommended for the beginning student. 224pp. Tar 73

_____. **THE PROGRESSED HOROSCOPE**, c$9.35 This is the most detailed examination of progressions available. Includes a great deal of background information on the why of progressions in addition to detailed instructions on calculating the progressed horoscope, directions, the progressed ascendant, solar and lunar positions and aspects, solar revolutions and transits, and primary directions. Index, oversize, 353pp. Fow 69

_____. **SATURN THE REAPER**, $2.50. Leo stresses the planet's individualizing influence and its relationship to the last three signs of the zodiac. Saturn is seen as the bridge between higher and lower self. 108pp. Wei 73

LEWI, GRANT. ASTROLOGY FOR THE MILLIONS, c$10.00. *Here is astrology applied to daily living; astrology applied to history; and astrology applied to your future.* Includes an extensive discussion of transits, explains how to cast a horoscope and interpret, how to project the horoscope into the future, and explains planetary influences in daily life. Also has the positions of the planets from 1870–1970, and planetary projection tables through 1980, with explanations. 266pp. LIP 69

_____. **HEAVEN KNOWS WHAT**, c$10.00. Lewi has developed a method for casting complete natal charts without learning complicated mathematics. Tables are included here which explain the technique and provide all the necessary material. Extensive interpretative material is also provided. A very popular beginning text. 203+pp. Llp 35

LIBRA, C.A. ASTROLOGY: ITS TECHNIQUES AND ETHICS, $3.95. This is a recent reprint of a classic text on astrology. We don't know the original publication date, but the text appears to date from the late nineteenth or early twentieth century. The interpretations tend to be negative, as is true with many books from that period, although this one is not as bad as many. All the basic material is included along with a great deal of information that is usually only found in more advanced texts. The presentation is spiritually oriented, and religious and karmic ideas are interspersed throughout. There's a lot of interesting material here—although we recommend it only for supplementary reading. Illustrations, charts, tables. 271pp. NPC 76

LILLY, WILLIAM. AN INTRODUCTION TO ASTROLOGY, $3.75. A comprehensive astrological classic, written in 1647. Covers all the basic material and forms an interesting contrast to modern astrological manuals for the beginning and more advanced astrological student. 346pp. NPC 72

LINDANGER, ALFA. YOUR SUN'S RETURN, $2.00. *The technique of computing a Solar Revolution Chart with thirteen chart illustrations together with the noon date method of finding an unknown birth time and an accurate method of rectification by arcs of events.* 47pp. Mac 49

LINDSAY, JACK. ORIGINS OF ASTROLOGY, c$10.00. This is by far the most complete study in English, covering the first stages in Babylonia, and developments by the Greeks, Egyptians and Romans. It also brings out the important role played by astrology in the evolution of ancient thought from Plato onwards. This detailed, illuminating work is fully indexed and includes definitions and 43 pages of notes and bibliography. 480pp. H&R 71

LITTLEJOHN, FRANCES. THE DUODENARY SYSTEM OF ASTROLOGY, $5.25. The duodenary system is useful in pinpointing the influences which lead to certain events. The author developed this system and uses it extensively in her personal practice. It is especially useful in rectification. The book includes many cycle charts including ones for the solar monthly return, lunar returns, and various duodenary charts. There are also complete tables, formulas, examples, and a dictionary of aspect interpretations. LjP

_____. **SIMPLIFIED ASTROLOGY**, $3.75. Simplified astrology is right! In eighteen pages, Ms. Littlejohn covers the meanings of the planets, signs, and houses as well as aspects and the meanings of the transiting planets. Her summaries are generally fairly good, however there is not much depth here. LjP 68

_____. **WHAT IS IN THE FUTURE FOR AMERICA OR THE WORLD?**, $3.25. Predictions about world events and the lives of well known individuals based on sidereal astrology. 15pp. LjP 69

LIVINGSTON, PETER. ON ASTROLOGY, c$5.95. This is an excellent introductory astrology text for young people covering the history of astrology and separate analyses of the planets, signs, and houses. The text is very graphically written so that all readers can get a good feeling for the meaning of the signs, planets, houses, and many other fundamental aspects of astrology. Though the book is obviously oriented toward youths in

its language and illustrations, it also makes a good introduction for anyone who wants a brief overview and does not want to be overwhelmed by detail. Glossary, index, 143pp. PrH 74

LLEWELLYN PUBLICATIONS. MOON SIGN BOOK, $2.95. An annual almanac that helps people plan their activities in accordance with the monthly lunar cycle. Packed with information including monthly weather forecasts, stock market forecasts, a farming and gardening guide, plus articles of special interest. 378pp. LIP

LOWELL, LAUREL. PLUTO, $2.95. A source book on Pluto, with charts detailing Pluto aspects arranged by planet; Pluto in the houses and the signs; transits; Plutonian correspondences, alphabetically arranged, with aspects; and a Pluto ephemeris 1851-2000. 150pp. LIP 73

_____. **SECONDARY PROGRESSIONS—USING THE ADJUSTED CALCULATING DATE**, $4.75. A technical text by a noted astrologer, with all the necessary tables. 91pp. Mac 73

LUNTZ, CHARLES. VOCATIONAL GUIDANCE BY ASTROLOGY, $3.95. This is the most comprehensive work on the subject, including material on selecting an occupation; determining the most favorable time to start a new enterprise; how to approach and understand employer-employee relationships; and other related topics. A working knowledge of astrology is necessary to utilize the tools and rules suggested. Index, 213pp. LIP 62

LYNCH, JOHN. THE COFFEE TABLE BOOK OF ASTROLOGY, $7.95. This is a profusely illustrated oversized compilation of writings on astrology. It begins with a history of astrology and study of the planets, both by John Lynch. The major portion of the book is devoted to an analysis of the 12 signs of the Zodiac, compiled from the writings of Alan Leo and Isabelle Pagan. There's also an essay on spiritual astrology by Zoltan Mason and a section relating palmistry to astrology. In addition, the text ends with a table of ascendents and ephemerides of the moon between 1900-74. The book is not recommended to anyone who wants an in-depth study, it does serve a function as a pictorial overview for the general reader. Includes many color plates. 326pp. Vik 67

LYNDOE, EDWARD. ASTROLOGY FOR EVERYONE, c$7.95. A basic text that includes everything for casting a chart (including ephemerides, tables of houses) and interpretative and instructional material. Not a complete presentation, but a beginning book for the interested student. 212pp. Dut 70

McCAFFREY, ELLEN. ASTROLOGICAL KEY TO BIBLICAL SYMBOLISM, c$7.95. A study of the esoteric wisdom in the Bible as it relates to astrology. *In this book I desire to show the different landmarks that should be passed by each believer who is on the Path . . . . Generally speaking the steps in spiritual progression may be grouped into four—corresponding to Initiation by Water, Air, Fire and Earth.* An examination of each of these steps is followed by a discussion of each of the signs of the zodiac from Biblical and psychological viewpoints. A meditation exercise of scriptural readings on the inner meaning of each sign is also provided. 192pp. Wei 75

_____. **GRAPHIC ASTROLOGY**, c$5.75. A good primer for the beginning astrologer. Explains all the basic concepts and shows in great detail how to put together a natal chart and begin basic interpretation. 303pp. Mac 52

McCORMICK, JOHN. THE BOOK OF RETROGRADES, $5.00. A graphic, statistical analysis of retrograde planets between 1880 and 1980 and including the following special features: what is a retrograde planet?, interpretation of the planets in retrograde, planetary group interpretation, and four sets of related tables. 84pp. AFA 75

_____. **DEDUCTIVE INTERPERETATIONS OF THE NATAL HOROSCOPE**, $4.50. This is a very helpful review of the houses, planets, and signs combined with a case study demonstrating *deductive interpretation*. The case study is quite lengthy and is very clearly presented. The approach is positive and the emphasis is on the inner meaning of the signs, houses, and planets and their synthesis. A good book for those who are learning interpretation. 68pp. AFA 76

MACCRAIG, HUGH. DESTINY TURNS THE WHEEL: HOW TO INTERPRET THE NATAL AND THE DESTINY CHART WITHOUT MATHEMATICAL CALCULATIONS, $3.50. An interesting effort. 163pp. Mac 70

MACKEY, SAMSON. "MYTHOLOGICAL" ASTRONOMY OF THE ANCIENTS DEMONSTRATED, c$12.00. An offset reprint of an 1822 treatise on the spiral precession of the equinoxes, Hindu time cycles, and the zodiacal origin of myths, with a rotating dial, new notes and bibliography and definitions. Also includes *The Key of Urania*. The text is very mythologically oriented, and often seems full of obscure references. It is one of the books referred to often by Blavatsky in **The Secret Doctrine**. 342pp. Wiz 74

MACLEOD, CHARLOTTE. ASTROLOGY FOR SKEPTICS, c$6.95. An excellent presentation of the basics of astrology. The author set out to write a debunking book and ended up with a rational presentation of astrology as a practical and challenging way of approaching life. The major part of the book is devoted to explanations of the planets and the signs. 297pp. McM 72

MAC NEICE, LOUIS. ASTROLOGY, c$6.95. The major portion of this oversized book is devoted to a survey of the history of astrology. The text is replete with photographs and drawings, many in color. Chapters on the planets and the individual signs are also included along with general instructions for erecting a chart. There is also an appendix containing tables of sidereal time (for finding ascendants) and extremely simplified tables of houses and ephemerides. Index, 351pp. Dou 64

MANILIUS. THE FIVE BOOKS OF M. MANILIUS, $3.75. Written originally at least a century and a half before Ptolemy, this work points out the influence of the Greek and Roman civilizations on astrology. All the major features of astrology as we know it today are apparent in Manilius' books, although couched in very different language. Much of the work is in the form of a poem. The translation is by *T.C.* Spiral bound, 179pp. AFA 1697

MANOLESCO, JOHN. SCIENTIFIC ASTROLOGY, $.95. An overview of 20th century scientifically-oriented researchers and discoveries, with brief summaries of the major books and theories and of some of the major periodical references. A scattered treatment, containing nonetheless some interesting information. 188 pp. Pin 73

MANTHRI, CHANDRA. THE DEGREES OF LIFE, $7.00. Manthri has deeply studied the astrological methods of the ancient Egyptian and Hindu schools. The material in this volume was first printed in *Wynn's Astrology Magazine* as a series and is reprinted here for the first time. The author says that he obtained these degree readings from an old Sanskrit text. The description of each degree is full of poetic insight and the material differs considerably from all the other books on degree-by-degree analysis. Oversize, 97pp. AsA 74

MARK, ALEXANDRA. ASTROLOGY FOR THE AQUARIAN AGE, $3.95. The chart, how to construct it, its division, and the meaning of each is explained simply. Differentiates between the solar chart and the natal chart and offers interpretations that even the newest student of astrology can understand. 400pp. S&S 70

MATTHEWS, E.C. THE ASCENDING SIGN, $3.00. Contains complete readings for twelve ascending signs, 144 portraits, profiles and cartoons of the types. Also includes the sun and ascending signs of many famous people and for those who cannot erect a chart, a simplified table of ascending signs. 126pp. MDC 70

_____. **FIXED STARS AND DEGREES OF THE ZODIAC**, $3.00. Exact readings for the 360 different degrees based on a careful analysis of more than 500 horoscopes. Each degree has a keyword, or characteristic name, along with the delineation. Also points out the mathematical, musical, literary, artistic, and eccentric degrees and the planetary natures and longitudes of important fixed stars in the signs. 78pp. MDC 68

_____. **STARS OF THE BIBLE**, c$10.00. The main feature of this book is eighty full page illustrations from the Bible illustrated by Gustave Dore. These woodcuts are not to be found anywhere else except in long out of print editions. The rest of the text consists of vaguely related biblical quotations and general, quite antiquated, astrological analysis. Oversize, 162pp. MDC nd

MAYO, JEFF. THE ASTROLOGERS' ASTRONOMICAL HANDBOOK, c$4.20. An informative reference book which is a guide toward a clearer understanding of the derivation and elements of the basic factors of astrological charting and theory. 126pp. Fow 65

_____. **ASTROLOGY**, $3.00. An excellent introduction to the basics of astrology. Includes material on the signs, planets, and aspects, as well as a section on chart erection and brief essays on interpretation and progressions. Some of the deeper aspects of astrology are covered and the text is generally quite clear. Recommended. 214pp. EUP 64

_____. **HOW TO CAST A NATAL CHART**, c$4.00. A very clear step-by-step presentation of natal chart calculations which includes exercises at the end of each chapter (with answers) and many examples. Mayo, a student of Margaret Hone, is one of Britain's top traditional astrologers. Here he takes advantage of his many years of teaching, clearly pointing out the most common errors made by students and presenting the most detailed method of calculation and erection he has been able to devise. The mathematical sections are especially well written. Includes many sample tables and charts. Vol. 3 in his Astrologers's Handbook series. Index, 194pp. Fow 67

_____. **HOW TO READ THE EPHEMERIS**, c$3.35. Excellent, comprehensive instructions for reading and interpreting the information in an ephemeris and a table of houses. 108pp. Fow 66

_____. **THE PLANETS AND HUMAN BEHAVIOR**, c$5.00. Explains what the sun, the moon, and the planets represent in terms of human behavior, and also correlates each cosmic body with the contemporary psychological factors and the Jungian concepts of the psychic structure of man. Practical guidance in interpretation is given with the help of an example birth chart. 172pp. Fow 72

MEYER, MICHAEL. THE ASTROLOGY OF CHANGE, $3.50. This is a self-contained guide to horary astrology, including an in-depth discussion of the factors involved in interpreting a chart (with material on houses, signs, planetary patterns, the lunation cycle, and the Sabian symbols). Meyer also includes an actual case study showing the value of horary astrology in personal problem-solving, and an extended series of appendices containing all the tables and instructions necessary to cast a horary chart. The horary (literally *of the hour*) chart is cast for the time and place that a specific crisis arises in the life of an individual and is used to uncover the potential for growth which may be found at the heart of any personal problem. Following as he does in the tradition of Marc Edmund Jones and Dane Rudhyar, Meyer's approach is spiritual and his book sheds a positive light on an aspect of astrology which so often speaks of disasters and unworkable situations on the individual level. The book is aimed at a psychological, humanistic understanding of incidents and problems in the best sense of these words. If you are interested in horary astrology, this is as good a place to learn as any we can think of. Biblio., 280pp. Dou 75

_____. **A HANDBOOK FOR THE HUMANISTIC ASTROLOGER**, $4.95. A handbook for the new astrologer who is more concerned with human growth than with isolated single events. By correlating the phenomenon of the cyclic motions of the planet

with the inevitable cycle of human existence, Meyer describes the unique potential focused in man and deciphers the instructions for realizing this potential. Charts of modern personalities are used as examples. An important new book by a close associate of Dane Rudhyar. Definitely not suggested for the beginning astrologer, despite the beguiling title. It is an excellent and a difficult book. 141 illustrations, bibliography, 380pp. Dou 74

HOROSCOPE by Erhard Schon

MIHIRA, VARAHA. BRIHAT JATAKA, $3.50. Principal source reference book of such exponents of Hindu astrology as Sepharial and DeLuce, this is a translation with commentary of the original Sanskrit work, written about 2,000 years ago. Sym

MILBURN, LEIGH HOPE. PROGRESSED HOROSCOPE SIMPLIFIED, c$5.25. The progressed horoscope indicates—for that particular time for which it is set up—the relative activity of the influences indicated in the natal chart. It is a very difficult aspect of astrology to master. This is a good, comprehensive text. 170pp. AFA 28

MILLER, PAT. ASTROLOGY: AN ILLUSTRATED MANUAL FOR TEACHERS AND STUDENTS, $5.00. Ms. Miller covers an amazing amount of material in this volume and in general she covers it well. There's all the basic information on planets, houses, signs, aspects, and chart erection along with more advanced information on finding aspects, progressions, transits, lunations and eclipses, and solar returns. The instructional material is uniformly clear and well presented and the author's approach is positive. 58pp. P&M 75

MISHRA, BHAWANI. ASTROLOGY FOR ALL, $2.00. This is the simplest of all the books on Hindu astrology. The material is taken from ancient Sanskrit texts, adapted to the interests of the modern day. Includes information on what astrology is; on the birth chart; on the signs, houses, and planets; on the planets in the signs and in the houses; on judging the chart; on the timing of events; and on transits. 200pp. JPH 73

MOORE, MARCIA and MARK DOUGLAS. ASTROLOGY: THE DIVINE SCIENCE, c$20.00. This unique book will instruct the newcomer and illumine the expert. It contains information necessary to become an expert astrologer including instructions for casting and interpreting a soul map. Lucid and explicit, this book is a ready reference of astrological information. An excellent compilation of insightful analysis and straightforward computation. This is the best overall text we have seen. Highly recommended for the beginning astrologer. Bibliography. 850pp. ArB 70

_____. **ASTROLOGY IN ACTION**, c$7.00. Illustrates the application of astrology by means of astrotypes, keywords, forty-two horoscopes, chart comparison, and discussions of transits and progressions as means of predicting the future. The material is based on the charts of Jacqueline Kennedy Onassis, her family and friends. 336pp. ArB

MORIN, J.B. THE MORINUS SYSTEM OF HOROSCOPE INTERPRETATION, $5.00. In the early seventeenth century, Morin attempted to purge astrology of many of its medieval superstitions. His work (newly translated here by Richard Baldwin) forms the basis of all horoscope interpretation since his lifetime. This is a difficult work, but quite valuable for the advanced astrologer. 109pp. AFA 74

MORIN de VILLEFRANCHE. ASTROSYNTHESIS, c$10.00. This translation of the above (by Lucy Little) is generally considered the clearer of the two. 192pp. Mas 75

MORRISON, AL. JOHNDRO'S THEORY OF PLANETARY RULERSHIP OF ASPECTS PER SE, $2.25. Selections from notes taken during a series of lectures W. Kenneth Brown gave in the early 1950's on the Johndro material. 14pp. AFA

MUIR, ADA. BOOK OF NODES AND THE PART OF FORTUNE, $1.25. 46pp. Mac 30

_____. THE HEALING HERBS OF THE ZODIAC, $1.00. A nicely illustrated little book which discusses the ailments common to zodiacal signs and reviews the herbs that are most beneficial to each sign. 63pp. LIP 59

MULKINS, ROBERT. DOWN TO EARTH ASTROLOGY, $2.50. A sketchy discussion of controversial astrological topics—along with analyses of the planets, signs, and moon in the houses. 39pp. Cos

_____. MIRACLES OF THE MIND AND ASTROLOGY, $5.95. This is an introduction to psychological astrology from a non-professional point of view. Houses, planets. and signs are briefly analyzed and examples are cited along with a generalized discussion. 94pp. Cos 74

_____. SECRETS OF TEACHING AND INTERPRETING ASTROLOGY, $4.95. This is a sketch of what topics an astrology teacher should cover in basic natal classes— giving an idea of how best to approach the various subjects considered. Mulkins is director of an astrological center which offers classes and correspondence courses. 85pp. Cos 74

NACCARATO, SHARON. ONCE UPON A ZODIAC, $6.00. An astrology book for children. Beautiful pictures and a story which reveals each sign of the zodiac to the child. Sha 73

NAYLOR, P.I.H. ASTROLOGY: A FASCINATING HISTORY, $2.00. An illustrated, non-technical account. 242pp. Wil 72

NOONAN, GEORGE. SPHERICAL ASTRONOMY FOR ASTROLOGERS, $3.00. *There is a definite need for a book to instruct astrologers in the theory and application of spherical astronomy. ... This booklet as written will* **not** *achieve the objective mentioned. What is presented here is a collection of formulae that will be useful to those interested in the theory of astrology. Examples are given of the use of these formulae, but no attempt is made to develop or prove them; there has been no attempt at a systematic discussion of the subject matter and its astrological implications. However this potpourri will enable those familiar with it to translate readily between the various coordinate systems in use in astronomy, and to compute such important astrological points as the MC and Ascendent without having to use out-of-date and inaccurate tables. The knowledge of elementary algebra and trigonometry ... is required to read this booklet.* 62pp. AFA 74

NORELLI-BACHELÉT, PÀTRIZIA. THE GNÒSTIC CIRCLE, c$12.90. This is a very personal exploration of esoteric astrology by a disciple of Sri Aurobindo and the Mother: *It is our intention to give as clear a picture as possible of the true purpose of astrology, and in which ways it can be an asset in the development of the spirit .... The zodiac gives us a picture of this outer movement of evolution which has as its support the inherent spirit.* The emphasis here is on sacred geometry and numbers, especially three and four and combinations thereof. Many intricate diagrams illustrate the text. The presentation is complete in itself and the reader does not need a depth of astrological knowledge to be able to appreciate and understand the text. We get a very nice feeling from the book and the philosophy it expounds and we recommend it to all who seek a deeper understanding of the true meaning of astrology. Index, 317pp. Aeo 75

_____. THE MAGICAL CAROUSEL, $3.75. Subtitled *A Zodiacal Odyssey*, this is a story of two children's adventure. *The children represent two complementary poles within the individual. It is also a treatment of astrology, each image evoked being a key to the deeper meaning of the signs.* The author is a resident of Pondicherry, the Aurobindo ashram in India (see Aurobindo section), and the spirituality of her life is fully revealed in her discussion of each sign. 146pp. AAP 73

NORRIS, A.G.S. TRANSCENDENTAL ASTROLOGY, c$8.95. Deals with the spiritual implications of astrology. The planetary numerals and glyphs and the lessons of the signs are delineated to enable an astrologer to link the soul to the astrological chart. An inspiring text. 288pp. Wei 30

OKEN, ALAN. AS ABOVE SO BELOW: A PRIMARY GUIDE TO ASTROLOGICAL AWARENESS, $1.95. An excellent introduction which gives the reader a good feeling of what astrology is and how it has evolved. A fascinating section is devoted to *Astrology, Astronomy, the Earth and You*, the sidereal as well as the tropical zodiac is discussed, and the material on the signs, houses and planets is very well presented. Of all the inexpensive general texts we've seen this seems to be the most enlightening. Recommended. 344pp. Ban 73

_____. ASTROLOGY: EVOLUTION AND REVOLUTION, $1.95. This is the third and final volume in Oken's series. *The basic theme ... is to point out that we are at an important shift in space and time, brought about by the transition from one World Age... to another. ... Part I tries to place the present stage of human revolution in a historical setting and gives a brief history of these Age Changes. Part II (The Sexual Revolution) and III (The Religious Revolution) focus upon two areas of human interest. ... Part IV explores Hindu astrology for the Western reader and attempts to resolve the question of the two Zodiacs.* Index, 252pp. Ban 76

_____. THE HOROSCOPE, THE ROAD AND ITS TRAVELERS, $1.95. *The purpose of the present work is to present astrology, both as a spiritual path toward the expansion of one's understanding of Universal Law and as a practical tool for helping others through the use and interpretation of the horoscope.* This book (Vol. 2 in the author's Astrological Series) is far and away the best value that we know of as well as an enlightening addition to any astrologer's library. Includes a general section on astrology with material on the planets in the signs and houses; information on chart erection and interpretation;

exercises; and analyses and sample charts for eight famous people ranging from Carl Jung and Edgar Cayce to Joseph Stalin. Fully indexed and illustrated. Highly recommended. 402pp. Ban 74

OMARR, SYDNEY. MY WORLD OF ASTROLOGY, $3.00. General instructions for casting and interpreting your birth chart, interpretations of every sign, the planets, the transits, and cusps, by one of America's most noted astrologers, as well as a personal view of how astrology influences his life. 378pp. Wil 65

_____. SIDNEY OMARR'S ASTROLOGICAL REVELATIONS ABOUT YOU, $1.25. General newspaper-type sun sign analyses, more detailed than most. Also gives approximate rising signs, with commentary. 239pp. NAL 73

PAGAN, ISABELLE. FROM PIONEER TO POET OR THE TWELVE GREAT GATES, c$8.95. A fascinating, instructive introduction to the study of the science of astrology. Details the twelve signs at great length and gives summary material and an analysis of selected horoscopes of historical personages. 318pp. TPH 69

PALMER, LYNNE. ABC BASIC CHART READING, $5.75. As the title suggests this is a guide to reading the horoscope. The material is more clearly and succinctly presented than in Ms. Palmer's other books. The material covered includes the houses, the aspects, and the planets (viewed in terms of discordant and harmonious). Basically the information is given in terms of key words and phrases. The author's point of view seems to be that key-words provide the kernel of an idea of the chart pattern without locking the reader into too firm a conception of each particular aspect, house, or planet. Oversize, 52pp. Qua 74

_____. ABC OF CHART ERECTION, $5.50. A very comprehensive manual, well presented but the very amount of information may be confusing for the beginning student. We suggest it as a good book to have around to review procedures (advanced as well as beginning ones) rather than something to start with. Graphically illustrated, with numerous examples, and many helpful tables. 212pp. AFA 71

_____. ABC OF MAJOR PROGRESSIONS, $5.50. A very technical work which clearly details the procedures for progressing, giving a few alternate methods and many tables. Numerous practical examples assist the student. Recommended for the advanced student. 162pp. AFA 70

PARCHMENT, S.R. ASTROLOGY—MUNDANE AND SPIRITUAL, c$10.00. Good astrology text which blends its spiritual teachings with a knowledge of cosmogenesis, anthropogenesis, esoteric philosophy, and astrology and how to relate it to mundane affairs, as well as how to erect and interpret birth charts. 680pp. AFA 33

PARKER, ELANOR. ASTROLOGY AND ITS PRACTICAL APPLICATION, $5.00. A reprint of a 1927 spiritually-oriented basic astrology text including chapters on the houses, the planets, the signs ascending, the planets in the signs and the houses, the part of fortune in the houses, aspects, and information on progressions. 204pp. HeR 70

PARKER, JULIA and DEREK. THE COMPLEAT ASTROLOGER, $6.95. A beautifully illustrated volume which contains the following parts: a history of astrology, guide to the astronomy behind astrology, interpretations and progressions of the birth chart, as well as astrological tables, including ephemerides from 1900 to 1975. Oversize, not very technical. Ban 71

PEARCE, A.J. TEXTBOOK OF ASTROLOGY, c$8.00. For those who desire only to gain a general knowledge of the subject, this book is easily intelligible, though it will be chiefly useful to the student whose aims are deeper. It is enriched with many interesting notices of nativities illustrating the different rules and doctrines of the science. There is something like an attempt at inductive verification in the many cases the author gives us with the view of justifying some of Ptolemy's teachings. Very scholarly. 468pp, 40 are charts, graphs, etc. AFA 70

PELLETIER, ROBERT. PLANETS IN ASPECT, c$10.00. Aspects are the relationship between planets in a chart. Most of the astrology texts do not devote much space to aspects so this definitive text is a much welcomed addition to the literature. Every major aspect— conjunction, sextile, trine, opposition, inconjunction—is covered. In all over 300 aspects are discussed in in-depth analyses. The general meanings of each major aspect are also presented. The text is fully indexed and forms an invaluable aid to the student seeking guidelines and material for chart interpretation. 346pp. PaR 74

PENFIELD, MARC. AN ASTROLOGICAL WHO'S WHO, c$10.00. 500 full page natal charts of well-known personalities, especially calculated, checked, and, where necessary, rectified for this volume. Includes a chart of the aspects in each horoscope, and other explanatory material. 567pp. ArB 72

PENN, ENOCH. PLANETARY INFLUENCES, $3.50. Attempts to show that the changes and processes in the lives of men are impelled by the various and varying influences received from the heavenly bodies, and which influences play upon man's body. Explains the planets as centers of forces and how these planetary forces work through our bodies. 64pp. EsF 68

PERRY, INEZ and GEORGE CAREY. THE ZODIAC AND THE SALTS OF SALVATION, c$12.95. A definitive work which explains the relation of the mineral salts of the body to the signs of the zodiac, and esoterically analyzes and synthesizes the signs and their physicochemical allocations. 352pp. Wei 71

PRATT, LAURIE. ASTROLOGICAL WORLD CYCLES, $3.95. Ms. Pratt's aim is to demonstrate the profound connection of the precession of the equinoxes with the history of mankind and the great cycles of the world. Many little known ancient records and scriptures are cited and explored. Oversize, 57pp. Hug

RAPHAEL. **HORARY ASTROLOGY**, $1.50. This was one of the first *modern* works on horary astrology written—it is of interest more as a historic document than for the information contained within, much of which is quite archaic and overly moralistic. 103pp. HeR 1897

_____. **THE KEY AND GUIDE TO ASTROLOGY**, $1.50. A small, complete text skimming over all aspects, but not going into any detail. 132pp. Fou 05

_____. **MUNDANE ASTROLOGY**, $2.00. Mundane astrology is the effects of the planets and the signs upon nations. 80pp. Fou 1897

RECHTER, CHRISTINE. **ELECTIONAL ASTROLOGY**, $4.25. Electional astrology is the art of choosing the proper moment or birth time for any particular project or event. There is very little material written in this area (please note that electional astrology is not the same as horary astrology). Ms. Rechter has studied and practiced electional astrology and here she draws on her experience to present a set of workable rules in casting and interpreting an electional chart. Many sample charts and case studies are included. Oversize, 56pp. Lor 75

_____. **FINE POINTS OF DELINEATION**, $4.25. This oversize pamphlet is designed as an aid for the student who already knows the basics of chart erection and now wants some tips on interpretation. Many themes to look for and specific topics are touched on in outline form. Though by no means a comprehensive presentation, this volume does present some useful hints. 65pp. Lor 75

Prediction of a great fire in London, woodcut after Thomas Lilly's forecast, 1651

REID, CHARLES. **PLANETARY EMOTIONS**, $2.50. A detailed study of planetary influences. 113pp. HSP 64

REID, VERA. **TOWARDS AQUARIUS**, $1.45. Traces each of the great ages through its 2,000 year cycle, interpreting the cataclysmic events of each age in the light of the zodiac and its symbols. A large portion of the text is devoted to the coming Aquarian Age. 124pp. Arc 71

REIDER, THOMAS. **ASTROLOGICAL WARNINGS & THE STOCK MARKET**, c$7.95. A study of astrology and the correlation between planetary cycles, investor confidence, and stock market patterns. All the astrological assumptions are tested against the historic performance of the Dow Jones Industrial Average from 1899 to 1971 and only those which meet the statistical test are accepted. The ideas and concepts utilized in this study are clearly explained and the reader is provided with all the necessary information to do his own market forecasting over the next decade. The author's research and analysis is condensed in a 34 inch fold-out graph. Bibliography, 116pp. PPL 72

RICHARDSON, DALE. **PLUTONIAN PHOENIX**, $7.00. Dale Richardson is an astrological writer who is especially noted for his stock market analyses. Though this book appears from the title to be on the influence of Pluto it is this only in part. The text is a compilation of articles Richardson has published in *Horoscope Magazine* over the last 15 years, with updating notes appended. Many of the articles do relate to Pluto and the transits of Pluto as they have affected individuals and public events. As a unified presentation, the book does not succeed—but as a collection of randomly presented ideas, there is much of interest. 166pp. AFA 74

ROBERTS, PRESS and IMA. **TRANSITS IN PLAIN ENGLISH**, $4.50. This is one of the most comprehensive and newest books on transits. Each planet is studied in a separate chapter which begins with a listing of keywords and goes on to analyze each transit connected with that planet and the various aspects related to each particular transit. Includes transits of the full and new moon, the nodes, the moon, and the part of fortune. 120pp. Vul 74

ROBERTSON, MARC. **COSMOPSYCHOLOGY: THE ENGINE OF DESTINY**, $5.45. Describes the 8 types of human personality, the supporting mechanisms in the personality that deal with self-definition, self-expansion, self-propagation, self-transformation, and self-maintenance. Cosmopsychology focuses on the concept of a cycle of energy-flow within which the aspects of astrology operate. It also deals with the idea of reincarnation and how the personality types are a clue to where the individual is in a cycle of incarnations. As is the case with Robertson's other books, the material is provocative, unusual, and very clearly presented. The emphasis is on the positive benefits to inner development to be gained through the study of astrology. 100pp. ANW 74

_____. **NOT A SIGN IN THE SKY BUT A LIVING PERSON**, $3.00. This booklet presents an analysis of the basic impulses moving through the eight personality types (as defined by the time in the month an individual was born) as they related to the inner self. This analysis is derived from the Lunation Cycle expounded by Dane Rudhyar. Robertson also discusses the progression of the Moon phases and the *natural outlets* by sign and house for expressing the energy flow and the personality type. As is the case with all of Robertson's books, the material in this volume seems to be excellent—but the organization is so terrible that it is often hard to follow what is being presented. This is the first volume in Robertson's *Cosmopsychology* Series. ANW 75

_____. **SEX, MIND, HABIT COMPATIBILITY**, $3.00. Reveals how individuals attract or repel one another on the basis of their birth charts. Emphasizes the factors that show quickly whether two people will be compatible. Robertson's books are well thought of by professional astrologers. ANW

_____. **TIME OUT OF MIND**, $3.50. *Reincarnation means something different to me than it does to most people who are first confronted with the idea. It shows me that I am connected to a heritage that I can call upon in my own personal growth. I have become so thankful for this—it has helped me so many times when crisis could have demolished me—that I decided there must be some way to see where it came from and for what reason. That's what this book is about. It's a way of going back into the past to tie the knot between the present and the future. I don't know what it will do for you except this: It could show you WHY your're facing what you are now and make sense of a lot of things that have been haunting you that an ordinary astrological analysis will never touch.* 47pp. ANW 72

_____. **TRANSITS OF SATURN**, c$5.00. Considers Saturn from every conceivable viewpoint. Gives suggestions on what you can do when Saturn is moving through a sign of the zodiac, a quadrant, a house and conjunction cycle with a birth planet. 73pp. ANW 73

ROBSON, VIVIAN E. **AN ASTROLOGICAL GUIDE TO YOUR SEX LIFE**, $.95. Examines the wide field of astrology and its relation to the sex life of the individual man and woman. Work is illustrated by seven horoscope charts including those of Oscar Wilde and Tchaikovsky. 140pp. Arc 63

_____. **ELECTIONAL ASTROLOGY**, c$7.50. Shows how to choose the best time, as far as astrological influences are concerned, to start a venture or undertaking. Includes general rules and principles of electional astrology, personal election, i.e., cutting hair, buying clothes, etc.; domestic election, i.e., employing servants, buying food, cooking; commerce and finance; friendship; medical elections and much more. Knowledge of the basics of astrology needed. 224pp. Wei 72

_____. **THE FIXED STARS AND CONSTELLATIONS IN ASTROLOGY**, $7.95. This is a systemized and as complete as possible compilation of all the information ever written about fixed stars since the Middle Ages. Includes chapters on the influence of constellations, fixed stars in natal astrology, influence of the stars and nebulae, and a chapter on the fixed stars and medieval magic. 225pp. Wei 69

_____. **THE RADIX SYSTEM**, $5.00. An amplification of the system introduced by Sepharial in 1918 to estimate the direction of progress of an astrological chart. Ms. Robson here describes and exemplifies the Radix system, with directions on calculating a directional and minor directional chart, cuspal directions, background material on each type of direction; information on midpoints and parallels, and on converse directions. Half of the text is devoted to an analysis of the effects of directions in the signs and the planets. Includes example readings and tables. 110pp. Dar 74

RODDEN, LOIS. **THE MERCURY METHOD OF CHART COMPARISON**, c$7.95. This is the method of chart comparison between two people by using the planet Mercury. Deals exclusively with the aspects of Mercury in one person's chart to the planets in another person's chart and shows that relationships can be defined with consistent accuracy by this method. The necessary requisites to using this book are a knowledge of the planets, signs and symbols, and a knowledge of how to read the ephemeris. 200pp. PAs 73

DANE RUDHYAR

To me, astrology has no meaning or value except it helps man to understand better his innate potentialities, the unfoldment of these potentialities, and the development of humanity through the centuries and with reference to the planet's biosphere within which it should operate as a harmonious force for further evolutionary growth. Indeed, as I see it, there is no such thing as astrology per se, as an independent entity having strictly defined methods of operation absolutely valid under any circumstances.

At the end of the cycle of the year all that belongs to the realm of the leaves of the yearly plants inevitably decays; but the seeds remain, as hidden centers

from which the new life will spring. What humanity needs now are seed—men and women willing and ready to assume the sacred task of self-metamorphosis, individually yet in constant relation to one another . . . .

————————◆————————

RUDHYAR, DANE. THE ASTROLOGICAL HOUSES—THE SPECTRUM OF INDIVIDUAL EXPERIENCE, $2.95. Analyzes the twelve houses in detail. They are considered to be the basic astrological frame of reference from whence all else derives. 208pp. Dou 72

_____. AN ASTROLOGICAL MANDALA—CYCLE OF TRANSFORMATIONS AND ITS 360 SYMBOLIC PHASES, $2.45. A reinterpretation of the Sabian symbols, a symbolic collection of images for each degree of the yearly cycle. It is an attempt to give meaning and significance to life experiences. *The symbols can be applied to any cycle of experience that can be conveniently divided into 360 phases.* Rudhyar feels that the book may be profitably used in the same fashion as the I Ching. 392pp. RaH 73

_____. AN ASTROLOGICAL STUDY OF PSYCHOLOGICAL COMPLEXES AND EMOTIONAL PROBLEMS, c$4.50. Rudhyarian philosophy delving into the astrological roots of parental, social, mental, emotional, and sexual complexes. RaH 66

_____. ASTROLOGICAL THEMES FOR MEDITATION. $1.50. See section on Meditation. CSA 72

_____. ASTROLOGICAL TIMING: THE TRANSITION TO THE NEW AGE, $3.45. An excellent philosophical work, originally entitled **Birth Patterns for a New Humanity.** A presentation of historical developments in the Western world combined with an account of the cycles of the precession of the equinoxes. One of the best statements of Aquarian Age philosophy that we've read. 246pp. H&R 69

_____. THE ASTROLOGY OF AMERICA'S DESTINY, $2.45. In this newly published, controversial work Rudhyar provides an astrological key to the social and political problems confronting our government and people. Contrary to other astrologers, he finds that the ascendant of the U.S. is Sagittarius, and this observation makes his analysis of the chart and the future of the U.S. very different from that of most other astrologers. Rudhyar provides a new context for the understanding of the events that marked the establishment of the American national identity, and for both their esoteric and exoteric meanings. Many contemporary events and future trends are discussed in the light of his examination of the birth chart. A very detailed, graphic study. 209pp. RaH 74

_____. THE ASTROLOGY OF PERSONALITY, $2.95. Rudhyar's most important philosophical work. He seeks to present astrology mainly as a symbolic language; by reformulating its basic concepts and stressing the importance of the study of the chart-as-a-whole rather than merely piecing together many small bits of memorized information and traditional data, he attempts to reorient and modernize the science of astrology. Highly recommended for the advanced astrologer. 500pp. Dou 70

_____. DIRECTIVES FOR NEW LIFE, $2.25. An enlightened view of the individual and how he fits into the society of the great transition. 73pp. See 71

_____. FIRE OUT OF THE STONE, $3.95. A reinterpretation of the basic images of the Christian tradition. Ser

_____. FROM HUMANISTIC TO TRANSPERSONAL ASTROLOGY, $2.50. This is an expanded version of Rudhyar's earlier pamphlet, **My Stand on Astrology.** *This new material introduces the concept of Transpersonal Astrology, which develops on the foundation that Humanistic Astrology has built, but refers to a new, because more inclusive approach to life. On the Transpersonal Way, everything in a birthchart is used for transformation, and the outermost planets of our known solar system—Uranus, Neptune, and Pluto—act as guides, pointing the way beyond the limits of the known....Within the context of this greater Whole, and for the persons able to answer the challenge it reveals, what matters most is not fulfillment at the personality level, but consecration to the Whole in terms of effectively focused and transforming action.* 77pp. See 75

_____. THE LUNATION CYCLE, $3.50. *The cyclic relationship of the moon to the sun produces the lunation cycle; and every moment of the month and day can be characterized significantly by its position within this lunation cycle* . . . . 138pp. ShP 71

_____. NEW MANSIONS FOR NEW MEN, c$7.50. This poetic, beautiful work treats the science of astrology as a system of symbols by which man can understand himself and the processes of life. 273pp. Ser 71

_____. OCCULT PREPARATIONS FOR THE NEW AGE, $3.25. This book is not about astrology per se. Rather, it is a study of man and his universe, a study that recognizes that not only the heavens affect us, but also that we affect the heavens, but also that the evolution of life is a cyclical process; that to evaluate correctly the condition of the world today, it is necessary that we retain the long, aeonic, evolutionary view. He includes a 1975 overview of Blavatsky's **Secret Doctrine** and a discussion of the *occult brotherhood.* Notes, 275pp. TPH 75

_____. PERSON CENTERED ASTROLOGY, c$8.95. Six essays. The title is derived from Rudhyar's person-centered approach to astrology as opposed to the *event-oriented* approach. He distinguishes between the two and establishes a psychological and philosophical basis for humanistic astrology. A psychologically oriented interpretation of man's relationship to himself, other people, and his environment as dictated by planetary influences. A compilation of his humanistic astrology series. 375pp. CSA 72

_____. THE PRACTICE OF ASTROLOGY AS A TECHNIQUE IN HUMAN UNDERSTANDING, $2.50. This book explains clearly the basic methods and facts of astrology and shows how they can be used to attain the ultimate goal of that study: the development of human understanding. 152pp. Pen 70

_____. THE PULSE OF LIFE: NEW DYNAMICS IN ASTROLOGY, $2.50. This book focuses on the signs of the zodiac and brings to our awareness our deep organic and instinctual roots in the rhythms of birth-life-death-new birth. 123pp. ShP 70

_____. RETURN FROM NO RETURN, $3.00. A *paraphysical novel* set in the twenty-second century which uses the medium of the novel to introduce us to a new concept of space and the possibility of integral existence beyond physical death. 167pp. See 73

_____. THE RHYTHM OF HUMAN FULFILLMENT: IN TUNE WITH COSMIC CYCLES, $2.25. Essay on flowing with nature through the doorways of great change. 81pp. See 73

_____. THE SUN IS ALSO A STAR, $3.95. Rudhyar's latest offering, subtitled *The Galactic Dimension of Astrology,* is an in-depth philosophical study of the trans-Saturnian planets: Uranus, Neptune, and Pluto. These planets, and especially Pluto, are the least understood of any of the planets (perhaps because they have been discovered the most recently). Rudhyar here begins with an insightful study of the solar system and of the differing scientific approaches to the universe throughout history. This theme reoccurs at various points in the book. The bulk of the material is devoted to in-depth analyses of the three planets including individual analyses, a study of them in Zodiacal sign, and an analysis of their interpenetrating cycles. Rudhyar has done a good job of integrating his philosophical concepts of the nature of the universe with an illuminating astrological analysis. The study of the trans-Saturnian planets is the best we know of. 209pp. Dut 75

_____. TRIPTYCH, c$6.95. Inspiring writing upon the spiritual nature and challenge each sign presents to the individual seeking fulfillment. Ser 68

_____. WE CAN BEGIN AGAIN TOGETHER, $4.95. Subtitled *A Re-evaluation of the Basic Concepts of Western Civilization in Terms of an Emergent Future for Mankind,* this is Rudhyar's latest philosophical attempt to explain where we have come from and where we are going. 233pp. Ome 74

WHITE, JOHN, ed. DANE RUDHYAR: SEED MAN, $2.50. A selection from some of the many books and articles Rudhyar has written over the years along with a full biographical study—and including some of Rudhyar's art (in color) and music. 28pp. HDI 75

————————◆◆◆————————

RUSSELL, LESLEY. BRIEF BROGRAPHIES, $5.00. This is a very interesting collection of natal charts of noted artists and writers which also includes birth data, family, physical characteristics, physical illnesses, psychological character, relationships, and a chronology of important life events. 94pp. AAs 73

SAINT-GERMAIN, COMTE de. PRACTICAL ASTROLOGY, $2.95. The author was a noted occultist. This work, first published in 1901, presents the basic astrological principles, including chart erection, and then goes into the relationships betwen astrology and the tarot. Graphically illustrated. 257pp. NPC 73

SAKOIAN, FRANCES and LOUIS ACKER. THE ASTROLOGER'S HANDBOOK, c$10.95. An impressive and complete introductory text on the subject of astrology. It includes the necessary information for casting the horoscope and interpreting the chart. The major portion of the work is given to delineations of each aspect. This is the best basic text that we know of for the beginning student and an invaluable aid for all astrologers. Includes a general index and a cross index of aspects. Highly recommended. 461pp. H&R 73

_____. THE ASTROLOGY OF HUMAN RELATIONSHIPS, c$10.95. This is the only major textbook that discusses the comparison of natal charts in depth. The book begins with a review of the basic principles of astrological analysis, especially as they apply to chart comparison. The bulk of the book is a study of comparative influences of the planets, by house placement and by aspects. Each of the planets is discussed individually, and at length. There's also a glossary and an excellent long index. This seems to be an excellent book of its type and we imagine it will be very popular. 401pp. H&R 76

_____. THE IMPORTANCE OF MERCURY IN THE HOROSCOPE, $2.00. A very popular series of pamphlets. This one begins with a general discussion of Mercury and then goes on to analyze Mercury in each of the elements, retrograde Mercury, and Mercury in each of the houses. 41pp. NES 70

_____. LADDER OF THE PLANETS, $2.50. This is a comprehensive essay on the correct planetary sign rulerships and exaltations, including material on the outer planets, Uranus, Neptune, and Pluto. 27pp. NES 74

_____. MAJOR AND MINOR APPROACHING AND DEPARTING ASPECTS, $2.75. This is an analysis of the following aspects: conjunction, opposition, sextile, square, trine, semi-sextile, decile, semi-square, quintile, tridecile, sesquiquadrate, bi-quintile, quincunx, and vigintile. First the aspect itself is discussed and then the approaching and departing and applying and separating of each aspect. 38pp. AFA 74

_____. THAT INCONJUNCT—QUINCUNX, $3.00. Most of the books on aspects do not discuss quincunxes, or do so only very briefly. This is the only book that discusses them in detail through the planets. 57pp. NES 72

_____. **TRANSITS OF JUPITER**, $3.00. Each of these pamphlets on transits first discusses the planet transiting each of the houses and then explores the transiting planet conjunct, sextile, square, trine, and in opposition to each of the natal planets. 72pp. NES 74

_____. **TRANSITS OF MARS**, $3.00. 55pp. NES 74

_____. **TRANSITS OF MERCURY**, $3.00. 80pp. Sak 75

_____. **TRANSITS OF THE MOON**, $3.00. 60pp. Sak 75

_____. **TRANSITS OF NEPTUNE**, $3.00. 78pp. NES 72

_____. **TRANSITS OF PLUTO**, $3.00. 64pp. NES 72

_____. **TRANSITS OF SATURN**, $3.00. 75pp. NES 72

_____. **TRANSITS OF THE SUN**, $3.00. Sak 75

_____. **TRANSITS OF URANUS**, $3.00. 78pp. NES

_____. **TRANSITS OF VENUS**, $3.00. NES 75

_____. **THE ZODIAC WITHIN EACH SIGN**, $6.00. *Astrologers have often noticed the differences in personal mannerisms of people who have the same planets prominent in the same signs of their horoscopes. . . . It is not difficult to recognize that, in terms of its quality of influence, a sign of the zodiac is not an undifferentiated continuum, but that different parts or sections of each sign have slightly, and sometimes noticeably, different influences. Several methods are used to determine the different qualities of natives born with planets placed in the same sign. The most widely known and publicized of these is the system of decantes. According to the decante system, a sign consisting of 30º of arc is subdivided into three segments of 10º each. Each of these segments has been found to have the sum influence or overtone quality of one of the signs of the Triplicity (or Element) to which the sign in question belongs. . . . Another important and highly useful method of subdividing the signs is by duads. By this approach each sign is divided into twelve segments of 2½º each, each segment having the subinfluence of one of the twelve signs of the zodiac.*—from the introduction. A detailed description of the decants and duads of each sign is presented in this manual, along with some helpful charts and general explanatory material. 142pp. Sak 75

SAMPSON, WALTER. **THE ZODIAC: A LIFE EPITOME**, c$15.00. An effusively written study of the inner meaning of the signs of the zodiac based upon the teachings of Christianity and upon the ancient mystery teachings. The presentation is a bit hard to follow, but illuminating insights are offered and the esoteric aspects of astrology are emphasized. 450pp. ASI 26

SARGENT, LOIS. **HOW TO HANDLE YOUR HUMAN RELATIONS**, $3.50. A manual giving practical pointers for living in a more harmonious manner with family, friends and associates. The suggestions and theory presented are based upon astrological considerations in conjunction with the finding of modern psychology. 77pp. AFA 58

_____. **YOU'RE IN GOOD ZODIAC COMPANY**, $3.00. The personalities and careers of notable persons born in the same sign are discussed, so that the reader may discover tendencies and traits that are common among those of the same sign. 120pp. AFA

SAWTELL, VANDA. **ASTROLOGY AND BIOCHEMISTRY**, c$3.60. All the parts and organs of the body have an analogical correspondence with one of the signs of the zodiac. This book explains the personality and physical characteristics of persons born under each sign and their associated physical weaknesses. 86pp. HSP 70

SCHULMAN, MARTIN. **KARMIC ASTROLOGY: THE MOON'S NODES & REINCARNATION**, $3.95. Many astrologers believe that the Moon's Nodes represent karmic influences at work in an individual's current life. The South Node is symbolic of the past and the North Node represents the future potential. In this volume Schulman gives a delineation of the Nodes by sign and house position and also discusses aspects to the Nodes. He also presents several sample delineations, ilustrating the natal charts and discussing the Nodal positions. Yogananda, Gandhi, and Edgar Cayce are among the samples chosen. This volume should by no means be considered a definitive work—Schulman is a young astrologer-psychic just beginning his exploration—however it deos delve into areas untouched by other books and the information Schulman comes up with is quite interesting. An appendix gives Nodal positions from 1850-2000. 133pp. Wei 75

SCHWICKERT, GUSTAV. **RECTIFICATION OF THE BIRTH TIME**, $4.50. A good attempt at elucidation of the difficult task of rectification. 163pp. AFA 54

SCHWICKERT, FRIEDRICH and ADOLF WEISS. **CORNERSTONES OF ASTROLOGY**, c$10.00. Teaches the analytical and systematic approach to horoscope interpretation developed by Morin de Villefranche. Much of the material here is unique to this book. Includes many explanatory charts. 342pp. PaB 72

SEHESTED, OVE. **THE BASICS OF ASTROLOGY**, c$12.95. This is a basic textbook for the beginning student, including extensive material on chart erection and interpretation and a long section of tables and reference material. The coverage is very comprehensive—too comprehensive we feel. Some selective editing would have improved the book—this is especially true of the chart erection instructions. However some people find the abundance of material helpful. Ura 73

SEISS, JOSEPH A. **THE GOSPEL IN THE STARS**, $7.00. An offset reprint of an old (1882) Christian-oriented spiritual text, covering each of the signs in depth and relating them to the Biblical tradition. Index, 522pp. HeR 1884

SEPHARIAL. **ASTROLOGY AND MARRIAGE**, c$3.50. The influence of planetary action in courtship and married life is explained. Sepharial discusses harmonizing factors, signs of happiness, signs of discord, the domestic circle, multiple marriages, and children. Case histories of assorted marriages are recorded. 59pp. Wei 70

_____. **ECLIPSES**, $2.95. The only complete treatise on eclipses in print which covers all phases of astrological significance and interpretation for application to mundane and individual affairs and charts. 112pp. Sym 73

_____. **GEODETIC EQUIVALENTS**, $2.00. Geodetic equivalents are used in Mundane Astrology as aids in prediction. It has been found that the longitude and latitude of a place affects the Midheaven and Ascendent. The Geodetic Equivalent measures and adjusts these effects. This is a short exposition of the G.E.s of principal towns, and a study of a sign rulership. 61pp. AFA nd

_____. **NEW DICTIONARY OF ASTROLOGY**, c$1.49. Definitions of hundreds of terms—from the everyday to the most obscure and controversial—used in the works of astrologers, past and present. Information on Pluto and tables of time differences are also included. 158pp. Arc

_____. **THE SCIENCE OF FOREKNOWLEDGE**, $3.00. Sepharial is often not the clearest writer, but his knowledge of the astrology of the ancients is unequaled. In this volume he discusses the astrology of the Hebrews and the ancient Hindus. He also focuses on Lilith and on Neptune and on the Radix System as a method of future forecasting. 160pp. HeR 18

_____. **THE SILVER KEY**, $3.00. This is an attempt of Sepharial's to see how accurate astrological prediction could be in relation to horse racing. Includes tables and detailed instructions. 94pp. HeR

_____. **THE SOLAR EPOCH: A NEW ASTROLOGICAL THESIS**, c$3.50. Sepharial claims that man is endowed with an organism capable of responding to impulses from the solar, lunar, and terrestrial planes of existence. If we accept the validity of a horoscope applied to terrestrial life, we must also accept the reality of a further horoscope corresponding to the solar epoch. It is the latter thesis that he explores in this book. 90pp. Wei 70

_____. **TRANSITS AND PLANETARY PERIODS**, c$3.50. An examination of the problems of transits: their continuity, duration, and the reasons for perceptible breaks in their action. 94pp. Wei 70

_____. **THE WORLD HOROSCOPE**, c$7.50. Points out Biblical references to the influences of stars and lays down the key to the study of scriptural prophecy. Includes interpretations of the world horoscope and period charts of the U.S.A. 70pp. Fou 65

SHIL-PONDE. **HINDU ASTROLOGY**, c$5.00. A comprehensive basic text with calculation instructions and a great deal of interpretative material. 333pp. Sag 75

SIMMONITE, W.J. **THE ARCANA OF ASTROLOGY**, $4.95. This is a recent reprint of one of the most noted astrological texts of the previous century. Unlike many of the other early texts, there is a great deal of valuable information here for the experienced astrologer. We don't recommend this book to the beginner since both the writing style and the abundance of detail would be confusing. Each chapter is followed by a section of related questions—with the answers given—and many of the items discussed are hard to find elsewhere. Over 100pp of mathematical and astronomical tables are also included. 434pp. NPC 74

_____. **HORARY ASTROLOGY**, $4.00. A nineteenth century horary text, revised in the late nineteenth century, by John Story, and revised again by Ernest Grant (of the A.F.A.) in 1950. 171pp. AFA 50

SMITH, HERBERT. **TRANSITS**, $4.00. Dr. Smith was Evangeline Adams' teacher. Although this volume suffers from the negative language so often found in nineteenth and early twentieth century works it is still a fairly good, in depth study of the aspects of the transiting planets. The style and the words used are unusual to say the least. 42pp. AFA nd

STAHL, CARL. **BEGINNER'S MANUAL OF SIDEREAL ASTROLOGY, BOOK I**, $5.00. The only instructional manual in sidereal astrology chart erection available. Includes all the logarithms. The detailed instructions are quite helpful but the student would have to be very good at math to catch on to the intricacies of the system without a teacher. Many examples of the various charts are given. The section of instructional material and charts is 70pp and the one with the tools is 66pp. Oversize. Sol 69

_____. **BEGINNER'S MANUAL OF SIDEREAL ASTROLOGY, BOOK II**, $7.00. Detailed lessons in sidereal natal interpretation gleaned from the author's eighteen years of experience with the system. Questions follow each chapter. Oversize, 133pp. Sol 73

_____. **THOUGHTS ON SIDEREAL ASTROLOGY**, $2.00. A collection of articles from **Spica, A Review of Sidereal Astrology**: *Personally Speaking, House Meanings in Sidereal Astrology, Thoughts on Pluto, Thoughts on Neptune, Thoughts on Uranus and Thoughts on Saturn.* Oversize, 52pp. Sol 73

_____. **VULCAN**, $6.00. Arguments seeking to prove the existence of Vulcan, *the intra-Mercurial planet* along with detailed tables for the calculation of its zodiacal position, published in the hope that by providing these tables more astronomers and astrologers would accept Vulcan as an actual planet. 104pp. Sol 72

STEARN, JESS. **A TIME FOR ASTROLOGY**, $1.95. A well written, chatty narrative, touching on many astrological subjects in a topical vein. Includes sample charts and analyses of famous people. The charts of the U.S. and of many of its presidents are also illustrated and analyzed and the whole is related to contemporary events. Includes ascendant, moon tables, and an abbreviated ephemeris for 1900–1975. A good book for those with a general interest in astrology who don't want to get bogged down in detail. 435pp. NAL 71

STONE, KEN. **ASTRODYNES**, $3.50. Numerical method of deciding important factors in chart interpretation. 75pp. ChL 68

_____. **DELINEATION WITH ASTRODYNES**, $3.95. Gives the basics in the delineation and interpretations of astrodynes in the horoscope, concerning health, vocational selection, harmony, temperament and compatability. Includes charts. 60pp. ChL 72

STRINGER, SHIRLEY. **INFLUENCE OF FIXED STARS: PISCES**, $2.00. The position of each fixed star is given in longitude, latitude, right ascension, declination, and magnitude. This is followed by a summary of all that each of the astrological experts have to say about the influence of each fixed star. The astrologers quoted include Robson, Weston, Matthews, Keane, Devore, Cockbain, Ebertin, Deluce, and Daiger. The encyclopedia comments are followed by a general summary. AsA

_____. **INFLUENCE OF FIXED STARS: TAURUS**, $2.00. The approach here is the same as in Ms. Stringer's book on Pisces. AsA

SUN, RUTH. **ASIAN ANIMAL ZODIAC**, c$7.75. In much the same way as people in the West analyze their personalities and predict the future by studying the position of the stars when they were born, Asians use the ancient animal zodiac to explain the individual personalities and predict the course of the future. According to legend, the twelve years in the Asian animal cycle were named for the twelve animals who visited the Buddha on his deathbed. This book examines in turn each of the zodiacal cycle and describes its history, its characteristics, and relates traditional tales that illustrate each animal's personality. Bibliography, 218pp. Tut 74

TAYLOR, MAXINE. **NOW THAT I'VE CAST IT, WHAT DO I DO WITH IT?** $4.50. Ms. Taylor is an astrology teacher and she has successfully applied the material presented here with many of her students. Her basic approach tends toward an intuitive understanding of the whole chart through key words and basic sentences. The main topics include the following: the houses, signs on cusps, planets in houses, planets in signs, aspects to planets, aspects to angles, and linking planets with signs. This is a useful interpretative aid for the beginning student. 86pp. Tay 75

_____. **WHAT'S A DIURNAL?** $3.50. The diurnal chart is an event chart which does not show the actual event or activity but rather reveals the true nature of the event and our subjective reaction to it and takes into consideration the natal, progressed, and transiting planets. This pamphlet begins with a short discussion of diurnals followed by instructions on casting a diurnal chart. The bulk of the book is devoted to twenty-six example charts, with interpretations. 50pp. Tay 76

_____. **WHAT'S A RELOCATED CHART?**, $1.50. An individual's natal chart relocates itself every time s/he leaves her or his place of birth. The farther one goes, the greater the changes. This pamphlet gives directions for casting a relocated chart along with three example charts with interpretations. 11pp. Tay 76

TAYLOR, C. TOUSLEY. **ASTROLOGICAL HOROSCOPES: HOW TO CREATE AND READ THEM**, $2.50. A general work, with an overwhelming number of adjectives. Gives the basic interpretation material as well as the charts of some noted 1930's figures. The analyses tend to be simplistic. 46pp. Hug 34

TESSIER, ELIZABETH. **THE MEANING OF THE HOUSES AND THE PLANETS**, $4.75. A general survey of the houses and the planets, emphasizing the basic ideas they represent. The presentation is psychologically and symbolically oriented and the mythological background of each of the planets is fully reviewed. A good introductory overview. 102pp. IAS 76

THIERENS, A.E. **ASTROLOGY AND THE TAROT**, $2.95. See the Tarot section. NPC 75

THOMPSON, DORIS. **CHART YOUR OWN STARS**, c$15.00. This is a very detailed chart erection instructional manual. Many examples are given for each step, and all the aspects of chart erection and the special terms involved are very fully explained. Much of the book can be used as a workbook. Samples are shown and there is space for the student to fill in his/her own details. The approach seems to be good and the explanations clear. It's a good book—however it is a good deal more expensive that similar manuals and we are not sure that the content is significantly better. Oversize, 286pp. Mac 75

TITSWORTH, JOAN. **CASE STUDIES IN HORARY ASTROLOGY**, $5.50. This book opens with a discussion of how to place the horary question by house and the strictures to reading certain charts (with example charts). This is followed by two example case studies of questions for each of the 12 houses. Each case is illustrated by the horary chart used followed by the background for the asking of the question, the actual question asked, and an in-depth delineation of the horary chart for the answer to that question. The cases themselves are taken from the actual practice of several of New Jersey's leading astrologers. AsA 75

TOBEY, CARL. **AN ASTROLOGY PRIMER**, $2.50. A sun sign analysis by one of America's most noted astrologers, with some additional material. 125pp. She 65

_____. **ASTROLOGY OF INNER SPACE**, $5.95. Results of a mathematician's fifty years devoted to astrology. Describes signs and houses and gives helpful hints and good esoteric views on the subject. 400pp. Ome 73

TOWNLEY, JOHN. **THE COMPOSITE CHART**, $2.95. A composite chart is a horoscope of the mutual midpoints of two natal charts. It seems to describe the relationship between two (or more) people. This is the only book that we know of on this system. Townley explains the how's and why's of composite technique and its possibilities and illustrates his exposition with many sample charts, including Hitler and Eva Braun, Nixon and the U.S., the U.S. and the U.S.S.R. 47pp. Wei 74

TUCKER, WILLIAM J. **ASTROLOGY AND YOUR FAMILY TREE**, c$6.75. A detailed study of the astrological structure of a family of forty members, showing the inter-relationship of related horoscopes, and in particular how the configurations on the day of ovulation point out the sign and degree which will rise at the moment of birth. 169pp. Pyt 60

_____. **ASTROLOGY FOR EVERYMAN**, c$9.50. This is Tucker's basic textbook, designed for beginning and intermediate students and including information on the houses, planets, and signs, the planets in the houses and signs, aspects, transits, and a great deal of supplementary material. There is also information on casting a horoscope and astronomical sections. Even the advanced student can find a great deal of interpretive material here. Dr. Tucker's writing is not the clearest we've read, but he is thorough and does give a good scientific presentation. Oversize, index. 333pp. Pyt 60

_____. **ASTRO-MEDICAL RESEARCH**, c$9.00. Dr. Tucker conducts the student through a modern hospital to introduce him/her to the sick and the dying. The clinical reports on each of the several hundred patients are presented and the malady afflicting the individual is studied in relation to his personal horoscope. Cases examined cover a wide spectrum. As with all of Tucker's books, this is only recommended to knowledgeable astrologers since an understanding of the material requires a great deal of technical competence. Oversize, mimeographed, 218pp. Pyt 62

_____. **ASTRONOMY FOR STUDENTS OF ASTROLOGY**, c$9.00. This text does a better job than any other we know of in presenting the basics of astronomy and its mathematical underpinnings for the astrologer. All of the material is graphically illustrated and Tucker succeeds in his aim of imparting a vital understanding of the dynamics of the universe. Each aspect of astrology is analyzed and explained and all astrologers will find that their understanding of how astrology has developed historically greatly enhanced. The why's and how's of chart erection and calculation are detailed at great length. Oversize, mimeographed, index, 211pp. Pyt 63

_____. **ASTROPHARMACOLOGY**, c$9.00. This is the latest of Tucker's medical manuals. He presents the principles of the science of prescribing drugs to match the requirements of the individual patient gleaned from the data to be found in his/her horoscope. 170pp. Pyt 66

_____. **AUTOBIOGRAPHY OF AN ASTROLOGER**, c$10.00. Tucker's life story. 380pp. Pyt

_____. **DESTINY, CYBERNETICS, AND ASTROLOGY**, c$8.00. Explains the programming of computers for use in astrology. 200pp. Pyt 67

_____. **THE FIXED STARS AND YOUR HOROSCOPE**, c$9.50. This seems to be the most detailed study of fixed stars available. The text begins with preliminary material relating the fixed stars to one's horoscope and classifying the stars. Then Tucker turns to detailed analyses of the effects of the three classes of stars (white, yellow, and red) through the houses. He ends with detailed analyses of the solar charts of historical personages, including Rudolf Steiner, H.P. Blavatsky, Annie Besant, and Sir Arthur Eddington. An appendix catalogues the birthstars, giving their right ascension, formulae of spectra, color, chief elements, and magnitude. Oversize, mimeographed, 268pp. Pyt 63

_____. **FORECASTING WORLD EVENTS**, c$9.50. Presents an entirely reconstructed method for the prediction of political and world events from the configurations of the heavens. This work also introduces a totally new method for establishing the sign-rulerships of countries. Tucker analyzes the salient historical events connected with the lives of people of various countries, and shows how an *authentic* national chart for each country is to be elicited. He then uses these national charts to show how past events can be understood and future events can be predicted. 350pp. Pyt

_____. **GENETICS AND ASTROLOGY**, c$8.00. Dr. Tucker reviews the creation of the universe and the evolution of man. He goes on to show the radiation methods whereby the stars govern and direct the activities of an individual and discusses how particular aspects forming at the instant of birth can cause genetic mutations. He also relates how to avoid these risks. 127pp. Pyt 71

_____. **THE HOW? WHAT? AND WHY? OF ASTROLOGY**, c$9.00. Dr. Tucker is a very well known English astrologer. His writing style is not the best, but the material is clearly presented and the scientific validity of each point is stressed. This is his most basic book, covering the fundamentals of astrology: the meanings of the signs, houses, and planets; the aspects; and chart erection. 161pp. Pyt 36

_____. MAN AND HIS DESTINY, $8.00. An analytic survey. 200pp. Pyt 67

_____. THE PRINCIPLES OF SCIENTIFIC ASTROLOGY, c$9.00. Analyzes all the facets of astrology from a scientific point of view, and shows how they evolved historically. Also includes chapters on the history of astrology and on the psychological aspects of astrology. Index, 327pp. Pyt 73

_____. PTOLEMAIC ASTROLOGY, $8.00. This is the only modern commentary on the Tetrabiblos of Ptolemy. 236pp. Pyt 72

_____. STUDY BY THE STARS, c$8.00. Subtitled, *A Refresher Course of Instruction in Modern Astrology*, this is a good short review of all major aspects of chart erection and interpretation, much more clearly written and organized than is true of most of Tucker's books. 200pp. Pyt 68

TUCKER, WILLIAM & ELIZABETH TESSIER. ASTROLOGICAL STUDIES: CASTING HOROSCOPES PAST AND PRESENT, $4.75. This is a good introduction to the basics of chart erection. All the tools are described and the major terms are defined. The chart erection instructions are clearly presented and examples are given using several types of systems and ephemerides. There are also interesting sections on ancient astrology, Ptolemy's contributions, the original Table of Houses, Tucker's system of equal house division, great quadrangles, and Tessier's sundial system. 94pp. IAS 75

TURNBULL, COULSON. THE SOLAR LOGOS, $4.00. An inspirational, intuitive study of the planets as they relate to the ancient mystery teachings. Oversize, 62pp. Hug nd

TYL, NOEL. THE HOROSCOPE AS IDENTITY, c$10.00. This is not part of Tyl's series. It is his first book, newly reprinted. The material is more general than in the other books and it is equally clearly written. The approach is an understanding of the psychological basis of astrology and the text is illustrated with 58 charts. Also includes extensive material on the meaning of Saturn and guidelines for interpretation. The material covered does not overlap the presentation in the series. 279pp. Llp 74

_____. THE PRINCIPLES AND PRACTICE OF ASTROLOGY

VOL. I: HOROSCOPE CONSTRUCTION, $3.95. This is a self-contained volume, with tables and practice horoscope blanks. Includes step-by-step instructions on casting the chart, with details on the use of materials and examples; material on placing the planets and measuring the houses; and a calculation review. For the money this is one of the best erection manuals available, though it is not our favorite. 250pp. Llp 73

VOL. II: THE HOUSES: THEIR SIGNS AND PLANETS, $3.95. Presents the rationale of house demarcation; the meaning of the signs and planets in each house; and derivative house readings. Llp 74

VOL. III: THE PLANETS: THEIR SIGNS AND ASPECTS, $3.95. A good concentrated study including material on the reading of aspects and dignities *at a glance* (not as easy as he makes it sound) and a brief analysis of all major aspects and sun-moon combinations. Graphically illustrated. 175pp. Llp 74

VOL. IV: ASPECTS AND HOUSES IN ANALYSIS, $3.95. Much of this book is devoted to aspect patterns, hemisphere emphasis and retrogradation, and to parallels, nodes, and parts of fortune. 144pp. Llp 74

VOL. V: ASTROLOGY AND PERSONALITY, $3.95. This volume systematically translates psychological theories of personality into astrological terms and techniques. Tyl's theory is illuminated through analyses of many horoscopes of well known people. This forms a valuable addition to the available material on interpretation. 158pp. Llp 74

VOL. VI: THE EXPANDED PRESENT, $3.95. Tyl begins with a discussion of prediction and then goes on to clarify the main techniques of prediction: radix methods, rapport measurements, secondary progressions, and his own discovery, factor-7 time-scan. He explains procedures for quickly estimating and corroborating important developments in the horoscope, and shows how to integrate the various predictive systems. A large part of the text is devoted to an analysis of progressed aspects. As with all Tyl books, the exposition is well presented and illustrated with sample charts. 183pp. Llp 74

VOL. VII: INTEGRATED TRANSITS, $3.95. A definitive work, modernizing the rationale, analysis, and application of transit theory. Astrology is translated into behavior with many case studies illustrating every major transit. Also includes studies of solar revolution, rectification, eclipse theory, and accidents. 237pp. Llp 74

VOL. VIII: ANALYSIS AND PREDICTION, $3.95. Tyl has produced a comprehensive, clearly written series. Each of the volumes covers its topic quite well and is self-contained. The books are a valuable addition to a beginning student's library and an important set of books for all astrologers. Each volume has a number of illustrative charts. This volume sets out each step of deduction, analysis, and projection—illustrated with case studies. Radix methods, progressions, and transits are fully interpreted. In addition, there is an introduction to horary and electional astrology. 171pp. Llp 74

VOL. IX: SPECIAL HOROSCOPE DIMENSIONS, $3.95. Presents a good overview of the following topics: vocation, relocation, opportunity, elections, chart comparison, creativity, health problems, vitality. 206pp. Llp 75

VOL. X: ASTROLOGICAL COUNSEL, $3.95. This is a detailed look at the psychodynamics of the astrologer-client relationship, with examples showing the astrologer's

consideration of the horoscope and the individual. Difficulties are analyzed, and communication techniques are explored. 171pp. Llp 75

VOL. XI: ASTROLOGY: ASTRAL, MUNDANE, OCCULT, $3.95. Covers the following topics: the fixed stars, the individual degrees and decanates; considerations of mundane astrology; study of death and reincarnation. 165pp. Llp 75

VOL. XII: TIMES TO COME, $3.95. An investigation into the potential of astrology. Also includes a complete subject index for all twelve volumes. 197pp. Llp 75

_____. TEACHING AND STUDY GUIDE TO THE PRINCIPLES AND PRACTICES OF ASTROLOGY, $15.00. Noel Tyl's latest work takes the concepts of astrology, translates them into human terms, and frames them within effective teaching techniques. The teacher learns how to present all astrological material; the student discovers intriguing ways to learn the material. In his characteristically lucid and dramatic style, Tyl covers an enormous amount of material in addition to the traditional techniques: the Key Cycle, eclipses, the minor aspects and harmonics, composite charting, planetary hours, the philosophy and technique of counseling, mundane astrological prediction, and much more. Over 190,000 words tell how every astrological concept from beginning to advanced can be taught and learned. A glossary of over 350 terms is also included. An important new work which we recommend highly. 650pp. LlP 76

URANIAN ASTROLOGY

Uranian Astrology, originally formulated by Alfred Witte and the Hamburg School, uses eight Transneptunian plants in addition to the classical ten and is basically a technique of structuring contacts between them called *planetary pictures*. These can and usuallly do occur without the classical aspects being involved and are written and understood much like algebraic equations (i.e., Moon + Pluto — Sun = Mars). These equations use not only natal, solar arc and transiting planets but antiscions of the above and so can become quite complex, but they are extraordinarily accurate. Although it seems difficult to learn, Uranian Astrology is precise and very descriptive and is coming into wider use. (Our thanks to Martha P. Taub for this description and the following Uranian reviews.)

AMBJORNSON, K. H. THE HANDBOOK OF THE 90° DISC. $9.75. *This Handbook has been especially prepared to teach the 90 degree disc technique for finding, simply and quickly, all planetary pictures and midpoints in the natal chart. Not only is it profusely illustrated with drawings to show the methods for deriving these patterns, but it also takes the astrologer step-by-step from the simplest to the most complicated structures. An added feature . . . is the inclusion of practice problems with answers . . . . While this Handbook has been prepared with Uranian Astrology in mind, the material is equally useful in finding the midpoint data from the cosmic structural pictures of Ebertin cosmobiology.* ——from the Introduction. 218pp. AMB 74

_____, DELINEATIONS OF MUNDANE EVENTS. $2.50. Presents a technique for delineating mundane events through investigation of the axes of Midheaven, Sun, Ascendent, Moon, Moon's Node, or their respective 45° angles. Planetary equations found on these axes, or combinations of planets forming a midpoint connection with these axes, will provide accurate information when precise timing has been ascertained. Planetary equations utilizing the transneptunian planets are emphasized. This pamphlet presents two case studies, analyzed in depth in an instructional fashion. 22 pp. Amb 74

BRUMMUND, RUTH. TRANSNEPTUN—EPHEMERIDES 1890—1990, $12.60. Gives positions of the Transneptunian planets every ten days. Important to have and easy to use once you accustom yourself to the European method of notation for the date: day first and month second. 209pp. AFA 72

CERS, ALFONS. NEW HORIZON ASTROLOGY, PART 1, $5.00. Cers believes that Uranian astrology and Cosmobiology are the astrology of the future and that the traditional techniques are obsolete. His books are instructional texts in the use of halfsums and planetary pictures. Each contains a number of guided lessons, with solutions. The instructions are not as clear as they might be. however some of our customers have found them to be useful. The material is keyed to the basic Uranian and Cosmobiological texts. This book covers the interpretation of a natal chart and also includes introductory material. 46pp. Cer 72

_____. NEW HORIZON ASTROLOGY, PART 2, $5.00. Covers natal chart calculations, directions, transits, investigations, interpretations, and determinations. 45pp. Cer 73

JACOBSON, ROGER. THE LANGUAGE OF URANIAN ASTROLOGY, c$11.05. This textbook is the best so far available on this complex subject, and most of the information needed to begin to understand Uranian Astrology is here. The Transneptunian Planets are well explained as are the Uranian house systems. The information on *planetary pictures*, the basic technique, is really excellent. Included are some simple meanings of planetary combinations. No index, unfortunately. This book has been badly needed for some time. Approx. 250pp. UrP 75

KICKBUSCH, ARTHUR. SOLAR ARC TABLES, $2.35. AFA

RUDOLPH, LUDWIG. MEANING OF THE PLANETS IN THE HOUSES, $3.50. Goes into the meanings of the planets in the houses of the various Uranian house systems, using equal houses on a 360° dial. 35pp. UrP n.d.

RUDOLPH, UDO. **THE HAMBURG SCHOOL OF ASTROLOGY**, $2.55. A useful and inexpensive explanation of the basic of Uranian Astrology: planetary pictures. Goes into the house systems as well. Worth having. 23pp. UrP 73

WITTE, ALFRED. **PERPETUAL EPHEMERIS OF THE TRANSNEPTUNIAN PLANETS**, $2.55. Less expensive than the Ruth Brummund Ephemeris, but requires calculation to use. (Gives only one position per year.) UrP

WITTE—LEFELDT. **RULES FOR PLANETARY PICTURES**, $16.65. This is the basic tool for Uranian Astrologers and should be bought as soon as Jacobson's book begins to be understood. It presents the basic meanings of planets (including the Transneptunians) in pairs and in combination with any third planet. Essential. 339pp. UrP 59

TOOLS

360° METAL DIAL, 150mm, $4.50

90° METAL DIAL, Solar Arc (in German), $4.50

BOARD CENTER SCREW, $2.00

VAN STONE, HENRY. **STUDY IN ZODIACAL SYMBOLOGY**, $2.95. Scholarly esoteric treatise synthesizing ancient Egyptian and Buddhist origins and significance of the symbols of the planets and zodiacal signs. 109pp. Sym 74

VAUGHN, RICHARD. **ASTROLOGY IN MODERN LANGUAGE**, c$8.95. A comprehensive basic text covering signs, planets, houses, chart erection, interpretation. The emphasis is on psychological understanding of character. A well-respected, well-written account. 351pp. Put 72

VOLGUINE, ALEXANDRE. **LUNAR ASTROLOGY**, c$7.95. Volguine is of the school of astrologers who feel that the role in astrology assigned to the moon is far smaller than it should be, taking into account the nearness of the moon and its influence on our lives. The astrology of antiquity recognized a lunar zodiac, as well as lunar houses, thus portioning out the influence of the moon into three systems similar to those of solar influence. Volguine believes that the twenty-eight *Moon Mansions* of the ancients is a system with a great deal of validity and he presents it in depth in this volume. Notes, bibliography, 130pp. ASI 74

_____. **THE RULER OF THE NATIVITY**, c$6.00. Volguine is considered France's most noted twentieth century astrologer. This is the first translation of his work into English. This book is devoted to an exposition of his system for finding the strength of each planet, house, sign, aspect, etc. and assigning to each a series of coefficients derived from multiple criteria, astronomical as well as astrological. His ideas are related to Hindu astrology and the book is only recommended to the expert astrologer. 152pp. ASI 73

WADE, ELBERT. **ASTROLOGY DIAL-A-SCOPE**, $3.50. Tables and a colored wheel for finding your ascendant and moon and material on the ascendant, sun, and moon in the signs. Seems to be generally accurate, although not very detailed. 79pp. Arc 70

WATTERS, BARBARA H. **THE ASTROLOGER LOOKS AT MURDER**, $1.95. Entrancing analyses of seven famous murders. 173pp. Val 69

_____. **HORARY ASTROLOGY AND THE JUDGMENT OF EVENTS**, c$13.50. Elucidates the science of horary astrology with enormous clarity, precision, and style. Case histories that inspire study, along with definitions and guidelines, make this definitely one of the best. 220pp. Val 73

_____. **SEX AND THE OUTER PLANETS**, $4.95. A very well presented, unusual study. 222pp. Val 71

_____. **WHAT'S WRONG WITH YOUR SUN SIGN**, $4.50. An instructive and unusual book by a noted astrologer which presents little known facets of the sun signs. 290pp. Val 70

WEST, J.A. and TOONAER, J.G. **THE CASE FOR ASTROLOGY**, $1.65. A well written and substantial account of where astrology has come from and why it has grown so in our time. Highly recommended for all who seek to comprehend the scientific basis of astrology. A very important introductory work. 310pp. Pen 73

WESTON, H.L. **THE PLANET VULCAN**, $1.50. This is an analysis of all that's known about the history and nature of this *unknown* planet. Also includes tables. 35pp. AFA

WHITE, G. **THE MOON'S NODES**, $1.50. A comprehensive account of the nodes and their importance in natal astrology. 74pp. AFA 27

WHITMAN, EDWARD. **ASPECTS AND THEIR MEANINGS: ASTRO-KINETICS, VOL. III**, c$7.95. The effects of the major and minor aspects in their differing locations, together with the meanings, are dealt with in detail. Also contains a detailed description of the influence of a progressed moon and its progressed aspects as well as a chapter on world time differences. This series is highly recommended. 178pp. Fow 70

_____. **THE INFLUENCE OF THE HOUSES: ASTRO-KINETICS, VOL. I**, c$7.95. First of a series of three books on applied astrology. The influence of each individual house of the zodiac has been analyzed and explained so that the reader may see just how to set about the delineation of a horoscope. 200pp. Fow 70

_____. **THE INFLUENCE OF THE PLANETS: ASTRO-KINETICS, VOL. II**, c$7.35. Explains how each of the signs of the zodiac has a definite planetary ruler and

each planet is more favorably placed in certain signs and less in others. However, the planets possess both negative and positive attributes and therefore, of necessity, must rule over two signs in order that both attributes shall have full expression. Fow 70

WILLIAMS, DAVID. **ASTRO-ECONOMICS**, $3.00. A detailed study of astrology and business cycles, emphasizing the development of an astrological tool to predict the turning points in mass psychology as applied to the economic field. Williams includes an extensive review of the development of economic thought regarding the business cycle in addition to his analysis of the planetary aspects as they relate to actual economic cycles. The text is illustrated with charts and diagrams, and a long bibliography is included. Oversize, 54pp. Llp 59

_____. **SIMPLIFIED ASTRONOMY FOR ASTROLOGERS**, $3.00. More than simply a study of astronomical data useful to astrologers, this is a presentation of the historical ages involved in the precession of the equinoxes. Many details of each age are reviewed and related to astrology. The development of various technical aspects of astrology is also explored. Oversize, 88pp. AFA

WILLIAMS, KATALIN. **ASTROLOGY STUDY GUIDE**, $5.75. Fine simple aid in understanding the symbolisms of planets, signs, decants, and aspects. It is presented in the form of a workbook, with blank space left for the student to fill in his own information. Includes many fold-out pages. Highly recommended for the beginning student. 49pp. Fos 72

_____. **CONSTRUCTING THE NATAL HOROSCOPE**, $5.75. A pretty clear presentation of the mechanics of chart construction, but without many of the samples from astrological tools which are included in several of the other books. Ms. Williams' step-by-step method is well organized and seems to be a good one. Oversize, 59pp. Fos 74

WILLIAMSON, JAMES AND RUTH. **ASTROLOGER'S GUIDE TO THE HARMONICS**. c$17.95. This is a reference work which serves first as a comprehensive catalog of harmonic intervals in astrology, and second as a manual and index defining the meaning, application and scope of harmonic analysis. Over 16,000 harmonics are listed, cross-tabulated and indexed. The volume is assembled in a steel ring binder with heavy plastic covers. 435 pp. CCL 75

WILSON, JAMES. **DICTIONARY OF ASTROLOGY**, c$12.95. The definitive work, which gives explicit definitions of every aspect of astrology. 406pp. Wei 1880

WILSON-LUDLAM, MAE. **HORARY: THE GEMINI SCIENCE**, $3.50. Fourteen examples of horary delineation. 65pp. Mac 73

_____. **INTERPRET YOUR CHART**, $6.00. A detailed presentation of an excellent method for learning chart interpretation. Very comprehensive and easy to follow. 141pp. Mac 73

WITTINE, BRYAN. **DO WHAT IT SAYS**, $5.95. This is a *hip* chart erection manual, integrating humanistic astrological concepts. Many graphic examples are included along with sample pages from some of the reference books. The step-by-step examples are pretty clear and the amount of material covered is extensive, including the calculation of progressions, transits, directions, and solar returns. MBS 74

WYNN. **THE KEY CYCLE**, $2.50. The key cycle is an aid to interpretation of daily, weekly and monthly influences upon an individual's chart. The details of the cycle and how it was developed are presented here as well as many examples of specific interpretations using this technique. Oversize, 55pp. AFA nd

ZAIN, C.C.

The Brotherhood of Light Lessons, presented by C.C. Zain (pseudonym for Elbert Benjamin) form a complete presentation of the hermetic teachings, whose evolution stems fron ancient Egypt. Each volume is illustrated with relevant horoscopes.

ZAIN, C.C. **ANCIENT MASONRY**, $5.75. The three-fold interpretation of every ritual and symbol of ancient Masonry is fully explained. The astrological meaning and derivation of each symbol and its meaning, as applied to the individual and to mankind as a whole, are given along with the principle it contains as used in the unfoldment of the powers of the soul. 416pp. ChL 73

_____. **COSMIC ALCHEMY**, c$6.75. Discusses how man is not an isolated intelligence, but rather a soul undergoing special training to perform a definite function in the cosmos. Many practical hints. 288pp. ChL 46

_____. **DELINEATING THE HOROSCOPE**, $4.25. Explains how to read a horoscope, how to make the most of whatever natural talents are present and how to select environmental conditions that are especially favorable. It analyzes the thirty-six decants, the keywords, and the qualities of the signs and planets. 256pp. ChL 73

_____. **DIVINATION**, $4.25. A complete analysis of every aspect of the subject, and every type of divination. Includes practical how-to suggestions. 224pp. ChL 40

_____. **ESOTERIC PSYCHOLOGY**, c$8.25. Explains how the mind is formed and how the laws that govern its working are created. 384pp. ChL

_____. **EVOLUTION OF LIFE**, c$6.50. An account of each important evolutionary step on earth which shows the important part played by inner-plane (astrological) weather, ESP and psychokinesis in adaptation and natural selection. 256pp. ChL 49

_____. **EVOLUTION OF RELIGION**, $4.95. Discusses the processes by which both primitive and modern religions have developed. 256pp. ChL

_____. **HORARY ASTROLOGY**, $4.25. Presents the math involved in erecting a horary chart as well as extensive interpretive material. 256pp. ChL

_____. **IMPONDERABLE FORCES**, $4.25. Explains the destructive uses of occult forces, and how to avoid their effect when directed toward you. The forces and their antidotes are discussed in great detail. 224pp. ChL 45

_____. **LAWS OF OCCULTISM**, $4.25. A complete presentation of the energies used by man and the substances through which they function. Topics include: occult data, astral substance, astral vibrations, doctrine of nativities, doctrine of mediumship, and spiritism. 224pp. ChL 73

_____. **MENTAL ALCHEMY**, $4.25. Explains how what we have within ourselves is attracted from without. In order to change a diseased condition, the discord within the astral body, of which it is an external manifestation, must be healed. This course explains how to apply specific thoughts to accomplish this. 224pp. ChL 36

_____. **MUNDANE ASTROLOGY**, c$7.25/4.25. Shows how to judge the trends of large groups of people and how to erect and read cycle charts. Text includes almost two hundred horoscopes. 320pp. ChL 39

_____. **NEXT LIFE**, $4.95. Gives a great deal of information about the conditions to be met in *The Next Life*, and the activities of life after physical death. 320pp. ChL 64

_____. **OCCULTISM APPLIED TO DAILY LIFE**, c$8.25. A very practical guide. 384pp. ChL

_____. **ORGANIC ALCHEMY**, $4.25. Sets forth the formula of the *Universal Law of Soul Progression*, the Brotherhood of Light's answer to reincarnation. 224pp. ChL 44

_____. **PERSONAL ALCHEMY**, $4.95. Sets forth the steps and methods best used to attain enlightenment. Half of the book is devoted to stellar healing. 320pp. ChL 49

_____. **PROGRESSING THE HOROSCOPE**, $4.25. A complete explanation of how to progress and a discussion of major and minor progressions of the sun, moon, planets, and angles; transits; and rectification. 256pp. ChL 73

_____. **THE SACRED TAROT**, $4.25. See section on tarot. ChL

_____. **SPIRITUAL ALCHEMY**, c$5.25. Topics include the doctrine of spiritual alchemy, seven spiritual metals, purifying the metals, transmutation, and higher consciousness. 160pp. ChL

_____. **SPIRITUAL ASTROLOGY**, c$8.75. Gives a full picture of each of the forty-eight ancient constellations, and sets forth the stories associated with each, the outstanding characteristics of those born under each sign, and the appropriate spiritual texts. 416pp. ChL

_____. **STELLAR HEALING**, $5.95. Gives the birthchart constants and the progressed constants for 160 of the most prevelant diseases and indicates the specific stellar treatment for each disease. 384pp. ChL 47

_____. **WEATHER PREDICTING**, c$6.00. Explains how to predict the oncoming weather by astrology by using temperature, moisture, and air movement charts—and how to draw up the charts. 224pp. ChL 49

ZOLAR. **THE HISTORY OF ASTROLOGY**, c$7.95. A complete illustrated history from the Chaldean astrologers of 5,000 years ago to the present day. Traces the origins of astrology through many civilizations. 308pp. Arc 72

_____. **IT'S ALL IN THE STARS**, $1.95. Mainly concerned with sun sign characteristics. Gives an interpretation for the degree in each sign, compatibility with other signs and a description of each sign as a marriage mate. Also includes a short history of astrology and a short explanation of the planets and houses. 318pp. Arc 62

GENERAL TOOLS

ARCANE. **6" PLASTIC WHEEL FOR CHART CONSTRUCTION**, $2.50. Arc

ASTRO NUMERIC SERVICE, ed. **AFA ASTROLOGICAL ATLAS OF THE UNITED STATES**, c$15.00. The title is deceptive for no maps are included. The latitudes and longitudes for over 30,000 towns and cities are given along with time conversions. Personally, we feel that the book is overpriced and that the student would be better off with a good atlas which contains maps and which also covers the entire world—although the time conversion is a helpful feature. 336pp. AFA 76

CIRCLE BOOKS. **ASPECT FINDER**, $2.25. This is the nicest of the aspectors. It has a large, easy-to-read dial and is made of heavy cardboard with protective coating. Includes Opposition, Conjunction, Square, Trine, Sextile, Semi-Square, Semi-Sextile, Quincunx, Quintile, Septile, Novile, Bi-quintile, and Sesquiquadrate. All clearly marked with orbs given for all major aspects. Reverse side gives aspect and interpretation keywords. Cir

DERNEY, EUGENE. **LONGITUDES AND LATITUDES IN THE U.S.** c$6.00. AFA

_____. **LONGITUDES AND LATITUDES IN THE WORLD**, c$6.00. AFA

DIGICOMP RESEARCH CORPORATION. **TRUE LUNAR NODES**, $4.95. Daily tables of the true lunar nodes computed for Midnight Greenwich and covering the years 1850–2000. 156pp. DRC 75

DOANE, DORIS CHASE. **TIME CHANGES IN CANADA AND MEXICO**, $5.00. PAs

_____. **TIME CHANGES IN THE U.S.A.**, $8.95. Qua

_____. **TIME CHANGES IN THE WORLD**, $5.30. PAs

EBERTIN, REINHOLD. **AUXILIARY TABLES FOR THE CALCULATION OF THE STELLAR POSITIONS**, $1.75. These tables allow the student to calculate the stellar positions for a particular point in time, without the use of logarithms. 32pp. EbV

_____. **90° DIAL**, Cardboard, $7.50. EbV

_____. **TABLES OF EVENTS—FOR THE CORRECTION OF BIRTHTIME AND FOR PROGNOSTICATIONS**, $2.50. Facilitates the correction of the solar arc directions. EbV

ESPENSHADE, EDWARD and JOEL MORRISON, eds. **GOODE'S WORLD ATLAS**, c$12.95/9.75. In addition to being a fine atlas, this book contains the largest selection of latitudes and longitudes available anywhere. Many more areas are listed than in both of the Dernay books combined. Oversize, 372pp. RMN

GRANT, ERNEST. **TABLES OF DIURNAL PLANETARY MOTION**, $5.00. The purpose of this time-saving tool is to provide the necessary calculations in order to find the exact positions of the planets for the given time of birth. If this table is used the student will not have to use logarithms—which are rather uncomplicated but do add extra steps and can be a source of arithmetic error. 165pp. AFA

_____. **TABLES OF MIDHEAVENS, ASCENDANTS, AND SIDEREAL TIME**, $4.25. AFA

HARDSIL, GEORGE. **ECLIPSES**, $1.50. Background material plus tables covering the years 1865–2000. AFA

HOFFMAN, GEORG. **SIDEREAL TIME, MERIDIAN, ASCENDANT TABLE**, $4.50. These tables give the values for the midheaven, those for the ascendant for all the degrees from 0°–67° North latitude and can be used also for south latitude by simple inversions. Introduction and explanations of how to use are written in both English and German. EbV

HUGHES, DOROTHY. **INSTANT ASPECTARIAN**, $2.00. Hug

_____. **INSTANT HOROSCOPE DELINEATOR**, $2.00. A quick—though not always totally accurate—way to find the ascendant. Hug

JONES, ALLEN. **EASY TABLES**, $3.00. Includes the following: 1, Diurnal Logarithms; Terrestrial Longitude to Longitude Time and/or Sidereal Time to Right Ascensions and Celestial Longitude; 3, Minutes and Seconds of Arc to Decimals of a Degree and/or Decimals of a Degree to Minutes and Seconds of Arc; 4, Corrections for Longitude time and G.M.T. Interval. All with examples. 38 pp. GSR 73

_____. **MECHANICS OF TABLES·OF HOUSES**, $6.00. Shows all necessary angles and arcs with explanations of the necessary math for Placidus, Regiomontanus, and Campanus methods of house division, with examples and diagrams. Also included in this volume is the procedure for calculating Placidian cusps for above the Arctic Circle. Oversize, 65 pp. GSR 74

KOCH, WALTER. **INTERPOLATION–PROPORTIONAL LOGARITHM TABLE**, $3.00. Sch

LIBIN, ARTHUR. **TABLES OF DIURNAL PLANETARY MOTIONS**, $2.00. This is a very complete set of tables, recently produced by computer and hopefully very accurate. Includes 3 sets of tables: I, used for calculating the apparent motion of the Sun for each minute of the day and for every 3 seconds of longitude within the range of the Sun's apparent motion; II, covers the range of diurnal motion of the Moon and all the planets; III, allows for a more precise calculation when the Moon's position is given for seconds of arc (used in Solar and Lunar Returns and Cyclic Charts). 186 pp. ASI 75

LOGARITHM CARDS, $.45. A large table on heavy paper. AFA

LOWELL, LAUREL. **TABLE OF ASPECTS**, $6.00. Comprehensive, detailed tables, with explanatory material. Oversize, LIP

MAYNARD, JIM. **DIURNAL PLANETARY MOTION**, $2.00. Contains diurnal proportional logarithms and tables of diurnal planetary motion. The tables are in 3 groups: Solar Motion, Lunar Motion, and Planetary Motion. The tables of Solar Motion are calculated in minutes and seconds of arc; the tables of Lunar Motion and Planetary Motion are for calculations to the nearest minute of arc. 32 pp. QPr 75

ORBIMETRIX CO. **ASTROLOGERS PLANETARY SLIDE RULE**, $4.00. An accurate, timesaving tool for the computation of intermediate planetary positions (longitude, latitude, declination) that takes the place of the more cumbersome diurnal logarithms or interpolation tables. It shows the proportional motion of the moon and the planets according to one minute of an arc and that of the sun to one to three seconds of an arc. Includes an instruction booklet. OrC

PRESSTYPE ASTROLOGICAL SYMBOLS, $3.75/sheet. Assorted sizes from about 1/8" to 1/2". AFA

QUICK SPECS. **MUNDANE TABLES OF FIXED STARS IN ASTROLOGY**, $14.95. Gives the cusps positions of 110 stars every 5° latitude from 60°N to 60°S and usable for every 100 years. The magnitude of each star and its influence is also given. The tables are very clear. There's also an index/chart which gives a quick way to locate Fixed Stars in the house where a planet is located arranged according to astrological signs. QSp 75

RAND McNALLY. **THE INTERNATIONAL ATLAS**, c$35.00. Over 300 pp. of maps and the longitudes and latitudes for more than 160,000 places in the comprehensive index. We looked up the most obscure places we could think of and they were all listed! 11" x 15", 557 pp. RMN 74

RAPHAEL. **GEOCENTRIC LONGITUDES AND DECLINATIONS**, $2.00. For Neptune, Herschel, Saturn, Jupiter, and Mars for the 1st of each month from 1900-2001. 35 pp. Fou

REY, RONALD. **ASPECTOR KIT**, $6.95. This is by far the most accurate of all the aspectors. It consists of a durable carboard wheel with a smaller tri-colored plastic wheel attached, and worksheets. You set your chart up on the worksheet and file the worksheet behind the plastic wheel. Then you move the pointer on the wheel to the planet you wish to aspect and then, following the directions given, find all the aspects in your chart. The worksheets can be used for natal charts, progressions, transits, chart comparisons, or whatever you like. It's a handy tool–though you have to know how to erect a chart to fill in the work sheet (or at least be able to transfer over an erected chart). Rey

STAHL, CARL. **TABLES OF ASCENSIONAL DIFFERENCES**, $2.00. Gives a step-by-step procedure for calculating tables of ascensional differences for any latitude along with tables for Washington D.C. (38°44' N Lat) and for Bay City, Michigan (43°18'). 35pp. Sol

_____. **MINI AND MICRO-DWADASHAMSA TABLES**, $6.95. A new method based on the Dwadashamas (subdivisions of the signs) of Hindu astrology and adapted to both personal charts and cyclic charts by the Paracelsus Research Society. 160+pp. Sol

CALENDARS

The prices listed below and the descriptions are for the 1976 editions. In later years the price may vary slightly and the format may also be different—although the changes usually are not significant.

BUSICK, ARMANDO. **THE SUN WHEEL**, $5.95. This is a beautifully written and illustrated new calendar. *In this calendar the year is divided zodiacally . . . aspects and events are plotted on a time grid to indicate the hour of their happening. Each vertical line repre-*

sents a two hour division of the day . . . . The motions of the sun, moon, and planets are plotted here on the zodiacal chart . . . . Until you get used to the format this calendar is harder to read at a glance than the more traditional ones-but for the experienced astrologer it seems more useful since you can look at the graphic illustration of the heavens and see where each of the planets is. Includes full directions and explanations of the symbols. Calculated for Greenwich Mean Time. HMC

CIRCLE BOOKS. **CALENDAR**, $1.75. Includes an ephemeris (with declinations of sun and moon), moon's sign, moon's phases, lunar aspects, lunation charts, important phenomena, upper transit time of moon for every day and angle between sun and moon for every day. Also has a short introduction to basic chart configurations and explanations of symbols. Calculated for Washington, D.C. time. Cir

LLEWELLYN. **ASTROLOGICAL CALENDAR**, $2.00. This is the oldest of the astrological calendars. For each day there is data on the moon's sign, phase, and time of change, as well as the best fishing and planting dates. There's also a sun sign forecast based on the individual lunar cycle, a chart of the planetary transits for each month along with a section containing charts of the new and full moons and solar ingresses and a table of time zone conversions. In addition, there are several articles. LIP

_____. **MOON SIGN BOOK**, $2.95. LIP

MACGREGOR, MARCIAN. **THE ASTROLOGY ANNUAL CALENDAR**, $1.95. This is the calendar we like best. Includes all the regular information as well as many additional tables. Lists all the major aspects, tables of time of solar and lunar ingress and new and full moons, along with special dates such as eclipses, solstice dates, etc. Also includes weekly planet position charts and a listing of monthly special phenomena and a chart of the symbols and elements of astrology. Calculated for Greenwich Mean Time. Sym

MAYNARD, JIM. **CELESTIAL INFLUENCES CALENDAR**, $2.50. In addition to the calendar there is a 1976 ephemeris presented in two ways: the traditional numerical tables giving sidereal time, daily longitudes, and declinations: and a graphical presentation with plotted monthly planetary motions and directions for superimposing a natal chart over the graph to see the transiting aspects. The calendar includes moon phases, times of sign change for sun and moon, times when the moon is void of course, best days for planting root and above-ground crops, and daily planetary aspects. There's also a lunar planting guide along with a general introduction to the planets and aspects and how they might influence our daily lives along with many planetary tables. A pocket version is available for $1.25. Calculated for Pacific Standard Time. QPr

_____. **ASTROLOGY ANNUAL REFERENCE BOOK, 1976**, $4.95. An excellent tool, equally valuable to both professional and beginning student. It is in the form of a daily diary containing the following information: all the current data for the year, graphically portrayed; space for recording daily events with daily aspectarian and weekly flat chart with planets' places, times of moon's phases and change of signs; a graphic preview of 1976 consisting of flat chart for the first day of each month; a miscellaneous reference data section; and two fold-out charts. A deluxe version (with blue leatherette cover) is available for $5.50. Sym

EPHEMERIDES

ARIES PRESS. **THE ASTROLOGER'S EPHEMERIDES**, c$8.00/each. Handy-sized ten-year volumes covering the following years:1890-1900,1900-10, 1910-20,1920-30, 1930-1940. Calculated for Midnight Greenwich and considered to be accurate. ArP

BACH, ELEANOR. **EPHEMERIDES OF THE ASTEROIDS**, c$8.00. The only book available so far on the asteroids, plus an ephemeris from 1900–2000 on four of them. CeC

DIE DEUTSCHE. **BAND I: 1850–1899**, c$19.50. These volumes are known for their accuracy and their handy size and cloth binding. No knowledge of German is required to read them. The two main drawbacks to them are that the position of Pluto is not listed before 1960 (though separate Pluto ephemerides are available from several sources) and they do not have as many supplementary tables as Raphael's and the Rosicrucian ones. Calculated for noon, Greenwich until 1930, after which they are calculated for midnight, Greenwich. Ott

_____. **BAND II: 1890–1930**, c$19.00. Ott

_____. **BAND III: 1931–50**, c$17.00. Ott

_____. **BAND IV: 1951–60**, c$16.00. Ott

_____. **BAND V: 1961–70**, c$16.00. Ott

_____. **BAND VI: 1971–80**, c$16.00. Ott

EBERTIN, REINHOLD. **PLUTO TABELLE: 1851–2000**, $1.50. 24pp. Ebv

ERLEWINE, MICHAEL . **THE SUN IS SHINING**, $5.00. *Heliocentric charts have neither houses nor ascendents and consist largely of the various aspects and whole chart configurations formed by the planets in relation to their center...the sun....Heliocentric astrology lends itself to quick sketches to bring out the basic configurations in effect at a given time...and the absence of a precise birthtime is not felt so strongly as with the geocentric natal chart....The tables of positions for the outer planets from 1653-2050 were taken from the Astronomical Papers prepared for the use of The American Ephemeris and Nautical Almanac.* Introduction, instructions, 53pp. Cir 75

GOLGGE. **1961–1965**, $7.65. These are very clearly presented ephemerides, calculated for midnight Greenwich Mean Time. Excellent for daily reference. Bav

_____. **1966–70**, $7.65. Bav

_____. **1971–75**, $7.65. Bav

_____. **1976–80**, $7.65. Bav

GRANT, E. **EPHEMERIDES**, $1.75 each. 1776, 1777, 1781, 1789, 1792. AFA

HIERATIC. **COMPLETE PLANETARY EMPHEMERIS, 1950–2000 AD**, c$25.00. This long-awaited ephemeris is calculated for midnight Greenwich and includes longitudes and latitudes tables, right ascension, and declinations. Hie

KEANE, JERRYL. **EPHEMERIS, 1775, 1776**, $2.00 each.

LANDSCHEIDT, THEODOR. **TRANSPLUTO**, $2.25. Graphic ephemeris of its tropical zodiacal position between 1878 and 1987, geocentric and heliocentric. EbV 72

MACCRAIG, HUGH. **THE EPHEMERIS OF THE MOON**, c$5.50. Computed for Greenwich noon, covering the years 1800–2000. Mac

_____. **THE 200 YEAR EPHEMERIS**, c$15.00. A month-by-month presentation of the position of the planets. This is not an ephemeris and *cannot* be used for calculating accurate charts: it is useful as a means for finding the approximate degrees of the planets. Includes selected longitudes and latitudes. Computed for Greenwich noon. 427pp. Mac

METZ, MAX. **SWISS EPHEMERIDEN, 1890–1950**, c$20.00. Positions of planets and the moon's nodes every day, Pluto's positions every eight days, latitudes, longitudes and time zones of major world cities. The best deal for the money and generally considered quite accurate. Calculated for Greenwich noon. Mtz

MICHELSEN, NEIL. **THE AMERICAN EPHEMERIS, 1931 TO 1980, AND BOOK OF TABLES**, c$25.00. Michelsen is well known for his excellent astrological computer programs. This new ephemeris is a masterwork. It gives daily longitude, latitude and declination of sun and planets at midnight, moon at midnight and noon, all moon phenomena including mean and true nodes, and a complete aspectarian. Also included are complete Placidus tables of houses, time tables, interpolation tables, and complete instructions on casting a natal horoscope. Highly recommended. 8½x11, 726pp. ACS 76

OMEGA ASSOCIATES. **PLUTO EPHEMERIS, 1773–2000**, $5.00. Longitude, latitude, and declination at ten day intervals, calculated for Greenwich midnight. OmA

_____. **SIDEREAL EPHEMERIDES**, $3.00/each. Gives the longitude (in the sidereal zodiac), latitude, right ascension and declination for the sun and planets daily at midnight and for the moon at both midnight and noon. Calculations done by computer. Each also includes fifteen pages of diurnal and twelve-hour logarithms. Extensive explanations and examples show how to make interpolations, calculate solar and lunar returns and progress the solar return. Available for the years 1970–1976. 80pp. OmA

PALMER, LYNNE. **PLUTO EPHEMERIS**, $10.00. This is by far the most complete Pluto ephemeris available, giving daily positions for the years 1900–2000. AFA 74

RAMUS, CARL. **EPHEMERIS OF THE GREAT COMETS**, $3.00. Covers the years 1402–1948. AFA

RAPHAEL. **ASTRONOMICAL EPHEMERIS**, $2.00/each. Single years, 1860–present. Calculated for noon, Greenwich. Considered more accurate than the Rosicrucian ephemerides and also contain more supplementary tables. The more recent tables include a daily listing for Pluto. Fou

ROSICRUCIAN FELLOWSHIP. **EPHEMERIS 1973–2000**, $1.00. Shows approximate positions of the planets on the first day of each month. Ros

_____. **SIMPLIFIED SCIENTIFIC EPHEMERIS**. Single years, 1857–present, $1.50. each; ten years, 1880–89, 1890–99, etc., $5.50 each. Calculated for noon Greenwich. Our most popular ephemerides. Ros

STAHL, CARL. **SOLUNAR SIDEREAL EPHEMERIDES**, $3.50/each. Single years 1960–69 available. Moon positions for every six hours; right ascensions of the sun, moon, and all the planets included with logarithms. Sol

STAHL, CARL and GARTH ALLEN. **SYNETIC VERNAL POINT EPHEMERIDES**, $1.50. Tables for the years 1761–2000. Oversize, 25pp. Sol

TABLES OF HOUSES

ARIES PRESS. **TABLES OF HOUSES EQUATOR TO 66° NORTH LATITUDE**, $4.00. Similar to the Rosicrucian Tables in format, complete from 0° to 60° North latitude. ArP

COPRIVIZA, R.C. **CAMPANUS TABLES**, $8.50. This oversize, spiral-bound book is the only complete Campanus table and it is very clearly laid out and printed. Calculations were done by an IBM computer from Equal Division of the Prime Vertical, complete from 1° to 60° North latitude. Mag

DALTON, JOSEPH. **TABLES OF HOUSES**, c$5.50. Covers 22°–60° North latitude. This is the table of houses that we recommend: it is the easiest to read and is very accurate. Includes instructions. Mac

KOCH **BIRTHPLACE TABLE OF HOUSES**, c$10.00/7.50. This is the house system that is used most frequently in Europe. Astrologers who use it find that they can make aspects to the house cusps. 0°–66° North latitude, with calculations for southern latitudes. ASI

LORENZ, DONA. **TOOLS OF ASTROLOGY: THE HOUSES**, $3.50. One of the biggest arguments in astrology today is which house system to use. This book discusses nine methods of house division: Alcabatius, Campanus, Morinus, Placidus, Porphry, Regiomontanus, and Equal House. Each method of house division is defined and the house sizes of different methods of division are compared and illustrated. Also included are the latitudes and longitudes of over 200 urban areas of the world; sidereal time for the years 1800–2045; and separate tables for determining the longitude of the ascendant, the longitude of the medium coeli, the longitude of the sun, and the size of semi-arcs. 127pp. EGP 73

MARR, ALEXANDER. **CAMPANUS TABLE OF HOUSES**, $2.50. Covers 35°–46° North latitude. Mimeographed text is sometimes faint, but readable. 60pp. Sol

OCCIDENTAL DATA. **THE OCCIDENTAL TABLE OF HOUSES**, $8.95. Latitudes 66° North—according to the systems of Campanus, Regiomontanus, and Placidus. Can be used for the equal house system and tables are also valid for the southern hemisphere. The text was done by a computer. 135pp. Occ 72

RAPHAEL. **TABLE OF HOUSES FOR NORTHERN LATITUDES**, $2.50. 0°–60°. Incredibly small print. Fou

ROSICRUCIAN FELLOWSHIP. **SIMPLIFIED SCIENTIFIC TABLE OF HOUSES**, $4.50. 0°–66° North latitude. The most popular table. 313pp. Ros 49

STAHL, CARL. **STAHL'S OCTOSCOPE TABLE OF HOUSES, CAMPANUS DOMNIFICATION**, $4.00. 0°–60° North latitude. Gives midheaven for each minute; ascendants for each four minutes for each degree of latitude; together with a set of tables for the Octopus House Cusps and meridians (as well as tables for the the twelve-fold houses and medians). Oversize, 75pp. Sol 74

Relationship between the zodiacal signs and the human body

SUBJECT INDEX

ASPECTS
Carter - Astrological Aspects
Jansky - Interpreting the Aspects
Jayne - Aspects to Horoscope Angles
Leinbach - Planets and Asteroids
Pelletier - Planets in Aspect
Sakoian and Acker - Major and Minor
Sakoian and Acker - That Inconjunct Quinconx
Tyl - Aspects and Houses in Analysis
Whitman - Aspects and Their Meanings

CHART COMPARISON
Burroughs - Astrology Reveals Life and Love
Darr - Comparisons
Darr - Keys to Inter-Relations
Ebertin, E. - Astrology and Romance
Ebertin, R. - Contact Cosmogram
Ebertin, R. - Cosmic Marriage
Goodman - Astrology and Sexual Analysis
Hand - Planets in Composite
Harding - Synastry
Jansky - Synastry
Manik - Astrology in Marriage Counselling
Robertson - Sex, Mind, Habit Compatibility
Robson - An Astrological Guide
Sakoian and Acker - Astrology in Human Relationships
Sargent - How to Handle Your Human Relations
Sepharial - Astrology and Marriage
Townley - The Composite Chart

CHART ERECTION
Benjamine - Beginners' Horoscope Maker
Crossley - Let's Learn Astrology
Davison - Astrology
Hall - Student's Calculation Form
Heindel - Simplified Scientific Astrology
Jacobson - Foundation of the Astrological Chart
Keyes - Master Guide
Leo - Casting the Horoscope
Mayo - How to Cast a Natal Chart
Palmer - ABC of Chart Erection
Thompson - Chart Your Own Stars
Tucker and Tessier - Astrological Studies: Casting
Tyl - Horoscope Construction

Weingarten - Manual for Erecting Horoscopes
Williams - Constructing the Natal Horoscope
Wittine - Do What It Says

DEGREES
Carelli - The 360 Degress of the Zodiac
Jones - The Sabian Symbols in Astrology
Koparkar - Degrees of the Zodiac
Kozimsky - Zodiacal Symbology
Leinbach - Degrees of the Zodiac
Leo - Degrees of Zodiac Symbolized
Manthri - Degrees of Life
Matthew - Fixed Stars and Degrees
Rudhyar - An Astrological Mandala

ESOTERIC
Bacher - Studies in Astrology
Bailey - Esoteric Astrology
Baker - Esoteric Astrology
Leo - Esoteric Astrology
Norris - Transcendental Astrology
Pagan - From Pioneer to Poet
Parchment - Astrology—Mundane and Spiritual
Sampson - The Zodiac
Schulman - Karmic Astrology
Zain - Astrological Signatures
Zain - Spiritual Astrology

FIXED STARS
Ebertin and Hoffman - Fixed Stars
Jain - The Signs and Your Future
Johndro - The Stars
Matthew - Fixed Stars and Degrees
Robson - Fixed Stars
Stringer - Influence of Fixed Stars: Pisces and Taurus
Tucker - Fixed Stars and Your Horoscope

HISTORY AND SCIENTIFIC BASIS
Cumont - Astrology and Religion
Gauquelin - Cosmic Clocks
Gauquelin - Scientific Basis of Astrology
Gleadow - Origin of the Zodiac
Goodavage - Astrology
Hall - Story of Astrology
Kenton - Astrology
Lindsay - Origins of Astrology
McCaffrey - Astrology
Manolesco - Scientific Astrology
Naylor - Astrology
Reid - Towards Aquarius
Rudhyar - Astrological Timing
Russell - Astrology and Prediction
Tucker - Principles of Scientific Astrology
Van Stone - Studies in Zodiacal Symbology
West - The Case for Astrology
Zolar - History of Astrology

HORARY
Davis - Horary Astrology
George - Powerful Planets
Jacobson - Simplified Horary
Jones - Horary Astrology
Knapp - Horary Art
Meyer - Astrology of Change
Raphael - Horary Astrology
Simmonite - Horary Astrology
Titsworth - Case Studies
Watters - Horary Astrology
Wilson-Ludlam - Horary
Zain - Horary Astrology

HOUSES
Leo - How to Judge a Nativity
Rudhyar - The Astrological Houses
Tyl - The Houses
Whitman - Influence of the Houses

INTRODUCTORY
Davis - Astrologers' Condensed Manual
Goodavage - Write Your Own Horoscope
Goodman - Sun Signs
Hiroz - Astrological Chart
Hodgson - Wisdom in the Stars
Hughes - Basic Elements
Jocelyn - Meditations on Signs of Zodiac
Jones - How to Learn Astrology
Kriyananda - Your Sun Sign as Spiritual Guide
Leo - Astrology for All
MacLeod - Astrology for Skeptics
MacNeice - Astrology
Mayo - Astrology
Oken - As Above So Below
Oken - The Horoscope, the Road, and Its Travellers
Omarr - My World of Astrology
Parker - The Compleat Astrologer
Stearn - A Time for Astrology
Tobey - An Astrology Primer
Tucker - The How What and Why
Tyl - The Horoscope as Identity
Wade - Astrology Dial-A-Scope

Watters - What's Wrong
Williams - Astrology Study Guide
Zolar - It's All in the Stars

INTERPRETATION
Adams - A Practical Approach
Carter - Astrology of Accidents
Carter - Some Principles
Dobyns and Roof - Astrologers' Casebook
Escobar - Side Lights
Hone - Applied Astrology
Jacobson - All Over the Earth
Jacobson - Here and There
Jacobson - Way of Astrology
Jansky - Planetary Patterns
Jansky - Selected Topics
Jayne - Horoscope Interpretation
Jinni and Joanne - Your Cosmic Mirror
Jinni and Joanne - The Spiral of Life
Jones - Essentials of Astrological Analysis
Jones - Guide to Horoscope Interpretation
Leo - Art of Synthesis
Leo - How to Judge a Nativity
Leo - Key to Your Own Nativity
McCormick - Deductive Interpretations
Meyer - Handbook for the Humanistic Astrologer
Moore - Astrology in Action
Oken - The Horoscope, the Road, and Its Travellers
Palmer - ABC of Basic Chart Reading
Robertson - Cosmopsychology
Robertson - Not a Sign in the Sky
Sakoian and Acker - Zodiac Within Each Sign
Taylor - Now That I've Cast It
Tobey - Astrology of Inner Space
Tyl - Astrology and Personality
Weingarten - The Study of Astrology
Wilson-Ludlam - Interpret Your Chart
Zain - Delineating the Horoscope

MEDICAL
Cornell - Encyclopedia of Medical Astrology
Culpeper - Astrological Judgment of Disease
Davidson - Medical Astrology Lectures
Duz - Practical Treatise
Garrison - Medical Astrology
Heindel - Astro-Diagnosis
Jansky - Introduction to Nutritional Astrology
Jansky - Modern Medical Astrology
Jenkyn - Astrology and Diet
Kayhle - Astrology Guide to Good Health
Perry and Carey - Zodiac and the Salts
Sawtell - Astrology and Biochemistry
Tucker - Astromedical Resurvey
Tucker - Astromedical Research
Tucker - Astropharmacology
Zain - Stellar Healing

MUNDANE
Blackman - Astrology
Blackman - So You Want to be President
Boyd - True Horoscope of U.S.
Carter - Introduction to Political Astrology
Dodson - Horoscope of U.S. Cities and States
Duane - Horoscopes of U.S. Presidents
Jain - Mundane Astrology
Johndro - Earth in the Heavens
Jones - Mundane Perspectives
Pratt - Astrological World Cycles
Raphael - Mundane Astrology
Robson - Electional Astrology
Rudhyar - Astrology of America's Destiny
Tucker - Forecasting World Events
Zain - Mundane Astrology

PLANETS
Benjamine - Influence of Planet Pluto
Dalton - Pluto in Libra
Ebertin - Focus on Pluto
Hickey - Pluto or Minerva
Holley - Pluto/Neptune
Jayne - Unknown Planets
Leinbach - Planets and Asteroids
Leo - Art of Synthesis
Leo - Jupiter
Leo - Mars
Leo - Saturn
Lowell - Pluto
McCormick - Book of Retrogrades
Reid - Planetary Emotions
Robertson - Transits of Saturn
Rudhyar - Sun Is Also a Star
Sakoian and Acker - Importance of Mercury
Sakoian and Acker - Ladder of Planets
Solunar - Influence of Moon
Stahl - Vulcan
Tyl - The Planets
Watters - Sex and Outer Planets
Weston - Planet Vulcan
Whitman - Influence of Planets

PROGRESSIONS AND PREDICTION
Bradley - Solar and Lunar Returns
Davison - Technique of Prediction
Dobyns - Progressions, Directions and Rectification
Green - Directions and Directing
Jayne - Progressions amd Directions
Jones - Scope of Astrological Prediction
Kemp - Progressions
King - Progression Formulas
Leo - Progressed Horoscope
Lindanger - Your Sun's Return
Lowell - Secondary Progressions
Milburn - Progressed Horoscope
Palmer - ABC of Major Progressions
Robson - Radix System
Tyl - Analysis and Prediction
Tyl - Expanded Present
Zain - Progressing the Horoscope

PSYCHOLOGICAL
Arroyo - Astrology, Psychology and Four Elements
Carter - Encyclopedia of Psychological Astrology
Darling - Astro-Psychiatry
Goodman - Psychological Astrology
Dobyns - Finding Person in Horoscope
Mulkins - Miracles of Mind
Rudhyar - Astrological Study
Rudhyar - Astrology of Personality
Rudhyar - Person Centered Astrology
Tyl - Astrology and Personality

RECTIFICATION
Bailey - Prenatal Epoch
Dobyns - Progressions, Directions and Rectification
Gordon - Rectification
Howell - Cyclic Astrology
Jayne - Technique of Rectification
Schwickert - Rectification of Birth Time

SIDEREAL, HINDU, AND COSMOBIOLOGY
Ayer - Everyday Astrology
Escobar - 144 Doors
Fagan - Astrological Origins
Fagan - Primer of Sidereal
Gleadow - Origin of Zodiac
Gleadow - Zodiac Revealed
Koparkar - Mathematical Astrology
Koparkar - Moon Mansions
Landscheidt - Cosmic Cybernetics
Logan - Your Eastern Star
Mihara - Brihat Jataka
Mishra - Astrology for All
Shil-Ponde - Hindu Astrology
Stahl - Beginners' Manual of Sidereal
Stahl - Thoughts on Sidereal
Volguine books

TEXTBOOKS
Adams - Astrology: Your Place in Sun
Adams - Astrology: Your Place Among Stars
Carter - Principles of Astrology
Evans - New Waite's Compendium
George - A—Z Horoscope Maker
Green - Astrologer's Manual
Hayes - Introduction to Natal Astrology
Heindel - Message of Stars
Hickey - Astrology
Hone - Modern Textbook
Jones - Astrology
Keane - Practical Astrology
Laurence - Foundation Book of Astrology
Lewi - Astrology for Millions
Lewi - Heaven Knows What
Libra - Astrology
Lyndoe - Astrology for Everyone
McCaffrey - Graphic Astrology
Mark - Astrology for the Aquarian Age
Moore - Astrology: Divine Science
Murchery - Astrological Tarot
Parker - Astrology
Sakoian and Acker - Astrologers' Handbook
Sehested - Basics of Astrology
Tucker - Astrology for Everyman
Vaughn - Astrology in Modern Language

TRANSITS
Dalton - World Transits
Darr - Transits
Ebertin - Transits
Elsnau - Astrologers' Notebook
Foelsch - Transits
Hand - Planets in Transit
Hiroz - Planetary Activity
Roberts - Transits
Robertson - Transits of Saturn
Sakoian and Acker - Transits booklets
Sepharial - Transits
Smith - Transits
Tyl - Integrated Transits

ASTRONOMY AND SCIENCE

Modern physics has had a profound influence on almost all aspects of human society. It has become the basis of natural science, and the combination of natural science, and the combination of natural and technical science has fundamentally changed the conditions of life on our earth, both in beneficial and detrimental ways. . . . [T]he influence of modern physics goes beyond technology. It extends to the realm of thought and culture where it has led to a deep revision in man's conception of the universe and his relation to it. The exploration of the atomic and subatomic world in the twentieth century has revealed an unsuspected limitation of classical ideas, and has necessitated a radical revision of many of our basic concepts. . . .

These changes, brought about by modern physics, have been widely discussed by physicists and by philosophers over the past decades, but very seldom has it been realized that they all seem to lead in the same direction, towards a view of the world which is very similar to the views held in Eastern mysticism. The concepts of modern physics often show surprising parallels to the ideas expressed in the religious philosophies of the Far East. Although these parallels have not, as yet, been discussed extensively, they have been noticed by some of the great physicists of our century when they came in contact with Far Eastern culture during their lecture tours to India, China and Japan. . . .

[T]he two foundations of twentieth-century physics—quantum theory and relativity theory—both force us to see the world very much in the way a Hindu, Buddhist or Taoist sees it, and this similarity strengthens when we look at the recent attempts to combine these two theories in order to prescribe the phenomena of the submicroscopic world: the properties and interactions of the subatomic particles of which all matter is made. Here the parallels between modern physics and Eastern mysticism are most striking, and we often encounter statements where it is almost impossible to say whether they have been made by physicists or by Eastern mystics.

When I refer to *Eastern mysticism*, I mean the religious philosophies of Hinduism, Buddhism and Taoism. Although these comprise a vast number of subtly interwoven spiritual disciplines and philosophical systems, the basic features of their world view are the same. This view is not limited to the East, but can be found to some degree in all mystically oriented philosophies. . . . Mystical traditions are present in all religions, and mystical elements can be found in many schools of Western philosophy. The parallels to modern physics appear not only in the *Vedas* of Hinduism, in the *I Ching*, or in the Buddhist *sutras*, but also in the fragments of Heraclitus, in the Sufism of Ibn Arabi, or in the teachings of the Yaqui sorcerer Don Juan. The difference between Eastern and Western mysticism is that mystical schools have always played a marginal role in the West, whereas they constitute the mainstream of Eastern philosophical and religious thought. . . .

If physics leads us today to a world view which is essentially mystical, it returns, in a way, to its beginning, 2,500 years ago. It is interesting to follow the evolution of Western science along its spiral path, starting from the mystical philosphies of the early Greeks, rising and unfolding in an impressive development of intellectual thought that increasingly turned away from its mystical origins to develop a world view which is in sharp contrast to that of the Far East. In its most recent stages, Western science is finally overcoming this view and coming back to those of the early Greek and the Eastern philosophies. This time, however, it is not only based on intuition, but also on experiments of great precision and sophistication, and on a rigorous and consistent mathematical formalism.

The roots of physics, as of all Western science, are to be found in the first period of Greek philosophy in the sixth century B.C., in a culture where science, philosophy and religions were not separated. The sages of the Milesian school in Ionia were not concerned with such distinctions. Their aim was to discover the essential nature, or real constitution, of things which they called *physis*. The term *physis* is derived from this Greek word and meant therefore, originally, the endeavour of seeing the essential nature of all things. . . .

The monistic and organic view of the Milesians was very close to that of ancient Indian and Chinese philosophy, and the parallels to Eastern thought are

even stronger in the philosophy of Heraclitus of Ephesus. Heraclitus believed in a world of perpetual change, or eternal *Becoming*. For him, all static Being was based on deception and his universal principle was fire, a symbol for the continuous flow and change of all things. Heraclitus taught that all changes in the world arise from the dynamic and cyclic interplay of opposites and he saw any pair of opposites as a unity. This unity, which contains and transcends all opposing forces, he called the Logos.

The split of this unity began with the Eleatic school, which assumed a Divine Principle standing above all gods and men. This principle was first identified with the unity of the universe, but was later seen as an intelligent and personal God who stands above the world and directs it. Thus began a trend of thought which led, ultimately, to the separation of spirit and matter and to a dualism which became characteristic of Western philosophy.

A drastic step in this direction was taken by Parmenides of Elea who was in strong opposition to Heraclitus. He called his basic principle the Being and held that it was unique and invariable. He considered change to be impossible and regarded changes we seem to perceive in the world as mere illusions of the senses. The concept of an indestructible substance as the subject of varying properties grew out of this philosophy and became one of the fundamental concepts of Western thought.

In the fifth century B.C., the Greek philosophers tried to overcome the sharp contrast between the views of Parmenides and Heraclitus. In order to reconcile the idea of unchangeable Being (of Parmenides) with that of eternal Becoming (of Heraclitus), they assumed that the Being is manifest in certain invariable substances, the mixture and separation of which gives rise to the changes in the world. This led to the concept of the atom, the smallest indivisible unit of matter, which found its clearest expression in the philosophy of Leucippus and Democritus. The Greek atomists drew a clear line between spirit and matter, picturing matter as being made of several *basic building blocks*. These were purely passive and intrinsically dead particles moving in the void. The cause of their motion was not explained, but was often associated with external forces which were assumed to be of spiritual origin and fundamentally different from matter. In subsequent centuries, this image became an essential element of Western thought, of the dualism between mind and matter, between body and soul.

As the idea of a division between spirit and matter took hold, the philosophers turned their attention to the spiritual world, rather than the material, to the human soul and the problem of ethics. These questions were to occupy Western thought for more than two thousand years after the culmination of Greek science and culture in the fifth and fourth centuries B.C. The scientific knowledge of antiquity was systematized and organized by Aristotle, who created the scheme which was to be the basis of the Western view of the universe for two thousand years. But Aristotle himself believed that questions concerning the human soul and the contemplation of God's perfection were much more valuable than investigations of the material world. . . .

Further development of Western science had to wait until the Renaissance, when men began to free themselves from the influence of Aristotle and the Church and showed a new interest in nature. In the late fifteenth century, the study of nature was approached, for the first time, in a truly scientific spirit and experiments were undertaken to test speculative ideas. As this development was paralleled by a growing interest in mathematics, it finally led to the formulation of proper scientific theories, based on experiment and expressed in mathematical language. Galileo was the first to combine empirical knowledge with mathematics and is therefore seen as the father of modern science.

The birth of modern science was preceded and accompanied by a development of philosophical thought which led to an extreme formulation of the spirit/matter dualism. This formulation appeared in the seventeenth century in the philosophy of Rene Descartes who based his view of nature on a fundamental division into two separate and independent realms; that of mind (*res cogitans*) and that of matter (*res extensa*). The *Cartesian* division allowed scientists to treat matter as dead and completely separate from themselves, and to see the material world as a multitude of different objects assembled into a huge machine. Such a mechanistic world view was held by Isaac Newton who constructed his mechanics on its basis and made it the foundation of classical physics. From the second half of the seventeenth to the end of the nineteenth century, the mechanistic Newtonian model of the universe dominated all scientific thought. It was paralleled by the image of a monarchical God who ruled the world from above by imposing his divine law on it. . . .

In contrast to the mechanistic Western view, the Eastern view of the world is *organic*. For the Eastern mystic, all things and events perceived by the senses are interrelated, connected and are but different aspects or manifestations of the same ultimate reality. Our tendency to divide the perceived world into individual and separate things and to experience ourselves as isolated egos in this world is seen as an illusion which comes from our measuring and categorizing mentality. . . .

Although the various schools of Eastern mysticism differ in many details, they all emphasize the basic unity of the universe which is the central feature of their teachings. The highest aim for their followers—whether they are Hindus, Buddhists or Taoists—is to become aware of the unity and mutual interrelation of all things, to transcend the notion of an isolated individual self and to identify themselves with the ultimate reality. The emergence of this awareness—known as *enlightenment*—is not only an intellectual act but is an experience which involves the whole person and is religious in its ultimate nature. For this reason, most Eastern philosophies are essentially religious philosophies.

In the Eastern view, then, the division of nature into separate objects is not fundamental and any such objects have a fluid and ever-changing character. The Eastern world view is therefore intrinsically dynamic and contains time and change as essential features. The cosmos is seen as one inseparable reality— for ever in motion, alive, organic; spiritual and material at the same time.

—from **THE TAO OF PHYSICS** by Fritjof Capra

The medieval concept of the sky as a star-studded globe, through which a fortunate traveller might poke his head and view the glories of Heaven beyond. (Bettman Archive)

ALLEN, RICHARD HINCKLEY. **STAR NAMES: THEIR LORE AND MEANING**, $5.00. Interesting, comprehensive study. 563pp. Dov 63

ALLER, LAWRENCE. **ATOMS, STARS, AND NEBULAE**, c$17.50. This is a revised and up-dated version of an earlier highly praised edition of the same name, by Aller and Professor Leo Goldberg. The text is fairly technical, being geared toward the knowledgeable layman and the beginning student of astronomy. The author explains how the astronomical explorer finds the distances of stars and nebulae, and how, on the basis of atomic structure, the constitution of stars can be determined. After a brief, nonmathematical excursion into the principles of atomic physics and of optics, Aller explains in nontechnical language the physical processes at work in the interiors and exteriors of stars and discusses the evolution of stars, the production of novae and of supernovae, the interstellar medium, quasars, and pulsars. Includes many technical drawings, graphs and photographs. Indexed, 359pp. HUP 71

ASIMOV, ISAAC. **ASIMOV'S GUIDE TO SCIENCE**, c$15.50. This is an updated edition of Asmiov's classic **New Intelligent Man's Guide to Science**, revised to include the latest developments in every field. This is generally considered the finest layman's account of modern science. It is an encyclopedic work, in non-technical language, which offers a comprehensive picture of the whole of modern science, explaining the basic ideas, highlighting the important developments, and pointing out the meaning of recent scientific discoveries. With wit, enthusiasm, and clarity, Dr. Asimov tells what has been learned of the earth and its atmosphere and the space beyond; the nature of matter and the atom; the natural laws and phenomena that have shaped our technology, the living cell and the chemistry of life; the biological heritage of mankind; the human brain and human behavior. For all who are interested in understanding individual areas of science this is a volume without equal and it is one that we have found immensely helpful. It's hard to understand how Asimov can produce the quantity of books that he does and still keep the quality uniformly high, but he does. And his gift for simplifying the complex is a rare and valued one. Includes an excellent chapter-by-chapter bibliography and subject and name indices, as well as many illustrations. 945pp. H&R 72

_____. **ASIMOV ON ASTRONOMY**, $3.50. The seventeen chapters in this book have been selected from earlier essays, updated and enhanced with new photographs. They represent Asimov at his best. Index, illustrations, 238pp. Dou 75

_____. **ASIMOV ON PHYSICS**, c$9.95. A collection of seventeen essays, selected from Asimov's earlier articles on physics and updated for this volume. As usual, Asimov's presentation is amazingly clear despite the complexity of the material. Illustrations, index, 206pp. Dou 76

_____. **FACT AND FANCY**, $1.25. Asimov is one of the most prolific writers today. He is a noted scientist and his books are aimed at the layman and are very clearly written and illustrated. His inventive mind has led him into science fiction and into many other areas. All of his books are recommended. Here he begins with statements that are solidly rooted in accepted truth and then gives rein to his ingenious imagination and constructs hypothetical situations that are at once fanciful and completely reasonable. Topics include *What lies beyond the planets* and *When can you escape the reach of gravity*. Photographs, 206pp. Avo 72

_____. **FROM EARTH TO HEAVEN**, $1.25. Here the reader is taken on an intriguing journey through basic scientific questions dealing with the earth, physics, and the universe. 253pp. Avo 72

_____. **SOLAR SYSTEM AND BACK**, $1.25. In his clear, instructive manner Asimov examines the riddles of our solar system. Then he returns to Earth to explore the vagaries of certain metals; the clues behind the disappearance of the dinosaurs; the causes and effects of chromosome aberrations; and many other areas. 253pp. Avo 72

_____. **THE UNIVERSE, FROM FLAT EARTH TO QUASAR**, $1.95. Asimov's most comprehensive explorations of astronomy. Topics include the earth, solar system, stars, galaxy, age of the earth, energy of the sun, stellar evolution, galactic evolution, receding galaxies, beginning of the universe, and the edge of the universe. Well-illustrated with photographs and drawings. Index, 315pp. Avo 68

BAADE, WALTER. **EVOLUTION OF STARS AND GALAXIES**, $5.95. *An astonishing complex of facts and the relations between them is presented with unusual clarity and lucidity, in a lively, spirited tone that is, I think, unrivaled in astronomical literature.... (This volume) is pervaded by the spirit of great adventure: to grasp and to comprehend for the first time the evolution of a whole galaxy. Dr. Baade's approach was basically simple. He concentrated on detailed study of nearby systems, especially the local group of galaxies, trying with inexhaustible invention to fit together a multitude of facts....It is a pleasure to read the full story of some spectacular Baade discoveries.*—**Sky and Telescope**. This is an edited transcription of a series of lectures given by Dr. Baade at Harvard Observatory in 1958. A highly technical presentation. Index, 334pp. MIT 63

BROWN, G. SPENCER. **LAWS OF FORM**, c$9.00. John Lilly calls this book one of the most important recent works. Many other scholars, mathematicians, and philosophers have acclaimed it. The **Whole Earth Catalog** said it *should be in the hands of all young people*. We, however, can't begin to understand it—although I'll admit, we haven't really tried. If you're a whiz at math and calculus perhaps you'll acclaim this as a work of genius also. Intense concentration is a prerequisite. 141pp. Jul 69

BROWN, HUGH. **CATACLYSMS OF THE EARTH**, c$11.25. Brown has spent over fifty years collecting material which led to the formulation of the theories presented here. He believes that the continual growth of the South Polar icecap, interacting with gravitational force, first produces a wobble in the earth's normal spin. Eventually, every 6000 to 8000 years, a sudden and radical shift of the earth's axis is caused. Continents and sea areas are rearranged, and the once tropical areas become lands of snow and ice. The great flood of Noah resulted from the last careening of the globe. This is a detailed scientific investigation of this phenomenon. Illustrations, index, 281pp. Twa 67

BOVA, BEN. **THE NEW ASTRONOMIES**, $1.95. This is a discussion of some of the new developments in astronomy such as quasars, pulsars, neutron stars, and black holes. Bova has woven his story around basic physical principles and current knowledge of astronomy to provide a look into the future and to show the posture of astronomy in the last third of the twentieth century. A good presentation for the general reader. Chapter-by-chapter bibliography, index, illustrations. 214pp. NAL 72

BUTLER, S. T. and ROBERT RAYMOND. **THE FAMILY OF THE SUN**, $2.50. This is a full exploration of the star that we call the sun, probing its effects on the earth, the moon, and the other planets. It is written in the form of a cartoon strip and is designed by the authors (a physicist and a writer/filmmaker) to present the most up-to-date information about the sun and the planets in a format which people of all ages can understand. The drawings are not the clearest we've seen, but the idea is an interesting one and is often effective. Oversize, 84pp. Dou 75

CALDER, NIGEL. **THE RESTLESS EARTH—A REPORT ON THE NEW GEOLOGY**, $4.95. Calder explores a bold new theory of the earth based on the theory of plate tectonics. Earthquakes, volcanoes, mountain ranges, are all connected to a single comprehensive process—the movement of huge plates that are said to make up the earth's outer shell. The account can be understood by the layman and is beautifully illustrated with color and black-and-white photographs, drawings, and tables. Oversize, 152pp. Vik 73

_____. **THE VIOLENT UNIVERSE—AN EYEWITNESS ACCOUNT OF THE NEW ASTRONOMY**, $3.75. A superbly written, illustrated book which presents the current state of knowledge, investigation and speculation concerning quasars, pulsars, neutron stars, anti-matter, exploding galaxies and gravity holes. Oversize, 160pp. Vik 69

CAPRA, FRITJOF. **THE TAO OF PHYSICS**, c$12.50/5.95. This is an amazing book which explores the parallels between the underlying concepts of modern physics and the basic ideas of Eastern mysticism. Dr. Capra gives a clear account, supplemented by diagrams and photographs, of the theories of atomic and subatomic physics, of relativity theory and of astrophysics, up to and including the most recent research, and relates the world-view emerging from these theories to the mystical traditions of Hinduism, Buddhism, Taoism, Zen, and the I Ching. Dr. Capra has a remarkable gift for making the complex understandable. From his text emerges a picture of the material world not as a machine made up of a multitude of objects, but a harmonious *organic* whole whose parts are determined by their inter-relations and which reflects a reality behind the world of ordinary sense-perception involving spaces of higher dimensions and transcending ordinary language and logical reasoning. We are fascinated by Capra's presentation and, despite the technical nature of the material, it has been extremely popular. Notes, bibliography, index, 330pp. ShP 75

CALLATAY, VINCENT de and AUDOUIN DOLLFUS. **ATLAS OF THE PLANETS**, c$15.00. This is a profusely illustrated account which begins with a review of the historical record of the planets and the ideas people have held about the heavens, beginning with the origins of astronomy in China and Babylon. A detailed description of the development of modern concepts of the solar system is also given. The 2nd section describes the fundamental principles of the planetary system and the methods of determining a planet's characteristics, and it reviews major astronomical terms. The authors explain the classification of planets, planetary symbols, the celestial sphere, both true and apparent motion of planets, their brightness, and methods of measuring distance and mass. The final section (the bulk of the book) is devoted to a study of each planet. Emphasis is placed on recent discoveries made by Russian and American space probes and recent observations from all over the world. Hundreds of diagrams and photos, some in color, illustrate the text. The material is clear enough for the layman to understand yet sophisticated enough to be of value to the specialist. 160 pp. UTo 74

CHARON, JEAN. **COSMOLOGY**, $2.95. An excellent book for the general reader which first traces the development of scientific ideas about the universe from the Greeks to the present day, and then discusses the possible meanings of space, time, distance, and man's uniqueness in the universe. Charon reviews the controversies and gives what he feels are reasonable explanations. Many fine illustrations in black-and-white and color are included. Bibliography, index, 255pp. MGH 73

CLAIBORNE, ROBERT. **SUMMER STARGAZER**, c$7.95. Subtitled *astronomy for absolute beginners* this is a good book for people who want to know more about what they can see in the skies. Claiborne takes the reader into observational astronomy by easy

stages—first with the naked eye, then with the simple optical aid of binoculars, and finally with the assistance of small to medium-size telescopes. He tells the stargazer what are the objects s/he can see and where to look for them during the four summer months. Some clearly presented related astronomical information is included. There's also a section giving practical advice on equipment, and appendices, catalog marker stars, some folklore and a glossary. Simple sky maps and diagrams supplement the instructions in the text. Index, bibliography, 222 pp. CMG 75

CLAYTON, DONALD. **THE DARK NIGHT SKY**, c$9.95. This is a very personal, simply written account of the history of cosmology and the men who made the revolutionary steps. The author is himself an astronomer and he relates the impact these discoveries had on him intellectually. Dr. Clayton seeks to share the sense of adventure that has led him to dedicate his life to the pursuit of the meaning of the universe. The book is, as the subtitle indicates, *A Personal Adventure in Cosmology*. Many photos illustrate the text. 218pp. Qdr 75

CORNELL, JAMES and NELSON HAYES. **MAN AND COSMOS**, c$8.95. A collection of 9 Guggenheim Lectures on the Solar System sponsored by the Smithsonian Institution: A.G.W. Cameron, *History of the Solar System*; Owen Gingerich, *The Sun*; John Wood, *TheMoon*; Carl Sagan, *The Planets*; S.I. Rasool, *Planetary Atmospheres*; John Lewis, *The Outer Planets*; Myron Lecar, *The Asteroids*; Brian Marsden, *The Comets*; and Fred Whipple, *Perspectives: Past, Present and Future*. The selections are well illustrated and should be understandable to the educated layman. Bibliography. 191pp. Nor 75

DITFURTH, HOIMAR von. **CHILDREN OF THE UNIVERSE**, c$10.95. This is not merely a book of popular science. Underlying the scientific data is a philosophical premise and even an evangelical intent. Von Ditfurth has presented a very animated narrative that actually seems to ensoul the vast machinery of the universe. Nature here is often personified, and always has implications for human life. Just beneath the surface of twentieth century scientific fact we find the preoccupation with immortality; the ancient concepts of *microcosm and macrocosm*; and echoes of the *As above, so below* of hermetic philosophy. Sober as the facts may be, underlying them is von Ditfurth's recognition that science is *merely the continuation of metaphysics in another form*. This is a fascinating exploration of stars and atoms, moons and fossils, earth and man, and the reaches of the cosmos. Von Ditfurth is a noted German scientist and this book was Number One on the German best seller list when it was first published there in 1972. Recommended. Illustrations, index, 301pp. Ath 74

EDDINGTON, SIR ARTHUR. **THE EXPANDING UNIVERSE**, $1.75. A detailed pioneering work by one of this century's most noted astronomers which deals *with the view now tentatively held that the whole material universe of stars and galaxies of stars is dispersing; the galaxies scattering apart so as to occupy an ever-increasing volume.* This is a brilliant exposition of the theory of the structure of the universe, not intended for the general reader. Index, 128pp. UMP 58

_____. **THE NATURE OF THE PHYSICAL WORLD**, $3.25. *To any intelligent and thoughtful reader who would know something of the trend of the finest scientific thought of today [1928], and of the bearing of the new theories of the nature of the phenomenal world on the eternal problems of philosophy and theology, it would be difficult to suggest a better or nobler introduction than this brilliant book.*—**Saturday Review.** Index, 380pp. UMP 58

ALBERT EINSTEIN

BARNETT, LINCOLN. **THE UNIVERSE AND DR. EINSTEIN**, $.95. A very clear explanation of Einstein's theories, endorsed by Einstein himself. 128pp. Ban 68

EINSTEIN, ALBERT. **IDEAS AND OPINIONS**, c$1.98. This is the most definitive collection of Einstein's popular writings, gathered under the supervision of Einstein himself. The subjects include relativity, atomic war or peace, religions and science, human rights, economics and government. 377pp. Out 54

_____. **THE MEANING OF RELATIVITY**, $2.95. A comprehensive paper on general relativity, including appendices on related matters including one on the Relativistic Theory of the Non-Symmetric Field. 168pp. PUP 74

_____. **THE PRINCIPLE OF RELATIVITY**, $2.80. A collection of original papers on the special and general theories of relativity. Contributors include H.A. Lorentz, H. Weyl and H. Minkowski. 216pp. Dov 52

EINSTEIN, ALBERT and LEOPOLD INFELD. **THE EVOLUTION OF PHYSICS**, $3.95. *A masterly exposition of physical thought since Galileo. To have presented a clear, penetrating account of the main stages in the evolution of modern physics without the use of mathematics is an extraordinary feat, and one possible only to complete masters of their subject. . . . Einstein and Infeld's book should do much to spread an understanding and appreciation of one of the great dramas in the evolution of human thought.*—**Saturday Review.** This is probably the clearest, most understandable of Einstein's works and is recommended to the general reader. Index, 315pp. S&S 38

HOFFMANN, BANESH. **ALBERT EINSTEIN—CREATOR AND REBEL**, $2.95. The author of this biography is a noted scientist who collaborated with and was a friend of Einstein. This is a very readable work, tracing his personal life from childhood and showing the development of his creativity. Illustrations, index, 272pp. NAL 72

ENGELBREKTSON, JUNE. **STARS, PLANETS AND GALAXIES**, $1.95. This is as good an introduction to the basics of the stars, planets, and galaxies as we know of for the reader who knows little or nothing about the subject and is curious, but does not want to be overwhelmed with details. Part of Bantam's *Knowledge Through Color* series and illustrated with 132 color photographs and maps. Index, 159pp. Ban 75

FANNING, A. E. **PLANETS, STARS AND GALAXIES**, $2.50. This is a well-written introductory survey of astronomy, with the bulk of the volume being devoted to the earth, the sun, and the other planets. There are also sections on the stars and the galaxies. The book is written for the beginner and all the material is very clearly presented, with a number of diagrams where they seem helpful and a section of photographs. Donald Menzel has completely updated the text and has included the latest discoveries. Index, 189pp. Dov 66

FLAMMARION, CAMILLE. **THE FLAMMARION BOOK OF ASTRONOMY**, c$29.95. Camille Flammarion was a distinguished astronomer and one of the great scientific popularizers of the late nineteenth century. This book was first published in France in 1880, and has since been brought up to date several times by noted astronomers and physicists. It contains nearly 1000 illustrations, diagrams, and rare scientific photographs of astronomical phenomena, each linked to the text, each fully explained. There are several full-color plates, and two full-color planispheres of the celestial sky, which fold out to a size of two by one-and-a-half feet. Divded into eight main parts, the book provides a total synthesis of astronomical learning, logically arranged so that the reader can first study the anatomy of our planet, then the laws and dimensions of our solar system, and then, in gradual steps, move on to the study of the vast reaches of space. The sequence of the main topics is as follows: I, the Earth; II, the Moon; III. the Sun; IV, the Planets; V, Comets, Meteorites, and Meteors; VI, the Sidereal Universe (stars, constellations, nebulae, and galaxies); VII, the Instruments of Astronomy; and VIII, Space Vehicles. This is an amazingly complete and readable synthesis of astronomical knowledge from antiquity to the modern era. Oversize, index, 700pp. S&S 64

GAMOW, GEORGE. **ONE, TWO, THREE, INFINITY**, $1.95. *The book originated as an attempt to collect the most interesting facts and theories of modern science in such a way as to give the reader a general picture of the earth in its microscopic and macroscopic manifestations, as it presents itself to the eye of the scientist of today. . . . The subjects to be discussed have been selected so as to survey briefly the entire field of basic scientific knowledge, leaving no corner untouched.*—George Gamow. 128 of Gamow's own drawings illustrate the text. Recommended. 340pp. Ban 71

GOLDEN, FREDERIC. **QUASARS, PULSARS AND BLACK HOLES**, c$7.95. In spite of the title, this is basically a clear introductory survey of astronomy by the science editor of **Time** magazine. The text is simply written and many photographs are included. The last few chapters are devoted to quasars, pulsars, and black holes. Bibliography, index, 205pp. Scr 76

GRIBBIN, JOHN and STEPHEN PLAGEMANN. **THE JUPITER EFFECT**, $1.95. Two young scientists present a chilling hypothesis with astrological overtones: the forthcoming Grand Alignment of all the planets in 1982, the first such in 179 years, may well trigger a California earthquake far worse than the San Francisco catastrophe of 1906. In establishing this link between planetary motion and accumulating strain in the San Andreas Fault, the authors examine findings on the role of continental drift in earthquake tensions and the latest research into storms on the earth and on the sun. Dr. Gribbin is an editor of **Nature**, the international journal of science, and Dr. Plagemann is currently working on a NASA study of upper atmosphere phenomena. Diagrams, notes, bibliography, index, 136pp. RaH 74

GUILLEMIN, VICTOR. **THE STORY OF QUANTUM MECHANICS**, $3.95. Beginning with brief sketches of the background against which quantum theories were developed, this book presents a detailed account of the discovery of the principles of quantum mechanics as well as an evaluation of their validity and significance. The book also portrays the men whose insight and imagination led to the creation of quantum mechanics. A concluding section stresses the strong influence of quantum mechanics on metaphysics, ethics, and theology. The material is geared toward the reader who has a foundation in basic physics. Illustrated, glossary, index, 348pp. Scr 68

HAPGOOD, CHARLES. **MAPS OF THE ANCIENT SEA KINGS**, c$14.50. Hapgood has been researching the material presented in this fascinating narrative for many years. He has collected a large and convincing amount of data and ancient maps to illustrate his thesis, and it is well presented here. Highly recommended for the serious student, and fascinating reading for all. 315pp. Chi 66

_________. **THE PATH OF THE POLE**, c$10.00. A completely revised version of Hapgood's **Earth's Shifting Crust**. By making use of thousands of radio-carbon datings of climatic events of the last 100,000 years, Hapgood shows that the earth's outer shell has slipped over its interior—changing the relative positions of the poles—three times during that period. The last such change came at the end of the Ice Age, between 18,000 and 15,000 years ago. Good scholarship, and not an overly technical presentation. Index, 439pp. Chi 70

HARE, MICHAEL. **MICROCOSM AND MACROCOSM**, c$15.00. This book introduces a cosmology based on a conservative, spherical, and oscillating universe which has three Euclidian dimensions in space and three in time, where time is viewed as an enduring sphere through which we flow. The author reviews a variety of organic and parapsychological phenomena in this light, and speculates on the philosophical consequences of his cosmology. 291pp. Jul 68

_________. **THE MULTIPLE UNIVERSE: ON THE NATURE OF SPIRITUAL REALITY**, c$15.00. Presents a new view of parapsychology and the physical sciences in the projection of a more inclusive picture of reality using related mathematical equations. It holistically describes the relationships of mystical experience to physical law, and includes the concept of three dimensional time in a universe which is infinitely conservative of its energy. Hare explores the implications of such a cosmology in terms of some aspects of mystical experience, extrasensory phenomena, and life after death. Extensive bibliography. 188pp. Jul 66

HEBWYND, J.D. and V.A. RYTOV. **THE LIVING UNIVERSE**, c$3.15. A study, written jointly by an American and a Russian scientist, which purports to demonstrate that life on other planets is possible—and that highly evolved civilizations exist on Mars and Venus. Many related scientific studies are cited and the text is extensively illustrated. 120pp. Spe 63

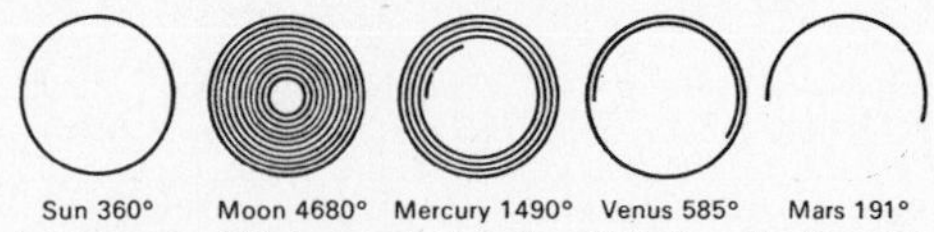

Orbital speeds. The planets move at differing speeds along the ecliptic from the Moon (13 complete tours a year) to Pluto (1°) annually.

HEISENBERG, WERNER. **ACROSS THE FRONTIERS**, $2.95. *The present collection of essays and addresses, which have sprung, directly or indirectly, from the author's concern with atomic physics, repeatedly leads beyond the frontiers of this domain. The reason lies in the universal character of the science of the atom. Anyone who takes it seriously, with all its consequences in philosophy, technology, and politics, has no other choice, when reflecting on these implications, than to trespass far beyond the boundaries of the field of physics proper . . . . The most important topics can perhaps be indicated by way of the following questions: Where is technology taking us? . . . . What content of truth do scientific assertions possess? . . . . What can we learn from modern science to assist in the solution of ancient philosophical problems?*—from the Preface. 248pp. H&R 74

_________. **PHYSICS AND PHILOSOPHY: THE REVOLUTION IN MODERN SCIENCE**, $3.95. *A fascinating and stimulating work. In the main, Heisenberg's remarks comprise a presentation of his view of the historical roots of atomic science, of the current status of quantum theory and the extent to which it constitutes a radical break with antecedent physical theories, and of the consequences of quantum theory on society as well as on science. . . . It is a book which every scientist, every person interested in the history of ideas, will find profitable and enjoyable.*—**Science** magazine. 212pp. H&R 58

HOWARD, NEALE. **THE TELESCOPE HANDBOOK AND STAR ATLAS**, c$14.95. This is a complete introduction to stargazing which combines a comprehensive discussion of telescopes with a star atlas featuring transparent map overlays. The maps show the stars seen by the naked eye, and the transparencies show those visible through the telescope. An accompanying celestial gazetteer groups objects by type and the characteristics of each—color, magnitude, right ascensions and declinations—are correlated with map numbers, catalog numbers, and names. Many astronomical study techniques are also outlined. Oversize, bibliography, glossary, index, 226pp. Cro 75

HOYLE, FRED. **FROM STONEHENGE TO MODERN COSMOLOGY**, c$8.10. A collection of 4 essays by one of the greatest astronomers of our day which demonstrate how astronomical knowledge is one of the main indices of human culture. The first is entitled *Science and Society in Modern Times*; the second, *Stonehenge*, reviews the scientific debate concerning the significance of this astronomical marvel and advances evidence for some startling new possibilities. In the third and fourth essays, Hoyle outlines the latest developments in the continuing research into the origin of the universe. Index, 96pp. Fre 72

_________. **FRONTIERS OF ASTRONOMY**, c$8.95. Beside being one of the most noted astronomers of recent times, Dr. Hoyle is also an excellent writer. This is one of the finest astronomy books that we know of. It opens with chapters on the Earth and a review of the discoveries in physics which have contributed to astronomy's advance. There are chapters on the Earth-Moon system and the origin of the planets. Then follow chapters on the Sun and the physical composition of the stars—with special reference to the stars as manufacturers of chemical elements and to exploding stars. The evolution of the stars and galaxies is discussed and this leads into the question of the origin of the universe. Much of the information in the book has been obtained through radio astronomy. Includes over 100 photos and line drawings. Even though the book is old, it is still an excellent survey. Index, 360pp. H&R 55

HOYLE, FRED. **HIGHLIGHTS IN ASTRONOMY**, $8.00. Hoyle's latest book is an introduction to astronomy for the layman—a lucid overview of what astronomers know and what they seek to know. This oversize volume presents the full scope of the science: from the structure of the Earth to the latest cosmological speculations; from the phases of the Moon to such phenomena as pulsars and black holes. Closely integrated with the text are 142 illustrations, including nearly 100 photographs (many in color). Hoyle writes extremely well and he is thorough and yet concise. This volume presents the best general survey of astronomy that we know of. Recommended. 179pp. Fre 75

JAKI, STANLEY. **SCIENCE AND CREATION**, c$16.15. A systematic analysis of the birth of science. Professor Jaki begins with a detailed analysis of ancient Hindu, Chinese, Maya, Egyptian, Babylonian, and Greek cultures—all of which made significant advances in science. This is followed by studies of science in the early Christian and Arabian cultures when science came to play an increasingly larger role in society. This is a scholarly study which offers the reader a wealth of information not generally available detailing the philosophy and civilization of the various cultures as much as their cultural achievements. Notes, index, 375pp. WAP 74

JASTROW, ROBERT. **RED GIANTS AND WHITE DWARFS**, $1.50. An excellent account by a very noted scientist-astronomer, utilizing the latest in scientific theory and discovery and profusely illustrated with photographs and drawings. Every aspect of the universe is discussed. Topics include the size of things, the forces of nature, alchemy, the beginning and the end, the origin of the solar system, the earth and the planets, the dawn of life, UFO's, DNA and Darwin. Recommended. 242pp. NAL 67

JONES, G.O., J. ROBLAT and G.J. WHITROW. **ATOMS AND THE UNIVERSE**, $3.60. Three physicists and astronomers survey the whole field of sub-atomic physics and modern astronomy, giving a complete guide to the structure of matter and to the age and origins of the universe. This is considered by many the outstanding book in its field and will appeal to laymen as well as to scientists. Pen 73

KAUFMANN, WILLIAM. **RELATIVITY AND COSMOLOGY**, $4.50. *A new vision of what astronomy is and what it can be unfolds to the reader of this book. From black holes to the primordial cosmic fireball radiation, from gravitational radiation to quasi-stellar sources, the reader sees the subject through the eyes of one close to the observational evidence and becomes aware of what rapidly evolving techniques can do to clear up some of the great of the outstanding mysteries.*—John Wheeler, Princeton University. *Kaufmann has done a magnificent job of exposition; it is one of the best-written scientific books I have ever had the chance to read. It is remarkable how the fundamental ideas of such complicated, difficult subjects can be so lucidly explained by skillfully drawn analogies, without the usually encountered penalty of loose and sloppy thinking.*—L.H. Adler, U.C.L.A. Includes many photos and line drawings and a glossary and index, 134pp. H&R 73

KILMISTER, CLIVE. **THE NATURE OF THE UNIVERSE**, $3.95. A well written, comprehensive introductory account of contemporary cosmology. Includes over 150 illustrations, 19 in color. Glossary and bibliography. 216pp. Dut 71

KOESTLER, ARTHUR. **THE SLEEPWALKERS**, $3.45. This is a generalized account of the men whose discoveries led to a radical reformulation of our vision of the universe. It is written in a lively style and is definitely designed for the non-technical reader. The historical development of each of the movements and the prime movers is fully covered. Extensive chapter notes are included along with a bibliography and an index, 624pp. G&D 59

KOPAL, ZDENEK. **MAN AND HIS UNIVERSE**, $3.95. Dr. Kopal is a noted scientist who has been Professor of Astronomy at the University of Manchester in England since 1951 and before that taught at Harvard and MIT. Here he has written a majestic survey of our universe and man's place in it. He interprets what is generally known about stars, their origin and evolution. He discusses our planetary system, and suggests why life developed only on the earth. And he speculates on where astronomical exploration may take man in centuries to come. A good book for the general reader. Illustrations, index, glossary, 313pp. Mor 71

LEVITT, I.M. **BEYOND THE KNOWN UNIVERSE—FROM DWARF STARS TO QUASARS**, c$10.00. Dr. Levitt is Director Emeritus of the Fels Planetarium and the author of many books on astronomy. Here he tells about many of the new astronomical discoveries and relates how scientists are attempting to solve the riddles they pose. Topics include white dwarfs, supernovae, neutron stars, black holes and white holes, pulsars, and quasars. The text is written for the general reader and over 48 pages of color illustrations help the reader understand the material. Index, 179pp. Vik 74

LEWIS, JOHN, ed. **BEYOND CHANCE AND NECESSITY**, c$10.35. This is a critical inquiry into Professor Jacques Monod's **Chance and Necessity**. Monod feels that *anything can be reduced to simple, obvious, mechanical interactions. The cell is a machine. The animal is a machine. Man is a machine.* The authors represented here disagree strongly with Monod's theory (Monod is a Nobel Prize-winning molecular biologist) and feel that seeing people once more as living beings in a world of living beings constitutes the major task of philosophy today. Contributors to this volume include Arthur Koestler, Joseph Needham, C.H. Waddington, and other noted philosophically-oriented scientists. Notes, 141pp. GaP 74

MENZEL, DONALD. **A FIELD GUIDE TO THE STARS AND THE PLANETS**, $5.95. This is the most complete pocket guide to the night sky ever published. The authoritative text by Dr. Menzel, former director of the Harvard College Observatory, and numerous charts, photographs, drawings, and astronomical tables convey the basic information needed by amateur astronomers. Each of the charts and sky maps appears twice, once as seen in the telescope and again on the facing page with the names of the stars, nebulae, clusters, and other objects superimposed. These charts and the accompanying text provide the reader with a pictorial road map to sky watching with binoculars or telescope. Other sections of the book cover the solar system, the planets, and other bodies such as comets, meteors, and asteroids. There's also material on using the telescope and camera in astronomy. Tables, glossary, bibliography, index, 397pp. HMC 64

_____. **ASTRONOMY**, c$20.00. A beautifully presented oversize pictorial survey of astronomy and the universe. Dr. Menzel's opening chapters are a thoughtful review of the gropings and later disproved *systems* of the early astronomers. The next chapter—on atoms, atomic energy, and radiation—lays the groundwork for an understanding of the universe. The remainder of the book is a masterly description of the sun, moon, planets, asteroids, meteors, comets, stars, nebulae, galaxies, eclipses, and auroras. All the latest theories are presented and analyzed. One interesting section is devoted to an account of a star from its prenatal state to its decline. Supplementing the text are 319 photographs, diagrams, and star maps. Glossary, index, 320pp. RaH 75

MENZEL, DONALD, FRED WHIPPLE, and GERARD de VANCOULEURS. **SURVEY OF THE UNIVERSE**, c$22.75. The authors of this comprehensive text are three of the most noted contemporary astronomers. This is a well-written scholarly account which includes chapters on the following areas: Astronomy and the Origins of Science, Ancient Astronomy, The Copernican Revolution, The Law of Gravitation, The Motions of the Earth, Some Tools of Astronomy, Measurements in the Solar System, Radiation and Atomic Structure, The Sun and Its Radiations, The Earth as a Planet, The Moon, The Terrestrial Planets, The Giant Planets, Asteroids and Comets, Interplanetary Debris, Space Exploration, Origin and Evolution of the Solar System, Extraterrestrial Life, Stellar Distance and Luminosities, The Spectra and Temperatures of Stars, Double Stars and Stellar Masses, The Diameters and Densities of Stars, Stellar Atmospheres, The Nucleus of the Atom, Sources of Stellar Energy, Nuclear Reactions and Atomic Evolution, Variable Stars, The Cataclysmic Variables, Stars with Atmospheric Shells, Interstellar Matter, Star Clusters and Associations, The Milky Way, Galaxies, Radio and X-Ray Sources, Relativity and Cosmology, Cosmic Evolution and Time Scales. This is basically a textbook and the format and style are in that vein. The whole work is illustrated with countless photographs, line drawings, and graphs. There is also an extensive chapter-by-chapter bibliography, name and subject indices, and chapter textbook questions. An overwhelming amount of information in one fat book for the serious student. 877pp. PrH 70

MOORE, PATRICK. **CONCISE ATLAS OF THE UNIVERSE**, c$19.95. This immense beautiful volume (11x15") is a revised and updated version of **The Atlas of the Universe**, which was published in 1970 to widespread critical acclaim. The contents include: ATLAS OF THE EARTH FROM SPACE (The phases of the Earth, the Earth's magnetosphere and atmosphere, weather systems from space, and panoramas of the entire globe taken from space); ATLAS OF THE MOON (The surface of the Moon, the Lunar landscape, and 14 pages of Moon maps and panoramas); ATLAS OF THE SOLAR SYSTEM (50 pages covering the Copernican revolution, maps of the solar system, sun-spots, solar eclipses, the planets, the asteroids, comets, meteors and meteorites); and ATLAS OF THE STARS (60 pages on such topics as stellar evolution, the motion and distances of the stars, unstable stars, double and multiple stars, star clusters and nebulae, mapping the galaxy, galaxies beyond our own, the radio sky, mapping the constellations, seasonal star maps, the northen sky, and the southern sky). The text forms a complete guide to the universe as we know it today. It is geared toward the general reader and all the technical material is very clearly explained and illustrated with countless full color and b/w photographs, drawings, and diagrams. A very well organized, fascinating compilation which we recommend highly to all who seek an understanding of the mysteries of our Earth and of the universe beyond. 190pp. RMN 74

_____. **THE OBSERVER'S BOOK OF ASTRONOMY**, c$3.30. This is a cute little book, 4x6"—just the right size to put in your pocket or purse when you go off stargazing. Moore is a leading astronomer and has written many books. Here he describes the stars visible at each season of the year, and in separate chapters deals with the sun, moon, and planets—together with such irregular occurrences as aurorae, comets, and shooting stars. The text is concise and clear and includes 64 plates, 14 in color, and numerous text illustrations. Index, 222pp. FWC 74

MOORE, PATRICK and IAIN NICHOLSON. **BLACK HOLES IN SPACE**, $2.05. This is the least technical account we know of. The authors explain how Black Holes are formed from the collapse of large stars, how they can be detected, and how they might be the explanation for some of the mysterious occurrences in the Universe, such as quasars, that continue to baffle astronomers. Index, 126pp. Oce 74

MUIRDEN, JAMES. **GUIDE TO ASTRONOMY**, $2.29. This is a good overall look at astronomy—well written and comprehensive but not overwhelming to the interested non-professional. Includes chapters on each of the planets; an overall look at man and the universe; an introduction to theories of cosmology; current topics in astronomy; and the problems of quasars and transient lunar phenomena. A final section gives hints and practical advice to the amateur astronomer. Illustrations, glossary, index, 320pp. Pan 72

MURCHIE, GUY. **MUSIC OF THE SPHERES, VOL. I**, $3.50. The material universe—from atom to quasar, simply explained. Fascinating volumes that delve into astronomy and physics in a way that is understandable to the layman. Recommended. Vol.I: The Macrocosm: Planets, Stars, Galaxies, Cosmology. 225pp. Dou 67

_____. **MUSIC OF THE SPHERES, VOL. II**, $3.00. Vol. II: The Microcosm: Matter, Atoms, Waves, Radiation, Relativity. Index, 599pp. Dou 67

NELSON, J.H. **COSMIC PATTERNS**, $5.50. Nelson was employed to study sunspots by RCA Communications because sunspots were believed to be the cause of magnetic storms which from time to time would disrupt shortwave radio communications. He spent almost thirty years doing detailed research and has produced very strong evidence that the planets do, when in certain arrangements, cause changes in the particular solar radiations that are associated with magnetic storms in the earth's atmosphere. Illustrations, notes, 76pp. AFA 74

NICOLSON, IAIN. **ASTRONOMY**, $1.95. A simple account, profusely illustrated in color. Ban 71

_____. **EXPLORING THE PLANETS**, $1.95. Traces the development of astronomy and includes a comprehensive planet-by-planet account. Written for the general reader and profusely illustrated in color. 159pp. Ban 71

OTTEWELL, GUY. **ASTRONOMICAL CALENDAR**, $4.95. There are a few astronomical calendars available but this one far surpasses all the others. It is designed to be useful to both advanced and beginning astronomers. There is a sky map for each month which is exceedingly clearly drawn and represents the whole of the sky that you can see, at the convenient time for viewing in the evening. There's also a monthly solar system diagram and on the page facing each map there's a comprehensive day-by-day listing of events. Extensive explanatory information is included to help the beginning astronomer and separate sections detail the following information: position, time, constellations, star designations, ecliptic, zodiac, precession, magnitudes, elongations, sun, young moon, tides, Jupiter's satellites, comets, meteors, brightest stars. There's also an excellent glossary. If you are interested in astronomy and star viewing you'll definitely enjoy using this calendar. Issued yearly. ACa 75

PENSEE EDITORS. **VELIKOVSKY RECONSIDERED,** c$8.95. A collection of the best articles out of the many **Pensee** has published as special features on Velikovsky. Some review the history of the case, re-examine the criticism and the claims, and in the light of subsequent scientific discoveries show not only how and wherein Dr. Velikovsky was right, but also how the critics are still claiming *ad hoc* explanations of Dr. Velikovsky's predicted phenomena, or pretending *they knew it all along.* A number of new articles by Velikovsky himself are also included along with many charts, diagrams, and graphs. It must be remembered that **Pensee** is very pro-Velikovsky, so this is not a balanced presentation of both sides. Dou 76

RAND MCNALLY. **STAR FINDER,** $1.95. The large, simplified star map shows the constellations, stars to the fifth magnitude, nebulae, the Milky Way. It is easy to use and the stars shine in the dark for night observation. Planets may be marked on the plastic surface and then erased. A zodiac dial locates constellations at various times of the year. Instructions and planet location tables are included. Laminated heavy board, 11x11"

RAND McNALLY. **THE STARFINDER,** $24.95. A map of the heavens in the form of a globe which adjusts easily to place the stars in positions relating to any given time and place. Double-ring mounting. Rings are tinted to match zodiac. Base is chrome-plated, contrasting the dark blue globe and yellow stars. With Starfinder Handbook and Official Map of the Moon. 16" high.

REISER, OLIVER. **COSMIC HUMANISM AND WORLD UNITY,** $6.95. *The cosmology of a cosmic humanism would weld into one world-view the pantheism of the Stoics as this was further developed by Giordano Bruno, Spinoza, and others, and give poetic expression by such writers as Goethe, Emerson, Thoreau, Whitman, and contemporary scientists like Albert Einstein.... Beyond that, it also makes contact with certain forms of Oriental religions and philosophy.... Briefly stated, this world-view asserts that the cosmos extends without limits in space and time and matter. The unbegotten cosmos is infinite and eternal.* This is a fascinating exploration of Reiser's cosmology. It's not light reading, and many gems are included. Index, 286pp. G&B 75

SCIENTIFIC AMERICAN. **THE NEW ASTRONOMY,** $2.95. A collection of twenty articles first published in **Scientific American** between 1948–55, written for the general reader. Topics include: structure of the universe; the shape and dynamics of space; our own galaxy; stars; the sun and its satellites; and photocell and radio telescope. Bibliography, 246pp. S&S 55

SCIENTIFIC AMERICAN. **THE SOLAR SYSTEM,** $4.50. A bound, fully indexed reprint of the September, 1975 issue of **Scientific American**—devoted to a survey of our current scientific knowledge of the Sun, the planets, and interplanetary space. The articles are extraordinarily clear and are accompanied by a profusion of charts, drawings, and some of the finest photographs (many in color) we have ever seen. The selections are uniformly excellent and are appropriate for the general reader as well as for the specialist who wishes to keep up with the latest discoveries and theories in the field. Recommended. Oversize, 145pp. Fre 75

SHAPLEY, HARLOW. **GALAXIES,** c$13.45. This very detailed study of galaxies is the second (updated) edition of the most noted book on the subject. In addition to new sections, chapters, and a revision of terminology, there is fresh material on galactic structure, galaxies as sources of radio signals, emitting and absorbing clouds of gas and dust in and among galaxies, and quasars. The text is enhanced by many fine photographs and drawings. . Index, 242pp. HUP 72

SHIPMAN, HARRY L. **BLACK HOLES, QUASARS, AND THE UNIVERSE,** c$12.95. Black holes and quasars are the latest developments in astronomy and an incredible amount of material has been written on them. This is a clearly written study of new developments in astronomy and of the new view of the universe that is emerging. The presentation is geared toward the general reader and though the topic is highly technical by nature Shipman's exposition should be understandable to the reader who has little or no scientific background. Each topic is very fully discussed and the text is supplemented by a profusion of photographs, tables, diagrams, and line drawings. Bibliography, notes, index, 309pp. HMC 76

STROMBERG, GUSTAV. **MAN, MIND, AND THE UNIVERSE,** $3.00. This noted scientist applies his knowledge of the physical world to a further understanding of the nature of life, mind, the immortality of the human soul, and God. 120pp. ERI 66

_____. **THE SEARCHERS,** $4.00. A fine series of essays which delve into the fields of science, medicine, and philosophy and which explore many aspects of the physical and non-physical world. Topics include gravitation, vibrating atoms, expanding waves and small particles, the roots of our consciousness, the immortal soul. 242pp. ERI 48

_____. **THE SOUL OF THE UNIVERSE,** $6.00. The author is a noted astronomer. He describes in simple language the scientific discoveries concerning the nature of matter, life and mind, and their bearing on the problems of the existence of God (or, as he calls it, a World Soul), and on the age-old ideas of the immortality of the soul. 312pp. Sci 70

SULLIVAN, WALTER. **CONTINENTS IN MOTION,** c$17.95. Sullivan, Science Editor of **The New York Times,** reveals how a variety of seemingly disparate discoveries were brought together to form the revolutionary theory of *continental drift – the view of our planet as everliving, ever in flux, its continents in motion with respect to one another, carried by the creeping movements of gigantic plates of the earth's crust, clashing with one another from time to time to produce the great mountain ranges.* It casts new light on the topo-

graphy of every part of the world. This is a well written account of the vast panorama opened up by the new discoveries. Oversize, with illustrations, notes, and index. 399pp. MGH 74

TAYLOR, JOHN. **BLACK HOLES: THE END OF THE UNIVERSE?** $1.50. Dr. Taylor is Professor of Mathematics at Kings College, University of London and has held Chairs of Physics at the University of Southampton and at Rutgers University in New Jersey. This is the most authoritative study available on black holes. He defines black holes as burned out stars that have undergone gravitational collapse. The fate of objects, however distant from the black hole, is ultimately to fall into it, and at a later time to be crushed to death at its center. Dr. Taylor explores various theories and attempts to put the entire question into perspective. Bibliography, index, 175pp. Avo 73

TOBEN, BOB. **SPACE-TIME AND BEYOND,** $5.95. This is one of the best and most important books on psi theory, on physics, and on the relation of the two areas. It is good because it is written by a person with an understanding of modern physics and ancient knowledges (and in conversation with physicists Jack Sarfatti and Fred Wolf who share the same orientation) and is able to explain the world of sense experience, the world of matter and of energy, as understood in quantum physics as it is connected to the world beyond sense experience, the world of psi phenomena. It is a quantum mechanical explanation of ESP, time travel and space warps. It deals with the space-time structure of consciousness with the universal patterns that relate galaxies, planets, humans, and particles. And, though it goes into these subjects deeply, it does so in a way that is helpful in understanding them—in pictures. Over eighty percent of the central part of the book is pictures. It is the only book on advanced physics that might be mistaken for a coloring book (which it also can be). It has a technical commentary by Dr. Sarfatti, and a good annotated bibliography. Recommended. 8½x11. 175pp. Dut 75

TOMAS, ANDREW. **ON THE SHORES OF ENDLESS WORLDS,** c$7.30. The story of the origin of life on this planet and some of the discoveries of modern science are woven into an entrancing tale, full of speculation and folklore. A well written account that seems a bit less scattered and a great deal more serious than most of the countless books on this topic. Includes illustrations, bibliography, and index, 230pp. Sou 74

TOULMIN, STEPHEN and JUNE GOODFIELD. **THE FABRIC OF THE HEAVENS,** $3.75. *Drawing not only from scientific but also from historical and literary sources, [Dr. Toulmin and Ms. Goodfield] have illustrated the often halting, always uncertain progress of man's knowledge of the universe and its laws through half-a-dozen representative figures: Aristotle, Aristarchos, Ptolemy, Copernicus, Tycho Brahe, Kepler, and Newton.... they have reconstructed the cultural milieu of the ancient and medieval worlds, the intellectual, emotional and social limitations that frequently misled scientists and philosophers to theories that may seem merely ridiculous to us....It is the best exposition of the subject.*—E. Nelson Hayes, Astrophysical Observatory, Smithsonian Institute. Illustrations, index, 285pp. H&R 61

VELIKOVSKY, IMMANUEL. **EARTH IN UPHEAVAL,** c$8.95. Documents the assertations in **Worlds in Collision.** Presents evidence from the natural sciences which indicate that these great disturbances which rocked our globe were caused by forces outside the earth itself. The evidence is assembled from mountains and oceans, deserts and tundras and jungles, and establishes the Velikovsky theory as of prime importance in man's understanding of the earth's past and man's own origins. 308pp. Dou 55

_____. **WORLDS IN COLLISION,** c$10.00. A very controversial book which propounds the theory that more than once within historical times the order in our planetary system was disturbed and caused enormous cataclysms; the earth became a primeval chaos lashed by tornados of cinders; the skies darkened; land masses were destroyed and large portions of the human race perished. 401pp. Dou 50

VLASTOS, GREGORY. **PLATO'S UNIVERSE,** $3.95. A distinguished Platonic scholar discusses the impact of the Greek discovery of the *cosmos* on man's perception of his place in the universe, describes the problems this posed, and interprets Plato's response to this discovery. Starting with the Presocratics, Vlastos describes the intellectual revolution that began with the cosmogonies of Thales, Anaximander, and Anaximenes in the sixth century BC and culminated a century later in the atomist system of Leucippus and Democritus. In a detailed analysis of the astronomical and physical theories of the **Timaeus,** Vlastos demonstrates Plato's role in the reception and transmission of the discovery of the cosmos. This is a fairly technical analysis. Notes, bibliography, index, 143 pp. UWa 75

WHITNEY, CHARLES. **WHITNEY'S STAR FINDER,** $5.95. A field guide to the heavens created by Dr. Whitney, Professor of Astronomy at Harvard. It clearly tells, explains, and shows what is up there. And it provides a removable locator wheel that enables the user to identify every prominent star in the sky, on any day of the year, all over North America. Includes very detailed instructional material and an index. The locator wheel is of very durable plastic. 103pp. RaH 74

WHIPPLE, FRED. **EARTH, MOON AND PLANETS,** $2.75. This is a very well-written account; the approach is non-mathematical and the scientific arguments are advanced in a simple but sound way. The illustrations are uniformly good and the photographs of the Earth, Moon, and Mars, taken from space vehicles, are truly remarkable. This is the third edition of this noted book and the material has been almost completely revised and up-dated to keep abreast of the rapid changes and discoveries in the field. Index, 296pp. HUP 68

ZIM, HERBERT and ROBERT BAKER. **STARS,** $1.95. A pocket-sized guide to the stars, illustrated with 150 color paintings showing the location and appearance of almost all the generally recognized constellations and tables for helping to locate the planets. An easy-to-use introductory handbook. Index, 160pp. Gol 56

BAHA'I

ABDU'L-BAHA. **SOME ANSWERED QUESTIONS**, c$5.00. Informal explanations of a wide variety of spiritual and philosophical questions, including the station and influence of the Prophets, the nature of man, and certain Biblical subjects. BPT 30

BAHA'U'LLAH. **EPISTLE TO THE SON OF THE WOLF**, $5.00. BPT 41

_____. **GLEANINGS FROM THE WRITINGS OF BAHA'U'LLAH**, c$5.00. Explains the meaning of true religion, the spiritual nature of man, and the transformation of human society. BPT 39

_____. **THE KITAB-I-IQUAN: THE BOOK OF CERTITUDE**, c$5.00. Sets forth the grand redemptive scheme of God, reveals the oneness of religion and explains abstruse passages of Jewish, Christian and Muslim scriptures. BPT 31

_____. **PRAYERS AND MEDITATIONS**, c$5.00. A treasury of prayers and devotional passages revealing the infinite bounty of God's purpose for man in this day. BPT

_____. **TOKENS FROM THE WRITINGS OF BAHA'U'LLAH**, c$4.95. A good selection of Baha'u'llah's major writings. BPT 76

BALYUZI, H.M. **BAHA'U'LLAH**, $2.00. The first part offers a short account of the life of Baha'u'llah, describing his background and his chief writing. The second part is an essay on the eternal manifestations of God, entitled _The Word Made Flesh_. 134pp. Nat nd

ESSLEMONT, J.E. **BAHA'U'LLAH AND THE NEW ERA**, $.95. An introduction to the Baha'i faith, covering its history and teachings. Includes many quotations from Baha'i writings. Pyr 23

BIBLES

ADDINGTON, JACK. **THE HIDDEN MYSTERY OF THE BIBLE**, c$5.95. A study guide to understanding the spiritual and psychological messages in the Old Testament. The result of many years' search for meaning while teaching Bible classes, this volume makes a fine companion for the Holy Book. 276pp. DMd 69

ANONYMOUS. **THE BOOK OF JASHER**, c$6.00. This is one of the long lost and long sought for sacred books which is contemporary with the Old Testament and which many think should have been included with the other books of the Bible. The original author was born during the lifetime of Moses and lived in association and companionship with him. Therefore, the first part of this edition was written by Jasher from the records and traditions that had been preserved by his ancestors. The latter part is based upon what he observed himself. For all interested in Biblical history this book presents another record of the events recorded in the Old Testament. This is a photographic reproduction of the 1751 edition, with an introduction and notes. Oversize, 83pp. Amo

THE INTERNMENT OF CHRIST from a fresco by Cimabue, thirteenth century

ANONYMOUS. **THE LOST BOOKS OF THE BIBLE AND THE FORGOTTEN BOOKS OF EDEN**, $4.95. _You will find between these covers all the ecclesiastical writings of early Christian authorities that are known to exist, and yet were omitted from the authorized New Testament._—from the preface. 269pp. NAL 27

THE APOCRYPHA

Twelve books of the Bible, dating from the time of the Old Testament, not found in the Hebrew Bible and removed from the King James version by the Puritans in the seventeenth century. It is a collection of histories, romances, books of devotion, and edifying sayings and discourses, which bridges the period between the Old and New Testaments.

GOODSPEED, EDGAR, tr. **THE APOCRYPHA**, $3.45. A translation into contemporary English, part in prose, part in poetry. This is the most popular edition and includes a good introduction. 519pp. RaH 38

THE NEW ENGLISH BIBLE: THE APOCRYPHA, c$4.95. See review of **The New English Bible** for a critique of this edition. 462pp. CUP

OESTERLEY, W.O.E. **AN INTRODUCTION TO THE BOOKS OF THE APOCRYPHA**, c$6.75. Oesterley is a well-known Old Testament scholar. Here he discusses the importance of Apocryphal literature from the literary, historical, and doctrinal points of view and gives the reader some background information on the individual books. Notes, bibliography, index. 345pp. SCK 35

BATES, ERNEST, ed. **THE BIBLE DESIGNED TO BE READ AS LIVING LITERATURE**, $4.95. This is a modernized arrangement of the Bible, basically following the King James version. Bates has edited the material for reading and enjoyment and is not overly concerned with strict theology. Over the years _The Bates Bible_ (as this book is generally called) has been extremely popular. All the spelling is modernized. Glossary, 1300pp. S&S 36

BEST, SHABAZ BRITTEN. **GENESIS REVISITED**, $2.85. While most people have assumed that the version of Genesis common to most Bibles is a correct translation, there is substantial evidence that this is merely a veiled version of Moses' original work. The early Hebrew in which it was written became a dead language about 500 BC. Ptolemy II possessed a copy and asked several Essene mystics to translate it into Greek. However when they encountered its mystery doctrines which they considered sacred, they refused to reveal them and so veiled in their translation the deeper doctrines; this became the basis of our present version. The Vatican had a copy of the original script which was published in 1515 and later translated by a remarkable genius, linguist and mystic, Fabre D'Olivet. In this translation the original spiritual teaching of Genesis is regained, touching on esoteric symbology, numerology, astrology, vegetarianism, Atlantis, the esoteric meaning of Adam and Eve, the Serpent, the Garden of Eden, Noah and the rams, as well as the purpose of creation of life itself. 96pp. Ser 64

BLAKE, WILLIAM, illustrator. **BOOK OF JOB**, $4.95. The full text of the Book of Job accompanied by excellent reproductions of Blake's illustrative plates. The introduction discusses Blake and the Bible and Blake as a visual artist. Oversize, 73pp. TCP 76

BUTTRICK, GEORGE, ed. **THE INTERPRETER'S DICTIONARY OF THE BIBLE**, c$49.95. This four volume set is a work of impeccable scholarship. It is the most comprehensive work imaginable and includes over 7500 entries, 163 maps, over 1000 plates (some in color), bibliographical material, and ample cross-referencing. While we imagine that only scholars or libraries would be interested in owning this set, it is generally well written. 3903pp. Abi 62

CAIRD, G.B. **SAINT LUKE**, $1.80. The Gospels all tell the story of Jesus and his ministry—each one giving the narration from a different point of view and using different sources. _Luke_ was a second generation Christian who had ample opportunity to associate with those who had first-hand knowledge of the Gospel story. He was an educated man who could adapt his diction to different occasions, writing sometimes formal, classical prose, sometimes a racy narrative style, and sometimes the _Bible Greek_ in which the Septuagint was written. This Gospel is notable for its insistence on the life, death, and teaching of Christ as a message of universal salvation addressed to all men. Included are detailed accounts of the working of the Spirit and the ministry of the angels. This book is part of the _Penguin New Testament Gospel Commentaries_. These new paragraph-by-paragraph commentaries have been written by modern scholars who are in touch with contemporary Biblical theology and also with the interests of the layman. The words of the Gospel are interpreted in a very clear way in the light of the latest archaeological, historical, and linguistic research. Also includes indices of references, subjects, and authors, more commentary on the verses than there are verses, and a long introduction. 271pp. Pen 63

CHAMBERLIN, ROY and HERMAN FELDMAN, eds. **THE DARTMOUTH BIBLE**, $9.95. A good, modern King James with the Apocrypha. Voluminous commentary on the historical background is included. 1260pp. HMC 50

CLAREMONT, LEWIS de. **THE TEN LOST BOOKS OF THE PROPHETS**, $3.50/set. A set of ten tiny books which purport to reveal the secret knowledge used by Moses, Solomon, and Jesus to cure the ill and perform other miracles. 320pp. DPC 59

DAVIES, W.D. **THE SERMON ON THE MOUNT**, $2.95. This is a detailed study of the Sermon on the Mount, a portion of the book of Matthew. Professor Davies examines the sermon in the light of how he perceives Matthew intended it to be understood, and in the settings of Jewish Messianic expectations, contemporary Judaism, the early Church, and the ministry of Jesus. The author quotes frequently from original sources to back up his assumptions. Index of references. 163pp. CUP 66

SAMSON SLAYING THE LION by Gustave Dore

DORE, GUSTAVE. **THE DORE BIBLE ILLUSTRATIONS**, $5.00. 241 beautiful plates which capture the dramatic intensity of the Scriptures. 9x12", 256pp. Dov 74

EDGE, HENRY TRAVERS. **ESOTERIC KEYS TO THE CHRISTIAN SCRIPTURES AND THE UNIVERSAL MYSTERY LANGUAGE OF MYTH AND SYMBOL**, $2.50. Two books in one. The first discusses the true esoteric meaning of certain key events in the Bible while the second discusses the esoteric meaning of a number of universal symbols. Edge was a theosophist and his presentation reflects theosophical cosmology. 93pp. PoL 73

ENOCH

There are two books generally attributed to Enoch: the first, generally known as **The Book of Enoch**, was unearthed in Ethiopia in 1773, while the second, usually known as **The Book of the Secrets of Enoch**, is a Slavic manuscript which was found in Russia in 1895. The Slavonic **Enoch** contains material which is similar to the Ethiopian, as well as some additional information. **The Book of Enoch** is generally considered the most notable extant apocalyptic work outside the canonical Scriptures. While it is attributed to Enoch most scholars feel that it was written over a long period of time and by more than one individual. The ideas contained in the manuscripts form the basis for much of the later Christian mystical doctrines.

CHARLES, R.H., tr. **THE BOOK OF ENOCH**, $2.20. Charles' original translation of the Ethiopian **Enoch**, with introductory and background material provided by W.O.E. Oesterley. 182pp. SCK 17

_____, tr. **THE BOOK OF ENOCH**, $5.00. This edition contains Charles' translation of the Ethiopian **Enoch**. Charles also provides 110pp of introductory material and an incredible amount of textual notes. Selections from the Greek Enochan fragments are also included. Index, 441pp. HeR 12

_____, ed. **THE BOOK OF THE SECRETS OF ENOCH**, $2.50. A translation by W.R. Morfill of the original Slavic manuscripts. Charles supplies a 48pp introduction and extensive notes. Index, 148pp. HeR 1896

LAURENCE, RICHARD, tr. **THE BOOK OF ENOCH THE PROPHET**, $6.50. A translation of the Ethiopian **Enoch**. This is the translation that H.P. Blavatsky refers to in **The Secret Doctrine** and she, at least, considers it the definitive one. Includes a long introduction and an index. 235pp. Wiz nd

WORK OF THE CHARIOT. **BOOK OF ENOCH**, $12.00. Consists of the R.H. Charles translation of **Enoch**, the **Book of the Secrets of Enoch**, and the Odeberg **Hebrew Book of Enoch**, along with the Hebrew text and critical notes. Also the *Shur Qoma*, *The Measure of the Divine Body*, from the **Book of the Angelic Secrets of the Great One**. WKC 70

FENTON, J.C. **SAINT MATTHEW**, $2.45. Part of the *Penguin New Testament Gospel Commentaries* (see full description under review of G.B. Caird). The author of **St. Matthew's Gospel** is often regarded as the most ecclesiastical and concise of the evangelists. He records Christ's teaching very fully, and shows special interest in the relation of the Gospel to Jewish law. Of the four Gospels, his is probably the best known and the one best adapted to the general reader. 487pp. Pen 73

FILLMORE, CHARLES. **METAPHYSICAL BIBLE DICTIONARY**, c$10.00. A complete index of names and places which are written about or mentioned in the Bible, with extensive definitions of who or where and the allegorical meaning they hold in the story they come from. 709pp. USC nd

FORRESTER-BROWN, JAMES. **THE TWO CREATION STORIES IN GENESIS**, $3.95. Forrester-Brown suggests some keys to understanding the symbolic meaning of the two distinct stories of the creation contained in the first three chapters of Genesis. He also analyzes the creation stories in the light of the ancient esoteric wisdom. Index, 302pp. ShP 74

FRIELING, RUDOLF. **HIDDEN TREASURE IN THE PSALMS**, c$4.80. A study of the mystical and esoteric meaning of the sacred poetry attributed to King David by an anthroposophist (see the Steiner section) who was also an Old Testament scholar. 190pp CCP 67

FROMM, ERICH. **YOU SHALL BE AS GODS**, $1.25. A radical interpretation of the Old Testament and its tradition by a noted psychologist which explores the evolution of the basic concepts of God, man, history, sin and repentance. 191pp. Faw 66

GASTER, THEODOR. **MYTH, LEGEND AND CUSTOM IN THE OLD TESTAMENT**. $9.90/set. *This book is an attempt to gather into one place all that can be derived from Comparative Folklore and mythology for the interpretation of the Old Testament. It grew out of the publishers' invitation to me to prepare an updated edition of Sir James G. Frazer's Folklore in the Old Testament on the lines of what I had previously tried to do for his Golden Bough. Very soon after I set to work, however, it became increasingly apparent that, to produce a work of any real use, I should have to go beyond that specification. . . . What I have done, then, is to go through the Old Testament from cover to cover and pick out, verse by verse, anything on which Comparative Folklore or mythology may throw light. In this effort, I have kept my sights not only on elucidating the overt sense of the text but also on recovering by the aid of such material the under currents of thought and the subliminal elements of the writers' minds. . . . Introduction notes. Two volumes, 1018pp. H&R 69*

GESENIUS, WILLIAM. **A HEBREW AND ENGLISH LEXICON TO THE OLD TESTAMENT**, c$37.50. The most comprehensive edition available, edited by Francis Brown S.R. Driver and C.A. Briggs, translated by Edward Robinson. 1144pp. Oxf nd

GINZBERG, LOUIS. **LEGENDS OF THE BIBLE**, c$7.95. This is an abridged edition of Ginzberg's **Legends of the Jews**, originally published in seven volumes. All the major Biblical stories are retold here in novelistic prose. The book provides a fine means of learning about the Biblical stories without having to plod through the Bible. Introduction 685pp. Jew 56

GRAVES, ROBERT and RAPHAEL PATAI. **HEBREW MYTHS—THE BOOK OF GENESIS**, $2.75. The authors have analyzed sixty-one stories of cosmic forces, deities, angels and demons, giants and heroes from Genesis and other Hebrew and Aramaic sources in the light of modern anthropology and mythology. 311pp. MGH 64

GREGORY, DICK. **DICK GREGORY'S BIBLE TALES**, c$6.95. Biblical stories retold in a modern, hip way by one of the U.S.'s greatest humorists and political activists. Gregory's commentaries interpret the lessons for the contemporary reader: the trumpets of civil rights protesters and grape boycotters blow down the walls of Jericho; the Tower of Babel is the first high-rise; Sodom and Gomorrah are destroyed for the sin of benign neglect; and so on. 187pp. S&D 74

GREENLEES, DUNCAN. **THE GOSPEL OF ISRAEL**, c$3.50. A topically arranged selection of Old Testament material, bound together with a 144pp exploration of the history of the Jewish people and the Biblical prophets. This is part of the Theosophical Society's *World Gospel Series*. Bibliography, index. 521pp. TPH 55

GROVE, DAISY. **THE MYSTERY TEACHING OF THE BIBLE**, c$2.50. A theosophist's look at the Bible, which explains the significance of certain archetypes, numbers, and names, and shows how the stories relate to man's need for God. 120pp. TPH 25

HALL, MANLY P. **OLD TESTAMENT WISDOM**, c$7.50. This is the result of years of careful Biblical research. Mr. Hall gives not only facts, but also his masterful interpretation of the deeper meanings contained in the Holy Scriptures. The approach is always within the framework of comparative religion, mysticism, and their practical application. For more background on Manly Hall, see the Mysticism section. Index, 312pp. PRS 57

HEBREW-ENGLISH LEXICON OF THE BIBLE, $2.95. A handy, concise dictionary designed to assist the student reading the Bible in the original Hebrew and Aramaic 287pp. ScB 74

HEIDENREICH, ALFRED. **THE UNKNOWN IN THE GOSPELS**, c$5.55. A collection of seven lectures given recently by a follower of Rudolf Steiner: *The Place of the Gospel in the Religious Literature of the World; The Contrasting Stories of the Childhood of Jesus in the Gospels of Matthew and Luke and their Meaning; The Dead Sea Scrolls and the Historical Background of the Gospels; Stages of the Incarnation of Christ in Jesus Spiritual Healing in the Gospels; Miracles; The Raising of Lazarus.* The material is fascinating and very clearly presented. 150pp. CCP 72

HELINE, CORINNE. **THE BIBLE AND THE STARS**, $3.50. Explores spiritual relationships between the zodiac and important books and stories of the Bible—Genesis, Abraham saac, Jacob, the Ten Commandments, Solomon, Job, the Prophets, the Apostles, and Revelation, to name but a few. 128pp. NAP 71

_____. MYSTIC MASONRY AND THE BIBLE, $3.75. Many mysteries of Masonry openly and clearly revealed. NAP nd

_____. MYTHOLOGY AND THE BIBLE, $2.00. A study of Biblical myths as related to those of Greece and Rome. 75pp. NAP 62

_____. NEW AGE BIBLE INTERPRETATION: AN EXPOSITION OF THE INNER SIGNIFICANCE OF THE HOLY SCRIPTURES IN THE LIGHT OF ANCIENT WISDOM. . . . *Not representative of any one school or system of thought. The Bible, the supreme spiritual textbook of life, is above all creeds, dogmas, and differences in religious beliefs. So also, this, a deeper and larger interpretation of its meaning, is offered as a manual of study for all groups, organizations, and individuals who seek to know the inner Christ and to develop increasingly the consciousness of the kingdom of Heaven within.* Old Testament: Volume I, c$8.50, 513pp; Volume II, c$8.50, 469pp; Volume III, c$8.50, 336pp. New Testament: Volume IV, c$3.75, 139pp; Volume V, c$6.00, 237pp; Volume VI, c$6.00, 262pp. NAP 73

_____. OCCULT ANATOMY AND THE BIBLE, c$6.00. Elaborates upon the idea that the mystery of the universe is expressed through the formation and birth of a child, and extended throughout the physical life of spiritual rebirths. 365pp. NAP 37

_____. QUESTIONS AND ANSWERS ON THE BIBLE, $2.00. 100pp. NAP 61

_____. TAROT AND THE BIBLE, $4.50. Although the title only mentions Tarot, this study also encompasses the Qabala and the mystic significance of the Hebrew alphabet. 267pp. NAP 69

HIEBEL, FREDERICK. TREASURES OF BIBLICAL RESEARCH AND THE CONSCIENCE OF THE TIMES, $.95. Brief but detailed historical survey of the time of Christ based on the writings found in the Dead Sea Scrolls. Traces the identity of the Essene *Teacher of Righteousness*, and describes Jesus' life with his parents and their connection with the Essenes. 42pp. API nd

HODSON, GEOFFREY. THE CHRIST LIFE FROM NATIVITY TO ASCENSION, $5.50. Hodson continues the exploration he began in **The Hidden Wisdom in the Holy Bible**. Here he focuses on the New Testament, interpreting the four Gospels in the light of their allegorical meaning. His text is based on the King James version. *Ever must it be remembered that the wondrous story [of Jesus the Christ] was never intended to be read as a record of external events alone, but rather as a revelation of the divine within man.* Glossary, bibliography, index. 466pp. TPH 75

_____. THE HIDDEN WISDOM IN THE HOLY BIBLE, VOLUME I, $1.95. As with the scriptures of all religions, many profound meanings lie hidden beneath the literal interpretations of the Bible, and Geoffrey Hodson has shown that these can be discovered through an understanding of the sacred language of allegory and symbol. The more incredible and baffling some of the myths and stories appear, he points out, the more important it is to search for the underlying truths which can bring genuine insight and inspiration. For almost fifty years Hodson has lectured for and contributed to the literature of the Theosophical Society. He has carried out significant research in collaboration with physicians, physicists, anthropologists, and archaeologists, and has made many other major contributions to mankind's understanding of his unique place in the universe. This volume is a discussion of allegory and symbol in both the Old and New Testaments with a look at the life of Jesus. Index, 250pp. TPH 67

_____. THE HIDDEN WISDOM IN THE HOLY BIBLE, VOLUME II, $2.95. This is an excellent, detailed study of the Book of Genesis, incorporating theosophical wisdom, the symbolism of mystic Christianity, and many insights from the Qabalistic tradition. Glossary, bibliography, index. 493pp. TPH 67

_____. THE HIDDEN WISDOM IN THE HOLY BIBLE, VOLUME III, $2.95. While the second volume deals with the first twenty-five chapters of Genesis, this one concludes the discussion of Genesis. The approach is the same as in the previous volume and there's also a glossary and an index. 365pp. TPH 71

HOLLADAY, WILLIAM, ed. A CONCISE HEBREW AND ARAMAIC LEXICON OF THE OLD TESTAMENT, c$18.90. 443pp. Eer 71

JONES, ALEXANDER, ed. THE JERUSALEM BIBLE: READER'S EDITION, $5.95. First published in English in 1966, this is a modern translation in clear, faithful and beautiful language. Single column pages. Old and New Testaments, including the Apocrypha, with chronological table, measure and money tables, and maps. A recommended translation. 1698pp. Dou 66

KING JAMES VERSION, THE HOLY BIBLE, $14.98. This is a 9½x11½" Bible, with large print and about fifty color plates of Biblically-related art and maps. A 300pp Biblical encyclopedic index is also included. Bound in black leatherette with gold embossing. 1164+pp. Nel 71

KINGSLAND, WILLIAM. THE GNOSIS OR ANCIENT WISDOM IN CHRISTIAN SCRIPTURES, $1.95. Kingsland outlines an esoteric interpretation of Christianity which, he contends, is the same root teaching contained in the more ancient scriptures of other religions. His work is well documented and is valuable to anyone interested in a deeper study of Christianity. Bibliography, index. 230pp. TPH 70

KLUGER, RIVKAH. PSYCHE AND BIBLE, $7.50. See the Jungian Psychology section.

LAMBDIN, THOMAS. INTRODUCTION TO BIBLICAL HEBREW, c$14.75. This is generally considered the best contemporary Biblical Hebrew grammar. The lessons are

very well organized and the text can be used either with a teacher or without. It is designed for a full year's course in elementary Hebrew at the college level. Lambdin is a Harvard professor. Oversize, 373pp. Scr 71

LAMSA, GEORGE, tr. HOLY BIBLE, $10.95. A translation from ancient Eastern (mainly Aramaic) manuscripts. Aramaic is the language of the Eastern church and it is generally felt that the Aramaic manuscripts are more authentic than those which are usually used. Lamsa himself is a native Assyrian and his translations from the Aramaic and comments on the Scriptures have aroused tremendous interest both in the U.S. and in Europe. 1262pp. Hol 40

_____. OLD TESTAMENT LIGHT, c$9.75. Detailed scriptural commentary based on passages selected from Dr. Lamsa's own translation and from the King James version. Index, 991pp. ABS 64

LEARY, WILLIAM. THE HIDDEN BIBLE, c$7.50. An understandable guide to the underlying psychological messages contained in familiar Bible stories. 112pp. Aty 52

MARSH, JOHN. SAINT JOHN, $4.75. Part of the *Penguin New Testament Gospel Commentaries* (see full description under review of G.B. Caird). Professor Marsh begins by debunking the traditional view that the author of this Gospel was John, the apostle. He feels that it must have been written by a later figure (this is the fourth and last Gospel). The main body of the commentary is an endeavor to locate John's central purpose, which was to enshrine, for a wide circle of readers, the living word of God. In this attempt he examines John's conception of history and takes a look at the similarities and the notable differences between this record and that of the synoptic Gospels. 705pp. Pen 68

MC CAFFERY, ELEN. AN ASTROLOGICAL KEY TO BIBLICAL SYMBOLISM, c$7.95. See the Astrology section.

MATTHEWS, E.C. STARS OF THE BIBLE, c$10.00. See the Astrology section.

MAY, HERBERT and BRUCE METZGER, eds. THE NEW OXFORD ANNOTATED BIBLE WITH THE APOCRYPHA, c$14.95. First published in 1967, this is the first edition of the English Bible to receive both Protestant and Catholic approval. Many aids for reading and study are provided, including introductions and page-for-page annotations. Also includes many supplementary articles and a full-color map section. All articles and notes have been recently revised and cross-referenced and an index to annotations is included. Based on the Revised Standard version, this is designed to be an aid to all who desire a modern translation combined with outstanding study aids. 1936+pp. Oxf 67

MEAD, G.R.S. THE GOSPELS AND THE GOSPEL, c$5.00. A collection of essays examining various aspects of the Gospels from a metaphysical/historical viewpoint by a noted nineteenth century scholar. 215pp. HeR nd

NEIL, WILLIAM. HARPER'S BIBLE COMMENTARY, $3.95. An aid to serious Bible study which follows the chronology of the Bible and presents commentary and background information. 544pp. H&R 62

NEW ENGLISH BIBLE WITH THE APOCRYPHA, c$9.95. English scholars have painstakingly collaborated on this Bible since 1946, comparing meaning, discussing wording and language forms, going sentence by sentence in an attempt to produce an edition best suited to many readers. This edition includes introductions to each part; footnotes throughout; descriptive subheadings for major divisions within each book; single-column format with text printed in paragraph form and set in verse form whenever poetry occurs. The language used is that of today. 1824pp. Oxf 71

NINEHAM, D.E. SAINT MARK, $4.95. Part of the *Penguin New Testament Gospel Commentaries* (see full description under review of G.B. Caird). This Gospel is generally acknowledged as the one which comes nearest to the events described. Although it is the least cultured and grammatical of the four, St. Mark's talent for writing narrative is indisputable. His Gospel, written around the themes of the Church's preaching, evinces his desire to witness Christ as the Messiah. 477pp. Pen 69

NOAH, MORDECAI, tr. THE BOOK OF YASHAR, c$12.30. One of the most fascinating and controversial books of early Hebrew literature, the **Sefer Ha-Yashar** is a chronicle of Biblical history from Adam to the Judges replete with colorful episodes. Although originally it was believed to be one of the lost books of the Bible, modern scholarship places its origin in twelfth century Spain or Italy. This is a photographic copy of the original 1840 edition, including the original introductory material by the printer and the translator. This work is also known as the **Book of Jashar**. 290pp. SHP 72

PRYSE, JAMES. THE APOCALYPSE UNSEALED, $3.75. To most of us the Book of Revelations of John is exactly what it pretends to be, the hallucinations of Jesus' beloved apostle. But to James Pryse it is far more. He interprets and untangles the riddles and puzzles John devised to shield the sacred knowledge from the eyes of the profane. This book is beautiful in that, as in alchemy, the true hidden meaning and solution lies within the divine center of the self. 222pp. Sym 74

_____. THE MAGICAL MESSAGE ACCORDING TO IOANNES, $4.50. Annotated literal translation of John's Gospel from the Greek, with half the book containing highly mystical commentary on the esoteric substance. HeR nd

_____. REINCARNATION IN THE NEW TESTAMENT, $2.00. A short work that points out possible references to Old Testament characters reincarnated in New Testament stories. 90pp. HeR 1899

_____. THE RESTORED NEW TESTAMENT, $10.00/set. Pryse wants to emphasize in his translation the mystical quality of the Biblical literature that can lift man's spirit above the illusions of his ego and connect him with the depth of his divinity. Many

RUTHERFORD, ADAM. **BIBLE CHRONOLOGY**, c$18.00. The most comprehensive work imaginable, covering every Biblical period from Genesis to Revelations in detail. It also explains and demonstrates every known method of testing a chronological system and establishing accuracy: astronomical fixing, recorded synchronisms, observed cycles, archaeological data, and radioactivity determination. The enormous data presented here throw light on related chronologies, especially the Egyptian. Includes a great deal of background material in addition to the tables. Index, 555pp. IPy 57

SINGH, CHARAN. **ST. JOHN THE GREAT MYSTIC**, c$3.50. An Indian yogi-master has written an inspiring commentary on the verses of John's Gospel. He explains the spiritual motivations and instructions of the words and deeds of Jesus as described.

STRONG, JAMES. **STRONG'S EXHAUSTIVE CONCORDANCE OF THE BIBLE**, c$21.95. This is the most complete concordance of the English Bible available. It includes a main concordance which lists each word in the King James version, and all passages in which it occurs; a comparative concordance which compares the King James version with the English and American revisions of 1885 and 1901; a dictionary of the Hebrew Bible; and a dictionary of the Greek Testament. Every word in the Bible and every passage in which it occurs is listed. Considered the standard reference work since its publication. Oversize, 1808pp. Abi 1894

SUARES, CARLO. **THE CIPHER OF GENESIS**, $1.75. See the Jewish Mysticism section.

BIORHYTHMS

Biorhythms are the cyclic patterns of change in your body's energy mechanism. There are three cycles: physical, intellectual, and emotional. Each runs in varying cycles, and is usually charted on a curve. The biorhythm is the same for all people born on the same day in the same year—which makes us wonder how accurate it can be. Biorhythms have become increasingly popular over the last few years and are now being widely used to chart people's *up and down and critical days*. Various airlines are using them to determine when pilots should and should not fly and they are also being used in industry.

BIOMATE COMPUTER, $10.00. The Biomate is a plastic slide rule especially designed to show at a glance the three biorhythms controlling your life. It consists of four gear wheels which you set into position following guidelines. Once set, the Biomate will show your personal biorhythms for a complete year. Each year a small adjustment will update it for the next year. The Biomate can also be used for a number of people by individually setting it each time it is used. It is easy to use and seems to work quite well—though occasionally the gears slip.

CASIO. **BIOLATOR**, $29.95. This biorhythm calculator is in the form of an electronic calculator and all the standard calculator functions are available. The electronic brain has been especially programmed to work out with a few simple key touches all three biorhythm cycles. This is the simplest and most exact method we know for calculating the biorhythms—and the calculator itself is a handy pocket size. It is battery operated and a recharger is available for an additional fee. In addition to the biorhythm function it will also give any day of the week and the elapsed time to or from a date. Works for all dates between 1901 and 1999. Rsn

COHEN, DANIEL. **BIORHYTHMS IN YOUR LIFE**, $1.50. A good historical discussion of biorhythms, with information on the initial research and all the current studies. There's also instructional material and addresses of the major sources for biorhythm supplies. Index, 192pp. Faw 76

DEWEY, EDWARD R. **CYCLES—THE MYSTERIOUS FORCES THAT TRIGGER EVENTS**, $3.95. The study of cycles is a new science dealing with the behavior of events recurring at reasonably regular intervals throughout the universe. It may ultimately enable us to predict, scientifically and accurately, the events of tomorrow. Dewey, president of the Foundation for the Study of Cycles, formerly chief economics analyst for the U.S. Department of Commerce, presents here the results of thirty years of research. He examines literally thousands of cycles in many areas. Extensively illustrated. 201pp. Haw 71

GITTELSON, BERNARD. **BIORHYTHM: A PERSONAL SCIENCE**, c$8.95. This is the best of the books on biorhythms. The background data, proofs, and explanations are clearly presented and complete tables are included, with instructions for casting your own biorhythm. Oversize, 186pp. Arc 76

LEWIS, H. SPENCER. **SELF MASTERY AND FATE WITH THE CYCLES OF LIFE**, c$6.60 See the Rosicrucian section.

LUCE, GAY. **BIOLOGICAL RHYTHMS IN HUMAN AND ANIMAL PHYSIOLOGY**, $3.00. Recent scientific research has shown that man, along with the rest of the animal and plant world, feels, grows, and reacts in time to various rhythms, the most common being the twenty-four-hour solar day. Hundreds of experiments and observations are cited in this book, a survey of all that was known about biological rhythms as of 1970. This is a technical survey, originally prepared for the National Institute of Mental Health. Includes over 50pp, double column, of references. Oversize, 183pp. Dov 71

_____. **BODY TIME**, $1.75. An intriguing report on man's inner time clocks and the new scientific discoveries about them that could revolutionize our lives. Tells how our highs and lows can be predicted—our peaks of strength and productivity, our valleys of stress and illness. Excellent chapter on the relation of body cycles to earth and moon cycles. 411pp. Ban 73

MALLARD, VINCENT. **BIORHYTHMS AND YOUR BEHAVIOR**, $4.95. A brief explanation of the biorhythm cycles combined with a section of step-by-step instructions for computing biorhythms and many tables and blank graphs. There are also sections on comparing two or more people's biorhythms and case studies of biorhythmic data for well-known public figures. Most of the book is devoted to the workbook sheets and the book is illustrated throughout. Oversize, glossary, bibliography, 68pp. MAm 76

PSI RHYTHMS. **BIO-KIT**, $4.95. A kit containing complete instructions for charting biorhythms, bio-curve plastic templates for the actual charting, a pad of bio-chart paper, and mathematical calculation tables. PSI 74

SMITH, ROBERT E. **THE COMPLETE BOOK OF BIORHYTHMS**, $5.95. As the title suggests, this is a very complete volume, including explanatory material and a series of charts covering the years between 1800 and 2001. The presentation is easy to follow and the instructions are clear. A number of case studies of famous people are also included. 7x10", index. Aar 76

STEIGER, BRAD. **A ROADMAP OF TIME**, c$7.95. In the early 1900's, astronomer Selby Maxwell discovered the rhythm of *tides* in the earth's jetstream that allowed him to predict weather years in advance. Independently, Richard Wheeler devoted twenty years and a staff of over two hundred to compiling detailed charts of 3000 years of world weather and the exact dates of significant events in world history. This book reviews and documents the Maxwell/Wheeler discoveries. Fully illustrated with charts and graphs. Index, 246pp. PrH 75

STILL, HENRY. **OF TIME, TIDES, AND INNER CLOCKS**, $1.50. As the title suggests this is a general survey of biological rhythms and how they affect the individual. Includes material explaining astrology, natural clocks, sleep, disorientation due to changes in time zones or work shifts, theories of disease and aging and how this affects the biological rhythms, and meditative and other ways of altering the body's rhythms. This is a very easy-to-read account. Notes, bibliography. 224pp. Pyr 75

THOMMEN, GEORGE. **IS THIS YOUR DAY?**, $1.75. This was the first extensive exploration of biorhythms published in the U.S. and it remains the most popular one. General background and explanatory information is presented along with a history of the development of the biorhythm theory. Also included are complete directions for charting biorhythms and calculation tables up to 1984. Bibliography, 160+pp. Avo 73

WARD, RITCHIE. **THE LIVING CLOCKS**, $1.95. A well written study of biological clocks which link all living things with the rhythm of the earth, the moon, the sun, and the stars. Profusely illustrated and geared toward the general reader—and also a work of good scholarship. Notes, index. 368pp. NAL 71

WINKLESS, NELS and IBEN BROWNING. **CLIMATE AND THE AFFAIRS OF MEN**, c$8.95. The authors believe that they have discovered the common denominator of all cyclical epochal weather change. Climate is directly related to the amount of particulate matter (dust) in the atmosphere. The amount of that particulate matter is determined by how much has been spewed up through volcanic activity. Volcanic activity is a direct function of tidal forces pulling at the earth: the higher the pull, the greater the volcanic activity. By plotting the complex factors that go into tidal force, one can predict when earthquake and volcanic activity will be high and, therefore, when periods of severe weather change will occur. And when weather changes, the authors postulate, so do the affairs of men: migrations occur, war breaks out, crime goes up, civilizations rise and fall. This interesting thesis is well backed up with tables and graphs. Bibliography, 228pp. H&R 75

BODY MOVEMENT

ARICA INSTITUTE. **PSYCHOCALISTHENICS**, $3.95. Presents a sequence of well-tested exercises of the rapid and simultaneous development of mind, body and spirit. These exercises have been used and refined over the years by thousands of students in the Arica schools. S&S 76

BARTAL, LEA and NIRA NE'EMAN. **MOVEMENT, AWARENESS AND CREATIVITY**, $7.95. The authors are Israelis who have worked extensively with dancers, actors, drama students, and children. They learned that bodies can be trained to be more effective tools of expression by applying inner discipline, intelligence, and awareness, and that uninhibited use of the body can develop imagination and the creative potential of the individual. This book sets out their approach to movement. It is a complete teaching program, with chapter-by-chapter descriptions of their own techniques. The book should be useful to both professionals and everyone interested in the development of creativity and imagination through movement. Illustrated throughout with photographs and line drawings. 179pp. H&R 75

BROOKS, CHARLES. **SENSORY AWARENESS**, c$12.95. The term *sensory awareness* was first coined by Charlotte Selver as a name for the work she has been actively developing in the U.S. since 1938. Here Charles Brooks, her husband and collaborator, presents us with a written equivalent of her workshops and an understanding of her lifework—which is not a technique but a practice based on distinguishing what is natural from what is conditioned. The workshops themselves evolve around the close study of the simplest aspects of our functioning—sitting, standing, lying, breathing—and are concerned with breaking down the barriers that have come between our consciousness and the world around us, so that these barriers have a chance of dissolving, thus opening the way to a clear perception of ourselves as whole beings and to a more authentic sense of the nature of our experience. Many illustrations, 265pp. Vik 74

CHENG MAN-CH'ING and ROBERT W. SMITH. **TAI-CHI**, c$10.00. Professor Cheng is a true renowned master of tai chi, an ancient Taoist exercise stressing mind and body relaxation; Robert Smith was a student of Cheng for thirteen years and is an expert on the martial arts of the Orient. Designed to introduce tai chi for health, sport, and self defense, this book provides step-by-step directions in Cheng's thirty-seven solo exercise postures with 275 photographs (of Cheng and his associates) and 122 foot weighting diagrams, plus a fold-out diagram of postures. Also contains excellent chapters on Yang Cheng-Fu (Professor Cheng's teacher), tai chi history, and **Tai Chi Ch'uan Classics**. This book excellently communicates the philosophy inherent in the practice of this ancient Chinese art. Highly recommended. 112pp. Tut 66

DE SOLA, CARLA. **LEARNING THROUGH DANCE**, $7.95. *This book is written for ... teachers who want to explore with their students the depths of energy and communication, freedom and understanding, to be released in each one of us through the dance. This is for the teacher who senses, if only in a dim way, how fundamental dance is to the human spirit and who wants assistance for tapping this energy in order to help unify the bodies, minds, and spirits of her students.* The dances are organized according to themes and step-by-step directions are provided along with photographic illustrations of the movements. Oversize, 244pp. Pau 74

DOWNING, GEORGE. **THE MASSAGE BOOK**, $4.95. A large, illustrated presentation of Esalen message. *The core of massage lies in its unique way of communicating without words.... When receiving a good massage a person usually falls into a mental-physical state difficult to describe. It is like entering a special room until now locked and hidden away; a room the very existence of which is likely to be familiar only to those who practice some form of daily meditation.* Recommended. 184pp. RaH 72

_____. **MASSAGE AND MEDITATION**, $1.65. Downing's point of view is that massage and meditation are in key aspects very much alike. In his earlier book he spelled

out specific techniques for giving a massage. Here he gives a few general pointers and then quickly moves on to show how massage can have deeper possibilities as a gateway to non-verbal communication between partners and to one's own changing awareness of him/herself on a bodily level. Here he first describes a number of short meditative experiments which can be used before, during, or after a massage; he then includes a number of meditations which one can use to heighten his/her ability to receive a massage; and finally, he adds a number of meditations which partners can practice together. Illustrations, 85pp. RaH 74

FELDENKRAIS, MOSHE. **AWARENESS THROUGH MOVEMENT**, c$6.95. Dr. Feldenkrais teaches practical exercises for posture, eyes, and imagination to build better body habits and invoke new dimensions in awareness, self-image and human potential. His philosophy offers specific lessons for individual dynamic development by integrating physical and mental equipment and inducing a better human relationship with our physical environment. One of our most popular books. 171pp. H&R 72

_____. **BODY AND MATURE BEHAVIOR**, $3.45. An important, technical book, advancing the thesis that study and re-education of muscular behavior patterns are important in understanding and treating emotional problems. The whole self, diet, breathing, sex, muscular and postural habits must be tackled directly and concurrently with emotional re-education, he believes. 167pp. Int 49

FISHER, SEYMOUR. **BODY CONSCIOUSNESS**, $2.45. A scholarly account which probes the way we go about making psychological sense of our bodies. It provides insights into the role body feelings play in the development of our personalities, with numerous examples, and offfers practical suggestions. 176pp. PrH 73

GALLWEY, W. TIMOTHY. **THE INNER GAME OF TENNIS**, c$7.95. *It is the thesis of this book that neither mastery nor satisfaction can be found in the playing of any game without giving some attention to the ... skills of the inner game.... The player of the inner game comes to value the art of relaxed concentration above all other skills.... He aims at the kind of spontaneous performance which occurs only when the mind is calm and seems at one with the body, which finds its own surprising ways to surpass its own limits again and again. Moreover, while overcoming the common hang-ups of competition, the player of the inner game uncovers a will to win which unlocks all his energy and which is never discouraged by losing.... All that is needed is to un learn those habits which interfere ... and then to just let it happen. To explore the limitless potential within the human body is the quest of the Inner Game; in this book it will be explored through the medium of tennis.*—from the introduction. Gallwey has taught the techniques and ideas he describes in this book and the response has been overwhelmingly good. It's a very popular book and people who buy it often come back for additional copies to give to friends. We haven't read all of it, but as tennis aficionados, what we have read sounds like excellent advice both from a spiritual and technical viewpoint. Oversize, 141pp. RaH 74

_____. **INNER TENNIS**, c$8.95. Inner tennis is based on the concept that the key to winning tennis lies in every player's head—in his or her ability to concentrate, to trust his/her body to do what comes naturally, and to let the game just happen. In this book Gallwey presents tested exercises and techniques which are designed to help a player increase awareness of the body, concentrate on muscles, physical reactions, and to improve the relationship to ball and racket, and much else. 192pp. RaH 76

GEBA, BRUNO HANS. **BREATHE AWAY YOUR TENSIONS: AN INTRODUCTION TO GESTALT BODY AWARENESS THERAPY**, $3.95. *Geba Therapy is a method to help you bring your body and your awareness back together.... Through this book you can learn how to have Gestalt Body-Awareness and how to integrate this new lifestyle awareness into everyday living.... The book is divided into five weeks. During each weekly session you will be introduced to a new routine. Although the book presents the routines over a five-week time period, your individual progress may vary.... The only true criterion ... is your own experience.* A large, illustrated manual. 188pp. RaH 73

GLUCK, JAY. **ZEN COMBAT**, $1.25. This is a general book for the beginning student which reviews many of the Japanese arts including karate, aikido, kendo, kongo and jitte, and kyudo. It is illustrated with many small drawings. The most interesting part of the book is the anecdotes about the arts and the masters who developed them. The latter material forms the major part of the book. Bibliography, 218pp. RaH 62

GUNTHER, BERNARD. **SENSE RELAXATION—BELOW YOUR MIND**, $4.95. Techniques developed and used at Esalen which enable you to turn on to your senses—to enhance direct sensory reality in the here and now. These are joyful experiences to have alone, with a lover, or with a group. Beautiful photographs, 191pp. McM 68

HAINES, BRUCE. **KARATE'S HISTORY AND TRADITIONS**, c$4.95. In this reference book, written expressly to counteract the Western trend toward misinformation about Asian martial arts, Haines offers the benefits of his thorough knowledge of Asian history, the origin of karate, and its close connection with Zen Buddhism. 192pp. Tut 68

HOWARD, BLANCHE. **DANCE OF THE SELF**, c$8.95. **Dance of the Self** is the only book we know of that expresses the heart of modern dance—and yet is geared to the nonprofessional. It opens by reawakening the senses to the concept of man as a primal being composed of earth, fire, water, and air, and it reorients the body in space as a completely interrelated network of energy lines and centers of force. This awareness of the body provides the groundwork for the experience of natural, rhythmic movement. Preliminary exercises concentrate on specific muscle toning and body strengthening, with breathing exercises, stretches, etc., and the fifty-three lesson plans that follow integrate these in harmonious, unrestricted expressions. Many line drawings illustrate the text. Oversize, 157pp. S&S 74

HUANG, AL CHUNG-LIANG. **EMBRACE THE TIGER, RETURN TO MOUNTAIN—THE ESSENCE OF T'AI CHI**, $3.50. *Huang teaches in a way that is unusual for an Asian master and . . . for Western masters as well. He begins from the center and not from the fringe. He imparts an understanding of the basic principles of the art before going on to the meticulous details, and he refuses to break down T'ai Chi movements into a 1-2-3 drill so as to make the student into a robot.*—from the foreward by Alan Watts. Huang teaches at Esalen. Many illustrations RPP 73

HUANG, WEN-SHAN. **FUNDAMENTALS OF TAI CHI CH'UAN**, $12.00. This is essential reading for serious students of tai chi ch'uan. It includes translations of some of the most important classics and is subtitled *An Exposition of its History, Philosophy, Technique, Practice and Application.* Professor Huang is a well known sociologist and has taught at universities in China and the U.S. for many years. The principles of both Chinese philosophy and oriental medicine are incorporated into the text. There is also a section devoted to technical directions for the postures, with photographic illustrations. A fine work in every sense, and a welcome addition to the small number of truly excellent works on the internal arts. Bibliography, index. 569pp. SSk 73

JOHNSON, LELAND. **BIOENERGETICS**, $3.00. *This monograph has been vibrating in our experience for the past several years as we [in the Houston Center for Human Potential] have worked with each other and ourselves in our own growth and expansion. . . . We have drawn on techniques, modes and methods from a variety of sources as we continue to explore what we can become.* The first pages explore energy, both in terms of flow and blockages and include many illustrations and quotations. The rest of the book details specific exercises to increase body awareness and is illustrated with photographs. Oversize, bibliography. 32pp. Esp 74

JONES, FRANK. **BODY AWARENESS IN ACTION: A STUDY IN THE ALEXANDER TECHNIQUE**, c$9.95. A vivid introduction to Alexander and his teaching which draws on Alexander's own writings and on the author's own long association with Alexander and with his brother. Jones supplements the Alexanders' findings with his own carefully designed research at Tufts University Institute of Experimental Psychology. He measured bodily movement in action and thereby provided scientific proof for the discoveries of Alexander. Notes, index. 224pp. ScB 76

KAUZ, HERMAN. **TAI CHI HANDBOOK**, $3.95. Kauz, a former student of Cheng Men-Ching, has spent most of his life studying the martial arts of the East. With the exception of Professor Cheng's definitive book on tai chi ch'uan, this is considered by experts to be the best exercise manual. The postures are explained and demonstrated in large clear photographs; and material is included on tai chi as a meditational technique. Includes a section of continuous sequence photographs. Tai chi cannot easily be learned from a book, but the material presented here can be a good introduction for the interested beginner and a good review of techniques and philosophy for the student. 183pp. Dou 74

KIPNIS, CLAUDE. **THE MIME BOOK**, c$12.50/$6.95. Claude Kipnis has been performing and teaching mime all over the world since 1960. Presently he heads the mime section of the American Academy for Dramatic Arts in New York. This is a very functional book, specifically concerned with the mechanisms and techniques of mime. The exercises and background material presented here can be very useful to all interested in body work. The illustrations are excellent and the material is clearly written. The edge of this oversize book is constructed like a flip-book, so that as you flip its pages, you will see a series of exercises performed. Kipnis defines mime as *the art of recreating the world by moving and positioning the human body* and says that *left to himself, with nothing and nobody around him, the mime acts in such a way that his audience not only understands but actually sees the world of objects and beings created before him.* This is an excellent presentation, and a beautiful artistic creation. Oversize, glossary. 226pp. H&R 74

LANGERWERFF, ELLEN and KAREN PERLOTH. **MENSENDIECK—YOUR POSTURE AND YOUR PAINS**, c$7.95. Dr. Mensendieck was a sculptor who became a physician in order to find out exactly what man would have to do to sculpt his own body into a sculpture he could be proud of and that would serve him well. During many years of research she analyzed in detail the individual functions of every bone, joint, and muscle as well as their intricate interactions. She became convinced that the primary exercise any one need is the maintenance of correct posture during normal daily activities. She designed numerous techniques, many of which are illustrated and explained here. The authors are trained practitioners of her method. 236pp. Dou 73

LEONARD, GEORGE. **THE ULTIMATE ATHLETE**, c$8.95. *The athlete that dwells in each of us is more than an abstract ideal. It is a living presence that can change the way we feel and live. Searching for our inner athlete may lead us into sports and regular exercise and thus to the health promised by physical fitness organizations—and that might be justification enough. But what I have in mind goes beyond fitness. It involves entering the realm of music and poetry, of the turning of the planets, of the understanding of death.* Leonard explores all aspects of games and sports—mythology, history, and evolution—as he delves into the true meaning (as he sees it) of athletics: the potentialities of the human body to transcend itself in reaching for the goal of the spirit. Along the way he describes some new games, designed to develop the energy body. An unusual account. Index, 283pp. Vik 75

LIU, DA. **TAOIST HEALTH EXERCISE BOOK**, $3.95. See the Oriental Medicine section.

LU KUAN YU (CHARLES LUK). **THE SECRETS OF CHINESE MEDITATION**, $3.95. See the Meditation section.

_____. **TAOIST YOGA**, $2.95. See the Chinese Philosophy section.

MAISEL, EDWARD, ed. **THE RESURRECTION OF THE BODY: THE WRITINGS OF F. MATTHIAS ALEXANDER**, c$5.95. This is the most comprehensive edition available of Alexander's writings. In the early twentieth century Alexander developed a practical technique for restoring the body to its optimum functioning as a means toward better health, greater awareness, and freedom from habit. Alexander's students included Bernard Shaw, John Dewey, and Aldous Huxley. Notes on the technique are included along with a variety of case studies. The editor provides an excellent long introduction. Notes, 252pp. UnB 69

MILLER, ROBERTA. **PSYCHIC MASSAGE**, $3.95. *This book describes a method of healing. It evolved from massage, yet it is more than massage. The addition of psychic awareness makes it possible to heal or balance a person's mind and emotions through his body. Psychic massage cannot be learned by reading. It can only be learned by doing—very much like playing a musical instrument. Therefore, this book is organized in a how to format, so that those who wish may try out the techniques. The primary purpose, however, is to inform rather than to instruct—to present the possibilities and potentialities of a new approach to personal growth.* Oversize, illustrated. 213pp. H&R 75

MOREHOUSE, LAURENCE and LEONARD GROSS. **TOTAL FITNESS IN THIRTY MINUTES A WEEK**, $2.95. Dr. Morehouse is a seminal figure in the world of physiology and exercise. He is the author of the standard text on the subject and he is the founding director of the Human Performance Laboratory at UCLA. This book presents his revolutionary techniques to the general public for the first time. The hardcover edition of the book was a best seller and the book is well regarded in all quarters. At the heart of Dr. Morehouse's fitness plan is the concept of effortless exercise which can be incorporated into an individual's daily schedule. The book itself is clearly written and is illustrated with many case studies. 220pp. S&S 75

MORRIS, MARGARET. **CREATION IN DANCE AND LIFE**, c$7.35. As a pioneer of modern dance techniques Margaret Morris is comparable to Isadora Duncan and Martha Graham. In this book she describes, with many diagrams and photographs, her choreographical and teaching methods as well as many ways of group improvisation. Ms. Morris is also a trained physiotherapist and has taught eurhythmics and dance movement to the physically handicapped. This volume also includes her therapeutic techniques for the aged and disabled. 125pp. Owe 72

MUSASHI, MIYAMOTO. **A BOOK OF FIVE RINGS**, $8.95. Born in 1584, Musashi was one of Japan's most renowned warriors. He was a samurai and, by the age of thirty, had fought and won more than sixty contests by killing all of his opponents. Satisfied that he was invincible, Musashi then turned to formulating his philosophy of *the Way of the sword.* This might sound like a strange area to cover in a spiritual book catalog, however, in addition to being the premier book on kendo, **A Book of Five Rings** is also one of the most perceptive psychological guides to strategy ever written, and the philosophy behind it—influenced by Zen, Shinto, and Confucianism—can be applied to many areas of life. This is an extraordinary book which gives the reader a good idea of the philosophy which influenced and guided the Japanese civilization for centuries and in which one can often find striking parallels with contemporary Western civilization. This is the first time this classic has appeared in the West, and the book includes many beautiful illustrations. 96pp. OvP 74

NAGAI, HARUKA. **MAKKO-HO: FIVE MINUTES PHYSICAL FITNESS**, $5.95. Presents a complete system of simple exercises which, when practiced over a long period of time, restore and retain physical fitness. The exercises are well illustrated and are quite different from traditional yogic practices. They have been successfully used in Japan for many years. The directions are detailed but quite clear. Practiced correctly, the system does take only five minutes. 83pp. Jap 72

NITOBE, INAZO. **BUSHIDO: THE SOUL OF JAPAN**, c$4.95. This neat little volume offers a thoughtful view of the ways and traditions of the Japanese samurai and the intrinsic relationship between the martial virtues of Bushido (*precepts of knighthood*) and the soul of Japan. 203pp. Tut 69

OESTERLEY, W.O.E. **THE SACRED DANCE**, $5.40. *Our study is concerned with the sacred dance.... Its extreme importance in the eyes of early man, who regarded it as indispensable at all the crises of life—initiation, puberty, marriage, burial—who used it as one of the essentials in worship, who saw in it a means of propitiating whatever supernatural powers he believed in, a means of communion with the deity, a means of obtaining good crops, fruitful marriages, and of communicating with the departed—to mention only its more important uses, shows that it is a subject worth investigating.—from the introduction. Index, 234pp. DaH 23

ROHE, FRED. **THE ZEN OF RUNNING**, $3.95. A beautiful photographic study on the joy of running, with poetic hints on what to do and how to be—but always understated and emphasizing the individuality of each being on this planet. What running means to Rohe is clearly stated and what it can mean to anyone else is discussed. Oversize. RaH 75

RUSH, ANNE KENT. **GETTING CLEAR: BODY WORK FOR WOMEN**, $5.95. See the Women section.

SCOTT, BYRON. **HOW THE BODY FEELS**, $2.95. The most useful feature of this book on massage is the collection of anatomical line drawings of all parts of the body. All the basic information on massage is here, including general instructions and directions on massaging specific body areas. The step-by-step instructions are illustrated with photographs of actual massage and the presentation, while not the best we've read, is adequate. 159pp. RaH 73

SHIODA, GOZO. **DYNAMIC AIKIDO**, c$7.95. Shioda is the chief instructor of the Yoshinka Aikido Dojo. Here he presents the history, basic movements, and fundamental techniques of theoretical and applied aikido. 500 photographs and line drawings. 160pp. H&R 68

SIOU, LILY. **CH'I KUNG: THE ART OF MASTERING THE UNSEEN LIFE FORCE**, c$14.50. While ch'i kung is the oldest of the Chinese martial arts, it is not widely practiced today. Ch'i kung calls upon the ch'i or universal life energy that every person possesses. It directs this energy, stimulates, controls it. In doing so an inner balance is achieved. Primary catalysts of ch'i kung are slow, disciplined breathing and a series of carefully prescribed movements. Together these set the unseen ch'i force into motion causing it to travel throughout the body providing rejuvenation and relaxation along with spiritual and self-awareness. Lily Siou is a master of ch'i kung and here she gives us a detailed presentation of the philosophy along with step-by-step photographic illustrations of the postures and movements. Oversize, 174pp. Tut 76

SMITH, ROBERT W. **CHINESE BOXING—MASTERS AND METHODS**, c$8.95. This is a revealing study of the men and methods Smith encountered in his study and practice of Chinese boxing. He explores the individual techniques of various masters and in the process describes various types of boxing. Among the men discussed are Hung I-Hsiang, Liao Wu-Ch'ang, and Cheng Man-Ch'ing. Includes many illustrations and a glossary, notes and bibliography. 141pp. Kod 74

_____. **HSING-I**, c$8.95. Hsing-i is one of the three ancient Chinese internal boxing arts, the other two being tai chi and pa-kua. Like the other two arts, it is essentially moving meditation. Here, for the first time in any Western language, every step is described in detail and fully illustrated with photographs of hsing-i masters. Smith himself is a well known teacher of the internal arts and he has studied with the leading masters throughout the world. He also includes the advice of masters from hsing-i's three centuries of scantily recorded history. 112pp. Kod 74

_____. **PA-KUA: CHINESE BOXING FOR FITNESS AND SELF-DEFENSE**, c$8.95. This is the first book on pa-kua in other than the Chinese language. It offers a complete introduction to the essence of pa-kua circling movements and to the benefits of disciplined study and practice. Using over 400 photographs (many of which show Kuo-Feng-Ch'ih, Smith's teacher in Taiwan) plus many diagrams, Smith demonstrates the flexibility of the self defense aspects; the accompanying text provides detailed instructions and enlightening insights into the spiritual qualities of this ancient Chinese art. 160pp. H&R 67

_____, ed. **SECRETS OF SHAOLIN TEMPLE BOXING**, c$5.95. Shaolin temple boxing is the father of all Chinese boxing forms and the close ancestor of Okinawan and Japanese karate. This is an English presentation of an anonymous Chinese work that Smith found during his study in Taiwan and which he feels presents the fundamental core of Shaolin. It is essential reading for those interested in these arts. 71pp. Tut 64

SO, DOSHIN. **SHORINJI KEMPO**, c$19.50. Shorinji kempo is a martial art developed simultaneously with seated Zen meditation by the monks at the temple Shorinji in China in the sixth century. It was taught only to Buddhist priests until recently. Though deeply imbued with the theory of calm in action Shorinji thought maintains that neither of these aspects of the whole can exist independently. This definitive study is written by the present head of the Shorinji and is a thorough introduction which combines detailed photographic explanations of all basic techniques with some of the profound philosophical truths of Shorinji thought. 8½x11", over 1000 illustrations. 256pp. Jap 70

_____. **WHAT IS SHORINJI KEMPO**, $3.25. This is an abridged edition of the **Shorinji Kempo**, greatly reduced in size. Many of the techniques are not included and the pictures, being smaller, are much harder to follow. The philosophical explanations are not abridged though. 128pp. Jap 70

SOLLIER, A. and Z. GYORBIRO. **JAPANESE ARCHERY: ZEN IN ACTION**, c$7.50. See the Zen sub-section of Buddhism.

SPINO, MIKE. **BEYOND JOGGING: THE INNERSPACES OF RUNNING**, $3.95. Mike Spino, physical fitness counselor and director of the Esalen Sports Center in San Francisco, presents individual training programs in this book along with information on his techniques and case studies. *After Mike Spino, running will never be the same. Renouncing the monotonous jog at a single tempo. Spino introduces his students to an imaginative variety of tempos, styles, and visualization techniques that can make running a carnival of delights. His suggestions, ranging from meditation and energy awareness to the methods of Olympic coaches, can benefit beginners and skilled runners alike.*—George Leonard. Illustrations, bibliography. 111pp. CeA 76

SWEIGARD, LULU. **HUMAN MOVEMENT POTENTIAL**, c$13.35. *How does movement proceed, and how can it be performed with greater efficiency? In striving to answer these questions, this book focuses on the interdependence of postural-alignment and the performance of movement. It provides an educational method which stresses the inherent capacity of the nervous system to determine the most efficient neuromuscular coordination for each movement. Through this book, I hope to offer my method of teaching body balance and efficient movement—which has been developed during many years of research and teaching.* This is an incredibly detailed study. Each part of the body is discussed in its own chapter and various specific exercises are offered. The whole work is clearly written and well illustrated. Many anatomical drawings are included. Bibliography, index. H&R 74

TANAKA, MINORU, tr. **BUSHIDO: WAY OF THE SAMURAI**, $3.50. This is the first English translation of a Japanese classic, **Hagakure**, which discusses the philosophy of the samurai. The text is made up of a number of short illustrative stories and aphorisms. 85pp. Sun 75

TOHEI, KOICHI. **AIKIDO IN DAILY LIFE**, $5.25. This is our most popular book on aikido, the art that stresses the necessity of mastering one's own spirit. Aikido is in strict accord with the laws of nature and offers the opportunity for mental and physical growth. In the first section, Tohei teaches how to breathe properly and how to concentrate one's spirit; while in the second part he shows the application of aikido to daily living. 48 illustrations, 220pp. Jap 66

_____. **THE BOOK OF KI**, $5.95. Tohei presents the philosophical framework and specific disciplines by which an individual can attune him or herself with the ki, or universal life energy. This book has been long awaited by those who have followed Tohei's work and have read his books on aikido. Oversize, 150 illustrations, index. 128pp. Jap 76

_____. **THIS IS AIKIDO**, c$15.50. This is the definitive text on aikido as a spiritual discipline and Tohei's first book. The first part discusses the psychology of aikido in detail and includes a glossary. The second and largest section is devoted to techniques, all of which are illustrated with step-by-step photographs laid out in the circular format in which an aikido practitioner moves. The descriptive material is clear and excellent and the illustrations are very well done. Recommended. 8½x12", over 1000 illustrations. 180pp. Jap 68

_____. **WHAT IS AIKIDO?** $3.25. This text was prepared under the supervision of the originator of aikido, Professor Uyeshiba. *The purpose of Aikido lies not in trying to make people strong in the arts of self-defense, but in helping them learn the eternal paths that form the basis of Aikido and manifest themselves in its practice.* This is an authoritative manual, emphasizing aikido's fundamental spirit. 70 photographs, many line drawings. 118pp. Jap 62

URBAN, PETER. **THE KARATE DOJO: TRADITIONS AND TALES OF A MARTIAL ART**, c$5.95. Discusses in detail the dojo, or school, where karate is taught, with vivid stories from karate's rich history. Tut 67

UYESHIBA, KISSHIMARU. **AIKIDO**, c$12.95. This is a combined edited version of two earlier Japanese works by aikido master Morihei Uyeshiba's only son, Kisshimaru, now Director of Aikido International. Well illustrated, covering technique and the development of aikido by Uyeshiba, this book presents the master's life experience and as such is essential reading for all aikido and martial arts aficionados. 190pp. Jap 70

WEISS, PAUL. **SPORT: A PHILOSOPHICAL INQUIRY**, $2.95. *The present study makes but a beginning in a new enterprise, the examination of sport in terms of principles which are at once revelatory of the nature of sport and pertinent to other fields—indeed, to the whole of things and knowledge.*—from the preface. This is an interesting inquiry which covers a broad spectrum of sports-related ideas and activities. Bibliography, index. 283pp. SIU 69

WESTBROOK, A. and O. RATTI. **AIKIDO AND THE DYNAMIC SPHERE**, c$12.75. This is an excellent full scale treatment of the art of aikido, in which its goal of neutralizing aggression is pursued through over 1200 illustrations and thirty-three charts and tables. 375pp. Tut 70

BUDDHISM

Like all other great religious movements, Buddhism has experienced its schisms, internal debates, and permutations (there are more than twenty separate schools of Buddhist teaching). Buddhism cannot be discussed as though it were a simple, consistent movement. . . . Buddhism has always evolved as a local phenomenon in countries and regions that knew nothing of sophisticated technological transportation and communication. Thus, for instance, after the death of a Buddhist teacher, the village in which he taught might continue his practices for years, while the disciples who had actually received the Master's transmission had left for far-off places. Centuries later, another enlightened teacher might arrive at the same village and condemn the degenerated practices there but employ a few of the old forms, adapting them to his newer communication. And so on. In light of this, all general statements about Buddhism have to be understood not as a way of absolutely categorizing every single Buddhist, but as a way of characterizing certain general movements in Buddhist history.

The various schools of Buddhism prescribe different forms of practice and stress different doctrinal points, and some even strongly criticize other Buddhist schools. Enlightenment is characterized in widely varying terms, and the enlightened man of the various traditions possesses a wide range of contrasting qualities. Nevertheless, fundamental to Buddhism itself is a characteristic orientation. If love is the cornerstone of the Christian gospels, and absorption in the Divine is the characteristic theme of Hinduism, the basic thrust of Buddhism is intuitive insight into one's own nature.

The orthodox historian might point out that Zen and Tantra are both aspects or at most elaborations of the inclusive Mahayana tradition. That is true enough, but that information is not particularly central to someone primarily interested in seeing the inner dimensions and dynamics that are the core of practice. . . . The Mahayana sutras represent a spiritual orientation that is characteristically distinct from both Tantra and Zen, each of which exemplify particular forms of spiritual practice that are in no way identical to each other.

At the beginning of any survey of Buddhism must be Gautama Shakyamuni, the *original Buddha*. He lived about 500 B.C., and the accounts of his life are so intermingled with legends about him that it is almost pointless to speculate about his personal example. The oldest teachings attributed to him are in Pali, a now-obsolete language very similar to Sanskrit. This Pali Canon forms the central scripture of the Theravadin (Teaching of the Elders) tradition, the only remaining school of Hinayana, a pejorative name meaning *Lesser Vehicle* and applied by Mahayanists. This tradition emphasizes the monastic *sangha*, or community, the attainment of personal liberation, and a generally conservative, literal interpretation of the Pali texts, most of which enumerate rules of conduct and spiritual practice.

When we hear about this tradition in the West, it is usually only briefly referred to and dismissed as something of an anachronism, long-debunked and now surviving only on the strength of its own stubbornness. But in fact there is a health Theravadin tradition, even though the Theravadins themselves do little to dispute their negative reputation. One must understand, theirs is a uniquely uncritical tradition. Primary attention is given to the importance of practice, the study of the basic teaching, and the attainment of liberation. There are exceptions to this—extraordinary or eccentric individuals supply exceptions to nearly any general statement. But it is fair to say that the overall mood of Theravada is austere, doctrinally simple, independent, and nonmystical, even mortal. Nirvana is rarely described in positive terms. Rather, it is the quenching of desire, the end to suffering. As a rule, this tradition is more concerned to identify and eliminate the binding influences in life than it is to indicate an ideal consciousness to which one should aspire. In other words, it is generally a *negative* path. Theravadins employ intense techniques of comprehensive self-inspection and other behavioral and meditative disiplines, all intended to bring about the elimination of desire and the sense of self.

Although the ancient Pali writings are relatively simple and basic, the Theravadins have clarified their teachings over the centuries, coming to emphasize

Vipassana—insight meditation. This is a practice of intelligence, in which the meditator recognizes the nature of karmic existence and thus enjoys a kind of freedom from its limiting force. Theravada emphasizes wakefulness, observation, and a loving, unruffled outlook on the world. All these practices relate primarily to life, to bodily and mental areas of perception, cognition, and impulse. There is very little mysticism in this path, very little orientation to higher, subtle, or visionary forms of realization. The Hinayana path is concerned with attaining a freedom from suffering in this life, in this world. It doesn't engage in making doctrinal distinctions.

The enlightened man of Theravada is called an *Arhat*, and he seeks and enjoys his own nirvana, primarily on the basis of his own efforts. The principal and necessary goal here is personal liberation; service to others may or may not follow. In any case, everything depends upon that realization. In ancient and modern times, this form of practice was criticized by Mahayanists for being private, selfish, and exclusive, devoted only to personal nirvana. The Mahayanists offered a contrasting ideal: the compassionate Bodhisattva. Arguing that the emphasis on personal liberation reinforced dualistic distinctions between self and others, and also between enlightenment and the ordinary world, the Mahayanists rejected the Arhat ideal. The Bodhisattva cannot separate his personal spiritual life from that of others. He vows not to enter into nirvana until all sentient beings can join him.

Where Theravada is spare, direct, negative in approach, and primarily interested in practice, the Buddhism of the Mahayana scriptures is flowery, doctrinally complex, and full of positive, even emotional excitement about the moment of enlightenment. Mahayana can be seen as in some ways a primarily exoteric reaction to the extreme esotericism or inwardness of Theravada. The Mahayanists idealized compassion, involved themselves in complex doctrinal distinctions, and spoke in the most elaborate terms of subtle Buddha-realms, visionary beings, and miracles. Highly critical of the emphasis on personal release which they identify with Hinayana, the Mahayana texts emphasize instead an enlightenment which is always turned outward to *all beings* rather than inward to *me*.

Mahayana thrived in India, and its literature and art reflect the characteristically Indian life of the *higher mind*—the superconscious, mystical, and visionary possibilities which flourish in Hinduism. These possibilities are not presented in Mahayana literature as the goal or ideal of spiritual endeavor, but they are seen as a perfectly natural aspect of things. Thus, subtle worlds are a very fine place for Buddhas and ascended Bodhisattvas to have long and interesting conversations, usually in verse. This broad spiritual ecology was not merely a playground for the imagination. The physically-embodied practitioner is a part of their same world, and the ascended ones may actually participate in his awakening to consciousness. So the emphasis on self-effort that we find in the Theravada tradition is somewhat mitigated in Mahayana. We find Mahayana schools as simple as the *Pure Land* faith school in which devotees simply recite the name of Amitabha Buddha in order to receive his saving grace.

But there were other schools, too, most of them a great deal more doctrinally complex and more involved in mental discrimination than in esoteric practice. Sutras recording conversations between disembodied deities often contain some of the most elaborate systems of doctrinal distinction in Eastern religion. The great North Indian Buddhist University of Nalanda came to stress scholarship and academic knowledge as the groundwork for intuitive insight in meditation. The complex dialectic of Nagarjuna, the founder of the non-dualistic Madhyamika school, and the elaborate psychological systematizing of the Yogachara school contrast dramatically with the simplicity of the Pali Canon. Paradoxically, all of this intellection brings the Mahayanists to the conclusion that enlightenment is not somewhere else, not at the end of an elaborate argumentation, nor even the result of superconscious experiences. To the Mahayanist, *nirvana and samsara are the same*.

In Tantra . . . the elaborate forms of Mahayana become grounds for esoteric spiritual practices which are equally elaborate. Buddhist Tantra developed most significantly in Tibet, which lay on trade routes between North India and China. Tantra has two main thrusts: transforming yoga and conscious insight. Many Tantric practices involve manipulating one's internal energies and ultimately developing expert control over them. Here we have the complex systems of deities and elaborate living relationships between them and the Buddhist practitioner. He invokes them, visualizes them, receives their grace, and uses their power as a tool of his own spiritual development. The native magical and animistic Tibetan Bon religion and Hindu Kundalini yoga both influenced Tibetan Buddhist yoga, but these forms are described by the Tibetan Buddhist as tools of an enlightenment which is ultimately a matter of insight, not control of internal energies.

So, in Tantric or Vajrayana Buddhism, the most inclusive *yana* according to the Tibetans, yoga harmonizes and integrates the individual, also developing his sensitivity to and responsibility for the internal processes which sustain his physical, mental, and psychic existence. At the same time, the radical intelligence represented by the profound *Mahamudra* teachings brings him into a position of humor and freedom from all these practices. Mahamudra manifests when all techniques and methods of attainment have relaxed in perfect emptiness, *shunyata*.

Despite the wealth of spiritual techniques, the notion of independent, individual attainment is not only de-emphasized in Tantra—it is heretical. Naropa, Marpa, Milarepa, and the other great spiritual figures of Tibet all underwent their spiritual development through the agency of a Guru, a man who represented the enlightened condition to them, transmitting it directly through their relationship. This became an essential aspect of Tantric practice.

At the same time that Tantra was developing most in Tibet, an entirely different form of Buddhism was developing in China and later in Japan. Here, the elaborate images and doctrinal distinctions of Mahayana fell away, and Ch'an or Zen emerged. Comparatively austere, Zen teaches through paradoxes instead of lengthy discussions; it is as profound as the Tibetan tradition, and as thoroughly grounded in practice, but comparatively elusive and enigmatic. Here life is described directly. *Ch'an* is the Chinese equivalent of the Sanskrit *dhyana*, or meditation, and *Zen* comes from the Japanese *zazen*, to sit in meditation. The emphasis in the written teaching is upon direct intuitive penetration of all conventions.

Like Theravadins, the Zen monks simply sit, wakeful to whatever arises, perhaps paying attention to breath or working with *koans* (mental riddles designed to frustrate the mind to the point of conscious awakening). Both schools seem simple, direct, and austere. And both have been described as negative paths. But there the resemblance ends. Zen literature is highly critical of less direct forms of practice, and compassion is emphasized in Zen as much as it is Mahayana and Tantra. The Zen description of satori or enlightenment is not really negative. Zen offers an inclusive vision of the world as illumined and transformed. The literature speaks in delighted, almost surprised terms about the simple things of the natural world. To the Zen man, all of it, presently, is nothing but Bodhi (the enlightened Mind).

As in Tantra, the fundamental means of instruction is the relationship to the enlightened Master, the *transmission of Mind* described by Huang Po and other Ch'an or Zen masters was a direct communication which could not be contained in words or images, but which was an actual transmission from the Master to his disciple. The means are characteristically paradoxical—the *koan* riddles, or *just sitting*. Such paradoxes are also used in Tantra to some extent, but nowhere are they so central to practice, so pervasive as in Zen.

In spite of their differing characters, these four forms of Buddhism do form a kind of unity. The essential statement of the Buddha is reflected in each of them: Life as conventionally lived is suffering and un-True; there is a way to end suffering and limited existence; in the extinguishing of desire and the knowledge of one's own real nature there is freedom. And they all agree that enlightenment, nirvana, is the real, original, and ultimate condition of all sentient beings.

—from **THE LAUGHING MAN MAGAZINE** by Crane Montano, Saniel Bonder, and Terence Patten, eds.

❖

ANONYMOUS. **THE WAY OF THE BUDDHA**, c$9.00. This oversize volume was issued by the Indian government to commemorate the 2500th anniversary of the Buddha's death Following an introduction by Gandhi, the album is divided into seven sections covering: the background against which the Buddha's life and teachings have to be viewed; his life, his mission; how Buddhism spread in India; in Asia; the Buddhist pantheon; and how the principles of his teachings have permeated Indian life and thought. Each section begins with Sanskrit and Pali quotations, has English translations, and is profusely illustrated in black-and-white and color with the best specimens of art from different countries. 330pp. PuD nd

ARNOLD, SIR EDWIN. **THE LIGHT OF ASIA**, $1.25. Sir Edwin Arnold has rendered in exquisite poetic form the story of the Buddha's search, enlightenment, and teaching. First published in 1879, the book has become a classic. 154pp. TPH 69

ASVAGHOSA

Asvaghosa was the first expounder of Mahayana Buddhism. Very little is known of his life, and the exact date of his birth is unknown. He is thought to have lived in the first century AD. He was brought up as a Brahman and converted to Buddhism late in life. Asvaghosa was a poet and a musician as well as a philosophical mystic, and he composed the words and music of many hymns used in Buddhist monasteries. The most celebrated work attributed to him is the **Mahayana Shraddotpada**, or **The Awakening of Faith in the Mahayana**.

BEAL, SAMUEL, tr. **THE FO-SHO-HING-TSAN-KING: A LIFE OF THE BUDDHA**, c$7.50. A translation, from the Sacred Books of the East series, of an important early source document, attributed to Asvaghosa, translated from Sanskrit into Chinese in 420 AD. Introduction and many notes. For the serious scholar. 417pp. MoB 1883

HAKEDA, YOSHITO, tr. **THE AWAKENING OF FAITH**, $2.95. A translation from Columbia University's Oriental Classics. Prof. Hakeda has supplied words which were only implied in the original and has also drawn upon the commentaries of ancient scholars, notably that of Fa-tsang. Includes extensive notes, a long valuable introduction, and annotated bibliography. 182pp. Col 67

JOHNSTON, E.H., tr. **THE BUDDHACARITA OR ACTS OF THE BUDDHA**, c$11.80. This work celebrates the life and teachings of the Buddha. Included here is a translation and the Sanskrit text as well as a profusion of notes and 98pp of introductory material. Index, 515pp. MoB 36

_____. **THE SAUNDARANANDA OF ASVAGHOSA**, c$11.80. This book celebrates the conversion of Nanda, half-brother of Gautama the Buddha, to Buddhism. It is written in verse. This edition includes the Sanskrit text, with an English translation, notes, introductory material, commentary, glossary, and index. 294pp. MoB 28

RICHARD, TIMOTHY, tr. **THE AWAKENING OF FAITH**, c$5.90. A profound and beautiful work which formulates the fundamental doctrines of the Mahayana school of Buddhism. It is considered one of the five most valuable Buddhist scriptures, occupying a place not dissimilar to the New Testament. This is a very readable translation and includes a long, excellent introduction. 96pp. Ski 60

SHRINE OF WISDOM EDITORS, trs. **THE AWAKENING OF FAITH IN THE MAHAYANA**, c$2.65. A nicely written, flowing translation. Introduction includes biographical material on Asvaghosa, as well as a discussion of Mahayana Buddhism, nirvana, and adoration. 59pp. ShW 64

AUNG, MAUNG, tr. **BURMESE MONK'S TALES**, c$14.00. The Monk's Tales were collected in the nineteenth century as part of the general effort to strengthen the national religion and the Burmese way of life under British rule. They were told by the Thingazar Sayadaw, one of the great monks of the era. These tales were modeled on the traditional Burmese folk tale and they dealt with the current problems and difficulties of the clergy and laity. The Thingazar Sayadaw usually introduced his tales into his short, informal addresses, inventing the tale on the spot to illustrate a point or give advice. Other monks soon began to tell similar tales of their own. A sampling of these is given here, following the fifty-seven tales and two groups of anecdotes and dialogues attributed to the Thingazar. Aung provides an abundance of introductory and background information. Bibliography, 181pp. Col 66

BAHM, A.J. PHILOSOPHY OF THE BUDDHA, $2.75. A basic introduction to Buddhist thought for the general reader. Bibliography. 166pp. Put 58

BARY, WILLIAM de. THE BUDDHIST TRADITION IN INDIA, CHINA, AND JAPAN, $2.45. An anthology, compiled from basic Buddhist writings, covering central doctrines and practices and including introductions and commentary on each selection. Bibliography, 401pp. RaH 69

BERRY, THOMAS. BUDDHISM, $2.95. A comprehensive survey of Buddhism aimed at the general reader. It begins with a review of the life of the Buddha, Buddhist doctrine and scriptures and the schisms. This is followed by an exposition of the changes that Buddhism underwent during its evolution and the schools and scriptures that developed. The book ends with explorations of Buddhism in Asia and Buddhism and the West. An adequate treatment, but not inspired. Bibliography, 188pp. Cro 67

BEYER, STEPHEN. THE BUDDHIST EXPERIENCE, $8.00. This is an excellent anthology of Buddhist writings by a young scholar. Many of the pieces presented here have never been translated and most of the others are only available in archaic editions. All aspects of the Buddhist experience are well covered by the selections, and the translations themselves are uniformly good. Both prose and poetry are included; there's introductory and background material; and the text is very well organized. The book forms both a fine primer on Buddhism and a wonderful sourcebook. Illustrations, 274pp. Dic 74

BLOFELD, JOHN. BEYOND THE GODS, $2.45. See Chinese Philosophy section.

BRUN, VIGGO. SUG, THE TRICKSTER WHO FOOLED THE MONK, $6.50. A translation of a trickster cycle containing about twenty-seven episodes, recorded in Northern Thailand in 1971 and never before translated in a Western language. The cycle is presented in parallel text and a vocabulary contains all the Thai words in the text. A long introduction discusses the trickster cycle and its variants along with notes on the social setting and an analysis of the trickster's development throughout the tale. 179pp. Cur 76

BURTT, E.A., ed. THE TEACHINGS OF THE COMPASSIONATE BUDDHA, $1.25. An excellent collection of the best translations of the basic texts, with introduction and commentary. A good basic book. Glossary, bibliography. 247pp. NAL 55

BYLES, MARIE B. FOOTPRINTS OF GAUTAMA THE BUDDHA, $1.75. A narrative of the Buddha's day-to-day ministerial life, related in the first person by one of his disciples. In researching this story the author retraced the Buddha's pilgrimage. All sources are cited. 224pp. THP 57

CARUS, PAUL. BUDDHA: HIS LIFE AND TEACHINGS, c$2.98. This edition includes two books: The Gospel of the Buddha by Carus and The World of the Buddha by a German who adopted the name Nyanatiloka. The author's purpose in the latter work is to assemble and codify the teachings known as the Eightfold Path to Deliverance from Suffering. The book is a guide to the practice of Buddhism as a way of life rather than as a religion. The two works complement each other. Illustrations, 269pp. Crn nd

_____. THE GOSPEL OF THE BUDDHA, $4.95. Carus' purpose here is to compile the life story and the teachings of the Buddha into the equivalent of a New Testament gospel. Part of this purpose is to emphasize the *many striking coincidences in the philosophical basis as well as in the ethical applications* of Christianity and Buddhism. But the book is actually in the form of a series of stories: first the story of the birth, life, and enlightenment of Prince Siddhartha who renounced the world and became the Buddha; then the stories of the first disciples; the establishment of the order; the first schism; the great questions and Buddha's answers; his parables; and his last days. Illustrations, glossary. 287pp. OpC 1894

_____. KARMA/NIRVANA, c$5.95. Each of these two stories revolves around the Four Noble Truths preached by the Buddha. And each story contains a tale-within-a-tale, showing that good actions lead to good karma. The stories were written over seventy years ago and have been translated into many languages. They were often attributed to Leo Tolstoy (who wrote the introduction to this volume and translated them into Russian). The stories are simple and strike to the heart of Buddhist philosophy. Illustrated, 135pp. OpC 73

CHANG, GARMA. THE BUDDHIST TEACHING OF TOTALITY, $6.65. This is a study of the philosophy and literature of the Hwa Yen School of Buddhism in China. *The Chinese word Hwa Yen means the flower-decoration or garland, which is originally the name of a voluminous Mahayana text: The Garland Sutra. Therefore, the teaching of this School is based mainly upon this text and draws inspiration from it.... Inspired by the revelation of the all-embracing Totality in this Sutra, the pioneer Hwa Yen thinkers... taught that the correct way of thinking is to view things through a multiple or total approach. Nothing is rejected, because in the round Totality of Buddhahood there is not even room for contradiction; here the inconsistencies all become harmonious.... The three major concepts of Mahayana—namely the Philosophies of Totality, of Emptiness, and of Mind-Only—are all merged into a unity.... Hwa Yen has been regarded as the crown of all Buddhist teachings, and as representing the consummation of Buddhist insight and thought*

....As any pioneer work, this book does not claim to be an exhaustive study of the stupendous Hwa Yen literature. But it is my humble opinion that the gist and the essential elements of Hwa Yen teachings, especially the philosophical aspects are all included in this volume. The philosophical presentation is very clear and quotations from the literature abound throughout the text in addition to the reading selections. This is a very important work. Notes, glossary, index. 300pp. PSU 71

CHATTERJEE, ASHOK. THE YOGACARA IDEALISM, c$15.00. An exposition of the metaphysics of the Yogacara school of Buddhism combined with an analysis of its logical implications. A complete picture of the school is presented and the system is seen as an original and constructive philosophy, not merely as a phase of Buddhism. Introduction, glossary, index. MoB 76

CH'EN, KENNETH. BUDDHISM, $2.25. This is one of the best overall works we have seen. The topics include the life and teachings of the Buddha, Mahayana Buddhism, the *sangha* or monastic community, the spread of Theravada Buddhism, Buddhism in China, Japan, and Tibet, Buddhist literature and art, and Buddhism in the modern world. Each chapter is well presented and clearly written and the text includes an excellent chapter-by-chapter bibliography. The emphasis is academic but not overly so. This would make a good book for the student who wants a general introduction. Ch'en is a religion professor at Princeton University and the author of several more technical books on Buddhism. Glossary, index. 297pp. BES 68

_____. BUDDHISM IN CHINA: A HISTORICAL SURVEY, $4.45. Treats the entire history of Buddhism in China up to the present century and concludes with an excellent chapter on the contributions of Buddhism to Chinese culture. A scholarly work which contains an extensive bibliography as well as a glossary of Chinese, Sanskrit, and Pali terms. 548pp. PUP 64

_____. THE CHINESE TRANSFORMATION OF BUDDHISM, $12.75. A very scholarly work investigating Buddhism's role in the ethical, political, literary, educational, and social life of the Chinese. Extensive bibliography and glossary. 330pp. PUP 73

CONZE, EDWARD. BUDDHISM: ITS ESSENCE AND DEVELOPMENT, $2.50. This is universally considered the best introductory volume in English. Here's what two noted scholars have to say about it. *There is not at present in English or in any other language so comprehensive—and at the same time so easy and readable—an account of Buddhism as is to be found in Dr. Conze's book. ... To Dr. Conze the questions that Buddhism asks are actual, living questions, and he constantly brings them into relation both with history and with current actuality.—Arthur Waley. Mr. Conze's Buddhism is perhaps the best book on the subject published so far in a European language. It is a brilliant piece of work, beautifully written and dramatically successful in presenting the essentials of Buddhism, from the beginnings to the Japanese Zen schools, in less than 200 pages.—Mircea Eliade.* Index, bibliography, chronology. 212pp. H&R 51

_____. BUDDHIST MEDITATION, $2.50. See the Meditation section.

_____. BUDDHIST SCRIPTURES, $1.95. Most of the writings chosen for this anthology were recorded between 100 and 400 AD, the Golden Age of Buddhist literature. They include passages from the Dammapada, the Buddhacarita, the Questions of King Milinda, and the Tibetan Book of the Dead. The collection is divided into topics. Glossary, 250pp. Pen 59

_____. BUDDHIST THOUGHT IN INDIA, $3.25. A careful, clear exposition of the development of the fundamental ideas of Buddhism and in what form each sect adopted them. Deals with three forms of Buddhism: Archaic, Hinayana (scholastic), and Mahayana (the more metaphysical school). Many references. 297pp. UMP 62

CONZE, EDWARD, I.B. HORNER, et al, eds. BUDDHIST TEXTS THROUGH THE AGES, $2.25. A comprehensive translation, topically arranged. Many of the excerpts are quite brief, but the reader is referred to important translations available elsewhere. All translations are new and some have never before appeared in English. Glossary. 322pp. H&R 54

CONZE, EDWARD, MAX MULLER and J. TAKAKUSA. BUDDHIST MAHAYANA TEXTS, $4.00. Translations originally published in the Sacred Books of the East Series: the Buddha-karita of Asvaghosa, the Larger and Smaller Sukhavativyuha, the Vagrakkhedika, the Larger and Smaller Pragnaparamitahridaya Sutras, the Amitayurdhyana Sutra. 201pp. Dov 69

COOMARASWAMY, ANANDA. BUDDHA AND THE GOSPEL OF BUDDHISM, $4.35. A lucid exposition of the Buddhist system and of all aspects of life related in any way to Buddhism. Very well written, highly recommended for both the scholar and the general reader. Glossary, bibliography, and many beautiful plates. 357pp. H&R 16

_____. THE ORIGIN OF THE BUDDHA IMAGE, c$19.15. 73 illustrations, 46pp. MuM

DAYAL, HAR. THE BODHISATTVA DOCTRINE IN BUDDHIST SANSKRIT LITERATURE, c$13.50. This is a very comprehensive study which reviews the Bodhisattva doctrine. The text begins by recounting the different factors that contributed to the rise and growth of the doctrine. The next section discusses the concept of enlightenment for all sentient beings. A third chapter describes thirty-seven practices and principles conducive to the attainment of enlightenment while a fourth explains the ten perfections (paramitas) that lead to welfare, rebirths, serenity, and supreme knowledge. A fifth chapter describes the different stages of spiritual progress and a final one relates the events of Gautama Buddha's past lives as Bodhisattva. The text is well written, with many Sanskrit words interspersed throughout. Notes, index, 411pp. MoB 35

THE DHAMMAPADA

Consists of twenty-six poems or chapters, attributed to the Buddha himself. These verses are an almost complete presentation of Buddhist ethics, much of it in actual practice today. As the Buddhist *way of truth* (*pada*, meaning path or way; *dhamma*, the teaching), **The Dhammapada** thus offers an invaluable insight into the nature of the Buddhist mind and its response to life.

ANONYMOUS. c$2.00. *Just as a fletcher makes straight his arrow, the wise man makes straight his crooked thinking. This is difficult to guard. This is hard to restrain.* A faithful Indian translation. Notes and commentary. 139pp. CuN 55

AUSTIN, JACK. $.85. *As a fletcher straightens his arrow, so the wise man straightens his unsteady mind, which is so hard to control.* This is a nice pocket edition, with a translation by a member of the Buddhist Society, London. 72pp. BuS 45

BABBIT, IRVING. $1.50. *As a fletcher makes straight his arrow, a wise man makes straight his trembling and unsteady thought, which is difficult to guard, difficult to hold back.* A revision of Max Muller's translation. Includes an essay by the translator on *Buddha and the Occident.* 126pp. NDP 36

BURLINGAME, E.W. **BUDDHIST LEGENDS (DHAMMAPADA COMMENTARY),** c$26.00/set. Three volumes, a Pali Text Society edition. PTS

LAL, P. $3.45. *Like an archer and arrow, the wise man steadies his trembling mind, a fickle and restless weapon.* This is our favorite translation. It is the most concise of the lot and was intended by Lal as a *transcreation* rather than merely another translation. Includes an introduction on the Buddha in two parts: his life and his teaching. All highly readable. Annotated bibliography. 184pp. FSG 67

MASACRO, JUAN. $1.25. *The mind is wavering and restless, difficult to guard and restrain: let the wise man straighten his mind as a maker of arrows makes his arrows straight.* Penguin Books' translation. Verse numbers are given. A clear, nice job. Includes an excellent long introduction. 93pp. Pen 73

MULLER, F. MAX. c$7.50. *As a fletcher makes straight his arrow, a wise man makes straight his trembling and unsteady thought, which is difficult to guard, difficult to hold back.* Critical introduction and notes. Sacred Books of the East Vol. 10. 269pp. MoB 1881

NARADA, VEN. c$4.00. *The flickering, fickle mind, difficult to guard, difficult to control, the wise person straightens, as a fletcher an arrow.* Narada is a distinguished Ceylonese Buddhist scholar. His translation is faithful to the original and his extensive notes provide valuable insights from his first-hand knowledge. Introduction, 88pp. Mur 54

RADHAKRISHNAN, S. c$3.80. Excellent translation, introductory essay, copious notes, and the Pali text. Bibiography. 202pp. Oxf

Eight-spoked wheel (Horin)

DHIRAVAMSA. **A NEW APPROACH TO BUDDHISM,** $1.95. The author is a Thai meditation master currently teaching in England. This book is a collection of discourses he has given on the following topics: life and death; integration of the intellectual and the spiritual life; freedom and love; Anatta—no-self; the meditative way of life; what Buddhism has to offer the West; and the problem of conflict. He writes very clearly and his aim is to present a new approach to Buddhism and the possibilities of integrating meditational techniques into daily life. He leans toward the vipassana form of meditation popular in South Asia. Dhiravamsa has lectured at many universities in the U.S. and Canada in addition to his work in England. 67pp. DHP 72

_____. **THE WAY OF NON-ATTACHMENT,** $7.80. See the Meditation section. 156pp. Tur 75

DONATH, DOROTHY. **BUDDHISM FOR THE WEST—THERAVADA, MAHAYANA, VAJRAYANA,** $2.45. A comprehensive review of Buddhist history, philosophy, and teachings including an interesting section on Vajrayana (or Tibetan) Buddhism and the influence of Marpa and Milarepa. Written in a very personal style that is easy for the student to understand. Bibliography. 146pp. MGH 71

DRUMMOND, RICHARD. **GAUTAMA THE BUDDHA,** $3.95. This is an unusual treatment of the life and teaching of the Buddha. Professor Drummond interprets the man and his thought in the light of Christianity, pointing to significant relationships between Gautama's teaching and the basic tenets of Christianity. After describing the religious background out of which Gautama arose, Drummond discusses such important themes in Buddhism as the Four Noble Truths, the Eight-fold Path, the Middle Way, Dharma, and Nirvana. In all cases the author draws a parallel between the Buddhist teaching and the teachings of Christ. Index, notes, bibliography. 239pp. Eer 74

DUTT, SUKUMAR. **BUDDHISM IN EAST ASIA,** c$13.50. This is a good book for the general reader which reviews Buddhism and its development in Ceylon, Burma, Siam, Cambodia, Vietnam, China, Chinese Turkestan, Japan, and Tibet. The text is accompanied by numerous photographs and emphasizes the culture and important individuals and movements. Index, 225pp. BTK 66

_____. **BUDDHIST MONKS AND MONASTERIES IN INDIA,** c$17.35. Though India is no longer a Buddhist country, Buddhism held its place among Indian faiths for nearly seventeen centuries (500 BC–1200 AD). During this long stretch of time the Buddhist monks were organized in *sanghas* in most parts of the country and their activities and achievements have profoundly influenced India's traditional culture. This volume presents the first connected history of the Buddhist monks of ancient India—their activities, their monastic establishments and their contributions to Indian culture. Dr. Dutt is a well known Buddhist scholar and he has based this study on original source material in Pali, Sanskrit, Chinese, and Tibetan. 24 full page plates accompany the text; also notes, a bibliography, and an index. 397pp. A&U 62

EDGERTON, FRANKLIN. **BUDDHIST HYBRID SANSKRIT GRAMMAR AND DICTIONARY,** c$50.65. Buddhist Hybrid Sanskrit is the language in which most North Indian Buddhist works are composed. This two-volume set is the first systematic attempt that has been done. 898pp. MoB 53

FOUCHER, A. **THE LIFE OF THE BUDDHA,** c$22.85. This is perhaps the definitive modern study of the life of the Buddha, based mainly on primary Indian sources, and divided into the following sections: The Nativity, Childhood and Youth, The Search for Enlightenment, Enlightenment, The First Sermon, The First Conversions, Duties of a Buddha, The Four Secondary Pilgrimages, and The Fourth Great Pilgrimage. The material on the nativity includes information on the Buddha's earlier lives, some early predictions, and an analysis of his horoscope. The book is extremely well written, with photographs interspersed. Both the general reader and the scholar should appreciate this text—although the price makes it unlikely that anyone but a scholar or a library will buy the book, which is too bad, because we recommend it highly. This is a well-bound, limited edition reprint. Notes, bibliography, 286pp. Gre 63

FOZDAR, JAMSHED. **THE GOD OF BUDDHA,** c$13.45. A topically arranged presentation of the major ideas of the Buddha, showing how they relate to traditional Hindu thought. The material is organized as follows: each page is divided into two columns; the right hand one presents quotations from the Hindu sacred literature; on the left there's a parallel selection from the sacred literature of Buddhism. Connective commentary is interspersed, and each topic is introduced. There's also an abundance of background and explanatory material to back up the author's thesis that the Buddhist does believe in divine revelation and an eternity of divine bliss. Glossary, index, 194pp. APH 73

FRAZIER, ALLIE, ed. **BUDDHISM,** $3.50. An excellent book of readings on Buddhist religious thought and practice which brings together both interpretative essays on the Buddhist tradition such noted scholars as Joseph Campbell, Edward Conze, D.T. Suzuki, Ananda Coomaraswamy, and Heinrich Zimmer, and selections from the sacred literature of Buddhism. The commentaries are spaced throughout the selection of primary sources and the principle governing the selection of materials has been to include those original sources and commentaries which illuminate the fundamental themes of Buddhist thought and experience. In this regard Ms. Frazier has produced an excellent work. Glossary, bibliography, 304pp. Wes 69

GETTY, ALICE. **THE GODS OF NORTHERN BUDDHISM,** c$32.50. This study has been recognized for almost half a century as a landmark achievement of unsurpassed excellence. Since its publication it has become a rare and costly collector's item and this edition is a beautifully produced unabridged reprint of the second edition. Ms. Getty discusses in detail the major deities of the Mahayana pantheon, their symbols, and their characteristics, at the same time giving attention to the minor gods and deified historical personages. The presentation of the gods themselves is preceded by an introduction in which Joseph Deniker provides the reader with a general survey of Buddhism and its evolution and prepares him for the discussions that follow. Almost two hundred works of Northern Buddhist art are illustrated in plates (eight in color) and there's also a glossary, bibliography, and index. Oversize, 341pp. Tut 62

GODDARD, DWIGHT, ed. **A BUDDHIST BIBLE,** $5.95. The first Buddhist anthology and still one of the most comprehensive and scholarly. Includes selections from all areas of Buddhism. 667pp. Bea 38

GOVINDA, LAMA. **PSYCHO-COSMIC SYMBOLISM OF THE BUDDHIST STUPA,** $4.95. Throughout the Buddhist cultures, the stupa has been the most pervasive and symbolic form of architecture. In early times stupas were symbols of illumination—memorials which were intended to inspire later generations to follow the path to enlightenment. Like the Egyptian pyramid, the Buddhist stupa evolved not only as a repository for the relics of revered persons, but as a universal symbol, the embodiment of all knowledge contained in a single picture of architecture. Much of Lama Govinda's knowledge about the stupa comes from his personal pilgrimages to various stupas in Ceylon, India, Nepal, and Tibet. Often he took measurements of the stupas by counting on his beads the number of steps required to circumambulate the structures. In this volume he discusses and illustrates his findings and he also reviews the relationship of the stupas to the chakras and to the traditional Buddhist stages of meditation. Index, 120pp. Dha 76

_____. **THE PSYCHOLOGICAL ATTITUDE OF EARLY BUDDHIST PHILO-SOPHY**, c$3.50. Shows not only what the ideas of early Buddhism were, but how they came into existence and why they took the form in which we now know them. It is a brilliant summary of Pali Buddhism, and in addition it constitutes a logical approach to the problems of Mahayana and Tantric philosophy. The text is clarified by a series of diagrams and charts. A very interesting interpretative work. Definitely not recommended for the student who desires simply an introduction. 176pp. Wei 61

GRIMM, GEORGE. **DOCTRINE OF THE BUDDHA**, c$10.50. Translation of a very scholarly German philosophical work on truth as the theme and basis of the doctrine of the Buddha. The study is prefixed with an introduction answering the questions: who was the Buddha, and what is a Buddha? The Appendix deals with the doctrine and the metaphysics of Buddhism. Includes bibliography and a general index as well as an index of quotations from Pali texts. 413pp. MoB 58

GUENTHER, HERBERT. **BUDDHIST PHILOSOPHY IN THEORY AND PRACTICE**, $2.45. An excellent philosophical treatise which traces the growth of Buddhist thought. Guenther is especially noted for his studies of the Tibetan school and the Tantras. The emphasis is apparent here although all schools are treated. Clearly written, but definitely not a broad introductory work. Many references and notes, bibliography. 230pp. Pen 71

_____. **PHILOSOPHY AND PSYCHOLOGY IN THE ABHIDHARMA**, $4.95. The study of the Abhidharma is indispensible for understanding the history of Buddhist philosophy and practice. Originally a summary of terms according to subject matters, it became systematized into a philosophical analysis of man and his world. This book summarizes the significance of the Abdhidharma and analyzes the concepts of mind and its states with reference to healthy and unhealthy attitudes toward life. Theories of perception are discussed together with the interpretation of the world on the basis of these theories as well as their critiques. The volume ends with a discussion of the Path, as conceived by the various schools. Six tables analyze the structure of mind in Buddhist psychology. Notes, index. 279pp. ShP 76

HALL, MANLY P. **THE ARHATS OF BUDDHISM**, $3.00. Volume II of Hall's series **The Adepts in the Eastern Esoteric Tradition**. 112pp. PRS 53

_____. **BUDDHISM AND PSYCHOTHERAPY**, c$5.00. Interpretative explanations of the psychological meanings of the beliefs and practices of the Mahayana Buddhists. Non-technical, illustrations, 324pp. PRS 67

HEROLD, A. FERDINAND. **THE LIFE OF BUDDHA**, $2.95. The story of the Buddha's life told in the form of a novel and based on the author's study of Indian legends, poems, history, and literature in translation. This account is translated from the French. 285pp. Tut 54

HESSE, HERMANN. **SIDDHARTHA**, c$7.50/1.75. A simple and beautiful story of a man's long quest of the ultimate answers to existence. A classic, an excellent introduction to the basic philosophy of Buddhism, and reading to savor for all. 122pp. NDP 51

HORNER, I.B. **WOMEN UNDER PRIMITIVE BUDDHISM**, c$15.20 A detailed study based on early Pali sources including the Canonical literature and commentaries. The book is divided into two parts. The first depicts the lay woman in her role as mother, daughter, wife, widow, and worker. The second deals with the almswoman and reviews her admission into the order, the eight chief rules of conduct, life in the order, and **Therigatha**. Notes, index, 415pp. MoB 30

HUA, HSUAN, tr. **ESSENTIALS OF THE SRAMANERA VINAYA AND RULES OF DEPORTMENT**, $5.00. Translation of an instructional treatise written in the Ming dynasty by Lien Ch'ih and derived from the Vinaya texts to serve as a guide to novice monks. Commentary and introductory material are also included. Index, 103pp. SAB 75

_____. **A GENERAL EXPLANATION OF THE BUDDHA SPEAKS OF AMITABHA SUTRA**, $7.00. We are really at a loss how to evaluate Master Hua's books. The introductions to all of them make great claims and say that he is the only one who has fully understood the texts. This is a bit hard to take. But it needs to be kept in mind that all the books are published by his disciples who of course feel that he is the greatest. We don't know anyone personally who has studied under him. The books have a nice feeling to them—although we do not like the elaborate claims—and the translations seem adequate. This is a translation with elaborate and extensive commentary of the Sutra in which the Buddha said that all living beings who recited his name with faith would be reborn in his Buddhaland, the **Land of Ultimate Bliss**. Illustrations and a great deal of background material are also included. Index, 179pp. SAB 74

_____. **A GENERAL EXPLANATION OF THE VAJRA PRAJNA PARAMITA SUTRA**, $7.00. The **Prajnaparamita Sutra** comprises many volumes, of which the **Vajra Sutra** is just one. **Vajra** is a Sanskrit word which essentially means an indestructible substance, usually represented by a diamond—and this **sutra** is usually called the **Diamond Sutra**. This is a translation of the **Sutra**, with extensive commentary and translations of some of the traditional commentaries. Illustrations, index, 186pp. SAB 74

_____. **RECORDS OF THE LIFE OF THE VENERABLE MASTER HSUAN HUA**, $5.95. Volume I of a projected three part work tracing the early life of the Master and presenting a vivid glimpse of the religious life of China in the first half of this century. Photographs, 96pp. SAB 73

_____. **THE TEN DHARMAREALMS ARE NOT BEYOND A SINGLE THOUGHT**, $2.00. A description of the realms of being as Buddhism teaches them—from Buddhas and Bodhisattvas to gods, men, animals, ghosts, and beings in hell. A short text is presented, followed by commentary and illustrated throughout. 34pp. SAB 73

HUMPHREYS, CHRISTMAS. **BUDDHISM**, $2.25. Traces the history and development of Buddhism and the teaching of the various schools, as well as its condition in the world today. An excellent primer. Humphreys is as qualified as any man in the West to write this material. He has been studying Buddhism and interpreting it to the West for over fifty years and has been President of the Buddhist Society of London for most of that time. Glossary and extensive subject-indexed bibliography. 252pp. Pen 51

_____. **BUDDHIST POEMS**, $4.20. A collection largely inspired by Buddhist themes, selected from Humphrey's finest poems over a fifty year period. 59pp. A&U 71

_____. **THE BUDDHIST WAY OF LIFE**, $2.45. Humphreys directs his attention to the interaction between Buddhism and its growing Western following. Designed as **An Invitation for Western Readers**, the book provides an introduction to Buddhism, both its basic doctrine and its adaptability in new contexts. 224pp. ScB 69

_____. **EXPLORING BUDDHISM**, $2.50. As the title suggests, this is an exploration of a variety of aspects of Buddhism. Each of the selections is fairly short and all schools of thought are reviewed. The text begins with essays on the Buddha and his enlightenment. This section includes a review of Mme. Blavatsky and Buddhism (Humphreys has been active in the Theosophical movement). Next comes a discussion of various Buddhist doctrines. This is followed by a survey of Buddhism in the West and the volume ends with a discussion of Buddhist practices. There's no great depth to the presentation it simply gives a taste of Buddhism. Glossary, index, 191pp. TPH 74

_____. **A POPULAR DICTIONARY OF BUDDHISM**, c$10.50. A dictionary and glossary of terms covering the entire field of Buddhism. Revised and enlarged editon. 224pp. Cur 74

_____. **SIXTY YEARS OF BUDDHISM IN ENGLAND (1907–67)**, c$4.40. A history and a survey of the Buddhist movement in England by the current President of the Buddhist Society. 84pp. BuS 68

_____. **STUDIES IN THE MIDDLE WAY**, c$6.50. Subtitled **being thoughts on Buddhism applied**, this work emphasizes the inner life as a constant moving on and the mover as a pilgrim travelling along an ancient Way. The Buddha called this way to ultimate reality the Middle Way, the path between the introverted life of contemplation and the extroverted life of action in the world of men. In this volume Humphreys aims toward an understanding and also an application of Buddhist principles in Western society, and a means whereby the Way may be traversed. Each chapter expounds a facet of life in relation to Buddhism. 180pp. Cur 76

_____. **THE WAY OF ACTION**, $1.25. A record of the author's personal experience. It concerns the analysis of action, in the sense of right acting rather than right action, and the emphasis is therefore on the how and why of action rather than the theoretical what. Many quotations from Buddhist texts illustrate Humphrey's practical treatise. Glossary and bibliography. 195pp. Pen 60

_____. **THE WISDOM OF BUDDHISM**, $2.65. A readable and interesting anthology drawn from a variety of older translations and containing material on all the schools of Buddhism. Very well organized. Recommended. Glossary, 274pp. H&R 60

IIJIMA, KANJITSU. **BUDDHIST YOGA**, $6.95. See the Yoga section.

IKEDA, DAISAKU. **THE LIVING BUDDHA**, c$7.95. This is subtitled **An interpretative Biography**. The Buddha emerges as a man, living in a turbulent period, who was confronted with the same kinds of personal problems and social conflicts that we all face. The description of how he conquered these obstacles, the nature of his great enlightenment, and the secret of his success as a religious teacher and leader makes this an engrossing and inspiring account. The author is leader of one of the most dynamic Buddhist renewal movements in the world. His image of the Buddha grows out of his own living experience as a Buddhist and as a man of action. This is a very successful work which we appreciate enormously. Translated by Burton Watson. Illustrations, glossary. 158pp. Wea 76

IRIE, TAIKICHI and SHIGERU AOYAMA. **BUDDHIST IMAGES**, $3.25. A beautiful pocket book containing 104 images of the Buddha, most of them in color. The plates are briefly described and there's a good section on Buddhist art and images. Glossary, 136pp. Hoi 70

JATAKA TALES

These tales are stories of the Buddha's previous lives when he was still a bodhisattva, striving (that doesn't sound very Buddhist, does it—but you get the idea) to accumulate a sufficient store of merit and wisdom to be able to achieve Buddhahood. They are based on traditional folklore and, whatever their intrinsic value, they illustrate the main tenets of Buddhism and are also just plain good stories.

COWELL, E.B. **JATAKA STORIES**, c$42.00/set. These volumes are the longest in the whole collection of suttas. The Jatakas or Birth stories contain the stories of the former rebirths of the Buddha. In these stories the Buddha is referred to as the Bodhisattva, since he was not yet enlightened, and he is presented sometimes as the hero, sometimes a secondary character, and at times a mere spectator. The story usually begins with the words, **At such and such a time, the bodhisattva was reborn in the womb of so and so**, and this permitted any story to be converted into a Buddhist jataka by merely changing some human being, animal, or deity in it into the Bodhisattva. Of the 547 jatakas in the collection, probably more than half are of non-Buddhist origin. They are notable as more than edifying tales to entertain audiences. They are valuable for the information which they provide concerning the early history of Buddhism as well as the social, political, and economic conditions in India. They also served as the inspiration for numerous scenes in Buddhist art (see **Ten Lives of the Buddha** by Wray for examples). PTS

DEROIN, NANCY, tr. **JATAKA TALES**, c$5.95. This is a lovely rendition of thirty of the tales, and it is our favorite version. It's a children's book—but like so many children's books it will probably enjoy it as much as the children, at least this adult does! The drawings are delightful and the stories themselves are told in a wonderful manner. Each is a couple of pages long and there are illustrations on almost every page. Ms. DeRoin is a Buddhist. Oversize, 84pp. HMC 75

FRANCIS, H.T. and E.J. THOMAS. **JATAKA TALES**, $2.60. A selection of some of the most important Jataka tales, translated in a simple, clear manner. For a fuller description of these tales see the review of E.B. Cowell's definitive edition. Introduction, glossary. 313pp. JHP 56

GELLEK, NAZLI. **THE KING AND THE MANGOES**, c$4.75. This is a new series of children's books, with beautiful color illustrations. They are extremely well done and have been very popular. The story line in this one is as follows. Wanting to save his herd of 80,000 monkeys, the Monkey King stretched his own body as far as possible to make a bridge from the mango tree to a bamboo grove nearby. But as the last monkey crossed over to safety he jumped with all his might on the king's back. Giving his own life to save his herd, the Monkey King died of a broken heart. Oversize, 24pp. Dha 75

_____. **THE PROUD PEACOCK AND THE MALLARD**, c$4.75. Having no modesty the Proud Peacock is spurned by King Mallard's daughter who turns to a young mallard wise enough not to show his feathers. The peacock is so ashamed that his voice turns hoarse. Squawking unhappily, he flies away into the forest. 24pp. Dha 76

_____. **THE SPADE SAGE**, c$4.75. *In that instant, as he looked into the river, the Spade Sage found within himself the secret of happiness and became a very wise man. The king and his people looked in wonder as the Spade Sage rose into the air and called to them to follow him and learn great truths. They did indeed follow him and were taught by him how to conquer their greediness and find the secret of happiness locked within their own minds. And so it happened that a poor gardener named the Spade Sage became a wiseman and a great teacher.* 24pp. Dha 76

WRAY, ELIZABETH, et al. **TEN LIVES OF THE BUDDHA**, c$15.00. Beautiful color reproductions of wall paintings illustrating ten of the most important Jataka tales. Every detail in the pictures means something. Each of the tales is an allegory of the ten cardinal virtues to be perfected in attaining Buddhahood. Two lengthy and informative background essays complement the stories and paintings. Glossary, extensive bibliography, oversize, 154pp. Wea 72

JAYATILLEKE, K.N. **THE MESSAGE OF THE BUDDHA**, c$17.25. The author was one of the best known contemporary Buddhist scholars in Asia and was a professor of philosophy at the University of Ceylon until his recent death. This volume is a culmination of his life's work. Writing for both the layman and the scholar, Professor Jayatilleke provides a historical perspective on the central events in the life of the Buddha and on the roots and rise of Buddhism, and he examines the Buddha's teachings in the light of contemporary understanding. The presentation is basically devoted to Theravada Buddhism. The material is topically organized and all the major scholars are cited. Index, 262pp. McM 74

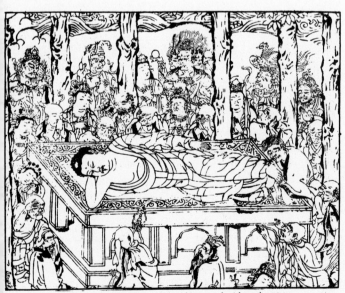

Buddha entering into Nirvana—artist unknown, early eighteenth century

JOHANSSON, RUNE. **PSYCHOLOGY OF NIRVANA**, c$6.15. An attempt to fit all the diffuse explanations and pronouncements on Nirvana of the scriptures together into a consistent picture, and to relate this picture to modern psychology. A fascinating, scholarly comparative study by a trained Swedish psychologist who has also extensively studied Sanskrit and Pali. 138pp. A&U 69

KALUPAHANA, DAVID. **BUDDHIST PHILOSOPHY**, $3.95. A fairly technical analysis of the basic philosophical teachings and historical development of Buddhism. Part I outlines the historical background out of which Buddhism arose, and examines the early teachings in both the Pali Nikayas and the Chinese Agamas. Topics such as epistemology, causality, existence, karma, morality, ethics, and nirvana are discussed in detail. Part II examines developments in the history of Buddhist thought and the emergence of the various schools of Buddhism. The development of Abhidharma is studied through analysis of the Mahayana sutras. Two chapters examine Madhyamika Transcendentalism and Yogacara Idealism. Appendices review the Buddha's attitude toward metaphysics and the relationship between early Buddhism and Zen. Source quotations, notes, index, bibliography, 209pp. UHa 76

_____. **CAUSALITY: THE CENTRAL PHILOSOPHY OF BUDDHISM**, c$12.00. A scholarly articulation, analysis, and interpretation of the doctrines of causation in Buddhist philosophy. Special attention is given to early Buddhist teachings as found in the Pali Nikayas and Chinese Agamas. *In early Buddhism, Kalupahana maintains, a cause is defined as the sum total of several factors that gives rise to a consequent—the consequent being the entire universe as well as a specific thing or event.* Notes, bibliography, index. 298pp. UHa 75

KERN, H. **MANUAL OF INDIAN BUDDHISM.**, c$7.50. This is a reprint of one of the earliest European studies of Buddhism. The text does not read very easily. It is based on Nepalese, Chinese, and Simhalese original sources and includes a general survey of the early literature; a study of the Buddha's life and his fundamental doctrines; a review of the Sangha and its disciplinary and ascetic rules; and an outline of the theological and philosophical history of Buddhism. Extensive notes accompany the text. Index, 145pp. MoB 1898

_____. **SADDHARMA-PUNDARIKA OR THE LOTUS OF TRUE LAW**, $4.50. Perhaps the single most important Mahayana Buddhist text, described as the *crown-jewel* in which *all Buddha-laws are succinctly taught*, it's almost required reading for every serious Buddhist student. This translation comes from the Sacred Books of the East series. Extensive introduction and notes. 442pp. Dov 1884

KING, WINSTON L. **IN HOPE OF NIBBANA: AN ESSAY ON THERAVADA BUDDHIST ETHICS**, $2.95. *Nibbana* is the Pali word for *Nirvana*. This is a very complete treatment of the topic. 284pp. OpC 64

KLOPPENBORG, RIA, tr. **THE SUTRA ON THE FOUNDATION OF THE BUDDHIST ORDER**, $5.75. A translation of the **Catusparisat Sutra**, giving an account of the foundation of the *fourfold order*, consisting of monks, nuns, and male and female lay-disciples. It describes that part of the Buddha's life that starts with his enlightenment and ends with the ordination of his two main disciples, Upatisya and Kolita. The text describes the meditations preceding enlightenment; the attainment of the six higher knowledges and of enlightenment; the acceptance of the first lay-disciples; and the Buddha's decision to preach the dharma. Notes, bibliography, index. 137pp. Bri 73

LEGGE, JAMES. **A RECORD OF BUDDHIST KINGDOMS**, $2.00. Early fifth century account of Buddhism in India and Central Asia; interesting source document. Extensively annotated, full Chinese text is reproduced. 168pp. Dov 1886

LESTER, ROBERT. **THERAVADA BUDDHISM IN SOUTH EAST ASIA**, $2.95. Describes both the scriptural and traditional ideal, and the contemporary reality of Buddhist practice. The author's portrayal combines insights of the religious historian and the cultural anthropologist. Theravada Buddhism is seen as a way of life. An interesting study, extensive notes and bibliography. 198pp. UMP 73

LING, TREVOR. **THE BUDDHA**, c$10.00. A comprehensive new study. Ling describes the India into which the Buddha was born, recounts what is known of his life and the development of his teaching, and then follows the course of Buddhism through succeeding centuries in India and Ceylon. His emphasis is on the links between religious thought and the society in which it exists. Extensive notes, bibliography, 287pp. Scr 73

_____. **A DICTIONARY OF BUDDHISM**, $2.95. Over two hundred entries provide a detailed introduction to the history, doctrine, and practice. Most entries are cross-referenced and contain a bibliography. Clear and concise. 277pp. Scr 72

LOUNSBERRY, G. CONSTANT. **BUDDHIST MEDITATION**, $2.95. See section on Meditation. 183pp. Ome 35

LU K'UAN YU. **PRACTICAL BUDDHISM**, c$5.95. A very clear outline of the Buddha's doctrine from the point of view of both the Hinayana and Mahayana schools in China, together with various methods of meditation and practice. The author also describes two cases of spiritual awakening by Western Buddhists. Other sections present translations of ancient texts, stories, and koans which demonstrate how various masters over the ages attained enlightenment. This is an excellent manual for all who are interested in Buddhism. The author, formerly Charles Luk, studied with various Chinese masters and now lives in Hong Kong and is devoting his life to presenting as many Chinese Buddhist texts to the West as possible. Glossary, 167pp. TPH 71

_____. **THE SURANGAMA SUTRA**, $8.85. This Sutra is considered one of the most important sources for the Ch'an or Zen school. In the Sutra the Buddha begins by stripping Ananda of his attachment to the illusory body and mind before revealing the One Mind. To teach how this One Mind can be realized he asked twenty-five Bodhisattvas to describe the different methods by which each had attained enlightenment. Avalokitesvara's method of turning inward the organ of hearing was judged the most suitable for mankind today. The Buddha also discloses the cause of transmigration through the six worlds and of the attainment of the four saintly planes, describing these ten regions in some detail. Finally, he details and warns against clinging to the various mental states experienced when practicing the Surangama Samadhi and he describes how man and his world came into being. This translation is based on Ch'an Master Han Shan's late sixteenth century commentary, portions of which are included in the footnotes. Index, notes, glossary, 284pp. Rid 66

_____. THE VIMALAKIRTI NIRDESA SUTRA, $3.95. This is one of the most important texts of Zen and Mahayana Buddhism. The sutra was produced in India probably around the beginning of the Christian era. It is a philosophical-dramatic discourse, full of marvelous episodes. The Boddhisattva path—the dedicating of one's energies toward the benefit of all living things—is introduced with critical insight and rare humor. It reveals the importance of inner commitment to the spiritual life. Glossary. ShP 72

MADHYAMIKA

Ideas concerning the non-dual nature of phenomenal existence and *nirvana* were first discussed in a group of Mahayana scriptures known as the *Prajna* or Wisdom Sutras, which developed about the beginning of the Christian era. They were further expounded in the writings of Nagarjuna, who is said to have established the Madhyamika, or the School of the Middle Way. Nagarjuna lived during the second century AD. Although there is no doubt that he is a historical person, very little is known about him, other than that he was of brahman parentage, and that he studied all the Hindu branches of knowledge before he was converted to Buddhism. The School he founded takes its position between the extremes of existence and non-existence, affirmation and negation, pleasure and pain. However, he also related this middle path to the Hinayanist doctrine of dependent origination, which he paraphrased by means of the eight-fold negation: *Nothing comes into being, nor does anything disappear. Nothing is eternal, nor has anything an end. Nothing is identical or differentiated, nothing moves hither, nor moves anything thither.* By means of this negation, he sought to explain the truth of emptiness and the unreality of all elements of existence. However, the word *sunya*, which is usually translated as empty, is also interpreted as relative. That is to say, a thing is *sunya* in that it can be identified only by mentioning its relation to something else: it becomes meaningless without these relations. Madhyamika accepts the truth that relations and dependence constitute the phenomenal world, but it also contends that one is unable to explain these relations intelligibly. In his writings, Nagarjuna proceeds to demonstrate that all relationships are false and erroneous, and on the assumption that any contradiction is proof of error, he finds contradictions in every concept. By a merciless system of logic, he proves that the whole phenomenal world is empty or unreal because it is based on relations which cannot be explained satisfactorily. He also points out that genuine realization of the emptiness of the phenomenal world is at the same time a religious awakening, a direct intuition of the highest truth, and this spiritual intent gives the real meaning to the doctrine of emptiness. To Nagarjuna, the doctrine of emptiness is taught not as a theory but as a means (*upaya*) to get rid of all theories, thus freeing one from the world around us. By getting rid of the ignorance that binds us to the phenomenal world through the realization that this world is empty and unreal, we achieve *prajna* or intuitive wisdom, that enables us to realize the absolute truth which is unconditioned, indeterminate, and beyond thought and word.

CONZE, EDWARD. **BUDDHIST WISDOM BOOKS: THE DIAMOND SUTRA, THE HEART SUTRA**, $3.30. The two sutras contained in this book were written between 1500 and 2100 years ago, and are considered by Buddhists to be the loftiest of the Buddhist writings called **Prajnaparamita**, which means the *perfection of wisdom*. The author spent twenty years translating these profound texts and writing a worthy commentary. 107pp. H&R 58

_____. THE LARGE SUTRA ON PERFECT WISDOM, c$25.00. The earliest and most influential of the Mahayana Sutras had the *perfection of wisdom* as its main subject matter. Of these texts, the famous *Diamond* and *Heart* Sutras have been known in the West for many years, but they are merely condensations of the original **Large Sutra on Perfect Wisdom** that took shape between 50 and 200 AD in southern India. The *Wisdom Sutras* continued to be composed over a period of 600 years, and in their entirety form a large and complex body of religious literature. The present volume makes the Sutra available for the first time in an annotated translation and is the result of thirty-five years of close study by Dr. Conze. This is a deeply philosophical work, filled with esoteric terminology, and is recommended only to those familiar with the Buddhist tradition. Glossary, notes, index, 697pp. UCP 75

_____. THE PERFECTION OF WISDOM, $5.00. Composition of this work extended over a period of 700 years. It is considered one of the world's most important spiritual documents. It was written to be memorized by monks, and for this reason this translation is a literary rather than a literal one—aimed at bringing forth the true meaning of the document. The text is presented in two versions, verse and prose. Includes glossary and cross-referenced index of topics. 325pp. FSF 73

_____. SELECTED SAYINGS FROM THE PERFECTION OF WISDOM, $5.15. An abundance of translations of **Prajnaparamita Sutras** has appeared in the last few years, most of them by Dr. Conze. This anthology contains selections from all important aspects

of the teaching arranged under three main headings, according to whether they deal with the Buddha, the Dharma, or the Samgha. The most readable passages have been selected and technicalities have been avoided. Usually the translation is quite literal. The selections are topically arranged within the main headings. This version is probably the best introduction to Prajnaparamita and a helpful introduction is also included. 131pp. BuS 55

_____. THE SHORT PRAJNAPARAMITA TEXTS, c$13.00. Translations of the following texts: *The Questions of Suvikrantavikramin (Perfect Wisdom in 2,500 Lines), The Perfection of Wisdom in 700 Lines,* and *The Perfection of Wisdom in 500 Lines.* In addition Dr. Conze provides summaries of the following texts: *The Diamond Sutra (Perfect Wisdom in 300 Lines), The Heart of Perfect Wisdom, The Perfection of Wisdom in a Few Words, Perfect Wisdom and the Five Bodhisattvas, The Holy and Blessed Perfection of Wisdom in 50 Lines,* and *The Perfection of Wisdom for Kausika.* In addition there are selections from **The Questions of Nagasri** and a summary of **The Sutra on Perfect Wisdom**. A final section is devoted to translations of four related Tantric texts. Notes, glossary, indices. 224pp. Luz 73

_____. THIRTY YEARS OF BUDDHIST STUDIES, c$10.95. A collection of the most important articles written by Dr. Conze over the last thirty years, including both translation and original essays: a report on recent progress in Buddhist studies; a survey of Mahayana Buddhism, based on original sources; a comparison of Buddhist and European philosophy; an essay on Buddhist saviors; and a variety of articles and translations of the **Prajnaparamita**. Notes, index, 277pp. Cas 67

HOPKINS, JEFFREY and LATI RIMPOCHE, trs. **THE BUDDHISM OF TIBET AND THE KEY TO THE MIDDLE WAY**, c$5.95. See the Tibetan sub-section.

_____. THE PRECIOUS GARLAND AND THE SONG OF THE FOUR MINDFULNESSES, c$5.95. See the Tibetan sub-section.

INADA, KENNETH, tr. **NAGARJUNA**, c$12.00. A translation of Nagarjuna's major work, the **Mulamadhyamakakarika** (generally known as the **Karika**), with notes, the Romanized Sanskrit text, an introductory essay on Nagarjuna's philosophy, and a long glossary. Bibliography, 214pp. Hok 70

KAWAMURA, LESLIE, tr. **GOLDEN ZEPHYR**, $4.75. See the Tibetan sub-section.

MURTI, T.R.V. **THE CENTRAL PHILOSOPHY OF BUDDHISM**, c$12.60. A very scholarly treatise detailing the system of the *Madyamika*, or the Middle Way, with great thoroughness. This is a highly regarded work. Glossary. 356pp. A&U 55

RAMANAN, K. VENKATA. **NAGARJUNA'S PHILOSOPHY**, c$15.20. Dr. Ramanan states in the introduction that his purpose is *to give as far as possible an objective and complete picture of the Madhyamika philosophy as it can be gathered from the whole of this text.* The text he refers to is the **Mana-prajna-paramita-sastra**, which is a commentary on the **Prajnaparamita Sutras** and is traditionally attributed to Nagarjuna. The original Sanskrit version of the **Sastra** has been lost and the text is preserved only in a Chinese translation. The author's main aim is not a translation—though in his exposition a great deal of the text is translated—but a deep study of the philosophical concepts found in the **Sastra**. The material is topically arranged and the author has made a valuable contribution to Buddhist studies with this volume. Notes, index. 409pp. MoB 66

STRENG, FREDERICK. **EMPTINESS: A STUDY IN RELIGIOUS MEANING**, $5.55. This is a fine in depth study of Nagarjuna and his interpretation of ultimate reality. Also included are translations of Nagarjuna's **Fundamentals of the Middle Way** and **Averting the Arguments**. The first two chapters on the relevance of studying *emptiness* and the implications of emptiness for understanding some basic Buddhist concepts are good scholarship and fairly dry going. The rest of the book is an excellent presentation of basic Indian Mahayana Buddhism (known generally as Madhyamika) and Nagarjuna's contribution to its development. They should be accessible to the general reader and we suggest that the reader reverse the order of the chapters and read the latter two first unless s/he has excellent grounding in Indian Buddhism. Very complete annotated bibliography, notes, index. 252pp. Abi 67

MALASEKERA, G.P. **ENCYCLOPEDIA OF BUDDHISM**, c$49.95. The most comprehensive, scholarly account available of every aspect of Buddhism. Illustrations. 1486pp. MoB

MATASUNAGA, ALICIA. **THE BUDDHIST PHILOSOPHY**, c$18.75. This is a detailed study of the rise and development of a theory of assimilation of the native gods in early Buddhism, particularly noting the developments occurring as this philosophy spread to China and Japan. This phenomenon is known in Japan as the *honji-suijaku* theory (the native Japanese gods are considered to be manifestations of the true nature of the various Buddhas and Bodhisattvas). Ms. Matasunaga examines the reasons why a unity between Buddhism and the indigenous faith occurred, the results of this unity, and the specific reasons why the Japanese developed their theory. An analysis is made of the principal deities involved as well as an investigation of the theory's impact upon other aspects of Japanese culture. An oversize volume, with many illustrations, extensive notes, bibliography, index. 310pp. Tut 69

MATICS, MARION, tr. **ENTERING THE PATH OF ENLIGHTENMENT**, $2.95. Contains the first complete English translation of Santideva's **Bodhicaryavatara**, a Mahayana classic which describes the Bodhisattva vow, one of the major Buddhist concepts. Included also is an interpretation and extensive notes as well as background material which places the text within the framework of Buddhist thought. It is a beautifully written piece and the translation is excellent. Bibliography, glossary, 318pp. McM 70

MOOKERJEE, SATKARI. THE BUDDHIST PHILOSOPHY OF UNIVERSAL FLUX, $20.35. A systematic exposition of the philosophy of critical realism as expounded by Dignaga and his school. Notes, index. 495pp. MoB 35

NANANANDA, BHIKKU. CONCEPT AND REALITY IN EARLY BUDDHIST THOUGHT, $4.00. *The analysis of the nature of concepts constitutes an important facet of the Buddhist doctrine of Anatta (not-self). Buddhism traces the idea of a soul to a fundamental error in understanding the facts of experience. This ignorance . . . is reflected to a great extent in the words and concepts in wordly parlance. . . . The Buddha's teachings on this particular aspect of our phenomenal existence can best be appreciated with the aid of two key words,* papanca *and* papanca-sanna-sankha, *an evaluation of which is the aim of this work.* Notes, index. 143pp. BPS 71

NIKAM, N.A. and RICHARD McKEON, trs. THE EDICTS OF ASOKA, $1.50. Asoka was a remarkable Indian ruler in the third century BC who not only renounced the warlike policies of his early career and converted India to Buddhism, but actually made a public proclamation of his errors and left a record of his teachings which he hoped would endure forever. It was inscribed on stone, not as a monument to himself, but as a record of moral law. This volume includes a full translation of the edicts along with a great deal of background and explanatory material. 94pp. UCh 59

NYANAPONIKA, VEN. THE HEART OF BUDDHIST MEDITATION, $3.95. A basic treatise, divided into three parts. The first explains the basic Buddhist meditation practices This is followed by a full translation, with explanatory notes, of **The Greater Discourse on the Foundations of Mindfulness** (the **Maha-Satipatthana-Sutta**), a review of the Buddha's teaching on the subject. There's also an anthology of translations from Pali and Sanskrit texts dealing with right mindfulness. A lucid exposition. Notes, glossary, 223pp. Wei 62

_____. **PATHWAYS OF BUDDHIST THOUGHT,** c$11.90. A collection of some of the most important essays from **The Wheel**, a series of short, authoritative paperbacks dealing with all aspects of Theravada Buddhism. Over 140 of them have been published over the years and a high standard has consistently been maintained. They include translations of portions of scriptures and commentarial works, as well as original essays on Buddhist themes related to modern life. The present essays cover some of the most important aspects of Buddhism and include discussion of such basic themes as the nature of Buddhism, Buddhist ethics and philosophical concepts, Buddhism and science, the power of mindfulness, *Anatta* and *Nibbana*. The Venerable Nyanaponika's writings form the central section of the book. Notes, index, 256pp. A&U 71

_____. **THE POWER OF MINDFULNESS,** $2.25. *This is a commentary on the Satipatthana mindfulness meditation, an inquiry into the scope of bare attention and the principal sources of its strength. Satipatthana, or the practice of mindfulness, was recommended by the Buddha for all who seek to grow spiritually and eventually attain the realization of enlightenment. . . . The method here described is the foundation of all Buddhist meditation practice.*—from the introduction. This is a very clear presentation, without the excessive use of capitalization that characterizes the Ceylonese texts. 56pp. UnP 72

NYANATILOKA. BUDDHIST DICTIONARY, c$7.00. A manual, in dictionary form, of Buddhist terminology and doctrine. All the Pali words are Romanized and many English words are given Pali equivalents. The text is fully cross-referenced and seems to be quite complete. Often original sources are quoted in the explanations. This is the third edition, revised and enlarged by Nyanaponika. 225pp. Fwn 72

_____. **THE WORD OF THE BUDDHA,** $2.20. A systematic exposition of all the main tenets of the Buddha's teachings as found in the **Sutta-Pitaka** of the Pali Canon. The selections have been grouped topically and the original texts themselves are translated and presented, with little commentary. The translator provides a Pali pronunciation guide and a short introduction as well as a fairly lengthy bibliography. Index, 113pp. BPS 71

OLCOTT, HENRY S. THE BUDDHIST CATECHISM, $1.00. A classic work which contains the essence of Buddhist teachings. 138pp. TPH 1881

THE PALI CANON

The Pali Canon is a compendious term for the Scriptures of the Theravada— Teaching of the Elders—School of Buddhism, sometimes called the Southern School, which today may be found in Ceylon, Thailand, Burma, and Cambodia. The language is Pali, which was the language of Magadha, where the Buddha taught, and was carried by missionaries at some stage to Ceylon . . . . The Canon is the slow product of an oral tradition handed down by generations of bhikkus or monks, as agreed in form, so the Canon itself claims, at a Council of Elders convened soon after the Buddha's death. What happened, in the 400 years of that handing down to this large collection of remembered discourses and conversations and to the written word as edited, no doubt, in the course of further centuries of commentary and argument, it is impossible to say.—Introduction to **Some Sayings of the Buddha** translated by F.L. Woodward. The Canon relates the life and teachings of the Buddha in the forty-five years of his ministry after reaching enlightenment. Virtually all of the material now available has been translated by the Pali Text Society, founded in 1881 by Dr. and Mrs. Rhys Davids. The following titles are mainly selected from the Society's list. If you would like a complete list of the available works, please write to us. See the sub-sections on Jataka Tales and the Dhammapada for more Pali texts.

ANDERSEN, DINES and HELMER SMITH, eds. SUTTANIPATA, c$7.00. An early work which presents Buddhism not as an established monastic system, but only as an ethical religion stressing the simple virtuous life. The recluse is called upon to adhere to the moral virtues, to subdue his desires for sensual pleasures, to turn his mind away from material possessions, to have no dealings in gold and silver, and to eat only moderately. Commentaries on the **Suttanipata** edited by Helmer Smith are also available (Vol. I, c$9.00; Vol. III, c$15.00). PTS

GEIGER, WILHELM. PALI LANGUAGE AND LITERATURE, c$12.00. Translated into English by Dr. Batakrishna Ghosh. 264pp. MuM

HORNER, I.B. THE BOOK OF THE DISCIPLINE, Vol. I, II, III, c$12.60/each; **Vol. IV,** c$10.00; **Vol. V,** c$12.60; **Vol. VI,** c$19.00. These volumes (I, II, III: Vinaya, Suttavibhanga; IV: Mahavagga; V: Cullavagga; VI: Parivara) contain the rules which govern the conduct of the monks and nuns in the Buddhist order. They cover such things as the admission of nuns and monks, their daily activities, their communal life, their food, clothing and shelter, and their relations with the laity. PTS

_____. **THE MIDDLE LENGTH SAYINGS (MAJJHIMA-NIKAYA),** c$20.00/each. A collection of discourses which exemplify the philosophy of the dhamma. Every point in this doctrine is discussed over and over again and in the process some of the greatest literary works in Buddhist literature are presented. Three volumes. PTS

JOHANSSON, RUNE. PALI BUDDHIST TEXTS, c$8.40. A simple and practical introduction to the language, consisting of texts, vocabularies, translations, and notes, and a systematic treatment of grammar. 160pp. Cur 76

MAHATHERA, A.P. BUDDHADATTA. ENGLISH-PALI DICTIONARY, c$12.00. PTS

NANAMOLI, VEN. THE LIFE OF THE BUDDHA, c$13.00. This **Life** has been translated and compiled by a scholar-monk and it is based on the oldest authentic records as found in the Pali Canon. The material is presented in the form of *Narrators* and *Voices* who quote the Canonical material. The Bhikkhu has organized the material chronologically and cites his sources. The narration often lacks cohesion and we would not recommend this book as a primary account of the Buddha's life and teachings. However, it is a good supplementary volume since a great deal of the material is not available in English translation elsewhere, or else is not easily obtainable. Index, notes, bibliography, 375pp. BPS 72

_____. **MINDFULNESS OF BREATHING,** $4.00. Anapanasati, *or* Mindfulness of Breathing, *is among the Buddhist methods of mind training given most prominence in the Pali Canon. It was originally for his own use that the translator collected the material that follows from the Pali Canon and its commentaries. The idea was to have under one cover, for the purpose of study, the Pali teaching of this meditation subject, omitting nothing important and eliminating repetitions.*—from the introduction. Notes and background information accompany the selections. 125pp. BPS 73

_____. **THE PATH OF PURIFICATION: VISUDDHI MAGGA,** c$19.30/$9.90set. This book, written in the fifth century, systematically summmarizes and interprets the teaching of the Buddha contained in the Pali **Tripitaka**, which is generally regarded as the oldest and most authentic record of the Buddha's words. This is one of the most important, if not the most important, Pali texts. It contains clear, detailed instructions on Buddhist doctrine and meditation. The translator was a member of a Ceylonese Buddhist monastic order for eleven years and is well known for his excellent critical translations of difficult texts. This volume is recommended to all serious students of Buddhism. Glossary, index, notes, 935pp. ShP 76

NANANANDA, BHIKKHU. THE MAGIC OF THE MIND, $4.00. An exposition of the **Kalakarama Sutta,** a canonical discourse on the illusory nature of consciousness centering on a discussion of the Law of Dependent Arising as a *golden mean* which freely transcends the dualities of existence and non-existence and mind and matter. An annotated translation of the discourse is presented, followed by a detailed exposition of the psychological and philosophical implications of the text. Notes, index, 92pp. BPS 74

NARADA, VEN. THE BUDDHA AND HIS TEACHINGS, $6.40. The author of this study is a member of the Order of the Sangha and he has based his account on the Pali texts, commentaries, and traditions prevailing in Buddhist countries (especially in Sri Lanka). The first part of the book deals with the life of the Buddha; the second with the Dhamma, the Pali term for his doctrine. The section reviewing the Buddha's life is quite vividly written and often reads like a novel. All of the terms used are clearly defined and a great deal of background information in presented. The book seems to be designed for the general reader and is easy to read. The material is presented in many short sections. All the references are cited. Notes, index, 730pp. BPS 73

_____. A MANUAL OF ABHIDHAMMA, $9.00. A translation of the **Abhidhammattha Sangaha**, with extensive commentary and notes on virtually every word and a Romanization of the Pali text. *Abhidhamma . . . is the Higher Teaching of the Buddha. It expounds the quintessence of His profound doctrine. . . . In the Abhidhamma both mind and matter . . . are microscopically analyzed. Chief events connected with the process of birth and death are explained in detail. Intricate points of the Dhamma are clarified. The Path of Emancipation is set forth in clear terms. . . . Consciousness is defined. Thoughts are analyzed and classified chiefly from an ethical standpoint. All mental states are enumerated. The composition of each type of consciousness is set forth in detail.* Index, 458pp. BPS 75

NYANAPONIKA, VEN., ed. **SELECTED BUDDHIST TEXTS FROM THE PALI CANON**, c$10.50/set. More selections from **The Wheel**. This three-volume set is devoted to translations from Pali texts. Many of the texts presented here are not available anywhere else and all the translations are by noted Buddhist scholars. Essential reading for all who are seriously interested in Theravada Buddhism. Many notes accompany the texts. About 1400pp. BPS 74

PIYADASSI, VEN. **THE BOOK OF PERFECTION**, $4.00. This is a translation of an anthology of selected discourses of the Buddha which was compiled centuries ago and was intended to be a handbook for the newly ordained novice. The idea was that those novices who are not capable of studying large portions of the **Discourse Collection** (*sutta pitaka*) should at least be conversant with the Book of Perfection. The twenty-four discourses presented here have been selected from the five **Nikayas** (the original Pali collections of the Buddha's discourses). This is the most widely known Pali book in Sri Lanka today. It is given an important place in the Buddhist home, and is even treated with veneration and is kept in the household shrine so that the residents can refer to it during their devotional hour. Notes, introductory material, 123pp. BPS 75

_____. **THE BUDDHA'S ANCIENT PATH**, c$7.00. This is a well written account by one of the leading monks in Sri Lanka today. It is based on the Buddha's teachings as expounded in the Pali Canon and is basically an in-depth discussion of the Four Noble Truths and the Noble Eightfold Path—with a full chapter devoted to an exposition of each of the Truths and Paths. There's also a concise account of the Buddha's life and an informative survey of Buddhist meditation. *This makes interesting and instructive reading, and the validity of the interpretations is not open to question. On the contrary, these interpretations, authoritative and unimpeachable, may be taken as a trustworthy guide.*—I.B. Horner, President, Pali Text Society. Notes, index, 239pp. BPS 64

RHYS DAVIDS, CAROLINE, tr. **BUDDHIST PSYCHOLOGY**, c$22.50. This is a translation of **Dhamma-Sangani**, the first of the seven books of the **Abhidhamma-Pitaka**. The text reviews the elements and objects of consciousness according to Buddhist doctrine and provides an *enumeration of the Dhammas*, i.e., an inquiry into the mental elements or processes. The text is accompanied by numerous long notes and the translator connects the material with the rest of the **Pitakas**. Mrs. Rhys Davids also provides an excellent 95pp introduction. Glossary, index, 488pp. OrP 75

_____. **PSALMS OF THE SISTERS (THERAGATHA).**, c$13.00. PTS

RHYS DAVIDS, CAROLINE and F.L. WOODWARD. **THE BOOK OF KINDRED SAYINGS (SAMYUTTA-NIKAYA)**, Vol. I, c$13.00; Vol. II, c$10.00; Vol. III, c$5.00; Vol. IV, c$13.25; Vol. V, c$7.00. Another collection of discourses which makes an attempt to divide the suttas according to different categories: a chief point of doctrine, or a class of demon or deity, or some prominent disciple of the master. PTS

RHYS DAVIDS, T.W., tr. **BUDDHIST SUTTAS**, $3.00. The Pali Suttas, third and fourth centuries BC, form the earliest essential part of the Buddhist scriptures. This selection, originally published in the Sacred Books of the East series, presents translations of seven of the most important ones. The gospel of the life, works, and death of the Buddha takes up almost half the volume. Introductions discuss the age, form and authenticity of the Suttas. 307pp. Dov 1881

_____. **THE QUESTIONS OF KING MILINDA**, $15.00/set. Ancient Buddhist dialogues, probably written in the second century. They provide an important supplement to the Pali Canon and help explain many of the philosophical ideas found there. Part of the Sacred Books of the East Series. Two volumes. 708pp. Dov 1894

RHYS DAVIDS, T.W. and CAROLINE. **DIALOGUES OF THE BUDDHA**, c$9.60/each. These two volumes, constituting in the Pali text, the **Digha** and **Magghima Nikayas**, contain a full exposition of what early Buddhists considered the teaching of the Buddha to have been. Each volume includes an index of principal subjects and proper names and of Pali words discussed, and averages over 350pp. PTS 1899

RHYS DAVIDS, T.W. and WILLIAM STEDE, eds. **THE PALI TEXT SOCIETY'S PALI-ENGLISH DICTIONARY**, c$31.00. This is the definitive Pali dictionary. Romanized, oversize, 738pp. PTS 21

SOMA, VEN. **THE WAY OF MINDFULNESS**, $6.00. Translations of **The Discourse on the Arousing of Mindfulness**, with commentary, **The Contemplation of the Body, The Contemplation of Feeling and of Consciousness**, and **The Contemplation of Mental Objects** (the **Satipatthana Sutta** and commentary). These are advanced texts, designed for the practicing student. The presentation is often abrupt—but this is a conscious design of the original author. Many practical topics are discussed in depth and the material here is not available elsewhere. Notes, introduction, 207pp. BPS 75

WOODWARD, F.L. **MANUAL OF A MYSTIC**, c$7.00. This is a translation of the Yogavachara's Manual, a practical working text for the aspirant in which systems of preparation and of meditation are set forth. Included are eight meditations and two exercises, all but one drawn from the **Sutta Pitaka**. This text is recommended only to the advanced student. Introduction by Mrs. Rhys Davids. Index, 179pp. PTS

_____. **MINOR ANTHOLOGIES, VOL. II**, c$6.00. A fifth collection of discourses which consists of a number of miscellaneous works including some of the earliest pieces of Buddhist literature. The two included here are *Udana: Verses of Uplift* and *Itivuttaka. As It Was Said.* Index of names and of words and subjects in each. 208pp. PTS

_____. **SOME SAYINGS OF THE BUDDHA**, $1.95. A selection (the only material available in paperback) of major portions of the Pali Canon. The selections were chosen and topically arranged by F.L. Woodward, a scholar who spent the last thirty years of his life translating the most important volumes of the Canon, and editing the commentaries to many others. The only way for the beginning student to even begin to approach the innumerable suttas contained in the Canon seems to be through the material presented here. A very well organized collection. An introduction by Christmas Humphreys discusses the Canon, and sketches the life and teachings of the Buddha. Index, 249pp. Oxf 25

WOODWARD, F. L. and E. M. HARE, trs. **THE BOOK OF THE GRADUAL SAYINGS (ANGUTTARA-NIKAYA)**, Vol. I, c$9.00; Vol. II, III, c$10.00/each; Vol. IV, c$7.00, Vol. V, c$10.00. A collection of discourses which consists of a classification according to numerical categories: that is, Section One consists of suttas dealing with things of which only one exists; Section Two, of things in which there are two; and so on until Section Eleven. PTS

PREBISH, CHARLES, ed. **BUDDHISM**, $10.00. Subtitled *A Modern Perspective*, this is a clearly written in depth introductory text written by eight leading scholars. The volume begins with a comprehensive survey of fundamentals and goes on to include topics previously untouched in introductory texts. The Buddha's life, basic Buddhist doctrines and practices, the Hinayana and Mahayana sects, Buddhist literature, schools of thought, and meditation are all thoroughly discussed. Each basket of the **Tripitaka** or Buddhist canon is discussed individually, and several of the most important Mahayana sutras are considered in detail. Much of the book is devoted to Indian Buddhism, and discussions of Buddhism in China, Japan, Ceylon, Tibet, Southeast Asia, and Korea are also included. An appendix gives the location of Buddhist groups in the U.S. and there's a 52pp glossary. Bibliography, index. 345pp. PSU 75

_____, tr. **BUDDHIST MONASTIC DISCIPLINE**, c$18.15. Translations from the Sanskrit of two important Buddhist monastic disciplinary texts, the **Pratimoksa Sutras** of the Mahasamghikas and Mulasarvastivadins, printed on facing pages. Introductory chapters give an overview of the rise of Buddhist monasticism, analyze Vinaya, that portion of the Buddhist canon regulating the life of monks and nuns; provisionally identify the problems inherent in Pratimoksa study; and describe how the Sutras were found and edited. The texts themselves are thoroughly annotated. Notes, bibliography, 156pp. PSU 75

PRICE, A.F. and WONG MOU-LAM, trs. **THE DIAMOND SUTRA AND THE SUTRA OF HUI NENG**, $2.95. Translations of two classic texts. The **Diamond Sutra** is a subtle scripture which forms a part of the **Prajnaparamita** (or Wisdom texts). **The Sutra of Hui Neng**, also known as the **Platform Sutra**, is one of the basic texts of Zen Buddhism. The translations are of fine quality and the translators also supply an abundance of notes. 114pp. ShP 69

RAHULA, WALPOLE. **THE HERITAGE OF THE BHIKKHU**, $3.95. This is an account of the Buddhist monk's life as a servant of the people's needs in his role as follower and teacher of the principles of the Buddhist doctrine. Buddhism here is seen as a religion of monks and laymen cooperating to improve the spiritual and material conditions of humanity rather than as a mere monastic discipline. Rahula himself received the traditional monastic training in Ceylon and held a high position in one of the leading monastic institutes there. Includes extensive notes, glossary, and index. 176pp. RaH 74

_____. **WHAT THE BUDDHA TAUGHT**, $2.95. The best presentation of the fundamental principles of the Buddha's teachings that we know of. Rahula is a Ceylonese Buddhist monk and scholar and he has based his book on the original Pali texts, which are universally accepted by scholars as the earliest extant records. A very readable book, highly recommended. This is a new, revised and expanded edition which includes texts from the **Suttas** and the **Dhammapada** as well as a glossary, index, and bibliography. Illustrations, 151pp. RaH 59

RAWDING, F.W. **THE BUDDHA**, $2.75. A pictorial introduction to the Buddha's life, main teachings, and times. 48pp. CUP 75

REYNOLDS, FRANK and MANI, trs. **THE THREE WORLDS ACCORDING TO KING RUANG**, c$18.95. This work was completed about 1345 AD by the heir apparent to the throne of a central Thai kingdom. Though the sermon is little known outside Thailand, and has never before been translated into English, it is a comprehensive, colorful, and popular presentation of the most profound message of Theravada Buddhism. Color and black-and-white illustrations, index, notes. 456pp. SUP 76

ROBINSON, RICHARD. **THE BUDDHIST RELIGION**, $6.65. This book seems to have been designed as a text for a course on comparative religion. It begins with a survey of Buddhism today in the East and West. This is followed by a discussion of the life and teachings of the historical Buddha. The last two chapters review the development of Indian Buddhism and developments outside India. The material is well written and organized, although it tends to be somewhat dry. The book is quite well thought of, especially in the academic community. All the major schools of thought are covered and an excellent topical annotated bibliography is included. Index, 136pp. Dic 70

_____. **THE LIFE OF THE BUDDHA**, $3.25. A well written account of the Buddha's life, based on Pali texts. The author is a Buddhist monk/scholar who is proficient in Pali and Sanskrit. Illustrations, 88pp. A&U

ROERICH, HELENA. **FOUNDATIONS OF BUDDHISM**, c$10.00. A version of the life of the Buddha and his teachings on the problem of human existence and the cessation of suffering by one of the founders of the Agni Yoga Society in New York. 146pp. AgY 71

SADDHATISSA, H. **THE BUDDHA'S WAY**, $1.95. This is a good clear presentation of Buddha's teachings and Buddhist practices. Part I describes the life and teachings of the Buddha, what it means to become a Buddhist, and both the negative and positive aspects of Buddhist morality. Part II explains the *Four Noble Truths* which form the foundations of Buddhist philosophy. Part III is devoted to meditation with preliminary instructions for meditation, and sections on Samatha and Vipassana meditation. Dr. Sadhatissa also includes selections from the Pali scriptures, details of the main Buddhist festivals, and a chronological table of Buddhist history in both the East and West. Illustrations, glossary, bibliography, and index. 139pp. Brz 71

_____. **BUDDHIST ETHICS**, $2.95. A very complete scholarly work which draws heavily from the scriptures of Theravada Buddhism. Bibliography, 197pp. Brz 70

SAYADAW, MAHASI. **PRACTICAL INSIGHT MEDITATION**, $2.25. An exploration of the Satipatthana mindfulness meditation, its basic and progressive stages. Sayadaw is a Burmese meditation master and has played an important part in the revitalization of interest in Insight Meditation. This book is an advanced study of the elements of mind and an in-depth investigation. It includes an abridged translation of the original **Maha Satipatthana Sutra**, with commentary. 65pp. UnP 72

_____. **THE PROGRESS OF INSIGHT**, $2.50. The translation by Nyanaponika Thera of an advanced treatise: *The foremost concern in this work is with a stage where, after diligent preliminary practice, the insight knowledges have begun to emerge, leading up to the highest crest of spiritual achievement, Arahantship (Sainthood).* This edition includes a Romanized version of the Pali original in addition to the translation. Introduction by Thera. 67pp. BPS 73

Mantra written in Tibetan script

SCHUMANN, HANS. **BUDDHISM**, $2.45. This is a systematically arranged study which outlines the distinctions between the three main Buddhist systems: Theravada, Mahayana, and Tantrayana. Schumann has used original Pali and Sanskrit texts, and his work contains material on karma, conditioned orientation, meditation, dharma, nirvana, and the Yogacara School. The most unique feature of the book is a Tabulated Synopsis of all the systems with which the book deals, showing the source, the method, the Interim Goal, and the Ultimate Goal of each. The material is clearly presented, but is intended for students with some previous knowledge of Buddhism. The detail included could be overwhelming to a beginning student. Illustrations, index, bibliography. 200pp. TPH 73

SHAFTEL, OSCAR. **AN UNDERSTANDING OF THE BUDDHA**, c$8.50. This is a fairly critical Western view of the Buddha's teachings and of Buddhist beliefs over the centuries. Shaftel appears to be trying to see what there is in Buddhism that can be useful to Western man. He begins with a general review of Buddhism and the Buddha's teachings and goes from there to a more detailed analysis of Tantra, Zen, and nirvana. Extensive notes follow the text. Bibliography, index, 247pp. ScB 74

SCHUON, FRITHJOF. **IN THE TRACKS OF BUDDHISM**, c$5.90. An excellent introduction to Buddhism which emphasizes the unity rather than the diversity. The forms may differ, but there is the thread of a common ideal. The author is a comparative religion scholar, especially noted for his work on Islam, and he freely cites other religious parallels and relates Buddhist wisdom to contemporary situations and assumptions. His aim is to present Buddhism not merely as an historical phenomenon or a philosophical system, but as a still living spiritual force and in this he succeeds admirably. Highly recommended. 165pp. A&U 68

SILCOCK, T.H., tr. **A VILLAGE ORDINATION**, $7.35. Translation of a Thai poem which describes the ordination of a Buddhist monk in a rural monastery, and also discusses Thai rural culture, Buddhist religion, and life in a Thai monastery. Parallel Thai-English texts, notes, introductory material, and photographs of the ceremony. 264pp. Cur 76

SINNETT, A.P. **ESOTERIC BUDDHISM**, c$7.95. See Theosophy section. 241pp. Wiz 1883

SOOTHILL, W.E. and LEWIS HODOUS. **A DICTIONARY OF CHINESE BUDDHIST TERMS**, c$14.80. An oversize text, with Sanskrit and English equivalents and a Sanskrit-Pali index. The Chinese is not Romanized. 531pp. CWP 75

SPIRO, MELFORD. **BUDDHISM AND SOCIETY**, $8.00. A comprehensive anthropological study of Burmese Theravada Buddhism. Very well documented, extensive bibliography. 593pp. H&R 70

STCHERBATSKY, T.H. **BUDDHIST LOGIC VOL. I**, $6.00. The most important work on Buddhist logic ever published. This volume covers the history of Indian and Tibetan logic up through the system of Dignaga. 559pp. Dov 30

_____. **BUDDHIST LOGIC VOL. II**, $6.00. A translation of Dharmakirti's **Nyaya-bindu**, with Dharmottara's commentary. Appendices contain translations from various other treatises. Plentiful reading for the scholar. 437pp. Dov 30

STRYK, LUCIEN. **WORLD OF THE BUDDHA: A READER, FROM THE THREE BASKETS TO MODERN ZEN**, $2.95. Translations come from many sources and Stryk has tried to pick out the clearest texts available. Material is included on all types of Buddhist teachings and Stryk has written a long introduction and commentaries on the primary source material. We recommend that a beginning student read some of the selections presented here in addition to one of the books giving an overall picture of Buddhism to give him/her a good basic foundation in Buddhist studies. This is an excellent source book, one of the most complete available. 479pp. Dou 68

SUJATA, ANAGARIKA. **BEGINNING TO SEE**, $2.50. See Meditation Section. UnP 75

SUZUKI, D.T. **ON INDIAN MAHAYANA BUDDHISM**, $3.90. An anthology of the best of Suzuki's essays from a variety of books, edited by Edward Conze. Conze also provides a long, illuminating introduction and a glossary. 284pp. H&R 68

_____. **OUTLINES OF MAHAYANA BUDDHISM**, $2.95. A very complete introductory work. Mahayana Buddhism is known as the *Greater Vehicle* in contrast to Hinayana, which is known as the *Lesser Vehicle*. In the latter the stress is on individual salvation, while Mahayana is concerned with social compassion. Alan Watts provides a long preface and gives an annotated listing of followup reading in various areas. 371pp. ScB 63

_____. **STUDIES IN THE LANKAVATARA SUTRA**, c$24.00. An attempt to elucidate the teachings presented in the Sutra systematically, at the same time analyzing the contents of the Sutra itself. Includes long introduction and extensive Sanskrit-Chinese-English glossary. 458pp. RKP 30

_____. **THE LANKAVATARA SUTRA**, c$18.00. The first complete translation of this important Mahayana text. The Sutra consists of a memorandum kept by a Mahayana master, in which he put down all the teachings of importance accepted by the Mahayana followers of his day. He did not try to keep them in any order—and so the text is a bit disorderly. But it can be understood with effort. A long introduction describes the general teaching of the Sutra, and the appendix contains the Sanskrit text, the three Chinese and the Tibetan versions, with their respective English translations. Many notes, 300pp. RKP 32

SWEARER, DONALD. **BUDDHISM IN TRANSITION**, $2.65. This is a sociologically-oriented study of Buddhism as the major religious force in Southeast Asia, analyzing its role as a focus for change and adaptation and its important role in nationalism. Swearer shows how, in the quest for a viable social ethic, Buddhist concepts are being emphasized, applied to different contexts, or transformed—especially in the areas of education and social thought. He also offers some suggestions as to how Buddhism might provoke religious reflection and renewal in the West. Notes, 160pp. Wes 70

_____. **SECRETS OF THE LOTUS**, $1.95. See section on Meditation. McM 71

_____. **TOWARD THE TRUTH**, $2.95. Selections from the writings of Buddhadasa, a widely acclaimed Thai Bhikkhu, which contribute to an understanding of contemporary Theravada Buddhism. He explains Buddhist doctrine as a practical system, open to all and his particular genius as an interpreter of Buddhism has been to relate ancient truths to our era, stressing the importance of individual personal experience. Notes, glossary, 189pp. Wes 71

TACHIBANA, S. **THE ETHICS OF BUDDHISM**, c$12.00. A didactic work, emphasizing the idea that Buddhism is a religion of moral stature—and has been since its origin—and that the morality which Buddhism particularly emphasizes is a practical one. Notes, bibliography, index. 304pp. Cur 26

TAKAKUSU, JUNJIRO. **THE ESSENTIALS OF BUDDHIST PHILOSOPHY**, c$9.00. This is a scholarly study of Buddhist philosophy in Japan. Professor Takakusu was the author, editor, and translator of monumental works on Buddhism. In this volume, his only major work in English, the summation of his lifetime study of Buddhist philosophy is presented. The material originally was delivered as a series of lectures at the University of Hawaii and was edited for publication by Wing-tsit Chan and Charles Moore. Divided into fifteen chapters, the book deals with different schools: Kusha, Jojitsu, Hosso, Sanron, Kegon, Tendai, Shingon, Zen, Jodo, Nichiren, and New Ritsu. Each of the schools is discussed very fully and the major individual figures and movements are analyzed in depth. A long introductory section gives the background necessary to appreciate the text. This is an excellent work for the serious student. Notes, index, 243pp. MoB 56

TAMBIAH, S.J. **BUDDHISM AND THE SPIRIT CULTS IN NORTH-EAST THAILAND**, $6.95. *This volume represents the most extensive—and, on balance, the best—account of Thai religion published to date in English . . . . [T]he author addresses himself at length to Buddhist cosmology, the initiation of manhood (both historically and locally), primary* *religious concepts* that emerge from the observation of thought and deed in the village, *the expression in contemporary religious institutions of the great literary and historical traditions of Buddhism, and, finally, the belief and ritual complexes that constitute the working substance of local religion.*—**American Anthropologist.** Index, notes, bibliography, 388pp. CUP 70

TAMURA, YOSHIRO and MIYOSAKAI KOJIRO. **THREEFOLD LOTUS SUTRA**, $7.95. The **Lotus Sutra** is revered by millions of Buddhists as containing the core and culmination of the Buddha's teaching. Together with the two shorter sutras that traditionally accompany it, **Innumerable Meanings** and **Meditation on the Boddhisattva Universal Virtue**, it comprises one of the most important scriptures of Mahayana Buddhism. Here all three scriptures are presented together for the first time in English. The latter two have never before been translated into English, while this version of the **Lotus Sutra** itself is based on the translation made by Bunno Kato and W.E. Soothill, thoroughly revised and annotated in the light of present scholarship. This excellent, readable translation is a welcome addition to the literature. Glossary, 399pp. Wea 75

TERWIEL, BAREND. **MONKS AND MAGIC**, $9.45. The narrative describes the practice of Buddhism in a Thai rural community. The children and young adults appear largely interested in esoteric spells and magical diagrams. Full ritual knowledge is obtained by many men in their twenties. The older people practice a more traditional Buddhism. Daily life and the role that Buddhism plays in it is discussed at length and there's also an analysis of Buddhist rituals. Glossary of Thai, Pali, and Sanskrit words, illustrations, bibliography. 303pp. Cur 76

THOMAS, EDWARD. **THE LIFE OF BUDDHA**, $7.50. This is a scholarly, authoritative **Life**, based on Sanskrit sources and on Chinese and Tibetan material in addition to the more traditional Pali source books. As is true with most studies of the Buddha's life, legend and history are intertwined. Thomas has updated the earlier material presented by such scholars as the Rhys Davids, Kern, and Oldenberg in the light of new findings in recently translated Pali texts. He presents many translations throughout this volume. An important work for all seriously interested in Buddhism, but not one that we recommend to the reader who seeks only a general survey. Notes, bibliography, index. 321pp. RKP 49

WALTERS, JOHN. **THE ESSENCE OF BUDDHISM**, $1.75. A clear, excellent primer by a British journalist who studied Buddhism in Ceylon. Includes chapters on the Buddha's life, his teachings (including a selection from the words of Buddha), Asoka, meditation, as well as a chapter on the solutions offered by Buddhism to outstanding problems of life. Bibliography. Recommended. 164pp. Cro 61

WARREN, HENRY, tr. **BUDDHISM IN TRANSLATIONS**, $6.65. This volume was first printed in 1896 as part of the **Harvard Oriental Series** and remained for many years the only authoritative collection of translations from the Pali which was generally available. Warren did all the translations himself and while they are stylistically dated, this volume remains an important sourcebook for those who seek translations of the Pali texts. 102 texts of varying length are included. 502pp. Ath 1896

WAYMAN, ALEX and HIDEKO, trs. **THE LION'S ROAR OF QUEEN SRIMALA** c$14.00. This text is the chief scriptural authority in India for the theory that all sentient beings have the potentiality of Buddhahood. It was a source of inspiration for both the **Lankavatara Sutra** and the **Awakening of Faith**. The original work was written in South India in the third century AD. This is the first modern translation into English, and it has been pieced together from many existing editions and commentaries. Also included here is a very detailed 57 page introduction and extensive textual notes. Glossary, bibliography of Chinese, Japanese and Western sources, and index, 142pp. Col 74

WEI TAT, tr. **DOCTRINE OF MERE CONSCIOUSNESS**, c$53.75. This is the first complete English translation of the **Ch'eng Wei-shih Lun**, the masterpiece of the charismatic seventh century **Tripitaka** master Hsuan Tsang. The text is a thorough and profound exploration of the human mind by introspection, meditation, and contemplation. Its central theme is that all sense impressions of the phenomena of the universe are illusory and that nothing exists except in the consciousness. The material is based on the insights of the ancient Buddhist scholars and mystics. Wei Tat provides an excellent long introduction and the text itself is reproduced in both Chinese and English on facing pages. Oversize, bibliography. 957pp. CWL 73

WELCH, HOLMES. **THE PRACTICE OF CHINESE BUDDHISM, 1900–50**, $6.95. A detailed, careful study which brings together a large amount of documentary material and the results of innumerable interviews Mr. Welch held with refugee monks during the four years he spent assembling material for this book. Bibliography. 584pp. HUP 67

WRIGHT, ARTHUR. **BUDDHISM IN CHINESE HISTORY**, $1.95. A balanced, well written account. Includes a long section of selected further readings and some illustrations. 138pp. SUP 59

TIBETAN BUDDHISM

ANURUDDHA, R.P. **AN INTRODUCTION INTO LAMAISM**, c$6.15. A general survey of the mystical aspects of Tibetan Buddhism, written in a non-technical manner. The book begins with a general survey of the teachings of the Buddha and the schism in Buddhism. Then there is a chapter on the introduction of Buddhism into Tibet and one on the Guru Tsongka-pa, founder of the Yellow Cap sect. This is followed by a detailed investigation of the Tibetan Buddhist iconography. Another section reviews the Lamaistic ritual and various features of Tantric Buddhism. The volume ends with a discussion of Tibetan yoga, yogis, and lamas. Notes, bibliography, index. 212pp. VVR 59

BEYER, STEPHAN. **THE CULT OF TARA—MAGIC AND RITUAL IN TIBET**, c$21.50. Dr. Beyer spent fourteen months in one of the few remaining Tibetan monasteries (in northern India). Here he draws on his experience as he attempts to formulate the processes and presuppositions of Tibetan ritual and to generalize therefrom to the fundamental structures of Tantric meditation. The book sets out from a consideration of the cult of the goddess Tara, and demonstrates its ramifications in monastic ceremony, folklore, literature, and magic. In thus outlining the fundamentals of the Tantric vision, Beyer deals as well with poetry, drama, medicine, divination, and art, trying to create a full statement of the life of Tibetan Buddhism. Many quotations from primary source material are included, and a feeling of the living ritual of Tibetan Buddhism can come out of a careful reading of the text. The text includes profuse chapter notes, an excellent long bibliography, illustrations, and it is fully indexed. This is one of the most important new books on Tibetan Buddhism that has been written since the Chinese take-over. 542pp. UCP 73

BLOFELD, JOHN. **THE TANTRIC MYSTICISM OF TIBET**, c$1.00/$3.25. An excellent review of the practice of Tibetan Buddhism, with an emphasis on their meditation techniques. The Mahayana background is given together with details of the techniques, purpose, and underlying theory of Tantric meditation. Ninety percent of the material in the book is based on the author's first-hand experience studying under Tibetan Lamas. The book forms an excellent introduction to the Buddhism of Tibet. It is very clearly written and includes both an introductory survey of the main features of the religion and a detailed presentation of the actual practices. Recommended. 257pp. Dut 70

BROMAGE, BERNARD. **TIBETAN YOGA**, c$6.00. Bromage, who spent years studying the Tibetans, gives revelations of the Tibetan as priest and magician, with absorbing explanations of his spells, magical rites, and the exercises by which he produces powers and faculties which are regarded as inexplicable by the Western mind. 238pp. Wei 52

BURANG, THEODORE. **TIBETAN ART OF HEALING**, $3.90. See the Healing section.

CHANG, GARMA. **TEACHINGS OF TIBETAN YOGA**, $2.45. An excellent, extremely concentrated book which provides an introduction to the spiritual, mental, and physical exercises. Includes an extensive discussion of *Dumo*, the generating of heat in one's body, which is a major part of Tantric Buddhism. Chang is a Chinese scholar who studied in Tibet for eight years and is very well respected. 128pp. Cit 63

CSOMA DE KOROS, ALEXANDER. **A GRAMMAR OF THE TIBETAN LANGUAGE IN ENGLISH**, c$16.15. This is a recent reprint of one of the earliest Tibetan grammars. *I have enumerated only those articles which I thought to be essentially required for a fundamental knowledge of this . . . language. I have gone through all the parts of speech and have given lists of them as fully as it was in my power to do, together with their derivations and variations, etc., that the learner might at once see and perceive all the constituent parts of the Tibetan language.* Appendices illustrate and explain the letters of the Tibetan language and the alphabet. Oversize, 251pp. Alt 1834

CONZE, EDWARD, tr. **THE BUDDHA'S LAW AMONG THE BIRDS**, $6.30. According to Buddhist belief the Dharma of the Buddha is not confined to men, but is taught to all kinds of beings, including animals. There is a legend that the great Bodhisattva of Mercy, Avalokitesvara, had taken among the birds the form of a cuckoo—an animal which recommends itself to the Buddhist mind by its attitude toward family life. About three centuries ago a Lama wrote a charming little book describing how the birds of the Himalayas met under the leadership of the cuckoo on a holy mountain and how they were instructed in the Buddhist way of living and thinking. Though it is a simple and unsophisticated book, it brings home to us, better than many scholarly treatises, the overtones of the faith in Tibet. This translation has been made from the Tibetan original and includes an introduction by Dr. Conze which sketches the background of the story and gives extracts from another Tibetan work which describes the spiritual antecedents of the cuckoo. Notes, commentary, 65pp. Cas 74

DAS, SARAT CHANDRA. **AN INTRODUCTION TO THE GRAMMAR OF THE TIBETAN LANGUAGE**, c$13.50. This is the newest and generally is considered the best grammar available. Most of the text is in Tibetan (not Romanized) and it includes exercises in the grammatical rules and specimens of composition from the standard works. Oversize, 340pp. MoB

_____. **INDIAN PANDITS IN THE LAND OF SNOW**, $6.00. This is a dated transcription of a series of lectures that Das gave in the late nineteenth century which discusses Tibetan history and religion. 162pp. Muk 1883

_____. **JOURNEY TO LHASA AND CENTRAL TIBET**, c$14.00. Das was an educator and scholar who made two trips into Tibet in 1879 and 1881-2. The account here is of his second, more extended trip. He was well-versed in the Tibetan language, history, religion and folklore and attempted to take in as much as he could in his travels. He visited Tibet at a time when foreign visits were very limited and was one of the first to report in detail on the country. He describes in the first person his travels and the people, secular and non-secular, whom he encountered as well as the rites and ceremonies he witnessed. The text includes many fold-out maps and explanatory notes. Index, 301pp. PBR

_____. **A TIBETAN-ENGLISH DICTIONARY**, c$30.00. The newest and most useful available. A reproduction of the 1902 edition. 1384pp. MoB

DASGUPTA, SHASHI. AN INTRODUCTION TO TANTRIC BUDDHISM, $3.95. See the Tantra section.

DAVID-NEEL, ALEXANDRA. INITIATIONS AND INITIATES IN TIBET, $5.20. The author, who died in 1969 at the age of 103, was a major force in spreading knowledge of the mystical and philosophical thought of Tibet. This book is a record of her observations on Tibetan Buddhist teachings and initiatory practices. 224pp. Rid 58

_____. MAGIC AND MYSTERY IN TIBET, $3.50/2.95. Ms. David-Neel wandered through Tibet for fourteen years observing what is reported in this fascinating narrative: how Tibetan mystics acquire the ability to live naked in zero temperatures, how they communicate with each other over vast distances by telepathy, how they learn to float on air and walk on water, how they create animate objects by thinking them into existence, and much else. She hoped by her account to elicit scientific inquiry which will help elucidate the mechanism of these *miracles*. 320pp. Pen 29

DAVID-NEEL, ALEXANDRA and LAMA YONGDEN. THE SECRET ORAL TEACHINGS IN THE TIBETAN BUDDHIST SECTS, $2.00. This is a fine short presentation of the essential features of Tibetan Buddhism which is non-academic and designed for practical use. The *Madhyamika* (Middle Way) school is emphasized and meditational methods are described. 128pp. CiL 64

DOUGLAS, NIK and MERYL WHITE. KARMAPA THE BLACK HAT LAMA OF TIBET, c$25.50. Karmapa has been honored as a living Buddha in his sixteen successive incarnations. Traditionally the coming of the first Karmapa fulfilled a prophecy made by the Buddha that this emanation would appear in the world in order to alleviate the sufferings of humanity in the dark age of materialism. The Karmapa life-stories—compiled from authentic Tibetan biographies and diaries and presented here for the first time in English— cover 800 years of events of great cultural and historical importance. The Karmapas were the teachers of emperors and kings and established many important monasteries and hermitages in Tibet and neighboring countries. Sixteen color and many black-and-white plates illustrate the text. Notes, bibliography, glossary, index, 7½x9½". 247pp. Luz 76

DOWMAN, KEITH, tr. THE LEGEND OF THE GREAT STUPA AND THE LIFE STORY OF THE LOTUS BORN GURU, $2.95. The Life Story is *the life story of the Guru Padma Sambhava, mendicant, tantrika, magician, scholar, exorcist, priest, missionary, visionary, and saint.... [He] traveled throughout eighth century India before being invited to Tibet.... The Guru's magical power was his primary instrument in turning the Tibetans away from the primitive fantasies of the Shamans. He brought Tibet the highly evolved techniques of yoga and meditation developed by Mahayana India and founded the original lineages of the Nyingma tradition. In addition, The story surrounding the Great Stupa is a legendary Tibetan tale of incarnation, adoration, disaster and rebirth. It is a Tibetan means of instructing the visionary along the spiritual path.... The method is given in a narrative between Guru Padma Sambhava and his entourage of aspirants.... The text has been used in ritual for several centuries to eradicate habitual mental reaction patterns of distortion and stupour by causing a faithful concentration upon both sound and meaning.* Glossary, 139pp. Dha 73

DRIESSENS, GEORGES, ed. THE PRELIMINARY PRACTICES OF TIBETAN BUDDHISM, $2.95. A clear transcription of an oral commentary on an eleventh century text by the Venerable Geshe Rabten, a contemporary Tibetan meditation master. The text begins with the *Four Contemplations*—preliminaries which set the stage for the teaching which follows. The second part presents detailed instruction in four actual practices which are especially designed for the dedicated beginning student. Tibetan teaching is immensely practical and this small volume is an excellent presentation of some basic techniques. Notes, 62pp. Tus 74

EKVALL, ROBERT. RELIGIOUS OBSERVANCES IN TIBET, c$16.80. Ekvall approaches Tibetan society anthropologically and in this study he is concerned with the Tibetan's subjective response to the particular form of Buddhism he has developed. Six religious attitudes are characteristic of the Tibetan form of Mahayana Buddhism: faith, prayer, offering, salutation, circumambulation, and divination. In this volume the function of religious belief and ritual are studied in terms of these six attitudes and acts. The history of each is outlined and related to traditional beliefs and practices derived from the pre-Buddhist Bon cult. Notes, bibliography, 362pp. UCh 64

EVANS-WENTZ, W.Y. THE TIBETAN BOOK OF THE DEAD, c$10.00/2.95. Evans-Wentz is one of the best known Tibetan scholars. This volume, originally published in 1927, was the first book that brought Tibetan Buddhism to the general Western public. This volume, known as the **Bardo Thodol**, is a basic sourcebook for the teachings concerning the Clear Light, the Void, and other major features of the religion. Although the book is used in Tibet as a breviary, and read or recited on the occasion of death, it was originally conceived as a guidebook for initiates who must *die in order to be reborn*. All the basic material is here for an understanding of the inner meaning of Tibetan Buddhism, and Evans-Wentz' scholarship is excellent—however, the book is often hard to read and the translation is not as flowing as we would like. Carl Jung has contributed a Psychological Commentary to this edition and Evans-Wentz himself has written a number of prefaces. Notes, index, 333pp. Oxf 60

_____. THE TIBETAN BOOK OF THE GREAT LIBERATION, c$10.00/3.95. Expounds the quintessence of the Supreme Path, the Mahayana, and reveals the yogic method of attaining enlightenment by means of knowing the One Mind, without recourse to the postures, breathings, and other techniques commonly associated with the lower yogas. This work is attributed to Padma Sambhava, and an account of his life and doctrines precedes the text. Another treasure brought to us by Evans-Wentz. Psychological commentary by Carl Jung. Many beautiful plates. 254pp. Oxf 54

_____. TIBETAN YOGA AND SECRET DOCTRINES, $3.95. Texts of seven treatises on yoga, the Seven Books of Wisdom of the Great Path, with extensive commentary. 364pp. Oxf 58

FIELDS, RICK. LOKA, $4.00. See the Conscious Expansion section. Dou

GOLDSTEIN, MELVYN and NAWANG NORNANG. SPOKEN TIBETAN: LHASA DIALECT, c$16.15. A manual originally prepared for use in an introductory university course. The book is in three parts: the first contains twenty lessons that comprise the basic patterns of spoken Tibetan and a working vocabulary of about seven hundred words, the second consists of a series of folk tales and conversations, and the third presents a Tibetan-English and English-Tibetan glossary—both of which give the written Tibetan forms—and various charts and lists. All the material in the first two sections is romanized. Oversize, 409pp. UWa 70

GORDON, ANTOINETTE. TIBETAN RELIGIOUS ART, c$16.00. Ms. Gordon is in charge of the Tibetan, Chinese, and Japanese collections at the American Museum of Natural History and she has catalogued the Museum's entire Tibetan collection which is probably the largest in the West. She speaks Tibetan, has studied Tibetan paintings and artifacts throughout the West, and is the author of several books on the subject. This is a good general survey. Temple paintings, images, books, wood blocks, tablets, ritual objects, robes, masks, jewelry, and calligraphy are illustrated and described in detail. The reproduction is excellent and the text is short and quite clear. The author also includes translations she has made from Tibetan texts which show the type of invocation used in the rituals. Oversize, bibliography, index. 104pp. PBR 63

GOVINDA, LAMA. THE WAY OF THE WHITE CLOUDS: A BUDDHIST PILGRIM IN TIBET, $5.95. This magical book is the autobiography of Lama Govinda. It is a rich mixture of beautiful prose, drawings, and photography. *Pilgrims are religious nomads, people who go with a purpose, think as they go, move for a reason. They have a constancy in flux, patterns in a variety, knowledge of the void.* 297pp. ShP 70

_____. FOUNDATIONS OF TIBETAN MYSTICISM, $4.50. This is the most valuable book written on the subject of Tibetan mysticism. Lama Govinda has spent over twenty years of his life at the feet of masters in Tibetan hermitages and monasteries and his direct experience has given him a clear insight into much that has so far remained totally obscure to the outside world. Highly recommended for the serious student. Bibliography. 297pp. Wei 74

GUENTHER, HERBERT, tr. THE JEWEL ORNAMENT OF LIBERATION, $4.50. A fine translation of a complex text which describes the special training necessary to win enlightenment—explaining how the enlightened attitude is strengthened by practicing the six perfections. The text closes with a definition of Buddhahood and a commentary and guide to the Bodhisattva tradition. 333pp. ShP 59

_____. KINDLY BENT TO EASE US, $5.95. A translation of Part I of **Ngal-gso-skor-gsum**. *Until now, there has been no authentic translation describing the Dzogchen teachings of the Nyingma school which are the most sophisticated and effective practices of Vajrayana Buddhism.... The subject of this book is how to attain Enlightenment. By interweaving the teachings of the Sutras and Tantras, Longchenpa beautifully summarizes all Buddhist thought. Longchenpa's presentation is very deep and meaningful, so read and study each word and sentence carefully.... Traditionally it is said that Padmasambhava pointed to the door and Longchenpa opened it. Through his omniscient insight and untiring compassion, he inspired many followers to practice the Dzogchen teachings and to attain Enlightenment in one lifetime.*—Tarthang Tulku Rinpoche. Notes, index, introductory material, 346pp. Dha 75

_____. THE LIFE AND TEACHINGS OF NAROPA, $3.95. *In the history of Tibetan Buddhism, the Indian Naropa (AD 1016–1100) occupies a unique position. To the present day his life is held up as an example to anyone who aspires after spiritual values, which are never realized the easy way but only after years of endless toil and perseverance. It took Naropa twelve years of ardent devotion and indefatigable service to his Guru Tilopa (AD 988–1069) to attain his goal: overwhelming experiences of the Real in direct knowledge.... Naropa's biography, which has been translated here from hitherto unknown sources, contains a number of strictly historical data, but it is pre-eminently an account of the inner development of this scholar-saint.*—from the introduction. The text includes extensive notes and commentary, technical appendices, indices of Tibetan and Sanskrit terms, a subject index, and a bibliography. 308pp. Oxf 63

_____. THE ROYAL SONG OF SARAHA, c$10.65. Little is known about Saraha, a poet-philosopher who is believed to have lived between 100 and 1000 AD. According to legend, he was a Brahmin who composed his **Three Cycles of Dohas**—the **King, Queen,** and **People Dohas**—to make clear the meaning of reality. This is an annotated translation of **King Dohas** (known also as **Song on Human Action**). *The elusiveness of the man is matched by that of his teaching,* writes Guenther. *This is partly because the song form in which Saraha's thought is expressed renders the whole representation into little fragmentary pictures which seem to stand independently by themselves. The progression of thought goes from image to image . . . and therefore seems to lack the logical clarity of a didactic treatise.* Elusive as Saraha's thought may seem today, it had a powerful influence on the Tibetan scholars who translated and interpreted his poems. Two of these commentators are translated here and there is also an extensive analysis of the tradition of Saraha and his work, the method of his teaching, and the Tibetan philosophical thought that grew out of the interpretation of the verses. The annotations provide translations from relevant Tibetan sources in addition to commentary on the verses. Glossary, index, 214pp. UWa 69

_____. TREASURES ON THE TIBETAN MIDDLE WAY, $4.50. Prof. Guenther wrote this study of the foundations of Tibetan Buddhism at the request of the Dalai Lama. His aim is to present information about Buddhism as an inner experience. ShP 76

GUENTHER, HERBERT and LESLIE KAWAMURA, trs. MIND IN BUDDHIST PSY-CHOLOGY, $4.75. A translation of Ye-shes rgyal-mtshan's **The Necklace of Clear Understanding**, a text which *belongs to that group of literature called Abhidharma which concentrates on the training of one's critical cognition by methods of proper inspection. The Abhidharma . . . is a systematic approach to understanding the world as man's horizon of meaning.*—from the preface. As Tarthan Tulku Rinpoche says, *The subject of this book is self-knowledge. That is, until we thoroughly examine the nature of our mind, we cannot really be aware of who we are or why we are here.* This is a difficult text, suggested only for those with a firm grounding in Tibetan Buddhism, although it probably would be of interest to all students of psychology. Introduction, notes, glossary, index, 162pp. Dha 75

GUENTHER, HERBERT and CHOGYAM TRUNGPA. THE DAWN OF TANTRA, $3.50. See the Tantra section.

GYATSHO, TENZIN. THE OPENING OF THE WISDOM EYE, c$7.50. An authentic account of the teachings of Tibetan Buddhism is given here by the fourteenth Dalai Lama. A short account of the spread of Buddhism in Tibet is also included. Extensive notes. 178pp. TPH 66

HAGEN, TONI. NEPAL, c$19.95. Hagen was commissioned by the United Nations to undertake the first complete geological survey of Nepal in 1950. He was, and still is today, the first and only foreigner to be allowed to travel the entire countryside with no restrictions. Here he presents a dramatic panorama, in word and picture, illustrated with black-and-white and color photographs and diagrams. Oversize, 266pp. RMN

HARRER, HEINRICH. SEVEN YEARS IN TIBET, $2.30. Harrer is an Austrian mountaineer who was climbing the Himalayas when World War II broke out. He was interned by the British in India. In 1943 he escaped and crossed the Himalayas into Tibet. After a long desolate march and many adventures, he and his companion reached the *forbidden city* of Lhasa, where they were allowed to remain. In the process they learned Tibetan and became advisers on many subjects. Harrer became a close friend of the Dalai Lama as well as his tutor. He remained in this position for almost five years; then accompanied the Dalai Lama on his flight to India after the Chinese invasion; and then returned to Europe. This is a fascinating account of his experiences, illustrated with photographs. 269pp. PnB 53

HOPKINS, JEFFREY and LATI RIMPOCHE, trs. THE BUDDHISM OF TIBET AND THE KEY TO THE MIDDLE WAY, c$5.95. This is the first volume in a new series, **The Wisdom of Tibet**, in which each volume has been chosen by the Dalai Lama and bears his own seal, certifying that it reveals a true oral tradition. The first essay contains an official introduction to Tibetan Buddhism for non-specialists, while the second presents a meditation on emptiness. This series is an important addition to the burgeoning literature on Tibetan Buddhism both because of the clarity of its presentation and the authenticity of the textual material. Professor Hopkins has prepared the translations at the direct request of the Dalai Lama and a close associate of the Dalai Lama has carefully reviewed it for accuracy. Notes, bibliography, index, 104pp. H&R 75

_____. THE PRECIOUS GARLAND AND THE SONG OF THE FOUR MIND-FULNESSES, c$5.95. Book Two in **The Wisdom of Tibet** series makes available two classic poetic Buddhist texts, often memorized by monks. **The Precious Garland** is a lay person's guide to enlightenment, written for a king by Nagarjuna some 400 years after the Buddha. It is famous for its description of the Bodhisattva path of compassion, together with its clear, concise analysis of the Buddha's teaching on emptiness. **The Song of the Four Mindfulnesses** contains a short summary of the meditational approach to enlightenment by Kaysang Gyatso, the seventh Dalai Lama (1708–57). Both of the texts are in poetic form and the first one occupies the major part of the book. Notes, 119pp. H&R 75

JASCHKE, H.A. TIBETAN-ENGLISH DICTIONARY, c$19.50. Includes an English-Tibetan vocabulary. 671pp. Ung 1881

_____. TIBETAN GRAMMAR, c$10.00. This is a well known text, first published in the late nineteenth century. This edition includes a reading exercise, with vocabulary. 126pp. Ung 54

JERSTAD, LUTHER. MANI-RIMDU: SHERPA DANCE DRAMA, c$9.35. The colorful and ancient Cham, a traditional Tibetan Buddhist dance-drama, has been noted by travelers in Tibet since the eighteenth century. Here Jerstad describes the Nepalese form of Cham as he observed it among the Sherpas of northeastern Nepal. He focuses on the reli-

gious and historical message which the dances convey and he includes a discussion of the Sherpas themselves. The text is liberally illustrated with photographs and line drawings. Glossary, bibliography, index. 208pp. UWa 69

KAWAMURA, LESLIE, tr. GOLDEN ZEPHYR, $4.75. Translations from the original Tibetan of two classic works, Nagarjuna's **A Letter to a Friend** and Lama Mipham's commentary, **The Garland of White Lotus Flowers.** Nagarjuna originally wrote his **Letter** to a close friend, instructing and encouraging him to practice the Dharma in his daily life. The enduring insight and conciseness of Nagarjuna's presentation prompted Lama Mipham, one of the most brilliant Tibetan lamas of the nineteenth century, to expand the original text for the edification of his own students. In his commentary the Lama interweaves an explanation of the Buddhist path, which refers to a continual unfolding of our inner potential. Introduction, glossary, bibliography, index. 185pp. Dha 75

KAZAMI, TAKEHIDE. THE HIMALAYAS, $3.50. A pictorial travel guide to Nepal, with 110 beautiful color pictures. 154pp. Kod 68

KAZI, LAMA DAWASAMDUP. AN ENGLISH-TIBETAN DICTIONARY, c$19.50. About 20,000 entries. 1003pp. MuM

LAUF, DETLEF. TIBETAN SACRED ART, c$37.50. This is the finest presentation of Tibetan art and imagery that we know of. The author is a well known Swiss Tibetologist and Professor of Religion who teaches at the Jung Institute in Zurich. The text explains the system of beliefs which integrates polar opposites found in Tibetan art, such as the representations of multi-armed, flaming guardian deities and sublimely composed Buddhas appearing together in the same painting. These explanations open up the remarkable paradoxes of Tibetan iconography. The volume includes eighty-six magnificent color plates and eighteen line drawings. A concise history of the development of Buddhism in Tibet supplements the text. 10x12", 131pp. ShP 76

MILAREPA

Milarepa has been an inspiration to Tibetans for almost ten centuries. Wronged in childhood, he left home to become apprenticed to a sorcerer, quickly became proficient in the black arts, then returned and destroyed his enemies. Struck with remorse he turned towards truth and started on the search for a teacher who would liberate him from his violent past. After various false starts, he found Marpa and persevered despite appalling hardships until Marpa eventually relented and gave him his teaching. He spent many years receiving instruction and finally returned to Tibet where he was widely recognized and gathered a large group of disciples around him. Milarepa was not only a great yogi, he was also a poet and singer—and his songs are both instructive and among the finest literature ever produced in Tibetan.

CHANG, GARMA, tr. THE HUNDRED THOUSAND SONGS OF MILAREPA, c$25.00/ 4.65. The life and teaching of the greatest poet-saint to appear in the history of Buddhism. These stories have provided solace and a source of inexhaustible joy and inspiration to Tibetans for many centuries. This is a lovely translation and the long introduction and explanatory notes provided by Chang are very helpful. Glossary, fully indexed. Highly recommended. Two volumes, 730pp. The paperback edition is very abridged (287pp). UnB 62

EVANS-WENTZ, W.Y., tr. TIBET'S GREAT YOGI MILAREPA: A BIOGRAPHY FROM THE TIBETAN, $2.95. In Milarepa's life, the teachings of all the great yogis of India, including Gautama the Buddha, are exemplified. He is considered the prototype of everything that a great saint should be. Dr. Evans-Wentz contributed a highly informative introduction and liberal explanatory notes to this edition. 309pp. Oxf 28

JIVAKA, LOBZANG. THE LIFE OF MILAREPA, c$3.50. This is a skillful retelling of Evans-Wentz' original translation, designed to bring the story of Milarepa to as many people as possible. The songs, some of the most obscure references, and some of the teaching have been omitted, but the bulk of the story remains. Jivaka's rendition is certainly more readable than Evans-Wentz' often awkward prose. A fairly long introduction summarizes the salient features of Tibetan Buddhism. 185pp. Mur 62

OLSCHAK, BLANCHE, tr. SPIRITUAL GUIDE TO THE JEWEL ISLAND, c$10.00. Translation of an important text by Konchog Tanpa Donme on the spiritual experience. Included are practical instructions and the language itself is simple and insightful. *In our technical over-civilized phase of life, such texts, guiding to an island of spiritual jewels,*

may help to bring about the longed-for balance between material and spiritual values and to create mental peace and serenity, whenever the tormented mind grows restless.—from the preface. On the left-hand pages the original Tibetan calligraphy is printed, followed by the orthographical letter-by-letter transcription and the phonetical transcription. On the right-hand pages, the English translation is given, followed by the German. 224pp. BPu 73

PALLIS, MARCO. **THE WAY AND THE MOUNTAIN**, c$8.65. This is a highly acclaimed survey of the Buddhism of Tibet. Pallis travelled extensively through the Himalayas in the 1930's and 1940's and did a great deal of scholarly research. This volume was written after his trip to Tibet in 1947 and is basically a series of personal impressions rather than an academic study. The following chapter headings should give the reader a good idea of the contents: *The Way and the Mountain; The Active Life, On Crossing Religious Frontiers, On Soliciting and Imparting Spiritual Counsel, The Place of Compassion in Tibetan Spirituality, Sikkim Buddhism Today and Tomorrow, The Dalai Lama,* and *The Tibetan Tradition.* Many illustrations accompany the text. 216pp. Owe 60

PAL, PRATAPADITYA. **THE ART OF TIBET**, c$16.50. The catalogue of what is said to have been the most extensive exhibition of Tibetan art ever presented in America. Many of the pieces came from the Dalai Lama's own collection and the rest were gathered from museums and private collections in both Europe and the U.S. The text includes a detailed interpretation of each plate and a 46 page survey of Tibetan religion, culture, and art. The reproductions are excellent. Oversize, bibliography, 163pp. Asi 69

_____. **NEPAL**, c$19.95. Dr. Pal is the Curator of Indian and Islamic Art, Los Angeles County Museum of Art. This is the catalogue of the exhibit he recently put together at the Asia House Gallery in New York City. It includes about 100 paintings and bronzes gathered from all parts of the U.S. Each of the pieces is illustrated (many in full color) and a full description of each item is supplied. An introduction discusses Nepali art. 10x10". bibliography, 136pp. Wea 75

RECHUNG, RINPOCHE. **TIBETAN MEDICINE**, c$16.00. English translations of the most important Tibetan medical texts, and a history of Tibetan medicine. A very extensive, illustrated treatment. Bibliography. 327pp. UCa

RICHARDSON, E.H. **A SHORT HISTORY OF TIBET**, c$6.95. Richardson spent eleven years as a diplomat in Tibet. His aim here is to provide a guide to Tibetan history which takes the Tibetan background and character into consideration. His study begins with the earliest recorded times and continues through the Chinese invasions to a discussion of the proceedings at the United Nations and of Tibetans in exile. Includes explanatory material and a topical bibliography. Illustrations, index, 308pp. Dut 62

RINJING, DORJE, tr. **TALES OF UNCLE TOMPA**, $3.95. *Many people in the world, especially in the West, believe Tibet is a land of magic saints where all people spend their time meditating. . . . While all the stories in this book deal directly with Tibetan Buddhist culture, they also reflect the ways in which Tibetans laugh and enjoy life. The stories*

were told to me while I was a yak herder boy. . . . Until now, none have ever appeared in print. They were all written down by me from memory. . . . This book was written informally using plain language about sexual matters as Tibetans always do when joking in their own tongue. Sample chapters include *Uncle Tompa Sells Penises at the Nunnery, Uncle Tompa Paints a Bull, Uncle Tompa Plays a Trick on His New Wife.* The book is beautifully produced, with many lovely illustrations. Oversize, 78pp. Lng 75

SHERRING, CHARLES. **WESTERN TIBET AND THE INDIAN BORDERLAND**, c$22.50. This is a detailed description of the area, with a full discussion of all the important tribes inhabiting the area, and the religions and customs of the people. The account was first written in 1906, at the time of the British hegemony—and since this text was written by an Englishman the attitudes prevalent at that time are readily apparent. Still, there is much of interest here both as a historical document and as a description of many customs and beliefs which retain their importance in the Himalayas and among the Tibetan refugee communities. Many photographs illustrate the text. Index, 391pp. Csm 74

SNELLGROVE, DAVID, tr. **FOUR LAMAS OF DOLPO**, c$18.90. Translations of the autobiographies of four Tibetan lamas in the land of Dolpo, which was part of Western Tibet until the end of the eighteenth century. Three of them were born in the fifteenth century, and one in the seventeenth. In every case the substance of these biographies was dictated by the lamas themselves in response to the entreaties of their disciples. They are of great importance in that they provide a direct and spontaneous account of Tibetan religious life as seen from the inside. An introduction provides the general background of conditions in Dolpo, including an account of religious beliefs. Many photographs, line drawings, and maps are included. Index, 352pp. A second volume contains the original Tibetan texts, commentary, and glossary, and sells for $27.00. Cas 67

STEIN, RA. **TIBETAN CIVILIZATION**, $3.95. A comprehensive survey, founded on a wide knowledge of the relevant European studies and the available Chinese and Tibetan literature. Divided into five sections: habitat and inhabitants, historical survey, society, religion and customs, arts and letters. Very well organized and presented, extensive bibliography and illustrations. 316pp. SUP 62

TARTHANG TULKU, ed. **CALM AND CLEAR**, $4.75. See the Meditation section. Dha

_____. **CRYSTAL MIRROR, VOL. I**, $3.95. *Crystal Mirror* is a periodical put together by the Tibetan Nyingmapa Meditation Center (2425 Hillside Avenue, Berkeley, California 94704). It includes excerpts from talks by Tarthang Tulku and this issue describes the cultural and historical context of Vajrayana Buddhism, and contains biographies of Tibet's greatest teachers and is illustrated with many block prints. Oversize, 82pp. Dha 71

_____. **CRYSTAL MIRROR, VOL. II**, $3.95. Includes an interview with Tarthang Tulku; translations of the Vajra Guru Mantra and of the Teaching of the Essential Point in Three Worlds; the following philosophical articles: *Fact and Fiction in the Experience of Being* by H.V. Guenther, and Tarthang Tulku's *Judgement, Skillfull Means* and *Entering the Mandala.* This issue also has information on the Center's projects and other related material. Illustrated with many block prints and line drawings, oversize. 89pp. Dha 72

_____. **CRYSTAL MIRROR, VOL. III**, $4.75. See the Meditation section.

_____. **CRYSTAL MIRROR, VOL. IV**, $6.95. This compilation seems to get better with each year. Vol. IV is divided into four parts: History, Teachings, Culture, and Practice. Part I presents three essays by Tarthang Tulku: *The Life and Liberation of Padmasambhava, The Twenty-five Disciplines of Padmasambhava,* and *Buddhism in Tibet: The Early Chronicles.* Part II is composed of a series of essays by Tarthang Tulku on various aspects of the practice entitled *Bring the Teachings Alive* and a translation by Herbert Guenther of Long-chen-pa's **The Natural Freedom of Mind.** Part III includes an essay by Tarthang Tulku, *Tibet: The Land, People, and Culture,* and two by Lama Govinda: *A Tibetan Buddhist Looks at Christianity* and *Pilgrims and Monasteries in the Himalayas.* In the last part Tarthang Tulku answers some questions on the practice and discusses some other things in *Opening to the Dharma.* Illustrated throughout. 281pp. Dha 75

_____. **REFLECTIONS OF MIND**, $4.75. In the summers of 1973 and 1974 the teachings of Tibetan Buddhism were introduced to a group of psychologists and mental health professionals during intensive eight-week seminars. This is a collection of essays by a number of the participants, including Charles Tart, Gay Luce, and Claudio Naranjo. They combine their professional training in Western therapeutic practices with their experiences in Tibetan Buddhism to present a picture of the vast psychological expertise of Tibetan Buddhism. Tarthang Tulku contributes a long introductory article. Notes, 198pp. Dha 75

TIBETAN NYINGMA MEDITATION CENTER. **SACRED ART OF TIBET**, $5.45. The catalog of an exhibition held a few years ago, with a nice introduction on Tibetan art. 36 beautiful plates. Dha 72

_____. **TIBETAN THANKA PORTFOLIOS**, c$25.00. Reproduced in full color and packaged in a gold-stamped, cloth-bound portfolio, these twenty paintings are a visual representation of Tibet's deeply spiritual culture. Examples of both ancient and modern styles of painting. The reproductions are fairly good. Dha

TRUNGPA, CHOGYAM. **BORN IN TIBET**, $3.50. A moving story of the early life and escape from Tibet of the author, a young tulku (an incarnate lama of high rank). His narrative includes an account of Tibetan wisdom and culture as well as his experiences in India, Britain and America. He now has two extremely popular meditational centers in the U.S. and is highly respected. Photographs and an extensive glossary. 267pp. Pen 66

_____. **CUTTING THROUGH SPIRITUAL MATERIALISM**, c$8.95/4.25. The record of two series of lectures given by Trungpa Rinpoche in 1972. They present an overview of the path and some warnings as to the dangers along that path. *Walking the spiritual*

path properly is a very subtle process. . . . There are numerous sidetracks which lead to a distorted, ego-centered version of spirituality. . . . This fundamental distortion may be referred to as spiritual materialism. . . . These talks first discuss the various ways in which people involve themselves with spiritual materialism. . . . After this tour of the sidewalks along the way, we discuss the broad outlines of the true spiritual path. —Chogyam Trungpa. Highly recommended. 250pp. ShP 72

_____. **FIRST THOUGHT BEST THOUGHT**, $3.95. This is a collection of poetry composed and based on Tibetan models as well as secular poetry originally written in English. Some of the poems show the deep influence Tibet's great poet/saint Milarepa has had on all Tibetan poetry while others are clearly the result of Trungpa's own intuitive insights into new forms and mediums offered to him by the English language and psychology. 108pp. ShP 76

_____. **THE FOUNDATIONS OF MINDFULNESS**, $3.95. This is the fourth volume of the Garuda series which is intended to constitute an ongoing encyclopedia of Buddhism. Mindfulness is the basic technique used for 2500 years in the tradition of Buddhist meditation. Trungpa teaches an understanding of mindfulness and why it is important and very alive in the modern world. Most of the selections were written by Trungpa himself and also included is a translation of the *Satipatthana-Sutta*, one of the earliest Buddhist meditation texts. The book is heavily illustrated with photographs and line drawings. Oversize, 88pp. ShP 76

_____. **MEDITATION IN ACTION**, $2.25. See section on Meditation.

_____. **MUDRA**, $2.95. Mudra is a symbol, in the sense of a gesture or action. It arises spontaneously, as an expression of apparent phenomena. It is not separate from that which it symbolizes. It is self-evident. *Mudra* is a selection of some songs and spontaneous poems written in Tibetan and English. Also, a presentation of the nine yanas, an illustrated commentary on the classic Zen Oxherding pictures, and a translation of a Maha Ati meditation text are included. 105pp. ShP 72

_____. **THE MYTH OF FREEDOM AND THE WAY OF MEDITATION**, $3.95. This volume is based on a series of talks given by Trungpa between 1971 and 1973. Here the idea of freedom is set in the context of Tibetan Buddhism. Spanning the gulf between the most esoteric tradition of the East and the everyday realities of American life, Trungpa shows how our attitudes, preconceptions and even our spiritual practices can become chains that bind us to repetitive patterns of frustration and despair. He also explores the significant role that meditation plays in bringing into focus the cause of frustration and in allowing these negative forces to become aids in advancing toward true freedom. The volume ends with Trungpa's translation of a classic text: Tilopa's instructions on Mahamudra meditation to his disciple Naropa. As usual, Trungpa expresses himself clearly and the text is an excellent blend of irony and seriousness. We recommend it highly to all those on the path. Illustrations, index. 190pp. ShP 76

_____. **VISUAL DHARMA**, $7.95. This is a catalogue of an exhibition of the Buddhist art of Tibet held at M.I.T. Fifty-four plates are reproduced, along with a very full discussion of each plate. Trungpa contributes an essay on the art of Tibet and he and his people helped organize the exhibit. Unfortunately only a few of the plates are in color. Oversize, glossary, 140pp. ShP 75

TUCCI, GIUSEPPE. **TIBET: LAND OF SNOWS**, c$20.10. Professor Tucci is one of the few Europeans able to speak of Tibet from personal experience. Here he presents a comprehensive survey of the nation's spiritual, artistic, and social achievements divided into the following sections: history, religion, art, daily life, birth, marriage, sickness and death, Tibetan literature, and administration. The oversize text is illustrated with 106 plates, about half in full color. This is much more accessible than Tucci's more scholarly works

and forms an excllent introduction to Tibetan civilization. Bibliography, index, 216pp. Ele 73

_____. **TO LHASA AND BEYOND**, c$10.20. An illustrated reproduction of the diary Tucci kept on his expedition to Tibet in 1948. He writes vividly and includes a description of his extended visit with the Dalai Lama. An appendix contains Dr. Regolo Moiso's *Remarks on Medicine and the State of Health in Tibet*. Oversize, index, 195pp. IPS 56

_____. **THE THEORY AND PRACTICE OF THE MANDALA**, $2.95. Mandalas are complex arrangements of patterns or pictures used in Hindu and Buddhist Tantrism to give expression to the infinite possibilities of the human subsconscious. In this book Prof. Tucci conducts a survey into the basic doctrines of the mandala. He shows that mandalas are used in religious ceremonies as a means of integration. An excellent presentation, which is generally considered the finest work ever written on mandalas. 141pp. Wei 61

_____. **TRANSHIMALAYA**, c$26.25. Professor Tucci has travelled extensively in Tibet and is the twentieth century authority on Tibetan culture. In this volume he reviews the present state of archaeological knowledge about Tibet and suggests possible lines of investigation once archaeological work again becomes possible in Tibet. 210 plates (33 in color) illustrate the text. Bibliography, notes, index. 239pp. Nag 73

WADDELL, L. AUSTINE. **TIBETAN BUDDHISM WITH ITS MYSTIC CULTS, SYMBOLISM, AND MYTHOLOGY**, $4.50. A scholarly, very complete text. Abounds with translations of Indian and Tibetan documents and texts, summaries of important works, annotated pictorial representations and a wealth of data. Bibliography, notes, 583pp. Dov 1895

WANGYAL, GESHE. **DOOR OF LIBERATION**, c$6.95. A very important, comprehensive work which contains authentic Tibetan Buddhist teachings as handed down through a lineage beginning with the Buddha himself. According to the Tibetan tradition, the translations were made by a lama in this lineage. The English rendering is therefore consistently true to the Tibetan, without the interpolation of Western concepts often found in other works in this field. Rather than being another collection of merely theoretical discourses, it is a comprehensive handbook that can be directly applied by anyone who wishes to investigate and experience the profound teachings of the Buddha. Good introduction and glossary. 323pp. Gir 73

WAYMAN, ALEX. **BUDDHIST TANTRAS**, c$12.50. A detailed work by a renowned Sanskrit and Tibetan scholar. An introductory section discusses the Buddhist Tantra within Mahayana Buddhism and analyzes the nature of Buddhist esotericism and the early literary history of the Tantras. The second section reviews the main features of this school, and the symbolism involved in its teaching. A final section presents some little known aspects of the subject including Tantric teachings on astrology, on the orifices of the body, on female energy and symbolism, the five-fold ritual symbolism of passion, and an analysis of the Tibetan canon. This is a difficult text, recommended only to those with an excellent background in the Tibetan esoteric teachings. Illustrations, bibliography, notes, index, 255pp. Wei 73

WILLIS, JANICE. **THE DIAMOND LIGHT**, $2.45. An introduction to Tibetan practices, especially meditation. The terminology is explained and defined, thus clarifying the significance of the technique. The instructions are quite clear and a great number of actual practices are described in detail. This is not a profound book, but it does provide a more than adequate introduction to the subject. 124pp. S&S 72

YONGDEN, LAMA. **MIPAM**, $3.95. A faithful description of the Tibetan people and their ways, in the form of a novel, by a Tibetan lama who was the adopted son of Ms. David-Neel and accompanied her on many of her travels. Complete with twelve original woodcuts. 349pp. Mud 38

ZEN BUDDHISM

ANESAKI, MASAHARU. **HISTORY OF JAPANESE RELIGION**, c$10.50. The standard one-volume history, chronologically arranged, which ties the religions in with the political and historical events of each era. It is somewhat dated. The text is oriented toward the general reader—although one would have to have a deep interest in Japanese culture to want to read so much about it. Notes, illustrations, index, 423pp. Tut 30

_____. **RELIGIOUS LIFE OF THE JAPANESE PEOPLE**, $3.75. This is a dry survey, sponsored by the Japanese Cultural Society, with chapters on Shinto, Confucianism and Taoism, Buddhism, and Christianity—with some more general sections and background material. Illustrations, bibliography, 122+pp. KBS 70

ASTON, W.G. **NIHONGI**, $5.75. This volume, often called the **Nihonshoki**, is generally considered among the most important Japanese histories. It provides a vivid picture of a nation in formation and we see the growth of national awareness following the assimilation of Buddhism and the general Chinese and Indian influence on Japanese culture. Ritual, myth, superstition are mingled in this account which was written down in the eighth century. Introduction, notes, 465pp. Tut 72

BAYARD, EDWIN. **KYOTO: JAPAN'S ANCIENT CAPITAL**, c$11.95. Kyoto is the ancient capital of Japan. The imperial epoch, which began in 794 and lasted for more than one thousand years, witnessed the emergence of a civilization that is considered one of the most refined and elegant in the world. To this day Kyoto remains the religious and aesthetic center of Japan. Imposing Buddhist temples and Shinto shrines can be found in every quarter of the city. This beautifully produced oversize book contains a text reviewing Kyoto's history and 115 illustrations (half in color). A final section presents descriptions of the city by Westerners and Japanese written between the twelfth century and the present. Chronology, bibliography, index, 172pp. Nsw 74

BENOIT, HUBERT. **LET GO!** $3.50. Subtitled *Theory and Practice of Detachment According to Zen*, this is a practical work which details an exercise by which a viewpoint similar to that which the Zen Buddhists call *satori* is achieved. The book represents a culmination of the material presented in **The Supreme Doctrine** and consists of theoretical material in the areas of *letting go* and *ultimate realization* followed by the exercise which is based on the analysis of language and which presents the necessary conditions for the exercise to be effective. The theoretical concepts presented throughout this book are often difficult to grasp—but once understood they become illuminating. 277pp. Wei 62

_____. **THE SUPREME DOCTRINE—PSYCHOLOGICAL STUDIES IN ZEN THOUGHT**, $1.85. This approach to Zen is not so much a philosophical system as a hygiene of intelligent living. Dr. Benoit, a practicing psychoanalyst, shows how it can liberate us from some of the sickness and anxiety that plague contemporary civilization. As Aldous Huxley states in his introduction, *this should be read by everyone who aspires to know who he is and what he can do to acquire such self-knowledge*. 248pp. Vik 51

BLOFELD, JOHN, tr. **THE ZEN TEACHING OF HUANG PO ON THE TRANSMISSION OF THE MIND**, $2.95. A historical text from the direct teaching of a Zen Master—considered one of the key works in Zen teaching. The dialogues recorded use the technique of a paradox to show how the experience of intuitive knowledge reveals to a man what he really is and illustrates the impossibility of communication through words. Blofeld provides an excellent translation, as well as an introduction and explanatory notes. 135pp.

_____. **THE ZEN TEACHING OF HUI HAI**, $2.75. Part I gives the Mahayana Instruction for self-realization of mind, for perception of self-nature, and consequent attainment of Buddhahood. Part II contains the dialogues between Hui Hai and those who came to him for instruction. Foreward by Charles Luk, long introduction and notes by Blofeld, glossary. 160pp. Wei 62

BLYTH, R.H. **GAMES ZEN MASTERS PLAY**, $1.50. Selections from Blyth's books. Contents include a translation, with commentary, of the **Hsinhsinming** (setting forth the basic Zen approach); a selection of the most famous *mondos* (questions and answers which differ from *koans* in that an immediate answer is demanded) of the great Zen masters; and an important selection of *koans* from the Mumonkan, perhaps the most widely used instrument for the teaching of Zen. It's nice that Blyth's excellent work is finally available at a reasonable price. Edited and with an introduction by Robert Sohl and Audrey Carr. 169pp. NAL 76

_____. **HAIKU**, c$15.95/each. A wonderful collection, divided into The Seasons, Sky and Elements, Fields and Mountains, Gods and Buddhas, Human Affairs, Birds and Beasts, Trees and Flowers. Haiku from its beginnings up to and including Shiki, 1867–1902. **Vol. l, Eastern Culture**, 440pp. **Vol. 2, Spring**, 382pp. **Vol. 3, Summer–Autumn**, 462pp. **Vol. 4, Autumn–Winter**, Index, 442pp.

_____. **A HISTORY OF HAIKU**, c$15.95/each. This is the best full length history available. Vol. I covers the period from the beginnings up to Issa and Vol. II covers from Issa up to the present. Blyth has chosen the best haiku of as many writers as possible, enabling the reader to learn by considering the failures and near-hits rather than just the successes. Text includes the Japanese characters, a Romanized transcription, and a translation and commentary. Brief biographical material is included on each poet. Haiku are poems of 16 syllables, usually about nature. **Vol.I**, 427pp. **Vol. 2**, index, 375pp. Hok 64

_____. **ZEN AND ZEN CLASSICS, VOL. I**, c$7.25. This series presents the most comprehensive picture of Zen–its background, history, philosophy–available. Each volume contains extensive quotations from the major thinkers as well as topical information and some illustrations. Highly recommended. Vol. I is a general introduction from the Upanishads to Huineng. 125pp. Hok 60–70

_____. **ZEN AND ZEN CLASSICS, VOL. II**, c$7.25. History of Zen, 713–867, Hanshan. 244pp.

_____. **ZEN AND ZEN CLASSICS, VOL. III**, c$7.25. History of Zen, 867–1260, Piyenchi. 244pp.

_____. **ZEN AND ZEN CLASSICS, VOL. IV**, c$8.50. Mumonkan. 352pp.

_____. **ZEN AND ZEN CLASSICS, VOL. V**, c$8.50. 25 essays on every aspect of Zen. 225pp.

BUCHANAN, DANIEL. **ONE HUNDRED FAMOUS HAIKU**, $3.25. Selections from Basho and Issa to the present, each presented in its original version, a Romanized version, and translation, including a note on the poet. 120pp. Jap 73

BUNCE, WILLIAM. **RELIGIONS IN JAPAN–BUDDHISM, SHINTO, CHRISTIANITY**, $2.95. A general survey. 194pp. Tut 55

CASAL, U.A. **THE FIVE SACRED FESTIVALS OF ANCIENT JAPAN**, c$6.60. A fascinating account of the development of the five festivals from their origin as primitive fertility rites. Oversize, illustrations, index, 122pp. Tut 67

CASTILE, RAND. **THE WAY OF TEA**, c$15.00. The most complete book available on the tea ceremony and its relation to Japanese history, aesthetics, philosophy and life. Lavishly illustrated, oversize, glossary, bibliography. 392pp. Wea 71

CHAN, WING-TSIT, tr. **THE PLATFORM SCRIPTURE**, $3.50. A fine translation of the basic Zen classic, given by the Sixth Patriarch, Hui-neng. Includes the Chinese text, an excellent long introduction, and many text notes. Recommended for all who desire an understanding of Zen. 193pp. SJU 63

CHANG, GARMA. **THE PRACTICE OF ZEN**, $1.50. This is an excellent primer on Zen. The first part surveys the main aspects of Zen Buddhism and gives Chang's suggestions and comments on Zen practice. The next section presents a number of short autobiographies and discourses of the Zen masters, from both ancient and modern sources. From these the reader can get a picture of the lives and works of the masters, thus getting a clearer picture of Zen. This section includes discourses on Hsu Yun, Tsung Kao, Po Shan, and Han Shan. The last two sections are *The Four Problems of Zen Buddhism* and *Buddha and Meditation*. Recommended. Notes, index, 256pp. H&R 59

CHUNG-YUAN, CHANG. **ORIGINAL TEACHINGS OF CH'AN BUDDHISM**, $2.95. The Trasmission of the Lamp, from which the texts in this book are taken, consists mainly of more than a thousand *kung-an* (koan), expressions of the inner experience and illumination of enlightened men. It is one of the earliest of the historical records of Ch'an Buddhism and is also the best source for the study of Ch'an. The parts of this translation are arranged to show a progression from basic tenets to methods of transmission. A very helpful work. Excellent long bibliography and notes. 333pp. RaH 69

CLEARY, THOMAS and J.C., trs. **THE BLUE CLIFF RECORDS, VOL. I**, $4.95. The **Blue Cliff Records** is a classic Chinese collection of Zen koans with commentary. It has been one of the major sources of meditation topics for Rinzai Zen schools for centuries. The translation will appear in three volumes. 300pp. ShP 76

DUMOULIN, HEINRICH S.J. **A HISTORY OF ZEN BUDDHISM**, $3.45. A comprehensive illustrated account by a Jesuit professor at Sophia University in Tokyo. Extensive bibliography and notes. 335pp. Bea 59

DURCKHEIM, KARLFRIED **HARA**, $3.95. See the Meditation section. Wei 62

_____. **THE JAPANESE CULT OF TRANQUILITY**, $2.95. See the Meditation section. Wei 60

EARHART, H. BYRON. **JAPANESE RELIGION**, $6.65. This book was designed as a survey of Japanese religion for a college course. It is well written and chronologically arranged, beginning with the earliest religious traditions and continuing through the postwar period. Selected readings are given for each chapter and there is a long annotated bibliography and an index. 158pp. Dic 74

_____, ed. **RELIGION IN THE JAPANESE EXPERIENCE: SOURCES AND INTERPRETATIONS**, $8.00. An excellent collection of fifty-two essays on all aspects of Japanese religion from a variety of books and authors. All of the selections are quite short and recommended readings follow each one. Illustrations, 282pp. Dic 74

Bodhidharma

ELIOT, CHARLES. **JAPANESE BUDDHISM**, c$21.00. Sir Charles was the British Ambassador to Japan for a period of time. He wrote this volume after his return to private life. Earlier he had written a monumental tome, **Hinduism and Buddhism**, based on his years of residence in the East and on his extensive study. Despite its title, this volume traces Buddhism from the time of the early canons through India and China and its introduction into Japan. The conditions in Japan throughout the ages and the various sects are discussed in depth. There's an incredible amount of information packed into this volume and it does not seem very outdated. It's also not overly technical, though the scholarship seems to be excellent. Notes, index, 485pp. RKP 35

ELLWOOD, ROBERT. **THE EAGLE AND THE RISING SUN**, c$7.95. This is an exploration of five *new religions* of Japan: Tenrikyo, *the religion of heavenly wisdom*; Nichiren Shoshu; The Church of World Messianity; Seicho-no-Ie; and Perfect Liberty. The emphasis is on how these religions are practiced in the U.S. and on the experience of Occidental converts. Notes, index, 224pp. Wes 74

FRANCK, FREDERICK. **THE BOOK OF ANGELUS SILESIUS**, $4.95. Angelus Silesius was a seventeenth century Christian mystic who described his four days and nights of illumination in 302 Zen-like epigrams. Franck has newly translated more than half of these deceptively simple verses and he also provides a running commentary of observations by the ancient Zen masters. In an introduction Franck shows how the verses of the Silesian poet form a bridge between Eastern and Western mysticism. Delicate drawings in the style Franck used so successfully in **Zen of Seeing** ornament each page. Oversize, 145pp. RaH 75

_____. **THE ZEN OF SEEING**, c$7.95/3.45. Subtitled *Seeing/Drawing as Meditation*, this lovely handwritten and drawn book presents a way of contemplation by which all things are made new, by which the world is freshly experienced at each moment. *What I have not drawn, I have never really seen*, says Franck, and he goes on to show that *once you start drawing an ordinary thing, a fly, a flower, a face, you realize how extraordinary it is—a sheer miracle....* Joseph Campbell says: *Even reading it, I could feel myself getting ready for a change. It is a beautiful book—a pure book—something good to have at hand, to be opened again and fed upon.* 8x11", 164pp. RaH 73

FROMM, ERICH, D.T. SUZUKI, and RICHARD de MARTINO. **ZEN BUDDHISM AND PSYCHOANALYSIS**, $2.45. A series of lectures from a symposium on the title subject. 180pp. H&R 60

FUNG, PAUL and GEORGE, trs. **THE SUTRA OF THE SIXTH PATRIARCH ON THE PRISTINE ORTHODOX DHARMA**, c$5.00. This Sutra gives an account of the life and thought of the monk Hui Neng (638–713), who is regarded as the true founder of Chinese Ch'an (Zen) Buddhism. Hui Neng is best known for his poem declaring that the way of sudden enlightenment is the essence of Buddhism. He is reputed to be the Sixth Patriarch in line from Bodhidharma and this Sutra was written down soon after his death by several of his disciples. Many of the master's discourses are recorded here along with a series of answers to questions put to him about his form of Buddhism. This is a new translation and the translators provide extensive notes and an English/Sanskrit/Chinese glossary. 187pp. BUC 64

GRAHAM, DOM AELRED. **ZEN CATHOLICISM**, $2.95. The author, a noted Benedictine monk, has reflected upon Zen and Catholicism—usually considered divergent in their rituals and philosophies—and has found many points of contact between them. Many quotations. 228pp. HBJ 63

HAKEDA, YOSHITO, tr. KUKAI MAJOR WORKS, c$15.10. Kukai (774–835), the man who introduced Esoteric Buddhism into Japan, greatly influencing the culture of Heian Japan and setting the tone for all subsequent artistic expression, is generally considered the father of Japanese culture. In the first two parts of this book Professor Hakeda examines the life and thought of Kukai both in relation to his times and to his influence down the ages. The third part consists of translations of eight of Kukai's major works. A definitive study which establishes Kukai's place in Japanese cultural history. Notes, index, 303pp. Col 72

HAKUIN, ZENJI. THE EMBOSSED TEA KETTLE—ORATE GAMA AND OTHER WORKS, c$9.90. Hakuin's teaching, as contained in this, his most important work, may be summed up as follows: (1) he suggests that meditation is not an *affair of the cloister* alone; it is rather the spirit that should pervade the whole life of men; (2) neither meditation nor any other religious practice is sufficient without a strict observation of the moral law; and (3) those who aim at spiritual maturity should take care to preserve the health of the body. This is one of the most important practical Zen handbooks and is universally highly regarded. Translated by R.D.M. Shaw. 197pp. A&U 63

_____. THE ZEN MASTER HAKUIN—SELECTED WRITINGS, c$15.10. Translated here are three works: the Orategama, Hebiichigo, and Yabukoji—the latter two have been unavailable in English. Written in the form of letters to various acquaintances, the works are in effect sermons and lectures on the study of Zen, its relationship to other schools of Buddhism, and exhortations to feudal lords to promote humane government, and other matters. Yampolsky provides, when they are readily determinable, explanations of difficult references and allusions in the texts as well as a valuable introduction. Translated by Philip Yampolsky. 253pp. Col 71

HANH, THICH NHAT. ZEN KEYS, $1.95. The author is a leading spokesman of the Vietnamese Buddhist peace movement and his teaching, as presented in this book, is a living tradition which he has modified in response to the needs of the society and culture in which he lives. Nhat Hanh begins this account with a discussion of the daily regime of life in a Zen monastery and the character of Zen as practiced in Vietnam. Drawing from both historical and personal examples, he explains the central philosophical concepts of awareness, impermanence, and not-I. Many major Zen concepts are discussed in a short paragraph and some relevant teaching stories are presented. The text often seems to skip around and this leads to confusion. Many fine insights are revealed, and the masters are quoted, but the book is not as useful as it might be. Phillip Kapleau provides a long introduction, 185pp. Dou 74

HASEGAWA, SEIKAN. THE CAVE OF POISON GRASS, $3.95. This is a profound exposition of the Hannya-shin-gyo Sutra, a one-page summary of the Mahaprajnaparamita Sutra which is widely known in Japan. Many Mahayana Buddhists chant this *sutra* on religious occasions. The volume begins with a translation of the *sutra* accompanied by a Romanized transliteration of the Chinese as it is chanted in Japan. Then Hasegawa analyzes virtually every word and concept at great length and relates the material to many other Zen source texts and to other aspects of Buddhist philosophy. The author is a young Rinzai Zen monk who has founded a Buddhist temple near Washington, D.C. Notes, index, 182pp. GOP 75

HENDERSON, HAROLD, tr. AN INTRODUCTION TO HAIKU: AN ANTHOLOGY OF POEMS AND POETS FROM BASHO TO SHIKI, $2.50. 190pp. Dou 58

HERRIGEL, EUGENE. THE METHOD OF ZEN, $1.95. Herrigel was a German professor who taught philosophy at the University of Tokyo between the wars. In endeavoring to become a Zen mystic he subjected himself to the rigorous discipline of training with a Zen master for six years. An account of this experience is given in his now classic book, Zen in the Art of Archery. He died in 1955. Among his papers were found voluminous notes on various aspects of Zen. They were selected and edited in the form of short pointed essays and collected here. This is an excellent primer on Zen culture and training. Topics include: Zen contrasted with European mysticism; How the Master sees whether the pupil has *satori*; Man's fall and fulfillment; The art of compassion. Recommended as an excellent introduction to *the method of Zen*. 124pp. RaH 60

_____. ZEN IN THE ART OF ARCHERY, $1.95. *In the case of archery, the hitter and the hit are no longer two opposing objects, but are one reality. The archer ceases to be conscious of himself as the one who is engaged in hitting the bull's-eye which confronts him. The state of unconsciousness is realized only when, completely empty and rid of the self, he becomes one with the perfecting of his technical skill. . . .* This is a wonderful book which illumines what very often must seem to be a strange and somewhat unapproachable Eastern experience. One of our most popular Zen books. Introduction by D.T. Suzuki. 109pp. RaH 74

HERRIGEL, GUSTIE. ZEN IN THE ART OF FLOWER ARRANGEMENT, $4.30. This is a charming book which reveals the significance and symbolism underlying flower arrangement. Ms. Herrigel studied under a contemporary master of the art, Bokuyo Takeda. The book is illustrated throughout, including copies of the ones made by the master. Introduction by D.T. Suzuki. 138pp. RKP 58

HIRAI, TOMIO. ZEN MEDITATION THERAPY, $3.25. See the Meditation section.

HOFFMAN, YOEL, tr. THE SOUND OF ONE HAND, $4.95. The subtitle of this book, *281 Zen Koans with Answers*, describes it as well as anything we can say. The author of the original Japanese version (published in 1913) considered contemporary Zen masters and most of their followers to be fakes and he hoped to reveal their *true face* through this account. The answers given here seem to fit and the translator provides a long introduction and extensive commentary. It's a strange book, but one which may be of interest to those who seek a deeper understanding of Zen and of *koans* in particular. Bibliography, 323pp. BaB 75

HOLMES, STEWART and CHIMYO HORIOKA. ZEN ART FOR MEDITATION, c$10.00. Reproduced here are thirty-one *landscapes of the soul* created by the great masters of ink

painting in China and Japan. For the artists who painted them, they represented acts of intense contemplation, attempts to comprehend the essential nature of the universe and to penetrate to the very core of individual existence. The commentaries and the translated haiku accompanying the paintings are designed to work at the nonverbal level, stimulating readers to similar *transactions with the universe*. The plates are arranged by subject, with two plates illustrating each perception. 115pp. Tut 73

HOOYKAAS, ELSE and BERT SCHIERBEEK. ZAZEN, $6.95. Ms. Hooykaas presents an artist's view of the life in a Zen monastery in Kyoto. The book takes the reader through a typical day including photographs of meals, daily chores, worship and devotion, and tending the gardens. The author's diary runs throughout the book, interspersed with quotations from masters. A beautiful study, 6½x11½", 80 plates. Ome 71

HORI, ICHIRO. FOLK RELIGION IN JAPAN, $4.25. An examination of the organic relationship between the Japanese social structure—the family and kinship system, village and community organizations—and *folk religion* as practiced by the majority of the Japanese populace. Professor Hori discusses the Pure Land Buddhist Practice called Nembutsu and the magical custom of reciting the holy name of Amitabha. The significance of sacred mountains as the focus of beliefs in the other world, Japanese shamanism, and the survival of shamanistic tendencies in the contemporary *new religions* are also studied. Glossary, index, bibliography, 278pp. UCh

HUA, HSUAN. PURE LAND AND CH'AN DHARMA TALKS, $3.00. A collection of discourses on Zen practice given at an extended retreat. 70pp. SAB 74

_____, tr. THE SIXTH PATRIARCH'S DHARMA JEWEL PLATFORM SUTRA AND COMMENTARY, c$10.00. A collection of lectures on the *sutra* and its commentary together with a fresh translation of the passages discussed. The presentation is often a bit scattered, however it is the fullest discussion that we know of and many interesting points are raised and examined. This text should be of interest to all who are seeking a deeper understanding of the *sutra* and its personal applications. 380pp. SAB 71

HUBER, JACK. THROUGH AN EASTERN WINDOW, $2.95. A beautifully written, personal account of the author's experience in a Zen monastery in Japan. *Probably one of the best efforts of an American to convey to Westerners what Zen discipline is all about.*—Thomas Merton. 121pp. SMP 65

HUMPHREYS, CHRISTMAS. WALK ON! $1.25. An inspiring and yet practical book which contains hints on meditation and suggestions for understanding some of the difficulties which face the aspirant. Christmas Humphreys was the founder of the Buddhist Society of England and has been one of the most influential and prolific Western interpreters of the East. 101pp. TPH 47

_____. A WESTERNER'S APPROACH TO ZEN, c$5.95. A clear, detailed analysis —perfected over years of practical teaching. Advocates deep study of the Buddha's teaching, some meditation allied to character-building, and then and only then, a course of mind control and development. 212pp. TPH 71

_____. ZEN—A WAY OF LIFE, $2.65. Presents an excellent basic account of the nature of Zen, its philosophy, and the ultimate goal of its teaching—including an extensive treatment of the doctrine of karma and of concentration and meditation, as well as quotations from the scriptures. The latter portion of the book offers a practical system of training for the Zen way of life. Detailed bibliography and glossary. Recommended. 199pp. LBC 62

_____. ZEN BUDDHISM, $1.95. Humphreys has attempted to transfer the life of Zen to the receptive reader by *leading the . . . mind to the precipice which lies between the highest thought and the humblest truth and then, by a jerk or joke, tries to push it over.* Liberal use of quotations as well as an extensive bibliography. 175pp. McM 67

HYERS, CONRAD. ZEN AND THE COMIC SPIRIT, $3.95. *Zen is the only religion that finds room for laughter,* said D.T. Suzuki. In the sayings of Zen masters one soon discovers that the object of laughter is really oneself, trapped in the predicament and folly of mankind. The purpose of wit, in Zen teachings, is to reveal the rational approach as a false trail. Hyers surveys Zen literature to reveal the direct experience of reality beneath the seeming playfulness and lightheartedness of Zen writers and masters. Notes, illustrations, index, 192pp. Wes 73

JAPAN TIMES PHOTO BOOK. ZEN BUDDHISM, c$10.50. Life of Zen monks, Zen temples, paintings, calligraphy, the practice of Zen, and many other aspects of Zen life are treated in photographs and text in this work prepared expressly for Westerners. 112pp. Jap 70

JOHNSTON, WILLIAM. CHRISTIAN ZEN, $2.25. *Thomas Merton and others have pleaded for the need of those of us brought up in the West to expose our Christian orientation to the insights to be found in Zen. William Johnston has responded with a workbook on the actual use of Zen meditation for precisely this purpose. The book is clear, personal, and practical. It is a personal testament that has been practiced before it was written.—Douglas Steere.* This small book includes material on *koans*, the body, breathing and rhythm, and about how Zen and Christianity have met in the author and what this meeting has evoked. 109pp. H&R 71

KAPLEAU, PHILIP. THE THREE PILLARS OF ZEN, $3.95. One of the best introductions as well as all-round books available, this rich source book includes Yasutaniroshi's introductory lectures on Zen practice and his private instructions to ten Westerners studying Zen, letters and a sermon by Bassui, eight contemporary enlightenment letters, passages from Dogen, illustrations of Zazen postures and the oxherding pictures, and notes on Zen vocabulary and Buddhist doctrine. Highly recommended. 363pp. H&R 67

_____. THE WHEEL OF DEATH: A COLLECTION OF WRITINGS FROM ZEN BUDDHIST AND OTHER SOURCES ON DEATH-REBIRTH-DYING, $2.25. An anthology which enables the reader to view death through the eyes of great Buddhist, Taoist, Hindu, and Western masters. The sections on rebirth and karma deal succinctly with those complex and often misunderstood doctrines. Glossary. 110pp. H&R 71

KATO, GENCHI. **A STUDY OF SHINTO**, c$10.00. A historical study of Shinto, from its origins to the present day, along with a review of its principal doctrines and practices. A scholarly presentation, which cites the major studies. Topically arranged. Bibliography, index. 259pp. Cur 26

KENNNETT, JIYU. **SELLING WATER BY THE RIVER: A MANUAL OF ZEN TRAINING**, c$5.95 Intended as a practical handbook for those wishing to study Soto Zen, either as laymen or for the purpose of entering the priesthood. It provides a wealth of heretofore untranslated material. Excellent glossary. 317pp. RaH 72

KUBOSE, GYOMAY. **ZEN KOANS**, $4.95. The most complete collection available in one volume. The *koans* are arranged in categories, although the editor admits that there are no real categories of *koans*; all are about finding the true self. This selection includes extensive commentary from ancient and modern sources as well as many brush paintings by Ryozo Ogura and a glossary. 274pp. Reg 73

LASSALLE, H.M. **ZEN MEDITATIONS FOR CHRISTIANS**, c$7.95. See Meditation section.

LEGGETT, TREVOR. **A FIRST ZEN READER**, $3.75. An anthology of texts discussing Zen theory and practice for the layman. The backbone of the books is two sessions of lectures by contemporary masters: Takashina Rosen and Amakuki Sessan, representing the two main surviving transmissions of Zen: Soto and Rinzai. Also includes selections from Zen literature and a valuable *Note on the Ways* by Leggett, in which he points out how *the student keeps his Zen practice in touch with his daily life*. Beautiful illustrations help to clarify the text. 236pp. Tut 60

LEVERANT, ROBERT. **ZEN IN THE ART OF PHOTOGRAPHY**, $2.00. This work goes back to the essential question of why—not just why we take photographs but why we do anything. It is a beautiful, poetic reminder that How is only important when there is a Why. ImP 67

LINSSEN, ROBERT. **LIVING ZEN**, $3.45. Linssen presents Zen as *neither simply a religion nor a philosophy . . . but as Life itself*. The essence of Zen thought consists in suppressing mental activity—the author says that the only way to live fully is to be detached from it. This work scientifically explains various Zen concepts and shows how they can be introduced into everyday living. Grv 58

LU K'UAN YU (CHARLES LUK), tr. **CH'AN AND ZEN TEACHING, FIRST SERIES**, $4.95. Charles Luk studied under two of the most noted Ch'an masters of his day. He now lives in Hong Kong and devotes himself to presenting *as many Chinese Buddhist texts as possible so that Buddhism can be preserved . . . in the West, should it be fated to disappear in the East as it seems to be*. In this series, Luk has translated the most significant literature. He clearly defines the hidden meanings and clearly describes the practices. Luk's translations are often criticized both in terms of their accuracy and readability—however he is doing a yeoman's job with them and is making many works available to the general public that would otherwise be lost. Vol. I contains: the practice as taught by Hsu Yun, the best known modern master; translations of six representative stories (*kung-an*) of Ch'an masters—each fully explained; and a translation of **Diamond** and **Heart Sutras** with the commentary of Ch'an master Han Shan. Extensive glossary. 255pp. ShP 60

_____. **CH'AN AND ZEN TEACHING, SECOND SERIES**, $8.25. Contains a summary of the different methods of teaching used by the five Ch'an sects; translations and explanations of the forty gathas by which the essence of Ch'an was transmitted verbally from the Buddha to Patriarch; and translations of the biographies of the seven founders of the five Ch'an sects, together with explanations of the *kung-ans* (or *koans*) they contain. Luk has provided an enlightening preface and a glossary. 254pp. Rid 61

_____. **CH'AN AND ZEN TEACHING, THIRD SERIES**, $3.95. Translations of three important texts: **The Sutra of the Sixth Patriarch**; **The Song of Enlightenment**; and **The Sutra of Complete Enlightenment** with the Ch'an master Han Shan's illuminating commentary. The latter, translated into English for the first time here, is the key *sutra* on which the meditational technique of all five Ch'an and Zen schools is still based. Preface and glossary. 306pp. ShP 62

_____. **TRANSMISSION OF THE MIND OUTSIDE THE TEACHING**, $2.95. This is the first volume of a projected ten-volume translation of the **Ku Tsun Su Yu Lu**, a compilation of Ch'an sayings and dialogues gathered by a number of disciples of each master during their stay at his monastery. The present volume contains biographies and teachings of the masters of the first, second, third, fourth, fifth, and sixth generations of the Nan Yo lineage of Dharma descendants of the Sixth Patriarch Hui Neng, with explanations and annotations. 191pp. Grv 75

MASUNAGA, REIHO. **A PRIMER OF SOTO ZEN**, $2.45. Soto Zen is a gentle, intellectual approach to enlightenment which relies on deep meditation—a *sitting in awareness*—rather than the *sudden*, direct method, with *koans* and *mondos*, as in Rinzai Zen, the method popularized in the West by D.T. Suzuki. This text is a translation of the Soto Zen master Dogen's (1200–1253) brief talks and instructional comments collected together in the **Shobogenzo Zuimonki**, or *simplified eye of the true law*. This is an excellent introduction to the form of Zen most popular in Japan today, in the words of the founder of the school. Introduction and notes. 119pp. UHa 71

MATSUSHITA, TAKAAKI. **INK PAINTING**, $7.95. A good study, enhanced by 170 black-and-white and color illustrations of the most vital form of Japanese painting. Oversize, glossary, bibliography, index, 124pp. Wea 74

MERTON, THOMAS. **MYSTICS AND ZEN MASTERS**, $3.25. See Meditation section.

_____. **ZEN AND THE BIRDS OF APPETITE**, $1.75. Merton believed the study of Zen to be an attempt to reach the ground of pure, direct experience which underlies all creative thought and activity. These essays approach this experience through Japanese art and philosophy, through the Zen of Suzuki, and through the classic Zen masters themselves. 141pp. NDP 68

MITCHELL, ELSIE. **SUN BUDDHAS, MOON BUDDHAS**, c$6.95. This is an engrossing story of the author's continuing quest for her true nature, a quest that has carried her from her Unitarian roots in New England to Japan and the living tradition of Zen Buddhism. The basis of the book is the tenet that all human beings are capable of enlightenment, so that all are potential Buddhas. Ms. Mitchell describes the myriad ways in which people experience the quest for true self and tells of the people she encountered in her personal quest. The text is interspersed with quotations and the entire work is a literary exhibition of Zen in its most vital form. 214pp. Wea 73

MIURA, ISSHU and RUTH SASAKI. **ZEN DUST**, c$15.00. An indispensable book for serious students and practitioners of Rinzai Zen. It is a greatly expanded version of the authors' **The Zen Koan**. Detailed notes have been added to the text of their former work; extended biographies of more than fifty major Zen masters set the historical background and trace the characteristic styles of the masters. Includes a set of drawings by Hakuin Ekaku. The text is carefully annotated and the bibliography is the most extensive we've seen. 574pp. HBJ 66

_____. **THE ZEN KOAN**, $2.95. *Koans* are used to bring the student, without recourse to the mediation of words or concepts, to direct, intuitive realization of reality. This work first considers the nature and origin of the *koan* itself, then traces the tradition of *koan* study. A final section comprises translations from the most important *koans*, giving the Chinese calligraphy, a phonetic transcription, and an English translation. 156pp. HBJ 65

MOORE, CHARLES, ed. **THE JAPANESE MIND**, $3.95. A collection of essays on the essentials of Japanese philosophy and culture written by noted Japanese scholars. The topics range from the strictly philosophical to economics and sociology. Index, notes, 357pp. UHa 67

NELSON, ANDREW. **MODERN READER'S JAPANESE-ENGLISH CHARACTER DICTIONARY**, c$19.50. Beautifully produced, and universally considered the most authoritative dictionary available. 1109pp. Tut 62

NISHIMURA, ESHIN. **UNSUI: A DIARY OF ZEN MONASTIC LIFE**, $4.95. Lovely watercolors by Giei Sato and a warm, handwritten text by Nishimura present Western readers with a realistic, non-technical introduction to every aspect of Zen monastic life. Nishimura also gives us a fine introduction and a glossary. Recommended. 152pp. UHa 73

OGATA, SOHAKU. **ZEN FOR THE WEST**, c$14.10. This is a well written, comprehensive general survey of Zen thought and culture. The book has a nice feeling and it is very well bound. Included are full translations of the **Mumonkan** and the **Tao Te Ching**, a chapter on *koans*, and an account of life in a Zen monastery. It is unfortunate that the book is so expensive, because it is a good introductory work. Illustrations, index, 182pp. Gre 59

OKAKURA, KAKUZO. **THE BOOK OF TEA**, c$5.25/1.25. An attempt to make understandable, through the tea cult, the essence of Japanese culture, to reveal to the West *a unified concept of art and nature, nature and art blended into a harmony of daily living.* A boxed, illustrated edition. 133pp. Tut 06

_____. **THE IDEALS OF THE EAST**, c$3.25. A treatise on Asian civilization, with special reference to the art of Japan. 244pp. Tut 70

ONO, SAKYO. **SHINTO—THE KAMI WAY**, c$4.50. A comprehensive, scholarly, illustrated treatment of Shinto, often called *the way of the gods.* As a religion, it is relatively unknown in the West, although for the Japanese it is as old as time and is both a personal faith in the *Kami* (the sacred spirits) and a communal way of life. 116pp. Tut 62

POWELL, ROBERT. **ZEN AND REALITY**, $2.45. Transcription of a series of lectures given to the Buddhist Society in London. Most of the selections are only a few pages long. Powell is a scientist who has written and lectured widely on Zen philosophy, consciousness, Krishnamurti, and science. His style is fairly dry; however, he does present some unusual insights. Bibliography, 142pp. Vik 61

REPS, PAUL. **BE!—NEW USES FOR THE HUMAN INSTRUMENT**, c$3.95. The newest Reps—more delightful picture poems, more personal prose and poetry. All deal with ways of rediscovering our natural being. 63pp. Wea 71

_____. **GOLD AND FISH SIGNATURES**, $4.25. Spontaneous picture poems, light and gay. 94pp. Tut 69

_____. **SIT IN: WHAT IT IS LIKE**, $2.50. Here Reps illustrates his thoughts on Zen sitting meditation. The drawings are done with brush and ink in the Oriental style. The poems and drawings are on facing pages. 18pp. ZCe 75

_____. **SQUARE SUN, SQUARE MOON**, $3.95. Reps' essays on centering throughout the world, personal experiences related, illustrated. 101pp. Tut 67

_____. **TEN WAYS TO MEDITATE**, c$4.95. See Meditation section. Wea 69

_____. **UNWRINKLING PLAYS**, $3.25. Short illustrated plays. 59pp. Tut 65

_____. **ZEN FLESH, ZEN BONES**, c$5.75/1.95. This is actually four books in one, books that would surely rank high in the canon if Zen were so non-Zen as to have scriptures. *101 Zen Stories* recounts actual Zen experiences; the *Gateless Gate* is a thirteenth century collection of the mind problems used in attaining Zen; *Ten Bulls* is a twelfth century commentary upon the stages of awareness leading to Zen. Illustrated with woodblock prints. Recommended as a delightful and enlightening introduction to Zen. 207pp. Dou 57

_____. **ZEN TELEGRAMS**, $3.50. Picture poems—if Zen works as a sudden flash of insight, so do these. Very much in the Zen tradition. 101pp. Tut 59

REXROTH, KENNETH, tr. **ONE HUNDRED POEMS FROM THE JAPANESE**, $1.75. Excellent translations of important poems, drawn chiefly from the traditional **Manyoshu**, **Kokinshu**, and **Hyakunin Isshu** collections. In addition there are examples of haiku and later forms. A romanized version of the poems is also reproduced along with calligraphy of the poet's name. Rexroth also supplies an introduction giving basic background on the history and nature of Japanese poetry, notes on the individual poets, and an extensive bibliography. 170pp. NDP 55

ROSS, NANCY. **THE WORLD OF ZEN: AN EAST-WEST ANTHOLOGY**, $3.95. The most comprehensive, accessible anthology we've seen. Includes illustrated sections on every aspect of the Zen way of life: the arts, science, psychology—as well as extensive selections from translations of the basic source material. Highly recommended. 362pp. RaH 60

SALAJAN, IOANNA. **ZEN COMICS**, $2.75. A collection of Zen stories and *koans* in comic strip form. When we first got this book in we wondered whether it was any good. Some of our customers whose opinion we trusted told us that the book was really insightful and as we looked through it more carefully it did seem to be an interesting volume. One of the main tenets of Zen is not to take anything very seriously and so Zen often expresses its essence best in humor. 88pp. Tut 74

SAN, TENKO. **A NEW ROAD TO ANCIENT TRUTH**, c$5.95. Tenko San is the founder of Ittoen, a spiritual community in Japan that has had a rapid growth in the past couple of decades. He attempts to present, through parables and anecdotes, the inner meaning of the movement (whose name translates as *garden of the light*). The aspect of Ittoen which most deeply impresses visitors is the loving kindness which pervades the community where no harsh word breaks the harmony. The main concept in Ittoen is *sange*, which is not

only a taking of responsibility for one's own acts, but a surrender of the sense of selfhood which is conceived as the source of evil—thus the life becomes one of selfless service and profound peace. Many personal accounts are also included. This book has been a best seller in Japan. Glossary, 183pp. Hor 72

SASAKI, JOSHU. **BUDDHA IS THE CENTER OF GRAVITY**, $3.00. Transcription of a series of lectures given by a Rinzai master who has taught at many centers in the U.S. The lectures are based on the **Mumonkan**, a thirteenth century compilation of forty-eight Zen *koans* and commentary. Excerpts from an English translation of the text are included along with many illustrations. Also included is a series of questions and answers between Sasaki Roshi and individuals at the Lama Foundation, where the talks were given. The volume is beautifully produced and a pull-out insert on rice paper reproduces the **Heart Sutra** in the original Chinese characters. 95pp. LaF 74

SATO, KOJI. **THE ZEN LIFE**, c$6.50. 120 pages of striking photographs and a succinct text by a Japanese psychology professor present an absorbing account of the everyday life of monks in Japan today. The text discusses the tradition and creativity of the Zen monk's life and the way of enlightenment. Included also is an account of life in a Zen-influenced Tokyo commune. 190pp. Wea 66

SAUNDERS, E. DALE. **MUDRA**, c$22.20. This is a detailed study of mudra (symbolic gestures or hand postures) with particular reference to the Buddhist sculpture of Japan. Saunders discusses the history and symbolism of each mudra in a text, illustrated with line drawings, diagrams, and half-tone plates. The eight principal and six secondary mudra are emphasized and the volume is copiously annotated, with bibliography and index, oversize. 319pp. PUP 60

SAWA, TAKAAKI. **ART IN JAPANESE ESOTERIC BUDDHISM**, c$12.50. Esoteric Buddhism flowered in ninth century Japan and upheld the doctrine that the essence of Buddhism was never directly understandable to mankind through pure teaching. It relied greatly on ritual and magical practices concealed from all but the initiate. Its numerous and remarkable deities, however, became well known to the populace and were represented over and over again in painting and sculpture. In fact, it was through the worship of sacred images and mandalas that devotees of the Esoteric sects learned the concepts of their faith and sought salvation in the present world. This book presents the most outstanding of these art treasures, revealing their aesthetic values as well as their religious connotations, and exploring the historical background from which they derive. The text includes 182 illustrations, 38 in color. Oversize, 151pp. Wea

SCHLOEGL, IRMGARD. **THE WISDOM OF THE ZEN MASTERS**, $1.95. Dr. Schloegl is the librarian at the Buddhist Society, London. This small volume presents a fine sampling of the stories and sayings of both Japanese and Chinese Zen masters. It's a good way to get a good feeling for Zen. 80pp. NDP 76

_____, tr. **THE ZEN TEACHING OF RINZAI**, $3.50. Rinzai was a ninth century Chinese Zen master. His teachings were considered eccentric, harsh, and shocking—but were intensely dynamic in their effect. He broke attachments to any ideal directly and fiercely, destroying complacency by using outrageous contradictions. He founded one of the principal schools of Zen Buddhism which flourished in China for eleven centuries, migrated to Japan in the thirteenth century, and to America in the twentieth. This record of Rinzai's training, teachings, and teaching career was written by his disciples and is translated into English for the first time in this volume. ShP 76

SEKIDA, KATSUKI. **ZEN TRAINING METHODS AND PHILOSOPHY**, $4.95. *For Mr. Sekida the unquestioned basis of any serious practice of Zen is zazen, the exercise in which the student sits and learns to control his body and his mind. A substantial part of the book is devoted to describing how zazen is performed and what its effects are....Posture, breathing, the function of the abdominal muscles, muscle tone, the mechanisms of wakefulness and attention—all are discussed in detail in the language of the physiologist.... [Sekida] goes on to present an account of the aims of zazen, and of Zen training in general, that differs markedly from most of those we have hitherto been offered.—from the introduction.* The author goes beyond the earlier stages and discusses *kensho, samadhi,* and how one lives as well as trains in Zen. This is an excellent work which we recommend highly to those seriously interested in the practice of Zen. Some of the author's personal experiences are included. Index, introduction, 258pp. Wea 75

SEKIGUCHI, SHINDAI. **ZEN: A MANUAL FOR WESTERNERS**, c$5.75. Contains many illustrations and thorough explanations that help the reader in achieving true *zazen* meditation even when the benefit of further guidance is unavailable. The author is a Buddhist priest and university professor. A comprehensive, well developed treatment. 111pp. Jap

SHAKU, SOYEN. **ZEN FOR AMERICANS**, $2.95. Formerly titled *Sermons of a Buddhist Abbot,* this is a collection of lectures given by the author on the **Sutra of 42 Chapters,** one of the most important canonical books—put together in book form and translated by D.T. Suzuki. The lectures present traditional thought in modern form. Also includes the complete text of the Sutra. Index, 226pp. OpC

SHIBAYAMA, ZENKEI. **A FLOWER DOES NOT TALK**, $3.95. Introductory essays by a Japanese abbot. He describes the basic characteristics of Zen, the training it calls for, and the Zen personality and then presents three typical Zen writings along with copious explanatory notes. The book is exquisitely illustrated. 264pp. Tut 70

_____. **ZEN COMMENTS ON THE MUMONKAN**, $2.25. The basis of this book is the **Mumonkan**, a classic collection of forty-eight *koans* commonly used in monastic training. The *koans* themselves were gathered by the thirteenth century Chinese master Mumon and discussed first by him. Mumon also appended short poems to each of his discussions. Sharing the insights of a long life of disciplined religious seeking and teaching, Shibayama has added his own comments on the *koans* themselves and on the commentaries and poems by Master Mumon. This is an excellent work for the serious student. Through concentrated attention first to the words of Master Mumon and then to those of a modern commentator, s/he is led as near to a sense of what *satori* implies as is possible without actual Zen discipline and training. The English translation is done by Sumiko Kudo, a student of Shibayama. Includes an introduction, long glossary, and an index. 377pp. NAL 74

SMITH, ARTHUR. **THE GAME OF GO**, $3.75. The game of Go is probably the oldest intellectual game in the world. First developed in China over 3,000 years ago, the game was introduced to Japan in the eighth century. *Go is not merely a picture of a single battle like chess, but a whole campaign of a modern kind, in which the strategical movements of the masses in the end decide the victory. Battles occur in various parts of the board, and sometimes several are going on at the same time . . . and far reaching strategy alone assures victory.* Smith was one of the first Westerners to make a scientific study of the game, and his classic work has never been surpassed for completeness, lucidity, and all-round excellence. This volume includes a glossary, and detailed instructions. 237pp. The game (with wooden board) is available for $10.00. Tut

SOHL, ROBERT and AUDREY CARR, eds. **THE GOSPEL ACCORDING TO ZEN**, $1.25. This is an interesting collection of essays on Zen and translations of some of the important works of Zen masters, designed to give the beginning reader a feel for what Zen is. 133pp. NAL 70

SOLLIER, ANDRE and ZSOLT GYOBIRO. **JAPANESE ARCHERY**, c$7.50. Archery (*kyudo*) in Japan is more than a sport, it is also a spiritual discipline. The many step-by-step photographs and clear, expert illustrations, and the presentation of *kyudo* terminology in both English and Japanese make the book eminently practical. Includes two introductory chapters, one on Zen and its role in the evolution of judo, karate, and *kyudo*, the other on the development of archery in the West and in the Orient. Glossary, oversize, 94pp. Wea 69

Sengai.
Banana plant and frog, with a haiku.
Late eighteenth century

STEWART, HAROLD, tr. **A CHIME OF WINDBELLS**, c$10.00. This is Stewart's second collection of haiku. Here we find 365 haiku, with the same delicate, fragile beauty in translation as the originals written centuries ago. They are divided into the traditional four seasons, with a short section on the New Year. Haiku try to express what the Japanese call *mono no aware*, the *ah!-ness of things*, a feeling for natural loveliness tinged with sadness at its transience. Thirty-three haiku paintings help create the mood and atmosphere of the seasons. Mr. Stewart also provides an essay which discusses the spiritual and religious tradition of haiku. A beautifully printed and bound book. Notes, bibliography, index, 236pp. Tut 69

_____. **A NET OF FIREFLIES**, c$11.75. 320 haiku over a span of five centuries by many of Japan's foremost poets, as well as thirty-three color paintings—swiftly brushed sketches which provide the reader with a new dimension for understanding the elusive essence of the haiku. This book is quite special in its beauty and content and includes a deeply perceptive essay by the translator. Tut 60

STISKIN, NAHUM. **THE LOOKING-GLASS GOD**, c$4.95. A lucid synthesis of three seemingly irreconcilable elements—Shinto, the dogma-free pantheism of Japan; the Chinese principle of yin and yang; and Western scientific rationalism. With the aid of many graphic illustrations, Stiskin has presented a new cosmology for modern man, merging *the analytic prowess of the West with the intuitive heritage of the East.* 157pp. Wea 71

STRYK, LUCIEN and TAKASHI IKEMOTO, trs. **AFTERIMAGES: ZEN POEMS**, $1.95. Translations of some of the poems of Shinkichi Takahashi, the foremost Zen poet of this century, which communicate the experience of Zen and illustrate the harmony of Buddhist thought and poetic imagery. The translators provide an excellent long introductory essay. 153pp. Dou 72

_____. **THE CRANE'S BILL: ZEN POEMS OF CHINA AND JAPAN**, $1.95. An annotated selection grouped under general subject headings. 143pp. Dou 73

_____. **ZEN: POEMS, PRAYERS, SERMONS, ANECDOTES, INTERVIEWS**, $1.95. A well regarded, illustrated anthology which conveys the essence of both the Soto and Rinzai schools of Zen. 160pp. Dou 63

SUZUKI, D.T. **ESSAYS IN ZEN BUDDHISM, FIRST SERIES**, $2.95. In 1927, when Suzuki published the first volume of his **Essays**, the Western world had little knowledge of Zen Buddhism. He, more than anyone else, is responsible for the increase in interest. He is the author of more than 100 works on Zen and Buddhism in both Japanese and English. Included here are essays on aspects of Zen training, on the doctrine of enlightenment and on *satori*, a history of Zen, and his commentary on the *ox-herding pictures*, which have long been used to illustrate the stages of spiritual progress, as well as a long introduction. 388pp. Grv 49

_____. **ESSAYS IN ZEN BUDDHISM, SECOND SERIES**, $5.95. Includes a long essay on *The Koan Exercise*, as well as shorter pieces on *The Secret Message of Bodhidharma*, two Zen textbooks: *Pi-yen-chi* and *Wu-men-kuan*, and *Passivity in Buddhist Life.* Many illustrations, 367pp. Wei

_____. **ESSAYS IN ZEN BUDDHISM, THIRD SERIES**, $5.95. A collection of profusely illustrated essays which show the evolution of Indian metaphysical ideas into a form more compatible with Chinese psychology. Includes a section on the relationship between Zen and the chief Mahayana *sutras*, the **Prajanaparamita** and the **Gandavyuha**. 396pp. Wei

_____. **THE FIELD OF ZEN**, $1.25. A selection of articles and recorded talks on a variety of subjects which were published in the **Journal** of the Buddhist Society of England. 105pp. H&R 69

_____. **INTRODUCTION TO ZEN BUDDHISM**, c$3.98. Two books bound in one: **Introduction to Zen Buddhism** and **Manual of Zen Buddhism**. The two books together make a complete introduction for the beginning student, the former being devoted to an academic presentation of what Zen is and topics in Zen study, and the latter an excellent selection of some of the most important *sutras* and texts of the Zen masters. See the review of each book for more information on them. Recommended. Index, 330pp. Cau 74

_____. **AN INTRODUCTION TO ZEN BUDDHISM**, $1.95. A general treatment of the same material contained in the first volume of Suzuki's **Essays**, aimed at the reader who wishes a preliminary knowledge of Zen. Long forward by C.G. Jung. 132pp. Grv

_____. **MANUAL OF ZEN BUDDHISM**, $2.95. A comprehensive anthology of Zen's most important original sources. Included are the *sutras* or sermons of the Buddha; the *gathas* or hymns; many *koans*; and the *dharanis*, or invocations to expel evil spirits—all translated by Dr. Suzuki. In addition, there are numerous reproductions of drawings and paintings and the recorded conversations of some of the great monks. 192pp. Grv 60

_____. **LIVING BY ZEN**, $2.50. This book was regarded by Suzuki as his second *introduction* to Zen, written many years after the first. It reinterprets Zen in the light of his later experience and reflection. Includes a general survey of Zen as well as detailed studies of *satori* and the *koan*. 187pp. Wei

_____. **SENGAI**, c$15.00. Gibbon Sengai (1750–1837) was one of the great Japanese Zen masters. Calligraphy and ink drawing were part of his training and it is for his art that he is most noted. D.T. Suzuki considered his texts and comments on Sengai's drawings and sayings as the summing-up of his own work (this is his final work). This book contains Suzuki's explanatory notes and texts to 127 scrolls, as well as the scrolls themselves, and makes it possible to look at authentic Zengas together with an explanation of the historical and spiritual background of the pictures. Oversize, 191pp. NYG 71

_____. **SHIN BUDDHISM**, $1.65. An in-depth exploration of Shin Buddhism—a way of enlightenment which stems from the writings and teachings of Shinran, a remarkably charismatic thirteenth century Japanese religious prophet. 93pp. H&R

_____. **STUDIES IN ZEN**, $2.45. A collection of articles and lectures covering a forty-seven year period. Selections include general treatises on Zen, an interpretation of the Zen experience, the role of nature in Zen, *mondo* (questions and answers as a way of teaching), reason and intuition in Buddhist philosophy, and an attempt at an explanation of the Zen movement. 210pp. Del 55

_____. **THE TRAINING OF THE ZEN BUDDHIST MONK**, $3.00. A precise, scholarly picture of Zen in life—including forty-three illustrations by Zenchu Sato—designed to present the practical aspect of Zen. 161pp. Win 34

_____. **WHAT IS ZEN?** $1.25. Three essays: *What is Zen?*, *Self and the Unattainable*, and *The Essence of Buddhism*. 116pp. H&R 71

_____. **ZEN AND JAPANESE CULTURE**, $.95. After briefly examining what Zen is, Suzuki considers in detail the various aspects of Japanese art and life that Zen has influenced: the cult of swordsmanship, the tea ceremony, haiku, the Japanese love of nature, the tradition of the *Samurai*, and its relation to Japanese art. A delightful work, pervaded with the spirit of Zen. Bibliography and 69 illustrations, some of them fold-outs. 478pp. PUP 59

_____. **ZEN BUDDHISM**, $2.50. A sampling, chosen from various Suzuki works covering the following topics: meaning of Zen; its historical background; *satori* (enlightenment); techniques; *The Zen Doctrine of No Mind*; Zen and philosophy; and Zen and Japanese culture. An excellent introduction to Suzuki and to Zen. 294pp. Dou 56

_____. **THE ZEN DOCTRINE OF NO MIND**, $2.95. This is an excellent discussion of the teachings of Hui-neng, the Sixth Chinese Zen Patriarch, and the school he founded. Most of what we know of his philosophy comes from the **Platform Sutra** and Suzuki discusses this text at length and includes quotations from it as part of his exposition. Suzuki is at his best when he is either translating or discussing a specific individual or movement and this is certainly one of his finest works. It is essential reading for all who seek an understanding of the Chinese roots of Zen Buddhism. Index, 160pp. Wei 49

SUZUKI, SHUNRYU. ZEN MIND, BEGINNER'S MIND, c$4.95/2.95. This book is about how to practice Zen as a workable discipline and religion, about posture and breathing, about the basic attitudes and understanding that make Zen practice possible, about non-duality, emptiness and enlightenment. Here one begins to understand what Zen is really about. Suzuki-roshi says: *The world is its own magic*—a feeling that pervades the entire book. Here indeed is a book of intense, profound, joyous reflection. Highly recommended. 138pp. Wea 70

TAKADA, KOIN. THE SPIRIT OF BUDDHISM TODAY, c$9.95. Koin Takada is one of the most influential men in Japan today. He is abbot of the Yakushi-ji and the head of the Hosso Sect of Buddhism. He feels that Buddhism is a religion of the people and that it is his duty to bring his religion to them. The essays translated here reflect a preaching directed toward the people in general, discussed in terms of the current state of the world. They reveal a side of Buddhism that is not well known to Western readers. 125pp. Tok 73

TANAKA, SEN'O. THE TEA CEREMONY, c$22.50. This magnificently illustrated volume by one of Japan's contemporary tea masters is written specifically to provide the Western world with a deeper understanding of the complexities and inspiration of this art form, and to reveal how the discipline of the ritual leads the individual to greater understanding and appreciation of the world around him. Beginning with the twelfth century origins, Mr. Tanaka traces the practice to the present day. All the elements of the ceremony—art, architecture, *kaiseki*, occasions for the ceremony, the utensils, incense, and flowers used, and the connections between Zen and the ceremony—are discussed. Beautiful black-and-white and color photographs add an important dimension to the text. Index, 9½x11", 214pp. Kod 75

THICH THIEN-AN. BUDDHISM AND ZEN IN VIETNAM, c$12.50. A comprehensive account of the history, traditions, and practices of the various Zen Buddhist schools in Vietnam and their relation to Buddhism in other Asian countries. Thich is a monk and scholar who has studied Vietnamese history in depth and who intimately experienced his country's recent upheaval and chaos. He now teaches Oriental philosophy at a number of California colleges and he has written extensively. Index, notes, 301pp. Tut 75

_____. **ZEN PHILOSOPHY, ZEN PRACTICE**, $4.75. Dr. Thich Thien-An is one of Vietnam's most influential contemporary Buddhist scholar and religious leaders. He has lived in the U.S. since 1970 and is presently the founder/president of the College of Oriental Studies in Los Angeles. Here he presents a comprehensive survey of Zen theory and technique. He begins by tracing Zen from its historical origins, viewing it within a more general context of Buddhist thought, and from there moving on to a discussion of the union between theory and practice, sitting and action, wisdom and compassion. Each of the fourteen chapters describes a specific meditation practice, ranging from relatively simple to more complex techniques as taught by the various Zen traditions. The material is presented as clearly as Zen can be in words, and reflects the author's extensive experience as both a teacher and a practitioner. Dr. Thich relates his material to contemporary American society and each chapter includes some traditional, applicable Zen stories or one of his own discourses. A good study for both beginning and experienced students. Illustrations, glossary, 191pp. Dha 75

TREVOR, M.H., tr. THE OX AND HIS HERDSMAN, c$5.50. The ten *Oxherding Pictures* outline the whole of the Zen training and what Zen is about. They are still considered important in Japan today. This edition includes translations to all three sets of poems that were written to accompany the pictures, the forewards to these poems, and the commentary and pointers by a contemporary Zen master, D.R. Otsu. The reproductions are of the original pictures. 102pp. Hok 69

TSUNODA, RYUSAKU, et al. SOURCES OF JAPANESE TRADITION, $8.95/set. A massive two-volume sourcebook, illustrating Japanese thought from the earliest times and covering not only religious and philosophical speculations, but also political, economic, and aesthetic questions. The work consists of translations from a variety of sources (including some made especially for this book) as well as extensive introductory essays and commentary and a bibliography. Index, 928pp. Col 58

UCHIYAMA, KOSHO. APPROACH TO ZEN, $3.95. A practical guide, intended as a manual for the actual practice of *zazen*. It is written specifically for Westerners by the

roshi of a Soto Zen temple in Kyoto. It offers the reader practical instruction and encouragement to go on sitting, and minimizes the use of technical Buddhist terminology. Illustrations. 122pp. Jap 73

WATANAGE, SHOKO. JAPANESE BUDDHISM: A CRITICAL APPRAISAL, $3.75. A survey which focuses on the men who helped to formulate Japanese Buddhism, and on the state of Japanese Buddhism today—with a discussion of various sects. Oversize, bibliography, 177pp. KBS 68

WATTS, ALAN. THE SPIRIT OF ZEN, $2.45. A detailed philosophical examination of Zen as a way of life. Many quotations are included, as well as illustrations. A less technical, less comprehensive treatment of the same material covered in Watts' earlier work, **The Way of Zen**. Bibliography, 128pp. Grv 58

_____. **THE WAY OF ZEN**, $1.95. A concise, lucid, and comprehensive introduction to the history and philosophy of Zen. Very rewarding reading. The best single introduction to Zen that we know of. Excellent bibliography, as well as a section of notes to the text in Chinese. 236pp. RaH 57

WEI, WU WEI. ASK THE AWAKENED—THE NEGATIVE WAY, $3.45. Mixing parables and gentle teaching, the author presents and interprets the teachings of the six Ch'an Patriarchs and the great masters of the T'ang dynasty, stressing throughout the need for subjective awareness rather than objective understanding. An enlightening undertaking. 282pp. LBC 63

WETERING, JANWILLEM van de. THE EMPTY MIRROR, $3.95. An absorbing account of the year that the author spent in a Japanese Zen Buddhist monastery. The narrative is vivid, often humorous, and sometimes disillusioning. 145pp. HMC 73

_____. **A GLIMPSE OF NOTHINGNESS**, c$6.95. Subtitled *Experiences in an American Zen community*, this is the story of the two weeks that van de Wetering spent in an intensive retreat. It is narrated in the first person and his experiences are recounted very vividly. Unlike his earlier account of struggle toward enlightenment in a Japanese monastery, he here seems to reach more of an intuitive understanding of *satori*. The reader can get a good feeling of Zen from this narrative without being overwhelmed by details which s/he cannot relate to his or her own existence. The book has been very well received and many feel that this is the best account of Zen they have read. 184pp. HMC 74

WIENPAHL, PAUL. A MATTER OF ZEN, $2.95. *Zazen* is an intense form of sitting meditation practiced by the Rinzai Zen Buddhist sect. The author is a Westerner who has studied *zazen* in Japan, and he explains the discipline in step-by-step detail. He describes each of the aspects: sitting quietly; breathing in a certain way; counting; *koans*; as well as the role of the *roshi*, or teacher, and the Zen moral code. This is one of the few books which specifically directs the student in *zazen* and although not the most enlightened study possible, it is adequate. Wienpahl includes chapters on the history of Zen and the relation of Zen to traditional Western metaphysics. Extensive chapter notes, 162pp. NYU 64

_____. **ZEN DIARY**, c$6.95. Wienpahl was a university philosophy professor who concluded that Western philosophical thought had exhausted its potential and seemed to be leading toward the death of values. He went to Japan and entered a monastery. This is an intensely personal account of his day-by-day experiences which describes the daily temple routine, the position for meditation, *koan* work, and interviews with the master. Throughout the book Wienpahl attempts to integrate Zen training with Western philosophy. 255pp. H&R 70

WOOD, ERNEST. ZEN DICTIONARY, $3.25. A comprehensive, practical work covering all aspects of Zen as taught and practiced both in China and in Japan. Each entry is concise and clear. 165pp. Tut 57

WU, JOHN C.H. THE GOLDEN AGE OF ZEN, $4.15. An exposition of Zen as experienced and taught by the great Zen masters of the T'ang dynasty (619–906). Includes an excellent long introduction by Thomas Merton, as well as many notes in Chinese. 322pp. NWC 67

YAMPOLSKY, PHILIP, tr. THE PLATFORM SUTRA OF THE SIXTH PATRIARCH—THE TEXT OF THE TUN-HUANG MANUSCRIPT, c$15.10 A new translation of this *sutra*, the summation of Hui-neng's teachings. Yampolsky furnishes a lengthy and detailed historical introduction, which provides the context essential to an understanding of Hui-neng's work, as well as biographical information on Hui-neng, and a discussion of the contents and the various texts of the **Platform Sutra**. The translation is supplemented by many textual notes, a glossary, full bibliography, and the Chinese text of the *sutra*. This is the definitive edition. 25pp. Col 67

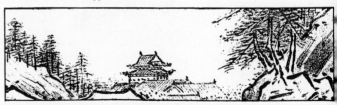

YASUDA, KENNETH. THE JAPANESE HAIKU. $3.50. This is a very complete study of the nature of haiku and its history, with illustrative examples throughout and a selection of haiku. Notes, bibliography, 252pp. Tut 57

ZAEHNER, R.C. ZEN, DRUGS, AND MYSTICISM, $1.95. See Conscious Expansion section.

CAYCE, EDGAR

The story of Edgar Cayce's life is quite remarkable and the results of his work have had far-reaching and proliferating effects. He will always be known for the trance-like state that he entered into over 16,000 times during his life and the wealth of information he gave humanity while in this state.

He had very little education as a young boy and was never very intellectual. However, even at a young age he had the amazing ability to acquire information during sleep which he retained in his memory and could reproduce verbatim. In this way, he could memorize whole texts but not know the meaning of what his mind recorded.

At a later time, but still early in his life, Cayce began entering into an unconscious trance state where he apparently had access to a universal storehouse of knowledge on all matter of subjects, including prognostications of the future. His revelations became known as *readings*. His first several thousand readings concerned medical diagnosis and therapeutical remedies. These were often done for patients suffering hundreds of miles from Cayce and whom he'd neither met nor knew of in any fashion. His medicinal prescriptions were extraordinarily accurate and showed an insight into the healing processes of the body which even today is lacking in the traditional medical profession.

Later in his life Cayce began giving life readings concerning the needs of individuals and the solution of their problems. It was during one of these readings that he casually mentioned that an individual had lived a previous life in another country. Thus began a new dimension of Cayce material as much relating to the law of rebirth was delivered during his state of trance. His prophecies relating to future events and *earth changes* have received much public attention. He accurately predicted every major international occurrence over a period of four decades and has prophesied much for the planet into the next century. Among his accurate forecasts were the death while in office of two American presidents and the emergence of the continent of Atlantis off the coast of Bimini in the late 1960's.

Another result of the Cayce material, of practical benefit to the lives of all mankind is the synthesis and integration of the philosophy of the East with the Western and Christian traditions of dynamic living.

In his last years Cayce located his headquarters in Virginia Beach, Virginia. Today the Association for Research and Enlightenment (A.R.E.), the organization founded by Cayce and continued by his son Hugh Lynn and others, is very active in many disciplines. Lectures and research projects are ongoing at the Headquarters (A.R.E., P. O. Box 595, Virginia Beach, Virginia 23451) and there are study groups in almost every major city in the U.S. and a few in other countries. Complete transcripts of every reading Cayce made are kept on file at the Association and are available to the public.

ADRIANCE, ROBERT. **HIGHLIGHTS FROM THE EDGAR CAYCE READINGS**, $1.75. A selection from the 254 readings which discuss how the A.R.E. should best be organized and its work conducted. The material is topically organized and can be used as a model for those wishing to start other organizations. 73pp. ARE 68

AGEE, DORIS. **EDGAR CAYCE ON ESP**, c$1.98. Details how Cayce was able to tune in to his subject's unconscious mind as well as the universal unconscious, how he developed his psychic ability. Other topics include telepathy, clairvoyance, auras, and prophecy. 224pp. War 69

ALLEN, EULA. **BEFORE THE BEGINNING**, $1.75. These three books by Ms. Allen form a trilogy which chronologically covers the Cayce material on creation. 76pp. ARE 66

_____. **THE RIVER OF TIME**, $1.75. 76pp. ARE 65

_____. **YOU ARE FOREVER**, $1.75. 74pp. ARE 66

A.R.E. **A COMMENTARY ON THE BOOK OF REVELATIONS**, $5.95. ARE

_____. **ECONOMIC HEALING**, $.50. An investigation of the reasons for *economic illness* in individuals and in society coupled with a detailed plan for *economic healing*. 29pp. ARE 74

_____. **GEMS AND STONES**, $1.25. See the Gems and Stones section.

_____. **THE HANDBOOK FOR A.R.E. STUDY GROUPS**, $1.00. 42pp. ARE 57

_____. **A SEARCH FOR GOD**, c$2.50/each. These two volumes are the outcome of eleven years of work by Edgar Cayce and a study group. They represent a distillation of the practical lessons coming through in Cayce's readings and arranged topically. They are meant to be used in present day Cayce study groups. 266pp. ARE 50

_____. **A SEARCH FOR GOD READINGS, BOOK I**, $6.95. ARE 45

_____. **A SEARCH FOR GOD READINGS, BOOK II**, $11.95. ARE 45

BAKER, M.E. PENNY. **MEDITATION—A STEP BEYOND WITH EDGAR CAYCE**, $1.25. See the Meditation section.

BOLTON, BUTT. **EDGAR CAYCE SPEAKS**, $2.25. A compilation of the Cayce readings on food, beverages, and physical health, topically arranged. 664pp. Avo 69

BRO, HARMON. **EDGAR CAYCE ON DREAMS**, $1.25. See the Dreams section.

_____. **EDGAR CAYCE ON RELIGION AND PSYCHIC EXPERIENCE**, $1.50. 265pp. War 70

_____. **HIGH PLAY: TURNING ON WITHOUT DRUGS**, $1.25. Dr. Bro, an experienced psychotherapist, draws on his own case notes and on the work of Edgar Cayce to present a guide to the varieties of consciousness-altering experience. 286pp. War 70

CARLSON, VADA. **THE GREAT MIGRATION**, $1.50. See the Ancient Americas subsection of Ancient Civilizations.

_____. **THE VISION AND THE PROMISE**, $1.25. The story of the childhood and youth of Edgar Cayce, told especially for children and illustrated. 35pp. ARE 72

CARTER, MARY. **EDGAR CAYCE ON PROPHECY**, $1.50. A comprehensive account of all the life readings connected with prediction as well as general material on Cayce's life and work. The material from the readings is arranged topically. 207pp. War 68

CARTER, MARY ELLEN and WILLIAM McGAREY. **EDGAR CAYCE ON HEALING**, $1.50. See the Healing section.

CATALDO, GERALD. **A DICTIONARY**, $2.00. Definitions and comments from the Cayce readings arranged in alphabetical form. 81pp. ARE 73

CAYCE, EDGAR. **AFFIRMATIONS**, $1.25. Inspirational affirmations for each day of the year. 60pp. ARE 63

_____. **AURAS**, $.75. See the Color and Aura section.

_____. **CHANGE: EDGAR CAYCE ON THE I CHING**, $1.75. See the I Ching subsection of Chinese Philosophy.

_____. **WHAT I BELIEVE**, $1.50. This autobiographical account is one of the few things that Cayce actually wrote himself. 48pp. ARE 46

CAYCE, EDGAR EVANS. **ATLANTIS: FACT OR FICTION**, $1.25. See the Ancient Civilizations section. 35pp. ARE 62

CAYCE, EDGAR EVANS and HUGH LYNN. **THE OUTER LIMITS OF CAYCE'S POWER**, $1.25. Hugh Lynn and Edgar Evans Cayce recount several instances when their father's predictions were either misleading or hopelessly wrong. Theirs is not, however, an attempt to discredit the psychic ability of their father, but to clarify those factors that are involved in the accuracy of psychic data. 170pp. H&R 71

CAYCE, HUGH LYNN. **DREAMS: THE LANGUAGE OF THE UNCONSCIOUS**, $2.25. See the Dreams section.

_____. **THE EDGAR CAYCE READER NO. 1**, $1.25. A selection of readings on various topics. 187pp. War 67

_____. **THE EDGAR CAYCE READER NO. 2**, $.75. 206pp. War 69

_____. **FOR THESE TIMES**, $1.25. Transcriptions of five lectures by the President of the A.R.E.: *This Man Sought First the Kingdom, Clairvoyance and the Bible, Where Karma Ends and Grace Begins, Faith and Miracles,* and *Can We Break the Time Barrier.* 62pp. ARE 64

_____. **VENTURE INWARD**, $1.25. An extensive discussion of various aspects of psychic phenomena including chapters on life after death, possession, hypnosis, telepathy, automatic writing, dreams, and drugs. Each chapter is followed by suggested readings. *I would place this book high on any required reading list for people interested in psychic matters.*—Gina Cerminara. 207pp. H&R 64

_____. **GOD'S OTHER DOOR**, $1.50. A study of the Cayce readings on life after death combined with the transcription of a lecture, *The Continuity of Life,* which Edgar Cayce gave in 1934. 48pp. ARE 58

CAYCE, J. GAIL. **OSTEOPATHY**, $3.00. See the Healing section.

CERMINARA, GINA. **MANY MANSIONS**, $1.50. See Reincarnation and Karma section.

CHURCH, W.H. **A GARLAND OF WISDOM**, $1.25. Topically arranged short quotations from the Cayce readings, in an illustrated gift book format. 35pp. ARE 75

CRAIG, PAULA. **BUILD YOUR OWN DREAM HOUSE**, $1.25. See the Dreams section.

FURST, JEFFREY. **EDGAR CAYCE'S STORY OF ATTITUDES AND EMOTIONS**, $1.25. A selection and interpretation of the Cayce readings on attitudes and emotions, this study examines the entire range of human feeling—its origins, manifestations, influences of daily life and physical and spiritual health—to present the first guide to self-knowledge and balanced living according to the ideals of Edgar Cayce. Provides both inspirational advice from the Cayce readings and a very practical guide to love that is the source of all spiritual growth. 206pp. Ber 72

_____. **EDGAR CAYCE'S STORY OF JESUS**, $.95. See the Christianity section.

GAMMON, MARGARET. **ASTROLOGY AND THE EDGAR CAYCE READINGS**, $2.00. See the Astrology section.

HATT, CAROLYN. **THE MAYA**, $1.75. See the Ancient Americas sub-section of Ancient Civilizations.

HERITAGE STORE. **MEDICINES FOR THE NEW AGE**, $1.50. See the Healing section.

JOHNSON, RAYNOR. **THE SITUATION OF MODERN MAN**, $2.00. Transcription of a series of lectures on the importance and unimportance of life and the re-orientation of being. 76pp. ARE 71

KAHN, DAVID. **MY LIFE WITH EDGAR CAYCE**, $.75. Kahn was one of Cayce's closest personal friends. 175pp. Faw 70

KETCHUM, WESLEY. **THE DISCOVERY OF EDGAR CAYCE**, $1.25. 52pp. ARE 64

KIDD, WORTH. **EDGAR CAYCE AND GROUP DYNAMICS**, $2.00. Practical suggestions for A.R.E. group organization and leadership. 54pp. ARE 71

KITTLER, GLENN. **EDGAR CAYCE ON THE DEAD SEA SCROLLS**, $.95. See the Christianity section.

KRAJENKE, ROBERT. **STAND LIKE STARS**, $1.75. A presentation of four case histories which illustrate the influence of past lives in the karmic patterns of these individuals. 59pp. ARE 70

LANGLEY, NOEL. **EDGAR CAYCE ON REINCARNATION**, $1.25. See the Reincarnation and Karma section.

LEHNER, MARK. **THE EGYPTIAN HERITAGE**, $2.95. See Ancient Egypt sub-section of Ancient Civilizations.

LEWIS, ROGER. **COLOR**, $1.50. See the Color and Aura section.

McGAREY, WILLIAM. **EDGAR CAYCE AND THE PALMA CHRISTI**, $4.95. See the Healing section.

McGAREY, WILLIAM and GLADYS. **THERE WILL YOUR HEART BE ALSO**, $1.95. Subtitled *Edgar Cayce's Readings About Home and Marriage,* this is an examination of Cayce's readings on almost every aspect of love and marriage—from choosing one's mate and forming one's own marriage vows, to the proper guidance of adolescents. Cayce's advice, above all, is practical and the Drs. McGarey have been practicing medicine and counseling for over twenty years, while raising a family of their own. They dramatize

Cayce's theories of choice, growth, and forgiveness with actual events from their own household and from their patients' experiences. The material is better integrated than most of the works drawn from the Cayce material. The McGareys run the A.R.E. Clinic in Arizona. Index, 264pp. War 75

MILLARD, JOSEPH. **EDGAR CAYCE, MYSTERY MAN OF MIRACLES**, $1.25. A simply written retelling of Edgar Cayce's story. 224pp. Faw 67

PATTERSON, DORIS. **THE UNFETTERED MIND**, $2.00. Subtitled *Varieties of ESP in the Edgar Cayce Readings.* 77pp. ARE 68

PATTERSON, DORIS and VIOLET SHELLEY. **BE YOUR OWN PSYCHIC**, $2.00. Selections from the readings, with commentary, which explain how to use your psychic abilities safely in accordance with your spiritual growth. 83pp. ARE 75

PURYEAR, HERBERT and MARK THURSTON. **MEDITATION AND THE MIND OF MAN**, $2.50. See the Meditation section.

QUEST, LINDA. **PEACE BY CHOICE**, $2.00. A political scientist applies the Cayce readings to the contemporary world. ARE 74

READ, ANNE. **EDGAR CAYCE ON JESUS AND HIS CHURCH**, $.95. See Christianity section.

REILLY, HAROLD and RUTH BROD. **THE EDGAR CAYCE HANDBOOK FOR HEALTH THROUGH DRUGLESS THERAPY**, c$10.95. See the Healing section.

ROBINSON, LYLE. **EDGAR CAYCE'S STORY OF THE ORIGIN AND DESTINY OF MAN**, $1.25. See the Ancient Civilizations section.

ROCHE, RICHARD. **EGYPTIAN MYTHS AND THE RA TA STORY**, $1.75. See the Ancient Egypt sub-section of Ancient Civilizations.

RUNNELS, RACHEL. **MARRIAGE AND THE HOME**, $1.75. A study of the readings approach to marriage, home, sex, parenthood, and being single. 74pp. ARE 73

SECHRIST, ELSIE. **DREAMS: YOUR MAGIC MIRROR**, $1.25. See the Dreams section.

_____. **MEDITATION—GATEWAY TO LIGHT**, $1.50. See Meditation section.

SHARMA, I.C. **CAYCE, KARMA, AND REINCARNATION**, $3.95. See Reincarnation and Karma section.

SHELLEY, VIOLET. **SYMBOLS AND THE SELF**, $1.75. A study of numbers and symbols based loosely on the Cayce readings, showing how symbolism surrounds us and enters into every aspect of our lives. 63pp. ARE 65

SPARROW, GREGORY. **LUCID DREAMING**, $2.25. See the Dreams section.

STEARN, JESS. **EDGAR CAYCE—THE SLEEPING PROPHET**, $1.75. A presentation of many of Cayce's predictions and prophecies, both those that have been accurate in the past and those forecast for the future. Many incidents in Cayce's life and some of his unorthodox but effective medical diagnoses and remedies are also described. A good introduction to the Cayce material, and the edition we prefer. 287pp. Ban 67

_____. **A PROPHET IN HIS OWN COUNTRY**, $1.75. Subtitled *The Story of the Young Edgar Cayce.* 309pp. RaH 74

STEINHART, LAWRENCE. **EDGAR CAYCE'S SECRETS OF BEAUTY THROUGH HEALTH**, $1.25. See the Nutrition section.

SUGRUE, THOMAS. **STRANGER IN THE EARTH**, $.95. The story of the years Sugrue spent with Cayce, including a transcript of his life reading. 367pp. War 48

_____. **THERE IS A RIVER—THE STORY OF EDGAR CAYCE**, $1.85. The closest, most intimate portrayal of the the life of America's greatest psychic clairvoyant and modern day prophet. The author was the only writer who actually knew Cayce personally and observed his activities. The writing style and information is very folksy, but the essential information is there. This is the first Cayce book that most people read. 384pp. Del 42

TURNER, GLADYS and MAE ST. CLAIR. **123 QUESTIONS AND ANSWERS FROM THE EDGAR CAYCE READINGS**, $1.25. Topically arranged. Index, 59pp. ARE 66

WINSTON, SHIRLEY. **MUSIC AS THE BRIDGE**, $1.75. See the Music section.

WOODWARD, MARY ANN. **EDGAR CAYCE'S STORY OF KARMA**, $1.50. See the Reincarnation and Karma section.

CHILDREN'S BOOKS

Most of the children's books we have selected for review have beautiful illustrations. That plus a good story are the chief features that we are looking for. So many hundreds are published each year that it is hard to choose. We have also tried to find books that have a genuinely positive message and something of a spiritual emphasis. At times we will select a book because we think it is especially neat, even though it has little or no message (**Harold and the Purple Crayon** is an example). We have also included the classic books which we feel fit best with our approach. If you readers have any suggestions as to what we might consider for our next edition, please write and let us know. Outstanding children's books seem harder to track down than books in almost any other category. We've found some that we really like and hope you agree with our choices.

AARDEMA, VERNA. **WHY MOSQUITOES BUZZ IN PEOPLE'S EARS**, c$6.95. Magnificent illustrations by Leo and Diane Dillon combined with a simple African legend make for a story that should hold a child's interest. The illustrations are unlike anything we have seen before and have a definite African feeling. The chief colors are pastel blues, pinks, and purples on a black background. Winner of the 1976 Caldecott Medal for the most distinguished picture book for children and recipient of a number of other citations. 10½x10½". Del 75

BARKER, CECILY. **FLOWER FAIRY BOOKS**, c$1.95/each. This series of books has delighted children and adults alike for many years. Each picture of the fairy is full page and beautifully colored. The personality of each fairy comes across and each one is totally unlike the others. A poem accompanies each drawing. The following books are available: **A Flower Fairy Alphabet, Flower Fairies of the Autumn, Flower Fairies of the Garden, Flower Fairies of the Spring, Flower Fairies of the Summer, Flower Fairies of the Trees, Flower Fairies of the Wayside.** Each book is about 50pp. TcP nd

BELLEROPHON. **COLORING BOOKS**, $1.95/each. These books are 8½x11" and contain reproductions of illustrations from the artists of the periods covered. The illustrations often contain a lot of detail so they are recommended only for older children. Once colored the illustrations become nice works of art and the books are a good way for a child to learn about other cultures. Titles available include **Ancient Egypt, Ancient Near East, Incas-Aztecs-Mayas, Ancient Greece, The Renaissance, The Middle Ages, American Indians.** BIB

BURKERT, NANCY. **SNOW-WHITE AND THE SEVEN DWARFS**, c$6.95. Ms. Burkert has painted a series of magical visions of this story. The illustrations can be studied endlessly and new forms and creatures pop out of the amazing detail work. Our favourite is a forest scene where the animals are camouflaged—the more you look at the pictures, the more animals you see. The drawings are extraordinary and the colors well chosen. The translation is by Randall Jarrell. The only complaint we have heard is that the pictures and text are not on facing pages and parents feel that children enjoy having a story read to them more when they can simultaneously look at related pictures. 9x12", FSG 72

CARROLL, LEWIS. **ALICE'S ADVENTURES IN WONDERLAND**, c$6.95. **Alice in Wonderland** is one of those classic tales which, while it is generally considered a children's story, has as much appeal to adults as it does to children. This edition includes Arthur Rackham's wonderfully detailed illustrations in color and black-and-white. Another hardcover edition, illustrated with line drawings, is available for $1.95. Oversize, 162pp. Vik 07

CHINMAYANANDA, SWAMI and KUMARI BHARATHI NAIK. **BALA BHAGAVATAM**, c$5.75. *The entire art and literature of India is moulded in the beauty and divinity of the* **Bhagavat** *. . . which narrates the childhood stories of Lord Krishna. . . . The devoted young hearts of the children loved the stories of Krishna's early childhood, full of pranks and mischiefs, meaningful adventures and purposeful jokes. . . . The ever-smiling, never-weeping Krishna should be the ideal for the modern world of children everywhere.* This is an oversize, illustrated volume, translating selected stories in short sections designed to be read by the parents (but it can also be easily read by older children). The translations are done in language easily understood by children. 153pp. CPT 69

Children of Odin

COLUM, PADRAIC. **THE CHILDREN OF ODIN**, c$6.95. A recreation of the Norse myths. These myths are very different from the classical Greek myths. The gods and the giants battle and there are witches and dragons and all kinds of mythological beasts. The

stories are exciting and keep the reader's interest. The print is fairly large and delightful line drawings accompany the narration. This volume has been extremely popular over the years and is our favorite retelling of these myths, most versions of which seem incredibly dry. All the important stories are included. 271pp. McM 20

CUMMINGS, E.E. **FAIRY TALES**, $1.75. *These four exquisite little stories might have sprung from the consciousness of a child. They are fragmentary and luminous, delicate, and blissfully unresolved. . . . John Eaton's illustrations are quite perfect for the book, combining line with soft washes of color.*—New York Times Book Review. 39pp. HBJ 75

DE ROIN, NANCY. **JATAKA TALES: FABLES FROM THE BUDDHA**, c$5.95. See the Jataka Tales sub-section of Buddhism.

EPSTEIN, PERLE. **ORIENTAL MYSTICS AND MAGICIANS**, c$5.95. This is an excellent book for parents who would like their children to learn about Eastern philosophy. A chapter each is devoted to the religious ideas and movements of India, Japan, Tibet, and China. There are also separate chapters on Sri Chaitanya, the Zen master Hakuin, Milarepa, and Sri Ramakrishna. The book is well illustrated with photographs and drawings. 151pp. Dou 75

GAER, JOSEPH. **THE FABLES OF INDIA**, c$4.95. The fables retold here have been selected from three collections: **The Panchatantra, The Hitopadesa,** and **The Jatakas.** All the stories are beast fables, about animals with human emotions and human failings. Gaer has done a fine job of recreating the ancient fables. The narrative reads well and older children should enjoy the book. There are nice illustrations throughout. The introduction discusses fables. Bibliography, 175pp. LBC 55

_____. **HOLIDAYS AROUND THE WORLD**, c$5.95. This is a lively discussion of the major holy days of the Chinese, Hindu, Jewish, Christian, and Muslim faiths. The folklore surrounding each holy day is fully discussed and its historical origin is also presented. Illustrations, index. 212pp. LBC 53

GELLEK, NAZLI. **TALES OF THE BUDDHA**, c$4.75/each. This is a new series of brightly colored tales of the Buddha's adventures in earlier incarnations. The stories can be read on a number of levels and the seemingly simple happenings have a deep symbolic meaning. See the Jataka Tales sub-section of Buddhism for a description of each of the individual volumes. Personally, we prefer the retelling in the DeRoin version, but this format is more appropriate for young children. The following books are now available: **The Golden Foot, The King and the Mangoes, The Proud Peacock and the Mallard, The Spade Sage, Three Wise Birds.** 11½x9", Dha

GINSBURG, MIRRA. **HOW THE SUN WAS BROUGHT BACK TO THE SKY**, c$6.95. This is an adaptation of a Slovenian folk tale. Grey clouds have shut out the sun for days. A family of chicks accompanied by a variety of other small animals set out to find the sun and bring it back to the sky. A series of beautifully colored full page illustrations parallel the text and spill over onto the page that has the writing. We love drawings of the sun and this book contains some of the finest we have seen along with a delightful set of animals. 8½x10½", McM 75

_____. **MUSHROOM IN THE RAIN**, c$5.95. It's raining and all the animals hide under the mushroom. They are amazed that there is room for them all until they realize what happens to a mushroom when it rains—it multiplies! Adapted from a Russian folk tale and beautifully illustrated with a variety of animals, rainbows, multi-colored mushrooms, and much more. 8½x10½". McM 74

GRAHAME, KENNETH. **THE WIND IN THE WILLOWS**, c$1.95/$1.25. This is one of our all time favorite children's books and it's one that can be read and appreciated by people of any age. Grahame brings Mr. Toad, the Mole, the Badger, and all their friends to life in a way that few other authors have done. Reading it is a wonderful way to get a finer appreciation for the role that animals play in the balance of nature. Grahame is guilty of creating anthropomorphic characters, but that does nothing to detract from the appeal of the story. Illustrated with line drawings. 244pp. G&D nd

GREEN, ROGER. **KING ARTHUR**, $1.50. See the Grail and King Arthur section.

_____. **TALES OF ANCIENT EGYPT**, $1.50. Green has a wonderful faculty for retelling ancient tales in a way that children can appreciate and still retain the underlying meaning of the stories. Here he begins with the story of Amen-Ra, the father of gods and men who created all the creatures of the world, and follows it with the story of how Isis searched the waters of the world for the body of her dead husband Osiris. Here, too, you will find the legends concerning the source of the Nile, journeys to the land of the dead, and much more. Illustrations, 185pp. Vik 67

_____. **TALES OF THE GREEK HEROES**, $1.50. An exciting retelling of the tales and legends of the Greek heroes and a history of the Golden Age of Greece up to the Trojan War. Illustrations, 205pp. Vik 58

HARRIS, JOEL CHANDLER. **THE COMPLETE TALES OF UNCLE REMUS**, c$14.95. There has been a strong backlash against the Uncle Remus stories recently as people have become more aware of stereotypes in literature. The popularity of the stories has certainly been affected by this change in public consciousness. When we were first looking for children's books to stock our bookshop a customer whose opinion we respect said that we should definitely have Uncle Remus because these stories represent one of the purest forms of African folklore available today, despite the dialect and the Southern trappings. This edition includes complete tales of Brer Rabbit, Brer Fox, Brer B'ar, and all the other animal tales which Harris made famous. All the fine original line drawings are also included. Introduction, glossary, 907pp. HMC 55

HAUFF, WILHELM. **THE ADVENTURES OF LITTLE MOUK**, c$6.95. This is one of our favorite books. The illustrations give the feeling of a beautifully colored tapestry from a century and a half. Little Mouk is orphaned and sets off in his father's baggy clothes to seek his fortune. Fortune does not come easily to him, however, and he has a series of adventures before his luck changes and he becomes the owner of a pair of magic shoes and an old walking stick that has the power to find buried treasure. He flourishes and is taken into the household of the king where his good luck creates jealousy and leads him deep into trouble. It all ends happily after another series of adventures. 10x11", McM 74

HODGSON, JOAN. **ANGELS AND INDIANS**, c$5.50. This is a strange book which is more obviously spiritual than most children's books. The first part presents a series of photographs of fairies purported to be real and discusses the young girl who made contact with the fairies. The next section is devoted to a story which illustrates what the American Indians knew about the fairies and angels in the world of light and discusses American Indian children's contact with the *Great White Spirit*. A final section discusses how Indians and others from the past influence our lives today. Many brightly colored illustrations are included, but these are not of the best quality. 48pp. WET 74

_____. **HULLO SUN**, c$3.50. This book is designed to help children reach spiritual understanding and encourage them to take full advantage of their natural fantasies. Here's an example: *Hullo Sun! You give us light. You make us warm. You make the trees and flowers grow. You make us happy. Thank you, Sun. Now shut your eyes and think of the Sun. Can you see the Sun with your imagination—with your inside eyes? It is shining so brightly. It makes us feel lovely and warm and happy inside. God is like the Sun. God is the Great Spirit behind the Sun. God is everywhere. God is everything but you cannot see Him with your outside eyes.* Fully illustrated with bright colors, again poorly drawn, but here it is the message that counts and not the pictures. Large print. 8½x10½". WET 72

HOLY ORDER OF MANS. **THE HEAVENLY TWO**, $3.00. An oversize picture book which is drawn in lines and designed to be colored in. Facing pages tell the story of creation and of mankind's fall from perfection and eventual regaining of grace. The pictures are lovely and contain subtle symbolism and the whole book is hand drawn. Here's a sample of the message: *Having pulled the sword of spirit out of the anvil of base metal, as King Arthur once had done, man dropped everything he had been doing, and appeared to tip himself upside down, in order to empty out all his old ways of thinking and to change everything, before starting anew.* It's hard to say how children will respond, but the idea is lovely. 43pp. HOM 75

HUME, LOTTA, ed. **FAVORITE CHILDREN'S STORIES FROM CHINA AND TIBET**, c$7.50. This is an extraordinary collection of traditional legends and stories. Ms. Hume lived in China for twenty-two years and immersed herself in the culture. She was especially impressed by the stories her neighbors told their children. Nineteen of them have been collected here in a format designed to appeal to children. A well known Chinese artist has supplied over ninety illustrations, twelve in color. We love to read these stories, many of which are filled with animals that speak and play tricks on each other and with humans who perform magical acts. There's a delightful illustration on almost every page that children can look at while the story is read to them. 7x8", 119pp. Tut 62

JOHNSON, CROCKETT. **HAROLD AND THE PURPLE CRAYON**, c$2.95. This is one of our all-time favorite books. It is an ingenious story, unlike any other we have ever seen. Harold, a small boy, goes out for a walk with his purple crayon and thinks of a variety of things he would like to do. Whatever he thinks of he draws and follows the adventure through until he decides to do something else. So then he draws his next idea with his purple crayon. The adventures continue from page to page. It's a simple story which children of almost any age can enjoy. 5x6", H&R 55

KENNEDY, PAUL. **STAINED GLASS WINDOWS COLORING BOOK**, $1.75. This coloring book is designed for older children. Kennedy has selected and reproduced a number of actual windows from Europe. He uses translucent paper so that, when colored, the sheet can be mounted on a window. 8x10½", 16 plates. Dov 72

KIPLING, RUDYARD. **JUST SO STORIES**, $2.75. This is a collection of modern fables which Kipling originally created for his own daughter. They are simple tales designed to be read aloud. The language is archaic and many of the images come from outside a child's normal world, but all the tales are exciting and involve the child in a wonderful fantasy world. Some of the titles: *How the Camel Got His Hump, How the Leopard Got His Spots, How the First Letter Was Written, The Elephants's Child.* This edition contains Kipling's own illustrations, with captions. 248pp. ScB 02

LA FONTAINE, JEAN de. **THE HARE AND THE TORTOISE**, c$5.95. Jean de la Fontaine created his fables in the seventeenth century and they have remained among the best loved children's books. The stories have been told and retold to countless generations of children and each generation has its own illustrators. The contemporary illustrator that we like best is Brian Wildsmith and all the La Fontaine Books that we list are illustrated by him. Every child knows the story of the swift hare who was so sure of winning the race that he dawdled on the way. The wise tortoise just plodded steadily along, won the race, and taught the conceited hare a lesson. Wildsmith has done a wonderful job of making the animals and nature scenes come to life in vivid color. 9½x11½", Wts 66

_____. **THE LION AND THE RAT**, c$5.95. This is a retelling of the classic fable which is beautifully illustrated. The lion is a magnificent beast, a true king of the jungle and golden as the sun. A rat accidentally walked between the lion's paws and the lion allowed him to escape unharmed. The rat promised to repay the kindness and repay it he did. Many other animals come into the illustrations and all of them are brightly drawn. It's a simple story, suitable for the youngest children. 8½x11", Wts 63

LEE, VIRGINIA. **THE MAGIC MOTH**, c$5.95. This is a story about death and its aftermath which is designed to help older children understand and accept death as a natural part of life. It is written in a direct, unsentimental way. Illustrations, 6½x8½", 64pp. Sea 72

LEWIS, RICHARD, ed. **IN A SPRING GARDEN**, $1.75. *This picture book for all ages is a collection of classic Japanese haiku, exquisitely illustrated by Ezra Jack Keats, winner of the Caldecott Medal, who uses with full effectiveness his familiar style of watercolor and collage. The book, both in text and illustrations, shimmers and glows with sensitivity, reverence for life, and earth-wise humor. . . . Here indeed is a book to enjoy over and over again in the viewing and the reading.*—**Los Angeles Times**. 8½x10½", Del 65

LIVINGSTON, PETER. **ON ASTROLOGY**, c$5.95. See the Astrology section.

McDERMOTT, GERALD. **ARROW TO THE SUN**, c$6.95. McDermott has adapted a Pueblo Indian tale. The color hues are bright and strong and the illustrations are bold, almost geometric; they really fill up the pages and the story itself is told in only a few simple words. It is a vibrant rendering of the universal myth of the hero's quest and it illustrates the Indian reverence for the source of life—the sun. A Caldecott Award book. 9½x 10½", Vik 74

_____. **THE STONE-CUTTER**, c$5.95. An adaptation of a Japanese folk tale in which a man's foolish longing for power becomes a tale of wishes and dreams that can be understood on many levels. It it the story of a stonecutter who is happy with his life until a prince passes by him in a lavish procession. He wishes aloud for great wealth and the spirit who lives in the mountain hears him and transforms the stonecutter into a wealthy and powerful prince. He is happy for a while until his desire causes him to make another wish, which the spirit again grants. And so it goes until he has his final wish, desiring to become a mountain. This too is granted and the story ends as the mountain trembles while a lowly stonecutter chisels away at its feet! The moral should be obvious. The illustration style resembles McDermott's earlier book. 7x11", Vik 75

MACAULAY, DAVID. **CATHEDRAL**, c$7.95. See the Sacred Geometry section.

_____. **PYRAMID**, c$7.95. See the Ancient Egypt sub-section of Ancient Civilizations.

MACLEOD, MARY. **KING ARTHUR AND HIS NOBLE KNIGHTS**, c$5.95. A retelling of Malory's **Le Morte d'Arthur**, aimed at young people. Illustrations are interspersed. 341pp. Lip 49

MAESTRO, BETSY. **FAT POLKA-DOT CAT AND OTHER HAIKU**, c$6.95. Well drawn simple illustrations of animals and nature scenes accompany haiku which seem to reflect a child's-eye view of the world of nature. Suitable for the very youngest children. 8x8", Dut 76

MATSUTARI, MIYOKO. **HOW THE WITHERED TREES BLOSSOMED**, c$3.95. This children's book was printed in Japan and both the illustrations and the story line seem

from Kipling's Just So Stories

ery Japanese. To start with, the book begins at what Westerners would consider the back. The paper is a facsimile of rice paper and the illustrations are delicate and lovely. The people are all very well drawn. The main character, a kind and honest old man, has a jealous neighbor who is always trying to take advantage of him. The nastier the neighbor treats the old man, the more bad things happen to him. All ends well as goodness triumphs and evil is punished. The Japanese characters of the text are included and the pictures are on facing pages. 9x11", 40pp. Lip 69

from Four Frogs in a Box by Mercer Mayer

MAYER, MERCER. **FOUR FROGS IN A BOX**, c$5.95. A set of four tiny books with engaging pictures which tell a story that even the smallest child can enjoy. No words. The stories tell about a boy, a dog, and a frog. 4¼x3½", Del 73

MILLER, J.P. **TALES FROM AESOP**, $.95. This is a retelling of six of the fables. The book is very fully illustrated and they are brightly colored and simple enough to be enjoyed by even the smallest child. There's a fair amount of text, and it is designed to be read to the child. Each of the stories has a moral and the stories themselves are universal in appeal. 8x8", RaH 76

MILNE, A.A. **POOH'S POT O' HONEY**, c$5.95/set. A boxed set of four little books, 3-3/4 x2-3/4": **Pooh Hears a Buzzing Noise and Meets Some Bees, Pooh Goes Visiting and Gets into a Tight Place, Pooh and Piglet Go Hunting and Nearly Catch a Woozle,** and **Eeyore Loses a Tail and Pooh Finds One.** Kids love both the stories and the size of the books and we've found that it's hard to part a little kid from these books once s/he has seen them. The vocabulary is simple enough for a beginning reader and there are illustrations throughout. Dut 68

MOSEL, ARLENE. **THE FUNNY LITTLE WOMAN**, c$7.95. This book has some of the most unusual and delightful illustrations we've ever seen. It takes place in Japan and the leading human is an amazing little old woman in a kimono with chopsticks in her hair. She's great, but our favorites are the wicked *oni* whom she accidentally meets when chasing a dumpling down a hole which leads to the middle of the earth. She is captured by the *oni* and made their cook until she finally escapes. She likes to laugh and her tee-he-he-he resounds on each page. The *oni* themselves are magnificent beasts, part troll, part dwarf, and truly unlike any creature we've ever seen. They live in a magical land. We know from experience that this is a story that children will never tire of. At first they are frightened of the *oni*, but soon they become transported into the enchanted realm that Ms. Mosel and Blair Lent, the illustrator, have created. A Caldecott Award book. 9x10", Dut 72

MUSGROVE, MARGARET. **ASHANTI TO ZULU: AFRICAN TRADITIONS**, c$8.95. Delightful vignettes describe the ceremonies, celebrations, and day-to-day customs of twenty-six African tribes. Dramatic illustrations by Leo and Diane Dillon capture the tone. 10x12½", 48pp. Del 76

NIVEDITA, SISTER. **CRADLE TALES OF HINDUISM**, c$2.75. A collection of traditional Indian nursery tales whose authenticity has been carefully checked by the translator, a disciple of Swami Vivekananda. The collection includes most of the best-loved tales and the language is well suited for reading to children. Illustrated, 319pp. AdA 07

PETRICH, PATRICIA and ROSEMARY DALTON. **THE KID'S GARDEN BOOK**, $3.95. A hand drawn, brightly colored book which gives simple instructions for a number of things that kids can do both with outdoor gardening and with houseplants. Lots of excellent hints are included as well as basic information about the tools needed and how to care for a great variety of plants. Index, 8½x5½", Nit 74

RAMAYANA

The **Ramayana** is one of the two great epics of India. To the Hindus, the story of Rama is the story of their god Vishnu (the preserver) who incarnated in the form of Prince Rama to save mankind from evil, embodied in the form of the King of the Giants. One of the reasons for its great popularity is that it is also a wonderful love story. Rama's wife Sita is captured by the Giants, and much of the story is devoted to Rama's attempts to rescue her with the aid of Hanuman, the monkey, who is worshipped by the Hindus as the embodiment of the perfect servant.

BAPU. **RAMAYANA: THE STORY OF RAMA**, $3.50. Comic book style and color illustrations, accompanied by a short, simple text. For the youngest readers. Follows Valmiki. 7¼x8¼", 71pp. ICA 74

BHOOTHALINGAM, MATHURAM. **CHILDREN'S RAMAYANA**, c$1.00. A nice retelling of some of the major stories. Each of the incidents is told in a separate chapter and there are nice line drawings on virtually every page. The book follows the Valmiki version and was prepared by the Publications Division of the Government of India. 6¼x9½", 91pp. PuD 67

CHINMAYANANDA, SWAMI and KUMARI BHARATHI NAIK. **BALA RAMAYANAM**, c$7.00. A more detailed retelling by one of India's most noted translators of scriptural texts. It is designed to be read to children since, historically, the epic was transmitted orally from one generation to another. Storytelling instructions are included along with a number of line drawings. 8x11", 170pp. CPT 68

CHOUDRY, BANI ROY. **THE STORY OF RAMAYAN**, c$6.30. A vibrantly illustrated rendition which retells the major stories and is designed for young readers. There's a bit more detail here than in the other **Ramayanas** which are published in India. 7x9-3/4", 104pp. HeP 70

GAER, JOSEPH. **THE ADVENTURES OF RAMA**, c$4.95. Gaer has done a wonderful job of making the story of Rama come alive for Western readers. He follows the original Valmiki version and tells the story in prose. This is our favorite rendition. Gaer has managed to get most of the story into his book and he has kept it simple. For older children. Nicely illustrated, bibiliography, index. 210pp. LBC 54

RAOUL-DUVAL, FRANCOIS. **PETALI AND GURIGOO OR HOW THE BIRDS GOT THEIR COLORS**, c$3.35. An Amazonian legend, with some amazing illustrations. A baby snake in the jungle ate up all the vegetation and most of the denizens. He thereby acquired a truly beautiful skin, stripping the jungle of all its colors. The birds, who had never been colorful, appealed to the snake to give the jungle back its colors, and he did. The birds all split up his skin and wrapped themselves in it. Magically their feathers turned the bright colors that we associate with jungle birds. 7½x10", MTI 71

RAY, IRENE and MALLIKA GUPTA. **TALES FROM RAMAKRISHNA**, $1.50. When Sri Ramakrishna was teaching people he often used to tell them stories to help them grasp his point. He loved telling these stories and at that time his room would be filled with joy and laughter. Adults enjoy them as good stories, and they also enjoy the inner teaching. Children enjoy them as good stories, teaching or no teaching. This is a delightful retelling of some of the most loved stories, designed with many joyful illustrations for children and meant for readers of all ages. Large print. 58pp. AdA 75

ROSE, ELIZABETH and GERALD. **HOW ST. FRANCIS TAMED THE WOLF**, $.50. This is a cute little book which retells the legend of how St. Francis tamed a ferocious wolf that was terrorizing a village. It's a simple story, colorfully illustrated, well drawn, and suitable for the youngest child. 7x5", Fab nd

SAINT-EXUPERY, ANTOINE de. **THE LITTLE PRINCE**, c$5.95/$1.25. This is an enchanting, elusive fable which is loved by children and adults alike. The Little Prince lived alone on a tiny planet no larger than a house. He owned three volcanoes, two active and one extinct. He also owned a flower, unlike any other flower, of great beauty and inordinate pride. It was this pride that ruined the serenity of the Little Prince's world and started him on the interplanetary travels that brought him to Earth, where he learned the secrets of what is really important in life from a talking fox. Fully illustrated. 113pp. HBJ 43

SAKADE, FLORENCE, ed. **JAPANESE CHILDREN'S FAVORITE STORIES**, c$6.25. A collection of twenty of Japan's most popular children's stories. These delightful tales are true expressions of Japanese character and customs and the more than ninety illustrations (twelve in color) by one of Japan's most noted illustrators of children's books add to the appeal. There's an enchanting illustration on virtually every page, helping to hold the child's interest while the story is read to him. A beautifully produced volume. 7x8", 120pp. Tut 58

SEDGWICK, PAULITA. **MYTHOLOGICAL CREATURES**, c$6.95. A remarkable book which includes illustrations and descriptions of over 400 fantastic mythological creatures. Each of the entries is a story in itself and the language and style are geared toward children. An amazing series of illustrations which should delight older children. Bibliography, HRW 74

SENDAK, MAURICE. **NUTSHELL LIBRARY**, c$4.95. A boxed set of four little books (2-3/4x3-3/4") which is a favorite of our youngest friends. The stories are extremely simple. One describes the months, another tells two rhymed stories about each of the ten numbers, a third teaches the alphabet, while the last one tells a tale *with a moral air*. H&R 62

SHERLOCK, PHILIP. **ANANSI, THE SPIDER MAN**, c$5.50. Anansi was a man and he was a spider. When things went well he was a man, but when he was in great danger he became a spider, safe in his web. By trickery and guile he always got the better of those who were much bigger than himself. Anansi's home was in the villages and forests of West Africa—and when the Africans were brought to the West Indies they brought with them the stories that they loved, the stories about Br'er Anansi and his friends. As a child growing up in Jamaica Sherlock listened to these stories, and his retelling of them reflects the authentic tradition. The illustrator also lived in Jamaica and knows well the background and atmosphere for these tales. 9x6¼", 112pp. Cro 54

SINGH, MALA. **THE STORY OF GURU NANAK**, c$3.75. Guru Nanak is the founder of the Sikh religion and is revered by millions of Indians. This book retells in simple form some of the main incidents in his life and presents a bit of his teaching. The big print and vivid color illustrations make it suitable for young readers. 64pp. HeP 69

STEIG, WILLIAM. **SYLVESTER AND THE MAGIC PEBBLE**, $1.95. This is a neat story about Sylvester, a humanized donkey, and his parents. One of Sylvester's main hobbies was collecting unusual pebbles. One day he found an especially beautiful one which he soon realized had the power to grant the wishes of the possessor. By accident he wished he was a rock and this was his final wish. His parents deeply mourned his disappearance and after a year or so came upon the rock and found the pebble. By chance they wished the rock would turn into a donkey—and it did! The illustrations are especially fine. All the animals are delightfully drawn and Steig has chosen beautiful bright colors. A Caldecott Award book. 8x11", Dut 69

SWIFT, JONATHAN. **GULLIVER'S TRAVELS**, c$1.95. This famous book was not originally written for children—but many of the tales have been retold in a simple fashion and have become children's classics. This is such a retelling. Gulliver's adventures with tiny people and giants have fascinated generations of children. 248pp. G&D 63

UNESCO. **FOLK TALES FROM ASIA FOR CHILDREN EVERYWHERE, BOOK 1**, c$4.95. This is an excellent series. Through the stories children in Western cultures can get a good feeling for the other cultures. The selections presented in this series are entirely authentic, having been selected, retold and illustrated by writers and artists from each of the Asian countries. The stories are simple and timeless and present the real flavor of Asia. Each of the stories is beautifully illustrated in bright colors. The stories in this volume come from Bangladesh, India, Iran, Korea, Laos, Singapore, Thailand, and Viet Nam. 7½x10", 53pp. Wea 75

_____. **FOLK TALES FROM ASIA FOR CHILDREN EVERYWHERE, BOOK 2**, c$4.95. Stories from Indonesia, Japan, Khmer, Malaysia, Nepal, Pakistan, Philippines, and Sri Lanka. 7½x10", 53pp. Wea 75

_____. **FOLK TALES FROM ASIA FOR CHILDREN EVERYWHERE, BOOK 3**, c$5.95. Stories from Afghanistan, Burma, Indonesia, Iran, Japan, Pakistan, Singapore, Sri Lanka, and Viet Nam. This volume has our favorite stories. 7½x10", 59pp. Wea 76

_____. **FOLK TALES FROM ASIA FOR CHILDREN EVERYWHERE, BOOK 4**, c$5.95. Tales from Bangladesh, Cambodia, India, Korea, Laos, Malaysia, Nepal, Philippines, and Thailand. 7½x10", 64pp. Wea 76

VAVRA, ROBERT. **LION AND BLUE**, c$6.95. The two books by Robert Vavra are highly acclaimed and are the most unusual picture books we have ever seen. Vavra saw Fleur Cowles' paintings and was convinced they would make wonderful illustrations for a book. He convinced her too, and she agreed to the idea. The paintings are bold and bright and filled with a wonderful series of animals and of nature scenes. Vavra's story matches the brilliance of the illustrations. One of the most amazing features of the books is Vavra's use of cut-outs to make one illustration serve a number of purposes. This book tells the story of a magnificent lion who grieves because he has lost his friend the butterfly and who searches the world until he and Blue, the butterfly, are reunited. We recommend these books highly for children and adults alike. 8½x11", Mor 74

_____. **TIGER FLOWER**, c$6.95. An enchanting book which is the favorite of many people we know. It tells the story of Tiger Flower, King of the Grass, who lives *where everything that should be small is big, and everything that should be big, is small.* Craig Claiborne calls this *a volume I have read with uncommon pleasure, and I wish I could give it to every child and adult that I love. It should be required reading for everyone else.* 8½x11", Mor 68

from Charlotte's Web by E.B. White

WHITE, E.B. **CHARLOTTE'S WEB**, $1.25. In all of White's books the animals come magically to life and there is an underlying moral. This one tells the story of a little girl who loved a little pig named Wilbur, and of Wilbur's close friend Charlotte, a beautiful gray spider who lived with Wilbur in the barn. As the story progresses Charlotte saves the life of Wilbur with the aid of a rat who never did anything for anybody unless there was something in it for him. It's a good story, and one that children love. Nicely illustrated, 184pp. H&R 52

_____. **STUART LITTLE**, $.95. The adventures of Stuart Little, a mouse that was born into a human family. It's an endearing story for young and old, full of wit and wisdom and amusement. Wonderful illustrations add to the appeal. 131pp. Del 45

WILLIAMS, MARGERY. **THE VELVETEEN RABBIT**, c$3.95/$1.75. This is an extraordinarily popular book. *What is real? asked the Rabbit one day. . . . Real isn't how you are made, said the Skin Horse. It's a thing that happens to you. When a child loves you for a long long time, not just to play with, but really loves you, then you become Real. It doesn't happen all at once. You become. It takes a long time. Generally, by the time you are Real, most of your hair has been loved off, and your eyes drop out and you get loose in the joints and very shabby. But these things don't matter at all, because once you are*

Real you can't be ugly, except to people who don't understand. We love this strange and wonderful story and we know you will too. 6x9", 44pp. Avo 75

YOLEN, JANE. **THE BIRD OF TIME**, c$4.50. Jane Yolen is our favorite storyteller (as you can see by the number of her titles we list!). She weaves original, enchanting tales, each one different and each one magical in its own way. She has the remarkable quality of picking exactly the right illustrator each time and so each book has an entirely different feeling. We recommend all of her books highly. Once you've read one, you are sure to want to read all the rest. They are magical enough to interest even the smallest child and older children can't get enough of them. Time is the theme of this tale. A miller's son is given the power to make time move faster and slower. He was a dreamer and believed in miracles, so he wasn't overawed by the gift. He used the power to rescue the king's daughter who had been captured by a fierce giant. It all ends happily: the giant is vanquished, the lad marries the king's daughter, and the bird of time is safely hidden away, never to be used again. The illustrations are in the classical style of fairy tales, with browns and greens predominating. 8½x10½", Cro 71

_____. **THE BOY WHO HAD WINGS**, c$5.50. Long ago in a small Greek village a boy was born with a beautiful set of wings. His family was amazed and uneasy and feared that the wings were a sign of the gods' disfavor. The boy was warned to keep them covered always so that others would not know of his differentness. One day his herdsman father was trapped in the high mountain snows and only Aetos, with his wings, was able to save him. He almost killed himself in the process and during his recovery his wings fell off—but for an enchanted moment, he glimpsed the meaning of his gift. The illustrations are magnificent and subtle. 9x12", Cro 74

_____. **THE GIRL WHO CRIED FLOWERS AND OTHER TALES**, c$5.95. Five masterful tales, each with an underlying message. There is the bittersweet story of the beautiful Olivia, who could not be happy herself, but whose sorrows brought happiness to others as her tears turned magically to flowers. There is the giant who hid the sun from the world; the proud lad who challenged the king to a contest; Vera, who had an insatiable desire for the truth; and silent Bianca whose wisdom outwitted an army and won her the hand of the king. The illustrations are by David Palladini and are stylized and quite unlike any other drawings we have seen. Again, they seem perfect for the stories. 7¼x9½", Cro 74

_____. **THE GIRL WHO LOVED THE WIND**, c$4.50. An incredible set of illustrations fill these pages. The border is tawny yellow and the pictures themselves are reminiscent of Persian miniatures in their richly patterned design and beautiful colors. A king surrounds his daughter with every possible luxury and comfort and gives her an abundance of love so that she would never be sad. And lest any of the world's sorrows reach her, he had great protective walls built around the palace and the garden. But for all his care, the king could not keep the wind's voice from his daughter's ears. It sang of the world that she had never seen. Its song was sometimes harsh and sometimes sweet, like life itself. After she had heard it the palace walls seemed to be imprisoning her, so she accepted the wind's challenge and set forth to discover the real world for herself. 8x10", Cro 72

_____. **AN INVITATION TO THE BUTTERFLY BALL**, c$5.50. This is the most inventive counting book we have seen. The illustrations are delightful and the rhymes equally so. A different set of animals is used for each number and the work is beautifully produced. It's an excellent way to introduce even the smallest child to the numbers. 8¼x 10¼", PMP 76

_____. **THE LITTLE SPOTTED FISH**, c$7.95. This is a much simpler tale than most of Jane Yolen's books and therefore suitable for the youngest children. It tells of a fisherlad and of the little spotted fish that three times saved the lad's life. The tale is inspired by folklore of the British Isles. The bright illustrations complement the mood of the narrative. 8½x10", Sea 75

_____. **MILKWEED DAYS**, c$5.95. Milkweed days are the long, lazy late summer days that children in this story love best. These are the days when they like to play in the sunny fragrant meadow behind the old barn. Beautiful photographs and a concise text evoke the sights, smells, and sounds of a summer day. A simple book for the beginning reader. 8x10", 32pp. Cro 76

_____. **RAINBOW RIDER**, c$5.50. In this volume Jane Yolen has written an original creation myth that evokes those of the Indians of North and South America. *In the time before time . . . there lived Rainbow Rider*, the only person in all the brand new world. Sometimes, just for fun, he would jump on a rainbow and ride the glittering arch into the sky, singing all the way. But after a while he grew tired of being all alone. He needed a friend and he tried to make one out of a variety of materials, with little success until he finally found his friend. Luminous watercolors glow with the ever-changing colors of the desert landscape and Western sky, providing a radiant setting for the story. 9½x 10½", Cro 74

_____. **THE SEVENTH MANDARIN**, c$6.95. A dramatic story, sumptuously illustrated by Ed Young. Both the text and the illustrations evoke a feeling of the Orient. The king's dragon kite is the carrier of the king's soul. One night when it was the seventh mandarin's turn to fly the kite high above the terrors of the night, a wild wind entered the kingdom and wrenched the kite out of his hands. Since it was death to fail the king and death to damage his kite, the seventh mandarin ran after it as it sailed far beyond the Palace gates. And for the first time he saw the harsh reality of life in the kingdom. He saved the kite and went back to tell his king the horrors of what he had seen. The king listened and for the first time became responsive to the people. 7x11¼", Sea 70

_____. **THE WIZARD ISLANDS**, c$4.95. Mysteries and island seem to be natural companions. In this book Jane Yolen brings her storytelling gift to both fact and fancy as she tells of ghost-haunted islands, of pirate islands, and of legendary islands such as Atlantis. Two excellent chapters tell of the Galapagos Islands and Easter Island. The illustrations include photographs, old documents, and newly drawn maps. For older children. 7¼x 10¼", bibliography, index. 115pp. Cro 73

CHINESE PHILOSOPHY

The great fundamental concepts of Chinese philosophy, religion, and culture were present in remote antiquity—and even then were considered ancient. As in most early cultures they did not exist as separate entities, but shared the recognition of a unifying spirit that animated all life. Distinctions were blurred, boundaries between objects, people, and animals were permeable. Animals often possessed divine attributes; and divine beings, spirits, and even legendary figures were all part of a system that saw life as an extremely intimate, interrelated, and interdependent force.

A deep and abiding love of nature is evident throughout the earliest religious and philosophical writings of the Chinese. Their abundant ancient literature is full of the beauty of crystal streams, placid lakes, and sharp angulated mountains that so dominated the landscape that their earliest religious symbolism developed around nature themes—mountain, wind, trees, fire, heaven. In this early literature we can see a world slowly humanizing, but retaining its original primordial knowledge of natural forces at work. This was a world where the night sky was not a distant or strange place but an extension of animal and earth; where a blessing was bestowed upon those who could sense best the knowledge of *Hsuan P'in* (the animal goddess), and *Ti* (the earth-goddess); who could identify the ways of nature as early man dwelt in the mists of a fertile earth that contained a vital spirit in every bird, stone, or murmur of spring rain. . . .

Unlike early Judaism and Christianity, Chinese nature worship did not take on the aspect of a God-rejected religion, but was incorporated into elaborate pantheistic rituals—eventually surfacing as simply a natural force, or dynamic, that existed in all living things, including humankind. In their earliest religious books one finds constant emphasis on a natural force or life-energy (*Ch'i*). In this way people were never divorced from the power of nature, or even of God, for identification with the rhythms of life meant partaking of it to the Chinese. As all life continued effortlessly, coming from no spring and moving to no ocean, so could mankind drink of immortality. For the seasonal destructions were observed to be never final. The tree that lost its greening luster, that appeared dead and gray during winter, was resurrected in the spring. And so all life was a manifest of this dynamic rhythm. The ancient Chinese believed that a man seeking salvation had simply to shed the self-imposed delusions of his character and stand in the stream of life. The Chinese philosophers believed that they thereby became masters of their own condition and partners of their gods. . . .

The Taoist sage Chuang Tzu wrote: *The heavens and the earth and I have come into existence together, and all creations and I are one*. This supreme reality Chuang Tzu speaks of is the Tao, and is the foundation upon which all Chinese mystical religion and philosophy was built. All the schools of Chinese thought can be said to have held the concepts of Tao in common, for all the old deities were their common origin.

The ancient Chinese also recognized the close relationship between the poetic function and the exalted life. Arthur Waley has pointed out that Chuang Tzu's method of communicating the Taoist *no-knowledge* was essentially that of the poet. The capacity of poetry to excite religious feelings in regard to both people and nature was used by the Chinese mystics not only to communicate what we in the West consider basically ineffable; they also developed it into a technique for exciting the awareness that stimulated the *ineffable* religious experience.

The Tao in its utter neutrality means simply *Way*—not even **the** *Way*—which would imply directionality or exclusivity. And it is this concept of Tao, which has been rendered in the West as equivalent to the vague concept of *natural law*, that is at the heart of all Chinese religious thought. But, and this is often forgotten, Confucius also incorporated Tao into his teachings. Most people popularly consider Confucius a strictly ethical and social philosopher. But the basis of Confucian philosophy can be seen as the ethical aspect of Tao, the Way of man rather than the metaphysical Tao or an abstract law drawn from nature. The Confucian concept of *Ju*, which was a humanist, personalist, and ethical doctrine, differs from the Tao in its emphasis, but retains the premise of finding the *Reality* of life through the action or non-action of man in relation to the world around him. The Taoist teaches that the *superior man* finds his ultimate reality in the center of *self*. But this cannot be obtained except through placing oneself in harmony with *Heaven* or the rhythms of the universe.

Lao Tzu spoke of, and Taoism came to mean, an acceptance of the spiritual oneness of all that exists, of action without assertion, and of a natural man instead of a conditioned, striving man seeking illusory, unnecessary goals. Quiet and peace within the soul would be accomplished, Lao Tzu taught, by a natural honesty rather than an educated shrewdness, of non-interference with the rhythms of life and rather a joining, a union with all nature. Such a philosophy lies at the heart of all pantheist and mystical religions, and extols the mystic's essential belief in the soul of living things in direct communion with a universal reality.

The classical Chinese philosophers-mystics continually emphasized the basic premise which underlies all early Chinese thought (especially Taoist)—the idea of Nature as a dynamic spiritual principle, and man's relationship with natural order as the foundation of his salvation. The sublime order of the Universe and Nature, of both *T'ien* (Heaven) and *Ti* (Earth), can be clearly found in early Chinese writings, especially in the *I Ching* or *Book of Changes*, the *Tao Teh Ching*, the *Chung Yung*, and the other ancient classics.

Nature was seen as an extension of universal order, and if man was to be happy and find his true self, he must conform to the *ways of Heaven*.

—from **CHINESE MYSTICS** by Raymond Van Over, ed.

The three star gods of happiness, affluence and longevity, with auspicious emblems

ANONYMOUS. CHINESE FOLK TALES, c$5.95. See the Fairy Tales section.

BASKIN, WADE, ed. CLASSICS IN CHINESE PHILOSOPHY, $4.95. A sourcebook which traces Chinese philosophy from the time of Confucius to the present. Selections from forty-eight individuals are included and the editor provides an introduction to each selection. The translations are from a variety of sources. The volume is a good introductory survey and in terms of the number of different selections it is as comprehensive as any we know of. Chronologically arranged. 737pp. LtA 72

BINYON, LAURENCE. THE FLIGHT OF THE DRAGON, c$3.50. Binyon's theme is that in the East art is an approach to an understanding of life. For the Chinese there was much more to life than could immediately be seen on the surface, and the artist sought continually with the utmost economy to suggest the inner form and rhythm of things. Here Binyon presents a collection of essays on the theory and practice of art in China and Japan, based on original sources. Notes, 86pp. Mur 11

BLOFELD, JOHN. BEYOND THE GODS, $2.45. Subtitled *Buddhist and Taoist Mysticism*, this is Blofeld's account of his extensive travels in China and on the fringes of Mongolia and Tibet before the Communist takeover. *I have sought to describe something of what I found; for amidst much that was merely colorful rather than spiritually inspiring, I came upon certain teachings and practices that bore witness to impressive soarings of the human spirit. As far as possible I have woven into my material stories heard and per-*

sonal experiences so as to offer the reader a series of insights just as I acquired them. . . . I use [the term mysticism] to mean all that pertains to the search for intuitive experiences inaccessible to ordinary understanding and to the merging of one's being into something so vast as to be beyond all human conceptions of divinity. The text includes details on mystical practices and illuminating dialogue. Recommended, glossary. 164pp. Dut 75

_____. **THE SECRET AND THE SUBLIME**, $3.25. Surveys all aspects of Taoism: popular Taoism with its lavish ceremonies, demon exorcism, oracles, and ghosts; yogic Taoism with its emphasis on rejuvenation; the ancient teachings of philosophical Taoism; and the mystical Taoism which aims at direct experience of the reality that lies behind the confines of conceptual thought. Recommended. 217pp. Dut 73

BYNNER, WITTER. **THE JADE MOUNTAIN**, $2.45. A definitive anthology of the 300 best poems of the T'ang era (618–906). Extensive introduction discusses Chinese poetry. 300pp. RaH 29

CARUS, PAUL. **CHINESE ASTROLOGY**, $2.95. Much more than an astrological tract, this is a study of the major systems of Chinese occultism and thought. He includes many illustrations and detailed analyses of the Yih system, P'an-Ku, Feng-Shu, Lo Pan, joss sticks, as well as of astrology. This is a scholarly work which gives the historical and philosophical background of the systems discussed and includes comparison with the systems of other civilizations. 135pp. OpC 07

CHAN, WING-TSIT, tr. **INSTRUCTIONS FOR PRACTICAL LIVING AND OTHER NEO-CONFUCIAN WRITINGS**, c$13.25. This volume contains the major works of Wang Yang-ming, an important Neo-Confucian writer. Neo-Confucianism arose in the eleventh century and developed and transformed Confucianism under the influence of Buddhism and Taoism and dominated Chinese thought for 800 years. Wang lived in the fifteenth century and represented the idealistic wing of the tradition. The radical difference between Wang and his predecessors is that he considered knowledge and action to be one thing while they had felt the two were separate. This innate knowledge he equated with the *principle of nature*. This edition includes a detailed introduction, notes and bibliography, and an index. 407pp. Col 63

_____. **REFLECTIONS ON THINGS AT HAND**, c$19.60. Translation of the **Chin-ssu lu**, *an anthology of Neo-Confucianism, giving in clear outline its doctrines of metaphysics, learning, ethics, literature, government, and its evaluation of great men in Chinese history and of heterodoxical systems, notably Buddhism and Taoism. Since it is the forerunner and model of the Hsing-li ta-ch'uan (Great Collection of Neo-Confucianism) which was for five hundred years the standard text for Chinese thought, its tremendous influence on Chinese philosophy can easily be imagined. In addition, just as Wang Yang-Ming's* Instructions on Practical Living *is the major work of the idealistic wing of Neo-Confucianism, so is the* Chin-ssu lu *the major work of the rationalistic wing.* Introductory material and extensive notes are provided by the translator. Glossary, bibliography, index. 482pp. Col 67

_____. **A SOURCEBOOK IN CHINESE PHILOSOPHY**, c$18.50/4.95. This massive volume covers the entire development of Chinese philosophy from pre-Confucianism to present times. The theme is Chinese humanism. Professor Chan has translated many of the selections himself (including the **Tao Te Ching**) and he provides extensive and excellent commentary on the extracts. The selections themselves are fairly lengthy. Chan is a leading scholar and this is the definitive anthology. Includes a long bibliography and a glossary of Chinese characters. Recommended. 831pp. PUP 63

CHANG, CHUNG-YUAN. **CREATIVITY AND TAOISM: A STUDY IN CHINESE PHILOSOPHY, ART, AND POETRY**, $2.50. A gentle, sensitive work which makes the elusive principle of the Tao available to the Western mind. Beautifully illustrated. 214pp. H&R 63

CHUANG TZU

Chuang Tzu (399–295 BC) lived 200 years after Lao Tzu. Using parable and anecdote, allegory and paradox, he set forth the early ideas of what was to become Taoism. Central in these is belief that only by understanding Tao (the Way of Nature) and dwelling in its unity can man achieve true happiness and be truly free, in both life and death. *To him, nature is not only spontaneity but nature is a state of constant flux and incessant transformation. This is the universal process that binds all things into one, equalizing all things and all opinions. The pure man makes this oneness his eternal abode, in which he becomes a companion of nature and does not attempt to interfere with it by imposing the way of man on it. His goal is absolute spiritual emancipation and peace, to be achieved through knowing the capacity and limitations of one's own nature, nourishing it, and adapting to the universal process of transformation. He abandons selfishness of all descriptions, be it fame, wealth, bias or subjectivity. Having attained enlightenment through the light of nature, he moves into the realm of great knowledge and profound virtue. Thus he is free.*

FENG, GIA-FU and JANE ENGLISH, trs. **CHUANG TZU: INNER CHAPTERS**, c$7.95/ $3.95. A companion volume to the translators' earlier book on Lao Tzu, also including lovely photographs and calligraphy. The format does not seem to work quite as well as in the earlier book since the material translated here is much longer than Lao Tzu's chapters but it is still a beautiful work which would make a fine gift and is a good introduction to the inspired writings of Chuang Tzu. The seven *inner chapters* presented here are accepted by scholars as being definitely the work of Chuang Tzu; another twenty-six chapters are of questionable origin—they are interpretations and developments of his teaching and may have been added by later commentators. Oversize, 162pp. RaH 74

GILES, HERBERT, tr. **CHUANG TZU—TAOIST PHILOSOPHER AND CHINESE MYSTIC**, c$12.25. This is the most complete edition of his works with an extensive introduction and notes. Prose translation. An edition that is not as nicely bound or typeset is also available for c$8.95. 325pp. A&U 1889

MERTON, THOMAS, tr. **THE WAY OF CHUANG TZU**, c$4.00/1.75. Working from existing translations, Father Merton has composed a series of personal versions from his favorites among the sayings of Chuang Tzu—a recreation of an ancient sage by a contemporary poet. Includes an introduction on the meaning of Taoism for the West today. Illustrated with early Chinese drawings. 159pp. NDP 65

WATSON, BURTON, tr. **CHUANG TZU—BASIC WRITINGS**, $3.30. A relatively new translation, prepared for the *Oriental Classics* Series from Columbia University. Includes the seven *inner chapters*, which form the heart of the book, three of the *outer chapters* and one of the *miscellaneous chapters*. An excellent long introduction places the philosopher in relation to Chinese history and thought. Prose. 140pp. Col 64

_____. **THE COMPLETE WORKS OF CHUANG TZU**, c$16.50. An excellent translation, probably the most scholarly and also most readable available. Watson also provides extensive annotations and an enlightening introduction. 397pp. Col 68

CONFUCIUS

Confucius (551–479 BC) is known as the molder of Chinese civilization. He believed that man *can make the Way (Tao) great,* and not that *the Way can make man great.* To this end he advocated a good government that rules by virtue and moral example rather than by punishment or force. For the family he particularly stressed filial piety and for society in general, proper conduct or *li*, (propriety, rites).

Confucius during his ministry: receiving a visitor and encouraging agriculture.

BAUM, ARCHIE, tr. THE HEART OF CONFUCIUS, c$4.50. Not a literal translation but an interpretation of the two most basic Confucian classics—**Genuine Living** and **Great Wisdom.** Nearly half the book consists of Bahm's clear explanations of key Confucian terms. Written for the inquiring layman rather than the scholar. Many illustrations. Recommended. 153pp. Wea 69

CH'U CHAI and WINBERG CHAI. CONFUCIANISM, $1.95. This is an excellent survey of Confucianism, with material on its origins, its development, its great exponents, and its domination of Chinese thought for over 2500 years. Introductory material characterizes Confucianism in Chinese history and briefly discusses the Confucian classics. The body of the book consists of nine chapters, in chronological and historical sequence, each being devoted to a major exponent or phase of the Confucian school. In addition, each chapter is preceded by a general survey of the background against which the individual developed his version of what Confucius taught. The text also includes biographical studies of the leading exponents and a critical commentary of their writings and doctrines. Notes, glossary, bibliography, index. 208pp. BES 73

CREEL, H.G. CONFUCIUS AND THE CHINESE WAY, $4.40. A fine portrait of Confucius, the teacher, scholar, and philosopher-reformer. Indispensible for all interested in fully understanding Confucian thought. Very extensive footnotes; bibliography, index. 354pp. H&R 49

FINGARETTE, HERBERT. CONFUCIUS—THE SECULAR AS SACRED, $1.95. A scholarly attempt to discern the deepest meanings of Confucian thought and apply it to our own time. 82pp. H&R 72

GREENLESS, DUNCAN. THE GOSPEL OF CHINA, c$2.50. A topically arranged translation of the major writings of Confucius and Mencius, based in main part on Dr. Pauthier's French translation. This edition is part of the *World Gospel* series put together by theosophists. Notes, index. 177pp. TPH

KAIZUKA, SHIGEKI. CONFUCIUS, c$3.80. This is a very readable review of Confucius the man, his life, philosophy, and times. It seems to cover all the material a general reader would want to know about Confucius and Confucian ideas and the scholarship seems to be good. If you just want to read one book on this subject, this is the one we would recommend. Chronological table, index. 192pp. A&U 56

LEGGE, JAMES, tr. CONFUCIUS—CONFUCIAN ANALECTS, THE GREAT LEARNING, AND THE DOCTRINE OF THE MEAN $4.50. It contains the entire Chinese text of each work in large characters, and beneath this Legge's full translation, which has been accepted as the definitive English version. More than 125 pages of introduction give excellent background. Also included is a complete dictionary of all the Chinese characters in the book, with meanings, grammatical comments, and place locations. The most scholarly translation, but not the most readable. 503pp. Dov 1893

_____. **THE PHILOSOPHY OF CONFUCIUS,** c$2.98. An extensively illustrated, very nicely put together presentation of Legge's translations of the **Confucian Analects, The Great Learning, and The Doctrine of the Mean.** This version is much easier to read than the more formal edition mentioned previously, and all of the background material and notes are not included. Large print, 220pp. Out 1893

McNAUGHTON, WILLIAM, ed. THE CONFUCIAN VISION, $2.95. The editor has done new translations of the crucial passages from the **Five Classics** and the **Four Books** as well as selections from royal proclamations, folk songs, and literature. The volume is organized to reveal the central ideas of the *Confucian vision.* Dr. McNaughton also provides background material and commentary as well as extensive notes. 168pp. UMP 74

POUND, EZRA. THE CONFUCIAN ODES, $2.45. The 305 odes of this *Classic Anthology* are considered among the greatest poetry of ancient China. Confucius held that no man was truly educated unless he had studied the odes; and in one of his works said that the odes serve to exhilarate, to stimulate awareness, to preach dissociation, and to kindle resentment against evil. Pound's translation is the culmination of forty years of Chinese study and his aim here is to make the poetry come alive for the modern reader. The edition is well arranged and includes a good introduction. 242pp. NDP 54

_____. **CONFUCIUS,** $3.75. Pound's noted translations, with commentary, of three basic Confucian texts: **The Great Digest (Ta Hsio), The Unwobbling Pivot (Chung Yung), and The Analects (Lun-yu).** For the first two the Chinese characters are printed. Introduction, 288pp. NDP 47

SOOTHILL, WILLIAM. THE ANALECTS OF CONFUCIUS, $7.50. An unabridged reprint of the 1910 edition which includes long essays on the ancient history of China and on the life and times of Confucius. The Chinese text is presented, along with a translation and extensive commentary. Soothill was President of the Imperial University in China and a very noted early Chinese scholar. An added feature of this text is the 93pp index of characters arranged according to their radicals—with the characters themselves, Romanization, translation, and cross-reference to the **Analects.** 1033pp. PBR 68

WALEY, ARTHUR, tr. THE ANALECTS OF CONFUCIUS, $2.45. Waley is the translator of a vast body of Oriental classics. This is thought of as the best English version of the **Analects.** It is more readable than Legge's, though perhaps not as scholarly. An extensive introduction gives the social and political background of this work, analyses of key terms, and a careful study of the book and its interpretations. Many footnotes, 252pp. RaH 38

_____. **THE BOOK OF SONGS,** $3.95. **The Book of Songs** is one of the five Confucian classics and is more generally known as **The Confucian Odes.** Confucius and his followers used the songs as texts for moral instruction and as examples of the highest wisdom. The songs deal with a variety of subjects, including courtship, marriage, warriors, agriculture, dynasties, and friendship. Waley is generally considered the foremost twentieth century translator of Chinese poetry and philosophy. Introduction, notes, index. 358pp. Grv 37

WARE, JAMES, tr. THE SAYINGS OF CONFUCIUS, $.75. Translation of 450 brief conversations and observations of the great sage, together with an introduction and index. 127pp. NAL 55

WILHELM, RICHARD. CONFUCIUS AND CONFUCIANISM, $1.65. A translation of **The Life of Confucius** from a second century BC text, the **Shih Chi,** or the **Historical Records** by Sse-Ma-Ch'ien—including commentaries on the text. Gives the reader a concise survey of the man and his teachings. 181pp. HBJ 31

WRIGHT, ARTHUR, ed. THE CONFUCIAN PERSUASION, $3.45. *This extensive survey maintains a balanced perspective in its diagnosis of the degree of Confucian inspiration or influence in social, cultural, and political attitudes and developments in the course of Chinese history.... By virtue of its content and format this is a welcome addition to any collection of works relating to China.*—Journal of the Royal Central Asian Society (London). Notes, index. 400pp. SUP 60

_____. **CONFUCIANISM AND CHINESE CIVILIZATION,** $3.95. *These essays are meant to illustrate the effects of the Confucian world view and its associated patterns of behavior on the development of Chinese civilization. They also suggest the Confucian tradition's capacity for adaptation, as well as some of its inner variety.*—from the introduction. This volume is a selection of the best essays from the three books Wright edited on Confucianism. Extensive notes, 381pp. SUP 64

YUTANG, LIN, ed. THE WISDOM OF CONFUCIUS, c$3.95. This is the best overall collection of Confucius' writings available. The text includes material on education, music, ethics and politics, and social order, as well as his aphorisms, and some of Mencius' writing. This edition also has 100 pages of introductory material on the life of Confucius and the character of Confucius and Confucian ideals by the editor. 290pp. RaH 38

COOPER, ARTHUR, tr. LI PO AND TU FU, $1.95. Li Po (701-762) and Tu Fu (712-770) are traditionally regarded by the Chinese as their two greatest poets. Includes 100 pages of material on Chinese poetry. Also, analyses of each poem. 249pp. Pen 73

COOPER, J.C. TAOISM: THE WAY OF THE MYSTIC, $2.95. An enlightening and easily read discussion of the teachings of Lao Tzu, Chuang Tzu and the essential Taoist philosophy. Amid the knowledgeable commentary on the Tao, yin/yang, Taoist art and symbolism are the brilliant aphorisms of numerous Taoist mystics. 128pp. Wei 72

CREEL, HERRLEE. WHAT IS TAOISM? AND OTHER STUDIES IN CHINESE CULTURAL HISTORY, c$12.00. A collection of eight papers published between 1954 and

1968: *What Is Taoism, The Great Cloud, On Two Aspects of Early Taoism, On the Origin of Wu-wei, The Meaning of* Hsing-ming, *The Fa-chai: Legalists or Administrators?, The Beginnings of Bureaucracy in China: The Origin of the Hsien,* and *The Role of the Horse in Chinese History.* Dr. Creel is one of the most distinguished contemporary Chinese scholars. Index, notes. 192pp. UCh 70

DAWSON, RAYMOND, ed. **THE LEGACY OF CHINA**, c$11.95. An unusual, very interesting collection of essays covering the following general topics: Western concepts of Chinese civilization, philosophy and religious thought, literature, the heritage of Chinese art, science and China's influence on the world (a 75 page essay by Joseph Needham), the Chinese and the art of government, and China and the world. Notes, illustrations, index. 411pp. Oxf 64

DE BARY, WILLIAM et al. **THE UNFOLDING OF NEO-CONFUCIANISM**, c$22.40. The fourteen essays collected here explore the range and variety of Neo-Confucian thought in the seventeenth century China with special attention to the new growth that emerged in the transition from the Ming to the Ch'ing periods. Emphasis is placed on the flowering of Confucian thought and scholarship which occurred partly as a result of interaction with Buddhism and Taoism. These papers were originally presented at a conference on seventeenth century Chinese thought. Notes, index. 607pp. Col 75

An imperial palace in the eighteenth century

DE BARY, WILLIAM, WING-TSIT CHAN and BURTON WATSON, eds. **SOURCES OF CHINESE TRADITION**, $8.95/set. Translations from Chinese sources that illustrate Chinese thought since earliest time. Most were made especially for this book. Selections in this comprehensive sourcebook cover political, economic and social questions, as well as philosophical and religious speculations. There is also much supplementary material provided by the editors. Bibliography, two volumes. 976pp. Col 60

FUNG, YU-LAN. **HISTORY OF CHINESE PHILOSOPHY**, c$20.00/each. By far the most comprehensive and authoritative survey. Highly recommended for the serious student. Two volumes. PUP

_____. **A SHORT HISTORY OF CHINESE PHILOSOPHY**, $3.95. A comprehensive adaptation of Dr. Fung's monumental two volume history. Attempts to give a systematic account of Chinese thought as a whole, from its beginnings to the present day. Dr. Fung is a scholar who is extremely well thought of by his countrymen. Extensive topic-by-topic bibliography. Recommended. 350pp. McM 48

_____. **THE SPIRIT OF CHINESE PHILOSOPHY**, c$14.80. This is a good survey of Chinese philosophy. Many of the individuals discussed are not well known and the presentation is uniformly excellent. The following chapter headings should give you an idea of the contents: Confucius and Mencius, the philosophers Yang Chu and Mo Ti, the dialecticians and logicians, Lao Tzu and Chuang Tzu, the Yi Scripture Amplifications and the Chung Yung, the Han Scholars, the Mystical School, the Inner Light School (Ch'an Tsung) of Buddhism, and the Neo-Confucianist philosophy. Notes, index. 238pp. Gre 47

GRAHAM, A.C., tr. **THE BOOK OF LIEH-TZU**, c$4.50. Lieh Tzu is a legendary Chinese sage revered by Taoists. The first mention of him was about 300 BC and the book which carries his name is one of the most important as well as one of the most entertaining of the Taoist classics. It is a collection of sayings and stories, most of them written about 300 AD, some borrowed from earlier sources, on such themes as reconciliation with death, the value of spontaneity, dreams and reality, limitations of natural knowledge. This is the first complete English translation. Notes, bibliography. 183pp. Mur

GROSIER, J.B. **THE WORLD OF ANCIENT CHINA**, c$3.95. See the *World of Ancient Civilizations* Series in the Ancient Civilizations section.

HALL, MANLY P. **THE SAGES OF CHINA**, $3.00. An exploration for the general reader of some of the most important sages. Many handsome line drawings and wood block prints

illustrate the text. 113pp. PRS 57

_____. **THE WAY OF HEAVEN**, c$5.00. A collection of nine Oriental fantasies told in the manner of Chinese literature of the classical period, based on Buddhist and Taoist philosophy. Many nice wood block prints illustrate the stories. 185pp. PRS 4?

_____. **THE WHITE BIRD OF TAO**, $3.75. A metaphorical treatise that gives the reader a true feeling for Taoism. 51pp. PRS 64

HAN FEI TZU. **BASIC WRITINGS**, $2.80. Han Fei Tzu was a third century BC philosopher of the Legalistic school who produced the final and most readable exposition of its theories. His handbook for the ruler deals with the problems of preserving and strengthening the state. There are sections on the way of the ruler, on standards, on the use of power and of punishment and favor and dangers to be avoided. This is an excellent translation by Burton Watson. Introduction, notes, index. 142pp. Col 64

HSUN TZU

Hsun Tzu was a fourth century Confucian who differed from Mencius by asserting that the nature of man is originally evil. His philosophical works outline methods of self-improvement to counteract this evil.

DUBS, HOMER, tr. **THE WORKS OF HSUNTZE**, c$5.60. *This work contains a translation of all the writings of Hsuntze that are both important and genuine.... To be sure to give a complete view of Hsuntze's teaching, I have not hesitated to include some writings whose authenticity is doubtful, and some which are not so important.... I have felt that it is more important to make the translation accurate and even literal than to make it literary.* The selections are topically arranged and extensive notes are provided. Index, 336pp. CWP 28

WATSON, BURTON, tr. **HSUN TZU: BASIC WRITINGS**, $3.35. An extremely readable and authoritative translation, and the one we prefer. Introduction, many notes, index. 187pp. Col 63

I CHING

The **I Ching** or **Book of Changes** is an oracular work dating back more than 3,000 years. Its core is a series of sixty-four symbolic figures called hexagrams, each of which is one of the possible combinations of six broken and/or unbroken parallel lines. Broken lines stand for yin, the dark, feminine, receptive, negative principle; while unbroken lines stand for yang, the light, masculine, creative, positive principle. Each hexagram is an aspect of life or a life situation. Each line shows a different aspect of the situation, pictured by the hexagram. Associated with each hexagram are commentaries which expound on its meaning.

Carl Jung considered the **I Ching** to be based on as valid an experimental method of investigation as Western science. He called the principle involved synchronicity, which means the occurrence at the same time of two events which though unconnected by cause and effect are nonetheless related.

The **I Ching** transcends its divinatory function to become a philosophical guide to Chinese thought, both Confucian and Taoist.

BLOFELD, JOHN. **I CHING**, $1.65. Emphasis is on the divining aspects of the oracle. Traditional commentaries are omitted. Blofeld succeeds in his stated purpose and his rendering is exceptionally clear. The introductory material is perhaps the best anywhere. However, without the commentaries this version cannot stand alone for the serious student. 228pp. Dut 65

CAYCE, EDGAR. **CHANGE—THE I CHING**, $1.75. Apparently Edgar Cayce never commented on the **I Ching**. Some of his followers herein compare pertinent extracts from the Cayce readings with the concepts of the sixty-four hexagrams. 70pp. ARE 71

DA LIU. **I CHING COIN PREDICTION**, $3.50. Translations of the judgment and symbol of each hexagram and the text of each line plus Da Liu's own interpretations drawn from his own experience and from the **Ch'un Ch'iu**, attributed to Confucius. Despite the image the title might evoke, this is one of the better modern versions, especially for those basically interested in the divinatory aspects. Clear directions are provided for throwing the coins. Introduction, 183pp. H&R 75

DHIEGH, KHIGH ALX. **THE ELEVENTH WING**, $3.25. Despite the author's presumption in entitling this work, this volume fills a long-standing need. It goes significantly beyond the scope of a how to or introductory volume and conveys a real sense of the inner dynamics of the **I Ching** as a universal prototype. Moreover, the final chapter, notes and the extensive bibliography afford a view of current interest in the **I Ching**. Mechanical devices and many visual aids are used. Highly recommended. 295pp. Del 74

HOOK, DIANA. **THE I CHING AND MANKIND**, c$10.95. This is a deep study of the philosophy of the **I Ching**, pointing out its significance in today's world. Ms. Hook discusses the connections between the **I Ching** and the Qabala, numerology, astrology, Tarot, and world religions. She also deals with the laws governing growth and decay, health and sickness, attraction and repulsion—both magnetic and sexual, and the general pattern of fe as set out in the **I Ching**. By means of charts and diagrams, she clearly and simply explains the two fundamental arrangements of the trigrams. The sequences of the hexagrams are also fully dealt with, as are the mutations of one hexagram into another. Many difficult concepts are well presented here. Index, 172pp. RKP 75

_____. **THE I CHING AND YOU**, c$6.75/$2.95. A thorough guidebook and introduction to the **I Ching**, a must for any reference shelf. This book is chiefly distinguished by its many and varied diagrams and appendices. Especially useful for interpretation is the extended appendix on the nature and qualities of the eight trigrams as seen under various experience headings. Very helpful work. 149pp. Dut 73

LEE, JUNG YOUNG. **THE I CHING AND MODERN MAN**, c$8.95. A survey of the metaphysical and cosmological implications of the **I Ching** in various areas of contemporary life. Notes, oversize, index. 236pp. UnB 75

_____. **THE PRINCIPLE OF CHANGES: UNDERSTANDING THE I CHING**, c$10.00. A workmanlike effort to expose the principle of change which underlies the working of the **I Ching**. Much emphasis is given to understanding how meaning is derived from the structure of the original written characters of the Chinese language. Pedantic and ponderous at times, the effort is broad in scope and remains worthwhile. 302pp. UnB 71

LEGGE, JAMES, tr. **I CHING**, $1.75. The original version of the Legge translation from the *Sacred Books of the East* Series. The structure and format of the volume are faithful to the ancient rather than the modern arrangement of material. This translation was aimed at nineteenth century Sinologues and those who desire to read the **I Ching** as pure literature. A serious student can approach this version by way of the study guide appended by Ch'u Chai and Winberg Chai. Not suitable for divination or causal use. 448pp. Ban 1899

The legendary Emperor Fu Hsi inventing the eight trigrams

McCLATCHIE, CANON. **CLASSIC OF CHANGE**, c$14.50. This is a photographic reproduction of the first English translation of the **I Ching**—of interest more as an historical document than for its literary merit, though it appears as if Wilhelm drew from the text for his definitive translation. The author was an American missionary in China and his introductory material (as well as aspects of the texts) reflects the *white man's burden* approach to intercultural understanding. The Chinese text (in large characters) and the translation are presented on opposite pages, and many traditional commentaries are included, also with parallel texts. Includes a good deal of background material. 473pp. CWP 1876

REIFLER, SAM. **I CHING**, $1.50. A modernized transcreation which loses virtually all its symbolic meaning in the process. For divination only. Introduction, 285pp. Ban 74

SCHOENHOLTZ, LARRY. **NEW DIRECTIONS IN THE I CHING**, c$7.95. An exploration of geometry, mathematics, and metaphysical meanings in the **I Ching**. This is not a translation—rather, it is an exploration of themes and patterns which are presented in an informal manner. Some interesting ideas are presented, although this is by no means a deep study. Illustrations, index. 157pp. UnB 75

SHIMANO, JAMES. **ORIENTAL FORTUNE TELLING**, $3.75. A parlor game approach to the **Book of Changes**. Translated from the Japanese to English. 170pp. Tut 56

SIU, R.G.H., tr. **THE PORTABLE DRAGON: THE WESTERN MAN'S GUIDE TO THE I CHING**, $5.95. A brilliant new translation aimed specifically at the modern Westerner. Illustrative literature is substituted for the traditional commentaries and provides excellent reading in its own right. Useful for a meditative approach to the **I Ching**. Although not a definitive rendering, the quality of this effort is very high. 463pp. MIT 68

SUNG, Z.D. **THE SYMBOLS OF YI-KING**, c$7.00. An attempt by the author to demonstrate logically how the **I Ching** *works*. Heavy going. CWP

_____. **THE TEXT OF THE YI-KING**, c$7.25. The original Chinese text of each line, with the Legge translation, and extensive commentary. The characters in the original text have a direct bearing on the symbolism of the lines, so this edition should be helpful to those familiar with Chinese. The appendices are also included. Introduction, 395pp. CWP 35

VAN OVER, RAYMOND, ed. **I CHING**, $1.75. An excellent back-up volume to the Wilhelm/Baynes version. Van Over lifts the scholarly Legge translation from its difficult format and renders it accessible to the ordinary reader. In addition, the running commentary, entitled *Legge's Notes*, is based essentially on sources not covered in the Wilhelm/Baynes version and adds significantly to the total expository material available. The only way to go with Legge. NAL 71

WILHELM, HELLMUT. **CHANGE—EIGHT LECTURES ON THE I CHING**, $2.45. **I Ching** basics by the son of the master translator. He reveals something of the spirit of the book and affords a perspective for learning to interpret the oracle. Required reading for all who desire a deep understanding of the **I Ching**. 111pp. PUP 60

WILHELM/BAYNES, trs. **I CHING—BOOK OF CHANGES**, c$9.50. A truly inspired translation: Wilhelm surely tapped the same levels of inspiration as did the original authors. This is the principal, definitive English language version and the most complete in its running commentaries. Extensive introduction by Carl Jung. Without equal. 802pp. PUP 61

ISHIHARA, AKIRA and HOWARD LEVY. **THE TAO OF SEX**, $1.25. The Tao of sex was regarded by the ancients not as an end in itself but as a means to enrich the body and enlighten the spirit. This translation of an ancient manual sets forth in plain words and diagrams the most beneficial ways to have intercourse, the way to prepare for it, the things to do, and the things to avoid. Annotated bibliography of over 100pp is included. 311pp. H&R 68

KALTENMARK, MARK. **LAO TZU AND TAOSIM**, $1.95. A well written, comprehensive account for the general reader. Includes biographical information and philosophical analyses of Lao Tzu, Chuang Tzu, and other major Taoist masters, as well as a clear presentation of the Taoist religion. Bibliography, 158pp. SUP 65

KUO, LOUISE and YUAN HSI, trs. **CHINESE FOLK TALES**, $4.95. See the Fairy Tales section.

LAO TZU

No one can hope to understand Chinese philosophy, religion, government, art, medicine . . . without a real appreciation of the profound philosophy taught in this little book. [Tao] is the One, which is natural, eternal, spontaneous, nameless and indescribable. It is at once the beginning of all things and the way in which all things pursue their course. When this Tao is possessed by individual things, it becomes its character or virtue. The ideal life for the individual, the ideal order for society, and the ideal type of government are all based on it and guided by it. As a way of life, it denotes simplicity, spontaneity, tranquility, weakness, and most important of all, nonaction (wu-wei). By the latter is not meant literally inactivity but rather taking no action that is contrary to Nature—in other words, letting Nature take its own course.

All this philosophy is embodied in a small classic of about 5,250 words called the **Tao-te ching** *(Classic of the Way and Its Virtue). More commentaries have been written on it than on any other Chinese classic. It is a combination of poetry, philosophical speculation, and mystical reflection. Lao Tzu tells of the deep harmony of life and how we may attune our beings into it, and of the way of life one in tune with the Tao would have: Always calm, always clear, he opens the dreamworld to eyes newborn. After 2000 years and hundreds of translations, Lao Tzu remains our friendly companion.*

BAHM, A.J., tr. **TAO TEH KING—INTERPRETED AS NATURE AND INTELLIGENCE**, $1.95. *That which is most yielding eventually overcomes what is most resistant. That which is not becomes that which is. Acting without coercing or being coerced is best. Guiding by example rather than by words or commands is most successful. Such simple truths are hard to understand.* Bahm provides a long interpretative section in which he discusses key ideas as well as an arrangement of quotations which summarized Lao Tzu's theories on various topics. Extensive bibliography, 126pp. Ung

BLAKNEY, R.B., tr. **THE WAY OF LIFE: LAO TZU**, $1.25. *The softest of stuff in the world penetrates quickly the hardest; insubstantial, it enters where no room is. By this I know the benefit of something done by quiet being; in all the world but few can know accomplishment apart from work, instruction when no words are used.* Each chapter is paraphrased directly underneath the translation. Includes long introduction which places the text in historical perspective and discusses key concepts. 134pp. NAL 55

BYNNER, WITTER, tr. **THE WAY OF LIFE ACCORDING TO LAO TZU**, $1.25. *As the soft yield of water cleaves obstinate stone, so to yield with life solves the insoluble: To yield, I have learned, is to come back again. But this unworded lesson, this easy example, is lost upon men.* Our all time favorite translation—a perfect rendering of a perfect work. Many beautiful illustrations and a fine introduction. 76pp. Put 44

CHAN, WING-TSIT. THE WAY OF LAO TZU, $3.00. *The softest things in the world overcome the hardest things in the world. Non-being penetrates that in which there is no space. Through this I know the advantage of taking no action. Few in the world can understand the teaching without words and the advantage of taking no action.* This is the most scholarly edition available. It begins with ninety-three pages of introductory material surveying the philosophy of Tao, Lao Tzu the man, and **Lao Tzu** the book. Then there's a translation, with commentary and extensive notes. And finally there are bibliographies of books in Western languages and in Chinese and a glossary of Chinese names and terms and a lengthy index. Dr. Chan is an eminent scholar. 285pp. BoM 63

CHANG CHUNG-YUAN. **TAO: A NEW WAY OF THINKING**, $3.95. *The meekest in the world penetrates the strongest in the world. As nothingness enters into that-which-has-no-opening. Hence, I am aware of the value of non-action, And of the value of teaching with no words, As for the value of non-action, Nothing in the world can match it.* The translation of each chapter is accompanied by a lengthy commentary on the application of the thoughts to contemporary life. Chang draws many parallels between the **Tao Te Ching** and the philosophy of Martin Heidegger. Introduction, bibliography, notes. 253pp. H&R 75

CH'U TA-KAO, tr. **TAO TE CHING**, $2.00. *The non-existent can enter into the impenetrable. By this I know that non-action is useful. Teaching without words, utility without action—Few in the world have come to this.* This translation was originally issued by the London Buddhist Society and was made from a hitherto unused edition of the text. A terse, beautiful rendition—one of our favorites. Many footnotes. 96pp. Wei 37

FENG, GAI-FU and JANE ENGLISH, trs. **LAO TSU: TAO TE CHING**, c$7.95/3.95. The **Tao Te Ching** has been translated more frequently than any work except the Bible. This fresh translation of the ancient Chinese classic offers the essence of each word and makes Lao Tzu's teaching immediate and alive. The philosophy is simple: accept what is in front of you without wanting the situation to be other than it is. Study the natural order of things and work with it rather than against it, for trying to change what is only sets up resistance. If we watch carefully, we will see that work proceeds more quickly and easily if we stop *trying*, if we stop putting in so much extra effort, if we stop looking for results. In the clarity of a still and open mind, truth will be reflected. In other words, simply be. This is an 8½x11" album, illustrated with delicate full-page nature photographs and the Chinese calligraphy of the text. It is one of the most beautiful works we have seen. 176pp. RaH 72

GILES, LIONEL, tr. THE SAYINGS OF LAO TZU, c$3.50. *The softest things in the world override the hardest. That which has no substance enters where there is no crevice. Hence, I know the advantage of inaction. Conveying lessons without words, reaping profit without action—there are few in the world who can attain to this.* Translation is divided into topical chapters, each incorporating a few of the original ones. It is part of the *Wisdom of the East* series. Introduction, 60pp. Mur 05

LAU, D.C., tr. **TAO TE CHING**, $1.95. *Do that which consists in taking no action, pursue that which is not meddlesome, savour that which has no flavour. Make the small big and the few many; do good to him who has done you an injury. Lay plans for the accomplishment of the difficult before it becomes difficult; make something big by starting with it when small.* Almost 100pp of supplementary material: glossary, analysis of text, nature of work, historical discussion. Excellent scholarship. 192pp. Pen 63

MACKINTOSH, CHARLES, tr. **TAO**, $1.25. *The weakest thing in all the world is water; yet its play, between the rocky ledges whirled, grinds the hard rock away.* Poetic translation by a theosophist. 79pp. TPH 26

MEDHURST, C.S., tr. **THE TAO-TEH-KING**, $2.25. *The world's weakest drives the world's strongest. The indiscernible penetrates where there are no crevices. From this I perceive the advantages of non-action. Few indeed in the world realize the instructions of the silence, or the benefits of inaction.* Extensive comments and notes follow each chapter and there is a good deal of introductory material. The translator was a missionary in China. 166pp. TPH 05

SHRINE OF WISDOM. **THE SIMPLE WAY OF LAO TSZE—AN ANALYSIS OF THE TAO TEH CANON**, c$2.35. A flowing, clear rendition, in which the stanzas are regrouped according to subject matter, and short commentaries are appended. The Shrine of Wisdom is a group which publishes the classics of East and West in an effort to show the universal teaching underlying all religions. 55pp. ShW 24

SUZUKI, D.T. and PAUL CARUS, trs. **THE CANON OF REASON AND VIRTUE**, $1.95. *The world's weakest overcomes the world's hardest. Non-existence enters into the impenetrable. Thereby I comprehend of non-assertion the advantage. There are few in the world who obtain of non-assertion the advantage and of silence the lesson.* This is a traditional translation, well done, but not inspired. This edition has several unique features: the complete Chinese text; full commentary on the text; a biography of Lao Tzu by Sze-Ma-Ch'ien, the Chinese Herodotus; and a table of references. There's also introductory material and an index. 209pp. OpC 13

_____. **LAO TZE—TREATISE ON RESPONSE AND RETRIBUTION**, $1.95. A generally unknown work, attributed to Lao Tzu. The main thrust of the work can be seen in the title which translates to mean that *in the spiritual realm of heaven there is a response to our sentiments, finding expression in a retribution of our deeds.* This text contains a long introduction, the Chinese text with parallel verbatim translations of each character, a rendition in English, and explanatory notes. Several Taoist folk tales are also translated. 139pp. OpC 06

WALEY, ARTHUR, tr. **THE WAY AND ITS POWER: A STUDY OF THE TAO TE CHING AND ITS PLACE IN CHINESE THOUGHT**, $3.95. *What is of all things most yielding can overwhelm that which is of all things most hard. Being substanceless it can enter even where there is no space; That is how I know the value of action that is actionless. But that there can be teaching without words, value in action that is actionless, few indeed can understand.* An excellent long introduction gives a sketch of Chinese prehis-

tory, early philosophy and literature. Much commentary. Considered the definitive translation by scholars. 257pp. RaH 58

WU, JOHN and PAUL SIH, trs. **LAO TZU—TAO TEH CHING**, $2.00. *The softest of all things overrides the hardest of all things. Only nothing can enter into no-space. Hence, know the advantages of non-Ado. Few things under heaven are as instructive as the lesson of silence, or as beneficial as the fruits of non-Ado.* The text in Chinese characters is on the left-hand page and the translation is on the right. 115pp. SJU 61

LEGEZA, LASZLO. **TAO MAGIC**, $4.95. A collection of full page (8½x11") plates illustrating Chinese calligraphy and Taoist magic diagrams, talismans and charms. In his commentary Legeza explores the Taoist belief in the spiritual powers of calligraphy and the beautiful secret scripts which were designed to protect the *mystery* of the Tao. 126pp. RaH 75

LEGGE, JAMES, tr. **THE FOUR BOOKS**, c$20.00. The definitive translation of the most important Confucian texts. Each page is divided into three parts: in the key section is the original Chinese text in large characters; the middle contains Legge's English translation; and on the bottom are his extensive textual notes. We recommend Legge only to the serious student. PBR 23

_____. **THE TEXTS OF TAOISM, PART I**, $4.00. A long introduction by Legge discusses the differences among Taoism, Confucianism, and Buddhism; the authorship of the **Tao Te Ching**, and the meaning of Tao in Chinese thought. Also contains the complete text of the **Tao Te Ching** and selections from Chuang Tzu. These two volumes are part of the **Sacred Books of the East** series. The translations are not the most readable available. Many notes, 395pp. Dov 1891

_____. **THE TEXTS OF TAOISM, PART II**, $4.00. More selections from the writings of Chuang Tzu, the **Thai-Shang Tractate of Actions and their Retributions**, plus several shorter works—many of which are to be found in translation only in this collection. This collection is indispensible for serious Orientalists. Index in this volume, 340pp. Dov 1891

LI CHI. **THE BEGINNINGS OF CHINESE CIVILIZATION**, $2.95. The archaeological site of Anyang is the largest and most important in China. Dr. Li Chi was the director of excavations at the site. This volume is a transcription of three lectures which describe the findings of his thirty-year effort. Fifty plates, bibliography, index. 130pp. UWa 57

Illustration from an early Ming edition of the TAO TE CHING, showing Li Tan riding away into the West and meeting the frontier official Kuan Yin.

LIU, WU-CHI and IRVING YUCHENG LO, eds. **SUNFLOWER SPLENDOR**, $6.95. This has been widely acclaimed as both the most comprehensive and the finest anthology of Chinese poetry in English. The volume presents the writings of over 140 poets—the chief exponents of the major schools of Chinese poetry within each major genre and period and covers 3000 years from the twelfth century BC to the present day. Over fifty individuals worked on the translations, the majority of which have been especially commissioned for this volume. A general introduction, textual notes, biographical introductions for each poet, and a bibliography provide a thorough background for the reader. 694pp. Dou 75

LU K'UAN YU (CHARLES LUK). **THE SECRETS OF CHINESE MEDITATION**, $3.45. See the Meditation section.

_____. **TAOIST YOGA—ALCHEMY AND IMMORTALITY**, $3.50. Translation of a comprehensive course of Taoist yoga with instructions by ancient patriarchs and masters—a very clear step-by-step presentation for readers to follow Taoist alchemy. Involves techniques similar to kundalini yoga—whereby the body's sexual energy is retained and thereby transmuted into higher consciousness. Luk provides a good explanatory introduction, an extensive glossary, and many diagrams. 199pp. Wei 70

LU YU. **THE CLASSIC OF TEA**, c$8.50. Lu Yu lived in the eighth century in China. He is so deferred to throughout Chinese history in the matter of tea that sacrifices have been made to him as the *god of tea*. In this, his major work, he teaches the reader how to manufacture tea, how to lay out the equipage, and how to brew it properly. This edition by Francis Carpenter is the first full translation. Illustrations, 177pp. LBC 74

McCURDY, JOHN. **OF ALL THINGS MOST YIELDING**, $6.95. Full color nature photographs are set off with Chinese poetry from all traditions and all ages. The photograph are some of the most beautiful we've seen and each poem is very successfully matched to a photograph evoking an equivalent mood. Oversize, 128pp. RaH 75

McNAUGHTON, WILLIAM, ed. **THE TAOIST VISION**, $1.95. Translations which illuminate Taoist concepts. Included are the most relevant passages from the **Tao Te Ching** and **Chuang Tzu**, and a selection of Chinese, Japanese, and Western philosophy. 90pp. UMP 71

McNEILL, WILLIAM and JEAN SEDLAR, eds. **CLASSICAL CHINA**, $2.60. An anthology of texts, with introductory material, covering the following topics: ethics, politics, history, Confucianism, Taoism, Buddhism, and poetry. Selections from all the major works are included and there's an introduction to each along with a general preface. 288pp. Oxf 70

MENCIUS

Mencius (372–289 BC) is second only to Confucius in reputation as a moralist and philosopher. The record of his teachings and his conversations with princes who sought his counsel, or disciples who gathered around him for instruction, forms the fourth of the Confucian **Four Books**. He drew out the implications of Confucius' moral principles and reinterpreted them for the harsh conditions of the time in which he lived, when Confucian doctrine was threatened by the doctrines of Legalism. His stress is on the individual conscience.

DOBSON, W.A.C.H., tr. **MENCIUS**, $6.40. A topical arrangement of Mencius, annotated and written in modern prose. The entire text has been translated in its entirety. *A new translation of this great classic has long been wanted and Mr. Dobson was especially qualified to make it.... [He] has produced an excellent rendering.*—**Journal of Asian Studies**. Introduction, 233pp. UTo 63

LEGGE, JAMES, tr. **THE WORKS OF MENCIUS**, $6.00. Mencius drew out the implications of Confucius' moral principles and reinterpreted them against the threat of the doctrines of Legalism. Its stress was on the *thinking heart* (or individual conscience). This translation is in three parts: large Chinese characters at the top of the page, English translation in the middle, and explanatory notes at the bottom. Includes a long index of Chinese characters and phrases as well as a wealth of introductory material including historical background and quotations from Confucian and anti-Confucian texts. The definitive edition. 587pp. Dov 1895

RICHARDS, I.A. **MENCIUS ON THE MIND**, c$9.70. This is a very scholarly study which review Mencius' psychological thought and discusses the problems of translating his ideas (and Chinese, non-Western ideas in general) into terms comprehensible by and useful to the Western *rational* thinker. An appendix presents psychological passages from Mencius, with characters followed by Romanization and an English translation. 190pp. RKP 64

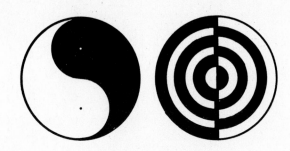

MOORE, CHARLES. **THE CHINESE MIND**, $3.95. An anthology of articles on the essentials of Chinese philosophy and culture written by noted modern scholars. Appears to have been produced for the college trade. 377pp. UHa 67

MORGAN, EVAN, tr. **TAO: THE GREAT LUMINANT**, c$5.50. This is a collection of translations of essays by Huai Nan Tzu, a noted Taoist commentator who wrote extensively on the **Tao Te Ching**. This is the only edition of his work that we know of in English. Notes, commentary. 399pp. CWP 33

MO TZU. **BASIC WRITINGS**, $3.30. Mo Tzu (fifth century BC) was an important political and social thinker and, at least until the third century BC, a formidable rival of the Confucianists. he advocated universal love, honoring and making use of worthy men in government, and identifying with one's superior as a means of establishing uniform moral standards. This is a translation by Burton Watson, who also supplies an introduction. Index, 146pp. Col 63

NEEDHAM, JOSEPH. **THE GRAND TITRATION: SCIENCE AND SOCIETY IN EAST AND WEST**, c$15.00. Needham has been studying the history of Chinese science for more than thirty years. Between the first and fifteenth centuries the Chinese, who experienced no *dark ages*, were generally far in advance of Europe. Throughout those centuries and ever since, the West has been profoundly affected not only in its technical processes but in its very social structures by discoveries and inventions emanating from China and East Asia. In a series of essays, reprinted here with over fifty illustrations, Dr. Needham explores the mystery of China's early lead and Europe's later overtaking. 350pp. A&U 69

_____. **SCIENCE AND CIVILIZATION IN CHINA, VOL. II, HISTORY OF SCIENTIFIC THOUGHT**, c$47.50. An extremely original and thought-provoking, though sometimes controversial, analysis from the point of view of science. CUP 74

_____. **SCIENCE AND CIVILIZATION IN CHINA, VOL. V:2, CHEMISTRY AND CHEMICAL TECHNOLOGY**, c$35.00. From a mass of hitherto obscure and puzzling source materials, Dr. Needham constructs a chart and provides an overview. He traces the rise of the ancient Chinese alchemical tradition from three roots: the pharmaceutical-botanical search for macrobiotic plants; the metallurgical-chemical practices for making artificial gold; and the medicinal-minerological use of inorganic substances in therapy. He and his collaborators try to reconstruct exactly what the old Chinese alchemists were doing in their laboratories, what they thought they were doing, and what general theories they developed about the physico-chemical world. This is the most detailed, scholarly account we know of. It is an indispensable reference work for scholars, but seems to have little value for the general reader. Notes, plates, and almost 200pp of bibliography, oversize, index. 542pp. CUP 75

RAWSON, PHILIP and LASZLO LEGEZA. **TAO**, c$4.98. This is an excellent pictorial presentation of the major elements of Taoism, with 196 illustrations, 33 in full color. The illustrations are drawn from artifacts, landscape and portrait paintings, and other forms of symbolic art. Each is fully commented upon and they are arranged topically according to the following order: the natural world, the moving spirit, cycles of change, heaven and earth, ritual, the mystical power of calligraphy, secret practices, and the realm of the immortals. An excellent general introduction gives some of the background necessary for a full appreciation of the plates. Oversize, 128pp. Out 73

REXROTH, KENNETH. **LOVE AND THE TURNING YEAR**, $2.25. Subtitled *One Hundred More Poems from the Chinese*, and including works by sixty different poets, from the third century to the present. The translations themselves are uniformly excellent and retain the flavor of the original. Introduction, biographical and explanatory notes on the poets and poems. Bibliography, 140pp. NDP 70

_____. **ONE HUNDRED POEMS FROM THE CHINESE**, $1.95. Thirty-five poems by Tu Fu (713–770) make up the first part of this volume. Rexroth follows with a selection of poets from the Sung Dynasty (tenth through twelfth centuries), much of which is not available elsewhere in English. There's also a general introduction, biographical and explanatory notes on the poets and poems. Bibliography, 160pp. NDP 71

ROWLEY, GEORGE. **PRINCIPLES OF CHINESE PAINTING**, $4.95. See the Sacred Art section.

SASO, MICHAEL. **TAOISM AND THE RITE OF COSMIC RENEWAL**, $5.40. *The first chapter of this study describes the annual cycle of events in the religious and social life of a Chinese town or city. In the second chapter, I examine the Chiao festival as the villagers see it.... The third chapter attempts to show something of the theology of the Chiao festival, by quoting from early Taoist works and classical sources. The fourth chapter gives an... inside description of the Chiao festival as the Taoist [priest] and his entourage witness it. Finally, the fifth chapter is devoted exclusively to Taoists themselves, describing their various ranks and orders, the lists of gods, the mudras and mantras, which the Taoist must know in order to function. The last section... presents a series of illustrations showing the visible aspects of what was described in chapter four.*—from the introduction. Notes, bibliography. 120pp. WSU 72

SCHARFSTEIN, BEN-AMI. **THE MIND OF CHINA**, c$12.00. *The China of this book is the China of tradition.... The book therefore has a soberly magical aim, to enter into the consciousness that traditional Chinese art, literature, history, and philosophy have kept alive.... I have hardly dealt with the early, formative philosophies of China, with Buddhism, or with the popular literature.... I have concentrated instead on a few subjects and a limited time, roughly the second millennium AD.* This is a detailed study of this millennium, analyzing the customs, cultures and beliefs of the educated ruling class. Scharfstein is an Israeli philosophy professor. Illustrations, notes, bibliography, index. 181pp. BaB 74

SHRINE OF WISDOM. **THE CLASSIC OF PURITY**, $.75. This is an important early Taoist text, attributed to Ko Hsuan, which is a treatise on the Way of Attainment through the purifying of the mind and the stilling of desires. 7pp. ShW 34

_____. **THE HISTORY OF GREAT LIGHT**, $1.95. A classic Taoist text. 36pp. ShW 60

_____. **YIN FU KING**, $.85. Another important early Taoist text, attributed to Huang Ti, the Yellow Emperor. Its theme is the importance of integrating man's inner and outer natures. As usual the Shrine of Wisdom has given us a beautiful translation, with commentary. 21pp. ShW 60

SIU, R.G.H. **CH'I, A NEO-TAOIST APPROACH TO LIFE**, $4.95. The form of this book suggests a Chinese classic. A brief, epigrammatic synoptic text is followed by a series of more extended commentaries in which the cryptic assertions of the text are explicated, as if later scholars sought to reveal their full meanings and the *ineffable essence* that holds them together and relates each to the others. The ultimate goal is to reveal the *ch'i*, an untranslatable word whose essence can be thought of as an ever-changing but never-ceasing flowing and confluence of time, light, and life. Dr. Siu examines its three components in separate commentaries. The commentaries on time recapitulate man's progressive or cyclically recurring musings from ancient philosophical traditions to modern physics. The commentaries on light deal with the attempts to reconcile its corpuscular and wave aspects. Those on life embrace such aspects as the origin and evolution of body and mind, the manifestations of rhythm, the anatomy of memory, and parabiological speculations. This is a fascinating, very well done work, recommended to all serious students who have enough background to understand the scientific aspects of the work and who also have sympathy with mystical insights. Includes over 50pp of notes and index. 352pp. MIT 74

_____. **THE TAO OF SCIENCE**, $2.95. Written by a Chinese-American scientist, this is an excellent essay on the nature and limitations of Western science and Eastern wisdom, considering in practical detail the theoretical basis of each and the best means of integrating the two. Siu advocates the cultivation of intuitive aesthetic sensitivity synthesized with Western *rational* methods of cognition. Bibliography, index. 192pp. MIT 57

SIVIN, NATHAN. **CHINESE ALCHEMY**, c$20.00. Prof. Sivin is a professionally trained historian of science, specializing in the Chinese scientific tradition. He begins with a discussion of which questions about Chinese alchemy are likely to be most fruitful and what attempts have been made to solve them, follows with a study of Taoist hagiography, and then presents a definitive edition, translation, and background study of an important seventh century handbook of alchemical recipes—a collection of formulas for the preparation of elixirs and methods for making scarce natural products. This is an important work in the history of science; it does not deal with alchemy from a spiritual point of view. Bibliography, notes, index. 363pp. HUP

The Three Pure Ones of the Taoist Trinity

SNYDER, GARY, tr. **COLD MOUNTAIN POEMS**, $4.00. A hand written edition, with translations of twenty-four of Han-Shan's poems. 8 x 12" and including the preface to the poems by Lu Ch'iu-Yin. **Cold Mountain Poems** expresses the essence of both Taoism and Zen. FSF 65

SOOTHILL, W.E. **THE THREE RELIGIONS OF CHINA**, c$9.35. An examination of the inter-relationship between Buddhism, Confucianism, and Taoism, and their effects upon Chinese life and thought. Notes, index. 272pp. Cur 29

SUN TZU. **THE ART OF WAR**, $2.95. Sun Tzu's essays on the art of war, written in China more than a thousand years ago, are the earliest of known treatises on the subject. They have never been surpassed in comprehensiveness and depth of understanding, and might well be termed the concentrated essence of wisdom on strategy and the conduct of war. This translation by Samuel Griffith is considered definitive and the translator also contributes an explanatory introduction and selections from the many commentaries in the Chinese language. Notes, bibliography, index. 214pp. Oxf 63

SUZUKI, D.T. and PAUL CARUS, trs. **YIN CHIH WEN**, $1.00. A translation of the **Tract of the Quiet Way**, an important Chinese religio-ethical tract, little known in the West but widely read and studied in China. Text includes notes, commentary, introductory and background material, and an index. 48pp. OpC 06

SWITKIN, WALTER. **IMMORTALITY**, $3.95. *The present translation includes Chapters 2 and 3 of the first part of the text of* **Yang-hsing Yen-ming Lu (Nourishing the Vital Principle and Prolonging Life)** *by T'ao Hung-Ching.... The text as a whole discusses the methods by which the aspirant of immortality sustains himself thereby achieving a long life and ultimately immortality.* The translation is annotated and there are extensive references. The Chinese calligraphy of many of the words is also included. 66pp. HSD 75

SZE, MAI-MAI. **THE WAY OF CHINESE PAINTING**, $2.95. See the Sacred Art section.

THOMPSON, LAURENCE. **CHINESE RELIGION**, $6.65. A well written, textbook-type survey, divided into the following sections: the world view of Chinese philosophy, protoscience and animistic religion, the family—kindred and ancestors, the community—Gods and temples, the state—emperors and officials, the individual—Buddhism and Taoism, the festival year, disruption of the tradition. Each section is clearly divided to make reading easier and is followed by an annotated list of recommended readings. Notes, index. 157pp. Dic 75

_____. **THE CHINESE WAY IN RELIGION**, $8.00. Selected readings and translations divided into the following general topics: the ancient native tradition, Taoism, Buddhism, religion of the state, family religion, popular religion, and religion under Communism. The selections are uniformly excellent and the volume itself is well organized. A great variety of points of view are represented. Notes, 241pp. Dic 73

VAN OVER, RAYMOND. **TAOIST TALES**, $1.95. This is a wonderful collection of Taoist tales, parables, anecdotes, *koan*, and poems written over many centuries by Taoist masters. They provide an understanding of Taoism in the one manner that Taoism recognizes—direct experience with its living nature. In so doing, they provide invaluable insight into Chinese philosophy in addition to some compelling literature. Van Over has selected translations from many sources in putting together this anthology and he also provides a good long introduction and bibliography. 250pp. NAL 73

WALEY, ARTHUR, tr. **DEAR MONKEY**, c$7.35. This is an abridgment by Waley's wife, Alison. The story really comes alive in this retelling and we actually like it better than Waley's original version. A profusion of delightful woodcuts illustrates the text. Bla 73

_____. **MONKEY**, $2.95. This classic combination of picaresque novel and folk epic, which mixes satire, allegory and history, is one of the most popular books in China. It is the story of the roguish Monkey and his encounters with major and minor spirits, gods, demigods, demons, monsters, and fairies. Waley has given us a wonderful translation of Wu Ch'eng-en's novel. 306pp. Grv 43

_____. **THE NINE SONGS**, $2.50. In ancient China the shaman was prophet, healer, dancer and singer, sometimes regarded as an outcast, though treated always with high consideration. In these songs, known in China for well over 1000 years, the always fleeting relationship of shaman and spirit is seen as that of lovers who come together and then part. Waley includes a commentary on the various deities whom the shaman served, and gives a general account of shamanism in China in addition to his translations. Index, 65pp. CiL 55

_____. **TRANSLATIONS FROM THE CHINESE**, $1.95. This volume contains all the poems from Waley's two famous collections, **170 Chinese Poems** and **More Translations from the Chinese**. The poems translated here are both ancient China's finest and Waley's most evocative work. One can get a good feeling for the essence of ancient China from this collection. Illustrations, notes. 325pp. RaH 19

_____. **THREE WAYS OF THOUGHT IN ANCIENT CHINA**, $1.95. Consists chiefly of extracts from Chuang Tzu, Mencius, and Han Fei Tzu, illustrating the three conflicting points of view in Chinese philosophy in the fourth century BC—the Taoist, the Confucianist, and the Realist. A very good selection by a noted scholar. 209pp. Dou 39

THE POET SU TUNG-P'O

WANG WEI. **POEMS OF WANG WEI**, $1.95. Wang Wei (699–761) was one of China's greatest poets, especially noted for his descriptions of landscape and the beauties of country life. Translated with an introduction by G.W. Robinson. 144pp. Pen 73

WARE, JAMES, tr. **ALCHEMY, MEDICINE AND RELIGION IN THE CHINA OF AD 320: THE NEI P'IEN OF KO HUNG**, c$20.15. In the China of the fourth century AD, alchemy, medicine and religion were so closely interrelated as to form a single study. This work, in effect, is a compendium of the state of knowledge and the mode of life open to the initiated in Ko Hung's time. In particular, it recounts the actual ways of Taoism as they have existed until fairly recent times—an extraordinary amalgam of mystical insight, wild speculation, superstition and legend, disciplined observation, and intellectual control. Ko Hung was apparently the first to break the taboo against putting this strictly oral tradition of a secret qabala into writing. A monumental work. 388pp. MIT 66

WATSON, BURTON, tr. **BASIC WRITINGS OF MO TZU, HSUN TZU AND HAN FEI TZU**, c$15.10. Watson's translation of the most important writings of these three philosophers along with an introduction which discusses the place of each in Chinese history and thought. This volume is also available in three separate parts (see them under the name of each philosopher in this section). Notes, 452pp. Col 63

_____. **COLD MOUNTAIN**, $2.45. A collection of 100 poems by Han-Shan. It is one of the earliest and most important works of Chinese Buddhist poetry and is especially influential in the later literature of Zen. The poems are important both as vivid descriptions of the wild mountain scenery in Han-Shan's home, and as metaphors of the poet's search for spiritual enlightenment and peace. Introduction, notes. 118pp. Col 62

WATTS, ALAN. **TAO: THE WATERCOURSE WAY**, c$8.95. Watts draws upon the ancient writings of Lao Tzu, Chuang Tzu, and the **I Ching** as well as the modern studies of Joseph Needham, Lin Yutang, and Arthur Waley. This final book written in collaboration with Al Chung-liang Huang is a survey of Taoism, documented with many examples from the literature and illustrated with Chinese calligraphy. Opening with a chapter on the Chinese written language, he goes on to explain what is meant by Tao (the flow of things), *wu-wei* (not forcing things), and *te* (the power which comes from this). There are long chapters on each of these important concepts. When Watts died in 1973 the book was almost completed, and was finished by Huang—a friend and colleague who attended and co-directed the discussions and lectures out of which the book came. Huang has also supplied much of the extensive calligraphy presented throughout the book. This is by no means the definitive textbook that the publishers claim it to be, but it is an interesting exposition of selected major topics and is geared toward both the general reader and the specialist. Notes and bibliography of works in Chinese and English. 180pp. RaH 75

WELCH, HOLMES. **TAOISM: THE PARTING OF THE WAY**, $3.95. An analytical, comprehensive discussion of Taoism, as well as a study (though not a translation) of Lao Tzu. The best overall account available. Bibliography and chronological chart. 188pp. H&R 57

WILHELM, RICHARD. **THE SECRET OF THE GOLDEN FLOWER**, c$6.95/$2.45. Essentially a practical guide to the integration of personality—hailed by Carl Jung as a link between the insights of the East and his own psychological research. The original text is translated and there is extensive commentary, including almost eighty pages by Jung. Also includes the **Book of Consciousness and Life**, a Chinese meditation text, with commentary. Numerous plates and illustrations. One of the most important basic texts. Recommended. 149pp. HBJ 31

WILLIAMS, C.A.S. **OUTLINES OF CHINESE SYMBOLISM AND ART MOTIFS**, c$12.50. A beautifully produced, alphabetically arranged handbook of Chinese symbolism based on the early folklore and illustrated throughout. All the important terms are accompanied by their Chinese version. Notes, introduction, index. 501pp. Tut 41

YANG WAN-LI. **HEAVEN MY BLANKET, EARTH MY PILLOW**, $4.95. A translation by Jonathan Chaves of nature poems from Sung Dynasty China, accompanied by lovely illustrations and a long interpretative introduction. Index, 118pp. Wea 75

YAP, YONG and ARTHUR COTTERELL. **THE EARLY CIVILIZATION OF CHINA**, c$15.95. A pictorial history of China from prehistoric times to the Mongol conquest. The art and culture and emphasized and the volume is oversize and beautifully produced. Over one hundred beautiful plates, many in color. Notes, bibiliography, index. 256pp. Put 75

THE CHINESE LANGUAGE

CREEL, HERRLEE, ed. **LITERARY CHINESE BY THE INDUCTIVE METHOD, VOL. I**, c$7.40. This set of books is generally considered the best instruction manual on learning the Chinese written language ever produced in English. First the text itself is printed in very large, clear characters and each character is numbered. The bulk of each volume is devoted to notes which analyze in detail each of the characters—taking them apart and discussing their formation, the other characters that they are composed of, a translation, and extensive explanatory and etymological information. Exercise sentences and essays using vocabulary introduced by the text and notes are also presented along with an index of first occurrences of characters and compound expressions, and general index in English. Introductory material is also included. The text in this volume is **The Hsiao Ching** (a classic of filial piety). Oversize, 228pp. UCh 48

_____. **LITERARY CHINESE BY THE INDUCTIVE METHOD, VOL. II**, c$11.45. This volume studies selections from the **Lun Yu**. 261pp. UCh 39

_____. **LITERARY CHINESE BY THE INDUCTIVE METHOD, VOL. III**, c$10.75. The text here is **Mencius, Books I–III**. 338pp. UCh 52

FENN, C.H. **THE 5000 DICTIONARY, CHINESE-ENGLISH**, $5.95. Words are arranged in the alphabetical order of their Romanized form. Six columns on each page present the characters in their various forms. Very extensive presentation. It seems easy to follow—

although we can't be sure since our knowledge of Chinese is nil. This is the one that most students use. 696pp. HUP 42

LAI, T.C. **CHINESE CALLIGRAPHY**, $4.95. To the Chinese calligraphy is one of the highest forms of art, the progenitor of brush painting and seal engraving, and a heritage as old as the culture. This is a visual collection of samples of the calligraphy drawn from many periods and styles and chronologically arranged. Each of the selections is identified. Glossary, introduction. 269pp. UWa 73

MATHEWS, ROBERT H. **CHINESE-ENGLISH DICTIONARY**, c$24.00. 1226pp. HUP

PEKING UNIVERSITY FACULTY. **MODERN CHINESE**, $3.50. This overall course in modern Chinese was designed by the faculty of Peking University and has been used successfully for the past decade in teaching English-speaking students basic Mandarin Chinese. Assuming no previous training in Chinese, this course is excellent for self study, with full explanations and ample pronunciation and grammar drills throughout. The official transcription of mainland China is used, and a conversion table to the Yale and Wade systems is provided, along with a vocabulary. A set of records designed to go along with the course is also available for $12.50—this price includes the book. 269pp. Dov 71

POUND, EZRA, ed. **THE CHINESE WRITTEN CHARACTER AS A MEDIUM FOR POETRY**, $1.50. 45pp. CiL

QUONG, ROSE. **CHINESE WRITTEN CHARACTERS**, $2.95. A lovely analysis and presentation of several hundred Chinese characters, grouped under key-characters known as radicals which, in composition, give a clue to meaning. Ms. Quong interprets the meaning of the characters and shows how conceptions of the material and spiritual world are given visible form by simple strokes arranged in an infinite number of combinations. The essence of each character is illuminated with quotations from Chinese sages. 78pp. Bea 68

SIMON, W. **1200 CHINESE BASIC CHARACTERS**, $9.00. This is an elementary textbook, adapted from one of the most popular manuals in use in China over the past century, consistently revised. The material is organized in the form of lessons and about fourteen new characters are introduced in each lesson, along with Romanization and English translations. Appendices, index. 332pp. LuH 57

WEIGER, DR. **CHINESE CHARACTERS**, $7.95. Their origin, etymology, history, classification and significance. 820pp. Dov 15

WILDER, G. and J. INGRAM. **ANALYSIS OF CHINESE CHARACTERS**, $4.00. An examination of about one thousand Sino-Japanese characters, beginning with simple words like I, you, he, and working through a high-frequency vocabulary of characters. For each character the text offers a printed form, and, where such exists, a seal form; a transcription of the pronunciation into modern Mandarin, including tonal indications; and an English translation. This is followed by an examination of the historical origin of the character, its semantic content, its components, including its radical in the traditional system. Indices, 375pp. Dov 34

WILLIAMSON, H.R. **TEACH YOURSELF CHINESE**, $3.95. An excellent teach-yourself manual for both written and spoken Mandarin Chinese. An introductory section covers the sounds and spelling of the language and grammar is presented through a series of dialogues. Forty dialogues (first in Roman script then in Chinese) introduce and illustrate every aspect of everday Chinese. Grammar notes and vocabulary are included at the appropriate points in the text and all the grammatical information is summarized at the end. 638pp. McK 47

WOLFF, DIANE. **AN EASY GUIDE TO EVERYDAY CHINESE**, $3.50. *This book is designed to enable anyone to appreciate Chinese for the magnificent language it is, or to begin learning it. You can browse in it and read what interests you in any order. The English section provides background information, history of the language, discussion of calligraphy, and technical information, such as pronunciation and sentence patterns. The Chinese section contains common everyday words, their meanings, many word derivations, and the stroke order (which is the instruction for writing each character.)* This is the most introductory of all the books on the Chinese language. Bibliography, 231pp. H&R 74

YEE, CHIANG. **CHINESE CALLIGRAPHY**, $5.95. This is a very highly regarded classic introduction to Chinese calligraphy, exploring the aesthetics and the techniques of this art in which rhythm, line, and structure are perfectly embodied. The illustrations alone make the book worth owning for all who are interested in calligraphy. This third edition includes two new chapters: *Calligraphy and Painting* and *Aesthetic Principles*. Oversize, index. 270pp. HUP 73

YUTANG, LIN. **LIN YUTANG'S CHINESE-ENGLISH DICTIONARY OF MODERN USAGE**, c$47.50. This is a handsomely produced dictionary with a number of important innovations. Dr. Lin considers this his life's work. Each of the characters is clearly reproduced, with Romanization. He is especially proud of his *instant index* system for both Chinese and English which reduces the 214 Kanghsi radicals to fifty. It is especially valuable as a literary dictionary, though it should be extremely useful to all serious students of Chinese. Oversize, 1786pp. CHK 72

CHRISTIANITY

ABHISHIKTANANDA. **PRAYER**, $1.95. This small book is a distillation of Christian wisdom on the union of God through prayer. The author was a French Benedictine monk who spent much of his adult life in India. The book is widely read by Indian Christians who find it a good combination of traditional Indian teachings and Christianity. Notes, 81pp. Wes 67

AJIBOLA, J.O. **THE SECRET SCHOOL OF JESUS**, $1.20. A selection of quotations from the gospels on the title theme, with commentary. *The phrase* Secret School *is used in the sense that after Jesus had preached in synagogues and in other public places where his twelve disciples had listened to him, he still called them separately to some secret and lonely places where he gave them more intensive instructions concerning the secrets of the Kingdom of heaven.* 75pp. Day 72

AKHILANANDA, SWAMI. **HINDU VIEW OF CHRIST**, $3.75. Christ is accepted as God incarnate in Hinduism as well as in Christianity. Swami Akhilananda stresses the agreement of the two religions on the model of life imparted by Christ—a model that each individual can grasp through his own experience. This way of life is considered throughout the book's chapters on Christ in connection with his teachings, spiritual practices, the Cross, the spirit of Easter, and the dynamics of spiritual power. Notes, bibliography, index, 291pp. BrP 49

ATTWATER, DONALD. **A DICTIONARY OF SAINTS**, $3.95. An alphabetical reference book detailing the lives and legends of over 750 saints, from Christ's apostles to the men and women who have been canonized in recent times—with full details of their work, their feast days, emblems, and dates of canonization. 362pp. Pen 65

ST. AUGUSTINE. **CITY OF GOD**, $7.95. Saint Augustine incorporated Platonism (as interpreted by Plotinus) into Christianity. The **City of God** was inspired by the fifth century sacking of Rome, an event which Augustine regarded as retribution for the worship of false gods by *educated pagans*. God's real purpose in creating the world, Augustine maintains, was the building of the Heavenly City and the events of history are mere moments in the implementation of a divine plan. The first half of the book reviews the sufferings of Rome throughout history, with Augustine asking where the Roman gods were during these bloody events. In the second half he turns from history to the need to found another city based on Christian love. Countless digressions present his ideals of social order in a universal religious society. This is an unabridged translation by Henry Bettenson. An abridged version translated by a group of Jesuits is available for $2.95. The complete version is indexed, 1148pp., and includes a 51pp. introduction. Pen 72

_____. **CONFESSIONS**, $2.45. St. Augustine of Hippo (350—430 AD) was one of the outstanding figures of the declining Roman Empire. From his own account he lived a life of sin until his conversion to Christianity at the age of 32. Twelve years later he gave a personal account of his search for truth in the **Confessions**, where his analysis of the emotional side of Christian experience in the face of sin remains unsurpassed. This edition is translated and has an introduction by R.S. Pine-Coffin. 347pp. Pen 61

The Holy Trinity (detail) by Albrecht Dürer

BABOCK, WINIFRED. **THE PALESTINIAN MYSTERY PLAY**, $2.95. An exploration of Jesus and Christianity in the form of a play. Some startling ideas emerge from the exposition and the play is designed to force readers to rethink their beliefs about Jesus. Some of the topics: was the crucifixion/resurrection drama a *plot* that failed, did the miracles really happen, are the Gospels true, did Jesus believe himself to be a Messiah. The text of this book is also contained in **The Shining Stranger**. Notes, 142pp. Hal 71

BAILEY, ALICE. **FROM BETHLEHEM TO CALVARY**, $2.75. See Theosophy section.

_____. **THE REAPPEARANCE OF THE CHRIST**, $2.25. See Theosophy section.

BARRETT, C.K. **JESUS AND THE GOSPEL TRADITION**, $5.90. Professor Barrett looks through the teaching of the Gospels to the teaching of Jesus himself about his person, his mission, his suffering, and his hopes for the future. He argues that Jesus was in some respects mistaken in his predictions about his death, but insists that he was thereby more effectively shown to be right in all that really mattered. Barrett is one of the foremost British New Testament scholars. Indices, 127pp. SPK 67

BESANT, ANNIE. **ESOTERIC CHRISTIANITY**, $1.95. Discourses on the esoteric background and spiritual meanings in the Christian legends by this noted Theosophist. Ms. Besant also relates Christianity to Indian philosophy. Notes, index, 284pp. TPH 01

BLAKNEY, RAYMOND. **MEISTER ECKHART**, $3.95. Eckhart was a medieval link in the long but narrow chain of men and women who see the truth, speak the truth, and live and die to keep the truth. He was a prime mover in the European Reformation. This book contains up-to-date versions of a full selection of his sermons, as well as the first modern rendering of Eckhart's defense at being branded a heretic, and notes and some historical perspective. 330pp. H&R 41

JACOB BOEHME

BOEHME, JACOB. **MYSTERIUM MAGNUM**, c$40.25/set. This book was written by Boehme the year before he died and at a time when his powers of expression had developed to their full. Taking the general form of an interpretation of Genesis, it far outstrips those confines, touching among other matters upon the meaning of the New Testament, and, from the first sentence, leading to the heart of the universal experience of all mystics: *When we consider the visible world with its essence and consider the life of the creatures, then we find therein the likeness of the invisible, spiritual world, which is hidden in the visible world as the soul in the body; and we see thereby that the hidden God is nigh unto all and through all, and yet wholly hidden to the visible essence.* 2 vols., 840pp. Wat 24

_____. **THE SIGNATURE OF ALL THINGS**, c$8.40. A collection of selected writings, including the title piece, *Of the Supersensual Life*, and *A Dialogue Between Two Souls*. Introduction, 295pp. Cla 69

_____. **SIX THEOSOPHIC POINTS**, $2.25. Philosophic discussion of aspects of the growth of good and evil and mystical points such as *the blood and water of the soul*. Includes an introductory essay by Nicholas Berdyae, *Unground and Freedom*, on Boehme. 208pp. UMP 70

HARTMANN, FRANZ. **THE LIFE AND DOCTRINES OF JACOB BOEHME**, $6.00. This is a very useful edited compilation of Boehme's writings, topically organized, combined with a study of his life and work. 337pp. HeR 29

BOYD, ANNE. **THE MONKS OF DURHAM**, $2.75. A pictorial description of life in a fifteenth century monastery. 48pp. CUP 75

BRIANCHANINOV, IGNATIUS. **ON THE PRAYER OF JESUS**, c$3.90. Bishop Brianchaninov was one of the greatest theologians of the Russian Orthodox Church. This volume contains his thoughts on the Prayer of Jesus, a method of thought control and concentration in the form of a spiritual exercise. The first references to this prayer are contained in the **Philokalia**. The Jesus Prayer is first repeated aloud again and again, making it a continuous background to one's life; the next step is to say the prayer silently, and concentrate on it as it is being thought; when complete concentration has been attained the prayer enters the heart and lives itself with every heart beat. Alexander d'Agapeyeff provides an illuminating introduction. Translated by Father Lazarus. 114pp. Wat 65

BUNYAN, JOHN. **THE PILGRIM'S PROGRESS**, $1.75. Penning the lines of characters such as Mercy, Christian, Obstinate, Good-will, etc., Bunyan searches through the land of the Bible to try to find answers to the thoughts that trouble his mind. First published in 1678, this book has remained a classic of religious and allegorical literature. Edited, with a long introduction by Roger Sharrock. Notes, 377pp. Pen 65

CAUSSADE, JEAN-PIERRE de. **ABANDONMENT TO DIVINE PROVIDENCE**, $1.45. A great Christian spiritual classic in which Caussade outlines the means to attain holiness through total surrender of the soul to God and complete cooperation with his will in all things. He emphasizes that we must embrace the present moment, for it provides *an ever-flowing source of holiness*. Total acceptance of the present moment and all the activities of that moment is the single most important concern of the soul seeking God. All things are sent by God, writes Caussade, and however troublesome they are, they will—if accepted gladly—lead us surely and quickly to holiness. The translation is by John Beevers, who also supplies introductory remarks. 119pp. Dou 75

THE CLOUD OF UNKNOWING

The unknown author of this classic work was probably an English country parson of the late fourteenth century. The book's main theme is that *all thoughts, all concepts, all images must be buried beneath in a cloud of for-*

getting, while our naked love (naked because divested of thought) must rise upward toward God hidden in the cloud of unknowing. —William Johnston.

JOHNSTON, WILLIAM. **THE CLOUD OF UNKNOWING,** $1.75. This is the translation we like best. The Middle English has been rendered into modern English without losing the flavor of the original. Father Johnston is an authority on fourteenth century spirituality and especially on the writings of this particular author. He provides a lengthy introduction and this edition also includes a translation of the same author's other principal work, **The Book of Privy Counseling**—a short but moving treatise on the way to enlightenment through a total loss of self and consciousness only of the being of God. Notes at the end cross reference the works to the **Collected Works** of St. John of the Cross. 195pp. Dou 73

PROGOFF, IRA, tr. **THE CLOUD OF UNKNOWING,** $2.95. Progoff, a student of Jung, provides up-to-date psychological comments and interpretation of this classic. He has studied **The Cloud** in scholarly detail, and here shares his knowledge of idiomatic expression and the various subtleties of meaning in the original to help us feel more clearly the writer's wisdom and understand his advice on transcending that cloud and finding the true God. 243pp. Del 57

UNDERHILL, EVELYN, ed. **THE CLOUD OF UNKNOWING,** c$4.70. An edited, modernized version of the British Museum manuscript. For those who want the edition most like the original. Includes an introduction by Ms. Underhill. 270pp. Wat 12

WOLTERS, CLIFTON, tr. **THE CLOUD OF UNKNOWING,** $2.25. This edition of the classic includes a long introduction and a listing of related recommended readings. 144pp. Pen 65

CHADWICK, HENRY. **THE EARLY CHURCH,** $3.50. A detailed study of Christianity from earliest times through the fourth century focusing on important individuals and movements. Index, topical bibliography. 304pp. Pen 67

CUMMINS, GERALDINE. **THE CHILDHOOD OF JESUS,** c$5.25. Ms. Cummins was a noted English psychic who had a great deal of information and wisdom revealed to her through automatic writing. Here she presents the material she has received on the early years in the life of Jesus in a manner which brings the countryside and people to life vividly. The years discussed here are not recorded in the Bible. 224pp. PsP 37

_____. **THE SCRIPTS OF CLEOPHAS,** c$7.50. These scripts were produced by automatic writing. The ultimate source is Cleophas, a Christian convert of the first century who drew on writings put together in the century after Christ's death. The narrative is transmitted by a *messenger* who lived some centuries later. The material supplements the Acts of the Apostles and the Epistles of St. Paul. It furnishes an account of the early Church and the Apostles from immediately after Christ's death to St. Paul's departure from Berea to Athens. The account seems not to be based upon the traditional scripture and therefore supplements incomplete Biblical material. The scripts have been well received academically. Index, 299pp. BrP 28

DALBY, JOSEPH. **CHRISTIAN MYSTICISM AND THE NATURAL WORLD,** c$3.35. The author argues that the mystics, while transcending the life of nature, do not neglect or despise the natural. He quotes extensively from the Christian mystics and especially from St. John of the Cross in making his case. 147pp. Cla 49

The artifix as priest. On the left is Earth suckling the Mercurius-child. From Maier, Symbola aurea mensae (1617)

DIONYSIUS THE AREOPAGITE. **THE DIVINE NAMES,** c$5.35. *In this treatise the writer gathers together and explains a number of the symbolic Names by which the nature of the Supreme and Absolute God is revealed in the Scriptures of the Old and New Testaments. . . . Dionysius speaks of two aspects of the nature of the Supreme God—the undifferentiated and the differentiated. . . . The consideration of each of these Attributes or Names is accompanied by a philosophical exposition of its nature and its relation to the universe and the human soul which, by turning to the Divine in prayer, opening the mind to true illuminations of His nature, and imitating, as far as possible, the Divine activity, may ultimately be led upward to union with God.*—from the introduction. No one knows who Dionysius was—however, nearly every great medieval scholar made use of his writings and his authority came to be almost final. 91pp. ShW 57

_____. **MYSTICAL THEOLOGY AND THE CELESTIAL HIERARCHIES,** c$6.70. This is a great classic which is little known today and which contains the very essence and foundation of true Christian mysticism. 73pp. ShW 65

DUNCAN, ANTHONY. **THE LORD OF THE DANCE,** c$5.20. A look at the *inner side of creation* divided into five parts. *The Great Dance* places man in his relationship to the Creator and the rest of creation, visible and invisible. *Light* discusses the devil and his demonic agencies. *Contemplation* contains a resume of *initiated symbol projection*—a use of the creative imagination that can bring awareness of other states of existence. *The Silence of Heaven* is centered on the Eucharist and the hierarchies of angels. *I Am, the Mind of All* calls the individual to a life of active communion with *the resurrected and living Lord of the Dance.* 109pp. Hel 72

ELLIOTT, MAURICE. **THE PSYCHIC LIFE OF JESUS,** c$5.00. A radical look at the healing powers and miracles of Jesus. Reverend Elliott says we all have these powers latent within us and gives examples and recounts experiences to convince the reader. 168pp. Spi 38

THE DEAD SEA SCROLLS

The Dead Sea Scrolls are manuscripts left by an obscure cult of scholars known as the Essenes. Discovered unexpectedly in 1947 near the Dead Sea, these writings give significant new information about the life, religious trends, and beliefs of the Jewish people about the time of Jesus. Since the discovery, scholars have been piecing together fragments of the brittle parchments and translating and interpreting the contents. The following studies are among the best.

ALLEGRO, JOHN. **THE DEAD SEA SCROLLS: A REAPPRAISAL,** $2.25. Allegro, a linguist and secretary of the Dead Sea Scrolls Fund, discusses the discovery of the scrolls, what they indicate about the life of the Jewish monastic community at Qumran, and some of the significance for reinterpretation both of early Christian history and of the New Testament. 200pp. Pen 56

CHANEY, ROBERT. **THE ESSENES AND THEIR ANCIENT MYSTERIES,** $2.00. This is an exploration of the Essenes: who they were, their teachings, and what happened to them. Other than the Dead Sea Scrolls, virtually no information on them exists (with the exception of the writings of Edmud Bordeaux Szekely: refer to the section on his work). Chaney here attempts to summarize all that is known. 48pp. Ata 68

DAVIES, A. POWELL. **THE MEANING OF THE DEAD SEA SCROLLS,** $1.25. This is the most comprehensive analysis of the scrolls available, including detailed accounts of the discovery, their dating, the Essenes, the scrolls and Christian origins, and the scrolls and Jesus. The material is clearly presented and illustrated. Recommended as the best overall book on the scrolls. Notes, 144pp. NAL 56

GASTER, THEODORE. **THE DEAD SEA SCRIPTURES,** $3.50. A complete English translation. There is very little interpretation included, but the text is well annotated. It is designed for the layman to read and come to his own conclusions. 420pp. Dou 56

HELINE, THEODORE. **THE DEAD SEA SCROLLS,** $1.95. Very good short work outlining the main points of significance about the famous find. 87pp. NAP 57

KITTLER, GLEN. **EDGAR CAYCE ON THE DEAD SEA SCROLLS,** $1.95. Along with Edgar Cayce's incredibly interesting information on historical detail surrounding the birth of Jesus, Hugh Lynn Cayce has enlisted the help of scholars and experts on the period to compile an accurate reference frame in which to examine and place in perspective what Edgar Cayce has to tell. 205pp. War 70

VERMES, G. **THE DEAD SEA SCROLLS IN ENGLISH,** $3.50. Faithful English translation and sensitive and scholarly interpretation of the non-Biblical scrolls from the Qumran cave. 250pp. Pen 62

DECHANET, J. M. **CHRISTIAN YOGA,** $1.50. A priest advocates the combination of peace of mind and communion with God. He explains the deep meanings of yoga and gives practical advice. 245pp. H&R 60

ST. FRANCIS OF ASSISI (1182-1226)

Born to comfort and a world of ease; he rejected both—embraced poverty, disease, suffering, with ecstasy and joy. And so he caught the imagination of

the world that had to believe that the weak, the sick, the hungry would in-
herit heaven, that there was virtue in suffering. And in his own lifetime St.
Francis became a mythic figure, curing the sick, feeding the hungry, gloating
almost in his own pain as a precious gift of God. He reidentified the Christian
message in a vivid human way with the teaching of Christ. Also he managed—
just—to stay within the confines of the Catholic Church and therefore helped
to generate one of its periods of reform and renewal. He and his little band
of brothers, and his sister, St. Claire, lived haphazardly the life of religious
ecstasy and practice. But he, too, had his St. Paul in Brother Elias, who
formalized the movement, turning St. Francis into the Franciscans—one of
the great crusading powers of the late Middle Ages.—Morris Bishop, from the
introduction, **St. Francis of Assisi.** A recording of **The Little Flowers** is available. See the Records section for a description.

ARMSTRONG, EDWARD. **ST. FRANCIS: NATURE MYSTIC,** c$12.00. Though St.
Francis is closely identified with the love of nature, this interest has been dealt with only
incidentally by previous scholars. Mr. Armstrong's study of the nature stories and the
manner of their incorporation in the Franciscan legend sheds light on our understanding
of the saint, the outlook of his age, and the character of the movement he created. The
author contends that the Church, both before and after St. Francis, failed to understand
the contribution that nature mystics could make to it. He stresses that delight in nature
as God's handiwork and compassion for all living things are integral parts of the Christian
heritage. Each of the animals that St. Francis came in contact with is detailed in legend in
a chapter devoted to it, as well as in the more general material. Notes, index, 270pp.
UCP 73

BISHOP, MORRIS. **ST. FRANCIS OF ASSISI,** c$6.95. This is a very well written biograph-
ical study, aimed at giving the general reader a feeling for St. Francis and the environment
in which he lived. Bishop was a classical scholar, specializing in French and Italian history
and literature. Index, introduction, 237pp. LBC 74

BROWN, RAPHAEL, tr. **THE LITTLE FLOWERS OF ST. FRANCIS,** $2.45. This book
was written a hundred years after the death of St. Francis to try to capture the true spirit
of his life and the Franciscan way for the followers of that time. It has come to us as the
classic gospel of the great saint. This edition contains twenty chapters never in English
before, and is considered the definitive presentation of these legends. It also includes a
long, enlightening introduction on the background of the book and its historical significance; a biography of St. Francis as well as biographical sketches of the principal characters in the book; and notes, appendices, and a bibliography. In addition the following
texts are included: *The Five Considerations on the Holy Stigmata, The Life of Brother
Juniper, The Life of Brother Giles,* and *The Sayings of Brother Giles.* Recommended.
359pp. Dou 58

CHESTERTON, G.K. **ST. FRANCIS OF ASSISI,** $1.45. A biographical study which brings
the saint and his times alive. The author's own feelings and interpretations are intermingled
with the narrative of St. Francis' life. This has been a consistently popular book and it is
quite well regarded. 158pp. Dou 24

CUNNINGHAM, LAWRENCE, ed. **BROTHER FRANCIS,** $1.25. This is an anthology of
writings by and about St. Francis, grouped topically. The book begins with some interpretations of St. Francis and then goes on to give selections from **The Little Flowers.** Other
topics include *Francis of Assisi and Nature, Francis on Poverty and Solitude, Francis and
Women, Francis the Mystic,* and *The Prayers of St. Francis.* Each is illustrated by several
essays, all from different authors. Cunningham's tapestry gives the reader an excellent feeling for St. Francis the man, his teachings, and his life. Introduction, 201pp. Pyr 72

EVERYMAN'S LIBRARY. **SAINT FRANCIS OF ASSISI,** c$5.30. Translations of **The
Little Flowers, The Mirror of Perfection,** and **St. Bonaventure's Life of St. Francis.** It is
not made clear who did the translations, but they seem to be works of good scholarship,
and the complete text of each is offered. Introduction, bibliography, 410pp. Dut 73

GOUDGE, ELIZABETH. **ST. FRANCIS OF ASSISI,** $2.25. A novelistic reconstruction
of the life, work, and thought of St. Francis. *My only excuse is that I wanted to write it
so much that I had to, my hope is that it may serve to introduce St. Francis to a few who
do not know him well and perhaps make them want to know him better.* The narrative
reads well and this is probably the easiest way to get a feeling for the man. 288pp. Hod 59

JORGENSEN, JOHANNES. **ST. FRANCIS OF ASSISI,** $1.95. This is the most detailed of
all the countless biographies of St. Francis. Jorgensen, one of Europe's most distinguished
authors, spent years researching this material. Detailed notes accompany the text. In addition to being a work of impeccable scholarship, the biography reads well. Index, 354pp.
Dou 12

KAZANTZAKIS, NIKOS. **ST. FRANCIS,** $3.95. This is a highly personal re-creation of
the life of St. Francis by one of this century's most passionate writers. The presentation is
more dramatic than in the other biographical studies. 379pp. S&S 62

MOORMAN, JOHN. **SAINT FRANCIS OF ASSISI,** $2.50. This is the only biography of
Francis by an ecclesiastic. He gives the facts of Francis' life and focuses on his Christian
teachings. Annotated bibliography. 118pp. SPK 50

SMITH, JOHN HOLLAND. **FRANCIS OF ASSISI,** $2.95. This is a very detailed major
biographical study, aimed less at the general reader than at the scholar and those wishing
further details on St. Francis' life and times, especially his ecclesiastical relationships.
Notes, bibliography, illustrations, index. 210pp. Scr 72

TIMMERMANS, FELIX. **THE PERFECT JOY OF ST. FRANCIS,** $1.95. A biography
which reveals a deep understanding of the man Francis and offers a penetrating interpretation of the ideals and humor which have made Francis so appealing throughout the ages.
It reveals the whole man: poet, ascetic, servant of the poor, miracle worker. Translated
by Raphael Brown. 276pp. Dou 55

ST. FRANCIS de SALES. **INTRODUCTION TO THE DEVOUT LIFE,** c$6.65. A seven-
teenth century classic of Christian mystical and devotional literature. *My intention is to
write for those who have to live in the world, and who, according to their state, to all
outward appearances have to lead an ordinary life; and who, often enough, will not think
of undertaking a devout life, considering it impossible.* St. Francis shows how *a strong
and resolute person may live in the world without being tainted by it, find spiritual spring
amid its salt waters.* 261pp. Dut 54

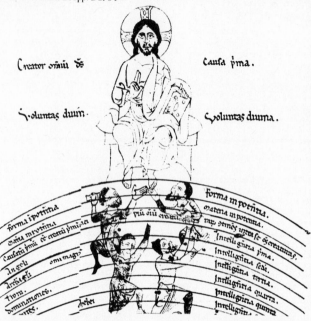

FRENCH, R.M. **THE WAY OF THE PILGRIM,** c$3.95/1.50. Written by an unknown
nineteenth century Russian, this classic has a special purity and simplicity of spirit. Recounts his ministry of love to his fellow men, his wrestlings with the problem of how to
pray continuously, and his receptiveness to the promptings of God. An important book,
giving us glimpses of the soul of Eastern Christianity. Notes, maps, 244pp. Sea 65

FRIELING, RUDOLF. **THE ESSENCE OF CHRISTIANITY,** $.85. A mystical presenta-
tion of Christian cosmology written by a follower of Rudolf Steiner's Anthroposophy.
31pp. CCP 71

FULLERSON, MARY C. **BY A NEW AND LIVING WAY,** $2.50. An interpretation of
the inner meaning of the sacrament of the Last Supper. 88pp. ShP 63

_____. **THE FORM OF THE FOURTH,** $2.50. A sequel to **By a New and Living
Way,** discussing how man can combat the inimical forces in the world and focusing on the
Book of Daniel. 86pp. ShP 71

FURST, JEFFREY. **EDGAR CAYCE'S STORY OF JESUS,** $.95. This arrangement brings
together the story of Jesus, as found scattered throughout the Cayce readings (see the
Cayce section for more background material). Furst also supplies commentary on the selections. Topics include *In the Beginning, On Soul Development, The Essenes, The Nativity,
The Early Years and Ministry, Crucifixion and Resurrection, The Early Church,* and *The
Church of Laodicea.* The very nature of the scattered readings and the language used in
them does not make this work the clearest story available, but many insights are offered.
413pp. Ber 68

GARDNER, EDMUND. **THE CELL OF SELF-KNOWLEDGE,** c$5.40. A collection of
seven mystical treatises by Richard of St. Victor, St. Catherine of Siena, Margery Kemp,
and Walter Hilton—first printed in 1521. Introduction, index, 157pp. CSq 66

GIBRAN, KAHLIL. **JESUS, THE SON OF MAN,** c$6.95. Gibran extends his sensitive
imagination into the realm of Jesus' day to day life, writing stories as they might have
been told to him by people who knew and loved and learned from Jesus in the flesh.
216pp. RaH 28

GOSWAMI, SHYAM SUNDAR. **JESUS CHRIST AND YOGA,** c$6.00. An examination
of Christ's life by an Indian yogi, pointing out the disciplines and ways in which Jesus sustained and developed his life force and great power of love in order to lead us to that divine inner being where we can truly be ourselves. 143pp. Fow

GWATKIN, HENRY. **SELECTIONS FROM EARLY CHRISTIAN WRITERS,** c$3.60.
Subtitled *Illustrative of Church History to the Time of Constantine.* The texts are quoted
with the original Greek and Latin on facing pages with the English translation. Index,
219pp. Cla 1897

HALL, MANLY P. **THE MYSTICAL CHRIST**, c$7.00. A presentation of the ministry of Christ and of his principal teachings. Hall draws on the ancient mystery teachings in his presentation. Index, 253pp. PRS 51

HAROLD, PRESTON. **THE SHINING STRANGER—UNORTHODOX INTERPRETA-TIONS OF JESUS AND HIS MISSION**, $3.95. The author's intention is to integrate the Christian legend with the understanding capacity of the modern mind. A religion is proposed where the participants realize Jesus rather than worship him. 443pp. DMd 67

HARTON, F.P. **THE ELEMENTS OF THE SPIRITUAL LIFE**, c$7.75. *Part I deals with the action of God in the soul by grace; Part II with the human resistance to the divine will and the means whereby that resistance may be overcome; Part III is a brief outline of the divine economy of the sacraments; Part IV is concerned with the life of prayer; and in Part V we consider the end of the spiritual life and the ways by which that end may be reached, concluding with a chapter on the guidance of souls with some consideration of the qualities of the ideal director. The author is an Anglican minister. Index, notes, 357pp.* SCK 32

HEER, FRIEDRICH, ed. **THE FIRES OF FAITH**, c$10.00. A study of the period between 312 and 1204 AD, emphasizing the turbulent spiritual leaders and movements of the time. Sixteen are studied in depth and these include St. Patrick, who strengthened the Christian Church in Ireland; William the Conqueror; Muhammad; Eric the Red, who introduced Christianity to Greenland; and St. Benedict, who provided a lasting model for monasticism. Supplementing the text are about 300 illustrations, nearly one third in full color, as well as numerous charts, maps and diagrams. Index, 160pp. Nws 73

HEINDEL, MAX. **THE ROSICRUCIAN CHRISTIANITY LECTURES**, $4.50. Twenty far ranging lectures on diverse topics relating to a central theme of Christianity and personal evolution. Of interest mainly to mystical occult metaphysicians. See Rosicrucian section for more Heindel. Index, 374pp. Ros 39

HELINE, CORINNE. **THE BLESSED VIRGIN MARY**, c$5.95. Beautiful volume showing the person of Mary as well as the eternal feminine archetype. Included are mystical evaluations of meaningful parts of her life along with a section connecting Zodiac symbolism with the infinite significance of herself. 125pp. NAP 71

_____. **THE MYSTERY OF THE CHRISTOS**, c$4.95. Deals with the Christ in his several aspects: cosmic, planetary, historical and mystical. In these various treatments references are made to the foremost events between the Annunciation and the Ascension, since each one has a specific meaning relative to progressive attainment in these different phases of spiritual unfoldment. 320pp. NAP

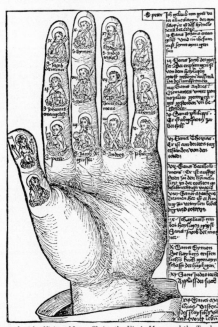

Hand decorated with effigies of Jesus Christ, the Virgin Mary, and the Twelve Apostles

HOLY ORDER OF MANS. **BOOK OF THE MASTER JESUS, VOL. I-III**, $3.50/each. This is a very spiritual interpretation of the life and ministry of Jesus, vividly written. The individuals who were intimately involved with Jesus and the times come alive. Many quotations from the Scriptures are included and the material is presented in chronological order. Volume I covers Jesus' early life, Volume II begins with his ministry, and Volume III traces his life as a teacher through his Ascension. About 230pp. each. HOM 74

_____. **THE GOLDEN FORCE**, $3.00. An integrated selection of teaching on living in harmony with the universe that God created and understanding one's purpose in the universal scheme. 120pp. HOM 75

_____. **THE GOLDEN NUGGETS**, $3.50. An anthology of insights into the *Reality of the Experience of Life* by a metaphysical Christian order. The format is topical, and each section is short, so many areas are covered. The subjects discussed are wide-ranging. 266pp. HOM 72

HOWARD, FATHER. **THE PERSONAL LIFE OF JESUS**, $1.25. A clairvoyant medium channels the words of a French preacher, along with those of Mary, Mary's other son and daughter, a Persian sage, a Brahman priest, and a Tibetan lama, all of whom knew Jesus personally and impart to us inside information so we can better understand him. The format may or may not be pretentious, but the material is thought provoking and very good. 140pp. Pee 72

HUGEL, FRIEDRICH von. **THE MYSTICAL ELEMENT OF RELIGION AS STUDIED IN SAINT CATHERINE OF GENOA AND HER FRIENDS**, c$14.00/set. *I was attracted at first, and I became more and more interested later on, in the saint of Genoa, not because of any immediately practicable suggestions furnished by her for my own life or that of others, but by certain rich and spiritual graces and deep and delicate doctrines hardly to be found elsewhere in as clear an articulation. Then, too, there was her outlook . . . which raised the whole great question as to the need and place of history and institutions in the spiritual life. And, finally, I here found rarely clear contrasts between genuine contemplative states and the more or less simply psycho-physical conditions which dogged them—conditions clearly perceived by the Saint, and by her alone, to be maladif and merely the price paid for the states which alone were of spiritual worth and significance.* Evelyn Underhill calls it *the best work on mysticism in the English language.* Two volumes, index, 923pp. Cla 23

ST. IGNATIUS. **THE SPIRITUAL EXERCISES OF ST. IGNATIUS**, $1.45. This volume, one of the great masterpieces of ascetical theology, is the fruit of the saint's own experiences and meditations and was used to guide himself and others toward spiritual perfection. Since St. Ignatius completed the **Exercises** in 1533, they have been universally recognized as a brilliant and inspired guide to the development of a deeper Christian spirituality. They were intended to be useful to people in all states of life and spiritual conditions. This is a modern translation by Anthony Mottola. Introduction, 200pp. Dou 64

JASPERS, KARL. **ANSELM AND NICHOLAS OF CUSA**, $3.50. The bulk of this volume is devoted to Nicholas of Cusa; the section on Anselm covers only twenty-five pages. The basic ideas of Nicholas are very fully discussed in an organized, textbook-like manner and a great deal of background information on the man and the times is offered. An excellent work of scholarship. Extracted from Jaspers' **The Great Philosophers**, Volume II. Bibliography, index, 188pp. HBJ 66

ST. JOHN OF THE CROSS (1542—1591)

St. John of the Cross was a close associate of St. Teresa of Avila and was one of the first members of the Discalced Order of Carmelite Friars which she founded. During his life he was noted for the rigor of his conduct and for his emphasis on internal meditation and silent prayer. He is regarded by many as Spain's major poet as well as one of the greatest Catholic mystics.

St. John gives witness to the sublime realities of the mystical life and of experiential union with God. However, John was also a theorizer and was able to make use of his philosophical, theological, and scriptural background in constructing a doctrinal synthesis of the spiritual life. But the purpose of his theory was to help clarify the issues for his readers and assist them in their journey up the mount of perfection to the perfect union with God. For John, God is like fire and man like a cold, damp, and dark log of wood. Through a process of purification and transformation effected by the fire of God's life, man can be gradually converted from his darkness and take on the properties of God's own fire, the light of His wisdom and the heat of His love. . . . In his major works . . . St. John of the Cross treats mainly of how one reaches perfection (or union with God), and of the life of divine union itself. In brief, this union is reached through the practice of the theological virtues, which purify the soul and unite it with God. The life of union with God is a life of perfect faith, hope, and charity.—Kieran Kavanaugh.

A recording of some of St. John's poetry is available. See the Records section for a description.

BARNSTONE, WILLIS, tr. **THE POEMS OF ST. JOHN OF THE CROSS**, $1.95. Barnstone provides an illuminating introduction in addition to his translation of the poems. The original Spanish version is on the facing page. Notes, bibliography, 124pp. NDP 68

BRENAN, GERALD. **ST. JOHN OF THE CROSS**, $5.95. This is the only full biography available which includes the complete poems in both Spanish and English. Brenan covers St. John's childhood and education, his association with St. Teresa, his imprisonment, torture and escape, and his final official disgrace and death. The account is written with great sensitivity and always with an eye to the following exposition and criticism of the poetry which introduces the translations of St. John's poems by Lynda Nicholson. The translations give the reader something very near the poems' literal prose sense, yet catch in many places the rhythm and intonation of the original. The Spanish version is on the facing page. Bibliography, notes, index. 233pp. CUP 73

CAMPBELL, ROY, tr. **POEMS OF ST. JOHN OF THE CROSS**, $1.95. A bi-lingual collection. 90pp. G&D 67

KAVANAUGH, KIERAN and OTILIO RODRIGUEZ, trs. **THE COLLECTED WORKS OF ST. JOHN OF THE CROSS**, $5.95. Kieran Kavanaugh is professor of spiritual theology at the Carmelite College of Theology and Otilio Rodriguez is a Spanish scholar who has a thorough familiarity with the works of St. John. This is a very carefully prepared volume which the two men spent years preparing and editing. The introduction is comprehensive and incorporates the most recent historical, doctrinal, and literary studies, mostly in French and Spanish. Included here are full translations of all the major works: **The Ascent of Mount Carmel, The Dark Night, The Spiritual Canticle,** and **The Living Flame of Love;** the minor works; and his poetry, with parallel Spanish/English texts. This is the translation for any reader seeking a clear, understandable statement of St. John's teachings. Includes extensive commentary. Recommended. 740pp. ICS 64

PEERS, E. ALLISON, tr. **ASCENT OF MOUNT CARMEL,** $1.95. Peers is the most noted translator of the works of both St. John and St. Teresa of Avila. His translations are considered very faithful and well written; and he supplies excellent introductions and notes. *On the opening page of* **The Ascent** *St. John indicates the nature of his treatise by declaring his intention to explain how one reaches the high state of perfection. This assertion at the outset plainly marks the practical character of the book. It is a work which describes the path to be followed in order to reach perfection, which he chooses to call union with God. . . . In addition to setting down rules,* **The Ascent** *gives a keen analysis of the principles which support them.*—Kieran Kavanaugh. Peers' introductory material is almost 100pp. 478pp. Dou 58

JERUSALEM by William Blake—detail

_____. **DARK NIGHT OF THE SOUL,** $1.25. A great and lasting work in the mystical tradition dealing with various stages experienced by the contemplative aspirant and the accompanying characteristics of each progressive stage. St. John's most famous work. 193pp. Dou 58

_____. **THE LIVING FLAME OF LOVE,** $1.45. This is a poem with a commentary. The poem is the song of a soul that has reached a highly perfect love within the state of transformation. Its stanzas refer to transient intense actual unions experienced by one advanced within this state of transformation. The commentary by St. John gives a general summary of each stanza, a detailed explanation of each verse, and many doctrinal explanations. 272pp. Dou 62

_____. **SPIRITUAL CANTICLE,** $2.95. *This book is a gift of God to man . . . one of the loveliest poems that the human heart has ever conceived, or the human mind expressed. . . . All can find much in it to instruct and inspire them; and many who have devoted their lives to the love of God count it among the dearest of their possessions.*—E. Allison Peers. 520pp. Dou 61

ZIMMERMAN, BENEDICT, ed. **THE DARK NIGHT OF THE SOUL,** $6.70. The works of St. John have at times been suppressed and there are various manuscripts, differing slightly in content. The editor has attempted here to present all the text in the most ancient copies of the **Dark Night,** with notes in both Spanish and English. The translation is not as flowing as Peers' or Kavanaugh's, but the introductory and background material are often useful for the serious student. General index and index to Biblical passages. 210pp. Cla 24

JOHNSTON, WILLIAM. **CHRISTIAN ZEN,** $2.25. See Zen Buddhism section.

KADLOUBOVSKY, E. and E.M. PALMER. **THE ART OF PRAYER,** c$10.60. This is a collection of texts on prayer, drawn from Greek and Russian sources. The spiritual teaching of the Orthodox Church appears here in its classic and traditional form, but expressed in unusually direct and vivid language. This material was compiled by Igumen Chariton of Valamo. 287pp. Fab 66

KADLOUBOVSKY, E. and G.E.H. PALMER, trs. **EARLY FATHERS FROM THE PHILOKALIA,** c$12.60. This book is drawn from the great collection of writings of Fathers of the Orthodox Church which was compiled in the eighteenth century under the title **Phil-**

okalia. This volume contains a representative collection of writings from the third to the seventh century, embracing the immense scope of the doctrines, knowledge and practice of saints who reached the highest levels of spiritual attainment. 421pp. Fab 54

_____. **WRITINGS FROM THE PHILOKALIA ON PRAYER OF THE HEART,** c$15.75. Shows the way to awaken and develop attention and consciousness; provides the means of acquiring training in what the Fathers, who reached the highest levels, called the art of arts and the science of sciences, leading a man toward the highest perfection open to him. 420pp. Fab 51

KAZANTZAKIS, NIKOS. **THE LAST TEMPTATION OF CHRIST,** $4.95. *In order to mount to the cross, the summit of sacrifice, and to God, the summit of immateriality, Christ passed through all the stages which the man who struggles passes through. This is why his suffering is so familiar to us; that is why we share it. . . . Every part of Christ's life is a conflict and a victory. He conquered the invincible enchantment of simple human pleasures; he conquered temptations, continually transubstantiated flesh into spirit, and ascended.* This is a fascinating novelistic rendition of the last years of Jesus' life. 506pp. S&S 60

_____. **SAVIORS OF GOD,** $1.95. *I am writing* **Spiritual Exercises,** *a mystical book wherein I trace a method by which the spirit may rise from cycle to cycle until it reaches the supreme Contact. There are five cycles, Ego, Humanity, Earth, the Universe, God. I describe how we ascend all these steps, and when we reach the highest how we live simultaneously all the previous cycles. . . . The search itself—upward, and with coherence—perhaps this is the purpose of the Universe. Purpose and means become identified. . . God is the supreme expression of the unwearied and struggling man.* This book is a collection of poetic aphorisms on the spiritual life and on union with God. Translation, notes and a long introduction, by Kimon Friar. 146pp. S&S 60

KEMPIS, THOMAS a. **THE IMITATION OF CHRIST,** $1.75. For more than five centuries, **The Imitation of Christ** has been acclaimed by men of every faith and belief as one of the greatest spiritual writings of all time. Next to the Bible, probably no other work in the Christian tradition has been as widely read nor has had such an influence. Written with the avowed intention of pointing the way by which all would be able to follow Christ's teachings and by so doing imitate his life, the timeless message of the humble monk is as inspiring in our era as the day it was written. Matthew Arnold called it *the most exquisite document, after those of the New Testament, of all that the Christian spirit has ever inspired.* Father Harold Gardiner has adapted Richard Whitford's classic translation of 1530 for this edition, and has supplied an introduction and notes. 236pp. Dou 55

_____. **THE IMITATION OF CHRIST,** $2.50. *My purpose in attempting a completely new version is to provide an accurate, unabridged, and readable modern translation, and thus to introduce this spiritual classic to a wider public.*—Leo Sherley-Price. Introduction, notes, 217pp. Pen 52

_____. **THE IMITATION OF CHRIST,** c$5.30. The Everyman's Library edition. 227pp. Dut 60

LAMSA, GEORGE. **THE MAN FROM GALILEE,** c$6.95. With the same devotion to linguistic and historical accuracy that made his translation of the Bible internationally famous, Dr. Lamsa has now applied his knowledge of Aramaic (the language of Jesus) to a new presentation of the life of Jesus through a skillful blending of the four Gospels. This is a very vivid presentation, which reads like a novel. Introduction, 308pp. Dou 70

_____. **MY NEIGHBOR JESUS,** $1.65. Subtitled *In the Light of His Own Language, People, and Times.* Introduction, 166pp. ABS 32

LANG, D.M. **THE BALAVARIANI,** c$8.00. Throughout medieval Christendom, the *Edifying Story of Balaam and Josaphat* was accepted as the classic exposition of the ideals of Christian monasticism and asceticism, renunciation of the world and of all human desires and passions. Modern research over the last century has shown that this legend is in reality an adaptation of the legendary biography of Gautama the Buddha, in particular the episodes of his miraculous birth, the Four Omens, the Great Renunciation, and his last mission and death. This is a translation of the full Georgian text of the oldest Christian version, with notes, introductory material, and illustrations. Index, 187pp. UCa 66

WILLIAM LAW

LAW, WILLIAM. **A SERIOUS CALL TO A DEVOUT AND HOLY LIFE,** $2.45. An edited and abridged version of an eighteenth century devotional classic which was designed to prod indifferent Christians into making an honest effort to live up to what they professed to believe. 158pp. Wes 75

_____. **THE SPIRIT OF PRAYER—THE SPIRIT OF LOVE,** c$6.15. The timeless communication between God and man is reasonably, practically, and encouragingly discussed by a deep thinker and true believer of the eighteenth century. 310pp. Cla 69

WALKER, A.K. **WILLIAM LAW: HIS LIFE AND HIS WORK,** c$13.90. A detailed study of Law's character and the whole of Law's work. Notes, bibliography, index, 287pp. SCK 73

LAWRENCE, BROTHER. **PRACTICE OF THE PRESENCE OF GOD,** c$1.95/.75. The value of this book lies in its Christian humility and simplicity. Brother Lawrence's one desire was for communion with God. This little record of his mind and heart is made up of notes of several conversations with him and letters written by him, set in order by a Cardinal of his time. There have been countless editions of this uplifting work. *[Brother Lawrence] showed us how, at any moment and in any circumstance, the soul that seeks God may find Him, and practice the presence of God.*—from the introduction. 63pp. PPP 63

LEVI. **AQUARIAN GOSPEL OF JESUS THE CHRIST**, c$5.95/2.95. The result of forty years of dedicated meditation and diligent probing into the Akashic record, this powerful work sheds invaluable light and revealing clarity upon the life and works of Jesus including vivid accounts of his ministry between childhood and Jordan Baptism. 270pp. Dev 07

C.S. LEWIS

GREEN, ROGER and WALTER HOOPER. **C.S. LEWIS—A BIOGRAPHY**, $3.95. This is the first biography of C.S. Lewis, written with full access to family papers and to Lewis' diaries, letters, and manuscripts. It provides a complete record of his life. It is also an account of Lewis' intellectual life, discussing the books that molded him and the genesis of his own writings. Throughout Lewis' career runs the theme of his conversion from atheism to Christianity. The narrative reads well. Index, 329pp. HBJ 74

LEWIS, C.S. **THE BEST OF C.S. LEWIS**, c$9.95. Contains the full text of the following five books: **The Screwtape Letters, The Great Divorce, Miracles, The Case for Christianity, and Christian Behavior**. 520pp. Cno 69

_____. **THE FOUR LOVES**, $2.45. A warmly personal book which describes the four basic kinds of human love—affection, friendship, erotic love, and the love of God. *The Four Loves deserves to become a minor classic as a modern mirror of souls, a mirror of the virtues and failing of human loving.* — **The New York Times Book Review**. 192pp. HBJ 60

_____. **THE GREAT DIVORCE**, $1.25. *Blake wrote* **The Marriage of Heaven and Hell**. . . . *I have written of their divorce.*—C.S. Lewis. Philosophy in the form of a novel. 128pp. McM 46

_____. **A GRIEF OBSERVED**, $1.95. A very revealing personal account of the desolation that Lewis felt after the loss of his wife and the inner turmoil that he went through on his way back to life. 151pp. Ban 61

_____. **MERE CHRISTIANITY**, $1.95. A revised and enlarged edition, with a new introduction, of three books: **The Case for Christianity, Christian Behavior**, and **Beyond Personality**. 190pp. McM 52

_____. **MIRACLES**, $1.45. An extended study of the possibility and probability of miracles, which cites the available historical evidence and incorporates Lewis' own beliefs. Index, 192pp. McM 47

_____. **REFLECTIONS ON THE PSALMS**, $1.95. Lewis relates the Psalms to their triple background: to the ancient Judaic religion which produced them, to the age of Christ when they took on new meanings, and to our daily experience in the modern world. This was the first religious book Lewis wrote after an interval of ten years. 128pp. Fon 58

_____. **THE SCREWTAPE LETTERS**, $1.25. Screwtape is a professional devil and self-described undersecretary of the Department of Temptation. The **Letters** gradually unfolds as a series of explicit directives and plans through which Screwtape's nephew Wormwood may subvert and twist human strivings toward love, charity, and wisdom, manipulating the human soul to his own diabolical ends. This edition is bound with **Screwtape Proposes a Toast**. Introduction, 187pp. McM 61

_____. **SURPRISED BY JOY**, $2.95. A frank autobiography which tells of Lewis' conversion from atheism to Christianity and discusses the early part of his life. 247pp. HBJ 55

_____. **THE WORLD'S LAST NIGHT**, $1.95. Seven essays discussing the efficacy of prayer, the various usages of the phrase *I believe*, the meaning of words like *culture* and *religion*, the interplay of *good work* and *good works*, the religious implications of life on other planets, and the doctrine of the Second Coming. **Screwtape Proposes a Toast** is also included. 113pp. HBJ 60

LEWIS, W.H., ed. **LETTERS OF C.S. LEWIS**, $4.95. Also includes a memoir by the editor, C.S. Lewis' brother. 308pp. HBJ 66

LEWIS, H. SPENCER. **THE MYSTICAL LIFE OF JESUS**, c$6.65. Detailed history of Jesus' background and activities, not spoken of in the New Testament writings. The information purports to come from ancient, well cared for secret records kept by the Rosicrucians since before the appearance of Jesus. Index, 320pp. Amo 37

_____. **THE SECRET DOCTRINES OF JESUS**, c$6.60. Insights into the being and personality of Jesus. Outlined is Jesus' role in the larger drama of undercover organizations attempting to free man's soul from eternally repressive power structures. Index, 237pp. Amo 37

LOSSKY, VLADIMIR. **MYSTICAL THEOLOGY OF EASTERN CHURCH**, c$10.80. *It is our intention, in the following essay, to study certain aspects of eastern spirituality in relation to the fundamental themes of the Orthodox dogmatic tradition. In the present work, therefore, the term* mystical theology *denotes no more than a spirituality which expresses a doctrinal attitude.* Notes, index, 252pp. Cla 57

MAINE, G., ed. **LIFE AND TEACHINGS OF CHRIST**, c$1.75. Selections from the New Testament, topically arranged. Introduction, index. 160pp. Dev 53

MARTIN, RALPH. **WORSHIP IN THE EARLY CHURCH**, $3.45. An examination of how the earliest Christian worshiped God. Notes, index, 144pp. Eer 64

MASSEY, GERALD. **THE HISTORICAL JESUS AND THE MYTHICAL CHRIST**, $5.00. An exceptionally mystical book dealing with the symbolism and allegory of the gospels, and incorporating Gnostic insights. Glossary, notes, index. 233pp. HeR nd

MEAD, G.R.S. **APOLLONIUS OF TYANA—THE PHILOSOPHER REFORMER OF THE FIRST CENTURY AD.**, c$5.00. A fascinating and scholarly piece of research into the life of one of the most influential individuals of the early Christian era. Reveals the personality, teaching, circumstances and events of this mystery-enshrouded figure, traces his travels, and probes into the influences which helped mold his philosophy. 168pp. UnB 66

_____. **THE HYMN OF JESUS—ECHOES FROM THE GNOSIS**, $1.00. An excellent set of verses believed to be among the earliest of Christian literature. These were very possibly the basis for communal services among the original families of Christ. 75pp. TPH07

McNEILL, JOHN. **THE CELTIC CHURCHES**, c$10.00. A comprehensive study of Celtic Christianity from 200—1200 AD. The major saints are discussed in detail and the missionary activities are also examined. Bibliography, index, notes. 289pp. UCh 74

THOMAS MERTON

Thomas Merton (1915—68) was a promising poet and writer during his college and post-collegiate years, but, on his own admission, he was a disorganized personality searching for meaning in life. After a rather sudden conversion to Catholicism . . . he entered a Trappist monastery in 1941, seeking to isolate himself completely from society in the hope of finding God in solitude and prayer. He did, however, under monastic obedience, continue his writing from within the monastery. For close to 27 years he maintained this isolation despite the fact that publication of his autobiography, **The Seven Storey Mountain** *(1948), brought him great literary prominence. His early monastic writings were on strictly religious and monastic themes. . . . Though he remained a strictly cloistered monk until just before his sudden death in 1968, from about 1958 on his writings disclose a vastly expanded social consciousness, and a much broader awareness of man's place and function in the world. The general context of his life shifted so that he became publicly concerned about social problems and the impact of social change on man's relationship to God and to his neighbor. From the vertical, other-wordly devotion of his earlier works, Merton shifted his emphasis to a direct, horizontal, deeply engaged, often militant concern for the critical situation of man in the world.—* F.J. Kelly, **Man Before God.**

In his later years Merton also moved away from the strict Catholic viewpoint and into more sympathy with the Buddhist way of life. This was due in part to the influence of his close friend, D.T. Suzuki. Merton was one of those rare Western minds which was entirely at home in Asian experience. The Asian trip during which Merton had his fatal accident was, many thought, an attempt to break out of the cloister and become more actively involved in the world. Some even felt that he was prepared to renounce his Catholicism and become a Buddhist. For his works in this area see the Zen Buddhism section and his selections from Chuang Tzu in the Chinese Philosophy section. Also see his **Asian Journal**, reviewed with Comparative Religion.

HART, PATRICK, ed. **THOMAS MERTON, MONK**, $1.95. Hart was Merton's private secretary, and is therefore uniquely qualified to bring together this composite monastic view of the man. The result is a moving, forceful, and honest appraisal of Merton. *The articles and poems chosen for this volume were written by monks and nuns from Europe and America, most of whom knew [Merton] personally. They bear witness to Merton's contemplative vision, and reflect the monastic frame of reference for his influence as a spiritual force in the fifties and as a social critic and bridge-builder between East and West in the sixties.*—from the introduction. Includes an essay by James Fox, Merton's Abbot for twenty years, and a bibliography of all his works. Woodcuts, 230pp. Dou 74

HIGGINS, JOHN. **THOMAS MERTON ON PRAYER**, $1.75. A comprehensive study of Merton's thoughts on prayer which reflects the full scope of his contemplative life and his writings on every aspect of prayer. To place Merton's idea of contemplative prayer in its full perspective, Higgins explores the two central forces of Merton's spirituality: man's search for God and his discovery of God through love shared with other individuals. Bibliography, notes, 200pp. Dou 75

KELLY, FREDERICK. **MAN BEFORE GOD**, c$7.95. Subtitled *Thomas Merton on Social Responsibility*, this is an in depth study which reveals Merton's concept of religious man and also the shift in his concerns from religious ones to contemporary secular porblems such as the threat of nuclear annihilation, war and peace, non-violent alternatives for social change, modern trends towards de-humanization, Christian renewal and ecumenism, and Oriental spirituality. Topics include an excellent study of the man and his writings. Merton as a social critic, religious man in his writings, and the social dimensions and concerns of religious man. Notes, 301pp. Dou 74

McDONNELL, THOMAS, ed. **A THOMAS MERTON READER**, $2.95. Here in one volume are important selections from Merton's major works and lesser known writings, beginning with his first book, **The Seven Storey Mountain**, and concluding with selections from his **Asian Journal**. The anthology clearly reflects Merton's own personal spiritual growth and development. Merton speaks on many themes: war, love, peace, Eastern thought and spirituality, monastic life, art, the psalms, contemplation, and solitude. This new edition of the **Reader** is a most welcome volume and is an excellent way to gain exposure to Merton's thought. 516pp. Dou 38

MERTON, THOMAS. **CONTEMPLATION IN A WORLD OF ACTION**, $2.45. *In this book, Merton presents his finest and clearest statements on the monastic life.... His concern was for the fullest and most complete contemplative life and, though his other writings discussed the results of that life, it is in the 21 essays of this book that we are asked to consider directly the contemplative life.* —**The New York Times Book Review**. 396pp. Dou 71

_____. **CONJECTURES OF A GUILTY BYSTANDER**, $1.95. Merton describes his book as *a personal and monastic meditation, a testimony of Christian reflection in the mid-twentieth century, a confrontation of twentieth century questions in the light of a monastic commitment, which inevitably makes one something of a bystander*. 350pp. Dou 65

_____. **CONTEMPLATIVE PRAYER**, $1.45. Looking from many sides, Merton wants to show the value of this *non activity* in breaking through the barriers of over-organized rituals into spiritual reality and meaning. 115pp. Dou 69

_____. **DISPUTED QUESTIONS**, c$3.45. Eleven essays, rich in meditative insights about various esoteric and exoteric aspects of Christian philosophy. Discusses love, government, spiritual art, and the views and doctrines of several well known historical personages. 216pp. FSG 53

_____. **EMBLEMS OF A SEASON OF FURY**, $2.45. In these poems Merton shows a deep awareness of the problems of the world beyond his monastery walls. He said that the twentieth century man who has not meditated on Auschwitz does not yet know the meaning of meditation or the meaning of his own times. These poems are often points for such meditation. There is also a section of translations from the works of several Latin American poets. 149pp. NDP 61

_____. **GEOGRAPHY OF LOGRAIRE**, $2.75. This is Merton's final testament as a poet, completed a few months before he set out on his final Asian journey. The text lacks final editing, but it is substantially a complete, self-contained work. *Lograire* is first of all a country of the imagination, but it is also a person—Merton himself— for its *geography* is the map of his mind. The charting in the poem is his search for self-location. Sections of personal experience are set against passages re-imagined from anthropological and historical texts, material that Merton chose for its character of myth to illustrate the general experience of mankind. Notes on sources, 153pp. NDP 68

_____. **THE LAST OF THE FATHERS**, c$12.10. This is a biographical study of the life and work of St. Bernard of Clairvaux, including a translation of the Encyclical Letter **Doctor Mellifluus**. St. Bernard (twelfth century) was one of the greatest Christian mystics, although he is not very well known today and virtually nothing of his is readily available. Bibliography, index, 123pp. Gre 54

_____. **MY ARGUMENT WITH THE GESTAPO**, $3.95. This is the earliest of Merton's full length prose works and it tells of the adventures of a young man, clearly identified by the name Thomas Merton, who travels from America to Europe to report on the war with Germany from the viewpoint of a poet. It is not, however, an autobiographical work. 259pp. NDP 68

_____. **NEW SEEDS OF CONTEMPLATION**, $2.45. A much enlarged, revised version of **Seeds of Contemplation**, one of Merton's most widely read and best loved works. For Father Merton, *Every moment and every event of every man's life on earth plants something in his soul.... Most of these unnumbered seeds perish and are lost, because men are not prepared to receive them: for such seeds as these cannot spring up anywhere except in the good soil of freedom, spontaneity and love*. 297pp. NDP 61

_____. **NO MAN IS AN ISLAND**, $1.45. Sixteen essays centering around the reality behind the quotation used as the title. 197pp. Dou 55

_____. **RAIDS ON THE UNSPEAKABLE**, $2.25. This paperback collection of Merton's prose writings reveals the extent to which he moved from the other-wordly devotion of his earlier work to a direct, deeply engaged, often militant concern with the

critical situation of man in the world. He looks candidly and without illusion at the world of the sixties, using many literary forms to vary the perspective—and though he sees dark horizons, his ultimate answer is one of Christian hope. Illustrations, 182pp. NDP 6

_____. **THE SEVEN STOREY MOUNTAIN**, $2.45. The autobiography of a man who turned his heart and soul inside out for the world. This masterpiece of expression is the chronicle of a totally dedicated and supremely successful attempt to realize the spirit of God in the life of man. This book could be used as a complete manual of introspective wisdom to help illuminate the path. 512pp. Dou 48

_____, tr. **THE WISDOM OF THE DESERT**, $1.50. This translation of the writings of the hermits who turned their back on a corrupt society remarkably like our own was one of Merton's favorites among his own books. Merton deeply identified with the legendary fourth century Christian Fathers who sought solitude and contemplation in the deserts of the Near East. 81pp. NDP 60

RICE, EDWARD. **THE MAN IN THE SYCAMORE TREE**, $1.95. This biography, subtitled *The Good Times and Hard Life of Thomas Merton* was written by one of Merton's closest friends. Rice not only tells the story of Merton from his childhood through his monastic years up to his fateful Far Eastern trip, but he writes more frankly and realistically than Merton, as a Trappist, was able to do. The reader can get a good feeling for Merton the man from this volume. It is full of photographs from all periods of Merton's life along with some of Merton's own drawings. 192pp. Dou 70

STONE, NAOMI, PATRICK HART and JAMES LAUGHLIN, eds. **THE ASIAN JOURNAL OF THOMAS MERTON**, $3.45. See the Comparative Religion section.

SUSSMAN, CORNELIA and IRVING. **THOMAS MERTON**, c$6.95. A moving biography based on Merton's published works and on discussions with those who knew him. The tone is personal and analytical and the authors' aim seems to be to make Merton come alive. Not a definitive study, but a highly readable, informative one geared toward the general reader. Bibliography, index, 175pp. McM 76

MONTGOMERY, RUTH. **COMPANIONS ALONG THE WAY**, $1.95. Dictated by Arthur Ford (in automatic writing) in 1973—after his death—this is the story of an incarnation Ford and Montgomery had shared 2,000 years ago when she was born as the third sister of Lazarus and Ford was their father, the Rabbi Jeremiah. The account is full of previously unpublished revelations of Jesus' life and ministry. The book also details group karma, the transmigrations of groups or clusters of souls to physical bodies at approximately the same time. Ford also tells of nine other meetings on earth from the Palestinian incarnation to the nineteenth century. 256pp. Pop 74

NICHOLAS OF CUSA. **THE VISION OF GOD**, $1.45. Nicholas was an ordained churchman dedicated to reform. As one might imagine in fifteenth century Europe, this turned out to be an extremely taxing chore. Fortunately, as his writing clearly shows, suffering and discouragement strengthened him in faith, hope, and great love of God. 152pp. Ung 28

NICOLL, MAURICE. **THE MARK**, c$6.50. See section on Gurdjieff. Wei

_____. **THE NEW MAN**, $2.00. See section on Gurdjieff. Pen

Early portrait of St. Paul

ST. PAUL. **A SYNTHESIS OF THE TEACHINGS OF ST. PAUL**, $2.00. The teachings are topically arranged and cover the following areas: the Holy Trinity; spirit, soul, and body; the law; and the redemptive graces and virtues. 39pp. ShW 22

PHILOSTRATUS. **LIFE OF APOLLONIUS**, $1.75. *Not a scrap of secure contemporary evidence survives to illuminate the career of Apollonius, the wise man of Tyana. It is extraordinary that this minor mystic, from a remote city, ... should have acquired long after his death no less a reputation than that of an anti-Christ. Apollonius raised the dead, healed the sick, and ascended bodily into heaven: so, at least, his biographer Philostratus affirms.... Apollonius was a neo-Pythagorean ... whose pursuit of truth and sincerity brought him into conflict with the established government of his time. Philostratus saw in this eccentric worker of miracles a magnificent subject for romantic and legendary biography. For Philostratus Apollonius was not an anti-Christ, but in his biography he provided the stories which made him one.* —from the introduction. Philostratus wrote in the third century AD. Index, 255pp. Pen 70

the Flemish mystics, and must take high rank in any list of Christian contemplatives and saints. This is the only edition currently in print and the only English translation extant of this fourteenth century mystic. It is important reading for all who are deeply interested in mystical insights and in contemplation. In addition to the translations, there is a long introduction by Ms. Underhill. Notes, 291pp. CCI 74

SADHU, MOUNI. **THEURGY**, c$12.10. A collection of Christian-oriented prayers which the author has garnered from a variety of religious traditions and which he feels are especially effective. The prayers are topically organized. 263pp. A&U 65

SARAYDARIAN, HAROUTIN. **CHRIST–AVATAR OF SACRIFICIAL LOVE**, c$6.00. **Christ–Avatar of Sacrificial Love** *is written to show the uniqueness of Christ, as the World Teacher, as the Path leading to the Brotherhood of men, and to innermost Reality within man and universe.* The work is very inspirationally written with many quotations from the works of Alice Bailey. For a full description of Sarayadarian, see the Mysticism section. Oversize, 128pp. AEG 74

SCHWEITZER, ALBERT. **THE MYSTICISM OF PAUL THE APOSTLE**, $2.95. A detailed survey, topically organized and including an extensive number of quotations from the New Testament and from other Christian writers. Indices, 411pp. Sea 31

ST. SERAPHIM. **SPIRITUAL INSTRUCTIONS OF ST. SERAPHIM OF SAROV**, $1.95. St. Seraphim (1759–1833) is one of the greatest saints of the Eastern Orthodox tradition. He applied himself to Christian and, in particular, Eastern Christian, spiritual techniques, including the *prayer of the heart*, but the intensity of his life, realization and spiritual work places him among those transcendent spiritual beings who stand outside tradition, orthodoxy, dogma and history. This volume includes an introduction to his life and work by A.F. Dobbi-Bateman and a translation of the **Conversation of St. Seraphim with Nicholas Motovilov.** This text is a report of an actual experience, written by a devotee which describes direct transmission of spiritual consciousness and force. 94pp. DHP 73

SQUIRE, AELRED. **ASKING THE FATHERS**, $7.00. This book attempts to trace the main lines of the teaching of the great spiritual masters of the past in terms of both form and method. The material is arranged into major topics and each subject is discussed at length, with quotations from many of the masters. Notes, index, 249pp. SCK 73

STEINER, RUDOLF. **CHRIST IN THE TWENTIETH CENTURY**, $.95. Translation of a lecture discussing the differing views of Christ over the centuries. Rudolf Steiner has written extensively on Christianity and Christian themes and he is probably the best twentieth century exponent of the mystical aspects of Christianity. We have just included a few of his works here; see the Steiner section for the rest of his books. 20pp. API 71

_____. **CHRISTIANITY AS MYSTICAL FACT**, $2.95. Steiner's interpretation of many famous ancient myths, with half the book explaining how the writings of Christianity restate and personalize the message of the old stories. 195pp. Ant 47

_____. **FROM JESUS TO CHRIST**, c$5.50. This is the favorite book of some of the people we know who are deeply into Steiner. Steiner sees the Christ-event as a continuous happening, something that becomes different in the twentieth century from what it was in the first, and which will be still different in the future. This idea is developed here in a variety of ways. An especially interesting selection discusses the characteristics of the two different Jesus children spoken of by St. Luke and St. Matthew. Another one studies the whole relation of the Christ-Being to that of Jesus the man. Ten lectures are transcribed here. 184pp. RSP 73

_____. **THE MYSTERIES OF THE EAST AND OF CHRISTIANITY**, $2.25. These four lectures given by Steiner in Berlin in 1913 delve into the realm of spiritual realities underlying life on the earth (or any other place for that matter) and how and why we should strive to see them more clearly as our main life's activity; and how most of us in one way or another get wrapped up and tied down in life's illusions rather than its truth. As always there is also plenty of far ranging speculation and teaching on broad cosmic and universal levels. 77pp. RSP 43

SUARES, CARLOS. **THE PASSION OF JUDAS**, $2.95. According to Suares, Judas was not weak and sinful; on the contrary, he was strong and selfless in fulfilling his destiny as Christ required. This work, written as a play following very closely the gospel of John, dramatizes this point. 116pp. ShP 73

PIERRE TEILHARD DE CHARDIN

Teilhard (1881–1955) was a French priest-scientist who spent much of his life in China. He achieved a remarkable unity between his spiritual life and his scientific pursuits, but his spiritual writings never received the approval of the Church; consequently none of his books were published until after his death. He was exiled from France by the Church because of his heretical ideas and travelled to sites of geological and paleontological interest, developing his theories about man and his place in the universe. He finally settled in China, as Director of the Peking Geological Service, where he remained for twenty years. Throughout his life he was a prolific writer. As there were few intellectually compatible people in Peking at this time he often found himself experiencing deeply the meaning of solitude. He also conducted a voluminous correspondence with several friends in the West. In 1946 he returned to Paris, where he lived and worked with his fellow Jesuits. He was allowed to publish only his scientific papers and forbidden to lecture in public except on purely scientific matters. In spite of this he became one of the most sought out and

---

PRABHAVANANDA, SWAMI. **THE SERMON ON THE MOUNT ACCORDING TO VEDANTA**, $1.25. See section on Indian Philosophy.

RAMACHARAKA, YOGI. **MYSTIC CHRISTIANITY**, c$7.00. A detailed examination of historical events and perspectives surrounding Jesus, and their meaning in terms of man's ultimate realization. See Indian Philosophy section for more of Ramacharaka's work. 268pp. YPS 07

READ, ANNE. **EDGAR CAYCE ON JESUS AND HIS CHURCH**, $.95. This is a retelling of the narrative pieced together from the readings, rather than quotations from the readings themselves. Occasional quotations are included. The material is from many of the same readings as Furst's book, but the presentation here is quite different. No commentary is included. 188pp. War 70

REICH, WILHELM. **THE MURDER OF CHRIST**, $2.75. See the Reich section.

REINHOLD, H.A., ed. **THE SOUL AFIRE–REVELATIONS OF THE MYSTICS**, $2.45. Presents a wide view of the feelings and thoughts of the most mystical Christians who have ever lived. Selected writings from a magnificent collection of souls, arranged into relevant categories can be a real tune-in to the history and depth of spiritual devotion in the West. 480pp. Dou 73

RINALDI, PETER. **IT IS THE LORD**, $1.50. Rinaldi has made a hobby of studying the shroud of Christ for some forty years and has written twenty-five possible explanations to disprove its validity. In each case he tells of his research along that line, and why the objection doesn't hold up. This is a most convincing book. The shroud of Christ has been preserved through the years as the linen that the body of Jesus was wrapped in after the Crucifixion, and it contains a remarkable likeness of a crucified man that is, according to Fr. Rinaldi, Jesus. 124pp. War 72

ROBERTS, ALEXANDER and JAMES DONALDSON, eds. **THE ANTE-NICENE FATHERS, VOL. I**, c$11.25. This is an excellent series. The books are beautifully bound and quite reasonably priced, and the translations are not readily available elsewhere. This volume includes the writings of the following Fathers: St. Clement, Mathetes, Polycarp, Ignatius, Barnabas, Papias, Justin Martyr, and Irenaeus (the first six of whom are generally known as the Apostolic Fathers). Double column, notes, indices. 610pp. Eer 1885

_____. **ANTE-NICENE FATHERS, VOL. II**, c$11.25. This volume presents the writings of the Fathers of the second century: Hermas, Tatian, Athenagoras, Theophilus, and Clement of Alexandria. 442pp are devoted to Clement's writings. Double column, notes, indices, 629pp. Eer 1885

_____. **THE ANTE-NICENE FATHERS, VOL. III**, c$11.25. This volume is devoted to the writings of the founder of Latin Christianity, Tertullian. Notes, indices, double column. 745pp. Eer 1885

ROLLE. **THE FIRE OF LOVE**, $2.95. The writing of a pious fourteenth century hermit. He describes a purity of love so powerful it burns away all material attachments stopping the realization of eternal life. 192pp. Pen 71

RUYSBROECK, JOHN OF. **JOHN OF RUYSBROECK**, $16.80. This is a recent reprint of Evelyn Underhill's edited version of C.A. Wynschenk Dim's translation. Three of his most important works (**The Adornment of the Spiritual Marriage, The Sparkling Stone,** and **The Book of Supreme Truth**) are included here. Jan van Ruysbroeck is the greatest of

discussed men in Paris, and his books were circulated in scientific and religious circles in manuscript form. He spent most of his last years in the U.S. After his death his written works were no longer under the jurisdiction of the Church and they began to be released for publication. Since then his position as a seminal thinker has been proclaimed worldwide.

The primary concern of Teilhard's life was to study *the area where God and the cosmos come together*, to seek and reveal the unity underlying religion and science, spirit and matter. Moreover, his experience and reflection during fifty years of professional research on five continents impelled him to formulate and then project into the future the laws that he believed have governed evolution in the past. *The past*, he wrote in 1945, *has revealed to me how the future is built.*

Our human task is to build that future. Evolution, said Teilhard, is in man's hands. Indeed, without our strenuous and immediate cooperation evolution on this planet, and with it life itself, may come to an end. The direction of the future revealed to Teilhard by the unfolding of the past is: more being in closer union. Heightened consciousness will always accompany increasing complexity. As the process of creative union continues, aided by sophisticated modern communications, people will be united in a timeless and richly diversified community. The force that propels us from below, that works in us and through us, is love. Thus Teilhard challenged us to do our utmost to increase consciousness, union, love.

Looking into the future Teilhard saw the long ascent, matter-life-thought-spirit, coming to its consummation in a radiant and loving supra-personal center on which the whole of evolution converges. He called that center Omega.

Some who wish to learn more about Teilhard may be tempted to take up his masterwork, **The Phenomenon of Man**, first. We would advise against this. A wiser plan would be to start in low gear with an introduction to his life and work by another author, then move on to some of his correspondence, after that to one of his more introductory writings on his spiritual thought and his scientific vision. Only after all this background reading would we recommend tackling **The Phenomenon of Man**.

BRUTEAU, BEATRICE. **EVOLUTION TOWARD DIVINITY**, c$10.00. In developing his synthesis of contemporary science and traditional religion, Teilhard developed a number of ideas and images which find more or less close parallels in the various strands of Hindu philosophy. Teilhard, however, was not only unaware of these similarities but even denounced Hinduism as a system and an outlook fundamentally inimical to the world-view he was setting forth. Dr. Bruteau has been Director and Vice President of the American Teilhard de Chardin Association and did her doctoral dissertation on the philosophy of Sri Aurobindo. In this volume she refutes Teilhard's criticisms and produces a brilliant comparison of the points of view represented by Teilhard and by Hindu thought. Includes many quotations and reference notes. Index, bibliography. 270pp. TPH 74

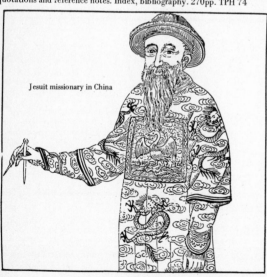

Jesuit missionary in China

CUENOT, CLAUDE. **SCIENCE AND FAITH IN TEILHARD DE CHARDIN**, c$4.40. This volume consists of four parts. The first two are lectures, expanded for this edition, given by Dr. Cuenot at the first annual conference of the British Teilhard de Chardin Association, under the titles: *The Spirituality of Teilhard* and *Science and Faith in Teilhard*. Then follows *A Comment* by Professor Garaudy, also from the conference. The book concludes with an original essay by Dr. Cuenot entitled *Teilhard de Chardin: A Tentative Summing-up*. Dr. Cuenot has written extensively on Teilhard and is a member of the Administrative Council of the French Teilhard Association. Index, 112pp. GaP 67

KNIGHT, ALICE. **THE MEANING OF TEILHARD DE CHARDIN**, $3.95. Subtitled *A Primer*, this is the best overall introduction to Teilhard's philosophy that we have seen. It is well written and covers all aspects of Teilhardian thought in a relatively easy to under-

stand fashion. The text also includes the most complete Teilhard bibliography we have seen and a biographical chapter entitled *Who Was Teilhard*. Recommended. DAC 74

KOPP, JOSEPH. **TEILHARD DE CHARDIN**, $1.45. Subtitled *A New Synthesis of Evolution*, this is a clear and careful examination of Teilhard's life and works as they relate to the subject. This is a good first book to read, well written and presented. 72pp. Pau 64

MOONEY, CHRISTOPHER. **TEILHARD DE CHARDIN AND THE MYSTERY OF CHRIST**, $1.45. The brilliant, formative and creative thinking of this philosopher and religious scientist is presented in order to construct a vision of his world view and the relation of the world and man to Christ. 318pp. Dou 64

O'CONNOR, CATHERINE. **WOMAN AND COSMOS**, c$8.95. This is an in depth exploration of *The Feminine* and the role of women in the thought of Teilhard. The text includes numerous quotations and the material presented is not explored elsewhere in other books on Teilhard. This looks like Sister O'Connor's doctoral thesis. Notes, bibliography, 188pp. PrH 74

SIMON, CHARLIE. **FAITH HAS NEED OF ALL THE TRUTH**, c$5.95. This is a popularized account of the life of Teilhard, written for the general reader. Index, bibliography, 180pp. Dut 74

TEILHARD de CHARDIN, PIERRE. **ACTIVATION OF ENERGY**, $2.95. Essays from 1939 to 1955 which extend and develop the theme begun in **Human Energy**. 410pp. HBJ 63

_____. **BUILDING THE EARTH**, $1.25. A collection of six essays: *We Must Save Mankind, The Spirit of the Earth, Human Energy, Thoughts on Progress, On the Possible Basis of a Common Credo*, and *The Psychological Conditions of Human Unification*. The material is well translated and the beginning reader can get a good feeling of Teilhard's philosophy from the essays. Also includes a good basic study of Teilhard's life and work by John Kobler and a bibliography. 116pp. Avo 69

_____. **CHRISTIANITY AND EVOLUTION**, $2.95. Nineteen essays which blend theological speculation with practical applications. Index, 255pp. HBJ 71

_____. **THE DIVINE MILIEU**, $2.95. This is considered Teilhard's most important spiritual work, and the key to his religious and meditational ideas. The vision presented here is universal in its application. The book includes a long essay on *The Man*, which presents important background material. Index, 160pp. H&R 68

_____. **THE FUTURE OF MAN**, $2.95. As the title suggests, this book presents a view of man, his evolution, and his relations with the earth and the universe. The material here is more approachable than most of Teilhard's writing and it includes a seminal chapter on the formation of the Noosphere. Index, 332pp. H&R 69

_____. **HOW I BELIEVE**, $1.25. *I have tried to pin down, in what follows, the reasons for my faith as a Christian, with the shades of emphasis it bears, and also its limitations or difficulties.* 91pp. H&R 69

_____. **HYMN OF THE UNIVERSE**, $1.95. In this, the most mystical of Teilhard's works, we see the poetic and visionary side of this man of prayer more intensely revealed than in his more scientific works. Teilhard glorifies and praises matter as the incarnate divine substance veiling the Christ principle of divinity. 164pp. H&R 61

_____. **LET ME EXPLAIN**, $2.45. J.P. Demoulin has selected and arranged this compilation of central passages from Teilhard's most important works in an effort to summarize the whole of Teilhard's thought in one volume. In 1948 Teilhard himself drew up an outline of what he considered the stages, the directions, and the major elements of his thought and this outline has guided M. Demoulin in his choice of extracts. The material is topically arranged and this edition includes an introduction, notes on Teilhard's vocabulary, an annotated bibliography, and an index. Presents a good overview for the beginning reader. 189pp. H&R 70

_____. **LETTERS FROM A TRAVELLER**, $2.45. These letters, written mainly from China but also during Teilhard's worldwide travels, form a wonderful introduction to the man and his thought. This edition also includes over sixty pages of background material in three essays by Sir Julian Huxley, Fr. Pierre Leroy, and Claude Aragonnes. Illustrations, index, 380pp. H&R 68

_____. **LETTERS TO TWO FRIENDS: 1928-52**, $3.95. Here two of Teilhard's correspondents presently living in the U.S. have chosen from a long series of letters those passages dealing with the author's daily life and the development of his thought. This edition includes a prologue by Rene d'Ouince and an essay on Teilhard as a scientist by Theodosius Dobzhansky. Index, 236pp. NAL 69

_____. **MAN'S PLACE IN NATURE**, $1.95. The aim of this work is to try to define experientially the phenomenon of the human mind by determining structurally and historically the human's present position in relation to the other forms the cosmos has assumed. 120pp. H&R 56

_____. **ON HAPPINESS**, c$3.95. Happiness comes through personal growth, through love and union with another (or with others) and through commitment to a larger cause, says Teilhard. This small book contains a lecture given on happiness in Peking in 1928, plus three wedding addresses. 93pp. H&R 66

_____. **ON LOVE**, c$3.95. Excerpts from most of Teilhard's major works briefly but thoroughly outline his thoughts on the subject. 95pp. H&R 67

_____. **ON SUFFERING**, c$4.95. Extracts from Teilhard's writings on the title theme, bound into a little gift book. 120pp. H&R 75

_____. **THE PHENOMENON OF MAN**, $2.50. A probing and insightful look into the life and philosophy of this great modern thinker, who made it his task to reinterpret the profound and eternal concepts of Christianity in the light of science and man's continuous evolution. 320pp. H&R 55

_____. **THE PRAYER OF THE UNIVERSE**, $1.25. A selection of essays from the larger work *Writings in Time of War* (World War I) including *In the Form of Christ, Cosmic Life, The Mystical Milieu, The Eternal Feminine,* and *The Priest.* This mystical and philosophical contemplation of the works of God was written while Teilhard was a stretcher bearer in the War and edited later. Notes, 191pp. H&R 73

_____. **TOWARD THE FUTURE**, $3.95. Essays which derive from Teilhard's concern to reveal the true meaning of our age and to stimulate *the sense of man and the sense of the Christian.* Index, 224pp. HBJ 75

TOWERS, BERNARD. **TEILHARD DE CHARDIN**, $1.75. An introduction to Teilhard's life, thought, and significance. Part of a series entitled **Makers of Contemporary Theology.** Bibliography, 46pp. Kno 66

ST. TERESA OF AVILA

St. Teresa and St. John of the Cross lived and worked in close co-operation with each other. They took it as their mission in life to reform the existing monasteries, to found new ones, and to reintroduce the full rigor of the religious life which they considered proper for the cloister. To this end they worked in collaboration against the most determined opposition. The two saints lived to see the subsidence of the opposition to their work and to bring it to a successful conclusion. St. Teresa is probably the best known female saint and is considered one of the greatest women in history. She was a prolific writer and is best known for her autobiography in which she observed the different stages of her mystical life.

She is a mystic—and more than a mystic. Her works, it is true, are well known in the cloister and have served as nourishment to many who are far advanced on the Way of Perfection, and who, without her aid, would still be beginners in the life of prayer. Yet they have also entered the homes of millions living in the world and have brought consolation, assurance, hope and strength to souls who, in the technical sense, know nothing of the life of contemplation. Devoting herself, as she did, with the most wonderful persistence and tenacity, to the sublimest task given to man—the attempt to guide others toward perfection—she succeeded so well in that task that she is respected everywhere as an incredibly gifted teacher, who has revealed, more perhaps than any who came before her, the nature and extent of those gifts which the Lord has laid up in this life for those who love Him.—E. Allison Peers.

PEERS, E. ALLISON. **THE AUTOBIOGRAPHY OF ST. TERESA OF AVILA**, $2.45. This autobiography, written at the express command of St. Teresa's confessors to give an accurate and detailed account of her spiritual progress, has been a treasured spiritual legacy since its publication. The first part of the book is autobiographical in the ordinary sense: it describes the author's early life and education, the inner conflicts which she experienced, and finally the crisis which ended in her resolve to *seek perfection and walk in the way of prayer.* After a section which describes the contemplative life under the figure of the *four waters,* each of which corresponds to one stage of spiritual progress, St. Teresa returns to her description of her inner life. Her concern is not to theorize, but to attract others to love of God. 399pp. Dou 60.

_____. **INTERIOR CASTLE**, $1.75. This is one of the most celebrated books on mystical theology in existence. It is the most sublime and mature of St. Teresa's works, and one reads in it the full blossoming of a thoroughly humble and exquisitely divine nature, whose inspiration touches even those who don't know her name or anything she did. **Interior Castle** tells the story of a soul as one travels through the mystical mansions and nears the center of life, which is love, and the innermost truth, which is God. 235pp. Dou 61

_____. **THE WAY OF PERFECTION**, $1.75. In an attempt to reform the order of nuns to which she belonged, St. Teresa set down, although she always said she was not a writer and would only do the best she was capable of, one of the finest and most sublime of the timeless classics of spiritual prayer for a life lived for pure love of the Divine. One who follows closely St. Teresa's example will discover that humility and self sacrifice are more potent forces than any illusions imaginable. 280pp. Dou 46

ST. THERESE OF LISIEUX

BEEVERS, JOHN, tr. **THE AUTOBIOGRAPHY**, $1.45. Therese lived to be only twenty-four, a nun from the age of fifteen. Twenty-eight years after her death she was officially canonized, and almost immediately recognized as one of the most holy of the saints. Obviously the light of love which she displayed in such a short life was of incredible quality, and will undoubtedly grow and grow in the mind of anyone who is interested. 125pp. Dou 57

CLARKE, JOHN, tr. **STORY OF A SOUL: THE AUTOBIOGRAPHY OF ST. THERESE OF LISIEUX**, $3.95. A full edition of the **Autobiography** taken from an unedited version of the original work. A fresh new picture of the saint is presented here and much valuable information is added to that previously available. This translation reads very well and is accompanied by many notes and an introduction. 306pp. ICS 75

SHEED, F.J., tr. **COLLECTED LETTERS OF ST. THERESE OF LISIEUX**, $9.35. Fully indexed, introduction. 364pp. S&W 72

TRANTER, GERALD. **THE MYSTERY TEACHINGS AND CHRISTIANITY**, $1.75. As religion has become over-organized and indoctrinated, many of our most valuable spiritual guides have lost their original abstract or mystical meanings and thus their ability to help man find his true happiness. This neat little book, written for the *man on the street* examines Bible stories and clearly shows how they are written as psychological aids to the person looking for truth in his/her being. 208pp. TPH 69

EVELYN UNDERHILL

ARMSTRONG, CHRISTOPHER. **EVELYN UNDERHILL**, c$8.95. Subtitled *An Introduction to Her Life and Writings,* this is a full study which also discusses the influences on Ms. Underhill's thought and contains a good deal of previously unpublished material. There's also an extensive bibliography. 326pp. Eer 75

UNDERHILL, EVELYN. **MYSTICISM**, $3.75. See the Mysticism section.

_____. **MYSTICS OF THE CHURCH**, c$10.05. A classic work which not only shows the historic development of Christian mysticism and its influence on the Church, but also gives a deep insight into the spiritual growth of the individual mystics, their struggles, achievements, and influence. The book covers the whole development of the Christian Church from St. Paul to this century. This is as good a review of the Christian mystics as we know of and we welcome its recent reprinting. Bibliography, index, 260pp. Cla 25

_____. **PRACTICAL MYSTICISM**, $1.45. See the Mysticism section.

WADDELL, HELEN, tr. **THE DESERT FATHERS**, $2.25. The Desert Fathers were fourth century Christians who fled from the tyranny of organized religion into the desert, where they founded their own movement based on gentleness and mercy. This volume contains introductory material along with translations of the major writings of the Fathers and their history. This is the fullest collection that we know of. It is beautifully written. Notes, 209pp. UMP 36

WAITE, ARTHUR EDWARD. **THE UNKNOWN PHILOSOPHER**, c$3.00/2.95. Steiner said of Louis Claude de St. Martin: *We must realize the deep incisive significance of this man, without whom Herder, Goethe, Schiller, and the German romantics cannot be imagined.... One feels that in his works there is an enormous amount of still undiscovered wisdom, and that much might still be brought out of them.... They contain a wonderful wealth of imaginative ideas, of true imaginations.* 464pp. Mul 70

WATTS, ALAN. **MYTH AND RITUAL IN CHRISTIANITY**, $3.95. This is a retelling for modern readers of many of the most noted Christian myths. Chapters include *In the Beginning, God and Satan, Advent, Christmas and Epiphany, The Passion, From Easter to Pentecost,* and a final one on death and judgment, heaven and hell, and eschatology. The material is well written and the reader gets a good feeling for the festivals of the Christian year. Many illustrations, including reproductions of some illuminated manuscripts, as well as an extensive glossary and index. 262pp. Bea 68

WESTERMANN, CLAUS. **CREATION**, $3.00. An examination of the relevance of the Book of Genesis to contemporary man together with a review of creation as outlined in Genesis. 123pp. SCK 71

COLOR AND AURA

Psychologically and physically we are affected by color. We are cheered by vivid colors, while drab colors give us a correspondingly dull feeling. Red warms us; blue is a cold color, soothing to the eyes and mind alike; green harmonizes us; and yellow acts as a mental stimulant. The sayings *seeing red* and *feeling blue, green with jealousy* and *black with rage*, all relate to actual changes which take place in the colors of our own electro-magnetic field due to changes in our emotions. This electro-magnetic field which surrounds everything, not only human beings, is often referred to as the aura. To some people the aura appears to be white at first, but with practice, the colors will appear. This aura, which is usually visible to sensitives, is the means by which the color healer diagnoses. The affected organ or part will show a dark or discolored mark in the aura over the place where the disharmony exists. The color healer, having diagnosed the condition, or in some instances having been told by the patient and having checked this by his/her own observations, will proceed to apply remedial colors where there is a deficiency, or contrasting colors where there is an excess.

ANDERSON, MARY. **COLOUR HEALING**, $1.50. This is an excellent booklet summarizing many aspects of color healing. Ms. Anderson writes very clearly and incorporates historical, practical, and descriptive material. She includes discussions of the auras, chakras, and subtle bodies, the seven major rays, diagnosis and treatment by color, colors specific to certain diseases, and general material on the scientific background of color research. Recommended for all seeking a general review. 62pp. Wei 75

ANONYMOUS. **THE AURA AND WHAT IT MEANS TO YOU**, $5.50. Summarizes information about the aura as given by many different individuals at different periods of time from their own personal knowledge and experience. No attempt has been made to comment on the material reported and the names of the individuals whose observations are recorded are not given. Topics include: physical properties of the aura, how science looks at the aura, where the aura comes from, what it looks like, what it is made of, how thought and emotion affect the aura, meaning of the colors, and much else. This is the most comprehensive study available. Oversize, index, 108pp. HeR 55

ANONYMOUS. **COLOR HEALING**, $5.50. This is an exhaustive compilation from the works of leading practitioners of chromotherapy. Includes articles by Edwin Babbit, Corinne Heline, Roland Hunt, Walter Kilner, Olver Reiser, George Starr White, and Gladys Mayer. Topics include: chromotherapeutics; colors and their effect on health; the alchemy of light and color; lectures to physicians; and much else. Oversize, 177pp. HeR 56

BAGNALL, OSCAR. **THE ORIGIN AND PROPERTIES OF THE HUMAN AURA**, $2.95. Except for Kilner's pioneering efforts, this is the only major study of the aura. It is a generally more readable work than Kilner's and incorporates newer research. It describes how to construct apparatus for viewing the aura, and gives a clear scientific explanation of the phenomenon, based upon accepted biological and physiological principles. Illustrations, 160pp. UnB 70

BESANT, ANNIE and C.W. LEADBEATER. **THOUGHT FORMS**, $3.95. Two noted, clairvoyant theosophists on their observations of thought and the forms which it creates. Includes material on the meaning of colors and the effects of various forms. The authors present us with over fifty color plates of illustrative thought forms created by emotions, music, meditation, and various kinds of feelings. An excellent presentation. 77pp. TPH 25

BIRREN, FABER. **COLOR—A SURVEY IN WORDS AND PICTURES**, c$15.00. A comprehensive survey of the mysteries of color, explored through many fields of learning including history, anthropology, archaeology, geology, religion, mythology, mysticism, art literature, culture, tradition, symbolism, astrology, alchemy, science, natural history, and much else. A fascinating, profusely illustrated account. 223pp. UnB

_____. **COLOR IN YOUR WORLD**, $1.25. Birren, the most influential modern color consultant, sets forth his theories of the interrelation of color preferences and personality and presents some fascinating points about color and the human psyche in this detailed introductory analysis. 121pp. McM 62

_____. **COLOR PSYCHOLOGY AND THERAPY**, c$8.95. Birren presents his most comprehensive analysis of the historical, scientific, and biological aspects of the influence of color on human life. He includes the most recent findings as well as quotations from many older works which have color-related material. He cites the sources not for the theoretical material presented but rather for the possible practical applications. Birren makes his living by prescribing color to the government, to educational institutions, to the armed forces, to industry, and to architects and designers. This is a clearly written, informative book. Good bibliography, index. 302pp. UnB 61

_____. **LIGHT, COLOR AND ENVIRONMENT**, c$26.80. The first four chapters bring together an exhaustive review of technical research into the significance of light, and the biological, visual, and psychological effects of color. The next chapters study biological lighting, good vision lighting, appearance lighting, and psychic lighting. The following chapters present recommended color specifications—practical suggestions

drawn from Birren's experience. All colors mentioned in the text are shown in mounted chips on accompanying charts. Finally, there are two lengthy chapters, one devoted to historical uses of color and the other to the authentic colors of period styles. Oversize, bibliography, index. 132pp. VNR 69

_____. **PRINCIPLES OF COLOR**, c$6.95. An elementary book on color dealing with traditional principles of harmony as well as advanced principles derived from modern studies of the psychology of perception. Many color plates and illustrations. 96pp. VNR

BOOS-HAMBURGER, HILDE. **THE CREATIVE POWER OF COLOR**, $7.80. A collection of exercises and affirmations based on Rudolf Steiner's approach to color in art. The sixty-six exercises are illustrated in full color. Topics include material on the basis for color experience, mainly based on the work of Goethe and Steiner, and selections on the creative aspects of color, including an analysis of each individual color. This is the most spiritually-oriented of all the works on color and the only one with supplementary exercises. Also contains an extensive bibliography of works by Steiner and others on the *pictorial arts* (as he labels them). Oversize, 63+pp. NKB 73

BUTLER, W.E. **HOW TO READ THE AURA**, $1.25. The aura is a luminous atmosphere consisting of an electro-magnetic field which surrounds every living thing. This is an excellent introduction which covers the nature of the aura, its structure, the circuit of force, and the emotional-mental aspects of the aura. Also includes instructions on developing auric sight. 64pp. Wei

CLARK, LINDA. **COLOR THERAPY**, c$6.95. Linda Clark is a reporter who has written on many aspects of natural healing and nutrition. This book is the result of twenty years of research into the subject, and it is both the newest and the most comprehensive review that we know of. Topics include the effects of light, how light and color work, the psychological impact of color, color and physical health, color and nutrition, color therapy for eye problems, how to apply color therapy, properties of individual colors, gem therapy, auras, and breathing color. The book is well written and organized. Recommended. Bibliography, 145pp. DAC 75

CLARK, LINDA and YVONNE MARTINE. **HEALTH, YOUTH, AND BEAUTY THROUGH COLOR BREATHING**, $4.50. While working on her book on color therapy Linda Clark heard about Yvonne Martine's remarkable techniques for using colors to rejuvenate and to heal. This book presents a survey of a variety of Ms. Martine's color breathing techniques. A number of specific treatments are outlined and many case studies are cited. The book is written in the *you can do it too* vein. Notes, bibliography, index. 95pp. CeA 76

COLVILLE, W.J. **THE HUMAN AURA AND THE SIGNIFICANCE OF COLOR**, $1.50. A collection of three spiritually oriented lectures on the force of color, including analyses of individual colors and a great deal of material on color and the aura in Eastern thought. 70pp. HeR 70

CRABB, RILEY. **COLOR—THE BRIDGE TO THE NEW AGE**, $1.50. An analysis of new developments in color research, especially as they apply to life energy research. Also includes some clairvoyant interpretations of color. Oversize, 29pp. BSR

FINCH, ELIZABETH and W.J. **PHOTOCHROMOTHERAPY**, $2.00. An analysis of the technique developed by the authors for using color in healing. Includes chapters on the history of color healing, on what photochromotherapy is, on how it works (how to apply the colors and the effects they have), on the properties of the colors, and also some case histories. 52pp. EsP 72

GOETHE, JOHANN. **THEORY OF COLORS**, $5.95. Goethe, as artist and scientist, probed the phenomena of color to their origins in the interplay of light and darkness. His investigation of the moral qualities evoked in human feeling by color laid the foundation for an aesthetic of color and the theories he presents in this volume have been very influential up to the present day (although not among the more traditional scientists). Goethe felt that a knowledge of physics was an actual hindrance to understanding and he based his conclusions exclusively upon exhaustive personal observation of the phenomena of color. Using simple equipment—vessels, prisms, lenses, and the like—the reader is led through a demonstration course not only in subjectively produced colors, but also in the observable physical phenomena of color. The material here is fascinating, but not recommended to the casual reader. It's slow going. Notes, 485pp. MIT 70

GRAHAM, F. LANIER. **THE RAINBOW BOOK**, $8.95. *A collection of essays and illustrations devoted to rainbows in particular, and spectral sequences in general, focusing upon the meaning of color (both physically and metaphysically) from ancient to modern times.* It is a veritable encyclopedia of rainbow lore, including myth, magic, paintings, prints, poems, the physics of the spectrum, the metaphysics of color, and exploring the colors of consciousness and auras. Includes poems by Virgil, Dante, Blake, Keats, Wordsworth, and others; paintings by Giotto, Bosch, Van der Weyden, Durer, Rubens, Turner, as well as the sacred art of Tibet. Ideas and images are presented that tell what a rainbow can mean, not only to the painter, printmaker, and poet, but also the scientist and the theologian. Each section includes essays offered at increasing levels of complexity. ShP 75

HELINE, CORINNE. **COLOR AND MUSIC IN THE NEW AGE**, $2.95. A fascinating volume which includes chapters on the color significance of the zodiacal signs, the presence and absence of color, color therapy (an extensive account), the cosmic aspects of color, the psychology of color in everyday living, color and music correlated with the seasons and the time of day, and occult effects of music. More of Heline's books are in the Christianity section and the Mysticism section. 139pp. NAP 64

_____. **HEALING AND REGENERATION THROUGH COLOR**, $1.95. All the experiences of life can be deciphered in terms of color. This book is an esoteric study of color which is presented in a clear and beautiful manner. 69pp. NAP

HUNT, ROLAND. **THE EIGHTH KEY TO COLOR: THE MASTER KEY TO THE PREVIOUS SEVEN**, c$5.35. A companion volume to **The Seven Keys**, written twenty-two years later. Sets out and analyzes the attributes of the rays in an effort to arrive at a do-it-yourself technique that students can use. Clearly presented and well illustrated. 101pp. Dan 65

_____. **THE SEVEN KEYS TO COLOR HEALING**, $5.40. A correlation of all the known methods and many new and essentially practical techniques for diagnosis and treatment through the radiancy of color. Analyzes each color individually. A very useful textbook. 124pp. Dan 71

ITTEN, JOHANNES. **THE ELEMENTS OF COLOR**, c$9.95. A condensed version of **The Art of Color**, edited and evaluated by Faber Birren. Itten examines both the subjective experience and the objective rationale of color and develops an important color theory. Illustrations (some in color), 96pp. VNR 75

JAEGERS, BEVERLY. **THE HUMAN AURA**, $2.00. Subtitled *How I teach my students to see it [the aura]*. This is a simplified, rather general study of the attributes of the aura and experiments designed to help an individual see it. Bibliography, 55pp. LuP 71

JOHNSON, KENDALL. **THE LIVING AURA**, c$15.00. Kendall was the first American to discover the process known generally as Kirlian photography. He has worked closely with Thelma Moss. Here he details his research and discoveries. This is the most comprehensive modern study of the aura. Illustrated with over 125 black and white photographs and 8pp of color plates. Oversize, 256pp. Haw

KILNER, WALTER J. **THE AURA**, $2.95. In 1908 Kilner, an English physician, conceived the idea that the human aura might be made visible if viewed through a suitable substance, and he experimented with dicyanin, a coal-tar dye. This dye appeared to have a definite effect upon eyesight, making the observer temporarily short-sighted and therefore more readily able to perceive radiation in the ultra-violet band. After many experiments Kilner published his findings in a book entitled **The Human Atmosphere** (this is the study, with a new title). He described techniques for viewing the aura, which he claimed had inner and outer components. The inner aura followed the body outlines, while the outer aura was more nebulous. Kilner said that there were marked changes in the appearance of the aura in states of health and sickness, and that his viewing screen could be used for diagnosis. 329pp. Wei 75

_____. **THE HUMAN AURA**, c$7.50. A completely revised edition, published nine years after the pioneering work and containing many additional observations and inferences. 318pp. UnB 65

KRIPPNER, STANLEY and DANIEL RUBIN, eds. **THE KIRLIAN AURA**, $3.95. This is the most important study yet done of material related to the recent scientific research and experimentation on the human aura. The material presented is generally technically written and the sources are usually cited. The following are among the selections presented: *Photography by Means of High-frequency Currents* by the Kirlians, *Bioplasma or Corona Discharge?* by Thelma Moss and Kendall Johnson, *Some Energy Field Observations of Man and Nature*, by William Tiller, *Chinese Acupuncture and Kirlian Photography* by Jack Worsley, *Phenomena of Skin Electricity* by Viktor Adamenko, and *The Art of the Aura* by Ingo Swann. Also includes a good bibliography and many photographs and line drawings. Index, 208pp. Dou 74

KUPPERS, HARALD. **COLOR: ORIGIN, SYSTEM, USES**, c$20.00. Kuppers provides a new and comprehensive approach to color. He begins with a discussion on the origins of color and its physical characteristics. He then explains the physiological process of sight and the problems such an approach raises in relation to the everyday acceptance of color, and more particularly the need to define the ways in which a color is affected by different circumstances. Such questions in turn affect the attitude to color mixing. Kuppers proposes a new model for color mixing—the *Rhombehedral System*—and illustrates how to use it. The model explains the laws of color mixing and the relationships between the colors themselves. This text includes many beautiful explanatory color diagrams, with explanatory notes. It's designed for those with a great deal of interest and some previous background. Oversize, bibliography. 155pp. VNR 73

LANE, EARLE, ed. **ELECTROPHOTOGRAPHY**, $4.95. This is a handbook on psycho-energetics developed for the generalist who is interested in building and using a Kirlian electrophotographic generator. Complete instructions are given (with schematics) and addresses for buying parts are also listed, along with various suggestions. There are also sections on electro-acupuncture and biofeedback—explanations, charts, and techniques—as well as a bibliography and addresses for additional information. A high point of the text is the eighteen pages of full color Kirlian photographs. The text is certainly not excellent, but with the paucity of material in the field all efforts are welcome—and the photographs are beautiful! 8x12", 57pp. AOP 75

LEADBEATER, C.W. **MAN, VISIBLE AND INVISIBLE**, c$5.25/$4.50. A very detailed analysis which records the observations of a clairvoyant investigator who described different auras as he saw them and endeavored to illustrate them with the aid of an artist. Contains material on all aspects of consciousness. Many beautiful color plates. 126pp. TPH

LEWIS, ROGER. **COLOR AND THE EDGAR CAYCE READINGS**, $1.50. Lewis is an artist who has studied the Cayce material on color at great length. First, he sets the stage with the scientific examination of color. Then, using the Cayce booklet **Auras**, he shows how Cayce interpreted various colors when they appeared in the emanation of light around an individual. Because the Cayce readings associated various colors with the seven spiritual centers in the body, Lewis traces the colors on the path of the kundalini, describing the influences of the endocrine glands. Finally he looks at color from the point of view of the color psychologist. Includes many quotations from the Cayce readings. Bibliography, 488pp. ARE 73

LUSCHER, MAX. **THE LUSCHER COLOR TEST**, $1.95. The principle of the test is that accurate psychological information can be gained about a person through his choice and rejections of colors. This book explains how to take the test and interpret and includes color cards. 188pp. S&S

MATTHAEI, RUPPRECHT, ed. **GOETHE'S COLOR THEORY**, c$27.50. Matthaei is director of the Goethe archives and his principle work for almost half a century has been the analysis of Goethe's scientific theories. Goethe's works on color fill 2000 pages of small print. Professor Matthaei has carefully selected and annotated the material and arranged it so that readers can follow Goethe's reasoning, examine his illustrations, conduct his experiments, and judge the color theory for themselves. The 1820 translation of part of Goethe's work by Charles Eastlake is reproduced in its entirety, following Professor Matthaei's selections. Most of the rest of the selections have not appeared in English before. This oversize book includes many full color illustrations. Notes, 275pp. VNR 70

MAYER, GLADYS. **COLOUR AND HEALING**, $1.90. A very spiritual essay by an English anthroposophist. 63pp. NKB 60

OUSLEY, S.G.J. **COLOUR MEDITATIONS, WITH A GUIDE TO COLOR HEALING**, $1.60. Meditations which explain how the different wavelengths of color function in the body, soul, and spirit, and how they can be utilized. The healing section outlines the system of chromotherapy. Fow

_____. **THE POWER OF THE RAYS: THE SCIENCE OF COLOR HEALING**, $1.60. A sequel to **Color Meditations** which explains the methods of using the *cosmic color rays* in the treatment of disease. Ousley also discusses the aura, the etheric body and the physical body. Fow

_____. **THE SCIENCE OF THE AURA**, $1.35. An introduction to the study of the human aura including the scientific basis, color aspects of the aura, developing auric sight. 32pp. Fow

PANCHADASI, SWAMI. **THE HUMAN AURA**, $1.00. A very nice introduction to the aura, especially its spiritual aspects. YPS 72

RAMADAHN. **COLOR HEALING IN NEW AGE**, $1.50. An inspirational treatise given through the mediumship of Ursula Roberts. 27pp. Whi

_____. **SPIRITUAL VIRTUES IN THE AURA**, $2.00. An inspirationally written account of various virtues, received through the mediumship of Ursula Roberts. 32pp. Rob nd

REGUSH, NICHOLAS. **THE HUMAN AURA**, $1.25. This is a very good selection of writings on auras and the energy field compiled from among the works of the most noted observers. It begins with a section entitled *The Pioneer Work*, which includes selections from Mesmer, von Reichenbach, Kilner, Bagnall, and Ousley. The next section, *Man's Inner Structure: The Psychic Experience*, relates what noted clairvoyants including Edgar Cayce, C.W. Leadbeater, Muldoon and Carrington, and researchers including A.E. Powell and Robert Monroe have had to say. The final section, *The Scientific Trajectory*, presents the writings of Charles Tart, Shafica Karagulla, William Tiller, W.E. Mann, and others of similar bent. Good overall introductory material. Recommended. Bibliography, 237pp. Ber 74

ROBERTS, URSULA. **THE MYSTERY OF THE HUMAN AURA**, $1.00. A straightforward discussion of what the aura is, how it is formed, types of auras, and the aura's relation to disease and to psychic phenomena. 34pp. Wei

SCHINDLER, MARIA. **GOETHE'S THEORY OF COLOR**, c$12.90. Secrets of color and their living spiritual reality. Colors as real forces which speak to our sensations and feelings and imprint their dynamic qualities on our inner life. Includes discussion of physiological colors, combinations, the balanced color circle, moral effects of color, Goethe's theory of color as image of world evolution. A valuable textbook with graduated exercises leading the student directly into the living realm of color. 210pp, 41 color. NKB 64

SHARPE, DEBORAH. **THE PSYCHOLOGY OF COLOR AND DESIGN**, $2.95. A concise study of the psychology of color. Dr. Sharpe is a well-known color consultant. A great deal of practical information is imparted here. Notes, indices. 174pp. LtA 75

WHITE, GEORGE STARR. **THE STORY OF THE HUMAN AURA**, $7.50. This is a very detailed study of research done by Dr. White in the early part of the twentieth century. It includes much scientific material not found elsewhere on the aura as a manifestation of the life force and many case studies of healing specific ailments using the energy of the aura. This is not a terribly readable study, but the material presented here has been the basis of much of the later work. Index, illustrations (with some color). 215pp. HeR 69

TOOLS

AURA GOGGLES, $13.25. Sturdily made goggles, developed along the guidelines set out by Dr. Kilner, with exchangeable coal-tar dicyanine filters and ventilating frame. AuE

COMPLETE AURA RESEARCH KIT, $45.00. Contains the following tools: a set of aura goggles with fitted 2X filters, soft face fitting of foam rubber, and screw rims; six pairs of color filters for study of inner aura striations; inner aura; outer aura; three pairs, basic set filters (graded diminishing shades); extra dark filters; spare frames. The kit is made by the Metaphysical Research Group in England to the specifications established by Kilner. MRG

COMPARATIVE RELIGION

ABHEDANANDA, SWAMI. GREAT SAVIORS OF THE WORLD, c$3.00. Lives and teachings of Krishna, Lao-Tze, Buddha, Christ, Muhammad, and Ramakrishna. VdP 47

ADAM, MICHAEL. WANDERING IN EDEN, $4.95. This oversize volume is divided into three sections: *The Way of the Body, The Way of Emptiness* and *The Way of Things*. The volume as a whole represents Adam's attempt to relate traditional Eastern concepts to Western religion, art, and modern science. The text itself is beautifully produced and 109 illustrations illuminate the narrative. Many quotations from sacred texts and masters are also included. 115pp. RaH 76

ANDERSON, NORMAN, ed. THE WORLD'S RELIGIONS, $3.95. An academic survey by a number of Christian scholars of the following religions: Judaism, Islam, Hinduism, Buddhism, Shinto, and Confucianism. The essays are well organized and they delve deeper into the scholarly aspects of the religions than most general surveys. Index, 244pp. Eer 75

ANGUS, SAMUEL. THE MYSTERY RELIGIONS AND CHRISTIANITY, c$10.00. When Alexander the Great completed his conquest of the Near East in 331 BC, one world died and another was born. The spiritual climate of the age found expression especially in the development of new types of religion. *The Mystery Religions consisted essentially in the performance of rites aimed at achieving the rebirth of the spiritually dead or moribund individual and providing a means whereby he might surmount the limitations of the human condition and be released from the trammels of mortality.*—from the introduction. This book remains, after fifty years, the classic volume on the mystery religions and their connection with the development of Christianity. Notes, extensive bibliography, index. 383pp. UnB 66

BAHM, ARCHIE. THE WORLD'S LIVING RELIGIONS, $3.25. This is a dry, factual presentation of the basic features of the following religions: Hinduism, Jainism, Buddhism, Shintoism, Judaism, Christianity, Islam, and Humanism. He also includes materials on what religion is and on primitive religion. The book is keyed toward giving the general reader a feeling for the religions without overwhelming him/her with details. Bibliography, index. 384pp. SIU 64

BALLOU, ROBERT, ed. THE BIBLE OF THE WORLD, $4.95. An excellent compilation presenting the reader with the essential scriptures of the world's eight major religions. The only explanatory material consists of notes at the end of the selections, along with source references and a glossary. Recommended. 1415pp. Abridged edition (605pp) available for $2.95. Avo 39

Dance of Shiva.

BANCROFT, ANNE. RELIGIONS OF THE EAST, c$12.95. This is a beautifully illustrated, clearly written presentation of the essence of Hinduism, Buddhism, Tibetan Buddhism, Zen Buddhism, and Sufism. The mystical aspects of these religions are emphasized and Ms. Bancroft makes use of poetry and legends to convey the essence common to their teachings. We feel that this book is the best introduction to the religions of the East available. Oversize, fully indexed, with chapter notes and a good topical bibliography. 256pp. SMP 74

_____. **TWENTIETH CENTURY MYSTICS AND SAGES**, c$12.95/$4.95. A nicely written survey of nineteen contemporary spiritual leaders: Aldous Huxley, Alan Watts, Thomas Merton, Teilhard de Chardin, Krishnamurti, Gurdjieff, Sak Subuh, Meher Baba, Maharaj Ji, Ramana Maharishi, Maharishi Mahesh Yogi, Chogyam Trungpa, Dhiravamsa, Martin Buber, Dion Fortune, Rudolf Steiner, Douglas Harding, Don Juan, and Mother Teresa. Each individual is fully discussed—some at greater length than others—and the presentation is definitely more enlightened than is usually the case with surveys of this type. We like Ms. Bancroft's style very much. Well illustrated, glossary, bibliography, index. 352pp. SMP 76

BOWMAN, JOHN, ed. COMPARATIVE RELIGION, $12.70. Transcriptions of the following lectures: *Accents of the World's Religions*—Huston Smith, *Common Denominators of Asian Thought*—Abbot Sumangalo, *Christian Theology and Two Asian Faiths*—E.G. Parrinder, *Religious Atheism? Early Buddhist and Recent American*—W. Cantwell Smith, *Methods of Yoga in Japanese Buddhism*—Carmen Blacker, and *Sufism and the Perennity of the Mystical Quest*—S.H. Nasr. Notes, index. 134pp. Bri 72

BURCKHARDT, TITUS. SACRED ART EAST AND WEST, c$8.60. See the Sacred Art section.

CAPRA, FRITJOF. THE TAO OF PHYSICS, $5.95. See the Astronomy section.

DE BARY, THEODORE and AINSLIE EMBREE, eds. A GUIDE TO ORIENTAL CLASSICS, $2.45. Classics of the four major traditions—Islamic, Indian, Chinese, and Japanese—are included in this bibliographic guide. The works listed range from history, philosophy, and religion to poetry, drama and fiction. Under each classic there is a list of translations, complete or partial, into English and other Western languages, with annotations, followed by a list of secondary readings and a series of topics for discussion. 199pp. Col 64

MIRCEA ELIADE

ELIADE, MIRCEA. DEATH, AFTERLIFE, AND ESCHATOLOGY, $2.50. Eliade is Chairman of the Department of the History of Religions at the University of Chicago Divinity School and is a very noted scholar. **From Primitives to Zen**, one of his best known works, was recently put out in four paperback volumes, of which this is Part Three. Included in each of the source books are the essential documents from all the important religious traditions (excepting Judaism and Christianity) arranged according to major recurrent themes. *It seems to me that only by reading a certain number of religious texts related to the same subject (cosmogony, initiation, myths on the origin of death, etc.) is a student able to grasp their structural similarities and their differences.* Bibliography, 120pp. H&R 74

_____. **FROM MEDICINE MEN TO MUHAMMAD**, $2.50. Part Four of **From Primitives to Zen**. Bibliography, 232pp. H&R 74

_____. **GODS, GODDESSES, AND MYTHS OF CREATION**, $2.50. Part One of **From Primitives to Zen**. Bibliography, 174pp. H&R 74

_____. **IMAGES AND SYMBOLS**, $2.95. *We have seen that myths decay and symbols become secularized, but that they never disappear, even in the most positivist of civilizations. Symbols and myths come from such depths: they are part and parcel of the human being, and it is impossible that they should not be found again in any and every existential situation of man in the Cosmos*—from the foreword. This book is a collection of studies in religious symbolism. The essays are enlightening as they show both how man has been influenced by these archetypes throughout history and their continuing role in the psyche of modern man. Notes, index. 189pp. S&W 52

_____. **MAN AND THE SACRED**, $2.50. Part Two of **From Primitives to Zen**. Bibliography, 186pp. H&R 74

_____. **OCCULTISM, WITCHCRAFT, AND CULTURAL FASHIONS**, c$8.95. Six essays: *Cultural Fashions and the History of Religions; The World, The City, The House; Mythologies of Death; The Occult and the Modern World; Some Observations on European Witchcraft;* and *Spirit, Light, and Seed*. Notes, index. 148pp. UCh 76

_____. **PATTERNS IN COMPARATIVE RELIGION**, $4.95. This is a study of the nature of religion based on the beliefs and systems of individuals and groups rather than on historical, categorical, or chronological approaches. Topics include: *The Sky and Sun Gods; The Structure and Morphology of the Sacred; The Sun and Sun-Worship; The Moon and its Mystique; The Waters and Water Symbolism; Sacred Stones; The Earth, Woman and Fertility; Agriculture and Fertility Cults; Sacred Places; Sacred Time and the Myth of Eternal Renewal;* and *The Structure of Symbols*. Notes, name and subject indices. 501pp. NAL 63

_____. **THE QUEST**, $2.95. Subtitled *History and Meaning in Religion*, this is a collection of essays on themes common to different religious experiences and beliefs. His hope in writing this work (and all his others) is to develop an awareness of the place of the history of religion in a secularized society. All of Eliade's work is considered the finest modern scholarship in the fields of religious history and mythology. However, the material is only recommended for serious students who will not be bogged down in all the reference material included in the main body of the books. Index, 180pp. UCh 69

_____. **THE SACRED AND THE PROFANE**, $1.95. Eliade traces manifestations of the sacred from primitive to modern times, in terms of space, time, nature and the cosmos, and life itself. He shows how the total human experience of the religious man compares to that of the non-religious and observes that even modern men who proclaim themselves to live in a completely profane world are still unconsciously nourished by the memory of the sacred, in camouflaged myths and degenerated rituals. Chapter-by-chapter bibliography. 256pp. HBJ 57

KITAGAWA, JOSEPH and CHARLES LONG, eds. MYTHS AND SYMBOLS, c$15.45. Subtitled *Studies in Honor of Mircea Eliade*, this is a collection of important original ays focusing on Eliade's continuing effort to delineate the multidimensional charac- r of myths and symbols as specific forms of the religious perception of mankind. The lume is divided into three sections: phenomenological and methodological studies; storical studies; and literary studies. Also included is a short account of Eliade's life, as ell as a complete bibliography of his works in many languages. The contributors, well- own scholars from all over the world, include Guiseppe Tucci, Gershom Scholem, eorges Dumezil, Ernst Junger and E.M. Cioran. Index, 438pp. UCh 69

LIADE, MIRCEA and J.M. KITAGAWA, eds. **THE HISTORY OF RELIGIONS**, $2.45. collection of detailed, scholarly essays on methodology for the study of religion, pecially on the university level. Many notes. 172pp. UCh 59

LLWOOD, ROBERT, JR. **RELIGIOUS AND SPIRITUAL GROUPS IN MODERN MERICA**, $7.95. A broad and general sympathetic survey of the vast range of non- ideo-Christian religions, from theosophists and Rosicrucians to transcendental meditation id Krishna consciousness. Useful reading for anyone who wants to get his bearings nong all the cults and movements in our present spiritual renaissance. Up-to-date bib- ography, addresses of some groups. Many references. 334pp. PrH 73

PSTEIN, PERLE. **ORIENTAL MYSTICS AND MAGICIANS**, c$5.95. See the Children's ooks section.

ARUQI, ISMAIL, ed. **HISTORICAL ATLAS OF THE RELIGIONS OF THE WORLD**, $17.50. This is the most extensive historical atlas of religion ever published. Sixty-five iaps, including material never before mapped, portray practically everything which lends self to cartographic interpretation. Maps illustrate the origins and distribution of religions, nd the locations of sacred cities, sites and temples. Also highlighting the material are umerous photographs and drawings. Accompanying essays by noted scholars present the istory of each religion, its growth and interaction with space and time, and the relation f one religion to another. The material is very well organized and each section includes xtensive bibliographic references. An appendix traces the chronology of each religion iscussed. Oversize, fully indexed. 368pp. McM 74

'RANCK, FREDERICK. **PILGRIMAGE TO HERE/NOW**, $3.95. This is the interior and xterior travelogue of Dr. Franck through the East. Franck has used his artistic gifts to elp illuminate what he saw—whether it be the eyes and hands of beggars in Madras or ie Dalai Lama and his entourage. He also recounts his conversations with the Dalai Lama nd leading Buddhist and Hindu thinkers as well as the events he witnessed in his personal uest, exploring the spiritual resonances between Christ and Buddha *at the deep level vhere they change men's lives, rather than on that level where their followers have too often snared them in the nets of theology and ritual.* Many illustrations. 156pp. OrB 74

'RAZIER, ALLIE. **CHINESE AND JAPANESE RELIGIONS**, $4.40. This is **Volume III** f the editor's *Readings in Eastern Religious Thought.* Here Ms. Frazier is mainly con- erned with the major movements in China and Japan. The book is designed to bring ogether in one volume the primary religious texts of the two countries along with signifi- ant secondary readings that shed light upon these traditions. The translations are chosen or their clarity and the emphasis is on those selections that would be of most value to he beginning student. Background material on each selection is included along with a survey of each of the religions discussed. The contributors are noted scholars from within he religious systems. Glossary, bibliography. 272pp. Wes 69

FROST, S.E., JR., ed. **THE SACRED WRITINGS OF THE WORLD'S GREAT RELI- GIONS**, $2.95. This selection covers the following religions: Hinduism, Zoroastrianism, Taoism, Confucianism, Jainism, Buddhism, Judaism, Christianity, Islam, Shinto, Sikhism, Mormonism, and Christian Science. The treatment of each religion begins with a general introduction describing the religion's origin, its founder, the location and number of its adherents, and the great books that constitute its scripture. This is followed by selections from the scripture itself. Passages of some length are included rather than brief excerpts, so that the reader can grasp the context and thereby appreciate the full message of the teaching. A topical index enables the reader to make comparisons between the views of the various faiths on specific matters. 416pp. MGH 72

GAER, JOSEPH. **WHAT THE GREAT RELIGIONS BELIEVE**, $1.25. This is a brief account of the basic beliefs of Hinduism, Jainism, Buddhism, Taoism, Shinto, Judaism, Christianity, Islam, Zoroastrianism, Confucianism, and Zen Buddhism—with selections from their sacred literature. This is the most simplified account we have seen. Bibliog- raphy, index. 205pp. NAL 63

GRAHAM, DOM AELRED. **THE END OF RELIGION**, $2.85. An exploration of the meaning and nature of religion and the role of the church in the contemporary world. Dom Graham is one of the few theologians in the West who, over a long period of time, has sought to bring to Christians an awareness and understanding of Hinduism and Buddhism. This volume is subtitled *Autobiographical Explorations.* Notes, index. 292pp. HBJ 71

HICK, JOHN, ed. **TRUTH AND DIALOGUE IN WORLD RELIGION**, c$5.95. This is an analysis of the conflicting truth-claims among religions—all of which purport to have the final answer. The book consists of a series of essays by noted scholars both in the field of comparative religion (e.g. R.C. Zaehner, Geoffrey Parrinder) and in specific religious areas (e.g. Trevor Ling, Kenneth Cragg) discussing the views of various religions toward the truth represented by all religion as well as by the individual religion studied. Index, 164pp. Wes 74

HUNTSMAN, B.W., ed. **WISDOM IS ONE**, c$2.25. A collection of topically organized quotations from all the major religious traditions. Each of the selections is very short. Bibliography, 175pp. Wat 69

JASPERS, KARL. **SOCRATES, BUDDHA, CONFUCIUS, JESUS**, $1.75. A scholarly overview of these four individuals. Each one is considered individually and the appraisal is divided into sections on life, thought, influence, and personality. A good summary, though on the dry side. Bibliography, index. 104pp. HBJ 62

KAUFMAN, WALTER. **RELIGIONS IN FOUR DIMENSIONS**, c$25.00. The four di- mensions Professor Kaufman refers to are: existential, aesthetic, historical and compara- tive. 240 illustrations—183 in color—represent the aesthetic and existential dimensions of the ten religions he discusses. The historical and comparative dimensions are presented in a series of chapters on the religions. The focus is mainly on Asia, since that is where most of the religions were born, and the approach is evocative. This is an excellent work of scholarship which also deeply involves the reader. Oversize, notes, bibliography, index. 448pp. Cro 76

KITAGAWA, JOSEPH. **RELIGIONS OF THE EAST**, $3.95. This is a sociologically- oriented study of religion, discussed within the framework of the national community. Topics include: *Chinese Religions and the Family System; Hinduism and the Caste Sys- tem; Buddhism and the Samgha; Islam and the Ummah;* and *Japanese Religions and the National Community.* Dr. Kitagawa is a Professor of the History of Religions both in the Divinity School and the Department of Far Eastern Languages and Civilizations at the University of Chicago. This is not an overly technical work but is rather designed to give a general orientation to the religions discussed, relating the structure and develop- ment of the *holy communities* to general historical events and cultures. Notes, bibliog- raphy, subject and author indices. 351pp. Wes 68

KOESTLER, ARTHUR. **THE LOTUS AND THE ROBOT**, $3.00. This is a very personal account of Koestler's pilgrimage to India and Japan. He desribes the contemporary scene and shows how spirituality infuses mundane life. 297pp. H&R 60

MERTON, THOMAS. **THE ASIAN JOURNAL OF THOMAS MERTON**, $3.45. The personal remarks, observations and thoughts of this modern mystic and humanitarian thinker as recorded by himself during his travels in Asia prior to his untimely death. The deeply spiritual understanding of this evolved soul is revealed in his inclusive and synthetic grasp of the underlying unity of the world's religions and all genuine approaches to a more enlightened consciousness. Includes his last letters and written thoughts before his death. Also contains an excellent descriptive glossary and a bibliography. Recom- mended. 353pp. NDP 73

MIDDLETON, JOHN, ed. **GODS AND RITUALS**, $9.35. A scholarly collection of readings in religious beliefs and practices basically devoted to articles on primitive religions. The selections focus on Africa and many of the religions discussed are little known in the West. Notes, bibliography, index. 478pp. UTx 67

MUELLER, F. MAX, ed. **SACRED BOOKS OF THE EAST**, c$11.50/$7.50 each volume, fifty volumes. Various entries are listed in the appropriate section. Write us for a com- plete list of the series if you're interested. These volumes have been written by twenty leading authorities in their respective fields. Their publication covered a period of thirty- four years. They include the translation of all the most important works of the seven Asian religions. Each volume is carefully translated, contains a good introduction and many notes as well as the text in its original language. MoB

MURPHY, GARDNER and LOIS, eds. **ASIAN PSYCHOLOGY**, $3.95. An exploration of the main currents of psychological thought in the East which illustrates the special insights and contributions of Asia through a judicious selection of both ancient and modern writings. The editors link the various passages with explanatory introductions, setting them in historical perspective, and providing interpretations. The book is divided into sections on the psychology of India, of China, and of Japan. It's an unusual compila- tion, which includes a great amount of source material. We recommend this highly to those who are interested in the psychology of religions. Index, 253pp. H&R 68

NAKAMURA, HAJIME. **PARALLEL DEVELOPMENTS**, c$28.00. Nakamura is a well- respected philosopher who has taught at many of the leading universities in the world. In this volume he presents an unusual approach to the history of thought in a variety of cultures. *These cultures are not treated separately, one after another, as is usually done in histories of thought. Rather the emphasis is upon such problems as the concept of God, the question of immortality, the controversy over universals, the nature of ortho- doxy and heterodoxy, the problem of moral values, and many others. The thought of the various cultures is then collected around such problems. The discussion is carried on with amazing erudition. There are thousands of quotations and references. And yet the work is not ponderous or directed solely to the specialist.*—Charles Morris. Notes, 587pp. Kod 75

__________. **WAYS OF THINKING OF EASTERN PEOPLES**, $5.95. *Professor Naka- mura . . . sets out to analyze, with rigor and objectivity, the characteristic thought- patterns of four Asian peoples as these are revealed in their languages, their logic, and their cultural products. In this analysis he speaks neither of an Oriental mind nor of an undifferentiated West. Rather he speaks of the Indians, the Chinese, the Tibetans, and the Japanese out of an understanding of their distinctive cultures and histories.* Extensive notes. 712pp. UHa 64

NEEDLEMAN, JACOB. **THE NEW RELIGIONS**, $1.50. In lucid and informative terms, Needleman, Chairman of the Department of Philosophy, San Francisco State College, examines the ways in which the traditional Western religions have failed modern man and the ways in which Eastern religions offer their followers the practical means for improving the quality of their lives. He offers a comprehensive picture of the most significant new movements, portraits of their leaders, and a glimpse into the experience of some of their adherents. 245pp. S&S 72

__________. **A SENSE OF THE COSMOS**, c$6.95. *Needleman presents a critical evaluation of modern science against the background of the ancient spiritual traditions . . . .There are several points on which I disagree with Needleman, but I have found al- most every page of his book thought provoking and stimulating, and many of his ideas extremely lucid and enlightening. . . .I want to strongly recommend* **A Sense of the Cos-**

mos to every reader seriously interested in our present cultural situation.—Fritjof Capra, author of **Tao of Physics.** Index, 178pp. Dou 75

_____, ed. **THE SWORD OF GNOSIS**, $4.95. A collection of essays first printed in the respected English quarterly **Studies in Comparative Religion** by noted continental scholars including Frithjof Schuon, Rene Guenon, Marco Pallis, Abu Bakr Siraj Ad-Din, Martin Lings, Titus Burckhardt, Seyyed Hossein Nasr, and Leo Schaya. Topics include: *The Spiritual Function of Civilization; Cosmology and Modern Science; Discovering the Interior Life; Remarks on the Enigma of the Koran; Livings One's Karma; The Language of the Birds; Perennial Values in Islamic Art; The Influence of Sufism on Traditional Persian Music; The Meaning of the Temple;* and much else. The mission of the contributors is to illuminate the universal truths upon which all authentic religions are based and this they do very well. The articles tend to be scholarly, so beware. Notes, 464pp. Pen 74

NEEDLEMAN, JACOB and DENNIS LEWIS, eds. **SACRED TRADITION AND PRESENT NEED**, c$10.00. This volume presents excerpts from a lecture series given in San Francisco in 1973. The general topic was the following: *Has the spiritual revolution lost its direction in a profusion of innovations? In our haste to reject outworn religious forms, customs, and ideals, have we overlooked the truths that have guided traditional life and thought since time immemorial? Can the ancient traditions cut through our present confusion and speak anew to Western man's need?* These were the lectures: *The Used Religions*—Jacob Needleman, *Christianity in Dialogue with Zen*—William Johnston, *Tibetan Buddhism: The Way of Inward Discovery*—Lobsang Lhalungpa, *The Samkhya of India*—Lizelle Reymond, *Sufism and the Spiritual Needs of Contemporary Man*—S.H. Nasr, *Contemplative Christianity*—Dom Graham, *Myth, Symbol, and Tradition*—P.L. Travers, and *Two Vedantas*—Philippe Lavastine. 146pp. Vik 75

NORTHROP, F.S.C. **THE MEETING OF EAST AND WEST**, $4.95. The contents of this classic work by a noted American educator fall into two major parts: the one, a determination of the differing ideological assumptions of the major peoples and cultures of the West, culminating with a chapter on the meaning of Western civilization; the other, a similar study of the peoples and culture of the East. Many references. 531pp. McM 46

OCTOPUS BOOKS. **ENCYCLOPEDIA OF WORLD RELIGIONS**, c$9.98. A pictorial survey of world religions with hundreds of color and black and white plates, divided into the following topics: the dawn of belief, primitive religion, the ancient world, the great faiths, the problem of evil, man and his destiny, the elements of religion, and new movements. The plates are exquisite and the written material is more than adequate for a general introduction. 9x12", index. 252pp. Crn 75

PARRINDER, GEOFFREY. **ASIAN RELIGIONS**, $2.95. A clearly written introductory survey of Islam, Indian religion, Buddhism, Chinese religion, and Japanese religion. All the important information is presented in succinct form and the individuals, main movements, and texts are all discussed. Bibliography, index. 138pp. SCK 57

_____. **AVATAR AND INCARNATION**, c$12.95. This is the only full length study of this topic. Parrinder first examines the Hindu beliefs in avatars—especially those of Krishna and Rama—in the classical texts, medieval devotion, and modern criticism, and he brings out the special characteristics of avatar doctrine. Next he examines other Indian beliefs relevant to the formation of avatar doctrine, beliefs in the Buddhas and the jinas. A brief discussion of Islamic teaching leads on to Christian belief. In the latter section he examines the parallels between the doctrine of the incarnation and avatar doctrine and makes a comparative study of the leading figures in the religions previously discussed. Notes, bibliography, index. 296pp. H&R 70

_____. **A DICTIONARY OF NON-CHRISTIAN RELIGIONS**, c$10.95. This is a very useful, comprehensive compilation, covering the whole field of religions of the world (with the exception of Christianity). It enables the student to find instant definitions, provides him/her with cross references that connect many of the subjects, shows common themes of religious perception, and links theology, religion and mythology. Thousands of entries define and explain deities, beliefs, practices, philosophies and philosophers, sacred objects, rituals, names and places, gods and goddesses, and a myriad of other topics. We found this an excellent tool in putting the catalog together. The concise explanations offered here are often either not available elsewhere or else require a lot of digging to come up with. Illustrations, bibliography. 320pp. Wes 71

_____. **WORSHIP IN THE WORLD'S RELIGIONS**, $3.50. Professor Parrinder sets out to answer the following questions about various religions: *What is the nature of their*

worship? What is their faith and prayer? How do they appear to their worshipers? He is concerned not with histories or philosophies but with worship as seen and shared by the laity: the temples, concepts of God and other spirits, objects of reverence, sacred books, festivals, pilgrimages, and prayers—both public and private. All the major Eastern sects are covered along with several lesser known ones. Bibliography, index. 239pp. LtA 6

POPE, HARRISON. **THE ROAD EAST**, $3.45. This is the result of Pope's travels throughout the U.S. talking with practitioners of disciplines such as yoga, Zen, Transcendental Meditation, Krishna Consciousness. He has previously written on the drug culture and this angle is heavily emphasized here through his view that most of the people practicing these disciplines come from a background of drugs. The book includes many long quotations from the people involved, discussing both how they got into the *trip* and what the main features of each discipline are. A rather scholarly, sociological study. Notes, bibliography, index. 158pp. Bea 74

RADHAKRISHNAN, S. **EASTERN RELIGION AND WESTERN THOUGHT**, $5.30. Radhakrishnan, distinguished statesman, educator, and philosopher, is the author of many books on Indian philosophy. He has served as President of India. This book describes the leading ideas of Indian philosophy and traces the probable influence of Indian mysticism upon Greek and Christian thought. 402pp. Oxf 39

_____. **RELIGION AND CULTURE**, $1.80. This great philosopher-statesman discusses the various facets of religion and culture and their application to life in the present-day world. 176pp. JPC 68

RAMAKRISHNA VEDANTA CENTRE. **WOMEN SAINTS OF EAST AND WEST**, $4.95. Each selection describes the struggles and difficulties, the spiritual disciplines and realizations, of the women saints portrayed, so that the reader might feel drawn to the divine ideal which they attained, and glimpse their fervor of soul. The life of the Holy Mother Sri Sarada Devi, who like Ramakrishna taught that all religions are paths to God, is the inspiration behind this volume. Each selection is written by an individual who has been devoted to Hinduism, with additional sections on Buddhism and Jainism, Christianity Judaism and Sufism. Index, 274pp. RVC 55

ROSS, NANCY WILSON. **THREE WAYS OF ASIAN WISDOM: HINDUISM, BUDDHISM, AND ZEN, AND THEIR SIGNIFICANCE FOR THE WEST**, $3.95. Our personal favorite. This is a layman's explanation of three religions, and the arts that grew from them. The text is beautifully written and profusely illustrated. Includes many references to the literature, a glossary and an extensive bibliography. Highly recommended. 222pp. S&S 66

SHAH, SIRDAR IKBAL ALI. **ORIENTAL LITERATURE**, $7.20. An anthology of literature (mainly poetry) from Afghanistan, Arabia, China, India, Iran, Japan, and Turkey. Mystical philosophy is emphasized in the selection. 416pp. Oct 37

_____. **THE SPIRIT OF THE EAST**, $5.00. The author is a noted Sufi scholar, the father of Idries Shah. This is a collection of some of the most important source material from Muslim, Parsee, Hindu, Hebrew, Confucian, and other traditions. He has presented just the translations without any further explanatory material. The selections were chosen not only for their particular worth but also for the way they each illuminate the particular virtues of each tradition. 276pp. Oct 73

SMITH, HUSTON. **THE RELIGIONS OF MAN**, $3.50. This is generally considered the best overall study available, emphasizing the meaning these religions carry for the lives of their adherents. The traditions emphasized include Hinduism, Buddhism, Confucianism, Taoism, Islam, Judaism, and Christianity. *This is a book about religion that exists . . . not as a dull habit but as an acute fever. It is about religion alive. And whenever religion comes to life it displays a startling quality; it takes over. All else, while not silenced, becomes subdued and thrown without contest into a supporting role.*—from the introduction. A fascinating account, ideal for both the general reader and the student of comparative religion. Recommended. Notes, annotated bibliography, index. 371pp. H&R 65

STAAL, FRITS. **EXPLORING MYSTICISM**, $4.95. Staal argues that mysticism can best be explored through mystical experiences. Relating mystical phenomena to drugs, ritual, religion, and philosophy, he concludes that we are only beginning to explore a domain of the mind as complex as many areas of physics or biology, but as yet barely touched by psychology and the humanities. 242pp. UCP 75

STRENG, FREDERICK. **UNDERSTANDING RELIGIOUS MAN**, $6.65. An academic study of the religious experiences divided into the following main sections: methods used to understand religious life, four traditional ways of being religious, modes of human awareness used to express religious meaning. Annotated bibliographic selections are included following each chapter. Index, 132pp. Dic 69

STROUP, HERBERT. **FOUNDERS OF LIVING RELIGIONS**, $4.25. This is an excellen introduction to the lives and teachings of Vardhamana (Jainism), Gautama (Buddhism), Nanak (Sikhism), Lao Tzu (Taoism), Confucius (Confucianism), Zoroaster (Zoroastrianism), Jesus (Christianity), and Muhammad (Islam). Dr. Stroup focuses on biography rather than theology or philosophy. He reports in detail on what is known or believed regarding the founder's birth, his family connections, early life experiences, education and calling, his gathering of disciples and converts, and his journeys to promulgate the new faith. In addition, Dr. Stroup includes descriptions of each religion and its relationship to other religions. Glossary, bibliography, index. 256pp. Wes 74

TAGORE, RABINDRITH. **THE RELIGION OF MAN**, $3.95. Very personal thoughts on human life in its relation to the divine, and the nature and being of God. A document of the spiritual life. 239pp. Bea 31

TANNER, FLORICE. **THE MYSTERY TEACHINGS IN WORLD RELIGIONS**, $2.45. Drawing from the inner doctrines of all the world's religions, the author shows that man's sic truth—which is the way to full self-consciousness at every level of his being—lies hid-n in every world faith, whatever the superficial differences might be. This is a very ent work, and the references cited include such books as **Psychic Discoveries Behind e Iron Curtain, Chariot of the Gods**, and Manly Hall's **Secret Teachings**. 192pp. TPH 73

OMLIN, E.W.F. **THE ORIENTAL PHILOSOPHERS**, $2.75. *The aim of this book is wo-fold: to provide a straightforward account of the life and work of the great thinkers f the Orient, and to attempt to show, in terms intelligible to the ordinary reader, with hat remarkable insistence the greatest of these thinkers dwell upon common themes. riental here includes the Egyptians, Babylonians, and Israelites as well as the Asian ligious leaders.* 323pp. H&R 63

ALAN WATTS

Over the past twenty-five years, Alan Watts has become widely recognized as he most penetrating and above all readable interpreter of Eastern religions or Western readers. The author of some twenty books, he is considered one f the outstanding philosophical writers of our day. His life and work reflect he thought of a whole generation in an amazingly varied and stimulating ange of activity and interests: Zen, meditation, psychedelics, Growth Cen- ers such as Esalen, ecology and alternative life ways. He died in 1974.

TUART, DAVID. **ALAN WATTS**, c$8.95. A bland, journalistic account of *The Rise and ecline of the Ordained Shaman of the Counterculture.* Most of Watts' writings are sur- eyed and evaluated and the major events and influences in his life are reviewed. To get real feeling for the man the reader is better off with Watts' autobiography. Index, 50pp. Chi 76

WATTS, ALAN. **THE ART OF CONTEMPLATION**, $2.95. An oversize manuscript hand- ritten by Watts, with his doodles—a reprint of a limited edition work. 18pp. RaH 72

_____. **BEHOLD THE SPIRIT**, $1.95. Calls for a reconciliation between Western nd Eastern religions. F.S.C. Northrop calls it *one of the best—in fact the only first-rate ook in recent years in the field of religion.* Extensive bibliography. 257pp. RaH 47

_____. **BEYOND THEOLOGY—THE ART OF GODMANSHIP**, $1.95. *The reader ust be assured that it is far from my intention to debunk, to give offense, or to hold acred things up to ridicule. For your author is acting, not in the role of the Devil, but in he capacity of the Court Jester....The function of the Fool was to keep his monarch uman and, with luck, even humane, by a judicious unstuffing of his pomposity and by eeping alive his sense of humor—the essence of which is laughter at oneself.* This is a heological work which aims at an understanding of what religion, and especially Christi- nity, truly means to the individual. Notes, index. 244pp. RaH 64

_____. **THE BOOK ON THE TABOO AGAINST KNOWING WHO YOU ARE**, $1.65. Probably the most popular and famous of all Watts' works, **The Book** delves into he cause and cure of the illusion that the self is a separate ego, housed in a bag of skin, which *confronts* a universe of alien physical objects. Watts here restates Vedanta philos- phy in terms understandable to the Western mind. Recommended first reader on Watts. 46pp. RaH 66

_____. **CLOUD-HIDDEN**. $1.95. Watts intends this to be a bedside book which an be read backwards, forwards, or any way one likes. He discusses following the Tao flowing where the stream takes you), the nature of ecstasy, karma and reincarnation, strology, tantric yoga, and much else. 179pp. RaH 68

_____. **THE COSMIC DRAMA**, $3.95. This is the final volume in Celestial Arts' eries *The Essence of Alan Watts.* The content of each of the nine titles can be under- tood simply by referring to the title. The books are gift books with a short quotation rom Watts on the right hand page and a photograph on the left. The content is skimpy to ay the least and the books are very overpriced. 63pp. CeA 75

_____. **DEATH**, $3.95. 63pp. CeA 75

_____. **DOES IT MATTER**, $1.65. Essays on man's relation to materiality. 25pp. RaH 68

_____. **EGO**, $3.95. 63pp. CeA 75

_____. **GOD**, $3.95. 63pp. CeA 74

_____. **IN MY OWN WAY**, $2.45. This fascinating autobiography is an absorbing iscussion of Watts' ideas, beliefs, and inward and outward experiences—all brought togeth- r with a whimsical lack of concern for chronology or tiresome statistics. 388pp. RaH 72

_____. **THE JOYOUS COSMOLOGY: ADVENTURES IN THE CHEMISTRY OF CONSCIOUSNESS**, $1.95. The best description we have seen of drug trips. The height- ening of consciousness ranges all the way from aesthetic insights into nature to a philo- ophical view of existence as a comedy at once diabolical and divine. 101pp. RaH 62

_____. **THE MEANING OF HAPPINESS**, $1.50. A very early book dealing with he quest for freedom of the spirit, modern psychology and the wisdom of the East. Extensive bibliography. 213pp. H&R 40

_____. **MEDITATION**, c$3.95/$1.25. See the Meditation section.

_____. **MYTH AND RITUAL IN CHRISTIANITY**, $2.95. See Christianity section.

_____. **NATURE, MAN AND WOMAN**, $1.95. Watts feels that hostility to nature is characteristic of our culture, and is at the root of our personal anxiety and loneliness, our fear of feeling and our reluctance to love. He discusses the origins of this alienation in Christian and Western thought, contrasted with the Chinese philosophy of the Tao and its vision of nature as an organic whole in which man is fully included and feels at home. Bibliography, 209pp. RaH 58

_____. **THE NATURE OF MAN**, $3.95. 63pp. CeA 75

_____. **NOTHINGNESS**, $3.95. 63pp. CeA 74

_____. **PHILOSOPHICAL FANTASIES**, $3.95. 63pp. CeA 75

_____. **PSYCHOTHERAPY EAST AND WEST**, $1.95. This is an excellent dis- cussion of the common ground between Western psychology and Eastern mysticism. As usual Watts writes clearly and expresses his ideas through a great number of examples. This is one of our favorite Watts books. Notes, bibliography. 206pp. RaH

_____. **THE SPIRIT OF ZEN**, $2.45. See the Zen Buddhism section.

_____. **THE SUPREME IDENTITY**, $1.95. An essay on Oriental metaphysics and the Christian religion. Bibliography, 199pp. RaH 72

_____. **THIS IS IT AND OTHER ESSAYS**, $1.95. The six essays in this volume all deal with the relationship of mystical experience to ordinary life. Also included is Watts' pamphlet **Beat Zen, Square Zen and Zen.** Notes, 158pp. RaH 60

_____. **TIME**, $3.95. 63pp. CeA 75

_____. **THE TWO HANDS OF GOD**, $1.95. See the Mythology section.

_____. **THE WAY OF ZEN**, $1.95. See the Zen Buddhism section.

_____. **THE WISDOM OF INSECURITY**, $1.65. *This book proposes a complete reversal of all ordinary thinking about the present state of man. The critical condition of the world compels us to face this problem: how is man to live in a world in which he can never be secure, deprived, as many are, of the consolations of religious belief? The author shows that this problem contains its own solution—that the highest happiness, the supreme spiritual insight and certitude are found only in our awareness that impermanence and in- security are inescapable and inseparable from life....*—**Book Exchange** (London). 152pp. RaH 51

WEDECK and BASKIN. **DICTIONARY OF PAGAN RELIGIONS**, $3.95. The cults, rites and rituals associated with polytheistic religions, from the Stone Age to the present. Many listings, generally quite brief. 363pp. CiP 71

WOODS, RALPH. **WORLD TREASURY OF RELIGIOUS QUOTATIONS**, c$3.98. More than 15,000 quotations are grouped by subject in some 1500 quick-reference categories. Each category brings together the most significant statements on the subject by important religious figures and thinkers. Author index, 1106pp. GaB 66

ZAEHNER, R.C., ed. **THE CONCISE ENCYCLOPEDIA OF LIVING FAITHS**, $4.95. The term encyclopedia in the title is deceptive. This volume presents a fairly complete introductory survey of the world's religions, with each chapter written by authorities. The articles are concise and tend to be fairly lively. The bulk of the book is devoted to the Eastern religions and sects, and many of the selections are not covered in most general texts. There's also an excellent five-part discussion of Christianity, and chapters on Judaism, Islam, and Zoroastrianism. 8x10", double column, illustrations, topical bibliography, index. 431pp. Bea 59

_____. **HINDU AND MUSLIM MYSTICISM**, $2.45. A comparative analysis of the major tenets of Hinduism and Islam. The two are discussed separately, but with constant reference to each other, as well as to Western thought. All the important individuals in each religion are reviewed along with the major texts. Professor Zaehner's presentations tend to be scholarly and dry, with an emphasis on the dry and the reader should not ex- pect to get a feeling for either of these mystical traditions. It's an academic study, albeit a good one. Notes, index. 242pp. ScB 60

ZARETSKY, IRVING and MARK LEONE, eds. **RELIGIOUS MOVEMENTS IN CON- TEMPORARY AMERICA**, c$25.00. This is a collection of twenty-eight academic papers, mostly written from a sociological viewpoint. The general aim is to understand the varieties of human behavior within these institutions and to point out their relationship to society in the United States. The volume considers three categories of religious movements: those churches such as Afro-American Spiritualist and Mormon with a long history and tradition in this country; recently founded religious groups such as Scientology; and synchretistic groups based on imported traditions such as the Krishna people and Meher Baba groups. Definitely recommended only to those wishing to read scholarly research papers. Notes, long bibliography, index. 837pp. Pri 74

CONSCIOUSNESS EXPANSION

What Is Consciousness?

In a recent review of research on the psychology of consciousness, Robert Ornstein emphasizes the fallacy of assuming that personal consciousness is a perfect mirror of some external reality. He points out that man is aware of only a tiny bit of what is usually called *reality*. The human's sensory systems are not even capable of receiving many energy forms. For example, the spectrum of electromagnetic waves extends from less than one billionth of a meter to more than a thousand meters. Yet the range of vision, that which can be seen, is only a small portion of this: that between 400 and 700 billionths of a meter. What is *seen* by infrared photography, for example, lies outside our range of vision and some animals such as dogs can hear sounds that are beyond our hearing.

Our usual waking consciousness, as we have seen, is principally a product of the functioning of the sensory-motor mind. The limits of this consciousness are the boundaries of the ego-level *I-ness*. It is outwardly oriented, involving action, and seems to have been evolved primarily for the purpose of ensuring individual survival. From the variety of sensory inputs and the information they present, a multi-leveled process filters out that which is related to survival. It is from this that we construct or create a consciousness which will permit us to maintain the integrity of the *I*.

We take the chaos and make sense out of it. Our notion of the world *out there* is based on how we select and process incoming data. This is a personal system which varies from one individual to the next. Our agreement on what *reality is* results from our similar limitations: for example, physical traits and common cultural training. Our eyes are restricted to the same spectrum; our conceptual categories are conditioned by common languages and traditions. Learning to take in and handle information in similar ways, we arrive at similar notions of *what reality is*. But alternate ways of constructing reality are also possible. A well-known passage from William James emphasizes this:

Our normal waking consciousness, rational consciousness as we call it, is but one special type of consciousness, whilst all about it, parted from it by the filmiest of screens, there lies potential forms of consciousness entirely different. We may go through life without suspecting their existence; but apply the requisite stimulus, and at a touch they are there in all their completeness, definite types of mentality which probably somewhere have their field of application and adaptation. No account of the universe in its totality can be final which leaves these other forms of consciousness quite disregarded. How to regard them is the question—for they are so discontinuous with ordinary consciousness. . . . At any rate they forbid a premature closing of our accounts with reality.

Consciousness as a Filter

Information coming into the mind is flashed onto a screen called the *lower mind*. This information is picked up from the outside world by the senses, which serve as a sort of scanning device. However, many things are filtered out. The senses are tuned to take in only certain stimuli while ignoring others, just as a radar antenna is set to pick up only certain signals from the outer world. This protects us from being overwhelmed by limiting the quantity and intensity of data that comes in. But there is also a process of selection. Certain inputs are chosen and others ignored, according to the area of concern outlined by the current self-definition. On this basis some stimuli are accepted as *meaningful* and interpreted in such a way as to fit with the *I*'s current notion of *reality*. Other stimuli which cannot be made to fit and do not serve the purposes of the *I* are rejected. When the radar of the senses is pointed towards the external world, the way in which incoming data is selected and filtered determines to a great extent what is present in the conscious mind at that point. In this fashion then, a *waking consciousness* is created.

There is another aspect to this scanning mechanism. Not only can it reduce the quantity of incoming data desired, it can also turn in different directions to focus on different things. An attractive scene may *catch one's eye*. An interesting comment can cause him to *prick up his ears*. The scanning device of the senses turns and tilts, aiming in first this direction and then tha

This is an action which, at least potentially, can be coordinated by high structures. However, it is not always done with the purposefulness and del beration that indicates coordination from above. Certain customary ways scanning the environment are simply the result of habit. Although original the result of an instinctual urge or a decision, through repetition they com to be carried out almost automatically. For example, one may have a hab of staring out the window while he eats breakfast rather than reading a new paper. Getting in the car, he absent-mindedly turns the radio dial until h finds his favorite program. One person may customarily look at the clothe of a new acquaintance; another notices his posture or speech. Our sensor scanner is governed much of the time by habit and comes to operate in nearly automatic way. In this fashion, *scanning habits* often determine th content of our waking consciousness, changing it from moment to momen They play a key role in shaping the state of the mind. Despite the fact tha such habits were often formed casually, and for no particular reason or pu pose, they persist, essentially unnoticed, automatically and aimlessly shapin and re-shaping our conscious minds from moment to moment.

But more than the momentary waking consciousness is affected by such sca ning habits. The content of the unconscious mind is also greatly affecte Much of the information that is brought in by the senses is never acknowledge consciously. It is stored directly in those areas of the mind that lie outsid normal awareness. Under hypnosis one is able to recall details about his su roundings of which he had not seemed aware at the time they were happen ing. Some information, then, while *meaningful* to the *I*, cannot be comfortabl handled by waking consciousness. It is filed away reflexively in the storag bank of the unconscious. One *hides it from himself* so to speak. Such exper iences tend often to be those which are emotionally charged, too *hot* to b held in awareness—so they are dropped into the unknown mind.

Moreover, even those things which are consciously acknowledged leave last ing imprints in the unconscious. A television drama depicting violence ma have an indelible mark on the impressionable child, but less striking sight and sounds are also taken in, quietly and continuously, slowly transformin the inner world throughout life. Though the habits of scanning and attentio that determine daily routine input may seem trivial and the stimuli may ap pear *meaningless,* by virtue of their quantity they become important. Con sciousness is enormously affected in this slow, undramatic fashion. Much o the process of meditation and the discipline of yoga is aimed at transformin awareness through a gradual but persistent reshaping of such seemingly inno cuous habits of attention.

The Unknown Mind

Notions about how normal waking consciousness is constructed and main tained are not so very different in yoga and Western psychology. Processes o filtration, selection and repression are common to both. Moreover, in bot the East and West there is the notion that a large part of the mental field cus tomarily lies outside awareness. These ideas are basically the same. But ther is disagreement about exactly what it is that is *excluded* from ordinary aware ness. Contrasting ideas about what lies outside ordinary consciousness consti tutes the major difference between yoga and modern psychology. In the Wes this is an unknown territory because it, by definition, lies beyond what i known. It is assumed to contains the instincts and bits and pieces of wha would not fit into one's ego-level activity.

But in yoga psychology this territory is not unknown. Those who formulate the yoga system of psychology did so by virtue of having familiarized them selves experimentally with these inner spaces. Meditation developed as a tech nique for entering these areas and discovering just what lay there. The resul is a systematic and detailed conceptualization of the *unknown mind*.

Collective vs. Transpersonal

As personal evolution advances, one comes to find that his consciousness ha more in common with that of others who have developed themselves. As the sense of *I* expands, personal definitions of *I-ness* increase until they eventually overlap. Then they become *transpersonal*.

People who function at the level of the sensory-motor mind exist more in a state of disparity. When the mind flits from one subject to another, the pattern of impressions is vastly different from one person to another. At that level man is very different from his fellow man. One person may be concerned with sensory stimuli that relate to sex, another with those related to food. The attention of each is drawn towards these desires through paths that are quite different from one another. At this level, disparity is predominant and consensus and agreement are reached only with difficulty, necessarily through compromise, with its inherent struggle and conflict.

But as consciousness expands, it reaches levels where more is held in common. At the highest states of consciousness, as described in yoga, experience is not only similar, it is shared. In other words, we might think of the hierarchy of consciousness as similar to a pyramid. At the base there's a wide area where diversity exists. But ascending through different levels of the hierarchy we begin to approach others who are clinging to the same step-wise fashion. At the peak of the pyramid all paths must come together and the consciousness and perspective that is gained there is identical. This is not a loss of *consciousness* nor slipping back into an indifferentiated state. From this point any part of the surrounding area can be viewed clearly.

As the ego level of *I-ness* is transcended, for instance, and the diversity which is a property of that level is dropped, then the impediments to experiencing a non-personal, encompassing consciousness begin to fall away. Higher consciousness is experienced, then, as *above* the personality, though the personality remains intact below to serve as its tool. For this reason, those who have attained a higher consciousness may continue to be quite different from one another in their outward behavior, even though their underlying consciousness has become identical. This contrasts with the attempt to gain identity through altering the ego or the grosser aspects of the personality. Social conformity, uniform behavior and uniform dress are, in a sense, polar opposites of the unity that is experienced through advanced awareness.

—from **YOGA AND PSYCHOTHERAPY** by Swami Rama, Rudolph Ballentine and Swami Ajaya.

ANDERSON, MARIANNE S. and LOUIS M. SAVARY. **PASSAGES**, $5.95. This large, extensively illustrated book gives many practical exercises for reaching altered states of consciousness without drugs. The exercises are clearly presented and relatively easy to follow. The techniques, involving mainly relaxation and self-hypnosis coupled with fantasy, are similar to those used by Silva Mind Control. Innumerable quotations add to the reader's enjoyment. Recommended. 221pp. H&R

ANONYMOUS. **FROWN STRONG: A CONVERSATION WITH MERLIN**, $2.25. *A series of remarkable conversations between an illumined man and his pupil. These exchanges, thirty-two in number, mark the passage of the student from his day-dream madness into a man, strong and gentle, of quality, substance and some very great account. Frown Strong's insistent teachings push and pull his pupil through the pitfalls of development.* 76pp. Rai 74

ARKLE, WILLIAM. **A GEOGRAPHY OF CONSCIOUSNESS: A PHILOSOPHY OF HUMAN COMMUNICATION**, c$9.25. See the Gurdjieff section.

ARTAUD, ANTONIN. **PEYOTE DANCE**, $2.45. Artaud's experience with the primitive Tarahumara Indians in 1936 was a psychic ordeal and a spiritual revelation: *I have not come to visit the Tarahumara as a tourist but to regain a truth. . . . I should go back to the source and expand my pre-conscious to the point where I could see myself evolve and desire. And Peyote led me to this point.* This is the story of Artaud's visit, refracted through varying states of mind, and documenting his struggle to integrate an overwhelming mystical experience. 105pp. FSG 76

BACH, RICHARD. **JONATHAN LIVINGSTON SEAGULL**, c$5.95/$1.50. An illustrated account of a seagull everyman's quest for self-identity. This was the great hit of a few years ago and if you are one of the few who are not familiar with the book, the photographs and accompanying text have been a delight to millions of people. 127pp. McM 70

BATESON, GREGORY. **STEPS TO AN ECOLOGY OF MIND**, $2.25. *The central idea in this book is that we create the world that we perceive, not because there is no reality outside our heads . . . but because we select and edit the reality we see to conform to our beliefs about what sort of world we live in. . . . For a man to change his basic, perception-determining beliefs . . . he must first become aware that reality is not neces-*

sarily as he believes it to be. This is an integrated collection of some of Bateson's most important essays. The writing style is fairly technical and Bateson has developed his own vocabulary. The book is often slow going, but many important insights are presented. 530pp. RaH 72

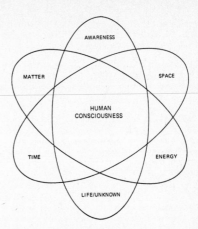

The underlying, interacting dimensions from which human consciousness arises.

BIOFEEDBACK

BOXERMAN, DAVID and ARON SPILKEN. **ALPHA BRAIN WAVES**, $4.95. This is the most comprehensive study of alpha for the layman available (not on a par with Brown's definitive **New Mind, New Body**). First the authors review what alpha is and how individuals respond to it. They then go on to discuss the potentials of alpha and its major uses to date. A final section gives diagrammatic instructions for building biofeedback machinery. Bibliography, index. 116pp. CeA 75

BROWN, BARBARA. **NEW MIND, NEW BODY**, $2.50. Dr. Brown is Chief of Experiential Psychology at the VA Hospital, Sepulveda, Calif. and a lecturer in the Department of Psychiatry at the UCLA Medical Center. She opened up the field of biofeedback research eight years ago and since then she has done most of the pioneering research. Her concept of biofeedback is simple: body processes generate specific electrical waves. These can be measured by electronic sensors and reported by an indicator. By watching the indicator we can follow what goes on inside us. Some sensors feed back temperature and other body changes, but the electrical indicators do most of the work. This sensory feedback to the mind amounts to intimate communication with the body, says Brown, but it does not stop there. As she and others have discovered, we seem to be able to control any activity that we can monitor. Brown's excitement over her findings led her to become the clearinghouse for many able researchers who came rushing in as the word spread. In this definitive study Dr. Brown reports her own and others' work in biofeedback research and describes many experiments in detail. Fully indexed, with a 31pp bibliography and references. 477pp. Ban 74

KARLINS, M. and L. ANDREWS. **BIOFEEDBACK**, $1.50. Biofeedback training is the procedure that allows us to tune into our bodily functions and, eventually, to control them. In a typical session a subject is given this feedback by hooking up with equipment that can amplify one or a number of his body signals and translate them into readily observable signals: a flashing light, the movement of a needle. This is the only comprehensive report for the layman yet published. Extensive bibliography. 183pp. Lip 72

LAWRENCE, JODI. **ALPHA BRAIN WAVES**, $1.75. An exposition—one of the few in print—of the scientific research into the brain waves. Details on what the alpha state is, how it can be attained and controlled, and its potential uses in medicine, education and psychiatry. A layman's guide, references. 248pp. Avo 72

BOONE, J. ALLEN. **KINSHIP WITH ALL LIFE**, $3.95. A presentation of the author's experiences with animals ranging in size from a camel to a fly. Each of the thirty-four chapters discusses a different animal. 157pp. H&R 54

_____. **THE LANGUAGE OF SILENCE**, c$5.95. More stories of Boone's communication with animals. 139pp. H&R 70

BROWNE, HARRY. **HOW I FOUND FREEDOM IN AN UNFREE WORLD**, $1.95. Discussion of the various traps we fall into which keep us from being free, followed by detailed recommendations on how to break free. *From this man's love of freedom, then, has come this book, a gift of power and of joy for whoever yearns to be free.*— Richard Bach, author of **Jonathan Livingston Seagull**. Very practical suggestions. 368pp. Avo 73

BRY, ADELAIDE. **EST**, $1.95. A not terribly informative summary account of the est experience as seen through the eyes of participants and the news media. Also included are opinions and commentary from various psychology and mental health experts. Glossary, 181pp. Avo 76

CALDER, NIGEL. **THE MIND OF MAN**, $4.25. A wide-ranging, clear, thoughtful report on current research on the brain and human nature, written for professionals as well as laymen, by a noted science writer. Topics include brain physiology discovered through sleep and dream research; influence of drugs on behavior; perceptual illusions; and a yogi's mental control over basic bodily functions. Many illustrations. 285pp. Vik 70

CALDWELL, W.V. **LSD PSYCHOTHERAPY: AN EXPLORATION OF PSYCHEDELIC AND PSYCHOLYTIC THERAPY**, $3.95. Divided into two parts: the first, based on the author's interviews and research, is a survey of modern treatment in the U.S. and abroad. The second part is devoted to the description and classification of basic universal images and fantasies as they manifest themselves under the hallucinogens. Very extensive bibliography. 319pp. RaH 68

CASTANEDA, CARLOS. **JOURNEY TO IXTLAN**, c$2.95/$1.75. The third volume in the continuing saga of Don Juan. **Teachings** was very good, **A Separate Reality** was even better and this one transcends them both. It has nothing to do with drugs—it's about the basic spiritual lessons Don Juan was trying to show Carlos; earlier Carlos was too busy trying to see everying in terms of drugs to see them. *When you see there are no longer any familiar features in the world. Everything is new. Everything has never happened before. The world is incredible! . . . there is really no way to talk about it. Seeing . . . is learned by seeing.* 315pp. S&S 72

__________. **A SEPARATE REALITY: FURTHER CONVERSATIONS WITH DON JUAN**, c$2.95/$1.50. At the end of the first book Carlos was so freaked by the world of *non-ordinary reality* that he decided to go back to UCLA and his academic womb and never resume his apprenticeship. That resolve did not last long and in this volume he resumes going deeper into Don Juan's world of mystical sensation and perception, learning to *see* beyond the surface realities of life. 317pp. S&S 74

__________. **TALES OF POWER**, $2.95. The fourth (and final?) book in Don Juan's continuing re-education of Carlos. All of the material presented in the previous books has been merely the preparation for **Tales of Power**, in which Don Juan's task of making Carlos *a man of knowledge* and *a man of power* is brought to a conclusion in a series of dazzling exploits, visions and lessons, ending in *the sorcerers' explanation*, which is at once an initiation and a deeply moving farewell. Castaneda here presents the culmination of his extraordinary initiation. 287pp. S&S 74

__________. **THE TEACHINGS OF DON JUAN: A YAQUI WAY OF KNOWLEDGE**, c$3.95/$1.95. An account of non-ordinary states of reality experienced through natural psychedelic substances, in the deserts of Mexico, with a strange and profound old man, who has become a legend, myth and teaching power among the flexible minds of America and the world. In this first book the text reads a bit like an anthropology Ph.D. dissertation (which it was an attempt at)—and there are technical appendices. But Carlos' apprenticeship makes fascinating reading. 276pp. S&S 68

__________. **DON JUAN QUARTET**, $11.95/set. A boxed set. S&S

CHAPMAN, RICH. **HOW TO CHOOSE A GURU**, $1.25. Spells out for novices, old and new, variations on the guru game and other traps for sleepwalkers on the road to enlightenment. A few chapter titles: *Compassion, Human and Divine; Consciousness, Planes of; Egonanda, Swami; Gnosis; Guru, Acid; Healing, Psychic; Mysticism; Meher Baba; Nepotism, Spiritual; Ouija Boards and Psychic Gurus; Saints, the Lives of; Yoga and Bhoga (Union and Ignorance).* An enlightening compendium by a follower of Meher Baba. 146pp. H&R 73

COHEN, SIDNEY. **DRUGS OF HALLUCINATION**, $3.25. The results of a twelve year objective research. Topics covered include the early use of LSD as an inducer of *model psychoses* and its present use in psychotherapy; its effects on subjects under controlled conditions; many first-hand accounts of LSD-induced transcendental experiences. Includes a chemical breakdown of the hallucinogens. A very scientific study. 217pp PaL 65

DUNNE, J.W. **AN EXPERIMENT WITH TIME**, $4.25. As a result of numerous dreams which appeared to anticipate the future, Dunne made a thorough study of the nature of time and found it to be something of an illusion, based on our differing perceptions of it. This book was first published in 1927, and has had considerable influence since then. Most of the text is written for the layman, but there are appendices for those with a more technical background. 254pp. Fab 58

DUSEN, WILSON van. **THE NATURAL DEPTH IN MAN**, $1.75. *Van Dusen writes out of his own wide experience with others, and out of his much more personal experience within himself. He explores the limits of consciousness, the expansion of consciousness through mysticism or drugs, the hypnagogic state (before you fall asleep), dreams and their significance. . . . Throughout it all he makes gentle suggestions to the reader. His description of how to meditate, for example, is the best I have ever seen. I predict this book will be highly popular with all those who wish to pioneer in inner space.*—Carl Rogers. H&R 72

FERGUSON, MARILYN. **THE BRAIN REVOLUTION**, $2.25. A comprehensive account. Among the topics covered are biofeedback training, electronic stimulation of the brain, the biochemistry of mental illness, theories about learning and the nature of consciousness; and how the brain responds to psychedelics, alcohol and other drugs. Includes information on planetary influences. Excellent bibliography and notes. 380pp. Ban 73

FIELDS, RICK. **LOKA**, $4.00. **Loka** is an oversize, profusely illustrated compendium of articles, essays, poetry, and images which grew out of the first session of Naropa Institute in the summer of 1974. Inspired by Chogyam Trungpa, Rinpoche, Naropa brought together some of the leading figures in contemporary East/West thought. Contributors to this volume include Miriam and Jose Arguelles, Gregory Bateson, Agehananda Bharati, John Cage, Ram Dass, Allen Ginsberg, L. Gyatso, Thich Thien-An, Chogyam Trungpa, and many others. 144pp. Dou 75

FREDERICK, CARL. **EST: PLAYING THE GAME THE NEW WAY**, $3.95. Frederick took est and has remembered his experience phenomenally well. This is a retelling of the high points of est and should provide an excellent review for those who have taken the training and a taste of the training for those who are curious. All the philosophy is here and some of the exercises. The est organization tried to prevent the publication of thi volume because it reveals many details of the training. The message is simply presente and basically is the following: you are perfect and have full control over what happen to you. Those who have reacted well to books like **Handbook to Higher Consciousnes** should appreciate this volume. 215pp. Del 74

FRENCH, PETER, ed. **PHILOSOPHERS IN WONDERLAND**, $9.95. This volume i hard to classify. It is subtitled *Philosophy and Psychical Research* but we do not fee that it fits in very comfortably with the parapsychology books. It is basically an anthology of classical and contemporary philosophical writings on consciousness. It is a interesting, albeit technical study, which covers many little-discussed and less understood areas. Notes, 388pp. LlP 75

FURST, PETER, ed. **FLESH OF THE GODS: THE RITUAL USE OF HALLUCINOGENS**, $4.95. Ten essays, all by highly respected scholars, covering the various hallucinogens currently in use in non-Western society. A fascinating study, excellent bibliography 304pp. Pra 72

GOLAS, THADDEUS. **THE LAZY MAN'S GUIDE TO ENLIGHTENMENT**, $2.00. A small jewel. Don't be put off by the title—it is a trusted companion for thousands. Recommended. *There is a paradise in and around you right now, and to be there you don't have to make a move. . . . You can open yourself to the diamondlike perfection of everything you see and feel. If you don't think it can happen that easily, just be loving, moment by moment, and trust that it will come to you . . .* 80pp. See 74

GREENFIELD, ROBERT. **THE SPIRITUAL SUPERMARKET**, $3.95. Greenfield has written extensively for **Rolling Stone** and the general writing style of that publication is apparent in this narrative. Nonetheless it is a frank, open look at some of the best known spiritual gurus in the U.S. today. A large part of the book is devoted to a detailed critique of Guru Maharaj-ji. A fascinating section explores Millenium 73—the gathering that took place in Houston. Other chapters discuss Stephen Gaskin, Sri Chinmoy, Ram Dass, Kriyananda, and the Lama Foundation. The account is all in the first person and all the leading characters come to life in the narrative. It makes for interesting reading. 277pp. Dut 75

GROF, STANISLAV. **REALMS OF THE HUMAN UNCONSCIOUS**, c$15.00. This is probably an important technical contribution to the literature in the field of human potential especially as seen through the extensive LSD research that has recently taken place. It's a bit hard for us to judge since something about the format of the book and its general style does not invite casual perusal and no one around here is interested enough in the subject to wade through the mass of material presented. But if you are, this seems to be a definitive volume by one of the pioneering academic researchers. Dr. Grof supplies countless case histories, especially his experiences utilizing LSD for emotional therapy and for terminal cancer patients. Illustrations, bibliography, index. 255pp. Vik 75

HALL, BRIAN, JOSEPH OSBURN and DONNA GRIFFIN. **NOG'S VISION**, $4.95. An adult illustrated *children's story* about a *pricklie* who had mystical vision and was born into a very mundane society and tried to infect the populace with his vision. Oversize, 141pp. Pau 73

HARNER, MICHAEL, ed. **HALLUCINOGENS AND SHAMANISM**, $1.95. Ten studies explore the widespread practice of invoking a trance state to perceive and manipulate supernatural forces. The researchers have succeeded in penetrating the mystical experience by taking the hallucinogens themselves, and participating in the native ceremony. Primitive cultures in various parts of the world are explored. 196pp. Oxf 73

HATTERSLEY, RALPH. **DISCOVER YOURSELF THROUGH PHOTOGRAPHY**, $7.95. This is a very unusual photographic technique book which uses 239 photographs to illustrate the points made. The main subjects include the following: *Free Your Creative Mind, Understand Your Aesthetic Sense, Discover Both Sides of Yourself, Discover Your Own Secret Symbols,* and *Photography May be a Practice of Religion for You.* An emphasis is also place on analyzing your feelings toward others from the pictures you take of them. Hattersley suggests many practice exercises, based on his years of teaching experience, and these are clearly presented and all are geared toward *self-discovery through photography*. We know people who have taken classes from Hattersley and his method has been well received. Oversize, 320pp. AsP 71

HEISEL, DORELLE. **THE BIOFEEDBACK EXERCISE BOOK**, $3.95. An epic poem in the stream-of-consciousness vein, designed to bring one gradually into the meditative state and to explore that state. 390pp. NAL 74

HENDERSON, C. WILLIAM. **AWAKENING**, $3.95. Subtitled *Ways to Psycho-Spiritual Growth*, this is an in-depth exploration of the most important growth groups, metaphysical schools, and Eastern spiritual organizations in the U.S. It is topically arranged and within each topic there is an introductory section and then a four- to ten-page write-up of each group describing its history, specifying what is taught, their training methods, how much they cost, and where to find local training centers. The material has been gathered from interviews with members and leaders of these groups, and from the author's personal experience. The expositions are objective, and, at least for the groups that we know of personally, factual. A fascinating account for those on the path who want to know more about specific groups and even find out about ones that they have not heard of before. 255pp. PrH 75

HISEY, LEHMANN. **KEYS TO INNER SPACE**, $1.95. Half of this book is devoted to brief analyses of the following topics: self-hypnosis and meditation; the Tarot; rhythmic breathing; color and sound; astrology; polarity vs. duality; the Tao and acupuncture; Gurdjieff's teachings; the LSD experience; and the chakras. The material presented in this section is too scanty to be of value to anyone but a beginning student who wants a rvey of the field. The fascinating material is in the second section where Mark Prophet, a deep-trance medium, gives an account of life after death reproduced and documented om actual tapes. Bibliography, 252pp. Avo 74

HUMAN DIMENSIONS INSTITUTE. **CONSCIOUSNESS**, $2.00. This is the summer, 1974 sue of the quarterly publication. It focuses on consciousness research and the nature of uman consciousness and the explorations presented are both theoretical and applied. ontributors include John White and Lama Govinda. Notes, 52pp. HDI

ALDOUS HUXLEY

BEDFORD, SYBILLE. **ALDOUS HUXLEY—A BIOGRAPHY**, c$15.00. Ms. Bedford was n intimate friend of the Huxleys through four decades. Here, in this definitive biography, e gives us not only the private Huxley and the literary Huxley, but the entire intellec- al and social era to which he was central. Huxley at first was primarily known as a ovelist. After coming to the U.S. in the late 1930's, his novels became increasingly hilosophical and utopian, and he began the experiments with mescalin and other con- ciousness expanding techniques that gave him an entirely new perspective. He became a ioneer explorer of the frontiers of the human mind and also delved deeply into Eastern eligion, especially Vedanta. In preparing this book the author spoke with hundreds of eople who knew Huxley throughout his life; she also drew from his letters and diaries. ndex, 789pp. RaH 74

HUXLEY, ALDOUS. **ISLAND**, $1.50. Huxley's final major work, the summation of his fe's views on what an ideal society would be like. It incorporates the realizations he ame to through the use of LSD. The form is a utopian novel, and the island described is South Seas paradise, Pala, which is isolated from the rest of the world. 295pp. H&R 62

_____. **THE DOORS OF PERCEPTION AND HEAVEN AND HELL**, $2.25. Huxley explores the mind's remote frontiers and the unmapped areas of human conscious- ess in this analysis of his psychedelic experience. A classic in the field. 185pp. H&R 54

_____. **THE PERENNIAL PHILOSOPHY**, $3.50. _Perennial Philosophy is pri- arily concerned with the one, divine Reality substantial to the manifold world of things nd lives and minds ... it cannot be directly and immediately apprehended except by ose who have chosen to fulfill certain conditions, making themselves loving, pure in eart, and poor in spirit._ Huxley traces this philosophy through East and West through xcerpts from texts and his own excellent bibliography. 306pp. H&R 44

HUXLEY, LAURA. **THIS TIMELESS MOMENT**, $4.95. A glimpse of Aldous Huxley's ast years. Includes material on psychedelics and a fascinating chapter on his use of LSD hile dying. 308pp. CeA 68

HUXLEY, LAURA. **BETWEEN HEAVEN AND EARTH**, c$8.95. This is a sequel to aura Huxley's **You Are Not the Target: Recipes for Living and Loving:** _The purpose f these Recipes ... is to stimulate a keener insight into our multiple nature and a reali- ation that our conflicting characteristics are desirable advantages rather than burdens._ One group of recipes shows that it is the synchronization of will, imagination and body hat gives meaning to life. Another, _All Living is Relationship_ explores the author's fun- amental interest. _Nutrition, Transformer of Consciousness_ is the title of another group nd additional recipes develop an awareness of vibrations and auras, and of the powerful nfluence of our thoughts. Ms. Huxley's writing style is very clear and the _recipes_ are enerally quite practical. Bibliography, 320pp. FSG 75

_____. **YOU ARE NOT THE TARGET**, $3.00. Recipes, (exercises) for living and oving. Very practical stuff. 277pp. Wil 63

JANOV, ARTHUR and E. MICHAEL HOLDEN. **PRIMAL MAN: THE NEW CON- SCIOUSNESS**, c$10.00. A major exploration of the levels of consciousness and how they operate. The results of Janov's research at the Primal Research Laboratory and the latest esearch in both psychology and neurology are reviewed. Each of the chapters is a sep- arate, albeit related, essay. An important topic is the effect of neurosis on the brain and what happens to the brain and body during a primal. Many case studies are cited. This hould be an interesting study for those who are deeply interested in the brain and its unctioning. Notes, illustrations, index. 532pp. Cro 75

JOHARI, HARISH. **LEELA: THE GAME OF SELF-KNOWLEDGE**, $4.95. See the ndian Philosophy section.

KARAGULLA, SHAFICA. **BREAKTHROUGH TO CREATIVITY**, c$6.95. An impor- ant study by a neuro-psychiatrist. Presents experimental evidence of _sensitives_ who could see into and through the human body, observing states of health and disease that correlated with medical findings. Others could see energy exchange among individuals in a group, and observe the giving or sapping of others' energy. Many fascinating examples. Good bibliography. 286pp. DeV 67

KEEN, SAM. **VOICES AND VISIONS**, $1.95. A collection of interviews Keen did for **Psychology Today** over the last few years and originally printed in the magazine. His subjects include Norman O. Brown, Herbert Marcuse, Joseph Campbell, John Lilly, Carlos Castaneda, Oscar Ichazo, Stanley Keleman, Ernest Becker, and Roberto Assagioli. Keen's style, as he expresses it, is _asking questions, posing problems, talking, listening._ He begins each conversation with a background essay on the individual—and the material presented in these essays is some of the best in the book. All in all the conversations provide a great deal of insight into some of the most important contemporary philos- ophers. 218pp. H&R 74

KEYES, KEN. **HANDBOOK TO HIGHER CONSCIOUSNESS**, c$4.95/$2.95. One of the best step-by-step guidebooks we have encountered. We recommend it highly as a basic textbook for all who are seeking ways to overcome addictions and become loving, peace- ful, wise, and free of a constant barrage of unpleasant emotional feelings. Its message is _love everyone unconditionally—including yourself._ It combines the spiritual insights of the East with the concepts of Western humanistic psychology, particularly Maslow and Perls and is therefore recommended for people in the human potential movement who are interested in moving on. 160pp. LLC 72

KOBERG, DON and JIM BAGNALL. **THE UNIVERSAL TRAVELLER**, $3.95. Subtitled _A Soft-Systems guide to creativity, problem-solving and the process of reaching goals._ Oversize, scattered, with lots of pictures. Index, 128pp. Kau 74

THE ORPHIC EGG. The ancient symbol of the Orphic Mysteries was the serpent-entwined egg, which signified Cosmos as encir- cled by the fiery Creative Spirit. The egg also represents the soul of the philosopher; the serpent, the Mysteries. At the time of ini- tiation the shell is broken and man emerges from the embryonic state of physical existence wherein he had remained through the fetal period of philosophic regeneration.

KOESTLER, ARTHUR. **ACT OF CREATION**, $2.75. Koestler argues that the scientist's insight is similar to the artist's act of creation, and that they share certain psychological conditions. Examining the common factors in scientific, artistic, and comic creations, he draws examples from psychology, Eastern mysticism, biology and literature which yield _the moment of truth_ in the creator's achievement. Discussing the nature of genius, he defines the process by which ability evolves into a completed work, and finds similarities to the creative process throughout the entire animal kingdom. This is a valuable compen- dium of psychological and scientific information for the layman. Notes, bibliography, index. 751pp. Del 64

_____. **THE HEEL OF ACHILLES**, c$8.95. A collection of Koestler's essays, 1968–73, about which he has written: _In spite of their diversity, these essays were inten- ded as variations on certain themes, and are grouped accordingly. The first section has as its leitmotif the predicament of man ... the section called_ Nothing But ...? _attacks the prevailing materialistic philosophy.... The last essay, dealing with certain distastrous aspects of Gandhi's life and philosophy—which are largely unknown to the public—is in- tended to redress the balance by stressing the dangers of taking shortcuts from Western materialism to Eastern mysticism._ Notes, 273pp. RaH 74

_____. **THE ROOTS OF COINCIDENCE**, $1.95. See the Parapsychology section.

LAMB, F. BRUCE. **WIZARD OF THE UPPER AMAZON**, $2.95. _Wizard ... is an extra- ordinary document of life among a tribe of South American Indians at the beginning of the century. For many readers the most compelling sections of the book will be the descriptions of the use of ... the yage or ayahuasca of the Amazon forests. This powerful hallucinogen has long been credited with the ability to transport human beings to realms of experience where telepathy and clairvoyance are commonplace....Manuel Cordova, the narrator..., is now an old man, well-known as a healer in Peru. He attributes his powers to his time as a captive among the Amahuaca Indians, in particular to intensive training sessions conducted under the influence of ayahuasca.—Andrew Weil._ This is an illuminating, entertaining tale which should especially appeal to Castaneda aficionados. 233pp. HMC 74

LEARY, TIMOTHY. **THE PSYCHEDELIC EXPERIENCE—A MANUAL BASED ON THE TIBETAN BOOK OF THE DEAD**, c$6.00. The classic trip-guide. Analyzes the stages one passes through during the psychedelic experience. A recording of Leary reading this manual is available. For a description see the Records section. 191pp. Stu 64

LEONARD, GEORGE. **THE TRANSFORMATION—A GUIDE TO THE INEVITABLE CHANGES IN HUMANKIND**, $2.75. Deals with an alternate system of perceiving and being. _After all the journeying,_ says Leonard, _all the pain and joy, we may discover that the transformation was difficult to grasp, not because it was so far away, but because it was so very near. To find the immense world of delight, is, in the end, to come home again, where it always was._ A beautifully written book which will appeal to all who see our culture dying, and who are experiencing a new way of being. It is a book of hope. 258pp. Del 72

LEWIS, HOWARD, et al. **GROWTH GAMES**, $1.75. See the Humanistic Psychology section.

LILLY, JOHN. **THE CENTER OF THE CYCLONE**, $1.95. Lilly continues his explo- rations into the human mind and the communication system begun in his research with dolphins. Through his own personal experience and experiments under conditions of solitude, confinement, LSD and mystical inspiration, he provides a scientific account of how the mind operates on various levels of consciousness. He demonstrates how an individual can self-program such spaces and create the principles that govern thoughts and behavior. The last chapters detail his experiences in Arica, Chile with Oscar Ichazo. We recommend this volume to all seekers. Our only reservations stem from Lilly's ten- dency to use mechanistic language. 200pp. Ban 72

_____. **LILLY ON DOLPHINS**, $3.50. This is a revised one-volume edition of **Man and Dolphin** and **The Mind of the Dolphin**. Here Lilly describes his ground-breaking attempt to communicate with dolphins and discusses his findings. Illustrations, notes, bibliography, index. 515pp. Dou 75

_____. **PROGRAMMING AND META-PROGRAMMING IN THE HUMAN BIO-COMPUTER**, c$4.95/$1.95. Deals with the theory and methods behind Lilly's personal work as expressed in **Center of the Cyclone** and the Dolphin books. The text was originally written as a summary report to a government agency and therefore the language is quite dry. An interesting, well-organized presentation if you can relate to the language used. 160pp. Jul 67

_____. **SIMULATIONS OF GOD**, $2.25. *My purpose is to present the simulations, the models, the belief structures of others as objectively and as accurately as I can....If you will agree to look for and explore basic beliefs with me, I can, despite my own limits, point out ways to take off on your own search, directions to look in, and methods of integrating the new as you find it... I ask you to consider and think about what I write, make what you can yours, and let the rest go for a while....We shall enter the sacred realms of self, religion, science, philosophy, sex, drugs, politics, money, crime, war, family, and spiritual paths. We shall enter with no holds barred, with courage, and a sense of excitement.*—from the introduction. This is a fairly technical exploration, which needs to be read slowly and carefully. 288pp. Ban 75

LOW, ALBERT. **ZEN AND CREATIVE MANAGEMENT**, $3.50. *Out of his considerable experience in management and Zen, Albert Low brilliantly diagnoses what lies behind the dilemmas and conflicts bedeviling the world of management...I know of no other book that so capably reconciles the seemingly disparate worlds of industry and Zen, or that speaks with the authority of this one. [This] is a profoundly wise book that needs to be read by managers, executives and manual workers alike.*—Phillip Kapleau. Notes, bibliography, index. 255pp. Dou 76

LOZOWICK, LEE. **BEYOND RELEASE**, $3.95. Lee is a spiritual teacher who runs a community called HOHM in New Jersey. His teachings are presented here in the form of short discourses and a series of questions and answers. His way to enlightenment for his followers is simply to experience. Lee Lozowick and his teaching style and message resemble that of Franklin Jones. *My act is to take over the world through the spiritual process of Satsang. That's my act and that's the same act as every other guru's act. Some admit it and some don't. See, I already am the world. I'm just claiming my heritage.* Many photographs, 223pp. HOH 75

MC CARROLL, TOLBERT. **EXPLORING THE INNER WORLD**, $1.95. A manual of growth techniques for individuals and groups, that bridges contemporary humanistic psychology and ancient spiritual traditions, East and West. Among the topics covered are: the use of a daily journal; working with inner imagery and dreams; listening to ourselves through art experiences and other tools of self-exploration; an introduction to meditation; working in self-exploration groups; and the relationship of self-knowledge to spiritual growth. Illustrations, chapter notes, and a long topical list of suggested readings. 223pp. Jul 74

MARTIN, MALACHI. **THE NEW CASTLE**, $3.95. This is a fascinating study of a few times in history when a transcendental vision came to a number of societies. Martin, a former Jesuit scholar well versed in Oriental philosophy, describes what people and places were like before the vision touched them, the nature of each vision, the tangible changes it wrought, and what remains of its promise. It includes penetrating critiques of the central artistic creations that were the concrete manifestations of each vision: the Islamic Arabesque, Byzantine mosaics, Gothic cathedrals, the temple of Angkor Wat, and even the American sky-scrapers. Martin also provides insights into the character, feelings, and actions of the leaders and the general populace who shared their vision. The cities discussed include Mecca, Jerusalem, Constantinople, Rome, Peking, Angkor Wat, and Wittenberg. 209pp. Dut 74

MASTERS, ROBERT and JEAN HOUSTON. **MIND GAMES**, $2.75. Authors describe and instruct the reader-player in the mental exercises they have developed scientifically to alter, explore, and regulate human consciousness. Includes exercises of entertainment, education, ecstasy, self-exploration, powerful games of growth. 246pp. Del 70

_____. **VARIETIES OF PSYCHEDELIC EXPERIENCE**, $2.45. *The effort will be made to detail means by which the average person may pass through new dimensions of awareness and self-knowledge to a transforming experience resulting in actualization of latent capacities, philosophical reorientation, emotional and sensory at-homeness in the world....We will also try to make... clear the enormous potential importance of psychedelic research.* One of the best introductions to psychedelia. 326pp. Del 66

METZNER, RALPH. **THE ECSTATIC ADVENTURE**, c$6.95. Thirty-eight people from a broad spectrum of backgrounds and beliefs discuss their experiences with hallucinogenic drugs. Some of the trips are hell, others ecstasy. Metzner introduces each account and explains the religious, sociological and historical background of psychedelics. 306pp. McM 68

_____. **MAPS OF CONSCIOUSNESS**, c$7.95/$3.95. *Down the ages, man has devised ways to free his consciousness from exterior limitations. These ancient ways, once known to only a few, have now become routes well-traveled by many modern adventurers. This book shows how to use these ways, and why they operate as maps of consciousness.* The maps discussed include the I Ching, tantra, Tarot, alchemy, astrology and actualism. Extensive treatment of each topic. Recommended. 160pp. McM 71

MISHLOVE, JEFFREY. **ROOTS OF CONSCIOUSNESS**, $9.95. As the title suggests, this is an exploration of consciousness throughout the ages divided into three increasingly more technical sections. Section I, *History of the Exploration of Consciousness*, includes discussions of the rituals and major figures in ancient civilizations (primarily Western),

the medieval period, the Renaissance (when alchemy and the original Rosicrucian flowered), the Age of Reason, and the nineteenth century. Section II, *Scientific Approaches to Consciousness*, presents the principal individuals, research, and findings in the following areas: extra-sensory perception, out-of-body experiences, psychic healing, fire walking, psychokinesis, life within death and death within life, other worlds, and the physiological mechanisms of consciousness. Section III, *People, Places, and Theories*, is more scientifically oriented. It includes some fascinating material by Arthur Young under the general heading of The Reflexive Universe along with a detailed overview of modern physics; and it ends with *Practical Applications of Psi*. This is a well organized, up-to-date sourcebook. An incredible amount of material is presented in a lively, instructive manner. Roots of Consciousness can be considered a textbook of consciousness as it has evolved from the esoteric teachings of ancient and medieval man down to present-day scientific and quasi-scientific explorations. The text is oversize with 300 photographs and diagrams and sixty-six color illustrations. 375pp. RaH 75

MURPHY, MICHAEL. **GOLF IN THE KINGDOM**, $2.65. Murphy founded the Esalen Institute. This is the story of time he spent with a Scottish golf pro for whom *the hidden but accessible meaning of the game becomes a metaphor for all the possibilities of transcendence that reside in the human soul....A revelation of all in golf that connects with the inner spirit of a player, and the personal record of a man brought into transforming touch with his own expanding awareness.* One doesn't have to be a golfer to find this journal enlightening. 205pp. Del 72

MUSES, CHARLES and ARTHUR YOUNG, eds. **CONSCIOUSNESS AND REALITY**, $2.45. Muses is the editor of the **Journal for the Study of Consciousness** and Young is the founder of the Foundation for the Study of Consciousness. Together they have assembled an extraordinary collection of articles on the developments in human consciousness. The selections span many scientific disciplines and cultures and are written by the most knowledgeable researchers available. Sample topics and authors include: *Trance Induction Techniques in Ancient Egypt*—C. Muses; *Recognition of Reincarnation and the Supra-Physical Body*—D. Kelsey and Joan Grant; *The Place of Consciousness in Modern Physics*—Eugene Wigner; and *Man's Potential*—Charles Lindbergh. This is far and away the best collection of articles that we know of and we recommend it highly, both to the layman and the professional. Notes, 472pp. Avo 72

NARANJO, CLAUDIO. **THE HEALING JOURNEY**, $1.50. Describes Naranjo's recent healing work using several new drugs in combination with more traditional forms of psychotherapy. These drugs—MDA, MMDA, harmaline, ibogaine—are *mind-manifesting* in that they facilitate access to otherwise unconscious processes, feelings and thoughts without the changes in thinking characteristic of the hallucinogens. They accelerate the process of analysis and allow the patient to see the problems which have made him ill. 235pp. RaH 73

NELMS, HENNING. **THINKING WITH A PENCIL**, $3.25. Subtitled *692 Illustrations of Easy Ways to Make and Use Drawings in Your Work and in Your Hobbies*, this is an excellent drawing technique book for the non-artist. Techniques reviewed include creative tracing; proportion, measurement, alignment; fixed-line construction; constructions for free-line drawings; visualizing numerical data; mechanical aids; adding the third dimension; controlling distortion; people and animals; lettering and layout. All of the material is well-explained and, at least according to the raves on the back cover, easy for anyone to follow. Includes a descriptive equipment and materials supplement. Index, 348pp. H&R 64

NEUMANN, ERICH. **THE ORIGINS AND HISTORY OF CONSCIOUSNESS**, $3.95. See the Jungian Psychology section.

OATLEY, KEITH. **BRAIN MECHANISMS AND THE MIND**, $3.95. Includes a description of the current study of the brain, an exposition of the elements of neurobiology, and analyses of forms of perception, behavior, learning, memory, language and thought, and an essay on artificial brains. Very clearly written. Glossary, 180 illustrations, and detailed bibliography. 216pp. Dut 72

O'CONNOR, ELIZABETH. **OUR MANY SELVES: A HANDBOOK FOR SELF-DISCOVERY**, $2.50. The author is on the staff of a liberal church—however, her exercises are quite eclectic and go far beyond traditional Church doctrine. They are not meant to guide the reader along someone else's path, but to help one find one's own. Also included are various essays by Ms. O'Connor and selections from writings she has found helpful, grouped with the appropriate exercise. Recommended. 201pp. H&R 71

ORNSTEIN, ROBERT, ed. **THE NATURE OF HUMAN CONSCIOUSNESS**, $8.75. Articles and essays are included from such diverse sources as the **I Ching**, Sufi literature, neurophysiological essays on the brain, and linguistic analysis. Among the contributors are William James, Michael Polanyi, Charles Tart, Aldous Huxley, Lama Govinda, Idries Shah, Robert Assagioli, Carl Jung and David Sobel. The tone is generally pretty academic and the selections run the gamut from sheer technocratic language which only an expert in the field could comprehend to more philosophical essays. All of the contributors are considered tops in their field. This is basically a textbook on the *new consciousness*. Oversize, extensive bibliography, index. 514pp. Fre 73

_____. **ON THE EXPERIENCE OF TIME**, $2.95. Dr. Ornstein is a research psychologist in neuropsychiatry who is especially noted for his right hemisphere, left hemisphere brain research. Here he discusses some of his earlier research on experimental analyses of the time experience. He disavows the generally assumed *inner clock* explanation and postulates a cognitive information processing approach. This is a technical work which basically recounts several experiments and summarizes the findings. Notes, bibliography, index. 126pp. Pen 70

_____. **THE PSYCHOLOGY OF CONSCIOUSNESS**, $1.95. Analyzes thought in terms of empirical research which has indicated that there are significant differences in the functioning of the two hemispheres of the brain. Western thought is seen as left-hemisphere dominated, oriented toward verbal mathematic rationality; Eastern thought, particularly as manifested in yoga and Zen, is seen as primarily influenced by the right hemisphere. Ornstein uses this theme and integrates it with meditative exercises and other ways of expanding awareness, such as biofeedback, as well as with tools of scientific inquiry. Extensive listing of sources for further reading. An excellent book for the serious student. 243pp. Pen 72

OSTRANDER, SHEILA and LYNN SCHROEDER. **PSYCHIC DISCOVERIES BEHIND THE IRON CURTAIN**, $1.50. See the Parapsychology section.

PAULUS, TRINA. **HOPE FOR THE FLOWERS**, $4.95. This is a delightful, beautifully illustrated tale of a caterpillar who has trouble becoming what he really is (a butterfly!)—and in allegorical form it is the story of all of us who must die to the old before being born anew. The story is a wonderful one to read and then to pass on to a friend, an underground classic along the lines of Jonathan Livingston Seagull—but much better done. Oversized, 152pp. Pau 72

PEARCE, JOSEPH CHILTON. **THE CRACK IN THE COSMIC EGG**, $1.95. A moving personal voyage of discovery. It emphasizes the similarity of processes which produce discovery and invention in the physical sciences to such phenomena as fire-walking, the dream life of the Australian aborigine, the transformation of reality evidenced in the life of Jesus, the teaching of a Yaqui Indian sorcerer, etc. It proves that significant learning and achievement emerge out of the vast reservoirs of human experience, vision, and potential, and not from the repeating of formulas of obsolete data parading as scientific truth. Extensive notes and bibliography. Recommended. 219pp. S&S 71

_____. **EXPLORING THE CRACK IN THE COSMIC EGG**, $1.75. In this sequel to The Crack in the Cosmic Egg, Pearce deals with the despair, anxieties and confusion modern man suffers. He identifies this dilemma as an attempt to live according to the imposed abstract programming that allows thinking and living only in culturally evaluated terms of reality. Here he presents other viable approaches emerging out of man's history and evolution, demonstrating that man has found and can achieve wholeness and a more expansive and fulfilling existence. Many of his examples come from the *teachings of Don Juan* as presented by Carlos Castaneda, and others from the concepts of individuals who have broken with the rigid rules of our limited quasi-scientific establishment. Good chapter notes and bibliography. 173pp. S&S 74

PELLETIER, KENNETH and CHARLES GARFIELD. **CONSCIOUSNESS EAST AND WEST**, $4.95. *This is the most comprehensive array of Western scientific approaches to altered states of consciousness. Anyone interested in psychology can learn a great deal from this review of the Western literature and scientists, themselves, will begin to see some of the major changes in approach and method that are needed for the next step in the study of consciousness.—Gay Luce.* Most of the essays are fairly technical. An excellent bibliography is included. 318pp. H&R 76

PENFIELD, WILDER. **THE MYSTERY OF THE MIND**, c$8.95. A scientific study by a leading researcher which describes the current state of knowledge about the brain and asks to what extent recent findings explain the action of the mind. The central question, he points out, is whether man's being is determined by his body alone or by mind and body as separate elements. Before suggesting an answer, he gives an account of his experience as a neurosurgeon and scientist observing the brain in conscious patients. Bibliography, index. 142pp. PUP 75

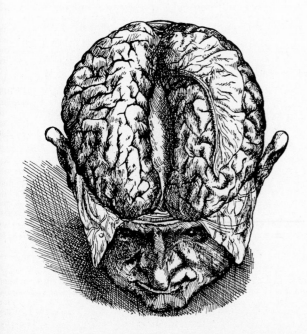

Drawing after the woodcut by Andreas Vesalius in DE HUMANI CORPORIS FABRICA

PINES, MAYA. **THE BRAIN CHANGERS**, $1.75. A journalistic report on brain research being done all over the U.S. by biologists, chemists, psychologists, surgeons and engineers. Includes material on controlling brain waves, on memory, and on actual ways of altering brain functions. Many case studies are cited and explored. Index, 223pp. NAL 73

PIRSIG, ROBERT. **ZEN IN THE ART OF MOTORCYCLE MAINTENANCE**, $2.25. This is a remarkable, moving autobiographical account that has been acclaimed in rave reviews throughout the country, including **Psychology Today** and **The New York Times Book Review**. On one level it is the story of a cross-country motorcycle trip taken by the author and his son. While they ride, Pirsig delivers an old-time series of popular talks which cover many topics, from a search for how to live, an inquiry into *what is best*, through the creation of a philosophical system that reconciles science, religion and humanism. On another and connecting level, the book is the story of Pirsig's visit to the forgotten tomb of his past and his confrontation there with the ghost of his former self, a brilliant questioning man who under the burden of his pursuit of ideals went mad, was institutionalized, underwent shock therapy, died—and has now returned. 412pp. Ban 74

PORTER, JEAN. **PSYCHIC DEVELOPMENT**, $1.75. *The most important experience which I want for you is that of joyousness as you move through these various journeys, inwardly and outwardly. Become, again, like a little child eager to explore new worlds of experience, looking for the positive and the beautiful and accepting what you find there as a discovery of a new treasure. Use this book to guide you through your explorations. Trust the experiences you have, and own them. And remember, this is only a beginning of a process of your own development. Your psychic abilities will increase as you use them.—from the introduction.* This book details, in clear, simple fashion, ways to develop the psychic abilities that all of us have. Ms. Porter has used all of the explorations detailed here in her classes. Illustrations, 55pp. RaH 74

PORTUGAL, PAMELA RAINBEAR. **A PLACE FOR HUMAN BEINGS**, $5.75. This is a lovely, hand written and hand colored account of being in the world and living, loving. Here's a quotation: *Truth does not last, it reoccurs, like blades of grass, almost always similar. almost always different. almost always new and changing. and quite often beautiful.* Oversize, about 150pp. Pop 74

PROGOFF, IRA. **AT A JOURNAL WORKSHOP**, c$12.50. Dr. Progoff is a depth psychologist, trained in analytical (Jungian) psychology. He has *evolved a remarkable method that uses the intensive journal to unify the personality and effectively achieve a kind of self-therapy. He begins by eliminating the idea of the journal as a literary achievement so that anyone from any walk of life with any degree of education could complete a mirror image of his life and character, make a synthesis of experiences and dreams and arrive at a self-creation....With this book anyone can learn to extract meaning from his life.—Anais Nin.* The book is a basic text on the method. It presents the concepts and techniques as they have emerged over the years and details the exercises which individuals can practice. All terms and principles are fully explained. 320pp. DHL 75

PUHARICH. **THE SACRED MUSHROOM: KEY TO THE DOOR OF ETERNITY**, $2.95. An early classic concerning the famous sacred mushroom known by botanists as *Amanita Muscaria*, used for thousands of years as a psychedelic and religious agent. Puharich describes his own investigation as well as his extraordinary association with Harry Stone, a sensitive, who, in a deep trance, defined the long lost ritual of the mushroom and its effects on human consciousness. Dou 59

RAM DASS, BABA. **BE HERE NOW**, $3.33. There are now over 250,000 copies in print of this combination manual, bible, sacred cookbook and printed friend. To know it is to love it. Richly illustrated, glossaried and bibliographied, it exists as one of the most complete books dealing with the transformation. It's divided into several sections: the transformation of Richard Alpert, who had it made with all the status symbols, through LSD and Timothy Leary, through inner space and outer spaces of mind, and at last to India, ending up at the feet of his guru; *From Bindu to Ojas—the Core Book*, 108pp of pure energy and light, unravelling the lessons we must share, on our journey into consciousness; *Cookbook for a Sacred Life*, insights into daily life, yoga, sex, what to eat, and much, much more. Glossary of terms and a very complete list of supplementary books. A magnificent document. Over 300pp. Cro 71

RAM DASS, BABA. **THE ONLY DANCE THERE IS**, $2.95. This book contains transcripts of lectures Ram Dass gave at the Menninger Foundation in 1970 and at Spring Grove Hospital in Baltimore in 1972. The style is very personal and there are also sections of questions and answers. Much of the material covered here is not included in **Be Here Now**, so this volume is well worth reading. The teaching, as usual, is clear and enlightening. Indexed, 180pp. A hardcover English edition (**Doing Your Own Being**) is available for $4.40. It contains the Menninger lectures and a bibliography updated through 1973. Dou 74

RAMA, SWAMI, RUDOLPH BALLENTINE, and SWAMI AJAYA. **YOGA AND PSYCHOTHERAPY**, c$11.95. An in-depth study by three men who have spent their adult lives integrating modern psychology and psychotherapy with Eastern, and especially Hindu, philosophy. Chapter I deals with the physical body and how working with it through various kinds of exercises affects the psychological makeup. The second chapter covers breath and energy. The third chapter contrasts the Western method of observing the mind by observing behavior with the yogic method of studying it through the direct experience of introspection using meditational techniques. Chapter IV goes beyond the mind to take a look at the systems of Western psychology that have studied altered states of consciousness. The fifth chapter discusses various states of bliss, while the sixth compares this consciousness with the state of psychosis with which it is sometimes confused, since both depart radically from ordinary awareness. The last chapter is a detailed study of the *chakras*, seven energy centers in the body. The *chakras* are defined and there is a discussion of the behavior manifested when energy is focused at each. An unusual and very interesting study. Illustrations, notes, index. 359pp. Him 76

REGUSH, JUNE and NICHOLAS. **PSI—THE OTHER WORLD CATALOGUE**, $5.00. This is a scattered collection of bits and pieces from books and catalogs pasted up without a great deal of care and little or no artistic input. There's a great deal of useful information contained here, material that is hard to find elsewhere—but it's difficult to know where in the book to find what you're looking for. The material is basically taken verbatim from the primary sources with no opinions appended by the editors. Illustrations are mainly from the book covers. It's a good idea but the execution leaves a lot to be desired. Oversize, 320pp. Put

RICHARDS, M.C. **CENTERING IN POTTERY, POETRY, AND THE PERSON**, $3.95. *In a marvelous Zen-like melange of jokes, proverbs, anecdotes, poems, folk-tales, myths and personal experiences, the author reaches directly and disturbingly toward inert portions of ourselves, which we suddenly find to be vulnerable, mysterious, and naive.* Unusually sensitive and beautiful. 159pp. WUP 62

_________. **THE CROSSING POINT**, $3.95. This new volume brings together a major selection of Ms. Richards' more recent statements. Prepared at different times for different audiences, they are one in their central concerns: the ongoing quest for total understanding of self and universe, for mutual respect and love, for integrity and fulfillment. She includes material on the concept of karma, the nature of language, the growth of the non-materialistic consciousness and much else. A gift for all those who loved her first book. 245pp. WUP 66

ROPP, ROBERT de. **CHURCH OF THE EARTH**, $2.95. This is the most personal book that de Ropp has written. It is a journal, cast in the form of essays, chronicling the life in his spiritual community in northern California. This book also reflects his religious and philosophical thoughts: man's position in the universe; ways of inner development along the lines suggested by Gurdjieff; the need to know death and challenge; and the spiritual benefits of living close to the earth. The later chapters clearly reflect the same theme developed in **The Master Game**: the continuing search for a higher state of being. Subtitled *The Ecology of a Creative Community*, this work is highly recommended to all those who seek to leave the city and find a more fulfilling life in the country. 280pp. Del 74

_________. **DRUGS AND THE MIND**, c$10.00. This is a revised edition of de Ropp's classic work, incorporating a great deal of new information (it was first published in 1957) and rearranging the subject matter. De Ropp is a biochemist who has carried out extensive research in the fields of mental health and drugs which affect behavior. Bibliography, index. 302pp. Del 76

_________. **THE MASTER GAME: PATHWAYS TO HIGHER CONSCIOUSNESS BEYOND THE DRUG EXPERIENCE**, $2.25. See the section on Gurdjieff.

ROSE, STEVEN. **THE CONSCIOUS BRAIN**, $4.95. An important and fascinating new scientific work which discusses in detail the functioning of the brain and the brain's relationship to the human mind. The author is a noted neurobiologist who makes clear what he and his colleagues are finding out about the way in which man thinks, knows, remembers, feels, sleeps and wakes. Extensively illustrated with superb diagrams and visualizations. A very well-organized and clearly presented work. We recommend it highly. Many, many references are cited, glossary. 343+pp. RaH 73

ROSENFELD, EDWARD. **THE BOOK OF HIGHS**, $4.95. A compilation of 250 ways to alter your consciousness without drugs. The methods are derived from every conceivable source (including some we've nevery heard of). They involve: just yourself, help from others, and devices and machines. A fascinating surface account. Most of the entries include a section on access which details the best material (books, etc.) on the subject; and the bibliography is one of the best we've seen. Qdr 73

ROSZAK, THEODORE. **UNFINISHED ANIMAL**, c$10.00. *We are in the midst of a religious renaissance, but it is religion by any other name and every other name that binds our attention. The spiritual impulse of the time steps beyond the boundaries of religious tradition altogether to become psychotherapy, sensory awareness, parapsychology, consciousness research, psychedelic tripping, bioenergetics, occult science.* Roszak calls these phenomena the *Aquarian frontier* and feels that the exploration of this frontier represents *a transformation of the human personality which is of* evolutionary *proportions, a shift of consciousness fully as epoch-making as the appearance of speech or the tool-making talents. . . .* This is an interesting, albeit scattered, exploration of this frontier. Index, 271pp. H&R 75

RUBIN, JERRY. **GROWING (UP) AT 37**, c$7.95. This is a very personal, candid account of Rubin's experiences in the human potential movement which details many of the therapies he went through including est, rolfing, and the Fischer-Hoffman process. Rubin discusses who he was and why he was that way as well as who he is today and where he is going. 208pp. Lip 76

RUSSELL, EDWARD. **DESIGN FOR DESTINY**, $1.25. A synthesis and interpretation of the work of many scientists, providing a link between science and religion, intellect and perception, man and his universe. Russell was especially close to Harold Burr, whose pioneering work with L-Fields (the permanent electro-magnetic fields which mold the constantly changing material of the cells) is described in great detail. Other scientists discussed include L.L. Vasiliev, J.B. Rhine, Wilder Penfield. An important book for the layman. Well-researched and annotated. 213pp. RaH 71

SAMUELS, M. and N. **SEEING WITH THE MIND'S EYE**. $9.95. The human mind is a slide projector with an infinite number of slides in its library, an instant retrieval system and an endlessly cross-referenced subject catalog. The inner images we show ourselves form our lives, whether as memories, fantasies, dreams or visions. Inner images supply the creative force in art, spirituality, psychology, healing, parapsychology and daily life, but they have never been studied comprehensively. Here Dr. Samuels, the author of the **Well Body Book**, presents such a study, subtitled *The History, Techniques and Uses of Visualization*. The book itself is 8½x11 and filled with illustrations. The material is topically arranged and each chapter is followed by bibliographic entries. Visualization, a presented in this book, is a set of concepts and techniques drawn from historical as we as contemporary sources, in every aspect of life, that seeks to reinstate the reader to a understanding of the nature of his visual processes and their importance in his life. This an exciting, important new book and we recommend it. 348pp. RaH 75

SAMUELS, MIKE and HAL BENNET. **SPIRIT GUIDES**, $1.45. *For centuries peopl have called their feeling and secret thoughts* inner voices. *I will discuss how these inne voices can have their own personalities, called* spirit guides, *and how these guides can b used to tap energies which are in all people. . . . You go to your inner world all the time when you pause to think; when you daydream; when you ponder a complex questior Often a kind of mental conversation takes place. There is a voice which you associat with you, your self, and a second voice that responds to you. The second voice is a spiri guide. These inner conversations take you on a journey into your imagination. On thes journeys, your spirit guide can help you make full use of your inner world.* 55pp. RaH 7

SINGER, MICHAEL. **THE SEARCH FOR TRUTH**, $2.45. *This book is for those wh . . . cannot look at this view of our planet without asking* WHY? *The search conducte within these pages is a logical journey into the fields of biology, psychology, physic parapsychology, yogic science, and Eastern and Western religious philosophies. Are the merely viewing different aspects of the same Truth?* Singer presents some interestin material, although he jumps around a lot and does not write terribly clearly. Index 153pp. Anh 74

SMITH, ADAM. **POWERS OF THE MIND**, c$10.00. This new book by the author o **The Money Game** and **Supermoney** has been welcomed with a lot of fanfare. We wondere how an individual who did not seem to know anything about or have any interest i our area would portray it in his *sure-fire best seller*. The title of the book and the chap ter headings did not alleviate our doubt. However the content does, once the reader get beyond the flashy words. Smith is an excellent writer and he seems to have delved quit seriously into this new (to him) world. He comes out with an enjoyable, informative in-depth analysis of these movements. He has explored and personally experienced eacl of the things that he writes about. We might not always agree with his impressions, bu we are glad that he is getting involved and turning many other people on in the proces (or off, as the case may be). Some of the areas covered include Transcendental Meditatio biofeedback, est, Arica, rolfing, Zen Buddhism, and parapsychology. Includes notes an an excellent long bibliography. 418pp. RaH 75

STEARN, JESS. **MIRACLE OF THE MIND**, c$8.95. Subtitled *The Power of Alpha Think ing*, this is an exploration of Stearn's own experiences with alpha-thinking and a presen tation of techniques. A journalistic work, replete with case studies. Index, 251pp. Mor 7(

STEVENS, JOHN. **AWARENESS: EXPLORING, EXPERIMENTING, EXPERIENCING** c$3.50/$1.95. See the Humanistic Psychology section.

TART, CHARLES, ed. **ALTERED STATES OF CONSCIOUSNESS**, $4.95. A classic The first major serious treatment of human consciousness. Tart collected articles from a wide range of sources to show the broad scientific dimensions of this field. Topics includ drugs, yoga, self-hypnosis, meditation, brain wave research, dream consciousness. A scholarly book with forty pages of references. Recommended. 570pp. Dou 69

_________. **ON BEING STONED—A PSYCHOLOGICAL STUDY OF MARIJUANA INTOXICATION**, c$7.95. A very complete study—the first in which the subjects, 150 experienced marijuana smokers, were in a natural social situation. Bibliography, 328pp S&B 73

_________. **STATES OF CONSCIOUSNESS**, $4.95. Tart's writing style always seem overly academic. Nevertheless, he is without question one of the leaders in the field o consciousness research and this is an important new work which outlines the researcl that he has been doing in a variety of areas and discusses the implications of the findings Basically he is presenting a systems approach to altered states of consciousness and th presentation itself is definitely geared to the sophisticated reader. Bibliography, index 316pp. Dut 75

_________, ed. **TRANSPERSONAL PSYCHOLOGIES**, $6.95. This is an excellent collection of eleven essays including the following: Charles Tart—*The Physical Universe, the Spiritual Universe, and the Paranormal* and two other long essays; Claire Owen—*Zen Buddhism*; Daniel Goleman—*The Buddha on Meditation and States of Consciousness* Haridas Chaudhuri—*Yoga Psychology*; Kathleen Riodan—*Gurdjieff*; John Lilly—*The Arica Training*; Robert Ornstein—*Contemporary Sufism*; William McNamara—*Psychology and Christian Mystical Tradition*; and William Gray—*Patterns of Western Magic*. Each contributor has practiced the area discussed as a personal discipline and presents it for its psychological rather than religious significance. The individual essays are very well done and present a good overview of the areas discussed. Bibliography, name and subject indices. 502pp. H&R 75

TEXLER, TIMOTHY. **ALTERED STATES OF AWARENESS**, $5.30. A collection of technical articles published in **Scientific American** between 1954 and 1972 divided into three sections: Brain and Awareness; Altered States of Awareness: Internal Control; Altered States of Awareness: External Control. Each selection is very fully illustrated in the usual **Scientific American** manner and complete with notes. Some of the more interesting selections for the layman include *Experiments with Goggles*—a detailed study of color and vision; *Learning in the Autonomic Nervous System*; *The Physiology of Imagination*; and *On Telling Right from Left*. Oversize, bibliography, index. 140pp. Fre 54

THOMPSON, WILLIAM IRWIN. AT THE EDGE OF HISTORY, $2.45. Thompson is a noted historian/philosopher who has taught at several major universities in the U.S. and Canada. After this book was written he dropped out of the university system and founded his own alternative community, Lindisfarne (P.O. Box 1395, Southampton, N.Y. 1968) incorporating educational and spiritual techniques and teachings from many disciplines, East and West. *At the edge of history the future is blowing wildly in our faces, sometimes brightening the air and sometimes blinding us. To get a sense of where we are going, I tried to see out through the geographical limits of my own experience to the spaces of our contemporary culture where the millennial imagination of the future is interrupting the daily news of the present*. Notes, index. 252pp. H&R 71

_____. **EVIL AND WORLD ORDER**, c$7.95. A collection of the following essays: *Meditation on the Dark Ages, Past and Present; We Become What We Hate; Three Wise Men of Gotham; Occulture: Out of Sight, Out of Mind; Introductions to Findhorn; Freedom, Evil, and Comedy; The Ends of Art*; and *Evil and World Order*. The general tone of all the selections is negative. Notes, 116pp. H&R 76

_____. **PASSAGES ABOUT EARTH**, $1.95. Continuing the searching study of contemporary society Thompson began in **At the Edge of History**, he now discusses the new planetary culture he sees emerging from the cracks in the old industrial civilization. *Passages* begins with the author's decision to leave the bureaucracy of modern university life (his material here is the most illuminating we have read anywhere on the problems of the university) and it ends with his founding a new cultural and educational center, Lindisfarne. In between it explores and analyzes some of the most important alternative cultures present today. Two of the most fascinating chapters recount the author's experiences during visits to the ancient British monastery of Lindisfarne and the New Age Scottish colony, Findhorn. Notes, index. 206pp. H&R 73

TOBEN, BOB. SPACE-TIME AND BEYOND, $4.95. See the Astronomy and Science section.

TOMPKINS, PETER and CHRIS BIRD. THE SECRET LIFE OF PLANTS, $1.95. An excellent, comprehensive account. The authors begin by describing the latest discoveries in plant research, including the latest Russian work, Cleve Backster's studies in plant communication, and the work of scientists from various disciplines. They go on from there to trace and analyze experiments and theories from the past, including extensive surveys of the pioneers of plant research. Their narrative is extensively documented. Long bibliography, 402pp. Avo 73

TRUNGPA, CHOGYAM. CUTTING THROUGH SPIRITUAL MATERIALISM, $4.25. See the Tibetan sub-section of Buddhism.

WASSON, R. GORDON. SOMA: DIVINE MUSHROOM OF IMMORTALITY, $7.50. See the Indian Philosophy section.

WATSON, LYALL. SUPER NATURE, $1.95. *The supernatural is usually defined as that which is not explicable by the known forces of nature. Supernature knows no bounds. Too often we see only what we expect to see; our view of the world is restricted by the blinkers of our limited experience; but it need not be this way. Supernature is nature with all its flavors intact, waiting to be tasted. I offer it as a logical extension of the present state of science, as a solution to some of the problems with which traditional science cannot cope, and as an analgesic to modern man.* Watson is a scientist and naturalist who here demonstrates a sound, scientific basis for many psychic and supernatural phenomena. He documents his case with an impressive array of scientific literature. An utterly fascinating book for the layman and scientist alike. We recommend it highly. Extensive bibliography and references. 335pp. Ban 73

WEIL, ANDREW. THE NATURAL MIND: A NEW WAY OF LOOKING AT DRUGS AND HIGHER CONSCIOUSNESS, $3.95. The author is a physician who has been studying mind-altering drugs for more than ten years in settings as diverse as Harvard University, Haight-Ashbury, the National Institute of Mental Health and the Amazon basin. His thesis: *altered states of consciousness, consciously entered, seem to be doors to ways of using the mind that are better than those we follow most of the time*. A discussion of various means of expanding the consciousness using psychedelics as a temporary catalyst. Recommended. 219pp. HMC 72

WEIL, G., R. METZNER, and T. LEARY. THE PSYCHEDELIC READER: THE BEST FROM THE PSYCHEDELIC REVIEW, $3.95. Cit 73

WELLS, BRIAN. PSYCHEDELIC DRUGS, $1.95. A detailed technical study of the properties and effects of the better-known psychedelics—LSD-25, mescalin, cannabis, and others. Wells covers the therapeutic uses of these drugs as well as the chances they may precipitate brain or chromosomal damage. He goes on to consider how they influence sexuality, aggression, crime, and creative and religious experience. *The most concise, yet at the same time balanced and detailed book which I have come across*—Humphrey Osmond. Many notes, index. 250pp. Pen 73

WHITE, JOHN, ed. FRONTIERS OF CONSCIOUSNESS, $2.50. A very readable, comprehensive collection of twenty-two articles on the full spectrum of consciousness research. Among the contributors are psychologists, physicists, parapsychologists, philosophers, and behavioral scientists. The topics discussed include transpersonal psychology; the nature of madness; biofeedback; meditation research; psychic research; paraphysics; biotechnology; the neurosciences; ecological consciousness; space travel and extra-terrestrial life; and death as an altered state of consciousness. All of the articles are written by experts and each topic is introduced by White, who also supplies a listing of suggested reading for each area. Notes, 366pp. Avo 74

_____, ed. **THE HIGHEST STATE OF CONSCIOUSNESS**, $3.50. A collection of essays by a great variety of people, which attempts to find the common denominators of the experience. Some of the thinkers approach the subject as a mystical religious experience; others describe it in physiological or psychological terms. The juxtaposition of these essays establishes a meaningful dialogue. Includes an excellent introductory piece by the editor on *What is the highest state of consciousness*. Recommended. 484pp. Dou 72

WHYTE, LANCELOT. THE UNIVERSE EXPERIENCE, $3.45. Subtitled *A World View Beyond Science and Religion. This is an essay in unity. There is nothing said here which has not its aesthetic, religious, moral, philosophical, and scientific aspects, for this work traces everything to its common source: the human imagination and its organic roots. . . . The author's view is that the only hope lies in the emergence of a potentially world-wide consensus of heart, mind, and will . . . [to achieve an awareness] of the ordering process at all levels in nature, without and within*. Notes, index. 155pp. HaR 74

WILLIAMS, PAUL. DAS ENERGI, $3.95. A collection of epigrams about living and being that has been very popular with our customers. Like most books of its type it is hard to describe. The tone and the message are more serious than most we have seen. A sample: *And one day, like any other day, finally tired of waiting for the help that never comes, make a rope, tie it to a rock throw it up pull yourself out and walk away.* 150pp. War 73

WOLFF, FRANKLIN MERRELL. PATHWAYS THROUGH TO SPACE—A PERSONAL RECORD OF TRANSFORMATION IN CONSCIOUSNESS, c$7.95. *For anyone who is generally seeking to experience the spaces of higher consciousness, I know of no other single work which so beautifully instructs and describes the pathways and the discipline* —John Lilly. The author is a scientist, but he has written in language that laymen can understand. This is a guide to be read a little at a time and slowly digested. It's arranged in the form of a diary and each entry is literature. 228pp. Jul 73

_____. **PHILOSOPHY OF CONSCIOUSNESS WITHOUT AN OBJECT**, $2.25. Reflections on the nature of transcendental consciousness. Because the author is well versed in both Oriental and Occidental schools of philosophy and in addition is quite familiar with the domain of higher mathematics characteristic of our Western scientific spirit, his philosophical presentaton is an integration of East and West. In fact, this book might be regarded as a pioneer effort in clearing the way for Western man to rediscover the truth of his own cultural heritage. The narrative is very personal as Merrell-Wolff shares with the reader his lifelong search for *Realization*. 265pp. Jul 73

WRIGHT, AUSTIN. ISLANDIA, $5.95. This is an underground classic, only recently reprinted, of a Utopian country and the experiences of a young American there. This isn't exactly the type of book we normally stock, but the ideals expressed by the characters here and their ancient civilization should be of interest to all those looking for alternative ways to live and be. 954pp. NAL 44

ZAEHNER, R.C. ZEN, DRUGS AND MYSTICISM, $1.95. The author, a noted writer, discusses the nature of various mystical states and seems to find little of value in contemporary states which have been induced by psychedelics, Zen, Krishna consciousness, etc. He calls for a return to more traditional, Western approaches and illustrates his argument with quotations from literature. 212pp. RaH 73

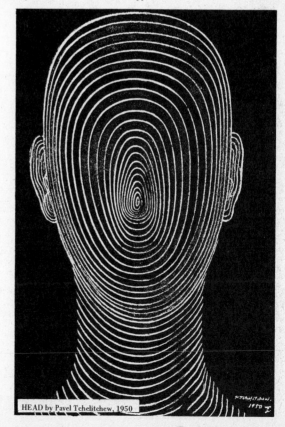

HEAD by Pavel Tchelitchew, 1950

COOKBOOKS

from the Tassajara Bread Book by Edward Brown.

ALTH, MAX. **MAKING YOUR OWN CHEESE AND YOGURT**, c$5.95. This is the most complete book of its type that we know of. The directions are carefully given and some illustrations are included. All aspects are discussed and some recipes are given. Bibliography, 239pp. Cro 73

BROWN, EDWARD. **TASSAJARA COOKBOOK**, $4.95. This is a beautifully produced book which contains simple-to-prepare recipes. Many of the recipes give tips for substitutions to add to the variety and the instructions are clear and easy to follow. Directions on cutting and cooking are also given and there are illustrations throughout. Many of the recipes are for raw items. Index, 255pp. ShP 73

BREAD

DWORKIN, FLOSS and STAN. **BAKE YOUR OWN BREAD**, $1.25. This is a good bread book that contains the widest variety of recipes of any of the books. The Dworkins begin with general instructions on bread baking and suggest some new method breads. This is followed by clear, detailed instructions on making kneaded breads. A number of different whole wheat recipes are offered and variations are suggested. Other sections include sourdough, spiral breads, rye breads and pumpernickel, challah and brioches, pizza and pitta, and batter breads. Very clear instructions. Index, 211pp. NAL 72

BRAVE, JOHN. **UNCLE JOHN'S ORIGINAL BREAD BOOK**, $3.95. A collection of over 200 unusual bread, biscuit, and muffin recipes. Many of the recipes seem to be variations on the traditional German breads. The ingredients are not strictly natural, but they are pretty generally healthful. Good, clear instructions. Well illustrated. 8x5", index. 192pp. Pyr 65

BROWN, EDWARD. **TASSAJARA BREAD BOOK**, c$6.95/$3.95. This is practically everybody's favorite bread book. The instructions for basic whole wheat bread are the best we have seen anywhere and they are illustrated with line drawings. The author tries to be as clear as possible and every possible aspect of bread making is reviewed. Many variations are included. Brown also includes recipes for yeasted pastries and yeasted breads as well as unyeasted breads, sourdough bread and pancakes, muffins and quickbreads, and desserts. The book itself is beautifully produced and we recommend it highly. 145pp. ShP 70

HUNTER, BEATRICE. **WHOLE GRAIN BAKING SAMPLER**, $2.25. Ms. Hunter provides a wide variety of recipes. She emphasizes unusual breads and desserts and over half the book is devoted to cookies and pastries. The instructions are clear and easy to follow and all natural ingredients are used. Many hints are offered for the beginner. The recipes we have tried have turned out great. Glossary, index. 312pp. Kea 72

ROSENVALL, VERNICE, MABEL MILLER and DORA FLACK. **THE CLASSIC WHEAT FOR MAN COOKBOOK**, $3.95. This book was written by a group of Mormons who hoped to turn their community on to natural foods and especially to natural grain baking. It is far from purist and both meat and sugar are included in some of the recipes. But the recipes are clearly presented and the cakes and cookies are especially good. It also includes good recipes for quick breads and muffins. 9x6", index. 162pp. WoP 75

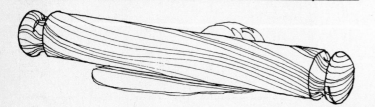

CADWALLADER, SHARON. **COOKING ADVENTURES FOR KIDS**, $4.95. A collection of simple, basic recipes of foods that kids both like to eat and can make fairly easily with some supervision. Basic information on terms and weights and measures is also included and there are illustrations throughout. 8½x8¼", index. 101pp. HMC 74

_____. **THE WHOLE EARTH COOKBOOK 2**, $4.95. A second collection of recipes. This one emphasizes soups and stews and casseroles, and is not strictly vegetarian. Spiral bound, index. 123pp. HMC 75

CADWALLADER, SHARON and JUDI OHR. **WHOLE EARTH COOKBOOK**, $4.95/ $1.50. This was one of the first natural foods cookbooks to come out and it remains a favorite for many people. The dishes are varied and the recipes are easy to follow and not overly complicated. Also includes suggestions for converting old recipes. The $4.95 edition is spiral bound. HMC 71

COURTER, GAY. **THE BEANSPROUT BOOK**, c$2.95. Complete directions for sprouting and discussions of the major grains and seeds that are sproutable. Some recipes are included too. This is the most popular of the sprouting guides. Illustrations, bibliography. 96pp. S&S 73

DAVIS, ADELLE. **LET'S COOK IT RIGHT**, $1.95. A very complete cookbook, emphasizing healthful (and not necessarily tasty) recipes. Not vegetarian and not very purist (sugar and additives are often included). Definitely not one of our favorites, but a classic nonetheless. Detailed instructions. Index, 573pp. NAL 70

DWORKIN, STAN and FLOSS. **BLEND IT SPLENDID**, $1.25. Over 200 blender recipes of every type imaginable. Clear instructions. Index, 230pp. Ban 73

_____. **THE GOOD GOODIES**, $4.95. This is the best all-around natural food dessert book that we know of. The recipes are imaginative and the instructions are clear. Many other baked items (such as pizza) are also included. Oversize, Rod 74

EWALD, ELLEN. **RECIPES FOR A SMALL PLANET**, $5.95/$1.95. This is one of our favorite cookbooks. Not many recipes are included, but all of the ones that we have tried have come out very well. The recipes are simple and they follow the principles of grain combining outlined by Frances Moore Lappe in **Diet for a Small Planet**—although they are far tastier than the recipes in the latter book. All types of recipes are included. The $5.95 edition is spiral bound. RaH 73

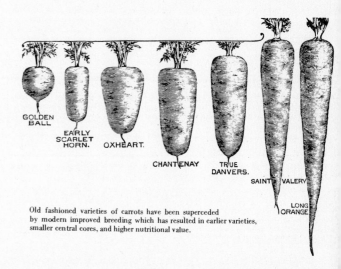

Old fashioned varieties of carrots have been superceded by modern improved breeding which has resulted in earlier varieties, smaller central cores, and higher nutritional value.

FORD, MARJORIE, SUSAN HILLYARD and MARY KOOCK. **DEAF SMITH COUNTRY COOKBOOK—NATURAL FOODS FOR FAMILY KITCHENS**, $4.95. This is an excellent overall cookbook and is one of the best natural foods cookbooks to buy if you only want to buy one. It includes descriptions of natural food staples and directions for their care and storage as well as information on sprouting and sample menus. Special sections present recipes for Mexican foods, baby and children's foods, and breads and desserts. The recipes are good and the directions are clear and easy to follow. 352pp. McM 73

GERRAS, CHARLES, ed. **NATURAL COOKING, THE PREVENTION WAY**, $4.95. A collection of over 800 recipes from the pages of **Prevention Magazine**, the U.S.'s leading nutritional magazine. Most were sent in by readers, so the quality is somewhat uneven. Some non-vegetarian dishes are included. Index, 357pp. NAL 72

GOODWIN, MARY and GERRY POLLEN. **CREATIVE FOOD EXPERIENCES FOR CHILDREN**, $4.00. More than a cookbook, this book is designed to turn kids on to natural foods and get them involved in the experience of making the foods themselves. Some useful suggestions are offered, although the book is not entirely successful. Oversize. CFS 73

GOULART, FRANCES. **THE ECOLOGICAL ECLAIR**, $3.50. A variety of recipes for *sugarless treats*. The directions are very complete. Descriptions of major natural sweeteners and homemade sweeteners are given. The tone of the book is a little cutesie for our taste. Index, 196pp. McM 75

HANNAFORD, KATHRYN. **COSMIC COOKERY**, $4.95. This is a very useful collection of recipes and general information on making natural foods. The recipes are not very unusual, but they all come out well and are simple to follow. The book itself is beautifully produced. All the basic areas are covered and special features include a glossary, sample menus, and descriptions of basic utensils and basic procedures. Oversize, index. 264pp. Brm 74

HEINDEL, MAX. **NEW AGE VEGETARIAN COOKBOOK**, c$6.75/$4.50. This is probably the oldest vegetarian cookbook that is still generally available and it remains one of the best. The presentation is exceedingly simple and the recipes all work. The book begins with some information on basic foods and vitamins and then presents a long table of food values. This is followed by many menu suggestions and then there's a topically organized collection of recipes—probably the most comprehensive collection available anywhere. There are also sections on high altitude cooking and on canning and preserving. A final section discusses herbs. Fully indexed. 492pp. Ros 68

HEWITT, JEAN. **THE NEW YORK TIMES NATURAL FOODS COOKBOOK**, $4.95. The best feature of this book is the variety of recipes it offers. We do not know of another book that has such a wide variety. Most of the recipes we have tried are easy to follow and come out well and often there are variations that can be tried. Every conceivable area is covered in depth. Bibliography, index. 434pp. Avo 71

HOBSON, PHYLLIS. **MAKING HOMEMADE CHEESE AND BUTTER**, $2.95. Simple directions for making a wide variety of cheeses. Also includes ways of making yogurt and butter. Index, 45pp. Gar 73

HOOKER, ALAN. **VEGETARIAN GOURMET COOKERY**, $4.95. As the title suggests, this is a beautifully produced book which gives detailed directions for the preparation of a number of gourmet dishes. The recipes are complicated and the dishes tend to be heavy—but they are delicious if you like this kind of food. Very clearly presented. Entrees, salads, soups, vegetables, sauces, and desserts are included. Oversize, index. 191pp. One 75

HUNTER, BEATRICE. **FAVORITE NATURAL FOODS**, c$7.95. A collection of recipes and tips for better eating by one of America's best known advocates of natural foods. The discussion is topically organized according to item discussed. 219pp. S&S 74

_____. **THE NATURAL FOODS COOKBOOK**, $2.95/$1.25. This has long been considered one of the basic natural foods cookbooks. Over 2000 recipes are included and, while Ms. Hunter often goes overboard including healthy items (brewer's yeast is a staple feature of her recipes!), she gives excellent instructions and the recipes we have tried have come out fine. Not vegetarian. Very fully indexed. 312pp. S&S 61

JENSEN, BERNARD. **BLENDING MAGIC**, $4.40. 650 unusual blender recipes combined with a review of the importance of raw foods and drinks in digestion and in healing. Many food items are critiqued and the principles of general nutrition are reviewed. 235pp. Jen nd

_____. **VITAL FOODS FOR TOTAL HEALTH**, $5.50. An unusual cookbook which combines basic facts about nutrition with a series of recipes. Over half the book is devoted to Jensen's exposition of *food chemistry and body chemistry*—detailing the effects of various foods on the body. Many raw recipes are included along with sample menus. Spiral bound. Index, 382pp. Jen 66

JONES, DOROTHEA. **THE SOYBEAN COOKBOOK**, $1.45. Over 350 recipes suggest the varied uses of soybeans. The recipes are generally simple. This is the best book of its type. Sample menus, glossary, index. 249pp. Arc 63

LAPPE, FRANCES MOORE. **DIET FOR A SMALL PLANET**, $5.95/$1.95. When this book first came out in 1971 it created a stir throughout the country. It was the first scientific study of vegetarianism and of the economic benefits of grains over meat that had been produced in recent times. Over half the book presents Ms. Lappe's arguments for non-meat protein. The recipes themselves often tend to be heavy, and we like those in Ewald's **Recipes** better. But as a document it is must reading for all those who are interested in natural foods. Newly revised. The $5.95 edition is spiral bound. Notes, bibliography, index. 411pp. RaH 75

LEE, GARY. **THE CHINESE VEGETARIAN COOKBOOK**, $3.95. This is a beautifully presented book which begins with a discussion of Chinese cooking and also examines the utensils. Each of the vegetables is then discussed individually and recipes are suggested. The recipes themselves are not terribly imaginative, but they cover the essentials and you can improvise from there. 5¼x8", index. 181pp. Nit 72

_____. **THE WOK COOKBOOK**, $3.95. This is a beautifully produced and illustrated book which begins with a detailed discussion of Chinese cooking—including information on the utensils and on the special foods and condiments. There's also a glossary. Most of the recipes call for meat—but this can be left out if desired. The instructions are extensive and more than adequate. This is the most popular book on Chinese cooking. 8½x5¼", 162pp. Nit 70

LO, KENNETH. **CHINESE VEGETARIAN COOKING**, $3.95. This is our personal favorite among the Chinese cookbooks. All of the recipes that we have tried have come out very well. The directions are more than adequate and all aspects of Chinese food are covered. The recipes tend to be fairly mundane, but it's easy to improvise once you get the general idea. All the terms are defined. Index, 182pp. RaH 74

LOEWENFELD, CLAIRE and PHILIPPA BACK. **HERBS, HEALTH AND COOKERY**, $1.95. See the Herbs section.

SACHAROFF, SHANTA. **FLAVORS OF INDIA—RECIPES FROM THE VEGETARIAN HINDU CUISINE**, $4.95. This is a wonderful cookbook. Not only does it offer a number of excellent Indian recipes, it also gives excellent detailed instructions on preparing the unusual items in the Indian menu. The reader is taken step by step through the preparation and everything we have tried has been both authentic and successful. Beautifully illustrated and produced. Oversize. One 74

SANTA MARIA, JACK. **INDIAN VEGETARIAN COOKERY**, $2.95. Hundreds of excellent recipes, but only useful as a supplement to the Sacharoff book—or for someone who is familiar with Indian cooking. Preparation instructions for basic Indian foodstuffs are not included. Wei 74

THOMAS, ANNA. **THE VEGETARIAN EPICURE**, c$8.95/$4.95. This is one of the most popular vegetarian cookbooks. It is beautifully produced and contains gourmet recipes. People seem to enjoy it even if they are not into natural foods. A perfect gift for those whom you want to turn on to natural foods. Some of the recipes include sugar, so it is not entirely purist. Index, 317pp. RaH 72

TURNER, MARY and JAMES. **MAKING YOUR OWN BABY FOOD**, $1.25. This is our favorite baby food cookbook. All the recipes are clearly presented and the authors have come up with a number of unusual ideas. Ban 70

WEINER, JOAN. **VICTORY THROUGH VEGETABLES**, $2.95. This is a very satisfactory collection of vegetarian recipes, all of which are easy to prepare. The recipes are not entirely pure and contain some additives and sugar. The book contains a number of useful hints also. Index, 163pp. HRW 70

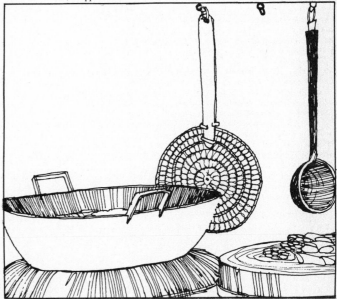

DEATH

BECKER, ERNEST. **THE DENIAL OF DEATH**, $2.95. . . . *a brilliant and desperately needed synthesis of the most important disciplines in man's life. It puts together what others have torn in pieces and rendered useless. It is one of those rare masterpieces that will stimulate your thoughts, your intellectual curiosity, and last, but not least, your soul.* . . .—Elisabeth Kubler-Ross. This book was a Pulitzer Prize winner in 1974. Notes, index. 329pp. McM 73

BUDGE, E.A. WALLIS. **THE EGYPTIAN BOOK OF THE DEAD**, $4.95. See the Egypt subsection of the Ancient Civilization section.

CORNISH, JOHN. **ABOUT DEATH AND AFTER**, $.90. A spiritual inquiry based on the teachings of Rudolf Steiner. 16pp. NKB 75

DRAKE, STANLEY. **THOUGH YOU DIE**, $4.80. **Though You Die** . . . *endeavors to show that there is more that is knowable about death than many people think. There are experiences of the brink of death which are not much spoken about. There are sources of knowledge which are not very widely known, and, above all, there is the central Christian mystery of Christ's overcoming of death.*—from the introduction. Drake is an anthroposophist (see the Steiner section). 102pp. CCP 62

EVANS-WENTZ, W.Y. **THE TIBETAN BOOK OF THE DEAD**, $3.95. See the Tibetan subsection of the Buddhism section.

GOLD, E.J. **THE AMERICAN BOOK OF THE DEAD**, $4.95. A modern restatement of the esoteric teachings on death and on dying to this life and being reborn. AOP 74

GROLLMAN, EARL. **TALKING ABOUT DEATH: A DIALOGUE BETWEEN PARENT AND CHILD**, $3.95. Since its original publication this book has been recognized as a sensitive and helpful dialogue about death. Thousands of parents have used it to explain the meaning and reality of death to their children. In this edition the beautifully illustrated dialogue between parent and child is accompanied by a greatly expanded *Parent's Guide* which suggests a variety of ways for parents to use this book, and helps parents themselves to come to terms with the sorrow of death. Also included is a fully annotated listing of resources for those seeking further help. 111pp. Bea 76

HAMPTON, CHARLES. **THE TRANSITION CALLED DEATH**, c$3.00. A theosophical treatise. 106pp. TPH 43

HENDERSON, JOSEPH and MAUD OAKES. **THE WISDOM OF THE SERPENT**, $1.95. See the Jungian Psychology section.

JURY, MARK and DAN. **GRAMP**, $5.95. A striking photographic portrayal of an elderly man's last year and of his family's reaction to his decline. This moving portrait was put together by the man's grandson and includes portions of the grandson's diary and verbatim transcriptions of dialogues between Gramp and various members of his family. Vik 76

KELEMAN, STANLEY. **LIVING YOUR DYING**, $3.95. *A warm and wise book. It will do much to strip away the superfluous terror and helplessness we feel in the presence of death. Keleman shows how our styles of dying are linked to our styles of living and how this makes dying an activity that can be lived creatively rather than an accident that merely happens to us. But the book is more than a handbook for dying. It is a guide to dealing with loss, anger, pain, excitement, grief and endings.*—Sam Keen. Keleman explores all aspects of being fully alive, expanding, and dying to the old in this well written evocative account. This has been an extremely popular book. Keleman runs the Center for Energetic Studies, exploring the human condition from the perspective of how we inhabit our bodies and embody our emotions. He is the leading West Coast bioenergetic practitioner. 162pp. RaH 74

KUBLER-ROSS, ELISABETH. **DEATH**, $2.95. Ours is a death-denying society. We hide death behind the sterile walls of the hospital and the cosmetic mask in the funeral home. But death is inevitable and we must face the question of how to deal with it. Why do we treat death as a taboo? What are the sources of our fears? How do we express our grief and accept the death of a person close to us? How can we prepare for our own death? From her own personal views and experiences and from comparisons with how our culture and other ones view death and dying, Dr. Kubler-Ross provides some answers to these and other questions by offering a spectrum of viewpoints from ministers and rabbis, doctors, nurses, sociologists, and personal accounts of those near death and their survivors. She shows how we can grow, through an acceptance of our finiteness; for death provides a key to the meaning of human existence. A provocative, evocative book, written by a psychiatrist who has made an extensive study of death and whose work is very well thought of. Index, bibliography. 203pp. PrH 75

_____. **ON DEATH AND DYING**, $2.25. Based on work of a seminar on dying which met with many terminally ill people, this book is filled with interviews and case histories showing the stages the dying person goes through: anger, bargaining, depression, acceptance. Offers insight and understanding so that all those who have contact with the terminally ill can do more to help them. 287pp. McM 69

_____. **QUESTIONS AND ANSWERS ON DEATH AND DYING**, $1.50. This sequel to Dr. Kubler-Ross' earlier book consists of the most frequently asked questions and her answers. Introduction, index. 189pp. McM 74

LIFTON, JAY and ERIC OLSON. **LIVING AND DYING**, $1.95. *Robert Jay Lifton and Eric Olson have produced one of those monumental usable and reusable, readable and rereadable works which promises to produce major shifts in all thinking and teaching about*

the care of the dying.—**Omega**. A very clearly written manual. Bibliography, index. 155pp. Ban 74

MATSON, ARCHIE. **THE WAITING WORLD: OR WHAT HAPPENS AT DEATH**, c$8.50. Almost dying is not an uncommon experience, particularly on the operating table. Many people who have returned from the edge have told extraordinary tales about what they saw—extraordinary, that is, when judged by conventional scientific and religious theories. Here Reverend Matson presents a varied collection of these descriptions drawn from acquaintances, from parapsychological sources, from medical eye witness accounts, and from literature. 151pp. Tur 75

MOODY, RAYMOND. **LIFE AFTER LIFE**, $2.45. This book has created a sensation. Elisabeth Kubler-Ross feels that it is one of the most important documents on death that has ever been published and countless readers agree. It presents a series of case studies of people who have come back from the dead—individuals who almost died and were saved and brought back to this world. In addition to the case studies, the author discusses the meaning of death and cites the impressions of the individuals whose cases are discussed. Stk 75

from Esoteric Anatomy by Baker

PELGRIN, MARK. **AND A TIME TO DIE**, $2.95. This is a moving account of the meditations of a man whose wife has died of cancer and who then learns that he too is suffering from the disease and has only eight months to live. It tells of his search for meaning in his own life and his thoughts as he approaches death. 173pp. TPH 62

PINCUS, LILLY. **DEATH AND THE FAMILY**, $2.95. Death has long been the last remaining taboo in Western society. Now, with new psychological and medical exploration into dying and the acceptance of death, the personal meaning of death has become an area of public concern. In this book a therapist examines the experience of coping with life after a loved one has died. Through detailed case histories of her patients, her friends and her own life, Ms. Pincus shows how ways of grieving are related to ways of loving and to the nature of the relationship that is mourned. Notes, 289pp. RaH 74

RUITENBEEK, HENDRIK, ed. **DEATH: INTERPRETATIONS**, $2.45. A collection of essays on death, e.g., *Death and the Pleasure Principle*, *On Dying Together* and *Death, the Giver of Life*. 286pp. Del

SHEPARD, MARTIN. **SOMEONE YOU LOVE IS DYING**, c$7.95. This is a helpful, practical guidebook which discusses how to cope with the mixed emotions of anxiety, resentment, guilt, despondency, aversion, and helplessness which are a natural reaction to death. Dr. Shepard, a well-known psychiatrist, offers specific suggestions on the everyday details involved in preparing for death—including ways of minimizing fear and grief. He also presents a number of case studies and includes information on realistic alternatives to the traditional ways in which we treat individuals who are dying. Bibliography, 220pp. Crn 75

WATSON, LYALL. **THE ROMEO ERROR**, $1.95. The author discusses the biology of life, the problem of deciding when death occurs, psychological and social attitudes toward death, and the idea that life and death may be indistinguishable, with death merely being a change of state, often temporary and sometimes even curable. Bibliography, index. 275pp. Del 75

WYSCHOGROD, EDITH, ed. **THE PHENOMENON OF DEATH**, $3.45. This is another collection of essays about death. It goes beyond the problem of individuals to explore also the question of the dying of a civilization. 235pp. H&R 69

DIVINATION

ANDERSON, MARY. **DIVINATION**, $1.00. A concise study of many methods of divination with chapters on divination by the elements, the shape of things to come, signs and omens from plants, and divination by stones and bones. Part of the **Paths to Inner Power** Series. Bibliography, 63pp. Wei 74

ATKINSON, WILLIAM WALKER. **PRACTICAL PSYCHOMANCY AND CRYSTAL GAZING**, $1.00. Atkinson was later known as Yogi Ramacharaka (see section on Yoga). Here he gives a series of practical lessons. 93pp. YPS 08

FABIA, MADAME. **THE BOOK OF FORTUNE TELLING**, $3.50. This is a detailed study of four techniques: palmistry, fortune-telling by cards, phrenology, and dream analysis. Each of the techniques is discussed at length, though it does not appear that a great deal of depth or insight is incorporated into the analyses. Illustrations, index, 510pp. Arc 72

GIBSON, WALTER and LITZKA. **THE COMPLETE ILLUSTRATED BOOK OF DIVINATION AND PROPHECY**, $2.25. The Gibsons have written many volumes on psychic phenomena, witchcraft, and other similar areas. This is their newest effort. Like their other volumes, this is basically a how-to-do-it, self-help book. Topics covered include use of the mystic oracle, divination by numbers, what today can mean to you, tasseomancy, Tarot, divination with playing cards, and palm reading. Glossary, index, 268pp. NAL 73

HALL, MANLY P. **STUDIES IN CHARACTER ANALYSIS**, $2.50. Sections on phrenology, palmistry, physiognomy, and graphology. Includes many diagrams and gives a good general view of each subject. An excellent introduction. 87pp. PRS 58

LEFAS, JEAN. **PHYSIOGNOMY—THE ART OF READING FACES**, c$3.98. Books on face reading seem to be gaining in popularity these days. This is the latest one. It's oversize, aimed at the general reader, and includes hundreds of illustrative photographs and line drawings along with instructional material. 111pp. A&W 75

MAR, TIMOTHY. **FACE READING**, $1.50. A clearly written exposition of Chinese physiognomy. Each of the parts of the face is analyzed in detail and many line drawings accompany the text. The last third of the book is devoted to a photo analysis of noted individuals. This book has been surprisingly popular. 175pp. NAL 74

MELVILLE, JOHN. **CRYSTAL GAZING AND CLAIRVOYANCE**, $2.00. Clear instructions for the use and care of the crystal. 92pp. Wei 1896

MIALL, AGNES. **THE BOOK OF FORTUNE TELLING**, c$2.98. Another general account. It's a bit hard to review these divination books and say anything since the books themselves do not seem to differ greatly from each other and none of them excites us in the least. This one seems to cover a broader range than the others, with chapters on palm reading, astrology, divination by the cards, name and number, handwriting analysis, face reading, dreams, crystal gazing, precious stones, and names. Index, 334pp. Ham 72

OPHIEL. **THE ORACLE OF FORTUNA**, $3.50. Presents a system of divination through and by symbols. Four symbols, each with a key word, are presented and thoroughly explained. Appendix contains color plates of the planet symbols and directions for drawing them. 129pp. Pea 70

RANDALL, EDITH and FLORENCE CAMPBELL. **SACRED SYMBOLS OF THE ANCIENTS**, $9.95. This is a fascinating study of the mystical significance of the fifty-two *playing cards*. Each card is analyzed at length. The study forms a method of character analysis based on numerical and astrological correspondence using the playing cards as keys, each of the fifty-two cards symbolizing a particular type of person. A complete description of the different types, their birthdates and variants is detailed in addition to the significance of suit, number, astrological rulership, etc. Includes spread charts. 198pp. Sym 47

RICHMOND, OLNEY. **THE MYSTIC TEST BOOK**, c$7.50. A Masonically-oriented text, claiming Atlantis as the place of origin of the pack of playing cards, and disclosing them to embody an astronomical-numerological and symbolical system. Gives meanings, astrological correspondences, permutations, and many illustrated card spreads. 340pp. Ric 1893

DREAMS

ALEX, WILLIAM. **DREAMS, THE UNCONSCIOUS AND ANALYTICAL THERAPY**, $1.25. Subtitled *A Jungian Approach to Dreams*, this is an edited transcript of a paper presented at a seminar on *Dreams and Vision*. It was originally published by the C.G. Jung Institute. It is a very good summation of dream symbols and myths as expounded by Jung. 32pp. Lod 73

BLACKER, THETIS. **A PILGRIMAGE OF DREAMS**, $4.55. *[T] he dreams which I have recorded here seem to come from a source which is not merely personal to me: they seem to come from other worlds, and it is because, on telling them to a number of my friends, these dreams of mine have been recognised by other people as significant to them also, that I have enscribed them in this book. For me they seem to be a kind of pilgrimage, and from them I have learned much of the meaning of life.* Ms. Blacker is a British artist who specializes in batik. 164pp. Tur 73

BRO, HARMON. **EDGAR CAYCE ON DREAMS**, $1.25. Many related selections from the seemingly endless library of Cayce readings. This volume should be read after Hugh Lynn Cayce's; it builds on the material presented there and includes many practical exercises. Dr. Bro himself provides a number of insights based on his work in depth psychology and he is the only trained social scientist to have written on Cayce. There is less direct quoting here than in most of the books which makes this one more readable than many of them. 223pp. War 68

BRUCE, ROBERT D. **LACANDON DREAM SYMBOLISM, VOL. I: DREAM SYMBOLISM AND INTERPRETATION**, $9.25. The Lacandon Indians live in the Yucatan Peninsula in Mexico and are descended from the Mayas. They have an intricate system of dream interpretation which they consider prophetic. The author is an anthropologist who spent a few years living in the Lacandon Jungle. In his study he hopes to illuminate the nature of symbolism itself among the Lacandones and thereby gain a deeper understanding into the mindset and belief systems that created the great Maya civilization. Bruce begins this study with a review of the general principles of dream interpretation and symbolism. This is followed by a series of actual dream/prophecies, with interpretation and confirmation. The bulk of the volume is devoted to an analysis of the cosmological meaning of the symbolism. Extensive notes, 132pp. EdE 75

CAYCE, HUGH LYNN. **DREAMS, THE LANGUAGE OF THE UNCONSCIOUS**, $2.25. Includes some of the material derived from the Cayce readings as well as other essays by A.R.E. researchers: *A Psychic Interprets His Dreams*, and *Working with Dreams as Recommended by the Edgar Cayce Readings*. 94pp. ARE 62

COULTON, ANN REE. **WATCH YOUR DREAMS**, c$10.00. Ms. Coulton has been actively researching the spiritual significance of dreams for many years. In this book she thoroughly explains the various types of dreams and their accompanying symbols. A detailed, highly instructive account. 414pp. NAP 73

COXHEAD, DAVID and SUSAN MILLER. **DREAMS: VISIONS OF THE NIGHT**, $5.95. A beautifully presented pictorial exploration of dreams and *visions of the night* in various cultures and through the ideas of analytical psychology. 110 illustrations, 24 in color. Part of the **Art and Cosmos** Series. 8x11", 96pp. Avo 76

CRAIG, PAULA. **BUILD YOUR OWN DREAM HOUSE**, $1.25. A dream book for children, based in part on the Edgar Cayce readings. The first part is a general analysis of dreams, the second contains topically arranged blanks for the child to fill in the words or symbols that pertain to a specific object, and the third is a form for making a simplified dream diary. 44pp. ARE 74

DEMENT, WILLIAM. **SOME MUST WATCH WHILE SOME MUST SLEEP**, c$5.95. *I do feel that my book is a satisfactory and authoritative introduction to the sleep field, readable in an evening or two without inducing drowsiness. At the end, the reader will have some awareness of the major problems of sleep research and the overall complexity of sleep and dream processes as well as a few ways in which knowledge of sleep might be personally helpful. If the book stimulates a desire for further exploration, the Reader's Guide at the end of the book contains a fairly substantial number of suggestions for additional reading.* Dement has done extensive sleep research at Stanford University and he reports on his findings in detail along with the other major research. Index, 160pp. Fre 72

DOWNING, JACK and ROBERT MARMORSTEIN, eds. **DREAMS AND NIGHTMARES**, $1.50. A detailed account of Gestalt dream therapy sessions conducted by Downing and others at the Esalen Institute in California. Includes a transcription of the session and a bit of commentary. 186pp. H&R 73

DUDLEY, GEOFFREY. **DREAMS, THEIR MYSTERIES REVEALED**, $1.00. An overview. 64pp. Wei 69

_____. **HOW TO UNDERSTAND YOUR DREAMS**, $2.00. A general account of the symbolism in different types of dreams, aimed at the individual who wants the simplest exposition possible. Index, 109pp. Wil 57

FARADAY, ANN. **THE DREAM GAME**, $1.95. Dr. Faraday is a noted psychologist. She has written this book in response to many requests for a comprehensive, step-by-step manual on how to understand and use dreams. The first two parts set out the ground rules for keeping a dream diary and understanding the symbolism of dreams. The third part, *Games for Advanced Players*, is based mainly on the author's research over the past two years. Her approach to dreams is based on the pioneering work of Freud and Jung as well as the techniques developed by Calvin Hall, Edgar Cayce, and Fritz Perls. Her bibliography on dreams and related areas is the most complete we've seen (with the exception of our catalog!). Indexed, 398pp. H&R 74

_____. **DREAM POWER**, $1.75. This is an excellent exploration of dreams by a British dream researcher who has trained in hypnotherapy, Freudian analysis, and Jungian depth psychology. The book begins with an outline of modern experimental dream research relevant to dream interpretation and goes on to review the theories of Freud and Jung in this light, drawing from Dr. Faraday's own experiences with patients. She also reviews the more modern approaches to dreams of Calvin Hall and Fritz Perls, who, in very different ways, sought to make dream interpretation more accessible to the average person. Against this background, she describes the method she herself developed in her dream study groups. The book concludes by showing how dreams may be used in all realms of life for greater self-awareness. Bibliography, index. 334pp. Ber 72

FREUD, SIGMUND. **THE INTERPRETATION OF DREAMS**, $2.65. This book, first published in 1900, marked the beginning of dream interpretation as we know it today. Many of the theories advanced by Freud in this seminal exploration are still well considered today and are the basis for much of the later work. This translation by James Strachey is the definitive one, incorporating all the alterations, additions, and deletions Freud made over a thirty-year period. The detailed commentary and scrupulous cross referencing enable the reader to understand clearly the development of Freud's thought. Index, notes, bibliography. 768pp. Avo 65

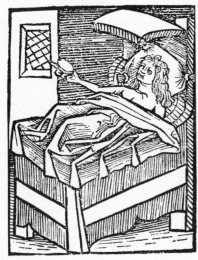

"He or she who looked at Zizaa, a precious stone, was said to have marvellous dreams." Woodcut from ORTUS SANITATIS, 1491

FROMM, ERICH. **THE FORGOTTEN LANGUAGE**, $2.95. Interesting discussion by an important modern thinker of Jung's, Freud's and his own concepts of the nature of the language of the dream. Fromm also relates his concepts to the interpretation of myths, fairy tales, rituals, and the novel. Recommended. 263pp. Grv 51

GARFIELD, PATRICIA. **CREATIVE DREAMING**, $1.75. This is a very popular recent book. Dr. Garfield explains how to keep a dream diary, develop control over what you dream, plan for *creative dreaming*, practice self-suggestion, and how to learn from the experiences of people in other cultures. *You can start dreaming creatively tonight.... As you succeed in establishing creative dreaming you will increase your capacity for concentration and recall. You will build a capacity for coping with fear-producing dream situations that carries over into the waking state. You will experience pleasurable adventures in your dreams. You will understand yourself better.... You will find support and help for waking problems.... And all this may be just the beginning.* Includes extensive notes and an index. 281pp. RaH 74

GIBSON, WALTER. **DREAMS**, c$1.49. A general introductory account, with material on dream interpretation, common dream patterns, and a dream dictionary. 127pp. G&D 69

GREEN, CELIA. **LUCID DREAMS**, c$5.90: A dream is called lucid when the dreamer is aware that he is dreaming and has some degree of voluntary control over the subsequent course of his dream, similar to out-of-the-body experiences. This book is based on case material in the possession of the Institute of Psychophysical Research, and on published accounts of lucid dreams and related phenomena. The sources are all cited. 194pp. HHL 68

HALL, CALVIN. **THE MEANING OF DREAMS**, $3.50. Dr. Hall, Director of the Institute of Dream Research, shows how the dreamer transforms his inner thought into symbols, into a play in which he is author, director, properties man and actor. Dr. Hall's work is quite highly regarded and he writes simply and clearly. This book is a good overview. Notes, index. 244pp. MGH 66

HALL, CALVIN and VERNON NORDBY. **THE INDIVIDUAL AND HIS DREAMS**, $1.50. A good presentation of techniques for scientifically recording and analyzing dream sequences, developed by the authors from years of research. Includes chapters on types of dreams, content, symbols, consistencies, dreams and waking behavior, and a section on analyzing one's own dreams. 207pp. NAL 72

HALL, MANLY P. **AN INTRODUCTION TO DREAM INTERPRETATION**, $1.50. A transcription of one of Mr. Hall's lectures. 33pp. PRS 55

_____. **STUDIES IN DREAM SYMBOLISM**, $4.00. Transcriptions of a series of classes given by this noted philosopher (see section on Mysticism). Topics include the dream process, sleep, self instruction through dreams, dream symbols, dreams as mystical experience and as warnings. Highly recommended. 70pp. PRS 65

HARTMANN, ERNEST. **THE FUNCTIONS OF SLEEP**, $2.95. Hartmann begins with review of historical and contemporary theories of the functions of sleep and of recent research in sleep deprivation and synchronized (non-dreaming) and desynchronized (dreaming) sleep. Citing his own studies, he investigates the reasons for variable sleep patterns and finds that sleep requirements are influenced by differences in personality, as well as age, life style, and mental state. He then explores the effects on sleep of psychological stress, physical and intellectual activity, and the use of drugs and of other chemicals. The different kinds of tiredness and the role of dreaming in sleep are also studied. This is a sophisticated theoretical presentation, not intended for the layman. Bibliography, index. 198pp. YUP 73

HEARD, VIDA. **THE SLEEP GAME: HOW TO WIN A NIGHT'S SLEEP**, $2.10. A *Repose Recipe* developed by the author. 92pp. TPL 72

HOLZER, HANS. **THE PSYCHIC SIDE OF DREAMS**, c$7.95. A general discussion, with many case studies, and covering the following topics: psychic dreams, prophetic dreams, warning dreams, ESP dreams, out-of-the-body experiences, survival dreams, and reincarnation dreams. 169pp. Dou 76

JONES, RICHARD. **THE NEW PSYCHOLOGY OF DREAMING**, $2.95. Jones here sets out to re-evaluate Freud's original dream theory in the light of the current use of sophisticated laboratory instruments and test the theory against subsequent theoretical and empirical developments. In effect he has modern psychologists such as Ullman, Angyal, Erikson, Lowy, Piaget, and Hall in a dialogue with Freud, Jung and Adler. Index, notes, 238pp. Vik 70

JUNG, C.G. **DREAMS**, $3.95. This is a collection of some of Jung's most important dream-related writings, composed of selections from **Freud and Psychoanalysis, The Structure and Dynamics of the Psyche, Psychology and Alchemy,** and **The Practice of Psychotherapy.** The book is divided into four parts: Dreams and Psychoanalysis, Dreams and Psychic Energy, The Practical Use of Dream Analysis, and Individual Dream Symbolism in Relation to Alchemy (including material on the symbolism of the Mandala). Fully illustrated throughout, with a very complete index. See Jung section for more background on his theories. 356pp. PUP 74

LEADBEATER, C.W. **DREAMS**, $1.25. A detailed study—one of the author's Theosophical Manuals—on what dreams are and how they are caused. Includes reports of the author's experiments on the dream state. 67pp. TPH 1898

LINDE, SHIRLEY and LOUIS SAVARY. **THE SLEEP BOOK**, $5.95. This is a guided photographic essay through the world of sleep and dreams which draws on recent discoveries in dream experiments and scientific research and quotations from many sources. It offers suggestions and information on achieving rest, treating insomnia, programming dreams, and performing memory tasks during sleep. A large part of the book is devoted to detailed practical exercises. **The Sleep Book** was created by some of the same people who put **Passages** together, and the format is the same. Oversize, 223pp. H&R 74

CRIME AND PUNISHMENT, wood engraving after J.J. Grandville, published posthumously in LE MAGASIN PITTORESQUE, France, 1847

MAHONEY, MARIA. **THE MEANING IN DREAMS AND DREAMING**, $2.95. This is the best non-technical review of Carl Jung's work interpreting dreams according to the formulations of analytical psychology. Ms. Mahoney begins by reviewing Jung's basic dream theories. She goes on to an analysis of archetypes and symbols as seen by Jung and an interpretative analysis of Jung's theories on persona, shadow, anima and animus. The next section outlines techniques for dreaming and integrating dreams. Final chapters discuss compensatory, or complementary, dreams; reductive dreams; reactive dreams; prospective dreams; somatic dreams; telepathic dreams; and archetypal dreams. Index, 256pp. CiP 66

SABIN, KATHERINE. **ESP AND DREAM ANALYSIS**, c$6.95. Ms. Sabin is a well known psychic, most noted for her Associative Card Code (a system of card reading using computer cards). In addition she has been recording and studying her dreams for years and interpreting them in the light of traditional Freudian and Jungian dream theory. Here she provides a practical handbook which teaches the reader how to recognize and interpret the ESP content of dreams, how to isolate certain symbols and themes in dreams, and how to train your subconscious mind to present ESP content in your dreams. Various other systems of dream interpretation are also reviewed. Index, 214pp. Reg 74

SANFORD, JOHN. **DREAMS: GOD'S FORGOTTEN LANGUAGE**, c$7.95. This is an exploration of the relationship between dreams and religious experience, drawing on modern psychology and Biblical scholarship. The case material is drawn from the author's counseling (he is an Episcopal Rector). A great deal of attention is also devoted to Jungian dream theories. The author's intention is *to show the extraordinary at work in the ordinary—to point out the spiritual overtones of meaning which are inherent in the simplest dreams of the most ordinary people.* Originally published by the Jung Institute in Zurich. Notes, 223pp. Lip 68

SECHRIST, ELSIE. **DREAMS: YOUR MAGIC MIRROR**, $1.25. An excellent, comprehensive account based on a study of the Edgar Cayce dream readings, explaining the moral, spiritual, and practical meanings of dream incidents and symbols, and giving practical step-by-step instruction in dream interpretation. Includes interpretations of hundreds of actual dreams on a great variety of subjects. Recommended. 255pp. War 68

SHERWOOD, JANE. **THE FOURFOLD VISION**, c$2.80. An interesting study of dreaming and verge-of-sleep experiences. The author uses psychological and scientific discoveries and combines them with information learned by her automatic writing to suggest a coherent theory of the nature of consciousness. 224pp. Spe 65

STREET, NOEL. **DREAM TIME**, $1.95. Rev. Street is a well know spiritually-oriented healer and psychic. He has written numerous general books on various topics, including several on dreams. This one analyzes the phenomena of sleep and dreams, gives meditation instruction for dreaming, and has an interpretative section. 79pp. LoA 74

_____. **DREAMER AWAKE**, $1.95. Subtitled *A Guide to Dream Study,* this book

includes chapters on the intent of dreams, the purpose of dreams, preparing to dream, experiments for the beginner, directing dreams in a particular manner, penetration of light into the consciousness, color dreams, friendship during dreams, interpretation, prophecy, and blessing from dreams. A clearly written, spiritually-oriented account for the general reader. Written with Judy Dupree. 98pp. LoA 72

ULLMAN, MONTAGUE and STANLEY KRIPPNER. **DREAM TELEPATHY**, $2.95. See section on Parapsychology.

WEBB, WILSE. **SLEEP: THE GENTLE TYRANT**, $3.95. A study of the psychology of sleep. The first two chapters are descriptions of the *dimensions and organization of sleep.* The next seven report on and analyze variations in sleep under different conditions. This is followed by two chapters on insomniacs and their treatment and an evaluation of the effects of variations in sleep on behavior. Final chapters are devoted to dreams, a review of why we sleep, and answers to the most frequently asked questions about sleep. Index, 180pp. PrH 75

WHITE, ROBERT. **THE INTERPRETATION OF DREAMS**, c$18.90. A translation with commentary on the **Oneirocritica** by Artemidorus, a second century AD work on dreams which was frequently mentioned by both Freud and Jung. The author was a dream interpreter by profession and the most outstanding characteristic of this volume is its rational, practical approach. The exposition is quite serious and while the examples are clearly mythological and classical today's dreamer can find much to relate to. The exposition is an excellent one and the material is well organized. This edition includes an introduction and many notes. Index, 259pp. Noy 75

WOODS, RALPH and HERBERT GREENHOUSE. **THE NEW WORLD OF DREAMS**, c$12.95. This is the most comprehensive anthology of material on dreams and sleep available. One unique aspect of the book is that it discusses the thoughts on dreams held by poets and philosophers, theologians, sociologists, and anthropologists as well as psychologists and medical doctors. The 130 selections are divided into three parts: what people dream about, the many dream theories throughout history, and scientific research on dreams. The book is a necessary part of the library of anyone seriously studying the area. The selections are well chosen and the whole is well organized. Bibliography, index, 458pp. McM 74

ECKANKAR

Eckankar is the science of soul travel or the ability to lift one's consciousness to higher dimensions or planes where one may realize the divine consciousness of his soul. This knowledge has been preserved since ancient times in the body of teachings known as Eck and has been revealed through the instrumentality of a living Eck Master. Eckankar was delivered to the west by just such a master whose name was Paul Twitchell. Eckankar means *co-worker with God* and supplies many answers to the deeper questions of human life and the possibility for direct experience of spiritual truth.

TWITCHELL, PAUL. **ANITYA**, c$6.95. A hand written, illustrated compilation from Twitchell's writings, designed especially for contemplation. Topics include love, truth, God, light, sound, soul and Eck spirit. 89pp. IWP 69

_____. **COINS OF GOLD**, c$7.95. A collection of mystical poems. IWP 39.

_____. **DIALOGUES WITH THE MASTER**, $5.95. A series of spiritual discourses dictated to Twitchell by Rebazar Tarzs, an ageless emissary for Eckankar. They give advanced training in the secret science of Eckankar. 256pp. IWP 70

_____. **THE DRUMS OF ECK**, $5.95. A historical novel, telling of a man's search for God, and of how he finally finds the path of Eckankar. 220pp. IWP 70

_____. **ECKANKAR: COMPILED WRITINGS, VOL. I**, c$6.95. Designed as an introductory volume and including the texts of **Introduction to Eckankar, All About Eck,** and **Eck and Music** along with a number of other essays. 195pp. IWP 75

_____. **ECKANKAR: ILLUMINATED WAY LETTERS, 1966–1971**, c$6.95. Discussions of many topics written monthly by Twitchell and sent out to members and friends. 270pp. IWP 75

_____. **ECKANKAR: KEY TO SECRET WORLDS**, c$4.95/2.00. The basic guide to the mastery of the ancient science of soul travel as well as the most popular Twitchell book. Step-by-step techniques. Extensive glossary of Eckankar words and terms. 254pp. IWP 69

_____. **ECKANKAR DICTIONARY**, c$4.95. Alphabetically arranged definitions of terms used in the Eckankar books. 160pp. IWP 73

_____. **THE ECK-VIDYA—THE ANCIENT SCIENCE OF PROPHECY**, $8.95. Practical instructions on the ancient method of reading the akashic records and predicting the future. Also contains information on the cycles of man, chemical affinities between people, sacred symbols and numbers. Extensive index and cross-references. 237pp. IWP 72

_____. **THE FAR COUNTRY**, $5.95. A discourse by the Eck Master Rebazar Tarsz on how to get beyond the physical world. Includes information on overcoming materialistic attachments, gaining God-realization, and finding oneself in this world. 247pp. IWP 70

_____. **THE FLUTE OF GOD**, $5.95. The first in a series of books which are essential reading in Eck, the others being **Tiger's Fang** and **The Far Country.** Lays down the fundamental philosophy of Eck. 173pp. IWP 70

_____. **HERBS**, $1.95. See the Herbs section.

_____. **IN MY SOUL I AM FREE**, $1.95. A biography of Twitchell by Brad Steiger. Includes material on Eck as an organization as well as a discussion of its elements and procedure. 190pp. IWP

_____. **LETTERS TO GAIL**, c$9.95. A collection of letters Twitchell wrote to his wife prior to their marriage instructing her in the spiritual works of Eckankar and covering a great many other topics also. One letter consists of a diverse collection of recommended readings. 170pp. IWP 73

_____. **THE SHARIYAT-KI-SUGMAD, BOOK 1**, $6.95. The title of these books is translated as *The Way of the Eternal.* It is the ancient scripture of Eckankar. *Every phase of life in both matter worlds and the highest planes is discussed. One will find within these pages an answer to every question man has ever devised to ask the greater ones. All that which is Truth is here now, within these pages.* 192pp. IWP 71

_____. **THE SHARIYAT-KI-SUGMAD, BOOK 2**, $6.95. 208pp. IWP 71

_____. **THE SPIRITUAL NOTEBOOK**, $5.95. Discusses the theoretical and practical doctrines of Eckankar and gives a history of the movement and its offspring. 219pp. IWP 71

_____. **STRANGER BY THE RIVER**, $5.95. A dialogue between Rebazar Tarzs and one of his chelas (followers). The chela raises questions and his master answers them and reveals *the divine light of Eck.* 175pp. IWP

_____. **TALONS OF TIME**, $2.95. In **Talons of Time,** *Peddar Zaskq describes an amazing journey undertaken with Sharir, the Magician of Lo. Their mission is to rescue the soul of John Skally, being held prisoner by Kal Niranjan, and to retrieve the Secret Diary which contains the secret of Time. They travel to the land of the Time Makers, a land beyond time and space, encountering fascinating beings and adventures, until Peddar alone faces Kal himself and the Talons of Time.* 188pp. IWP 74

_____. **THE TIGER'S FANG**, $3.95. An autobiographical account of Paul Twitchell's initiation into Eckankar and his experiences as an initiate. 175pp. IWP 67

_____. **THE WAY OF DHARMA**, $3.95. A novel which gives the fundamentals of Eckankar. 244pp. IWP 70

_____. **THE WISDOM OF ECK**, $2.00. A collection of quotations taken from Twitchell's writings and covering the basic precepts of Eckankar. 87pp. IWP 72

EDUCATION

ALLISON, LINDA. **THE REASONS FOR SEASONS**, $3.95. This is a neat book, a hundred or so different exercises written and designed for kids and adults to work at together— or just for kids to work with. *This is a book about the trip that the earth makes around the sun. It explains the reasons for seasons. Plus a whole lot more. Inside you will find stuff to do, things to make, ideas to think about, stories to read, and things to inspect, collect, and give away.* All the instructions are clear and the book is illustrated throughout. The material is roughly organized according to things to do in different seasons. Oversize, recommended. 125pp. LBC 75

Spore Rain

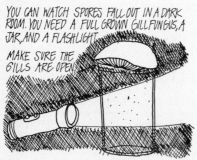

YOU CAN WATCH SPORES FALL OUT IN A DARK ROOM. YOU NEED A FULL GROWN GILL FUNGUS, A JAR, AND A FLASHLIGHT.

MAKE SURE THE GILLS ARE OPEN.

A GIANT PUFF BALL FUNGUS MAY HAVE 2,000,000,000,000 SPORES LUCKILY ONLY A FEW WILL GROW.

from The Reasons for Seasons by Linda Allison

ASHTON-WARNER, SYLVIA. **SPEARPOINT**, $1.95. Ms. Ashton-Warner's **Teacher** has profoundly influenced the education of small children around the world and she has been invited to observe and consult with schools in England, Israel, and Asia. Recently she was invited to bring her *organic teaching* to an American experimental school in Colorado. In this book she pours out her impressions, feelings, and intuitions about the American children she worked with, their teachers, their schooling, their world. 222pp. RaH 72

_____. **TEACHER**, $1.50. *Miss Ashton-Warner believes that she has discovered a method of teaching that can make the human being naturally and spontaneously peaceable. Aggressiveness, an instinct without which wars could not arise or be conducted, is the name we give to mental or emotional reactions caused by the frustration of the child's inherited drives: self-preservation and sexual gratification. Education as normally practiced throughout the world ignores these main interests. By recognizing and even welcoming their presence in the child and making them the foundation of an organic method of teaching, these interests can be allowed expression and be at the same time moulded into patterns of constructive delight.* This is a first-person account of what happened in the classes that Ms. Ashton-Warner taught in New Zealand for twenty-four years. It is considered a landmark work. Illustrations, 191pp. Ban 63

SRI AUROBINDO and THE MOTHER. **SRI AUROBINDO AND THE MOTHER ON EDUCATION**, $2.00. They insist that one must understand human psychology in order to adequately teach and learn. This includes the understanding of the human mind in all its stages (infant, adolescent, adult) and an integration and development of the human personality equipment and its proper relationship to the divine soul within us all. 118pp. Mat 56

AXLINE, VIRGINIA. **DIBS IN SEARCH OF SELF**, $1.75. **Dibs** is a perceptive study of a disturbed adolescent in our society. It is the portrait of a little boy achieving under therapy a successful struggle for identity. To anyone who has, or expects to have, contact with small children, this book is a deeply moving experience. RaH 64

_____. **PLAY THERAPY**, $1.75. *Play therapy is based upon the fact that play is the child's natural medium of self-expression. It is an opportunity which is given to the child to play out his feelings and problems just as, in certain types of adult therapy, an individual talks out his difficulties.* This volume, although directed especially at psychologists, psychiatrists, and teachers, is an important and rewarding book for anyone who comes in contact with children. Dr. Axline has drawn a great many case studies from her experience with children ranging in age from four years to twelve, with problems covering a wide spectrum of *maladjustment*. The book gives specific illustrations of how therapy can be implemented in play contacts. Illustrations, index. 374pp. RaH 47

BAILEY, ALICE. **EDUCATION IN THE NEW AGE**, $1.50. See the Theosophy section.

BARATTA-LORTON, MARY. **WORKJOBS...FOR PARENTS**, $3.95. *During the past several years I have been making learning tasks for the children in my classroom built around a single concept I wanted my children to work with. These manipulative skills are designed to help children develop language and numbers skills, as well as more general skills such as hand-eye coordination, observing, seeing relationships, and making judgments.... I have selected those activities from the original classroom edition of* **Workjobs** *that seem to be the most appropriate for parents to make and use at home.* Each activity includes a general description, ideas for getting started, ideas for follow-up discussion, and a picture of a child doing the activity. Oversize, 115pp. AdW 75

BARAVALLE, HERMANN von. **INTRODUCTION TO PHYSICS IN THE WALDORF SCHOOLS**, $2.25. See the Waldorf Education sub-section of Steiner.

_____. **PERSPECTIVE DRAWING**, $2.25. See the Waldorf Education sub-section of Steiner.

_____. **TEACHING OF ARITHMETIC AND THE WALDORF SCHOOL PLAN**, $3.00. See the Waldorf Education sub-section of Steiner.

BARTH, ROLAND. **OPEN EDUCATION AND THE AMERICAN SCHOOL**, $3.95. Barth is the principal of an elementary school in Newton, Massachusetts, and was formerly Assistant to the Dean of the Harvard Graduate School of Education. This account is solidly rooted in the author's own personal experience and academic research and is considered one of the best accounts of open education available. He begins with a theoretical analysis of some assumptions about learning and knowledge. The next section is devoted to a discussion of the teacher and the open classroom. This is followed by a case study of what actually happened at the school where Barth works. A final section investigates the principal and the open classroom. There's also an excellent 50+pp annotated bibliography of books and curriculum materials (including addresses). Index, notes, 320pp. ScB 72

SAWBUCK TABLE

Build a frame 30" square out of 1'x 3's - use glue and nails. Add some 1'x3" spacers to one end. These are for the legs.

Place a piece of half inch plywood 30" square over the top of the frame. That is the top of the table.

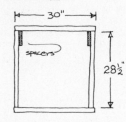

30"

spacers

28½

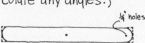

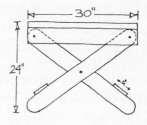

30"

24"

4"

Cut four 1'x 4's to 35½". Round the ends. (This way you will not have to calculate any angles.)

¼ holes

Drill ¼" holes and fasten with ¼" carriage bolts.

Use a 1'x 4" as a cross brace at the bottom.

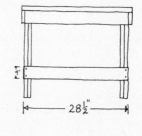

28½"

from No More Public Schools by Hal Bennett

BENNETT, HAL. **NO MORE PUBLIC SCHOOLS**, $2.95. A complete step-by-step guide and idea-book for providing alternative means of education. It includes materials and information one would need for withdrawing one's child from public school, starting one's own school, gathering essentials, structuring the day, how to operate efficiently, and a bundle of ideas and suggestions for operating a school on limited funds. The book breaks the crystallized patterns of public schools and provides concrete and practical suggestions for new modes of educating children. 137pp. RaH 72

BERENDS, POLLY. **WHOLE CHILD/WHOLE PARENT**, $6.95. Besides providing a sound philosophical interpretation of the early child-rearing years, **Whole Child/Whole Parent** offers practical guidelines for the construction, purchase, and use of specific toys, books, learning materials, and nursery equipment. Included are annotated bibliographies of direct-mail catalogs, toy-making and play-activity books, and nearly 500 books for children under four. The book is oversize and topically organized under the following headings: spirit; happiness and fulfillment; freedom; unity; beauty; truth; and love. The material is garnered from a wide variety of sources and the text includes many relevant quotations. A well done, unusual book. Index, 301pp. H&R 75

BLESSINGTON, JOHN. **LET MY CHILDREN WORK**, $2.95. An informally written account of the state of formal and informal education in the U.S. today. Blessington, an educator and a parent, feels that the changes that have taken place are basically cosmetic and much still remains to be done. The book suggests the major flaws and presents some constructive and creative plans for resolving them. 184pp. Dou 74

BORTON, TERRY. **REACH, TOUCH AND TEACH**, $3.95. The title of this book, by one of the most sane and humane teachers around, could not be more apt. This is a powerful description of a way of teaching that really does have the personal development of kids as its central purpose. Moving and practical. Includes an excellent selection for firms and resources. Illustrated. 213pp. MGH 70

BOSTON CHILDREN'S MEDICAL CENTER. **WHAT TO DO WHEN THERE'S NOTHING TO DO**, $1.25. Child-care experts suggest 601 play ideas for babies, toddlers, and two-to-six year olds using ordinary household items. The ideas are illustrated and arranged according to age groups. Index, 186pp. Del 68

BRADY, MARGARET. **CHILDREN'S HEALTH AND HAPPINESS**, c$4.70. Ms. Brady is the mother of three children. Her aim here is to give mother-to-mother advice about the phases that all growing children go through. Allowance is made for the variations which distinguish individual children. This is an interesting, useful account, topically arranged as follows: *Mother's Potential Power; Food; Fresh Air, Sunshine, Water; Physical Environment, Sleep, and Exercise; Spiritual and Emotional Environment; General Management and Training; The Child and His Habits; Children and Ill-Health; Children and Accidents.* Index, 223pp. TPL 48

BRAGA, JOSEPH and LAURIE. **CHILDREN AND ADULTS**, c$10.95. A fine idea book of *activities for growing together* arranged according to recommended ages and covering the period from birth to six years. Each of the ideas is very fully explored and the descriptive material is divided into the following parts: participants, material, explanation (in steps), purpose, and variations. A very creative, well thought-out presentation. Includes an annotated resource list as well as a chapter on learning and growing with children. We get a very good feeling from this book. The Bragas are both developmental psychologists. Index, 310pp. PrH 76

_____. **GROWING WITH CHILDREN**, $2.95. A humanistically-oriented study of childrearing relating the parents' growth to their children's development. The needs, capabilities, and limitations of children from birth to six years are studied—the most noted authorities are cited along with many practical hints developed from the authors' own experiences as parents and as development psychologists. Bibliography, 205pp. PrH 74

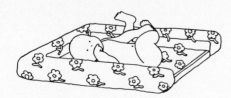

BRAZELTON, T. BERRY. **INFANTS AND MOTHERS**, $4.95. This is a pictorial month-by-month study of the development of a baby in its first year. Three general types are individually studied: quiet, active, and average. Individual infants are traced, giving continuity to the narrative. The aim is to show parents different ways that an infant can develop. Oversize, index. 296pp. Del 69

_____. **TODDLERS AND PARENTS**, $4.95. Utilizing the format that was so successful in his earlier work, Dr. Brazelton explores the period between one year and two and a half years when children are struggling for independence and often challenging the patience and understanding of everyone around them, as well as growing, changing, and learning very swiftly. Each chapter is a realistic family profile, recreating with tenderness and humor the life of one particular small child and the brothers and sisters, parents or other adults shaping his or her life. Woven into the narrative are Dr. Brazelton's professional insights and advice. Many photographs, oversize, index. 267pp. Del 74

BROWN, GEORGE, ed. **THE LIVE CLASSROOM**, $3.50. *The book contains theory illustrated by practice underlined by theory or explanation.* These teaching/learning practices take as their philosophical base a combination of several theories of learning and growing: Gestalt therapy (here termed Gestalt Awareness Training) and Robert Assagioli's Psychosynthesis. The authors share their own classroom experiences. The range is from first grade through high school and covers a variety of subjects including science, social studies, mathematics, English, art, and foreign languages. Bibliography, 306pp. Vik 75

BURNS, MARILYN. **THE I HATE MATHEMATICS BOOK**, $3.95. *This book is for non-believers of all ages. It was written especially for kids who have been convinced (by the attitudes of adults) that mathematics is (1) impossible, (2) for those smart kids who can't play stickball, and (3) no fun anyhow. But this book will also do wonders for parents, teachers, or any adult who likes kids. This book says that mathematics is nothing more (nor less) than a way of looking at the world and is not to be confused with arithmetic. The content of mathematics is the same as the content of any kid's life. Why not? In this*

book you'll find several hundred mathematical events, gags, magic tricks, and experiments to prove it. Beautifully produced, with an abundance of drawings, oversize, 127pp. LBC 75

From THE I HATE MATHEMATICS BOOK

CANEY, STEVEN. **STEVEN CANEY'S PLAY BOOK**, $4.95. Caney is a well-know designer and consultant on toys and educational materials. *The book contains more than seventy activities and projects to do, to make, and to play with wherever children are. They use only discards and inexpensive material found around the house, or at places kids often visit—things like straws, paper cups, cardboard, old tires, pencil and paper, wood scraps, playing cards, and art materials. . . . While all are complete projects in themselves, each provides incentive, and stimulates the imagination for further self-starting play.—*from the foreward. Oversize, many photos and drawings. 230pp. WPC 75

_____. **TOY BOOK**, $3.95. This was Caney's first book. Here he tells how to make a variety of toys. He supplies information on the materials needed and instructions on the construction as well as a general description of the toy. Fully illustrated with photographs and line drawings. This has been a very popular book. 176pp. WPC 72

CAPLAN, FRANK and THERESA. **THE POWER OF PLAY**, $3.95. An exposition of the belief, supported by leading psychologists, that play is a child's natural way of life, developing the child's intelligence, skills and general capacity to grow besides encouraging self-discovery and self-confidence. Also covers the various phases of physical and mental development throughout childhood. The authors were the founders of Creative Playthings. Bibliography, index, 334pp. Dou 73

CARDOZO, PETER. **THE WHOLE KIDS CATALOG**, $5.95. Mainly designed for older kids, this catalogue discusses where to write and get certain kinds of information, where to go, and things to do. The material is topically organized and illustrated throughout. Some of the areas covered include the following: crafts, art, games, theater and puppets, films, photography, music, hobbies, cooking, gardening, children's museums, sports, science, space, history, free or almost free. Oversize, 218pp. Ban 75

CASS, JOAN. **HELPING CHILDREN GROW THROUGH PLAY**, c$6.95. Delves into the meaning and significance of child's play and its major role in the formation of personality and character. *Play is as necessary and important to a child as the food he eats, for it is the very breath of life to him, the reason for his existence and his assurance of immortaliy.* Different methods and styles of play are discussed with suggestions for stimulating and improving the quality of child's play and enhancing the materials used. 166pp. ScB 71

CASTILLO, GLORIA. **LEFT-HANDED TEACHING**, $3.95. Traditionally, public schools have had as their main focus the development of cognitive skills. But today many educators insist that we must also consider the affective dimension—the interests, concerns, fears, anxieties, joys, and other personal and emotional reactions the child brings to the learning situation. This book provides a model that allows for the development of the whole child, taking both cognitive and affective dimensions into consideration. A humanistic study, in lesson form. Annotated bibliography, 223pp. Pra 74

CENTER FOR CURRICULUM DESIGN. **SOMEWHERE ELSE: A LIVING—LEARNING CATALOG**, $3.00. A directory to non-school learning: places that will let you get your hands dirty and places that will leave you alone to work out your struggle between you and whatever hunk of the world you're grappling with. Its 400 entries are an extensively annotated guide to people, places, networks, centers, books and groups. 213pp. Swa 73

COFFIN, PATRICIA. 1, 2, 3, 4, 5, 6—HOW TO UNDERSTAND AND ENJOY THE YEARS THAT COUNT, $4.95. A lovely 8x11" photo and word essay about the development of the author's daughter from one to six. The daughter, now eighteen, offers her own comments. The theme is how the human traditions of family love are the sources of the child's own humanity, his capacity to love and to embrace the values of the human community. 159pp. McM 72

COHEN, DOROTHY. THE LEARNING CHILD—GUIDELINES FOR PARENTS AND TEACHERS, $2.45. Gives commendable answers to such questions as: How does a child learn? Why is the seventh year such a turning point in the child's life? What are the limits to learning at any given age? etc. The entire presentation is stimulating and challenging and the research and qualified resources utilized, such as Piaget and the author's own experience as a child development instructor, lend credibility and authoritativeness to the author's conclusions. A highly recommended guideline for both parents and teachers. 360pp. RaH 72

COLE, ALAN, et al. I SAW A PURPLE COW AND 100 OTHER RECIPES FOR LEARNING, $2.95. A multi-colored delightfully illustrated workbook containing many innovative ideas for pre-schoolers and elementary students. 96pp. LBC 72

_____. A PUMPKIN IN A PEAR TREE, $4.95. *Ideas for Twelve Months of Holiday Fun* is the subtitle. *Holidays have always been times of feasting, singing and dancing, and exchanging gifts, but they have a serious side, too, and understanding something about their true origins will help us to appreciate how and why each is celebrated. A* **Pumpkin in a Pear Tree** *offers a chance to sample a variety of ways to enrich our holiday enjoyment.... [It] is an imaginative activity book that...features an easy-to-follow recipe format. The materials required are generally found around the house.... We have searched for activities that involve the whole family, bridging the generations by offering something for everyone, from toddlers to grandparents. A delightful presentation, in the same format and style as* **Purple Cow**. Many colorful illustrations, oversize, bibliography. 112pp. LBC 76

DeMILLE, RICHARD. PUT YOUR MOTHER ON THE CEILING, $2.95. This is a collection of imaginative children's games (printed in large type so children can use the book themselves). The games are designed for two people, only one of whom may be a child. Each game has a short introduction that gives some idea of what the game is about and establishes a reference point in reality for that game. The game ends with questions which allow the child to complete the game in a way that satisfies him. The individual games progress from easy to hard, but they can be done in any order and we have gotten excellent reports from our customers who have used the book with children. This is a unique book which puts the participating adult in touch with the most neglected and enjoyable parts of his/her children and his/herself. 175pp. Vik 73

DENNISON, GEORGE. THE LIVES OF CHILDREN, $1.95. A journal of the author's experiences with twenty-three children in a small New York private school where he taught. *[T]here is no book that I know of that shows so well what a free and humane education can be like, nor is there a more eloquent description of its philosophy.*—Herbert Kohl. 308pp. RaH 69

DOMAN, GLENN. HOW TO TEACH YOUR BABY TO READ, $2.50. Doman is the Director of Institutes for the Achievement of Human Potential, which has had unprecedented success in treating brain-injured children over the last twenty-five years. Here he discusses why young children want to, can, and should learn to read. He also reviews the controversies surrounding his position and gives detailed instructions for teaching a child to read—with suggested books and an easy-to-follow, step-by-step method. 192pp. Dou 64

EDMUNDS, FRANCIS. RUDOLF STEINER'S GIFT TO EDUCATION: THE WALDORF SCHOOLS, $3.95. See the Waldorf Education sub-section of Steiner.

ELIZABETH CLEANERS STREET SCHOOL PEOPLE. STARTING YOUR OWN HIGH SCHOOL, $2.45. This is the unadorned story of an attempt to create an alternative high school by ten New York City high schoolers age twelve to seventeen and their parents and teachers, filled with dialogue, photographs, and the actual content of the school life. Many of the articles were written by the students and the difficulties and satisfactions of the school are honestly revealed through the eyes of all participants. 236pp. RaH 72

ELLIS, ALBERT. HOW TO RAISE AN EMOTIONALLY HEALTHY, HAPPY CHILD, $2.00. Argues that it is the child's unique and largely inborn way of viewing the world and the people around him that importantly contributes to what happens to him. Shows parents how to assess their child's unique genetic endowment, how to firmly teach him the difference between his desires and his needs, and how to realistically accept rather than make himself angry over the realities of a harsh world. Plays down the importance of the first years of life and streesses what can be done after the child reaches the age of reason—from five on. 247pp. Wil 66

EMERY, DONALD. TEACH YOUR PRESCHOOLER TO READ, c$7.95. There have been a number of books lately on teaching preschoolers to read. This seems to be the best one. The author has had over thirty years' experience as an educator in top positions and has worked with many precocious children. He was also the director of the National Reading Center. Here he discusses why four-year-olds are ready to read and presents detailed instructions for teaching the child to read and to enjoy reading. Very clearly written. Notes, index. 191pp. S&S 75

FABER, ADELE and ELAINE MAZLISH. LIBERATED PARENTS, LIBERATED CHILDREN, $1.75. This is a description of the practical application of Dr. Haim Ginott's non-violent method of communication: instead of threats, choices are offered; cooperation

is invited, not demanded; children's feelings are accepted rather than denied. Index, 238pp. Avo 74

FIAROTTA, PHYLLIS. STICKS AND STONES AND ICE CREAM CONES, $4.95. A step-by-step presentation of more than 120 craft projects, toys, and games for children. Fully illustrated with photographs and line drawings throughout. This is a very popular book. Oversize, 319pp. WPI 73

FLYNN, ELIZABETH and JOHN LAFASO. DESIGN IN AFFECTIVE EDUCATION, $10.00. It continually surprises us how many copies of this teacher resource program we sell. It is organized in terms of 126 different teaching strategies in a recipe-like format (purpose, group size, time suggested, general directions, materials required, and procedure). Selections include themes of communication, freedom, happiness, life, peace, love, valuing, responsibility, work, prejudice, dreaming, futuring, ecology, senses, conflict, family, communication, meditations, marriage, death, life styles. This is a clearly organized, very well presented innovative book for junior and senior high school teachers. Oversize, index, 358pp. Pau 74

FOUKE, GEORGE. FIRST BOOK OF SPACE MAKING, $2.95. An oversize book containing step-by-step instructions for making various kinds of geometric forms. The illustrations are large and the directions are clear. 64pp. GeB 74

FREIRE, PAULO. EDUCATION FOR CRITICAL CONSCIOUSNESS, $2.95. The first English translation of two of Freire's major studies: *Education as the Practice of Freedom* and *Extension or Communication*. These were developed as the result of his efforts in the field of adult literacy in Brazil and his studies of the practice of agricultural extension in Chile, but they extend in reference to all social helping relationships. 164pp. Sea 73

_____. PEDAGOGY OF THE OPPRESSED, $3.95. Freire evolved a theory for the education of illiterates, especially adults, based on the conviction that every human being, no matter how ignorant or submerged in the *culture of silence* is capable of looking at his world in a dialogical encounter with others, and that provided with the proper tools for such an encounter he can gradually perceive his personal and social reality and deal critically with it. As the illiterate learns, his world becomes radically transformed and he is no longer willing to be a mere object responding to changes occurring around him. This is Freire's basic book, outlining his theory and his experiences. 186pp. Sea 68

GINANDES, SHEPARD. THE SCHOOL WE HAVE, $2.75. *I find this to be a fascinating account of the way in which a school has gradually been built which really meets the needs of young people today. While the group at the School is composed primarily of disturbed adolescents and young people, the principles evolved in working with them contain highly significant lessons for everyone in all of the helping professions and for teachers of young people.*—Carl Rogers. Dr. Ginandes is a psychiatrist who is director of the School. His study is based on case histories and actual scenes from day-to-day operations of the School. Bibliography, 272pp. Del 73

GLASSER, WILLIAM. SCHOOLS WITHOUT FAILURE, $2.95. Working from the premise that today's schools are designed for failure, the author deals with the teaching process and ways to make the classroom more relevant. He examines the shortcomings of the education system itself and the role it plays in causing the failure of its students. He offers practical suggestions towards introducing involvement, relevance, and thinking to the school. 255pp. H&R 69

GOODELL, CAROL, ed. THE CHANGING CLASSROOM, $1.95. A wide selection of a variety of pioneering classroom techniques and educational philosophies in the words of numerous authors and leading figures in the field. 340pp. RaH 73

GOODLAD, JOHN, et al. TOWARD A MANKIND SCHOOL, c$7.95. Dr. Goodlad and his coauthors organized an experimental school at the University Elementary School, UCLA, to find ways to put their humanistic concepts into schooling. This book identifies some of their basic ideas and their possible meaning for education and schooling, and contains the authors' reflections on the project and its implications for the future. The project was aimed at both a group of elementary school children and a group of teachers. This is a dry, scholarly, descriptive text. Includes almost 50pp of annotated bibliography, index. 204pp. MGH 74

from Active Learning by Cratty

GORDON, IRA. **BABY LEARNING THROUGH BABY PLAY**, $3.95. A collection of exercises designed to develop a baby's motor skills and awareness of his or her environment. We're not really sure that a baby needs these exercises, but if you want a book like this, this one seems as good as any. The exercises are arranged according to age (the book covers the period up to age two). Many illustrations, oversize. 121pp. SMP 70

from Baby Learning through Baby Play by Ira Gordon

GORDON, IRA, BARRY GUINAGH, and R.E. JESTER. **CHILD LEARNING THROUGH CHILD PLAY**, $3.95. *The years between two and four are special because so much happens in the child's use of speech and language. The child uses language not only to extend his intellectual development but also as a way of knowing and handling his feelings. Of special importance at this time is the way in which parents and other adults play with, work with, and care for him. . . . The purpose of this book is to provide specific, concrete, realistic learning opportunities for you to present to a child in a positive and loving fashion . . . . Their primary aim is to foster intellectual and language development. Included are suggestions for involving other children . . . so that the child will have opportunities for both a one-to-one relationship with an adult and interaction with other children.* Oversize, well illustrated. 116pp. SMP 72

GORDON, THOMAS. **PARENT EFFECTIVENESS TRAINING**, $4.95. A new technique devised to assist parents in becoming responsive and skilled in their parental role. It has been successfully used by many thousands throughout the country and its effectiveness is acclaimed by parents everywhere. NAL 70

_____. **P.E.T. IN ACTION**, c$10.95. An investigation of what happens when P.E.T. is applied in the home. Includes interviews with parents and a variety of case studies. S&S 76

_____. **TEACHER EFFECTIVENESS TRAINING**, c$9.95. T.E.T. (Teacher Effectiveness Training) evolved from P.E.T. (Parent Effectiveness Training) which is now taught by over 5000 instructors. Teachers and administrators began to hear from parents about what they had learned in P.E.T., and asked that the course be given to their districts' teachers, so that they could apply the same communication skills and conflict-resolution methods to students in the classroom. A special course was designed for school teachers. This book presents the same principles, skills, and methods that were developed, refined, and tested in Dr. Gordon's in-service work with teachers in the T.E.T. course. Many of the illustrations and case histories have been drawn from these teachers. The orientation is on developing practical skills rather than on abstract educational concepts. 382pp. S&S 74

GRAUBARD, ALLEN. **FREE THE CHILDREN—RADICAL REFORM AND THE FREE SCHOOL MOVEMENT**, $1.95. The author has combined his knowledge and experience with the ideas of many other outspoken leaders of educational reform to penetrate into the triumphs and failures of the movement. He analyzes much of the current, well known literature on the subject written by such notables as John Holt, A.S. Neill, and George Leonard, and places the radical school reform movement in the context of a wide political and cultural viewpoint. 306pp. RaH 72

GROSS, BEATRICE and RONALD, eds. **WILL IT GROW IN A CLASSROOM?** $3.25. *The book is a joy. I started reading it sitting in an airport waiting room and that first gorgeous mad story made me laugh out loud. I get a great deal of mail from lonely, discouraged teachers who write me how defeated they feel in trying to change the established order. The book breaks through that anomie with encouragement and practical ideas and reinforcement. Thanks for a great experience!*—Eda LeShan. Every article was written by a teacher and every one was written out of personal experience. Among the contributors are some of the best known teacher/writers in the U.S.—John Holt, Herbert Kohl, Miriam Wasserman, for example. Bibliography, 332pp. Del 74

GRUNELIUS, ELIZABETH. **EARLY CHILDHOOD EDUCATION AND WALDORF SCHOOL PLAN**, $2.00. See the Waldorf Education sub-section of Steiner.

HALL, BRIAN. **THE DEVELOPMENT OF CONSCIOUSNESS**, $5.95. *This book is about values. It formulates a theory of values that offers you, the reader, an overall construct. . . a meaning structure out of which you can understand the nature of values and how they may be utilized within the educational process.* The book is the result of Dr. Hall's work at the Center for Exploration of Values and Meaning. A great deal of technical instructional material is included in this detailed analysis along with case studies. The emphasis is on an integration of affective and cognitive learning. Diagrams, annotated bibliography, index. 282pp. Pau 76

_____. **VALUE CLARIFICATION: A GUIDEBOOK**, $7.95. A basic manual of exercises and strategies: the companion volume to the **Sourcebook**. The book is divided into four parts: I, an introduction, giving definitions of a value, value ranking, and value indicators; II, presents forty-nine *strategies* (techniques) for students, teachers, and professionals; III, details six complete workshops for training people in the Value Clarification Process; and IV, deals with those issues which will enable Value Clarification techniques to be used in the classroom. The exercises are presented in a recipe-like format and the text is oversized and well illustrated. 253pp. Pau 73

_____. **VALUE CLARIFICATION: A SOURCEBOOK**, $7.95. The basic text for understanding the theory of values underlying Dr. Hall's methodology of Value Clarification. The book also contains a variety of practical techniques designed to engage the reader in the process of clarifying his or her own values. Many case studies are also presented along with supportive material previously written. Oversize, illustrations, annotated bibliography, index. 306pp. Pau 73

HALL, BRIAN and MAURY SMITH. **VALUE CLARIFICATION: A HANDBOOK FOR CHRISTIAN EDUCATORS**, $7.95. Provides a theological basis for understanding the possibilities and limitations of the effective use of Value Clarification in religious education. Includes case studies of the methodology, with applications for parish renewal, liturgy, and prayer life. Annotated bibliography, oversize. 269pp. Pau 73

HANSEN, SOREN and JESPER JENSEN. **THE LITTLE RED SCHOOL BOOK**, $1.25. This book was originally written and published in Danish. It tells the student many helpful things not normally revealed in a rigid and repressive school environment, which can be of practical immediate value. It tells about teachers and the school system, discusses homework, punishment, mobilizing for greater influence, the life of students, an explanation of sex with forthright, honest definitions, drug problems, grading system, and right representation of student interests. 255pp. S&S 69

HARWOOD, A.C. **THE RECOVERY OF MAN IN CHILDHOOD**, $8.40. See the Waldorf Education sub-section of Steiner.

HAWLEY, ROBERT, SIDNEY SIMON, and D.D. BRITTON. **COMPOSITION FOR PERSONAL GROWTH**, $4.95. *[This book presents] a program for teaching composition to students in grades 7 through 12. Through guided activities and a wide range of writing assignments, this approach attempts to promote the student's awareness of self, his ability to translate his values into meaningful actions.* The book includes many specific suggestions and techniques to stimulate students to exchange ideas about themselves and each other. The material is clearly presented and is designed for practical classroom use. Index, bibliography. 184pp. Har 73

HAWLEY, ROBERT and ISABEL. **HUMAN VALUES IN THE CLASSROOM**, $4.95. The Hawleys set forth a humanistic approach to teaching and learning which focuses on the prime values of love, trust, cooperation, and tolerance. To foster the development of values, the teacher creates learning opportunities where values come into play. This book presents practical ways to create such opportunities. The authors delineate a sequence of theoretical and practical ideas for creating a classroom climate which promotes personal and social growth. Included are scores of specific activities, procedures and suggestions which have proven their worth in classroom use. They also address such issues as the need for positive focus in teaching, the merits of grading as a means of evaluation, and what to do about discipline and behavior problems. Index, annotated bibliography. 282pp. Har 75

HENDRICKS, GAY and RUSSELL WILLS. **THE CENTERING BOOK**, $3.25. *There is a feeling of balance, a feeling of inner strength that we feel when we are centered. To feel centered is to experience one's psychological center of gravity—a solid integration of mind and body. . . . This book contains activities that people use to help themselves feel centered; all of the techniques can be used in the classroom and in the home, and then can be used by people of all ages. . . . Schools place a great deal of emphasis on the development of cognitive, rational, and intellectual processes. To balance this emphasis, The Centering Book provides the core of a curriculum for the development of affective, intuitive, and creative processes in students. . . . [In addition] this book can . . . be used in the home to provide a set of activities that parents and children can use to explore new levels of awareness together. The sources of the activities include yoga, Zen, movement, imagery, relaxation training, the Senoi people of the Central Malay Peninsula, and the Sufi tradition. This is a wonderful collection, very well put together and complete with detailed instructions, clear descriptions of the exercises and illustrations where applicable. The table of contents reads as follows: Basic Centering, Relaxing the Mind, Expanding Perception, Relaxing the Body, Working with Dreams, Imagery, Stretching the Body, Movement and Dance, and Storytelling.* There's also a topical listing of recommended books. 180pp. PrH 75

HERNDON, JAMES. **HOW TO SURVIVE IN YOUR NATIVE LAND**, $1.25. An informal exploration of the lives of several white students in middle class suburbia which, although it is basically about teaching, is also a wonderful record of growing up in America today which some reviewers have compared to **Huckleberry Finn**. 179pp. Ban 71

_____. **THE WAY IT SPOZED TO BE**, $.95. The personal record of one ill-fated year in a metropolitan ghetto school, 98% black, 99% *deprived*, and 100% chaotic. It tells how the educational bureaucracy, the schools, and life itself in our big cities are all rigged against the students who can't take it—the ones we call deprived. *The most accurate description so far in print of ghetto school-children and the forces lined up against them.—* Nat Hentoff. 198pp. Ban 68

HERTZBERG, ALVIN and EDWARD STONE. **SCHOOLS ARE FOR CHILDREN**, $2.45. Written by two American elementary school principals, this book is a valuable attempt to bring the reality of the *open school* method of learning into more extensive consideration and usefulness. The authors relate their experiences and communicate to the reader an understanding of the immense potential of this method. They suggest practical means of adapting the medium of the open classroom to the needs and temperament of American society. 232pp. ScB 71

JOHN HOLT

John Holt has been called a prophet in the educational wilderness. His books have created a great stir among all people concerned with the field of education and have caused many teachers, parents and educators to undergo a deep self-searching of methods, attitudes, and assumptions in their field. Holt has himself been a teacher for seventeen years, and has taught school in Colorado, Massachusetts and California. He has been an assistant to Harvard graduates as well as elementary school children. His insights and revelatory probes into our present educational system provide a deep critique of the whole system, and the whole of American society as well.

HOLT, JOHN. **ESCAPE FROM CHILDHOOD**, $1.75. Subtitled *The Needs and Rights of Children*, this is an examination of the way society systematically denies young people responsible choices, while expecting them to assume this same responsibility at an arbitrarily determined age. The material is very well presented and the questions raised are important ones for all parents whether they are specifically interested in the educational process per se or not. 225pp. RaH 74

_____. **FREEDOM AND BEYOND**, $2.75. Holt explores certain fallacies in human thinking and assumption, which create unreasonable behavior of the human species and irrational social perspectives. Excellent selection of recommended readings, films and other source material. 276pp. Del 72

_____. **HOW CHILDREN FAIL**, $1.95. Holt attacks the coercive, mindless, fear-producing techniques of our schools that blunt the normal drive to experience and learn which innately and normally impels the child. 181pp. Del 64

_____. **HOW CHILDREN LEARN**, $2.45. A series of observations about the mechanisms of learning as actually witnessed by the author. The obvious conclusion is that children most assuredly do come into the world equipped to explore, discover and learn if only their natural curiosity is not blunted by the pre-conceived notions of parents and would-be educators. 156pp. Del 67

_____. **INSTEAD OF EDUCATION**, c$8.95. Subtitled *Ways to Help People Do Things Better*, this book shows how we can turn our whole society into a place of genuine learning. Holt proposes expanding the creative uses of facilities we already have, adding new facilities that will serve more people for less money (such as neighborhood printing presses), and using people to their fullest capacity (for example, matching skilled people with those who want to learn that skill). A very positive approach to improving both our educational system and society in general. Notes, bibliography. 250pp. Dut 76

_____. **THE UNDER-ACHIEVING SCHOOL**, $2.25. A collection of short essays, lectures and insights written down by the author over several years. 207pp. Del 69

_____. **WHAT DO I DO MONDAY?** $2.45. Holt makes the reader look at himself and the world and his understanding of the world in new ways. He gives many practical examples of how the experience of learning might be made more meaningful and might retain more of its wondrous quality for both child and adult. 318pp. Del 70

HOWE, LELAND and MARY. **PERSONALIZING EDUCATION**, $5.95. Subtitled *Values Clarification and Beyond*, this is a clear practical explanation of just how and why the valuing process can be made to permeate the total educational process. The four-part elaboration of techniques for personalizing education focuses on (1) human relationships, (2) goals in the classroom, (3) the curriculum, and (4) classroom organization and management. The book contains well over 100 specific techniques and worksheets. This seems to be an excellent sourcebook for the teacher. Excellent long bibliography, index. 574pp. Har 75

IVAN ILLICH

Ivan Illich has had a deep impact upon the cultural and educational revolution with his visionary ideas. The value of his thoughts, as expressed by Erich Fromm, is *that they have a liberating effect on the mind by showing entirely new possibilities; they make the reader more alive because they open the door that leads out of the prison of routinized, sterile, preconceived notions.* Illich has led a varied life, was at one time a Roman Catholic priest, and is the co-founder of the Center for International Documentation in Cuernavaca, Mexico.

ILLICH, IVAN. **AFTER DESCHOOLING WHAT?** $1.50. The author probes into the possible consequences of the disestablishment of institutionalized schooling which he advocates as necessary to restrict and dissolve the inadequacies and miseries of the established

---

order. A number of critics add their own thoughts in this selection of essays. 162pp. H&R 73

_____. **CELEBRATION OF AWARENESS**, $1.95. Illich seeks to arouse man's sleeping consciousness to an appreciation of the potential for a wondrous future if humanity can break the shackles that hold us in bondage to an obsolete past. 181pp. Dou 69

_____. **DESCHOOLING SOCIETY**, $1.25. This is an important study which exposes the massive failures of our educational system and seeks to totally reform it. As usual, Illich is not easy to read, but his argument is clear and straightforward. Things must change. Rather than just complaining about what is wrong, he outlines what can and must be done—and his ideas are both visionary and immensely practical. 167pp. H&R 71

_____. **SCHOOLS FOR CONVIVIALITY**, $1.25. Illich chooses the term *conviviality* to designate the opposite of industrial productivity. He intends it to mean creative intercourse among persons, and the intercourse of persons with their environment, and this in contrast with the conditioned response of people to the demands made upon them by others, and by a man-made environment. 110pp. H&R 73

JONES, RICHARD. **FANTASY AND FEELING IN EDUCATION**, $3.30. The author, a psychologist, claims that it is now time to stress the importance of feeling, emotion and imagination in our educational methods. 276pp. H&R 68

JANOV, ARTHUR. **THE FEELING CHILD**, $2.95. Janov draws on his vast experience with patients in primal therapy and the research done at the Primal Institute to formulate ways of bringing up emotionally healthy children. Dr. Janov deals with a broad range of problems common to child-rearing, from daydreaming, excessive whining, and fear of the dark, to the consequences of divorce, punishment, and childhood sexuality. He shows how parents can fulfill the psychological and physiological needs of their children with their own feelings in an environment free from neurotic pain. 285pp. S&S 73

KHAN, HAZRAT INAYAT. **EDUCATION: FROM BEFORE BIRTH TO MATURITY**, $3.95. See the Islam section.

KIRSCHENBAUM, HOWARD, RODNEY NAPIER and SIDNEY SIMON. **WAD-JA-GET**, $2.95. A discussion of grading and its effects on students written by three professors of education who have had first-hand contact with this problem in all its manifestations. All possible alternatives are examined in detail. Notes, 315pp. Har 71

KOHL, HERBERT. **MATH, WRITINGS AND GAMES IN THE OPEN CLASSROOM**, $2.45. Kohl gives practical suggestions for teachers and parents on developing new and imaginative ways to teach. The section on writing describes the techniques that Kohl used in getting children to write stories, fables, and poetry by encouraging them to rely on their own experiences and their own language. The largest part of the book, *Games and Math*, is an analysis of the ways in which games can be used in teaching. He describes games and learning ideas and shows how playing these games can stimulate children's imagination and thinking so that they can comprehend complex concepts. He includes clear and practical suggestions on setting up a classroom game center, and a list of the materials needed. Also includes over 150 illustrations and an annotated list of recommended reading. 252pp. RaH 74

_____. **THE OPEN CLASSROOM**, $1.65. A clearly stated and practically presented guidebook for the inception of open classroom teaching techniques. Chapters are included on starting the year, actual operational classroom examples, discipline, and other specific problems. 116pp. RaH 69

_____. **READING, HOW TO**, $1.95. Proclaiming that reading is no more difficult than walking or talking, and that all persons can learn to read effectively or can improve their skills, the author proceeds to suggest techniques that will facilitate reading ability. 224pp. Ban 75

_____. **36 CHILDREN**, $.95. A first-person account of what it is like to be a white teacher in a public school in Harlem. Kohl really cares and this is obvious from the narrative presented here. 224pp. NAL 67

KONIG, KARL. **BROTHERS AND SISTERS**, $2.25. See the Waldorf Education subsection of Steiner.

_____. **THE FIRST THREE YEARS OF THE CHILD**, c$5.50. See the Waldorf Education sub-section of Steiner.

KOZOL, JONATHAN. **DEATH AT AN EARLY AGE**, $1.25. A heart-rending account of the psychologically crippling education processes involving black children in the Boston public schools. 240pp. Ban 67

KRAMER, EDITH. **ART AS THERAPY WITH CHILDREN**, $3.95. *Edith Kramer has worked as an art therapist in a variety of settings with children suffering from just about every known emotional or social disorder. . . . Her true and practical understanding stems from a deep knowledge of psychoanalysis combined with the skill and intuition of an artist and the humane love of a born teacher. The book deals with such subjects . . . as sense of identity, feelings of emptiness, interpretation of reality, ambivalence, aggression, defenses, sublimation. It is organized around these ideas, and richly documented with case material.* This is a useful study of a little-explored field. Bibliography, color and black-and-white plates, index. ScB 71

KRISHNAMURTI. **EDUCATION AND THE SIGNIFICANCE OF LIFE**, c$3.00. An exquisite book that penetrates to the core of the problems of education. The author's deep understanding and clear perceptions lead the reader to realizations about the role and purpose of the teacher, the interrelation of the school staff, and necessary qualities of the true teacher. See section on Krishnamurti. 125pp. H&R 53

ONARD, GEORGE. **EDUCATION AND ECSTASY**, $2.25. An incisive, boldly written
ok that at times seems to merge almost into romantic poetry only to slash suddenly and
eply into the existing *educational* techniques which are damming up the flood of human
tentialities. 259pp. Del 68

USING NEWSPAPERS

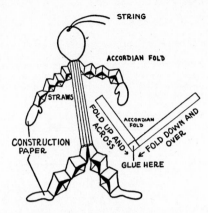

From ECOLOGY CRAFTSBOOK FOR THE OPEN CLASSROOM

IPSCHITZ, CEIL. **ECOLOGY CRAFTSBOOK FOR THE OPEN CLASSROOM**, c$13.35.
nit 1 spells out specific guidelines and materials for preparing your classroom for ecology
afts activities. Units 2–6 provide dozens of individual and group activities. . . . Every ac-
ity comes to you in a convenient . . . format that includes a descriptive title and sug-
sted grade level for use, a full list of necessary tools and materials, step-by-step directions
r carrying out the activity, an illustration of the construction object, and ideas for indi-
dual variation. The instructions are very thorough and many unusual ideas are presented.
versize, 208pp. PrH 75

cDIARMID, NORMA, MARI PETERSON, and JAMES SUTHERLAND. **LOVING AND
EARNING**, c$8.95. Working on the premise that it is the *emotional* component which
rovides the basis for a child's intellectual and social development, the authors show how
ve, physical contact, and simple interaction with a baby or toddler will foster the child's
riosity and lead to an emotional stability that will have a profound effect on his or her
ter life. The emphasis is on play as a learning stimulus and the book includes many acti-
ties, exercises, and games to stimulate a child from shortly after birth to the age of three.
describes yoga exercises, new reading techniques, feeling and touching games, and ways
make musical instruments, puppets, and books. The material is arranged according to
e age of the child. Glossary, bibliography, index. 309pp. HBJ 75

ANN, JOHN. **LEARNING TO BE**, $5.30. Subtitled *The Education of Human Potential*,
is book explores new learning methods such as psychosynthesis, tai chi ch'uan, tantric
oga, and breathing exercises in the hope of designing an *internal curriculum* which will
elp children develop their feelings as well as their intellects. Professor Mann has adapted
any humanistic awareness and sensitivity techniques for classroom use and related them
basic human functions. This is a dry, academic account which contains some good ideas
hich can be followed up in greater depth elsewhere. Notes, bibliography, index. 281pp.
cM 72

ARIN, PETER and KATHRYN, and VINCENT STANLEY. **THE LIMITS OF SCHOOL-
NG**, $2.45. Provides a close look at education's most radical departures by giving selec-
ons from the writings of some of the nation's most active alternative educators. Includes
ssays by George Dennison, Jonathan Kozol, Paul Goodman, Ivan Illich, John Holt, Her-
ert Kohl, Sylvia Ashton-Warner, and James Herndon. 150pp. PrH 75

ARSH, LEONARD. **ALONGSIDE THE CHILD**, $2.45. This is a warm, well written dis-
ussion of experiences in an English primary school modelled on the open classroom sys-
em. Included are chapters on specific areas such as painting, mathematics, writing, using
ooks, and discovery approaches. There is also information on using teaching areas, organ-
zation, and on the school and the community. Many photographs of classrooms and
hildren's work are included. Index, 154pp. H&R 70

ARTIN, J.H. and CHARLES HARRISON. **FREE TO LEARN**, $2.45. The main prob-
m with American education, according to the authors, is the boards of education that
rganize the schools around outmoded nineteenth century ideas, segregating children ac-
ording to age instead of ability. This is a handbook showing why and how to change the
oards. Index, 185pp. PrH 72

ARZOLLO, JEAN and JANICE LLOYD. **LEARNING THROUGH PLAY**, $2.95. **Learn-
g Through Play** *is an all-day, every-day book aimed at the parents of preschool children.
is a deft translation of the weightiest and most advanced findings of educational scientists
to a lighthearted collection of games, projects, amusements and conversational gambits
esigned to stimulate and satisfy the preschooler's twin appetites for fun and knowledge
. . . The dozens of activities listed in the book are divided into eleven chapters corres-
onding to what the authors call basic skill-families: The Five Senses, Language Develop-
ent, Pre-reading, Understanding Relationships, Sorting and Classifying, Counting and
easuring, Problem Solving, Exploring, Creativity, Self-Esteem, and Physical Growth.*
he activities are well described and the book is illustrated throughout. Index, 211pp.
&R 72

MARIA MONTESSORI

Maria Montessori was one of the most eminent and influential figures in the
field of education during the past century. She became a practicing physician
in Rome, one of the first women to achieve such a specialized status in her
country. She later left the field of medicine for what she felt was her true
life purpose, the study and improvement of the education of the child.

She patterned her philosophy and techniques upon her understanding of the
mysteries of childhood. Her methods revolutionized education throughout
the world and she introduced many new principles for her schools that were
based on the conception of the child as a soul with profound potential.

CRANDALL, JOY. **EARLY TO LEARN**, c$5.95. A photographic collection of portraits
of children's experiences, tied together with related text. Topics include *A Child Needs,
A Child Thrives On, School Gives, The Environment,* and *Developing Skills.* Oversize,
annotated bibliography, 128pp. DMd 74

KRAMER, RITA. **MARIA MONTESSORI: A BIOGRAPHY**, c$15.00. A long overdue
definitive biography of this definitive figure in the modern educational process. Ms.
Kramer draws on Montessori's own works, what others have written about her, and the
memories of those still living who knew and worked with her. This is a study of the Montessori method as much as of Montessori herself. Illustrations, notes, index. 410pp. Put 76

MALLOY, TERRY. **MONTESSORI AND YOUR CHILD: A PRIMER FOR PARENTS**,
c$4.75. The first three sections of this lovely hand drawn book ask simple questions:
What is your child really like? What does your child need? How can you help your child?
The last section describes ideas used in Montessori preschool education. An illustrated
appendix shows some of the Montessori materials mentioned in the text and gives concrete
guidance to parents. The author is director of a Montessori school in California. This is
the best primer for parents on the Montessori method that we have seen. Bibliography,
95pp. ScB 74

MONTESSORI, MARIA. **THE CHILD IN THE FAMILY**, $1.50. A chief principle of Mon-
tessori's techniques of education is that a child must have the liberty to mold his/her own
personality. This and other fundamental insights and beliefs developed by Montessori and
central to her approach are discussed in this volume. 160pp. Avo 56

_____. **CHILDHOOD EDUCATION**, $2.95. A general philosophical discussion of
the basic premises of the Montessori method and an attempt to answer both the criticisms
and the serious misconceptions that have arisen about it. 136pp. NAL 55

_____. **THE DISCOVERY OF THE CHILD**, $1.50. A basic book on the author's
methods with a selection of pictures of children at work in a Montessori school. 339pp.
RaH 62

_____. **THE MONTESSORI ELEMENTARY MATERIAL**, $3.45. An intensive
discussion of the body of knowledge that is to be put before the elementary school child.
Almost half the book is devoted to Ms. Montessori's original techniques for teaching grammar. The successive steps in learning reading meaningfully are also discussed in detail as
are arithmetic, geometry, and music, and the teaching materials for these subjects are
shown and their use described. 421pp. ScB 17

_____. **THE MONTESSORI METHOD**, $2.95. This book is perhaps the most com-
plete rendition of the application of Montessori's principles. It covers all phases of development and all areas of instruction. 376pp. ScB 12

_____. **THE SECRET OF CHILDHOOD**, $1.50. The author reveals her deep un-
derstanding of the childhood stage with precision and genuine compassion. She points out
that all children have an inborn urge to learn and that learning is a spontaneous action of
their growth. 216pp. RaH 66

_____. **SPONTANEOUS ACTIVITY IN EDUCATION**, $2.95. This is a fundamen-
tal text in the theory and practice of producing the right environment for children who
are learning through their own developing mastery of experiences. Key sections are devoted to *Experimental Science, Attention,* and *Intelligence* as fundamental problems in
education. The text includes many case studies based on the author's own experience.
The material was written after Dr. Montessori had been teaching for quite a while and
therefore contains some advanced material. This should not be considered an introductory
volume. 383pp. ScB 65

OREM, R.C., ed. **MONTESSORI**, $3.25. Orem has assembled a layman's guide to Montes-
sori that answers many questions parents have about the Montessori method. Both the
practical aspects (the day-to-day operations of a typical school) and the philosophical
roots are discussed in easy-to-comprehend terms. The first essay offers Montessori as a
strategy for much-needed educational reforms. In the second section, Montessori *tactics*
as employed in a variety of Montessori schools are described. The third section includes
six articles exploring topics such as the home, discipline, flexibility, public education,
language, and arts—each in relation to contributions made by the Montessori method.
263pp. Put 74

_____. **A MONTESSORI HANDBOOK**, $2.45. Half of this book consists of *Dr.
Montessori's Own Handbook,* the only authentic practical manual of the Montessori
method, and the other half of new material on current Montessori theory and practice.
The book integrates Dr. Montessori's writings with up-to-date commentary and is designed
to be useful for both practicing teachers and interested parents. Each section of the Montessori text is introduced by a brief essay relating that particular aspect of Montessori to

current education practices. An appendix provides a guide to what to look for in a good Montessori school. Recommended as a primer. 192pp. Put 66

STANDING, E.M. **MARIA MONTESSORI: HER LIFE AND WORK**, $1.50. The author was a close friend and associate of Montessori for many years. Photographs. 370pp. NAL 57

MOUSTAKAS, CLARK, ed. **THE CHILD'S DISCOVERY OF HIMSELF**, $1.75. Ten therapists talk about the times that they first made contact with individual children. Retaining portions of the actual dialogue and commentary, each contributor focuses on the actual transactions, the relationships, and the process in such a way that the reader has an opportunity to see the emergence of the child's self. Notes, index. 242pp. RaH 66

_____. **CHILDREN IN PLAY THERAPY**, $1.75. Moustakas presents the methods and materials used at the Merrill-Palmer School in Detroit—the playroom equipped with toys and materials chosen in part for their symbolic content, arranged in an unstructured fashion, and reserved for the child to use and interpret in his own way, without the judgment or interference of the supervising adult and without restrictions other than those of safety. He also discusses the attitudes and attributes of the therapists and illustrates them, and the techniques of play therapy, through a number of case histories containing both verbatim material and commentary. Index, notes. 237pp. RaH 53

_____. **PSYCHOTHERAPY WITH CHILDREN**, $1.95. Through verbatim dialogues the author takes the reader into the usually hidden world of the child at crucial moments of psychic development. Dr. Moustakas places special emphasis on growth and creativity in psychotherapy, parent counselling, relations with schools, and therapy of gifted and handicapped children. 365pp. H&R 56

_____. **WHO WILL LISTEN?** $1.75. An exploration of the communication problem between parents and children in which Moustakas contends that simply by listening to children parents can come to understand their hidden needs, fears, joys, and frustrations. Notes, bibliography. 147pp. RaH 75

MOUSTAKAS, CLARK and GRETA PERRY. **LEARNING TO BE FREE**, $2.95. The authors present guidelines for setting up an educational environment in which active learner participation, learner-initiated experiences, the one-to-one relationship of play therapy, and open-discussion groups make the child a decision-maker in his own education. Many case studies are included and there are bibliographies of children's books and of professional books, and a list of supplemental materials and resources, and an index. 184pp. PrH 73

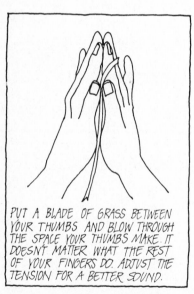

PUT A BLADE OF GRASS BETWEEN YOUR THUMBS AND BLOW THROUGH THE SPACE YOUR THUMBS MAKE. IT DOESN'T MATTER WHAT THE REST OF YOUR FINGERS DO. ADJUST THE TENSION FOR A BETTER SOUND.

from The Reasons for Seasons by Linda Allison

A.S. NEILL

Neill's famous Summerhill school, which was a unique experiment when it started, has greatly altered the approach to childhood education. Much has been written about Neill's ideas and his radical philosophy of child rearing, both critical and complimentary. His writings and his thoughts are practices which have deeply stirred thoughtful people everywhere. No doubt, the Summerhill school and its success has shattered many of the old assumptions about what is proper or necessary in education. His principal book, **Summerhill**, with an introduction by Erich Fromm, is very stimulating, and the provocative ideas are sure to evoke a strong response from the reader, either sympathetic or otherwise.

Neill's philosophy of Summerhill is really the belief that children must be free and unoppressed and that if they are allowed this liberty, within an environment of understanding, their innate impulse will be to interact and live cooperatively and constructively. They will, naturally and spontaneously, learn,

study, and grow. Thus coercion, punishment, suppression, and authoritarianism are removed and the child can be himself and express his individuality in an atmosphere of happiness without inhibiting psychological burdens being forced upon him. Neill died in 1973 at 89.

HEMMINGS, RAY. **CHILDREN'S FREEDOM—A.S. NEILL AND THE EVOLUTION OF THE SUMMERHILL IDEA**, $3.45. An absorbing examination which traces the progression of Neill's thought and the evolving manifestations of his ideas. Neill's ideas are discussed in relation to current education reform ideas and are placed in a sociological and political frame of understanding and influence. 218pp. ScB 73

NEILL, A.S. **FREEDOM, NOT LICENSE**, $2.45. Advice to parents and educators on how to raise their children and cope with common (and uncommon) problems of growing children. Written as answers to questions by Americans. His comments are often surprising and will certainly be helpful if for no other reason than to give a fresh outlook on problems and a new perspective at looking at the child and his relationship with parent, teacher and environment. 187pp. Har 66

_____. **SUMMERHILL**, $4.95. Har 60

NEWMAN, RUTH. **GROUPS IN SCHOOLS**, $3.95. Dr. Newman examines the group dynamics of the school world—the administration, the staff, the parents, and the children—to explain why some children thrive in the school, why some fail, and what can be done to change and transform the schools for the benefit of all children. The author has done a great deal of study of group behavior and has also done practical work with groups. She believes that an understanding of the groups in the schools is essential in providing an environment where change can take place. Bibliography, 286pp. S&S 74

NIEDERHAUSER, HANS and MARGARET FROHLICH. **FORM DRAWING**, $4.50 See the Waldorf Education sub-section of Steiner.

NYQUIST, E.B. and C.R. HAWES. **OPEN EDUCATION—A SOURCEBOOK FOR PARENTS AND TEACHERS**, $1.95. A comprehensive compilation of new American educational methods by a large number of contributors. A helpful and idea-stimulating collection that provides one of the best overviews available. 371pp. Ban 72

JEAN PIAGET

Jean Piaget is the Swiss psychologist whose name will forever be inextricably associated with the study of the crucial stage of childhood. He has perhaps done more than anyone else to clarify the complex psychology of the period of early growth in the human being. His research and conclusions are significant breakthroughs in understanding human personality development. The concepts Piaget has developed are somewhat complex and the terminology involved somewhat specialized. His work represents, however, the most scientifically precise and verifiable observation and theory on the developmental pscyhology of childhood.

FURTH, HANS G. and HENRY WACHS. **THINKING GOES TO SCHOOL**, c$9.60. Subtitled *Piaget's Theory in Practice*, this is an excellent manual showing how to prepare children to develop their full potential as thinking human beings. The book sets forth a curriculum which is based upon clinical work conducted since 1952, and upon a work study project carried out at the Tyler School in West Virginia. At the Tyler School the project classroom was marked by laughter, discussion, activity, and movement. There was freedom, but it was freedom within structure. The child was permitted to perform at the level which most challenged his ability and interest. This was accomplished through a series of specially designed activities or games. How to perform these games at home or in the classroom is the heart of this book. More than 175 games or activity situations are described in detail. This is generally considered the best practical manual on Piaget education. Recommended. Index, notes. 314pp. Oxf 74

PIAGET, JEAN. **THE CHILD AND REALITY**, $1.95. How do children learn to perceive the world around them? How do they learn to coordinate their muscles? To speak? To hold notions of right and wrong? Piaget has made answering these questions his life's work. This book comprises nine essays in which Piaget offers an exposition of his answers to those questions, his now famous theory of the stages of intellectual development through which all children pass. This is a good general overview of Piaget's major theories. Index. 182pp. Vik 73

_____. **THE CHILD'S CONCEPTION OF MOVEMENT AND SPEED**, $1.65. A thorough examination of the young child's thought processes. Provides a deep insight into the functioning process of reason. 340pp. RaH 46

_____. **THE CHILD'S CONCEPTION OF PHYSICAL CAUSALITY**, $2.50. An in depth exploration of the conception of material force and the system of physics peculiar to the child. The results of practical experiments are discussed and the volume is divided into sections on the explanation of movement, prediction and explanation, explanation of machines, and the child's conception of causality and reality. Index, 309pp. LtA 60

_____. **THE CHILD'S CONCEPTION OF TIME**, $1.65. The product of several years of work, originally inspired by the suggested questions of Albert Einstein: Is our intuitive grasp of time primitive or derived? Is it identical with our intuitive grasp of velocity? 360pp. RaH 27

_____. **THE CONSTRUCTION OF REALITY IN THE CHILD**, $1.65. In the words of Gardner Murphy, *The unique contribution of Jean Piaget seems to me to be in the sensitive and imaginative way in which he has explored the inner world of the child's*

...ought; the child's way of understanding the world, the social order and himself; and the ...ng process of development from the infantile to the adult way of thinking. This book is ...st such a contribution. 434pp. RaH 54

_____. **THE MORAL JUDGMENT OF THE CHILD**, $4.95. This classic study ex-...mines a problem that stands at the heart of society—how does a child distinguish between ...ght and wrong. Piaget and his co-workers conducted a number of experiments and the ...sults are reported here along with detailed analysis. The volume concludes with a com-...arison of Piaget's findings with related social psychology and sociology theories. Notes, ...dices. 410pp. McM 65

_____. **SCIENCE OF EDUCATION AND THE PSYCHOLOGY OF THE CHILD**, ...2.45. A biting attack upon the educational techniques in use today. Piaget criticizes the ...utmoded and obsolete methods of the public school systems which practically ignore the ...ental and emotional growth of the child. He feeels educators must concentrate on the ...hild they seek to help rather than upon educational theory. 180pp. Vik 69

...IAGET, JEAN and BARBEL INHELDER. **THE PSYCHOLOGY OF THE CHILD**, $3.95. ...Designed to serve as a definitive summary of Piaget's work. Concerned with the growth of ...onsciousness and behavior patterns up to the stage of adolescence. 159pp. H&R 69

...RICHMOND, P.G. **INTRODUCTION TO PIAGET**, $3.95. A clearly written short general ...ntroduction to Piaget's theories. Among the topics Professor Richmond discusses are the ...rocess of intellectual development, the development of thought from the sensorimotor ...o the operational stage, the progression from concrete to formal operations, and learning ...nd teaching from a Piagetian viewpoint. Index, 120pp. H&R 70

...HARP, EVELYN. **THINKING IS CHILD'S PLAY**, $1.45. A very useful presentation of ...iaget's learning and teaching games for pre-schoolers, modified by the author to take ...dvantage of current research. Unlike most of the books on Piaget's techniques, this is an ...npretentious volume which is a pleasure to read. Forty games are presented, with infor-...nation on purpose, materials, and a section of comments. A drawing accompanies each ...f the games. These can be used by parents and teachers alike. Recommended. Bibliog-...aphy, index. 143pp. Avo 69

...SIME, MARY. **A CHILD'S EYE VIEW**, c$6.95. This book examines the implications of ...Piaget's theories based on the author's years of experience working with the theories. It ...begins by outlining the fundamental tenets of Piaget's views of a child's intellectual growth ...nd basic concept development, and describes the reactions of some primary school child-...ren to some of his tests. The second section illustrates the paths by which young children ...learn to reason logically, while the third explores the progress of logical thinking as the ...child matures. Piagetian tests are used throughout to illustrate the stages of normal intel-...ectual development and to pinpoint their lack of synchronization with chronological age. ...Illustrated appendices describe projects carried out in junior high schools. The book is il-...ustrated throughout with diagrams, reproductions of children's work, and photographs. ...Oversize, index. 144pp. H&R 73

POSTMAN, NEIL and CHARLES WEINGARTNER. **LINGUISTICS**, $2.45. The linguistic ...approach is used extensively in today's schools. The book begins with a survey of linguistics ...and then goes on to an examination of linguistics and grammar, usage, semantics, lexicog-...raphy, and reading. A detailed study geared toward the English teacher. Bibliography, ...209pp. Del 66

_____. **THE SCHOOL BOOK**, $3.25. The first part of this book contains a history ...of school criticism in the past fifteen years; a discussion of ways school can change, has ...changed and is likely to change; and a series of questions for parents to ask in evaluating ...their children's schools. The second part is descriptions of people and terms important in ...the school world, recent important legal decisions, and resources for further study. A com-...plete guide for parents. 308pp. Del 73

_____. **THE SOFT REVOLUTION**, $1.95. A grab-bag of strategies for students. ...181pp. Del 71

from the Whole Kids Catalog

_____. **TEACHING AS A SUBVERSIVE ACTIVITY**, $2.25. A refreshing look at ...the subject of teaching and learning. A stimulating presentation which beautifully exposes ...the sham methods that have gone by the name of teaching and education and which are ...so dominant in our schools even today. The authors contribute numerous valuable and ...practical suggestions for introducing real discovery into our education methods. 218pp. ...Del 69

RASBERRY, SALLI and ROBERT GREENWAY. **RASBERRY EXERCISES**, $3.95. A classic on free schools and alternative educational movements. It's sure to get you high. It's written *to the millions of children still in prison in the United States and to the handful of adults trying to spring them.* Many photographs and illustrations. 125pp. FPC 70

RENFIELD, RICHARD. **IF TEACHERS WERE FREE**, $2.25. Contends that teachers might be entirely different if they saw their task as to help learning happen instead of trying to make it happen. 158pp. Del 69

REPO, SATU. **THIS BOOK IS ABOUT SCHOOLS**, $1.95. Contains essays first published in **This Magazine Is About Schools**, one of the most famous teaching periodicals in North America. It presents tactics and possibilities and projects for school-age children. 457pp. RaH 70

ROBERTS, THOMAS, ed. **FOUR PSYCHOLOGIES APPLIED TO EDUCATION**, $12.75. A massive tome. In four separate sections, four psychologies—Freudian, behavioral, humanistic, and transpersonal—are presented with some of their applications to education. The editor provides an introduction to each section and he has done an excellent job in choosing the selections. It's a technical volume designed for the professsional educator and as such it makes a fine contribution to the literature in the field. Oversize, notes, bibliography, index. 588pp. ScP 75

ROWEN, BETTY. **LEARNING THROUGH MOVEMENT**, $1.95. *The material for this booklet has been gathered from my experiences as a classroom teacher in the elementary school and in nursery school, and as a dance teacher.* Chapters include: *Developing Creativity through Movement, Language and Movement, Creative Movement as an Aid to Social Learnings, Movement as an Aid in Mastering Number Concepts, Creative Movement in the Science Program, Creative Movement and Personality.* Also includes recommended readings, songs, poems, and recordings to be used in conjunction with the movement techniques described. 87pp. TCP 63

RUBIN, THEODORE. **JORDI/LISA AND DAVID**, $1.25. Two essays which movingly reveal the inner life of mentally troubled children. 144pp. RaH 62

SAUVY, JEAN and SIMONE. **CHILD'S DISCOVERY OF SPACE**, $2.25. Topology is the study of the general properties of space, including nearness, connection, and continuity. The Sauvys have been working with topology in a school in France and they present an in depth introduction here including a discussion which can be done with children to broaden their awareness of the topological properties of space. Many detailed exercises are presented and explained, and the book is fully illustrated. 93pp. Pen 74

SAVA, SAMUEL. **LEARNING THROUGH DISCOVERY FOR YOUNG CHILDREN**, c$7.95. A practical, well written book, designed as a handbook for teachers as well as a guide for parents. Dr. Sava begins by tracing the pioneering efforts of Montessori, Gesell, Bloom, Hunt, Piaget, and others. The major part of the book is devoted to a section entitled *activity centers.* This is divided into eight chapters and it details practical activities in the following areas: creative play, art and sculpture, cooking, woodworking, language, numbers, music and movement, and nature and science. The book is well produced and photographs are interspersed. There's also an excellent 19pp bibliography. This is an excellent toolbook for the preschool teacher. 156pp. MGH 75

SCHMUCK, RICHARD and PATRICIA. **A HUMANISTIC PSYCHOLOGY OF EDUCATION**, $5.95. *In this book, we grapple with ways of humanizing schools by using theory and research available from the social sciences—social psychology in particular. . . . It is meant to be practical: to shed light on what humanized schooling means, what humanized schools look and feel like, and, most important, how such schools can be created. Although it undoubtedly will be used primarily in professional courses . . . we intend it to be read also by individual educators, parents, students, and citizens interested in our schools.* Index, bibliogaraphy. 399pp. MPC 74

SCHOOLS COUNCIL. **CHILDREN'S GROWTH THROUGH CREATIVE EDUCATION**, c$7.95. This book contains the findings that came out of a detailed observation of teachers, children, and schools. The project team, experienced teachers themselves, has examined the problems and possibilities that face every teacher. There are specific chapters on children and their patterns of behavior, on the teachers' relationships with children, and on the atmosphere and environment in which creative work can flourish. It seems to be a fairly dry, academic study with helpful material for the professional. The Schools Council is the principal organization in England concerned with the reform and development of curricula, teaching methods, and examination systems. Bibliography, 144pp. VNR 74

SCHRANK, JEFFREY. **TEACHING HUMAN BEINGS**, $3.45. An idea book filled with possibilities for making any classroom a real place of learning and discovery. It serves the purpose of being a resource catalog as well as a mine of practical ideas. This book takes for granted that schools and classrooms need to be greatly changed and makes a practical step in that direction. Recommended by teachers who have visited us. 192pp. Bea 72

EASEL

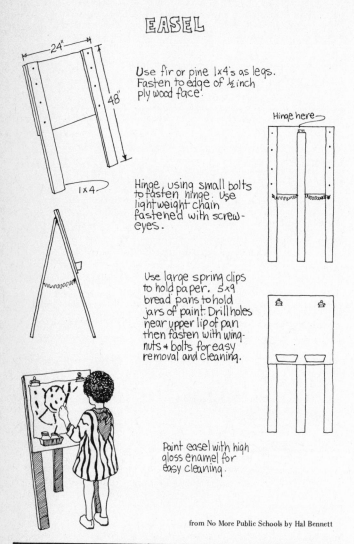

Use fir or pine 1x4's as legs. Fasten to edge of ½ inch plywood face.

Hinge here

Hinge, using small bolts to fasten hinge. Use lightweight chain fastened with screw-eyes.

Use large spring clips to hold paper. 5x9 bread pans to hold jars of paint. Drill holes near upper lip of pan then fasten with wingnuts & bolts for easy removal and cleaning.

Paint easel with high gloss enamel for easy cleaning.

from No More Public Schools by Hal Bennett

SHAKESBY, PAUL. **CHILD'S WORK**, $4.95. *In one sense, this is a book about home-made toys which offer sound education as well as good fun and enjoyable work for your child. Yet on another level, the true subject of these pages is the relationship between parent and child. For it is only through your involvement in making the toys and using them with your child that this book will fulfill its purpose.... If you enjoy being with your child, sharing the experiences of learning, growth and discovery, then you will appreciate the kind of involvement that this book demands.* This is a well laid out and extremely well illustrated manual with sections covering sensory awareness, manual dexterity, size, shape, and form, numbers, and language. Suggested age groups are given for the activities. Recommended. Oversize, 112pp. RuP 74

SILBERMAN, CHARLES. **CRISIS IN THE CLASSROOM**, $2.45. Subtitled *The Remaking of American Education,* this has been an extremely influential book. *One of the most significant statements on education since World War II. To one of the most important and urgent problems of modern society, Mr. Silberman has brought a unique combination of perceptive inquiry, broad scholarship, and deep personal concern.*—John Fischer, President, Teacher's College, Columbia University. Notes, index. 567pp. RaH 70

_____. **THE OPEN CLASSROOM READER**, $2.95. A companion to **Crisis in the Classroom** containing sixty-five selections from American, Canadian, and English sources, plus a general introduction by Silberman and his running commentary explaining why each selection was made and how it fits into the overall framework. Each selection presents practical explanations and detailed descriptions of classroom activities and methods, interspersed with theoretical discussions. 789pp. RaH 73

SIMON, SIDNEY, LELAND B. HOWE and HOWARD KIRSCHENBAUM. **VALUES CLARIFICATION**, $4.95. Designed to engage students and teachers in the active formulation and examination of values, this popular book is unique in content and format. There is no moralizing. The goal is to involve students in practical experiences, making them aware of their own feelings, their own ideas, their own beliefs, so that the choices and decisions they make are conscious and deliberate, based on their own value systems. Recommended. 397pp. Har 72

SKUTCH, MARGARET and WILFRID HAMLIN. **TO START A SCHOOL**, $2.45. The story of a housewife in Stanford, Connecticut who started an *Early Learning Center* devoted not only to learning, but to the awareness of how wonderful it is to learn. Many photographs. 147pp. LBC 71

STEINER, RUDOLF, et al. **EDUCATION AS AN ART**, $1.95. Essays by Steiner and other writers. Rudolf Steiner was one of the most innovative and creative thinkers of the twentieth century. His conception of man and universe (anthroposophy) has detailed explanations of the scientific application of spiritual principles to all areas of human endeavor. His ideas led naturally into the all important area of childhood education, for Steiner realized that there could be no regeneration of human civilization without a technique, philosophy, and practice of education that dealt with the whole human being—emotional, mental, and spiritual. The application of Steiner's ideas in education has come to be known as Waldorf education (after the first school with that name). The philosophy and approach is centered in the understanding of the child as an evolving human soul with unlimited potentiality. Education then becomes an art whereby the highest, truest and most beautiful is drawn out of the child and he learns to express his unique, divine individuality in a socially, artistically and creatively constructive manner. For a description of specific books see the Waldorf Education sub-section in the Steiner section.

TAYLOR, JOY. **ORGANIZING THE OPEN CLASSROOM**, $2.45. An English guidebook stressing that an open classroom must be even more highly structured and organized than its traditional counterpart. Bibliography, index. 116pp. ScB 71

ULMAN, ELINOR and PENNY DACHINGER, eds. **ART THERAPY—IN THEORY AND PRACTICE**, c$15.00. This collection brings together in book form the most important thinking, discussion, and experience in the field of art therapy. The articles are culled from **The American Journal of Art Therapy**. This is a very comprehensive presentation of every aspect of the field, with articles on the visual arts in education, rehabilitation, and psychotherapy. Many color and black-and-white plates illustrate the text. 415pp. ScB 75

WHITE, BURTON. **THE FIRST THREE YEARS OF LIFE**, c$10.00. Probably no living person knows more about what happens during the first three years of life than Dr. Burton White, Director of Harvard University's world famous Pre-School Project. And now, for the first time, Dr. White has made his knowledge available in book form to the general reader. The book is a detailed guide to the intellectual and emotional development of the very young child. Dr. White divides the first thirty-six months into seven successive developmental phases, paying special attention to the critical fifth and sixth phases. For each phase he provides both a comprehensive description of the characteristic physical, emotional, and mental developments of which parents must be aware and a detailed list of instructions concerning childrearing practices, parental strategies, and even toys and equipment. This is an excellent book which we can't recommend too highly. Annotated bibliography, index. 298pp. PrH 75

WICKES, FRANCES. **THE INNER WORLD OF CHILDHOOD**, $1.25. This is a revised edition of a classic examination of the crucial relationship between parent and child. *Her penetrating studies of children have opened up a new world of understanding. To her, the child is a person possessing innately the right to be individual and to experience the world about him in the light of his own subjective experience.... [The] child psychologist needs to have at least in some measure Frances Wickes' sensitivity, wisdom, and love.*—M. Esther Harding. The book is based on Dr. Wickes own experiences with her patients and many case studies are included. This revised edition follows up some of the cases from the first edition of more than forty years ago. Introduction by Carl Jung. Index, 325pp. NAL 66

WURMAN, RICHARD. **YELLOW PAGES OF LEARNING RESOURCES**, $1.95. A new look at how to learn about living from simply taking a closer look at all the many things that go on around us. The book opens up the sense of discovery and introduces a new way of looking at things, a new perspective and awareness of the many things in our culture from which we can learn. Contains information and suggestions about learning from such things as airports, restaurants, tree stumps, candy, money, telephones, cemeteries, libraries, etc. 94pp. MIT 72

YANES, SAMUEL. **THE NO MORE GYM SHORTS, BUILD-IT-YOURSELF, SELF-DISCOVERY, FREE SCHOOL TALKIN' BLUES**, $1.95. The title says it. Yanes has taken portions of interviews, letters and articles from the free school movement and woven them together with photographs, drawing and his own continous commentary. 111pp. Har 72

YANES, SAMUEL and CIA HOLDORF, eds. **BIG ROCK CANDY MOUNTAIN RESOURCES FOR OUR EDUCATION**, $4.00. A grand collection of resources for educational purposes. A **Whole Earth Catalog** for education. 188pp. Del 71

FAIRY TALES AND FANTASY

For a story truly to hold the child's attention, it must entertain him and arouse his curiosity. But to enrich his life, it must stimulate his imagination; help him to develop his intellect and to clarify his emotions; be attuned to his anxieties and aspirations; give full recognition to his difficulties, while at the same time suggesting solutions to the problems which perturb him. In short, it must at one and the same time relate to all aspects of his personality —and this without ever belittling but, on the contrary, giving full credence to the seriousness of the child's predicaments, while simultaneously promoting confidence in himself and in his future.

In all these and many other respects, of the entire *children's literature*—with rare exceptions—nothing can be as enriching and satisfying to child and adult alike as the folk fairy tale. True, on an overt level fairy tales teach little about the specific conditions of life in modern mass society; these tales were created long before it came into being. But more can be learned from them about the inner problems of human beings, and of the right solutions to their predicaments in any society, than from any other type of story within a child's comprehension. . . .

Through the centuries (if not millennia) during which, in their retelling, fairy tales became ever more refined, they came to convey at the same time overt and covert meanings—came to speak simultaneously to all levels of the human personality, communicating in a manner which reaches the uneducated mind of the child as well as that of the sophisticated adult. Applying the psychoanalytic model of the human personality, fairy tales carry important messages to the conscious, the preconscious, and the unconscious mind, on whatever level each is functioning at the time. By dealing with universal human problems, particularly those which preoccupy the child's mind, these stories speak to his budding ego and encourage its development, while at the same time relieving preconscious and unconscious pressures. . . . These tales, in a much deeper sense than any other reading material, start where the child really is in his psychological and emotional being. They speak about his severe inner pressures in a way that the child unconsciously understands, and—without belittling the most serious inner struggles which growing up entails—offer examples of both temporary and permanent solutions to pressing difficulties. . . .

Fairy Tales and the Existential Predicament

In order to master the psychological problems of growing up—overcoming narcissitic disappointments, oedipal dilemmas, sibling rivalries; becoming able to relinquish childhood dependencies; gaining a feeling of selfhood and of self-worth, and a sense of moral obligation—a child needs to understand what is going on within his conscious self so that he can also cope with that which goes on in his unconscious. He can achieve this understanding, and with it the ability to cope, not through rational comprehension of the nature and content of his unconscious, but by becoming familiar with it through spinning out daydreams—ruminating, rearranging, and fantasizing about suitable story elements in response to unconscious pressures. By doing this, the child fits unconscious content into conscious fantasies, which then enable him to deal with that content. It is here that fairy tales have unequaled value, because they offer new dimensions to the child's imagination which would be impossible for him to discover as truly on his own. Even more important, the form and structure of fairy tales suggest images to the child by which he can structure his daydreams and with them give better direction to his life. . . .

There is a widespread refusal to let children know that the source of much that goes wrong in life is due to our very own natures—the propensity of all men for acting aggressively, asocially, selfishly, out of anger and anxiety. Instead, we want our children to believe that, inherently, all men are good. But children know that *they* are not always good; and often, even when they are, they would prefer not to be. This contradicts what they are told by their parents, and therefore makes the child a monster in his own eyes. . . .

The message [of] fairy tales [is] that a struggle against severe difficulties in life is unavoidable, is an intrinsic part of human existence—but that if one does not shy away, but steadfastly meets unexpected and often unjust hardships, one masters all obstacles and at the end emerges victorious.

Modern stories written for young children mainly avoid these existential problems, although they are crucial issues for all of us. The child needs most particularly to be given suggestions in symbolic form about how he may deal with these issues and grow safely into maturity. *Safe* stories mention neither death nor aging, the limits to our existence, nor the wish for eternal life. The fairy tale, by contrast, confronts the child squarely with the basic human predicaments.

For example, many fairy stories begin with the death of a mother or father; in these tales the death of the parent creates the most agonizing problems, as it (or the fear of it) does in real life. Other stories tell about an aging parent who decides that the time has come to let the new generation take over. But before this can happen, the successor has to prove himself capable and worthy.

It is characteristic of fairy tales to state an existential dilemma briefly and pointedly. This permits the child to come to grips with the problem in its most essential form, where a more complex plot would confuse matters for him. The fairy tale simplifies all situations. Its figures are clearly drawn; and details, unless very important, are eliminated. All characters are typical rather than unique.

Contrary to what takes place in many modern children's stories, in fairy tales evil is as omnipresent as virtue. In practically every fairy tale good and evil are given body in the form of some figures and their actions, as good and evil are omnipresent in life and the propensities for both are present in every man. It is this duality which poses the moral problem, and requires the struggle to solve it.

Evil is not without its attractions—symbolized by the mighty giant or dragon, the power of the witch, the cunning queen in *Snow White*—and often it is temporarily in the ascendancy. . . . It is not that the evildoer is punished at the story's end which makes immersing oneself in fairy stories an experience in moral education, although this is part of it. In fairy tales, as in life, punishment or fear of it is only a limited deterrent to crime. The conviction that crime does not pay is a much more effective deterrent, and that is why in fairy tales the bad person always loses out. It is not the fact that virtue wins out at the end which promotes morality, but that the hero is most attractive to the child, who identifies with the hero in all his struggles. Because of this identification the child imagines that he suffers with the hero his trials and tribulations, and triumphs with him as virtue is victorious. The child makes such identifications all on his own, and the inner and outer struggles of the hero imprint morality on him.

The figures in fairy tales are not ambivalent—not good and bad at the same time, as we all are in reality. But since polarization dominates the child's mind, it also dominates fairy tales. A person is either good or bad, nothing in between. . . . Presenting the polarities of character permits the child to comprehend easily the difference between the two, which he could not do as readily were the figures drawn more true to life, with all the complexities that characterize real people. Ambiguities must wait until a relatively firm personality has been established on the basis of positive identifications. Then the child has a basis for understanding that there are great differences between people, and that therefore one has to make choices about who one wants to be. This basic decision, on which all later personality development will build, is facilitated by the polarizations of the fairy tale. . . .

The Fairy Tale: A Unique Art Form

While it entertains the child, the fairy tale enlightens him about himself, and fosters his personality development. It offers meaning on so many different levels, and enriches the child's existence in so many ways, that no one book can do justice to the multitude and diversity of the contributions such tales make to the child's life. . . .

The delight we experience when we allow ourselves to respond to a fairy tale, the enchantment we feel, comes not from the psychological meaning of a tale (although this contributes to it) but from its literary qualities—the tale itself as a work of art. The fairy tale could not have its psychological impact on the child were it not first and foremost a work of art.

Fairy tales are unique, not only as a form of literature, but as works of art which are fully comprehensible to the child, as no other form of art is. As with all great art, the fairy tale's deepest meaning will be different for each person, and different for the same person at various moments in his life. The child will extract different meanings from the same fairy tale, depending on his interests and needs of the moment. When given the chance, he will return to the same tale when he is ready to enlarge on old meanings, or replace them with new ones. . . .

As we cannot know at what age a particular fairy tale will be most important to a particular child, we cannot ourselves decide which of the many tales he should be told at any given time or why. This only the child can determine and reveal by the strength of feeling with which he reacts to what a tale evokes in his conscious and unconscious mind. Naturally a parent will begin by telling or reading to his child a tale the parent himself or herself cared for as a child, or cares for now. If the child does not take to the story, this means that its motifs or themes have failed to evoke a meaningful response at this moment in his life. Then it is best to tell him another fairy tale the next evening. Soon he will indicate that a certain story has become important to him by his immediate response to it, or by his asking to be told this story over and over again. If all goes well, the child's enthusiasm for this story will be contagious, and the story will become important to the parent too, if for no other reason than that it means so much to the child. Finally there will come the time when the child has gained all he can from the preferred story, or the problems which made him respond to it have been replaced by others which find better expression in some other tale. He may then temporarily lose interest in this story and enjoy some other one much more. In the telling of fairy stories it is always best to follow the child's lead.

Even if a parent should guess correctly why his child has become involved emotionally with a given tale, this is knowledge best kept to oneself. The young child's most important experiences and reactions are largely subconscious, and should remain so until he reaches a much more mature age and understanding. It is always intrusive to interpret a person's unconscious thoughts, to make conscious what he wishes to keep preconscious, and this is especially true in the case of a child. Just as important for the child's well-being as feeling that his parent shares his emotions, through enjoying the same fairy tale, is the child's feeling that his inner thoughts are not known to his parent until he decides to reveal them. If the parent indicates that he knows them already, the child is prevented from making the most precious gift to his parent of sharing with him what until then was secret and private to the child. And since, in addition, a parent is so much more powerful than a child, his domination may appear limitless—and hence destructively overwhelming—if he seems able to read the child's secret thoughts, know his most hidden feelings, even before the child himself has begun to become aware of them.

Explaining to a child why a fairy tale is so captivating to him destroys, moreover, the story's enchantment, which depends to a considerable degree on the child's not quite knowing why he is delighted by it. And with the forfeiture of this power to enchant goes also a loss of the story's potential for helping the child struggle on his own, and master all by himself the problem which has made the story meaningful to him in the first place. Adult interpretations, as correct as they may be, rob the child of the opportunity to feel that he, on his own, through repeated hearing and ruminating about the story, has coped successfully with a difficult situation. We grow, we find meaning in life, and security in ourselves by having understood and solved personal problems on our own, not by having them explained to us by others.

Fairy-tale motifs are not neurotic symptoms, something one is better off understanding rationally so that one can rid oneself of them. Such motifs are experienced as wondrous because the child feels understood and appreciated deep down in his feelings, hopes, and anxieties, without these having to be dragged up and investigated in the harsh light of a rationality that is still beyond him. Fairy tales enrich the child's life and give it an enchanted quality just because he does not quite know how the stories have worked their wonder on him.

—from **The Uses of Enchantment** by Bruno Bettelheim

AESOP. **AESOP'S FABLES**, c$2.98. The main difference between fables and fairy tales, other than sheer length, is that there can be no good fable with human beings in it and no good fairy tale without them. In a fable all characters must be totally impersonal and simple represent the stereotype of things that is being disdussed. Fables are also almost always about animals. Aesop's is the classic collection of fables and it set the style for all that were to follow. All the tales are short (no more than a paragraph), there is absolutely no character development, and each fable has its own moral. This edition is illustrated by Arthur Rackham and includes a fine introduction by G.K. Chesterton. 253pp. Crn 12

AFANAS'EV, ALEKSANDR. **RUSSIAN FAIRY TALES**, c$12.95/$5.95. This is the only comprehensive edition available in English of the classic Russian folk and fairy tales collected by Afanas'ev, the Russian counterpart of the brothers Grimm. This collection introduces the Russian versions of such universal fairy tale figures as witches and heroes, soldiers and fishermen, peasants and kings, beggars and thieves, as well as such unique Russian creations as Koshchey the Deathless, Baba Yoga, the Swan Maiden, and the splendid Firebird. These immortal tales are a storehouse of psychological and historical experience. An excellent commentary is included as well as many fine illustrations by Alexander Alexeieff. Notes, index. 662pp. RaH 45

ANDERSEN, HANS CHRISTIAN. **FAIRY TALES**, c$4.95. A beautifully produced over-size edition of many of Anderson's most loved stories. Anderson was a contemporary of the brothers Grimm. Unlike the latter he wrote his own tales, and while they reflect traditional Scandinavian folk themes, they are his own creations. Many delicate color illustrations accompany the tales. 207pp. Ham 59

THE ARABIAN NIGHTS

For descriptions of a variety of editions of the **Arabian Nights** see the Islam section.

BAIN, R. NISBET, tr. **TURKISH FAIRY TALES**, $2.50. The Turkish tales are a curious blend of Eastern and Western elements which turns them into stories that are extraordinarily bizarre and beautiful. The tales are sometimes reminiscent of the **Arabian Nights** and sometimes of the tales of the brothers Grimm. They are filled with magic carpets and magic mirrors, animals and birds with extraordinary powers, great journeys, and magical people—the peris. Seventeen tales from Asia Minor are followed by four from Rumania which reflect a blend of Magyar, Slavonic, Romance, and Turkish elements. This book was compiled at a time when Turkey's ancient oral tradition was still very much alive. Illustrations, introduction, 285pp. Dov 1896

BETTELHEIM, BRUNO. **THE USES OF ENCHANTMENT**, c$12.50. This is a masterful examination which opens the reader up to the real content of the great fairy tales. Dr. Bettelheim shows how, beneath their surface shimmer of palaces and princesses, fairies and witches, wishes and spells, they deal in the profoundest ways with the emotional turmoils of childhood—with feelings of smallness and helplessness, with the terrifying perceptions of outward dangers, with the even more terrifying anxieties the child feels possessed by, with the mystery of the outside world, and with the child's deepest questions about self and about the future. He also shows how fairy tales help children cope with their emotions and their world and how they reveal the child, subconsciously, to him or herself. Over half the book is devoted to a detailed examination and retelling of some of the best known stories. Here Dr. Bettelheim shows specifically how the tales work to support and free the child. Notes, bibliography, index. 339pp. RaH 76

BONNET, LESLIE. **CHINESE FAIRY TALES**, c$4.70. 208pp. MlI 58

BROCKETT, ELEANOR. **BURMESE AND THAI FAIRY TALES**, c$4.70. A collection of stories which are filled with dragons, goddesses, spells, enchantments, and talking animals. All are told with wit and humor and the collection is designed for young readers. It is characteristic of these tales that virtue is not always rewarded and it is not unusual for the fool to emerge better off than the wise man. Good luck may be valued more highly than intelligence and the hero is more often reluctant than not. Nicely illustrated. 208pp. MlI 65

_____. **PERSIAN FAIRY TALES**, c$5.80. Like Arabian tales, traditional Persian folk and fairy tales are filled with tales of vizars and kings, of the humor and guile of the bazaar, and of the fantastic world of giants, genies, and demons. This is a vividly written collection which includes many of the traditional tales as well as some of the great national legends recounted in the eleventh century by Ferdosi. Two color illustrations. 207pp. Mll 62

_____. **TURKISH FAIRY TALES**, c$5.95. These stories have an affinity with both the traditional legends and folklore of the Orient and the fairy tales of Europe. They have on the whole a background of peasant life and agricultural labor, rather than the piety of the mosque and the guile of the bazaar, although these too play their part in giving these stories their unique character. This is a varied collection, retold by Ms. Brockett and illustrated. 198pp. Mll 63

EAGER, EDWARD. **HALF MAGIC**, $1.75. Four young children who have been reading the magical books of E. Nesbit stumble on a magical world of their own. They take turns making wishes which lead them to incredible adventures. Illustrations, 217pp. HBJ 54

GRAY, NICHOLAS. **THE EDGE OF EVENING**, c$6.35. A series of magical tales. Our favorite is the one about a horrible witch who was not very clever. When she tried a spell to call up a demon slave she mistakenly called up demons who made her their slave. But as it turns out they were not really demons, their job was to make her more lovable—and in this they succeeded. Other stories are about accident prone demons, dragons, taking animals, and much more. Eight stories in all—and all evoking mysterious, enchanting worlds. Illustrations, 124pp. Fab 76

GREEN, ROGER. **MYTHS OF THE NORSEMEN**, $1.50. See the Mythology section.

from Grimm's Fairy Tales by Arthur Rackham

JACOB AND WILHELM GRIMM

The brothers Grimm were both lawyers who lived at the end of the eighteenth and beginning of the nineteenth century. They were serious, scholarly men who were fascinated by German history and particularly by the history of the German language, which contained many traces of the past in everyday speech. The land they lived in was very different from the Germany of today. Instead of one country, Germany was a mass of small kingdoms ruled by hereditary dukes and princes who lived in castles on the shores of lakes or in the beautiful dark forests. Almost every district had its own dialect and a special store of local wisdom and history contained in tales and folklore about former days. The brothers Grimm devoted much of their lives to collecting and transcribing many of these traditional tales. Their collections remain the best known and most authoritative to this day. *Told by generation after generation, the traditional stories projected the deepest wishes of the folk, generalized diverse characters into a few types, selected the incidents that would most strikingly illustrate what heroes and heroines, witches, enchanters, giants and dwarfs, the haughty, the envious and the unfaithful were capable of.*—from the introduction to the Pantheon edition. Today we think of these tales as mainly for children but down through the ages they have appealed to many adults.

MAGOUN, FRANCIS and ALEXANDER KRAPPE, trs. **GERMAN FOLK TALES**, $6.95. This is a highly acclaimed new translation of all the stories. The stories are presented with literal faithfulness and the original style is captured. People who have deeply studied the stories feel that this is the definitive collection. German and English title indices are included. Foreward, 682pp. SIU 60

PANTHEON BOOKS. **THE COMPLETE GRIMM'S FAIRY TALES**, c$12.95/5.95. For many years this was the only complete edition of the tales available. The stories have been presented in a lively style and the edition has been highly praised. Many fine line drawings are included and two noted mythologists, Joseph Campbell and Padraic Colum, supply illuminating commentaries and introductory material. 878pp. RaH 44

PUFFIN BOOKS. **GRIMM'S FAIRY TALES**, $1.75. A simple and accurate retelling of some of the best loved stories. The edition, translated by Sir Walter Scott, is designed for children. 268pp. Pen 48

RACKHAM, ARTHUR. **GRIMM'S FAIRY TALES**, c$6.95. Twenty stories, chosen especially for their appeal to young readers, and illustrated with Rackham's delightful drawings. Oversize, 127pp. Vik 73

SEGAL, LORE and RANDALL JARRELL, trs. **THE JUNIPER TREE AND OTHER TALES FROM GRIMM**, c$15.00/set. A beautiful boxed two volume set which includes fresh translations of twenty-seven of the tales which the translators and the illustrator, Maurice Sendak, felt were the most significant. The translations are faithful to the original text and are graceful. The selections include some of the best known stories as well as a number of lesser known ones. Sendak's amazingly detailed line drawings are quite possibly his finest work. 332pp. FSG 73

JACOBS, JOSEPH. **CELTIC FAIRY TALES**, $3.00. Jacobs (1854–1916) was the leading British folklorist. His two volume collection captures the special vision and color and the unique magic of the Celtic folk imagination. The twenty-six stories in this volume present many wonderful characters and incidents. The stories are often long and detailed and Jacobs has included characteristic samples of every type. The twenty-six stories in this volume present many wonderful characters and incidents. Eight full page plates and thirty-seven drawings are included. Preface, notes and references. 279pp. Dov 1892

_____. **ENGLISH FAIRY TALES**, $2.50. Forty tales, including many familiar ones like *Jack and the Beanstalk* and quite a few lesser known tales. The style of the retelling is excellent and this book has been loved by children and adults for generations. Preface, notes and references, sixty-five line drawings. 276pp. Dov 1898

_____. **INDIAN FAIRY TALES**, $3.00. A selection of stories from India. Included are many Jataka tales and tales from a variety of other collections. As usual, Jacobs has made a fine selection and the stories are geared toward children. Forty-six illustrations, preface, notes. 280pp. Dov 1892

_____. **MORE CELTIC FAIRY TALES**, $2.50. Twenty more tales. Illustrations, preface, notes, references. 237pp. Dov 1894

KUO, LOUISE and YUAN HSI, trs. **CHINESE FOLK TALES**, $4.95. A simple retelling of many of the most loved tales, with illustrations and a short introduction to each one. Also includes a glossary, map, and brief chronology. 175pp. CeA 76

KURTI, ALFRED, tr. **PERSIAN FOLKTALES**, c$5.95. Fine versions of twenty-nine folktales, anecdotes, and tales from Persian literature. The tales are well written and are based on scholarly collections of folklore made within the last hundred years. Notes, 216pp. Bel 71

LEEKLEY, THOMAS. **THE KING AND THE MERMAN AND OTHER MEDIEVAL STORIES**, c$3.15. A collection of tales from the Middle Ages, originally written in Latin by Walter Map in the twelfth century. Some of the stories are legendary and others throw a new light on famous historical figures. The illustrations are reminiscent of medieval woodcuts. 127pp. Bla 72

LEWIS, C.S. **THE CHRONICLES OF NARNIA**, $8.95/set. These seven books are the passport into an enchanted magical land and wonderous happenings. We recommend the books highly for people of all ages. In the first book the children enter through a wardrobe into Narnia and learn how Aslan, the noble lion, freed Narnia from the spell of the white witch. The second discusses Prince Caspian and his army of talking beasts. In the third Caspian, now king, sails through magic waters. The fourth book tells of Prince Rilian's escape from the emerald witch's underground kingdom. The next tale is about how a talking horse and a boy prince saved Narnia from invasion. The sixth tells how Aslan created Narnia and gave speech to its animals. And the final reveals how evil came to Narnia and Aslan led his people to a glorious new paradise. Boxed set. McM 56

LE GUIN, URSULA. **THE FARTHEST SHORE**, $1.50. The final volume in the Earthsea Trilogy, an award-winning classic of high fantasy that has been compared with Tolkein and with C.S. Lewis' *Narnia* stories. In this book the story of a hero's quest is repeated as the prince and the archmage set out to confront their own pasts, to meet unknown dangers, and to test the ancient prophecies. 197pp. Ban 72

_____. **THE TOMBS OF ATUAN**, $1.50. This is the second volume in the trilogy. The heroine is a young priestess who has had everything taken away from her. She becomes high priestess to the ancient and nameless powers of the earth. She is living in the middle of the desert when her vigil is interrupted by a thief seeking the great treasure that surrounds her in the tombs. The thief is in reality a young wizard on a quest. The join together and she escapes from her lonely life. 146pp. Ban 71

_____. **A WIZARD OF EARTHSEA**, $1.50. This is the first volume of the trilogy. It tells of a young boy who goes off on a quest and meddles with the dark forces before he is strong enough to withstand them. It is pure fantasy, with deep underlying siginificance, as is the case with the whole trilogy. 205pp. Ban 70

MACDONALD, GEORGE. **THE GIFTS OF THE CHILD CHRIST**, $7.95/set. MacDonald was one of the main figures in modern fantasy writing. He lived in the nineteenth century and he influenced C.S. Lewis, J.R.R. Tolkein, and Charles Williams. This edition includes all of his stories and fairy tales except for several longer ones which are readily available elsewhere. MacDonald himself said that *I do not write for children, but for the childlike, whether of five, or fifty, or seventy-five.* Glenn Sadler, the editor, provides an introduction. Two volumes, 593pp. Eer 73

_____. **THE PRINCESS AND THE GOBLIN**, $1.50. A story in the classic fairy tale style which tells of a little princess who lives in an ancient castle in a wild and lonely mountainous region. Her father has left her to go off on a serious mission and she is attacked by the goblins who live underneath her land. She is saved by a boy miner. A classic tale of the battle between good and evil. Pen

NESBIT, E. **FIVE CHILDREN AND IT**, $1.50. *It was a Psammead, which looked a little like a monkey but had eyes which came out on stalks like a snail's, and it was furry all over. Five children found it when they were digging in a sandpit. It was thousands of years old. It gave them a wish a day, but whatever they wished for was guaranteed to fade at sunset, when everything went back to normal. One difficulty was to think of really good wishes: another was to avoid saying thoughtlessly at the critical moment, Oh, I wish! and getting something they did not really want at all. Every wish brought them into difficulties. . . . This is an old and tried favorite. Between nine and twelve is a good first time for it, but plenty of children read and [have it read] at eight, and people in their sixties still reread it.*—from the preface. Nicely illustrated. 215pp. Pen 02

_____. **THE PHOENIX AND THE CARPET**, $1.25. The same children have more adventures with a magic carpet which transports them wherever they wish to go. Inside the carpet is a strange egg from which hatches the phoenix, an ancient and honorable bird, but not much easier to handle than the Psammead. Illustrations, 250pp. Pen 04

_____. **THE STORY OF THE AMULET**, $1.50. At the end of **Five Children and It** the children promised not to ask the Psammead for another wish as long as they lived, but expressed half a wish to see it again some time. They found it again, badly mistreated, in a pet shop and their adventures started all over again. They were led to an amulet—half of it actually—which contained strong magic and which they used to try to find the other half. The amulet took them back to ancient Egypt and Babylon; they visited Atlantis; and they saw Julius Caesar. But none of these adventures ran smoothly and they were always afraid of losing the amulet or forgetting the word of power and thus being stuck in another era. Illustrations, 281pp. Pen 06

OPIE, IONA and PETER, eds. **THE CLASSIC FAIRY TALES**, c$13.95. Designed primarily for adults, this book presents twenty-four of the best known fairy tales in the exact words in which they were first published in English. The stories are lavishly supported by illustrations—more than forty of them in color—that show how the tales have been visualized in popular and juvenile literature since the time of their first publication. The work of the finest illustrators of the nineteenth and twentieth centuries has been selected. For each tale, the Opies provide a historical introduction, showing the development of the story by citing parallels in other countries and other centuries and noting the changes in the tales over the ages. Oversize, bibliography, index. 255pp. Oxf 74

OZAKI, YEI. **THE JAPANESE FAIRY BOOK**, $2.50. Twenty-two stories, especially retold for young readers and beautifully illustrated. The Eastern mood is captured in these tales about magical animals, serpent-dragons, undersea kingdoms, magic chariots, and much more. 308pp. Dov 04

PERRAULT, CHARLES. **PERRAULT'S FAIRY TALES**, $2.50. The original eight stories from Perrault's 1697 volume. These were among the earliest versions of some of our most familiar fairy tales and are still among the few classic retellings of these perennial stories. This edition also includes thirty-four extraordinary full page engravings by Gustave Dore, which in many cases created the pictorial image we associate with the stories. Oversize, 117pp. Dov 69

PIGGOTT, JULIET. **JAPANESE FAIRY TALES**, c$5.80. The culture of Japan is one of the most ancient in the world, and the richness of its folklore is well represented in this collection of thirteen tales. Ms. Piggott grew up in Japan and is an authority on Japanese history and legend. This is a fine collection, nicely illustrated. 192pp. Mll 62

RACKHAM, ARTHUR. **FAIRY TALES FROM MANY LANDS**, c$6.95. Thirteen tales, each told in a form characteristic of the country it represents. The tales come from Japan, England, Belgium, Scotland, Serbia, Wales, Russia, Portugal, France, Italy, and Ireland. Many color illustrations and line drawings are included. Oversize, 122pp. Vik 16

_____. **ONCE UPON A TIME: THE FAIRY TALE WORLD OF ARTHUR RACKHAM**, c$14.95. A collection of Rackham's personal favorites, including 110 illustrations, 35 in color. 296pp. Vik 72

RYDER, ARTHUR, tr. **THE PANCHATANTRA**, $3.45. The word *Panchatantra* means the *Five Books*. Each of the five is independent, consisting of a framing story with numerous inserted stories, told by one or another of the characters in the main narrative. The majority of the main characters are animals who have a fairly constant character. The animals often quote verses from the sacred writings to justify their actions. It is now believed that the original work was composed in Kashmir about 200 BC—at this date, however, many of the individual stories were already ancient. The text that is translated here dates from 1199 AD. The fables have traveled the world and are the forerunners of many tales

that we associate with other cultures. They are noted for their realism and pervasiv humor. Introduction, 470pp. UCh 25

SHAH, AMINA. **ARABIAN FAIRY TALES**, c$5.80. Amina Shah is Idries Shah's sister She has traveled widely in the Arabic-speaking world and she retells these twenty-eight tales from the living oral tradition. Included in this volume are stories about caliphs and dervishes, fairies and jinn, rich men and poor men, and, as always, about the wily Grand Vizier. Ms. Shah has done a fine job of recapturing the original dialect and atmosphere Illustrated with wood engravings. Glossary, introduction. 175pp. Mll 69

_____. **FOLK TALES OF CENTRAL ASIA**, c$6.00. Eighteen tales compiled from the oral tradition of Central Asia and written in the same excellent style as her earlier work. Introduction, glossary. 148pp. Oct 70

SIE, CHEOU. **A BUTTERFLY'S DREAM AND OTHER CHINESE TALES**, c$5.50. An exquisite collection of simple universal tales. From romance to tragedy, from the emperor to the hermit, they run the gamut of human emotions and types. The renditions in this volume are excellent and they present a penetrating picture of ancient China. Each tale has an appropriate evocative color illustration by Chi Kang, China's greatest living classical artist. 91pp. Tut 70

TOLKIEN, J.R.R. **THE HOBBIT**, $1.95. The enchanting prelude to **The Lord of the Rings**, where Tolkien first created the imperishable world of fantasy called Middle-earth and the charming hobbits. The tale tells of Bilbo the hobbit's search for the ancestral home of the dwarfs, of Gandalf the Wizard, and of the magical ring that Bilbo acquires. 287pp. RaH 38

_____. **THE LORD OF THE RINGS**, $10.00/set. This is a boxed edition of this great fantasy classic which chronicles Middle-earth and tells of the ultimately successful attempt to save the land from the dark forces. A delightful series of creatures takes part in the tale: hobbits, wizards, dwarfs, elves, and men. The story should be well enough known that there's no need to repeat it here. Three volumes. Illustrations, index. 1530pp. RaH 65

WALEY, ALISON. **DEAR MONKEY**, c$7.35. This is a delightful abridgement of Arthur Waley's classic translation of one of China's most famous and best loved folktales. Monkey is an amazing character who is created out of a stone monkey and who somehow obtains great powers, including immortality. He challenges the gods and is eventually vanquished and punished and only set free as a companion on a dangerous quest to bring back the Buddhist scriptures from India to China. Monkey is valiant and intrepid and he and his compatriots have many strange and exciting adventures. A series of excellent woodblock prints illustrates the story. 223pp. Bla 73

WALTON, EVANGELINE. **THE FOUR BRANCHES OF THE MABINOGION**, $6.00/set. *These books are not only the best fantasies of the twentieth century, but also great works of fiction. They are actual retellings of the diverse legends of **The Mabinogion** in novel form . . . dealing with Good and Evil . . . and the nature of love.*—**The Saturday Review.** The **Mabinogion** is the classic Welsh book of mythology. Four volumes, introduction, 1006pp. RaH 36

WILHELM, RICHARD, tr. **CHINESE FOLKTALES**, c$5.95. A delightful collection of fifty tales, based on scholarly collections of folklore made within the last 100 years. These folktales belong partly to the myths of Confucianism and Buddhism and partly to historical times, when heroes, saints and rulers assumed magical powers. Other stories deal with the continual warfare between good and evil spirits, which can be resolved only with the help of humans. Notes, 215pp. Bel 71

WILLIAMS-ELLIS, AMABEL. **FAIRY TALES FROM THE BRITISH ISLES**, c$5.50. An illustrated collection, aimed at children, and including tales from England, Scotland, and Ireland. Most of the tales are not included in other collections. There are illustrations on almost every page and the narrative style is good. Notes, 344pp. Wrn 60

_____. **ROUND THE WORLD FAIRY TALES**, c$5.50. A collection of traditional tales from all parts of the world, aimed at children. Many of the favorites from all traditions are included. Many illustrations, some in color. Notes, 302pp. Wrn 63

YEATS, W.B. **FAIRY AND FOLK TALES OF IRELAND**, c$13.50. A representative collection of Irish folk tales, bringing together stories recorded by writers over the last 200 years which cover every aspect of Irish folklore: fairies, changelings, leprechauns, the Pooka, the Banshee, ghosts, witches, fairy doctors, Tir-na-n'og, Saints, priests, the devil, giants, animals, kings, queens, robbers, druids. The authors represented include Crofton Croker, Sir William and Lady Wilde, Lover, Carleton, Allingham, Hyde, and Yeats himself. Kathleen Raine has written a special forward to this volume tracing Irish folklore. 406pp. McM 73

YOLEN, JANE. **THE MAGIC THREE OF SOLATIA**, c$6.95. The magic three and three magical buttons which grant the wisher one desire apiece. They are the web that connects this haunting four-part novel of fantasy, magic, romance, and enchantment. The main characters are Dread Mary, part witch and part mermaid, who teaches her magic to Solatia, Solatia's son, and Blaggard, the evil king who is also a powerful sorcerer. We love this story and if you are moved by fantasy, you will love it too. Ms. Yolen is a great storyteller. Illustrations, 172pp. Cro 74

FASTING AND RAW FOODS

ne of the best ways of healing a diseased body is simply to fast and purify e whole system. Almost any body impurity, including cancer, can be minated from the system. Fasting is more than simply not eating, although is is a large part of it. Often juices are used to intensify the body's natural minative ability and to supply some nutrients. Fasting, at times, leads to mptoms of illness, as the toxins that have been buried in the system come t. It is the diseased tissues that the body breaks down first. Once these ssues are eliminated the natural healing power of the body comes into play ore strongly.

IROLA, PAAVO. **HOW TO KEEP SLIM AND HEALTHY AND YOUNG WITH JUICE ASTING**, $3.25. Dr. Airola considers juice fasting to be the number one healer and juvenator. He gives theory, case histories, fasting to reduce, how to fast, why juice sting is better than water fasting, advocates enemas and gives complete advice on what do while fasting. Bibliography, 79pp. HPP 71

NDREWS, SHEILA. **NO-COOKING FRUITARIAN RECIPE BOOK**, $5.45. A collec- on of imaginative recipes utilizing only raw foods. No sweeteners are included in any of em. A bit of fruitarian philosophy is also included. Index, 96pp. TPL 75

IRCHER-BENNER. **NUTRITION PLAN FOR RAW FOOD AND JUICES**, $2.75.

RAGG, PAUL. **THE MIRACLE OF FASTING**, $3.00. Bragg, who is now in his nineties, the best example of health through good diet principles that we know of, and this is ne of the most popular books on fasting. Contrary to most authors, he believes we hould fast on distilled water only (possibly with a little honey and lemon added) and hould not take enemas during fasts. He urges the reader to start with easy twenty-four to hirty-six hour fasts and gradually work up to longer ones. Bragg fasts a day a week and or seven to ten days four times a year. This book, in addition to giving much practical dvice on fasting, contains a lot of other Bragg advice about healthful eating and living. 97pp. HeS nd

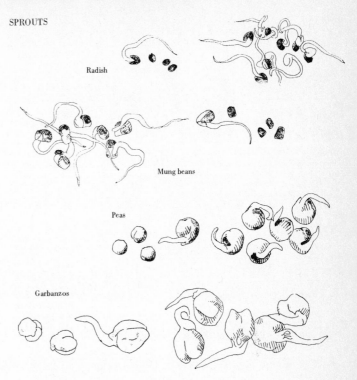

SPROUTS

Radish

Mung beans

Peas

Garbanzos

BRANDT, JOHANNA. **THE GRAPE CURE**, $1.95. Johanna Brandt was a South African who, in 1925, cured herself of cancer by fasting on nothing but grapes. She recommends eating one to four pounds of grapes a day, chewing the skins and seeds, and continuing for a week to a month. The grapes apparently act to break up diseased tissue and purify the blood. Later other fruits, buttermilk, etc. can be added. The grape cure for various diseases has a long history. Needless to say, it is controversial. However, it can't hurt you and if you like grapes as much as we do, you might want to give this idea a try next grape season for whatever good it might do you. 191pp. Lus 67

CARRINGTON, HEREWARD. **SAVE YOUR LIFE BY FASTING**, $3.25. This is a reprint of an old (pre-World War II) book by one of the best-known early hygienists. He makes an interesting case for not eating any more than the minimum amount of food needed to sustain life. (This has been corroborated by more recent studies with rats showing that those who ate twice as much lived half as long!) *We are not nourished by the amount of food we eat, but by the amount we can properly use and assimilate.* The last half of the book deals with fasting per se, although it is more concerned with arguing the merits of the case than with giving practical advice. 226pp. Prv 69

COTT, ALLAN. **THE ULTIMATE DIET**, $1.75. This is a book by a medical doctor for people from a more conventional background who may feel that fasting is a very strange activity. It attempts to set their minds at rest and make the case for fasting. It recommends that no one fast for more than a day without consultation with a doctor. Dr. Cott is a psychiatrist who specializes in megavitamin therapy. Extensive bibliography. 148pp. Ban 75

EHRET, ARNOLD. **MUCUSLESS DIET HEALING SYSTEM**, $1.25. Near the beginning of this century, Arnold Ehret came into prominence as an exponent of the mucusless diet. He argues that meat, dairy products, and starchy foods tend to produce large quan- tities of mucus which provide an ideal medium for germs. He favors fasting and a fruit diet. This book is his major statement and it continues to be extremely popular. His writing style (or perhaps it is the translation) is terrible and he tends to make outlandish claims which he does not back up with facts. Nonetheless, his work is important and al- most everyone that we know has at least sampled Ehret. Sample diets and menus are included. 194pp. Ehr 22

_____. **RATIONAL FASTING**, $1.50. This book gives useful information about fasting in addition to extolling its benefits. Professor Ehret favors use of lemon juice and enemas during fasts. 175pp. Ehr 25

GHAZALI, Al-. **THE MYSTERIES OF FASTING**, $1.50. The practice of fasting as a spiritual discipline is both ancient and widespread, found in virtually all religious tradi- tions. Al-Ghazali, a fourteenth century poet and mystic, wrote this piece to discuss fasting from the Islamic point of view, rather than strictly from a health standpoint. Fasting *stands alone as the only act of worship which is not seen by anyone except God. It is an inward act of worship performed through sheer endurance and fortitude . . . it is a means of vanquishing the enemy of God, Satan, who works through the appetites and carnal lusts.* Translated by Nabih Amin Faris. 52pp. MuA 68

JENSEN, BERNARD. **SEEDS AND SPROUTS FOR LIFE**, $1.75.

KIRSCHNER, H.E. **LIVE FOOD JUICES**, $3.00. Kirschner, an M.D., here cites many case histories of near-miraculous cures through the use of juices, including one woman who drank only carrot juice for eighteen months. There is a table of the nutritional con- tent of various juices, discussion of the values of individual juices, and a listing of condi- tions showing the juices considered helpful. Also includes a brief chapter on the virtues of a low protein diet. 120pp. WoP 74

KROK, MORRIS. **DIET, HEALTH AND LIVING ON AIR**, $3.50. This is briefer than the following book, but covers a wide range of ideas about natural foods, relating them to naturopathic practice and yogic philosophy. The most interesting section is at the end where he discusses the concept of ultimate fast—living on air only (see Yogananda's **The Autobiography of a Yogi** for two examples of this). Krok discusses the mechanisms of the body which may explain how this is possible. Pretty far out stuff for most readers but if you are into yoga and raw foods you'll probably find it fascinating. 95pp. EsH 69

_____. **FORMULA FOR LONG LIFE**, $5.80. Krok, a South African, favors a diet primarily of raw fruits and vegetables. In addition to reading what others have said, he has experimented on himself, eating one food at a time to determine its effects. There is a lot of interesting information in this book about the effects of different foods, cooking, fasts, about cleansing and diseases and acid/alkaline reactions. He has an interesting chapter on pregnancy, asserting that a woman with a clean body will not suffer from morning sickness and other symptoms usual in most pregnancies. 138pp. EsH 62

_____. **FRUIT THE FOOD AND MEDICINE FOR MAN**, $5.30. EsH

KULVINSKAS, VIKTORAS. **LOVE YOUR BODY—LIVE FOOD RECIPES**, $2.50. Kulvinskas is co-director of Ann Wigmore's Hippocrates Health Institute, where persons are cured by eating live (raw) foods and fasting on wheat grass juice. This book gives a few pages of theory; the rest is recipes—ways to make live food interesting, even delicious. We once spent a week with Kulvinskas sampling many of these recipes and can testify that he has done as much to elevate raw food cuisine as any man alive. The book has a subtitle, *complete organic diet on eight cents or less per day*. With recent inflation, that figure should doubtless be increased to at least ten cents. 90pp. Oma 74

LUST, JOHN. **DRINK YOUR TROUBLES AWAY**, $1.95. Lus

_____. **RAW JUICE THERAPY**, c$3.90. This is our favorite of the raw juice books. Provides the theory of raw juice therapy without oversell, and then goes on to give a great deal of useful information for anyone interested in juices: extensive listing of vitamin and mineral deficiency symptoms and the juices to take to overcome them, a table of the vitamin content of foods to be juiced, extensive juice recipes with discussion of the health values thereof, lists of ailments with juice formulas to treat them, menus, and many other assorted tables of useful information. Excellent index, 173pp. TPL 58

NEWMAN, L. **MAKE YOUR JUICER YOUR DRUG STORE**, $1.95. Dr. Newman is naturopath who spent some thirteen years compiling the information in this book. Aft a general treatment of raw juices, cleansing, etc., it considers a wide variety of diseases separate chapters, relating each to this diet. These include hardening of the arteri digestion, elimination, glands, circulatory troubles, respiratory troubles, female trouble nerves, eyes, teeth, weight, and children's ailments. Concludes with a discussion of vario juices, including alfalfa, clover and dandelion. 191pp. Lus 72

ROSS, SHIRLEY. **NATURE'S DRINKS**, $1.75. After a discussion of nutrients in ma fruits and vegetables and how to process them (e.g., never put garlic in your juicer—y can't get the smell out), Ms. Ross gives us some 200 mouth-watering recipes for prepari delicious, energizing, nutritious drinks, free of preservatives and sugar. If you have a juic and want ideas on new combinations to try, this is the book for you. The latter part the book deals in great detail with coffee and tea, how to buy, brew and use then 154pp. RaH 74

SHELTON, HERBERT. **FASTING CAN SAVE YOUR LIFE**, $1.75. This is the book th introduced us to the benefits of fasting. Dr. Shelton is top man in the American Natur Hygiene Society and this book includes a good deal about natural hygiene. It reviews th whole area of fasting, what it can accomplish and what problems to watch out fo Shelton favors plain water fasting, without enemas. The latter half of the book discuss therapeutic values of fasting in relation to many conditions, among them weight loss an gain, asthma and hay fever, arthritis, high blood pressure, psoriasis, multiple scleros and gonorrhea. Index, 200pp. ANH 64

_____. **FASTING FOR RENEWAL OF LIFE**, $2.25. Shelton's latest book is th most comprehensive and scholarly treatment of the subject we've seen. He gives a grea deal of historical background, analogies with animals, and information about fasting i other cultures. He also gives all the necessary advice about conducting a fast, though i is not as immediately accessible as in some of the briefer books. The last part of the boo discusses the use of fasts in many different kinds of diseases. Index, 314pp. NHP 7

SZEKELY, EDMOND BORDEAUX, trans. **THE ESSENE GOSPEL OF PEACE**, $1.00 This is a translation of a third century Aramaic manuscript, preserved in the Vatican an chives, which gives Christ's views on healing and health. *For I tell you truly, except yo fast, you shall never be freed from the power of Satan and from all diseases that come from Satan.... Seek the fresh air of the forest and of the fields, and there in the mids of them shall you find the angel of air. Put off your shoes and your clothing and suffe the angel of air to embrace all your body.... After the angel of air, seek the angel o water.... Think not that it is sufficient that the angel of water embrace you outward only.... Seek, therefore, a large trailing gourd, having the stalk the length of a man take out its innards and fill it with water from the river which the sun has warmed. Han it upon the branch of a tree and kneel upon the ground before the angel of water, and suffer the end of the stalk of the trailing gourd to enter your hinder parts, that the wate may flow through all your bowels.... Then let the water run out from your body that i may carry away from within it all the unclean and evil-smelling things of Satan.... Re new your baptising with water on every day of your fast, till the day when you see that the water which flows out of you is as pure as the river's foam. Then betake your body to the coursing river, and there in the arms of the angel of water render thanks to the living God that he has freed you from your sins.* Aca 75

_____. **TREASURY OF RAW FOODS**, $1.75. Szekely recommends a diet of 25% cereals and 75% raw foods. We found him a little rigid in this book, but there are a lot of interesting points in here about good foods and diet. He introduces us to the word *trophology* to describe the science of food combining. In addition to discussing body needs and the contribution of various foods, this book includes suggested menus and a number of raw food recipes. 42pp. Aca 73

WALKER, N.W. **DIET AND SALAD SUGGESTIONS**, $3.20.

_____. **RAW VEGETABLE JUICES**, c$3.10/$1.25. This book was first published in 1936 and ever since has been the bible of the juicer contingent. In fact, Dr. Walker is inventor of the Norwalk juicer—the most effective one on the market. The book begins with a discussion of the importance of juices and the reasons for drinking them in quanti ty, then follows with information on the values of many different kinds of juice from al falfa to watercress. Finally Walker discusses the therapeutic uses of juices in different ailments ranging from acidosis to varicose veins. These are keyed to eighty-seven different juice mixture formulas. (The $3.10 edition is larger and has bigger type.) 171pp. Pyr 70

GEMS AND STONES

YCE, EDGAR. **GEMS AND STONES**, $1.50. A comparative study of the scientific
perties and occult aspects of twenty-two gems, stones, and metals based on Cayce's
readings, and arranged topically. Includes a list of dealers and bibliography. 50pp.
E 60

OW, W.B. **PRECIOUS STONES**, $1.00. A popular account which details the history
uses of the stones and their healing and magical properties. 64pp. Wei nd

RNIE, WILLIAM. **OCCULT AND CURATIVE POWERS OF PRECIOUS STONES,**
95. This is our most popular book on gems and stones. Dr. Fernie was a physician
his life's work is reflected in this volume. The best known gems and metals are
cussed at length and a great deal of background information is also supplied. Folk-
e is incorporated into the discussion and the book is fully indexed. This is the most
prehensive treatment of precious and semi-precious stones and metals that we know
This edition is a reprint of a much earlier work. 486pp. Mul 07

THE TREE THAT EXUDES AMBER.
From the "Hortus Sanitatis," of Johannis de
Cuba [Strassburg, Jean Pryss, ca. 1483]; De lapidi-
bus, cap. lxx. Author's library.

Capitulum xc.

A PRACTICAL TEST OF THE VIRTUES
OF THE BLOODSTONE TO PREVENT
NOSE-BLEED.

From the "Hortus Sanitatis" of Johannis de
Cuba [Strassburg, Jean Pryss, ca. 1483]; De
lapidibus, cap. xc. Author's library.

KUNZ, G.F. **THE CURIOUS LORE OF PRECIOUS STONES**, $4.50. Dr. Kunz was
America's foremost gemologist and this is the definitive collection of traditional gem
lore. The material presented here is derived from a great number of sources—oral, ancient
lapidary manuals from the Middle Ages, Greek and Roman geographic accounts, archaeological discoveries in Egypt, oriental gem books, and much else. Among the topics covered
are the following: the use of gems as amulets and talismans, carved and engraved magical
stones (including scarabs), luminous stones, the astrological meaning of precious stones,
and the therapeutic value of gems. 410pp. Dov 13

MELLA, DOROTHEE. **THE LEGENDARY AND PRACTICAL USE OF GEMS AND
STONES**, $3.95. *The information in this booklet is the distillation of the stories and
legends of centuries. The practicing arts of the ages, as well as the knowledge of the mystics, have been synthesized into these pages in order to present a composite and practical
guide to the use of gems and stones in our world of here and now.* This is a neatly designed
pamphlet which discusses thirty-two different gems and stones in a simplified manner.
It's a fine short overview containing as much as most people would like to know. 8½x11",
spiral bound. Bibliography, 22pp. Dom 76

DGES, DORIS. **HEALING STONES**, $2.00. A discussion of the twelve most common
ecious stones followed by information on *four stones of hidden healing*: azurite,
alachite, lazurite and chrysocolla. Healing properties are emphasized. 72pp. Hia 61

GRAIL AND KING ARTHUR

he Grail legend is an especially stimulating subject for psychological con-
ideration because it contains so many features that are also to be found in

myths and fairy-tales. Moreover, it has lost far less of its fascination for contemporary men and women than have the latter, which may indicate that it
still embodies a living myth.

The story is known to everyone, at least in its general outlines. A mysterious,
life-preserving and sustenance-dispensing object or vessel is guarded by a King
in a castle that is difficult to find. The King is either lame or sick and the
surrounding country is devastated. The King can only be restored to health
if a knight of conspicuous excellence finds the castle and at the first sight
of what he sees there asks a certain question. Should he neglect to put this
question, then everything will remain as before, the castle will vanish and the
knight will have to set out once more upon the search. Should he finally suc-
ceed, after much wandering and many adventures, in finding the Grail Castle
again, and should he then ask the question, the King will be restored to health,
the land will begin to grow green and the hero will become the guardian of
the Grail from that time on.

So runs the story in its barest outline. It is one of those fairy-tales of which
there are many, in which the search for a *treasure hard to attain* and deliv-
erance from a magic spell form the principal themes. What is of special
interest about the Grail story, however, is that the fairy-tale is interwoven
with a Christian legend and the treasure that must be sought for is thought
to be the vessel in which Joseph of Arimathea received the blood of Christ
at the Descent from the Cross. This remarkable blend of fairy-tale and
legend gives the Grail stories their peculiar character, for through these
stories the eternal fairy-tale enters, as it were, the realm of the temporal
drama of the Christian aeon and thus reflects not only fundamental human
problems but also the dramatic psychic events which form the background
of our Christian culture.

—from **The Grail Legend** by Emma Jung and M.-L. von Franz

ASHE, GEOFFREY. **ALL ABOUT KING ARTHUR**, $1.45. Arthur, King of Britain, became a national hero in the twelfth century. The real ruler during most of that time was Henry II. But the legendary monarch was soon more widely renowned than the actual one, and his fame has continued ever since. Ashe explores the beginning of the Arthurian legend, the forms in which writers and poets have presented it over the ages. He traces the Arthur of fiction and also tells the historical and archaeological facts of all that is known about the King. This includes an account of the results of recent excavations in South Cadbury, now believed to be the site of the original Camelot. Written for the general reader, many illustrations. 173pp. Crg 69

BARBER, RICHARD. **KING ARTHUR**, $5.30. Arthur has emerged as a national hero in Great Britain who, it is believed, will return to lead his country in trouble. The author traced the development of this folklore from the twelfth century, when Geoffrey of Monmouth wrote of Arthur as the Emperor hero of a lost golden age, to his portrayal as the flower of chivalry by Malory and Tennyson. Includes many color and black and white manuscripts illustrating the Arthurian legend. Notes, bibliography, index. 192pp. Car 73

BEARDSLEY, AUBREY. **BEARDSLEY'S ILLUSTRATIONS FOR LE MORT D'ARTHUR**, $3.50. 171pp. Dov 72

BEDIER, JOSEPH. **THE ROMANCE OF TRISTAN AND ISEULT**, $1.65. This Arthurian romance is the most famous of the genre and it remains a classic love story. The ideals of the chivalric era are well set forth and the tragic tale retains its appeal over the centuries. Bedier has done the most noted modern retelling and this translation by Hilaire Belloc and Paul Rosenfeld retains the beauty and sense of fatality of the original tale. 151pp. RaH 65

CABLE, JAMES. **THE DEATH OF KING ARTHUR**, $2.50. Set at the end of the Arthurian world, this translation of **La Mort le Roi Artu**, is a French romance of the thirteenth century. The story begins with a Round Table depleted in numbers after the quest of the Holy Grail. It goes on to tell of Lancelot and Guinevere and the treacherous Mordred and ends with the last battle of Arthur and Lancelot at Salisbury. 235pp. Pen 71

ESCHENBACH, WOLFRAM von. **PARZIVAL**, $2.95. Parzival, an Arthurian romance completed by von Eschenbach in the first years of the thirteenth century, is one of the foremost works of German literature and a classic work on the Grail. The most important aspects of human existence, worldly and spiritual, are presented against the panorama of battles and tournaments and Parzival's long search for the Grail. The world of knighthood, of love, loyalty and human endeavor despite the cruelty and suffering of life, is constantly mingled with the world of the Grail, affirming the inherent unity of man's temporal condition and his quest for something beyond human existence. This translation by Hele Mustard and Charles Passage is the definitive one. The translators also provide a 56pp introduction. 493pp. RaH 61

EVANS, SEBASTIAN, tr. **HIGH HISTORY OF THE HOLY GRAIL**, c$10.05. A translation of the first volume of **Perceval le Gallois ou le conte de Graal**, the most complete book of the Grail known today, the original manuscript of which dates from the thirteenth century. Every aspect of the legend is discussed at length and the narrative is in the form of a story. The language is archaic. Introduction, 388pp. Cla 69

GREEN, ROGER. **KING ARTHUR AND HIS KNIGHTS OF THE ROUND TABLE**, $1.50. A retelling of twenty-two of the stories, aimed at children but fine for all who wish to read the stories. Green writes well and the enchantment of the stories is retained in his recreation. Beautifully illustrated. 282pp. Pen 53

HELINE, CORINNE. **MYSTERIES OF THE HOLY GRAIL**, $2.95. Expounds the roots of the Grail story and the legends that grew up around it. The story conveys deep esoteric and mystical symbolism concerning the *Ageless Wisdom Teaching* and the path of the human soul through various initiations into greater consciousness. The legend of King Arthur is revealed in its symbolic meaning. 128pp. NAP 73

JENKINS, ELIZABETH. **THE MYSTERY OF KING ARTHUR**, c$20.00 A sumptuously illustrated, well researched account of all that is known today about Arthur. Exploring every aspect of the myth, Ms. Jenkins discusses the Round Table, the Holy Grail, Glastonbury, the tragedy of Lancelot and Guinevere, and much else. She recounts the development of these concepts over the years and notes the political significance of the Arthur story. Fascinating reading for those who would like to learn more about Arthur. Ninety-six illustrations, sixteen in color. Index, 7½x9½". 224pp. Put 75

JUNG, EMMA and MARIE-LOUISE VON FRANZ. **THE GRAIL LEGEND**, c$9.35. Mrs. Jung devoted her last thirty years to an extensive study of the Grail legend. *It was not the intention of Emma Jung . . . to examine the Grail legend from a historical or literary point of view but to rely, in these respects, on the numerous and distinguished achievements of other scholars. Rather, the material provided by the Grail stories will be considered here from the standpoint of C. G. Jung's depth psychology. Like alchemy and its curious symbolic productions, these poetic fantasy creations and their symbolism are also illustrative of deep-seated, unconscious religious processes that are still of the greatest significance, for they prepare the way to, and anticipate, the religious problem of modern man.—M.-L. von Franz.* Dr. von Franz completed the work at the request of Dr. Jung after his wife's death. Notes, bibliography, index. 452pp. Hod 71

LANIER, SIDNEY, ed. **KING ARTHUR AND HIS KNIGHTS OF THE ROUNDTABLE**, c$3.95. See the Children's Books section.

MAC LEOD, MARY. **THE BOOK OF KING ARTHUR AND HIS NOBLE KNIGHTS**. See the Children's Books section.

MALORY, THOMAS. **LE MORTE D'ARTHUR**, c$3.98. Le Morte d'Arthur, originally published in 1485, was the first coherent history of Arthur from his magical birth to his

dramatic death. Malory collected all the legends and myths and attempted to judge their historical veracity. His account is still considered the definitive one and all later scholars have relied heavily upon it—although later research has shown it to be in error on a number of counts. It is a classic work which many have heard of but few have read due to the elaborate and obscure nature of medieval rhetoric. This edition is rendered in a modern idiom and includes an introduction by Robert Graves. 532pp. Crn 62

MALTWOOD, K.E. **A GUIDE TO GLASTENBURY'S TEMPLE OF THE STARS**, c$6.70. The author believes that it is now possible to localize the Arthurian Grail legends by means of air photographs of the area between Glastonbury and Somerton. The prehistoric earth works and artificial water courses in that area appear from the air to delineate enormous effigies resembling zodiacal creatures arranged in a circle. Maltwood studies each of the representational images as if they were a zodiacal sign and makes an in depth analysis of the symbolism and the legends that derived from the giant natural form. Appropriate quotations from **The High History of the Holy Grail** are included. Illustrations, bibliography. 129pp. Cla 64

MATARASSO, P. M., tr. **THE QUEST OF THE HOLY GRAIL**, $2.50. The translation of an important thirteenth century work which vividly discusses the adventures of Arthur's knights in their search for the Holy Grail. In the process, the author didactically presents the Christian ideals. The whole work is a fusion of Christian symbolism and Celtic legend. The translator provides a long introduction and extensive notes. 304pp. Pen 69

MORDUCH, ANNA. **THE SOVEREIGN ADVENTURE**, c$5.25. The Sovereign Adventure *endeavours to show that the story of the Grail in all its different versions is neither romantic fiction nor the property or tradition of one race. It belongs to mankind and every race of men has its own Grail story . . . . We hope that this book will send many of the young out as Grail knights of our time, strong, enlightened and tolerant . . . . The can all share in the sovereign adventure, the quest for man's goal and the finding of the way that leads to it.* 196pp. Cla 70

PYLE, HOWARD. **THE STORY OF KING ARTHUR AND HIS KNIGHTS**, $3.50. A vividly written retelling of the adventures of King Arthur and his knights. All the major stories are included. This is considered the definitive children's version of the Arthurian legend—though some of the more recent works probably speak better to contemporary youth. Forty-one excellent drawings by Pyle accompany the text. 329pp. Dov 03

STEWART, MARY. **THE CRYSTAL CAVE**, $1.75. This novel brings the legend of Merlin to life. It is the story of his childhood, his mystical visions, and the manner in which he developed. Ms. Stewart has given us a fascinating tale. She doesn't claim to be presenting a serious study—yet the reader can get as good (or better) a feel of fifth century Britain from this book as from any of the more scholarly works. 384pp. Faw 70

_____. **THE HOLLOW HILLS**, $1.75. This is our personal favorite of all the books on Arthur. Mary Stewart is an enthralling writer and she has created a wonderful story which takes us through Arthur's childhood and young manhood up to the time when he becomes king. And again Merlin plays a leading role. Must reading for all those who would like to know more about Arthur and Merlin. 447pp. Faw 73

STONE, BRIAN, tr. **SIR GAWAIN AND THE GREEN KNIGHT**, $1.95. The tale of Sir Gawain is one of the best known of the Arthurian romances. This version was written in the fourteenth century and is considered a masterpiece of medieval alliterative poetry. In the poem Sir Gawain triumphs against almost insuperable odds. This edition includes 68pp of interpretative and background material and a 20pp introduction. 185pp. Pen 59

WAITE, A. E. **THE HIDDEN CHURCH OF THE HOLY GRAIL**, c$17.50. *I am about to set forth after a new manner, and chiefly for the use of English mystics, the nature of the mystery which is enshrined in the old romance-literature of the Holy Grail . . . . The task will serve . . . on the one hand . . . to illustrate the deeper intimations of Graal literature and, on the other, certain collateral intimations which lie behind the teachings of the great churches and are, in the official sense, as if beyond their ken.* 724pp. YPS 09

WESTON, JESSIE. **FROM RITUAL TO ROMANCE**, $2.95. *The Grail Story is not . . . the product of imagination, literary or popular. At its root lies the record, more or less distorted, of an ancient Ritual, having for its ultimate object the initiation into the secret of Life, physical and spiritual.* Ms. Weston is an eminent medieval scholar and here she has applied the discoveries of cultural anthropology to the literature of medieval legend and romance. This book is best known as the one which inspired the basic symbolism of T. S. Eliot's **The Waste Land**. Notes, index, 217pp. Dou 57.

WHITE, T. H. **THE ONCE AND FUTURE KING**, $2.25. A novelistic recreation of Arthur's childhood and his reign as king. This is the most popular contemporary retelling and was the basis for **Camelot**. 639pp. Ber 39

GRAPHOLOGY

ndwriting is a permanent record of personality, a mirror in which are re-
cted character traits, abilities, emotions; orientation toward the environ-
nt and people in general; intellect; approach to tasks; values; strong points
d weak ones; even past experiences and present state of development; the
ount of physical strength and resilience—all are set down by the stroke of
en.

comparison of samples of handwriting, given by the same writer, over a
riod of years, frequently shows graphic changes. Samples from school days
ar little resemblance to present-day writing. Similarly, a letter during a
ppy, healthy period looks quite different from one that was penned when
e writer was sad, depressed, or ill. Just as the personality changes, so does
ndwriting.

e close association between personality and handwriting is due to the phys-
ogical fact that writing impulses emanate from the cortex of the brain,
m which they are conveyed into the muscles of the fingers via the nervous
stem. Actually the finished product could be considered *brain* rather than
nd writing. The hand merely holds the pen or the pencil; it is the brain
at directs the movements of the hand, which is thus responsible for the
nner in which the letters are formed or the lines are spaced.

ost of us sense instinctively this close connection between handwriting and
rsonality without giving it much thought. At times, we may have looked
riously at the strange handwriting of a letter and wondered what kind of
rson wrote it, perhaps even taken an instant like or dislike to our unknown
rrespondent just on the strength of his handwriting. However fleeting and
formulated these impressions may be, as we perceive them we are unwit-
gly trying to understand something about the writer's character.

rom **HANDWRITING** by Dr. Henry Teltscher

UNKER, M.N. **HANDWRITING ANALYSIS**, c$1.98. A very straightforward, instruc-
e account of how graphoanalysis identifies character and personality traits and tenden-
es. *These are based in the mind, follow the nervous system and inevitably show up in
ndwriting.* Includes many specimens. 256pp. NeH 59

_____. **WHAT YOUR HANDWRITING TELLS YOU**, $7.50. This was Bunker's
st book and it is a pioneering study by one of the leaders in the field of graphoanalysis.
ell known personalities of the thirties are used as case studies and the book is designed
teach the general principles so that they can be applied in daily life. 243pp. NeH 31

ALCON, HAL. **HOW TO ANALYSE HANDWRITING**, c$1.49. Dr. Falcon has been a
acticing graphologist for over thirty years. Here he explains the basic techniques he uses
d quotes from many basic sources. The text is directly written to the reader and seems
be a good overall survey of the basics. There seems to be more depth here than in
any of the general books. Many illustrations, index, 159pp. GaB 64

RENCH, WILLIAM. **GRAPHOANALYSIS**, $2.95. Formerly titled **The Psychology of
andwriting**: *Each chapter contains some of the underlying principles of handwriting
ychology as applied to some phase of human endeavor, commercial advancement, or
otection and such information as is relative to characteristic traits, aptitudes and talents
hich are revealed.* 240pp. NPC 74

ARDNER, RUTH. **A GRAPHOLOGY STUDENT'S WORKBOOK**, $4.95. Material
vered in detail includes strokes, margins, spacing, line and letter leaning, script size,
d pen pressure. Space is left for the student to add information as it is acquired. Also
cludes removable transparencies which assist in the calculation of the degrees of various
ctors. This is the best practical text we've seen both for self-study and group instruc-
on. 137pp. LIP 73

REEN, JANE. **YOU AND YOUR PRIVATE I**, $4.95. Ms. Green is a social worker who
ses graphology as a supplementary diagnostic tool, focusing on the personal pronoun *I*
s a unique expression of personality. Numerous case histories show how she does in-
epth personality analyses on the basis of handwriting samples. As with most graphology
ooks the author seems to get carried away with what she sees in each squiggle—however
s an additional psychological tool graphology has proven its usefulness. This is a serious
udy. Bibliography, 299pp. LIP 75

ACOBY, H.J. **ANALYSIS OF HANDWRITING**, c$6.50. A scholarly introduction to
e psychological analysis of handwriting. Every aspect is fully covered. Appendix includes
61 examples, some extensively analyzed. The best theoretical work. 285pp. A&U 39

ANN, PEGGY. **THE TELLTALE LINE**, c$6.95. A very simplified guide to the science
f handwriting analysis. Written for older children. Practical instructions are included.
2pp. McM 76

MARCUSE, IRENE. **GUIDE TO PERSONALITY THROUGH YOUR HANDWRITING**,
$1.45. Dr. Marcuse is one of the foremost contemporary graphologists and this book is
considered a classic. She tells us the history and development of graphology in the field of
child psychology, in vocational guidance, in marriage counseling, in personnel selection,
in criminal detection, and in abnormal psychology. There's also instructional material on
the technique of graphology. The text is illustrated throughout with handwriting samples.
Bibliography, index, 190pp. Arc 62

MARLEY, JOHN. **HANDWRITING ANALYSIS MADE EASY—A GUIDE TO CHAR-
ACTER AND HUMAN BEHAVIOR**, $2.00. A practical, comprehensive guide to charac-
ter and human behavior as discovered through graphology. 183pp. Wil 67

MEYER, JEROME. **THE HANDWRITING ANALYZER**, $3.95. A recent reprint of a
classic text, first written in 1927 and revised in 1953, which includes many samples
and techniques along with a series of *see-through* charts which can be used as diagnostic
aids. This is about as comprehensive a technique-manual as we have seen and even includes an index to characteristics. Recommended. Oversize, 101pp. S&S 53

OLYANOVA, NADYA. **HANDWRITING TELLS**, $3.00. Ms. Olyanova was one of the
pioneers in the science of graphology and was instrumental in getting it generally accepted as a significant tool in character and personality analysis. This is a classic volume
in which she illustrates the broad range of application the science covers. Includes many
illustrations. 37lpp. Wil 36

_____. **THE PSYCHOLOGY OF HANDWRITING**, $2.00 A much more recent
volume, covering the same material as the other, but adding many new insights garnered
from years of application. 224pp. Wil 60

ROMAN, KLARA. **HANDWRITING: A KEY TO PERSONALITY**, $4.95. Well-organized,
clear survey of the techniques used in handwriting analysis. Mrs. Roman is an interna-
tionally known psychologist and handwriting expert. Her approach can be utilized in
analyzing the chief features of both normal and disturbed personality. Many samples.
385pp. FSG 52

SAINTE COLOMBE, PAUL de. **GRAPHO-THERAPEUTICS: PEN AND PENCIL THER-
APY**, $3.95. The scientific technique of graphotherapy for solving psychological prob-
lems has been successfully used in Europe for the past thirty years and was introduced
into the U.S. by the author. This comprehensive volume is the only text on the subject.
It was written for the layman and can be practically applied to one's life. Very clearly
written, many illustrations. Recommended. 340pp. NPC 66

SINGER, ERIC. **A MANUAL OF GRAPHOLOGY**, $4.95. This is a reissue of three of
Singer's books, bound in one volume: **Graphology for Everyman, The Graphologist's
Alphabet** and **A Handwriting Quiz Book**. Singer writes very well and this volume is an
excellent introduction for the general reader. All aspects are well covered and the quiz at
the end should be helpful to those who seek to test their knowledge. Recommended.
244pp. Hip 49

_____. **PERSONALITY IN HANDWRITING**, c$6.95. Dr. Singer studied hand-
writing analysis and psychology under experts in Austria and Switzerland and has been
retained as handwriting consultant by several large industrial firms and has a large private
practice. His work is very well regarded and he is probably the foremost psychological
graphologist. Here he discusses the writer's conception of the visual pattern he wants to
put down on the paper. This guiding image is a mark of the writer's individuality and taste,
a sum of the shapes he likes and therefore remembers and repeats; to know why and how
he chooses these particular shapes is to penetrate to the core of his personality. In the
course of his study, Dr. Singer shows the reader some of the deductions that can be made
from such things as addresses, doodles, signatures, and the influence the subject matter
itself may have on a person's writing. Bibliography, 120pp. Hip 74

SOLOMON, SHIRL. **HOW TO REALLY KNOW YOURSELF THROUGH YOUR HAND-
WRITING**, $1.95. A new account, written in a very personal vein and apparently intended
for the general reader. Chapter headings include *The Physical You, You the Thinker, Your
Motivation Symbols, Are You Repressed, Your Self-Image.* Many examples. 189pp. Ban 73

Roosevelt Family Franklin Morak

Specimen 191   Specimen 195
Age nineteen   Age sixty-three

TELTSCHER, HENRY. **HANDWRITING—REVELATION OF SELF**, $3.95. Subtitled
A Source Book of Psychographology, this is the most complete book on handwriting
analysis as a branch of psychological interpretation. The material is comprehensive and
is very well put together. There is no biographical material on Dr. Teltscher included;
however he seems to have had extensive empirical experience and to have worked closely
with psychiatrists and neurologists in developing and testing his theories. He includes
chapters on psychographology—its background and practice, on method, analysis of
children's writings, marital compatibility, vocational skills, personnel selection, applications in medicine and psychology, symbolic imagery in writing, criminology, and
analyses of political leaders—domestic and foreign. An excellent work for someone
seriously interested in understanding and applying graphology. Recommended. Bibliography, indices. 350pp. Haw 71

GURDJIEFF AND THE WORK

Gurdjieff died on the 29th of October 1949. He was an extraordinary man who made a profound impact upon those who met him even casually. He attracted widespread attention when he first came to Europe in the early 1920's. He founded a school in France, popularly known as the forest philosophers, and attracted a circle of remarkable men and women whose lives were changed by their contact with him. Through them his ideas have penetrated into the world, particularly among the English-speaking people, and they have had more influence than many suspect.

Nevertheless, after 1935, he almost disappeared from view and remained an enigma till the end of his life. He was surrounded by a small circle of devoted followers, the majority of whom, after he died, pledged themselves to perpetuate his work and see to the publication of his books. Of his four books, only one, **The Herald of Coming Good**, was published during his lifetime and, within one year, repudiated and withdrawn from circulation. His great work consists of three books: the first, **Beelzebub's Tales to His Grandson**, was published a few months after his death, the second, **Meetings with Remarkable Men**, ten years later, and the third, now finally being published, **Life is Real Only Then, When "I Am."** These three were regarded by Gurdjieff as a single work with the title **All and Everything** but in practice this title was originally applied to the first.

His books and books about him have been widely sold, but it is doubtful if they have been equally widely read. Many people have admitted to me that they had *dipped into* Gurdjieff's **Beelzebub's Tales** without understanding what it was all about. Very few have read right through and fewer still have claimed to have understood his purpose in writing it. This may partly explain why it is that after his death, in spite of the publication of his books and the very wide circulation of Ouspensky's **In Search of the Miraculous**, which has come to be regarded as the most authoritative summary of Gurdjieff's ideas, he still remains an unknown quantity. His works are in libraries where they are usually classified under religion or occultism. They seldom appear under headings of philosophy or science, yet he claimed that his contribution was both scientific and philosophical. The truth is that it is a manifesto to humanity to which humanity is only now ready to listen.

This is indicated by the fact that now, nearly twenty-five years after his death, a new interest is being taken in him and his work. His books are being read and discussed differently. Appearing all over the world, especially in the English-speaking countries, are groups who set themselves to study his ideas and put them into practice. Many of those who are leading these groups have no acquaintance with his method except through what they have read. He himself asserted that it was not possible to transmit the essence of his teaching by books alone, which casts some doubt on the value of much that is going on.

We have here a not uncommon phenomenon: a strikingly original thinker, who is far ahead of his time, makes an impact upon his immediate followers, but is not understood or accepted by his contemporaries in general. A generation, or sometimes several, have to pass before an interest begins to awaken. This is what has happened with Gurdjieff. The resurgence has been most marked among the young people who are interested in his teaching, because they see in Gurdjieff a prophet of the New Age which they hope will come after the present crisis of mankind has passed. They see in him a break with the past and an understanding of the needs of the future. There is another side to this, which is the belief that in some way Gurdjieff is not a *lone wolf*, but that he belongs to a tradition that is timeless and is, therefore, unaffected by passing fashion and so capable of enlightening our changing world.

Scores of personal accounts of the impression made by Gurdjieff on those who worked with him for many years, or even met him only casually, have appeared in books and periodicals. Each is necessarily subjective, for Gurdjieff was an enigma presenting a different face to every person and to every occasion. His own account, that is to be found solely in the *Third Series* of his writings, **Life is Real Only Then, When "I Am"**, is more revealing than any other, and we are fortunate that this book is now to be published. The principal reason why personal impressions have so little value is that Gurd-

jieff was from start to finish a seeker experimenting with different ways living and behaving and with different means for accomplishing his lif work. I can affirm that in me he always inspired love and complete con dence. I never doubted that he wished to help me to fulfil my own lif work, and that we were linked together in a common aim, which was to p sent to humanity a more acceptable account of *Man, the World and G* than present-day psychology, science and religion could offer. He had devot the first half of his life to this greatest of undertakings, and in the second set himself to share with others the conclusions he had reached. In this was not wholly successful because nearly all who met him were obsess with their personal problems and needs and insisted upon looking at him *their* teacher. He had immense compassion and gave himself freely. Som times he revolted from the stupidity and narrowness of his own followe and shut himself away to find some better way of fulfilling his mission. must be added that the impression he made upon people was usually nee lessly distorted by the way of life he had deliberately set himself, of arousi hostility by *treading heavily on the most sensitive corn of everyone he me* What really mattered was Gurdjieff's message as it applies to the present-d world. It is also vital that we should form our own opinion as to whether h message was his own private affair or whether it was part of a greater me age coming from a higher source. . . .

One of the reasons why Gurdjieff and his life story have such a strong appe for young people is the feeling that he has opened a channel to let the wate of life flow again. Others have claimed to have known the Masters of Wisdo but Gurdjieff brought their teaching and converted it into a practical way life for the modern world, not only for individuals, but for the whole hum family.

In terms of his hopes and aspirations, Gurdjieff's life may appear to ha been a failure. His Institute collapsed; he left very few outstanding discip behind him. His books have been read as curiosities rather than harbingers the new world.

Gurdjieff took deliberate measures to ensure that he should not be made cult-figure. The very powerful effect on all who met him, he referred to *Zvarnoharno*, which is incidentally the same as the Avestan *hvareno*, mark a superior being or *aura of kingship*. His outrageous behaviour was one mea he adopted for deflecting incipient hero-worship. He followed this cour until he finally abandoned, in 1935, the hope of establishing his Institu After that time, until the end of his life, he was concerned primarily with i dividuals who could interpret his ideas. At first, he looked for writers who he specially trained. These included many who did not become famous li Kathryn Hulme, and Rene Daumal, but who wrote notable books. He h some remarkable pupils in America, but he took steps to ensure that no o ganization should be created. Everyone who had capacity for initiative w encouraged to form his or her own group. If he required something don he often entrusted the task to two, three or more people separately, th causing confusion and jealousy.

Yet another precaution taken was to give out his ideas in many differe forms, always incomplete and sometimes misleading. No one has the right say: *This is the teaching which we had from Gurdjieff. It is complete, sat factory and immutable. This is what we have to transmit.* Yet, unfortunatel this is just what some of his followers have said. He did not leave behind hi either an embryo organization, or a fixed teaching or a designated successo He did leave a small group of loving and devoted pupils who have set them selves to keep his work in the form in which they received it, passing it on t those who are prepared to accept it without modifying it or adding anythi from other sources.

—from **GURDJIEFF: MAKING A NEW WORLD** by J.G. Bennett

ANDERSON, MARGARET. **THE STRANGE NECESSITY**, c$7.50. This is the last vol ume in Ms. Anderson's autobiography, covering the period in which she worked closely with Gurdjieff. A very personal, literary account which discusses the people and thing the author knew. 223pp. Hor 69

________. **THE UNKNOWABLE GURDJIEFF**, $3.50. An evocation of Gurdjieff itten in a simple manner by one of his students which passes over the biographical facts out Gurdjieff and concentrates on his teaching. Ms. Anderson writes *of what he said en I was there to hear him say it; of what he taught us, how he taught it, and what eft it had not only upon me but upon my friends since each of us experienced it differently.* 2pp. Wei 62

KLE, WILLIAM. **A GEOGRAPHY OF CONSCIOUSNESS**, c$9.25. While Arkle is not urdjieffian the ideas he presents here about cosmology and man's mechanical nature quite similar to those taught by Gurdjieff. One of the most interesting features of this ok is Arkle's careful analysis of different *circuits* (corresponding to Gurdjieff's *centers*). ere's also an interesting discussion of consciousness and of the *self*. Other chapters dis-ss sin, justice, education, religion, astrology, the will, beauty, and the atomic field. any diagrams illustrate the text. Foreward by Colin Wilson. 240pp. Spe 74

NJAMIN, HARRY. **BASIC SELF KNOWLEDGE**, $3.50. A very simple introduction Gurdjieff, with some parallels to Krishnamurti's thinking. 167pp. Wei

NNETT, J.G. **CREATIVE THINKING**, $2.60. Bennett here explains the need to set e the instrument of thinking in order that creative thought can occur. Various tech-ques are interspersed throughout the book. One of the key ideas is that in order to think, u must not think—and here the use of the Zen *koan* is illustrated. CSP 64

________. **THE DRAMATIC UNIVERSE, VOL. IV**, $9.45. This is the only volume **The Dramatic Universe** that is still in print. It applies to history the conclusions of the rlier volumes regarding the nature of time and the Laws of Universal Transformation. e basic hypothesis is that Intelligent Direction distinguished history from mere happen-g. The evidence for this is examined for all stages of evolution. The book ends with a recast of the course of history in the next one thousand years. Glossary, 441pp. Hod

________. **ENERGIES—MATERIAL, VITAL, COSMIC**, $3.90. Scientific interpreta-ons of personal experiences which are a bit less complex than those presented in **The ramatic Universe.** *He shows how depth psychology, mysticism, and religious experience onnect with mother theories of Energy Field Forces and Vital Structures, and the later apters devoted to Consciousness, Creativity and Love open new vistas towards under-anding man and the universe as a complete harmonious structure.* 145pp. CSP 64

________. **THE ENNEAGRAM**, $1.95. The Enneagram is an ancient symbol of pro-und significance. The understanding of its use has passed down through spiritual broth-rhoods for over 2,000 years. During his travel in search of teachers of wisdom, Gurdjieff und the Enneagram used as a method of passing on traditional teachings. Since his first ontact with Gurdjieff, Mr. Bennett has studied and used the Enneagram for fifty years. ere he uses everyday situations to illustrate the working of this symbol as well as to ow its deeper significance, revealing possibilities of using the Enneagram to come to an nderstanding of the principles underlying the laws of the universe. Part of the **Transfor-ation of Man** series. 64pp. CSP 74

________. **GURDJIEFF—A VERY GREAT ENIGMA**, $2.75. Transcripts of three lec-ires dealing with (l) his background and the environment of his boyhood, (2) the sources f his ideals—the various secret societies that he encountered in his travels between 1885 nd 1910, and (3) Gurdjieff's teaching and methods. Bennett studied under Gurdjieff for any years and is as qualified as anyone to deal with him. 100pp. Wei 63

________. **GURDJIEFF—MAKING A NEW WORLD**, $3.95. This is a new major ork in which Bennett sets out to inquire whether Gurdjieff was an isolated phenomenon r part of a cultural tradition that for centuries has been concerned with the destiny of ankind. He presents many of Gurdjieff's ideas and describes the methods Gurdjieff used n trasmitting them. The theme of the work is summed up by *Gurdjieff's question: What s the sense and significance in general of life on the earth, and in particular, of human ife?* Illustrations, 320pp. H&R 73

________. **GURDJIEFF TODAY**, $2.65. This small book is part of the **Transforma-ion of Man** series. It is a reprint of a talk that Bennett gave in 1973 and expresses better han anything else how Bennett felt that the Work and the Gurdjieffian tradition relate o present-day world conditions and needs. The material is clearly presented and there is also a section of questions and answers which delve more deeply into several relevant areas. 47pp. CSP 74

________. **HOW WE DO THINGS**, $1.95. This book is based on a series of lectures on he human functions which discusses how our bodies are made and how their structure in-luences our behavior. Topics include automatism, sensitivity, spontaneity and conscious-ness, and the role of vital energies in our lives. CSP

________. **LONG PILGRIMAGE: THE LIFE AND TEACHING OF THE SHIVAPURI BABA**, $4.95. The Shivapuri Baba was one of the most remarkable sages of our time. Bennett met him for the first time when he was well over one hundred years old and had several remarkable discussions with him before he died in 1963 at the age of 137. These conversations are recorded here and they present a vital discipline and guide to *right living* hat incorporates many traditions. The book begins with the account of an amazing jour-ney the Shivapuri Baba set out on at the end of the nineteenth century which lasted for thirty-five years. It was undertaken after he had lived in seclusion for thirty years. During his travels he met personally with monarchs and heads of state including Queen Victoria and Theodore Roosevelt as well as with spiritual and cultural leaders. An important book for all seriously interested in work on themselves. Rai 75

________. **THE MASTERS OF WISDOM**, c$8.50. Mr. Bennett's long-awaited account of the historical esoteric brotherhood which has traditionally been the keeper of secret knowledge. These were the groups that Gurdjieff studied under and whose techniques he taught and that also directed Bennett's work throughout his life. 256pp. Tur 76

________. **THE SEVENFOLD WORK**, $2.60. The material in this monograph devel-oped out of talks given by Mr. Bennett at Sherbourne. The Work is resolved into a spec-trum of seven lines which are applicable to past and present practice and experience, and probably valid for the future. All the aspects of the Work are discussed, and while this is not a complete presentation there could never be a complete written presentation, since material such as this cannot be explained in books but must be transmitted from person to person. Index, 116pp. CSP 75

________. **SEX**, $1.95. *In this little book I will be talking about the action of sex in us with little reference to the power of love. We shall have to spend some time looking at how the sexual energy affects the workings of our bodily and physical apparatus, and the role that it plays in the transformation of the energies which constitute our being. . . . To understand something, we must try and see it as a whole in all its diversity. Sex in human life is all or any one of the following: a disease and a source of illusion; a means of repro-duction and the perpetuation of the species; a regulator of our psychic energies, or a way towards union of will. All of these must be taken into account if we wish to understand the operation of sex in our lives and what is possible in our human communities. The last chapter . . . is an attempt to sketch the requirements for right sexual life in the truly pro-gressive society.* 85pp. CSP 75

________. **A SPIRITUAL PSYCHOLOGY**, c$6.95. Presents a framework in which the spiritual and the natural elements in human experience can be distinguished and yet related and indicates the ways in which spiritual development can be realized. It is derived from three sources, Ouspensky's **In Search**, Gurdjieff's **All and Everything**, and the **Bhaga-vad Gita** and is basically an edited transcription of talks given at a seminar. It is more understandable than most of Bennett's writings. 251pp. CSA 74

________. **VALUES**, c$3.50. 38 essays collected together, chosen for reading in a study group and used as an exercise, reading one passage every week and ending with a meditation upon the theme: *Forms are different but Truth is One.* The selections are all from noted translations and include large extracts from Nicholson's **Mathnawi**, various **Upanishads**, the **Tao Te Ching**, and Suzuki's **Zen Essays**. 166pp. CSP

________. **WHAT ARE WE LIVING FOR?** $3.60. A searching look at the quality of contemporary life and a discussion of the necessity for the re-establishment of the balance between the inner and outer man. CSP 65

________. **WITNESS**, $5.95. A completely revised, updated version—including two new chapters which cover the past twelve years of Bennett's life and his work at Sher-bourne, his school in England. **Witness** is Bennett's autobiography. It is a chronicle of his search for what lies beyond. It is also a record of many of the great spiritual leaders of this century, including material on all of the people with whom Bennett has been associated and especially emphasizing his work with Gurdjieff. Among the clearest and most read-able of Bennett's works. 26 photographs, 381pp. Ome 74

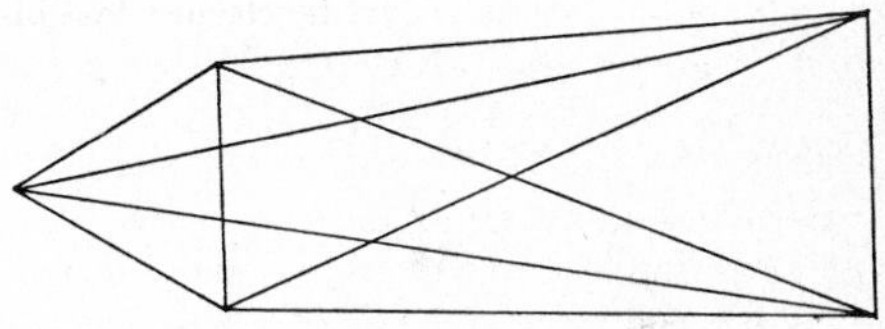

COLLIN, RODNEY. **THE THEORY OF CELESTIAL INFLUENCE**, $5.00. A complex scientific reconstruction in one particular form and in one particular language of the body of ideas given by Ouspensky, profusely illustrated with charts and diagrams. It is an at-tempt to assemble all the knowledge and experience of today into a single whole which would explain their relation to the universe and their possibilities within it. Collin's con-clusion is that the purpose of everything in the universe, from sun to cell, is the attain-ment of a higher level of consciousness. Without that, whatever the accumulation of *facts*, there is no growth in knowledge or real understanding. Collin's cosmology is clearly pre-sented and geared toward the scientific/intuitive mind of the person seeking to awaken and to understand. Highly recommended. 374pp. Wei 73

________. **THEORY OF ETERNAL LIFE**, c$5.95. A fascinating theoretical study of death and *man's being in the invisible worlds between life and death.* Collin has reviewed the ancient teachings on this subject and presented his view of the eternal recurrence. He illustrates his account with diagrams and quotations. Every word counts in this illuminat-ing study—and each rereading brings new insights. 134pp. Wei 74

DAUMAL, RENE. **MT. ANALOGUE**, $2.50. A symbolic mountain that represents the knowledge to be passed on to other seekers: *that between learning and teaching there exists no secure or stationary zone of knowledge. To know means to be learning or to be teaching; there is no middle way.* 106pp. Pen 74

DE HARTMANN, THOMAS. **OUR LIFE WITH MR. GURDJIEFF**, $2.50. A very personal account of the years 1917-1929 that de Hartmann and his wife spent studying under Gurdjieff. This is the only account of the first years of Gurdjieff's work. Its aim is to tell about the way Gurdjieff worked with his students and to convey an idea of the work and its relation to man. De Hartmann was a noted composer. 134pp. Pen 64

GAGE, ANNE. **THE ONE WORK—A JOURNEY TOWARDS THE SELF**, $4.70. A very personalized intuitive account of the author's visits to Banaras, Arunachala, Angkor, Bali, Ajanta, Borobodur. She is able to evoke real meaning from the shrines and temples of the past, and from the teachers of today, not only as a scholar, but as a human being on a quest for enlightenment. Includes long dialogues with the holy men and teachers she en-countered. 137pp. Wat 61

GURDJIEFF

Gurdjieff grew up in the Caucasus at the end of the nineteenth century. He was influenced in his youth by diverse traditions of Turkish and Persian Islamic Sufism, Greek and Russian Christian spirituality, Armenian secret societies, Assyrian Christianity, and Zoroastrian mysteries. He traveled widely from the mid-1880's to 1910 through Central Asia, Tibet and the Middle East. As he traveled he picked up bits and pieces of paths that he was later to use in his work.

Gurdjieff made an extraordinarily detailed examination of the conditioning process. He pointed out that the conditioning of each individual creates major distortions in the way that the mental, physical and emotional *centers* of a person interrelate. One or another of the *centers* comes to typify the conditioned personality, instead of all the *centers* being in harmonious balance. In other words, one person may be primarily intellectual, while another is primarily emotional or physical.

As this work on oneself was taking place, something called *self-remembering* would develop. The individual will have a growing direct relation with the universe, a ceaseless and growing intuition of the cause and effect relations which surround us and, among other things, determine the conditioning of ourselves and others.

When the centers were in balance—a very rare occurrence—new intuitive powers beyond the faculties of the rational mind would develop. Higher emotions would also develop, superceding the lower emotions of anger, jealousy, envy, fear.

The goal of Gurdjieff's work is to wake man up so that he does not sleepwalk through his life. To accomplish this, Gurdjieff and his students developed many exercises and techniques—most of which are described in the following books, although reading can never take the place of practical application.

Gurdjieff worked and taught in the West for about 30 years and his ideas have been very influential, especially in intellectual circles.

GURDJIEFF, GEORGE. **ALL AND EVERYTHING: BEELZEBUB'S TALES TO HIS GRANDSON,** c$11.95/8.95. First Series. Gurdjieff's purpose is *to destroy, mercilessly, without any compromises whatever, in the mentations and feelings of the reader the beliefs and views, by centuries rooted in him about everything existing in this world.* In the form of a myth on a cosmic scale, Gurdjieff's intention is to show how human life is growing steadily more empty of meaning. He traces, with compassion and often with humor, the causes of man's alienation from the real sources of life. He integrates his conception of man in a new and universal science, embracing all fields of thought and endeavor and every period of history. A monumental work. 1238pp. Dut 50

_____. **GUIDE AND INDEX TO GURDJIEFF'S ALL AND EVERYTHING,** c$9.95. This is an excellent aid for those who want to study certain topics in **Beelzebub.** Many ideas and words are listed in alphabetical order, with sub-headings under the main heading, explanatory phrases, and page references. There is also a page correlation for the paperback edition. The book was prepared by members of a Gurdjieff group in Toronto. 680pp. TrS 73

_____. **HERALD OF COMING GOOD: FIRST APPEAL TO CONTEMPORARY HUMANITY,** $3.50. Gurdjieff's first book, and the only one published (in 1933) during his lifetime. An early attempt to get his teachings into written form. 87pp. Wei 74

_____. **MEETINGS WITH REMARKABLE MEN,** c$7.50/2.25. **Meetings** consists of a series of stories, each bearing as its title the name of one of the men Gurdjieff knew in his early life, including his father and masters that he met in his travels. *As he grew his urge to understand the meaning of human life became so strong that he attracted a group of remarkable men—among whom were engineers, doctors, archaeologists. . . . In search of a knowledge which they were certain had existed in the past but of which almost all traces seemed to have disappeared, he set out with them to explore many countries in the Middle East and Central Asia. . . . If Gurdjieff speaks of himself, he does so to serve his life-long purpose. It is apparent that this is not an autobiography in the strict sense of the word. For him the past is not worth recounting except in so far as it can serve as example. In these tales of adventure what he suggests are not models for outward imitation, but a completely new way of facing life, which touches us directly and gives us foretaste of another order of reality.* The book also includes background prefaces and a long rambling introduction by Gurdjieff himself. In a final chapter, *The Material Question,* he reviews his activities, financial and otherwise, since coming to Europe. Many readers feel that this book is easier to read than **Beelzebub,** so, even though it is the Second Series, it is often read first. And it can be read on the surface as an entertaining narrative—although that certainly was not what Gurdjieff had in mind when he wrote it. 314pp. Dut 69

_____. **VIEWS FROM THE REAL WORLD,** $3.95. A collection of talks and lectures that Gurdjieff gave in the period 1917-33. Gurdjieff did not permit his pupils to take notes while they were working with him—so these selections are made up of carefully selected notes made up by various students shortly after the actual talks were made. Some of the selections are followed by questions and answers and the selections themselves allow the reader a glimpse of Gurdjieff's own techniques and how he applied his theory in various contexts. This should not be read as a first book by someone seeking to understand Gurdjieff and his system, but it is excellent supplementary reading for all who have had some exposure to the system. The talks are wide-ranging and, at least for this reader, many concepts are expressed and illustrated better in this selection than anywhere else. Also included is a translation of the aphorisms which Gurdjieff had inscribed above the walls of the study house at his Institute, as well as *Glimpses of the Truth,* a long essay on Gurdjieff and his ideas written by one of his Russian pupils around 1914. This contains germs of what is developed more fully in **In Search of the Miraculous,** along with a more personal approach toward the ideas and their application. 288pp. Dut 74

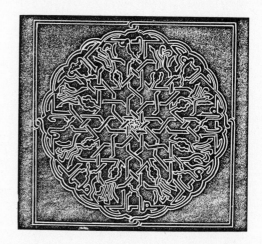

HODGSON, A.M. **BIRTH TO ADULTHOOD,** $1.95. A systematic study of child development based on Gurdjieffian principles by a close associate of J.G. Bennett. Many diagrams are included. 50pp. CSP 65

HULME, KATHRYN. **UNDISCOVERED COUNTRY— IN SEARCH OF GURDJIEFF,** $3.95. Another personal memoir of time spent studying with Gurdjieff in France during his last years. Ms. Hulme is a novelist, author of **The Nun's Story,** and she has brilliantly evoked the *very wise old man sitting in his rich pantry of foods and thoughts* telling his students *Know thyself.* 306pp. LBC 66

LEFORT, RAFAEL. THE TEACHERS OF GURDJIEFF, $2.45. A record of a journey which purports to trace the sources of Gurdjieff's teachings, following clues provided in his writings. Rumor has it that Idries Shah is the true author of this book. It is very anti-Gurdjieff, or at least anti the Gurdjieffian movements of today. Each of the stages that the author found stated that Gurdjieff's teachings—as interpreted by various disciples—are a dead end to today's seekers. Central concepts in Sufi philosophy are well described. 151pp. Wei 63

MAURICE NICOLL

Maurice Nicoll was a noted physician and an early believer in psychological medicine. He was a pupil of Carl Jung for a period. He met Ouspensky in 1921 and later studied directly under Gurdjieff as well as Ouspensky. He became a teacher on his own in 1931 and was formally named as Ouspensky's successor in his school. Nicoll's interpretations are especially valuable because he applied what he had learned from Gurdjieff to the interpretation of Christian scripture.

NICOLL, MAURICE. LIVING TIME AND THE INTEGRATION OF LIFE, c$6.50. Quotations, notes, and observations referring to the invisible side of things, taken from the standpoint of dimensions (not taken mathematically) and also from the related standpoint of higher levels of consciousness. The question of a new understanding of time, and of what life means in the light of this understanding is discussed. The possibility of a change in the time-sense, with a changed feeling of oneself, enters into this question. Also eternity and reincarnation are reviewed. Nicoll's major philosophical work. 245pp. Wat

_____. **THE MARK,** c$6.50. A companion volume to **The New Man** which discusses, in relation to the Gospels, the idea that real religion is latent but unborn in every man. The end of the transformation of a man is thought of as *the mark* to be aimed at. The word *sin* means in the literal Greek *missing the mark*. Here, in passages of great beauty, is the key for those who long for a greater understanding of the teaching of Christ and the meaning of our existence. 216pp. Wat 54

_____. **THE NEW MAN—AN INTERPRETATION OF SOME PARABLES AND MIRACLES OF CHRIST,** $2.00. *All sacred writings contain an outer and an inner meaning; behind the literal words lies another range of meanings, another form of knowledge.* Penetrating to this inner knowledge, Nicoll finds that the Gospels are about transcending the violence that characterizes mankind's present level of being. 184pp. Pen 50

_____. **PSYCHOLOGICAL COMMENTARIES ON THE TEACHINGS OF GURD-JIEFF AND OUSPENSKY.** Commentaries written from Dr. Nicoll's own understanding of the teaching of Gurdjieff and Ouspensky in its practical application to himself and to the members of his groups. They were begun during the years of the last World War and continued afterwards, taking the form of weekly papers to members of the groups who were scattered over the world. In these papers the fundamental ideas of the system of Gurdjieff and Ouspensky are expounded with clarity so that the reader is helped toward understanding the efforts required to reach that individual level of development indicated as the goal of all great religions—attainable only by practical work on oneself. They can be read in any order. We recommend them highly. Wat

_____. **VOL. I—1941-43,** c$9.50. 373pp.

_____. **VOL. II—1944-45,** c$9.50. 402pp.

_____. **VOL. III, 1945-48,** c$9.50. 449pp.

_____. **VOL. IV—1948-51,** c$8.50. 277pp.

_____. **VOL. V—1951-53,** c$8.50. 263pp.

NOTT, C.S. JOURNEY THROUGH THIS WORLD: MEETINGS WITH GURDJIEFF, ORAGE AND OUSPENSKY, c$6.95. It contains a summary of Gurdjieff's booklet **Herald**

of Coming Good. Throughout the narrative there runs as a central theme the teaching of Gurdjieff, its impact on Nott and his continuation of the Work. Wei 69

_____. **TEACHINGS OF GURDJIEFF,** c$6.95. This *Journal of a Pupil* is a sincere narrative of a young seeker who meets Gurdjieff in New York and is convinced by seeing the demonstrations of sacred dances that at last he has found the Way he is looking for. It is a record, compiled from hundreds of pages of notebooks and diaries, of the sayings and doings of Gurdjieff and their impact on Nott as well as descriptions of a pupil's life at Prieure, Gurdjieff's school near Paris. Much of the book consists of Orage's discourses to his Gurdjieff group in New York. These include commentary on **Beelzebub.** 228pp. Wei 62

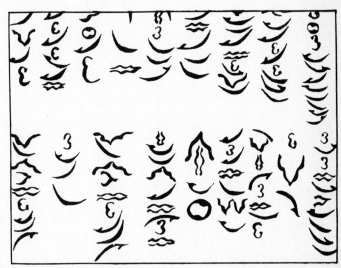

Transliteration: Always remember that you came here having already understood the necessity of contending with yourself, only with yourself, and therefore thank everyone who affords such opportunities (one of the Study House Aphorisms)

ORAGE, A.R. CONSCIOUSNESS, $1.95. This is a study of pure consciousness and an exploration of the differences between our inner and outer senses. The material originally was given in the form of four lectures on the nature of consciousness, and on animal, human, and superhuman consciousness. This is a very clear presentation, recently reprinted. 86pp. Wei 74

_____. **ON LOVE—WITH SOME APHORISMS AND OTHER ESSAYS,** $1.95. Four essays written after Orage came in contact with Gurdjieff's system: *On Love, On Religion, What is the Soul?* and *Talks with Katherine Mansfield at Fontainebleu.* The aphorisms were given out in his talks to the groups in New York, 1924-30. Includes a detailed biography or Orage, very clearly presented material. 72pp. Wei 74

_____. **PSYCHOLOGICAL EXERCISES AND ESSAYS,** $1.95. Over 200 *practical exercises which were used for years in classes consisting of students varying in age from 12 to 60. The results were observed and checked and the conclusion is that the exercises, at first utterly impossible, became with practice relatively easy; and that along with the increased facility in the exercises themselves, the facility in the use of the mind upon ordinary exercises is enormously increased. The fifteen essays are on topics such as How to Learn to Think, Can Intuition Be Acquired?, On Daily Dying, Doing as One Likes.* Recommended. 123pp. Wei 74

P. D. OUSPENSKY

P.D. Ouspensky was a noted Russian mathematician and writer. After journeying extensively through Europe, the Middle East, and South Asia in a quest for the *miraculous,* in 1915 he met Gurdjieff and began studying with him. From that time on his interest was centered in the practical study of methods for the development of consciousness in man. After the Revolution he moved to London and began a series of lectures which eventually led to the establishment of study groups concerned with working with Gurdjieff's ideas. Ouspensky continued his work in London until 1940, lecturing to many influential Englishmen and women. From 1940 until his death in 1947 he worked in the U.S.

OUSPENSKY, P.D. THE FOURTH WAY, c$10.00/2.95. Consists of verbatim extracts from talks and answers to questions given by Ouspensky between 1921 and 1946. The first chapter is a general survey of the fundamental ideas which in subsequent chapters are amplified subject by subject in the specific order followed by Ouspensky. This book is very helpful for those who wish to follow the *fourth way* (and not retire from the world) but do not have a teacher and therefore need lucid explanations of the practical side of the work. Very carefully indexed. 437pp. RaH 71

_____. **IN SEARCH OF THE MIRACULOUS**, c$12.00/3.25. The most complete rendition of intellectual aspects of Gurdjieff's teachings. Hardly anyone understands it on first (or even second) reading, but if you are interested in Gurdjieff, you'll be fascinated by his cosmology and his rendering of the ancient truths. There's an emphasis on math that you can skip if your mind is not so inclined and still have much to ponder about. Highly recommended. 387pp. HBJ 49

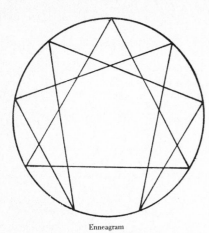

Enneagram

_____. **A NEW MODEL OF THE UNIVERSE**, c$8.95/2.95. Written directly after the time Ouspensky spent *in search of the miraculous*. He analyzes the ancient teachings and connects them with modern concepts of physics and philosophy. Includes in depth explorations of esotericism and modern thought, the fourth dimension, the idea of the superman, Christianity and the New Testament, the symbolism of the Tarot, yoga, dreams and hypnotism, experimental mysticism, reincarnation, sex and evolution. There also are sketches of various masters he met in his journey. It's easier reading than the rest of Ouspensky and quite fascinating. 467pp. RaH 71

_____. **THE PSYCHOLOGY OF MAN'S POSSIBLE EVOLUTION**, c$5.95/1.95. Five lectures which were delivered by Ouspensky from time to time as an introductory course for those who came to study with him in London and New York—revised shortly before his death, to be published after the general system of Gurdjieff's teaching should have appeared in print. They give a clear and simple account of Gurdjieff's teaching on man and his nature and make the concepts accessible to the uninitiated reader. The paperback contains some additional material. 114pp. RaH 73

_____. **STRANGE LIFE OF IVAN OSOKIN**, $1.65. The problems of duration, of infinity, of eternal recurrence were crucial to P.D. Ouspensky's thought. This is his only novel. 204pp. Pen 71

_____. **TALKS WITH A DEVIL**, c$5.95. The first translation of two stories, written in 1914, which express Ouspensky's belief that man's chief error is to believe that the material world is the only reality. Two problems are examined. The first is conscious evil and is illustrated by the story of an inventor who does harm particularly when he intends to do good and cannot bring himself to accept the disastrous consequences of his own work of genius. It is an allegory of modern man faced with the consequences of the miracles of science and technology. The second problem is brought out by the suggestion that the devils are interested in man only when he makes an effort to escape. Only a few people can recognize that the price of doing the right thing is inevitably to expose onself to opposition and even to the threat of destruction. Edited and introduced by J.G. Bennett. 155pp. RaH 72

_____. **TERTIUM ORGANUM—A KEY TO THE ENIGMAS OF THE WORLD**, c$12.00/2.95. Ouspensky's second book, written before his encounter with Gurdjieff. In it he formulates a philosophy based on the mathematical concept known as the fourth dimension, the fourth form of the manifestation of consciousness—the intuitional. This work is an attempt to formulate a new logic which will deal with this higher consciousness, a bold attempt to reorganize all knowledge. It is a heavy book that requires ability to handle mathematical concepts. 310pp. RaH 70

PAUWELS, LOUIS. **GURDJIEFF**, $5.00. A critical survey of various students' experiences with the work. Includes both positive and negative reactions as well as long extracts from diaries and letters. Pauwels himself had a terrible experience with Gurdjieff which almost led to his death, so this colors the reporting. 456pp. Wei 54

PETERS, FRITZ. **BOYHOOD WITH GURDJIEFF**, $1.65. Peters spent four years at Gurdjieff's Institute. This covered the period before, during, and after the auto accident that cut the work of the Institute short and led ultimately to Gurdjieff's writing. This is the only book that covers that period and although the reader does not get much feeling

for Gurdjieff's ideas, s/he can get a good picture of a young boy's impression of him, recalled years later. A very personal account. 175pp. Pen 64

_____. **GURDJIEFF REMEMBERED**, $2.25. Describes Peters' later encounter with Gurdjieff in Paris, New York, and Chicago. It is more a story of the man than the teaching, although a good deal of personal instruction comes through. 160pp. Wei 7

POPOFF, IRMIS. **GURDJIEFF: HIS WORK ON MYSELF WITH OTHERS, FOR THE WORK**, c$5.95. Ms. Popoff studied with both Ouspensky and Gurdjieff. She mainl worked with Ouspensky's group in New York and it is the experiences in that group an the work she continues to do today that she reconstructs here. This is a very subjective account and the experiences she recounts are not found in any of the other person accounts, most of which are by pupils who studied in Europe. Of special interest is th vivid picture she gives of the exercises and the meaning of the enneagram. Indexed, 198pp Wei 73

TRAVERS, P.L. **GEORGE IVANOVITCH GURDJIEFF**, $1.20. A brief biographic sketch which indicates some of the broad currents in his teaching. TsP 73

WALKER, KENNETH. **THE MAKING OF MAN**, c$5.95. An autobiographical account o the time Walker spent studying under Ouspensky and Gurdjieff as well as his encounter with Maurice Nicoll, published six years after **A Study**. He transcribes various talks as we as incidents. There are chapters on Special Movements and Dance, Gurdjieff as a Teache The Death of Gurdjieff, as well as a commentary on **All and Everything**. Another excellen presentation. 159pp. RKP

_____. **A STUDY OF GURDJIEFF'S TEACHING**, $3.50. Walker is a British phy sician who studied Gurdjieff's system for many years, first under Ouspensky, and the under Gurdjieff himself. He expounds in outline the ideas themselves, with the help o diagrams and compares them with kindred ideas obtained from scientific, religious, an philosophical sources, both Eastern and Western. Though he acknowledges that *formula tion and printing squeeze out of the spoken word* [Gurdjieff's teaching was essentially oral *almost all of its vitality*, Walker has made as clear and thoughtful a presentation as w have seen. Recommended as the best introduction to Gurdjieff for those who don't wan to plunge into the rigors of **In Search**. 216pp. Wei 74

Majlis and dhikr of the Mevlevi dervishes (from a nineteenth century woodcut)

REMDE, HENRY. **THE ART IN A CRAFT**, $4.95. A spiritual study of what is require to become a true craftsman. If a craft can be a vehicle for inner understanding, this book points the way. It draws us past technical competence towards an awareness—on anothe level—of the three inner laws of craftsmanship. Oversize, illustrated, 36pp. TsP 75

REYMOND, LIZELLE. **TO LIVE WITHIN**, $1.75. See the Indian Philosophy section

ROPP, ROBERT de. **THE MASTER GAME**, $2.25. **The Master Game**, *which involves the awakening of the powers latent in man, can no more be played by swallowing a pill than can a difficult mountain be ascended by sitting in an armchair drinking beer and indulging in daydreams*. De Ropp restates Gurdjieff's philosophy in a modern manner and integrates it with psychology. It offers a synthesis of many practical methods derived from different sources for attaining full awakening. 245pp. Del

_____. **SEX ENERGY**, $2.45. Examines the role of sex energy in human behavior (as well as in plants, insects, and animals) from both a physiological and a historical point of view. 227pp. Del

_____. **VENTURE WITH IDEAS**, c$5.95. Walker's first attempt, newly reprinted at presenting the impact Gurdjieff's and Ouspensky's ideas had upon him, trained as h was in the scientific method. The book *is the chronicle of a journey through the bewilder ing inner world of ideas, a journey in which I was fortunate enough to have two remark able men as guides*. A clear, personal presentation. 192pp. Wei 51

WELCH, LOUISE. **THE OLD MAN RIDES A BICYCLE**, $2.95. A children's book written by a member of the Toronto Gurdjieff group that presents a young boy's journey of ex ploration into reality. TsP 72

HEALING

here is a healing process, in which the sick matter, rediscovering the original
rm of nature, again becomes a channel for life; and is restored to health. . . .

plied here is the rediscovery of an original principle, and its adaptation to
e new or abnormal circumstance. For example, certain poisonous matters
gin to accumulate in the fleshy layers of the body. After a time the condi-
on becomes too acute to be relieved by the normal methods of excretion.
he white corpuscles of the blood, however, are perfectly endowed with the
ower and duty of eliminating poisons. Surrounding and isolating the poison
ith pus, they *invent* a form of excretion. A boil develops, comes to head, and
ursts. The poisons are expelled, and if the condition is not too general, the
ssue heals.

here are in the body healing agents of all kinds. But in some cases their
ork can be helped by the assistance of drugs and medicines of a similar na-
ure. . . . These are matters containing in concentrated essence that natural
rinciple, which is necessary to correct the abnormality and restore the heal-
y form. In the case of the boil, the doctor applies certain salts which con-
ain the natural tendency to draw out or suck the poisons from the flesh. He
tilizes the same principle on a molecular level by applying heat in the form
f a hot compress. In other words, he remembers and uses natural laws, to
vent a way of returning the organism to a form through which life and
lood can again flow freely.

lready in this example we see the process of healing working on two levels.
irst, there is the natural physiological healing in the body itself. Secondly,
his process is supported by human ingenuity, expressed in the art of medi-
ine. The two processes are the same: the scale and medium of their opera-
ion is different. In the first case we see the process operating in the cellular
vorld, in the second in the world of man. In the first it appears to us as heal-
ng power, in the second as invention, skill, or applied science, that is, the
ntentional use of natural laws.

The Physician Curing Fantasy (French School, Seventeenth century).

Healing, fundamentally, is that which restores to health things touched by
the corruptive or criminal process. When corruption begins to degenerate the
matters of his own body . . . [man] can not remain . . . indifferent, and must
strive to stop the rot and make them whole again. . . . Thus medicine is born.

In the Middle Ages a very elaborate and interesting system of medicine was
developed on the basis of classifying organs and organisms according to the
four *humours*—hot, cold, wet and dry—and after diagnosing an excess of one
or deficiency of another, trying to restore the balance by supplying the opposite *humour* through treatments and medicaments classified in a similar
way. The method of healing by balancing the four humours is still used, for
example, in applying *cold* compresses to a *hot* fever, or in prescribing a *dry*
climate for a *moist* condition like tuberculosis. And if this system as a whole
is now discredited, it is not because it was mistaken or superstitious in itself,
but only because the underlying principle has since been lost, and a completely different system of medicine constructed on another basis.

Old medicine was almost entirely based on treating the body as a whole, or
on treating individual organs. Besides being studied from the point of view of
the humours, these organs were classified according to their affinity with the
planets, and herbal medicines—classified in the same way—used to stimulate
the response to one or another planetary influence. Again, the principle used
in healing was the restoration of harmony—*in the world of organs.*

It was the study of the cellular structure of plants and animals in the 1830's,
the discovery of the dance of *active molecules* by Brown about the same
time, and the subsequent synthesis of organic compounds, which really led
to the overthrow of mediaeval medicine. For with this knowledge came the
possibility of a medicine which should restore harmony not only in the world
of organs, but in the world of cells and even of molecules. Such treatment
applied directly to lower cosmoses, and *utilizing the times of those cosmoses,*
could of course yield results very much faster than the old-fashioned treatment of organs. And its speed and exactness seemed literally miraculous in
comparison, as intervention of the laws of another cosmos must always seem
miraculous from the point of view of our own.

Study of the life of cells brought to light the role of bacteria, the accomplices
of corruption on a cellular level. And very much of the enormous progress of
medicine under Pasteur and Lister in the second half of the nineteenth century was based on asepsis or antisepsis, that is, the elimination or destruction
of these agents of disease *in the cellular world.*

Later, with the work of Ehrlich, who combined germicides with dyes which
were known to stain only specific tissues, chemists began to work in a still
smaller, a still faster world. Ehrlich created nearly a thousand different molecular combinations in an attempt to produce chemical messengers which,
introduced into the body, would perform one specific task, *in the molecular
world.*

This technique led to the discovery of the various *sulpha* drugs, with their
amazing power of penetration and speed of action. Acting thus directly to
restore balance in the world of molecules modern doctors can, in some cases,
effect cures in the course of hours, which old-fashioned medicine working in
the world of organs, might take weeks or even months to achieve. From the
point of view of speed and accuracy, this is an immense improvement.

What has not yet been taken into account, however, is the fact that by working directly in the world of molecules, modern medicine often bypasses and
undermines the *intelligence of organs.* Fundamentally, old medicine recognized that each organ has its own intelligence, capable—with help—of diagnosing its own malady and producing its own antidote. These intelligences of
different organs are in fact linked together in a general intelligence for the
whole instinctive function, which, if trusted and not thwarted, can save the
human organism from almost any ill which may befall it.

Modern medicine, working on a molecular level, for the most part ignores
this instinctive intelligence altogether, and by going below it, so to speak,

often undermines its authority and power. It is as if a patient, instead of entrusting himself to the responsibility of a large hospital, with its wise director and many subservient specialists and departments, went straight to the research laboratory and persuaded the assistant there to prescribe his latest drug. Although an occasional cure might prove startling, such a practice would soon make the healing work of the hospital as a whole completely impossible. In the same way, over-indulgence in molecular drugs working with startling power and speed, may undermine the organism's power of self-healing and recuperation in the future.

At the same time, it is quite clear that medicine can not go back on its own discoveries, cannot retreat from the world of molecules into which its healing has now penetrated. In fact, there is only one way out. For healing to be complete, that is, for it to achieve the real benefit of the whole man, rather than the killing of a particular germ or the stimulation of a particular hormone, the patient must himself make acquaintance with the intelligence of his own instinctive function. He must first listen within himself for its voice, and when he recognizes and distinguishes this voice, he must trust in its wishes and obey its commands. If he does this, the process of healing will begin in him on a scale which may in time make the intervention of external medicine unnecessary altogether.

In fact, the possibility exists that he may acquire the power of acting directly on instinctive intelligence with the mind; that is, he may place in the cellular organ an exact electronic image of health to which it must inevitably conform. This possibility lies behind true faith-healing, the methods of Christian Science, and so on. The problem is that it requires very great mental control, a completely positive attitude, and the knack of communicating with the organs in their own language. Moreover, it is often simulated by a kind of self-hypnosis, when the process of disease continues as before, but the patient persuades himself that he feels no symptoms. This is exactly putting instinctive intelligence to sleep.

It is instinctive intelligence, indeed, which provides the link between physiological healing and intellectual invention—those two main aspects of the process which we are studying. For above the level of cells and organs, what is invented by man's mind, and what is invented by his other functions, working through the instinctive intelligence, becomes increasingly mingled. We may even suppose that all the inventions of man's mind are the result of some subtle realization of the natural principles, laws or devices which are all the time operating in the mechanics of his skeletal movements, the chemistry of his digestion, the electric phenomena of his nervous system, and so on.

The aberrations of human ingenuity, however, should never make us overlook the fact that the true end-product of this process is indeed *life*—increased vitality, power, opportunity and so on. This is most clear in physiological and even psychological healing, where this process really means the correction of an abnormality, that is, it counters a tendency or secretion which has exceeded its function, or stimulates one which is deficient. Thus the goal of the healing process is to produce a *normal* or harmonious organism, for it is only in such an organism that life flows most abundantly.

Exactly the same process and the same agents in the body reorganize matter in a form to preserve life in changed circumstances. By it, the human organism miraculously adapts itself to extreme heat, extreme cold, long fasting or lack of sleep. By it the blind man begins to *see* with the skin of his face, the deaf man to *hear* with the bone of his skull.

This is the process by which errors and disasters can be repaired, a damaged organ return to health, and man approach normality by right understanding of natural law.

—from **THE THEORY OF CELESTIAL INFLUENCE** by Rodney Collin

ACADEMY OF PARAPSYCHOLOGY AND MEDICINE. **THE DIMENSIONS OF HEALING**, $10.00. Transcript of the Fall 1972 program, including individual research as well as theoretical constructs for viewing the *whole man*. It contains addresses of Drs. Puryear, Worrall, Grad, Chaudhuri, Green, Puharich, Tiller, McGarey, Moss, Bradley, Simonton, Sister Justa Smith, Mr. Dean and Mr. Johnson, and Edgar Mitchell. Includes questions and discussion as well as two lectures from the professional medical seminar on acupuncture by Drs. McGarey and Puharich. 172pp. APM 72

_____. **THE VARIETIES OF HEALING EXPERIENCE**, $5.00. The complete transcript of the Academy's October 1971 interdisciplinary symposium. Includes addresses of Drs. Holland, Lilly, Green, Puharich, Tiller, McGarey, and Bradley on a variety of healing phenomena related to the parapsychological capabilities of man. 112pp. APM 7

AIROLA, PAAVO. **HEALTH SECRETS FROM EUROPE**, $1.65. An excellent report by a Swedish naturopath reveals the nutrition and vitamin-mineral therapies now in use in some of Europe's leading natural health centers and progressive medical clinics. This book is composed of easy-to-follow, do-it-yourself instructions based on European studies and experiences. Fully indexed, with references. 224pp. Arc 70

_____. **HOW TO GET WELL**, c$8.95. This is Dr. Airola's *magnum opus*, a complete handbook of natural healing, written for professionals or informed laymen. This is the comprehensive reference work on therapeutic uses of foods, vitamins, food supplements, juices, herbs, fasting, baths, heat therapies and other nutritional and biologic modalities in the treatment of most common diseases. The first 160 pages provide the information in relation to a wide variety of diseases and conditions ranging from acne and alcoholism to warts and worms. This is followed by sections on protection against common poisons in our environment, directions for recommended therapies, recipes and charts and tables. Extensive references and index. This is our favorite home medical encyclopedia. 301pp. HPP 74

AMBER, R. **PULSE IN THE OCCIDENT AND ORIENT**, c$15.00. A detailed scholarly study of the pulse and pulse diagnosis in the East and West. The material is arranged in almost outline form and the text includes an abundance of footnotes. Index, 218pp. NYA 66

ARTHRITIS

The Arthritis Foundation, which is the leading authority in the United States, has flatly stated: *The relationship between diet and arthritis has been thoroughly and scientifically studied. The simple proven fact is: no food has anything to do with causing arthritis and no food is effective in treating or curing it.* Along with this view, conventional medicine has little to offer the arthritic except aspirin and sympathy.

Fortunately, there are a number of doctors who didn't accept the Foundation's simple proven fact and who have explored the relationship between arthritis—which is not one but many different diseases—and metabolic, nutritional and biochemical factors. They have frequently had remarkable success in treating arthritis by treating the whole person. If you are one of the twenty million in this country who suffer from arthritis and want more than aspirin and sympathy, you would do well to start reading among these books and decide if you wish to make the changes in eating and living habits that might bring the relief so desperately sought.

AIROLA, PAAVO. **THERE IS A CURE FOR ARTHRITIS**, $2.95. This is our most popular book on arthritis. Anything Dr. Airola writes, we find worth reading. PrH 68

CAMPBELL, GIRAUD W. **A DOCTOR'S PROVEN NEW HOME CURE FOR ARTHRITIS**, $2.95. Written by an osteopath, this book recommends avoidance of all processed and adulterated foods, use of raw and natural foods, good elimination, and a certain amount of osteopathic manipulation and exercise as needed. Although written with a little too much hype for our taste, the concepts appear sound and certainly worth trying by anyone suffering from arthritis. Bibliography, index. 224pp. PrH 72

DONG, COLLIN H. and JANE BANKS. **NEW HOPE FOR THE ARTHRITIC**, c$6.95. Dr. Dong, who has treated thousands of arthritics over forty years, hypothesizes that the inciting factors are food allergens. The Dong diet avoids milk products, most meats, and fruits and fruit juices, as well as the usual chemical additives, etc. It's not too different from the recommendations of many nutritionists for good health and long life. This book contains a review of standard treatments of arthritis, many case histories, discussion of the Dong diet, menus and several dozen recipes. There is also a chapter on use of acupuncture in arthritis. Extensive bibliography, index. 269pp. Cro 75

JARVIS, D.C. **ARTHRITIS AND FOLK MEDICINE**, $1.25. Dr. Jarvis is the M.D. who made an extensive study of folk medicine, observed the care of plants and animals, and reached many important conclusions for his medical practice that differed from what he had been taught in medical school. This book is fascinating reading because it goes back to basics and lets us see why things work the way they do. In particular, he advocates the use of vinegar and honey to keep blood calcium in solution so that it doesn't precipitate in the cells. How and why this works is explained in the text. In addition to any other book you read about arthritis, we think you'll find a great deal of interest in this one to help you understand how the body works. Index, 144pp. Faw 60

SPEIGHT, PHYLLIS. **OVERCOMING RHEUMATISM AND ARTHRITIS**, $1.10. 61pp. HSP 76

ARMBRAND, MAX. **HOW THOUSANDS OF MY ARTHRITIS PATIENTS. . . .**, $1.65. milar to the following book, but written in a somewhat more popular vein. Includes et, how to use water for relief of pain, exercises and helpful manipulative techniques, e role of vitamins and food supplements, recipes and a guide to meals and beverages. dex, 225pp. Arc 70

_____. **NEW HOPE FOR ARTHRITIS SUFFERERS**, c$4.95. Dr. Warmbrand oints out that the use of cortisone demonstrates that arthritis is a metabolic disorder; owever, cortisone, like other drugs, has undesirable side effects. His method of therapy lies primarily on proper diet as part of a new way of life that will bring into play the atural healing power inherent in the organism. This book covers the dietary and exer- se requirements, tells what to expect during the transition period (problems that may be ncountered) and also discusses related afflictions such as gout, rheumatic fever, bursitis nd slipped discs. 153pp. TPL 68

_____. **OVERCOMING ARTHRITIS AND OTHER RHEUMATIC DISEASES**, 8.95. This book presents an extremely positive, practical approach to treatment. etoxification and raw foods form the basis of his approach. The elimination of stress nd a life in harmony with nature are equally important, as is appropriate exercise. This is simply written account, replete with case studies which should inspire and aid all rthritic sufferers. Dr. Warmbrand is one of America's best known naturopathic physi- ans. 220pp. DAC 76

ELSH, PHILLIP. **HOW TO BE FREE FROM ARTHRITIS**, $7.95. Dr. Welsh is a dentist nd naturopath, with more than fifty years of experience treating people nutritionally. e considers white sugar, white flour and salt to be the three leading offenders in arthritis. ll additives must also be avoided. He prescribes a cleansing course and then a basic diet rimarily of fresh fruits and vegetables. This book is written in a simple style, and is easy follow. It also includes quotations from many other writers who have treated arthritis utritionally, plus a large number of recipes. Oversize, bibliography. 107pp. WoP 74

DWARD BACH

ach was an English physician who felt that sickness and disease were pri- narily due not to physical causes, but to some deeper disharmony within the ufferer himself. These conclusions were strengthened and confirmed by his bservations during sixteen years of practice. In 1930 he determined to de- ote all of his time to the search for a simple method of treatment and armless remedies among the wild flowers of the countryside. He worked ith them until his death in 1936 and found thirty-eight remedies; all, with ne exception, the flowers of plants, trees, and bushes. The remedies are pre- cribed not directly for the physical complaint, but rather according to the ufferer's state of mind, according to his moods of fear, worry, anger or de- ression. The patient himself decides which remedies he/she should take and ow long to continue taking them. The remedies are absolutely benign in heir action. Therefore they can be safely prescribed and used by anyone.

ACH, EDWARD. **HEAL THYSELF**, $.85. Dr. Bach's first book on his philosophy of ealing, subtitled *An Explanation of the Real Cause and Cure of Disease*. 56pp. Dan 31

_____. **TWELVE HEALERS**, $.60. Bach's basic book, in which he describes hirty-eight remedies, one for each of the most common negative states of mind, or noods that afflict mankind. He divided these negative states of mind into seven groups nder the following headings: fear, uncertainty, insufficient interest in present circum- tances, loneliness, oversensitivity to influences and ideas, despondency or despair, and verconcern for the welfare of others. In addition, he gives directions for preparation nd dosage. 30pp. Dan 33

HANCELLOR, PHILIP, ed. **HANDBOOK OF THE BACH FLOWER REMEDIES**, c$6.60. his is the newest and most comprehensive of the books on the remedies. Much of the naterial is taken from **The Bach Remedy News Letter**, published by Nora Weeks. In- ludes an excellent section, *Prescribing and the Interview: for Oneself, for Pregnancy and hildbirth, for Children, for Mental Distress, for Animals, for Plants*. There's also a separate hapter on each of the remedies and notes on prescribing, together with many case istories to illustrate the use of the remedies in the home as well as by the practitioner. ndex, bibliography. 251pp. Dan 71

VANS, JANE. **INTRODUCTION TO THE BENEFITS OF THE BACH FLOWER REMEDIES**, $.60. 19pp. Dan 74

WEEKS, NORA. **THE MEDICAL DISCOVERIES OF EDWARD BACH, PHYSICIAN**, $2.40. Ms. Weeks runs the Bach Healing Centre in England and is the editor of **The Bach Remedy Newsletter**. This is the only critical account of his work available. 144pp. Dan 40

WEEKS, NORA and VICTOR BULLEN. **BACH FLOWER REMEDIES**, c$9.25. Contains botanical descriptions and colored illustrations of the remedy flowers and the exact method of preparing each. 98pp. Dan 64

WHEELER, F.J. **THE BACH FLOWER REMEDIES REPERTORY**, $.60. A supplemen- tary guide to the use of the herbal remedies discovered by Dr. Bach, designed as an aid to those seeking to develop their own ability to choose and administer the right remedy. n outline form. 28pp. Dan 52

BAILEY, ALICE. **ESOTERIC HEALING**, $5.75. *In this book the seven ray techniques of healing are described, the laws and rules of healing are enumerated and discussed, the*

requirements for healing are given in detail, and basic causes of diseases are shown. We learn, for example, that much disease can be karmic in origin, that certain diseases are in- herent in the soil and the substance of the planet, and that many others are psychological, arising in the mental and emotional bodies. See our Theosophy section. 771pp. LPC 53

BAKER, DOUGLAS. **ESOTERIC HEALING**, $12.50. This is the most comprehensive treatise we have seen on the title subject. Baker is an English surgeon, among other things. This 11¾x8" tome is profusely illustrated, including many full color plates, and is divided into four parts: *The Origin and Nature of Esoteric Healing, Some Common Disorders, Some Esoteric Healing Methods,* and *Nutrition and Preventive Medicine*. The techniques and background material emphasize the energy centers and rays and the use of healing energy in general. The material is practical and well organized and the illustrations help illuminate the text. Bak 75

BENJAMIN, HARRY. **EVERYBODY'S GUIDE TO NATURE CURE**, c$11.70. A com- prehensive and illuminating treatise on the nature of disease and its treatment by natural methods by an English naturopath. Includes in depth discussions of diseases of all parts of the human organism, with specific as well as general treatments. Index, 487pp. TPL 61

BOYD, DOUG. **ROLLING THUNDER**, $3.45. Rolling Thunder is an American Indian medicine man. As a medicine man, or shaman, he is guardian of a wealth of knowledge that has been passed down through countless Indian generations. This knowledge includes the power to cure disease and heal wounds, to find and use medicinal herbs, to make rain, to transport objects through the air, and to communicate telepathically. These powers come out of his special relationship with nature, with what can only be called a *spirit of the earth*. This remarkable book is a record of an attempt to learn something about the sources of the medicine man's powers. With Rolling Thunder's full cooperation, Doug Boyd, on a research field trip for the Menninger Foundation, spent a long time observing him and he reports in detail on his observations here. A fascinating account. 283pp. Del 74

BRENA, STEVEN. **YOGA AND MEDICINE**, $2.45. This book contends that the average human has far too little control over his own mental and physical health. With this in mind, Dr. Brena, an American physician, reviews both the medical and the yogic concepts of anatomy, physiology, nutrition, respiration, sexual activity, pathology, and pain. In each case he makes a comparative analysis, stressing the many similarities as well as the fundamental differences. Notes and illustrations. 175pp. Vik 72

BRODSKY, GREG. **FROM EDEN TO AQUARIUS**, $1.95. This is a well written, excel- lent survey with chapters on mind and meditation, breath and energy, food as natural medicine, hydrotherapy, movement, Swedish massage, acupuncture, and Oriental massage. Brodsky has studied and practiced many of these disciplines and incorporates his spiritual training with the physical suggestions. Each aspect of the study is presented succinctly and with clarity and the whole presentation hangs together. This is a book to read and then go back and consult rather than merely a dry reference manual. The orientation is toward ways of becoming a whole person rather than toward remedies for specific symp- toms. Index, bibliography. 347pp. Ban 74

BURANG, THEODORE. **TIBETAN ART OF HEALING**, $3.90. *The medicine indigenous to Tibet is highly respected throughout Central Asia and has a remarkable record of suc- cess in healing. Its philosophy and curative methods transport us into a strange web of macrocosmic and microcosmic interrelations. In contrast to the standpoint of Western research, it acquaints us with unusual spiritual foundations . . . and often displays a mas- terful observation of nature. The material is divided into the following parts: The Cosmic Humours, The Second Body, Tibetan Medical Writings, Materia Medica, Tibetan Methods of Healing, About Cancer, Mental Illness and Possession* and *Co-operation Between West- ern and Tibetan Doctors.* The style is not overly technical and the general reader can gain much from the book. 117pp. Wat 74

CANCER

In the United States the only legal treatments for cancer are surgery, radiation or chemicals. Each of these is destructive to the body. Any other treatments, even though completely non-toxic, require approval by the FDA—a process that takes years and can be additionally hampered by the prejudices of the establishment. As the American Cancer Society has stated: *Research is to be strongly encouraged—but only in the framework of the accepted ideology.* The Government has gone to great lengths to prosecute non-orthodox researchers: witness the imprisonment of Wilhelm Reich and the burning of his books.

The unorthodox approach to cancer treatment swings away from the attempt to destroy cancer cells themselves (dealing with the symptoms) to a concerted effort to restore the sick host to a state of health by mustering up the inherent natural defense mechanisms of the body (dealing with the cause). Cancer is thus regarded as a degenerative disease of the entire system and much of the treatment (detoxification and nutritional improvement) is essentially the same as for any other degenerative disease. There is considerable evidence that these unorthodox methods work if the individual is willing to make the necessary changes in his/her living habits and the cancer is not too far advanced. For example, the author of **A Program for Prevention, Detection and Reversal of Pre-Cancerous Conditions** reports following some 400 cancer victims over a ten year period. Of 268 who followed their (orthodox) doctor's instructions and did not change their living habits, 7% survived. Of 57 early and precancer involvements who followed the recommended approach without professional help, 100% survived. Of 41 advanced cases who followed the recommendations (and in some cases got therapy outside the U.S.), 90% survived. And of 39 *terminal* cases who followed the recommendations, 46% were still alive at the time of writing.

Unorthodox cancer therapy—even by nutritional means—is largely illegal in the U.S. Fortunately, the First Amendment protects the right to publish books about it. Thus only the educated and/or rich have any real freedom of choice about cancer. The former can read the books listed below. The latter can go to Mexico or Europe for treatment.

There are two large organizations championing non-toxic cancer therapies and promoting public awareness of alternatives. The first is the International Association of Cancer Victims and Friends, Inc., PO Box 707, Solana Beach, CA 92075. It was started by a woman who lost a lot of her insides to the surgeon's knife before discovering laetrile therapy, and who was ultimately responsible for setting up a clinic in Tijuana for the use of laetrile and other non-toxic therapies. Several years later most of the leaders of the Los Angeles chapter split off and formed a new organization, the Cancer Control Society, 2043 N. Berendo, Los Angeles, CA 90027. Both groups hold large annual conferences with many speakers and exhibits, publish journals, and sell a wide range of books. Both are doing good work and deserve support. It's a pity they can't get together!

AIROLA, PAAVO. **CANCER: CAUSES. PREVENTION AND TREATMENT**, $2.00. An excellent overview of twenty-two causes of cancer, possible cures, and a discussion of the biological anti-cancer program. Includes many addresses of clinics and references to the literature. 40pp. HPP 72

BORDERLAND SCIENCES. **THE KOCH REMEDY FOR CANCER**, $4.45. Includes three separate parts: *The Koch Treatment* (involving blood purification); *The Occult and Karmic Causes of Cancer*; and *The Electro-Magnetic Approach to Health* (restoring the balanced polarity of body cells with soft radio waves and/or homeopathic remedies). This is a detailed, graphically illustrated account, designed for practical use and inspiration. Includes newspaper clippings, quotations, and comments by N. Meade Layne and Riley H. Crabb. Oversize, bibliography. 70pp. BSR 71

FERE, DR. MAUD. **DOES DIET CURE CANCER**, $4.70. Dr. Fere cured herself of cancer of the bowel. Her hypothesis is that cancer is a constitutional disease, like rheumatism or the common cold. She believes that it is almost always caused by excessive sodium, plus a constitution that has been debilitated through breaking the *Laws of Good Health*—which are listed and explained in detail. Dr. Fere is a medical doctor and she details her cure in terms other doctors as well as laymen can understand. In the process, she provides a succinct biochemical explanation of what causes cancer and how it starts forming in the body. 112pp. TPL 71

GERSON, MAX. **A CANCER THERAPY—RESULTS OF FIFTY CASES**, $8.10. A detailed, technical book by one of the great pioneers of nutritional therapy of cancer. Directed primarily to physicians with a theoretical discussion, complete dietary directions and fifty case histories. 402pp.

GRIFFIN, EDWARD. **WORLD WITHOUT CANCER**, $4.00. 526pp. AmM 74

HAUGHT, S.J. **HAS DR. MAX GERSON A TRUE CANCER CURE?** $1.00. The late Dr. Max Gerson developed a method of cancer treatment that relied heavily on diet and

body cleansing. He became controversial due to the apparent success of his method and the simultaneous obstruction and vituperation by the AMA and the American Cancer Society. This is a fascinating account by a journalist who planned an expose and the more he dug into the story the more he was convinced of the value of what Dr. Gerson was doing. 160pp. Par 62

INTERNATIONAL HEALTH COUNCIL. **A PROGRAM FOR THE PREVENTION DETECTION AND REVERSAL OF PRE-CANCEROUS CONDITIONS**, $1.50. This booklet is written by a layman who devoted himself to a thorough study of cancer after his son died from it. In addition to reviewing the literature, he interviewed several hundred cancer victims, following them to success or death. The booklet contains a good summary of the nutritional, detoxification, enzyme, and laetrile approaches. It also provides addresses and full details on obtaining urine and blood tests to diagnose cancer earlier than is possible by orthodox approaches. We recommend this as the best brief treatment of the subject we've seen. 44pp. IHC 74

ISSELS, JOSEF. **CANCER: A SECOND OPINION**, $15.00. Dr. Issels is a noted German cancer specialist who has treated over 8000 patients with considerably better than average results. He is known for his *ganzheitstherapie*—whole body treatment—which views cancer as a systemic disease and supplements surgery or other conventional therapies with whole array of methods to help the body build up its own resistance and immunities. This is an excellent, comprehensive book, which surveys much of the history of medicine provides a pointed short course in relevant physiology, and covers broadly the state of knowledge about cancer and its origins. It is written primarily for physicians but can be read with great profit by anyone else who can handle the technical terminology. Dr. Issels writes from a basis of extensive European research which is not hung up by our unfortunate American legalities. Recommended. Extensive bibliography, but mostly in German. 216pp. Hod 75

KELLEY, WILLIAM. **NEW HOPE FOR CANCER VICTIMS**, $1.45. An excellent simple discussion. Kelley, a dentist by background, cured himself of cancer and now studies cancer through his Kelley Research Foundation. Considers cancer a symptom of protein metabolism malfunction—a deficiency disease, which can be treated by detoxification, proper nutrition, and ingestion of pancreatic enzymes. 42pp.

_____. **ONE ANSWER TO CANCER**, $1.50. This is Kelley's latest book with the regimen he favors described in some detail. While he gives general recommendations regarding nutritional supplements and enzymes in the book, he is unable, for legal reasons to name specific brands recommended. For that, one can go to a series of three interviews with him printed in the **Cancer News Journal** of the International Association of Cancer Victims and Friends. Can

KITTLER, GLENN. **LAETRILE, CONTROL FOR CANCER**, $1.95. A journalist's account of the development of what has been called the most effective drug against cancer which is also harmless to other tissues, and the struggle with medical orthodoxy to have it tested and used. Includes case histories and evaluations from many research scientists. Can

KREBS, ERNST, ET AL. **THE LAETRILES-NITRILOSIDES IN PREVENTION AND CONTROL OF CANCER**, $3.00. Technical papers on laetrile treatment by the leaders in its development. Directed to physicians. 88pp.

LEROI, A. **THE CELL, THE HUMAN ORGANISM AND CANCER**, $.95. Leroi is a doctor at the Society for Cancer Research in Arlesheim, Switzerland. Here he points out that the causes of cancer should be sought in the entire organism, not just in the cells. The problem is not eradicating the diseased cells, but rather healing the diseased human being. Includes references, mainly from European sources. 24pp. NKB 61, 69

The rich doctor, cartoon by George Cruikshank, from Magic, Myth, Medicine by Joan Camp.

MC NAUGHTON FOUNDATION. **PHYSICIAN'S HANDBOOK OF VITAMIN B-17 THERAPY**, $2.00. Can

MEDEXPORT, V.O. **VITAMIN B-15 (PANGAMIC ACID)**, $5.00. Indications for use and efficacy in internal disease. 33pp. Can 68

REICH, WILHELM. **THE CANCER BIOPATHY**, $5.95. See the Reich section.

SCIENCE PUBLISHING HOUSE. **VITAMIN B-15**, $7.00. Can

SCOTT, CYRIL. **VICTORY OVER CANCER**, $3.60. Scott is a naturopath who believes that there are several prime causes of cancer, including oxygen starvation and the consumption of over-salted foods. In this volume he explains these causes and seeks to establish the concept that cancer is a blood disease. He advances reasons for the increase of cancer and reveals the failure of orthodox cancer research and treatment. Drugs, food, and chronic constipation are also discussed in relation to cancer. The second half of the book is devoted to a review of unorthodox cancer treatments. Notes, 168pp. HSP 39

SUN, WONG HON. **HOW I OVERCAME INOPERABLE CANCER**, c$6.00. Subtitled *The true account of a man who conquered the dread disease by using the principles of natural healing.* Wong Hon Sun is now a naturopath. 125pp. ExP 75

OBE, JOHN H. HOW TO PREVENT AND GAIN REMISSION FROM CANCER, $12.85. Tobe is an outspoken iconoclast who has written a great many books on dif-rent nutritional and naturopathic subjects. Here he takes on the whole cancer estab-shment, which he accuses of having a vested interest in cancer (it costs $13,000 to die om cancer) rather than its cure. Much of the book discusses the various foods and drugs avoid, some well recognized and some not fully established as carcinogenic, but prob-ly worth avoiding anyway. He reviews a number of the non-toxic cancer treatments ch as laetrile, but comes out most strongly in favor of an all raw food diet. Tobe has bviously done a great deal of research but the book is marred by a lack of footnotes or mplete citations and a tendency to quote from newspaper accounts or refer to un-nown (to us) persons as the famous Dr. So-and-So. For all our criticisms, there is a lot of alue for anyone doing serious reading on cancer. Bibliography, index. 402pp. Prv 75

AERLAND, EBBA. CANCER—A DISEASE OF CIVILISATION, $1.50. Brief discus-on of the biological basis of cancer, in particular disturbed cellular respiration. Advo-ates the Waerland diet (primarily raw food). 54pp. Prv 70

ARLSON, RICK, ed. THE FRONTIERS OF SCIENCE AND MEDICINE, $3.95. A col-ction of papers presented at a conference on the title theme. A wide variety of topics re included and the papers are fairly readable. The contributors are distinguished scien-sts, physicians, and people involved in the new consciousness. Reg 76

ARTER, MARY ELLEN and WILLIAM MC GAREY. EDGAR CAYCE ON HEALING, 1.50. *This book is about a psychic and his work in suggesting methods by which healing ight come to the human body. These suggestions centered on the field of medicine and pread out over osteopathy, chiropractic, physical therapy, herbal therapy, nutrition, piritual therapy, hypnotherapy, dentistry, and what is best described as other methods.* he major part of the book consists of Ms. Carter's narrative of the lives of several people some critically ill) who, through Cayce's suggestions, regained their health as well as a ifferent perspective on life. Each of Ms. Carter's accounts is followed by Dr. McGarey's iscussion of the physiological concepts and the various therapies which Cayce suggested. r. McGarey is Director of the A.R.E. Clinic. 205pp. War 72

AYCE, EDGAR. MEDICINES FOR THE NEW AGE, $1.50. This is the most detailed ccount of the remedies suggested in the Cayce readings (see our section on Edgar Cayce or information on his work). The material is alphabetically arranged by remedies. The naterial is paraphrased from the original readings and there's also background material on he remedy. The appropriate *Circulating Files* are cited by number (these files are avail-ble only to A.R.E. members) and manufacturers' product names for Cayce formulas are lso given. Appendices contain an alphabetical listing of publications and files on related ubjects, a cross-reference guide to selected conditions and recommendations, a partial isting of medical circulating files available from the A.R.E., and a list of products re-ommended in the readings that are not currently available. Her 74

AYCE, J. GAIL. OSTEOPATHY, $3.00. A comparison of various parallel concepts ex-ressed by A.T. Still, the founder of osteopathy, and Edgar Cayce. Excerpts from both ources are examined with brief comments between extracts. The material is topically rranged and an appendix explores several topics in further detail. *It is hoped that this urvey will serve as a tool and as a foundation for expansion of the various points presented the outline. . . .* Oversize, bibliography. 64pp. ARE 73

ERNEY, J.V. HANDBOOK OF UNUSUAL AND UNORTHODOX HEALING METH-DS, c$8.95. In the introduction Cerney summarizes his book as follows: *Section I tells he story of those amazing Z zones that not only treat you, but can be used to diagnose our own problems. Section II is composed of healing agents called herbs, cell salts, raw uice and fasting. Section III has to do with physical therapy procedures you can use in our home, procedures such as somatherapy, the body cure, spinal concussion, percus-ion, vibration, and aquatonics.* The orientation is toward the general reader and the em-hasis is on practical advice and case studies. Index, 217pp. PrH 76

_____. MODERN MAGIC OF NATURAL HEALING WITH WATER THERAPY, 8.95. Dr. Cerney has had over thirty years of experience with water therapy, mainly in he line of physical fitness for athletes. He devotes a separate section to water treatments or each of the following parts of the body: the head, the neck, the shoulder, the upper xtremities, the chest, the back, the abdomen, the lower extremities, and the skin. The reatments are clearly presented and can be followed with ease by the student. Index, 16pp. PrH 75

HAITOW, LEON. OSTEOPATHY, $3.90. A practicing osteopath explains the origin f osteopathy and its development. The ailments which respond well to osteopathic reatment (including lumbago, sciatica, brachial neuritis, neuralgia, slipped disc, migraine, nsomnia, asthma, cardiac conditions, and bronchial and catarrhal disorders) are discussed nd a selection of case histories drawn from the author's own experience is presented. He lso reviews the latest trends in osteopathic research and training. The text is very well llustrated and many exercises and techniques are presented. Glossary, 92pp. TPL 74

HALLONER, H.K. THE PATH OF HEALING, $3.95. A very inspiring book on the true ature and function of spiritual healing. 175pp. TPH 72

HERASKIN, E., W.M. RINGSDORF and J.W. CLARK. DIET AND DISEASE, c$8.95. r. Cheraskin, trained both in medicine and dentistry, is one of the leading academic utritional researchers today. Together with his colleagues at the University of Alabama Medical Center, he presents here a thorough review of findings about the relationship of iet and disease. Originally written as a college text, with voluminous footnotes, it has ecently been given wider circulation by the Rodale Press because of its value to con-erned general readers. Index, 369pp. Rod 68

HERASKIN, E. and W.M. RINGSDORF. NEW HOPE FOR INCURABLE DISEASES, 1.65. An easily understood, concise work which shows scientifically that nutrition and iet play a large role in the determination of a disease. The book presents the medical

findings showing that glaucoma, multiple sclerosis, schizophrenia, alcoholism and other problems, including aging, can be controlled or prevented with proper diet and nutrition. Footnotes, 187pp. Arc 71

CLARK, LINDA. GET WELL NATURALLY, $1.65. Ms. Clark is a reporter who has a deep interest in nutrition and alternative healing techniques. In this compendium she begins by presenting a good review of many healing techniques including homeopathy, Bach flower remedies, herbs, acupuncture and pressure therapy, radiesthesia, and material from the Edgar Cayce readings. From there she goes on to summarize the various *nutri-tional therapies*. The main body of the book is devoted to a section entitled *Treating Diseases Naturally*, in which she devotes a separate section to many ailments and reviews the applicable remedies and the literature on the subject and also cites sources (with ad-dresses) for many of the items and individuals mentioned in her survey. There's also a good, albeit outdated, bibliography. A well written, informative survey. Index, 406pp. Arc 65

_____. HELP YOURSELF TO HEALTH, $1.50. A very inspirational approach to healing through prayer and positive thinking as viewed by a leading nutritional repor-ter. Topically arranged and basically composed of case histories of countless individuals. Bibliography, index. 267pp. Pyr 72

COCA, ARTHUR. THE PULSE TEST, $1.45. Based on the fact that allergens speed up the pulse, this book provides a simple method by which the reader can conduct his own allergy tests simply and effectively. Dr. Coca was President of the American Association of Immunologists and founder of the **Journal of Immunology**, the foremost medical pub-lication in this field. 189pp. Arc 56

COOKE, GRACE. HEAL THYSELF, c$2.50. For nearly half a century White Eagle, through Grace Cooke, has been healing the sick in mind and body, as well as teaching others how to heal. This is a general, inspirational treatise on healing by letting the uni-versal love emanate from one's being. 61pp. WEP 62

CRABB, RILEY and JUDY. THE HEART TO HEART TRANSPLANT, $1.75. A scat-tered tract on the conscious use of the subconscious to promote health through positive thinking from a theosophical/metaphysical point of view with relation to the energy cen-ters and the etheric body. Oversize, 44pp. BSR

DAVIS, ADELLE. LET'S GET WELL, $1.95. This is our favorite Davis; we keep it on our shelf along with her **How to Get Well** as our two home medical encyclopedias. When anything ails us we look it up in the excellent index. It's all here, including fifty-five pages of medical references in small print! Her final chapter, *A Fortress Against Disease*, summarizes the unfortunate state of our national health as well as anything we've seen. Recommended. 476pp. NAL 65

DECKER, NELSON and RILEY CRABB. PSYCHIC SURGERY, $2.35. A collection of scattered material entitled fully **Psychic Surgery in the Philippines (and in Brazil), Bible 'Kahuna Healers in Hawaii, New Age Therapy in California**. Some interesting material is presented, none of it in any way verified. Oversize, illustrations. 51pp. BSR 74

DEXTREIT, RAYMOND. OUR EARTH, OUR CURE, $4.50. This book is compiled, edited and translated by Michel Abehsera from the forty-three books written by Dex-treit. *Mr. Dextreit brings something new to medical practice . . . for in addition to his authoritative use of food, herbs, and baths, and his extensive knowledge of the human organism, Mr. Dextreit has mastered the use of clay for curative purposes. . . . A basic principle in Mr. Dextreit's medicine is that when undertaking to heal ourselves, treating* *the general condition is more primary than relieving a specific manifestation, for a local disease is usually the consequence of a general disorder.* The clay remedies suggested here have been the rage in France and they have created quite a stir among natural healers in the U.S. This edition is oversize and beautifully illustrated. Includes many specific remedies and preparations. Index, 203pp. SwH 74

DIGESTIVE SYSTEM

BIRCHER-BENNER. **NUTRITION FOR DIGESTIVE PROBLEMS**, $2.75. Written by the staff of the Bircher-Benner Clinic, this is one of fifteen guides to diet for particular purposes. It includes both menus and recipes for a variety of digestive disorders. 142pp. Nas 71

FLATH, CARL. **THE MIRACLE NUTRIENT**, $1.95. One out of every two Americans is now, or is on the way to becoming, a laxative addict, and collectively they are shelling out about a quarter of a billion dollars to support the habit. Flath, a health care administrator, begins this book with a review of laxatives and the problems they create, and a basic discussion of the gastrointestinal tract, before going into a discussion of the values of bran. He covers all the usual ground. Despite the title, this is a good brief general book on good bowel health, not just a rehash on the case for bran. Recipes, glossary, index. 169pp. Ban 75

FREDERICKS, CARLTON. **HIGH-FIBER WAY TO TOTAL HEALTH**, $1.95. Fredericks has been advocating a high-fiber diet for years. One can expect, then, that this book will be more about Carlton Fredericks' views on health than just a resume for the high-fiber hypothesis. There's more background information, and a discussion of the dangers of sugar and the delights of yogurt and wheat germ. If you just want to learn about fiber, we'd recommend the Galton book. If you want to use the growing awareness of the importance of fiber as a handle to turn some of your friends on to better diet and better health habits in general, this book should do an effective job. In addition to an extensive medical bibliography, Dr. Fredericks lists eight all-time great books on nutrition. Three of them turn out to be his own! Index, 208pp. S&S 76

GALTON, LAWRENCE. **THE TRUTH ABOUT FIBER IN YOUR FOOD**, c$8.95. This, we think, is the best of the fiber books. Galton, an experienced writer on medical topics, has gone to the source—the various British doctors who did most of the basic research on the fiber hypothesis. Chief among them is Dr. Denis Burkitt, whose epidemiological data are derived from his communications with a network of 110 mission hospitals throughout Africa. Burkitt has contributed an introduction to this volume. Galton tells the full story of Burkitt's research and that of many others, so that the reader can follow the evidence as it unfolds and judge it for himself. One singular contribution of this book is a discussion of the importance of eating foods with their natural fiber, rather than merely adding bran to a refined diet. Appendices provide tables of fiber and caloric contents of over 1000 foods and some 130 high fiber recipes. Bibliography, index. 246pp. Crn 76

MOYLE, ALAN. **CONQUERING CONSTIPATION**, $4.55. Most of the basic causes of constipation, and the complaints associated with that condition, can be traced to modern methods of food production and consumption. Recently a rash of books has appeared suggesting that a major factor in constipation is the lack of suitable roughage in our food. In this book an experienced naturopath explains the nutritional deficiencies which precipitate constipation, and how to remedy them. All the related ailments are also discussed in some depth. Index, 126pp. TPL 76

REUBEN, DAVID. **THE SAVE YOUR LIFE DIET**, $1.95. Dr. Reuben gained widespread popularity with **Everything You Always Wanted to Know About Sex and Were Afraid to Ask**. Hopefully, that popularity will be translated into many readers for this important book about the role of fiber in health. Based on a study of over 500 medical authorities in 600 articles (and the book is extensively footnoted with special notes to other M.D.'s), Reuben points out the high correlation between our Western low-fiber diets and our high rates of cancer of the colon and rectum, heart attacks, diverticulosis, appendicitis, hemorrhoids and obesity. He recommends a natural food diet which avoids white sugar and white flour but holds out hope for those who insist on eating junk food if they take three teaspoons to three tablespoons of bran per day. Bibliography, 173pp. RaH 75

SUBAK-SHARPE, GENELL. **THE NATURAL HIGH FIBER LIFE SAVING DIET**, $1.95. This book begins with a review of the medical research that led to our understanding of fiber, treated somewhat like a detective story. It covers the various diseases related to fiber and gives considerable attention to the problem of weight reduction in general and in relation to a high fiber diet. Ms. Subak-Sharpe is editor of **Medical Opinion**; she is also a cook and some of her favorite recipes are included. This is the fiber book for the overweight reader. Bibliography, 190pp. G&D 76

TROY, MARIAN. **BETTER BOWEL HEALTH**, $1.50. All of us suffer from intestinal problems sometimes, many of us much of the time. This, therefore, is a book that should have a wide audience. Written by an M.D., it covers the whole range of bowel problems from infancy to old age, explaining why things happen as they do, what to worry about and what not to worry about, and what we can do through eating, exercise, etc., to avoid or alleviate our problems. A useful home reference work. Index, 223pp. Pyr 74

DINTENFASS, DR. JULIUS. **CHIROPRACTIC: A MODERN WAY TO HEALTH**, $.75. Presents a good overview of the subject. Pyr 66

DOOLEY, ANNE. **EVERY WALL A DOOR**, $2.95. An engrossing study of spirit healing and psychic surgery. Ms. Dooley traces the awakening of her interest in psychic phenomena and her study of various mediums. She was invited to a healing session given by Lourival de Freitas, a Brazilian psychic surgeon, and following it she went to Brazil to study his work more thoroughly. The bulk of the book is devoted to her recreation of De Freitas' remarkable healings and surgical operations. She herself underwent an operation. She also gives us a comprehensive picture of the Brazilian spiritualist scene and reports on the work of other healers. Photographs, bibliography. 206pp. Dut 74

DUZ, M. **ASTRAL MEDICINE AND THERAPEUTICS**, $5.00. See the Astrology sectic

EDMUNDS, H. TUDOR, ET AL., eds. **SOME UNRECOGNIZED FACTORS IN MEL CINE**, $3.25. A group of scientists, physicians, and clairvoyants present a philosophy medicine and healing based upon the concept of man as a complex being consisting a spirit, soul, and physical body. The authors suggest that health, in its fullest sens means the alignment of the whole of man's being to his spiritual nature. They also f that diagnosis can only be accurate if consideration is given not only to the effect of disease, but also to the cause of the disease. Here they discuss special diagnostic tec niques and include a complete section on the principles of the treatment of diseas Index, 209pp. TPH 76

EDWARDS, HARRY. **A GUIDE TO THE UNDERSTANDING AND PRACTICE O SPIRITUAL HEALING**, c$8.40. Harry Edwards is England's most noted spiritual heale In this book he has drawn upon his vast healing experience and his unparalleled kno ledge of spiritual science to explain how spiritual healing is accomplished and how we c develop our own healing potential. Edwards prepared a series of healing study cours for members of the National Federation of Spiritual Healers, and these courses are no embraced in this volume, which in itself is an extended and revised edition of his earli book, **A Guide to Spirit Healing**, which was considered to be the leading textbook f healers. Major sections include: *Absent Healing and the Seeking of Attunement wi Spirit, The Theory of Spirit Healing, Healing Practice, The Science of Spirit Healin Psychosomatic Conditions and Mental Healing,* and *An Enquiry into the Cause, Preve tion and Cure of Cancer.* Photographs, index. 360pp. SHS 74

_________. **THE HEALING INTELLIGENCE**, $2.50. In clear and precise languag the author explains the laws at work behind the experience widely known as *spiritu healing.* Drawing material and insight from numerous experiences in his own long care in the healing art he candidly and convincingly explains the inner spiritual factor in ma that may be released in order to vanquish disease and illness of both psychological an physical varieties. 189pp. Haw 65

_________. **THE POWER OF SPIRITUAL HEALING**, c$4.75. *This book is not s much a scientific appreciation of spiritual healing as an effort to present the healing stor in a simple way to enable everyone to have a measure of understanding of its power processes, and purpose and how all who are in need can benefit from it.* SHS 63

_________. **SPIRIT HEALING**, c$4.75. Outlines some fundamental principles c spirit healing, its relationship to the church and the medical profession and its actual a plication in cases of disease. 170pp. SHS 60

_________. **THIRTY YEARS A SPIRITUAL HEALER**, c$4.40. Edwards' autobio raphy, in which he discusses how he first realized his healing faculty and relates many c his healing experiences. Photographs, index. 167pp. SHS 68

EICHENLAUB, JOHN. **HOME TONICS AND REFRESHERS FOR DAILY HEALT AND VIGOR**, $1.25. A selection of natural tonics and remedies for various common ai ments—with instructions on how to prepare them. Also includes background materia Index, 221pp. ASC 63

_________. **A MINNESOTA DOCTOR'S HOME REMEDIES FOR COMMON AN UNCOMMON AILMENTS**, $2.95. This is an excellent collection of useful tips whic is well organized and covers every conceivable area. All the remedies are simple to prepare Dr. Eichenlaub writes in a simple down-home style and includes many anecdotes. We hav found this book very useful and we think you will too. Fully indexed. 262pp. PrH 7

FEINGOLD, BEN. **WHY YOUR CHILD IS HYPERACTIVE**, c$7.95. Dr. Feingold, noted pediatrician, received considerable newspaper publicity when he found that th problem of hyperkinesis—a learning disability which affects more than five million chi dren in the U.S.—could in many cases be traced to the additives in their food. By eliminatin all synthetic food colorings and flavorings from their diet, he found his patients becam much calmer, more responsive, less distractable, more able to cope, and their school wor improved markedly. What a contrast to the recent scandal in Iowa in which the schoo system was systematically drugging many of the children to try to get the same results. I this book, Dr. Feingold relates how his discovery came about and its scientific basis and provides details about the diet and how parents should apply it. Recipes included 211pp. RaH 74

FISHER, RICHARD. **DICTIONARY OF DRUGS**, $2.25. Describes the uses, effects chemical make-up and side effects of the fifty-six drugs most commonly used by physicians Not for self medication (dosages are not given) but will enable the serious reader to bette understand or question what his/her doctor is doing. Indexed by trade names, chemica names, and diseases. 252pp. ScB 71

FLAMMONDE, PARIS. **THE MYSTIC HEALERS**, c$8.95. This survey of spiritual healers through the ages is mainly a series of anecdotes and biographical material on the healers reviewed. The emphasis is on modern day healers beginning with Mary Baker Eddy and on Christian-oriented healers such as Oral Roberts and Katherine Kuhlman. Most of the individuals discussed were totally unfamiliar to us. The book lacks depth and serves merely as an introductory overview from which the reader can pick out those healers that interest him/her and get a more in depth study elsewhere. Glossary, bibliography index. 252pp. S&D 74

FLATTO, EDWIN. **REVITALIZE YOUR BODY WITH NATURE'S SECRETS**, $1.45. A treatise on natural therapies—the first third gives general natural health tips and the rest of the book is devoted to questions on various topics with detailed answers. Fully indexed. 174pp. Arc 73

FULLER, JOHN. **ARIGO: SURGEON OF THE RUSTY KNIFE**, c$7.95. Arigo had only a third grade education and no medical training, yet thousands flocked from all over

Brazil and South America, and from all over the world, to the small village where he lived, to be cured by him. He performed hundreds of operations daily, usually with an ordinary kitchen knife or jackknife, without anesthetics, without major bleeding, and without the benefits of modern science. He made thousands of correct diagnoses without even examining the patient. And, one after another, patients left his primitive clinic cured. He saved many from cancer and other fatal diseases who had been given up as hopeless by the leading medical authorities. He never charged for his services nor would he accept any remuneration. Arigo's healings were witnessed by both Brazilian and American doctors. Explicit motion pictures of his operations were taken, and stills from these illustrate the book. This is a spellbinding book in which John Fuller has reconstructed the story of Arigo, and has carefully researched and documented his presentation. Afterword by Henry Puharich. Bibliography, index. 282pp. Cro 74

GARTEN, M.O. **THE HEALTH SECRETS OF A NATUROPATHIC DOCTOR**, $2.45. This is a good, clear layperson's guide to naturopathy, covering many therapies and diet suggestions in detail. PrH 67

_____. **THE NATURAL AND DRUGLESS WAY FOR BETTER HEALTH**, $1.65. Garten's books are very good practical guides to living a more healthy life—this one specifically details exercises and remedies for every part of the body. 240pp. Arc 69

GUIRDHAM, ARTHUR. **OBSESSION**, c$5.60. Subtitled *Psychic Forces and Evil in the Causation of Disease*, this is a study based on the author's years of psychiatric and medical experience. Dr. Guirdham believes that obsessional symptoms are often due to the repression of psychic gifts and here he explores this thesis through many case studies and background theory. He writes very clearly and his work is useful both for the layperson and the professional. 181pp. Spe 72

_____. **A THEORY OF DISEASE**, c$5.90. *The aim of this book is to produce a comprehensive theory of disease. Proneness to disease is related to the degree of development of the personality and to the individual's awareness of it. The pattern of disease depends to a large extent on the religious and philosophical outlook of the community in which he finds himself.* 204pp. Spe 57

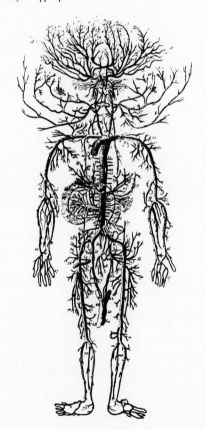

HALL, MANLY P. **HEALING**, c$7.75. A fascinating account which traces the history of healing from the earliest times and discusses the major figures in the field. Hall analyzes various types of healing and relates the whole to esoteric psychology, physiology and anatomy, including material on the etheric bodies of man and nature, the human will, the factor of conscience, and the energies underlying the physical processes of the body. There is a special section on the pineal gland and on the effects of mental attitudes on health. The book concludes with a group of case histories, showing how the individual causes many of his/her health problems, and discussing techniques for self help. See the Mysticism section for more background on Hall. 341pp. PRS 71

HAMMOND, SALLY. **WE ARE ALL HEALERS**, $1.95. Ms. Hammond is a reporter with an intense personal and professional interest in healing. She feels that the ability to heal psychically is innate in all humans—although dormant in most of us—and that it can be developed to greater or lesser degree. The only requirements for that develop-

ment are a sense of compassion and a willingness to acquire the necessary training. In researching this book Ms. Hammond visited the most noted healers and healing centers in the U.S. and the U.K. including the National Federation of Spiritual Healers, Harry Edwards, Gordon Turner, Mary Rogers, Ronald Beesley, the Academy of Parapsychology and Medicine, Rolling Thunder, and many others. It is a very personal account and includes many interviews. A well written account for the general reader. Index, 296pp. RaH 74

HAND, WAYLAND. **AMERICAN FOLK MEDICINE**, c$12.95. An exploration of the medical traditions of various ethnic groups: the Pennsylvania Dutch, Hispanic people of Mexico and the Southwest U.S., the blacks in Jamaica, and the American Indians. The discussion includes magical treatments in addition to natural medicine. UCa 76

HANSSEN, MAURICE. **CIDER VINEGAR**, $1.50. A comprehensive guide to the uses and properties of cider vinegar which begins with some general information and then goes into its effectiveness for specific ailments and ends with a series of recipes. Index, 128pp. Arc 75

HARTMANN, FRANZ. **OCCULT SCIENCE IN MEDICINE**, c$6.50. Reprint of a philosophical treatise first published in 1893. Hartmann wrote a number of things on Paracelsus, the pioneering alchemist/physician, and he incorporates many alchemical concepts into the material presented here. Material is included on the esoteric constitution of man, on the development of medicine through the ages (it is here that he delves most deeply into alchemy), on the causes of disease from the spiritual/theosophical point of view, and on the five types of diseases and the five related types of physicians and treatments. The material presented here seems to have been presented since Hartmann's time (and before!) in a clearer manner than he is able to convey. Definitely a work for those interested in *esoteric science* only. 100pp. Wei 75

HEINDEL, MAX. **ASTRO DIAGNOSIS: A GUIDE TO HEALING**, $4.50. An introductory text explaining certain fundamental principles of the methods of medical diagnosis based on an understanding of the astrological factors influencing the patient. Ros 29

_____. **OCCULT PRINCIPLES OF HEALTH AND HEALING**, $4.00. A treasury of material concerning the health and healing of the human organism as considered from the occult point of view. Discusses specific ailments as well as the origin, functions, and proper care of the physical vehicle. 248pp. Ros 38

HEWLETT-PARSONS, J. **ABC'S OF NATURE CURES**, $1.45. This is the best overall introduction to naturopathy that we know of. It is written for the layperson and includes sections on dietetics, hydrotherapy, fasting, vitamin therapy, and various specialty treatments such as mono diets and eliminative diets. It also contains a great deal of information on basic nutrition and on the role of the various micro-nutrients and minerals. Dr. Hewlett-Parsons is a practicing naturopath. He bases his work on the classic teachings of naturopathy and stresses a balanced lifestyle. Glossary, index. 192pp. Arc 68

HOLZER, HANS. **BEYOND MEDICINE**, $1.50. Presents the latest research about unorthodox and psychic healing, including documented case studies; a discussion of various healing theories; and a long section devoted to noted healers, including some in the medical profession. A fascinating study. 209pp. RaH 73

HOMOLA, DR. SAMUEL. **A CHIROPRACTOR'S TREASURY OF HEALTH SECRETS**, c$6.95. Each chapter of this excellent book outlines a complete self-help program for a specific ailment, along with general nutritional information. Includes many practical exercises, with illustrations. 224pp. PrH

_____. **DR. HOMOLA'S LIFE-EXTENDER HEALTH GUIDE**, c$7.95. Dr. Homola has been a practicing chiropractor, using natural methods, for nearly two decades, and he is a prolific writer. This book contains a wealth of good nutritional information and simple, practical home remedies for a wide variety of ills. It covers in detail ways to get rid of body poisons, restore good digestion, control weight and build energy. Index, 223pp. PrH 75

_____. **DR. HOMOLA'S NATURAL HEALTH REMEDIES**, c$6.95. Dr. Homola details here the practical home remedies for numerous ailments—combining naturopathy and chiropracty into what he calls naturomatic healing methods. This is an interesting study, fully indexed. 250pp. PrH 73

ILLICH, IVAN. **MEDICAL NEMESIS**, c$8.95. We believe this is one of the most important books of 1976, written by a man the **East-West Journal** calls a Western saint. Illich argues that modern medicine has reached the stage where it itself is a major threat to our health. With incredibly comprehensive documentation, he shows that during the past century doctors have affected epidemics no more profoundly than did priests during earlier times, and that, indeed, much of modern illness is doctor-caused. ...*one out of every five patients admitted to a typical research hospital acquires an iatrogenic disease (i.e., caused by the treatment there), sometimes trivial, usually requiring special treatment, and in one case in thirty leading to death. Half of these episodes result from complications of drug therapy; amazingly, one in ten comes from diagnostic procedures. Despite good intentions and claims to public service, a military officer with a similar record of performance would be relieved of his command, and a restaurant or amusement center would be closed by the police.* No wonder malpractice insurance rates are skyrocketing. But Illich's major attack on the medical establishment is even more basic. The doctors have mystified healing to such an extent that they have taken away from us the faith and ability to heal ourselves. Illich's attack on educators (see the Education section) has now been extended to the medical profession. Illich's concern is a profound humanism which would return to people control over the most basic elements of their own lives. This book has received wide acclaim and attention in the media. It may turn out to be one of the most important influences in hastening the revolution in attitudes and approaches to healing that we now see taking place. Difficult reading. Highly recommended. Subject and author indices. 294pp. RaH 76

JARVIS, I.C. **FOLK MEDICINE**, $1.50. This book has sold over three million copies. Dr. Jarvis is a respected physician who went beyond what he learned in medical school to observe the animal laws of health and the way native Vermonters used simple natural remedies: honeycomb, cider vinegar, kelp, etc. There is a lot of useful information here for those who are trying to wean themselves away from the AMA and drugs. 192pp. Faw 58

JENSEN, BERNARD. **CHART FOR IRIDOLOGY**, $8.40. This is a very well reproduced chart, 8½x14" and well laminated in heavy plastic. Both eyes are reproduced and the various points on the eyes can be clearly seen. Jen

_____. **THE SCIENCE AND PRACTICE OF IRIDOLOGY**, $20.75. Dr. Bernard Jensen, D.C., N.D., is the foremost exponent of iridology, a method of diagnosis by viewing the condition of the iris, which Dr. Jensen believes is more accurate than any other single method of diagnosis. The iridologist can determine the inherent structure and working capacity of an organ, can detect environmental strain, can tell if a person is anemic, can determine the nerve force, the responsive healing power of tissue and the inherent ability to circulate the blood. This is a technical book, for professionals, profusely illustrated, including many color plates. Index, 372pp. Jen 74

_____. **WORLD KEYS TO HEALTH AND LONG LIFE**, $6.65. This is a collection of forty observations about health that Jensen has made in his world-wide travels. The writing style is informal and case studies and photographs illustrate a variety of healing techniques. 305pp. Jen 75

_____. **YOU CAN MASTER DISEASE**, $5.50. Jensen is a well-known chiropractor who bases his work on preventive therapy and has developed the science of iridology (diagnosis of health through photographs of the eye). This book is subtitled *Lessons Dealing with the Causes of Disease and How They can be Prevented*. Includes chapters on *Starvation in the Midst of Plenty, What Determines Ideal Health, Intestinal Disorders, Fasting and Eliminative Diets, Surgery, Diabetes, Cancer, Colds, The Mental and Spiritual Aspects of Healing*, and much else. Dr. Jensen's approach emphasises purification of the body through good food (usually uncooked) and good thoughts. He includes case studies illustrating his experiences. 229pp. Jen

JOHARI, HARISH. **DHANWANTARI**, $4.95. *This is a book for anyone who is seeking a logical, scientific and practically tested set of principles for daily life. It is a book about waking up, cleansing, eating, drinking, massage, sex and home remedies. It is a book about right living, about synchronizing the individual organism with the cycles of the Cosmos which has given him birth. It is a book about becoming normal. There are chapters on meditation, exercises and the cycle of breath—for these are ways of tuning the system in shorter spans of time. . . . This is a book about techniques of centering, about stabilizing one's energy, about creating a place within one's being to which he can return at will. . . . This book is based upon my own cultural experience [Johari is a Hindu] and the ageless traditions of India. On the pages which follow are practices from Yoga, from Ayurvedic medicine, from the ancient Yunani system of the Greeks and Moslems, and from the timeless tribal cultures which people the plains, deserts and mountains of the Indian subcontinent. But the validity of these practices is not limited to Indians. There is nothing on these pages which has not been tried successfully on and by those born and raised in America. Truth, to be worthy of its name, must be universal.—from the preface.* Illustrations. RHI 74

KELLER, JEANNE. **HEALING WITH WATER**, $.95. Details the author's practical step-by-step methods. Fully indexed. 148pp. ASC 68

KERVRAN, LOUIS. **BIOLOGICAL TRANSMUTATIONS**, $2.75. The only English edition of Kervran's controversial research. He has shown that the mechanisms for the transmutation of biochemical elements exist within man. For example, if you need iron, you can take organic manganese and your body will convert this element into iron. The field of transmutations has been widely applied in France by both physicians and agronomists. This is a detailed account of Kervran's research and discoveries, suitable for the layperson who has some knowledge of the biological sciences. Bibliography, 183pp. SwH 72

KHAN, HAZRAT INAYAT. **THE BOOK OF HEALTH**, $3.95. See the Islam section.

_____. **SUFI HEALING**, $1.95. Inayat Khan was a great Sufi healer, and this newly discovered transcription of his 1925 healing seminar is his most lucid and succinct presentation of Sufi healing, from cause to cure, from disease to health. 40pp. Rai 75

KIEV, ARI, ed. **MAGIC, FAITH AND HEALING**, $2.95. A collection of anthropological papers on the beliefs, rituals, and symbols of the aborigines of Western Australia, the Sea Dayaks of Borneo, the Mescalero Apache of North America, and the Yoruba of Nigeria. Most of the material is dry and academic but there are occasional insights into the healing practices of the groups discussed. Notes, index. 475pp. McM 64

KORTH, LESLIE. **THE PYONEX TREATMENT**, $1.40. 64pp. HSP 68

_____. **SOME UNUSUAL HEALING METHODS**, $5.45. Dr. Korth was trained in traditional medical practices. However, he has devoted his career to the search for alternative practices. This book is a review of the therapies he himself encountered. The material is presented in terms of practical usage and background information is also given. Topics include respiratory therapy, osteopathy, foot reflexology, acupuncture and pulse diagnosis, iris diagnosis, colds and coughs, color therapy, magnetism, and much else. A specific chapter is devoted to each topic. 148pp. HSP 67

_____. **TENSIONS**, $2.40. A collection of short chapters which give a number of self-help techniques for relieving tension, including the use of color, word pictures, and various other relaxation techniques. 78pp. HSP 71

KROEGER, HANNA. **OLD TIME REMEDIES FOR MODERN AILMENTS**, $3.45. This little book, published by the author, is a remarkably interesting collection of natural remedies, modern nutritional knowledge, spiritual healing, fasting, magnetism, etc. One of our best informed alternative medicine enthusiasts speaks highly of it. 105pp. NAF 71

KRUGER, HELEN. **OTHER HEALERS, OTHER CURES**, c$8.95. This is a scattered survey of alternative forms of healing and other aspects of the new consciousness. The material is not well arranged and does not seem to be well researched. Almost every technique is mentioned somewhere in the volume and the format makes a general scanning possible, but those seeking any depth or good general information on a topic should look elsewhere for their information. Fully indexed. 403pp. BoM 74

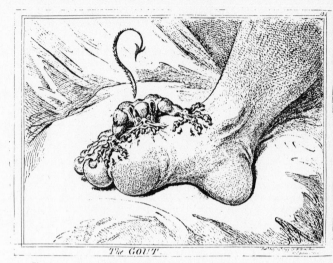

The Gout, by James Gillray, 1799, is an example of the visualization of illness as a demon.

KULVINSKAS, VIKTORAS. **SURVIVAL INTO THE TWENTY-FIRST CENTURY**, $8.00. This is a very popular new book which covers all aspects of alternative healing—albeit in a scattered fashion. The reader can dip into this volume and learn a bit about an incredible variety of things and go from there into more detailed discussions of the topics that interest him/her the most. The layout and general tone of the book is not very pleasing to us; nonetheless it is a welcome effort which should help to turn many people on to natural healing methods. Illustrated throughout and including many practical suggestions. 8½x11". Oma 76

LAW, DONALD. **A GUIDE TO ALTERNATIVE MEDICINE**, $3.95. This is the best encyclopedic work we have seen. We have referred to it often in writing background for the reviews. The material is alphabetically arranged and each entry is brief and informative. The more important topics are discussed at length. There is also a good topically arranged bibliography and a listing of where to go for further information (usually the addresses of related societies), also topically arranged. Every conceivable (to us, anyway!) area is surveyed. Recommended. 212pp. Dov 74

_____. **HOW TO KEEP YOUR HAIR ON**, $3.15.

LAWSON-WOOD, D. and J. **GLOWING HEALTH THROUGH DIET AND POSTURE**, $1.40. A collection of suggestions for ways of improving one's general health based largely on the principles of Oriental medicine and macrobiotics. Basic concepts such as yin-yang and the laws of the universe are discussed in the first chapters. The Lawson-Woods follow with some specific suggestions including a regime of self-massage. The information on yin-yang is the clearest we have read anywhere. Illustrations, 62pp. HSP 73

LOOMIS, EVARTS and J. SIG PAULSON. **HEALING FOR EVERYONE**, c$8.95. A physician and a minister blend their experience to explore the physical, mental, and spiritual elements that make up a complete human being. Both men have had extensive healing experience. The book begins with a conversation between the two and from there Dr. Loomis goes on to analyze man's being from a spiritual point of view. He devotes the next chapter to nutrition and gears his discussion toward the need for maintaining physical harmony. Other chapters review the diabetic and hypoglycemic states and provide advice on muscle use and breathing. Various alternative healing systems are also discussed and evaluated. Sig Paulson then follows up with the minister's view, with emphasis on the importance of proper mental and emotional attitudes. Notes, index. 234pp. Haw 75

MC GAREY, WILLIAM. **EDGAR CAYCE AND THE PALMA CHRISTI**, $4.95. A detailed study of the use of castor oil packs as suggested in the Edgar Cayce readings and as observed in case histories from the readings and in Dr. McGarey's own practice. Cayce suggested the packs as remedies for over fifty different ailments and the results have often been remarkable. Oversize, notes. 133pp. ARE 70

MC GINNIS, TERRI. **THE WELL CAT BOOK**, c$10.00. If you are a cat owner, this book will tell you just about everything you can handle about your pet's body, preventive medicine, diagnostic medicine, home medical care, and breeding and reproduction. It will save on vet bills and provide information halfway between that of the trained vet and the average cat owner. Many line drawings, index. 279pp. RaH 75

_____. **THE WELL DOG BOOK**, c$10.00. Just the same as the above, but for dogs. 237pp. RaH 74

MC GUIRE, THOMAS. **THE TOOTH TRIP**, $3.95. Our dentist doesn't like this book. He says it makes his patients too suspicious. If you think maybe you ought to be a little more suspicious, this is for you. Written by a dentist, it tells you all you'll need to know about your teeth and how to care for them (including good advice on nutrition), plus such chapters as: *A Manual for Survival in the Dental Office, Portrait of the Bad Dentist as Con Artist*, and *How to O.D. Your Teeth*. Written in hip style with many amusing illustrations. Recommended. 233pp. RaH 72

MAJNO, GUIDO. **THE HEALING HAND**, c$25.00. Illustrated with hundreds of photographs, many in full color, this is a well researched account of man's attempts over the centuries to promote good health and conquer pain and disease. Dr. Majno, Chairman of the Department of Pathology at the University of Massachusetts, spent over ten years researching the material. He reviews the techniques and documented experiences of physicians in Egypt, Greece, Rome, India, and China. A mammoth, oversize volume—well documented but still suitable for the general reader. Fully indexed, extensive notes. 594pp. HUP 75

MELLOR, CONSTANCE. **NATURAL REMEDIES FOR COMMON AILMENTS**, c$10.50. This is a modern and up-to-date encyclopedia of common ailments and their remedy by purely natural methods, including homeopathy, herbalism and biochemistry. The author is a physiotherapist and nutritionist. She discusses not only the general nature of disease but the specific treatment of its many signs and symptoms. Preventive suggestions and diets for specific ailments are given in great detail, as are other therapies. The book is alphabetically arranged by disease, and fully indexed. Recommended. 240pp. Dan 73

MENTAL HEALTH

In recent years, research has brought about a much greater awareness of the relationship between the chemical balance in our cells and our emotional and mental states. Most dramatic is the growth of orthomolecular medicine and megavitamin therapy in treating schizophrenia. While still vigorously opposed by many psychotherapists, this metabolic approach is finding new converts within the medical profession as further evidence of its effectiveness becomes known. The Canadian Schizophrenia Foundation found an 85% recovery rate and the Princeton Brain Bio Center found a 90% recovery rate using the biochemical approach, compared to a 35% spontaneous recovery rate and a 50% rate using traditional therapies. The leading organization promoting research and understanding in this field is the Huxley Institute for Biosocial Research (parent of the American Schizophrenia Association) at 56 W. 45th Street, New York, NY 10036. In addition to the books below, see also the section on Sugar, because hypoglycemia is involved in most cases of schizophrenia, alcoholism, etc., and is central to the whole problem of disturbed metabolism that underlies much mental and emotional disturbance.

ADAMS, RUTH and FRANK MURRY. **BODY, MIND AND VITAMIN B**, $1.75. If you get as confused about all the different B vitamins as we do, you will welcome this book. Clearly written, with a wealth of research findings, it details the effects of the various B vitamins on physical ills, mental illness, depression and the stresses of modern life. Lengthy foreword by Abram Hoffer. Bibliography, index. 258pp. War 75

_____. **MEGAVITAMIN THERAPY**, $1.95. This book is largely devoted to various forms of drug abuse and addiction—particularly alcohol and sugar—and their relationship to nutritional deficiencies. The cure includes but is not limited to megavitamin therapy. A good, occasionally rambling, account. Includes a list of addresses where further information on megavitamin therapy may be found. Index, 277pp. War 75

BLAINE, TOM. **MENTAL HEALTH THROUGH NUTRITION**, $3.45. Judge Blaine's interest in allergies led him to hypoglycemia and adrenal cortex insufficiency; these in turn led him to schizophrenia and alcoholism—all the various diseases that respond to diet and megavitamin therapy. Citing a wealth of medical evidence (but lacking footnotes, alas) he alleges that most mental disorders, major and minor, have their genesis in improper or inadequate nutrition. 203pp. CiP 69

CHERASKIN, E. and W. RINGSDORF, JR. **PSYCHO-DIETETICS**, $1.95. With the obvious help of Arlene Brecher, a popular writer on medical subjects, the authors here present their most up-to-date survey of the relationship of diet and psychological stress. Covers alcoholism, schizophrenia, hypoglycemia, depression, etc. Written in popular style, with lots of quizzes by which you can see how you rate on mental states or diet. Useful appendices with further sources of information and an excellent bibliography. Index, 228pp. Ban 74

HOFFER, ABRAM and HUMPHRY OSMOND. **HOW TO LIVE WITH SCHIZOPHRENIA**, c$8.95. This is a new edition of the classic book on schizophrenia by the two doctors who pioneered niacin therapy. Briefly, they view schizophrenia as basically a physical illness due to disturbances in the biochemical balance of the body. It appears to involve a defective adrenal metabolism which results in production of a subtle poison in the blood of the victims—a poison which is counteracted by megavitamin therapy. Written for lay readers, it should be the first book read by persons facing this problem. Index, 224pp. UnB 74

LILLISTON, LYNN. **MEGAVITAMINS**, $1.25. An excellent, up-to-date summary of the whole field: the development of megavitamin therapy for schizophrenia, alcoholism, hypoglycemia, heart attacks, senility, drugs. An interesting chapter details the use of fasting for treatment of schizophrenia and allergies. The final chapter discusses organiza-

tions in the forefront of research and publicity regarding this new therapy. Clear and readable. References, index. 224pp. Faw 75

NEWBOLD, H.L. **MEGA-NUTRIENTS**, c$11.95. This is a worthy addition to the do-it-yourself medical books. Dr. Newbold is a psychiatrist with excellent medical credentials who, like most of his profession, ridiculed or ignored nutritional medicine until he, himself, became hypoglycemic, which the best doctors he could find did not diagnose. He tells his own story in the book and that is one of its delights—the reader gets a good feeling about who the author really is. After hitting on an accurate self-diagnosis he began to read up on nutritional medicine and since then has been able to help his patients much more than he ever did before. In this book Dr. Newbold assumes you don't have access to a physician who is knowledgeable about preventive medicine so it tells you what you need to know (and your doctor ought to know), advising you what tests you can give yourself, and what ones you should ask your doctor to give or authorize. In particular, he gives details on how to establish your own vitamin and mineral regimen, what the minimum tests you need are, and how you can gradually step up dosages of each vitamin and tell when you have hit the right level. Other chapters deal with hormone deficiencies, alcoholism, beauty and weight control, the importance of the right kind of light, aging, and how to save money on your nutritional needs. A final chapter suggests some ways to go about finding a nutritionally-oriented doctor. Recommended. Index, 360pp. Wyd 75

WADE, CARLSON. **EMOTIONAL HEALTH AND NUTRITION**, $1.50. Carlson Wade is one of the most prolific of all the popular health writers. His writing is generally sound, although at times a bit overly enthusiastic for our taste. This book covers hypoglycemia, schizophrenia, megavitamin therapy, effects of caffeine, tension, fatigue and many related topics. 155pp. ASC 71

WATSON, GEORGE. **NUTRITION AND YOUR MIND**, c$1.95. This has been quite a popular book. Dr. Watson was Professor of Philosophy of Science at USC before devoting full time to psychochemical research and treatment. He contends that mental and emotional disorders are caused almost exclusively by physical malfunctioning of the body's metabolism. His unique contribution is the concept of fast oxidizers and slow oxidizers and he provides a simple test by which the reader can determine which metabolic type he is. This, in turn, greatly affects the kind of food each of us needs to be in best physical and mental shape. The book gives practical diet and vitamin suggestions for both types. 204pp. Ban 72

MESSEGUE, MAURICE. **OF MEN AND PLANTS**, c$6.95. An autobiography of the world's greatest plant healer with anecdotes about the thousands he has healed, and a full account of his actual methods and treatment. Even more engrossing than the anecdotes is the plant lore throughout the book. It has been a bestseller in Europe. 327pp. McM 70

MEYER, CLARENCE. **AMERICAN FOLK MEDICINE**, $3.95. A collection of early American remedies, arranged topically by ailment, from a wide variety of people, utilizing ingredients usually found at hand (at least back in the good old days!). Includes a listing of common and Latin names. 296pp. NAL 73

MICHELE, ARTHUR. **ORTHOTHERAPY**, c$6.95. One out of every three Americans is born with a musculoskeletal imbalance which ultimately puts stress on every muscle of the body—a stress that results in pain. Every painful muscle is a tightened and shortened muscle that can only be relaxed through exercise. The core of this book is a series of corrective exercises, each keyed to a particular muscular problem. There are exercises to help hip pain, exercises for sciatica, exercises for cricks in the neck, headaches, and leg cramps. To help ascertain which of them you need, Dr. Michele also includes a series of tests based on the diagnostic procedures he uses in his own private practice. Dr. Michele himself is an orthopedic surgon and in this book he summarizes the results of over thirty-five years of medical study. Illustrations, index. 223pp. EvC 71

MILLER, DON. **BODY MIND**, $1.50. Calling itself the *Whole Person Health Book*, this one, written by a martial arts instructor, deals with movement, breathing, flexibility and relaxation, centeredness, sex and love, and food. It's very general, so only suggested for people just beginning to take an interest in these things. 217pp. Pin 74

MONTGOMERY, RUTH. **BORN TO HEAL**, $1.95. Here Ms. Montgomery gives us the life story and experiences of Mr. A—who she says is one of the greatest healers of our time. Mr. A heals by *laying on of hands* and some of his most interesting cases are cited here along with his interpretation of his healing abilities. 224pp. Pop 73

MOYLE, ALAN. **NATURAL HEALTH FOR THE ELDERLY**, $4.55. Moyle, a British naturopath, begins this book with an explanation of the aging process and how it is complicated by such degenerative diseases as rheumatism, arthritis, bronchitis, emphysema, and asthma. He gives details of simple therapies and diets designed to overcome these and other disorders in the aged. Index, 128pp. TPL 75

MURPHY, JOSEPH. **HOW TO USE YOUR HEALING POWER**, $3.00. A discussion of Jesus' healing power and techniques and an explanation of how the same principles can be applied to every individual. 158pp. DeV

NOLEN, WILLIAM. **HEALING**, $1.75. Nolen, a surgeon, conducts an investigation into faith healing and psychic surgery. The book is in five parts, the first of which sets the stage and relates how Dr. Nolen got interested in these things. Then Nolen devotes three long chapters to analyses of Norbu Chen, Katherine Kuhlman, and Filipino psychic surgeons. A final section sums up his thoughts on healing and the healers previously discussed. Nolen presents interviews with each of the individual healers and does follow-up research on many of the healed patients. He attempts to be objective, but we get the feeling that he just does not believe that the type of healing he is investigating is possible—therefore he finds that most of the healing miracles are hoaxes. In the process he provides a fascinating narrative. 308pp. Faw 74

NULL, GARY. **THE COMPLETE QUESTION AND ANSWER BOOK OF NATURAL THERAPY**, $1.25. Arranged alphabetically by ailment, disease, or organ. Index, 287pp. Del 72

OKI, MASAHIRO. **YOGA THERAPY**, $5.95. In this volume Master Oki presents a series of techniques which are a combination of controlled breathing, mental concentration, and physical movement and which produce concentrated effects on specific organs, muscles, and bodily functions. Master Oki is Japan's foremost yoga teacher and is also adept at Oriental and North African healing arts. Oversize, 150 illustrations, index. 128pp. Jap 76

OYLE, IRVING. **THE HEALING MIND**, $4.95. Dr. Oyle organized New York City's first free clinic. More recently he founded a clinic in Bolinas, CA, which incorporates herbal medicine, osteopathy, traditional medicine, psychic healing, acupuncture, massage, sonopuncture (his own technique utilizing high frequency sound rather than needles), and many other ancient and modern techniques. This narrative relates his experiences in an informal style and emphasizes specific cases and practical self-healing instructions. A well written, informative account for the layperson. Illustrations, notes, bibliography. 125pp. CeA 75

PARAMANANDA, SWAMI. **SPIRITUAL HEALING**, c$2.75. A short religious treatise, with chapters on *Spiritual Healing, Control of Breath and Healing, The Source of Healing Power, Healing of Body and Mind*, and *Healing in Meditation*. 86pp. VdC 75

PFEIFFER, CARL. **MENTAL AND ELEMENTAL NUTRIENTS**, c$9.95. Subtitled *A Physician's Guide to Nutrition and Health Care*, this book will appeal not only to physicians but to educated laypeople who want a more in depth discussion of nutritional treatment of disease. Part I, *Nutritional Background*, contains a lot of material familiar to health food types, written at a fairly simple level (perhaps on the assumption that many physicians are abysmally ignorant in such matters). There is a good discussion of cholesterol and the widespread misunderstandings about it within the profession. Parts II and III deal in depth with the vitamins and trace elements, discussing effects on various conditions, dosages, overdosages, etc. Niacin and megavitamin therapy get first billing since Dr. Pfeiffer is Director of the Brain Bio Center in Princeton, NJ, a research-educational organization for the diagnosis and treatment of biochemical imbalances, with emphasis on mental illness. Part V, *Clinical Problems*, goes into milk problems, alcoholism, hypoglycemia, schizophrenia (good detailed treatment), insomnia, headache, aging and senility, arthritis, skin problems, nutrients for a better sex life, etc. This section is primarily for doctors, but any readers wishing to expand their repertory on drugless healing methods would doubtless find much of value here. This book should be regarded as a useful reference work, rather than a book to curl up with and attempt to read through. Bibliography, name and subject indices. 519pp. Kea 75

POWELL, ERIC. **HEALTH FROM EARTH, AIR , AND WATER**, $1.40. Health from the earth covers clay and mud treatments, from the air covers breathing exercises, and from water deals with the skin and a variety of baths and water packs. The final chapter outlines the Kneipp naturopathic presentation. 64pp. HSP 70

_____. **THE NATURAL HOME PHYSICIAN**, c$15.75. This is an encyclopedic handbook which contains remedies for a host of ailments. The treatments are taken from a variety of natural healing areas including herbalism, biochemistry, homeopathy, spiritual healing, and zone therapy. Powell himself is a naturopath and he brings years of experience to this compendium. The arrangement is alphabetical, with ailments and remedies mixed together; unfortunately there is no index. Nonetheless, this is one of the most useful handbooks that we know of. 284pp. HSP 75

PRENSKY, JOYCE, ed. **HEALING YOURSELF**, $1.50. This small, multilithed booklet contains a great deal of useful information about home remedies for a wide variety of ailments. It also covers babies and children, birth control, vitamins and minerals, and suggests a complete home remedy self-help kit. Written in hip style with a do-it-yourself layout (not always too readable), it is oriented toward good nutrition and natural remedies, but also contains up-to-date medical knowledge. It started with a printing of 500 copies and kept growing as people passed it on and word about it spread. Illustrated with line drawings and some photographs. Index, 65pp. HeY 75

QUICK, CLIFFORD. **NATURE CURE FOR CYSTITIS**, $1.45. A simply written explanation of cystitis—including information on how and why it occurs, its effects on the urinary and other vital body systems, and how to cure it and allied ailments by a combination of diet, exercise, and fasting. 64pp. TPL 75

_____. **SINUSITIS, BRONCHITIS AND EMPHYSEMA**, $1.95. Describes the nature of these diseases, why they happen, and how they can be treated with drugless, natural methods. A variety of diet suggestions, helpful breathing exercises, and other programs are included. Kea 75

RAMACHARAKA, YOGI. **THE PRACTICAL WATER CURE**, $1.00. A comprehensive survey of various water cures practiced in India and the Orient. 123pp. YPS 37

_____. **THE SCIENCE OF PSYCHIC HEALING**, c$5.50/$2.25. A simple introductory explanation of healing through the understanding of natural laws and cooperation with them. Many theories are introduced to acquaint the reader with various aspects of healing. See the Yoga section for more of Ramacharaka's books. 190pp. YPS

REILLY, HAROLD J. and RUTH HAGY BROD. **THE EDGAR CAYCE HANDBOOK FOR HEALTH THROUGH DRUGLESS THERAPY**, c$10.95. Dr. Reilly is a physiotherapist who was referred many cases by Edgar Cayce and has worked with Cayce methods for some forty-five years. In this book he presents a fusion of his own knowledge and experience and Cayce's recommendations. Subjects covered include diet and nutrition, exercise, hydrotherapy, massage, internal cleansing, weight reduction, com-

plexion and skin care, and how to age without growing old. The chapter on massage is particularly good, with extensive instructions and line drawings on how to give a massage. For followers of Cayce's health ideas, this is the most comprehensive, useful book to come along yet. Index, 348pp. McM 75

REYNER, J.H. **PSIONIC MEDICINE**, c$5.95. A new approach to orthodox medicine, involving the assessment and treatment of the underlying causes of clinical symptoms, is described here. Dr. George Laurence discovered that from the scientific application of medical dowsing, precisely determined homeopathic or allied remedies can be presribed to restore vital harmony to the body. Reyner, in collaboration with Dr. Laurence, describes the basis and practice of psionic medicine—including case histories and explanations of techniques. Bibliography, index. 139pp. Wei 74

RODALE, J.J., et al. **ENCYCLOPEDIA OF COMMON DISEASES**, c$12.95. A very comprehensive volume divided into the following general sections: diseases affecting specific parts of the body, general disorders of the body, and general discussions of diseases. Every conceivable area is covered in considerable depth and the discussion is quite specific. The orientation is toward the general reader. Fully indexed. 1008pp. Rod 62

ROSE, LOUIS. **FAITH HEALING**, $2.95. This is a dry review of healing through the ages by a British clinical psychiatrist who has investigated British faith healers such as Harry Edwards and Dr. Christopher Woodard for many years. Bibliography, index. 194pp. Vik 71

ROSSITER, FREDERICK. **WATER FOR HEALTH AND HEALING**, $2.00. The virtues of hydrotherapy or water treatment have been known since ancient times. *It is the purpose of this book to present a practical guide to the use of water for the promotion of health by simple methods which may be used in the home, and to present vital information about the marvels of water and its relation to human health. The book stresses the connection between water and the circulation of the blood and other fluids of the body, and its relations to functions of the mind.*—from the introduction. 112pp. Wte 72

ST. CLAIR, DAVID. **PSYCHIC HEALERS**, c$8.95. A chatty account of the lives and work of eleven American psychic healers: Dorie D'Angelo, Charles Cassidy, Rosita Rodriguez, Harold Plume, Ethel de Loach, the Fullers, Betty Bethards, Bob Hoffman, Dorothy Vurnovas, Reverend William Brown, Dr. Wiliam McGarey. A separate chapter is devoted to each individual and several cases are cited. The addresses of all the healers are also given. 328pp. Dou 74

SAMUELS, MIKE and HAL BENNETT. **BE WELL**, $3.95. The authors believe that each person contains inborn healing abilities which s/he can use to make her/himself well. This impulse toward healthiness represents a guiding force which is available to us every moment of our lives and which is manifest in many forms throughout the world in which we live. In this volume Samuels and Bennett suggest a variety of ways to recognize your inborn healing abilities and to learn what you can do to free them to work at their best. The techniques are simple and can be incorporated into your daily life patterns. It is a very positive message and it is well stated. Illustrations, glossary, bibliography, index. 164pp. RaH 74

_____. **THE WELL BODY BOOK**, $6.95. This is the most comprehensive home medical handbook we've seen. Samuels, a physician at the Headlands Clinic in California, describes in excellent detail how to do a complete physical exam, how to diagnose common diseases, how to practice preventive medicine and how to get the most from your doctor if you do need to go to one. Includes wonderful step-by-step illustrations and an annotated bibliography. Highly recommended. Oversize, 350pp. RaH 73

THE BOW

BOW ASANA: stretches abdomen and hip muscles; relieves stomach gas; reduces abdominal fat. From the Well-Body Book by Samuels-Bennett.

SCOFIELD, ARTHUR G. **CHIROPRACTIC: THE SCIENCE OF SPECIFIC SPINAL ADJUSTMENT**, c$7.80. A comprehensive, scholarly presentation of the principles and history for laypeople and doctors. Chiropractic consists of analysis by X-ray of interference with normal nerve transmission followed by manual adjustment of the vertebral column. This is the best overall book available. TPL 68

SELYE, HANS, M.D. **THE STRESS OF LIFE**, $2.95. This book is a classic. Dr. Selye has received eight honorary degrees and his pioneer work on stress has been compared with the contributions of Pasteur, Ehrlich and Freud. Presented in five parts: I, the discovery of stress; II, the dissection of stress, analyzing the mechanism through which our body is attacked by, and can defend itself against, stress-producing situations; III, the diseases of adaptation: maladies such as cardiovascular diseases, digestive disorders and mental derangements considered to result largely from failures in the stress-fighting mechanism; IV, a sketch for a unified theory; and V, implications and applications, not only in medicine but also as regards man's ability to devise a natural, healthy philosophy of life. Difficult reading for laypeople but has a good glossary and various helps by the author to make his findings accessible. This new revised edition is somewhat more readable than the original. It incorporates the findings of the last twenty years and eliminates some of the original lengthy arguments for matters which are now commonly accepted. Glossary, bibliography, index. 515pp. MGH 76

_____. **STRESS WITHOUT DISTRESS**, $1.75. In this book, Dr. Selye again takes us through a discussion of the mechanism of stress as a nonspecific response of the body to any demand made upon it. He goes on to develop a philosophy of life which is in harmony with the demands of nature and which uses stress as a positive force for personal achievement and happiness. He calls for an altruistic egotism which is both biologically sound and consonant with the teachings of most religions. For those of us who talk about living in harmony with nature, this book presenting the scientific views of a physician can reveal many valuable new perspectives. Glossary, excellent annotated bibliography, index. 171pp. NAL 74

SHEALY, C. NORMAN. **OCCULT MEDICINE**, c$7.95. When we first heard of this book we were put off by the title. Despite its title, this is a fine overview of contemporary healing movements. Dr. Shealy has held professorships in neurosurgery at three American medical schools and he has devoted himself to learning about these techniques and incorporating them into his practice. This book traces what Dr. Shealy has learned about alternative medicine and discusses his experiences with it. It is a personal account which often makes fascinating reading. Dr. Shealy begins with an account of faith healing and then he relates how he got interested in all this. The next section is devoted to an historical study of occult medicine. This is followed by surveys of the medical benefits of psi phenomena, astrology, palmistry, graphology, and much else. The final sections discuss when conventional medicine should be used and when alternative techniques should be applied. Bibliography, index. 214pp. Del 75

_____. **THE PAIN GAME**, $.4.95. Dr. Shealy is a neurosurgeon who believes that drugs and surgery should be used as little as possible in treating pain. In this book he discusses the games patients and doctors play, in transactional analysis terms, and shows how much the condition and the treatment are games. He has developed a clinic in which drugs are withdrawn and operant conditioning (learning to live normally despite the pain) and biofeedback and autogenics are used. The object is to help the patient understand where the pain is really coming from and what he/she can do to take responsibility for dealing with it. The book includes both a discussion of the theoretical aspects of pain, and practical exercises that the reader can do at home. Bibliography, index. 145pp. CeA 76

SHERMAN, HAROLD. **YOUR POWER TO HEAL**, $.95. An excellent overview of all the healing techniques and important healers, including practical suggestions and case studies. 223pp. Faw 72

_____. **WONDER HEALERS OF THE PHILIPPINES**, $5.25. The author investigated claims of psychic surgery being done by persons in the Philippines without drugs or instruments, and causing no pain to patients even though they remained in full consciousness. The operations were reported to have been accomplished only with the use of the surgeon's hands. The facts and results of these highly successful, unorthodox surgeries are presented, allowing the reader to decide for him/herself upon the evidence gathered. Included is a series of pictures of successful surgery being performed on a woman with an internal stomach growth. 328pp. DeV 66

SIMEONS, A.T.W. **MAN'S PRESUMPTUOUS BRAIN**, $2.95. This is the best book we have ever seen on psychosomatic disorders. Dr. Simeons contends that man's brain battles with and submerges his animal instincts and that this battle grows more serious with every advance of our civilization. The book begins with a review of the evolution of the body, psyche, and culture, and provides a medical and historical background for his thesis. Dr. Simeons next discusses the many physical complaints caused by the unceasing struggle between the cortex and the source of our instincts (the diencephalon). Included are disorders of the upper and lower digestive tracts, of the heart and blood vessels, the thyroid and metabolism (obesity), some forms of diabetes, arthritis, and sexual deviations. A fascinating, important contribution. Index, 290pp. Dut 60

STEARN, JESS. **DR. THOMPSON'S NEW WAY FOR YOU TO CURE YOUR ACHING BACK**, c$7.95. Jess Stearn has done it again. Plagued by lower back problems, he finally discovered Dr. Alec Thompson, a well-known Southern California osteopath who developed a simple exercise that anyone can do to relieve the many forms of misalignment which cause a variety of pains in the back and limbs. It seems unnecessary to write a whole book to explain this; a short article or even a couple of pictures would do. Nevertheless, anyone with lower back problems would probably consider $8.00 cheap enough for relief and possibly cure. Much of the book is case histories; the rest gives details that will help you to understand what it is all about and maybe convince you that you can indeed do something about your aching back. Illustrations, glossary. 203pp. Dou 73

STEBBING, LIONEL, ed. **MUSIC: ITS OCCULT BASIS AND HEALING VALUE**, $9.10. See the Music section.

STEINER, RUDOLF. **SPIRITUAL SCIENCE AND MEDICINE**, $6.95. The twenty lectures in this volume were given by a number of physicians. Their form and content were also determined by specific questions asked by those attending the course. Basically the lectures led to a deepened understanding of man's being, without which, in Steiner's words, *it has actually become impossible to investigate the true nature of health and*

disease. Many case studies included in the lectures show the importance of spiritual insights in true healing. The language is often technical. Illustrations, index. 277pp. RSP 48

SUGAR

A hundred years ago the average annual consumption of sugar in the United States was several pounds a year. Now it is over a hundred pounds—more than a teaspoon per hour, every hour of the day or night for every man, woman and child in this country. Virtually every food you buy in the supermarket has some sugar in it. White sugar is not a natural product, but is a highly concentrated form which our bodies were never designed to be able to handle. It goes right to the bloodstream, where it calls forth the production of insulin to balance it. Then it is quickly metabolized (quick energy!) and the insulin is left floating in the bloodstream, causing a low blood sugar condition. Overconsumption of sugar leads to hypoglycemia (low blood sugar) and often then to diabetes, which is increasing in incidence every year in this country. Hypoglycemia is possibly the most widespread and generally undiagnosed disease in America today. Estimates of those affected range from ten to fifty million persons. Hypoglycemia is implicated not only in alcoholism and schizophrenia—the two diseases that lead to more long-term institutionalization than any others—but also in allergies, heart disease, and probably most forms of degenerative disease. Thus we sometimes refer to sugar as America's number one drug addiction problem. And we are delighted to see so many books on the subject now being published. We hope that the general public will begin to wake up to the problem, despite the efforts of the sugar and processed foods industries to convince us that sugar is good for us.

ABRAHAMSON, E.M. and A.W. PEZET. **BODY, MIND AND SUGAR**, $1.50. This was the first book to alert the public to the problem of low blood sugar, here called hyperinsulinism, often called hypoglycemia. Written by a medical doctor, the book relates it to chronic fatigue and allergies, alcoholism and insanity. A thorough presentation of symptoms and effect, enlivened by many case histories. Dietary advice. 240pp. Pyr 51

ADAMS, RUTH and FRANK MURRAY. **IS LOW BLOOD SUGAR MAKING YOU A NUTRITIONAL CRIPPLE**, $1.65. Adams and Murray are two of the most prolific medical and health writers around and their books are balanced and well informed. This is an excellent review of the literature, not only concerning the diseases most often implicated in hypoglycemia, but also including toothache, neurasthenia, psoriasis, hyperactivity, epilepsy, peptic ulcers, gout and multiple sclerosis. If you have a problem with any of these, you'll be interested in the research reported herein. Bibliography, food value tables, index. 174pp. Lar 75

BRENNAN, R.O. **NUTRIGENETICS**, c$8.95. Dr. Brennan is past President of the American College of General Practitioners in Osteopathic Medicine and founder of the International Academy of Preventive Medicine. This book argues the case for better nutrition in preventive medicine. Hypoglycemia keeps coming into the picture because it is so central to virtually all of the problems our cells and organs face from inadequate nutrition. The title comes from Dr. Brennan's view that hypoglycemia results from the combination of genetic and nutritional factors. Appendices include food value tables, menus, recipes, and some suggestions for converting your favorite recipes to more nutritious ones. Index, 258pp. EvC 75

CLEAVE, T.L. THE SACCHARINE DISEASE, $4.95. Saccharine means related to sugar. Subtitled *The Master Disease of Our Time*, this book discusses illnesses resulting from the taking of sugar or via the digestion of starch in white flour, white bread and rice or other refined carbohydrates. And this includes coronary disease, diabetes, obesity, ulcers, bowel disorders. This book, by a British physician, must rank along with Dr. Yudkin's book as must reading for anyone seeking further information about America's number one form of drug addiction: sugar. Kea 75

DUFFY, WILLIAM. SUGAR BLUES, $1.95. Duffy was a pudgy sugarholic until he met Gloria Swanson to do an interview. She set him on the right path and he not only swore off sugar but got into macrobiotics as well. This is a fascinating account of the history of sugar consumption with as much data as the author (a journalist) could find in pretty extensive research of the subject. If you are already anti-sugar you'll love it. If you are not, we hope you won't be put off by Duffy's slam-bang, hyped-up style of writing or his somewhat unnecessary (from our point of view) plugging of macrobiotics at the end of the book. Duffy himself had a happy ending. He looks years younger than he did ten years ago, and after travelling around to plug the book, he and Gloria Swanson got married. 194pp. Faw 75

FREDERICKS, CARLTON. LOW BLOOD SUGAR AND YOU, $2.95. Dr. Fredericks is currently President of the International Academy of Preventive Medicine and one of the best-informed nutritional experts in the business. In this book he presents the basic material on hypoglycemia in a well written and detailed form, suitable to an educated layperson or and M.D. who wants to find out what this disease—belittled by the AMA—is all about. If your doctor pooh-poohs hypoglycemia, maybe you can get him to dip into this book and become aware of the facts his journals aren't giving him. No index, unfortunately. 190pp. CoI 69

HURDLE, J. FRANK. LOW BLOOD SUGAR—A DOCTOR'S GUIDE TO ITS EFFECTIVE CONTROL, $2.95. This is quite a comprehensive treatment. Dr. Hurdle deals with control of low blood sugar through diet, exercise and mind control. He also goes into a host of related conditions: heart disease, alcoholism, digestive problems, etc., showing their relationship to blood sugar and how they can be controlled or helped through blood sugar control. Index, 224pp. PrH 69

MARTIN, CLEMENT. LOW BLOOD SUGAR: THE HIDDEN MENACE OF HYPOGLYCEMIA, $1.65. Arc

SCHWANTES, DAVE. THE UNSWEETENED TRUTH ABOUT SUGAR, $2.95. In easy-to-read fashion, this brief review by a journalist gives the basic information about the growth in sugar consumption, how it acts in the body, its harmful effects, and how you can cut down and substitute honey, maple syrup, fruit, etc. Lots of recipes. Not a very deep book, but useful to give to a friend or relative who needs to be led gently into better eating habits. Index, 96pp. DTP 75

WELLER, CHARLES and BRIAN BOYLAN. HOW TO LIVE WITH HYPOGLYCEMIA, $1.90. 157pp. UPD 70

YUDKIN, JOHN. SWEET AND DANGEROUS, $1.95. This is *the* book about sugar. Dr. Yudkin, M.D., Ph.D., is Professor of Physiology at the University of London and has devoted much of his career to research on the connection between sugar and heart disease, diabetes, ulcers, and many degenerative conditions. Here he reports many of his findings as well as the pressures brought to bear by the sugar interests to see that these findings are not widely understood. Our favorite quotation: *If only a fraction of what is already known about the effects of sugar were to be revealed in relation to any other material used as a food additive, that material would be promptly banned.* Index, 209pp. Ban 72

SUTHERLAND, F. N. THE NATURAL WAY TO HEALTH AND HEALING, $2.25. A general overview of natural healing, with emphasis on *the real cause of disease.* 80pp. Fow 67

THAKKUR, CHANDRASHEKHAR. INTRODUCTION TO AYURVEDA, c$10.00. Ayurvedic medicine is the traditional medicine practiced in India. The system is derived from the Vedas, the most ancient Indian religious writings. Basically the illness is attributed to disorder in one of the four humors (air, water, phlegm, and blood) and the treatment recommended basically utilizes medicinal plants. This is a comprehensive text citing the modern practices and the teachings of the most noted ancient Ayurvedic physicians. Index. 196+pp. ASI 74

THEOSOPHICAL RESEARCH CENTRE. THE MYSTERY OF HEALING, $1.25. This is a sequel to **Unrecognized Factors,** edited by Edmunds, et al. Topics include: *The Healing process; Some Factors in Health and Disease; The Psychological Approach to Healing; Thought Power; Various Unorthodox Treatments and Methods of Diagnosis; Healing Centers and Rituals; The Practice of Self Healing.* An excellent overview, recommended. 95pp. TPH 58

THOMAS, LEWIS. THE LIVES OF A CELL, $1.75. Subtitled, *The Notes of a Biology Watcher,* this is an exploration of man's being—his health, germs and interior organism. Thomas is a noted physician and researcher and he expresses himself in a clear, engaging manner. Geared toward the general reader. Notes, 153pp. Ban 74

TILDEN, JOHN. TOXEMIA, $1.50. One of the basic principles of natural hygiene is that disease is caused not by the invasion of germs against an innocent body, but by toxemia of the body, which makes it attractive to germs which act as nature's scavengers. The solution, of course, is to watch what we put into our bodies and cleanse them as necessary. Dr Tilden, who died in 1940, was one of the most eminent of the natural hygienists, and his book still says much of value. Index, 119pp. ANH 74

TURNER, GORDON. AN OUTLINE OF SPIRITUAL HEALING, $1.25. Turner, a note spiritualist, explains what disease is, how spirit healing works and its relationship to reir carnation, and cites many case histories. 174pp. War 72

TURNER, R. NEWMAN. FIRST AID NATURE'S WAY, $2.75. Ailments such as colds influenza, acute indigestion and headache are dealt with here in addition to cuts, sprains bruises and other minor accidents. The injuries and ailments have been grouped togethe in chapters according to the system of the body affected. There is also a chapter of mis cellaneous conditions. Bibliography, 93pp. TPL 69

VISION

AGARWAL, J. CARE OF EYES, $1.50. This small pamphlet, illustrated with man photographs, contains a lot of good, practical advice on eye exercises and proper use o the eyes as developed by the author's father, Dr. R. S. Agarwal at his Eye Institutes i Delhi and Madras and his School for Pefect Eyesight in Pondicherry. It provides an intro duction to Agarwal's ideas—similar to those of Dr. Bates. 33pp. AAP 62, 71

This OM chart for Eye Exercises was found on Bhojpatra in Kashmir. From Mind and Vision, by R.S. Agarwal.

AGARWAL, R.S. MIND AND VISION, c$6.00. Subtitled, *A Handbook for the Cure o Imperfect Sight without Glasses,* this book first reviews the way the eye sees, the caus of errors of refraction, and then goes into detail regarding care of the eyes and treatmen methods such as eye baths, many relaxation methods, diet, etc. These natural method have become quite popular in India and this book can be used by any individual wh wants to try them out for him/herself. Illustrated with photos, diagrams, and eye chart 269pp. AAP 72

_____. **SECRETS OF INDIAN MEDICINE,** c$6.00. This book is primarily abou the eyes, drawing upon principles of allopathic and ayurvedic medicine. It will be of in terest to persons wishing to know more about Indian medicine and non-physical concept of healing, but is not for general readers since much of what it says is fairly specific t Indian culture. Dr. Agarwal has lived at the Sri Aurobindo Ashram in Pondicherry sinc 1955 and his ideas should appeal to many spiritual seekers. Illustrated, 240pp. AAP 7

_____. **YOGA OF PERFECT SIGHT,** $5.45. This is the most recent of Dr. Agar wal's books and the one we would recommend to most general readers. Not really abou yoga, but about improving your eyesight. Covers the whole range of theory and exercise Some of the basic principles (taken from Bates) are: 1. Reading fine print is beneficia while reading large print in not; 2. Reading in a dim light or in candle light is very useful 3. Reading at a closer distance is beneficial. Includes eye charts and a series of letters t and answers from Sri Aurobindo about Dr. Agarwal's work. 223pp. AAP 74

BATES, W. H. BETTER EYESIGHT WITHOUT GLASSES, $1.75. This is the classi book on the use of various eye exercises to improve eyesight without glasses, originall published in 1920. Dr. Bates was the pioneer in developing methods of mental relaxation focusing techniques and other aids that many since then (such as Dr. Agarwal) have con tinued to promote. This book explains how the eye works, the cause and treatment o errors of refraction and then runs through the methodology in such fashion that the reader can apply it him/herself. A large foldout eye chart is included. 175pp. Pyr 75

BENJAMIN, HARRY. BETTER SIGHT WITHOUT GLASSES, $1.70. This is anothe exposition of the Bates method by a well-known British naturopath. Clearly and simpl written and nicely illustrated. 106pp. Originally published in 1929. TPL 71

CORBETT, MARGARET. HELP YOURSELF TO BETTER EYESIGHT, $2.00. Margare Corbett was perhaps the best-known American disciple of Dr. Bates and she hersel taught many eye teachers through her Los Angeles School of Eye Education. Covers the basic principles of the Bates method with a number of additional drills of her own Nicely illustrated. 217pp. Wil 49

_____. **HOW TO IMPROVE YOUR SIGHT,** c$1.69.

EMEL, DIANA. **VISION VICTORY**, $3.00. This book goes considerably beyond the usual Bates method exercise books to cover also nutrition in relation to eyesight, homeopathic remedies for the eyes, the effect of light on the eyes and the glandular system, iridology (medical diagnosis from observing the condition of the iris), chiropracty and the eyes and much else. Includes several articles by others. A good round up. 193pp. ChP 72

HUXLEY, ALDOUS. **THE ART OF SEEING**, $4.95. In 1939, with eyes rapidly worsening, Aldous Huxley came in contact with the Bates method. He undertook the training, was able to do away with his glasses, and wrote this book in appreciation. It has just been reprinted after thirty-three years. Huxley presents a good review of the scientific argements pro and con and then explains the various exercises. 158pp. Mnt 75

JACKSON, JIM. **SEEING YOURSELF SEE**, $3.95. An oversize book which presents a series of eye exercises designed to help the individual become more conscious of his visual processes and the functions of his eyes. The exercises are easy to follow and are fully illustrated. They are not specifically aimed at improving poor vision—although Jackson discusses this area. Visual care exercises and massage techniques are included to add alertness, sharpen responses, and soothe tired eyes. An excellent work which everyone should find useful, no matter how bad or good their eyes are. Bibliography, 125pp. ut 75

SHEPPARD, HAROLD. **BETTER SIGHT WITHOUT GLASSES**, c$3.95. Another version of the Bates method, first published in 1936. Illustrations, including fold-out eye exercise chart. 153pp. Dou 36

ROSANES-BERRETT, MARILYN. **DO YOU REALLY NEED EYEGLASSES?**, $1.95. This is generally considered the best of the recent books on eyesight improvement. The author is well known in the human potential movement and she has conducted many workshops throughout the country. Her techniques are practical and are very clearly presented. The method is somewhat similar to Bates' but is refined and new ideas are included. Har 74

SIMPKINS, BROOKS. **OCULOPATHY**, $5.80. In this work, Mr. Simpkins argues against the theory that longsight, shortsight and astigmatism are incurable visual defects, portraying how refractive errors develop and how the eye actually adjusts its focus. Diagrams are included which explain to those who prescribe glasses the irregular activity of the intercranial processes of vision primarily responsible for the external refractive error. Remedial methods of treatment, other than glasses, are indicated. This is a technical book for professionals. Illustrated with many diagrams. 105pp. HeS 63

WADE, CARLSON. **ALL NATURAL PAIN RELIEVERS**, c$7.95. A copious grab bag of useful suggestions for relief from headaches, backaches, muscle pains and most every other kind of pain and ache. Wade covers herbal and nutritional remedies, exercises of many kinds, use of ice, water, sun, heat, etc. While we don't care for Wade's hype or agree with the claim in the foreword that the book *is the most treasured and desired reference manual for physicians, scientists, nutritionists...,* if you are trying to kick the drug habit you can doubtless find many ideas here worth trying. Pain-locator index, 227 pp. PrH 75

_____. **FACT BOOK ON HYPERTENSION (HIGH BLOOD PRESSURE) AND YOUR DIET**, $1.50. A useful compendium of information for the twenty-three million Americans who suffer from high blood pressure. Begins with a detailed explanation of the heart and circulatory system, and statistics about cardiovascular diseases. The bulk of the book discusses why and how to avoid salt, sugar, caffeine and fats, how to control stress and how to reduce. Glossary, 158pp. Kea 75

_____. **NATURE'S CURES**, $1.50. Natural methods for relieving headaches, healing colds, eliminating constipation, easing arthritis, sleeping better, increasing stamina, beautifying hair and skin, improving digestion, losing weight, etc. Index, 224pp. ASC 72

WAERLAND, ARE. **HEALTH IS YOUR BIRTHRIGHT**, $2.50. Waerland devoted most of his life to turning people in Scandinavia on to natural healing and especially the *Waerland System*—a systematic nutritional diet designed to cure illness and to prevent any further deterioration of the human organism. He studied medicine in London, Paris and Sweden for almost thirty years and carried out extensive experiments in nutritional physiology before beginning to spread his findings to the European populace. He was extraordinarily successful at spreading the word and was publicly hailed by the greatest scientists and authorities of his day. This book is a detailed presentation of the Waerland system and its underlying philosophy—including sample menus. The second half of the book is devoted to *Waerland Diet in the Treatment of Disease* by Are's wife, Ebba. Here the principles are systematically applied to various ailments and detailed menus, diets and remedies are given. 88pp. Hum (nd)

WAERLAND, EBBA. **REBUILDING HEALTH**, $1.45. This is the most detailed account of the Waerland system. It includes many case histories and outlines the nutritional program of treatment for various diseases. This approach has been used with great success in many European sanitoriums. 252pp. Arc 61

WARMBRAND, MAX. **THE ENCYCLOPEDIA OF HEALTH AND NUTRITION**, $1.95. Dr. Warmbrand is a naturopath and doctor of osteopathy. In this fat book he has collected a wealth of information about natural healing methods for a wide variety of conditions, among them: respiratory diseases, stomach ailments, diabetes, arthritis, rheumatism and gout, heart trouble, constipation, ulcers, liver problems, asthma, nervous tension, infec-

tious diseases and allergies. He ranges from folk medicine to modern health science, all woven around the proposition that the human body has its own natural curative powers and the goal is to find ways to help it maximize these powers without resorting to harmful drugs. A good value. Index, 496pp. Pyr 62

WESTLAKE, AUBREY. **LIFE THREATENED**, c$7.00. Dr. Westlake is a well-known British physician who has intensively studied alternative methods of healing and alternative methods of thinking. The concepts in this volume seem to be derived from the work of Rudolf Steiner and other anthroposophists. *In Part I I have endeavored to establish that a grave menace confronts us in the indiscriminate...use of all these chemical poisons ....In Part II I discuss what can be done about it....This resolves itself into two aspects. The first is how to restore the balance between matter and spirit....The second,...whether there is any way in which the long-term effects of paratoxic environment can be detected, and can be rectified before irreversible damage has been done, both in the world of nature and in man himself.* Index, 193pp. Wat 67

WHITEHOUSE, GEOFFREY. **EVERYWOMAN'S GUIDE TO NATURAL HEALTH**, $4.70. Despite the title, this is more of a guide to mothers-to-be than a general study of ailments peculiar to women. There is also, however, a great deal of information on specific female ailments including material on women's hormones, varicose veins, cervicitis, polyps and pruitus, ailments of the urinary system, prolapse of the uterus, breast disorders, menopause, and the pill. The material is presented in a straightforward manner and the suggestions are clearly put. Index, 159pp. TPL 74

WILBORN, ROBERT and JAMES and MARCIA TERRELL. **HANDBOOK OF IRIDIAGNOSIS AND RATIONAL THERAPY**, $16.50.

WINTER, RUTH. **TRIUMPH OVER TENSION**, $3.95. A collection of *100 Ways to Relax*. Each of the suggested remedies is briefly explained and the causes of tension are examined. Bibliography, index. 106pp. G&D 76

OLGA WORRALL

CERUTTI, EDWINA. **OLGA WORRALL**, c$7.95. Ms. Worrall is one of America's most renowned spiritual healers. Her ministry has mainly been in Christian circles and she often refers to the Bible in her healings. This is a moving biographical study of her life and ministry and many case studies are included. 169pp. H&R 75

WORRALL, AMBROSE and OLGA, **THE GIFT OF HEALING**, $3.95. This is the simple and factual account of the experiences of these two spiritual healers. 220pp. H&R 65

YALLER, ROBERT and RAYE. **THE HEALTH SPAS**, $2.95. This is a guidebook to the health spas, clinics and sanitariums in the U.S., Mexico, Europe, Israel and Japan. It begins with several brief chapters discussing types of institutions, what they do and what they are like, with special attention to fasting spas, special food spas, and the Ringberg Cancer Clinic in Germany. Then follow the country chapters with some general information plus a listing of many of the more important places. It is a useful guide for anyone who has the desire (or need) to visit such spas. Illustrated, glossary of health spa terminology. 158pp. WoP 74

YESUDIAN, S. and ELIZABETH HAICH. **YOGA AND HEALTH**, $1.50. Explains the achievement of physical and mental well-being by means of yoga. From a general discussion of principles the authors move on to practical hatha yoga, and in this section describe carefully the three essential factors to be combined: control of consciousness, breath control, and physical postures. The text is well illustrated and the exposition is excellent. This is the best work of this type that we've seen. 184pp. H&R 53

FISH ASANA: strengthens back and neck musles; helps sexual and abdominal muscles.

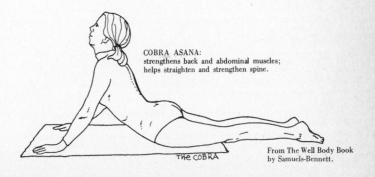

COBRA ASANA:
strengthens back and abdominal muscles; helps straighten and strengthen spine.

From The Well Body Book by Samuels-Bennett.

HERBS

Title page of THE GRETE HERBAL (Pierpont Morgan Library)

Herbalism is the oldest known method of healing. The oldest record of herbal treatment is Chinese, dating from 3000 BC and it was used extensively in the Egyptian, Babylonian-Assyrian, and Greek civilizations. Until the twentieth century the majority of healing throughout the world had an herbal basis. Herbalism is one form of healing which is impossible to control because anybody with a book can go out and collect the plants for him/herself, make the medicines and take them. Herbal medicine works upon the natural theory of correcting what is wrong with the body so that it may heal itself. It seeks to strengthen the natural functions of the body.

BECKETT, SARAH. **HERBS FOR CLEARING THE SKIN**, $1.25. Arranged according to herbs, with a line drawing of each, a description, the part used, and directions for use. Also includes some general information and a therapeutic index. 64pp. TPL 73

_____. **HERBS FOR FEMININE AILMENTS**, $1.25. Same format and content as Herbs for Clearing the Skin. 63pp. TPL 73

_____. **HERBS FOR RHEUMATISM AND ARTHRITIS**, $1.35. Same format as Ms. Beckett's other herbals. 59pp. TPL 75

_____. **HERBS TO SOOTHE YOUR NERVES**, $1.10. A useful, practical compendium, including descriptions (with line drawings) and directions for use. Also includes some background information on the effects of each herb along with an introduction explaining how herbs can heal. Alphabetically arranged by herb. 64pp. TPL 72

BERGLUND, BERNDT and CLARE BOLSBY. **THE EDIBLE WILD**, $3.45. Includes descriptions (with line drawings) of over fifty wild plants, trees, and shrubs that provide edible food, with recipes that have been adapted from those of the pioneers, early settlers and the Indians. Geared toward those whose knowledge of these plants is small. The authors are considered two of Canada's leading authorities on wilderness survival. Alphabetically arranged, index. 188pp. Scr 71

BETHEL, MAY. **THE HEALING POWER OF HERBS**, $2.00. An excellent book tracing uses of herbs and the properties of various herbs. Various diseases are discussed in detail and there are chapters on pregnancy and child care. Recommended. 160pp. Wil 74

CERES. **HERBS AND FRUIT FOR SLIMMERS**, $1.35. Twenty plants, alphabetically arranged, with information on their nutritive and healing properties and line drawings. 64pp. TPL 75

_____. **HERBS AND FRUIT FOR VITAMINS**, $1.25. Same format as Ceres' other books. 64pp. TPL 75

_____. **HERBS FOR FIRST-AID AND MINOR AILMENTS**, $1.25. A useful compendium, alphabetically arranged by herb (with line drawings of each) and including a therapeutic index. Includes information on usage as well as folklore. 64pp. TPL 72

_____. **HERBS TO HELP YOU SLEEP**, $1.45. A descriptive selection of herbs which help induce sleep, including line drawings of each one and a concise statement of the properties of the herb and the folklore surrounding it. Alphabetically arranged, and including a therapeutic index. 62pp. TPL 72

COON, NELSON. **THE DICTIONARY OF USEFUL PLANTS**, c$10.95. A compendium of information on hundreds of plants found in the U.S. Each plant is featured in an entry, arranged alphabetically within botanical families. Each entry describes the plant and its habitat and discusses the fact and folklore behind current and historic uses. Many practical details are included and most of the individual listings include line drawings. A clearly written account. Coon also includes a long introduction covering the

main uses of plants and a special section on American Indian uses of plants. Long bibliography, fully indexed. 304pp. Rod 74

CRESCENT BOOKS. **COLOR TREASURY OF HERBS AND OTHER MEDICIN**[A]**PLANTS**, c$1.98. Wonderful large pictures and practical instructions for their use. excellent value. Out 72

CROW, W.B. **THE OCCULT PROPERTIES OF HERBS**, $1.00. An overview of the use herbs in areas such as astrology, alchemy, magic, and religion. Also includes material herbs in healing and the symbolism of herbs. 64pp. Wei 69

CULPEPER, NICHOLAS. **COMPLETE HERBAL**, c$6.70. A comprehensive descripti[on] of many herbs with their medicinal properties. Includes color pictures of many of [the] herbs, descriptions of all of them, places they are found, and very complete directions [for] use. Includes a listing of diseases and the herbs that will cure them. This herbal is ov[er] 250 years old and has remained consistently popular. 430pp. Fou

_____. **CULPEPER'S HERBAL REMEDIES**, $2.00. An adaptation of Culpepe[r's] **Complete Herbal**, intended for modern use. Includes over 100 herbs, their description a[nd] modern uses. 128pp. Wil 73

ELBERT, VIRGINIE and GEORGE. **FUN WITH GROWING HERBS INDOORS**, $4.9[5] This is by far the best book on growing herbs we have seen. The Elberts tell how to sele[ct] the right plants and how to care for the seeded plants. With excellent how-to illustratio[ns] the authors demonstrate the step-by-step methods of growing an herb garden, includi[ng] informative directions for quarantining, potting, repotting, decanting the plant, p[ot] binding, cleaning the roots, multiplying plants, cutting, and growing the cuttings. T[he] second half of the book is devoted to detailed growing instructions for many herbs. Exot[ic] varieties are included (ginger, for example) along with the more well-known herb[s.] Oversize, index, some color plates. 192pp. Crn 74

EMBODEN, WILLIAM A. **BIZARRE PLANTS**, c$10.95. Folklore and descriptions [of] many highly unusual plants, illustrated with photographs. Index, 214pp. McM 74

FOLEY, DANIEL, ed. **HERBS FOR USE AND FOR DELIGHT**, $3.50. A collection [of] articles by amateurs and scientists, this book covers an extremely wide range of materi[al] from popular historical accounts of herb usage to personal accounts of cultivating herb[s] to analyses of specific herbs to scientific papers on the latest research. The articles we[re] selected from **The Herbalist**, the annual publication of the Herb Society of America. [In] all, sixty-four different articles are presented, with illustrations and tables. 323pp. Dov [71]

FOSTER, GERTRUDE. **HERBS FOR EVERY GARDEN**, c$7.50. Ms. Foster and he[r] husband have been publishing **The Herb Grower Magazine** for over twenty-five years[.] The articles in the magazine derive mainly from the Fosters' own herb garden in Con[necticut] where they grow over 300 species of herbs gathered from all parts of the globe[.] Ms. Foster is recognized nationwide as an authority on the history, cultivation, and use [of] herbs. She has organized and presented her knowledge very well in the volume. The con[tents] include all the information necessary to start a successful herb garden indoors o[r] outside, and special sections present the use of herbs for pest control in the garden an[d] the preparation of herbs for culinary and medicinal usage. A definitive volume. Illustra[tions], bibliography, index. 256pp. Dut 73

GABRIEL, INGRID. **HERB IDENTIFIER AND HANDBOOK**, c$6.95. Over 100 herb[s] are described and pictured (many in color). Each entry includes the following materia[l:] scientific name; popular names; where found; description; elements contained; medicina[l] use (with detailed instructions); and culinary use. Indexed by ailment, scientific name[,] popular name, and geographic location. The pictures (line drawings and color plates[)] are about the clearest we've seen. 256pp. Str 74

GEOGRAPHIC HEALTH STUDIES PROGRAM. **A BAREFOOT DOCTOR'S MANUAL**[.] $12.25. See the Oriental Medicine section.

GERARD, JOHN. **THE HERBAL, OR GENERAL HISTORY OF PLANTS**, c$50.00[.] Gerard's **Herbal** has long been the most famous English herbal. First published in 1597, i[t] was republished in 1633 in an edition in which Thomas Johnson revised and enlarged the original text. This is a photographic reproduction of the 1633 edition, which describe[s] 2850 plants and has about 2700 illustrations. In both text and illustration, it is a monu[ment] of Renaissance botany and at the same time it remains a remarkable compendium of Elizabethan folklore and naturalistic description. 8½x12", 1723pp. Dov 1633

GEUTER, MARIA. **HERBS IN NUTRITION**, $3.15. Ms. Geuter, an anthroposophis[t] (see Steiner section), begins with an extensive discussion of the importance of consciou[s] cooking. She explains how various herbs can be used to alter an individual's temperamen[t] in addition to his/her health. She then gives a deep analysis of the spiritual and physica[l] properties of twenty-six different herbs. An unusual, informative account. 108pp. Bio 62

GIBBONS, EUELL. **STALKING THE HEALTHFUL HERBS**, $3.95. A delightfully written book which discusses many of the culinary and medicinal herbs native to North America—kinds that were well known to the Indians and early settlers. His intimate knowledge of these plants is based on countless field studies as well as on painstaking research. Includes line drawings, descriptive and usage material. All of Gibbons' book[s] are very popular. 303pp. McK 74

GRIEVE, M. **A MODERN HERBAL**, $10.00. The most comprehensive herbal imaginable[.] Two large volumes containing the medicinal, culinary, cosmetic, and economic properties

tivation and folklore of herbs, grasses, fungi, shrubs and trees with their uses. Detailed scriptions as well as drawings of many of the plants. Recommended. 888pp. Dov 71

ARDING, A.R. GINSENG AND OTHER MEDICINAL PLANTS, $7.00. A 1908 book ich discusses the folklore of ginseng, gives comprehensive cultivation instructions, luding material on diseases and marketing. The same information is presented for her medicinal plants, including Golden Seal. Many illustrations. 367pp. HeR

ARPER-SHOVE, F. PRESCRIBER AND CLINICAL REPERTORY OF MEDICINAL RBS, $4.70. Provides leading symptoms of diseases and ailments, together with the rresponding herb or herbs for treatment by homeopathic medicine, and the exact dos- e to be prescribed in each case. The book is arranged according to parts of the body and ther subdivided into ailments. Also includes a list of herbal remedies, abbreviations, and act dosages (including time). There's also a section listing synonyms, common, or local mes of herbs. 240pp. HSP 52

ARRIMAN, SARAH. THE BOOK OF GINSENG, $1.50. A new book which presents cient lore, recent discoveries, and information on buying growing, and using ginseng. tes, bibliography. 157pp. Pyr 73

ARRINGTON, H.D. and L.W. DURRELL. HOW TO IDENTIFY PLANTS, $3.95. A ry thorough scholarly text on plant identification going over identification of each the plant and giving many keys to identification. Also includes questions following ch section. Each topic is extensively illustrated throughout. Only recommended to ose who are very serious about learning the subject. 203pp. Swa 57

ARRIS, BEN. BETTER HEALTH WITH CULINARY HERBS, $3.95. A detailed survey domestic and wild culinaries, their cultivation, collection, and uses. Also includes re- pes and formulas for home remedies. Harris identifies the nutritive and salutary ingred- nts in each herb and offers some dietary tips. Index, 163pp. BaP 71

_____. EAT THE WEEDS, $1.25. Detailed descriptions and recipes for about 150 ommon plants, including material on habitat, part used, preparation, and synonyms in ition to the more general material. There's also a long introduction incorporating Harris' any years of experience. The herbs described are especially prevalent in northeastern nited States. Bibliography, index. 240pp. Kea 73

ARRIS, LLOYD. THE BOOK OF GARLIC, $10.00. This is a humorous, comprehensive ook on garlic which includes sections on the history and folklore of garlic, a garlic herbal with many Russian remedies), and a scientific survey of garlic's composition and healing gredients. There's also a section of garlic culinary recipes. Oversize, extensively illus- ated, bibliography. 273pp. HRW 74

EFFERN, RICHARD. THE COMPLETE BOOK OF GINSENG, $3.95. A comprehen- ve presentation, divided into the following sections: botany, history, legends, grades, omparative values of Asiatic and North American varieties, early and contemporary re- arch, cultivation and marketing, collection of the wild plant. Illustrations, bibliography, dex. 127pp. CeA 76

_____. THE HERB BUYER'S GUIDE, $1.25. The only available guide to the pur- hase, processing and use of herbs. The appendix contains addresses of sources for addi- onal information. 187pp. Pyr 73

_____. SECRETS OF THE MIND-ALTERING PLANTS OF MEXICO, $1.50. A etailed study of a great number of plants, including line drawings, description, and infor- ation on their properties, uses, and the research that has been done with them. Also here's some folklore and background information. The text includes material from ancient layan and Aztec sources in addition to contemporary material. Index, 204pp. Pyr 74

_____. THE USE OF HERBS IN WEIGHT REDUCTION, $1.50. Pyr 75

ERMANN, MATT. HERBS AND MEDICINAL FLOWERS, c$4.98. The full color, arge drawings of herbs in this volume make this book the most valuable identification uide that we know of. 221 different plants are illustrated, with a brief accompanying ext highlighting the medicinal properties of each, along with a bit of folklore. Both the atin name and the common use are indicated and cross-referenced. There's also a short herapeutic index. Oversize, 128pp. GaB 73

EWLETT-PARSONS, J. HERBS, HEALTH AND HEALING, $2.05. A well-presented ynopsis of herbal uses for various ailments, with specific remedies and the directions for heir preparations and background information on each ailment. Chapters include: the irculatory system; digestive system; skin; respiratory system; nervous system; liver and all bladder; urinary system; women's complaints. Recommended as a good overview. Hewlett-Parsons is a naturopath. 94pp. ThP 75

OOKER, ALAN. HERB COOKERY, $4.95. A nicely laid out non-vegetarian cook- ook, utilizing herbs in the recipes and explaining the culinary uses of herbs. Index, 92pp. Scr 71

USON. PAUL. MASTERING HERBALISM, c$10.00. Huson has written extensively on witchcraft and his herbal emphasizes the folklore and traditional uses of herbs in witch- raft and astrology. There's also a great deal of material on herbal perfumes and incense nd on herbal beauty secrets along with more traditional sections on herbal remedies and ulinary herbs. There are chapters on growing herbs and planting and harvesting by the moon. Huson also provides an excellent annotated listing of mail-order herbal sources. lossary, illustrations, tables of weights and measures, index. A well written, unusual ccount. 371pp. S&D 74

UTCHENS, ALMA. INDIAN HERBOLOGY OF NORTH AMERICA, c$10.00. This is he definitive work on the subject. There's not another book that even comes close to pre-

senting the wealth of material contained here. The material presented comes from the author's years-long study of Anglo-American, Russian, and Oriental literature on Indian Medical Botanics. The textual order is alphabetical, according to the common name of the herb. All of the proper names are also included along with a drawing of the plant and the following information: features (what the plant looks like); medicinal part; solvents; bodily influence; uses (internal and external); dose; homeopathical clinical uses; uses throughout the world. The information is presented in a concise fashion, with no unnec- essary verbiage. There's also a 33pp bibliography, very well annotated, and a 29pp detailed index. Highly recommended for the serious student. 382pp. Mer 74

HYLTON, WILLIAM, ed. THE RODALE HERB BOOK, c$12.95. Over half of this weighty volume is devoted to an herbal encyclopedia, discussing more than 150 herbs, with many entries illustrated with photographs. The unique contribution of this volume, though, is not the herbal encyclopedia—helpful though it might be—but the specialized chapters. Each is written by an expert and the material is covered in depth. Chapters in- clude: *The Healing Herbs*—Nelson Coon (a disease-by-disease discussion); *The Culinary Herbs*—Louise Hyde; *The Aromatic Herbs*—Bonnie Fisher; *The Colorful Herbs*—Barbara Foust (dyeing with herbs); *Cultivating the Herbs*—Heinz Grotzke (Heinz runs the Mead- owbrook Herb Garden, source of some of the best quality herbs available); *The Com- panionable Herbs*—William Hylton. Also includes a glossary, list of sources, bibliography, and index. 653pp. Rod 74

MARJORAM: leaf stalk and flowering stem, with enlarged flowers and flower groupings of O. vulgare.

KADANS, JOSEPH. ENCYCLOPEDIA OF MEDICINAL HERBS, $1.00. Preparation and uses of hundreds of herbs. Gives alternate names of the herbs (there are many) and a unique *herb-o-matic* locator index which gives many ailments and the herbs which treat them. Very clearly presented. 256pp. Arc 73

KERR, RALPH. HERBALISM THROUGH THE AGES, c$6.55. Legends and folklore from antiquity to contemporary times. 226pp. Amo 69

KIMMERS, ANDREW, ed. TALES OF THE GINSENG, $3.95. Folklore about ginseng, mainly Confucian and Taoist, in the form of stories. Annotated bibliography, index. 218pp. Mor 75

KLOSS, JETHRO. BACK TO EDEN, c$7.95/2.25. The most popular herbal—over one million copies sold. We prefer Levy's **Herbal Handbook**, but this is the bible for many. There is material on all kinds of natural cures, a long section of diseases and suggested remedies, information on preparation, foods and a potpourri of much else. The organiza- tion leaves something to be desired, but there's certainly a lot of information here. 700pp. WoP

KROCHMAL, ARNOLD and CONNIE. A GUIDE TO THE MEDICINAL PLANTS OF THE UNITED STATES, $4.95. Dr. Krochmal has a Ph.D. in Economic Botany and is sidered an expert on medicinal plants. This is a well-organized account, profusely illus- trated with line drawings and photographs. Each entry (organized alphabetically by the common name) includes information on other common names; plant description; where the plant grows; what is harvested and when; and uses. Appendices cite sources of botanical supplies and meanings of plant names. Fully indexed and cross-referenced. Bibliography, 259pp. NYT 73

LAW, DONALD. **HERB GROWING FOR HEALTH**, $1.65. Law is an authority on botanic medicine. Here he tells how to grow, use and recognize over 150 healing herbs. Includes information on growing them indoors and a section on the medicinal value of the bark and leaves of over forty kinds of trees. 223pp. Arc 72

LEEK, SYBIL. **HERBS: MEDICINE AND MYSTICISM**, c$9.95. A straightforward, informative herbal, alphabetically arranged and giving the following information: botanical name, synonyms, habitat, description, action, medicinal uses, method of use, dosage, culinary uses, astrological rulership. Special sections cover the medicinal herbs of the Hopi Indians and extensive information on herbs and astrology. Despite our generally not very positive feeling about Sybil Leek, this seems to be a well-researched, well-organized and clearly written volume. The astrological sections are especially useful since there is so little written on the subject. Also includes an extensive listing of retail sources for herbs, with addresses. 255pp. Reg 75

CARAWAY: with variation of foliage, beginning with first leaf, lower right, slightly older above and on the left a mature leaf; also umbel, enlarged flower and dried seed.

LEVY, JULIETTE de BAIRACLI. **COMMON HERBS FOR NATURAL HEALTH**, $2.45. This is an excellent herbal, one of our favorites. The author is a practicing herbalist and botanist (and some say a gypsy). A long section is devoted to herbal *materia medica*, there are original cosmetic and curative recipes, a chapter on the uses of certain plants for the benefit of others, notes on herb preservation, planting with the moon, and much else. The material is alphabetically arranged by the common name of each herb and each entry includes an illustration, the Latin name, where found, use, and dosage, along with a bit of folklore. Two indices: names of herbs and recipes for herbal treatments, and disorders and diseases amenable to herbal treatment. 200pp. ScB 74

_____. **THE COMPLETE HERBAL FOR THE DOG**, $9.75. A handbook of natural care and rearing. 207pp. Arc 73

_____. **HERBAL HANDBOOK FOR FARM AND STABLE**, c$5.00. *Contains much sound advice on the general management of livestock and much wisdom on herbal remedies: The author gives useful information about the many herbs she lists and then sets out cures and preventions for ailments of sheep, goats, cows, horses, poultry, and sheepdogs.* – The Field. The text begins with a general materia medica, geared toward livestock and then goes on to specific sections on each of the animals discussed, subdivided into ailments pertinent to each animal. Index, 320pp. Fab 73

_____. **NATURE'S CHILDREN**, $1.25. A guide to organic foods and herbal remedies for children. 176pp. War 72

LEYEL, C.F. **ELIXIRS OF LIFE**, c$7.00. An English herbal which concentrates on those herbs which prolong life by rejuvenating the glands and repairing tissue wastes and keeping the digestive organs functioning normally. The material is alphabetically arranged. Each entry includes a line drawing and a great deal of folklore in addition to summarized basic materia medica. Many of the herbs are exotic and are not easily avail-

able. The presentation is often more chatty than informative. 221pp. Wat 70

LIGHTHALL, J.I. **THE INDIAN FOLK MEDICINE GUIDE**, $1.25. This survey, first published in 1883, was written by a lifelong student of the roots, flowers, barks, leaves and herbs that comprise the Indian pharmacopaeia. Over 100 remedies are discussed. big drawback is the lack of a coherent organization in the volume. 158pp. Pop

LOWENFELD, CLAIRE. **HERB GARDENING**, $3.15. Fab

LOEWENFELD, CLAIRE and PHILIPPA BACK. **HERBS, HEALTH AND COOKER** $1.95. This is a comprehensive survey of culinary herbs, including material on he use in special diets, directions for teas, descriptions of the twenty-four most common used culinary herbs, and recipes utilizing herbs. There's also a short section on the use a health properties of many individual herbs. Index, 441pp. ASC 67

LUCAS, RICHARD. **COMMON AND UNCOMMON USES OF HERBS FOR HEALTHF** LIVING, $1.65. Lucas' second book and the more comprehensive one. Detailed chapt on remedies, herb lore; chapters on specific plants such as dandelion, sage, nettle, onio sections on healing plants from the sea, herbal health secrets of the American India herbs and their effect on the emotions, and much else. Recommended. 208pp. Arc

_____. **GINSENG, THE CHINESE WONDER ROOT**, $2.15. Nut

_____. **THE MAGIC OF HERBS IN DAILY LIVING**, c$8.95. PrH 72

_____. **NATURE'S MEDICINES**, $2.00. A fascinating account of the folklo and value of herbal remedies. Chapter headings include: *The Intriguing Herb that Hid from Man, Strange and Mystic Plants, The Favorite of the Pharaohs, The Secret of Pe petual Youth.* Includes practical information. 224pp. Wil 74

LUST, JOHN. **THE HERB BOOK**, c$12.95/2.50. This is the most comprehensive ar best written of all the contemporary herbals and our favorite for the general reader. Ce tering on a comprehensive section describing medicinal uses for more than 500 plants nearly 300 of them illustrated—the book combines traditional herbal knowledge with t latest information from current research, especially research carried out in Europe whe herbal medicine is still a vital branch of the medical profession. Special sections on botan obtaining and keeping herbs, and making and using herbal preparations help you unde stand and use what you learn. There's also an extensive glossary of medicinal effects ar herbs that produce them, a listing of plants applicable to various conditions and body o gans, and three separate indices along with the most comprehensive bibliography we'v seen. A final section discusses herbal mixtures, drinking herbs, natural cosmetics, and pla dyes—along with material on plant legend and lore. 659pp. Ban 74

MABEY, RICHARD. **FOOD FOR FREE**, c$8.95. A guide to the edible plants in Britai with line drawings and color plates and very complete information. Scr 73

MEDSGER, OLIVER. **EDIBLE WILD PLANTS**, $3.95. A classic work which has guide several generations of nature lovers. Detailed line drawings of over 150 species, alor with information on where to find the plants, how to recognize them, and what parts eat. Included are fruits and berries, salad plants and herbs, roots and tubers, nuts, beverag and flowering plants, seeds and seed pods. Plants are listed by type and species as we as by region; descriptions include characteristics, when each is in season, and scientifi and common names. Fully indexed, 324pp. McM 72

MESCHTER, JOAN. **HOW TO GROW HERBS AND SALAD GREENS INDOORS** $1.50. A good, profusely illustrated (with line drawings and photographs) account wi step-by-step instructions. The material on salad greens is hard to find elsewhere in clear a form and for the price the book is the best value we know of. Index, 176pp. Pop 7

MEYER, JOSEPH. **THE HERBALIST**, c$5.95. This is one of the best regarded olde herbals. This is a revised and enlarged edition prepared by the author's son. The herba materia medica is one of the most complete we've seen and includes a shaded line drawin of each plant along with information on the botanic and common names, medicinal part description, properties and uses and dosage. There are also over 400 color illustrations o various plants. In addition, the book has the following special features: a section detailing medicinal uses of certain classes of herbs, a section on teas and one on culinary herbs material on potpourri, sachets, plant dyes, and wines. Index, 304pp. Str 60

MILLSPAUGH, CHARLES. **AMERICAN MEDICINAL PLANTS**, c$15.00/$10.00 This is an unabridged reproduction of the 1892 edition, considered the definitive herba of its day. After general descriptions of the order and genus, every plant is presented ir botanical sequence. Common and scientific names are given. Then follows a detailed description of the plant with full information on its size, color, shape, range, habitat The medicinal use of the plant is equally detailed; the author cites observations from the time of the Greeks to the end of the nineteenth century. Each disease or ailment the herb is reported to have an effect on is noted and methods of preparation are given alon with the chemical constituents extracted from each. Altogether 180 plants are covered— each with a full page illustration. There's also a therapeutic index which keys over 100 ailments to herbs. Many indices. 828pp. Dov 74

MUIR, ADA. **THE HEALING HERBS OF THE ZODIAC**, $1.00. In ancient times al herbalists studied the zodiacal sign and planetary ruler of each herb and saw that it was gathered under the most favorable planetary conditions. Often, Ms. Muir feels, herbs are combined irrespective of planetary laws and the active principle of one will counteract the active principle of another. This is a study of the herbs pertaining to each of the twelve signs of the zodiac, with descriptive material on each one. Some medical astrology as it pertains to each sign, is also included. Illustrations, index. 63pp. Llp 59

PAGE, NANCY and RICHARD WEAVER. **WILD PLANTS IN THE CITY**, $3.95. A use ful, color-coded guide to the most common wild plants found in abandoned lots and parks

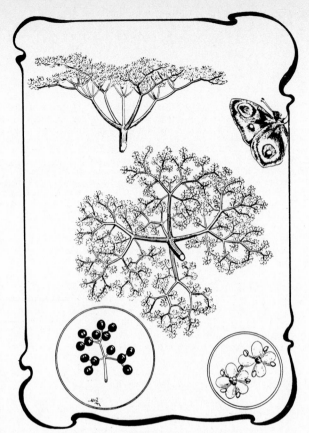

ELDER: flowering head, enlarged flowers showing variation in numbers of petals and berries.

in eastern U.S. cities. The authors have described each plant and include photographs and line drawings of each. Bibliography, index. 127pp. Qdr 75

PALAISEUL, JEAN. **GRANDMOTHER'S SECRETS**, c$7.95. A comprehensive record of the herbal folklore of the author's French grandmothers. Over 150 plants and their properties are described in detail, accompanied by line drawings. Common names are used. 292pp. Put 74

RAU, HENRIETTA. **HEALING WITH HERBS**, $1.50. An encyclopedic guide to the healing properties of a large number of herbs. The information on each herb is extremely complete and is also quite approachable. All the possible uses are detailed and the usable parts of each are noted. A final section lists the herbs which are useful in over three hundred ailments. An excellent all-round presentation which we recommend highly. The author is a naturopath who has worked extensively with medicinal herbs. Fully indexed, 235pp. Arc 68

ROSE, JEANNE. **HERBS AND THINGS**, $2.95. **Herbs and Things** is one of the most popular herbals among our customers. It is attractively designed and clearly written. It's also one of our favorites. The first part consists of an alphabetical list of human conditions and the herbs that affect them. The second part is a very well done materia medica. There's also a glossary, a table of weights and measures and their equivalents, and a listing of where to purchase botanicals. Various recipes for all types of things (including beautifying oneself) are also included and there's a good bibliography and a long index. Recommended. 323pp. G&D 74

_____. **JEANNE ROSE'S HERBAL BODY BOOK**, $4.95. As the title suggests, this herbal is devoted to recipes for cosmetic herbal preparations of all types. Every conceivable topic is fully covered and the instructions are clear and often humorous. About 100pp is devoted to descriptions of plants. There's also a cosmetic glossary and information on where to buy the herbs. This is far and away the best book of this type we know. Illustrations abound throughout. 400pp. G&D 76

ROWSELL, HENRY and HELEN MAC FARLANE. **HENRY'S BEE HERBAL**, $1.80. TPL

RUTHERFORD, MEG. **A PATTERN OF HERBS**, $2.95. This book has some of the nicest illustrations of any volume we know. The line drawings are clear and well made and often sections of the flowers and stems are shown in detail. The description of each herb is adequate, although we do not care for many of the suggested culinary recipes. The emphasis is not on the medicinal qualities—in fact this feature is hardly mentioned. Bibliography, 157pp. Dou 74

SANECKI, KAY. **THE COMPLETE BOOK OF HERBS**, c$9.95. This is a comprehensive account for the general reader, emphasizing the culinary properties and the folklore of each herb. Each entry is accompanied by an illustration, including some color photographs. The material is more extensive and better presented than most books of this type. Includes an index of common and botanical names. Oversize, 247pp. McM 74

SHEPHARD, DOROTHY. **PHYSICIANS POSY**, c$6.60. See the Homeopathy section.

SHIH-CHEN, LI. **CHINESE MEDICINAL HERBS**, $5.00. This work was originally published in 1578. The complete herbal comprises 1892 species of drugs, includes 8160 prescriptions, and was the product of twenty-six years of research. Two American physicians translated this massive work, added their personal observations, and annotated their translation. This is a new edition with additional references. The Latin name as well as the Chinese and English are given for each entry. 467+pp. GEP 73

SIMMONS, ADELMA. **THE ILLUSTRATED HERBAL HANDBOOK**, $2.50. Large line drawings are the chief feature of this handbook. The text includes folklore, a detailed description, uses, and the culture of the herb. The presentation is geared toward the general reader. Different varieties of each herb are discussed, giving the botanical name for each. Index, 124pp. Haw 72

_____. **HERBS TO GROW INDOORS**, $3.50. A comprehensive, illustrated text. 146pp. Haw

SMITH, WILLIAM. **HERBS FOR CONSTIPATION**, $1.20. Dr. Smith begins with some general advice and goes on to describe a series of herbs and their usage. Line drawings accompany each selection. A handy little book. 64pp. TPL 76

SZEKELY, EDMOND BORDEAUX. **THE BOOK OF HERBS**, $2.25. A brief compendium of diseases and remedies as well as an herbal *materia medica*. See our section on Szekely. 46pp. ACL 71

TOBE, JOHN. **PROVEN HERBAL REMEDIES**, $1.25. Includes a complete disease-by-disease listing of ailments and their remedies, discussions of herb teas, and gathering and preparing them. 176pp. Pyr 73

TOGUCHI, MASARU. **ORIENTAL HERBAL WISDOM**, $1.25. This is a good presentation of Oriental herbalism for the general reader. The author begins with an excellent section on the Oriental system of observing conditions and determining remedies—specific diseases are cited as examples and all the terms used are thoroughly explained. The second section, *Applications of the Herbal Way*, discusses ailments and the specific herbal treatments pertinent to each. A long glossary and many cross-referenced indices are included. 151pp. Pyr 73

TWITCHELL, PAUL. **HERBS: THE MAGIC HEALERS**, $1.95. A compendium of hundreds of herbs giving their ancient and modern uses, their health-giving and occult powers. A very complete account which relates herbs to the philosophy of Eckankar (see our section on Eckankar). 189pp. IWP

VENINGA, LOUISE. **THE GINSENG BOOK**, $4.95. This is the first comprehensive guide to ginseng in seventy-five years. The author has travelled in the U.S. speaking to cultivators, importers, exporters, doctors, pharmacologists, Chinese herbalists, and numerous ginseng enthusiasts. This book represents an encyclopedia of their ginseng knowledge. Beautifully illustrated and well laid out. Appendix includes a resource section and a comprehensive bibliography. 152pp. BTp 73

WEINER, MICHAEL. **EARTH MEDICINE—EARTH FOODS**, $4.95. An oversize, illustrated disease-by-disease listing of plant remedies, drugs, and natural foods of the North American Indians. Recommended. 214pp. McM 72

WESLAGER, C.A. **MAGIC MEDICINES OF THE INDIANS**, $6.50. This is a well written comprehensive survey of the herbal treatments and folklore used by the Indians of New Jersey, Pennsylvania, Delaware, and Maryland. It includes material on the plants and trees and specifics on various cures. The book seems to be a good research project, but a bit hard to use since it is a narrative rather than an organized manual. Index, bibliography, 262pp. MAP 73

WESLEY, JOHN. **PRIMITIVE REMEDIES**, $2.25. Recent reprint of an eighteenth century herbal manual by the noted Methodist reformer. The material is alphabetically arranged according to diseases and is mainly interesting because of its archaic nature. 142pp. WoP 73

WREN, R.W., ed. **POTTER'S NEW CYCLOPEDIA OF MEDICINAL HERBS AND PREPARATIONS**, $4.95. A very scholarly reference book prepared for practitioners. Hundreds of plants are listed and the following information is given for each one: synonym, habitat, description, medicinal use, preparations. There are appendices on the forms of medicinal preparations, herbal components, a glossary of botanical and medical terms, and a descriptive listing of plant families. Illustrations, 402pp. H&R 72

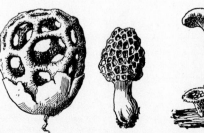

HOMEOPATHY

Homeopathy is the medical practice of treating like with like. The principle was known to Hippocrates and Paracelsus but the main debt of those who follow it is to Samuel Hahnemann, an eighteenth century physician. He believed that human beings have a capacity for healing themselves, and that the symptoms of disease reflect the individual's struggle to overcome the forces antagonistic to life. The physician's work is to discover, and if possible remove, the cause of the trouble, and to stimulate the vital healing force. For more information and a listing of homeopathic physicians in your area, write to the National Center for Homeopathy, Suite 428-31, Barr Building, 910 17th Street, N.W., Washington, D.C. 20006

Hahnemann Monument at Leipsic.

Hahnemann and his followers were so convinced of their theories that they carried out experiments upon themselves (called *Provings*) in which over long periods they took small doses of various reputedly poisonous or medicinal substances, carefully noting the symptoms they produced. Patients suffering from similar symptoms were then treated with these substances with very encouraging results.

Having thus established the principle of similarity, Hahnemann worked to establish the smallest effective dose, for he realized that this was the best way to avoid side effects. He found that, using a special method of dilution with milk sugar, the more the similar remedy was diluted, the more active it became, while dissimilar remedies were ineffective. He called his method potentization, to indicate the power that was developed. The materials are sometimes diluted to such an extent that no molecules of the original material remain. It appears that they transfer their energy to the milk sugar, thus suggesting that homeopathy works by affecting the energy body rather than the physical body.

Homeopaths treat the sick person rather than the disease. For this to be possible, a lot must be known about the patient: his past health and life circumstances, the pattern of health in his family, and his present condition, together with his personality characteristics.

The remedies can be animal, vegetable, and mineral. Homeopaths also use herbs and botanical medicines but usually only after potentization. They also use drugs, but again in their potentized form. Substances which in their natural state have little or no obvious effect upon the human body—sand, charcoal, common salt, pencil lead—develop in the potentized form powerful healing properties in the right patient.

Homeopathy is not a cure-all nor an instant means of curing symptoms. Rather it is an idea, a way of looking at people and helping them increase their harmony and spiritual and physical well-being. In the late nineteenth and early twentieth centuries it was a popular medical technique. But with the advent of *wonder drugs* and powerful quick-working alleopathic treatments, people turned away from it. In the last few years, as more attention has been paid to the treatment of the whole person, homeopathy has again been given serious consideration as an alternative method of healing.

Most of these books come from India and the prices of imported books tend to fluctuate with the exchange rate. The prices we list are as of the time we went to press. If you would like a current price on a specific title or titles, please write to us.

ALLEN, H.C. **BOENNINGHAUSEN'S THERAPEUTIC POCKET BOOKS**, $4.75. JPC

_____. **DISEASES AND THERPEUTICS OF THE SKIN**, $3.75.

_____. **KEYNOTES AND CHARACTERISTICS OF THE MATERIA MEDICA WITH NOSODES**, $3.75. A keynote is something that specifically identifies a particular remedy. This is the definitive work on keynotes and it is indispensable for the physician who desires to presribe exactly the right remedy. Dr. Allen continued to expand his original work to the end of his life, incorporating later findings of his own and his colleagues. This is a reprint of the sixth and final edition. Index, 388pp. JPC 75

_____. **MATERIA MEDICA OF SOME IMPORTANT NOSODES**, $.50. A very complete account. 67pp. JPC nd

_____. **THE MATERIA MEDICA OF THE NOSODES AND PROVING OF X-RAYS**, $9.50. SeD

ALLEN, J.H. **DISEASES AND THERAPEUTICS OF THE SKIN**, $3.50. SeD

_____. **CHRONIC MIASMS**, $5.75. Rin

_____. **INTERMITTENT FEVER**, $6.15. Rin

_____. **PRIMER OF MATERIA MEDICA**, $3.85. Rin

_____. **THE THERAPEUTICS OF FEVER**, $7.75. Rin

ALPH, TESTE. **A HOMEOPATHY TREATISE ON THE DISEASES OF CHILDREN**, $2.30. Rin

BERJEAU, J.P.H. **THE HOMEOPATHIC TREATMENT OF SYPHILIS, GONORRHOEA, SPERMATORRHOEA AND URINARY DISEASES**, $3.00. SeD

BHATTACHARJEE. **FAMILY PRACTICE**, $3.25. Rin

_____. **FIRST AID**, $.75. Rin

BLACKWOOD, A.L. **DISEASES OF THE LIVER, PANCREAS AND DUCTLESS GLANDS**, $3.50. SeD

BOENNINGHAUSEN, C. von. **MATERIA MEDICA AND REPERTORY**, $17.00. Rin

_____. **SIDES OF THE BODY**, $.85. Rin

_____. **THERAPEUTIC POCKET BOOK**, $9.50. Rin

BOERICKE, WILLIAM. **COMPENDIUM OF PRINCIPLES OF HOMEOPATHY**, $3.60. SeD

_____. **MATERIA MEDICA WITH REPERTORY**, c$7.20. This is a reprint of the ninth edition which includes a comprehensive reportory, revised and updated by Oscar Boericke. The main part of the text analyzes the preparations as used in specific ailments. This book is considered one of the best materia medicas available and is an essential aid to all practitioners. Includes many indices, 1105pp. JPC 27

BOERICKE, WILLIAM and W.A. DEWEY. **TWELVE TISSUE REMEDIES**, $5.00. SeD

BOGER, C.M. **BOENNINGHAUSEN'S CHARACTERISTICS AND REPERTORY**, $20.00. JPC

_____. **A SYNOPTIC KEY OF THE MATERIA MEDICA**, c$3.95. As the title suggests, this is a detailed guide to the use of various preparations intended for the serious practitioner. Also includes an index of symptoms and the related preparations. 350pp. JPC 31

BORLAND, DOUGLAS. **CHILDREN'S TYPES**, $1.20. This is an in depth discussion of the five principal types of children. Borland reviews the remedies that are especially efficacious for each type. 66pp. BrH nd

_____. **HOMEOPATHY FOR MOTHER AND INFANT**, $1.00. A useful discussion which considers the mental health and development of the infant (up to two years of age) and pregnant mother as well as the physical health. Specific remedies are discussed. 20pp. BrH nd

_____. **INFLUENZAS**, $.75. Transcriptions of a series of lectures discussing eight remedies. 20pp. BrH nd

_____. **PNEUMONIAS**, $1.80. A discussion of the prescribing for acute pneumonia divided into sections on the incipient stage, on fully developed pneumonia, on complicated pneumonia, and on late pneumonia. Specific remedies are advanced and discussed in each case. The appendix, which contains a repertory for pneumonia-related conditions, is topically arranged and exceedingly helpful. 76pp. BrH nd

BRITISH HOMEOPATHIC ASSOCIATION. **A GUIDE TO HOMEOPATHY**, $1.20. A small pamphlet prepared by the British Homeopathic Association containing articles on the history of homeopathy and a short review of several topics in homeopathic practice. 25pp. BrH 75

BURNETT, J.C. **CATARACT**, $2.70. Rin

_____. **CHANGE OF LIFE IN WOMEN**, $1.45. Rin

_____. **DELICATE AND BACKWARD CHILDREN**, $1.90. Rin

_____. **LIVER**, $1.50. Rin

_____. **ORGAN DISEASES OF WOMEN**, $1.50. Rin

_____. **SKIN**, $1.50. Rin

_____. **TONSILS**, $.75. Rin

_____. **VACCINOSIS**, $1.10. *By vaccinosis Burnett means the disease known as Vaccinia, the result of vaccination plus that profound and often long lasting morbid constitutional state engendered by the vaccine virus. To this state Thuja is homeopathic, and therefore curative of it.* This is a very complete discussion. 93pp. HSP 60

CHAPMAN, ESTHER. **HOW TO USE THE TWELVE TISSUE SALTS**, $.95. Gives specific instructions on tissue salt therapy for a large number of illnesses, details each salt's role, and shows how an imbalance in one or more can lead to persistent, troublesome illness. Also includes sections on the body's need for various vitamins and minerals along with many tables. 140pp. Pyr 74

CHAPMAN, J.B. **DR. SCHUESSLER'S BIOCHEMISTRY: A MEDICAL BOOK FOR THE HOME**, c$3.25. The biochemic system of medicine was originated by Dr. W.H. Schuessler who realized that within the body itself are found the most potent weapons in the battle against disease and that healing should be directed towards arousing and stimulating the natural recuperative forces. The twelve biochemic remedies, or tissue salts, correspond with the principal inorganic elements found in the human body. On this fundamental principle Dr. Schuessler based his carefully worked out theories, and the results he achieved led to the formulation of his system of cellular therapeutics, to which he gave the name Biochemistry. The author of this work was regarded by Dr. Schuessler as one of the most capable exponents of his therapy. This is an excellent, comprehensive disease-by-disease text, with information on causes and symptoms, treatment, and suggestions. Glossary, fully indexed. 185pp. TPL 61

CLARKE, J.H. **CATTARH, COLDS AND GRIPPE**, $1.50. JPC

_____. **CLINICAL REPERTORY**, c$8.50. This is an excellent supplement to the larger materia medicas. Part I gives clinical information such as the remedies for many disorders, alphabetically arranged by ailment. Part II deals with causation, i.e., bee stings, anxiety, acid food, cold air, etc.—also alphabetically arranged by cause. Part III examines temperaments, dispositions, constitutions and states, i.e., agitation, angry and excited persons, chubby children, peevishness, etc.—again alphabetically arranged. Part IV indicates clinical relationships: naming, when known, complementary remedies, what the remedy follows well, what it is followed well by, compatible remedies, incompatible remedies, remedy antidotes, what the remedy is antidoted by, and duration of action. This seems to be the most generally useful of the comprehensive books for the layperson and is certainly a necessity for all practitioners. 346pp. HSP 71

_____. **COLD**, $3.80. Rin

_____. **CONSTITUTIONAL MEDICINE**, $1.15. Includes a general discussion, examples, and material from the experiences of Grauvogl and Bojanus. Index, 182pp. JPC 74

_____. **DICTIONARY OF PRACTICAL MATERIA MEDICA**, c$57.00/set. This is far and away the most comprehensive materia medica available. It includes thousands of references and quotations and is considered a remarkably precise work. It is also the most clearly presented and well written of the materia medicas. Both the characteristics of the remedy and the symptoms are discussed in great detail. Highly recommended to all who are serious about homeopathic study and practice. Three volumes, 2585pp. Rin

_____. **HEART**, $1.15. Rin

_____. **HOMEOPATHY EXPLAINED**, $1.50. As the title suggests, this is an introductory book covering the careers and achievements of the major homeopathic doctors,

and general material on what homeopathy is and how it works. The organization is a bit scattered and the writing style is not as flowing as in some of the other books, so this is not an ideal introduction but rather a good supplement to some of the other introductory works. Index, 212pp. JPC 71

_____. **INDIGESTION**, $.95. Rin

_____. **NON SURGICAL TREATMENT OF DISEASES OF THE GLAND AND BONES**, $.75. JPC

_____. **THE PRESCRIBER**, c$4.80. This is the definitive prescriber, alphabetically organized by symptom or part of the body affected. Includes material on using the preparations, and specific advice on the potency of each medicine and the dosage. Edward Cotter, a practitioner with wide experience, has thoroughly revised and added to the treatment section of this edition. Also includes Clark's treatise, *How to Practice Homeopathy*. 382pp. HSP 72

CONQUEST, J.T., ed. **FIVE IN ONE**, $.75. Five basic essays: *Remedies related to Pathological Tissue Changes* by Kent, *Pathology Versus the Hahnemannian Homeopath* by Del Mas, *The Repetition of the Remedy* by R.G. Miller, *Homeopathy* by John Weir, and *What is Homeopathy* by Conquest. 48pp. JPC

COULTER, HARRIS. **HOMEOPATHIC MEDICINE**, $1.65. An exposition of the science of homeopathy by a noted practitioner. 73pp. AFH

COWPARTHWAITE. **TEXTBOOK OF GYNECOLOGY**, $5.75. JPC

_____. **A TEXT BOOK OF MATERIA MEDICA AND THERAPEUTICS**, $10.80. Rin

COX, DONOVAN. and JONES. **BEFORE THE DOCTOR COMES**, $1.30. TPL

DEARBORN, F.M. **DISEASES OF THE SKIN**, $9.00. JPC

DEWEY, W.A. **ESSENTIALS OF HOMEOPATHIC MATERIA MEDICA**, $3.60. Rin

_____. **ESSENTIALS OF THERAPEUTICS**, $2.70. Rin

_____. **PRACTICAL HOMEOPATHIC THERAPEUTICS**, c$3.95. This text is devoted exclusively to homeopathic prescribing. The indications for the remedies given have been culled from the experience of noted homeopathic prescribers. The book is topically arranged by ailment and each section is further divided into an analysis of the preparations efficacious for each ailment. Indices of ailments and subindices of remedies for each ailment plus a listing of the authorities quoted. 479pp. JPC 34

FARRINGTON, E.A. **CLINICAL MATERIA MEDICA**, c$10.80. This is one of the classic materia medicas and is often used as a text in college courses. Each of the major remedies is extensively discussed. Dr. Farrington expresses himself clearly and covers a great deal of material which is not available elsewhere. Index of remedies and therapeutic index. 826pp. JPC 08

_____. **THERAPEUTIC POINTERS AND LESSER WRITINGS**, $7.20. Rin

GIBSON, D.M. **ELEMENTS OF HOMEOPATHY**, $1.05. *This short text-book has been prepared primarily for the information of doctors and medical undergraduates who are interested in exploring the possibilities of homeopathy. It is intended as an introduction to the subject and is offered as such. The text is divided into the following chapters: basic principles, materia medica, diagnosis, remedy selection, small dose and potencies, the single remedy, and administration of the remedy.* 38pp. BrH nd

_____. **FIRST AID HOMEOPATHY IN ACCIDENTS AND AILMENTS**, $3.25. A very clearly written discussion of some of the most prevalent conditions resulting from accidents and injuries. All the relevant remedies are discussed and programs of usage are outlined. This is one of the most useful homeopathic books for the general reader and if you are interested in homeopathic treatments we suggest you buy this book. Index, 84pp. BrH 75

GROSS. **COMPARATIVE MATERIA MEDICA**, $7.20. JPC

GUERNSEY, H.H. **HAEMMORRHOIDS**, $1.50. SeD

_____. **KEYNOTES TO MATERIA MEDICA**, $3.80. Rin

_____. **MENSTRUATION**, $.80. Rin

_____. **OBSTETRICS AND DISORDERS PECULIAR TO WOMEN AND YOUNG CHILDREN**, $12.00. SeD

HAEHL, RICHARD. **SAMUEL HAHNEMANN—HIS LIFE AND WORK**, c$14.40/set. This is the definitive study (in two volumes) of Hahnemann's life and work. There's probably more information here than most people would like to know about his personal life, but also a great deal of material on how he developed his theories. Bibliography, index. 958pp. JPC 22

HAHNEMANN, SAMUEL. **THE CHRONIC DISEASES**, $18.00. This is the most comprehensive text available. 160 pages are devoted to an exposition of the *Nature of Chronic Diseases* and the rest of the book is a detailed analysis of fifty of the major medicines, including material on how to use them and what kind of reaction to expect. The latter section also includes a listing of most of the symptoms which are treated with each preparation. Index, 1620pp. JPC 1898

_____. THE CHRONIC DISEASES—THEORETICAL PART, c$2.50. The theory of chronic diseases explicated in this volume was something that came to Hahnemann late in his career after he found that the principles he outlined in the **Organon** did not always effect a permanent cure. The approach given here to the treatment of psora, syphillis, and syeosis serves as a guideline to the treatment of all types of chronic diseases. The material presented here is considered an invaluable aid to all practitioners. 269pp. JPC 72

_____. MATERIA MEDICA PURA, $23.50/Two volume set. Rin

_____. ORGANON OF MEDICINE, c$2.90. This is a translation of the sixth edition by William Boericke. It presents Hahnemann's most developed philosophical insights into the practice of medicine and incorporates his vast experience in the treatment of both acute and chronic diseases. Dr. Boericke, a noted homeopath himself, also supplies many reference notes. 314pp. JPC 21

_____. SPIRIT OF HOMEOPATHY, $.80. SeD

_____. THERAPEUTIC HINTS, $1.80. SeD

HANSEN, OSCAR. A TEXTBOOK OF MATERIA MEDICA AND THERAPEUTICS, $3.50. This is designed as a supplement to Dr. Cowperthwaite's text. The stress is on rare homeopathic remedies. 121pp. HeR 1899

HERING. THE GUIDING SYMPTOMS OF OUR MATERIA MEDICA, c$144.00/Ten volume set. JPC

JAHR, G.H.G. FAMILY PRACTICE WITH HOMEOPATHIC REMEDIES, $2.35. JPC

_____. THERAPEUTIC GUIDE. $5.75. SeD

JANSKY, ROBERT. HOW TO USE THE CELL SALTS, $1.50. Jansky is an astrologer and a biochemist. He is most noted for his work with nutritional and medical astrology. Here he presents the general reader with an introduction to the cell salts, discusses how they should be taken, and reviews the physiological use of each of the twelve cell salts together with the common ailments that they seem to influence most strongly. 10pp. ASA 74

KENT, JAMES. LECTURES ON HOMEOPATHIC MATERIA MEDICA, c$7.95. A series of informal lectures first delivered at the Post-Graduate School of Homeopathics and extensively revised for this volume. *The lectures are presented in the simple form to explain the author's plan of studying each remedy.... Not all of the Materia Medica has been brought out, but the leading and proven remedies ... have been presented for the purpose of showing how the Materia Medica must be evolved and used.... They are not offered as being complete digests of the various remedies, but simply as the examinations of some of the most salient points.* Topically arranged by remedy. Index, 1031pp. JPC 71

_____. LECTURES ON HOMEOPATHIC PHILOSOPHY, c$3.25. Transcription of a series of lectures originally delivered in the Post-Graduate School of Homeopathy as a commentary on the **Organon**. Each one elucidates a particular doctrine promulgated in the **Organon** and the intent is to help the student understand the concepts. 276pp. JPC 74

_____. NEW REMEDIES, CLINICAL CASES, LESSER WRITINGS, ETC., $10.00. SeD

_____. REPERTORY OF THE HOMEOPATHIC MATERIA MEDICA, c$12.60. This is considered the definitive general repertory of the homeopathic materia medica. Kent compiled it from many sources—both previous books and the experiences of practitioners. This is a reprint of the sixth American edition, edited, revised, and updated by Dr. Clara Kent, J.T. Kent's wife. The text is topically arranged by the part of the body and within each section, further broken down into symptoms and remedies. Includes a 77pp index. 1516pp. JPC 74

_____. USE OF THE REPERTORY, $.55. Includes Kent's essay *How to Study the Repertory* and *Repertorising* by Mary Tyler and John Weir. 36pp. JPC

_____. WHAT THE DOCTOR NEEDS TO KNOW, $.85. SeD

LILLIENTAL, SAMUEL. HOMEOPATHIC THERAPEUTICS, $21.00. Rin

MORGAN, W. PREGNANCY, $2.30. SeD

MUZUMDAR, K.P. PHARMACEUTICAL SCIENCE IN HOMEOPATHY AND PHARMACODYNAMICS, $3.80. JPC

NASH, E.B. HOW TO TAKE THE CASE, $1.70. Rin

_____. LEADERS IN HOMEOPATHIC THERAPEUTICS, c$3.10. An in depth discussion of the leading preparations. Each entry begins with a detailed listing of the symptoms related to each preparation. This is followed by a lengthy discussion of the effects of the preparation (related preparations are also cited). All of the material cited comes from the author's extensive experience as a homeopathic physician and the text is written in an informal style. Two indices: therapeutic and remedies. 493pp. JPC 72

_____. REGIONAL LEADERS, $3.25. SeD

_____. RESPIRATORY ORGANS, $2.90. Rin

_____. SULPHUR, $2.30. Rin

_____. THERAPEUTICS, $4.55. Rin

NEW ERA LAB. THE NEW BIOCHEMIC HANDBOOK, $1.40. Subtitled *An intr duction to the cellular therapy and practical application of the twelve tissue salts accordance with the Biochemic System of Medicine....* Includes descriptions of th salts, selecting a remedy, and specific remedies for many ailments. 127pp. Nut

PELIKAN, WILHELM. THE ACTIVITY OF POTENTIZED SUBSTANCES, $2.4 This is a very detailed statistical analysis of experiments on plant growth using certa remedies. Includes many charts and graphs and an analysis of this material. 33pp. PAV 6

PERRY, EDWARD. LUYTIES HOMEOPATHIC PRACTICE, $1.85. 153pp. FoI 2

POWELL, ERIC. BIOCHEMISTRY UP-TO-DATE, $3.15. In addition to listing an explaining the use of Schuessler's original twelve biochemical salts, also provides deta of thirty more elements now employed by modern biochemists. A quick-reference guic is given for over 250 disorders. Notes of potencies, frequency of doses, and examples dosage are presented. 66pp. HSP

_____. THE GROUP REMEDY PRESCRIBER, c$4.70. Indicates treatment fc a great variety of diseases by combinations of homeopathic and biochemic remedie supplemented by homeopathic remedies in higher potency. The right potency and th correct remedy are ascertained through radionic testing. Includes some explanator material, many examples and formulae, and a therapeutic guide. 144pp. HSP 70

PUDDAPHAT, NOBLE. CORRECT REMEDY, $2.55. Rin

_____. FIRST STEPS, $2.55. Rin

_____. MATERIA MEDICA, HOW IT SHOULD BE STUDIED, $1.40. Rin

QUAY, G.H. DISEASES OF NOSE AND THROAT, $3.00. SeD

Herb and plant press.

ROBERTS, HERBERT. ART OF CURE BY HOMOEOPATHY, $4.00. This is a well written basic text for the beginning student. It includes introductory material, chapters on vital force and vital energy, remedies and why they act, analyses of sample cases, the law of cure, the dosage and dynamic action of the drugs, and a great deal of specific material on disease classification. 286pp. JPC 42

_____. THE PRINCIPLES AND ART OF CURE BY HOMOEOPATHY—A MODERN TEXTBOOK, c$9.45. This is the best inexpensive (relatively) comprehensive text. TPL

_____. SENSATIONS AS IF, c$5.40. This is the most comprehensive index available of remedies for use in individual cases. The text is divided into major parts of the body and within these divisions specific, very detailed symptoms are listed and further subdivided, with remedies for each aspect of the symptom listed. An invaluable aid for all practitioners. 519pp. JPC 37

ROYAL, GEORGE. HANDY BOOK OF REFERENCE, $5.75. Rin

_____. TEXTBOOK OF HOMOEOPATHIC THEORY AND PRACTICE OF MEDICINE, c$5.75. This is a very comprehensive text for the practitioner. Dr. Royal was a Professor of Homeopathic Materia Medica and Therapeutics at the University of Iowa for thirty years and President of the American Institute of Homeopathy. The book covers blood and infectious diseases; diseases of the bones, the muscles, the mucous and serous membranes; the heart, arteries, and veins; the brain and nervous system; the urinary, digestive, and respiratory organs; the glands; and miscellaneous conditions. The section on each specific ailment is divided into the following parts: synonym, description, etiology, symptoms, complications and sequelae, diagnosis, prognosis, treatment, diet, remedies, and pathology. Separate comprehensive indices for both diseases and remedies. 688pp. JPC 23

RUDDOCK, E.H. THE COMMON DISEASES OF CHILDREN, c$1.25. This is an abridgement of the author's manual **The Diseases of Infants and Children**. Dr. Ruddock's expectation was that this book could be used in the home and he has tried to make the contents easily comprehensible to the non-professional. The book is topically arranged by disease and it begins with a section explaining many of the terms used. Each listing includes material on causes, symptoms, remedies, and accessory treatments. Index, 168pp. JPC

_____. THE POCKET MANUAL OF HOMOEOPATHIC VETERINARY MEDICINE, $2.00. JPC

Caricature of the homeopath's infinitesimal doses. "I should like a hundred thousandth of a decigram of magnesia please." "I'm sorry, madam, we don't sell such large quantities."

RUSHOLM, PETER, ed. COUNTRY MEDICINES, $1.10. A listing of over 100 ailments, with herbal and homeopathic remedies. All the ailments are common ones and the remedies are ones that can be given by the non-professional. 64pp. HSP 71

SCHUSSLER, W.H. ABRIDGED THERAPEUTICS, $5.00. An in depth discussion of the tissue salts and their uses in various ailments. Includes material on the theory and function of the salts, an extensive glossary, and an index. 226pp. HeR 74

SHADMAN, ALONZO. WHO IS YOUR DOCTOR AND WHY, c$10.00. This is the only comprehensive book on homeopathy written for the general reader which does not employ technical terms. It includes chapters on Hahnemann, the history of homeopathy and the reasons behind its decline in the U.S., and material on the following areas as they relate to homeopathy: vaccination, the common cold, arthritis, food and drink, constipation, eczema, injuries and burns, the heart, cancer, smoking, having a baby. The final 200pp are reprint of Pointers to the Common Remedies by M.D. Tyler, revised by D.M. Borland, a descriptive listing of remedies for frequent household ailments. Bibliography, 446pp. Mey 58

SHARMA, C.H. A MANUAL OF HOMOEOPATHY AND NATURAL MEDICINE, c$7.15. This is no ordinary book.... Dr. Sharma is far more than a successful homoeopathic physician. He has penetrated deeply into the medical systems of East and West. This combined with his own original research work and his vast clinical experience has given him a rare insight into the bases of health and disease that he seeks in this book to share with others. He has not written a treatise on homoeopathy for the practising physician, but rather an introduction to the fundamentals of natural healing addressed as much to the interested layman as to the specialist. It is also a work book that everyone can use—J.G. Bennett. Divided into two sections: The Essentials of Homoeopathic Therapy and Catalogue of Remedies. Bibliography, 154pp. Tur 75

SHEPHERD, DOROTHY. HOMOEOPATHY FOR THE FIRST AIDER, $2.40. Easily understandable homeopathic remedies for pain, aches and bruising; wounds; hemmorrhage; burns and scalds; poisons; boils; carbuncles; and other medical emergencies. Also includes material on potencies and an index. 72pp. HSP 45

_____. HOMEOPATHY IN EPIDEMIC DISEASES, c$7.00. This book has been edited from a series of papers written by Dr. Sheperd. It begins with a general discussion of epidemics and prophylaxis and then goes into a survey of homeopathic remedies for a variety of epidemic diseases. Index, 100pp. HSP 67

_____. THE MAGIC OF THE MINIMUM DOSE, $6.30. A collection of case histories taken from Dr. Sheperd's own experience. These cases feature many disorders and diseases, including arthritis, bronchitis, the common cold, epilepsy, influenza, kidney trouble, pneumonia, rheumatism, tonsilitis, and whooping cough. She also discusses homeopathy in dentistry, obstetrics, first aid, veterinary medicine, and women's ailments. The book is very clearly written. Index, 214pp. HSP 64

_____. MORE MAGIC OF THE MINIMUM DOSE, $7.00. Additional cases from Dr. Sheperd's wide experience, topically arranged by type of ailment (i.e., skin diseases, eye infections, etc.) along the lines of her earlier book with a glossary and a comprehensive index. As is the case with Dr. Shepherd's other books, this is a very readable account. 286pp. HSP 74

_____. A PHYSICIAN'S POSY, c$6.60. Homeopathic remedies utilizing herbs in addition to the more traditional remedies. 256pp. HSP 69

SHEPPARD, K. TREATMENT OF CATS BY HOMOEOPATHY, $2.50. A detailed discussion, arranged according to ailment, with an additional section on general hints. 62pp. HSP

_____. THE TREATMENT OF DOGS BY HOMOEOPATHY, $2.50. Sheppard is an experienced practitioner. Here he indicates proven remedies for common ailments to which dogs are prone. The material is topically arranged by ailment. HSP 72

SMALPAGE, E.H. CANCER, ITS CAUSE, PREVENTION, AND CURE, $2.30. SeD

SMITH, DWIGHT. HOMOEOPATHY, $.90. A general introduction by a noted homeopath. Includes chapters on pediatrics, dentistry, childbirth, and allergies. Very clearly written. 64pp. JPC 71

STEPHENSON, JAMES H. A DOCTOR'S GUIDE TO HEALING YOURSELF WITH HOMEOPATHIC REMEDIES, c$8.95.

TYLER, M.L. HOMOEOPATHIC DRUG PICTURES, c$20.50. Dr. Tyler is one of the most noted female homeopathic teachers and practitioners and this is considered her finest book. She presents essential details of the leading 125 remedies for the guidance of students who wish to learn the basic characteristics. Successful prescribing depends on a knowledge of the difference—often very slight—between remedies, and it is this area that Dr. Tyler emphasizes. The text includes material from the author's own practice along with many case studies. Topically arranged by remedy. 885pp. HSP 52

_____. POINTERS TO COMMON REMEDIES, c$4.35. Nine books bound in one: (1) Colds, Influenza, Sore Throat, Coughs, Croup, Acute Chest, Asthma; (2) Stomach and Digestive Disorders, Constipation, Acute Diarrhoea, Acute Intestinal Conditions and Colic, Epidemic Diarrhoea of Children, Acute Dysentery, Cholera; (3) Dentition, Rickets, Malnutrition, Tuberculosis, Diseases of Bones and Glands; (4) Convulsions, Chorea, Rheumatism of Children and of Adults, Common Heart Remedies; (5) Chicken Pox, Diphtheria, Erysipelas, Herpes Zoster, Measles and Mumps, Scarlet Fever, Smallpox, Typhoid, Vaccination, Whooping Cough; (6) Some Drugs of Strong Mentality, Fears with their Dreams, Indices; (7) Nephritis and Suppression, Renal Calculi and Renal Colic, Cystitis, Enuresis, Retention; (8) Vertigo, Headache, Apoplexy, Sleeplessness, Collapse, Sun Stroke; and (9) Organ Remedies. The books are also available in separate pamphlets for $1.05. each. 337pp. JPC nd

TYLER, M.L. and JOHN WEIR. SOME OF THE OUTSTANDING HOMOEOPATHIC REMEDIES FOR ACUTE CONDITIONS, INJURIES, ETC.—WITH SPECIAL INDICATIONS FOR THEIR USE, $2.25. In two parts, the first covering a series of conditions and ailments and the second discussing remedies and their uses. 44pp. BrH nd

VANNIER, LEON. HOMOEOPATHY: HUMAN MEDICINE, $2.40. This is an interesting philosophical discussion of homeopathy by one of the foremost European homeopaths. Dr. Vannier presents both his specific techniques and his philosophical outlook. He also discusses the human conception of medicine, the different constituents and temperaments, and various aspects of homeopathic therapeutics. 231pp. HSP nd

VERMA, S.P. PRACTICAL HANDBOOK OF GYNECOLOGY, $3.10. This is an excellent illustrated account, written for both the student and the practitioner. The material is clearly presented and the coverage is comprehensive. 255pp. JPC

_____. PRACTICAL HANDBOOK OF SURGERY, c$4.15. A comprehensive analysis including introductory material, sections on preoperative and postoperative care and a descriptive listing arranged topically by disease. 567pp. JPC 74

_____. TEXTBOOK OF GYNECOLOGY, $5.75. JPC

VITHOULKAS, GEORGE. HOMOEOPATHY—MEDICINE OF THE NEW MAN, $1.25. This is the best overall introduction available. It includes all the basic material on what homeopathy is and how the principles underlying it were discovered as well as chapters on diagnosis, how the remedies work, what diseases can be cured, and thoughts on the history and spread of homeopathy. There's also an extensive bibliography and a listing of the names and addresses of homeopathic pharmacies, societies, and lay organizations in the U.S. 143pp. Avo 71

WEIR, JOHN. THE SCIENCE AND ART OF HOMOEOPATHY, $.50. Transcription of a talk. 14pp. BrH 27

WHEELER, CHARLES. AN INTRODUCTION TO THE PRINCIPLES AND PRACTICE OF HOMOEOPATHY, c$10.40. This is one of the newest books on homeopathy available, written by the past president of the British Homeopathic Society. Topics include a discussion of the principles of homeopathy, the structure of homeopathic materia medica, homeopathic pharmacy, potentization, dosage, the choice and mode of administration of the remedy, a therapeutic index and repertory, and a materia medica of thirty-one leading remedies. Therapeutic index and general index, 371pp. HSP 48

WILLIAMSON, WALTER. DISEASES OF FEMALES AND CHILDREN AND THEIR HOMOEOPATHIC TREATMENT, $2.70. A detailed account including a description of the diseases, their symptoms, mode of administration of remedies, and the doses and repetitions according to Hahnemann's Law of Similars. Divided into three sections: diseases of females, treatment of children, and general diseases. Topically arranged by ailment. Index, 256pp. JPC 74

WOODS, H. FERGIE. ESSENTIALS OF HOMOEOPATHIC PRESCRIBING, c$3.60. 78pp. TPL

_____. HOMOEOPATHIC TREATMENT IN THE NURSERY, $.75. Includes some general information as well as specific sections on the ailments and the remedies. 12pp. BrH nd

YINGLING, W.A. ACCOUCHEUR'S EMERGENCY MANUAL, $3.80. SeD

HUMANISTIC PSYCHOLOGY

Humanistic psychology is a name applied to a broad spectrum of approaches to human experience and behavior, involving:

- the fundamental uniqueness and importance of human life
- the conviction that all people have the potential for being creative.
- an emphasis on what is characteristically human, (as opposed to thinking about people in mechanistic terms) such as choice, self-realization, spontaneity, love, creativity, valuing, responsibility, meaning and transcendental experience.
- an emphasis on the integration of the whole person: feelings and intellect, body and soul.

Humanistic psychology transcends the usual academic boundaries to include any of the disciplines which seek to understand human behavior and experience.

Many interested persons have joined together in the Association for Humanistic Psychology (325 Ninth Street, San Francisco, California 94103). It is also closely associated with the Human Potential movement and some one hundred fifty growth centers around the U.S., such as Esalen.

Freudian psychoanalysis is passe; more people than ever are involved in therapy, but now it is called growth. The movement is known for encounter, sensory awareness, altered or higher states of consciousness, many new forms of therapy and body work, and Eastern philosophies. Especially in very recent years, the movement seems to have become increasingly concerned with spiritual development. The same thing has happened to us, so we feel in the mainstream. We believe that a person just getting into encounter groups and a follower of Sri Aurobindo, for example, are both on the path, but just at different places.

The books that follow aren't exclusively about humanistic psychology but are mostly so, and most of the key people in that field are represented.

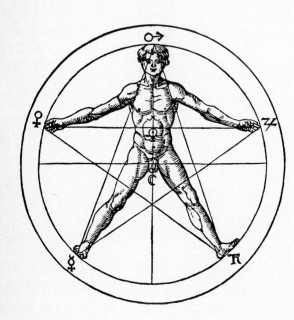

ABELL, RICHARD. **OWN YOUR OWN LIFE**, c$9.95. The techniques and exercises presented here are a synthesis of transactional analysis, Gestalt therapy, nonverbal technique, and traditional psychoanalytic procedures. Dr. Abell was a traditional psychiatrist who became dissatisfied with analytic methods and then participated in a number of experimental therapeutic workshops which changed him profoundly. He describes his own experiences and tells how he incorporated the techniques into his practice. Many case histories are included and special attention is given to the moments when therapeutic breakthroughs take place. Index, notes, 254pp. McK 76

AGEL, JEROME. **THE RADICAL THERAPIST**, $1.25. A collection of essays from the **Radical Therapist** magazine attacking therapy as a commodity or means of social control and discussing how therapists can be agents of social change. 292pp. RaH 71

_____. **ROUGH TIMES**, $1.65. More of the same, but the magazine has changed its name to **Rough Times**. 243pp. RaH 73

ANGYAL, ANDRIAS. **NEUROSIS AND TREATMENT: A HOLISTIC THEORY**, $3.75. Angyal argues that basic motivations are similar in sickness and health, that neurosis arises from an unrealistic philosophy of life, and that recovery is equivalent to acquisition of new orientation toward life. Newly reissued. Foreward by Maslow. 238pp. Vik 65

ASSAGIOLI, ROBERTO. **THE ACT OF WILL**, $2.95. A development of some of the concepts presented in **Psychosynthesis**. Here Assagioli emphasizes the human will, which he defines as a constructive force guiding intuition, impulse, emotion, and imagination toward complete realization of the self. He proposes a set of exercises that train the will for *optimum use at all levels of existence—from the personal to the transpersonal and reaching into the realm where the individual will merges with the universal will. Thus transfigured* the will becomes a central part of a *coherent psychology of joy.* Dr. Assagioli writes very clearly. Notes, index, 288pp. Pen 73

_____. **PSYCHOSYNTHESIS**, $2.75. *Psychosynthesis is a psychological and educational approach for recognizing and harmonizing the many, often conflicting, elements of our inner life. It is a developmental process based on a positive conception of man within in an evolving universe. Starting with each person's existential situation as he perceives it, personal growth is organized into a process aiming at the integration of personality and the emergence of an effective unifying center of being and awareness, the Self. The practical work of psychosynthesis chooses in each situation the appropriate progressive activities among many techniques and methods available. Some of these are: guided imagery, movement, self-identification, creativity, gestalt, meditation, training of the will, symbolic art work, journal-keeping, ideal models, and development of intuition. The emphasis is on fostering an ongoing process of growth that can gain momentum and bring about a more joyful, balanced actualization of one's life.—The Esalen Catalog.* Assagioli was an Italian psychiatrist who formulated the concept of psychosynthesis in response to what he felt was the partial answer provided by traditional psychoanalysis. This is the basic book and it includes both theoretical material and many practical exercises. We recommend Assagioli's work highly. Index, 323+pp. Vik 65

_____. **THE PSYCHOSYNTHESIST**, $2.00. A special issue of **Human Dimensions** magazine devoted to Assagioli and including the following articles by him: *The Impact of a Presence, Bio-Psychosynthesis, The Technique of Evocative Words, Life as a Game and Stage Performance (Role Playing), Symbols of Transpersonal Experiences, Smiling Wisdom, The Conflict between the Generations and the Psychosynthesis of the Human Ages.* Also includes some biographical material. Provides a good survey of Assagioli's major ideas. Illustrations, oversize, 28pp. HDI 74

BACH, GEORGE and RONALD DEUTSCH. **PAIRING**, $1.95. A book about intimacy, how to establish it and keep it going. A handbook for singles who want to learn to get along better with the opposite sex. 318pp. Avo 70

BACH, GEORGE and HERB GOLDBERG. **CREATIVE AGGRESSION**, $1.95. A popularly written account which details how individuals can express their natural anger constructively. This is Bach's newest book and is written in much the same tone as his others. The techniques are clearly presented and many people have found them extremely useful. Notes, index, 337pp. Avo 74

BACH, GEORGE and PETER WYDEN. **THE INTIMATE ENEMY**, $1.95. An original approach for using domestic quarrels constructively—how to fight with your mate but fight fair. 384pp. Avo 68

BACK, KURT. **BEYOND WORDS**, $1.75. A fairly academic survey of the encounter movement, which traces its development and growth, details the techniques that make it up, and assesses its over-impact and its meaning as a symptom of the state of society. Index, bibliography, 287pp. Pen 73

BANDLER, RICHARD and JOHN GRINDER. **THE STRUCTURE OF MAGIC**, c$7.95. This is an excellent manual for practicing therapists. *What we have attempted to do . . . is not to create a new school of psychotherapy but rather to make understandable and learnable some of the language skills of some of the world's most talented psychotherapists. We do this in a way which shows both the simplicity and the similarities of the techniques of these seemingly divergent therapists. Our hope is that this work will begin the long overdue process of sharing the resources of all those who are involved in finding ways to help people have better, fuller and richer lives and relationships with those they love. Our approach to this was to distill and formalize the patterns of therapeutic interaction which are common to some of the leading clinicians of the many schools of psychotherapy. By formalizing these patterns, our belief is that they will become available as a tool for people-helpers to have access to the resources of these therapeutic wizards. If you are someone who wishes to have more tools and resources as a people-helper, we wrote this book for you.* Glossary, bibliography, 225pp. S&B 75

BERNHARD, YETTA. **SELF-CARE**, $6.95. *I think that Yetta Bernhard addresses herself to the central issue which is how to define, to limit, and to make specific your everyday interpersonal negotiations with the people with whom you live. . . . Another outstanding contribution of her book is the specific and practical methods she offers. . . . Implied in her book is the assumption that human beings in daily work with one another will meet* *conflict and differences as part of the givens of being human. Coping with this difference in the way that Yetta demonstrates is a central point in the development of maintenance and self-care.*—Virginia Satir. Glossary, bibliography, index, 227pp. CeA 75

CASRIEL, DANIEL. **A SCREAM AWAY FROM HAPPINESS**, $2.95. An exploration of *scream therapy*—a technique developed by Dr. Casriel independently of Janov's primal therapy and utilized by him extensively in his practice. Many case studies are cited and the rationale for the therapy is developed in depth. There's also a section of exercises which allow the reader to actually practice the technique. The presentation is not overly technical. Bibliography, index, 307pp. G&D 72

Detail from a drawing
by Picasso

CLARK, TED. **GOING INTO THERAPY**, $1.95. Designed as an aid for those who are thinking of going into therapy and covering the following topics: what is therapy, why and when should I enter therapy, what kinds of therapy are there, how do I choose the right therapy and therapist, what if I don't like my therapist, how much should I pay, how long should I remain in therapy. 134pp. H&R 75

COSTER, GERALDINE. **YOGA AND WESTERN PSYCHOLOGY**, $2.45. See the Patanjali sub-section of Indian Philosophy.

CRAIG, JAMES and MARGE. **SYNERGIC POWER**, $2.50. *Beyond Domination and Permissiveness* is the subtitle. *This book is the product of the search we have pursued for the past eight years with many friends to understand the game and the rules, to discover which rules can be changed, and to devise ways for bringing people together to co-create a future which they choose.* Bibliography, index, 144pp. Pro 74

ELLIS, ALBERT. **HUMANISTIC PSYCHOTHERAPY**, $2.95. This is Ellis' latest and most complete statement of his method of therapy. More technical than the book listed above, it is recommended for therapists or those planning to enter therapy. 273pp. MGH 73

ELLIS, ALBERT and ROBERT HARPER. **A GUIDE TO RATIONAL LIVING**, $3.00. Ellis, best known for his sex books, is also founder of a school of therapy called rational psychotherapy, based on self-questioning. He believes that human emotions and feelings do not magically exist in their own right, but rather stem from ideas, attitudes and beliefs that can usually be radically changed by modifying the thinking processes that created them. Clearly written with many case histories. 241pp. Wil 61

FADIMAN, JAMES and DONALD KEWMAN, eds. **EXPLORING MADNESS**, $6.65. *This book presents many innovative and, in some cases, radical ideas for the investigation, understanding, and treatment of madness. Included are personal and literary accounts of madness, theoretical positions, and research findings. Our intention is to present the contributions of individuals who extend or go beyond current concepts in abnormal psychology—to survey alternative models that emphasize inner experience in the development of further theories and research. Many of the writers view madness as an altered state of consciousness that causes certain perceptual, emotional, and behavioral changes; however, each viewpoint is based on a different way of exploring and interpreting the experience.*—from the preface. Notes, index, bibliography, 236pp. Wad 73

FRANKL, VIKTOR. **MAN'S SEARCH FOR MEANING**, $1.50. Frankl is the founder of logotherapy or existential analysis, which grew out of his three years in Auschwitz where he survived because of the strength of his goals. His approach is based on man's search for and need for meaning in life and in whatever he does. *Logotherapy . . . makes the concept of man into a whole . . . and focuses its attention upon mankind's groping for a higher meaning in life.* The first half of this book is a chilling yet fascinating account of Frankl's concentration camp experience. The second presents the basic concepts of logotherapy. A good introduction. 226pp. S&S 59

_____. **PSYCHOTHERAPY AND EXISTENTIALISM**, $3.95. This volume of selected papers on logotherapy is the most comprehensive for serious students. 242pp. S&S

_____. **THE UNCONSCIOUS GOD**, $2.95. A central feature of logotherapy is the idea that an awareness, conscious or unconscious, of a God within him/herself is essential to wo/man's humanity. Through his own psychiatric practice Dr. Frankl has found that even the repression of religiosity in a patient does not conceal a belief within. In fact, a more intense denial frequently reflects an equally intense acknowledgement of God. This book is an up-dated translation of a volume originally written in 1948, including current empirical-clinical evidence. Notes, bibliography, index, 161pp. S&S 75

_____. **THE WILL TO MEANING**, $2.50. A survey of the foundations of logotherapy and its applications. 181pp. NAL 69

FROMM, ERICH. **THE ART OF LOVING**, $1.75. This is a small classic by one of the greatest psychoanalytically-oriented thinkers of our time. Fromm calls love the answer to the problems of human existence, and deals with self-love, brotherly love, motherly love, erotic love and God-love. Recommended. 148pp. H&R 56

_____. **ZEN BUDDHISM AND PSYCHOANALYSIS**, $1.95. See the Zen Buddhism section.

GEBA, BRUNO. **VITALITY TRAINING FOR OLDER ADULTS**, c$5.95. *We need to change our attitude about growing old. Through an invigorating attitudinal change, new values can be created. They can lay the foundation for a new mythology of aging. The initiative for this change must come from older adults. There is no time to look outside ourselves for help. The solution must come from within us. By allowing yourself to experience yourself growing old, you will discover your own solutions and will act accordingly. And that is what Vitality Training is all about: a method which assists in changing a person's defeatist attitude into a vital one. It is a gentle way—a way of going with life, of going with growing old and all that is associated with it.* Bibliography, 106pp. RaH 74

GESTALT THERAPY

Gestalt Therapy was originated by Fritz Perls (who died in 1970). It is more than a philosophy, it is a philosophy of life which involves needs and desires and being fully responsible for one's own actions. It centers on the reality of what is instead of the abstraction of what we think should be or might be. The philosophy is capsulized in Perls' Gestalt Prayer:

> *I do my thing, and you do your thing.*
> *I am not in this world to live up to your expectations.*
> *And you are not in this world to live up to mine.*
> *You are you, and I am I.*
> *And if by chance we find each other, it's beautiful.*
> *If not, it can't be helped.*

DOWNING, JACK, ed. **GESTALT AWARENESS**, $1.95. A collection of talks given at the San Francisco Gestalt Institute including a lengthy discussion by Ram Dass on attachment and perception, therapy and karma, love, dying, and emptying. The following are the others: *Gestalt Awareness in the Training of People Helpers*—John Enright, *Women and Gestalt Awareness*—Lois Brien and Cynthia Sheldon, *A Gestalt Way of Using Language*—Paula Bottoms, *Gestalt Art Groups*—Celia Thompson-Taupin, *Social Dreamwork and Gestalt Therapy*—Joel Latner, *Facial Therapy*—Jack Rosenberg. 174pp. H&R 76

DOWNING, JACK and ROBERT MARMORSTEIN, eds. **DREAMS AND NIGHTMARES: A BOOK OF GESTALT THERAPY SESSIONS**, $1.50. See the Dreams section.

FAGAN, JOEN and IRMA SHEPHERD, eds. **GESTALT THERAPY NOW**, $3.50. This is an authoritative collection of articles on the theory, techniques, and applications of Gestalt that has ever been published. This is probably the most extensive presentation of all the aspects of Gestalt that has ever been published. Twenty-two different practitioners present their ideas and experiences. The material is geared toward the practicing therapist. Portions of this book have been separately reprinted in **What is Gestalt Therapy?** and **Life Techniques in Gestalt Therapy** ($1.50 each). Index, notes, bibliography, 341pp. H&R 70

LATNER, JOEL. **THE GESTALT THERAPY BOOK**, $1.95. A holistic guide to the theory, principles and techniques of Gestalt therapy. In straightforward prose it shows the reader how Gestaltists understand human events, health and illness, and growth. Includes excellent up-to-date bibliography. Dr. Latner is a Gestalt therapist in San Francisco. 243pp. Ban 73

LEDERMAN, JANET. **ANGER AND THE ROCKING CHAIR—GESTALT AWARENESS WITH CHILDREN**, $1.95. Janet Lederman is one of the leading Gestalt therapists in North America, currently heading the Gestalt Institute founded by Fritz Perls in Vancouver. This short, well-illustrated book shows how the methods of Gestalt therapy can be used with children and in classroom situations. 63pp. Vik 69

PERLS, FRITZ, RALPH HEFFERLINE, and PAUL GOODMAN. **GESTALT THERAPY**, $3.75. This collaboration is perhaps the single most important book on Gestalt therapy. A unique feature is a series of eighteen experiments by which the reader can participate in the growth of self-discovery. They include: sharpening the body sense, integrating awareness, changing anxiety into excitement, mobilizing the muscles, etc. The second half is a stimulating and provocative but difficult exposition of the theory. 470pp. Del 51

PERLS, FRITZ. **EGO, HUNGER AND AGGRESSION**, $2.40. This is Fritz' first book on the theory behind Gestalt therapy. 273pp. RaH 47

_____. **THE GESTALT APPROACH AND EYE WITNESS TO THERAPY**, $1.95. These are Fritz' two last works, uncompleted at his death. He wrote **The Gestalt Approach** because he was no longer satisfied with his two earlier theoretical works, **Ego, Hunger and Aggression** and **Gestalt Therapy**. In the intervening twenty years he had integrated a great deal from Eastern religions, meditation, psychedelics, and body work. After the section on theory, **Eye Witness** consists of transcripts of films of Fritz working with patients, each with an introduction that highlights the lessons to be learned. 214pp. Ban 73

_____. **GESTALT THERAPY VERBATIM**, $3.50/1.95. In this book, Perls gives a clear explanation in simple terms of the basic ideas of Gestalt therapy, followed by verbatim transcripts of complete therapy sessions with explanatory comments. It is probably the best introductory book to this method of therapy, and is certainly one of the most interesting to read. 306pp. Ban 69

_____. IN AND OUT OF THE GARBAGE PAIL, $4.00/1.95. This is Fritz Perls autobiography, in which he applies his theory of focusing on awareness and writes *whatever wants to be written*. Partly in poetic form, often playful, sometimes theoretical, the book is a many-faceted mosaic of memories and reflections on this life—in the past and at the moment—and on the origins and continuing development of Gestalt therapy. 296pp. Ban 69

POLSTER, ERVING and MIRIAM. GESTALT THERAPY INTEGRATED, $2.95. The Polsters are among the group of second generation Gestaltists who learned from and further developed and refined the work of Fritz and Laura Perls. This book, subtitled *Contours of Theory and Practice*, has been widely acclaimed as probably the best current presentation of Gestalt therapy. It is a serious and scholarly work which is well written and very clearly organized. The authors explain the basic principles, develop new concepts, reformulate older ones, and show, through case studies, how all of these elements come together in the therapeutic practice. Notes, index, 347pp. RaH 73

PURSGLOVE, PAUL, ed. RECOGNITIONS IN GESTALT THERAPY, $1.60. This is a brief collection of writings by Laura Perls, Paul Goodman and others about Gestalt therapy. Says the editor: *It is not my central purpose as a compiler and editor to stimulate intellect or inspire debate. Rather, I would excite, enchant and haunt you with these writings.* 149pp. H&R

RHYNE, JANIE. THE GESTALT ART EXPERIENCE, c$12.50. Ms. Rhyne is an art therapist. Here she focuses on direct and immediate experiential insights gained through creating art that expresses and clarifies for participants their personal problems and potential. The emphasis is on exploring one's present life-style and discovering possibilities for self-actualization. The author presents simple directions for art activities designed for individuals and groups in therapeutic and educational settings. The book is divided into four sections: *Art Experience in Therapeutic Growth Processes, Art Experience for Contact and Communication, Using the Gestalt Art Experience for Yourself,* and *Using the Gestalt Art Experience with Others.* Oversize, illustrations index, 216pp. Wad 73

ROSENBLATT, DANIEL. THE GESTALT THERAPY PRIMER, $1.95. *This book is intended as a first taste, a small bite, a slice of what Gestalt therapy is like. In a real session with a Gestalt therapist, what happens is cooked up for just you. Here, since I don't know you, I will invent what might happen between us, so that you can gain some idea of the kind of thinking and the kind of techniques that are used to help you to grow, to get in touch with your feelings, to explore hidden parts of yourself, to become whole.... This book is deliberately small and short. That is because you are asked to do the experiments by yourself. If you will put the book down and do the experiments, much more will happen. The book is illustrated throughout.* 188pp. H&R 75

_____. OPENING DOORS, $7.95. *This book is a strong gestalt, a successful integration of theory and practice, of explanation and expression, into an intensely personal style of communication. Daniel Rosenblatt's precise and, at the same time, imaginative and flowing use of language in dialog and metaphor makes exciting and enjoyable reading. It is the most painless and least superficial introduction to Gestalt Therapy. I recommend this book to all serious students and practitioners of psychotherapy as well as to the general public.—Laura Perls.* 144pp. H&R 75

SCHIFFMAN, MURIEL. GESTALT: SELF THERAPY, $3.50. A very personal book that can be used by persons without any background in psychology. Helps you to know yourself, to be truly aware of the opposing forces within you, to deal with your search for identity, self-discipline, judgmental attitude, need to control, failure, depression, loneliness, etc. 223pp. STP

_____. SELF THERAPY, $2.45. An earlier work on the same subject. STP

SHEPARD, MARTIN. FRITZ, $3.95. Subtitled, *An Intimate Portrait of Fritz Perls and Gestalt Therapy,* this is a biographical study composed of the remembrances of those who knew Fritz best—his family, associates, patients, and lovers. The years covered are the ones in which he developed and practiced the techniques which became known as Gestalt therapy. This is a vividly written, informative, and often amusing study. Dr. Shepard is a psychiatrist. Bibliography, index, 251pp. Dut 75

STEVENS, BARRY. DON'T PUSH THE RIVER, $3.50. A first-person account of the author's use of Gestalt therapy and the ways of Zen, Krishnamurti and the American Indian to deepen and expand personal experience and work through difficulties. Her emphasis is on the flow. *We have to turn ourselves upside down and reverse our approach to life.* 268pp. RPP 70

STEVENS, JOHN. AWARENESS: EXPLORING, EXPERIMENTING, EXPERIENCING, $3.50/1.95. Detailed instructions lead you through more than a hundred experiments in exploring your awareness of yourself, your surroundings, and your interaction with others, and getting more in touch with your own flow of experiencing. 309pp. RPP/Ban 71

_____, ed. GESTALT IS, $3.50. *This book is a collection of writings on gestalt therapy. It contains all of Fritz Perls' previously published uncollected papers.... The Perls papers were originally published in the fifties and sixties, and Van Dusen's articles originally appeared in the sixties. These papers show important aspects of the development of gestalt during that period. All of the other articles were either published within the past five years, or were written for this book. They show some of the developments that are now taking place in the theory and practice of gestalt. These articles have been chosen simply on the basis of our preference. To us, they are the clearest, most interesting, original and vital of current writing on gestalt.* Stevens is the son of Barry Stevens, a well known Gestalt therapist, and he was the original publisher of Perls' books. 277pp. RPP 75

GLASSER, WILLIAM. THE IDENTITY SOCIETY, $2.95. This volume carries Dr. Glasser's ideas about Reality Therapy into the field of sociology. Here the author examines almost all varieties of human motivation and behavior, applying his theory and knowledge most specifically to aspects of modern life such as childrearing, criminal justice, hospitals, welfare, and maladjustment. Revised edition. Index, 254pp. H&R 75

_____. POSITIVE ADDICTION, c$7.95. A detailed presentation of Dr. Glasser's thesis that it is possible to become *addicted* to positive behavior. Those positive addictions can strengthen a person so that he can overcome negative addictions, and lead a more integrated and rewarding life. In his investigations Dr. Glasser found more *PA* devotees among runners and meditators, and so he explores these activities in depth. He also discusses the steps to positive addiction, its manifestations and benefits. Many case studies are examined. 159pp. H&R 76

_____. REALITY THERAPY, $2.95. Reality therapy has been developed over many years by Dr. Glasser. Its requirements—an intense personal involvement, facing reality, rejecting irresponsible behavior, and learning better ways to behave—bear little resemblance to conventional therapy and produce markedly different results. Whether the patient thinks he is Napoleon, is running berserk, or has nervous headaches, the common cause is inability to fulfill his two essential needs: to love and be loved, and to feel worthwhile to himself and to others. The first part of this book explains Reality therapy and contrasts it with conventional treatment. The second part illustrates it in practice and includes many case studies. 189pp. H&R 65

GREENBERG, IRA, ed. PSYCHODRAMA, c$25.50. Psychodrama is a therapeutic approach which involves acting out your significant *others* as well as yourself. By playing different roles, an individual gains new perspective on relationships. This anthology presents the most important articles and essays that have been written on the subject and on its creator, J.L. Moreno, M.D. Theory, history, biography, and practical methods are presented, and the approach itself is evaluated. Most of the selections are fairly technical and the book is oriented toward professionals. Index, 511pp. Beh 74

GREGORY, R.L. EYE AND BRAIN, $2.95. Brings together the experimental discoveries of both physiology and psychology to give a comprehensive account of how we see the world. Profusely illustrated. A good summary. 255pp. MGH 66

HARPER, ROBERT. THE NEW PSYCHOTHERAPIES, $2.95. Short summaries of the major systems that have arisen in recent years. The therapies are grouped by type and the individual therapies in each grouping are compared and contrasted, and a bibliography is given covering the major books in the field. The material is clearly presented. Index, 178pp. PrH 75

HOPER, CLAUS et al. AWARENESS GAMES, $3.50. A practical compilation of 115 suggestions and directions for games that can be played in groups of four or more and that aim at increasing social awareness and personal growth. The games are divided into five categories: making contact, communication and group formation, observation and perception, identification and empathy, aggression and self-assertion. The directions include guidelines as to size of group, duration of game, materials required, learning goals, and general suggestions. The authors have had extensive experience in group work, especially with young adults. 156pp. SMP 75

HOPSON, BARRIE and CHARLOTTE. INTIMATE FEEDBACK, $1.50. Subtitled *A Lovers' Guide to Getting in Touch with Each Other,* this is a collection of exercises and information on marital patterns based on the authors' extensive work with couples in the human potential movement. Quotations from various authorities are also included. Biliography, notes, 222pp. S&S 73

HOWARD, JANE. PLEASE TOUCH, $2.95. Jane Howard set out to experience every possible form of encounter. This is her report on what she saw happen to others—and what happened to her. 274pp. Del 70

HUDSON, LIAM. HUMAN BEINGS: THE PSYCHOLOGY OF HUMAN EXPERIENCE, $2.95. *This book is designed to serve as an introductory text; an invitation to approach the discipline of psychology in a certain way. The view of psychology that it advances seems to me to have two virtues that more conventional approaches lack. It has immediate human relevance, in that it is about people and the lives they lead.... And it is integrative, creating connections between traditions and styles of thought that have in the past been treated as separate: the artistic as well as scientific; the biological as well as the cultural. For the heart of psychology lies, I believe, in interpretative argument: in the effort to make sense of what people think and do.* Index, notes, 232pp. Dou 75

HUXLEY, LAURA. YOU ARE NOT THE TARGET, $3.00. See section on Consciousness Expansion. 293pp. Wil 63

HUYCK, MARGARET. GROWING OLDER, $2.95. A collection of essays on all aspects of aging, explaining the biological and psychological changes that take place and showing how to best deal with these changes. Bibliography, index, 191pp. PrH 74

JAFFE, DENNIS, ed. IN SEARCH OF A THERAPY, $3.25. *The contributors to this book all practice therapy in certain ways based on certain values, experiences, and commit-*

ents each of them will relate. The purpose of bringing their accounts together is, how-er, to shed light on the nature of the basic choices and definitions of the work we call erapy. . . . This book presents personal answers . . . not in theoretical form, but as they olved in the work and growth of each of the contributors.* 154pp. H&R 75

ANOV, ARTHUR and E.M. HOLDEN. **PRIMAL MAN: THE NEW CONSCIOUSNESS** $10.00. See the Consciousness Expansion section.

ANOV, ARTHUR. **THE PRIMAL REVOLUTION**, $2.95. An exploration of how primal erapy works, as seen through case studies and the thoughts of its founder. 285pp. S&S 72

_________. **THE PRIMAL SCREAM**, $3.45/1.50. Janov presents a revolutionary new pproach to psychological thinking—primal therapy—and, through case histories, gives ocumented evidence for the elimination of lifetime ailments, both psychological and hysical. Primal therapy forces a patient to relive core (primal) experiences, i.e., those oments in infancy and childhood which he found too painful to endure and took refuge the comfortable half-world of neurosis. 446pp. Del 70

OURNARD, SIDNEY. **DISCLOSING MAN TO HIMSELF**, $3.95. This is a continuation f material presented in **The Transparent Self**. Again, the thesis is the importance of re-ealing oneself and not hiding behind veils and personas. A technical study by one of the ajor figures in humanistic psychology. For professionals or well-read laymen only. Notes, ibliography, index, 245pp. Lit 68

_________. **HEALTHY PERSONALITY**, c$12.75. *Some ways of behaving in the world e life-giving to the person and not destructive to other people, to animals, or to the en-ironment which supports us all. These are ways I call healthy personality. Not only do hese ways enhance life and health for the person, they also stimulate, or at least do not npede, the growth and actualization of his more desirable possibilities. . . . In this book have presented what we have learned in psychology—through clinical experience and hrough research in laboratories and natural settings—about healthy personality. . . . The wo previous editions of this book were entitled* **Personal Adjustment**. This is a greatly xpanded version. Notes, index, 370pp. McM 74

_________. **THE TRANSPARENT SELF**, $4.25. A choice which confronts everyone f us at every moment is this: shall we permit our fellow man to know us as we now are, r shall we seek instead to remain an enigma, wishing to be seen as something we are not? 54pp. Lit 71

EEN, SAM. **BEGINNINGS WITHOUT END**, c$6.95. *During three years of intense inner urmoil and change I wrote, almost daily, memos to myself. Whenever I found a way to nove from despair to hope, or numbness to anger, or sorrow to laughter I tried to capture he insight in an aphorism, a paragraph, a story or an essay. This book began from notes nd fragments I left beside the trail to mark my journey. When I was past the crisis, I re-raced my steps and filled in descriptions of the roads and twisting lanes that led me from ne point to the next. I share this log of my travels because I think it may be helpful to thers who are on a similar adventure. Each person's journey involves both unique circum-tances and a common map. My particular path is only a variation of a way that is univer-al. . . . This book is offered to anyone who feels the need to begin again. It is not so nuch the story of my journey as it is a report of places where I found an oasis, a helping pirit, a devouring demon, a rushing river or a tree with magical apples.* 142pp. H&R 75

KEEN, SAM and ANNE VALLEY FOX. **TELLING YOUR STORY**, $1.50. *The tech-niques of storytelling and the psychology which underlies them rest on a discovery of the obvious: that what all persons have in common is their uniqueness. Every person has a story to tell. . . . We were all raised by an intimate group that had traditions, values, rites of passage, ceremonies and legends. We feel nameless and empty when we forget our stor-ies. . . . Find the unconscious and make it conscious, find an audience for the untold tales, and you will discover you are already living a rich mythical life. What most of us lack is only the permission to tell stories that are our own birthright. . . . Journey back into the past, ahead into your future, and out into cosmic time. Discover a few of your many selves.* Keen presents guidelines and sample stories. 159pp. NAL 73

KELEMAN, STANLEY. **THE HUMAN GROUND: SEXUALITY, SELF AND SURVIVAL**, $4.95. *Stanley Keleman is a teacher of awareness in the classic sense. Out of his own ex-perience he finds words and exercises to evoke insight and learning in others. . . . His es-sential message is simple: be yourself, experience your bodily life directly. . . . This book is an expanded and revised edition of* **The Human Ground** *and* **Sexuality, Self and Survival**, *which were originally compiled out of a number of weekend workshops. . . . In* **The Hu-man Ground**, *Stanley Keleman talks about the ways in which we take on self definition. . . and how this may or may not be grounded in one's natural being. In* **Sexuality, Self and Survival**, *using vignettes from workshops, he demonstrates how the central energy of our sexual nature becomes diverted, dissipated, blocked, and warped by conditioned responses that may begin in the cradle or with toilet training.*—from the introduction by Gay Luce. 191pp. S&B 75

_________. **YOUR BODY SPEAKS ITS MIND**, c$7.95. This is Keleman's most com-plete book on understanding the language of our bodies: *We do not have our bodies, we are our bodies . . . and your body is not only alive, but formative.* Using his experiences of working with people, he shows how they achieve formative experiences which put them in touch with the full range of human emotions. Through his program for *grounding and experiencing*, he tries to provide ways to deal with the anxiety and anger confined through years of denial in a tense musculature and to help people free themselves to ex-press the positive and loving feelings previously unavailable. Keleman writes clearly and directly and the reader can get a good feeling for the bioenergetic experience from his exposition and from the first person accounts he quotes. 189pp. S&S 75

KEYES, MARGARET. **THE INWARD JOURNEY**, $4.95. *My concern here is to describe in practical detail how I use art materials with the nonartist, the client who has come into therapy with some very specific questions and problems. Some of these questions are sim-ilar to your own for they are the questions of anyone who seeks to understand himself, his thoughts, his feelings and actions. These art processes, originally developed in work with troubled clients, I have used in workshops with teachers, students, ministers, and a range of people who simply wished to know themselves more deeply and who found these methods useful.* Ms. Keyes has made an excellent presentation. Her background is in Jung-ian psychology and she has also worked with Eric Berne and Fritz Perls. Many illustrations, index. 121pp. CeA 74

KOPP, SHELDON. **GURU**, c$6.95. In **Guru**, Washington psychologist Kopp distills the wisdom of gurus from many times and settings: from primitive tribes, ancient Greece and Rome, Judaism and Christianity, the Renaissance world and the Orient, even children's tales, science fiction and the psychedelic scene. In the closing chapters, Dr. Kopp takes his place as a latter-day guru with some profound thoughts on life and loving and change and death and rebirth. Kopp writes as he lives: directly yet with poetry, simply yet with profundity, mystically yet with immediacy, firmly yet with warmth. 180pp. S&B 71

_________. **THE HANGED MAN**, c$7.95. The theme of this highly personal account is that each of us has a dark side which we must get in touch with in order to become real-ized beings. *I would turn myself, my patients, and my readers toward those hidden uncon-scious recesses of ourselves, away from which we have been turned by science, civilization, and conventional wisdom.* Dr. Kopp uses a tarot card to highlight the subject of each chapter and he illustrates his narrative with myths, dreams, and stories from countless tra-ditions and ages. He also presents case studies from his psychiatric practice. A well written, moving account which has been extremely popular. Notes, bibliography, 256pp. S&B 74

_________. **IF YOU MEET BUDDHA ON THE ROAD, KILL HIM**, $1.95. This book, subtitled *The Pilgrimage of Psychotherapy Patients*, uses the framework of the Canterbury Tales to recount the spiritual pilgrimages of people today, as seen by their therapist, and, in the course of all this—Kopp's own pilgrimage. 183pp. Ban 72

_________. **NO HIDDEN MEANINGS**, $4.95. Photographs by Claire Flanders illustrate Kopp's *An Eschatological Laundry List: A Partial Register of the 927 (or was it 928) Eter-nal Truths.* Our poster of this (see illustration) has been one of our most popular items. 9x10", S&B 75

R.D. LAING

R.D. Laing is one of the best known and most influential of the *anti-psychia-trists*. In his first work, **The Divided Self** (1960), he viewed much of *madness* not as a disease but as a reasonable adjustment to an unreasonable environ-ment. In **Self and Others** and **Sanity, Madness and the Family**, he enlarged on this, looking at the schizophrenic family which created and cast out into a mental institution the young person who would not adapt to the double-bind situation forced upon him. By 1964 he began to view schizophrenia as one stage in a natural psychic healing process which, if successful, could lead to entry into a realm of *hyper-sanity*. Psychiatric medicine offered, at best, a mechanistic bungling of this potential process; at worst, it drove its patients insane with its chemicals, surgery and regimentation. Laing founded a thera-peutic community at Kingsley Hall in London to provide a sympathetic set-ting for the patients' inner voyage. In his more recent writings, Laing has become both more socially committed and more mystical. He compares psy-chotic and psychedelic experiences. It is not the psychotic who has the split personality, it is the so-called *normal* person: alienation and splitting are in-deed the basic conditions for our repressive normality and its apparatus of anti-human institutions. Laing thus can be seen as possibly the most influen-tial spirit behind the whole radical therapy movement.

BARNES, MARY. **TWO ACCOUNTS OF A JOURNEY THROUGH MADNESS**, $1.95. *What an extremely rich book this is—how it combines a personal drama of redemption from madness with a profound revolutionary statement on how a free community of souls can interact for the good of its individuals; how it sets forth the theories of the charismatic R.D. Laing without reducing them to sterile syllogisms. . . . But what I found particularly moving is the faith the book expresses in the resiliency of the human spirit; that no matter how damaged the soul, there remains a part of it that always grows toward wholeness . . . and that no behavior, however bizarre or seemingly empty it may seem, is without order and meaning or beyond the reach of love.*—**The New York Times.** Illustrations, notes, 374pp. RaH 71

BOYERS, ROBERT et al. **R. D. LAING AND ANTI-PSYCHIATRY**, $1.95. This collection of essays represents a great deal of the serious writing of the last few years about Laing and the ideas he has expounded. 310pp. H&R 71

EVANS, RICHARD. **R.D. LAING: THE MAN AND HIS IDEAS**, $3.95. Transcription of a long dialogue Evans had with Laing in which Laing covers a wide range of subjects—his debt to Freud and Gregory Bateson, his true position on schizophrenia, mysticism as an aid to understanding, his concept of therapy as practiced at Kingsley Hall. Also includes a biographical essay by Peter Mezan and a hitherto unpublished study by Laing of Kallman and Slater's genetic theory of schizophrenia. Evans also provides a long introduction. Index, 255pp. Dut 76

FRIEDENBERG, EDGAR. **R.D. LAING**, $1.95. A critical examination of Laing, part of the **Modern Masters** series, which discusses Laing's revolutionary theories and their impli-cations not only in psychiatry but in politics and culture as well. Bibliography, index, 118pp. Vik 73

AN ESCHATOLOGICAL LAUNDRY LIST:

A Partial Register of the 927 (or was it 928?) Eternal Truths.

1. This is it!
2. There are no hidden meanings.
3. You can't get there from here, and besides there's no place else to go.
4. We are all already dying, and we will be dead for a long time.
5. Nothing lasts!
6. There is no way of getting all you want.
7. You can't have anything unless you let go of it.
8. You only get to keep what you give away.
9. There is no particular reason why you lost out on some things.
10. The world is not necessarily just. Being good often does not pay off and there is no compensation for misfortune.
11. You have a responsibility to do your best nonetheless.
12. It is a random universe to which we bring meaning.
13. You don't really control anything.
14. You can't make anyone love you.
15. No one is any stronger or any weaker than anyone else.
16. Everyone is, in his own way, vulnerable.
17. There are no great men.
18. If you have a hero, look again; you have diminished yourself in some way.
19. Everyone lies, cheats, pretends (yes, you too, and most certainly I myself).
20. All evil is potential vitality in need of transformation.
21. All of you is worth something, if you will only own it.
22. Progress is an illusion.
23. Evil can be displaced but never eradicated, as all solutions breed new problems.
24. Yet it is necessary to keep on struggling toward solution.
25. Childhood is a nightmare.
26. But it is so very hard to be an on-your-own, take-care-of-yourself-cause-there-is-no-one-else-to-do-it-for-you grown-up.
27. Each of us is ultimately alone.
28. The most important things, each man must do for himself.
29. Love is not enough, but it sure helps.
30. We have only ourselves, and one another. That may not be much, but that's all there is.
31. How strange, that so often, it all seems worth it.
32. We must live within the ambiguity of partial freedom, partial power and partial knowledge.
33. All important decisions must be made on the basis of insufficient data.
34. Yet we are responsible for everything we do.
35. No excuses will be accepted.
36. You can run, but you can't hide.
37. It is most important to run out of scapegoats.
38. We must learn the power of living with our helplessness.
39. The only victory, lies in surrender to oneself.
40. All of the significant battles are waged within the self.
41. You are free to do whatever you like. You need only face the consequences.
42. What do you know ... for sure ... anyway?
43. Learn to forgive yourself, again and again and again and again.

By Shelly Kopp

(author of <u>GURU</u>: Metaphors from a Psychotherapist)

a "yes! poster
by I.K.P.
YES inc.
1039 31st st. N.W.
Washington 20007 D.C.

LAING, R.D. **THE DIVIDED SELF**, $1.95. Laing's first book (see above). Its basic purpose is to make madness, and the process of going mad, comprehensible. 218pp. Pen 60

_____. **THE FACTS OF LIFE**, c$7.95. *In this book I've tried to portray some facts of my life and world. What is here is sketches of my childhood, first questions, speculations, observations, reflections on conception, intra-uterine life, being born and giving birth: allusions to behavior and experience of adults which seem to belong to the same class as traumatic neuroses. They make us wonder: the adult content of the adult misery seems to have the form or mold of intra-uterine and birth catastrophes—can this be possible? I continue to muse over the ways in which structural configurations emerge into two sets of elements, mythological and embryological.* 153pp. RaH 76

_____. **KNOTS**, $1.65. *They are playing a game. They are playing at not playing a game. If I show them I see they are, I shall break the rules and they will punish me. I must play their game, of not seeing I see the game.* **Knots** is unlike any other book, consisting of a series of powerful, witty, unexpected, dialogue-scenarios, revealing Laing's insights into the intricacies of human relationships and the way we tie ourselves into knots. 90pp. RaH 70

_____. **THE POLITICS OF EXPERIENCE**, $1.75. *The condition of alienation, of being asleep, of being unconscious of being out of one's mind, is the condition of the normal man. Society highly values its normal man. It educates children to lose themselves and to become absurd, and thus to be normal. Normal men have killed perhaps 100,000,000 of their fellow men in the last fifty years. We are not able even to think adequately about the behavior that is at the annihilating edge. But what we think is less than what we know; what we know is less than what we love; what we love is so much less than what there is.* 90pp. RaH 67

_____. **THE POLITICS OF THE FAMILY**, $1.95. The basis of Laing's argument is that the concept of *family* lies in the mutual collusion of those who believe themselves to be its members. A family is threatened, then, when one or more of the constituting ideas of its existence is threatened. But since the family in turn gives each of its members his self-identity, we are left with a chain of interlocking chains, each of which can carry any number of interpersonal processes in which any member may be simultaneously involved. 133pp. RaH 69

_____. **SELF AND OTHERS**, $2.50. This book, exploring some aspects of relations between persons, is a thoroughly revised edition of a book originally published in America in 1962 but barely known in America at that time. The first part examines different modes of experience as forms of relationships. In the second part some key patterns of interaction are considered, especially those that characterize certain extreme forms of disturbance or breakdown of relationships. 192pp. Pen 61

LAING, R.D. and D.G. COOPER. **REASON AND VIOLENCE**, $1.95. This is an introduction to the thought of the great French existentialist, Jean-Paul Sartre. Laing and Cooper see in him one of the most radical thinkers of the century, a man who has brought about a revolution in man's understanding of himself. 184pp. RaH 64

LAING, R.D. and A. ESTERSON. **SANITY, MADNESS AND THE FAMILY**, $1.75. To prepare this report, Drs. Laing and Esterson conducted and recorded a series of interviews with eleven patients, drawing on parents and relatives. In this way the authors dramatically exposed the cross-currents of affection, hatred, and indifference within the family, which go far to explain the *why* of madness. 282pp. Pen 64

LAING, R.D., H. PHILLIPSON, and A.R. LEE. **INTERPERSONAL PERCEPTION**, $1.50. The theme of this book is the experiences, perceptions and actions which occur when two human beings are engaged in a meaningful encounter. Whatever the issue, love or hate, concern or neglect, the method presented comes to terms with the way in which one person's position is experienced by the other, so that he first may become aware of how he looks in the eyes of the other. 233pp. H&R 66

LEWIS, HOWARD et al. **GROWTH GAMES**, $1.75. A compendium of more than 200 of the best techniques of the human potential movement, usable by yourself, with a partner, or in a group. Many have been tested in leaderless groups. This is the best collection of this sort we've seen. 301pp. Ban 70

LIEBERMAN, MORTON A., IRVIN D. YALOM, and MATTHEW B. MILES. **ENCOUNTER GROUPS: FIRST FACTS**, c$21.45. Just how effective are encounter groups in changing people? What kind of personal growth do they achieve and how long-lasting is it? This comprehensive book, the first scientific study of the encounter movement, examines the major theories currently used in the U.S. and Europe and presents a theoretical and empirical analysis of leader behavior and other group conditions as they affect productive or counter-productive changes in individuals. 498pp. BaB 73

LOWEN, ALEXANDER. **THE BETRAYAL OF THE BODY**, $1.95. Lowen is the leading developer of bio-energetics, an outgrowth of the work of Wilhelm Reich. Lowen argues that the schizoid personality is the dominant one in America, manifested by a split between our feelings and our actions. This book traces this argument through many case studies and shows how we can reclaim our bodies through bio-energetics. 275pp. McM 67

_____. **BIO-ENERGETICS**, $2.50. Dr. Lowen is the founder of bio-energetic therapy and this is the definitive book on it. He presents a full explanation of the principles and techniques and a historical review of their development from the work of Wilhelm Reich. Bio-energetics believes that *you are your body*. How your body functions energetically determines what you feel, think, and do. Disturbances in the body's vital energetic processes affect both mental and physical health. Dr. Lowen explains why so many people lack energy, pointing out how chronic muscular tensions restrict breathing, limit movement, and reduce a person's effectiveness in dealing with life. The bio-energetic approach

leads to an understanding of these tensions as the direct result of the suppression of feeling and their release through direct body work. In addition, Dr. Lowen analyzes a number of common physical disorders such as headaches and lower back pain and shows how they can be overcome by unlocking the muscular tensions that create them. This account is more clearly written than Lowen's earlier work and is illustrated with line drawings of bio-energetic exercises. Index, 352pp. CMB 75

_____. **DEPRESSION AND THE BODY**, $2.50. Discusses how we can overcome depression by activating dormant life forces and by training mind and body to respond to each other. 318pp. Pen 74

_____. **LANGUAGE OF THE BODY**, $2.95. This is Lowen's first book, originally published as **The Physical Dynamics of Character Structure**. Contains a critique of conventional analysis, followed by extended discussion of various character types such as oral, masochistic, hysterical, phallic, narcissistic, etc. 404pp. McM 58

_____. **LOVE AND ORGASM**, $1.95. Explores the physical and psychic effects of orgasm and argues that full orgiastic release is only possible in mature heterosexual love. Brings love back to sex. 319pp. McM 65

_____. **PLEASURE**, $1.95. Defining pleasure as a *bodily experience*, Dr. Lowen states that *there is no such thing as pure mental pleasure* and points out that *the capacity for pleasure is also the capacity for creative self-expression.* In most adults, however, the struggle for power competes with the striving for pleasure, undermines creativity, and causes muscular tensions. This book describes a way out of this dilemma through a series of bio-energetic exercises. 251pp. Pen 70

LUCE, GAY GAER. **BODY TIME**, $1.50. See the Biorhythms section. Ban 71

LUTHMAN, SHIRLEY. **DYNAMIC FAMILY**, c$7.95. A practical text on family therapy by students of Virginia Satir, rich with examples, anecdotes and case histories drawn from the authors' professional experience. The book begins with a discussion of their theories on growth, both individual and within the family context. The next sections review treatment concepts and techniques. Final sections discuss the development of the family therapist and give many practical ideas. Bibliography, 250pp. S&B 74

ABRAHAM MASLOW

Maslow, who died in 1970, is regarded as the father of humanistic psychology and the human potential movement. He had the revolutionary idea of studying not neurotics—but people as psychologically healthy as he could find. They turned out to be not unlike Eastern ideals of realized men. Maslow also concluded that man's inner nature is not intrisically bad but good, or at least neutral.

Said Maslow, *. . . mankind, throughout history, has looked for guiding values, for principles of right and wrong. But he has tended to look outside of mankind, to a God, to some sort of sacred book perhaps, or to a ruling class. What I am doing is exploring the theory that you can find the values by which mankind must live, and for which man has always sought, by digging into the best people in depth. . . . If under the best conditions and in the best specimens, I simply stand aside and describe in a scientific way what these human values are, I find values that are the old values of truth, goodness and beauty, and some additional ones as well—for instance, gaiety, justice, and joy.*

GOBLE, FRANK. **THE THIRD FORCE—THE PSYCHOLOGY OF ABRAHAM MASLOW**, $1.50. This is a condensation of Maslow's ideas, distilled from his five books and over a hundred articles in language understandable to the layman. It is a good place to start in studying Maslow and humanistic psychology. Maslow coined the term *third force psychology* to distinguish it from the Freudian and behavioristic approaches. S&S 70

MASLOW, ABRAHAM. **THE FARTHER REACHES OF HUMAN NATURE**, $2.95. This first posthumous work serves as an extension of Maslow's classic **Toward A Psychology of Being**. It is a wide-ranging synthesis of his inspiring and influential ideas on biology, synergy, creativity, cognition, the hierarchy of needs, and the role of science in the expanding study of human nature. In this book he has touched upon all the key concepts of his work and life over the past forty years. 429pp. Vik 71

_____. **RELIGIONS, VALUES, PEAK EXPERIENCES**, $1.75. Argues that the religious experience is a rightful subject for scientific investigation and, conversely, the scientific community will see its work enhanced by acknowledging and studying the species-wide need for spiritual expression which, in so many forms, is at the heart of *peak experiences* reached by healthy, fully-functioning persons. 131pp. Vik 64

_____. **TOWARD A PSYCHOLOGY OF BEING**, $3.95. This is the basic book of Maslow's ideas. Should be read by anyone interested in self-actualization and growth. 250pp. Lit 68

WILSON, COLIN. **NEW PATHWAYS IN PSYCHOLOGY: MASLOW AND THE POST-FREUDIAN REVOLUTION**, $1.95. Wilson considers Maslow second in importance only to Freud among twentieth century psychologists. To place Maslow in his proper professional perspective, Wilson surveys the history of psychology from David Hume through Freud and Jung, placing special emphasis on Maslow's true forerunner, William James, who recognized that *higher* forms of consciousness are natural to man. After discussing Maslow's life and ideas, he also surveys the work of Frankl, Assagioli and other post-Freudian psychologists. 268pp. NAL 72

MAY, ROLLO. **THE COURAGE TO CREATE**, c$7.95. *All my life I have been haunted by the fascinating questions of creativity. Why does an original idea in art and science pop up from the unconscious at a given moment? What is the relation between talent and the creative act, and between creativity and death? . . . I have asked these questions not as one who stands on the sidelines, but as one who himself participates in art and science . . . . These chapters are a partial record of my ponderings. They had their birth as lectures given at colleges and universities. I had always hesitated to publish them because they seemed incomplete—the mystery of creation still remained. I then realized that this unfinished quality would always remain, and that it is part of the creative process itself.* Notes, 143pp. Nor 75

_________, ed. **EXISTENCE**, $2.95. Regarded as the most important, complete and lucid account of the existentialist approach to psychology. Classic case histories and writings of the leading spokesmen of the existential analytic movement have been selected to define the approach which seeks to understand mental illness not as deviations from the conceptual yardstick of the psychiatrist but as deviations in the structure of the particular patient's existence. 445pp. S&S 58

_________. **LOVE AND WILL**, $1.75. The heart of our dilemma, according to May, is our failure to understand the real meanings of love and will, their sources, and their interrelation. An important book. 352pp. Del 69

_________. **MAN'S SEARCH FOR HIMSELF**, $3.45. Examines the neuroses afflicting modern men and women in the age of anxiety. Neither a hydrogen bomb nor a sexual revolution can change the essential nature of man. With uncommon wisdom, the distinguished psychologist probes the hidden layers of personality to reveal the core of man's integration— the inborn sense of value which is basic to the human animal . . . the ability to choose, judge and act. 239pp. Del 53

_________. **POWER AND INNOCENCE**, $2.95. Dr. May argues that powerlessness is just as corrupting as is power: when people feel impotent they are likely to become either violent or sick. This lies at the root of the rise of violence in our society. We have made a virtue of powerlessness because we have been in the habit of thinking of power only in its negative forms—in terms of aggressors and victims. But, Dr. May shows, *power is the birthright of every human being. It is the source of his self-esteem and the root of his conviction that he is . . . significant.* Index, notes, 283pp. Del 72

MAYEROFF, MILTON. **ON CARING**, $1.25. *To care for another person, in the most significant sense, is to help him grow and actualize himself. . . . Through caring for certain others, by serving them through caring, a man lives the meaning of his own life. In the sense in which a man can ever be said to be at home in the world, he is at home not through dominating, or explaining, or appreciating, but through caring and being cared for.* This small book is destined to become a classic. 106pp. H&R 71

MISSILDINE, HUGH. **YOUR INNER CHILD OF THE PAST**, c$8.95. *Somewhere, sometime, you were a child. This is one of the great obvious, seemingly meaningless and forgotten common denominators of adult life. . . . Your childhood, in an actual, literal sense, exists within you now. It affects everything you do, everything you feel. These childhood feelings and attitudes influence, often actually determine and dominate your relations. . . . They can interfere with your ability to work or to love. Such feelings may be a significant part of your fatigue, your inability to relax, your irritating headaches, your upset stomach . . . . The child you once were can balk or frustrate your adult satisfactions, embarrass and harass you, make you sick—or enrich your life.* This is a detailed exploration, based on Dr. Missildine's extensive study and experience. 317pp. S&S 63

MISSILDINE, HUGH and LAWRENCE GALTON. **YOUR INNER CONFLICTS—HOW TO SOLVE THEM**, c$8.95. A development of the material in Dr. Missildine's earlier book. Patterns of living and being as well as of experience are identified and specific suggestions are made for counteracting each pattern. Guidelines are presented for achieving an awakened sense of self-confidence and the freedom to explore and develop abilities and talents and to pursue more meaningful relationships. 345pp. S&S 74

MONTAGU, ASHLEY. **TOUCHING**, $2.25. *A fascinating analysis of a long neglected and important subject; the skin regarded as a sense organ rather than as a simple bodily covering. . . . An attractive and wide-ranging volume which should be read by all students of human behavior.*—Loren Eiseley. 406pp. H&R 71

MOUSTAKAS, CLARK. **FINDING YOURSELF, FINDING OTHERS**, $2.95. *This is a treasure trove of nuggets which will enhance the reader. It is full of the wonder of life and persons.* This illustrated, oversize volume is composed of quotations from leading figures in the human potential movement. 120pp. PrH 74

_________. **LONELINESS**, $2.95. Loneliness is an intrinsic condition of human existence. This study of existential loneliness reveals that—beyond the first pangs of desolation, out of the terror of despair—human beings have found a key to deeper insight and keen perception of the world in which they live. Encourages the reader to make a penetrating investigation of his own solitude. 107pp. PrH 61

_________. **LONELINESS AND LOVE**, $2.45. Reveals how periods of loneliness and solitude can help a person move toward more authenticity, more honesty, and therefore more meaningful love relationships with his fellow human beings. 146pp. PrH 72

_________. **PORTRAITS OF LONELINESS AND LOVE**, $2.95. A blending of photographs and sensitive poetry and prose which evokes the depth and impact of the emotions we experience. Most of the writing is Moustakas'. Oversize, 95pp. PrH 74

_________. **THE TOUCH OF LONELINESS**, $2.45. Dr. Moustakas definitely seems be guilty of writing the same book over and over again. This is his newest attempt. It's collection of letters received by the author in response to his earlier books—letters whi detail many individuals' experiences of loneliness. Also included are some letters Moust kas wrote to himself in times of crisis and a review of his own recent experiences wi loneliness. 112pp. PrH 75

MURPHY, GARDNER. **HUMAN POTENTIALITIES**, $3.95. Dr. Murphy, a leading ps chologist, traces the development of man from the simple, biologically motivated mar malian, through the more complex organism evolving from interaction with its cultu mold, to the next stage of human growth—in which, Dr. Murphy foresees, man's creati drive will transcend his biological and cultural inheritances to open the way for a broa free expression of his capacity for love and knowledge. This is a fairly technical accou which is definitely not light reading. Notes, bibliography, index, 352pp. Vik 58

MURPHY, GARDNER and LOIS, eds. **ASIAN PSYCHOLOGY**, $3.95. This explorati of the main currents of psychological thought in Asia illustrates the special contributio and insights of Asia through a judicious selection of both ancient and modern writing The editors link the various passages with explanatory introductions, setting them in h torical perspective, and providing interpretations for the Western reader. Includes sectio on India, China and Japan. 238pp. H&R 72

MURPHY, GARDNER and MORTON LEEDS. **OUTGROWING SELF-DECEPTIO** c$8.95. An exploration of techniques for testing one's assumptions about oneself and t world—from everyday methods (such as logic and learning to listen to what others a telling you) to more specialized approaches, such as analysis, bio-feedback, sensitivi training, yoga, Eastern philosophy. In addition the authors examine the lives of men wl *changed the world*—Freud, Darwin, Einstein, and others—showing the methods they us to confront (and triumph over) their own self-deceptions. Index, bibliography, 175p H&R 75

NARANJO, CLAUDIO and ROBERT ORNSTEIN. **ON THE PSYCHOLOGY OF MED TATION**, $2.25. See section on Meditation. Vik 71

O'CONNOR, ELIZABETH. **OUR MANY SELVES: A HANDBOOK FOR SELF DISCO ERY**, $2.50. Written from a Christian activist point of view, this book contains a series practical exercises to help the reader understand his or her own life and evolve a progra of continuing growth. On the path to self-realization, the book moves from confession identification with those one has criticized, to creative suffering. The author's commen are buttressed by readings from a wide range of sources which integrate the findings contemporary psychology with ancient discoveries in the life of the spirit. 201pp. H&

O'NEILL, NENA and GEORGE. **OPEN MARRIAGE**, $1.95. This book came out a fe years ago when the idea of open marriage was just beginning to be discussed in the medi It was an immediate best seller and has remained a popular book. although the ideas expresses are today not the slightest bit revolutionary. The O'Neills got divorced recentl so their *open marriage* did not seem to work. Notes, bibliography, 286pp. Avo 72

_________. **SHIFTING GEARS**, $1.95. A popular account which gives practical guid lines and advice on achieving your full potential in today's rapidly changing world, b making crucial changes in yourself, your relationships, your job, and your whole way life. In short, how you can keep growing. The advice is often simplistic, but many hav found it to be helpful. Notes, bibliography, 280pp. Avo 74

OSMOND, HUMPHRY, JOHN OSMOND and JEROME AGEL. **UNDERSTANDIN UNDERSTANDING**, $1.95. An important book by a leading British psychiatrist. Discu ses ways of better understanding others' perceptions of the world; presents a new typolog of personalities. Much on schizophrenia (Osmond was one of the first to advocate niac therapy) and the use of a card text, HOD, to measure perception distortions in sick an well. Interesting discussion of psychedelics (Osmond introduced Huxley to mescaline Recommended for professionals and general readers alike. 216pp. Ban 74

OTTO, HERBERT, ed. **LOVE TODAY**, $2.75. **Love Today** had its beginnings when th American Psychological Association undertook the study of love in the twentieth centur and chose *Love as a Growth Experience* for the theme of a recent annual meeting. Twent professionals from various disciplines were invited to examine the meaning of love an this is a transcription of these papers. 272pp. Del 72

OTTO, HERBERT and JOHN MANN, eds. **WAYS OF GROWTH—APPROACHES T EXPLORING AWARENESS**, $2.45. A collection of various articles: general person expressions on the theme; accounts of new methods requiring professional backgroun and training before they can be successfully applied; and approaches that the reader ca directly apply to his own life. Most of the authors come out of the human potential mov ment. 229pp. Vik 68

PESSO, ALBERT. **EXPERIENCE IN ACTION**, c$13.10. A description of psychomoto therapy, a technique developed by Pesso and his wife Diane. Psychomotor can be describe as follows: movement is isolated into three modalities—reflex, voluntary, and emotional and accomodators, usually other group members, provide an appropriate responding envi onment that encourages emotional free association. Since most of the material that eme ges relates to the past and to parents, the negative accomodators represent negative aspec of the parents, while the positive accomodators represent new archetypal parents. Th provides a structure within which catharsis may be achieved followed by new and mor positive experiences. This volume presents psychomotor theories, illustrated with exar ples from actual sessions. 270pp. NYU 73

_________. **MOVEMENT IN PSYCHOLOGY**, c$13.10. The basic book on psych motor, outlining the theories and the techniques. Neither of the Pesso books is easy t read and we have a hard time following what is being presented. If you are familiar wit the technique the books will probably be quite helpful. 233pp. NYU 69

PIAGET, JEAN. **MAIN TRENDS IN PSYCHOLOGY**, $1.95. *Does the mind retain its own identity independent of its biological origins and its involvement with society, or is its reality inevitably confined to these two connecting areas? . . . These are the two problems which we shall find underlying all the perspectives and it is for me a great privilege to present them.* Small type. 72pp. H&R 70

PLECK, JOSEPH and JACK SAWYER, eds. **MEN AND MASCULINITY**, $3.45. In contrast to the proliferation of volumes on women's liberation, there is little or nothing written on the confining aspects of the traditional man's role. This volume fills the need. It is a collection of essays edited by two psychologists which presents psychological and sociological studies which show how suppression of emotions and anxiety about achievement restrict men's ability to work, play, and love freely. Most of the accounts read well and relate a great variety of experiences. Notes, 184pp. PrH 74

PRATHER, HUGH. **I TOUCH THE EARTH, THE EARTH TOUCHES ME**, $2.95. *This book, like the one which preceded it, (below) evolved. . . . The entries . . . exhibit the same curious pattern I saw in my last book: that every time I think I have learned something, my life seems to deliberately set about contradicting it. Yet the contradiction is never absolute; it is more a quarter turn than a whole. And so I am left with this belief: that there are no answers, only alternatives.* Dou 72

_____. **NOTES TO MYSELF**, $2.00. Cogent and incisive short paragraphs, personal yet general, about living, feelings and experience, behavior and relationships. These serve both as beginnings for the reader's exploration of his own experiences, and as thoughtful and insightful reminders about them. RPP 70

CARL ROGERS

EVANS, RICHARD. **CARL ROGERS: THE MAN AND HIS IDEAS**, $3.95. Rogers developed the technique of nondirective or client-centered psychotherapy and he is considered one of the founders of the human potential movement and one of its guiding lights. This volume includes a dialogue between Evans and Rogers which reveals the main tenets of Rogers' theories and gives the reader a feeling for Rogers the man; a long study of Rogers' work by Richard Farson, the president of the Esalen Institute; a famous *debate* between Rogers and B.F. Skinner; and an introductory sketch by Evans. Notes, bibliography, index, 283pp. Dut 75

ROGERS, CARL. **ON BECOMING A PERSON**, $3.95. In the few years since it was first published, this study of personal growth and creativity has established itself as a classic work, posing such fundamental questions as: What is the meaning of personal growth? Under what conditions is growth possible? How can one person help another? What is creativity and how can it be fostered? 424pp. HMC 61

_____. **ON ENCOUNTER GROUPS**, $2.50. *Clear, lucid, simple, evocative, Carl Rogers' book is the only one that I have seen that communicates to the layman what an encounter group is, what it looks like, what it feels like, what the different approaches are about. This is a beautiful and straightforward book. It is far and away the best general book on encounter groups in existence. Everything I ever wanted to say to a group leader or to a prospective member is here.*—Philip E. Slater. 174pp. H&R 70

ROGERS, CARL and BARRY STEVENS. **PERSON TO PERSON: THE PROBLEM OF BEING HUMAN**, $3.00/1.75. *This book is intended for anyone who is interested in it: anyone who is not interested should not read it. That is a simple statement of what this book is chiefly about: the importance of choosing for ourselves, regardless of what anyone else tells us is good or bad.* 293pp. S&S 67

ROPP, ROBERT de. **SEX ENERGY**, $2.45. Here the author of **The Master Game**, a noted bio-chemist, examines the sexual behavior of plants, insects and animals and the role of sex energy in human behavior from both a physiological and a historical point of view. He ends calling for a *sane sex society*. 236pp. Del

ROSE, ANTHONY and ANDRE AUW. **GROWING UP HUMAN**, $2.25. *This is primarily a practical book. Nonetheless there are some theoretical threads weaving through it. Foremost is our unbending faith in the worthiness of the person. . . . Out of this . . . grows a series of correlative assumptions: that the individual is educable, that relationships are resilient, that transcendence is within reach.* The book begins with chapters on seeking and on trust. These are followed by chapters on the individual and on relationships and on community. The material is well written and a great number of exercises accompany the text. The exercises themselves are clearly presented and quite unusual. 125pp. H&R 74

RUBIN, THEODORE. **THE ANGRY BOOK**, $1.50. This book by a former president of the American Institute of Psychoanalysis urges people to get out their anger rather than repress it and possibly cause depression, insomnia, psychosomatic illness, frigidity, etc. Simply and soundly written. 223pp. McM 69

SALTER, ANDREW. **THE CASE AGAINST PSYCHOANALYSIS**, $1.95. *A splendid and long-needed book. In a devastating analysis Salter exposes the shams and fakeries of Freud and the Freudians. This is a necessary book for all mature readers. It is easy reading, wise and witty.*—Catholic Digest. 183pp. H&R 52

SATIR, VIRGINIA. **PEOPLEMAKING**, $4.95. *The book is written so clearly, and with so much humanity, that it will be useful to the layman as well as the professional. In simple language free of jargon Satir here presents about self-worth, communication, and the family in the form of case histories, anecdotes, and a strikingly effective series of communication games that illuminate her research findings.*—**Psychotherapy and Social Science Review**. 306pp. S&B 72

_____. **SELF ESTEEM**, $2.95. Illustrated, schmaltzy poems like the following:

When I review later how I looked and sounded, what I said and did, and how I thought and felt, some parts may turn out to be unfitting. Handwritten. CeA 75

SCHEFLEN, ALBERT. **BODY LANGUAGE AND SOCIAL ORDER**, $3.45. Through text and many photographs, shows that body language, combined with spoken language, primarily serves to control human behavior and maintain the social order. Describes greeting, courting, and other social behavior and analyzes how territorial and dominance behavior determine the mobility of individuals and groups within the social hierarchy. 210pp. PrH 72

SHUTZ, WILLIAM. **ELEMENTS OF ENCOUNTER**, $1.50. Schutz is one of the most respected encounter group leaders in the world. This is a more scholarly approach to encounter than the ones he took in his earlier books. He begins with a history of encounter and describes various methods. This is followed by surveys of the principles of encounter, its physiological and psychological basis, theories of group development, a description of the encounter group, and a summary of the applications of encounter. Extensive bibliography, index, 118pp. Ban 73

_____. **HERE COMES EVERYBODY**, $1.25. The author of **Joy** here presents encounter as a culture and a way of life. *This is clearly Schutz' best book. . . . It's outlandish, outrageous, boisterous, wild, and a feeling of terror seizes you on turning each page for fear of what he's going to say next. But the fact is that it is the most intelligent, clear, honest, and joyous book about the encounter culture I've read.*—Warren G. Bennis. 370pp. H&R 71

_____. **JOY**, $1.95. One of the first books about encounter groups, largely concerned with methods or games which will help us to break through our defenses, rigidities and accustomed ways, and find joy in new ways of relating to ourselves and others. 252pp. Grv 67

SHAPIRO, STEPHEN and HILARY TYRKA. **TRUSTING YOURSELF: PSYCHOTHERAPY AS A BEGINNING**, $2.45. An exposition of the role of therapy and of the client-therapist relationship combined. *The biggest step we can take toward knowing and trusting ourselves is trusting another person to help us. This book is no substitute for that step. Rather, it helps clarify why we cannot just look at ourselves, read books, and change.* Bibliography, 127pp. PrH 75

❖

SHOSTROM, EVERETT. **FREEDOM TO BE**, $1.50. *Most of us, because of early experiences, have cut off one or more of the polarities in our attempts to experience and express ourselves. Whereas being self-actualized may be defined as the total expression of our unique beings, most of us are only partial in this ability to be fully ourselves. Hopefully, however, this book can help us to become more total in our expression, to become more and more self-actualizing.* Bibliography, index, 173pp. Ban 72

_____. **MAN THE MANIPULATOR**, $1.25. According to Shostrom, man is a manipulator who needs to become aware of the manipulative styles of relating to others. He is also a person who needs therapeutic goals which are comprehensible and which will motivate and excite him to live his life to its fullest potential. This book attempts to provide a model which meets these two needs. *I believe that this is a significant book. Laymen and professionals alike will find it interesting and challenging. I believe this book will serve as a layman's guide to many of the principles of Gestalt Therapy. . . . I am proud to have been [Dr. Shostrom's] teacher and therapist.*—Fritz Perls. Bibliography, index, 205pp. Ban 67

SHOSTROM, EVERETT and JAMES KAVANAUGH. **BETWEEN MAN AND WOMAN**, $1.75. This is a comprehensive survey of the dynamics of inter-sexual relationships, with guidelines on how to make a relationship work. It's a more serious volume than might be expected and some rather good insights are presented. Bibliography, 206pp. Ban 72

SIEGLER, MIRIAM and HUMPHRY OSMOND. **MODELS OF MADNESS, MODELS OF MEDICINE**, $2.95. *It is a valuable book for, like a good road map, it lays out before the reader all the alternative routes which may be taken to understanding* mental illness. . . . *The reader is left with the feeling that he understands more after finishing the book, something which can be said about few books in this field.*—E. Fuller Torrey. Notes, index, 254pp. H&R 74

SMITH, GERALD. **COUPLE THERAPY**, $1.95. Contains forty-seven exercises the author has used with married couples at Esalen and elsewhere. For example, asking a couple to plan something together, like what to do Sunday afternoon, reveals how they deal with power, who is in charge, how they communicate, etc. This last is a central concern of the book. 150pp. McM 71

STEINER, CLAUDE, ed. **READINGS IN RADICAL PSYCHIATRY**, $4.95. Dr. Steiner's **Manifesto** signalled the emergence of a new group of radical psychiatrists on the West Coast who challenge the most cherished beliefs and practices of extended individual psychotherapy still so widely used today. This group, which has been gaining increasing attention, developed its ideas and recorded its experiences in its own publication, **The Radical Therapist**. The most seminal of the writings which appeared in this publication have been collected in this anthology. Index, notes. 202pp. RaH 75

SZASZ, THOMAS. **THE MANUFACTURE OF MADNESS**, $3.45. *It is widely believed today that just as some people suffer from diseases of the liver or kidney, others suffer from diseases of the mind . . . and that* mental patients *because of their supposed incapacity* to know what is in their best interests, *must be cared for by their families or the state, even if that care requires interventions imposed on them against their will. . . . In vain does the alleged madman . . . reject treatment and hospitalization as forms of torture and* imprisonment; his refusal to submit to psychiatric authority is regarded as a further sign of his madness. In this medical rejection of the Other as a madman, we recognize . . . his former religious rejections as a heretic.—from the preface. Szasz and Laing are the two strongest voices urging us to view madness as a socially-determined disease. This is a serious, careful and well-documented study comparing our present treatment of madness with our former treatment of witches. In actuality, Institutional Psychiatry is a continuation of the Inquisition. All that has really changed is the vocabulary and the social style . . . . [T]he only hope for remedying the problem of mental illness lies in weakening—not strengthening—the power of Institutional Psychiatry. Only when this peculiar institution is abolished will the moral powers of uncoerced psychotherapy be released. Extensive bibliography, index, 383pp. Del 70

TORREY, E. FULLER. **THE DEATH OF PSYCHIATRY**, $2.50. Dr. Torrey presents a reasoned review of the mythology of mental illness and the persecutory practices of psychiatry. . . . His work should help to make psychiatric barbarities couched in the idiom and imagery of mental care morally more distasteful and hence politically less useful. I commend his courage and recommend his book.—Thomas Szasz. Notes, bibliography, index, 234pp. Pen 74

TRANSACTIONAL ANALYSIS

The unit of social intercourse is called a transaction. If two or more people encounter each other in a social aggregation, sooner or later one of them will speak, or give some other indication of acknowledging the presence of the others. This called the transactional stimulus. Another person will then say or do something which is in some way related to this stimulus, and this is called the transactional response. Simple transactional analysis is concerned with diagnosing which ego state implemented the transactional stimulus, and which one executed the transactional response. The simplest transactions are those in which both stimulus and response arise from the Adults of the parties concerned. . . . Next in simplicity are Child-Parent transactions. . . . Both of these transactions are complementary; that is, the response is appropriate and expected and follows the natural order of healthy human relationships. . . . The first rule of communication is that communication will proceed smoothly as long as transactions are complementary . . . [and] communication is broken off when a crossed transaction occurs.—Eric Berne, **Games People Play**

BERNE, ERIC. **GAMES PEOPLE PLAY**, $1.95. Subtitled The Psychology of Human Relationships, this was the first book that brought TA to the general public. It was on the **New York Times** best seller list for over two years. Most people, in most of their family and business relationships, are constantly playing games with each other. What's more, they are striving—often unconsciously—for an emotional payoff which is startling different from what they might rationally expect to get from wining or losing their game.—Eric Berne. Here Dr. Berne presents and explains 120 of these games, and describes the anti-game which liberates an individual from each game. Notes, index, 192pp. Grv 64

_____. **A LAYMAN'S GUIDE TO PSYCHIATRY AND PSYCHOANALYSIS**, $1.95. An entirely revised and updated edition of Berne's first book, **The Mind in Action**. As the title suggests the presentation is non-technical and the coverage is comprehensive; the book itself is about the human mind and the human being as the psychiatrist sees them. Glossary, index, 342pp. Grv 57

_____. **PRINCIPLES OF GROUP TREATMENT**, $4.95. A systematic treatise on the use of TA in groups which draws on the author's more than twenty years of clinical experience as well as information provided by hundreds of other group therapists. The first part of the book describes how to set up a group therapy program and discusses the four most common methods of group therapy. The second part focuses on TA: its principles and techniques and its relationship to other forms of treatment. This book is geared toward the professional. Glossary, index, 397pp. Grv 66

_____. **SEX IN HUMAN LOVING**, $1.95. A long look at the title theme based on the principles of transactional analysis. Every aspect of the subject is touched on. Diagrams, index, 270pp. S&S 70

_____. **TRANSACTIONAL ANALYSIS IN PSYCHOTHERAPY**, $3.95. A technical analysis for the practicing therapist. Includes a clear description of the process and its technical applications, diagrams, notes, and indices. 270pp. Grv 61

_____. **WHAT DO YOU SAY AFTER YOU SAY HELLO?** $1.95. Berne's latest bestseller talks about the scripts that people follow compulsively throughout their lives—and how they can break out of them to achieve true freedom and fulfillment. 458pp. Ban 72

BLACKSTOCK, RICHARD. **STUDY GUIDE FOR I'M OK, YOU'RE OK**, $1.50. 70pp. H&R 71

BRY, ADELAIDE. **T.A. FOR FAMILIES**, $1.50. Subtitled Using Transactional Analysis for a Happier Family Life. This is a simplistic series of books, all with the same format—a picture or drawing on the left-hand page, a TA-related saying on the right. 167pp. H&R 76

_____. **THE T.A. PRIMER**, $1.25. A profusely illustrated, basic introduction to the three personas—parent, adult, and child—that make up each of us, and how our personas interact with those of others to make us feel good or bad. 151pp. H&R 73

_____. **T.A. GAMES**, $1.25. Subtitled Using Transactional Analysis in Your Life. 115pp. H&R 75

FREED, ALVYN. **TA FOR KIDS**, $4.00. A manual to either be read to children between the ages of seven and eleven or which they can read themselves. The basic principles of TA are presented in short words and simple phrases and the text is illustrated with many cartoon-like drawings. Oversize, 82pp. Jal 71

_____. **TA FOR TOTS**, $5.95. TA for Tots is designed to help little boys and girls get acquainted with themselves, to find out that they are not frogs, but princes and princesses. By talking straight to their mothers and fathers and other important people, they will be able to stay princes and princesses and learn how to get rid of froggy feelings. Then they will be able to avoid some of the unhappiness that most grown-ups now experience. This is a very practical, oversize book—completely hand-lettered in big print and illustrated. Topics include: All About You, Feeling Good and Feeling Bad, Being Afraid and What to Do About It, and The OK Society of the World. 232pp. Jal 73

HALLETT, KATHRYN. **A GUIDE FOR SINGLE PARENTS**, $3.95. A family therapist shows how, by means of TA, personal loss such as divorce, separation, desertion, or death can provide growth rather than paralysis and despair. Glossary, bibliography, 122pp. CeA 74

HARRIS, J. **I'M OK, YOU'RE OK**, $2.95. Long a Number One bestseller, this is a clearly-written presentation of Transactional Analysis, developed by Eric Berne. 317pp. Avo 67

JAMES, MURIEL. **BORN TO LOVE**, $3.95. Applies TA to church activities and relationships. Can be read by one person or used in church study groups. Well illustrated. 209pp. AdW 73

_____. **TRANSACTIONAL ANALYSIS FOR MOMS AND DADS**, $3.95. Shows how a parent or teacher can use TA to recognize unpleasant feelings and behavior and turn them into pleasant ones and provides new insights into the giving and receiving of strokes among members of a family. Line drawings throughout. Bibliography, 148pp. AdW 74

_____. **WINNING WITH PEOPLE**, $3.95. Subtitled Group Exercises in TA. An oversize workbook designed to accompany **Born to Win**. AdW 73

JAMES, MURIEL and DOROTHY JONGEWARD. **BORN TO WIN**, $4.95. Primarily concerned with Transactional Analysis, the book also uses Gestalt-oriented experiments to show the reader a useful way to discover the many parts of his personality, to integrate them, and to develop a core of self-confidence. **Psychology Today** calls it the clearest and most up-to-date statement of current thinking in Transactional Analysis, and easily the best of the popular books. 301pp. AdW 71

JAMES, MURIEL and LOUIS SAVARY. **THE HEART OF FRIENDSHIP**, c$6.95. A guide to the art of making and keeping friends utilizing principles developed in TA. 205pp. H&R 76

_____. **THE POWER AT THE BOTTOM OF THE WELL**, $3.95. Subtitled TA and Religious Experience. Includes exercises which specifically apply the principles to life situations. Notes, 160pp. H&R 74

STEINER, CLAUDE. **SCRIPTS PEOPLE LIVE**, $2.25. Dr. Steiner was a close collaborator with Eric Berne in developing the principles of TA. This book has more substance to it than most of the TA books. Steiner begins with a survey of the development of TA and a biographical essay on Berne. The rest of the book is devoted to the transactional analysis of life scripts. Both theoretical material and practical exercises are presented. Bibliography, index, 394pp. Ban 74

TANNER, IRA. **LONELINESS: THE FEAR OF LOVE**, $1.50. Transactional Analysis applied to loneliness. 143pp. H&R 73

VERNY, THOMAS. **INSIDE GROUPS: A PRACTICAL GUIDE TO ENCOUNTER GROUPS AND GROUP THERAPY**, $3.95. I hope in the following pages to strike a balance between an objective assessment of what these groups are all about and how they function and a subjective expression of my own feelings about their strengths and shortcomings. I have sought to write a practical, straightforward guide for those who wish to find out about the different approaches to groups and to derive the most benefit from a group once they have joined it. Resource guide, with addresses, index, 262pp. MGH 74

WOOD, JOHN. **HOW DO YOU FEEL?** $2.95. This is a uniquely personal book. I believe anyone reading it will become more aware of the vast unknown world which lies within each one of us. He will find himself more able to be, and to express those fragile things we call feelings. It will encourage the reader to be more fully a person.—Carl Rogers. 203pp. PrH 74

ZUNIN, LEONARD. **CONTACT**, $1.95. What two people communicate during their first four minutes of contact is so crucial that it will determine whether strangers will remain strangers or will become friends, lovers or lifetime mates. This book deals with those four minutes: what often happens and what can happen. A useful how-to book. 271pp. RaH 74

HYPNOSIS

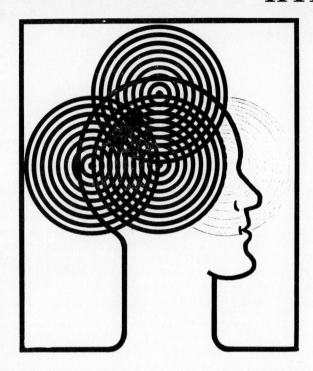

LYTHE, PETER. **HYPNOTISM**, $1.50. Blythe is a practicing hypnotherapist and psychology teacher. This account has been written specifically for the general reader. It explores the dynamics of hypnotism: what it is, how it works, who is most susceptible to it and what are its possible uses and dangers. 150pp. McM 71

OOKE, C.E. and A.E. van VOGT. **HYPNOTISM HANDBOOK**, c$6.95. This is the best practical manual we've seen, giving a good deal of philosophy and excellent step-by-step instructions. Our most popular hypnotism book. 262pp. Bor 56

OUE, EMILE and C. H. BROOKS. **SUGGESTION AND AUTO SUGGESTION**, $2.25. oue developed controversial healing techniques and worked in France during the 1920's. e used a method of conscious autosuggestions and was known as a miraculous healer. his is a collection of essays he wrote about his techniques and material written by several f his followers on his techniques and on Coue himself, along with case histories of some atients. 158pp. Wei 74

DMUNDS, SIMEON. **HYPNOTISM AND PSYCHIC PHENOMENA**, $2.00. This is a very omplete study which incorporates the author's own extensive research with a historical urvey and chapters on induction and on the general phenomena of hypnosis. The conction of hypnosis with paranormal phenomena is emphasized and various chapters disuss hypnosis in relation to different forms of psi. Notes, bibliography. 177pp. Wil 61

_____. **THE PSYCHIC POWER OF HYPNOSIS**, $1.25. A short survey of the title heme divided into the following chapters: *The Higher Phenomena of Hypnotism, Hypotism and Hypnosis, Psychic Phenomena and Psychical Research, The Background—Mesmerism, Hypnosis and Paranormal, Psuedo-Clairvoyance and Reincarnation*, and *The osition Today, the Prospect for Tomorrow*. 63pp. Wei 68

STABROOKS, GEORGE. **HYPNOTISM**, $2.45. A well written, comprehensive volume. Notes, index. 251pp. Dut 43

INDES, BERNARD. **NEW CONCEPTS OF HYPNOSIS**, $3.00. This is a serious study of ypnosis which traces its history, theoretical aspects, mechanisms, and characteristics. Dr indes then goes on to chapters on necessary conditions in hypnotic procedure, objective nd subjective methods of hypnotic induction, suggestive therapy, and hypno-analysis nd hypno-synthesis. Many case studies illustrate the exposition and references and good efinitions are included for all the material covered. 262pp. Wil 51

ILGARD, ERNEST and JOSEPHINE. **HYPNOSIS IN THE RELIEF OF PAIN**, c$10.00. wo distinguished researchers, a psychologist and a psychiatrist, present an assessment of he role of hypnosis in relation to pain—based both on studies in the experimental laboraory and on clinical practice. A detailed study, geared toward the general reader. Notes, ibliography, index. 271pp. Kau 75

OLLANDER, BERNARD. **METHODS AND USES OF HYPNOSIS AND SELF-HYPNOSIS**, $2.00. Subtitled *A Treatise on the Powers of the Subconscious Mind*, this book is result of the author's thirty years of experience with experimental hypnosis and hypnotic reatment. He discusses his techniques, gives case histories of some of the cures affected, nd talks about hypnosis as a technique for tapping into clairvoyance and thought transerence, and other supernormal phenomena. Index, 189pp. Wil 57

LE CRON, LESLIE, ed. **EXPERIMENTAL HYPNOSIS**, $2.95. Twenty articles by many of the world's leading authorities explaining what hypnotism is, why it is conducive to rapid psychotherapy, and how its utilization results in cures which might otherwise be difficult to achieve. The discussions are illustrated with case histories. The authors also report on research and set forth the technique and dynamics of hypnotic induction. 483pp. CiP nd

_____. **SELF-HYPNOTISM**, $2.95. This is our most popular hypnotism book. Readers seem to find the techniques outlined here easy to follow and successful in their application. The presentation is hardly subtle. Chapter titles include the following: *Eliminate Emotional Troubles from Your Life, Never Suffer from Headaches Again, Fears and Phobias Can Be Conquered*, and so on. Bibliography, 220pp. PrH 64

LONG, MAX FREEDOM. **SELF SUGGESTION AND THE NEW HUNA THEORY OF MESMERISM AND HYPNOSIS**, c$4.50. Max Freedom Long was instrumental in rediscovering the ancient psycho-religious system of the Polynesians called *Huna* or the secret. The system is fully outlined in his other books (see the Mysticism section). The ancient theories and methods have been tested by him as well as by many other researchers and the results of this research as well as practical applications are reported here. 117pp. DeV 58

MEARES, AINSLIE. **A SYSTEM OF MEDICAL HYPNOSIS**, c$15.00. Meares is a respected Australian psychiatrist. This is considered the definite text on the subject. It gives a good explanation of the principles and uses of hypnosis in medicine, explicit details of the five fundamental techniques of induction, and many case histories that vividly portray the problems and the successes that attend the use of hypnotism. A very detailed account, recommended for the serious student. 484pp. Jul 60

MORRIS, FRIEDA. **SELF HYPNOSIS IN TWO DAYS**, $3.50. Dr. Morris is a psychologist who has studied clinical and experimental hypnosis and has taught its use in psychotherapy at the UCLA Medical School. This seems to be a very well organized, useful book for those who wish to learn self-hypnosis. The method described here has been successfully used by the author and her students in many workshops and we have had good feedback on it from customers. Recommended. Index, 138pp. Dut 74

ROSA, KARL. **YOU AND A.T.**, c$6.95. *Autogenic training is an exact, clearly defined method of self-hypnosis, and the means to a new, relaxed enjoyment of one's physical existence.... More and more doctors are advising patients who suffer from functional disorders to take up autogenic training.* The technique was developed by Dr. Johannes Schultz in Germany in the 1930's and has been a standard tool in medicine and psychiatry in Europe since then. It has been gaining increasing renown in the U.S. This book, written by a student of Dr. Schultz, has been a best seller in its many German editions for twenty years and is considered the best popular account of the technique. Introduction, bibliography. 158pp. Dut 76

SAINT-GERMAIN, COMTE de, ed. **PRACTICAL HYPNOTISM**, $5.00. This is a recent reprint of a text compiled by the leading editor in 1901 from older papers written by leading authorities. It is arranged topically beginning with a history of hyphotism and its major practitioners and going from there to theoretical and practical sections. The material is quite comprehensive and includes essays not available anywhere else. 260pp. HeR 01

SALTER, ANDREW. **WHAT IS HYPNOSIS**, $2.45. This book is a classic in the field, recently revised and reprinted. It is concise and very clearly written. Topics include conditioning and hypnosis, hypnotic reaction patterns, experiments in authohypnosis, techniques in autohypnosis. Includes many references. 106pp. FSG 41

INDIAN PHILOSOPHY

It has been said that almost all thought in India is in a sense religious thought and Hinduism has not only influenced, throughout many centuries, India's intellectual life, but almost completely determined her social and cultural life as well.

Hinduism cannot be called a philosophy, nor is it a well defined religion. It is, rather, a large and complex socio-religious organism consisting of innumerable sects, cults and philosophical systems and involving various rituals, ceremonies and spiritual disciplines, as well as the worship of countless gods and goddesses. The many facets of this complex and yet persistent and powerful spiritual tradition mirror the geographical, racial, linguistic and cultural complexities of India's vast subcontinent. The manifestations of Hinduism range from highly intellectual philosophies involving conceptions of fabulous range and depth to the naive and childlike ritual practice of the masses. If the majority of the Hindus are simple villagers who keep the popular religion alive in their daily worship, Hinduism has, on the other hand, brought forth a large number of outstanding spiritual teachers to transmit its profound insights.

The spiritual source of Hinduism lies in the **Vedas**, a collection of ancient scriptures written by anonymous sages, the so-called Vedic *seers*. There are four **Vedas**, the oldest of them being the **Rig Veda**. Written in ancient Sanskrit, the sacred language of India, the **Vedas** have remained the highest religious authority for most sections of Hinduism. In India, any philosophical system that does not accept the authority of the **Vedas** is considered to be unorthodox.

Each of these **Vedas** consists of several parts which were composed at different periods, probably between 1500 and 500 B.C. The oldest parts are sacred hymns and prayers. Subsequent parts deal with sacrificial rituals connected with the Vedic hymns, and the last, called the **Upanishads**, elaborate their philosophical and practical content. The **Upanishads** contain the essence of Hinduism's spiritual message. They have guided and inspired India's greatest minds for the last twenty-five centuries, in accordance with the advice given in their verses. . . .

The masses of the Indian people, however, have received the teachings of Hinduism not through the **Upanishads**, but through a large number of popular tales, collected in huge epics, which are the basis of the vast and colourful Indian mythology. One of those epics, the **Mahabharata**, contains India's favourite religious text, the beautiful spiritual poem of the **Bhagavad Gita**. The **Gita**, as it is commonly called, is a dialogue between the god Krishna and the warrior Arjuna who is in great despair, being forced to combat his own kinsmen in the great family war which forms the main story of the **Mahabharata**. Krishna, disguised as Arjuna's charioteer, drives the chariot right between the two armies and in this dramatic setting of the battlefield he starts to reveal to Arjuna the profound truths of Hinduism. . . .

The basis of Krishna's spiritual instruction, as of all Hinduism, is the idea that the multitude of things and events around us are but different manifestations of the same ultimate reality. This reality, called *Brahman*, is the unifying concept which gives Hinduism its essentially monistic character in spit of the worship of numerous gods and goddesses.

Brahman, the ultimate reality, is understood as the *soul*, or inner essence, of all things. It is infinite and beyond all concepts; it cannot be comprehende by the intellect, not can it be adequately described in words. . . . Yet, peopl want to talk about this reality and the Hindu sages with their characteristi penchant for myth have pictured *Brahman* as divine and talk about it i mythological language. The various aspects of the Divine have been given th names of the various gods worshipped by the Hindus, but the scriptures mak it clear that all these gods are but reflections of the one ultimate reality. . .

The basic recurring theme in Hindu mythology is the creation of the worl by the self-sacrifice of God—*sacrifice* in the original sense of *making sacred* whereby God becomes the world which, in the end, becomes again God. Th creative activity of the Divine is called *lila*, the play of God, and the world seen as the stage of the divine play. Like most of Hindu mythology, the myt of *lila* has a strong magical flavour. *Brahman* is the great magician who tran forms himself into the world and he performs this feat with his *magic creativ power*, which is the original meaning of *maya* in the **Rig Veda**. The wor *maya*—one of the most important terms in Indian philosophy—has change its meaning over the centuries. From the *might*, or *power*, of the divine acto and magician, it came to signify the psychological state of anybody unde the spell of the magic play. As long as we confuse the myriad forms of th divine *lila* with reality, without perceiving the unity of *Brahman* underlyin all these forms, we are under the spell of *maya*.

Maya, therefore, does not mean the world is an illusion, as is often wrongl stated. The illusion lies merely in our point of view, if we think that th shapes and structures, things and events, around us are realities of nature, in stead of realizing that they are concepts of our measuring and categorizin minds. *Maya* is the illusion of taking these concepts for reality, of confusin the map with the territory.

In the Hindu view of nature, then, all forms are relative, fluid and ever-chang ing *maya*, conjured up by the great magician of the divine play. The world o *maya* changes continuously, because the divine *lila* is a rhythmic, dynami play. The dynamic force of the play is *karma*, another important concept o Indian thought. *Karma* means *action*. It is the active principle of the play the total universe in action, where everything is dynamically connected wit everything else. . . .

The meaning of *karma*, like that of *maya*, has been brought down from it original cosmic level to the human level where it has acquired a psychologica sense. As long as our view of the world is fragmented, as long as we are unde the spell of *maya* and think that we are separated from our environment an can act independently, we are bound by *karma*. Being free from the bond o *karma* means to realize the unity and harmony of all nature, including man and to act accordingly. . . .

To be free from the spell of *maya*, to break the bonds of *karma* means t realize that all the phenomena we perceive with our senses are part of th same reality. It means to experience, concretely and personally, that every thing, including our own self, is *Brahman*. This experience is called *moksha* or *liberation* in Hindu philosophy and it is the very essence of Hinduism

Hinduism holds that there are innumerable ways of liberation. It would neve expect all its followers to be able to approach the Divine in the same way and therefore it provides different concepts, rituals and spiritual exercises fo different modes of awareness. The fact that many of these concepts or prac tices are contradictory does not worry the Hindus in the least, because they know that *Brahman* is beyond concepts and images anyway. From this atti tude comes the great tolerance and inclusiveness which is characteristic o Hinduism.

The most intellectual school is the Vedanta which is based on the **Upanishad** and emphasizes *Brahman* as a nonpersonal, metaphysical concept, free from y mythological content. In spite of its high philosophical and intellectual [lev]el, however, the Vedantist way of liberation is very different from any [sch]ool of Western philosophy, involving as it does daily meditation and other [spi]ritual exercises to bring about the union with *Brahman*.

[An]other important and influential method of liberation is known as *yoga*, a [wo]rd which means *to yoke, to join*, and which refers to the joining of the [ind]ividual soul to *Brahman*. There are several schools, or *paths*, of yoga in[vol]ving some basic physical training and various mental disciplines designed [for] people of different types and at different spiritual levels. For the common [Hi]ndu, the most popular way of approaching the Divine is to worship it in [th]e form of a personal god or goddess. The fertile Indian imagination has [cr]eated literally thousands of deities which appear in innumerable manifesta[tio]ns. The three most worshipped divinities in India today are Shiva, Vishnu [an]d the Divine Mother. Shiva is one of the oldest Indian gods who can assume [m]any forms. He is called *Mahesvara*, the Great Lord, when he is represented [as] the personification of the fullness of *Brahman* and he can also impersonate [m]any single aspects of the Divine, his most celebrated appearance being the [on]e as *Nataraja*, the King of Dancers. As the Cosmic Dancer, Shiva is the god [of] creation and destruction who sustains through his dance the endless rhythm [of] the universe.

[Vi]shnu, too, appears under many guises, one of them being the god Krishna [in] the **Bhagavad Gita**. In general, Vishnu's role is that of the preserver of the [un]iverse. The third divinity of this triad is Shakti, the Divine Mother, the [ar]chetypal goddess representing in her many forms the female energy of the [un]iverse.

[Sh]akti also appears as Shiva's wife and the two are often shown in passionate [em]braces in magnificent temple sculptures which radiate an extraordinary [sen]suousness of a degree completely unknown in any Western religious art. [Co]ntrary to most Western religions, sensuous pleasure has never been sup[pr]essed in Hinduism, because the body has always been considered to be an [int]egral part of the human being and not separated from the spirit. The Hindu, [th]erefore, does not try to control the desires of the body by the conscious [wi]ll, but aims at realizing himself with his whole being, body and mind. Hin[du]ism has even developed a branch, the medieval Tantrism, where enlighten[m]ent is sought through a profound experience of sensual love. . . .

[Sh]iva was closely associated with this medieval form of erotic mysticism, and [so] were Shakti and numerous other female deities which exist in great num[be]rs in Hindu mythology. This abundance of goddesses shows again that in [Hi]nduism the physical and sensuous side of human nature, which has always [be]en associated with the female, is a fully integrated part of the Divine. Hindu [go]ddesses are not shown as holy virgins, but in sensual embraces of stunning [be]auty.

[Th]e Western mind is easily confused by the fabulous number of gods and [go]ddesses which populate Hindu mythology in their various appearances and [in]carnations. To understand how the Hindus can cope with this multitude of [di]vinities, we must be aware of the basic attitude of Hinduism that in sub[st]ance all these divinities are identical. They are all manifestations of the [sa]me divine reality, reflecting different aspects of the infinite, omnipresent, [an]d—ultimately—incomprehensible *Brahman*.

[f]rom **THE TAO OF PHYSICS** by Fritjof Capra

[A]BHEDANANDA, SWAMI. **HOW TO BE A YOGI**, c$2.75. This is an excellent presenta[tio]n of the science and practice of different types of yoga, along with their philosophy [an]d psychology. Two introductory chapters discuss the true religion and what yoga is. [Th]e next chapters are devoted to different types of yoga: hatha, raja, karma, bhakti, and [jn]ana. The two final chapters discuss the science of breathing and *Was Christ a Yogi?* [Sw]ami Abhedananda was a direct disciple of Sri Ramakrishna. 188pp. VdP 55

[A]BHISHIKTANANDA. **GURU AND DISCIPLE**, $3.60. This is one example of the recent [tr]end toward books which integrate the teachings of Christianity with Eastern philosophy. [Tw]o different accounts are presented here. The first tells of the author's visit with a Hindu [gu]ru and relates the teachings that he received. The second is an account of the author's [jo]urney with an Indian fellow priest to the sacred source of the Ganges in the company of [Hin]du pilgrims. It culminates in a moving description of the first Eucharist to be celebrated [the]re. Notes, 176pp. SCK 74

[A]KHILANANDA, SWAMI. **HINDU PSYCHOLOGY: ITS MEANING FOR THE WEST**, [$3].75. A comparison of Western and Eastern schools of thought, with emphasis on medi-

tation, intuition, extrasensory perception, and methods of superconscious experience. Swami Akhilananda emphasizes the importance of developing the superconscious state as a means of integrating the total personality. Notes, bibliography, index. BrP 46

_____. **SPIRITUAL PRACTICES**, c$8.50. Swami Akhilananda founded the Ramakrishna Vedanta Society in Boston and was well known as an active minister from 1926–62. In this book he stresses that in our scientific age verification of the existence of the ultimate reality or God is the main objective of real religion. He points out that only by this direct and immediate experience of God can our personalities be integrated and society harmonized. The handbook is illustrated with details from his personal experiences and from the lives of his spiritual teachers. 225pp. Sta 74

ANANDAMURTI, SHRII SHRII. **BABA'S GRACE**, $2.95. A collection of discourses by the spiritual leader of the Ananda Marga organization. Each of the selections is short and the translation is clearly done. The emphasis is on the journey of the soul. Glossary, illustrations. 197pp. AMa 73

_____. **THE GREAT UNIVERSE**, $3.25. Discourses discussing the problems that beset modern mankind: governmental corruption, economic injustice, overpopulation, crime—and offering practical solutions to them. Illustrations, 271pp. AMa 73

ARNOLD, EDWIN, tr. **LIGHT OF ASIA AND THE INDIAN SONG OF SONGS (GITA GOVINDA)**, $1.60. Two classic translations, bound in one volume. Introduction, glossary. 253pp. TPH 49

ASHBY, PHILIP. **MODERN TRENDS IN HINDUISM**, c$11.20. Ashby begins this survey with a historical discussion of Hinduism as a religious and philosophical system. The bulk of the book is devoted to its diversification in the nineteenth and twentieth centuries. The great modern and religious and social leaders—Aurobindo, Ramakrishna, Vivekananda, and Gandhi—are evaluated in terms of their liberalizing influence on Hinduism. The next two chapters are devoted to a study of contemporary Indian youth and their changing attitudes toward the Hindu faith and a study of the Radha Soami Satsang sect (followers of Charan Singh). Concluding chapters discuss the role of Hindu religion and culture in Indian politics and the promise of Hinduism for the future. Notes, glossary, index. 152pp. Col 74

ATMANANDA, tr. **WORDS OF SRI ANANDAMAYI MA**, $2.00. A selection of Sri Anandamayi Ma's replies to oral questions, topically arranged. Glossary, index. 250pp. SSA 71

Sri Aurobindo
by Sisirkumar Mitra

SRI AUROBINDO

Sri Aurobindo was a great knower of God who exemplified a way of spiritual integration that combined the noblest truths of the East and West into a practical and majestic mode of realization. Although born in Calcutta, he was given a Western education and was actually sheltered from the influence of mystic India by his Anglicized father.

At seven he moved to England where he lived and studied until the age of twenty. He manifested a brilliant intellect and copious aptitude for reading, devouring volumes of books with nearly verbatim comprehension. His fertile mind was nourished by the western rational tradition and he soon mastered Greek and Latin as well as English. Ironically he was forbidden to learn his native tongue and thus his mother country remained remote.

At twenty he went to India and was soon immersed in the task of liberating that country from foreign control. He was appalled at the condition of the masses and through the medium of newspaper articles he urged the immediate release of the proletariat from the bondage of oppression. His deep insight made him aware that India's political problems stemmed largely from her apathy, passivity, negligence and even cowardice. He was a man of action and he sought a means to rouse the languor of his sleeping countrymen.

During this time, he read the numerous sacred writings of India with the same relish and avid intensity that he had applied so masterfully in his studies of Western literature. But it was not until he had witnessed an actual demonstration of the powers wielded by the individuals proficient in the science of yoga that he was aroused to the possibility of using these less tangible means to accomplish his ends.

The young revolutionary plunged into the practice of yoga eager to find the key that would enable him to relieve the suffering of the people he loved. But his was a unique yoga formed from the practical, action-oriented side of his nature joined with the fathomless spiritual realizations that were soon to be his. His political activities led to his arrest and during the days of trial and imprisonment his diligent efforts led to supernal realizations and recognitions of divine unity. The integral yoga that this modern day rishi was to formulate scintillates with the wisdom of eternal ages coupled with the immediacy of instant divine revelation.

Aurobindo realized that true liberation was an experience of consciousness, but simultaneously he knew that the key to discovering the greatness of being was through diligent activity. This was not the restless cogitation of frenzied motion, but was rather the action of self-discovery. Unlike other systems of yoga that resulted in the upward surge of the kundalini energy from the base of the spine, Sri Aurobindo's integral yoga resulted in the downflow of creative, inspirational energies from supramental centers of one's being.

Later in his life, Aurobindo was joined by a French woman who soon became known as the Mother and who to this day has helped carry on the work. Sri Aurobindo and the Mother have become powerful forces for good in the world and their new age message of brotherhood and liberty have caught the imagination and the heart of people throughout the world. A city called Auroville has been started in India to embody their philosophy of human unity and to demonstrate the fact of the oneness of mankind. The message of Aurobindo and the Mother's life is a guarantee of the eventual spiritual destiny and divine consummation of all our lives. In the words of the Mother, *Sri Aurobindo's message is an immortal sunlight radiating over the future.* The Mother died in late 1973.

ACHARYA, K.D. GUIDE TO SRI AUROBINDO'S PHILOSOPHY, $1.50. Part I of a projected four part work. The book is divided into sections by subject. 88pp.

AUROBINDO, SRI. BASES OF YOGA, $1.50. Extracts from letters to disciples; selections chosen are considered especially helpful to aspirants seeking for an understanding of the practice of yoga. 168pp. SAA 36

_____. THE FOUNDATIONS OF INDIAN CULTURE, c$5.50. Systematically sets forth the true, spiritual basis, with reference to Western culture—religion and spirituality, art, literature, et al. 414pp. SAA 59

_____. THE FUTURE EVOLUTION OF MAN, $2.25. Extracts from The Life Divine, The Human Cycle and The Synthesis of Yoga. 157pp. TPH 63

_____. THE FUTURE POETRY AND LETTERS ON POETRY, LITERATURE AND ART, c$7.50. 561pp.

_____. A GATEWAY TO SRI AUROBINDO'S THOUGHTS, $1.25. Extracts from The Life Divine, The Human Cycle, and The Synthesis of Yoga, arranged to present Sri Aurobindo's vision of man's future. 61pp.

_____. THE HOUR OF GOD, $1.65. Compiled from manuscripts, consisting mainly of notes intended for fuller treatment. 74pp. SAA 73

_____. THE HUMAN CYCLE, THE IDEAL OF HUMAN UNITY, WAR AND SELF-DETERMINATION, c$7.50. A trilogy on the psychology of social development, mankind's search for true unity, mutuality and harmony, and how life and society may be remolded in the truth of the spirit to express the greatest harmony of individual freedom and social unity. 654pp. SAA 71

_____. LETTERS ON YOGA, VOL. I, c$6.00. These three volumes present a complete picture of Aurobindo's philosophy and its practical application. The short pieces presented here are often easier to comprehend than the material in The Synthesis. 502pp. SAA 71

_____. LETTERS ON YOGA, VOL. II, c$7.00. 587pp. SAA 71

_____. LETTERS ON YOGA, VOL. III, c$8.00. 686pp. SAA 71

_____. THE LIFE DIVINE, c$11.00/set. Aurobindo's philosophical magnum opus. 1070pp on his vision of the spiritual life. Sanskrit glossary, two volumes. SAA 73

_____. LIGHT ON YOGA, $1.50. Extracts from letters to disciples. Sanskrit glossary, 104pp. SAA 35

_____. MAN—SLAVE OR FREE, $1.00. Eight essays. 48pp. SAA

_____. THE MIND OF LIGHT, $2.25. The best general introduction to Sri Aurobindo's sytem, for it concentrates in a brief space his entire cosmic and transcendent vision. Includes an excellent introduction and long, annotated bibliography by Robert McDermott.

128pp. Dut 53

_____. MORE LIGHTS ON YOGA, $1.50. More extracts. 113pp. SAA 73

_____. THE MOTHER, c$8.50. An essay on the Mother, with Aurobindo's lett on the identity, purpose and working of the Mother, and his translation of her Pray and Meditations and interpretations of some of her prayers and Conversations. 495 SAA 72

_____. THE PROBLEM OF REBIRTH, c$3.50. See the Reincarnation secti

_____. RIDDLE OF THIS WORLD, $1.25. Originally issued as answers to qu tions raised by disciples and others. 98pp. SAA 33

_____. SAVITRI: A LEGEND AND A SYMBOL, c$8.50. His (unfinished) e poem is based on an episode in the Mahabharata and records in mantric poetry his v spiritual experience and Savitri's struggle with and final victory over Death. With his ters on the poem. 816pp. SAA 73

_____. THE SECRET OF THE VEDA, c$7.50. The significance and symboli of the Veda and the origins of Aryan speech, with translation and commentary of selec hymns from the Rig Veda, of the Atris and others. 581pp. SAA

_____, tr. SONGS OF VIDYAPATI, $1.50. Songs relating to the divine love Krishna and Radha. In English and Bengali. 46pp. SAA

_____. SRI AUROBINDO ON HIMSELF, c$7.00. Compiled from notes and ters. *It would be only myself who could speak of things in my past giving them their form and significance. In my view, a man's value does not depend on what he learns his position or fame, or what he does, but on what he is and inwardly becomes.* Inclu letters on himself and the Mother. 513pp. SAA 72

_____. SRI AUROBINDO ON THE TANTRA, $1.00.

_____. THE SYNTHESIS OF YOGA, c$10.00. *Each side of the Yoga dealt w separately with all its possibilities and indications as to how they meet so that one star from knowledge could realize Karma and Bhakti and so on with each path.* Presents four parts of integral yoga: the yoga of divine works; the yoga of integral knowledge; yoga of divine love; and the yoga of self-perfection, including the nature and gradati of supermind and the supramental (transformed human) instruments. 872pp. SAA

_____. THOUGHTS AND APHORISMS, $1.50. Reflectiosn on the yogas: jna karma, bhakti; on the *Delight of Being*, and on man. 125pp. SAA 58

_____. VEDIC GLOSSARY, c$5.00. Over 7,000 entries, grammatical notes. In duction on the Vedas extracted from Aurobindo's works. SAA

The Mother's

Sri Aurobindo's

AUROBINDO, SRI and the MOTHER. ART: REVELATION OF BEAUTY, $2.50. Print on both sides of unbound decorated pages in a cloth covered stiff wrapper, and tied. S

_____. CENTENARY BOOKLETS, $.60/each; $25.00/set. A series of fifty bo lets, each containing selected passages from Aurobindo and the Mother on a particu subject. Booklets are between twenty-eight and thirty-six pages. Illness, Parts I and Evolution; Meditation; Sleep and Dreams; Occultism; Truth; Prayer and Mantra; Scien Education, Parts I—III; Aspiration; Surrender and Grace; Religion; Food; Work; Den cracy and Socialism; Yoga; Helping Humanity; Beauty; Transformation; Happiness a Peace; On Themselves, Parts I and II; the Aim of Life, Parts I and II; Death; Rebir Human Unity; Art, Parts I and II; India; the Gita; Veda, Upanishads, Tantra; Planes a Parts of Being, Parts I and II; Nature; Self Perfection, Parts I—IV; Fate and Free W Love, Parts I and II; Supermind. SAA

_____. COLLECTIVE YOGA, $1.75. Extracts dealing directly with collective d cipline. 75pp. SAA

_____. THE DESTINY OF MAN, $3.00. A compilation covering the followi topics: evolution and spiritual transformation, reason, towards supermind, gnostic bei divine life, how man can realize his destiny, yoga. 269pp. SAA 69

_____. EDUCATION, $2.00. 118pp. SAA 56

_____. A PRACTICAL GUIDE TO INTEGRAL YOGA, c$6.00/$4.50. A comp tion on nearly all aspects of the yoga. Outlined are the aids and obstacles in Sadhana a other pertinent information. 345pp. SAA 55

_____. SRI AUROBINDO AND THE MOTHER ON LOVE, $1.50. 49pp. SAA

_____. THE TEACHING OF SRI AUROBINDO, $1.50. Extracts arranged to present the teaching in a clear manner, including chapters from **The Mother**, and extracts on meditation, psychological perfection, living from within, physical education, sex, food, prayers. 76pp. SAA 64

AUROBINDO ASHRAM TRUST. **AUROVILLE: CITY OF THE FUTURE**, $1.75. 37pp. SAA 74

AUROBINDO SOCIETY. **TOWARDS TOMORROW**, $1.85. SAA

AUROPUBLICATIONS. **AUROVILLE: THE FIRST SIX YEARS**, $3.75. 102pp. Aur 74

CHAUDHURI, HARIDAS. **BEING, EVOLUTION, AND IMMORTALITY**, $2.75. An outline of the author's Integral Philosophy which reinterprets the ancient teachings for the modern age. Portions of the book were originally published as **The Philosophy of Integralism**. Notes, index. 210pp. TPH 74

_____. **INTEGRAL YOGA**, c$4.95. The concepts of integral yoga were first presented by Sri Aurobindo. This volume presents an excellent analysis of integral yoga, discussing its principles and its relationship to other forms of yoga, to modern Western thought, and to other philosophical and religious systems. Notes, index. 160pp. TPH 65

_____. **SRI AUROBINDO—PROPHET OF THE DIVINE**, $3.75. An excellent introduction to the life and teaching of Sri Aurobindo for the serious student. Chaudhuri, President of the California Institute of Asian Studies, expounds with clarity and precision the fundamental principles of integrated living (purna yoga) based on Aurobindo's integral world-view (integral non-dualism). Also makes recent developments in the Aurobindo movement more meaningful in relation to the ideas from which it has emerged. 270pp. JF 51

CHAUDHURI, HARIDAS and FREDERIC SPIEGELBERG. **THE INTEGRAL PHILOSOPHY OF SRI AUROBINDO**, c$6.00. A symposium consisting of articles contributed by thirty eminent scholars who have discussed different aspects—philosophical, psychological, ethno-religious, political, etc.—of Sri Aurobindo's contribution to civilization. Also includes a complete list of all the books by Aurobindo published in English. 350pp. A&U 60

GUPTA, N.K., et al. **SRI AUROBINDO AND HIS ASHRAM**, $1.00.

_____. **THE YOGA OF SRI AUROBINDO**, c$11.00. Probably the best presentation of this subject. Twelve parts in six volumes. SAA

McDERMOTT, ROBERT, ed. **THE ESSENTIAL AUROBINDO**, $2.95. Extracts from some basic writings of Sri Aurobindo, giving his concept of spiritual and human evolution, his vision of man's destiny, the integral yoga, the implementation of his vision by the Mother, with extracts from her writings on education and Auroville. Includes a life sketch by McDermott, a passage from **Savitri**, bibliographical guide to further reading and a glossary. An excellent introduction. 200pp. ScB 73

MAITRA, S.K. **THE MEETING OF EAST AND WEST IN SRI AUROBINDO'S PHILOSOPHY**, $4.75. 470pp. SAA 56

MITRA, SISIRKUMAR. **SRI AUROBINDO—THE QUEST FOR DIVINE CONSCIOUSNESS**, c$10.00. InB 72

THE MOTHER. **ABOUT SAVITRI**, c$16.00. Forty color plates by Huta illustrating passages from **Savitri**, with the Mother's comments on lines from Book I, Canto I. 64pp. SAA

_____. **CONVERSATIONS**, $1.75. Talks with aspirants on yoga, adverse conditions, role of mind, art and yoga, illness, the general aim to be attained. 136pp. SAA 31

_____. **FLOWERS AND THEIR MESSAGES**, $6.50. A beautiful collection: the Mother's interpretation of the significance of various flowers; appropriate extracts from the writings of Aurobindo and the Mother; a note on color symbolism. Alphabetically arranged by botanical name, and cross-referenced. Color plates, drawings, bibliography, glossary, index of common names. Oversize, 236pp. Aup 73

_____. **MEDITATIONS ON SAVITRI, VOL. II**, c$16.50. Thirty-five color plates from images in Book I, Cantos 2 and 3. 72pp. SAA

_____. **MEDITATIONS ON SAVITRI, VOL. IV**, c$13.00. Twenty color plates, images from Book I, Canto 5. 36pp. SAA

_____. **THE MOTHER ON SRI AUROBINDO**, $2.00. The identity and purpose of Sri Aurobindo. SAA

_____. **PRAYERS AND MEDITATIONS**, $1.50. Selected and translated from the Mother's diaries by Sri Aurobindo. SAA

_____. **QUESTIONS AND ANSWERS**, c$10.00/each. Questions asked at the Mother's class for students and disciples at the ashram. Vol I: 1950–51; Vol II: 1956; Vol. III: 1957–58. Each volume is almost 400pp. SAA

_____. **WHITE ROSES**, $2.50. Letters to a disciple on various aspects of the yoga, and inspirational notes. 152pp. SAA

MOTWANI, KEWAL. **AUROBINDO ON SOCIAL SCIENCES AND HUMANITIES FOR THE NEW AGE**, $2.50. An anthology on social evolution, individual and community,

collective consciousness, occultism, astrology, psychology, etc. 188pp. SAA

NIRODBARAN. **CORRESPONDENCE WITH SRI AUROBINDO**, c$6.00. The author was a doctor who served as secretary and attendant to Aurobindo. The material covers a wide range of subjects. Photographs, 356pp. SAA

_____. **TALKS WITH AUROBINDO**, Material taken from the author's notebooks, covering the post-1938 period. Vol. I: 385pp., c$3.00; Vol. II: index, 256pp, c$4.50; Vol. III: index, 257pp, c$4.00. SAA

_____. **TWELVE YEARS WITH SRI AUROBINDO**, $4.00. Personal glimpses of Aurobindo, the Mother, the ashram, etc. from 1938 to 1950. 306pp. SAA

NORELLI-BACHELET, PATRIZIA. **THE GNOSTIC CIRCLE**, c$12.90. See the Astrology section.

_____. **SYMBOLS AND THE QUESTION OF UNITY**, c$7.25. See the Sacred Art section.

PANDIT, M.P. **DICTIONARY OF SRI AUROBINDO'S YOGA**, c$6.00. A comprehensive dictionary of the ideas, concepts, principles, Sanskrit and special English words used by Aurobindo and defined in his own words. 315pp. SAA 66

_____. **GEMS FROM SRI AUROBINDO**, c$7.50/set. Four volumes of brief extracts from Aurobindo's prose and poetry on a wide range of subject, arranged alphabetically. 913pp. SAA

_____. **GLOSSARY OF SANSKRIT TERMS IN SRI AUROBINDO'S WORKS**, $2.25. Excludes Vedic words, for which there is another glossary, and translations from the Upanishads. English equivalents are almost wholly in Aurobindo's own words. 84pp. SAA 66

_____. **SRI AUROBINDO ON THE TANTRA**, $1.00. Compiled from writings on integral yoga, kundalini, chakras, worship, mantra, japa, etc. 47pp. SAA

PRASAD, N. **LIFE IN SRI AUROBINDO ASHRAM**, c$5.50. SAA

PURANI, A.B. **EVENING TALKS WITH SRI AUROBINDO**. Recorded by one of the early disciples, covering a wide range of topics. Series I: index, 325pp, c$6.50; Series II: index, 351pp, c$5.65; Series III: 320pp, c$3.75. SAA

SATPREM. **SRI AUROBINDO OR THE ADVENTURES OF CONSCIOUSNESS**, $3.95. Written by a Westerner, this biography sets forth his spiritual realizations in terms of his own life and the life of man the mental being—the yoga, the supramental consciousness and transformation. Highly recommended as an introduction to Sri Aurobindo's vision and work. Photographs, 381pp. SAA 68

SRIVASTAVA, RAMA. **SRI AUROBINDO AND THE THEORIES OF EVOLUTION**, c$15.00. A detailed, scholarly study. Bibliography, index. 464pp. CSS 68

SHANKARANARAYANAN, S. SRI. **SRI CHAKRA**, $4.25. SAA

BANERJEE, P. **EARLY INDIAN RELIGIONS**, c$9.00. A comprehensive survey of India's religious history during the period between 185 BC and 300 AD. Index, bibliography, notes. 253pp. VPH 73

BASHAM, A.L. **THE WONDER THAT WAS INDIA**, $6.95. An encyclopedic all-around view of Indian culture, its cults and doctrines, its social structures, arts, languages, and literature. Over 200 illustrations, appendices on astronomy, medicine, the calendar, origin of the gypsies. Fully indexed, with a bibliography and references. 539pp. RaH 54

BASHAM, A.L. et al. **SOURCES OF INDIAN TRADITION**, $8.95/set. Source material that illustrates Indian and Pakistani thought since earliest times. The traditions represented include Buddhism, Jainism, Hinduism, Sikhism, and Islam. Recent movements such as nationalism, liberalism, socialism and the modern religious revivals are also included. A massive two volume collection with extensive bibliography. 946pp. Col 58

BEHARI, BANKEY. **MINSTRELS OF GOD**, $3.10/set. A presentation of writings by and about a variety of spiritual figures who are associated with Brindaban in India: the Gopis, Mira Bai, Andal, Jaideo, Bilwamangal, Surdas, Narsi Mehta, Chandidas, Vidyapata, Chaitanya, Tukaram, and Tulsidas. Most of the texts are not readily available elsewhere and Behari's translations read very well. The Sanskrit is included at the end of each volume and Behari also provides a long introduction. Two volumes, 342pp. BBU 70

_____. **SUFIS, MYSTICS AND YOGIS OF INDIA**, $1.75. *This book is meant to show the Path pursued by the Saints who realized God in one Life, and thereby to guide aspirants after God-realisation who have a similar desire to get His Vision and thereby emancipation in this present life.* Behari provides about 100 pages of excellent introductory material, a bibliography, and extensive quotes from saints such as Kabir, Nanak, Ramdas, Shankaracharya. The entire text is also presented in Sanskrit. 384pp. BBU 62

BENNETT, JOHN. **LONG PILGRIMAGE**, $4.95. See the Gurdjieff section.

BHARDWAJ, S.M. **HINDU PLACES OF PILGRIMAGE IN INDIA**, c$14.40. A very scholarly study of the nature of the interconnections between the Hindu sacred places of different levels and their pilgrim fields in both spatial and social dimensions. The work begins with a survey of pertinent literature on the Hindu holy places, and is followed by an attempt to establish a direct continuity of the broad spatial pattern of Hindu sacred places from the time of the **Mahabharata** to the modern period. Bibliography, index. 278pp. UCP 73

BHATTACHARYA, DEBON, tr. **LOVE SONGS OF CHANDIDAS—THE REBEL POET-PRIEST OF BENGAL**, $2.95. Extensive commentary, illustrations, bibliography. 170pp. RaH 67

_____. **LOVE SONGS OF VIDYAPATI**, $2.95. Extensive commentary, illustrations, bibliography. 144pp. RaH 63

_____, ed. **THE CULTURAL HERITAGE OF INDIA, VOL. I**, c$16.00. Early phases, background, prehistoric and Vedic India, Jainism and Buddhism. VdP 58

_____, ed. **THE CULTURAL HERITAGE OF INDIA, VOL. II**, c$16.00. Itihasas, Puranas, Dharmas, discussions of **Ramayana** and **Mahabharata, Gita**, Indian mythology, treatises on moral and social conduct. VdP 58

_____, ed. **THE CULTURAL HERITAGE OF INDIA, VOL. III**, c$16.00. The philosophies—including extensive discussion of Vedanta. VdP 58

_____, ed. **THE CULTURAL HERITAGE OF INDIA, VOL. IV**, c$16.00. The religions—origins, histories, leading ideas, and important saints. VdP 58

BOUQUET, A.C. **HINDUISM**, $2.65. This is an adequate survey of Hinduism which, while it is written in a popular vein, goes far beyond most introductory presentations in the depth of its presentation. The exposition is historical, beginning with the religion of the Vedic age and culminating with the political independence of the Indian state. All the major movements, deities, and spiritual leaders are discussed and quotations from the sacred texts and other source material are interspersed. Notes, bibliography, index. 160pp. HPG 49

BOYD, DOUG. **SWAMI**, c$10.00. Doug Boyd spent several months in India in 1973 and 1974, and over two months as a personal assistant to Swami Rama during a series of psychophysiological tests at the Menninger Foundation in Kansas. The first third of the book is devoted to a detailed study of Swami Rama and included are verbatim recordings of conversations between the Swami and others at the Institute as well as a discussion of the tests he underwent and the results. The rest of the book is devoted to a series of portraits of various Indians Boyd encountered in his travels. The account is vividly written and the main personages come alive in Boyd's portrayal. 350pp. RaH 76

BRUNTON, PAUL. **A SEARCH IN SECRET INDIA**, $3.50. The story of Brunton's quest for the truly sacred in India, which he found embodied in Ramana Maharshi. *I have titled this book* Secret India *because it tells of an India which has been hidden from prying eyes for thousands of years, which has kept itself so exclusive that today only its rapidly disappearing remnants are left.* 313pp. Wei 34

BUHLER, GEORGE, tr. **LAWS OF MANU**, $5.00. Presents the basic moral and social code for the Hindu way of life. Extracts from important commentaries included. Translation is from the *Sacred Books of the East* Series. Extensive notes. 582pp. Dov 1886

BUITENEN, J.A.B. van, tr. **TALES OF ANCIENT INDIA**, $2.45. *This admirably produced and well-translated volume of stories from the Sanskrit takes the Western reader into one of the Golden Ages of India.... The world in which the tales are set is one which placed a premium upon slickness and guile as aids to success.... Merchants, aristocrats, Brahmins, thieves and courtesans mingle with vampires, demi-gods, and the hierarchy of heaven in a series of lively or passionate adventures. The sources of the individual stories are clearly indicated; the whole treatment is scholarly without being arid.*—**The Times Literary Supplement**. 260pp. UCh 59

CAMERON, CHARLES, ed. **WHO IS GURU MAHARAJ JI**, $1.50. This is the only book on Guru Maharaj Ji in print. It is written by a premmie (disciple) and includes many verbatim transcripts of the Guru's discourses along with the story of the Divine Light Mission and the editor's involvement in and impressions of the movement. Also includes many photographs. 302pp. Ban 73

CARROLL, DAVID. **THE TAJ MAHAL**, c$11.95. See the Sacred Art section.

CHAKRAVARTI, PULINBIHARI. **ORIGIN AND DEVELOPMENT OF THE SAMKHYA SYSTEM OF THOUGHT**, c$28.70. A scholarly work which discusses some of the fundamental topics of Samkhya and traces the system's evolution and growth. This study is based entirely on a detailed examination of the original texts. Sanskrit words (not transliterated) are interspersed throughout and many of the notes are in Sanskrit. Bibliography, index. 343pp. OrB 75

CHAPMAN, TOM and ERIKA PETIGURA. **DELHI AND AGRA**, $3.50. A descriptive travel guide illustrated with eighty-two color photographs. Kod 74

CHINMAYANANDA, SWAMI, tr. **ASHTAVAKRA GEETA**, c$5.75. A translation of an illuminating text which records the *universal insight and spiritual experiences which a seeker gathers during moments of his intense meditation.* CPT 72

_____. **A MANUAL FOR SELF-UNFOLDMENT**, $2.95. Swami Chinmayananda has the wonderful ability to take complicated concepts and distill their essence. His translations of the the sacred scriptures are among our favorites and he writes clearly and well. This volume is an edited version of his teachings which was put together by a disciple, with the Swami's assistance. The bulk of the volume presents practical teachings on the spiritual path and on various techniques of self-discovery and self-awareness. Many Sanskrit terms are used and all are thoroughly defined. There is also a short review of Hinduism. 97pp. Chn 75

_____. **A THOUSAND WAYS TO THE TRANSCENDENTAL SAHASRANAAMA**, c$4.00. *The* Sahasranaama *are the thousand names of Sree Narayan, the Immutable Self, each one a pointer indicating the direction towards which the mind's attention should*

turn *in order to detect and apprehend the Divine Reality in the heart of everythi*. 266pp. CPT 68

_____, tr. **WANDERING IN THE HIMALAYAS**, c$3.00. A travelog, prepared Swami Chinmayananda's guru, Swami Tapovanam. Presents a panoramic view of the H alayas as well as a feeling of the philosophy of the Upanishads.

COOMARASWAMY, ANANDA. **THE ARTS AND CRAFTS OF INDIA AND CEYLO** $2.95. See the Sacred Art section.

_____. **THE DANCE OF SHIVA: ON INDIAN ART AND CULTURE**, $3.2 Fourteen essays, numerous illustrations, illuminating the Indian way of life by one of t most respected interpreters of the East to the West. 182pp. FSG 47

COOMARASWAMY, ANANDA and SISTER NIVEDITA. **MYTHS OF THE HINDU AND BUDDHISTS**, $3.95. A collection of the most important Indian myths, taken mai ly from the **Mahabharata** and the **Ramayana**, with additional tales from the Puranas a Vedas and from assorted narratives of Krishna, Buddha and Shiva. This is universally co sidered the finest one volume introduction to Indian mythology ever prepared. Illustr tions, 414pp. Dov 13

DANIELOU, ALAIN. **HINDU POLYTHEISM**, c$18.00. A detailed, scholarly work whi seeks to explain the significance of the most prominent Hindu gods as envisaged by t Hindus themselves. Principal topics are the polytheistic philosophy, the Vedic gods, t Great Trinity (Vishnu, Shiva, Brahma), the Goddess (Shakti) and the secondary go forms of worship, and representations. Numerous illustrations. Appendix contains tra scriptions of the Sanskrit texts which are quoted in translation. Bibliography, inde 491pp. PuP 64

_____. **YOGA: THE METHOD OF RE-INTEGRATION**, c$4.95. This is a tec nical book which differs from other yoga books in that it presents its subject exactly defined in the Hindu scriptures. Built up mainly with quotations from Sanskrit sourc (with original Sanskrit texts as an appendix), it gives an authentic account of the aim methods, results, and different forms of yoga. It explains the technical processes by whi the subconscious may be brought under control. The yogas discussed include the follow ing: hatha, raja, mantra, laya, shiva, karma, jnana, bhakti, kundalini. Appendices discu the chakras, the subtle body, and the siddhis. Illustrations, 172pp. UnB 64

DASGUPTA, S.H. **HINDU MYSTICISM**, $2.25. A systematic introduction, designed f the general reader. Dasgupta begins with an analysis of sacrificial mysticism in Vedic time and goes from there to chapters on the mysticism of the Upanishads, yoga mysticism Buddhistic mysticism, and classical forms of devotional mysticism. Numerous reference to the sacred literature are incorporated into the text. 188pp. Ung 27

_____. **A HISTORY OF INDIAN PHILOSOPHY**, $65.00/set. An exhaustiv study in five volumes. Every school of thought and movement is discussed at length. Th is universally considered the definitive study of Indian philosophy. Notes, bibliography index. MoB 75

_____. **INDIAN IDEALISM**, $3.95. *[For] students of philosophy who are at loss where to begin in their search for the main principles that have influenced philosop ical speculation in India ... this book will be of great value. The style is extremely luci and easy to read, with the result that so abstruse a subject is made not only interestin but also popular without being denuded of its peculiar depth.... We commend this boo to every student of serious thought.*—**Times** of India. The main topics are *Beginnings o Indian Philosophy, Upanishadic Idealism, Buddhist Idealism, The Vedanta and Kindre Forms of Idealism.* Index, 229pp. CUP 33

DASS, BABA HARI. **THE YELLOW BOOK**, $3.50. *These sayings were first collecte from the chalkboard of Baba Hari Dass during his first two visits to the Lama Foundatio ....Baba Hari Dass was first introduced to most of us by Baba Ram Dass in* Be He Now (Hari Dass Baba was my teacher. I was taught by this man with a chalkboard in th most terse way possible.).... *The teachings and stories have Ashtanga yoga as their four dation.* Included are the original quotes and later comments that Baba Hari Dass made o the quotations. Crn 74

DATE, V.H. **THE YOGA OF THE SAINTS**, c$10.05. Dr. Date's book, originally entitle **Analysis of Spiritual Experience**, is an elaboration of the thesis he presented as a PhD car didate at Bombay University. Here he traces all aspects of the spiritual life in a scholar manner, using his direct experience and the experiences of the great saints as his models Includes chapters on *Dogmas and Puzzles of Spiritual Life; Religious Belief, Sensual t Spiritual; From Idol-Worship to God-Realization; Moral and Intellectual Preparation Patanjala-Yoga and Bhakti; Types of Devotion; Methodology of Meditation; Surrende Prayer and Grace; Nature of Spiritual Experience; The Spirit Manifests in Man; The Karm of a Saint Culminates in Jnana; and The Other Six Aspects of the Saintly Life.* Ofte heavy going, but some good insights are presented. Index, 270pp. MuM 74

DAVE, H.T. **LIFE AND PHILOSOPHY OF SHREE SWAMINARAYAN**, c$8.95. This the only work in English which presents the history and philosophy of the Swaminaraya Mission, one of the most influential religious sects of India and East Africa. The move ment is basically a revised form of the traditional *visistadvaita* Vedanta of Ramanuj 274pp. Wei 67

DAYA, SISTER. **THE GURU AND THE DISCIPLE**, $3.30. *In April 1919, Georgin Jones Walton, the aristocratic daughter of a United States Senator, met Swami Parama nanda, a young monk of the Ramakrishna Order of India. Two months later she joine his small monastic community in Boston and became known as Sister Daya.* **The Gur and the Disciple** *is her personal account of her struggles and strivings and of the way he teacher dealt with them.*—from the introduction. 124pp. VdC 76

ECHANET, J.M. **CHRISTIAN YOGA**, $1.25. See the Christianity section.

MOCK, EDWARD et al. **THE LITERATURES OF INDIA: AN INTRODUCTION**, 16.80. Six experts review the representative genres of Indian literature. Each contributor writes in depth about the area of his particular interest, treating it in the light of traditional Indian canons of literary criticism and poetics and presenting the cultural background needed for its full understanding. The material is arranged topically and excerpts in translation are provided to clarify concepts, themes, and premises. 292pp. Ch 74

————. **THE THIEF OF LOVE**, $3.95. One of the richest of India's regional languages is Bengali, spoken today by over seventy-five million people. The medieval period of Bengali extended from the thirteenth through the eighteenth centuries and includes an immense oral literature as well as numerous manuscripts. For this collection, subtitled *Bengali Tales from Court and Village*, Professor Dimock has chosen stories representing two important genres: village poetry and court poetry. Folk legends combining the exotic, the homely, and the shrewd contrast strongly with the extract from a religious epic, **Man-sa Mangal**, which shows the gods afflicting but ultimately blessing their human victims. Good readable translations, glossary. 316pp. UCh 63

OWSON, JOHN. **A CLASSICAL DICTIONARY OF HINDU MYTHOLOGY**, c$10.00. It's not clear when this book was originally produced, but from the typeface it appears to have been in the late nineteenth or early twentieth century. It remains the standard work. The entries are quite extensive and all aspects of the mythology and religion are well covered. Short descriptions of the most frequently mentioned Sanskrit books are also included. Alphabetically arranged, Sanskrit and general indices. 430pp. RKP 72

WIVEDI, R.C., ed. **THE CONTRIBUTION OF JAINISM TO INDIAN CULTURE**, $15.20. India's leading Jainist scholars contributed to this volume and the areas covered include language and literature, religion, philosophy and ethics, fine arts and sciences, history and culture. Extensive quotations from the appropriate Jaina texts are included and the material is in both Sanskrit and English. Notes, indices. 323pp. MoB 75

LIADE, MIRCEA. **YOGA: IMMORTALITY AND FREEDOM**, $4.45. This is the most important and exhaustive single volume study of the major ascetic techniques available in English. It is a wide survey of the various phases of yoga: the yoga sutras and Patanjali; yogic techniques (e.g. concentration on a single point, postures, respiratory discipline); and yoga in relation to Brahmanism, Buddhism, tantra, Oriental alchemy, mystical eroticism, and shamanism. Fully indexed with a 50pp list of references cited and extensive annotation. Highly recommended for the serious student. 558pp. PuP 69

MBREE, AINSLIE, ed. **THE HINDU TRADITION**, $2.95. A comprehensive anthology of basic writings which range in time from the Rig Veda to the writings of Radhakrishnan. Selections are preceded by introductory material. Many sections deal with Indian social life, political relationships, love, as well as religion. Bibliography, index. 372pp. RaH 66

EURSTEIN, GEORG. **THE ESSENCE OF YOGA**, $3.95. A psychohistorical examination of yoga within the framework of its contribution to the development of Indian civilization. This is a scholarly discussion which focuses on the variety of ways in which yoga has been used to expand consciousness and on its philosophical and practical application to contemporary society. Translations from relevant texts are included. Bibliography, notes, index. 224pp. RaH 76

RAUWALLNER, ERICH. **HISTORY OF INDIAN PHILOSOPHY**, c$24.00/set. This is one of the most authoritative texts available by a noted German Indologist. It is built from the earlier sources with the addition of the author's independent research. Includes a complete bibliography, a glossary, and an index. 665pp. MoB 73

RAZIER, ALLIE, ed. **HINDUISM**, $3.50. A collection of readings on Hindu religious thought and practice, including both interpretative essays and selections from the sacred literature. The books begins with a general essay by Heinrich Zimmer on the meeting of East and West and goes from there to essays on the formative stages of the Hindu religion and selections from the Rig and Atharva Vedas, the **Bhagavad Gita**, and the Upanishads. There is also an essay on Samkhya yoga by Mircea Eliade and one on Vedanta by Paul Deussen and selections from the Jaina Sutras, with commentary. Most of the translations are from the nineteenth century, though not as flowing as some of the later ones. All in all, this is a good collection. Glossary. 272pp. Wes 69

ULLER, J.F.C. **YOGA**, c$6.00. An esoteric examination of yoga and Indian metaphysics by a student of Yogi Ramacharaka which discusses yogic practices in the light of the Western esoteric system and the Qabala. Includes chapters on Vedanta, raja yoga, mudras, and the esoteric bodies of man. There's also some reference to Buddhism. Illustrations, 148pp. PS 25

AER, JOSEPH. **THE FABLES OF INDIA**, c$4.95. See the Children's Books section.

MAHATMA GANDHI

In 1947, after centuries of foreign rule, India won its independence from Great Britain—not through violence, but through years of intense, patient opposition based on love. The architect of this was the professional revolutionary M.K. Gandhi, whom a reverent nation called *Mahatma*, or *Great Soul*: a little man in a loincloth, weighing less than 100 pounds and worth only two dollars in material possessions at the time of his death, who had managed to translate the perfect love of the Sermon on the Mount and the Bhagavad Gita into effective action.

BLACK, JO ANNE, NICK HARVEY and LAUREL ROBERTSON. **GANDHI THE MAN**, $4.95. *This is not another book about Gandhi's life or the details of his political career. It is a book about Gandhi the man, master of the art of living, as we have come to know him through the stories and spiritual perspective of our teacher, Eknath Easwaran.* This is a photographic essay, including many photographs not to be found elsewhere, direct quotations from Gandhi, and stories, all emphasing the warmth and gentle strength of Gandhi the man. Index, 157pp. GIP 73

CHAUDHURI, HARIDAS and LEONARD FRANK, eds. **MAHATMA GANDHI**, $1.00. Transcription of a commemorative symposium under the general heading of *His Message for Mankind*. The selections are very spiritually-oriented. 39pp. CIF 69

DUNCAN, RONALD, ed. **GANDHI: SELECTED WRITINGS**, $2.75. *In making this selection, I have tried to bear three things in mind: . . . to present material of permanent interest . . . to show the development and to give the essence of [Gandhi's] philosophy of satyagraha . . . to emphasize those ideas which, though they may not seem immediately applicable to Western life, should be of considerable relevance to contemporary thought.* Duncan includes a long introduction and the book is fully indexed. 288pp. H&R 71

FISCHER, LOUIS. **THE ESSENTIAL GANDHI**, $2.95. A detailed self-portrait, in Gandhi's own words, of his mind, heart and soul. Essays from all periods of his life. 369pp. RaH 62

GANDHI, MOHANDAS. **ALL MEN ARE BROTHERS**, $1.95. Life and thoughts as told in his own words. Glossary and bibliography. 186pp. WWW 58

————. **AN AUTOBIOGRAPHY**, $5.95. A highly personal, self-critical account, subtitled *The Story of My Experiments with Truth*. Its narrative goes only as far as 1921, and is primarily concerned with Gandhi's spiritual development rather than his public political activity. Index, 543pp. Bea 57

MERTON, THOMAS, ed. **GANDHI ON NON-VIOLENCE**, $1.50. Selections from Gandhi's **Non-Violence in Peace and War.** In a long introduction Merton shows how Gandhi linked the thought of the East and West in his search for universal truth, and how, for him, non-violence sprang from realization of spiritual unity in the individual. Index, 83pp. NDP 64

RAMACHANDRAN, G. and T.K. MAHADEVAN, eds. **GANDHI**, $2.95. A collection of essays under the general heading of *His Relevance for Our Times* published jointly by the World Without War Council and the Gandhi Peace Foundation. The orientation is toward theories of non-violence and movements for peace. Index, 393pp. WWW 67

VASTO, LANZA del. **WARRIORS OF PEACE**, $2.45. Lanza del Vasto is a disciple of Gandhi and the acknowledged leader of the non-violent movement in France. In 1948 he founded the Community of the Ark, a nonsectarian working order of men and women who put nonviolent principles into practice in their daily lives. **Warriors of Peace** contains his most important writings and discourses on the techniques of nonviolence. 236pp. RaH 74

VERMA, SURENDRA. **METAPHYSICAL FOUNDATIONS OF MAHATMA GANDHI'S THOUGHT**, $2.10. Notes, long bibliography and glossary. 177pp. OLL 70

WOODCOCK, GEORGE. **MOHANDAS GANDHI**, $1.95. A critical survey of Gandhi's life and work, including a great deal of biographical material. Bibliography, index. 133pp. Vik 71

BHAGAVAD GITA

The **Gita** is often called the Bible of India. It is a portion of the **Mahabharata**, the great Hindu epic, and is recognized as embodying the highest and noblest truths of Eastern philosophy. The scene is a battlefield and the contestants are symbolic of the struggle between the higher and lower self in every man.

Its form is that of a dialogue between Krishna and his disciple Arjuna. Emphasis is given to the discharge of spiritual duties as an effective discipline for the realization of God. Countless generations have been inspired and uplifted by the wisdom of the **Gita**.

A number of recordings of the **Gita** are available. See the Records section for descriptions.

ABHEDANANDA, SWAMI. THE BHAGAVAD GITA, c$14.75. In 1907 Swami Abhedananda delivered a series of sixty-four discourses on the **Gita** before sophisticated American audiences. Thirty-two of them have been collected here and critically edited and annotated. Virtually every idea expressed in the **Gita** is fully discussed here. Swami Abhedananda expresses himself very clearly and most of his analogies are derived from Western sources. He also keeps his usage of Sanskrit terminology to a minimum. 1028pp. RVM 69

ARNOLD, EDWIN, tr. THE SONG CELESTIAL: A POETIC VERSION OF THE BHAGAVAD GITA, $1.00. *The poets rightly teach that Sannyas is the foregoing of all acts which spring out of desire; and their wisest say Tyaga is the renouncing fruits of acts.* The classic rendition. 154pp. TPH 70

AUROBINDO, SRI. ESSAYS ON THE GITA, c$7.00. *Almost all spiritual problems have been dealt with in the Gita and I have tried to bring out all that fully in the* **Essays.** Highly recommended for the serious student. 575pp. SAA 70

_____. THE GITA, $6.00. *The sages have known as Sannyasa the laying aside of actions born of desire; Tyaga is the name given by the wise to the entire abandonment of the fruit of action.* This edition contains Sri Aurobindo's translation and his comments as well as the original Sanskrit text. There is also a selection from Aurobindo's **Essays on the Gita.** Glossary, SAA 75

BAHM, ARCHIE. THE BHAGAVAD GITA, c$6.45. *The ascetics regard renunciation as giving up all desire to exert effort which will bring rewards. Those able to discriminate clearly speak of abandonment as giving up all interest in rewards of such effort.* Professor Bahm's translation and study was the result of grave doubts he felt regarding the conflicting claims about doctrines attributed to the **Gita** by various authors and schools. In this book he reviews these claims and shows that a deep analysis of the text itself both justifies virtually all the conflicting claims and shows that the **Gita** itself transcends all such claims. Extensive notes accompany the text. Bibliography, 178pp. Som 70

BARBORKA, GEOFFREY. THE PEARL OF THE ORIENT: THE MESSAGE OF THE BHAGAVAD GITA FOR THE WESTERN WORLD, $1.95. A theosophical interpretation. 182pp. TPH 68

BESANT, ANNIE, tr. BHAGAVAD GITA, c$2.50. *Sages have known as renunciation the renouncing of works with desire; the relinquishing of the fruit of all actions is called relinquishment by the wise.* Noted for its close adherence to the original Sanskrit. Extensive index. 223pp. TPH 1895

CHATTERJI, MOHINI, tr. THE BHAGAVAD GITA, c$3.98. *The renunciation of all works for specific purposes is known by the wise as renunciation; the sages call the abandonment of the fruit of all actions the giving up of results.* This is the best of the nineteenth century translations. Both in the translation and in his notes, Chatterji showed a full awareness of the questions that were being asked in the West as to the character of the religious and philosophical structure of the **Gita.** At the same time, as a believing Hindu he made use of his own insights and also drew upon the writings of the great classical Indian commentators. This gives the copious notes a unique value, for they provide not only a comment on the **Gita** but also a summary of traditional views.—Ainslee Embree. Introduction, index, 304pp. Cau 60

CHINAMAYANANDA, SWAMI. GEETA FOR CHILDREN, $2.50. *Sannyasa is the Renunciation of Ego and its desire-prompted Activities while Tyaga is the abandonment of all anxieties to enjoy the fruits-of-action.* This translation is not written in a language that young children can easily understand but rather is intended as a guide to parents on explaining the **Gita** to their children. Each chapter recommends a few stanzas which the children may memorize and chant and there are questions suggesting areas for discussion at the end of each chapter. 171pp. CPT 67

_____. THE HOLY GEETA, c$12.00. *The sages understand SANYASA to be the renunciation of works with desire; the wise declare the abandonment of the fruits of all actions as TYAGA.* This is one of our favorite editions and combines an exceptionally careful textual analysis and commentary (with a great deal of background material integrating ancient Indian philosophy with modern psychological schools) with an excellent translation. There is a constant attempt to bring forth from each verse not only its obvious meaning, but also its hidden import. The Sanskrit text is included and the edition is beautifully bound and a great deal sturdier than most Indian books. Recommended. 1156pp. CMT nd

DATE, V.H. BRAHMA-YOGA OF THE GITA, c$22.50. *Renunciation of actions which are motivated by desires, the sages know as sannyasa. The wise have called the giving up of the fruits of all actions, as tyaga.* Dr. Date is a well known contemporary Indian scholar who has written a number of important volumes. Here he expounds at length on the philosophy of the **Gita.** Years of deep study went into this exposition and there are many valuable insights. Sankara's noted commentary on the **Gita** is cited and quoted often. Index, 687pp. MuM 71

DAVIS, ROY EUGENE, tr. THE BHAGAVAD GITA: GOD'S REVEALING WORD, $3.00. *Wise people know that true renunciation is a matter of giving up all actions which are prompted by desire; relinquishing of the results of all works is the highway of freedom.* A modern restatement, with commentary. 149pp. CSA 68

DEUTSCH, ELIOT. THE BHAGAVAD GITA, $6.00. *Sages know renunciation as the giving up of acts of desire; the surrendering of the fruits of all actions the wise call* abandonment. This is a very poetic rendition and the scholarship is excellent. An introduction discusses some of the main concepts employed in the **Gita** (which are kept in Sanskrit in the translation). There are also explanatory notes, and a small series of philosophical essays. This is a good version for the general reader. 203pp. HRW 68

EASWARAN, EKNATH. THE BHAGAVADGITA FOR DAILY LIVING, c$12.95. translation of the first six chapters. *Sri Easwaran's commentary on the Bhagavad Gita differs from any of those existing at present. Since, in common with Gandhi, he sees the battlefield described in the Gita as symbolic of interior warfare between narrow self-seeking and selfless divine realization, Easwaran's commentary is concerned not with textual criticism or historical exposition but with practical and specific ways whereby this spiritual battle may be won.—Elizabeth Nottingham.* Both the Sanskrit text and the translation of each stanza are presented. Index, 433pp. BMC 75

EDGERTON, FRANKLIN, tr. THE BHAGAVAD GITA, $1.95. *The renouncing of acts of desire sages call renunciation. The abandonment of action-fruits the wise call* abandonment. 100 pages of this edition are devoted to an extensive interpretation of the **Gita,** its origins and teaching. The translation is a bit dry but the explanatory material is excellent. 202pp. HUP 44

JOHNSTON, CHARLES, tr. BHAGAVAD GITA, c$3.25. *The renouncing of works done through desire, sages have called Renunciation; and the wise have declared that ceasing from all desire of personal reward for one's work is Resignation.* General introduction and an introduction to each chapter. 132pp. Wat 08

JUDGE, WILLIAM, tr. BHAGAVAD-GITA, COMBINED WITH ESSAYS ON THE GITA, $2.50. *The bards conceive that the forsaking of actions which have a desired object is renunciation or Sannyasa, the wise call the disregard of the fruit of every action true disinterestedness in action.* The essays analyze the first seven chapters in detail. 220pp. ThU 68

LAL, P., tr. THE BHAGAVADGITA, c$4.80/$1.20. *Renunciation means the giving-up of desire-laden action; it also means abandonment of action's fruits.* A terse, beautiful rendition. 107pp. WrW 65

LAL, R. THE GITA IN THE LIGHT OF MODERN SCIENCE, c$12.95. A lengthy discourse discussing the **Gita** chapter by chapter and relating it to the modern scientific approach rather than explaining it in terms of ancient Hindu scriptures and traditional beliefs. Includes many textual quotations. Index, 331pp. Som 70

MAHARISHI MAHESH YOGI. ON THE BHAGAVAD GITA, $2.95. The first six chapters with the original Sanskrit text, an introduction, and a commentary relating the text to meditational techniques. 494pp. Pen 67

MASCARO, JUAN, tr. THE BHAGAVAD GITA, $1.95. *The renunciation of selfish works is called renunciation; but the surrender of the reward of all work is called surrender.* Includes a long introduction but no textual commentary. Verses are numbered. 122pp. Pen 62

NIKHILANANDA, SWAMI, tr. THE BHAGAVAD GITA, c$3.00. *The renunciation of works induced by desire is understood by the sages to be sannyasa, while the surrender of the fruits of all works is called tyaga by the wise.* Introduction and glossary. 226pp. RVC 44

_____. THE BHAGAVAD GITA, c$5.95. The same translation as above with the following special features: an introduction to the philosophy of the **Gita,** a summary of the **Mahabharata,** of which it forms an integral part, and notes and comments based on the commentary of Sankaracharya. 382pp. RVC $4

PARAMANANDA, SWAMI, tr. SRIMAD BHAGAVAD GITA, $2.75. *The Sages declare that the renunciation of actions with desire (for fruits) is Sannyasa, and the learned declare that the relinquishment of the fruits of all actions is Tyaga.* This is a very clear translation and is a favorite of some of our more knowledgeable customers. Paragraphs are numbered and there is a short introduction. 162pp. VdC 74

PARRINDER, GEOFFREY. THE BHAGAVAD GITA, $2.95. *Renouncing actions of desire is what Renunciation meant, abandoning rewards of acts the wise have called Abandonment.* Includes textual notes and references, and an appendix summarizing the chapters. *The purpose is to provide a popular yet accurate rendering, which will help readers to memorize important verses and understand the teachings.* Parrinder is one of England's most distinguished scholars of Hindu literature. 124pp. Dut 75

PRABHAVANANDA, SWAMI and CHRISTOPHER ISHERWOOD, trs. THE SONG OF GOD, BHAGAVAD GITA, c$3.75/$1.25. *The sages tell us that renunciation means the complete giving-up of all actions which are motivated by desire. And they say that non-attachment means abandonment of the fruits of action.* An interpretation rather than a straight translation. The most popular **Gita,** it is highly recommended for its readability, clarity and insight. Introduction by Aldous Huxley. 191pp. VdP 44

PREM, SRI KRISHNA. THE YOGA OF THE BHAGAVAT GITA, $1.65. *The point of view from which this book has been written is that the Gita is a textbook of Yoga, a guide to the treading of the Path. By Yoga is here meant not any special system called by that name . . . but just the path by which man unites his finite self with Infinite Being. It is the inner Path of which all these separate yogas are so many one-sided aspects.* Glossary, 224pp. Pen 38

PUROHIT, SWAMI SHRI, tr. THE GEETA, $1.45. *The sages say that renunciation means foregoing an action which springs from desire; and relinquishing means the surrender of its fruit.* 95pp. Fab 35

ADHAKRISHNAN, S., tr. **BHAGAVAD-GITA**, $3.95. *The wise understand by renun-*
tion the giving up of works prompted by desire: the abandonment of the fruits of all
rks, the learned declare, is relinquishment. A classic work by one of the most noted
dian philosophers. Gives us the Sanskrit text, English translation and extensive com-
*ntary as well as an excellent long introductory essay. Recommended. 384pp. H&R 48

AMACHARAKA, YOGI, tr. **BHAGAVAD GITA OR THE MESSAGE OF THE MAS-**
:R, c$3.25. *The sages have told us that the principle of Sannyasa, or Abstaining from*
tion, lieth in the forsaking of all Action which hath a desired object; and that the prin-
le of Tyaga, or Renunciation of Fruits of Action, lieth in the forsaking of all the fruits
every Action. 184pp. YPC 30

AMDAS, SWAMI. **GITA SANDESH: MESSAGE OF THE GITA**, $1.00. A chapter-by-
*apter discussion of the philosophical message of the **Gita**. Krishna's message is restated
modern terms and the exposition is aimed at seekers on the path. 124pp. BBU 66

ELE, VASANT G. **BHAGAVAD-GITA—AN EXPOSITION**, $2.40. An interesting inter-
etation/translation from the standpoint of modern psychoanalysis coupled with the an-
ent Indian idealistic philosophy—Arjuna as the confused patient and Krishna as the ana-
st. 156pp. TSc 72

OY, DILIP, tr. **THE BHAGAVAD GITA**, c$1.75. *The sages hold that the repudiation/*
all acts motivated by desire/ Is renunciation (sannyasa) and the disclaimer/ Of the fruits
action is (tyaga) non-attachment. Dilip Roy is a singer and a musician and is one of
Aurobindo's leading disciples. In addition to the translation Roy offers the reader a
*ries of thoughts inspired by the message of the **Gita**.* Index, 190pp. IBC 74

ARAYDARIAN, H. **BHAGAVAD GITA**, c$6.00. *Renunciation is performed when a*
n acts without the desire of fruits. Abandonment is performed when all the fruits are
en up. Saraydarian says that *this translation was made in deep reflection and medita-*
n, pondering on each Sanskrit word and phrase until the spirit behind the words was
en, grasped, and put into form. For more on Saraydarian see the Mysticism section.
versize, introduction, numbered verses. 96pp. AEG 74

HASTRI, HARI PRASAD, tr. **TEACHINGS FROM THE BHAGAVAD GITA**, c$1.65.
rue renunciation consists in renouncing all selfish activities, and also the fruits of other
tivities such as offerings to God. Includes a nice introduction. 96pp. ShS 35

HRINE OF WISDOM. **A SYNTHESIS OF THE BHAGAVAD-GITA**, c$2.95. This version
specially prepared for the seeker of the significance of the Indian teachings in respect to
e Good Life, and therefore the passages in the poem are rearranged under the headings
the Five Margas or Paths to Perfection. A very interesting translation. 72pp. ShW 27

VANANDA, SWAMI. **THE BHAGAVAD GITA**, c$5.50. *The sages understand Sannyasa*
be the renunciation of action with desire; the wise declare the abandonment of the
its of all actions as Tyaga. This is an excellent edition. Sivananda supplies extensive
mmentary on each phrase as well as the Sanskrit text, an English translation of each
ord and an English translation of the stanza, as well as a good introduction. Swami Siva-
nda was one of the greatest exponents of the philosophy, religion and technique of the
hagavad Gita of this century, and his commentary is regarded as one of the most author-
ative expositions available. 630pp. DLS 39

_____. **THE BHAGAVAD GITA EXPLAINED**, $.90. An exposition of the philo-
phical meaning of each chapter of the **Gita** designed to aid seekers after spiritual under-
anding. 160pp. DLS 68

TEINER, RUDOLF. **THE OCCULT SIGNIFICANCE OF THE BHAGAVAD GITA**,
.50. Nine lectures. 142pp. API 68

WARUPANANDA, SWAMI, tr. **SHRIMAD BHAGAVAD-GITA**, c$3.50. *The renuncia-*
n of Kamya actions, the sages understand as Sannyasa; the wise declare the abandon-
ent of the fruit of all works as Tyaga. The Sanskrit text is presented and individual
ords are defined. The translator is a disciple of Swami Vivekananda. 430pp. AdA 72

ELANG, KASHINATH, tr. **THE BHAGAVAD GITA**, c$7.50. Vol. 8, *Sacred Books of*
e East. A very literal translation, with many scholarly notes and translations of classical
mmentaries. 446pp. MoB 1882

HOMAS, EDWARD J., tr. **THE SONG OF THE LORD: BHAGAVAD-GITA**, c$2.50.
he giving up of actions that involve desire the sages know as renunciation; the abandon-
ent of the fruit of all actions the wise call abandonment. Includes a good introduction.
28pp. Mur 31

IRESWARANANDA, SWAMI, tr. **SRIMAD BHAGAVAD GITA**, c$4.25. *Sages under-*
and the renouncing of actions that fulfill desires as renunciation (Sannyasa), and the
arned declare the abandoning of the fruit of all actions as relinquishment (Tyaga). This
dition includes the Sanskrit text and translation as well as Sridhara's gloss on the **Gita**
nown as **Subodhini**. Index, 536pp. RVM 48

AEHNER, R.C. **THE BHAGAVADGITA**, $4.95. *To give up works dictated by desire,*
ise men allow to be renunciation; surrender of all the fruits that accrue to works dis-
erning men call self-surrender. A transliterated version of each stanza accompanies the
anslation along with definitions and expositions of specific words and ideas and a lengthy
anza and chapter commentary. This is a very scholarly version, somewhat lacking in the
pirit of the original, but containing an abundance of valuable information for understand-
g the subtler points of the text. Also includes a lengthy introduction and an index.
39pp. Oxf 69

OETZ, HERMANN. **THE ART OF INDIA**, c$6.95. See the Sacred Art section.

HAICH, ELISABETH and SELVARAJAN YESUDIAN. **YOGA AND DESTINY**, c$4.50.
Transcripts of a series of lectures: *Yoga and Destiny, Yoga and Self-Healing, How to Be-*
come a Yogi, Yoga in Today's Struggle for Existence, and *A Few Words About Magic.*
80pp. ASI 66

HIRIYANNA, M. **THE ESSENTIALS OF INDIAN PHILOSOPHY**, $7.50. A scholarly,
thorough account of Indian philosophy, providing interpretation and criticism. An introductory chapter summarizes Vedic religion and philosophy, and then Indian thought is
considered in chapters dealing respectively with the early post-Vedic period and the age
of the systems. Recommended only to those students desiring a serious study. Glossary,
notes, index. 216pp. A&U 49

Vishnu, the Preserver   Shiva, the Destroyer

IONS, VERONICA. **INDIAN MYTHOLOGY**, c$4.95. See the *Hamlyn Mythology* Series
in the Mythology section.

JACOBI, HERMANN, tr. **JAINA SUTRAS**, $7.00/set. The Jain religion developed in India
at about the same time as Buddhism did, during a period of decline in the Hindu religious
tradition. It has had continuing importance in India to the present day—though it has
never been as important a movement as Hinduism or Buddhism. This two-volume set,
from the *Sacred Books of the East* Series, contains the most important classical sutras
along with an extensive introductory essay. 750pp. MoB 1884

JOHARI, HARISH. **LEELA: THE GAME OF SELF-KNOWLEDGE**, $4.95. *This ancient*
game is to the Hindu tradition what the I Ching is to the Chinese, and, in both, chance
plays a vital part. The game of Leela is centuries old. The version used as the basis for this
translation was brought to this country in 1969 by Harish Johari, a distinguished Sanskrit
scholar, poet, artist, and composer. He created the Commentaries on each of the seventy-
two squares of the gameboard in a form Western readers could understand. With them
American readers can now play the Leela game and discover through this unique Hindu
psychological tool, the nature of their hidden selves.—from the preface. A gameboard is
included. 143pp. CMG 75

JOHNSON, DONALD and JEAN. **GOD AND GODS IN HINDUISM**, c$4.40. An illustrated,
concise general presentation of the nature of God according to the Hindus and the role
played by deities in Hinduism throughout the ages. Each of the major deities is examined
and many related plates accompany the text. 88pp. AHI 72

JOHNSTON, E.H. **EARLY SAMKHYA**, c$6.00. The description of Samkhya before the
formulation of the classical system of Isvarakrisna are contained in a large number of contradictory, vague texts. Johnston begins this study with an introductory section which describes the sources and defines methods. The next sections are basically made up of original
source material in the following areas: origins, prakrti, life and the soul, and theoretical
principles of Samkhya philosophy. Extensive textual notes are included which help bring
the material together, and the author attempts to account for the contradictions. Index,
198pp. MoB 37

JONES, FRANKLIN. **THE KNEE OF LISTENING**, $3.95. Subtitled *The Early Life and*
Radical Spiritual Teachings of Franklin Jones. The first half is his autobiography. The second half contains his spiritual wisdom. He teaches that seeking by any means, even traditional spiritual, philosophical, religious, and yogic means is an inappropriate and fruitless

approach to truth. As he puts its, *Truth is not realized as a result of any action. Truth is always already the case.* Alan Watts says *It is obvious, from all sorts of subtle details, that he knows what It's all about . . . a rare being.* 271pp. DHP 72

_____. **THE METHOD OF THE SIDDHAS**, $3.95. A collection of Jones' discourses on the spiritual process of Satsang, which he says is the ancient method of teaching in the tradition of all the Siddhas or perfect spiritual masters. *All seeking is unnecessary. Only understand your own search. Bodies and worlds are only full. All power is at the Heart. Joyous Light surrounds your head. Truth is consciousness itself. The only one who has to come is always already here.* Topics include understanding, money, food, sex, relationship and association, meditation and Satsang, one-pointedness, the Gospel of the Siddhas, and other related areas. Good glossary, 381pp. DHP 73

_____. **NO REMEDY**, $3.50. *An Introduction to the Life and Practices of the Spiritual Community of Bubba Free John.* Life in the community is very fully discussed and the following topics are featured: study, money, food, sex, service, the community, satsang, meditation, and the ashram. 170pp. DHP 75

JOSHI, K.S. **YOGA IN DAILY LIFE**, $1.60. This is an Indian yoga treatise. Topics include: introducing yoga, a discussion of the different kinds of yoga, preparing for yoga, and analysis of various bodily systems, i.e., digestive, respiratory; yoga exercises; silencing the breath; silencing the mind; and questions and answers. 163pp. JPC 60

KABIR

Kabir was one of India's most beloved poets and mystics. He lived in the fifteenth century. Both Sufis and Hindus claim him as their own, but his joyous teachings transcend all such boundaries and categories. Kabir was not a recluse or an ascetic. He was a weaver and a family man and it was from out of the heart of the common life that he sang his rapturous lyrics of divine love. His dislike of all institutional religion was obvious. *The simple union with Divine Reality which he perpetually extolled, was alike the duty and joy of every soul, was independent both of ritual and of bodily austerities; the God who he proclaimed was neither in Kaaba nor in Kailash. Those who sought Him needed not to go far; for He awaited discovery everywhere, more accessible to the washerwoman and the carpenter than to the self-righteous holy man. Therefore the whole apparatus of piety, Hindu and Moslem alike—the temple and mosque, idol and holy water, scriptures and priests—were denounced by this . . . clear-sighted poet as mere substitutes for reality; dead things intervening between the soul and its love—*

The images are all lifeless, they cannot speak: I know, for I have cried aloud to them.
The Purana and the Koran are mere words: lifting up the curtain, I have seen.

—R. Tagore, from **Songs of Kabir**

BLY, ROBERT. **THE FISH IN THE SEA IS NOT THIRSTY**, $1.50. *The English of the Tagore-Underhill translations is hopeless, and I simply put a few of them, whose interiors I had become especially fond of, into more contemplative language, to see what they might look like. . . . I believe in translation being as accurate as possible. Kabir wrote the originals in Hindi; Tagore was working from a Bengali translation of that. Many errors may be built in.*—Robert Bly. 15pp. Rai 71

EZEKIEL, ISAAC. **KABIR, THE GREAT MYSTIC**, c$3.55. This is the only study available of Kabir's life and teachings. Translations of over 200 of his songs are also interspersed throughout the body of the text. The book quotes a large number of other spiritual teachers and masters and analyzes how their teachings relate to the philosophy expounded by Kabir. Glossary, 454pp. RSS 66

TAGORE, RABINDRANATH. **SONGS OF KABIR**, $1.95. Despite the criticisms quite justifiably made by Robert Bly and others, Tagore's translation of Kabir's songs remains the standard work. The reader can get a good idea of Kabir from the book and can always let his imagination and heart fill in the rest. 145pp. Wei 15

VAUDEVILLE, CHARLOTTE. **KABIR, VOL. I**, c$32.25. *There has been to this day no critical translation of the bulk of Kabir's verses and hardly any attempt at studying him for himself, against the background of his own time and tradition. The present work is a step in that direction. It aims at filling what is felt as a serious gap in our knowledge of Indian religious tradition and mysticism, by translating whatever can be considered authentic in Kabir's utterances and also by carefully sifting and analysing the various data which can be gathered to this day about Kabir himself, his words and his time.* Extensive notes, bibliography. 354pp. Oxf 74

KRISHNA

CHINMAYANANDA, SWAMI and KUMARI BHARATHI NAIK. **BALA BHAGAVATAM**, c$5.75. See the Children's Books section.

COHEN, S.S. **SRIMAD BHAGAVATA**, $2.00. This is a condensation of the original longer work, bringing out all the instructions and stories and cutting out some of the repetition. This book is basically a series of stories about the life (and loves) of Krishna and contains some of the most famous tales about him. There are also other stories interspersed. The translation flows well and is quite faithful to the original. 376pp. CPT 65

DIMOCK, EDWARD and DENISE LEVERTOV, trs. **IN PRAISE OF KRISHNA**, $1.9[...] Songs from the Bengali. The translators provide notes. 95pp. Dou 67

FRITH, NIGEL. **THE LEGEND OF KRISHNA**, c$7.95. A modern retelling of Krish[...] stories gathered together from nearly every major classic of Hindu literature and providi[...] a continuous narrative of Krishna's exploits. In novelistic style, Frith portrays Krishna [...] all his guises—mischievous youth, lover, mighty warrior, and great teacher. All the ma[...] Indian gods and Vedic myths are woven into the narrative. This is a welcome addition [...] the Krishna literature. Frith teaches poetry at Oxford University. 237pp. ScB 76

KEYT, GEORGE, tr. **GITA GOVINDA: SONG OF LOVE**, c$12.60/$1.60. The love [...] Radha and Krishna has been the inspiration for countless works of art, music, and liter[...] ture in India. The **Gita Govinda** is a twelfth century poem about their love and it is pr[...] ably the most popular account. The hardcover edition is on fine paper and is beautiful[...] illustrated. 123pp. HPB 40

MUKERJEE, RADHAKAM. **THE LORD OF THE AUTUMN MOON**, c$4.00. A trans[...] tion of part of the **Srimad Bhagavata** with two introductory essays (*The Place of the Bh[...]gavata in Indian Thought* and *Bhagavata-Dharma: The Religion of Man*) and exhausti[...] critical and interpretative notes on the text. The chapters translated deal with Krish[...] and his love play with the Gopi shepherdesses. Index, 177pp. APH 57

MUNSHI, K.M. **KRISHNAVATARA**, c$31.50/set. This is a seven volume compilation [...] all the stories about Krishna's life. Krishna's story has been told in epic, story, and so[...] by thousands of poets in every Indian language for centuries. Munshi has done a wonde[...] ful job of retelling all the old stories and making the characters and events come aliv[...] This is probably the best collection of Krishna stories for the general reader that has ev[...] been prepared. Introduction, a few notes, glossary, 1334+pp. BBU 71

PRABHAVANANDA, SWAMI. **SRIMAD BHAGAVATAM: THE WISDOM OF GO[...]** $3.65. By means of stories from the lives of avatars, sages, devotees, and kings, the **Srima[...] Bhagavatam** popularizes the truths contained in the Vedas. One section consists of th[...] teachings of Sri Krishna to his disciple, and this has been rendered without omissio[...] Good glossary. 340pp. Put 43

SANYAL, J.M. **THE SRIMAD BHAGAVATAM**, c$33.00/set. Two volumes. MuM 7[...]

SATHYA SAI BABA. **BHAGAVATHA VAHINI**, $3.60. Sathya Sai's retelling of the Sr[...] **mad Bhagavatam**. He also includes episodes from other ancient texts which detail even[...] in Krishna's life. Written in a novelistic style. Sathya Sai claims to be an incarnation [...] Krishna. 338pp. SSS 70

SINGER, MILTON, ed. **KRISHNA: MYTHS, RITES AND ATTITUDES**, $2.95. A colle[...] tion of essays which examine Krishna of Gokula—the divine herdsman, the mischievo[...] child, the lover, the paradox of flesh and spirit. The poetry, legend, myths, and rites whic[...] have dramatized his deeds and described his world are analyzed. Bibliography and notes [...] 277pp. UCh 66

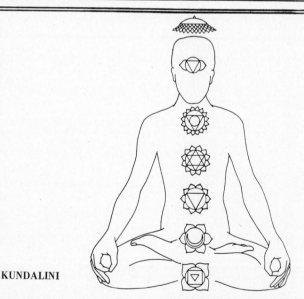

KUNDALINI

ARUNDALE, G.S. **KUNDALINI: AN OCCULT EXPERIENCE**, c$1.75. The author de[...] scribes the awakening of consciousness as Kundalini moves from its base in the human [...] body through the force centers, causing illumination of universal life, light, sound and [...] power.

BERNARD, RAYMOND. **THE SERPENT FIRE**, $4.00. Subtitled *The Awakening o[...] Kundalini: Secret Yoga Methods of Rejuvenation Through Awakening a Mysterious Power [...] at the Base of the Spine, Known as Kundalini or the Serpent Fire, and Causing It to As[...] cend to the Brain, Which It Energizes and Vitalizes.* Detailed instructions, but watch out [...] it can be dangerous. 100pp. HeR 59

KRISHNA, GOPI. **THE AWAKENING OF KUNDALINI**, $3.25. *Gopi Krishna believe[...] that planted in human beings is a powerful reservoir of psychic energy which, when rouse[...]*

activity in the state of Kundalini, can lead to transcendental states of consciousness, *nius, and supernormal psychic powers. In the state of Kundalini the reproductive sys- m recoils on itself and transfers energy to the brain. We can learn to activate Kundalini* *ly through devoted meditation and yogic exercises.* This book presents Gopi Krishna's llest exploration of the phenomena of Kundalini. He tries to make his exposition as ractical as possible and he emphasizes the scientific aspects. Introduction, 141pp. Dut 75

_____. HIGHER CONSCIOUSNESS, c$7.95. This book is written in the form of etailed answers to questions on the physiological and psychological changes accompany- g the awakening of the Kundalini. Topics include: what is higher consciousness, what is undalini and how does it work, is the sex act as we know it evolutionary or entropic, nd what can we do to change society. Gopi Krishna is unique among writers on the sub- ct of higher consciousness because what he has to say is from his own direct experience. nce 1937 when he first attained *cosmic consciousness*, he has lived in two worlds: *the* *comprehensible and infinitely marvelous universe within and the colossal but familiar* *orld without.* 208pp. Jul 74

_____. KUNDALINI: THE EVOLUTIONARY ENERGY IN MAN, $3.50. A fas- nating autobiographical account of what happens to the mind and body when the Kun- alini is aroused spontaneously, after many years of yogic discipline. It is told in a sincere nd simple way. Besides describing the perils, upheavals and final balanced entry into nother dimension, the book also gives some of the traditional Hindu theories about this rce. Highly recommended. 252pp. ShP 67

NARAYANANDA, SWAMI. THE PRIMAL POWER IN MAN OR THE KUNDALINI HAKTI, $3.00. An extremely detailed study, based on tantric teachings. It's good to ave some knowledge of Indian philosophy before beginning this volume, although the anskrit terminology is kept to a minimum. 155pp. HeR 50

ANDIT, M.P. KUNDALINI YOGA, c$2.75. See the Tantra section.

RELE, VASANT. THE MYSTERIOUS KUNDALINI, $2.10. *The chief interest in this* *ook consists in the description of the modification at will of certain physiological pro- esses by a Yogi. It has a distinct value as describing and illustrating the physical training f the Yogi, and interpreting the difficult pseudoanatomical descriptions of the Tantric* *exts.*—Sir John Woodroffe. Bibliography and glossary. 113pp. TSC 60

RIEKER, HANS-ULRICH. THE YOGA OF LIGHT: HATHA YOGA PRADIPIKA, $3.95. n Indian philosophy it is generally understood that hatha yoga is one distinct path to lib- ration and raja yoga another. This text shows a rare and fruitful combination of the two paths. This is the first time that the full text has been translated into English. This ancient ext is written in an extremely terse and often highly symbolic language. Rieker's excellent commentaries help a great deal. The text is concerned mainly with various postures and reathing exercises, and it also discusses Kundalini at greath length. Glossary, illustration. 203pp. DHP 71

SIVANANDA, SWAMI. KUNDALINI YOGA, c$3.80. This is the best exposition of the heory and practice of Kundalini yoga that we have seen. Includes an excellent summary chart of the chakras and many other clear, helpful illustrations. The first 120 pages pre- sent background and theoretical material and the last 200 give detailed, practical exercises or raising the Kundalini (along with preliminary exercises). Recommended. 272pp. DLS 35

WOODROFFE, JOHN. THE SERPENT POWER, $5.00. See the Tantra section.

KUNHAN RAJA, C. SOME FUNDAMENTAL PROBLEMS IN INDIAN PHILOSOPHY, c$15.00. This is a survey of Indian philosophy from the Vedas to the medieval period. The author's fundamental thesis is that, in essentials, there is no conflict between ancient philosophical thought and modern scientific thought, and that there is only a progression accompanied by appropriate revision of views with the change of time and environment. Part I discusses the three modes of knowing: direct experience, inference, and authority. Part II surveys the formation of the world and its constituent parts as expounded in dif- ferent systems of Indian philosophy. Part III reviews man and his destiny. Index, 430pp. MoB 74

LANNOY, RICHARD. THE SPEAKING TREE, $3.95. This is an excellent sociologically oriented study of Indian culture and society *with the chief aim of identifying the origins* *of the nation's contemporary problems. Though generally manifested in economic terms, these have their root causes in the historical development of India's system of values and thought, as reflected in its cultural and social organization.* The study traces Indian culture from antiquity to the present and is illustrated with many photographs. Lannoy has lived, studied and worked in India during much of the past two decades. Extensive bibliography and index. 492pp. Oxf 71

LE BON, G. THE WORLD OF ANCIENT INDIA, c$3.95. See the *World of Ancient Civi- lizations* Series in the Ancient Civilizations section.

McCARTNEY, JAMES. YOGA: THE KEY TO LIFE, $2.20. Provides a good, general outline of yoga philosophy, surveying first hatha yoga; then going on to a discussion of concentration, meditation and contemplation; and then reviewing the less familar aspects of karma, mantra, bhakti, raja, and jnana yoga. Each chapter concludes with appropriate exercises. Illustrations, 241pp. Dut

McDERMOTT, ROBERT and V.S. NARAVANE, eds. THE SPIRIT OF MODERN INDIA, $2.45. This book establishes the historical context in which Indian thinkers of the past 100 years have developed their ideas, and shows how these ideas comprise a coherent vis- ion which is at once Indian and contemporary. The volume focuses on a full treatment of these ideas and includes writings by Ramakrishna, Vivekananda, Tagore, Gandhi, Nehru, Radhakrishnan, and Sri Aurobindo. The selections are topically arranged and contain introductory and background material. Glossary, bibliography, index. 337pp. Cro 74

McNEILL, WILLIAM an JEAN SEDLAR, eds. CLASSICAL INDIA, $2.65. A collection of source readings classified according to subject under four heads: 1) *artha*, or the prac- tical skills of public and private life; 2) *kama*, or sense-gratification; 3) *dharma*, or law and righteousness; and 4) *moksha*, the means of transcending the common-sense world of things. The selection of readings is well made and the translations read well. 307pp. Oxf 69

THE MAHABHARATA

The **Mahabharata**, an ancient and vast Sanskrit poem that traditionally runs 100,000 couplets, is the most important Indian literary work in existence. This remarkable collection of epics, legends, romances, theology, and ethical and metaphysical doctrine is representative of the history and culture of the entire Hindu civilization. The **Bhagavad Gita**, for example, is but one of its component parts. Begun perhaps in the twelfth century BC by an unknown author, this epic spans a period of history that saw the rise and spread of Buddhism, Indian political and economic expansion, and the transformation of the ancient Vedic religion into Hinduism. This was also the period of the development of the principal philosophical schools and the rise of the worship of Vishnu and Siva. The core of the **Mahabharata** is formed by stories of an epical struggle between two branches of a royal family. The five Pandava brothers spend many years and experience countless adventures in vying with their one hundred contentious cousins for rule of the land.

BUCK, WILLIAM, tr. THE MAHABHARATA, c$10.95/$4.95. Buck's rendering is not a translation. Instead, he has retold the story so that the modern reader will be able to know the epic in terms of modern life as well as in terms of its origins. Although he greatly condensed the story, he remained faithful to its spirit and underlying truth, reflecting the original sequence of events, and conveying the flavor by using traditional narrative tech- niques. 370pp. UCP 73

BUITENEN, J.A.B. van, tr. THE MAHABHARATA: 1, THE BOOK OF THE BEGIN- NING, c$26.00. This is the first volume in what will ultimately become a multi-volume edition encompassing all eighteen books of the **Mahabharata**. Professor van Buitenen has based his translation on the definitive Poona edition of 1933—66. He provides the reader with a wealth of material for understanding the text including summaries of sections, notes, chapter-by-chapter cross references, and much else. This volume incorporates the first of the eighteen books and serves as an introduction to the ones that follow. Index, 539pp. UCh 73

_____. THE MAHABHARATA: 2, THE BOOK OF THE ASSEMBLY HALL AND 3, THE BOOK OF THE FOREST, c$44.35. Translations of the second and third books. Index, 875pp. UCh 75

LAL, P., tr. THE MAHABHARATA, c$3.25. A very complete translation, now in process. Of the 180 projected volumes, 64 are ready.

NARASIMHAN, C.V., tr. THE MAHABHARATA: AN ENGLISH VERSION BASED ON SELECTED VERSES, $3.95. The best scholarly one volume English translation. Includes a glossary of persons, places, and transliterated Sanskrit words, as well as genealogical tables which show the relationship of the Kauravas and the Pandavas, and also an index of chapters and verses correlated to the original Sanskrit text. Index, 254pp. Col 65

RAJAGOPALACHARI, C. MAHABHARATA, c$4.00/$2.95. A simple retelling which speaks to the readers in their own language. Recommended as the best introduction. 332pp. BBU 51

RAO, SHANTA RAMESHWAR. THE MAHABHARATA, $2.85. A novelistic recreation and condensation of the main story of the epic. Ms. Rao retells the story vividly and for those who wish to get a feeling for the content without being overwhelmed with details, this is as good a place to start as any. 229pp. OLL 74

SUBRAMANIAM, KAMALA. MAHABHARATA, c$12.00. A rendition in which the em- phasis is on character studies and the dramatic significance of the scenes. A very readable translation, including a glossary. 766pp.

MAHADERIAN, T.M.P. TEN SAINTS OF INDIA, $2.05. Short biographical studies of Tirujnana Sambandhar, Tirunavukkarasu, Sundaramurti, Manikkavackar, Nammalvar, Andal, Sankara, Ramanuja, Sri Ramakrishna, and Ramana Maharshi. All but one of the saints are from South India. Index, 159pp. BBU 65

MENEN, AUBREY. THE MYSTICS, c$15.00. This is a profusely illustrated account of major themes and individuals in Hindu religious philosophy. Menen begins with a discuss- ion of the early Indian religious philosophy and the Vedic and Upanishadic thinkers and goes from there to discussions of specific individuals such as Sankara, and to religious themes such as yoga, tantrism, and the **Gita**. Then he devotes chapters to several figures including Ramakrishna, Vivekananda, Krishnamurti, Rajneesh, and Chinmayananda. The book is designed to serve as an easy-to-read introduction to Hindu philosophy—a coffee table book that a person interested in Hinduism might give to his or her parents, for ex- ample. And for this purpose, it is successful. The whole book is full of Menen's opinions about the subjects, but it reads well and gives a fairly good, albeit scattered, overview. Oversize, index. 239pp. Del 74

MOFFITT, JOHN. JOURNEY TO GORAKHPUR, c$7.95. Moffitt was a monastic mem- ber of the Ramakrishna order for twenty-five years and is now a Catholic. He provides brief sketches of Indian saints, presents a large variety of popular forms of devotion, and describes his visits to holy men and participation in religious ceremonies. The major pre- sentation is through anecdotes, interviews, stories of chance meetings, poems, and short biographies. Subtitled *An Encounter with Christ Beyond Christianity*, this is a useful book for Christians seeking to understand Eastern spirituality. Notes, index. 318pp. HRW 72

MONIER-WILLIAMS, M. **RELIGIOUS THOUGHT AND LIFE IN INDIA**, c$22.50. First published in 1883, this is still the most comprehensive general survey that we know of. Monier-Williams is a well known Sanskrit scholar and while the reader needs to keep when the book was written in mind, s/he will find the text both informative and well written. The following table of contents should give a good idea of the coverage: Vedism; Brahmanism; Saivism; Vaishnavism; Saktism, or Goddess-Worship; Tutelary and Village Worship; Demon-Worship and Spirit-Worship; Hero-Worship and Saint-Worship; Death, Funeral Rites, and Ancestor-Worship; Worship of Animals, Trees, and Inanimate Objects; The Hindu Religion in Ancient and Modern Family-Life; Religious Life of the Orthodox Hindu Householder; Hindu Fasts, Festivals, and Holy Days; Temples, Shrines, and Sacred Places; Castes; and Modern Hindu Theism. Notes, 532pp. MuM 74

MOORE, CHARLES, ed. **THE INDIAN MIND**, $3.95. *This volume presents a middle-of-the-road explanation of the fundamentals of the Indian mind as expressed in its great philosophies, religions, and social thought and practices.* The essays in this volume were originally presented at four East-West Philosophers' Conferences between 1939 and 1964. Notes, index. 469pp. UHa 67

MUKERJI, A.P. **THE DOCTRINE AND PRACTICE OF YOGA**, c$5.50. A series of lessons based on the teachings of Yogi Ramacharaka, which includes *the Practices and Exercises of Concentration, both Objective and Subjective, and Active and Passive Mentation, an Elucidation of Maya, Guru Worship, and the Worship of the Terrible, also the Mystery of Will-Force.* 79pp. YPS 22

_____. **YOGA LESSONS FOR DEVELOPING SPIRITUAL CONSCIOUSNESS**, c$5.50. A collection of practical lessons and explanations on the title theme. 191pp. YPS 11

MUKTANANDA, SWAMI. **AMERICAN TOUR 1970**, c$2.95. Muktananda's style is especially informal in this series of talks. He includes many teaching stories and discusses aspects of the spiritual life. 114pp. SGA 74

_____. **GETTING RID OF WHAT YOU HAVEN'T GOT**, $1.45. The most recent collection available of Muktananda's talks and conversations, including a bit of personal advice given to individuals. The reader can get a good feeling of Muktananda's technique through the introductory material to each selection and there are also short pieces by Baba Ram Dass and Claudio Naranjo. Glossary, 45pp. SYD 74

_____. **LIGHT ON THE PATH**, $1.50. A collection of several short works, each dealing with specific aspects of the path of Siddha Yoga. Topics include spiritual initiation, the relationship of guru and disciple, the nature of God, the path of devotion to the guru, and meditation on oneness with the divine. 119pp. SYD 72

_____. **MUKTESHWARI II**, $1.50. A series of poems on the spiritual life as advocated by Muktananda and as practiced by his disciples. The same message as in his other books, only here delivered in verse. Long glossary, 200pp. SYD 73

_____. **THE NECTAR OF CHANTING**, $3.50. Contains both the Sanskrit transliteration and the English translation of all the chants, mantras, prayers, and texts sung in Muktananda's ashrams all over the world. Includes the *Guru Gita* and *Hymn to the Glory of Shiva.* Muktananda stresses chanting as one of the main aspects of spiritual practice because it has such a purifying effect on the entire atmosphere wherever chants are sung as well as on the person who is chanting. 151pp. SYD 75

_____. **PLAY OF CONSCIOUSNESS**, $3.95. The full presentation of Muktananda's autobiography, originally published in an abridged form as **Guru**. Here he relates his experiences on the path to realization: his fears, his physical contortions, his development of supernormal abilities, and his ecstatic states. It is the frank record of a fascinating spiritual journey. Long glossary, 295pp. SYD

_____. **SADGURUNATH MAHARAJ KI JAY**, $15.00. 110 black-and-white and 100 color pictures of Muktananda plus a text selected from Muktananda's 1974 talks in Australia. 216pp. SYD 76

_____. **SATSANG WITH BABA, VOL. I**, $3.95. Questions and answers between Muktananda and Western disciples living in his Indian ashram. The answers are specific and practical and the topics covered include work, marriage, meditation, and much else. 348pp. SYD 74

_____. **SATSANG WITH BABA, VOL. II**, $4.95. More questions and answers from the Ganeshpuri ashram. SYD 76

_____. **SIDDHA MEDITATION**, $3.00. *Siddha Meditation is understanding that everything you see, touch, hear, smell, taste, imagine, think, dream, or in any way experience is made of the same divine consciousness which is your Self.* In this volume Swami Muktananda comments on the Shivasutras and other ancient texts, all of which he feels reveal the essence of siddha meditation. 117pp. SYD 76

_____. **SO'HAM JAPA**, $.35. 31pp. SYD 72

_____. **SONGS OF GOD, GURU, SELF**, $2.25. SYD

_____. **THE SPIRTUAL INSTRUCTIONS OF SWAMI MUKTANANDA**, $1.50. The text of this book is in the form of an intimate letter written by Swami Muktananda to Franklin Jones in 1968 in which he describes the nature and goal of spiritual life, its experiences, and its benefits and also goes into the meditational techniques which he ad-

vocates. It is edited, with an introduction and epilogue by Franklin Jones (now Bubb Free John). 30pp. DHP 74

_____. **SWAMI MUKTANANDA IN AUSTRALIA**, $2.00. A series of lectures given in 1970, each printed with its original introduction by Baba Ram Dass. 152pp. SYD 7

_____. **SWAMI MUKTANANDA PARAMAHANSA**, $1.50. A biographical study written by one of Muktananda's close disciples and edited and revised by other disciples. Glossary, 104pp. SYD 69

MULLER, MAX. **SIX SYSTEMS OF INDIAN PHILOSOPHY**, c$6.00. Professor Mulle was the general editor of the *Sacred Books of the East* Series and was thus responsible for bringing the wisdom of the East into more general recognition in the West. Here he presents a scholarly study of Indian philosophy, with introductory material, a general study of the systems of philosophy in India, and detailed sections on the Vedas, Vedanta, Purva Mimamsa, Samkhya philosophy, yoga philosophy, Nyaya and Vaiseshika philosophy. The scholarship is excellent, but the text is often hard going—especially since this is a translation of the original German version. Index, notes. 510pp. CSS 71

NAKAGAWA, TSUYOSHI. **INDIA: CENTURIES OF YOUTH**, $3.50. A beautiful little travel guide with many color plates and an informative text. 154pp. Kod 73

NARADA BHAKTI SUTRAS

CHINMAYANANDA, SWAMI, tr. **NARADA BHAKTI SUTRA**, c$4.00. A presentation of each sutra, with extensive commentary. Includes the Sanskrit text of each sutra, translations of individual words, and a translation of the whole sutra. As usual, Chinmayananda's translation is excellent and his commentary is enlightening. 197pp. CPT 70

GREENLESS, DUNCAN, tr. **THE GOSPEL OF NARADA**, c$3.00. The complete text, with extensive notes as well as a very informative 180 page general introduction. 834pp. TPH

PRABHAVANANDA, SWAMI, tr. **NARADA'S WAY OF DIVINE LOVE: THE BHAKTI SUTRAS**, c$5.25. One of the world's great manuals on divine love as a means to God-realization. Sri Ramakrishna recommended the path of devotion as taught by Narada as the best and easiest for this age. By his clear translation of each sutra and commentary, illustrated by quotations from scriptures and examples from lives of holy men of many religious traditions, Swami Prabhavananda provides an invaluable aid for spiritual aspirants. Introduction by Christopher Isherwood. 189pp. VdP 71

SHASTRI, HARI PRASAD, tr. **THE NARADA SUTRAS: THE PHILOSOPHY OF LOVE**, $1.70. A full and original commentary by Shastri brings out the meaning of the text in simple language which can be readily understood. He has done a good job. 102pp. ShS 47

TYAGISANANDA, SWAMI, tr. **NARADA BHAKTI SUTRAS**, c$2.75. Each sutra is followed by a word-for-word translation and a sentence expressing the whole thought. A separate section contains extensive notes which discuss the aphorisms and recommended practices. 306pp. SRM 72

NIKHILANANDA, SWAMI. **HINDUISM: ITS MEANING FOR THE LIBERATION OF THE SPIRIT**, c$5.00. Gives the Westerner a complete survey of the beliefs of a Hindu regarding his religion and philosophy. A very clear presentation, based on Vedanta. 189pp. SRM 68

_____. **MAN IN SEARCH OF IMMORTALITY: TESTIMONIALS FROM THE HINDU SCRIPTURES**, c$4.95. Five articles bearing on the immortality of the soul. The scriptures cited (and quoted from) record the experience of the enlightened seers *who see truth directly, as fruit lying in the palm of one's hand can be seen. This experience is not the monopoly of any particular seer, but the heritage of all, irrespective of time, place and creed.* 107pp. RVC 68

NIVEDITA, SISTER. **CRADLE TALES OF HINDUISM**, $2.75. See the Children's Books section.

_____. **FOOTFALLS OF INDIAN HISTORY**, $1.00. An interesting study of some aspects of Indian history from the point of view of their impact on the Indian mind and the character of the Indian people. Sister Nivedita was an English disciple of Swami Vivekananda. 264pp. AdA 56

O'FLAHERTY, WENDY. **HINDU MYTHS**, $2.95. This new selection and translation of seventy-five seminal myths spans the wide range of classical Indian sources, from the serpent-slaying Indra of the Vedas (c. 1200 BC) to the medieval pantheon—the phallic and ascetic Siva, the maternal and bloodthirsty goddess Kali, the mischievous child Krishna, and the many minor gods, demons, rivers, and animals sacred to Hinduism. The traditional themes of life and death are set forth and interwoven with many complex variations which give a kaleidoscopic picture of the development of almost three thousand years of Indian mythology. Ms. O'Flaherty's translations could not be better. Glossary, introduction. 358pp. Pen 75

OMAN, JOHN. **THE MYSTICS, ASCETICS AND SAINTS OF INDIA**, c$13.50. A detailed, scholarly, early twentieth century study of Indian asceticism tracing the tradition through history up to the present. There is also a great deal of scholarly information on Hindu Sadhus and on various spiritual movements. Index, notes. 303pp. OrP 73

ORGAN, TROY. **HINDUISM: ITS HISTORICAL DEVELOPMENT**, $2.95. This is an excellent textbook presentation of Hinduism which traces its historical development and within this context reviews and summarizes the major religious and reform movements. Each of the important individuals and individual movements is dealt with in a clear way nd all the Sanskrit terms are well defined. The early background (up to the time of Sankara's Vedantist, non-dualist movement) is discussed in the greatest depth. There are extensive notes and an excellent chapter-by-chapter bibliography, as well as an index. Recommended to those desiring a readable, not overly detailed academic overview. 425pp. BES 74

OSBORNE, ARTHUR. **THE INCREDIBLE SAI BABA**, $2.50. Sai Baba was a very eccentric Indian saint who died in 1918, but is still worshipped daily by many. He taught neither specific philosophy nor any special means for God realization. He was especially known for the unending miracles he performed. This volume contains his life, teachings, miracles and anecdotes: *I give people what they want in the hope that they will begin to want what I want to give them.* This book discusses the original Sai Baba—not to be confused with the current Indian guru, Sathya Sai Baba. 128pp. Wei 58

PANIKKAR, RAIMUNDO, tr. **MANTRAMANJARI, THE VEDIC EXPERIENCE**, c$25.00. An annotated selection of texts from the **Rig Veda**, from the **Brahmanas** (prayers and rituals of sacrifice), from the **Aranyakas (Forest Treatises** which set forth the spiritual ideals and speculations of those who have renounced the world), and the **Upanishads.** Each of the sections is fully introduced and there is also a general introduction as well as a glossary. Indices, illustrations, 800pp. UCa 76

PARAMANANDA, SWAMI. **SECRET OF RIGHT ACTIVITY**, c$2.75. A modern restatement of the philosophy of karma yoga in practical religious terms written by a monk of the Ramakrishna Order. 84pp. VdC 64

_____. **SELF-MASTERY**, c$2.80. A treatise on how to gain control over our faculties and end internal discord through surrender to the *Supreme Will.* 84pp. VdC 61

PARRINDER, GEOFFREY. **THE INDESTRUCTIBLE SOUL**, $4.25. For over 3000 years much thought has been devoted in India to the idea of the soul or self of man. This is held to be eternal and indestructible. Transmigration into other existences, on earth or elsewhere, follows almost naturally, although the future state is conditioned by karma. This book discusses different Indian teachings about the soul and its destiny, its relationship to God or the absolute, its transmigration, and its final goal of nirvana or bliss. Prof. Parrinder illustrates the different teachings with quotations from many texts. He is the Professor of Comparative Study of Religions at the University of London, has studied Indian beliefs for over forty years, and is the author of countless books on the subject. Index, 116pp. H&R 73

PATANJALI

Patanjali's Yoga Sutras (aphorisms) are not the original exposition of a philosophy, but a work of compilation and reformulation. What he did was to restate yoga philosophy and practice for the man of his own period. But what was his period? And who was he? Hardly anything is known about him. As for the date of the Sutras, the guesses of scholars vary widely, ranging from the fourth century BC to the fourth century AD. *The simplest meaning of the word sutra is thread. A sutra is, so to speak, the bare thread of an exposition, the absolute minimum that is necessary to hold it together. . . . Only essential words are used. . . . There was a good reason for this method. Sutras were composed at a period when there were no books. The entire work had to be memorized and so it had to be expressed as tersely as possible. Patanjali's Sutras, like all others, were intended to be expanded and explained.—* from **How to Know God**. Patanjali's sutras remain the best exposition of raja yoga we have, and they are highly recommended.

ABHEDANANDA, SWAMI, tr. **THE YOGA PSYCHOLOGY**, c$3.95. A transcription of a series of lectures which Swami Abhedananda delivered to sophisticated American audiences in 1924. The material has been carefully edited and all facets of Patanjali's psychological system are fully discussed. 239pp. RVM 67

BAILEY, ALICE. **THE LIGHT OF THE SOUL: ITS SCIENCE AND EFFECT**, $3.50. See the Theosophy section.

BESANT, ANNIE. **AN INTRODUCTION TO YOGA**, c$2.25. A series of lectures designed to prepare students for the study of the Yoga Sutras. 167pp. TPH 08

COSTER, GERALDINE. **YOGA AND WESTERN PSYCHOLOGY**, $2.45. Ms. Coster presents a translation of the Yoga Sutras with commentary, and compares the psychology advanced by Patanjali with modern analytical psychology. A very interesting compendium. Notes, bibliography. 244pp. H&R 72

DASGUPTA, SURENDRANATH. **YOGA AS PHILOSOPHY AND RELIGION**, c$6.75. This volume is an exposition of the philosophical and religious doctrines found in Patanjali's Yoga Sutras, as explained by the commentaries of Vyasa, Vacaspati, Vijnana Bhiksu, and others. It is a comprehensive analysis which assumes that the reader is familiar with the content of the Sutras, with Sanskrit terminology, and with Hindu philosophy. An excellent work for the advanced student. 200pp. MoB nd

DAVIS, ROY EUGENE, tr. **THIS IS REALITY**, $3.95. A new, updated commentary on the eternal wisdom contained within the Yoga Sutras. It presents many illuminating ideas. See the Mysticism section for more on Davis. Glossary, 211pp. CSA 62

ELIADE, MIRCEA. **PATANJALI AND YOGA**, $2.95. This is a well produced survey of the Yoga Sutras and of their subsequent influence. All the major commentaries are cited and quoted from and various Indian theories of yoga are discussed. While Eliade's exposi-

tion is interesting, he seems to miss the heart of what the Sutras attributed to Patanjali express. This is an important, but disappointing, study. Beautifully illustrated. Chronology, annotated bibliography, index. 222pp. ScB 62

MISHRA, RAMMURTI, tr. **YOGA SUTRAS: THE TEXTBOOK OF YOGA PSYCHOLOGY**, $2.95. This is an authoritative recent translation, with thorough interpretation and commentary by Mishra, a respected Sanskrit scholar. He provides both the Sanskrit-transliterated text and the translations as well as a long introduction on the philosophy of yoga, and a glossary. The commentaries are very detailed and incorporate many Sanskrit terms. This is an excellent work for the serious student. 554pp. Dou 63

PRABHAVANANDA, SWAMI and CHRISTOPHER ISHERWOOD, trs. **HOW TO KNOW GOD: THE YOGA APHORISMS OF PATANJALI**, c$2.95/$1.25. This is a beautiful, absorbing translation, and our personal favorite by far. *In this translation we have not only provided a commentary but expanded and paraphrased the aphorisms themselves, so that each one becomes an intelligible statement in the English language. . . . Our commentary is mainly our own work. However we have followed the explanations of the two ancient commentators, Bhoja and Vyasa. We have also quoted frequently from . . . Swami Vivekananda.* Highly recommended. 166pp. NAL 53

TAIMNI, I.K. **THE SCIENCE OF YOGA**, $3.95. Sanskrit text, Roman transliteration, and English translation and extensive commentary. This is a clear, intelligible presentation of the Sutras from the spiritual and philosophical points of view in the light of both ancient and modern thought. This version is very well regarded. Excellent material for study. 461pp. TPH 61

VIVEKANANDA, SWAMI. **RAJA YOGA**, c$3.50/$1.75. A scientific treatment, describing the methods of concentration and psychic development, and the liberation of the soul from the bondage of the body. This small book forms an excellent commentary on the Yoga Sutras, since Vivekananda was probably the most enlightened twentieth century interpreter of them. Glossary, 305pp. RVC 55

WOOD, ERNEST. **PRACTICAL YOGA, ANCIENT AND MODERN**, $2.00. Wood has studied yoga and Sanskrit for over forty-five years. He has made his life's work the interpretation of ancient Indian wisdom to the West. In his presentation of the Sutras he has rearranged the order of the sections to make them more intelligible. His translation is clear and direct and his commentary is very enlightening. Next to **How to Know God**, we feel that this is the most illuminating version for the average reader—the two complement each other quite well. When reading an ancient text in translation it's often good to read more than one version as each translator has his own viewpoint and brings out nuances in the work. 244pp. Wil 48

WOODS, JAMES. **THE YOGA SYSTEM OF PATANJALI**, c$9.00. An extensive philosophical study, including a full translation of the Sutras and many references. This is the most scholarly of any of the translations, and also the most weighty. 424pp. MoB 14

POPLEY, H.A. **THE SACRED KURAL**, $1.50. A translation of portions of the most sacred text of the Tamil people. An introduction and extensive notes are included. Bibliography, index. 174pp. YPH 31

PRABHAVANANDA, SWAMI. **THE ETERNAL COMPANION—BRAHMANANDA, HIS LIFE AND TEACHINGS**, $3.45. Swami Brahmananda was regarded by Sri Ramakrishna as his spiritual son. The teachings given here are taken from diaries and private notes on informal talks. They are simple, direct, and full of practical counsel regarding meditation and the inner life. 301pp. VdP 44

_____. **RELIGION IN PRACTICE**, $2.95. Basic guide for anyone seeking to know the underlying reality of life. Explains the goals and methods to attain them. For persons of every faith. Good annotated bibliography. 253pp. A&U 68

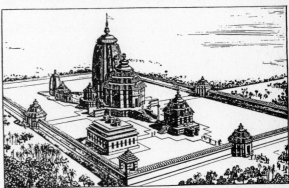

Temple of the Sun, Konarak, Orissa. From Basham's The Wonder That Was India.

_____. **THE SPIRITUAL HERITAGE OF INDIA**, $1.95. Comprehensive history of India's philosophy-religions. Illuminating discussions of the Vedas, Upanishads, **Bhagavad Gita**, Buddhism, Jainism, and India's six systems of thought (e.g., yoga and Vedanta). Includes liberal quotations from scriptures and supplemental writings. Also, presents the lives and ideals of the greatest Indian philosophers. Long bibliography. 361pp. VdP 63

_____, tr. **SWAMI PREMANANDA: TEACHINGS AND REMINISCENCES**, $2.95. Teachings which proceed directly from the heart of this close disciple of Sri Ramakrishna. 157pp. VdP

_____. VEDIC RELIGION AND PHILOSOPHY, c$2.00. A text on the wisdom of the Vedas, the Upanishads, and the Gita, together with a description of the general features of Indian philosophy. 172pp. SRM nd

_____. YOGA AND MYSTICISM, $1.25. Transcriptions of four lectures. 53pp. VdP 68

PRABHAVANANDA, SWAMI and CLIVE JOHNSON. PRAYERS AND MEDITATIONS FROM THE SCRIPTURES OF INDIA, c$3.75. More than 100 selections from the Vedas, the Upanishads, the **Bhagavad Gita** and other ancient and modern sources. Glossary, 136pp. VdP 67

S. RADHAKRISHNAN

Radhakrishnan, distinguished statesman, educator, and philosopher, is the author of countless books on Indian philosophy and he has done excellent translations of many of the sacred texts.

McDERMOTT, ROBERT, ed. **RADHAKRISHNAN**, $3.75. This is an excellent selection of Radhakrishnan's most significant writings. Includes essays on Tagore, Gandhi, and Nehru, selections on Radhakrishnan's personal philosophy, and surveys of major themes in Indian philosophy. McDermott provides extensive explanatory material as well as a fine annotated bibliography and glossary. 344pp. Dut 70

MUNSHI, K.N. and R.R. DIWAKAR, eds. **RADHKRISHNAN READER**, c$11.50. A representative selection of Radhakrishnan's writings, intended to give an idea of his thoughts on philosophy, education, and religion. This is the most comprehensive anthology available. Index, 680pp. BVB 69

RADHAKRISHNAN, S. **THE HINDU VIEW OF LIFE**, $1.45. A collection of four lectures. 92pp. McM 71

_____. INDIAN PHILOSOPHY, c$40.85/set. This two-volume set is Radhakrishnan's magnum opus and, as the title suggests, reviews every aspect of Indian philosophy from the Vedas through the Advaita Vedanta of Shankara and the theism of Ramanuja and the Vaisnava theism in great depth—with extensive citations and quotations from pertinent literature. This is a book that every good library should have, however the treatment of each topic is probably more extensive than most individuals would want. Voluminous notes accompany the text. Index, 1545pp. HuP 29

_____. OUR HERITAGE, $1.60. Dr. Radhakrishnan here examines Indian culture as a whole and shows how this heritage affects the India of today. His main topics include the legacy of Sanskrit, the **Mahabharata** and the **Bhagavad Gita**, Sankara, the Buddha, Ramakrishna and Vivekananda, Gandhi, and Nehru. 156pp. HPB 73

_____. RECOVERY OF FAITH, $1.80. *Our age is still in desperate need of that which religion alone can give.* Dr. Radhakrishnan gives his answer to man's need for a new faith. Examining a wide field of religious thought, he presents the faiths that men have lived by, and shows how, out of these enduring expressions, a faith can be achieved which transcends religious dogma and narrow sectarianism. 187pp. HPB 67

_____. RELIGION AND CULTURE, $1.50. An ecumenical view of the various facets of religion and culture and their application to life in the present-day world. 176pp. HPB 68

RADHAKRISHNAN, S. and CHARLES MOORE. **A SOURCEBOOK IN INDIAN PHILOSOPHY**, $4.95. A scholarly work which begins with the **Rig Veda** and ends with works written in the twentieth century. Includes Radhakrishnan's fine translation of the **Gita**, as well as selections from many lesser known works. The best source book available in English. Excellent bibliography. Highly recommended. 669pp. PuP 57

BHAGWAN SHREE RAJNEESH

Many consider Bhagwan Shree Rajneesh a tantric master. Others see him as a Taoist or Zen master, or even as a Sufi master. Scholars in India have written books comparing his teachings to those of Krishnamurti and Gurdjieff. Each of his disciples claims that he belongs to this school or that tradition that the disciple himself feels the greatest affinity towards. Bhagwan Shree has many doors for one to enter. He is not defined by any one of them. He incorporates them all.—The New Age Journal.

RAJNEESH, BHAGWAN SHREE. **THE BOOK OF THE SECRETS**, c$10.00/each. See the Tantra section.

_____. DIMENSIONS BEYOND THE KNOWN, $4.50. The only collection of discourses in which Bhagwan Rajneesh talks about himself—about his childhood, his rebellious adolescence, his spiritual experiences prior to enlightenment, and the ways in which these experiences affected his subsequent development. As Bhagwan rarely talks about himself, these discourses are the closest thing to his autobiography that will probably ever exist. 190pp. RaF

_____. EMPTY BOAT, c$10.00. Chuang Tzu says: *Such is the perfect man: his boat is empty. Empty of what? Bhagwan asks. Empty of the I. Empty of the ego. Empty of somebody there inside. My whole effort is to make you a nobody. Because unless you become nobody, you cannot be blissful, you cannot be ecstatic, you will go on missing life.* Edited as poetry. 400pp. RaF

_____. HAMMER ON THE ROCK, c$12.00. A remarkable book, first in a series that will record, in words and pictures, the unique experience of being with an enlightened master. Every evening Rajneesh holds darshans for disciples and visitors. *Darshan* literally means seeing but Bhagwan's are not passive sitting-in-the-presence-of-the-master. They are group therapy sessions, primal theatre, an experiential encountering with oneself. In the volumes in this series, the living response of an enlightened master is revealed in its infinite variety. Each disciple encounters his own master in the evening darshans—as each reader will—until each encounters his own uniqueness, his own divinity. Other books in the Darshan series will be **Above All Don't Wobble** and **Nothing to Lose But Your Head**. 450pp. RaF 76

_____. HIDDEN HARMONY, c$10.00. Talks based on **The Fragments of Heraclitus**. Rajneesh says if Heraclitus had been born in India, he would have been known as a Buddha. But because Greek philosphy is based on Aristotelian concepts of logic, he could not be understood. Instead he was known as Heraclitus the Obscure, for he spoke like a poet, reconciling opposites and creating mysterious out of the obvious. Bhagwan brings the poetry of Heraclitus' wisdom to light, reclaiming a part of Western heritage that has been obliterated by exclusive reliance on the rational, and brings us to that point where rational meets irrational, where dualities merge and the hidden harmony of opposites is revealed. 280pp. RaF

_____. I AM THE GATE, $3.95. On the meaning of initiation and discipleship. How Rajneesh works with his disciples, creating situations for their inner transformations. 230pp. RaF

_____. JUST LIKE THAT, c$10.00. For ten days Rajneesh was a Sufi, bringing rare insight to ten chosen Sufi stories. The true tradition of Sufi learning lies in the rapport between master and disciple. These talks, edited as poetry, give the reader an opportunity to experience this intimate transfer, a transfer that is beyond words. Bhagwan says: *Let me repeat the Sufi saying: Simply trust. Do not the petals flutter down just like that?* 450pp. RaF

_____. MEDITATION: THE ART OF ECSTASY, $3.95. The basic text on the teachings and meditation techniques of Rajneesh. The need for meditation techniques that start out from a psycho-therapeutic base is discussed and an extensive description and analysis is given of both traditional techniques and new methods that have been devised by Bhagwan specifically for the new needs of the modern seeker. 224pp. RaF

_____. THE MUSTARD SEED, c$15.00/$7.50. Based on selected texts from the newly discovered Gospels according to Thomas. These talks probe the enigmatic words of the Gospel and give a living explanation to their hidden meanings. Rajneesh not only makes Jesus' words intelligible, but he makes the teaching come to life again. Through Bhagwan, Jesus becomes real, relevant. 500pp. RaF

_____. THE MYSTIC WAY, c$10.00. The spontaneous responses of Rajneesh to more than twenty-five questions about the particular problems facing spiritual seekers in the West. Questions about: female energy, sex energy, love relationships, bringing up children, integrating spiritual seeking and living in the world, the human potential movement, the guru/disciple relationship, and other problems pertinent to those who are living in the world and trying to grow inwardly. 500pp. RaF

_____. NEITHER THIS NOR THAT, c$10.00. In these talks Bhagwan expands and illuminates the sutras of the Taoist master Sesan, the sixth Zen Patriarch. These brief scriptures, called **Verses on the Faith Mind**, are the only words Sesan ever uttered and as such are very powerful. Bhagwan illuminates these words in the light of present-day experience. *We will be talking about Sesan and his words. If you listen attentively suddenly you will feel a release of silence within you. These words are atomic, they are full of energy. Whenever a person who has attained says something, the word becomes a seed, and for millions of years the word will remain a seed . . . and will seek a heart.* 265pp. RaF

_____. ONE OPEN SKY, $3.45. Based on Tilopa's **Song of Mahamudra**, a rare document that is at the heart of tantra. Rajneesh shares with the reader the rich meanings of this miraculous text. Each part is unravelled to expose the intricate threads of paradox which weave the complex web of tantra. Bhagwan has said that the time is ripe now for a tantric explosion in the West. We are faced with a world that will move into either madness or meditation. In this climate Bhagwan speaks on tantra so that we can evolve towards the latter alternative. 250pp. Dut

_____. THE SUPREME DOCTRINE, c$10.00. In this series of discourses on the **Ken** Upanishad Bhagwan talks about Western psychology and its role in the awakening of higher consciousness. The direction in which Western psychology must move now—beyond Freud, Jung, or Reich—is discussed in the light of both Western contemporary thought and the ancient understandings of the East. 450pp. RaF

_____. THE ULTIMATE ALCHEMY, c$10.00/each. Two volumes on the **Atma Pooja** Upanishad. (Worship of the Self.) Most books on the Upanishads are scholarly commentaries about the possible meaning of these ancient scriptures. Bhagwan doesn't comment on them, he responds to them. And he says that he has chosen to repond to the **Atma Pooja** *simply because I have fallen in love with it. Firstly, it is the shortest of the Upanishads. It is just seedlike—potent, pertinent, with much in it. Every word is a seed with infinite possibilities, so you can echo it and re-echo it infinitely. And the more you ponder over it and allow it to enter you, the more new significances will be revealed.* Each volume is 420pp. RaF

_____. UNTIL YOU DIE, c$10.00. *The whole of my effort is to help you move toward the heart, because only through the heart will you be reborn. Nobody can be reborn until he dies. So the whole message of Sufism, Zen, Hassidism—these are all forms of Sufism—is how to die. The whole art of dying is the base. I am teaching you nothing here except that: how to die. That is the whole message of this series of talks: that until you die, nothing is possible.* 250pp. RaF 76

_____. **VEDANTA: SEVEN STEPS TO SAMADHI**, c$10.00. On the **Akshya** _panishad_, an ancient Hindu scripture which outlines a practical and life-affirming path for the spiritual seeker. Because these discourses were given at a meditation camp Bhagwan conducted, alternating with his discussion of the Upanishads is much practical information about meditation techniques. 420pp. RaF

_____. **WHEN THE SHOE FITS**, c$10.00. _When the shoe fits, the foot is forgotten. When the belt fits, the belly is forgotten. When the heart is right, for and against are forgotten._ Bhagwan uses **The Way of Chuang Tzu** by Thomas Merton as the text on which he bases these discourses. _Chuang Tzu is a rare flowering because to become nobody is the most difficult, most impossible, most extraordinary thing in the world. The ordinary mind hankers to be extraordinary. That is part of its ordinariness. The extraordinary starts only when you don't hanker after extraordinariness. Then the journey has started. Then a new seed has sprouted._ Edited as poetry. 400pp. RaF

AMA, SWAMI. LECTURES ON YOGA: EIGHT LESSONS ON YOGA, $3.00. A clear presentation of the following topics: what is yoga, yama and niyama, asanas and their therapeutic value, pranayama, nadhishodhanam, concentration, mind and its analysis, what is meditation, and samadhi. The Sanskrit terms are well defined in the text. 126pp. **am**

_____. **YOGA AND PSYCHOTHERAPY**, c$11.95. See the Consciousness Expansion section.

OGI RAMACHARAKA

These works are generally considered among the clearest and most comprehensive on the subject of Oriental Occult Philosophy ever offered to the Western World. **Fourteen Lessons** _and_ **Advanced Course** _may be read first to afford a basic understanding. However, the Yoga System is scientifically separated into a number of different branches or phases, i.e., Raja Yoga is mental development, Gnani Yoga is the development of intellect and wisdom, Hatha Yoga is physical development and well-being, Bhakti Yoga is spiritual development and Karma Yoga is development through deeds and work. The term Yoga is neither mystical nor mysterious in any sense. It is derived from the Sanskrit root_ yug, _literally meaning to_ yoke or unite _the separate, innate forces of Man._ Yogi Ramacharaka wrote under at least two additional names: William Atkinson and Bhikshu.

TKINSON, WILLIAM. MIND POWER, $6.00. This is Ramacharaka's most comprehensive **work** on the subject—it incorporates the material in **Secret of Mental Magic** and **Mental Fascination**. The material is clearly stated and very practical. This is one of his most popular books. 441pp. YPS

_____. **PRACTICAL MENTAL INFLUENCE AND MENTAL FASCINATION**, **1**.00. 96pp. YPS

_____. **PRACTICAL MIND READING**, $1.00. A course of lessons on thought transference, telepathy, mental currents, mental rapport, etc. 97pp. YPS

_____. **PRACTICAL PSYCHOMANCY AND CRYSTAL GAZING**, $1.00. 93pp. **PS**

_____. **REINCARNATION AND THE LAW OF KARMA**, c$4.50. See the Reincarnation and Karma section.

HIKSHU. BHAKTI YOGA, c$4.00. _Bhakti Yoga is that branch or form of the Yogi Philosophy specially suited to those whose religious nature is largely developed and who prefer to grow into an understanding and union with the Absolute by the power of Love—by the inspiration that comes from the love of some conception of God and some form of worship that may accompany that conception of Deity._ This is a series of twelve detailed lessons in every aspect of the yoga. 148pp. YPS

_____. **KARMA YOGA**, c$5.00. A detailed treatise in the form of a series of lessons, geared toward the general reader. 138pp. YPS 28

RAMACHARAKA, YOGI. ADVANCED COURSE IN YOGI PHILOSOPHY AND ORIENTAL OCCULTISM, c$5.50/$3.10. Lessons include: an extensive analysis of **Light on the Path**; a discussion of the branches of yoga; dharma, the yoga philosophy of ethics or right action; and a presentation of the higher yogic scientific and metaphysical principles. 337pp. YPS

_____. **FOURTEEN LESSONS IN YOGA PHILOSOPHY**, c$5.50/$3.10. Lessons include: the human aura, thought dynamics, clairvoyance, human magnetism, occult therapeutics, the astral world, spiritual cause and effect, and death and the afterlife. YPS

_____. **HATHA YOGA**, c$5.50. Hatha yoga is the yoga of physical well-being. Lessons include: prana absorption from food, yogi breathing, breathing exercises, pranic exercises, rules for relaxation, yogi physical exercises, the yogi bath, solar energy, et al. YPS

_____. **LESSONS IN GNANI YOGA**, c$5.50/$3.10. _What is known as_ Gnani Yoga _deals with the scientific and intellectual knowing of the great questions regarding Life and what lies back of Life—the Riddle of the Universe._ YPS

_____. **THE LIFE BEYOND DEATH**, c$5.50. See the Reincarnation and Karma section.

_____. **THE PHILOSOPHIES AND RELIGIONS OF INDIA**, c$5.50. The discussion is from the occult point of view. 359pp. YPS

_____. **PRACTICAL WATER CURE**, $1.00. See the Healing section.

_____. **RAJA YOGA**, c$5.50/$3.10. Raja yoga is the yoga method devoted to mental development. This book presents a series of lessons for development of mental concentration and development. The lessons include the following: the I, the ego's mental tools, the expansion of the self, mental control, cultivation of attention and of perception, and sub-consciousing. 248pp. YPS

_____. **SCIENCE OF BREATH**, c$3.25/$1.95. A complete manual of the Oriental breathing philosophy of physical, mental, psychic and spiritual development. 88pp. YPS 04

_____. **THE SCIENCE OF PSYCHIC HEALING**, c$5.50/$2.70. See the Healing section.

SRI RAMAKRISHNA

Sri Ramakrishna (1836–1886) devoted his life to an intense career of experimentation in the field of religious experience: he had a vision of Kali, an aspect of God worshipped by Hindus as the Divine Mother of the Universe; he ventured into other branches of Hinduism and experienced Sri Rama, Sri Krishna, and the Tantras, gaining insight into the non-dualism of Advaita Vedanta as expounded by Sankara. He never learned to read or write and his beliefs are known to us through **The Gospel**, notes taken by M., one of his disciples. He preached the message set down in the **Rig Veda**: _Truth is One but the Wise have given it different names_, a gospel of truly universal love and universal understanding of all religions. This _madman of God_ spent almost half his life in a state of religious ecstasy and each experience brought him new awareness of the absolute God. As his disciple quoted him: _I have practiced all religions—Hinduism, Islam, Christianity—and I have also followed the paths of the various sects of Hinduism . . . and I have found that it is the same God toward whom all are turned, along different roads. . . . You have to pass along these various roads in the practice of each religion once. Everywhere I see men who dispute in the name of religion. . . . But they do not stop to think that he who is called Krishna is also called Siva, and that he is also called Primal Force or Jesus or Allah. . . . The substance is One under different names, and each man is looking for the same substance._

ABHEDANANDA, SWAMI. SAYINGS OF SRI RAMAKRISHNA, c$2.25. 121pp. RVM 68

ADVAITA ASHRAMA. THE LIFE OF SRI RAMAKRISHNA, c$4.95. A comprehensive biography compiled from various sources by monks of the Ramakrishna Order. 511pp. AdA 24

_____. **TEACHINGS OF SRI RAMAKRISHNA**, $1.95. An excellent compilation, arranged topically and well edited. This is the most systematic and condensed presentation of Ramakrishna's teaching in his own words. 344pp. AdA nd

ISHERWOOD, CHRISTOPHER. RAMAKRISHNA AND HIS DISCIPLES, $4.95. An engrossing, very well written account. An excellent presentation of Indian thought and practice and the best introduction to Ramakrishna. Bibliography, photographs. Recommended. 432pp. S&S 64

M. THE GOSPEL OF SRI RAMAKRISHNA, c$12.95. M., one of the intimate disciples of Sri Ramakrishna, recorded his conversations with his disciples, devotees and visitors. M. was present during all of the conversations in the main body of the book and received first-hand reports of the ones in the appendix. He has produced a unique book which relates his master's teaching in detail, as well as the small happenings of each day—all with complete fidelity. Swami Nikhilananda has made a literal translation. He has purposely retained the repetitions of teachings and parables. Nikhilananda also includes a lengthy introduction in which he acquaints the reader with the Master's life, the systems of Indian religious thought intimately connected with his teaching, people who came into contact with him, and much else. The book is fully indexed and contains an extensive glossary. 1063pp. RVC 42

_____. **THE GOSPEL OF SRI RAMAKRISHNA**, c$5.00/abridged. The same fine translation, but abridged by one third. The continuity and completeness of the teachings remain unaffected, only the repetitions and unfamiliar references have been eliminated, and Nikhilananda has retained his excellent introduction and glossary. 615pp. RVC 42

NIKHILANANDA, SWAMI. **HOLY MOTHER—BEING THE LIFE OF SRI SARADA DEVI, WIFE OF SRI RAMAKRISHNA**, c$4.50. The Holy Mother came to Ramakrishna when she was five and later lived with him for fourteen years. He trained her for her future role as his spiritual successor. To her disciples she was mother and teacher, and also the embodiment of divinity. This book may be regarded as a companion volume to Sri Ramakrishna's **Gospel**. 334pp. RVC 62

RAMAKRISHNA, SRI. **TALES AND PARABLES OF SRI RAMAKRISHNA**, c$3.50. A delightful, exhaustive collection. Includes a long introduction on Ramakrishna's life and teaching. 316pp. SRM 43

RAY, IRENE and MALLIKA GUPTA. **TALES FROM RAMAKRISHNA**, $1.50. See the Children's Books section.

SARADANANDA, SWAMI. **RAMAKRISHNA: THE GREAT MASTER**, c$13.25. Interpretative account of Sri Ramakrishna's life, spiritual disciplines, and teachings, closely analyzed by one of his intimate disciples. Sourcebook for all other biographies. Fully indexed, glossary. 960pp. VdP

STARK, CLAUDE. **GOD OF ALL**, c$12.00. Subtitled *Sri Ramakrishna's Approach to Religious Plurality*, this is a detailed study of Ramakrishna's spiritual experiences (his *verification of God*) in different religious traditions, his role as a spiritual teacher, and the role of his major disciples. Stark provides an abundance of detailed footnotes (about one per page) which take up about one third of the text, as well as many quotations and a 17pp bibliography. Index, 253pp. Sta 74

YOGESHANANDA, SWAMI. **THE VISIONS OF SRI RAMAKRISHNA**, c$2.25. *Swami Yogeshananda has carefully, conscientiously, collected the records of Sri Ramakrishna's transcendental experiences that have heretofore lain scattered throughout the histories of his life, and presented all that are available—from the most profound to the seemingly slight. The result is a glowing, indeed dazzling, display.*—from the foreward. Index, 150pp. SRM 73

RAMANA MAHARSHI

Ramana Maharshi was born in 1879. In his seventeenth year he attained enlightenment through a remarkable experience. He underwent the death of his physical body while remaining in full consciousness. Following this transformation he left his home and was drawn to the sacred hill of Arunachala. He never left it. In the ashram which soon formed around him he taught the purest form of Advaita Vedanta (non-dualism) through the discipline of self-inquiry.

JONES, FRANKLIN, ed. **THE HEART OF THE RIBHU GITA, AS TAUGHT BY RAMANA MAHARSHI**, $1.75. The **Ribhu Gita** is a legendary mystical text which is said to represent the teaching given to the sage Ribhu by God in the form of the Lord Shiva. The texts given here are selected verses which represent a summation of its central teaching. Illustration, 34pp. DHP 73

MUDALIAR, A. DEVARAJA. **DAY BY DAY WITH BHAGAVAN**, c$3.75. A record of Maharshi's talks from the author's diary. 405pp. SRT 68

NARASIMHA, B.V. **SELF REALIZATION**, $2.05. A biographical study, which emphasizes Maharshi's teachings and includes quotations from his discourses. 271pp. SRT 68

OSBORNE, ARTHUR, ed. **THE COLLECTED WORKS OF RAMANA MAHARSHI**, $3.00. This is a collection of all of Maharshi's extant written works and includes his translation of classic texts including a number of Shankara's writings and a portion of the **Gita**. Glossary, 188pp. Wei 59

_____. **RAMANA MAHARSHI AND THE PATH OF SELF KNOWLEDGE**, $3.95. The most comprehensive and readable account of Maharshi's life and teachings. Glossary, 207pp. Wei 56

_____, ed. **THE TEACHINGS OF RAMANA MAHARSHI**, $3.95. Contains many actual conversations with those who sought Maharshi's spiritual guidance. They cover the whole religious and spiritual field from basic theories about God and the nature of man to advice about the conduct of our daily lives. Expressed in the form of questions and answers. The material is well arranged by subject and there are helpful editorial comments. 195pp. Wei 62

RAMANA MAHARSHI. **MAHARSHI'S GOSPEL**, $1.00. A series of topically arranged questions and answers on a variety of subjects related to the spiritual quest. The interchange is between Maharshi and some of his devotees. 92pp. SRT 69

SADHU, MOUNI. **IN DAYS OF GREAT PEACE**, $2.00. See the Meditation secti

SARASWATI, SWAMI, tr. **TALKS WITH RAMANA MAHARSHI**, c$4.50. An extens collection of questions an answers from 1935—39. 655pp. SRT 58

THE SPIRITUAL TEACHING OF RAMANA MAHARSHI, $2.95. Collection of practi answers to often asked questions. Topics include *Who Am I?*, *Spiritual Instruction*, a *Maharshi's Gospel*. Very clear communications. Introduction by Carl Jung. 125pp. ShP

RAMANUJAN, A.K., tr. **SPEAKING OF SIVA**, $2.25. A collection of lyric expressio of love for Siva written in the tenth century. Long introduction and notes. 199pp. Pen

RAMAYANA

The **Ramayana** is one of the two great Indian epic poems. It is estimated have been composed by the sage Valmiki about the fourth century BC. *may sound hyperbolic, but I am prepared to state that almost every indiv ual among the five hundred millions living in India is aware of the story the Ramayana in some measure or another. Everyone of whatever age, o look, education, or station in life knows the essential part of the epic a adores the main figures in it—Rama and Sita. Every child is told the story bedtime. Some study it as part of a religious experience, going over a certa number of stanzas each day, reading and rereading the book several times a lifetime. The Ramayana pervades our cultural life in one form or anoth at all times, it may be as a scholarly discourse at a public hall, a traditior story-teller's narrative in an open space, or a play or dance-drama on sta . . . . Everyone knows the story but loves to listen to it again. One accep this work at different levels; as a mere tale with impressive characters; as masterpiece of literary composition; or even as a scripture. As one's und standing develops, one discerns subtler meanings; the symbolism becom more defined and relevant to the day-to-day life. The Ramayana in the fu est sense of the term could be called a book of perennial philosophy.*—R. Narayan.

BAPU. **RAMAYANA: THE STORY OF RAMA**, $3.50. See the Children's Books sectio

BHOOTHALINGAM, M. **CHILDREN'S RAMAYANA**, c$1.00. See the Children's Boo section.

BUCK, WILLIAM, tr. **RAMAYANA**, c$14.95. A well written one volume retelling of t major episodes. Illustrations, 416pp. UCa 76

CHINMAYANANDA, SWAMI and KUMARI NAIK. **BALA RAMAYANAM**, c$7.00. S the Children's Books section.

COLLIS, MAURICE. **QUEST FOR SITA**, $1.95. This is a wonderful, novelistic retelli of the central section of the **Ramayana**. If we had to choose just one book to introduc friend to the **Ramayana** it would be this one. Collis has chosen the most exciting episod of the tale and has recreated them in an engrossing fashion. Accompanying the text are series of extraordinary line drawings of some of the main characters. 162pp. Put

DUTT, ROMESH, tr. **THE RAMAYANA AND THE MAHABHARATA**, $2.95. A ve condensed poetic version of the epics. 333pp. Dut 10

GAER, JOSEPH. **THE ADVENTURES OF RAMA**, c$4.95. See the Children's Boo section.

GITA PRESS. **SRIMAD VALMIKI RAMAYANA**, c$10.80/set. This two volume set a pears to be a complete translation of the **Ramayana**, including the Sanskrit text—althou it does not say anywhere whether it is a full translation or not. The books themselves a bound about as poorly as any Indian books we have ever seen, but the translation do seem to be adequate. If you are interested in the full **Ramayana** and do not want to sper much money this is the set for you. It even includes a number of full page color plat and *procedure of reading the full Valmiki-Ramayana in nine days*. 1370pp. Git 69

GRIFFITH, RALPH T.H. **RAMAYAN OF VALMIKI**, c$11.50. A translation into rhymi octo-syllabic couplets. Griffith wrote in the last half of the nineteenth century and is be known for his translations of the Vedic hymns. To say that this translation is dated is speak kindly of it. It's interesting as a document of the times, but it is hardly one that w would choose to read. Notes, index. 590pp. CSS 1875

KHAN, BENJAMIN. **THE CONCEPT OF DHARMA IN VALMIKI RAMAYANA**, c$9.0 *This study is calculated to show to the present generation how in this age of seethin doubts we may still draw inspiration from that ancient epic and how most of the problem that are baffling modern society can be solved by understanding and following the pr cepts held out by it. It also shows how the Western Ethics compare with the ancient ethic notions of the* **Ramayana**—*from the introduction*. Notes, bibliography, index. 287p MuM 65

NARAYAN, R.K. **THE RAMAYANA—A SHORTENED MODERN PROSE VERSIO OF THE INDIAN EPIC**, c$7.95. Narayan is considered India's leading novelist in Englis His **Ramayana** was inspired by a Tamil version written by an eleventh century poet calle Kamban. It is less a translation than a new retelling, in terms that will help the mode reader to appreciate its rich lore. Introductions, illustrations. 173pp. Vik 72

ama and the stag Maricha. From a bas-relief at Angkor. Drawing by Mlle Sappho Marchal, from ackin's *Asiatic Mythology*.

AJAGOPALACHARI, C. **RAMAYANA**, c$4.00/$2.00. Translation by Rajagopalachari f a Tamil version of the **Ramayana** done by him previously. This is probably the best inxpensive summary of this wondrous epic available. Glossary, 320pp.

HASTRI, HARI PRASAD. **THE RAMAYANA OF VALMIKI**, c$37.95/set. The most adable, complete edition available in English. Recommended for all who wish to get the ll flavor of the epic. Three volumes, 1797pp. ShS 62

AMDAS, SWAMI. **DIVINE LIFE**, $1.50. BBU 60

_____. **IN QUEST OF GOD**, $1.50. Swami Ramdas was a God-intoxicated folower of Ram who first wandered all over India in a frenzy with the Ram Mantra on his ps and then finally founded an ashram to guide and serve mankind in order to awaken to the awareness of God. His writings come from the depths of his soul and therefore o straight to the heart. He is especially loved by Sufis. This is his own narrative of his uest for enlightenment and his renouncement of the wordly life. 167pp. BBU 61

_____. **IN THE VISION OF GOD**, $1.50/each. *By the command of the almighty ord, Ramdas, His child, undertakes the task of continuing the story of his experiences rom the time and place where he broke off at the end of his first book* **In Quest of God.** *he narrative of* **In Quest of God** *extends over to one year after the great change came pon him. The purpose of the present book is to draw further the thread of the same narative, and it contains an account of his later experiences in the course of nine years that ave elapsed.*—from the preamble. Glossary, two volumes, about 270pp each. BBU 63

_____. **THE PATHLESS PATH**, $1.00. Helpful hints for aspirants. Topics include antra, meditation, samadhi, the divine name. Some of his aphorisms are jewels. The folowing is an example: *Mind is only a cloud that hides the sun of Truth. Man is, in fact, od playing the fool. When he chooses, He liberates Himself.* BBU 64

_____. **RAMDAS SPEAKS, VOLS. I–V**, $1.50/each. All the speeches and talks iven by Swami Ramdas, including answers to questions, during his world tour in 1954 nd 1955 are published in these volumes. BBU 57

_____. **STORIES AS TOLD BY SWAMI RAMDAS**, $1.75. A collection of 108 tories which are a source of instruction and enlightenment to the spiritual aspirant. 95pp. BBU 62

_____. **WORLD IS GOD**, $1.00. A chronicle of Ramdas' impressions during a ix month world tour. All the individuals he met are itemized and his descriptions are ivid. Also includes a number of his discourses. Glossary, 224pp. BBU 67

ANGANATHANANDA, SWAMI. **ETERNAL VALUES FOR A CHANGING SOCIETY**, 19.15. An excellent collection of lectures and writings. They deal with a wide variety f subjects—cultural and spiritual, scientific and philosophical, educational and biographal, and ethical and socio-political. But they all bear on the one dominant theme of man the modern age, his growth, development and fulfillment. This is a new edition of this ell known work. 884pp. BBU 71

ENOU, LOUIS. **RELIGIONS OF ANCIENT INDIA**, $1.95. M. Renou is Professor of anskrit and Indian Literature at the Sorbonne. This is a very concise discussion of the arly religious movements in India. The first two chapters are devoted to the Vedic India nd this section is especially valuable since there is so little written about the Vedas that suitable for the general reader. This material is followed by chapters on early Hinduism nd Jainism. The emphasis throughout is on an understanding of the major texts and of he mythology. Index, 147pp. ScB 53

EYMOND, LIZELLE. **MY LIFE WITH A BRAHMIN FAMILY**, $1.75. A firsthand reort. 202pp. Pen 57

_____. **SHAKTI**, $5.00. A moving description of the very nature of Shakti— a oncept at the heart of the Hindu tradition. It is, Ms. Reymond says, the active and concious force of God, the glory of the absolute; Shakti is the presence, invisible and con-

stant, which sustains the world, linking form and name. It is the strength and fullness of the living silence, where the whirlwind will be born—the whirlwind from which the sacred sound issues forth: *In the beginning was the Word, and the Word was with God, and the Word was God.* This is the first book to analyze Shakti and to speak of it in practical terms. Illustrated with Tantric drawings by Madhur Jaffrey. 64pp. RaH 74

_____. **TO LIVE WITHIN**, $1.75. The story of the five years Ms. Reymond spent in a Himalayan hermitage studying under a spiritual master, Shri Anirvan. A clear, beautiful account, written especially for the Westerner. The second half is devoted to the master's words. He discusses the path, consciousness, awakening, life-in-death. Recommended. 271pp. Pen 69

RIEPE, DALE. **THE NATURALISTIC TRADITION IN INDIAN THOUGHT**, c$9.35. This is a detailed study of a little explored area. Most books on Indian philosophy concentrate on the mystical and idealistic aspects of the Indian traditions. This is the only volume that we know of that is solely devoted to Indian early naturalistic tendencies. The Hindu, Jaina, and Buddhist schools are all included in this study. Notes, glossary, bibliography, index. 319pp. UWa 61

ROOF, SIMONS. **JOURNEYS ON THE RAZOR-EDGED PATH**, c$4.00. An attempt to reveal the changes in consciousness which occur in the quest for God. A first-person account of time Roof spent in India, replete with fables, parables and short stories. See the Mysticism section for more of his work. 204pp. Cro 59

ROY, DILIP and INDIRA DEVI. **PILGRIMS OF THE STARS**, $3.25. The authors are disciples of Sri Aurobindo and noted artists and spiritual leaders. Their respective autobiographies are presented here, including many vivid reminiscences of Tagore, Gandhi, Sri Aurobindo, Ramana Maharshi, Swami Ramdas, and others. Their inner experiences are emphasized in this fascinating account. This book resembles much of the material in **Autobiography of a Yogi**, and one gets the same feeling for India and its spiritual leaders. 362pp. Del 73

RYDER, ARTHUR, tr. **THE PANCHATANTRA**, $3.45. See the Fairy Tales section.

SAKSENA, SHRI KRISHNA. **ESSAYS ON INDIAN PHILOSOPHY**, $4.50. A varied collection, designed to clarify prevailing misconceptions. 127pp. UHa 70

SANSKRIT

APTE, V.S. **STUDENT'S ENGLISH-SANSKRIT DICTIONARY**, c$10.15. Apte's dictionaries are generally considered the best reasonably-priced volumes available. 501pp. MoB 20

_____. **STUDENT'S SANSKRIT-ENGLISH DICTIONARY**, c$7.50. A comprehensive compilation which covers virtually every discipline and field of study. 664pp. Mob 1890

BARBORKA, GEOFFREY. **GLOSSARY OF SANSKRIT TERMS**, $1.25. With a pronunciation key. 76pp. PoL 72

BLUE MOUNT CENTER OF MEDITATION. **A GLOSSARY OF SANSKRIT**, $2.00. A glossary of the terms that are most commonly found in the spiritual traditions of India. A clear presentation of the original Sanskrit is included, along with Romanization. There's also a bit of information on the Sanskrit alphabet. The explanations are clear. 24pp. BMC 70

EDGERTON, FRANKLIN. **BUDDHIST HYBRID SANSKRIT GRAMMAR AND DICTIONARY**, c$50.65/set. See the Buddhism section.

GONDA, JOHN. **A CONCISE ELEMENTARY GRAMMAR OF THE SANSKRIT LANGUAGE**, c$9.45. This is a very good grammar, translated and amended by Gordon Ford. The primary objective of the author was to make it possible for students to acquire a good measure of command over the Sanskrit language in as short a time as possible, either in the classroom or privately. With this in mind, they have provided twenty translation exercises and thirteen Sanskrit readings, together with a glossary of all words used. The Sanskrit is all transliterated. 152pp. UAl 66

KALE, M.R. **A HIGHER SANSKRIT GRAMMAR**, c$5.40. *The present Grammar has been prepared with a view to meet the growing wants of the Indian University students. The University examiners have been, of late, evincing a desire to exact a more thorough knowledge of the obscurer and therefore more difficult parts of Sanskrit Grammar, than was required formerly.* Mr. Kale has based his work on the style and format of the classical Sanskrit literature and his text includes the following special features: feminine bases, gender, indeclinables, an extensive chapter on the conjugation of verbs, and chapters on syntax and prosody. He has relied on many of the older works, and has tried to incorporate the best features of each in an attempt to present as complete a grammar as possible. 160pp. MoB 1894

LANMAN, CHARLES. **A SANSKRIT READER**, c$20.15. *In making my selections from the various Sanskrit writings, I have had two practical aims in view: first, to provide abundant material for thorough drill in the language of the classical period, and secondly, to furnish a brief introduction to the works of the Vedic period, Mantra, Brahmana, and Sutra. There is also a complete vocabulary which is more than a mere list of the actually occurring Sanskrit words with their English equivalents. Rather it aims at teaching the student how to trace every word back to its root and to trace every signification back to the radical idea. The words in the vocabulary are Romanized. There is also a long section of page-by-page textual notes.* This is generally considered one of the best readers available. 421pp. HUP 1894

MAC DONNELL, ARTHUR. **A PRACTICAL SANSKRIT DICTIONARY**, c$24.90. A well printed, clearly presented work, with transliteration, accentuation, and etymological analysis throughout. Excellent definitions. Oversize, 392pp. Oxf 24

_____. SANSKRIT GRAMMAR FOR STUDENTS, c$12.10. This has been considered the definitive introductory grammar for generations. All the usual features are included and the whole work is extremely well organized. Includes verb lists, information on Vedic grammar, and indices. 282pp. Oxf 27

MONIER-WILLIAMS, M. ENGLISH-SANSKRIT DICTIONARY, c$18.00. The most complete available. 872pp. MoB

_____. A SANSKRIT-ENGLISH DICTIONARY, c$45.00. The recommended dictionary for the serious scholar. 1370pp. MoB 1899

PERRY, EDWARD. A SANSKRIT PRIMER, c$11.20. *The Primer can be finished by earnest students in sixteen or seventeen weeks, reckoning three lessons per week, with here and there an hour for review. After that Lanman's* Sanskrit Reader, *an introduction to which this work is partly intended to be, should be taken up. Students are strongly recommended to provide themselves with Whitney's* Sanskrit Grammar *at the outset.* All the usual basic features are included and exercises follow each lesson. A Romanized Sanskrit-English glossary is included. 240pp. Col 36

SIVANANDA, SWAMI. YOGA VEDANTA DICTIONARY, c$3.00. This work contains technical terms pertaining to yoga and Vedanta systems of philosophy and therefore the meanings given are explicitly meant to help the spiritual aspirant to understand the yogic and Vedantic texts in which these terms occur. Includes a pronunciation guide. The Sanskrit words are given only in their transliterated form. 190pp. MoB 73

TYBERG, JUDITH. FIRST LESSONS IN SANSKRIT GRAMMAR AND READING, $4.50. A simplified yet comprehensive and inspiring text designed by a disciple of Sri Aurobindo for those who wish to delve into the ancient scriptures of India. Includes many verses from the Bhagavad Gita and Upanishads. Highly recommended. 240pp. EWC 64

_____. LANGUAGE OF THE GODS, c$6.50. Contains the interpretation of some 2000 Sanskrit spiritual, philosophical, and religious terms. A stress has been given to the verb roots of the words, they being the essential carriers of the meaning of the words as originating in the spiritual element of the universe. Designed for students who would like to become familiar with the meaning and symbolic truths contained in Sanskrit words. Highly recommended. 254+pp. EWC 70

USHA, BRAHMACHARINI. A RAMAKRISHNA-VEDANTA WORDBOOK, $1.35. *Six hundred terms and proper names most important in the vocabulary of today's student of Vedanta, defined and pronunciation indicated.* 87pp. VdP 62

WHITNEY, WILLIAM. SANSKRIT GRAMMAR, c$20.15. This is universally considered the definitive grammar. Every possible aspect of the subject is covered in depth and the instructional material is fairly clear—although the presentation is dated. Indices, 571pp. HuP 1889

SARASWATI, SWAMI. MEDITATIONS FROM THE TANTRAS, c$12.00. See the Meditation section. 314pp. Bih 74

SARMA, D.S. ESSENCE OF HINDUISM, $1.15. A concise survey of some of the major elements of the Hindu faith divided into the following general topics: Hindu scriptures, Hindu rituals and myths, Hindu ethics, Hindu theism, and Hindu philosophy. 121pp. BBU 71

_____. HINDUISM THROUGH THE AGES, c$3.00. Sarma begins with a general survey of Hinduism. The bulk of the book is devoted to late nineteenth· twentieth century individuals and movements. Included are separate chapters on each of the following: Ram Mohun Roy and the Brahmo Samaj, Ranade and the Prarthana Samaj, Swami Dayananda and the Arya Samaj, Tilak, Annie Besant and the Theosophical Society, Sri Ramakrishna, Swami Vivekananda, Tagore, Gandhi, Sri Aurobindo, Ramana Maharshi, and Radhakrishnan. 312pp. BBU 56

SATHYA SAI BABA

A very popular present-day guru who purports to be the reincarnation of the original Sai Baba, perhaps India's most loved saint. To some he is thought of as a god, to others he is a siddha (a man who performs miracles, but has little real power or spiritual distinction). Thousands follow him and his miracles are legendary.

MURPHET, HOWARD. SAI BABA, MAN OF MIRACLES, c$6.50. This is a journalistic survey which focuses on the miracles Sai Baba has performed since childhood. Many case studies are included. The account is entirely uncritical. Index, 211pp. Wei 73

SANDWEISS, SAMUEL. SAI BABA: THE HOLY MAN AND THE PSYCHIATRIST, $4.25. Sandweiss is an American psychiatrist who became dissatisfied with traditional therapeutic techniques and journeyed to India to see what he could learn from the approach of the Indian gurus. While there he became deeply involved with Sathya Sai Baba. *This book is an attempt to describe my direct observation and personal experience of some of these powers. It is the outcome of a soul's struggle to comprehend phenomena in which the West does not generally believe. I have tried to prepare the Western reader for the alien territory which he will encounter here and to relate what I observed to psychiatric concepts with which most of us are at least somewhat familiar. ... Who is Sai Baba? If his powers are genuine, how can he lead one deeper into the innermost mysteries of our existence? These were the basic questions with which I started my search. ... I invite you*

to join my journey toward this holy man ... to explore an exciting and inspiratio realm of human possibility through this enigmatic figure. This is a very personal accou The second half of the book is devoted to a reproduction, from Sathya Sai's writings a speeches, of key passages for an exploration of his teachings. Many color photographs a included. Glossary, 240pp. BDP 75

SATHYA SAI BABA. DHARMA VAHINI, $1.75. Teachings on morality. SSS nd

_____. DHYANA VAHINI, $2.25. Translation of a series of discourses on medi tion. 76pp. SSS nd

_____. GEETHA VAHINI, $2.00. Teachings of the Bhagavad Gita. SSS nd

_____. JNANA VAHINI, $1.75. Teachings on wisdom. SSS nd

_____. PREMA VAHINI, $2.25. Transcription of a series of discourses on bhak yoga or *inner peace through love,* as Sathya Sai phrases it. 97pp. SSS 70

_____. SATHYA SAI SPEAKS, VOL. I—VII. Verbatim transcriptions of discourse I (1956–60), $2.95; II (1960–62), $3.60; III (1963–64), $3.60; IV (1964–65), $4.5 V (1965-67), $4.50; VI (1967–68), $4.50; VII (1968–71), $4.95.

_____. SATHYAM SHIVAM SUNDARAM, PARTS 1–3. Sathya Sai's autobio raphy, in three parts. Part 1 covers the period from his birth to 1926, $3.60; Part 2, t years 1926–61, $3.60; Part 3, the years 1961–72, $3.95.

_____. SUMMER SHOWERS IN BRINDAVAN. Each summer Sathya Sai invit hundreds of high school students from all over India to Brindavan and has educators i struct them in matters relating to morality, spiritual living, and service to others. He al gives frequent discourses. Two sets of summer discourses have been transcribed. 197 $4.50; and 1973, $3.60.

_____. UPANISHAD VAHINI, $1.50. Spiritual discipline. SSS nd

SEN, K.M. HINDUISM, $2.95. A good introduction to the nature and functions of Hir duism designed for those who have no previous knowledge of the subject. Includes ex tracts from the scriptures. Recommended. 153pp. Pen 61

SERRANO, MIGUEL. THE SERPENT OF PARADISE, $2.95. A very readable accour of Serrano's pilgrimage through India. He discusses the people, holy places and saints tha he encountered and heard of, and reveals personal reactions. 184pp. H&R 72

SHANKARANARAYANAN, S. SRI CHAKRA, c$4.25. This is an obscure work based a least in part on the teachings of Sri Aurobindo. Shankaranarayanan discusses the tru meaning of the nine chakras that make up the *Sri Chakra.* He also includes chapters on S *Chakra and the Mantra, Sri Chakra and the Guru, Sri Chakra and the Human Body,* an on outer and inner worship. Many illustrations, notes. 123pp. SAA 73

SHARMA, CHANDRADHAR. A CRITICAL SURVEY OF INDIAN PHILOSOPHY c$6.00. An important treatise on the different systems of Indian philosophy based o original sources. Each system, from the Vedas to Sri Aurobindo, is analyzed in depth an Sharma has quoted from the original sources on almost all fundamental points to enabl the reader to compare the interpretations with the texts. Fully indexed, with an extensiv topical bibliography. 415pp. MoB 73

SHASTRI, HARI PRASAD. ASHTAVAKRA GITA, $1.75. 68pp. ShS 61

_____. AVADHUT GITA, $1.25. *The word Gita means a song. The Indian holy scriptures were written in songs, and each was attributed to a great sage, or to an Incarna tion of God, called an Avatara. ... The Avadhut Gita is a special classic which is mean for the use of those advanced students of Indian metaphysics who have learned self-contro to an appreciable extent. ... It is for those who practise detachment in daily life, an are eager to realise God at any cost.* —from the introduction. 40pp. ShS 68

_____. THE HEART OF THE EASTERN MYSTICAL TEACHINGS, $1.70. A account of the life of a modern Mahatma, Shri Dada of Aligarh. In dialogues with pupil he expounds his teaching in different ways, appropriate to their understanding. Glossary 320pp. ShS 48

_____. THE WORLD WITHIN THE MIND, $1.60. Extracts translated from the Indian classic, Yoga Vasishtha, a work of unusual charm. Both philosophical and practica teachings are given by the sage Vasishtha to his pupil Rama. 142pp.

_____. YOGA, c$.95. Shastri came from a long line of Brahmin scholars and wa well versed in Sanskrit and in the classical philosophy of India, as well as in the Chinese Japanese and Persian literatures. This is an excellent treatise on the philosophy and prac tice of yoga and includes illustrative passages from yoga literature, biographical sketche of three yogis and a glossary. Recommended as a good, clearly written overview. 96pp. Foy 57

SHASTRI, J.L., ed. THE LINGA-PURANA, c$30.00/set. A complete translation of the San skrit text, in two volumes. *It derives its name from the fact that it reveals the supreme lord, Siva in his niskala (attributeless) and sakala (qualified) forms, recounts his emblems, qual ities, exploits and incarnations, narrates legends on the origin and importance of the Linga— his phallic idol, dwells upon the merit of installing and consecrating it, describes the ritual and philosophical principles of the Linga cult and embodies sermons and dissertations on the glory of the Linga image.* —from the introduction. Notes, 841pp. MoB 73

_____. THE SIVA-PURANA, c$60.00/set. This is a complete translation of the Sanskrit text, in four volumes. Primarily concerned with Saivite religion, philosophy, and ethics, this purana is a source of ancient Indian geography, history and sociology.

he translation contains footnotes, an extensive introduction, and a general index. It is a valuable contribution for indologists. 2174pp. MoB 70

THE SIKH RELIGION

The Sikh Religion was founded in the fifteenth century by Guru Nanak. At that time India was ruled by Mogul princes. Nanank's family were Muslims and Nanak's teachings form a deliberate bridge between the Hindu and Muslim faith. It is ironic that Nanak himself preached non-violence since the Sikhs today are associated with militancy. The Sikh faith quickly grew in popularity and by the time of the fifth Guru, Gobind Singh, they began to be persecuted by the ruling Moguls. It was at that time that they took to arms to defend themselves. Today the Sikh religion remains one of the most popular faiths in India.

FRIPP, PETER. **THE MYSTIC PHILOSOPHY OF SANT MAT**, c$4.50. Presents all aspects of the ancient philosophy as taught by the present spiritual master, Charan Singh. The book is in the form of a very personal narrative with photographs. 174pp. Spe 64

GREENLEES, DUNCAN. **THE GOSPEL OF THE GURU GRANTH SAHIB**, c$4.50. TPH 52

JOHNSON, JULIAN. **PATH OF THE MASTERS**, c$4.60. Presents a comprehensive description of Charan Singh and his yogic system as well as details on the previous Sikh masters who presented the Radha Soami system to the world. This is also considered an excellent work for all who seek to understand the Indian spiritual tradition and what it is like to follow a master. Includes practical techniques. Unabridged edition. 617pp. RSS 39

_____. **WITH A GREAT MASTER IN INDIA**, c$3.95. Letters based upon the observations and experiences of the author during the year and a half he spent with Charan Singh. Includes a section on the Radha Soami system, the yoga of the sound current. 241pp. RSS 71

KAUR, PREMKA. **GURU FOR THE AQUARIAN AGE: GURU NANAK**, $2.95. Five hundred years ago this great teacher traveled from town to town singing songs of love and protest, bringing enlightenment to those who listened. A great Indian sage claimed by Hindus, Muslims, Sikhs and Sufis alike. His life and teachings are recorded here. 131pp. SpC 71

_____. **PEACE LAGOON**, $4.50. Sacred songs of the Sikhs: Guru Nanak, Guru Amar Das, Guru Ram Das, Guru Arjun and Guru Gobind Singh. 223pp. SpC 72

LEVERANT, ROBERT. **KIRPAL SINGH**, $2.95. A *visual biography* by a devoted disciple. A series of inspirational messages accompany the photographs. 47pp. ImP 74

McLEOD, W.H. **THE EVOLUTION OF THE SIKH COMMUNITY**, c$11.00. Sikh history has traditionally been regarded as a paradox. Beginning in the early sixteenth century as a system of interior devotion, Sikhism emerged into prominence during the eighteenth century as a clearly defined belief laying stress upon martial prowess and external symbols. This book seeks to demonstrate that there is in fact no paradox. In a series of five essays it examines the history and sacred literature of the Sikhs, showing that the evolution of the community has in reality been a logical and consistent process. Notes, glossary, bibliography, index. Oxf 76

PARROTT, L. GURNEY. **THE CELESTIAL MUSIC**, $4.00. The author is a devotee of Kirpal Singh. In this volume he discusses the life and teachings of the master and describes his own experiences with him. The material on Kirpal Singh's teachings is topically arranged. 208pp. SSB 74

SEADER, RUTH, ed. **THE TEACHINGS OF KIRPAL SINGH, VOL. II: SELF-INTROSPECTION MEDITATION**, $3.00. Teachings on the title theme, compiled and edited from the writings of Kirpal Singh. 188pp. SSB 75

SINGH, CHARAN. **DIVINE LIGHT**, c$6.00. *The book is in two parts—the first dealing with the Path of the Saints which all perfect Masters have revealed in all ages, climes and countries. . . . In the second part are excerpts from letters to seekers and disciples dealing with their day to day personal problems, material and spiritual.—from the introduction.* Charan Singh is the current master of the Radha Soami (or Sant Mat) sect of the Sikhs. 386pp. RaS 67

_____. **LIGHT ON SANT MAT**, c$4.50. The first section of this book contains Charan Singh's explanation of what Sant Mat truly is. The rest of the book is devoted to his correspondence with disciples throughout the world. Glossary, index. 432pp. RaS 58

_____. **THE PATH**, $.75. The first half of **Divine Light** is presented here. Devotees of this faith suggest that this volume is the best one to start with. 148pp. RaS nd

_____. **QUEST FOR LIGHT**, c$3.95. The most recent of Singh's books. Gives excerpts from letters written by the master to his disciples, and states the philosophy of Sant Mat. 321pp.

_____. **SPIRITUAL DISCOURSES**, c$3.70. Transcription of discourses on a variety of topics. 254pp. RaS 64

SINGH, GOPAL. **THE RELIGION OF THE SIKHS**, c$6.40. A topically organized compilation of selections from the sacred literature of the Sikhs, with commentary. 199pp. APH 71

SINGH, GURSARAN. **JAPJI: THE MORNING PRAYER OF THE SIKHS**, c$9.00. This work includes the full text of the *Japji*, in Gurmukhi script and in English translation—with an extensive interpretation in the light of modern thought. The author suggests that Guru Nanak's mission was not to found any new faith; what he wanted was to create a new society based on the principles of truth, tolerance, and equality. 291pp. ARS 72

SINGH, HARBANS. **GURU NANAK AND THE ORIGINS OF THE SIKH FAITH**, c$10.00. This is the most extensive biographical study available. Every aspect of Nanak's life and teachings is discussed at length. Also includes selections from his major writings. 247pp. APH 69

SINGH, HUZUR. **PHILOSOPHY OF THE MASTERS**, $3.75. 378pp. RaS 73

_____. **SPIRITUAL GEMS**, c$4.00. RaS 65

SINGH, KHUSHWANT, tr. **HYMNS OF GURU NANAK**, $2.00. 97 hymns, including the **Japji**. Khushwant also provides extensive introductory material on the life, times, and m message of Guru Nanak. 192pp. Ser 69

SINGH, K. and S.V. **HOMAGE TO GURU GOBIND SINGH**, $1.60. A short, popularized biographical study. 100pp. JPH 66

SINGH, KIRPAL. **THE CROWN OF LIFE: A STUDY IN YOGA**, $3.00. A complete textbook on yoga. Includes an exhaustive analysis of Pantajali's yoga system, studies of all yogas currently practiced in India, an explanation of Shankara's philosophy of Advaitism or non-dualism, and a complete presentation of the Surat Shabd yoga of which the author was an exponent. 255pp. RuS 61

_____. **GODMAN**, $2.00. A thorough study of the origin, mission and nature of masters of the highest order. 191pp. RuS 67

_____. **A GREAT SAINT: BABA JAIMAL SINGH**, $2.00. This great saint was the master of Baba Sawan Singh, the spiritual master of both Charan Singh and Kirpal Singh. Includes excellent glossary. 146pp. RuS 60

_____. **THE HOLY PATH**, $2.00. This is Volume I of **The Teachings of Kirpal Singh**. It includes essays on various aspects of the spiritual path which have been selected from his major writings. Notes, 94pp. SSB 74

_____. **JAP JI: THE MESSAGE OF GURU NANAK**, $2.25. The bulk of this volume is devoted to Kirpal Singh's introductory comments. The translation itself is more than adequate and extensive commentary is also included. In addition there are notes and a long glossary. 215pp. RuS 59

_____. **MORNING TALKS**, $3.00. Forty talks, transcribed from tapes, covering all aspects of the spiritual path. 268pp. SSB 74

_____. **THE NIGHT IS A JUNGLE**, c$8.95. A selection of discourses prepared especially for Western audiences. 358pp. SSB 75

_____. **NAAM OR WORD**, $3.00. A poetic, carefully drawn study of the expression of God, *Naam*, Word or *Logos*; the aspect of God that at once creates and sustains the universe and also because it is the essence of each individual, serves as the most natural means of reaching Him. Copious quotations from Hindu, Buddhist, Islamic, and Christian sacred writings demonstrate the universality of the concept. 335pp. SSB 60

_____. **PRAYER: ITS NATURE AND TECHNIQUES**, $1.50. All forms and aspects are discussed, from the most elementary and dualistic to the ultimate stage of praying without ceasing, where all life is a prayer. Includes specific prayers from all religious traditions. 153pp. SSB 59

_____. **SURAT SHABD YOGA: THE YOGA OF CELESTIAL SOUND**, $2.50. Surat Shabd yoga is translated as the yoga of celestial sound. This is the practice that Kirpal Singh taught and here he presents an introduction to the practice. 71pp. ImP 75

_____. THE THIRD WORLD TOUR OF KIRPAL SINGH, $2.50. Includes many photographs and personal recollections of disciples as well as some of the discourses that Kirpal Singh gave on the tour. 158pp. SSB 74

_____. WHEEL OF LIFE, $1.80. See the Reincarnation and Karma section.

SINGH, MARA. THE STORY OF GURU NANAK, c$3.75. See the Children's Books section.

SINGH, SANGAT. JAPJI, $1.60. A nice, concise translation, with a fair amount of introductory material. Notes, 128pp. HPB 73

SINGH, SARDAR. SCIENCE OF THE SOUL, c$3.30. A collection of discourses and excerpts from letters and talks. 287pp. RaS 59

SINGH, SAWAN. PHILOSOPHY OF THE MASTERS, VOL. I–V, c$4.95/each. RaS

_____. SPIRITUAL GEMS, c$4.55. RaS 65

SINGH, SHANTA, tr. NANAK THE GURU, c$3.40. A comprehensive account of Nanak, the man, reformer, and universal prophet. 180pp. OLL 70

SINGH, TRILOCHAN, et al. THE SACRED WRITINGS OF THE SIKHS, $3.50. This is the only paperback edition of major selections from the Adi Granth which is available. Also includes selections from the Dasm Granth. These translations are excellent and the volume is part of the UNESCO Collection. Glossary, index. 288pp. Wei 73

TRUMPP, ERNEST. THE ADI GRANTH, c$45.00. The Adi Granth is the most sacred book of the Sikhs and is the authoritative scriptural work. The present version includes writings by all the ten Sikh gurus and also the banis of thirty-six Hindu and Muslim saints who lived between the twelfth and seventeenth centuries. This is the only complete edition of the Adi Granth that we know of. It also includes extensive introductory material. A massive, oversize volume. 853pp. MuM 1877

WATSON, KATHRYN. THE LIVING MASTER, c$5.00. Ms. Watson's impressions of life with Charan Singh. 316pp. RaS 66

SIVANANDA, SWAMI. FOURTEEN LESSONS IN RAJA YOGA, $2.50. Swami Sivananda was one of the most noted gurus of this century. The two disciples he sent to the West, Swami Satchidananda and Swami Vishnudevananda, are two of the most popular and respected American spiritual leaders. Sivananda's teaching is excellent. DLS

_____. GYANA YOGA, $3.50. This book discusses each of the following topics: Sad Guru, Guru and Disciple, Guru and Initiation, Gyana or the Yoga of Wisdom, Brahmavidya, Upanishads, Creation, the Doctrine of Maya, Atman, as distinguished from the three bodies and practical aspects of yogic philosophy. The appendix contains the text of the Ribhu Gita, Sri Rama's instructions to Hanuman, and several ancient stories. 267pp. MoB

_____. JAPA YOGA, $1.50. Japa is the repetition of any mantra or name of the Lord. This is a comprehensive treatise on japa yoga. 192pp. DLS 72

_____. PRACTICAL LESSONS IN YOGA, $2.70. Swami Sivananda is without a doubt the most prolific writer on spiritual matters the twentieth century has produced. His books are extremely popular in India. In this book he presents twelve lessons on yoga and its objects, yoga sadhana, yogic discipline, yogic diet, obstacles in yoga, yoga asanas, concentration, meditation, and samadhi. 248pp. DLS 38

_____. PRACTICE OF KARMA YOGA, c$6.75/$4.25. A comprehensive treatise, discussing all aspects of the subject. 324pp. MoB 65

_____. PRACTICE OF YOGA, c$3.50. Subtitled A comprehensive introduction to the definition, ethics, psychology and the science of yoga in its various branches of approach. This seems to be the most complete of Sivananda's general yoga books, and includes a glossary. 479pp. DLS

_____. RELIGIOUS EDUCATION, $2.70. Despite the title, this book contains a series of essays on various aspects of the spiritual life. 365pp. DLS 60

_____. SADHANA, c$12.00. This is one of Swami Sivananda's major works. Here he discusses Hindu psychology and psychological processes. Information is included on all types of practices. A very complete account. 755pp. MoB 58

_____. THE SCIENCE OF PRANAYAMA, $1.50. A detailed work on the science and practice of pranayama, a very important aspect of yogic practice. 142pp. DLS

_____. SPIRITUAL EXPERIENCES, $2.10. A good overview of Swami Sivananda's view of spiritual development for the aspirant. Topics include the nature and states of consciousness, cosmic consciousness, the experiences the aspirant must pass through in the path of meditation, the different phases of experience found in samadhi and attained through the various paths of sadhana, psychic powers attained by Yogis, characteristics of spiritual progress, jnana yoga and the state of liberation; and a narrative of the experiences of some mystics. 317pp. DLS 57

_____. SURE WAYS FOR SUCCESS IN LIFE AND GOD-REALIZATION, $2.70. This is one of Sivananda's most popular practical works. Topics include culture of will and memory, raja yoga, psychic influence, cultivation of virtues, eradication of negative qualities, and a number of short guides for day-to-day life. 352pp. DLS 70

SLATER, WALLACE. RAJA YOGA, $1.75. Presents the basic technique of raja yoga in a graded practical do-it-yourself course divided into ten lessons. The instructions include

postures, breathing, right attitudes and methods of meditation. 106pp. TPH 68

STUTLEY, M.E.L. and J.D. HARPER'S DICTIONARY OF HINDUISM, c$30.00. An exhaustive study which concentrates on classical Hinduism through the fourteenth century when the religion became fully formulated and after it had absorbed Buddhism in India. Both major and lesser known terms, gods, goddesses, and legends are clearly explained. The presentation is comprehensive but not overwhelmingly detailed. Hinduism is seen not only in its religious aspects, but also in terms of the social, economic, and political conditions of the times. Many sources and parallels—both mythological and etymological—have been drawn upon. The authors devoted over seventeen years to the preparation of this definitive volume. Cross-references, maps, illustrations, notes, oversize. 416pp. H&R 7

TADDEI, MAURIZIO. INDIA, c$26.20. An archaeological study of early Indian civilization which incorporates the latest findings and, while it is a work of excellent scholarship, is not overly technical. 169 plates, many in color, notes, index, bibliography. 263pp. Nag 70

TAGORE, RABINDRANATH. GITANJALI, $1.45. Prose translations of a collection of Indian song offerings. Introduction by W.B. Yeats. 123pp. McM 13

_____. SADHANA: THE REALIZATION OF LIFE, $1.95. In the form of a great inspirational tapestry, Tagore reveals the relation of the individual to the universe, self consciousness, and how to realize love and beauty—through them, the infinite. 164pp. Ome 13

_____. A TAGORE READER, $4.95. Tagore (1861-1941) was hailed during his lifetime as the living embodiment of Indian culture and its greatest spokesman. This volume includes selections from his most important writings, including poetry, short stories, fables, drama, and philosophy. Some of his letters are also included. The selection was made by his former literary secretary. 414pp. Bea 66

TAIMINI, I.K. GAYATRI, c$3.25. The japa of Gayatri is an integral part of sandhya, the daily practice of the Hindus. . . . The Gayatri mantra which is the chief element of Gayatri upasana or sandhya as it is usually called occurs in all the four Vedas and also in Tantra and is referred to in superlative terms by many Rishis.—from the introduction. This is the fullest exploration in print of gayatri and the gayatri mantra. Taimini is a theosophist. 202pp. TPH 74

_____. GLIMPSES INTO THE PSYCHOLOGY OF YOGA, c$6.50. A very complete discussion which builds upon the material presented in Science of Yoga (see the Patanjali sub-section). The major topics are the nature of reality, the nature of consciousness, the nature of the mind, and the nature of matter. Taimini often uses Sanskrit terminology. 426pp. TPH 73

THAKUR, S.C. CHRISTIAN AND HINDU ETHICS, c$8.40. A systematic, detailed scholarly work which attempts to bring out both the differences as well as the similarities. Bibliography and notes. 213pp. A&U 69

SWAMI RAMA TIRTHA

SINGH, PURAM. THE STORY OF SWAMI RAMA, c$8.10. Swami Rama Tirtha was one of the greatest philosophers and humanitarians of modern India. He believed that the Indian people had lost touch with their ancient wisdom and worked with missionary zeal to help them regain the faith. He believed that this could be done by the six-fold path: action, love, knowledge or law, fearlessness, purity, and yoga (a word which he considered synonymous with contemplation or concentration). He also followed the religion of nature and looked upon the many aspects of nature as his co-religionists. This biography includes selections from his letters and writings. 297pp. Kly 74

TIRTHA, SWAMI RAMA. AIDS TO REALIZATION, c$1.50. Transcription of discourses on the mind, consciousness, and realization. 170pp. RTP 72

_____. COSMIC CONSCIOUSNESS, c$1.50. More discourses, this time on religion, spiritual laws, and the brotherhood of man. 269pp. RTP 66

_____. THE FOUNTAIN OF POWER, c$1.50. Discourses on the secret of success, the nature of inspiration, the way to fulfillment of desires, and the spiritual power that wins. 226pp. RTP 63

_____. IN WOODS OF GOD REALIZATION, c$16.00/set. The complete works of Swami Rama Tirtha in four volumes. 1514pp. RTP 56

_____. PARABLES OF RAMA, c$2.75. A topically arranged collection, each with its own moral. 330pp. RTP 72

_____. THE PALE STAR WITHIN, c$1.40. RTP

_____. RAMA: HIS NOTEBOOK, c$2.10. These notebooks are really the veritable treasure of perennial truths and experiences culled by Rama from among his vast and selective study.—from the preface. The material is topically arranged, but it's hard to figure out the order. 472pp. RTP 13

UPANISHADS

The Upanishads form the concluding the portion of the Hindu scriptures, the Vedas; and their philosophy, called the Vedanta (anta meaning the end of) is the basis of all Hindu systems of religious thought, both dualistic and nondualistic. Originating hundreds of years before Christ, they record the mysal experiences of saints and sages. All ask and answer one question: *What that, knowing which, everything else is known?* And all attempt to solve e problems of the origin, the nature and the destiny of man and the universe.

LSTON, A.J., tr. **REALIZATION OF THE ABSOLUTE**, c$7.00. This is a translation of e **Naiskarmya Siddi** of Sri Suresvara. Sri Suresvara was an immediate pupil of Sankara d lived in the eighth century. He called his work *a compendium containing the essence the entire Upanishadic teaching.* This edition contains the transliterated Sanskrit text d a full commentary. 285pp. ShS 69

UROBINDO, SRI. **A GUIDE TO THE UPANISHADS**, c$3.50. 143pp. SAA 67

_____, tr. **THE UPANISHADS**, c$7.00. A collection of essays on Upanishadic phil-ophy and translations of the thirteen major Upanishads as well as translations of some rly Vedantic texts. The Sanskrit is included and the translation is in simple, rhythmic nglish. Commentaries are included with each text. 541pp. SAA 72

ESANT, ANNIE. **THE WISDOM OF THE UPANISHADS**, $1.25. A collection of lectures y this noted theosophist. 95pp. TPH 07

HINMAYANANDA, SWAMI. **AITREYA UPANISHAD**, c$3.50. Swami Chinmayananda's anslations are especially noted for their clarity. He provides the original Sanskrit verses, ith transliteration accompanied by the meanings of individual words, followed by a com-lete discourse on each verse. 135pp. CPT nd

_____. **ISA VASYOPANISHAD**, c$3.50. 153pp. CPT nd

_____. **KAIVALYOPANISHAD**, c$3.50. 121pp. CPT nd

_____. **KATHOPANISHAD**, c$4.50. This is generally considered one of the major panishads. 273pp. CPT nd

_____. **KENOPANISHAD**, c$3.50. 158pp. CPT nd

_____. **MUNDAKOPANISHAD**, c$4.00. 150pp. CPT nd

_____. **PRASNOPANISHAD**, c$3.50. 166pp. CPT nd

_____. **TAITREYA UPANISHAD**, c$4.25. CPT nd

DEUSSEN, PAUL. **THE PHILOSOPHY OF THE UPANISHADS**, $3.50. A clear, detailed statement of the Upanishadic system of thought which is generally considered one of the finest works ever produced. Deussen includes a history of the Upanishads, a full exposi-tion of the system emergent from them, and a discussion of parallel Western concepts. A first-rate work for the scholar. Many notes, index. 429pp. Dov 06

EASWARAN, EKNATH, tr. **THE KATHA UPANISHAD**, $2.00. A beautifully written poetic rendition. Includes a short introduction. 28pp. BMC 70

_____, tr. **THREE UPANISHADS**, $2.00. Poetic renditions of the Isha, Mandukya, and Shvetashvatara Upanishads. Easwaran writes beautifully. 35pp. BMC 73

HUME, ROBERT, tr. **THE THIRTEEN PRINCIPAL UPANISHADS**, $4.95. This was con-sidered the definitive collection for many years. It seems a bit stiff and dated to us. This edition is fully annotated and includes an appendix of recurrent and parallel passages in the principal Upanishads and the **Gita** as well as a discussion of translation techniques. Bibliography, indices. 588pp. Oxf 31

MAHADEVAN, T.M. **UPANISHADS**, c$10.50. Brief, easy-to-read selections from all the 108 Upanishads. A summary of each precedes the selections. There's also a good introduc-tion. A fine way to get a taste of all the Upanishads and see which ones you would like to read more fully. The book itself is beautifully produced and of a quality almost never found in Indian books. 240pp. AGI 75

MASCARO, JUAN, tr. **THE UPANISHADS**, $1.95. Includes the full texts of six Upani-shads and parts of six others. Mascaro also gives us an excellent introductory essay. A good basic translation for the general reader. 143pp. Pen 65

MULLER, MAX, tr. **THE UPANISHADS, VOL. I**, $4.00. This is one of the most schol-arly translations available, and to our taste one of the least enlightening. This was a land-mark volume when it was first written in the nineteenth century, part of Muller's *Sacred Books of the East* Series. This volume contains a 100pp introduction and the Chandogya, Kena, Aitereya, Kausitaki, and Vejasaneyi Upanishads. 420pp. Dov 1878

_____. **THE UPANISHADS, VOL. II**, $4.00. Sixty page introduction plus the fol-lowing Upanishads: Katha, Mundaka, Taittiriya, Brhadaranyaka, Svetasvatara, Prasna, and Maitrayani. 401pp. Dov 1884

NIKHILANANDA, SWAMI, tr. **THE UPANISHADS, VOL. I**, c$6.50. This translation in four volumes is both literal and graceful, preserving the dignity and flavor of the original. The extensive accompanying notes, based on the commentaries of Shankara, explain ab-struse texts. Each Upanishad has its own introduction and a glossary is appended to each volume. Vol. I contains an outline of Upanishadic thought, the metaphysics, and the psychology of Hinduism. Includes Katha, Isa, Kena and Mundaka. Highly recommended. 319pp. RVC 49

_____. **THE UPANISHADS, VOL. II**, c$6.50. Contains a long study of Hindu ethics as well as the following Upanishads: Svetasvatara, Prasna, and Mandukya. The in-troduction discusses Hindu ethics. 390pp. RVC 52

_____. **THE UPANISHADS, VOL. III**, c$6.50. The Aitareya and the Brihadara-nyaka, the most the most extensive and, by general consideration, the most important Upanishad. 392pp. RVC 57

_____. **THE UPANISHADS, VOL. IV**, c$6.50. The Taittiriya and the Chandogya Upanishads. The Taittiriya is regarded as the source book of Vedanta philosophy and the Chandogya is one of the oldest and most authoritative. Both discuss meditation and ways to realize the true self. 406pp. RVC 59

_____, **THE UPANISHADS**, $4.25. An abridgement of Nikhilananda's fine trans-lations. Certain portions of the texts have been omitted and the notes and explanations condensed. An excellent comprehensive glossary and a long introduction discussing the nature of Brahman, the soul and rebirth, Hindu ethics, and other aspects of Vedanta phil-osophy have been added. 388pp. H&R 63

PANDIT, M.P., tr. **THE UPANISHADS: GATEWAYS OF KNOWLEDGE**, c$4.00. Gen-eral introduction to the Upanishads by a disciple of Sri Aurobindo as well as a translation and detailed study of the Isha, Kena and Taittiriya. 260pp. Gan 68

PARAMANANDA, SWAMI, tr. **THE UPANISHADS**, c$3.35. A fine concise translation of the Isa, Katha, Kena, and Mundaka, with commentary. Swami Paramananda was a disciple of Swami Vivekananda. 154pp. VdC 19

PARRINDER, GEOFFREY. **THE WISDOM OF THE FOREST**, $1.95. *In this new version I have tried to make things as plain as possible, in straightforward English and using the narratives fully. Some passages have been shortened and some of the repetition reduced. But in the main this book presents the most important teachings and nearly all the narra-tive . . . faithfully.* A fine introduction for the general reader. 94pp. NDP 75

PRABHAVANANDA, SWAMI and FREDERICK MANCHESTER, trs. **THE UPANI-SHADS: BREATH OF THE ETERNAL**, c$3.50/$1.25. Major portions of the twelve prin-cipal Upanishads. An eloquent translation which captures the sense, beauty and spirit of the original. Short introduction. Highly recommended. 210pp. VdP 47

PREM, SRI KRISHNA. **THE YOGA OF THE KATHOPANISHAD**, c$7.85. *The Katho-panishad is an exposition of the ancient road that leads from death to immortality. Being a real road, the knowledge of it is not confined to any one religious tradition. The aim of this commentary is to bring out the fact that it is a road known to a few over the world and that, though their descriptions have varied in detail, they all refer to what is recog-nisably the same experience.* —from the introduction. 264pp. Wat 55

RADHAKRISHNAN, S., tr. **THE PRINCIPAL UPANISHADS**, c$18.55. The most schol-arly and at the same time most readable text available. Eighteen of the principal Upani-shads are given here in Roman script, along with a very valuable introduction, English translation and illuminating notes. The introduction discusses every aspect of Upanishadic thought. Bibliography. 952pp. A&U 53

RAMACHARAKA, YOGI. **THE SPIRIT OF THE UPANISHADS**, c$3.25. A collection of texts, aphorisms, and sayings from the Upanishads compiled from over fifty translations. 85pp. UPS 07

SHASTRI, HARI PRASAD. **WISDOM FROM THE EAST**, c$5.25. A series of lectures which contain the essence of Upanishadic teaching. 238pp. ShS nd

SIRCAR, MAHENDRANATH. **HINDU MYSTICISM ACCORDING TO THE UPANI-SHADS**, c$15.00. A thoughtful collection of twenty-six essays on the title theme cover-in almost every aspect of Upanishadic and mystical thought. The author was a philosophy professor in Calcutta. Anyone deeply interest in Hindu mysticism will find a wealth of stimulating ideas in this volume. The essays themselves read well and virtually no Sanskrit terms are included in the text—so even students who have little knowledge of Hindu phil-osophy can easily immerse themselves in the text. Index, 344pp. MuM 74

YEATS, W.B. and SWAMI PUROHIT. **THE TEN PRINCIPAL UPANISHADS**, $2.30. A free translation of ten Upanishads by and English and an Indian poet. 159pp. McM 37

VARENNE, JEAN. **YOGA AND THE HINDU TRADITION**, c$12.50. This is an excel-lent work by a distinguished French scholar. Professor Varenne presents the theory of classical yoga through quotations from the sacred Hindu texts, with extensive commen-tary. He begins with a brief discussion of the history and structures of Indian religious thought. The cosmology is discussed and the strucutre of Indian society is analyzed. The next section is a topically arranged commentary on a variety of yogic exercises. There's also a fine discussion of kundalini yoga and of tantra. A final section contains a translation of the Yoga Darhsana Upanishad. Notes, bibliography, index, illustrations. 263pp. UCh 76

VASTO, LANZA del. **RETURN TO THE SOURCE**, $2.95/$1.50. An autobiographical account of the author's pilgrimage to India, to the source of the Ganges, and to Gandhi, who renamed him Shantidas, or servant of peace. *The book may and should be read as a religious quest, but even if it is read as an eccentric traveler's experiences of India, it is excellent.*—The Times Literary Supplement. 319pp. S&S 43

VATSYANA. **THE KAMA SUTRA**, $1.75. Richard Burton's translation of the Hindu classic on physical love. A long introduction is included with this edition. 252pp. Dut 64

THE VEDAS

The word veda means wisdom. Wisdom in this case means absolute, intuitive, and esoteric wisdom as distinguished from discursive knowledge, either rational or empirical. The word veda is used both to designate the entire early literature of the Hindus and the earliest collection of hymns, sacrifices, and prayers. We shall use the term only in the latter sense. The Vedas consist of four collections (*Samhitas*) known as the **Rig**, the **Sama**, the **Yajur**, and the **Atharva**. The first is the oldest, largest, and most important; indeed it is so important that it is sometimes simply known as **The Veda**. The Vedas are not the folklore of a primitive, animistic, and nature-worshiping people, as is sometimes thought. They are the work of sophisticated priests seeking riches, success, long life, power, safety, posterity, food, and women for their patrons. The formula is quite simple: praise the god, and then petition the god for benefits. The Vedas are hopelessly confusing if they are approached as encyclopedias of information about the earliest form of Hinduism, but if they are examined as records of the religious experiences, practices, experiments and thoughts of these early Hindus, they can prove to be immensely valuable. The Vedas are also interesting for the light they shed on the gods who came to the fore in later Hinduism.

AUROBINDO, SRI. **HYMNS TO THE MYSTIC FIRE**, c$10.00. Hymns to Agni from the **Rig Veda**, in Sanskrit with an esoteric English translation, and an introduction covering the problem of translating the Vedas and discussing the doctrine of the mystics. 607pp. SAA nd

_____. **KEY TO VEDIC SYMBOLISM**, c$4.00. A useful, topically organized study covering most of the major concepts, ideas, and individual figures. 123pp. SAA 67

BISSOONDOYAL, BASDEO. **THE ESSENCE OF THE VEDAS AND ALLIED SCRIPTURES**, $1.90. Includes long extracts, arranged topically, and a good introduction. 154pp. JPH 66

BLOOMFIELD, MAURICE. **A VEDIC CONCORDANCE**, c$12.00. Part of the Harvard Oriental Series. 1100pp. MoB

_____, tr. **HYMNS OF THE ATHARVA-VEDA**, c$7.50. The **Atharva Veda** is the last of the Vedas. It is mainly a book of spells and incantations designed to assist people who were possessed with a fear of evil spirits. Many of its stanzas or *suktas* are to be used with magical plants, potions, lotions, and drugs. The chief siginificance of this Veda in India today is as the basis of Ayurvedic medicine. The classic book of medicine and health is called the **Ayurveda**, and is a supplement to the **Atharva**. This translation is a part of the *Sacred Books of the East* series. Introduction, notes, 780pp. MoB 1897

BOSE, ABINASH, tr. **HYMNS FROM THE VEDAS**, c$16.15. We feel that this is the best single volume translation of the Vedas. Dr. Bose has translated selected hymns from all the four Vedas. The original Sanskrit text is also given on the facing pages. His emphasis is on the poetic and spiritual values, on the inner life of the early Aryans, and on their contact with the realities of material existence, and he shows no preoccupation with the external forms and rituals of Vedic worship. The selections are topically arranged and Dr. Bose also provides an excellent long introduction. Notes, index. 387pp. APH 66

CHATTERJI, J.C. **THE WISDOM OF THE VEDAS**, c$3.95. A systematic presentation of the Vedic system of thought, as simplified as possible. 99pp. TPH 73

CHINMAYANANDA, SWAMI. **THE UNIVERSAL PERSON—PURUSHA SOOKTAM**, $1.00. The **Purusha Sooktam** is a *Hymn of Praise adoring the Mighty Spirit Divine*. It is the most famous of all the similar hymns in the **Rig Veda** and is chanted at many important Hindu functions. The Swami presents the original hymn in Sanskrit, along with a translation, a transliteration of the text, and a great deal of commentary on the meaning of the verses. 68pp. CPT 69

GONDA, J. **THE VEDIC GOD MITRA**, c$25.40. An exhaustive study of all that can be surmised about Mitra's character, functions, and relationships with other gods and with various aspects of the natural world. Many quotations from the Vedic texts are included. Indices, 147pp. Bri 72

_____. **THE VISION OF THE VEDIC POETS**, c$27.35. This is a scholarly, technical study which discusses the major Vedic concepts and quotes from the hymns themselves—both the English translation and the transliterated text. Extensive notes accompany the text. For serious students only. Indices, 372pp. Mou 63

GOPALACHARYA, MAHULI. **HEART OF THE RIGVEDA**, c$16.00. Gopalcharya presents selections from the Rig Vedic hymns accompanied by his own translation of the stanzas and the translations of other scholars including Wilson, Griffith, Macdonell, Muller and Edgerton. At least four versions accompany each stanza and the Sanskrit text is also included. There's also a great deal of interpretative and background material. Indices 487pp. Som 71

GRIFFITH, RALPH, tr. **THE HYMNS OF THE ATHARVAVEDA, VOL. 1 AND** c$15.00/set. A comprehensive selection, with copious notes. The style is stilted, but there is no other edition that even comes close to this one in terms of completeness and excellence of scholarship. 1035pp. CSS 1894

_____. **HYMNS OF THE RIGVEDA**, c$27.00. A new, revised edition of this classic work—one of the few authentic translations available in English. 728pp. MoB 188

HALL, MANLY P. **THE ADEPTS IN THE EASTERN ESOTERIC TRADITION, PART THE LIGHT OF THE VEDAS**, $1.75. A summary study of the twentieth century's most prolific writers on these matters. 111pp. PRS 52

JOLLY, JULIUS, tr. **THE INSTITUTES OF VISHNU**, c$7.50. A translation of the Vishnu smriti, which many scholars feel is really the ancient Dharma sutra of the Karayaniya kathaka Sakha of the Black **Yajur Veda**. Part of the *Sacred Books of the East* series. Index, 348pp. MoB 1880

KAEGI, ADOLF, tr. **THE RIG VEDA**, c$10.50. A comprehensive, authoritative, and condensed manual of Vedic research including extensive quotations from the texts and commentary. Includes extensive notes. 198pp.

KEITH, A.B. **THE RELIGION AND PHILOSOPHY OF THE VEDA AND UPANISHADS** c$18.00/set. The most comprehensive, scholarly treatment available. Topics include the following: the sources, the gods and demons of the Veda, Vedic rituals, the spirits of the dead, the philosophy of the Veda. Many appendices. Highly recommended. Harvard Oriental Series. 708pp. MoB nd

_____, tr. **RIGVEDA BRAHMANAS**, c$12.00. The Brahmanas basically consist of instructions for priests, often for the performance of sacrifices. This volume consists of translations of the Aitareya and Kausitaki—with extensive explanatory and background material and a helpful introduction. Harvard Oriental Series. 568pp. MoB

_____, tr. **THE VEDAS OF THE BLACK YAJUR SCHOOL**, c$4.50. The **Yajur Veda** is a priestly handbook containing both mantras and prose directions for the performance of sacrifices. Here Keith provides a translation of a portion of it, the Taittiriya Samhita along with a running commentary and an elaborate introduction. 832pp. MoB

KNIPE, DAVID. **IN THE IMAGE OF FIRE**, c$10.50. This is an unusual, penetrating study of Vedic man's religious experience of fire and heat. It is a portrayal of the complex system of religious expressions that developed in ancient India from man's intimate relationship with the element fire. Utilizing the full corpus of Vedic literature, the author ranges from the mysteries of the great Vedic sacrifices through the brahmanical doctrine of correspondences to Upanishadic identities and yogic techniques, demonstrating that ritualized control of cosmic heat (*tapas*) which eventually became the hallmark of asceticism. Related expressions of fire and heat are drawn from ancient Iran and Scandinavia and from the mystics of European Christianity. This work was the author's doctoral thesis from the University of Wisconsin and reads like one, complete with extensive notation and a long bibliography. Index, 187pp. MoB 75

KUNHAN RAJA, C., tr. **ASYA VAMASYA HYMN (THE RIDDLE OF THE UNIVERSE)**, c$5.00. A translation of one of the finest hymns in the **Rig Veda**. The original Sanskrit text is included along with extensive notes. 223pp. Gan 56

_____. **POET-PHILOSOPHERS OF THE RIG VEDA**, c$7.95. A study of the lives and teachings of the most important Vedic poets along with a survey of the story of creation and evolution as described in the hymns. Thirteen important hymns are translated in an appendix, and the transliteration is given along with translations of individual words. Notes, 360pp. Gan 63

_____. **THE QUINTESSENCE OF THE RIG VEDA**, c$2.25. A prose summary of the narrative presented in the Vedas written in a novelistic vein and including a good general introduction. 160pp. Tar 64

LAL, P., tr. **WOMB OF THE SUN**, c$5.05. A beautifully written poetic transcreation of some Rig Vedic songs. 40pp. WrW 65

LE MEE, JEAN, tr. **HYMNS FROM THE RIG VEDA**, c$12.50/$5.95. The Vedic hymns are said by tradition to embody the laws of the universe, as seen by the rishis. There are over 1000 which have been preserved through an oral tradition, consciously designed to prevent any distortion. Above all, the **Rig Veda** is a glorious song of praise to the gods, the cosmic powers at work in nature and in man. This lovely oversize book presents translations of twelve hymns and is designed to make generally available for the first time one of the major scriptures of mankind, and to suggest something of its profundity and magnificence in a translation that reflects the quality, substance, and form of the original. The book was put together by the same people as the Gia-fu Feng edition of Lao Tzu and Chuang Tzu. It is illustrated with evocative full-page photographs facing each stanza. The Sanskrit text is also given, and there is an introduction to each hymn and a general introduction which tells of the Vedic tradition and sets the stage for the hymns which are presented. The unusual photographs make this a wonderful gift for all, even those not on the spiritual path. And the profundity of the photographs draws the reader into the hymns themselves. Oversize, 236pp. RaH 75

AC DONNELL, A.A. **THE BRIHAD-DEVATA, PARTS I AND II**, c$4.50/set. A summary of the deities and myths of the Rig Veda. Includes Sanskrit text, English translation, many notes. Harvard Oriental Series. 582pp. MoB 04

_____. **VEDIC MYTHOLOGY**, c$10.50. A detailed study which is almost impossible to follow due to the poor organization and poor typography of the text. An amazing amount of material is condensed into these pages if you can plow through them. We wish you luck! Good scholarship, extensive references, index. 189pp. MoB 1898

_____. **A VEDIC READER FOR STUDENTS**, c$2.15. Thirty hymns, comprising just under 300 stanzas, taken exclusively from the Rig Veda, with transliteration, translation, explanatory notes, introduction, and vocabulary. The Sanskrit text is also included. An adequate knowledge of classical Sanskrit is necessary before attempting this volume. Index, 294pp. Oxf 17

MAINKAR, T.G. **MYSTICISM IN THE RIGVEDA**, c$3.25. A scholarly work which quotes extensively from the Vedic hymns and is organized topically. Indices, 127pp. BD 61

MULLER, MAX. **THE VEDAS**, c$2.70. A survey written by the man who first brought the Vedas to the attention of the West. It remains one of the most comprehensive general presentations available—though it is far from stimulating. The text is organized under the following general headings: the Veda and the Zend-Avesta, what is the Veda, hymns of the Vedas (including some translations), the religion of the Veda, Vedic deities, and the Veda and Vedanta. 163pp. IBH'nd

_____. **VEDIC HYMNS**, c$24.00/set. An important early translation of the hymns, accompanied by a veritable profusion of notes. Part of the *Sacred Books of the East* series. Two volumes, 1180pp. MoB 1891

PETERSON. **A SECOND SELECTION OF HYMNS FROM THE RIGVEDA**, c$6.45. Sanskrit text and translation of a number of hymns, with extensive notes. Index, 401pp. MoB 1899

SAMPURNANAND, SRI. **THE ATHARVA VEDA: VRATYAKANDA**, $1.25. Sanskrit text and translation, with extensive commentary. An introduction discusses the Vedas. 57pp. Gan 56

VIDYALANKAR, SATYAKAM, tr. **WISDOM OF THE VEDAS**, $1.60. A simple modern translation of 108 hymns selected from the four Vedas. The Sanskrit text is also included. 130pp. HPB 74

WASSON, R. GORDON. **SOMA: DIVINE MUSHROOM OF IMMORTALITY**, $7.50. One of the key enigmas of cultural history has been the identity of a sacred plant called soma in the Rig Veda. Wasson has advanced and documented the thesis that soma was a hallucinogenic mushroom. In his presentation he throws fascinating light on the role of mushrooms in religious ritual. Careful scholarship, seventeen color plates, for the student and the layman. Much of the volume consists of translations of Vedic material. 381pp. HBJ nd

WHITNEY, WILLIAM D., tr. **ATHARVA-VEDA-SAMHITA, VOL. I AND II**, c$24.00/set. Original text, translation, and notes. Harvard Oriental Series. 1208pp. MoB nd

VEDANTA

Vedantic philosophy is probably the most influential of the Indian philosophical systems. It springs from the Upanishads and its central thesis is the upanishadic doctrine of the brahman. The founder of the system was Badarayana whose **Brahma Sutra** (also called the **Vedanta Sutra**) makes up, along with the Upanishads and the **Bhagavad Gita**, the foundation of the Vedanta system. In the 555 sutras an attempt is made to systematize the teachings of the Upanishads. These sutras, which consist of two or three words each, can not be understood without a commentary. The different commentators develop different interpretations in the light of their own preconceived opinions. The three outstanding commentaries on the **Vedanta Sutras** are those of Sankara (ninth century), Ramanuja (eleventh century), and Madhva (thirteenth century), and their forms of Vedanta are known respectively as *Advaita* (non-dualism), *vishishtadvaita* (non-dualism qualified by difference) and *dvaita* (dualism). Sankara's interpretation, because his commentary is one of the earliest and perhaps the most thorough, is usually assumed to be the Vedanta. All Vedantists agree that the world is the manifestation of *brahman*, that knowledge of brahman is the *marga* (path) which leads to liberation, and that brahman can be known only through the *sruti*, teachings of the Upanishads. They differed regarding the nature of brahman, how brahman causes the world to be, the nature of the world, the relation of the individual self to brahman, and the condition of the self in the liberated state.

CHINMAYANANDA, SWAMI, tr. **ATMA BODH**, c$3.50. A fine translation of Sankara's **Self Knowledge**. Chinmayananda writes beautifully and conveys the essence of the original. This work forms an excellent introduction to Vedantic thought. Swami Chinmayananda includes the Sanskrit text, transliteration, and a translation of individual words, along with a stanza-by-stanza translation of the text. He also provides extensive commentary. 137pp. CPT nd

_____, tr. **HYMN TO SRI DAKSHINAMOORTHY**, c$2.00. *Of all the hymns of Sri Sankara, Sri Dakshinamoorthy Stotra's is the shortest but, at the same time, in its philosophical import, subtlety of expression and confident assertion, it is one of the most inspired works of the Advaita philosopher. On a small canvas, Sankara has with unerring dexterity crammed all the arguments of the Nondualists against the preachers of Dualism.*—from the introduction. In addition to the translation Swami Chinmayananda supplies the Sanskrit text, transliteration, and an in depth commentary on each stanza. CMT 68

_____. **VEDANTA THROUGH LETTERS**, c$3.50. A collection of replies to letters from a variety of people. 231pp. CPT nd

_____, tr. **VIVEKACHUDAMI—THE CREST JEWEL OF DISCRIMINATION**, c$8.00. This masterpiece of Sankara is clearly translated and commented upon. Two volumes. 596pp. CPT nd

DATE, V.H. **VEDANTA EXPLAINED, VOL. I AND II**, c$30.00/set. A scholarly and faithful translation of Sankara's commentary on the **Brahma Sutras**. *The author has been able to do so because, in the first place, he has kept himself very close to the meaning and spirit of the interpretation of the Sutras as done by the great Acarya, and secondly, because he could adopt the mystical viewpoint ... which subsumes and goes beyond the view-point of the earlier theistic interpreters and translators.* Includes the original Sanskrit text along with transliteration and translation of key phrases. The translation is sutra by sutra and is very complete. Dr. Date is a noted contemporary Indian scholar. 958pp. MuM 54

DAVIS, ROY EUGENE. **THE PATH OF SOUL LIBERATION**, $1.95. A simple Westernized translation, with extensive commentary, of Sankara's classic **Atma Bodha**, along with a general survey of Sankara's non-dualistic Vedanta and a glossary. 78pp. CSA 75

DEUSSEN, PAUL. **THE SYSTEM OF THE VEDANTA**, $4.00. Vedanta is notoriously difficult to expound on, and the student is sometimes hard pressed to find an exposition that is both adequate and easily intelligible. In the opinion of many scholars Dr. Deussen, a noted German philosopher and Sanskritologist, has prepared one of the finest expositions of the Vedanta of Sankara by working with the **Vedanta Sutras** of Badarayana and Sankara's commentaries on them. The text is complete and authoritative, yet so clear in its organization and exposition that the reader can follow it without too much difficulty. This is an unabridged reproduction of the original edition, complete with indices of names, terms and quotations, as well as many notes. 513pp. Dov 12

DEUTSCH, ELIOT. **ADVAITA VEDANTA—A PHILOSOPHICAL RECONSTRUCTION**, $1.95. Covers the basic metaphysical, epistemological, and ethical ideas of Vedanta in an organized manner. Bibliography. 114pp. UHa 68

GAMBHIRANANDA, SWAMI, tr. **BRAHMA-SUTRA BHASYA OF SANKARACARYA**, c$10.75. A reliable unabridged translation of the sutras and of Sankara's commentary by a senior monk of the Ramakrishna Order. The Sanskrit text of each sutra is included. Sanskrit notes, index. 920pp. AdA 72

GRIFFITHS, BEDE. **VEDANTA AND THE CHRISTIAN FAITH**, $1.95. Griffiths is an English Benedictine monk who founded a contemplate community in India in 1955. His book is a capsulization of the spiritual and mystical tradition of India combined with a parallel description of the mystical and spiritual tradition of the Christian West. Includes quotations from the Gospels and the Upanishads along with the author's personal experiences. 99pp. DHP 73

ISHERWOOD, CHRISTOPHER. **AN APPROACH TO VEDANTA**, $1.00. In this volume Isherwood describes his impressions of the Vedanta Society in California in the 1940's and discusses what attracted him to Vedanta and how he became a devotee. He also discusses the translations he made with Swami Prabhavananda. 72pp. VdP 63

_____, ed. **VEDANTA FOR MODERN MAN**, $1.50. Vedanta philosophy is based on three propositions. First, that the real nature of man is divine; second, that the aim of human life is to realize this divine nature; and third; that all religions are essentially in agreement. Separate phases of the philosophy and techniques are treated in sixty-one chapters. Also included are essays on related subjects. This is the second of the compilations. 441pp. NAL 45

_____, ed. **VEDANTA FOR THE WESTERN WORLD**, $2.95. The scholars involved include Aldous Huxley, Tagore, Swami Prabhavananda, and many others. Isherwood provides a fine introduction. Excellent presentations. 452pp. Vik 45

LEVY, JOHN. **THE NATURE OF MAN ACCORDING TO THE VEDANTA**, c$3.00. A personal, non-technical introduction. 101pp. RKP 56

MAHADEVAN, T.M.P., tr. **THE HYMNS OF SANKARA**, c$4.25. Translations of the following hymns: Daksinamurti, Guru, Bhajagovindam, Siva, Totakastaka, and Manosolasa. The Sanskrit texts are included along with transliteration and extensive commentary. 256pp. Gan 70

MUDGAL, S.G. **ADVAITA OF SANKARA: A REAPPRAISAL**, c$12.00. This is an attempt to bring out the impact of Buddhism and Sankhya on Sankara's philosophical thought and account for the inherent contradictions in Sankara's two-tiered philosophy (transcendentalism vs. theism). This is a deeply philosophical work, suitable only for those with an excellent background in Indian thought. Notes, bibliography, index. 205pp. MoB 75

MURTY, SATCHIDANANDA. **REVELATION AND REASON IN ADVAITA VEDANTA**, c$12.00. *The author deals in great detail with texts from the earliest Upanisads of seventh or sixth century B.C., to the last great dialectic texts of sixteenth and seventeenth centuries A.D. This is of great interest since many of these texts have not been translated....*

The treatment is fair and adequate.... [The text] also discusses the treatment of revelation and reason in the other five most important Indian philosophical systems and their criticism of Advaita Vedanta... [and] contains the author's own criticism and rejection of the Advaita Vedanta and his arguments in favor of theism.—**The Journal of the Asia Society**. Index, notes. 384pp. MoB 59

NIKHILANANDA, SWAMI, tr. **SELF-KNOWLEDGE**, c$4.00. A translation of Sankara's **Atma Bodha** which sets forth the knowledge of the *atman* or the self, to which all other forms of knowledge are secondary. The long introduction gives a detailed account of Vedanta, both in its theoretical and practical aspects, covering different phases of man's progressive thought, beginning with dualism, passing through the qualified non-dualism, and ending in absolute non-dualism, in which one experiences the total identity of the soul, the universe, and the Godhead. 243pp. RVC 67

_____, tr. **VEDANTASARA**, $1.50. Sadananda's treatise on Vedanta, one of the best and most widely read introductory books on the subject. Sanskrit and English, glossary. 136pp. AdA 49

PARAMANANDA, SWAMI. **VEDANTA IN PRACTICE**, c$1.70. *The aim of these lectures is to show us how to avail ourselves of the great principles of Vedanta, so that they will become part of our daily lives; to teach us how we can put them into practice and live by them every moment of our existence.*—from the preface. Swami Paramananda was a direct disciple of Swami Vivekananda. 110pp. VdC 08

PRABHAVANANDA, SWAMI. **THE SERMON ON THE MOUNT ACCORDING TO VEDANTA**, c$2.95/$1.25. In the form of a part-by-part commentary on the entire Sermon. Christ's teachings are compared with those of the Vedanta. 110pp. VdP 63

PRABHAVANANDA, SWAMI and CHRISTOPHER ISHERWOOD, trs. **CREST-JEWEL OF DISCRIMINATION WITH A GARLAND OF QUESTIONS AND ANSWERS**, c$2.95/$1.95. Describes the transcendental knowledge of Brahman and the way to achieve it through discrimination and meditation. Includes a full introduction to Sankara's philosophy of non-dualism. This is probably the best introduction to his work, in the form of a dialogue between teacher and disciple. 162pp. VdP 71

PRATYAGATMANANDA SARASWATI, SWAMI. **THE FUNDAMENTALS OF VEDANTA PHILOSOPHY**, $6.00. Vedanta from the standpoint of Western philosophy. 310pp. Gar 28

SHARMA, B.N.K. **THE BRAHMASUTRAS AND THEIR PRINCIPAL COMMENTARIES**, c$25.00/set. This is the first work on the sutras to give parity of treatment to the three principal traditions of interpretation by placing them in close thematic relation to each other and allowing them to speak for themselves. Many minor commentators are also reviewed. This is an important work for all who seek a deep understanding of Vedantic philosophy. 938pp. BVB 71

TATTWANDA, SWAMI, tr. **THE QUINTESSENCE OF VEDANTA**, c$2.75. A translation of Sankara's **Sarva-Vedanta-Siddhanta-Sarasangraha** which, *as its name implies, is a compendium and a precise restatement of all that has been thought of and set down about the Self from a purely philosophical viewpoint.*—from the preface. The text is presented in both Sanskrit and English. 191pp. AdA 70

THIBAUT, GEORGE, tr. **THE VEDANTA SUTRAS OF BADARAYANA WITH SANKARA'S COMMENTARY**, $10.00/set. The definitive English translation, originally part of the *Sacred Books of the East* Series. Included also is a translation of Sankara's exhaustive commentary as well as a comprehensive 128 page introduction and summary by the translator as well as copious footnotes. Two volumes, 954pp. Dov 1890

_____, tr. **THE VEDANTA SUTRAS WITH THE COMMENTARY OF RAMANUJA**, $8.00. This is the only unabridged translation of Ramanuja's commentary that we know of. *The present translation... claims to be faithful on the whole, although I must acknowledge that I have aimed rather at making it intelligible and, in a certain sense, readable than scrupulously accurate.*—from the introduction. Many notes are included and the volume is fully indexed. 811pp. MoB 04

VIDYARANYA, SWAMI. **PANCHADASHI: A VEDANTA CLASSIC**, c$8.00. An exposition of the metaphysics of Vedanta on a logical and dialectical basis which also details practical methods of meditation which lead to the realization of the Advaita ideal. Translated by H.P. Shastri. 486pp. ShS 54

VIRESWARANANDA, SWAMI, tr. **BRAHMA-SUTRAS**, c$4.00. A fine, reasonably priced translation which also includes the Sanskrit text, a word-for-word English rendering, and

exhaustive notes based mainly on Sankara's commentary. The introduction contain exposition of *Adhyasa* (or superimposition) as well as a comparative study of Sank Ramanuja, and Nimbarka. Indices, 552pp. AdA 36

WOOD, ERNEST. **THE GLORIOUS PRESENCE**, $2.75. This is a topically organized tillation of Vedantic philosophy which is built around Sankara's commentaries on the **danta Sutras**, the **Gita**, the Upanishads, and some of his shorter works. Wood also inclu a translation of Sankara's **Ode to the South-Facing Form** which presents a series of m tations which Wood has translated and explained. 320pp. TPH 51

_____, tr. **THE PINNACLE OF INDIAN THOUGHT**, $1.45. Translation of S kara's **Crest Jewel**, with extensive commentary, by a noted Western scholar who sp many years studying in India. Includes a long introduction. 161pp. TPH 67

VIRAJANANDA, SWAMI. **TOWARD THE GOAL SUPREME**, $2.95. Swami Virajana was President of the Ramakrishna Math and Mission from 1938 until his death in 19 During his earlier years he was closely associated with many of Sri Ramakrishna's dir disciples. It was his habit to note down his thoughts and experiences on the subject spiritual practices and disciplines. He did this primarily for the guidance of his discip and he himself prepared this English edition of his thoughts. 155pp. VdP 50

SWAMI VIVEKANANDA

Swami Vivekananda was Ramakrishna's leading disciple and he is the gre interpreter of the eternal Vedanta for modern man in the West as well as t East. As the dynamic representative of Hinduism at the World Parliament Religions in Chicago in 1893 he proclaimed the truth of all religions, the di nity of the soul, and the oneness of all existence. He, more than any oth individual, introduced Indian philosophy to the U.S. In the course of a sho life of thirty-nine years (1863–1902), of which only ten years was devote to public activities, Vivekananda composed his four classic volumes on yog all of which are outstanding treatises on Hindu philosophy. In addition, I delivered innumerable lectures, wrote ceaselessly, acted as spiritual guide the many seekers who came to him for instruction, and organized and le the Ramakrishna Monastic Order.

ADVAITA ASHRAMA. **TEACHINGS OF SWAMI VIVEKANANDA**, $1.95. An excelle compilation of aspects of Vivekananda's teaching, in the form of direct quotes, topical arranged. An excellent introduction to the man and his philosophy. 298pp. AdA

ROLAND, ROMAIN. **THE LIFE OF VIVEKANANDA AND THE UNIVERSAL GO PEL**, c$2.95. A biographical study which presents a fascinating and graphic account Vivekananda's life and teachings. 382pp. AdA 53

VIVEKANANDA, SWAMI. **BHAKTI YOGA**, $1.00. This is a comprehensive treatise the yoga of love and devotion. 113pp. AdA nd

_____. **THE COMPLETE WORKS OF SWAMI VIVEKANANDA**, c$4.95/eac c$38.00/set.

VOL. I. Contains karma yoga, raja yoga, and twenty-one lesser lectures and discourse among them selections on the **Gita** and breathing. 543pp. AdA 54

VOL. II. Jnana yoga, reports on American newspapers, and practical Vedanta and othe lectures. 535pp.

VOL. III. Contains bhakti yoga, para-bhakti (or supreme devotion), reports in Americ newspapers, and lectures from Colombo to Almora. 558pp.

VOL. IV. Contains prose and poems, original works as well as translation, seventeen lec tures on bhakti yoga, discourses and six addresses. 534pp.

VOL. V. Contains epistles, interviews, notes from lectures and discourses, questions an answers, conversations and dialogues (recorded by disciples), and writings: prose an poems original and translated. 554pp.

VOL. VI. Contains ten lectures and discourses, notes of class talks and lectures, prose an poetic writings, and epistles. 535pp.

VOL. VII. Contains inspired talks, conversations, and dialogues; translation of writing notes of class talks and lectures; and epistles. 542pp.

VOL. VIII. Discourses on jnana and raja yoga; lectures on Buddha's message to the world women of India, discipleship, and Vedanta; original prose and poetry. 558pp.

_____. **INSPIRED TALKS**, c$3.50/$2.00. A lecture on Sri Ramakrishna, as wel as conversations with friends and disciples, and a glossary. 259pp. RVC 58

_____. **JNANA YOGA**, c$3.50/$1.75. Contains the essence of the Vedanta philo sophy, and describes the wisdom of the Vedas, the Upanishads, and the **Gita**. 317pp RVC 55

_____. **KARMA YOGA**, $1.00. 131pp. AdA nd

_____. **KARMA YOGA AND BHAKTI YOGA**, c$3.50. Describes the method o reaching perfection through daily work and of sublimating human affection into divine

_____. RAJA YOGA, $3.50/$1.50. See the Patanjali sub-section.

_____. WHAT RELIGION IS, c$2.50. The essence of his teaching in one unified whole, condensed from his lectures and writings. The comprehensive, well-organized volume reads like an original work. Biographical introduction by Christopher Isherwood. 224pp. Jul 62

_____. THE YOGAS AND OTHERS WORKS, c$14.95. Vivekananda provided rational interpretations of such eternal truths as the divine nature of the soul, the oneness of man, and the harmony of religions. The present volume includes the unabridged texts of works on jnana yoga, raja yoga, karma yoga, bhakti yoga; **Inspired Talks**, the Chicago address, lectures, poems, and letters, a glossary, and a biography of Swami Vivekananda by his disciple, Swami Nikhilananda. 978pp. RVC 53

WILLIAMS, GEORGE. THE QUEST FOR MEANING OF SWAMI VIVEKANANDA, 3.50. *We all know of that Swami Vivekananda who championed the cause of Hinduism in the external tension in which it was historically caught; Dr. George Williams has now drawn for us a portrait of Swami Vivekananda as caught in the internal tensions of Hinduism—of a religion which insists that there is a Reality but fights shy of saying what it is, which insists that the Reality can be reached . . . but shrinks from indicating one exclusive road to it. And in seeing Swami Vivekananda caught in these tensions one sees how the spokesmen of a tradition contribute as much to it by the honesty of their doubt as by the profundity of their faith.—from the foreword.* 158pp. NHP 74

WATTS, ALAN and ELIOT ELISOFON. EROTIC SPIRITUALITY: THE VISION OF KONARAK, $3.95. Magnificent photographs by Elisofon and the text by Watts illuminate the simultaneously erotic and spiritual manifestations of ancient Indian culture. 125pp. McM 71

WILKINS, W.J. HINDU MYTHOLOGY, c$10.65. This is a very complete study. The deities are described, discussed, and classified insofar as is possible according to the words of the Hindu scriptures and to the period in which they appear most often. The classification is designed to give the reader a good overview of Hindu mythology. Fully indexed, illustrations. 518pp. Cur 00

WILSON, HORACE. THE VISHNU PURANA—A SYSTEM OF HINDU MYTHOLOGY AND TRADITION, c$30.00. A monumental work by one of the greatest Sanskrit scholars of the mid-nineteenth century, recently republished. PPu nd

WINTERNITZ, MAURICE. A HISTORY OF INDIAN LITERATURE, c$40.00. A comprehensive account in two volumes covering the following topics: Vedas, national epics, puranas, tantras, Buddhist and Jaina literature. Translated from the original German by S. Ketkar and B. Kohn. Long introduction by the author. 1349pp. MuM nd

WOOD, ERNEST. YOGA, $1.75. A complete analysis of yogic philosophy based largely upon the leading classical books and supplemented by the author's own experiences. Bibliography and glossary are included. A scholarly work, yet useful for anyone interested in subject. 272pp. Pen 59

YESUDIAN, SELVARAJAN. SELF RELIANCE THROUGH YOGA, $5.25. An autobiographical account of the author's childhood and youth in India, the inner guidance which he received, and other memories. Within this loose framework, practical instruction, legends and ancient stories, and sequences of questions are gathered together. Many beautiful illustrations are included in this fascinating account. 243pp. A&U 75

YESUDIAN, SELVARAJAN and ELISABETH HAICH. RAJA YOGA, $4.70. This book was originally entitled **Yoga Uniting East and West**. It is a practical introduction to yoga as it actually is but definite laws by which yogis perform miracles rather than from the holy books of the Orient. It is very clearly written and illustrated and Sanskrit vocabulary is avoided. Topics include *What is Yoga?, The Path of the Orient, The Path of the Occident, The Two Paths Meet.* Other books by these authors can be found in this section under Ms. Haich's name. 160pp. A&U 56

PARAMAHANSA YOGANANDA

A variety of records by Yogananda and his disciples are available. See the listings under Sri Daya Mata in the Spoken Records sub-section of Records and the Yogananda listings in the Chanting and Singing sub-section.

KRIYANANDA, SWAMI. THE ROAD AHEAD, $1.50. Transcription of some of Yogananda's predictions of what is to come in the world by one of his most active disciples. AnP 74

_____. STORIES OF MUKUNDA, $3.50. A collection of true episodes from the early life of Yogananda. Kriyananda compiled these stories from reminiscences of Yogananda himself and first hand accounts gathered from his childhood friends. Illustrations, AnP 76

YOGANANDA, PARAMAHANSA. AUTOBIOGRAPHY OF A YOGI, c$5.95/$1.95. This is the first time that an authentic Hindu Yogi has written his life story for Western readers. Describing in vivid detail many years of spiritual training under Sri Yukteswar, the author has here revealed a fascinating and little-known phase of modern India. He explains with scientific clarity the subtle but definite laws by which yogis perform miracles and attain self-mastery. A book about Yogis by a Yogi. This *unusual life-document is certainly one of the most revealing of the depths of the Hindu mind and heart, and of the spiritual wealth of India, ever to be published in the West.*—W.Y. Evans-Wentz. Many photographs. One of our most popular books. 591pp. SRF 46

Portrait of Yogananda by Sundaram

_____. COSMIC CHANTS, $3.50. Chants for awakening man's consciousness of the omnipresent Lord. Words in English and music of sixty songs: original compositions by Yogananda and adaptations by him of ancient Hindu bhajans (devotional melodies). An introduction explains musical notation. Foreward by the author on the sacred art of chanting to God. 106pp. SRF

_____. HOW YOU CAN TALK WITH GOD, $.95. 32pp. SRF 57

_____. THE LAW OF SUCCESS, $.95. 32pp. SRF 44

_____. MAN'S ETERNAL QUEST, c$7.95. A collection of some of the weekly talks Yogananda gave between 1931 and his death in 1952 on a variety of subjects all related to seeking and knowing God within oneself and developing along the spiritual path. The messages are often inspirational and should be welcomed by the thousands who have read and absorbed his **Autobiography**. Footnotes and a lengthy glossary are included. In general no knowledge of Indian philosophy or of Yogananda's work is necessary for an understanding of the material presented here. 501pp. SRF 75

_____. METAPHYSICAL MEDITATIONS, $.95. *Thoughts that bestow divine peace.* An inspiring foreward on meditation by the author. Pocket-size edition. 115pp. SRF 74

_____. PARAMAHANSA YOGANANDA: IN MEMORIAM, $.95. 125pp. SRF

_____. SAYINGS OF YOGANANDA, c$2.95. Illuminating answers to questions about the meaning and purpose of life. A collection of sayings and wise counsel to his disciples. 126pp. SRF

_____. SCIENCE OF RELIGION, c$1.95. Happiness as the goal of all religions. A clearly written exposition of man's inescapable search for God. The four main paths to the goal. 101pp. SRF 53

_____. SCIENTIFIC AND HEALING AFFIRMATIONS, $.95. For awakening by scientific concentration the inner powers that free men from the consciousness of sickness. Explains healing potency of thought, will, feeling, and prayer. 76pp. SRF 74

_____. SPIRITUAL DIARY, $2.25. An inspiring quotation for each day taken from the writings of Yogananda and Sri Yukteswar. SRF

_____. WHISPERS FROM ETERNITY, c$3.00. *Heartfelt prayers that convey to man an infinite hope.* 274pp. SRF 35

YUKTESWAR, SWAMI SRI. THE HOLY SCIENCE, c$2.50. A profound treatise by the guru of Yogananda, on the underlying unity of the Bible and the Hindu scriptures. The Sanskrit rendition of each sutra (precept summarizing Vedic teaching) is followed by its English translation and then by the commentary of Sri Yukteswar. 77pp. SRF 74

ZIMMER, HEINRICH. MYTHS AND SYMBOLS IN INDIAN ART AND CIVILIZATION, $3.95. A comprehensive scholarly interpretation, for Western minds, of the key motifs of India's legends, myths, and folklore. Illustrated with 70 plates, notes, index. 318pp. PUP 46

_____. PHILOSOPHIES OF INDIA, $5.95. A monumental scholarly work, prepared by Joseph Campbell from the extensive notes left by Zimmer. Divided into three section: a discussion of Eastern and Western thought and their meeting; a discussion of success, pleasure, and duty; and finally the major portion of the book, discussing Jainism, Sankara, yoga, Brahmanism, Buddhism, tantra. Illustrations, notes, and a fine bibliography. 687pp. PUP 51

INSPIRATION

ACHAD, FRATER. **MELCHIZEDEK TRUTH PRINCIPLES**, $4.50. 196pp. DeV 63

ALLEN, JAMES. **AS A MAN THINKETH**, c$1.95. A classic inspirational book and one of the most popular. G&D nd

ANDERSON, U.S. **THE GREATEST POWER IN THE UNIVERSE**, $4.00. Anderson's books are considered to be among the clearest and best available. This is his latest, in which he delves into many new areas such as alpha waves, chakras, reading the aura, and generally expanding awareness. It seems to be his best. 270pp. A&U 71

_____. **THE MAGIC IN YOUR MIND**, $3.00. Wil 61

_____. **THE SECRET OF SECRETS**, $3.00. 252pp. Wil 58

_____. **SUCCESS CYBERNETICS: PRACTICAL APPLICATIONS OF HUMAN CYBERNETICS**, $2.00. 241pp. Wil 66

_____. **THREE MAGIC WORDS**, $3.00. People who are into inspirational literature love this book and often buy copies to give to friends. 318pp. Wil 54

ANONYMOUS. **CHRIST IN YOU**, $2.60. *The voice of Christ is fearless, all powerful, the voice of a conqueror; the voice of the shadow of good suggests limitation, sickness, death. Hold fast to the All-good, the only real.* 184pp. Wat 10

_____. **THE IMPERSONAL LIFE**, c$3.50. *This little book . . . is intended to serve as a channel or open door through which you may enter into the Joy of your Lord, the Comforter promised by Jesus, the living expression in you of the Christ of God.*—from the introduction. The book contains practical instruction on a variety of topics including thinking and creating, the word, good and evil, authority, mediums and mediators, masters, and much more. 167pp. Wll 44

_____. **THE WAY OUT**, c$3.50. Four essays written by the author of **The Impersonal Life**: *The Way Out, The Way Beyond, Wealth,* and *The Teacher*. More practical instruction. 154pp. Wll 71

_____. **THE WAY TO THE KINGDOM**, $4.00. Subtitled *Being Definite and Simple Instructions for Self-Training and Discipline, Enabling the Earnest Disciple to Find the Kingdom of God and His Righteousness*. By the author of **The Impersonal Life**. 345pp. DeV 32

BACH, MARCUS. **THE POWER OF PERCEPTION**, $2.75. Dr. Bach discusses the art of perception through an examination of such subjects as insight, reflection, awareness, perception, inspiration, recognition, intuition, receptivity, empathy, consciousness, expectation, and apprehension. He also provides hints for finding one's own potential. 156pp. Haw 51

BRISTOL, CLAUDE and HAROLD SHERMAN. **TNT—THE POWER WITHIN YOU**, $2.45. Many of our customers feel that this book (and its revised edition by Harold Sherman) formed the basis of Silva Mind Control and it contains a good detailed presentation of Mind Control teachings. 238pp. PrH 54

CRUM, JESSIE. **THE ART OF INNER LISTENING**, $1.25. *Jessie K. Crum speaks of inspirational listening through which she discovered and freed the soul of a poet—her own. In this fascinating book she explores her personal experiences, showing how, when and why she was able to tap heretofore unimagined wisdom, grace, even genius, which in her case found its expression in writing.*—from the foreword. 96pp. TPH 75

DAVIS, ROY EUGENE. **SECRETS OF INNER POWER**, $2.95. Davis was a disciple of both Yogananda and Neville and his books synthesize the philosophy of both. Most of his books are listed in our Mysticism section. 191pp. Fel 64

DUMONT, THERON. **ADVANCED COURSE IN PERSONAL MAGNETISM**, c$5.50. YPS

_____. **THE ART AND SCIENCE OF PERSONAL MAGNETISM**, c$5.50.

HOLMES, ERNEST. **THE SCIENCE OF MIND**, c$10.00. Holmes was the founder of the New Thought school of Christianity, an important early twentieth century movement which is still active today. This is the movement's bible.

HOWARD, VERNON. **ESOTERIC ENCYCLOPEDIA OF ETERNAL KNOWLEDGE**, c$7.15. Here Howard reveals how to achieve three objectives: solving daily problems, ending unwanted experiences, and winning self-command. In his discussion he presents and analyzes 200 *guides to a new life* which are arranged in alphabetical order. 256pp. TPL 74

_____. **THE MYSTIC MASTERS SPEAK!** c$7.50. *This book is for anyone who wants to escape from the trap. There is a way out. And you can find it. I assure you of this. This book contains the concentrated wisdom of the ages. In this power-packed volume are all the answers you need for winning a New Life. Its solutions are simple, accurate, helpful. . . . It shows you how to abolish fear and loneliness, what to do about painful problems with other people, how to achieve ease, confidence, and a self-independence beyond your fondest dreams.* Index, 283pp. TPL 74

_____. **THE MYSTIC PATH TO COSMIC POWER**, $2.95. 258pp. PrH 67

_____. **PATHWAYS TO PERFECT LIVING**, c$6.95. 200pp. PrH 69

_____. **PSYCHO-PICTOGRAPHY: THE NEW WAY TO USE THE MIRACLE POWER OF YOUR MIND**, $2.45. 202pp. PrH 65

MURPHY, JOSEPH. **THE AMAZING LAWS OF COSMIC MIND POWER**, $2.95. Murphy

is the most popular of all the inspirational writers. Once a customer buys one, he is usual[ly] back either for another or for the same title to give to a friend. 221pp. PrH 65

_____. **THE COSMIC ENERGIZER**, c$7.95. 214pp. PrH 74

_____. **THE COSMIC POWER WITHIN YOU**, $2.95. 203pp. PrH 68

_____. **LIVING WITHOUT STRAIN**, $2.50. 156pp. DeV 59

_____. **MAGIC OF FAITH**, $1.50. 35pp. MCP 54

_____. **MENTAL POISONS AND THEIR ANTIDOTES**, $1.00. 28pp. DeV 5[ ]

_____. **THE MIRACLE OF MIND DYNAMICS**, $2.45. 221pp. PrH 64

_____. **MIRACLE POWER FOR INFINITE RICHES**, $2.45. PrH

_____. **PEACE WITHIN YOU**, $3.00. The meaning of the Book of John. 221pp. DeV 56

_____. **THE POWER OF YOUR SUBCONSCIOUS MIND**, $2.95. The most pop[ ]ular of all Murphy's books. 224pp. PrH 63

_____. **PRAY YOUR WAY THROUGH IT**, $3.50. The inner meaning of the reve[ ]lations of St. John. 171pp. DeV 58

_____. **PRAYER IS THE ANSWER**, $2.50. The meaning of the sacraments. DeV 5[ ]

_____. **SPECIAL MEDITATIONS FOR HEALTH, WEALTH, AND LOVE**, $1.50[ ] 64pp. ChD 52

_____. **TELEPHYSICS: MAGIC POWER OF PERFECT LIVING**, $2.95. 230pp[ ] PrH 73

NEVILLE. **RESURRECTION**, $5.00. Neville was the teacher of many of the other author[s] in this section including Joseph Murphy and Roy Eugene Davis. 226pp. DeV 66

NICOLS, R. EUGENE. **THE SCIENCE OF HIGHER SENSE PERCEPTION**, c$7.95. A detailed presentation of ways to expand awareness—more serious than many in this sec[ ]tion. 214pp. PrH 72

OPHIEL. **THE ART AND PRACTICE OF GETTING MATERIAL THINGS THROUGH CREATIVE VISUALIZATION**, $3.50. 114pp. Wei 67

RUSSELL, LAO. **GOD WILL WORK WITH YOU—BUT NOT FOR YOU**, c$6.00. 270pp. DeV 55

RUSSELL, WALTER. **THE MESSAGE OF THE DIVINE ILIAD**, $20.00/set. Two volumes. DeV 48

SHERMAN, HAROLD. **HOW TO TAKE YOURSELF APART AND PUT YOURSELF TOGETHER AGAIN**, $.95. 192pp. Faw 71

_____. **HOW TO USE THE POWER OF PRAYER**, c$4.95.

_____. **KNOW YOUR MIND**, $.95. 160pp. Faw 53

_____. **THE NEW TNT MIRACULOUS POWER WITHIN YOU**, c$7.95. PrH 66

_____. **YOUR POWER TO HEAL**, $.95. 223pp. Faw 72

SKARIN, ANNALEE. **THE BOOK OF BOOKS**, $2.50. This is the newest of Ms. Skarin's books as well as the most comprehensive. 333pp. DeV

_____. **THE CELESTIAL SONG OF CREATION**, $2.75. 212pp. DeV 62

_____. **MAN TRIUMPHANT**, $2.75. 253pp. DeV 66

_____. **SECRETS OF ETERNITY**, $2.75. 287pp. DeV 61

_____. **THE TEMPLE OF GOD**, $2.75. 224pp. DeV 58

_____. **TO GOD THE GLORY**, $2.50. 196pp. DeV 56

TRINE, RALPH WALDO. **IN TUNE WITH THE INFINITE**, $1.95. 171pp. BoM 08

WEED, JOSEPH. **COMPLETE GUIDE TO ORACLE AND PROPHECY METHODS**, $2.95. Weed's books are very popular, practical manuals which deal with a great variety of subjects. This is his newest book. 222pp. PrH

_____. **PSYCHIC ENERGY—HOW TO CHANGE DESIRES INTO REALITY**, $2.95. 216pp. PrH 70

_____. **WISDOM OF THE MYSTIC MASTERS**, $2.95. The emphasis is on healing techniques as the author covers the panorama of information regarding the human body, karma, birth-death-reincarnation, the power of thought, the law of cycles, the power of prayer, telepathy, psychic energy, and psychic projection. 208pp. PrH 68

WIEHL, ANDREW. **CREATIVE VISUALIZATION**, $2.95. Subtitled *How to Unlock the Secret Powers of Mind and Body for Full Self-Realization and Happiness*. 112pp. LIP 58

ISLAM

every major religious community there exists a gap, more or less great, between the beliefs and practices of what may be called *official* or *orthodox* religion and the piety of common people. This is nowhere more true than in the Islamic case. While most Muslims are vaguely aware of the fundamental theological positions adopted by the community in the course of its development, only a small number, those who have had the privilege of advanced training in a traditional school of religious instruction, or *madrasah*, know these matters in detail from first-hand acquaintance with the works of the great religious leaders of the past. The Islamic community is second to none in the richness and depth of its intellectual heritage, and one of the areas where that legacy is the strongest is the field of religious speculation. There exist veritable macro-libraries of books dealing with Islamic theology, law, philosophy, mysticism and other subjects of religious relevance. Most of this treasury of writing and thought, however, is closed to the ordinary Muslim, not because he is in any way discouraged from the pursuit of learning, but because he does not have the training and background that would permit him to exploit it.

It may, therefore, with reason be claimed that there are two Islams, or more properly, two levels of Islamic life, that are of interest to one who wishes to know about the religion. On the one hand is the *high Islam* of the learned and the religious class, and on the other is the Islam of everyday life as it is appropriated and lived by the vast majority of members of the community. Both levels of religious expression are vital to an understanding of Islamic culture, the one showing the efforts of the community to be clear and firm about its spiritual foundations, and the other showing the way in which Islamic spiritual values affect the lives of people, what it means and how it feels actually to be a Muslim. The task here is to indicate some of the perceptions and feelings of ordinary people who have little concern for theology and who, in fact, may be ignorant of even the simplest doctrinal formulations but who are, nonetheless, animated by an Islamic spirit and vision of the world.

The reasons for the great difference between *high Islam* and the religion of ordinary Muslims are to be found largely in the sophistication and complexity of Islamic religious thought in its higher levels of development and in the consequent loss of emotional content. At some time in the late ninth or the tenth century a turning point was reached in the community's religious evolution. As the arguments of theologians and lawyers became more subtle and difficult to follow, the common people were left behind. A fierce competition for status existed among the learned class, and each theologian strove by always more clever arguments to outdo his fellows. In consequence religious writings became more and more difficult to comprehend and ever farther removed from normal daily life. As specialists, the theologians wrote for other specialists, endeavoring to achieve more subtle distinctions and greater refinement of thought. There was very little religious guidance for ordinary people to be gained from discussions that they did not understand. Although the class of men learned in the religious sciences has everywhere retained the respect of common people, the Muslim for many centuries now has found religious inspiration and leadership of a more immediate and relevant kind in the *murshids* (spiritual guides) of the Sufi (mystic) orders.

By the middle of the eleventh century, virtually all creative thought in the area of theology had ceased, and from that time to our own the theological literature which has been produced consists largely of commentaries on some of the authoritative writings of earlier times or of manuals and compendia that rehearse over and over again the great issues of the formative age. The same period witnessed the rise of the Sufi orders that eventually came to pervade the Islamic world. The congruence of dates is no coincidence. The success of the orders is due in large part to their ability to fill the religious vacuum created by the increasing intellectualism and specialisation of theology and the religious law. To all practical intents and purposes a kind of Sufism, mediated through the orders, especially the cult of the saints and their tombs, has been the real religion of large numbers of Muslims for the past six or seven centuries.

Let us now consider some of the characteristics of the Islamic faith as it is held and exercised by the great body of Muslim believers.

The first point to be made is at once complex and simple. It is that the Muslim dwells in a universe where religion has the central place. The consciousness remains, inchoate and vague though it may be, of a realm beyond the world of time and space where there dwell the powers that control events in this life and that determine human destiny in another world to come. The world in which we live is but a preparation for the other world, and life is to be lived in expectation of what follows it.

This lively sense of relation with a supernatural realm shows itself in many different ways. Perhaps the most evident is the operation of the religious law which has its basis in the will of the Sovereign Lord. The law determines the form of greeting that Muslims use toward one another, the types of food they eat or refuse, the manner of dress they adopt, the relations between the sexes, even so minor a thing as the method of cleansing the teeth. All of these aspects of culture, and many others beside, in addition to the specific obligations of worship, emerge from the religious teachings of the Islamic tradition, as mediated in the Qur'an itself, in the example of the Prophet or, most important of all, in the established custom of the community in the past.

The role played by established custom or tradition among Muslims is particularly important but somewhat difficult to understand, for tradition has a clear religious meaning in Muslim minds. In spite of their differences in attitude and behaviour, ordinary Muslims everywhere have a strong religious sense in common and hold the conviction that their way of life is an expression of *Islam*. In other words the most characteristic elements of daily life in the Islamic countries are seen by Muslims themselves to proceed out of their religion. These customs and mores are observed, and change is resisted, because ordinary people consider that in holding to their traditional mode of life they are acting in accord with the will of the power that controls the universe. The manner of living thus reflects a conception of human life under divine control and at the same time continuously reinforces that conception. Instinctively, the Muslim acts to preserve the spiritual foundation of his universe by clinging to the actions, attitudes and institutions that symbolise it.

For Muslims, the religious dimension of existence extends to encompass the whole of life and not only that small segment of activity concerned with specific acts of worship or the fulfilment of religious duties. This vivid religious awareness has several accompanying characteristics that are worth noting. One of these is the strong sense of community that Muslims have felt throughout their history. Part of the reform effected by the Prophet Muhammad was the creation of a band of followers, pledged to support one another as though they were kinsmen, but united only by their common religious faith. Even during the lifetime of the Prophet, this community was transformed into a kind of state with the Prophet as lawgiver, judge and commander-in-chief. After the Prophet's death, under the leadership of his Rightly Guided Successors, through military conquest the community founded an empire that quickly became the vehicle of one of the most brilliant civilisations of its time. Responding to the call of God through His Prophet meant gaining membership in a commonwealth of the faithful, where all were equal, and all were charged with upholding a common cause. This cause was nothing less than subjecting the world to the dominion of God by striving for the hegemony of the community of the faithful. The task of the community under the leadership of the Successor to the Prophet of God was to order human affairs according to the *shari'ah* or religious law that represented the specific formulation of the divine will for human life. Muslims thus had a sense of mission as a kind of chosen people, a Messianic community, who were to bring a new era of well-being to mankind by ensuring a social order that reflected the intentions of the Creator; this sense of community is very much alive among Muslims today.

Another characteristic of Muslim piety related to the feeling of community oneness is the great sense of confidence that being Muslim instils in the breasts of the faithful. There is an essential optimism in the Islamic outlook, both for the individual and for the community. This confidence grows out of the conviction that Islam is a divinely ordained path for men, the very will of God for human life, which in His mercy He sent down for men's guidance through the Prophet. For most Muslims, therefore, it is inconceivable that a man could be anything but a Muslim. For the Muslim himself there is neither doubt nor hesitation about the rightness of his perception of reality and of man's duty. The revelation guarantees, and the experience of the community testifies, to the absolute rectitude of a way of life in which one may feel certainty and also pride.

Much of the strength of Muslim certainty stems from the fact also that Muslims feel themselves part of a sacred history stretching back to the very foundations of the created world. The Prophet of Islam with his Revelation of Guidance to a generation that had gone astray was only the last in a long series of divine spokesmen who had appeared among different nations in different epochs, one for each people addressing it in its own language.

In thinking of themselves and the meaning of life, the matter uppermost in Muslim minds is the fact that human beings, like everything else in the universe, are created by forces which they neither understand nor control; men come into being and pass away, not from their own choice, but at the whim of overwhelming powers beyond their ken. Men do not know whence they came, where they are going, what they are to do while here, how the universe operates, or, indeed, why it exists at all. Men have a degree of intelligence, but it is flawed. Nothing in their native endowment will permit them to rise to an understanding of these profound mysteries, for their capacities are only those of creatures. The most telling aspect of creaturehood is its limitation. Correspondingly, the most challenging problem for mankind caught in this limitation is somehow to escape the fumbling, suffering and meaninglessness that are its consequences.

Given our native disability, what we men require is to be told in detail and with authority how we ought to live. We require to have guidance for the proper conduct of our lives and in order to distinguish between right and wrong. What the Muslim wants and what he expects above all else from his religion is guidance in respect to the myriad situations of life. Guidance, then, is perhaps the most basic word in the entire Muslim religious vocabulary. And it is guidance that Islam offers in abundance. The Revelation in the Qur'an is the divine method of letting men know what they need to know in order to live properly. Thus, the ignorance inherent in creaturehood and the consequences that it may breed are overcome by a divine act of mercy, and men, while still being men, can live rightly and anticipate happiness. The

ebullient assurance Muslims feel in the superiority and rightness of th[eir] religious attitudes springs from the knowledge that the community posses[ses] a divinely ordered map of the right kind of life.

Further, the guidance that Muslims have received in the Qur'an and the [ex]ample of the Prophet is practical, simple and clear. The Muslim knows exa[ct]ly what he is expected to do, and not to do. There are certain fundamen[tal] duties incumbent upon the Muslims, the so-called Pillars of Islam: confessi[on] of faith, the five daily prayers, alms-giving, fasting in the month of Ramad[an] and the pilgrimage to Mecca at least once in a lifetime if at all possible. No[ne] of these has any hidden element, and none, except perhaps the last, [is] beyond the capacity of every man. Nothing more is expected or neede[d]; there remains no striving toward an unattainable ideal, no demand for p[er]fection, no requirement that men should be like God. Content in the soun[d]ness of the guidance given him and in the knowledge that it is within [his] grasp to do what is required, the Muslim can feel himself a good man witho[ut] qualification and find happiness in doing so.

What most needs to be appreciated here in speaking of these Muslim attitud[es] is that one is not dealing merely with an intellectual construction, but wi[th] the way that Muslims actually feel.

Along with the feelings of confidence and assurance there is another eleme[nt] in the Muslim's basic religious response. It is the feeling of obligation that [is] accompanied on the one hand with the threat of punishment and on th[e] other with the promise of reward. Islam, it has been said many times, is e[s]sentially a religion of law. The basic content of its religious teaching is [a] series of commands and prohibitions that form the substance of the way [a] Muslim is to follow. The proper attitude toward these divinely ordaine[d] rules and their divine author should be *Islam*, obedience, submission, [or] commitment, which is the sense in Arabic of the name of the religion itse[lf]. In addition to assurance, therefore, the Muslim's religious experience is o[ne] of judgment, of being held accountable to a power in the unseen realm [of] the supernatural. Thus, both the confidence in the rightness of the way an[d] the awareness of being under judgment serve to strengthen the Islamic sen[se] of dependence upon the powers beyond that have created and ordered th[e] world.

To this point our discussion has dealt with what might be called *orthodo[x]* Islam; the time has now come to explore some other factors in the Islam[ic] religious picture. The first matter to be noted is that the supernatural or un[seen] realm plays a role in Muslim consciousness in ways that are not alway[s] reflected in *orthodox* religious thought or that may even be contrary to it[.] In the belief of common people in particular the universe is inhabited by [a] host of supra-human, normally invisible, beings, some of them beneficen[t] but the greater majority dangerous to mankind.

Sufism is one of the most important channels for the impingement of the[?] supernatural upon the Muslim and therefore one of the fundamental factor[s] in popular religion. In many respects Sufism, in both its higher expression[s] and its popular forms, stands in sharp contrast to *orthodox* Islam. The aim of the Sufi devotee is to draw nigh to God, to experience directly and im[me]diately something of the divine nature, even to attain union with God[.] This goal is much higher and more difficult to achieve than that of obedi[en]ce to exoteric rules that are clearly formulated. It also implies a radical[ly] different view of the nature of man and of human possibilities. The Suf[i] wants to know the mystery of God, to enter into the very nature of the Divine, and to do this he must forsake worldly life, overcome his own personality, and strive through an arduous discipline to be wholly transformed into that Other which is his aim. In the process he must traverse many mystical states and stages before achieving the culminating ecstasy of extinction in the reality of God. The major motif of the Sufi endeavour is thus that of the soul yearning for God, the spiritual element in man longing to return to its source in the all-encompassing Divine reality, the lover seeking the ecstasy of merging with his beloved. This motif is repeatedly symbolised in the literature of the Muslim peoples whose poetry is dominated by the theme of an all-consuming but unfulfilled love. The hero of this literature is the lover driven to distraction by his passion, eternally seeking the beloved but never able to possess her. For perhaps a fleeting second the frustrated lovers may have contact, only to lose one another again and be plunged back into the throbbing yearning. Erotic though the theme may appear at the superficial el, it is at the same time a description of the human situation and the man goal, for the lover is the soul, and the beloved whom he so ardently d unceasingly seeks is the Divine. Such is the religious outlook so often d so lovingly reiterated in familiar stories such as Layla and Majnun (the uth driven mad by love), which are known to every Muslim, literate and terate, lowly or exalted.

e contact of common people with the Sufi element in the Islamic religious ritage has come in largest part through the great Sufi orders or brother-ods which spread all over the Islamic world after the twelfth century and tained their significance until the present. These brotherhoods with their ystical doctrine and their organised centres, resembling monasteries, served any purposes for the common folk of the Islamic world. The Sufi teachers ere immediately accessible sources of counsel, guidance, spiritual instruc-on and succour. The centres were often the agencies of stability and order a local region, Sufi orders in several cases having become the holders of mporal power and their heads the founders of dynasties. The Sufi orders ere one of the most important features of Islamic society in the medieval d pre-modern periods, both in a religious sense and socially. Though less sible, they retain an importance even today, especially in the rural areas of e Islamic world, but they have come under severe criticism by reformers d secularised intellectuals.

e element in Sufi teaching that holds the greatest attraction for the com-on people of the Islamic world is the doctrine of the saints. A Sufi saint is individual with outstanding spiritual gifts, one who has himself successful-journeyed along the Pilgrim's Progress of the Right Way to the goal of im-ediate contact with the Divine. His success in penetrating to the very secret f Reality is to be accounted for by his having secured an esoteric knowledge the methods of spiritual discipline from another great spiritual figure, also saint, who was his teacher and preceptor in a relation of great and special timacy. Thus the Sufi saint stands in the line of a succession of spiritual achers who stretch back at least to the Prophet, Muhammad, and who rough him have direct access to the divine mysteries and divine power. very saint in consequence has about him the aura of holiness. He carries an ement of the very Divine Being in himself and is the locus of a peculiar ower or blessedness known as *barakah*. Even to be in the presence of such a an' or to touch his garment is to capture something of this blessing for neself, and the common people of the Islamic world pay the highest rever-ace to the men who are reputed to be among the friends of God. A saint ossesses also, by the grace of God, the capacity to perform miracles. In his piritual evolution he has passed the stage where all the secrets of nature and f being are known to him; it lies, therefore, within his ability to interfere ith the normal course of things in miraculous ways, though the true saint ill never do so for his own advantage or in conspicuous fashion. This mi-aculous power, however, may be used to benefit those who seek the assist-nce of the saint, and the ordinary folk of Islam come in their thousands to nese spiritual leaders seeking ways out of their difficulties. Even in death ne saint retains his sanctity and his power, so that his tomb will be a centre f pilgrimage for his devotees. Scattered throughout the Islamic world there re thousands of such tomb shrines. For the common understanding the aints are the links with that unseen world where human destiny is formed nd controlled. They are the mediators of divine power in the world, the hannel by which reality flows into all things and through which all things re sustained. The saints, their power and their shrines are the heart of eligion for a vast number of Muslims, even though much of the religious ractice connected with the cult goes sharply against the teachings of *high slam*.

is apparent after this long discussion that the religious outlook of Muslims ontains a number of different elements that are not easily describable in single formula. The reality of Islamic religious life is a great richness, an ffulgent diversity that seeks always new forms of expression. As a living eligion Islam has been a constantly changing spiritual perspective on human fe that through more than 1300 years of existence has shown itself capable f meeting the religious needs of a major segment of mankind.

-condensed from Charles J. Adams' article in R.M. Savory's **Introduction** o **Islamic Civilisation**.

ABDEL-KADER, ALI HASSAN, tr. and ed. **THE LIFE, PERSONALITY, AND WRIT-INGS OF AL-JUNAYD.** $4.45. A detailed study of this ninth century mystic. The Ara-bic text of some of his writings is included along with a translation and an in depth anal-ysis of his personality and writings. Gibb Memorial Series. Notes, 276pp. Luz 76

ABUN-NASR, JAMIL. **THE TIJANIYYA**, c$12.00. The Tijaniyya is a mystical Sufi order which has had considerable political activity and influence. This study covers the theological controversies over Tijani doctrines as well as the history of the movement up to the present. The order is most influential in Maghriban and West Africa. Index, biblio-graphy, notes, 204pp. Oxf 65

AHMAD, FAZL. **HEROES OF ISLAM SERIES**, $1.35/each. This is a nice series of short books, written especially for Muslim youth. Each one contains a biographical study of a major Islamic figure and is over 100pp. MuA 74

    1: Muhammad, The Prophet of Islam
    2: Abu Bakr, The First Caliph of Islam
    3: Omar, The Second Caliph of Islam
    4: Othman, The Third Caliph of Islam
    5: Ali, The Fourth Caliph of Islam
    6: Khalid Bin Walid, The Sword of Islam
    7: Muhammad Bin Qasim
    8: Mahmood of Ghazni

AHMED, ALI. **THE GOLDEN TRADITION**, $4.95. This is an anthology of Urdu poetry from the fourteenth to the beginning of the twentieth century. There is also an introduc-tion which contains a comparative study of Urdu and English poets and poetic movements; it discusses the techniques and characteristics of Urdu poetry, its particular forms and schools; and it surveys the literary and philosophical background of the eighteenth and nineteenth century. In addition, a short sketch of each poet is presented. Index, 286pp. Col 73

ALI, AMEER. **THE SPIRIT OF ISLAM**, c$10.95. *In the following pages I have attempted to give the history of the evolution of Islam as a world-religion; of its rapid spread and the remarkable hold it obtained over the conscience and minds of millions of people within a short space of time. The impulse it gave to the intellectual development of the human race is generally recognised. But its great work in the uplifting of humanity is either ignored or not appreciated; nor are its rationale, its ideals, and its aspirations properly understood. It has been my endeavour in the survey of Islam to elucidate its true place in the history of religions.* The first half of the book describes the life and ministry of Muhammad; the second discusses the religious spirit of Islam. This volume was originally published in 1890 and revised and enlarged in 1902 and 1922. It is a classic and not overly scholarly. Notes, index, bibliography, 586pp. C&W 22

ANONYMOUS. **THE SUFIC PATH**, $1.00. Quotations from the Qur'an, Hadis, Ibn 'Arabi, materials on the path of Tassawuff and many photographs, written/created by the people of Habibiyya who have given us both the **Book of Strangers** and the Habibiyya record. 36pp. Diw

ANONYMOUS. **PERSIAN FOLK TALES**, c$5.95. See Fairy Tales section.

MUHYID IBN 'ARABI

Ibn 'Arabi (1164–1240) is universally considered one of the greatest mystical Islamic philosphers. He was born in Spain during the height of the Golden Age of Islam and spent his early years there. He later lived in several Middle Eastern countries and traveled widely. He was a prolific writer, expounding a definite system, pantheism. His teaching has been a source of inspiration to practically every pantheistic Sufi that came after him. Even Rumi is said to have come under his influence. Outside the Islamic world 'Arabi's influence reached Christian philosophers and mystics of the Middle Ages.

AFFIFI, A.E. **THE MYSTICAL PHILOSOPHY OF MUHYID DIN IBNUL 'ARABI**, c$7.50. *This work is divided into four chapters dealing with the whole of Ibnul 'Arabi's mystical philosophy, i.e., his ontology, doctrine of the Logos, epistemology, psychology, mysticism, religion, ethics, eschatology and aesthetics, and an appendix in which a rough outline is given of the main sources which seem to have influenced Ibnul 'Arabi's thought .... The material on which the work is based is drawn from twenty-three works by Ibnul 'Arabi, principally his* Futuhat *and* Fusus. This volume was originally part of the Gibb Memorial Series and Affifi was a student of R.A. Nicholson. This is an excellent study, which helps to make many of 'Arabi's difficult philosophical doctrines understandable. It was the pioneering study of 'Arabi's work. Notes, index, 233pp. MuA 38

AUSTIN, R.W.J. SUFIS OF ANDALUCIA: THE RUH AL-QUDS AND AL-DURRAT AL-FAKHIRAH, c$8.75. Biographical sketches describing the lives and teaching of some Sufi masters of the twelfth and thirteenth centuries from Muslim Spain and North Africa. The sketches come from two works by the celebrated Muslim Sufi, Muhyid al-Din Ibn 'Arabi–these are among the few works of this great master available in English. There is, in addition, an extensive account of Ibn 'Arabi's life and work. This book provides, in a most inspiring way, many insights into the teachings and practices of the Sufis. Includes in-depth annotation. 173pp. UCa 74

BURCKHARDT, TITUS. WISDOM OF THE PROPHETS (FUSUS AL-HIKAM), $4.50. This is a translation of what is probably the most significant and influential of all 'Arabi's books. It is the nucleus of his teaching and expresses the particular standpoint and teaching of each of the major prophets from Adam to Muhammad. The work is beautifully written and the translation itself is as accurate and as evocative as any we could imagine. 'Arabi's concept of a totally unified and unifying spiritual perspective is well expressed and we urge all who are deeply interested in both Sufism and the mystical aspects of all religions to dip into this volume. Notes. Wei 76

CORBIN, HENRY. CREATIVE IMAGINATION IN THE SUFISM OF IBN 'ARABI, c$23.50. A penetrating analysis of the life and doctrines of the Spanish-born mystic and Arab theologian of the twelfth century. Through his text, introduction, and the numerous translations of Ibn 'Arabi's major works and other Sufi documents, Professor Corbin provides the reader with a scholarly approach to understanding the complexities of Sufism. Extensive bibliography and notes. 390pp. PUP 58

HUSAINI, S.A.Q. IBN AL 'ARABI, $1.05. This book begins with a biographical study of 'Arabi and then reviews his writings and his philosophy. While there is no depth of analysis, this is the only volume that briefly reviews 'Arabi's work. The scholarship seems to be adequate. 109pp. MuA 49

_____. THE PANTHEISTIC MONISM OF IBN AL-'ARABI, c$5.88. The bulk of this volume is devoted to topically arranged translations of 'Arabi's writings. Each section begins with introductory remarks by the author, followed by the Sanskrit text and then the translation. All of 'Arabi's major doctrines are included. The selections have been made from the Fu'uhat, the Fusus and 'Arabi's poetry. The volume begins with a short history of pantheism, including information on the Pantheistic schools which preceded 'Arabi. There is also a life study of 'Arabi and a good deal of background material. A number of the topics presented here are not dealt with in any other book on 'Arabi. Notes, index, 268pp. MuA 70

ARABIAN NIGHTS

DAWOOD, N.J., tr. TALES FROM 1,001 NIGHTS, $2.95. Folk tales from three distinct cultures: Indian, Persian, and Arab. Written in a simple, almost colloquial style, they are masterpieces of the art of story-telling, and, in their minute accuracy of detail and the vast range and variety of their subject matter, they constitute a comprehensive and intimate record of medieval Islam. The stories went through many versions until their final revision at the end of the eighteenth century. They remain delightful. Illustrations. 407pp. Pen 54

LANG, ANDREW, ed. THE ARABIAN NIGHTS ENTERTAINMENTS, $3.50. This edition of the Arabian Nights has been especially edited for children and told in a manner that they can enjoy. Twenty-six tales are presented here, including the full Voyages of Sindbad the Sailor, Aladdin and the Lamp, the Enchanted Horse, and some of the other most popular tales. The vivid illustrations which H.J. Ford provided for the original text have been retained here: there are 33 full page plates and 34 smaller drawings. 440pp. Dov 1898

WIGGIN, KATE and NORA SMITH, eds. THE ARABIAN KNIGHTS, $3.95. A well written, easy-to-read retelling of nine of the major tales, with illustrations by Maxfield Parrish. Technically, this is a handsome volume and the print is large. 350pp. Sri 09

WILLIAM-ELLIS, ANNABEL. THE ARABIAN NIGHTS, c$9.95. This is a beautifully produced volume, illustrated throughout with line drawings and color plates. Twelve stories are included, each in a complete version, and notes on the sources and history follow the narrative. 348pp. Bla 57

ARBERRY, A.J. ARABIC POETRY: A PRIMER FOR STUDENTS, $4.95. Professor Arberry begins with a long introduction on the development, nature, forms, and rhythms of Arabic poetry. The main body of the book is an anthology of Arabic poems in the original, ranging from the sixth century to the present day, and giving examples of the work of thirty of the greatest Arab poets. Each poem has a literal English translation on the facing page. The edition also includes textual notes and short biographical notes on the poets. 174pp. CUP 65

_____. ASPECTS OF ISLAMIC CIVILIZATION, $2.95. This selection of translated passages from the most highly regarded works of Islamic literature illustrates the development of Islamic civilization from its origins in the seventh century to the present. The anthology is made up of selections from Arabic and Persian writers such as Hafiz, Sa'di, Rumi, Omar Khayyam, Ibn al-Farid, Avicenna, and Ibn Hazm, and from such works as the Qu'ran and the Masnavi. This is a very good collection. 409pp. UMP 64

_____. THE DOCTRINE OF THE SUFIS, $5.40. This is a translation of the Kitab al-Ta'arruf li-madhhab ahl al-tasawwuf of Kalabadhi, a fourth century philosopher. This volume has been generally accepted as an authoritative textbook on Sufi doctrine, and commentaries have been written on it by a number of eminent writers. The text is divided into five parts. The opening section provides a general introduction to the subject, discusses the meaning and proposed derivations of the term Sufi, and enumerates the names of the great Sufis. The second section is a statement of the tenets of Islam, as accepted by the Sufis, which shows that Sufism as a system lies within and not without the bounds of orthodoxy. The third part illustrates the stations of the Sufis, such as fear, hop love, etc. The author illustrates his remarks with copious quotations from the literatur The fourth section, perhaps the most important, discusses the technical terms of the Su that is, the expressions used to designate the true mystical experience. The book conclud with descriptions of the various phenomena of Sufism, and of the miraculous dispen tions accorded to the Sufis by God. Professor Arberry provides notes and an introductic Index, 207pp. MuA 35

_____. FITZGERALD'S SALAMAN AND ABSAL, c$11.95. The poem, by Jar tells with much digression and courtliness of Salaman, born to Solomon without the aid a woman and meant to live the same way, and Absal, his nurse, who fell in love and elop with him to a desert isle. Solomon discovered them and subjected them to a trial by f in which Absal was consumed. This edition includes introductory material and th translations: a literal one by Arberry and two different ones by FitzGerald. 213pp. CUP

_____. THE MYSTICAL POEMS OF IBN Al-FARID, $4.80. Translations the major poems accompanied by notes summarizing the contents of each poem a elucidating the form and meaning of the individual verses. Ibn al-Farid was a twelf century Arabic poet who wrote some of the finest mystical poetry ever produced. Th volume does not include Nazm as-suluk. 130pp. HFC 56

_____. ORIENTAL ESSAYS, c$6.50. A collection of portraits (one a self-portrai of seven English Oriental scholars: Simon Ockley, Sir William Jones, E.W. Lane, E. Palmer, E.G. Browne and R.A. Nicholson. 261pp. A&U 60

_____, tr. THE POEM OF THE WAY, $2.75. A translation of Ibn al-Farid's Naz as-suluk, a poem whose theme is the mystic's quest for and realization of his identity wi the spirit of Muhammad, and thereby the absorption of his individual personality in the Unity of God. Introduction, notes, bibliography. 88pp. HFC 52

_____. POEMS OF AL-MUTANABBI, c$11.00. Al-Mutanabbi (915–965), thoug universally considered among the greatest of the Arab poets, has seldom been translate or discussed outside Arab countries. This study uses the same format as Arberry's Arab Poetry and is intended to supplement that text. The introduction discusses al-Mutanabbi life, style, influence, and critics. There follows a selection from his poems, in the origin Arabic, with a literal English translation on the facing page. There are also many textu notes. 155pp. CUP 67

_____, ed. RELIGION IN THE MIDDLE EAST, c$37.50/set. These two volum survey Judaism, Christianity, and Islam, and their relationships during the last hundre years. Since Arberry is an Islamic scholar he includes central Asia, Pakistan, and parts o Africa in his survey. While primarily concerned with religion, the survey also follows th interaction of ethnic, economic, political, social, and cultural factors. The backgroun and history of the three religions are described; the distribution of sects and communiti is studied; and each religion is discussed in terms of its doctrinal, legal, social, politica and cultural aspects. Arberry is the general editor of the work and the individual subjec editors are E.I.J. Rosenthal, Judaism; M.A.C. Warren, Christianity; and C.F. Beckingham Islam. Notes, bibliography, glossary, index. 1345pp. CUP 69

_____. REVELATION AND REASON IN ISLAM, c$6.55. A transcription o three lectures Arberry gave on the title topic. He reviews the conflict and examines th attempts made to resolve the dilemma. Many references are cited. 122pp. A&U 5

_____, tr. THE RUBAIYAT OF OMAR KHAYYAM AND OTHER PERSIA POEMS, $2.65. An anthology of verse translations from the classical period. Include passages by Rumi, Sanai, and Hafiz; and from the Shah-nama and the Rubaiyat. 223pp Dut 54

_____. SHIRAZ, c$3.95. Shiraz, an ancient Persian city, is known as the city o saints and poets. In these essays I have sought to isolate the elements which have mad Shiraz immortal, and I have diagnosed those elements to be the worship of beauty an the love of beautiful things; the vision of beauty as an eternal spirit transcending and ye informing phenomena, giving a purpose to life, and a consolation in the midst of life' incalculable calamities. I have tried to body forth these abstractions in the lives and work of saints and poets who are the great glory of Shiraz.... Bibliography, index, 191pp UOk 60

_____, tr. A SUFI MARTYR, c$5.00. A translation of The Apologia of Ain a Qudat al Hamadhani, composed by him in 1131 while in jail, in a vain attempt to over throw his death sentence. It gives a fascinating account of his life and works. Arberry pro vides explanatory notes. 101pp. A&U 69

_____. SUFISM, $2.15. This is the best short survey of Sufism that we know of Each of the major individuals and orders are reviewed and the development of its doctrine is traced. Professor Arberry illustrates his treatise with extensive quotations from the lit erature, including selections from all the major poets and philosophers. Index, notes 141pp. H&R 50

ARDALAN, NADER and LAZEH BAKHTIAR. THE SENSE OF UNITY–THE SUF TRADITION IN PERSIAN ARCHITECTURE, c$30.25. Despite its extraordinary rich ness, Islamic architecture has rarely been studied for its conceptual and symbolic signifi cance. The authors examine the architecture of Persia as a manifestation of Islamic trad ition and demonstrate the synthesis of traditional Persian thought and form. The mos fundamental principle of Sufism, the inner, esoteric dimension of Islam, is that of unity in multiplicity. The book's introductory sections present the metaphysical doctrine that supports Islam's unitary perspective. This leads to a discussion of the root concepts o space, shape, surface, color, and matter. The next section deals with the symbolism of the traditional forms of Persian architecture–garden, gateway, platform, porch, dome, and

inaret. The final section shows how these forms are combined in settlements which ex-
hibit three kinds of order: natural, geometric, and harmonic. The book is beautifully
illustrated with photographs, drawings, charts, and tables, which exemplify the principles
discussed in the text. A fascinating account. Oversize, index, 169pp. UCh 73

ARNOLD, SIR EDWIN. **PEARLS OF THE FAITH OR ISLAM'S ROSARY**, $1.25. A
verse enumeration of the ninety-nine names of Allah. Appended to each is an illustrative
legend, tradition, or comment, and occasionally a paraphrase of the Qur'an. 152pp.
TuA 61

ARYANPUR, MANOOCHEHR. **A HISTORY OF PERSIAN LITERATURE**, $7.65. *The
author has tried to give a general survey of Persian literature, complemented, on the one
hand, with brief sketches of relevant Persian history and, on the other, with longer sections in which the work of major writers is examined. Considerations of space have made
it necessary to bridge many areas and to omit many names. A detailed history of Persian
literature . . . demands several volumes and more than a single man's lifetime. All translations used in this book are by the author unless otherwise stated. As far as footnotes
are concerned, the policy has been to reduce them to a minimum and give them, whenever practical, within the text itself.* Despite the author's disclaimers, he has done an
excellent job on this volume. The major figures and many minor ones are surveyed at
some length and the quotations from the literature are abundant. Index, extensive bibliography, 347pp. Kay 73

FARID AL-DIN ATTAR

Attar (1142–1221) is one of the greatest Sufi poets. He was very prolific,
having written, according to one account, forty treatises and over 100,000
lines of poetry. Modern scholars usually consider between nine and twelve of
the works attributed to him to have actually been written by him. Rumi
knew Attar and was greatly influenced by his work. In a poem Rumi himself
states: *The Seven Cities of Love did Attar Traverse/ We are still in the curve
of one alley.* Attar's poetry was steeped in mystical love for the Creator and
His creations. Attar wrote in many forms.

ARBERRY, A.J., tr. **MUSLIM SAINTS AND MYSTICS**, c$13.25. A translation of the
Tadherat al-Auliya (Memorial of the Saints), Attar's best known prose work. This is an
account of the lives of 142 Sufi saints, accompanied by philosophical material. The beauty
of the work lies in the fact that it brings out the obstacles that often surmount mystics
when they tread the Path, and details how these saints met with these difficulties. In this
edition Arberry has shortened the work, only presenting the lives of 96 saints, and has
concentrated on the biographies. The selections start with Hasan of Basra (642–728)
and finish with al-Shebli (759–846), whose death marks the end of the formative period
of Sufism. Attar writes vividly and well, and all readers (even those not versed in Sufism)
should find the biographical studies entertaining and enlightening. And Arberry has provided an excellent translation, along with a bibliography and notes for each section and
an introduction, Persian Heritage Series. 287pp. RKP 66

BEHARI, BANKEY, tr. **TADHKARATUL-AULIYA OR, MEMOIRS OF SAINTS**, c$5.40.
This translation does not read quite as well as Arberry's, does not offer as many selections,
nor is it as well organized. However, more of Attar's philosophical speculations are presented, and some of the sixty-two selections in this edition are different from the ones
Arberry chose. The translation is definitely adequate and if we did not have Arberry's to
compare it to we would probably be very pleased with this one. Dr. Behari is a noted
scholar and translator and he supplies excellent introductory material. 245pp. MuA 65

NOTT, C.S., tr. **THE CONFERENCE OF THE BIRDS: A SUFI FABLE**, c$3.95/2.95.
*O you who have set out on the path of inner development, do not read my book only as
a poetical work, or a book of magic, but read it with understanding; and for this a man
must be hungry for something, dissatisfied with himself and with this world. He who has
not smelt the perfume of my discourses has not found the way of lovers.* This is probably
the most popular work in this section and it is one of our personal favorites. We recommend it highly to all on the path—whatever their individual path is! 147pp. ShP 54

BAKHTIAR, LALEH. **SUFI**, $5.95. An exploration of the inner world of Sufism in the
form of 120 illustrations, thirty in color, which focus on the forms and rhythms of Islamic
art and architecture. 9½x10". Avo 76

BAWA, GURU M.R. **THE DIVINE LUMINOUS WISDOM THAT DISPELS THE DARK-
NESS**, $4.00. A collection of answers that the Master gave to people of diverse backgrounds
who were visiting his Ashram in Ceylon. They are in the form of simple parables and
examples and deal with the most fundamental questions of life and death, truth, God,
and man. GBF 72

_____. **SONGS OF GOD'S GRACE**, $1.95. English translations of songs which
convey moments of ecstatic communion with God. 160pp. GBF 73

_____. **TRUTH AND LIGHT**, $2.50. Transcriptions of conversations Guru Bawa
held over the radio that distill his own brand of the universal wisdom teachings. Some
questions and answers are included. 143pp. GBF 74

BEESTON, A.F.L. **WRITTEN ARABIC**, c$5.95. This is a very clear introduction to the
essential features of modern written Arabic. Beeston excludes the mass of linguistic detail
contained in traditional Arabic grammars which assume the student wishes to master all
aspects of the language. Instead, the book provides for a sound understanding of abstract
literature on scholarly subjects, in contrast to manuals teaching a quick understanding of
journalistic Arabic. Index, 117pp. CUP 68

BEHARI, BANKEY. **SUFIS, MYSTICS, AND YOGIS OF INDIA**, $1.75. See Indian
Philosophy section.

BENY, ROLOFF. **PERSIA**, c$55.00. This is a beautifully produced volume, 10x12", dis-
tilling the essence of Persian culture with grace and sensitivity. The volume was commis-
sioned by the Empress of Iran, and so reflects a desire to make the Persian heritage as
significant as possible, which it does very well. The book is divided into four main themes:
Light, Life, the Sacred Place, and the Domain of Kings. The text is filled with exquisite
color photographs, drawings, and calligraphy. Much of the written material is on brown
paper with gold lettering. Seyyed Hossein Nasr, a leading Persian scholar, examines his
country's culture in an essay and anthology which trace the literary and spiritual development of the land, the people, and its artistic and cultural heritage. Illustrated with 228
color plates and many engravings. There are long notes on each of the plates along with
an index and bibliography. 367pp. NYG 75

BISSING, RONIMUND von. **SONGS OF SUBMISSION**, c$6.15. This is a mystical explo-
ration of the ecstasy of union with God expressed in a form which is rich in imagery. It
is subtitled *On the Practice of Subud* and the content reflects the heights of inner experience reached by followers of this path. 189pp. Cla 62

BLUNT, WILFRID. **SPLENDORS OF ISLAM**, c$10.95. This is a beautifully presented
survey of the arts and architecture of the entire Islamic world covering the period from
the seventh century to the present. The book is aimed at the general reader and, as could
be expected by the broadness of the coverage, each of the individual sections is quite
brief. The plates are magnificent and the text is adequate. Many color plates. 7x11",
bibliography, index. 152pp. Vik 76

BODROGLIGETI, A.J.E. **HALIS' STORY OF IBRAHIM**, c$16.35. *The Story of Ibrahim
is a literary-artistic exposition of the belief, widely held by the Sufis, that the believer's
attention must be turned entirely to Allah, that it cannot be divided or shared with anything but Allah. . . . The Lord, displeased by what he regards as Mohammed's excessive
love for his son Ibrahim, requests the Prophet to sacrifice his son if he wishes to retain the
guardianship of his Community and the concomitant right to intercede for it on the Day
of Resurrection. Mohammed . . . does not hesitate to carry out Allah's request, and yet,
like everyman, he finds it difficult to sacrifice the pleasures of this life—here represented
by Ibrahim—for the higher spiritual pleasures associated with the Divine Being.* This is a
religious legend which minstrels recited. The edition includes a large photographic reproduction of the original late Chagatay Turkic script, Romanized transcription, English
translation, introduction, glossary, and notes. 100pp. Bri 75

BROCKETT, ELEANOR. **TURKISH FAIRY TALES**, c$5.95. See the Fairy Tales section.

BROWN, JOHN P. **THE DARVISHES; OR ORIENTAL SPIRITUALISM**, c$23.50. The
most detailed account available, first published in 1868 and reprinted in this edition
(edited, with an introduction and notes by H.A. Rose). Illustrations, 520pp. Luz

BURCKHARDT, TITUS. **ALCHEMY—SCIENCE OF THE COSMOS, SCIENCE OF THE SOUL**, $2.50. See Alchemy section.

_________. **ART OF ISLAM: LANGUAGE AND MEANING**, c$25.00. This is far and away the most magnificent book on Islamic art we have ever seen. It is a large volume with over 200 color plates and 100 half tones and line drawings. The text itself is excellent and Burckhardt himself is one of our favorite authors. Here he states that Muslim art is a sacred art and its masterpieces are outward manifestations of the religious beliefs of Islam. From this standpoint he studies the flowering of Islamic art, its mosques, crafts and cities, illustrating his theme with carefully selected photographs. 228pp. WIF 76

_________. **AN INTRODUCTION TO SUFI DOCTRINE**, $4.10. Burckhardt's scholarship is excellent here, as usual. This is a very readable work for the layman as well as the scholar. He is *the* expert on Ibn 'Arabi of this century, and his presentations are heavily based on 'Arabi. 155pp.

_________. **LETTERS OF A SUFI MASTER**, $1.55. Mulay al-'Arabi ad-Darqawi, the author of these letters, was the founder of the Darqawi Order of Sufis, a Moroccan branch of the great Shadhili Order. The spiritual radiation of the Shaikh al-Darqawi brought about a sudden great flowering of Sufism in Morocco, Algeria, and beyond, and several of his direct disciples became outstanding Masters themselves. These letters were compiled by the Shaikh himself and this translation is based on two nineteenth century manuscripts. Introduction, 48pp. Prn 69

_________. **MOORISH CULTURE IN SPAIN**, c$18.50. A monumental study of the character and achievements developed during 800 years of the Muslim dominance of Spain. 200 Plates and illustrations. Burckhardt's newest work. 232pp. A&U 70

BURKE, O.M. **AMONG THE DERVISHES**, $3.95. Burke states in the preface that he *resolved to travel to as many Eastern lands as my resources would permit, to spend as much time as might be needed, to look for and record as much as possible* about the Sufis. Traveling as a dervish pilgrim and staying at Sufi monasteries, he learned a great deal about Sufism and this book is Burke's account of these experiences. A vividly written account which gives the reader a good feeling for Sufism and its practitioners. Bibliography, 203pp. Dut 73

BURTON, RICHARD. **THE KASIDAH**, c$5.00. The **Kasidah** or Lay of the Higher Law was composed by Sir Richard Burton in 1853 on his return journey from Mecca. Here he comments upon Western methods of thought, modern theories and philosophies, from the Sufi point of view. 128pp. Oct 74

_________. **PERSONAL NARRATIVE OF A PILGRIMAGE TO AL-MADINAH AND MECCA**, $7.00/set. Sir Richard (1821–90) was one of the great traveler-explorers of history. Successfully posing as a wandering dervish, he gained admittance to the holy Kaabah and to the tomb of the Prophet at Medina and participated in all the rituals of the Hadj (pilgrimage). He is still one of the very few non-Muslims to visit and return from Mecca. Above all, Burton was a sharp observer—of character, customs, and physical surroundings. These pages contain a treasury of material on Arab life, beliefs, manners, and morals; detailed descriptions of religious ceremonies and mosques; and a variety of ethnographic, geographical, and economic information. This two-volume edition gives us a vivid picture of the region and its people. Index, 955pp. Dov 1893

CHAPMAN, J.A. **MAXIMS OF ALI**, $1.35. Ali was a son-in-law of Muhammad's and was considered one of the great men of his day. A well known orator and spokesman, his sermons and speeches were collected soon after his death. This is a translation of some of the most popular ones, topically arranged. Introduction, 97pp. MuA 46

COWAN, DAVID. **MODERN LITERARY ARABIC**, $6.95. The lessons are written in non-technical language, and have many examples along with numerous exercises for translation from Arabic to English and vice versa. Since the fundamental grammar of written Arabic has hardly changed at all during the last thirteen centuries, this book also serves as an introduction to the classical language. This grammar is considered quite a good one. 215pp. CUP 58

COWAN, J.M., ed. **ARABIC-ENGLISH DICTIONARY**, $7.50. An unabridged edition of the highly acclaimed Hans Wehr **Dictionary of Modern Written Arabic**. *Its comprehensiveness and reliability as well as its clear presentation of the material have made it the principal aid for the study of written Arabic. Indeed, for the student and the younger (Western) scholar, it seems to have superceded—at least to a large degree—all other lexical aids.* —**Journal of the American Oriental Society**. Unfortunately the printing quality is not very good and the Arabic script is often hard to read. 1117pp. SLS 76

CRAGG, KENNETH. **THE CALL OF THE MINARET**, $3.95. Dr. Cragg presents an interpretation of Islam based on the phrases of the Muslim call to prayer. Islam is presented as a religious belief, as history, as a religious discipline, and as a social force. The political and ideological influence of Islam since 1945 is discussed, as is the Christian attitude toward Islam. Of special concern in this study is the relation of modern Christian and Muslim to one another. Dr. Cragg seems to be trying to present Islam to the non-Muslim Western world so it can be understood by providing points of reference within our own culture. Index, bibliography, 391pp. Oxf 56

_________. **THE HOUSE OF ISLAM**, $6.65. This is a good academic survey of the religious life of Islam with chapters on Islamic cosmology, Muhammad, the Qur'an, Law, Liturgy and the Sufic Path, and *Ummah* (the spiritual community of Islam). The chapters are divided well and the material is clearly presented. There are also questions for further study and discussion, a glossary, notes, and a bibliography. The format is definitely that of a textbook—but the material reads better than most textbooks. Chronology, index, 158pp. Dic 75

CRITCHLOW, KEITH. **ISLAMIC PATTERNS**, c$24.95. The geometric patterns of Islam art yield to the sensitive observer's eye an understanding of the cosmological laws a fecting all creation. Long misunderstood in the West as merely decorative, the wonderf abstractions of Islam were designed to lead the mind from the literal and mundane sphe toward the reality underlying worldly existence. Critchlow, through detailed analytic drawings, shows how Islamic art is inseparable from the science of mystical mathemati associated with the Pythagorean tradition. He shows clearly how the cosmos as exper enced by man is mirrored in the patterns created by Islamic art. Illustrating his analys with nearly 200 two color drawings, Critchlow has produced a fascinating, albeit specul tive study. 8½x10", index. 192pp. ScB 76

CROOKE, WILLIAM. **ISLAM IN INDIA**, c$13.50. An archaic study, written in the ear nineteenth century, of the manners, social habits, customs, and religious rites of the Mu lims in India. Every conceivable aspect of their life is discussed at length. Illustration glossary, notes, bibliography, index. 414pp OrB 21

DANNER, VICTOR, tr. **IBN 'ATA'ILLAH'S SUFI APHORISMS**, c$9.60. This is a tran lation of **Kitab al-Hikam**. *The main theme of the* **Hikam** *is . . . Gnosis. . . . In other word instead of being a purely objective exposition of Oneness of Being, that doctrine is her deliberately aimed at the reader so that he may experience it as a continual knocking o the doors of his intelligence. Bound up with this is the theme of* adab *which . . . may b translated* pious courtesy. *Gnosis is not merely an act of the intelligence; it demands total participation; and* adab *in its highest sense is the conformity of the soul, in all i different facets, to the Divine Presence. . . . We have here, in this little volume, one of th great basic texts of Islamic mysticism.*—Martin Lings. Danner also provides a study of th life and work of Ibn 'Ata'illah, background and introductory material, extensive note glossary, and bibliography. 102pp. Bri 73

DAR, B.A., ed. **RE-ORIENTATION OF MUSLIM PHILOSOPHY**, $4.50. A collection o short essays on the title theme by S.H. Nasr, B.H. Siddiqi, D.M. Azraf, and M.S. Shaikh together with an introduction by the editor which ties the selections together. 50pp PPC 65

DAVIS, F. HADLAND. **THE PERSIAN MYSTICS—JAMI**, c$2.85. Narrudin Abdur Rah man Jami (1414–92) was a great Persian mystical poet. This volume includes a shor biographical sketch followed by abridged translations and selected passages from his mos noted works: *The Story of Salaman and Absal, The Teaching of Lawaih, The Story o Yusuf and Zulaikha*, and *The Baharistian* or *Abode of Spring*. 103pp. MuA 46

DE BOER, J.J. **THE HISTORY OF PHILOSOPHY IN ISLAM**, $2.75. A very comprehen sive account, covering the major philosophers, their teachings, and the historical back ground of the Islamic system. 224pp. Dov 03

ELAHI, MAQBOOL, tr. **THE ABYAT OF SULTAN BAHOO**, c$3.00. Sultan Baho (1630–91) was a well known Indian mystic, author of well over 100 books on aspects o mysticism and religion. It is in his **Abyat** that his beliefs about the fundamentals of mysti cism find their most impressive expression. This is a bilingual (Punjabi/English) edition divided into parts and translated into verse, and expressing the true mystic's love of God The volume is the best technical production we have seen from a Pakistani publisher Introduction, notes, 398pp. MuA 67

EL-SAID, ISSAM and AYSE PARMAN. **GEOMETRIC CONCEPTS IN ISLAMIC ART** c$19.50. This volume shows how knowledge of simple geometric principles led Muslim craftsmen to produce intricate and beautiful patterns and provided a measuring system needed in other art forms. These patterns are illustrated by over 150 of the author's original drawings and by photographs of their architectural application. Oversize, 160pp WIF 76

ELWELL-SUTTON, L.P. **ELEMENTARY PERSIAN GRAMMAR**, $12.30. Provides a simple grammatical framework for contemporary written Persian based on the character istic idiom and phraseology of the language as it is used in newspapers, magazines, and novels. The student is introduced to Persian script from the first lesson. Words are fully vocalized in the early lessons, but vowels are progressively discarded—they are, however shown in the vocabulary. The letter forms of printed Persian are used in the exercises and two appendices give examples of commonly used cursive scripts. The example and exer cises require only a limited vocabulary of fairly commonly used words—about 1500 in all Pronunciation guides are also given and there is a key to the lessons at the end of the book, along with a Persian-English vocabulary. Index, 225pp. CUP 72

EPTON, NINA. **MAGIC AND MYSTICS OF JAVA**, c$8.40. A well written, travelogue-like account of Java. The author seems to have attended many ceremonies not usually accessible to the traveller and she reports her observations quite vividly. The reader gets a good feeling for the daily life of the Javanese people in addition to the magical side of the culture. Religious practices are also discussed. 212pp. Oct 74

ESIN, EMEL. **MECCA THE BLESSED, MADINAH THE RADIANT**, c$19.50. For thirteen centuries, the cities of Mecca and Madinah have been closed to non-Muslims, and this work contains the first comprehensive description and photographic documentation of them to appear in the West. The author and the photographer are both Turkish Muslims and were given special permission by the Saudi authorities to travel in the area and gather impressions and take photographs. Ms. Esin is an expert on Islamic art. Her text for this volume embraces all historical and cultural aspects of the holy cities, from the legends of prehistory up to the present day. 113 illustrations, over half in full color. Notes, index, 222pp. Ele 63

FAKHRY, MAJID. **A HISTORY OF ISLAMIC PHILOSOPHY**, c$19.60. A general survey of the development of Islamic thought from the seventh century to the present. In addition to philosophical and theological currents, Professor Fakhry discusses the legalism, rationalism, and mysticism in Islamic thought, the cultural impact of Islam on the diverse ects of Muslim life, and the nineteenth century rise of Pan-Islamism which attempted unite the politically disparate Islamic nations into a spiritual unity. All of the major ools and individuals are reviewed. The author is Chairman of the Department of Philophy at the American University of Beirut. Notes, index, bibliography, 442pp. Col 70

RAH, CAESAR. **ISLAM**, $2.75. This is a well written textbook-type analysis of Islam a religion as well as a system and ideology. It traces the history and growth of Islam, e role of Muhammad as Prophet and man, the significance of the Qur'an, the fundamens of Islamic beliefs and observances, the dynamism and resiliency of the religion, and status in the world today. Quotations from the sacred literature are interspersed oughout the text. Recommended.Notes, glossary, bibliography, index, 306pp. BES 68

ARUQI, BURHAN. **THE MUJJADDID'S CONCEPTION OF TAWHID**, $3.75. This is a reful, detailed study of the conception of Tawhid, or the unity of Being and of all ings, in the thought of Shaikh Ahmad Sirhindi (who is generally called the Mujaddid-i I-i-Thani). Shaikh Ahmad was the first and greatest among the mystics of Islam who exessly and strenuously opposed the Panthestic conception of Tawhid. This conception d become almost universal among Muslim mystics, especially since the time of Ibn 'Arabi, o wrote on it extensively and who has had enormous influence on the subsequent amic thought. Dr. Faruqi has been careful to define all the terms used and he provides tensive textual annotation. Introduction, index, 146pp. MuA 43

ARZAN, MASSUD. **ANOTHER WAY OF LAUGHTER**, $2.35. A collection of over 100 amples of Sufi humor in the form of short tales, written by such masters as Rumi, Attar, di, and Jami. The translator and editor is a native Persian now teaching Persian culture Columbia University. Dut 73

_____. **THE TALE OF THE REED PIPE**, $1.95. Professor Farzan has taught at iversities in the U.S. and here he provides a guide to the main concepts of Sufism. Part *What is Sufism, Who Is a Sufi*, includes a short general introduction and a selection om the writings of Al-Ghazali, Attar, Shams-e Tabrizi, Rumi, and Sa'di. Part II, *The actice of Sufism*, includes selections from some of the Sufi Masters discussing the folwing topics: *Repentance, Dreams, Zekr, Jami on the Practice of Sufism, Sufi Dance and usic*, and *Psychic Phenomena*. Part III, *Treasure in the Ruins*, presents some traditional aching stories. Part IV, *Sufism East and West*, is a translation of Mohammad Iqbal writgs on the Idea of Individuation. A very simple overview of some of the main Sufi ideas d writings. 104pp. Dut 74

RIEDLANDER, IRA. **THE WHIRLING DERVISHES**, $4.95. This photographic study a good introduction to the practice of Sufism. It is an account of the Sufi order known the Mevlevis (or whirling dervishes) and its founder, the poet and mystic Mevlana alalu'ddin Rumi. The author is an American Sufi, who is also a writer and an excellent ook designer and this oversize photographic study reflects both of those abilities well. It gins with a general study of the Sufi and goes on to an account of the life and spiritual evelopment of Rumi and ends with a detailed presentation of the whirling dervish ceremony and its background. The photographs are evocative of the ceremony's atmosphere d captions explain each one. A wonderful, moving study. Bibliography, glossary, 160pp. McM 75

_____, ed. **WISDOM STORIES FOR THE PLANET EARTH**, $1.75. A rare collection, compiled from Eastern and Western sources by an American who has travelled extensively in the East and has studied under several masters. Many of the stories are thousands of years old, some translated from ancient scriptures, others handed down in the oral tradition. These are tales for all those *who are interested in tapping the higher selves within them.* 108pp. H&R 73

FRYE, RICHARD NELSON. **BUKHARA**, c$3.95. Bukhara is in central Asia and was the center of the New Persian renaissance in the tenth century. It was the city of scholars, most notably Acicenna, and poets led by Rudaki. This is a description of the civilization of the city from its beginnings as a desert oasis up to and including the twefth century. Index, 209pp. UOk 65

FUZULI. **LEYLA AND MEJNUN**, c$12.60. In the Islamic world the love story of Leyla and Mejnun is as famous as Romeo and Juliet in the English speaking world. This edition is part of the UNESCO series. It provides a thorough introduction to the Leyla and Mejnun theme and the various forms in which the story has appeared by one of the leading authorities on the poem, Professor Alessio Bombaci and an extremely readable translation by Mme. Sofi Huri. 350pp. A&U 70

GEERTZ, CLIFFORD. **ISLAM OBSERVED**, $1.95.*In four brief chapters I have attempted both to lay out a general framework for the comparative analysis of religion and to apply it to a study of the development of a supposedly single creed, Islam, in two quite contrasting civilizations, the Indonesian and the Moroccan.*—from the Preface. The author begins his study by outlining the situation conceptually and providing an overview of the two countries. He then traces the evolution of their classical religious styles which, with disparate settings and unique histories, produced strikingly different spiritual climates. In Morocco, the Islamic conception of life came to mean activism, moralism, and intense individuality, while in Indonesia the same concept emphasized aestheticism, inwardness, and the radical dissolution of personality. Detailed bibliographical notes, index, 144pp. UCh 68

AL-GHAZALI

Al-Ghazali (1058–1111) was born in Persia and wrote in both Persian and Arabic. He studied under the greatest theologian of his age, al-Juwayni, and at 33 was appointed professor at the university in the capital—one of the most distinguished positions in the academic world of his day. A few years later he underwent an internal crisis and came to feel that his way of life was too worldly to have any hope of eternal reward. He left Baghdad and took up the life of a wandering ascetic. Though later he returned to the task of teaching, the change that occurred in him at this crisis was permanent. He was now a religious man, not just a worldly teacher of religious sciences.

Al-Ghazali has sometimes been acclaimed in both East and West as the greatest Muslim after Muhammad, and he is by no means unworthy of that dignity. His greatness rests above all on two things: (1) He was the leader in Islam's supreme encounter with Greek philosophy—that encounter from which Islamic theology emerged victorious and enriched, and in which Arabic Neoplatonism received a blow from which it did not recover. (2) He brought orthodoxy and mysticism into closer contact; the orthodox theologians still went their own way, and so did the mystics, but the theologians became more ready to accept the mystics as respectable, while the mystics were more careful to remain within the bounds of orthodoxy.—W. Montgomery Watt.

ALI, SYED, tr. **SOME MORAL AND RELIGIOUS TEACHINGS OF AL-GHAZALI**, $2.70. This small work includes a good study of Ghazali's life and work along with a topically divided list of his works. The bulk of the book presents extracts from **Ihyau-Ulum-id-Din (The Revival of Religious Sciences)**, one of his most important philosophical treatises, including chapters on The Nature of Man, Human Freedom and Responsibility, Pride and Vanity, Friendship and Sincerity, The Nature of Love, The Unity of God, The Love of God and its Signs, and Joyous Submission to God. The volume ends with some extracts from **Minhaj-ul-Abidin**, said to be Ghazali's final work. Index, 182pp. MuA 44

AVERROES. **THE INCOHERENCE OF THE INCOHERENCE**, c$25.60. A translation from the Arabic of **Tahafut al-Tahafut** by Simon van den Bergh. The two-volume set is a refutation of Al-Ghazali's major attack on philosophers and philosophy. The substance of Ghazali's attack is incorporated in this volume and Averroes follows point for point the arguments Ghazali uses and tries to refute them. Averroes is systematic. Introduction, notes, indices. 629pp. Luz 54

BAGLEY, F.R.C., tr. **GHAZALI'S BOOK OF COUNSEL FOR KINGS**, c$20.50. This is one of the masterpieces of Persian literature, though it was long known only in an Arabic version made some decades after his death. The book consists of two parts. The first sets forth the proper beliefs which a good ruler should hold, and contains a valuable Islamic creed. The second gives advice, mainly ethical but partly practical, concerning desirable qualities in ministers, secretaries, and wives. All these counsels are exemplified in anecdotes and aphorisms, attributed to famous Muslims, to kings and sages, and to Greek philosophers. A long introduction by the translator discusses the book's background and Ghazali's place in Muslim political thought. The text also includes extensive footnotes and a biographical index. 270pp. Oxf 71

FARIS, NABIH AMIN, tr. **THE BOOK OF KNOWLEDGE**, c$7.50. A translation of the **Kitab al-Ilm**, the opening part of **The Revival of Religious Sciences**. Here Ghazali defines what constitutes true *knowledge*, its relation to religious faith, and the abuses of academic learning. Introduction, notes, bibliography, index, 252pp. MuA 66

_________. **THE FOUNDATIONS OF THE ARTICLES OF FAITH**, c$4.50. The **Ihya 'Ulum al-Din** of al-Ghazali is divided into four quarters. The first deals with the acts of worship, the second with the usages of life, the third with the destructive matters of life, and the fourth with the saving matters of life. Each of these four quarters comprises ten books (*kitab*). The present work is the second book in the first quarter, the **Kitab Qawa'id al-Aqa'id**. It deals with the foundations of the articles of faith and is generally considered the most important part of the first quarter. The paper and the printing in this volume are unusually good for a Pakistani book. Index, bibliography, 146pp. MuA 63

_________. **THE MYSTERIES OF ALMSGIVING**, $6.30. A translation from the Arabic, with notes, of the **Katib Asrar al-Zakah** of al-Ghazali. The text details the different kinds of Zakah, or alms-giving, and goes from there to discuss the payment of Zakah and the inward and outward rules which govern that payment as well as the duties of the recipient. Indices of Arabic terms and proper names, bibliography, 106pp. AUB 66

_________. **THE MYSTERIES OF FASTING**, $1.80. See the Fasting section.

_________. **THE MYSTERIES OF PURITY**, $3.00. A translation of Book III of the first quarter of the **Ihya**. In his preface the translator states that this volume is not one of the more profound contributions of Ghazali—however, it is an integral part of the text and it is his desire to translate the entire **Ihya**. The material in this book should be especially valuable to those interested in cleansing and purifying their physical bodies. Part of the text gives detailed instructions on making ablutions. Bibliography, preface, 103pp. MuA 66

FIELD, CLAUD, tr. **THE ALCHEMY OF HAPPINESS**, $1.50. Ghazali was a practical mystic. His aim was to make men better by leading them away from a parrot-like repetition of orthodox phrases to a real knowledge of God. The constituents of alchemy are the knowledge of the self, the knowledge of God, the knowledge of the world as it really is, and the knowledge of the next world as it really is. 136pp. MuA 64

_________, tr. **THE CONFESSIONS OF AL GHAZZALI**, $1.05. This is a translation of a short autobiographical work in which Ghazali reviews many important events in his life and discusses many aspects of his philosophy and how he arrived at many of his major insights. 69pp. MuA nd

GARDNER, W.H.T., tr. **MISHKAT AL-ANWAR (THE NICHE FOR LIGHTS)**, $1.50. A translation of an intimate statement which reveals Ghazali's inner life and esoteric thought. MuA

HOLLAND, MUHTAR, tr. **AL GHAZALI: ON THE DUTIES OF BROTHERHOOD**, c$5.95. A translation of one of al-Ghazali's most important examinations of ethics and personal conduct. 95pp. OvP 76

KAMALI, SABIH, tr. **TAHAFUT AL-FALASIFAH (INCOHERENCE OF THE PHILOSOPHERS)**, c$7.20. *I decided to write this book in order to refute the ancient philosophers. It will expose the incoherence of their beliefs and the inconsistency of their metaphysical theories. . . . This book will set forth the doctrines of the ancient philosophers as those doctrines really are. . . . . This book is going to demonstrate that the ancient philosophers, whose followers the atheists of our day claim to be, were really untainted with what is imputed to them. They never denied the validity of the religious laws. On the contrary, they did believe in God, and did have faith in His messengers.* Index, notes, 267pp. MuA 58

MCKANE, WILLIAM, tr. **AL GHAZALI'S BOOK OF FEAR AND HOPE**, c$11.75. A translation of Book III of the fourth quarter of the **Ihya Ulum al-Din**. Bri

SHEHADI, FADLOU. **GHAZALI'S UNIQUE UNKNOWLABLE GOD**, c$17.95. Subtitled *A Philosophical Critical Analysis of Some of the Problems Raised by Ghazali's View of God as Utterly Unique and Unknowable*. This is a very scholarly work, which quotes extensively from Ghazali's work. Many notes, bibliography, index, 132pp. Bri 64

SHERIF, MOHAMED AHMED. **GHAZALI'S THEORY OF VIRTUE**, c$20.15. A study of Ghazali's ethical thought as shown in his extensive treatment of the virtues and their relation to the ends of life and to each other. This is a scholarly presentation which is exceedingly well organized and definitive and which includes extensive notes, a long bibliography, and an index. Clearly written. 218pp. SNY 75

STADE, ROBERT, tr. **99 NAMES OF GOD IN ISLAM**, $2.50. A translation of the major portion of al-Ghazali's **Al-Maqsad Al-Asna**. *Among Muslims and students of Islam it is common knowledge that the beads of the Muslim rosary (*subha*) are ninety-nine in number and that the individual adherent of the Islamic faith regularly uses them in his worship life. As he fingers the individual bead, he quietly and reverently repeats the ninety-nine names of God that are particularly familiar to him.*—from the introduction. In this work Ghazali discusses in detail the ninety-nine names that he regularly used. 138pp. Day 70

UMARUDDIN, MUHAMMAD. **THE ETHICAL PHILOSOPHY OF AL-GHAZZALI**, c$7.50. *The term Ethics . . . is used by al-Ghazzali . . . in a much wider sense than is usually done by modern ethical writers. It includes all the activities of man, religious as well as social, consequently there are many topics included in the present work which would have been omitted in a book dealing strictly with ethics. But such an omission would have presented a distorted picture of al-Ghazzali's ethical theory. My aim in this work is to present the basic principles and the practical implications of al-Ghazzali's ethical theory, and to reconstruct the whole system of his thought as presented in his works. . . . The presentation . . . in this book is based on al-Ghazzali's original works in Arabic, pa culary the* **Ihya** *and the* **Mizan al-'Amal**. This is a very carefully presented, clearly writt study, with ample notes. Preface, index, bibliography, 346pp. MuA 62

WATT, W. MONTGOMERY, tr. **THE FAITH AND PRACTICE OF AL-GHAZALI**, c$6.5 The first of the books here translated, **Deliverance from Error (al-Munqidh min ad-Dal** is the source for much of what we know about al-Ghazali's life. It is autobiographical, y not exactly an autobiography. It presents us with an intellectual analysis of his spiritu growth, and also offers arguments in defense of the view that there is a form of hum apprehension higher than rational apprehension, namely, that of the prophet when G reveals truths to him. The second selection is a translation of the introduction to the **Ihy** *The Beginning of Guidance*. It deals with the *purgative way* and directs the reader to t larger work for what lies beyond that. The ideal he establishes resembles that of a monast order with a very strict rule, and the forces of evil and superstition are prominent in h exposition. Watt supplies introductory material and notes. Index, 155pp. A&U 53

_________. **MUSLIM INTELLECTUAL**, c$8.50. This is an excellent biographical stu of Al Ghazali which looks at his life and thought as a whole within the context of th times in which he lived. Notes, bibliography, index. 223pp. EUP 63

ZAYD, ABDUL-R-RAHMAN abu, tr. **AL-GHAZALI ON DIVINE PREDICATES AN THEIR PROPERTIES**, c$6.00. In Islam, the question of the Divine Attributes has be treated from various perspectives. This volume presents a critical and annotated tran lation of the chapters of Ghazali's **Al-Iqtisad Fil-i'tiqad** which discuss the logical aspec of this question. It is one of Ghazali's most sophisticated presentations of his maj work on the subject. Introduction, index. 146pp. MuA 70

GIBB, H.A.R. **MOHAMMEDANISM**, $3.35. Dr. Gibb was Director of the Center for Mi dle Eastern Studies at Harvard University and the author of many books. Here he preser an historical survey of the growth and influence of Islam. The life of the Prophet, th teachings of the Qur'an, the expansion of Islam in Asia and Africa, Sufism, and the pro lems which Islam confronts in the modern world are all reviewed in this study. The to is dry and rather academic, and the presentation is designed not to overwhelm the read with a mass of details. This is as good a short overview as we know of. A chapter-by-chapt annotated bibliography is included. Index, 144pp. Oxf 70

GIBRAN, KAHLIL. **THE PROPHET**, c$5.00. *Islam* might seem a strange category f this Christian mystic. However, Gibran wrote in Arabic and came out of a tradition sin lar to many Sufis. And **The Prophet** seems to fit as well here as any other category (tha the advantage of an author index—we can put things where we feel they fit best, ar those who don't agree can still find their favorite works). **The Prophet** is Gibran's maste piece and it has sold over four million copies in the U.S. alone. It is mystical poetry at i finest and if you haven't read it, we recommend you do. You can't help but be moved b the majesty and beauty of the language and the imagery. Twelve mystical drawings b Gibran illustrate the text. 96pp. RaH 23

GILANI, HAZRAT. **FUTUH AL-GHAIB (THE REVELATIONS OF THE UNSEEN** c$1.95. Gilani was an important Sufi saint, known generally as the Saint of Baghdad. Th collection of eighty of his discourses is one of the most highly regarded works in the I lamic world. His teaching is both esoteric and exoteric and is directed toward aspirants o the Path. It is clear and eminently practical. This is a translation by M. Ahmad and th edition includes introductory material and a life sketch. 236pp. MuA 58

GILSENAN, MICHAEL. **SAINT AND SUFI IN MODERN EGYPT**, c$20.50. This is a d tailed study in the sociology of religion focusing on the Sufi orders of contemporar Egypt as the author observed them during two years in Cairo. He examines and attemp to explain the transformation of the order in Egypt since the turn of the century. Th bulk of the book is devoted to an analysis of the only modern Egyptian order which ha succeeded, in however limited a way, in expanding its membership and activities. Th order is known as the Hamidiya Shadhiliya. It differs from more traditional orders in i emphasis on comprehensive direction and control over its members. Notes, bibliography index, 248pp. Oxf 73

GOHLMAN, WILLIAM, tr. **THE LIFE OF IBN SINA (AVICENNA)**, c$26.90. This i the first complete Arabic text and English translation of the eleventh century philoso pher's autobiography, with its continuation by one of his pupils. The translation is base on recently discovered manuscripts; the Arabic text and English translation are on facin pages and there is a profusion of critical notes and annotations along with a long bil liography. Index, 163pp. SNY 74

GOICHON, A.M. and M.S. KHAN. **THE PHILOSOPHY OF AVICENNA**, c$4.50. Avicenn was a tenth century philosopher and physician, and the first Arab to create a philosophica system which is complete and whole. He had a profound and lasting influence on bot Eastern and Western philosophers. This book is an expanded version of a series of lectur the author gave. Its first chapter discusses the cultural background of tenth century Persi and Iraq, and gives an account of Avicenna's life and work. The second chapter deals wit the origin and development of Arabic philosophical vocabulary with special reference t the language used by Avicenna. The third chapter discusses the influence of Avicenna metaphysics on medieval Europe. The book is based entirely on Arabic and Persian origin sources. Notes, bibliography, 129pp. MoB 69

GOLDZIHER, IGNAZ. **MUSLIM STUDIES, VOLUME I**, c$20.15. This study, originall published in German at the end of the last century, is generally considered one of th works which laid the foundations for the study of Islam as a religion and a civilizatio This volume discusses the reaction of Islam to the ideals of Arabic tribal society and th attitudes of early Islam to the various nationalities that they conquered (especially th Persians). The volume culminates in a study of the Shu'ubiyya movement which represent the reaction of the newly converted peoples, again especially the Persians, to the ide of Arab superiority. The second volume of **Muslim Studies** is reviewed with the works o Hadith. A good third of this volume is devoted to annotations. Index, 254pp. SNY 6

UNEBAUM, GUSTAVE von. **MEDIEVAL ISLAM**, $4.65. *This book has grown out of ries of public lectures.... It proposes to outline the cultural orientation of the Muslim ddle Ages, with eastern Islam as the center of attention. It attempts to characterize the ieval Muslim's view of himself and his peculiarly defined universe, the fundamental ellectual and emotional attitudes that governed his works, and the mood in which he d his life. It strives to explain the structure of his universe in terms of inherited, bor- and original elements, the institutional framework within which it functioned, and place in relation to the contemporary Christian world.* Notes, index, 385pp. UCh 53

_____. **MUHAMMADAN FESTIVALS**, c$5.25. This presentation is concerned h the essential and typical elements of Islamic ritual, prayer, and pilgrimage. Illustra- ns, notes, bibliography, index. 140pp. Cur 76

ILLAUME, ALFRED. **ISLAM**, $2.25. Deals in turn with Muhammad; the Qur'an; the lution of Muhammadanism as a system of faith, law, religion, and philosophy; the ying schools of thought; the devotional life; and the changes taking place in the modern mic viewpoint. Bibliography. 210pp. Pen 54

ADITH

e Hadith consists of the sayings and practices of the Prophet and his im- ediate companions. Its contents not only complement the Qur'an and ex- ain the vague passages therein, but also provide guidance in matters on ich the Qur'an is silent; thus the Hadith has become the second source of v in Islam. The Hadith is also a source of information on the development Islamic thought and contains most of the basic ideas which later Muslim olars drew upon with regards to the conduct of daily life as well as social, litical, and cultural institutions.

BDUL, M.O.A. **THE PROPHET OF ISLAM**, $6.00. The text is aimed at students and the general public. The bulk of the text is devoted to a survey of the basic and most ortant traditions relating to law and theology which are known as Hadith. Included is iscussion of the origin, transmission, contents, and arrangement of Hadith, information the classification of Hadith collections, and a presentation of the **Forty Traditions of Nawari**, including Arabic text, transliteration, and translation. There's also a section th biographical information on the Prophet. 120pp. IPB 72

_____, tr. **THE SELECTED TRADITIONS OF AL-NAWARI**, $6.00. The selec- ns presented here consist of traditions from almost all the important, recognized Sun- e collections of Hadith and cover a variety of topics relating to every possible aspect of e life of a Muslim—religious, social, cultural. An introductory chapter reviews the de- lopment of Hadith literature and subsequent chapters contain the Arabic text, translit- ation, translation, and commentary on each of the forty selections. Abdul has at- mpted, through his commentaries, to make Hadith relevant to contemporary life. pp. IPB 73

OLDZIHER, IGNAZ. **MUSLIM STUDIES, VOLUME II**, c$30.90. A recent translation Goldziher's famous study on the development of the Hadith in which the Hadith is own to reflect the various trends of early Islam, and in which its collection, and the bsequent literature devoted to it, is described. An additional essay discusses the cult of nts, which though contrary to the spirit and the letter of the earliest Islam, played an portant part in its subsequent development. Extensive notes, index. 378pp. SNY 71

HAN, MUHAMMAD. **GARDENS OF THE RIGHTEOUS**, c$12.00. A concise collec- n of Hadith, which is well organized and well translated. Notes, index, 352pp. Cur 75

OBSON, JAMES, tr. **MISHKAT AL-MASABIH**, c$31.25/Two volume set. This set is ased on the most authentic and reliable Hadith literature and shows the Prophet's attitude wards various aspects of religious and social life. Virtually every imaginable topic is thoritatively presented and the discussion is in depth. This is an extremely important ok for all who are seriously interested in the Islamic way of life as taught by the Pro- het. Introduction, notes, glossary, bibliography, indices. 1473pp. MuA 75

DDIQI, ABDUL, tr. **SAHIH MUSLIM**, $55.00/Four volume set. This is a mammoth ur volume translation of one of the most authentic and exhaustive collections of the aditions of the Prophet, narrated by his companions and orginally compiled under the le **Al-Jami'-Us-Sahih** by Imam Muslim. This edition also includes extensive commen- ry and many notes based on original sources along with brief biographical sketches of ajor Hadith narrators. A welcome addition to the literature and a must for all serious Is- mic scholars and practitioners. Introduction, index. 1638pp. MuA 75

HAFIZ

afiz' spiritual greatness and mental power proceeded from that mystical onsciousness which in him attained perfection. That path of life of which na'i, Attar, Jalal-al-Din and Sa'di had spoken each in turn and in his own ay, was by Hafiz described in language that plumbs the depths of feeling

and soars to the heights of expression .... So deeply immersed was he in the mystical unity, that in every ode and lyric, whatever its formal subject, he in- cluded one or more verses expressive of this lofty theme.... His true mastery is in the lyric (ghazal). In Hafiz' hands the mystical lyric on the one hand reached the summit of eloquence and beauty, and on the other manifested a simplicity all its own.... In short words he stated ideas mighty and subtle .... It is evident that the master's lyrics come straight from the heart; each poem is a subtle expression of the poet's innermost thoughts.—from the in- troduction to Arberry's translation.

ARBERRY, A.J., ed. **HAFIZ: FIFTY POEMS**, c$9.50. Here Arberry presents poetical translations of Hafiz' poems done by fourteen different people. This has the double ob- ject of exhibiting the various aspects of Hafiz' style and thought, and of showing how various English scholars have translated his poetry. Professor Arberry also supplies a long introduction, biographical and critical, and extensive notes on the texts. The poems are presented in full in the original Persian script and then the translations follow. The trans- lations are considered among the finest available; though not as many poems are here as in Clarke's monumental work, they are generally much more readable. Index, 187pp. CUP 53

ARYANPUR, ABBAS. **POETICAL HOROSCOPE OR ODES OF HAFIZ**, c$14.70. This is a recent Iranian translation of the Odes which includes a biographical sketch, a glossary, and the English translation on facing pages with the Persian script. The translations are often quite literal and are certainly not the best we've read. Each poem is followed by a short interpretative paragraph. The tone seems more racy than mystical and the color il- lustrations interspersed throughout add to this impression. EPI 65

CLARKE, WILBERFORCE. **THE DIVAN-I-HAFIZ**, $45.00/set. The private life of a Persian is discovered. His turn of mind and his thoughts become clear. Hafiz' power was found in his originality, free from attempts at wit and obscure metaphors. His style was clear, unaffected, and harmonious. The shaikhs and Sufis agreed in considering the **Divan-I-Hafiz** as the heights of perfection. Written in the fourteenth century, this is the first English prose translation, and includes critical and explanatory remarks, an intro- ductory preface, notes on Sufism, and a life of the author. Limited edition, two volumes, boxed. 1011pp. Wei 1891

HAFIZ. **SELECTIONS FROM THE RUBAIYAT AND ODES TOGETHER WITH AN ACCOUNT OF SUFI MYSTICISM**, c$5.50. Collected from many old Persian manuscripts and rendered into English verse by a member of the Persia Society of London, who also supplies an excellent long critical introduction and a detailed glossary. A flowing, delight- ful translation—much more readable than Wilberforce Clarke's painfully literal English prose. 147pp. Wat 20

NAKOSTEEN, MEHDI, tr. **THE GHAZALIYYAT OF HAAFEZ**, c$17.50. Includes a long introduction on the life and times of Hafiz, his place in Persian literature and his philosophy; a section on the structure, contents and origin of the *ghazal* (sonnet); notes on the translation; bibliographical notes and sources; and the translator's calligraphy of the Persian text. Nakosteen is a noted Persian scholar. Edition limited to 300 copies. 390pp. EEP 73

HAIM, S. **SHORTER PERSIAN-ENGLISH DICTIONARY**, c$12.60. Covers 30,000 words and idioms used in modern Persian. The Persian words are in script. 814pp. Bkh 73

HALL, MANLEY P. **THE MYSTICS OF ISLAM**, $3.00. This is an excellent review of the Islamic mystical tradition. Hall begins with a discussion of mystical visions and insights of Muhammad and in the process gives us an informative summary of the main features of the Prophet's life and experiences—including a discussion of the Qur'an. The next sections discuss the rise of Islam and the Caliphs, religious philosophy in Islam, and the foundations of Islamic mysticism. Hall also surveys the Druses, the Dervishes, and the Sufis as well as the Arabian Nights and Rumi. 107pp. PRS 75

HALL, MANLEY P. and HENRY DRAKE. **MYSTICISM OF THE DIVINE UNION**, $1.50. This is a reprint from Hall and Drake's correspondence course which reviews Islamic mysticism and places an emphasis on the teachings of Rumi. Oversize, 17pp. PRS 53

HAQ, M. ANWARUL. **THE FAITH MOVEMENT OF MAWLANA MUHAMMAD ILYAS**, c$18.50. The Faith Movement originated in a small area south of Delhi, India in 1927 and has now spread across the world. It claims to be one of the largest religious movements in the history of Islam. Ilyas' simple goal was to teach Muslims true Islam: to revive the Islamic way of life prescribed by God and practiced by the Prophet and his Companions. He emphasized practice and personal involvement. Since he was a Sufi, he based his movement on Sufi teaching and ceremonies, though he made certain changes. He kept his movement free from political influences and it is a tribute to him that Muslims of different political views could work together in his movement. This book presents a detailed study of the life, work, and thought of Ilyas, and the technique of work and the organization of the Movement. Notes, bibliography, index. 210pp. A&U 72

HAWI, SAMI. **ISLAMIC NATURALISM AND MYSTICISM**, c$21.55. A detailed philosophical study of Ibn Tufayl's **Hayy Bin Yaqzan** divided into the following sections: *Philosophical and Literary Background and the Methodical Structure of the Treatise; Naturalism, The Beginning of All Philosophizing;* and *The Existence of God and His Attributes and the The Nature and Unity of the Phenomenal World.* Indexed, with extensive notes and bibliography. 295pp. Bri 74

HIRASHIMA, HUSSEIN. **THE ROAD TO HOLY MECCA**, c$3.50. A beautiful little travelguide, full of color plates. 130pp. Kod 72

HODGSON, MARSHALL. **THE VENTURE OF ISLAM, VOL. I: THE CLASSICAL AGE OF ISLAM**, c$26.85. This volume analyzes the world before Islam, Muhammad's challenge (570-624), and the early Muslim state of 625-692. Professor Hodgson then reviews the classical civilization of the High Caliphate, discussing such topics as the bloom of Arabic literary culture, Muslim personal piety, and the dissolution of the absolutist tradition. There's also a section on the Islamic vision in religion. This is a very detailed, scholarly study, which reads like a textbook (which it is, in a way, since it grew out of the course that Hodgson taught for many years at the University of Chicago). Glossary, bibliography, index. 544pp. UCh 74

HOURANI, GEORGE, tr. **AVERROES: ON THE HARMONY OF RELIGION AND PHILOSOPHY**, $4.05. Translation of an important work in which Averroes sets out to show that the scriptural law of Islam does not altogether prohibit the study of philosophy by Muslims, but, on the contrary, makes it a duty for those people gifted with the capacity for scientific reasoning. Introduction, notes, index. 128pp. Luz 61

HUGHES, THOMAS. **A DICTIONARY OF ISLAM**, c$24.00. A systematic exposition of the doctrines of the Muslim faith in the form of a concise and comprehensive account of the doctrines, rites, ceremonies and customs, together with the technical and theological terms, of the Islamic religion. Also includes biographical sketches of some of the most noted figures, many illustrations and appropriate quotations from the Qur'an. Oversize, 750pp.

HUSSAIN, AHMED. **THE PHILOSOPHY OF FAQIRS**, $1.80. A discussion of the two schools of **Tasawwuf**: the Monastics, who identify God with Nature; and the Positivistics, who differentiate God from Nature. 70pp. MuA 40

IQBAL

ARBERRY, A.J., tr. **COMPLAINT AND ANSWER OF IQBAL**, $1.20. Translations of the **Shikwa** and the **Jawab-i-Shikwa** of Iqbal in verse. These are among the most popular of Iqbal's poems and were the first to bring him fame. The central theme of both poems is the decay of Islam from its former greatness, and the measures to be adopted if it was to re-establish its authority and regain its vitality. 79pp. MuA 55

_____, tr. **JAVIA-NAMA**, c$5.25. This is an excellent translation of Muhammad Iqbal's (1873-1938) greatest work, **The Javia-nama.** In imitation of the Prophet of Islam, the poet soars through the spheres, encountering on his heavenly journey many great figures of history with whom he holds converse. Arberry provides an introduction, extensive notes, and a bibliography. 151pp. A&U 66

_____, ed. **NOTES ON IQBAL'S ASRAR-I-KHUDI (THE SECRETS OF THE SELF)**, $.60. These are notes by Iqbal himself which were not included in the revised edition of the **Asrar-i-Khudi** and which Professor Arberry feels throw light upon important aspects of the work. Introduction, 57pp. MuA 52

_____, tr. **PERSIAN PSALMS**, c$3.00. A translation of Iqbal's **Zabur-i-Ajam**, which was written through the medium of the Persian *ghazal* or lyric. Iqbal did an excellent job of making this ancient form express his philosophy with the simple language for which he is noted. Introduction, 135pp. MuA 48

HUSSAIN, M. HADI, tr. **THE NEW ROSE GARDEN OF MYSTERY AND THE BO OF SLAVES**, $1.95. **The New Rose Garden** (Gulshan-i-Raz-i-Jadid) was composed Iqbal in response to Shabistari's **The Secret Garden**. The latter was written in reply t series of fifteen questions on mystical philosophy propounded by an inquirer. Iqb poem has nine questions, covering the same material. This is a verse translation wh reads quite well. The second selection, **Bandagi Namah** is translated in blank verse describes the arts, music, and religion of slave nations and the architecture of free natio Introduction, 182pp. MuA 69

IQBAL, ALLAMA. **THE RECONSTRUCTION OF RELIGIOUS THOUGHT IN ISLA** c$2.25. This is the transcription of a series of lectures which Iqbal gave on the title ther In his *reconstruction* the great philosopher took both the philosophical traditions Islam and the more recent developments in human knowledge into consideration. T topical headings included the following: *Knowledge and Religious Experience, Philosophical Test of the Revelations of Religious Experience, The Conception of G and the Meaning of Prayer, The Human Ego—His Freedom and Immortality, The Spirit Muslim Culture, The Principle of Movement in the Structure of Islam,* and *Is Relig Possible?* Index, 207pp. MuA 75

MALIK, HAFEEZ, ed. **POET-PHILOSOPHER OF PAKISTAN**, c$16.80. As one of foremost Muslim thinkers of the twentieth century, Muhammad Iqbal in eleven volum of poetry as well as scores of essays and lectures, urged upon his followers spiritual generation based on the love of man and God. The first part of this study presents extensive biography of Iqbal by the editor and Linda Malik. Part II is a selection of essa on his political thought; Part III presents essays on his philosophy; Part IV discusses attitude toward Islamic mysticism; and Part V is devoted to essays on his poetry. None the selections in this volume are the work of Iqbal himself, although each is written by expert in the field and many quotations from his work are included. Notes, bibliograph index. 466pp. Col 71

NICHOLSON, REYNOLD, tr. **THE SECRETS OF THE SELF**, c$1.80. A translation Asrar-i-Khudi, a philosophical poem exploring the doctrine of unity—this edition was vised by Nicholson in the light of corrections suggested by Iqbal himself. The transla also supplies ample introductory material and notes. 179pp. MuA 40

JALBANI, G.N. **TEACHINGS OF SHAH WALIYULLA OF DELHI**, c$5.40. The Sh was an eighteenth century Indian reformer who was versed in both the esoteric and ex teric sciences. His slogan was *Back to the Qur'an* and he felt that he had been selected deal with a scientific age where people were not disposed to accept everything at fa value. He did not follow any of the established schools and subjected the findings of the schools to a thorough investigation based on the Qur'an and the Hadith—what ce forms to them both, he accepts; the rest he rejects outright. Notes, bibliography, inde 259pp. MuA 73

JAMES, DAVID. **ISLAMIC ART: AN INTRODUCTION**, c$3.98. See Sacred Art sectic

KAMAL, AHMAD. **THE SACRED JOURNEY**, c$8.50. *The volume includes the la pertaining to Pilgrimage, and whenever the author approaches a facet or aspect of t Pilgrimage he provides an insight into the origin and the rituals. In brief, within the pages, you will find the complete ceremony of Pilgrimage, its laws and observances, a implicit therein, an appeal to Muslims to unite and thrust out of bondage, with a wa ing against discord and its perils. Both the Arabic text and translation are included in t* volume. 216pp. A&U 61

KEDDIE, NIKKI, ed. **SCHOLARS, SAINTS, AND SUFIS—MUSLIM RELIGIOUS I STITUTIONS SINCE 1500**, c$19.50. A collection of sixteen scholarly papers deali with the social role of religious institutions in the Muslim world, this volume attemp to provide a view of these institutions as functional groups playing an important role Muslim society and politics. Many notes. 401pp. UCa 72

KHALDUN, IBN

Ibn Khaldun was a fourteenth century Arab historian who founded a speci science to deal with the problems of history and culture based on the philo ophies of Plato and Aristotle and their Muslim followers. He is known one of the fathers of modern social science and cultural history.

MAHDI, MUHSIN. **IBN KHALDUN'S PHILOSOPHY OF HISTORY**, $4.25. This is a d tailed investigation of Khaldun in the light of what he himself wrote and taught and in relations to modern science. A very scholarly account, with many notes, a bibliograph and a long index. 325pp. UCh 57

ROSENTHAL, FRANZ, tr. **THE MUQADDIMAH: AN INTRODUCTION TO HISTOR** c$60.50/set. This is the earliest critical study of history in the Muslim world, and one the earliest extant anywhere. It was written by Ibn Khaldun in 1377 as the preface to book of world history. It has since become known as a self-contained work, treating in most encyclopedic detail the general problems of the philosophy of history and relati the information to the Islamic tradition. This is the first English translation and it includ a long introduction, notes, bibliography, and index. Three volumes, boxed. 1698pp. PU

_____, tr. **THE MUQADDIMAH**, $4.95. Edited and abridged by N.J. Dawoo this version makes Khaldun's essential ideas more accessible to the general reader. 479p PUP 67

KHAN, EBRAHIM. **ANECDOTES FROM ISLAM**, c$7.50. A selection of short piec culled from a great variety of sources (the editors claim that over five hundred are repr

nted) from all parts of the Islamic world and from its major leaders. Basically the theme
teaching. The majority are teaching stories and are designed to serve as an inspiration.
Glossary, bibliography. 479pp. MuA 60

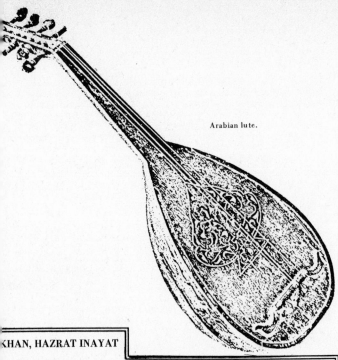

Arabian lute.

KHAN, HAZRAT INAYAT

Inayat Khan was born in 1882 in Baroda, in a family who had been well-known musicians for several generations. When he was twenty he began travelling all over India, giving concerts, lectures and private lessons. Even then he had begun to speak about the need to dissolve differences between people, such as those he had seen between Hindu and Moslem in his own country.

When he came to Hyderabad his aptitude to follow the spiritual path was recognized and he lived there from 1903 till 1907 as a disciple of his Sufi master. His sense of the brotherhood of men was deepened and connected to his religious foundations, for as a mystic he was able to understand the truth that all originate in one source. When his master died, Inayat travelled as a pilgrim throughout India, Ceylon and Burma, at the same time giving concerts, which met with an increasing measure of success. But his master had enjoined him not only to work to bring all Indians together, but also to unite people of East and West.

In 1910 he travelled to America with his brothers, musicians like himself. He gave concerts and lectures in America, France and Russia and met the prominent artists of the time. Between 1914 and 1920 he was in London, founding the universal Sufi Movement to make known the idea of unity, which is at the root of everything.

He expressed this truth in such a way that people from a Western background notwithstanding all outward differences could take the steps to understand his message. He had to give up his music, but his Movement grew.

From 1920 till 1926 he travelled in Europe and America, followed by an increasing number of disciples. He founded Sufi centres in twelve countries, meeting fame and admiration, but also misunderstanding and resistance.

Towards the end of 1926 Inayat Khan returned to India and he died the following year in Delhi.—from de Jong-Keesing's biography.

JONG-KEESING, ELISABETH de. **INAYAT KHAN**, $12.50. This is the most complete biographical study of Inayat Khan available. Ms. de Jong-Keesing worked closely with surviving members of his family and with his associates in the Sufi Movement. The material is well written and covers Inayat Khan's entire life, with the greatest emphasis being given to his mystical experiences. Unfortunately the volume is overpriced, but if one wants to know about the life and teachings of Inayat Khan we cannot think of a better book to read. Glossary, notes. 302pp. Luz 74

KHAN, HAZRAT INAYAT. **THE BOOK OF HEALTH**, $3.95. The material in this beautifully produced volume can also be found in the Sufi Message Books. **The Book of Health** is a collection of teachings on the spiritual aspects of healing, originally intended only for

Inayat Khan's pupils. In a long introductory section he discusses the basic laws governing the mind's influence over the body, which he considers greater than the physical body's influence on mental existence. In Part Two Khan presents an excellent review of healing. Part Three is devoted to the psychological nature of diseases; Part Four reviews the development of healing power; Part Five, the application of healing power; and Part Six, methods of healing. The material is not discussed in depth—however the spiritual philosophy behind the teaching is evident and the material is very clearly presented. SPC 74

_____. **EDUCATION**, $3.95. A collection of material from the Sufi Message Books. The volume is beautifully produced and includes a wealth of knowledge and insight into the upbringing of infants and children, leading to a greater understanding of the young soul on its journey to maturity. 127pp. SPC 75

_____. **HINDUSTANI LYRICS**, $1.50. A fine collection of the mystic poets of India. Mostly they are Sufis who scoff at the unenlightened orthodox. For them, God is All in All, symbolized as the beautiful and cruel Beloved; difficult to find, withdrawn behind the veil, inspiring and demanding all worship and devotion. 59pp. Rai 19

_____. **MUSIC**, $2.95. Touches on the themes of music as related to life, to man, to the universe and to creation. Topics include: *Music of the Spheres, The Mystery of Sound and Color, The Psychic Influence of Music, The Aid of Music in Spiritual Development.* 101pp. SPC 62

_____. **THE MYSTICISM OF SOUND**, $2.00. See the Music section.

_____. **THE PURPOSE OF LIFE**, $2.95. *The first thing that a seeker after Truth must realize, is the purpose of life. No sooner does a soul begin to feel sober from the intoxication of life, than the first thing it asks itself is: What is the purpose of my life? Each soul has its own purpose, but in the end all purposes resolve into one purpose, and it is that purpose which is sought by the mystic.* 127pp. Rai 73

_____. **THE SMILING FOREHEAD**, $2.95. Chapters on *The Symbol of the Cross, The Religion of the Heart, Unpublished Papers, Aspects of Sufi Mysticism, The Word That Was Lost, The Smiling Forehead,* and much else. A representative collection of his work. Introduction by Pir Vilayat. Illustrations, 128pp. Rai 73

_____. **SONGS OF INDIA**, $1.50. Beautiful songs rendered into English from Urdu, Hindi, and Persian. Glossary, 46pp. Ikh nd

_____. **THE SUFI MESSAGE BOOKS.**

The Sufi Message Books are the verbal teachings of Pir-O-Murshid Hazrat Inayat Khan, who brought the Sufi way of life to the West. The discourses cover a wide range of subjects, including the relationships of man and woman, education, life, happiness, psychology, religion, meditation, the raising of children, music and much else. Each relates ways in which people can better realize, shape, and direct the course of their lives. We recommend all of these volumes very highly. c$9.50/each. B&J

VOLUME I: THE WAY OF ILLUMINATION; THE INNER LIFE; THE SOUL, WHENCE AND WHITHER?; THE PURPOSE OF LIFE. These four books in one volume may be regarded either as an introduction to Sufism, or as representative of Sufi mysticism as developed by Inayat Khan.

VOLUME II: THE MYSTICISM OF SOUND; MUSIC; THE POWER OF THE WORD; COSMIC LANGUAGE. Contains most of his teachings on sound and music. Inayat Khan was a master musician and often expressed himself in musical terms, especially when speaking of the birth and evolution of matter.

VOLUME III: EDUCATION; RASA-SHASTRA (SEXUAL UNION); CHARACTER-BUILDING AND THE ART OF PERSONALITY; MORAL CULTURE. Teachings on human relationships.

VOLUME IV: HEALTH; MENTAL PURIFICATION; THE MIND WORLD. The relationship of mind and body; how to purify them, how to be healthy, how to be healed, how to be used as an instrument for healing, how to be harmonious within, how to be whole.

VOLUME V: SUFI MESSAGE OF SPIRITUAL LIBERTY; AQIBAT, LIFE AFTER DEATH; THE PHENOMENON OF THE SOUL; LOVE, HUMAN AND DIVINE; PEARLS FROM THE OCEAN UNSEEN; METAPHYSICS. Early teachings. 256pp.

VOLUME VI: THE ALCHEMY OF HAPPINESS. A collection of forty lectures on all aspects of the spiritual life—to be lived and practiced.

VOLUME VII: IN AN EASTERN ROSE GARDEN. This edition has been enlarged by eleven lectures never previously published. 271pp.

VOLUME VIII: THE SUFI TEACHINGS. Sixty-eight subjects, a wonderful introduction to Sufism. Material on *The Law of Attraction, Pairs of Opposites, History of the Sufis, The Awakening of the Soul,* and so much more.

VOLUME IX: THE UNITY OF ALL RELIGIOUS IDEALS. Perhaps the most important part of his teaching. 279pp.

VOLUME X: SUFI MYSTICISM; THE PATH OF INITIATION AND DISCIPLESHIP; SUFI POETRY; ART: YESTERDAY, TODAY AND TOMORROW; THE PROBLEM OF THE DAY. 270pp.

VOLUME XI: PHILOSOPHY, PSYCHOLOGY, MYSTICISM. Just prior to his death, he reviewed and rewrote many of his lectures on these subjects. It may be considered his *magnum opus.* This volume also contains his aphorisms. 259pp.

VOLUME XII: THE VISION OF GOD AND MAN; CONFESSIONS; FOUR PLAYS. 274pp.

_____. **VADAN GAYAN NIRTAN,** $3.95. A collection of aphorisms and poems on all aspects of the spiritual life. This is one of the most treasured of all Inayat Khan's works. They display spontaneous flashes of his soul faced with people's quandaries, aspirations, misgivings, heartbreaks, and ignorance. 285pp. Rai 74

STOLK, SIRKAR van. **MEMORIES OF A SUFI SAGE: HAZRAT INAYAT KHAN,** $4.95. *The purpose of the present work was simply to share with the reader some part, some breath, of the fragrance of Hazrat Inayat Khan's teachings, so that those who felt drawn to them might by moved to gather the real flowers from his own books.* EWP 67

KHAN, KHAN. **THE SECRET OF ANA'L HAQQ,** c$3.75. A topically arranged translation of **Irshadat-i-Shaykh Ibrahim,** the teachings of a tenth century Muslim saint which expound the secret doctrine of *how God is manifest in man,* in the form of short, detached sayings. These sayings are short commentaries on the esoteric teachings of some verses of the Qur'an. Glossary, notes. 199pp. MuA 35

KHAN, MUSHARAFF. **PAGES IN THE LIFE OF A SUFI,** c$5.80. A living journey into the life of a mystic, into the heart of spirituality and Sufism. He recounts his youth in India, of stories and experiences with Maharajas and wandering dervishes. He speaks of the relationship between master and disciple, of spiritual healing, of his travel experience with Inayat Khan, of the practices of Sufis, Hindus and Moslems, of mystical life, prayer and meditation. 155pp. SPC 32

KHAN, PIR VILAYAT INAYAT and GEORGE TREVELYAN. **NEW AGE MEDITATIONS,** $3.75. A collection of Pir Vilayat's lectures at a 1970 seminar which forms an excellent condensed course in Sufi techniques of breathing, mantra (wazifa), and meditation. There's also material on the history of Sufism and its underlying philosophy. 123pp. WHP nd

KHAN, PIR VILAYAT INAYAT. **SUFI MASTERS,** c$2.50. Details the lives of seven of the great Sufi teachers: Jelal-uddin Rumi; Al Hallaj; Ibn 'Arabi; Attar; Bastami; Suhrawardhi; and Hazrat Inayat Khan, the author's father. 43pp. Suf 71

_____. **TOWARD THE ONE,** $7.95. Pir Vilayat's *magnum opus,* an enlightening presentation of Sufi practices, his teachings, and transcripts of his lectures in Europe and America, as well as some completely new material. Filled with drawings, designs, and photographs, and printed on oatmeal paper. Includes a 24x36" poster folded into the book to reproduce the chapter entitled *Heart.* 9x9" format. 400pp. H&R 74

OMAR KHAYYAM

This **Rubaiyat** was written anonymously in the eleventh century by a poet who was known in his time as a highly skilled mathematician. It is a very popular philosophical and mystical work. A recording of the **Rubaiyat** is available. See the Records section for a description.

ARBERRY, A.J. **THE ROMANCE OF THE RUBAIYAT,** c$6.85. A facsimile reprint of Edward FitzGerald's first edition with notes by Arberry on its origin and step-by-step evaluation as well as an extensive introduction. 239pp. A&U 59

DASHTI, ALI. **IN SEARCH OF OMAR KHAYYAM,** $15.10. This is a biographical study of Omar Khayyam by a noted Persian scholar, translated into English by L.P. Elwell-Sutton. A major problem facing anyone seeking to study this twelfth century poet is that there is no conclusive evidence to prove which of the many quatrains attributed to Khayyam are authentic. Ali Dashti therefore constructs a picture of the poet from references found in the works of writers of his day or immediately after, and from Khayyams's own works on philosophy, mathematics, and astronomy, of which the authenticity is not questioned. Using this portrait as a touchstone, Dashti draws up a list of some hundred quatrains which are in keeping with Khayyam's character and translates them for this volume. A final section studies Khayyam's religious and philosophical beliefs. Glossary, bibliography, index. 276pp. Col 71

FITZGERALD, EDWARD, tr. **RUBAIYAT OF OMAR KHAYYAM,** c$4.50. FitzGerald, writing in 1859, has supplied an adaptation rather than a strict translation. It is the most popular version available. This edition includes biographical and critical introductions. 110pp. Dou

_____, tr. **RUBAIYAT OF OMAR KHAYYAM,** c$2.98. This edition of Fitz-Gerald's translation is fully illustrated by noted Persian artist Sarkis Kathchadourian in color and line drawings. The text itself is hand lettered and the book is oversize. 131pp. GAB 56

NAKOSTEEN, MEHDI, tr. **THE RUBAIYYAT OF OMAR KHAYYAM,** c$14.50. A new translation in quatrain form by a noted Iranian scholar. This is a lovely flowing translation and it includes Nakosteen's calligraphy of the original Persian facing each page, extensive notes and an excellent bibliography. Collector's edition, limited to 300 copies. 258pp. EEP 73

KLEIN, F.A. **THE RELIGION OF ISLAM,** c$9.35. A topically arranged study of the major doctrines of Islam. Each of the topics is explored at some length and more are discussed here than in any other book we know. The discussion is often hard to follow and Islamic terms are interspersed throughout. It seems that more space is devoted to notes than to

the text itself. The material is apparently derived from the original sources. Includes su things as contracts, marriage, debt, prayer, hell, and much else. Notes, 241pp. Cur

KRITZECK, JAMES, ed. **ANTHOLOGY OF ISLAMIC LITERATURE,** $4.95. As t title suggests, this is a comprehensive anthology of Islamic literature from the rise of Isla to the nineteenth century. The selections cover both prose and poetry and the translatio are interspersed with commentary and introduced by biographical information. T arrangement of the material is chronological. On the whole the quality of translati seems to be good, although this varies with individual selections. The translations da from both the nineteenth and twentieth centuries. Bibliography, 379pp. NAL 64

LAMBTON, A.K.S. **PERSIAN GRAMMAR,** $7.95. *With her unrivalled knowledge of t Persian language, Professor Lambton has produced a work that will long remain the sta dard textbook. As was to be expected, the treatment of pronunciation and the spoke language is particularly excellent...an extremely useful work for which student a teacher will be equally grateful.*—Journal of the Royal Asiatic Society. Although it primarily for the contemporary Persian language, the book also serves as an excelle introduction to the classical language. Index, 300pp. CUP 57

_____. **PERSIAN VOCABULARY,** $6.50. This is a companion to Professor Lam ton's **Persian Grammar.** It is mainly intended for the student of contemporary Persian a it will also be a useful handbook for those who wish to read classical Persian literatu The Persian-English and English-Persian sections contain a wide range of the more co mon words and phrases. 406pp. CUP 64

LANDAY, JERRY. **DOME OF THE ROCK,** c$10.00. Jerusalem's ancient Temple Mou now dominated by the Dome of the Rock, is sacred to Jews, Christians, and Moslem This is a study of the Holy City, focusing on its most famous monument. Manuscri illuminations, statuary, ancient maps, and modern diagrams complement the text—alo with numerous photographs. 120 illustrations are included in all—one half in full colo There's also a section *Jerusalem in Literature.* This volume will be especially appreciate by those who are interested in Islamic architecture. 172pp. Nws 72

LEACROFT, HELEN and RICHARD. **THE BUILDING OF EARLY ISLAM,** c$6.40. simply written study, designed for older children. All aspects of the buildings are discusse and the book is illustrated with many fine line drawings and a number of color plate 8x10", index. 40pp. Hod 76

LEBON, GUSTAVE. **WORLD OF ISLAMIC CIVILIZATION,** c$3.95. See the descri tion of the **World of Ancient Civilizations** series in the Ancient Civilizations sectio

LEFORT, RAFAEL. **THE TEACHERS OF GURDJIEFF,** $2.45. See the Gurdjieff sectio

LEVY, REUBEN. **AN INTRODUCTION TO PERSIAN LITERATURE,** c$13.45. Th volume is the first to appear in English in the UNESCO Introduction to Asian Literature Levy begins with the historical setting, discussing the various geographical, political, an religious forces that influenced the development of Persian literature. He goes on examine the main trends of that literature from ancient times to the present, illustratin his comments with his own translations of many of its forms. Levy begins his detaile survey by describing and giving examples of the verse forms composed in the Persia idiom—the *qasida, ghazal, rub'ai,* and *mathnavi*—then surveys the growth of prose. R turning to poetry, Levy gives detailed treatment to the classic poets Persians hold to b masters. A final chapter discusses modern writers. Appendices contain biographical an bibliographical information. Index, 194pp. Col 69

LEWIS, BERNARD, ed. **ISLAM AND THE ARAB WORLD,** c$29.95. A beautifu produced exploration of Islamic culture which contains nearly 500 illustrations—phot graphs, paintings, illuminated manuscripts, tapestries, and maps—almost half of them i full color. Thirteen eminent specialists discuss in turn the origins and history of the I lamic faith, the achievements of Islamic artists, architects, and poets, Islamic history and the great Islamic nations. 9¾x12", 360pp. RaH 76

LEWIS, SAMUEL. **DANCES OF UNIVERSAL PEACE,** $1.00. **Dances of Univers Peace** *is based on the work of the late Murshid Samuel L. Lewis....As such it is ne essary to use the first volume (***Introduction to Spiritual Dance and Walk***) as a backgroun for the dances presented here....We wish to present in this volume, not the fundamer tals, but a further application of these dances in the form of a dance for six of the majo religions of the world.* 10pp. Rai 74

_____. **AN INTRODUCTION TO SPIRITUAL DANCE AND WALK,** $1.00. detailed, beautiful little manual by *Sufi Sam,* the beloved Murshid of the San Francisc Sufis. Sam had been initiated into Buddhism, Vedanta and Sufism. He was recognized b Moslems as a Sufi and counted among his masters Nyogen Senzaki, Swami Ramdas, an Inayat Khan. 19pp. Rai

_____. **IN THE GARDEN WITH MURSHID SAM,** $5.00. This is a wonderful co lection of reminiscences about *Sufi Sam,* photographs, transcriptions of discourses whic he presented at teaching seminars at the Lama Foundation, selections from Sam's poetr and of his aphorisms. The text is illustrated throughout and the reader gets a good feelin for this American spiritual master who combined ancient techniques with modern ones i such a moving way. Glossary, bibliography. 288pp. Crn 75

_____. **THE JERUSALEM TRILOGY,** $5.95. Three long poems which Murshi Sam considered his most important literary effort. The volume is subtitled *Songs of th Prophets,* and this is just what they are. They are entitled *The Day of the Lord, Wha Christ? What Peace?* and *Saladin.* An introduction and an extensive glossary accompan each poem and there are many illustrations throughout. The book itself is beautifull produced. The content is biblically oriented, with elements of the quranic literatur added. Oversize, 335pp. PrP 75

_____. **THE REJECTED AVATAR**, $1.25. A Heart-Poem of the *awakened child* Krishna, including his spiritual practices and a beginning notation of the science of death. 24pp. PrP 68

_____. **SPIRITUAL WALK**, $.50. Transcription of ten papers discussing the attitude to be developed in the walk and the physiological functions involved in spiritual walk. 10pp. Ikh 73

_____. **SURAS OF THE NEW AGE**, $1.00. Ikh 73

_____. **THIS IS THE NEW AGE, IN PERSON**, $3.65. Sufis, it is said, adapt themselves to the time and place. Perhaps no man epitomized that phrase more than Lewis. A Sufi initiated into several dervish orders, a Zen Roshi, a Christian mystic, the offspring of wealthy Jewish parents, he exemplifies the Universal Mystic Brotherhood as developed in the U.S. These ten lectures are noted not only for their illumination of the mystic content of St. Paul's writing, but also for their revelation of the depth of the divine experience. 158pp. Ome 72

_____. **TOWARD SPIRITUAL BROTHERHOOD**, $2.50. The first portion traces the process of spiritual cooperation through the mineral, vegetable and animal kingdoms to its potential in mankind. Utilizing this perception as a key, the second portion examines the place of music, dance, psychedelics, communities, and much else in our contemporary civilization as vehicles for the balanced unfolding of spiritual brotherhood. PrP 72

LICHTENSTADTER, ILSE. **INTRODUCTION TO CLASSICAL ARABIC LITERATURE**, $6.50. The first section consists of a long introductory survey of the history of Arabic literature from pre-Islamic times through its high period in the Middle Ages. Both religious and secular literature is discussed. The rest is devoted to a representative selection of the literature itself, beginning with some pre-Islamic poetry and including, among many other things, a portion of Ishaq's **Life of Muhammad** (the definitive early study), philosophical writings of al-Ghazali, and much else. Notes, index. 416pp. ScB 76

LINGS, MARTIN. **THE QURANIC ART OF CALLIGRAPHY AND ILLUMINATION**, $25.00. A beautiful book which reveals the superb workmanship of quranic calligraphy, its history, and its differing styles. The color reproductions cover over 200pp and are all from the best manuscripts extant, include the use of gold and are of outstanding quality. Oversize, 256pp. WIF 76

_____. **A SUFI SAINT OF THE TWENTIETH CENTURY: SHAIKH AHMAD AL-'ALAWI, HIS SPIRITUAL HERITAGE AND LEGACY**, $2.95. The author allows the Sufis to speak for themselves and, in a series of unusual texts mainly translated from the Arabic, provides a vivid picture of life in a North African Sufi order. Against this background stands the Algerian shaikh who headed the order until his death in 1934. The final chapters reproduce selections from his writings. 242pp. UCP 61

_____. **WHAT IS SUFISM?**, $4.95. This is the best introduction to Sufism that we know of. Lings has written extensively on the subject and he presents his exploration in a clear, thorough, authoritative manner. He begins with a general discussion of the originality and universality of Sufism and goes from there to a study of The Book (the Qur'an) and The Messenger (Muhammad). Other chapters consider The Heart, The Doctrine, and The Method, and a final one traces Sufism through the ages. There are extensive references to the appropriate texts throughout. Index, 133pp. UCP 75

MC NEILL, WILLIAM and MARILYN WALDMAN, eds. **THE ISLAMIC WORLD**, $5.30. A sourcebook of political, historical, religious, and literary readings from 600 AD to the present day. The material is chronologically arranged and each historical epoch is introduced. Comments and notes for each selection are also included. The readings are well selected and give a good total picture of Islamic culture through the ages. 485pp. Oxf 73

MAKAREM, SAMI, tr. **ASH-SHAFIYA**, $6.00. An edited translation of an Isma'ili poem attributed to Shihab Ad-Din Abu Firas, with an introduction and commentary by the translator and also including the Arabic text. Notes, bibliography, index. 260pp. AUB 66

MANSUR AL-HALLAJ. **THE TAWASIN**, $3.95. This is the first volume in a new series of translations of classical Sufi texts. This volume is a translation of one of the greatest texts on Tawhid (The Unity of Reality) and a contemporary text by a renowned Sufi from Fez, Morocco. Also included is the Commentary on the Song *Purification*, by Sidi Fudul al-Hawari as-Sufi. The various Ta-Sins translated are arranged by subject and are in the form of short paragraphs. The teaching is very clear if the reader is familiar with Islamic terminology and philosophical ideas. The book is beautifully produced. 81pp. Diw 74

MEHER BABA

Meher Baba (his name means Father of Compassion) was born in India in 1894. Between the years of 1913 and 1921 the five Perfect Masters (Sadgurus) of that time led him to realize his identity and universal mission as the Avatar of the age. After working intensively with an intimate group of disciples for some years, Baba began to observe silence in 1925, and throughout the remaining four decades of his spiritual activities he never uttered another word. From his work in India and the East with the mad, infirm and poor and with spiritually advanced souls, to his contact with thousands of people in the West, Meher Baba has awakened innumerable persons to the quest for higher consciousness and their own ultimate reality.

Declaring that his work had been completed 100% to his satisfaction and that the results of that work would soon begin to manifest, Meher Baba dropped his body on January 31, 1969.

This all-comprehensive knowledge is obtained in a flash. But to know everything in a flash takes an eternity in the illusion of time while you gradually die to yourself. This dying to yourself means completely losing yourself in God to find yourself as God. The dying to your false self is no easy task; raising a corpse to life is child's play compared to it.

ADRIEL, JEAN. **AVATAR**, $2.95. This colorful biography, written by one of Baba's early disciples from the West, gives the reader a vivid acquaintance with Meher Baba the man. Besides telling Baba's life story, the author relates his personal experience with him. It includes Baba's visit to Hollywood and his encounters with all manner of seekers, both famous and ordinary. MBI 47

ANZAR, NAOSHERWAN. **THE BELOVED**, c$13.50. This is a pictorial biographical study of Meher Baba. The narrative is clear, readable, and interspersed with frequent anecdotes. Meher Baba is seen in his childhood; in his first contact with his spiritual masters; during his much-publicized visits to the West; on his travels by foot throughout India; in the periods of deep seclusion; and in his close contact with people of all classes and religions throughout the world. The text was put together by a disciple of Baba and reflects the love that his disciples feel for him. Oversize, glossary. 153pp. Shr 74

BARKER, ELSA. **SONGS OF A VAGROM ANGEL**, c$2.75. Spiritual poems by a disciple of Baba. 55pp. SRe 68

BRABAZON, FRANCIS. **IN DUST I SING**, $2.95. The poetry in this volume is based on material that Baba gave to Brabazon, his close disciple. The form is based on the Persian *ghazal*. The content is the relationship between the Lover and the Beloved—a relationship that is never wholly fulfilled until the loved ceases to exist in himself and passes away in the Beloved. 162pp. MBI 74

_____. **JOURNEY WITH GOD**, $1.25. A collection of love poems written to Baba by the author, selections from Baba's discourses in India, and a note on the *God-Man*. 35pp. Shr 71

DESHMUKH, C.D., ed. **SPARKS OF THE TRUTH FROM THE DISSERTATIONS OF MEHER BABA**, $1.75. Twenty dissertations: practical hints and guidance to aspirants; expositions of eternal truths concerning the nature of the soul and the meaning of life; and some hitherto unknown sayings of Baba. 95pp. Shr 66

DONKIN, WILLIAM. **THE WAYFARERS: MEHER BABA WITH THE GOD-INTOXICATED**, c$10.95. This is a meticulous account of Meher Baba's work with *God-Intoxicated*—spiritually advanced souls who, overcome by the power of their inner vision, are drowned in the ecstasy of the experience. This work took place from 1922-1946 during which time Meher Baba toured throughout India. 512pp. SRe 48

DUCE, IVY. **HOW A MASTER WORKS**, c$17.95. Murshida Duce is the present leader of the organization founded by Baba. In this book she presents answers to questions of interest to all spiritual seekers. Questions such as *Who am I? What am I doing here? How do I grow spiritually?* She also discusses authentic spiritual practice and integrating the mystical with the practical. The bulk of the book is an illustration of Baba's work with his disciples—both in India and the Western world. A long supplementary section contains excerpts from Meher Baba's writings which illustrate the principles with which she is concerned. A wide range of topics has been selected—from the dynamics of reincarnation to the poetry of divine love; from a spiritual perspective on the occult to the specifics of everyday spiritual practice. Glossary, bibliography. 778pp. SRe 75

_____, ed. **SUFISM**, $1.00. Four essays on various aspects of Sufism as seen by Meher Baba and his disciples. 58pp. SRe

_____. **WHAT AM I DOING HERE?**, $1.20. Murshida Ivy Duce, of Sufism Reoriented, draws here on the teachings of Meher Baba in her discussion of a variety of topics including the planes of existence, the bodies, reincarnation and karma, the spirit world, and the Avatar. 112pp. SRe66

FREDERICK, FILIS, ed. **THE LIFE DIVINE**, $2.00. This is a special photographic issue of **The Awakener**, a journal devoted to Meher Baba. Selected short essays accompany the pictures which show Baba in every imaginable (for him anyway!) situation. Photographic index, 79pp. Awa 71

HOPKINSON, TOM and DOROTHY. **MUCH SILENCE**, c$7.95. The Hopkinsons knew Meher Baba, and have been his disciples for many years. This is the most complete biographical study of him available. It is straightforward and is directed toward general readers who are curious about Baba but do not want to wade through some of the more detailed volumes of his teachings. The authors include a summary of the teaching along with their biographical study. Bibliography, 191pp. DMd 75

MEHER BABA, **THE ADVANCING STREAM OF LIFE**, $2.00. Compiled from a wide variety of Baba's published works, including some which are currently out of print. A comprehensive sampling of excerpts and discourses, it is thorough and includes a vast range of spiritual subjects. 200pp. MBI 69

_____. **BEAMS FROM MEHER BABA ON THE SPIRITUAL PANORAMA**, c$2.00. A collection of questions, answered by Baba, arising from ideas in **God Speaks**. The simplified responses in this volume illuminate some of the more difficult concepts in the latter work. 116pp. SRe 58

_____. **DARSHAN HOURS**, $1.95. Records conversations which took place between Meher Baba and some of his disciples who visited him in India in 1960. Baba, as was his custom, conducted his *conversations* through the use of gesture-language, which was translated by his closest disciples. *It is the heart of Baba's teachings addressed to the hearts of His lovers.* 72pp. Beg 71

_____. **DISCOURSES**, $5.95. A major work, dictated on Baba's alphabet board. They *are the practical guide for the aspirant as he slowly finds his way back to Oneness.* This is the standard edition of **Discourses**. The editing of each of the forty-five was carefully examined and approved by Meher Baba. Every aspect of Baba's teaching is contained herein, and the collection is arranged topically. **Discourses** and **God Speaks** are his major philosophical statements. Highly recommended for all seekers. Three volumes. 546pp. SRe 67

_____. **THE EVERYTHING AND NOTHING**, $1.45. These are in many ways the most vital and profound of all Baba's discourses. Certainly they are the most poetic. With frequent flashes of humor, Baba highlights the essence of spirituality through rich parables, anecdotes, and vibrant new images. 115pp. MBI

_____. **THE FACE OF GOD**, $1.25. A small volume which contains quotations from Baba faced with drawings of him. 14pp. Shr 71

_____. **GOD SPEAKS—THE THEME OF CREATION AND ITS PURPOSE**, c$15.00. This is Baba's most advanced philosophical statement. It deals with the mechanics of the universe and how consciousness develops through various stages. The material is illustrated with various charts to make it more comprehensible. This is a revised edition in which certain new points and corrections indicated by Meher Baba have been made. There are also some additions to the supplement; various of the charts have received minor but necessary changes and five more charts have been included. Further footnotes have been added as well as a complete glossary. 334pp. DMd 55

_____. **LIFE AT ITS BEST**, c$2.00. A collection of messages given by Meher Baba during his visit to the United States in 1956. The style is succinct and penetrating and touches on all aspects of Baba's teaching. 106pp. SRe

_____. **MEHER BABA IS LOVE: MESSAGES FOR CHILDREN 4 TO 100**, $2.25. Shr 61

PURDOM, C.B., ed. **GOD TO MAN AND MAN TO GOD**, $3.95. This is a reprinting of Purdom's edited and condensed version of the original edition of Meher Baba's discourses. It differs from **Discourses** by being more compact (thirty-two discourses in one volume as opposed to forty-five discourses in three volumes) and less authoritative (not benefiting from the review procedures used in the editing of **Discourses**). Shr 75

_____. **THE GODMAN: THE LIFE, JOURNEYS AND WORK OF MEHER BABA WITH AN INTERPRETATION OF HIS SILENCE AND SPIRITUAL TEACHING**, c$6.95. This is the most complete biography of Meher Baba available. It describes in detail the various phases of his life, journeys and spiritual work up to the 1960's: the early years, Baba's meeting with the Perfect Masters of the time; his work with his early disciples, the beginnings of his silence and his comments on it, through Baba's final declaration and the breaking of his silence. 464pp. Shr 64

_____. **THE PERFECT MASTER**, $3.95. A biography of the early years of Meher Baba, first published in 1937, and long out of print. This was the first biography of Baba to appear in the West. It discusses the period from 1911 to 1936 in a great deal of depth. Index, 333pp. Shr 76

SHIFRIN, ADAH FRANCIS. **THE FLOWER OF CONTEMPLATION**, $1.70. A small book of spiritual thoughts dedicated to Baba's forty years of silence and including a short biographical sketch. 66pp. Shr 65

STEVENS, DON, ed. **LISTEN, HUMANITY**, $3.45. An American businessman reports vividly his experience with Baba in India and Baba's answers to questions on life, death, suicide, war, love, avatarhood, and much else. Of all the books about Baba, this is probably the most comprehensible and interesting introduction. 262pp. H&R 57

WATSON, RICHARD. **MEHER BABA AND SUFISM: A PERSONAL VIEW**, $1.0[ ]
26pp. Sre

MILSON, MENAHEM. **A SUFI RULE FOR NOVICES**, $1.95. This is the first trans[ ]tion of a twelfth century guide to the Sufi way of life, the **Kitab Adab al-Muridin** of Su[ ]awardi, founder of one of the oldest and largest Sufi orders. A manual of ethics, address[ ]to novices and to laymen, this work spells out in detail the *adab* or rules of condu[ ]general rules on such matters as eating, companionship, hospitality, and specific or[ ]dealing with particular situations. A concluding section is on ethical dispensations—p[ ]mitted departures from the rules. The translator also includes a long introduction, gl[ ]sary, and a bibliography. 93pp. HUP 75

MOREWEDGE, PARVIZ. **THE METAPHYSICS OF AVICENNA**, c$16.80. A criti[ ]exposition of one text of Avicenna, the great Persian philosopher who lived from 980[ ]1037. The text is his **Metaphysica** in the **Danish Nama-i ala-i (The Book of Scienti[ ]Knowledge)**. In addition to a translation, this edition includes a critical commentary[ ]the major arguments found in the text, and notes and references to other texts of[ ]as well as to relevant texts of Greek philosophers, particularly Aristototle, Plotinus a[ ]Proclus. There is also a glossary of the key terms used in the **Metaphysica**, with th[ ]Persian, Arabic, Greek, and Latin equivalents where necessary. Indices, 371pp. Persi[ ]Heritage Series. Col 73

MORRISON, GEORGE, tr. **VIS AND RAMIN**, c$16.80. This Persian poem was compos[ ]in the eleventh century AD by Fakhr ud-Din Gurgani. It is a romantic epic and is one [ ]the earliest of its kind in Persian literature. The story bears a resemblance to the lege[ ]of Tristan and Isolde, following the adventures of a pair of lovers who go against cou[ ]less odds to be together. This is a prose translation, with notes and an introductic[ ]366pp. Col 72

MUHAMMAD

ANDRAE, TOR. **MOHAMMED—THE MAN AND HIS FAITH**, $2.60. This is a goo[ ]standard biography which, though published many years ago, has retained both its pop[ ]larity and its relevance. This was a pioneering book in that it was the first to apply th[ ]principles of the psychology of religion to the certain facts of Muhammad's life and cha[ ]acter. Andrae begins with a survey of Arabia at the time of Muhammad and then di[ ]cusses the period from Muhammad's childhood to his prophetic call. The next two se[ ]tions are devoted to Muhammad's religious message and his doctrine of revelation. Fro[ ]there the author reviews the conflict with the Quraish and Muhammad as the ruler [ ]Medina. A final section is a psychological study of Muhammad's personality. This volum[ ]reads well and remains the best general biography that we know of. Index, 194pp. H&R [ ]

'ABD AL-QADIR AS-SUFI, **THE WAY OF MUHAMMAD**, $5.95. This is a presentatio[ ]of the practice and teaching given to the world by Muhammad. It is topically arrange[ ]and numerous quotations from the Qur'an and from Islamic masters illuminate the con[ ]mentary. The book opens with a description of the nature of the *shadah*, the affirmatio[ ]and acceptance of how things are. The next section is devoted to an exploration of th[ ]Science of the Self—directed toward those who seek enlightenment and union with Alla[ ]The book then goes on to examine the *sunna*, or form of man and from there explore[ ]the Science of States which places man in harmony with himself, creation, and the tota[ ]universal Reality. After an examination of the nature of quranic revelation and langua[ ]itself, the book goes on to describe the creation process as a structured and unified fiel[ ]of Divine manifestation, before returning to its starting point, one's own reality and pat[ ]The picture that unfolds is that the genuine transmission of Sufism is a total psycholog[ ]of the human being based on a recognition of the illusory nature of the experiencing sel[ ]and all its practices are to enable one to turn away from this apparently real and trouble[ ]making identity that so persistently betrays us. A final section contains a fascinatin[ ]section of charts analyzing the letters of the Arabic language in depth in a manner simila[ ]to Qabalistic works. Each letter is analyzed in nineteen different ways. The book is wri[ ]ten by an English Muslim living in a community that follows the sunna and is from th[ ]line of transmission of the Habibiyya-Shadhiliyya Tariqa. This is an excellent work, pa[ ]of the Sufic Path Series. Its content is extremely complex (although clearly written) an[ ]only an experienced Islamic student could hope to understand much of it. 248pp. Diw 7[ ]

BODLEY, R.V.C. **THE MESSENGER: THE LIFE OF MOHAMMED**, c$19.85. Bodley [ ]a Westerner who lived among the Arabs of the Sahara Desert for seven years. He becam[ ]immersed in a culture which still follows Muhammad's teachings faithfully. Here he pres[ ]ents the picture of Muhammad which he absorbed and in the process he has given us th[ ]most readable account of the Prophet's life and work that we know of. Unfortunately[ ]this book is not yet available in paperback. In any event, this is one biography that li[ ]braries should have. The orientation is not toward oriental scholars or theologians—[ ]though the account seems to be a work of excellent scholarship. Glossary, bibliography[ ]index. 378pp. Gre 46

GABRIELI, FRANCESCO. **MUHAMMAD AND THE CONQUESTS OF ISLAM**, $2.9[ ]A general survey, illustrated with forty photographs (half in color) and five color maps[ ]which emphasize the political rather than the religious rise of Islam—although the two ar[ ]so intertwined that no account can fully separate them. The author is a professor o[ ]Arabic at the Institute for Islamic Studies at Rome University. Annotated chapter-by[ ]chapter bibliography, index. 253pp. MGH 68

GLUBB, SIR JOHN. **THE LIFE AND TIMES OF MUHAMMAD**, $2.95. Glubb spent al[ ]most sixty years in the Arab countries and he had a great deal of contact with illiterat[ ]tribesmen whose lives are not very different from their ancestors' in Muhammad's time[ ]With this in mind, Sir John has written a study of Muhammad which is designed to giv[ ]the general reader a good feeling for Muhammad the man: his trials, the wars he fough[ ]his exile, and his ultimate achievements. Many maps are included along with a great dea[ ]of background material. Glubb writes vividly and brings the times to life in this volume[ ]Bibliography, index. 416pp. S&D 70

GUILLAUME, A., tr. **THE LIFE OF MUHAMMAD**, $9.75. This is a translation of Ibn Ishaq's biography of Muhammad, **Sirat Rasul Allah**, written in the generation after the Prophet's death. Ishaq was closely associated with many of Muhammad's direct disciples and this remains the definitive biographical study to this day. Here Guillaume has given us an excellent translation and has also provided a long introduction and extensive notes. Ishaq's scholarship is meticulous and many first-person accounts are quoted. The study covers traditions from the pre-Islamic era, Muhammad's childhood and early manhood, his call and preaching in Mecca, his migration to Medina, his wars, triumphs, and death. The amount of material is immense and only those who desire an in depth study of Muhammad's life are encouraged to venture into this tome—excellent though it is. Indices, 862pp. Oxf 55

HUSAIN, ATHAR. **PROPHET MUHAMMAD AND HIS MISSION**, c$7.05. A study of the Prophet's life and work which aims at presenting the reader with as comprehensive a picture of his personality as can be seen through his message and his life. Husain uses passages from the Qur'an to illustrate the message of Islam and the personality of the Prophet. The reader can also get a good feeling for the times from this study. Notes, bibliography, index. 224pp. APH 67

LANE-POOLE, S., tr. **THE TABLE-TALK OF PROPHET MUHAMMAD**, $2.25. *The aim of this little volume is to present all that is most enduring and memorable in the public orations and private sayings of the Prophet Muhammad in such a form that the general reader may be tempted to learn a little of what a great man was and of what made him great.* Some of the material is derived from the Qur'an—but from a chronological and topical arrangement of material rather than the scattered way that Muhammad's message is presented in the Holy Book. The other material comes from his recorded speeches and from sayings traditionally attributed to him dealing with the most minute and delicate circumstances of life. Lane-Poole has done a good job of translating his material and he also has written an excellent long introduction. Notes, 206pp. MuA 66

RODINSON, MAXIME, tr. **MOHAMMED**, $3.95. This is basically a political biography of Muhammad which approaches Islam as an ideology which galvanized a fragmented and nomadic society. M. Rodinson reviews the major events of Muhammad's life in the light of this thesis and backs up his thesis with excellent scholarship and an assortment of notes. The text itself reads well and is not cluttered with too much obvious scholarship. For those interested in this aspect of Muhammad's life and work this is as good a survey as we know of. Glossary, annotated bibliography, index. 381pp. RaH 74

SARWAR, HAFIZ. **MUHAMMAD**, c$6.00. This is one of the few biographies of Muhammad available in English which was written by a Muslim. *This book attempts to show the path of success in life by most carefully collecting the facts of Muhammad's (peace be upon him) life and setting them up as an Example to all mankind....The learned author is an expert student of the Qur'an and the chief events of the Holy Prophet's life are explained by quotations from the Holy Qur'an....This biography depicts Muhammad as a man—the Greatest MAN who ever lived on this earth.* All the known facts of Muhammad's life are included along with the major events and the tone of the biography can be seen from the quotation. Index, 448pp. MuA 61

WAHAB, SYED. **THE SHADOWLESS PROPHET OF ISLAM**, c$3.00. Subtitled *A Treatise on the Spiritual Aspect of the Prophet's Life and Spiritualism of Islam as Taught By Him.* Muhammad's prophecies and the supernatural events surrounding his life are emphasized. 148pp. MuA 49

WATT, W. MONTGOMERY. **MUHAMMAD: PROPHET AND STATESMAN**, $3.95. This is an abridgement of Watt's fine study **Muhammad at Medina**, with some additional material. The book opens with a background chapter on the birth and early life of the Prophet in Mecca. Dr. Watt tells of Muhammad's call to prophethood as a result of his visions and recounts the writing down of the Prophet's revelations in the Qur'an (with an explanation of some of its passages); Muhammad's betrayal, expulsion from Mecca, and migration to Medina; and his rise to political power in Arabia. Throughout Dr. Watt makes clear the social and political background out of which Islam was born, especially the influence of Judaism and Christianity. This book is addressed to a wider public than Watt's more detailed and specialized earlier volumes and is written in a clear, interesting manner. Notes, bibliography, index. 250pp. Oxf 61

_____. **MUHAMMAD AT MEDINA**, c$18.50. An in depth scholarly study of the second half of Muhammad's life, mainly emphasizing the political and social aspects of his career. Watt is one of the most respected contemporary historians. Extensive notes, index. 432pp. Oxf 56

MYERS, EUGENE. **ARABIC THOUGHT AND THE WESTERN WORLD**, $1.45. This is a survey of Islamic philosophers and translators during the Golden Age of Islam. Myers points out that the philosophical traditions of the Greeks were not known in Europe during the Dark Ages and when they again became known in Europe it was only in Arabic translation. Myers discusses the major figures in the Islamic Golden Age and devotes special attention to Al-Ghazali, Ibn 'Arabi, and Ibn Khaldun. He begins with a survey of the early scholars (ninth and tenth century) and then goes on to discuss Islamic scholarship in the eleventh and twelfth centuries. Other chapters are devoted to the translations which were made into Arabic between the seventh and eleventh centuries and to the impact of these translations in the West. Bibliography, index. 156pp. Ung 64

NAIMY, MIKHAIL. **THE BOOK OF MIRDAD: A LIGHTHOUSE AND A HAVEN**, $6.25. *Between the covers of* **The Book of Mirdad** *lie answers to the whence, whither, and wherefore of man. The aim of Mirdad, the book's central figure, is to uncover God in man by dissolving man's sense of duality—the I and the Not-I. The Not-I he calls a shadow which must be cast away.* 185pp. Wat 62

NAKOSTEEN, MEHDI. **MULLA'S DONKEY AND OTHER FRIENDS**, c$20.00. Professor Nakosteen's adaptations of many of the shortest Nasrudin stories—most of which are not in the three Idries Shah Nasrudin books. EEP 74

_____, tr. **RETURN TIES OF EXISTENCE OF HATEF OF ISFAHAN**, c$25.00. Sayid Ahmad Hatef (eighteenth century) was among the last classical Sufi poets of Iran. His strophe poem translated here (**The Tarji'band**), is a pantheistic interpretation of existence. Edition limited to two hundred copies, numbered and autographed and beautifully bound. EEP 76

_____, tr. **THE RUBIYYAT OF BABA TAHIR ORYAN OF HAMADAN**, c$12.75. Oryan, an eleventh century Persian poet, was considered one of the most noted mystics of his time. Includes introductory and comparative material, and Persian calligraphy of the text. EEP

_____, tr. **A TALE OF CATS AND MICE**, c$12.75. A free and interpretive translation of the fourteenth century Persian satirist Obeyd of Zaakan, beautifully illustrated and including the Persian text and introductory material. Limited edition. EEP

The Last Judgment. From a Persian miniature of the eighth century, reproduced from The Lost Books of the Bible.

NASR, SEYYED HOSSEIN. **IDEALS AND REALITIES OF ISLAM**, $3.95. In six chapters dealing with Islam, the Qur'an, the Prophet, the Shari'ah or Divine Law, the Tariqah or Sufism, and Sunnism and Shi'ism, Nasr discusses the major aspects of the Islamic tradition, making frequent comparisons with other religions. In each case the traditional Islamic doctrines and beliefs are explained in the light of contemporary thought, and each chapter is accompanied by an annotated bibliography of the works of both Muslim and Western scholars. Nasr is a very noted Iranian scholar and educator. 184pp. Bea 66

_____. **ISLAMIC SCIENCE: AN ILLUSTRATED STUDY**, c$25.00. The first fully illustrated study of Islamic science published in the West. Professor Nasr examines many branches of science, including cosmology, geography, astronomy, alchemy, medicine, and agriculture, and discusses them and the role of science within the context of the quranic revelation. Includes 135 color plates and over 100 half tones and line drawings. Oversize, 272pp. WIF 76

_____. **SCIENCE AND CIVILIZATION IN ISLAM**, $3.50. This is the only one volume work in English which discusses every branch of Islamic science and approaches it not from the Western viewpoint but as it is understood by the Muslims themselves. Islamic science, known to the West principally for its influence on the development of European scientific thought, occupied a central position within the Muslim culture. Through historical and morphological analysis, as well as through excerpts from texts, Dr. Nasr conveys to Western readers the content and spirit of Islamic science. His introduction surveys the religious, metaphysical, and philosophical concepts of Islam. Succeeding chapters cover the entire scientific spectrum from cosmography, mathematics, and medicine to alchemy and theology, as well as the interaction of these with related schools of thought. Nasr writes very well and he is one of the most noted contemporary Islamic scholars. Notes, bibliography, index. 384pp. NAL 68

_____, tr. **SHI'ITE ISLAM**, c$20.15. A translation from the Persian of Muhammad Husayn al-Tabataba-i-'s comprehensive statement of the history and beliefs of the Shi'ite religion, edited and with an introduction, notes (many of which form a running commentary on the text), bibliography, and index. 267pp. SNY 75

_________. **SUFI ESSAYS**, c$16.10. This book combines scholarly research into certain aspects of Sufi doctrines with a penetrating account of the spiritual and metaphysical message and significance of Sufism as a living spiritual tradition. Nasr, probably the leading scholar of Sufism today, places special emphasis on the pertinence of Sufi teachings to the most acute contemporary problems and he draws on his intimate knowledge of Sufi literature in Arabic and Persian as well as his first-hand knowledge of the Sufi tradition itself in this excellent study. We recommend all of Nasr's books highly—although not on the introductory level. Notes, index. 184pp. SNY 72

NAZAMI. **LAILI AND MAJNUN**, c$11.70. A reproduction of James Atkinson's 1835 translation of this classic Persian love story. Atkinson's was the first English translation and it still remains a fine one. The translation is in rhymed couplets and notes and an introduction by Atkinson are included. 135pp. JRC 68

NICHOLSON, R.A. **IDEA OF PERSONALITY IN SUFISM**, c$4.10. *My chief purpose was to show by means of examples chosen from the literature, that Sufism is not necessarily pantheistic but often bears the marks of a genuine personal religion inspired by a personal God.* 105pp. MuA 64

_________, tr. **KASHF AL-MUHJUB OF AL-HUJWIRI**, $6.50. A translation of the oldest Persian treatise on Sufism. Al-Hujwiri discusses some of the basic concepts of Sufism, eminent Sufis, and Sufi sects. This is an excellent text and many of the ideas the author discusses have not been expressed better in any other place. Nicholson has done a fine job with the translation. Introduction, notes, index. 463pp. Gibb Memorial Series. Luz 11

_________. **A LITERARY HISTORY OF THE ARABS**, $6.95. The Arabs during a thousand years or more produced one of the richest and most extensive literatures of the world, embracing fine poetry on subjects as diverse as the fierce desert life and the sophistication of the royal court; *belles lettres* (learned essays and satires); religious, mystical, and philosophical writings; and a huge collection of works on history, biography and geography. For over sixty years, the best account in English of this vast output has been Nicholson's **Literary History**, and it is likely that its supremacy will long remain unchallenged. Bibliography, index. 537pp. CUP 07

_________. **THE MYSTICS OF ISLAM**, $2.45. Nicholson is one of the most noted Persian scholars of this country. He gives an outline of Sufism here and describes some of the basic principles, methods, and characteristic features of the inner life. Many quotations are given, mainly in the author's own fine versions from the original Arabic and Persian. 168pp. ScB 14

_________. **STUDIES IN ISLAMIC POETRY**, $17.50. Two essays on Persian and Arabic poetic literature. The first one is an anthology of early Persian poems, with a great deal of commentary. The second section is devoted to a textual analysis of **The Meditations of Ma'arri**, along with many selections from the text divided into the following parts: poems on life and death, on human society, on asceticism, and on religion and philosophy. An appendix contains the Arabic text of the translated pieces. 314pp. CUP 21

NIZAMI. **THE STORY OF LAYLA AND MAJNUN**, $13.50. This version of Islam's most famous classical love story is our favorite. There are a great variety of Arabic versions (see the listings under Fuzuli and Nazami for other editions), the oldest ones dating back to the seventh century AD and based, it is thought, on a true story. At the end of the twelfth century, Nizami, a Persian poet, forged the work into a great epic of 4,000 stanzas. His work was widely acclaimed and soon became the acknowledged prototype for numerous later poems throughout the Orient. It was Nazami who transformed an originally simple romantic episode into a work of great poetry and mystical experience. This is an excellent prose translation of a highly acclaimed Persian edition of W. Dastgerdi. Twelve lovely full color miniatures accompany the text. 221pp. Cas 66

_________. **THE STORY OF THE SEVEN PRINCESSES**, $13.50. The story of the Seven Princesses, the most important part of the **Haft Paykar (The Seven Images)** is a precious jewel of oriental narrative art which can be compared only with the most beautiful stories out of **Thousand and One Nights**. On the seven days of one week each of the seven princesses tells her tale to her husband, each tale being of the same magical beauty as the miniatures which illustrate the book. Each of the princesses comes from a different country, each has been born under a different star, and lives in a different colored pavilion of the royal palace. The symbolic meaning of the stars and of the colors of their pavilions is artfully interwoven with their stories and each of the stories is meaningfully connected with the others. Twelve full color miniatures accompany the text. Cas 76

NUMANI, SHIBLI. **AL-FAROOQ: LIFE OF UMAR THE GREAT**, c$4.80. *After the Holy Prophet. . . .Omar is universally acknowledged as the first great Conqueror, Founder and Administrator of the Muslim Empire. It was during his Caliphate that Islam planted its banners far beyond the confines of the Arabian peninsula. This great military and administrative genius is up til now believed to be a miracle in himself, for he not only founded a great Empire but gave that solidarity to it which remained unshaken for centuries.* This edition was translated by Maulana Zafar Ali Khan, a well known scholar. It is the only major biographical study of Omar available in English. Introduction, notes, index. 207pp. MuA 43

PALMER, E.H. **ORIENTAL MYSTICISM**, $5.00. *The following work is founded upon a Persian M.S. treatise by 'Aziz bin Mohammed Nafasi, but I have endeavoured to give a clearer and more succinct account of the system than would have been afforded by a mere translation.* This is a good presentation of the basic cosmological system of Sufism. A classic work, recently reprinted. Glossary, index. Oct 1867

PELLAT, CHARLES, ed. **THE LIFE AND WORKS OF JAHIZ**, c$10.00. Al-Jahiz, who lived in the eighth and ninth centuries, was one of the most famous and prolific of Arab prose writers. He is known for his works of *adab* and his religious and political polemics as well as his literary works of social satire. *For the majority of literate Arabs al-Jahiz remains, if not a complete buffoon, at least something of a jester . . . for he never fails even in his weightiest passages, to slip in anecdotes, witty observations, and amusing comments. . . .He deliberately aimed at a lighter touch, and his sense of humour enables him to deal entertainingly with serious subjects.* In this book Professor Pellat, indisputably the greatest Jahiz authority, has selected the best as well as the most characteristic of Jahiz's writings, prefacing them with an assessment of his life and works. Glossary 286pp. UCP 69

PERLMANN, MOSHE. **IBN KAMMUNA'S EXAMINATION OF THE THREE FAITHS** c$14.25. Written in 1280 by a Jew of Baghdad, this essay systematically examines the creeds, arguments and counterarguments of the three monotheistic religions—Judaism Christianity, and Islam. The book offers an excellent summary of the Arabic literature and lore of interfaith disputations and provides insight into the mentality of medieval scholars. The translator's introduction places Ibn Kammuna in his historical and theological context and he provides extensive interpretive notes. Index, 160pp. UCa 71

PETERS, F.E. **ALLAH'S COMMONWEALTH**, c$19.95. This is an excellent scholarly (and quite readable) history of Islam in the Near East, 600–1100 AD. *The format of this book is what the Arabs called an era work, the setting-down of deeds, chiefly those of a political nature, along a chronological line established by the succession of Caliphs, their vassals and the ministers. But I have attempted something more, an excursion into another literary genre known to the Arabs as the* book of refinement. *The Arabs'* refinement*. . . was a generous term in that it eventually came to embrace the sum of manners and learning appropriate to the Muslim gentleman. And although there is rich material available on the manners of the early Muslim, the emphasis here is upon his literary learning, what the educated Muslim knew and thought about man, the world and Islam. His culture is in his books . . . and some of the most important of them have been opened again here and their contents displayed in the appropriate context.*—from the preface. This is a secular history, and an excellent one. And since Islam itself has such a strong religious and philosophical basis, these elements play a large role in the narrative presented here. Chronology, glossary, notes, annotated bibliography, index. 800pp. S&S 73

PICKTHALL, M. **CULTURAL SIDE OF ISLAM**, $2.70. Pickthall is a very well respected Islamic scholar whose translation of the Qur'an is generally considered one of the finest available. This volume presents the transcription of a series of lectures which reveal important points about Islamic culture. The topics include the following: Islamic culture; causes of rise and decline; brotherhood; science, art and letters; tolerance; the charge of fatalism; relation of the sexes; and the City of Islam. Many pertinent quotations from the Qur'an and other writings of the Prophet are included in the talks. 202pp. MuA 61

PLANHOL, XAVIER de. **THE WORLD OF ISLAM**, $4.75. This is a not overly technical study divided into the following sections: the geographical mark of Islam, groupings and modes of life derived from religion in the countries of Islam, and geographical factors in the expansion of Islam. Includes a bibliography (wholly of French sources). 153pp. Cor 69

THE QUR'AN

The Qur'an (Arabic for The Recital) is the earliest and by far the finest work of Classical Arabic prose. For Muslims it is the infallible word of God, a transcript of a tablet preserved in heaven, revealed to the Prophet Muhammad by the Angel Gabriel. Except in the opening verses and some passages in which the Prophet or the Angel speaks in the first person, the speaker throughout is God.

The Qur'an preaches the oneness of God and emphasizes divine mercy and forgiveness. God is all-mighty and all-knowing, and though compassionate towards his creatures, He is stern in retribution. He enjoins justice and fair dealing. The most important duties of the Muslim are faith in Allah and His apostle, prayer, almsgiving, fasting, and (if possible) pilgrimage to Mecca.

It is unfortunate that in preparing the contents of the Qur'an for book form its editor or editors followed no chronological sequence. Its chapters were arranged generally in order of length, the longest coming first and the shortest last. Various scholars have attempted to arrange the chapters in chronological order, with varying success.

AHMED, NISAR, ed. **THE FUNDAMENTAL TEACHINGS OF THE QUR'AN AND HADITH, VOLUMES I, II, III**. $2.55/each. A topically organized presentation of the major teachings from Islam's two basic texts, with a great deal of commentary. The quotations are taken from a variety of translations and both the Arabic and the English is offered. This should be a useful volume for those who wish to live in accord with the precepts of the Prophet. Volume I covers basic religious and social concepts; Volume II, the state and government, and the economic, legal and ethical systems; Volume III, moral values and manners. About 115pp each. JFP 74

ALI, A. YUSAF, tr. **THE HOLY QUR'AN**, c$16.80. Far and away the most magnificent translation available. Extensive commentary on almost every line, and the Arabic text, fully indexed. This is *the* Qur'an for the serious scholar. It is highly recommended. 1862pp. Isl

AMIR-ALI, HASHIM, tr. **THE MESSAGE OF THE QUR'AN**, c$25.00. Dr. Ali is a noted Muslim scholar who has devoted his heart and intellect to transcribing the Qur'an into poetic English that would convey the depths of the quranic message to today's readers. In this volume he presents a complete translation of the Qur'an which combines his intelectual integrity with a wide knowledge and personal experience of the search for simple and unambiguous truth. Textual notes discuss certain quranic problems which have baffled scholars over the centuries and present the author's solutions. The text is accompanied by introductory material and appendices. The volume is beautifully bound, 7x10", with illustrations and the full Arabic text, and the translation reads very well. 500pp. Tut 74

_____. THE STUDENT'S QURAN, $4.00. A translation, with detailed commentary on the first twenty-five suras. Amir-Ali's aim is to help the student incorporate the teachings into his or her daily life. Blank sections for notes are interspersed throughout. An introductory section summarizes quranic thought and Muhammad's teaching. Notes, 184pp. APH 61

ARBERRY, A.J., tr. THE KORAN INTERPRETED, $6.95. Dr. Arberry is generally considered to be the leading Islamic scholar of this century and his translation of the Qur'an to be the finest one by a non-Muslim, and the one that comes closest to conveying the impression made on Muslims by the original. He follows the traditional arrangement of the Suras. An interesting preface compares the English translations of the Qur'an over the years. Index, 358pp. McM 55

CRAGG, KENNETH. THE EVENT OF THE QUR'AN, c$15.10. *Separate events in the Islamic Scriptures are not hard to arrange and to chronicle—a lonely brooding in the caves and hills of Mecca, a tenacious vocation in the teeth of heavy odds, emigration to a new city as the watershed of the story, energy in leadership, vindication, success. But what was the event of the whole? How should we understand the coming together of personal charisma, poetic eloquence, Arab consciousness, and vibrant theism, into the single phenomenon of the Qur'an? What is the inner story of the prophethood which Islam receives as the final, cumulative revelation from God? How did the setting of time and territory and tradition enter into its metaphors and condition its contents? How should its relation to the present time be read in its original time? These are the questions which make the theme of this study. In aiming to be scholarly they have a duty to more than scholarship.* The text includes many quotations from the Qur'an, along with detailed notes, a glossary, and indices. 208pp. A&U 71

_____. THE MIND OF THE QUR'AN, c$14.30. Takes up central quranic themes: life and time, God and man, mercy and forgiveness, death and eternity, and sets them within the context of the Qur'an itself. The object of this work is to determine how the Qur'an is received in contemporary Islamic society—whether its philosophy is integrated into the society. 209pp. A&U 73

DAWOOD, N.J., tr. THE KORAN, $2.25. A very readable translation in which the traditional arrangement of verses has been abandoned. The sequence presented here begins with the more Biblical and poetic revelations and ends with the much longer, and often more topical, chapters. A translation for the general reader. 431pp. Pen 74

GATJE, HELMUT. THE QUR'AN AND ITS EXEGESIS, c$20.00. A translation of key passages of the Qur'an (following Arberry's version) and its classical and modern commentaries. The book shows the teachings of the Qur'an and the views of later commentators on such topics as revelation, Allah, Muhammad, angels and jinn, eschatology, and Muslim beliefs and duties. It also discusses the quranic view of other religious communities, particularly the *People of the Book.* There are also chapters on mystical, philosophical, and Shi'ite quranic exegesis. This volume has been translated from the German and edited by Dr. Alford Welch. Notes, bibliography, index. 330pp. UCa 76

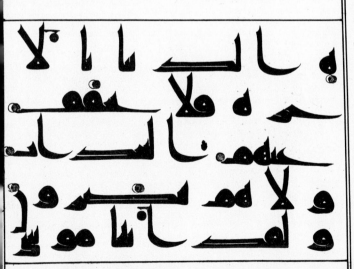

Kufic-Arabic leaf from the Qur'an / Mesopotamia 7th Century

GREENLEES, DUNCAN. THE GOSPEL OF ISLAM, c$4.00. **The Gospel of Islam** *is not a translation of the Glorious Qur'an....This little book is meant only as an introduction or a guide-book to the Scripture itself, whose arrangement does not make quick reference easy for the general reader. So I have chosen beautiful, striking and typical passages from all parts of the Book and woven them into a logical sequence in short sections, each on a certain topic, and then completely translated afresh from the Arabic original. To help the reader to refer to the original context of each passage, the reference to chapter and verse ... is printed after it.* 211pp. TPH 48

HINGORA, Q.I. THE PROPHECIES OF THE HOLY QURAN, $4.10. A presentation of the major prophecies, in composite form and topically arranged. 173pp. MuA 64

KHAN, MUHAMMAD Z., tr. THE KORAN, c$6.98. This is an excellent translation which is a great deal more readable than most. Rather than duplicating the verse patterns of the original, Khan structures the material through verse paragraphs that combine groups of verses which capture the feel of the Arabic but do not sacrifice clarity of meaning. The Arabic text and English description are printed in parallel columns to facilitate comparisons and cross-references. Khan has drawn upon the most up-to-date scholarship in Arabic and quranic studies to enrich the accuracy of the translation. The translator is not only a noted Islamic scholar but has also had a distinguished political career: first as Foreign Minister of Pakistan; then as head of the Pakistani delegation to the United Nations; and presently as President of the International Court of Justice. Beautifully bound, with excellent introduction and index. 673pp. Pra 70

LANE, EDWARD, STANLEY LANE-POOLE and A.H.G. SARWAR, trs. KORAN, c$2.98. This is an arrangement of prose selections from the separate translations of the three authors, with illustrations and a short note on Muhammad and the Qur'an. 200pp. Crn

MERCHANT, MUHAMMAD. A BOOK OF QURANIC LAWS, $5.10. A selection of verses on some of the fundamental principles of Islam arranged under the following subject headings: doctrine of the Unity of God; prayers and alms; fasts; hajj; food, drinks and games—lawful and unlawful; marriage; divorce; inheritance; usury; and purdah. 206pp. MuA 47

MERCIER, HENRY, tr. THE KORAN, $6.95. This is the only paperback translation which also includes the Arabic text and transliteration. The volume is also very nicely laid out and the translation appears to be a good one. Introduction, index. 349pp. Luz 56

PALMER, E.H., tr. THE QUR'AN, c$15.00/set. **Sacred Books of the East, Volumes VI and IX.** Extensive introduction and notes. 730pp. MoB 1880

PENRICE, JOHN. DICTIONARY AND GLOSSARY OF THE KORAN, $10.00. The Qur'an is one of the most complex and difficult works in any language. The wealth of commentaries and interpretations of individual passages testifies to the subtlety and complexity of both language and syntax and the resulting ambiguities of meaning. This volume was originally published in 1873. In it Penrice, a distinguished scholar, seeks to provide *a clue of elucidation to the intricate passages of the Koran.* Through painstaking and detailed analysis, he clarifies the more ambiguous passages, drawing upon grammatical as well as linguistic references. Revised edition, oversize. 174pp. Cur 76

PICKTHALL, MARMADUKE. THE GLORIOUS KORAN, c$43.55. This is a magnificent volume which combines Pickthall's fine rendering with an Arabic text reproduced from the original Hyderabad edition, based on the famous Royal Qur'an which many regard as the most beautiful example of Arabic script ever produced. The Arabic and English are on facing pages and the translator also provides extensive notes and an excellent introduction. Index, 1768pp. A&U 76

_____. THE MEANING OF THE GLORIOUS KORAN, $1.75. *The aim of this work is to present to English readers what Muslims the world over hold to be the meaning of the words of the Koran, and the nature of that Book....It may be claimed that no Holy Scripture can be fairly presented by one who disbelieves its inspiration and message; and this is the first English translation of the Koran by an Englishman who is a Muslim. Some of the translations include commentation offensive to Muslims, and almost all employ a style of language which Muslims at once recognize as unworthy. The Koran cannot be translated....The Book is here rendered almost literally and every effort has been made to choose befitting language. But the result is not the Glorious Koran....It is only an attempt to present the meaning of the Koran—and peradventure something of the charm—in English....Before publication the work has been scrutinized word by word and thoroughly revised in Egypt with the help of one whose mother-tongue is Arabic, who has studied the Koran and who knows English; and when difficulties were encountered the translator had recourse to perhaps the greatest living authority on the subject.* This is the most popular modern translation among the Muslims. Index, 456pp. NAL 70

ROBERTS, ROBERT. THE SOCIAL LAWS OF THE QUR'AN, $5.25. A straightforward presentation of quranic teachings as they affect everyday life and as a guide to social conduct. Index, 138pp. Cur 74

RODWELL, J.M., tr. THE KORAN, $2.50. The main feature of this translation is Rodwell's chronological arrangement of the *suras,* which enables the reader to trace the development of the Prophet's inspiration. The translation itself is a good work of scholarship, but not as good a work as some of the more recent versions. Rodwell himself was not a Muslim and this is reflected in his presentation. Introduction, notes, index. 517pp. Dut 09

SALE, GEORGE, tr. THE KORAN, c$5.50. George Sale's translation first appeared in 1734. It was only the second translation into English ever made and is still considered a good one, though not a very exciting rendition. It's interesting to see the differences over two hundred years of Islamic scholarship. Sale provides an extensive commentary in addition to his translation, some of which he got from original sources and some of which he picked up from Luigi Marraccini's pioneering 1698 Latin edition. Notes, index. 712pp. Wrn nd

WATT, W. A COMPANION TO THE QUR'AN—BASED ON THE ARBERRY TRANSLATION, c$9.25. Designed to help readers by giving them necessary background information and explaining allusions. An account is given of ideas peculiar to the Qur'an or to the Arabs, and phrases which might puzzle the occidental reader are elucidated. The main variant interpretations are noted. A full index of quranic proper names and an index of words commented on have been provided. The **Companion** is based on Professor

Arberry's translation but can be used with other translations or with the original text, since the verses are numbered. Professor Watt is a noted scholar. 355pp. A&U 67

RAHMAN, FAZLUR. **ISLAM**, $2.50. This is a quite good scholarly account which traces Islam through the fourteen centuries of its existence, commenting on the various political events that stirred its intellectual development and gave rise to its theory, its systems of law and administration, its sects, and its traditions. It includes a close look at the life and mission of Muhammad with a careful analysis of the Qur'an, and explains Islam's rapid spread in terms of its power structure rather than the sword. All the topics we are interested in seem to be covered, including chapters on Sufi doctrine and practice, Sufi orders and an examination of Islamic education. The book ends by examining the interaction between Western ideas and Muslim cultural tradition and confirms the strength of the religion today. The book reads well and many illustrations accompany the text. Notes, bibliography, index. 357pp. Dou 68

RAUF, MUHAMMAD ABDUL. **ARABIC FOR ENGLISH SPEAKING STUDENTS**, $16.15. *I assumed that the student is an absolute beginner, and I go along with him on the road very slowly in the early stages until he gradually builds up some basic knowledge for proceeding at a faster rate. The method adopted here is as follows: (a) The lesson begins by giving a sample for the uses of the topic to be discussed and taught, in a clear and tabulated form. (b) This is followed by Notes in which observations are derived from the examples in the table. (c) At the end of the Notes, a summary of information gained in the lesson is given to reinforce the student's understanding. (d) The lesson is concluded by an exercise to help in digesting the rules. . . .* This book is basically a work on grammar, not an Arabic reader. 444pp. Isl 75

RICE, CYPRIAN. **THE PERSIAN SUFIS**, c$5.05. An excellent little book which first traces the historical background of Sufism and then deals at length with the philosophy. Topics include the way and its goal, the seven stages, the mystical states, lost in God (Fana) and the vision of God. 103pp. A&U 64

RUMI, JALAL AL-DIN

Rumi, who lived during the thirteenth century in what is now Turkey, is the greatest mystical poet of Persia, and perhaps the greatest of any language. His vast body of poetry includes the **Mathnawi**, a lengthy epic of religious mysticism, and more than three thousand lyrics and odes, many of which came to him while he was in a state of trance.

Rumi lived the quiet life of a religious teacher until the age of thirty-seven, when he came under the influence of a wandering dervish, Shamsi Tabriz. After a time Rumi's jealous disciples drove Shamsi away, but Rumi's transformation into a state of religious ecstasy was permanent. Torrents of poetry poured from him. To symbolize the search for the lost Divine Beloved, now identified with Shamsi, Rumi invented the famous whirling, circling dance of the Mevlevi dervishes and under the impact of the passionate moment, uttered a stream of quatrains and lyrics which his disciples recorded. These poems were thereafter chanted as accompaniment to the dervishes' sacred dance. Rumi opens a new world of spiritual experience. *God is One but religions are many*, runs the Sufi teaching. The influence of his example, his thought, and his language has been powerfully felt through all the succeeding centuries.

ARASTEH, A. REZA. **RUMI THE PERSIAN, THE SUFI**, $2.25. Arasteh presents a systematic study of Rumi's rebirth into a total being who expressed the ideas of religious tolerance and presented the idea of love as the fundamental creative force. By studying the elements of Persian culture, as well as Rumi's writings, Dr. Arasteh reveals the characteristics of maturity, the qualities of final integration in identity, health and happiness that underlie Rumi's life and work. 196pp. Ome 65

ARBERRY, A.J. **THE DISCOURSES OF RUMI**, $3.95. These discourses, published for the first time in English, are the raw materials out of which the **Mathnawi** was fashioned and like the **Mathnawi** they *represent the impromptu outpourings of a mind overwhelmed in mystical thought, the multifarious and often arrestingly original and beautiful images welling up unceasingly out of the poet's overflowing consciousness.* Profoundly instructive stories and parables. Many notes, 276pp. Wei 61

_____, tr. **MYSTICAL POEMS OF RUMI**, $2.95. This is the best collection of Rumi's lyrics. Arberry has carefully chosen two hundred from the first 1,500 odes and lyrics—representing a planned selection which includes poems of various styles and degrees of difficulty. If you want to read just one book on Rumi this is the one we suggest. He was above all a mystical poet, and it is through these poems that he revealed his soul and the profundity of his thought. Introduction, notes, index. 202pp. UCh 68

DAVIS, F. HADLAND. **THE PERSIAN MYSTICS: RUMI**, $1.50. The first part of this monograph is devoted to an analysis of Sufism, with sections on its origins, nature, and influence as well as a study of the early Sufis and an analysis of the *Religion of Love*. The next part reviews the life and work of Rumi and discusses the main influences on him. This is followed by selections from the **Divani Shamsi Tabriz** and from the **Mathnawi**. 107pp. MuA 67

HAKIM, K.A. **METAPHYSICS OF RUMI**, c$3.80. This is a detailed scholarly study with extensive quotations from Rumi's own work (in Persian and in English translation)—with chapters on the nature of the soul, the problem of creation, evolution, love, freedom of the will, the ideal man, the survival of personality, God, and Sufi pantheism. Bibliography, 157pp. IIC 65

IQBAL, AFZAL. **LIFE AND WORK OF RUMI**, c$7.50. *Until the publication of th[e] present volume no attempt has been made to write for the general public a biography and aesthetic appreciation of the man who enriched humanity with such splendid and massiv[e] contributions to literature and thought. . . .The author of this excellent monograph . . . has read deeply the extensive writings of Rumi, and what others have said on the subjec[t] in ancient and modern times. . . .I recommend this book warmly; it is a pleasure to read and it holds the key to further delight for those many who will be encouraged by it t[o] study further the immortal poetry of Rumi.—A.J. Arberry.* Selections from Rumi's work are included in the text, along with notes, a bibliography, and an index. 321pp. MuA 7[?]

NICHOLSON, REYNOLD, tr. **DIVANI SHAMSI TABRIZ**, $2.95. *When Shamsi me[t] Rumi he took his books and threw them in a pool of water saying, Now you must liv[e] what you know. When a disturbed Rumi moved to save his books, Shamsi told him tha[t] the theoretical knowledge in his books was meaningless but if they meant so much to him he could remove them from the pool and they would be dry. Rumi declined and the two men embraced. To the jealousy of Rumi's students . . . the two merged as one being. . . Rumi was the teacher, the prophet, and Shamsi the enigmatic catalyst who knows and knows that he knows.* Shamsi was first driven from Konya by the students of Rumi and finally murdered by the students after Rumi in his loneliness brought him back to Konya. The poems in this volume were written after Shamsi's death in dedication to him, and they represent some of Rumi's finest work. This edition includes a good introduction and illustrations. Notes, 126pp. Rai 73

_____. **THE MATHNAWI**. This is the most comprehensive, scholarly edition. It was edited from the oldest available manuscript. Nicholson provides critical notes and commentary in addition to the translation. Gibb Memorial Series. Luz 37

VOLUME I, c$11.25. This is the Persian text of the first and second books. 390pp.

VOLUME II, c$17.30. English translation of the first and second books. 419pp.

VOLUME III, c$19.25. Persian text of the third and fourth books.

VOLUME IV, c$17.30. English translation of the third and fourth books. 496pp.

VOLUME V, c$20.00. Persian text of the fifth and sixth books. 602pp.

VOLUME VI, c$19.25. English translation of the fifth and sixth books. 529pp.

VOLUME VII, c$14.50. Commentary on the text of the first and second books. 373pp.

VOLUME VIII, c$17.30. Commentary on the text of the third to the sixth book with indices to the seventh and eighth volumes. 473pp.

_____. **RUMI, POET AND MYSTIC, 1207-1273: SELECTIONS FROM HIS WRITINGS**, c$6.50. Beautiful and faithful translations of Rumi's last works of poetry. Covers a variety of subjects, illuminated by Professor Nicholson's notes on Sufi Doctrine and experience. An introduction traces Rumi's life, literary output, and philosophy. 190pp. Wei 50

WHINFIELD, E.H., tr. **TEACHINGS OF RUMI: THE MASNAVI**, $3.95. This is the only abridged English edition of Rumi's masterpiece. The translation does not match Nicholson's—but the price difference is considerable. It is good to have an edition of the **Mathnawi** available at a low price. And the translation is all right. 342pp. Dut 73

SA'DI. **THE BUSTAN: MORALS POINTED AND TALES ADORNED**, c$26.85. Sa'di's **Bustan** is one of the best known major moralistic poems in the whole of Persian literature, and this translation by G.M. Wickens is the first fully annotated modern English edition. It is part of the Persian Heritage Series. The text mixes anecdotes with precepts and illustrations of the proper life in its presentation of moral lessons. There's a good deal of variety within the poems as each of the 160 are separate tales. The narrative reads well and the message is often cloaked within an entertaining tale. Sa'di lived in the thirteenth century and very little is known about him with the exception of the many autobiographical references and anecdotes in his writings. Wickens also provides introductory material and notes. 344pp. UTo 74

_____. **THE BUSTAN OF SADI**, c$1.50. This translation by A. Hart Edwards was originally prepared for Murray's **Wisdom of the East** series. The translation reads well and is probably a better edition to begin with than Wickens because you can read the stories straight through without being constantly interrupted by annotations—and the price difference is also considerable. Some introductory material and notes are also included. 147pp. MuA nd

_____. **THE ROSE GARDEN (GULISTAN)**, c$6.70. This is Sa'di's most popular work, and the one for which he is best known. It was written about the same time as the **Bustan** and complements the latter work. The book consists of a series of instructive and often humorous prose stories. The great beauty of Sa'di's style lies in its simplicity; his work (and especially this book) remains among the most read and the most beloved literature in the Islamic world. This is a reprint of Edward Eastwick's 1852 translation, with the original prefatory material. 267pp. Oct 74

SANA'I, HAKIM ABU. **THE ENCLOSED GARDEN OF THE TRUTH**, c$12.50. Sana'i (1118-1152) gives the reader a genuine taste of Sufi mysticism. The main core of the work is the interpretation of the Sufi philosophy regarding prayer and the adoration of God. This edition is edited and translated by Major J. Stephenson and is considered the best one available. A copy of the original Persian text is included. This is one of the most important ancient texts available today. 300pp. Wei 08

_____. **THE WALLED GARDEN OF TRUTH**, $5.40. This is an abridged translation by David Pendlebury, a student of Idries Shah, which gives a feeling of the original. It is based on the study of Stephenson's translation and is designed to appeal to modern readers. 74pp. Oct 74

SAVORY, R.M. ed. **INTRODUCTION TO ISLAMIC CIVILIZATION**, $5.95. A wide-ranging general introduction to Islamic civilization from its origins to the present day. The book begins with a section on the geographic, ethnic, and linguistic background of the Middle East, continues with an historical resume of the Islamic period, and moves on to the core chapters on the religious, philosophical, and legal foundations of Islamic society and its contributions to world civilization in the fields of literature, art, science, and medicine. The selections are written in clear and non-technical language and there are illustrations throughout. 7½x10", glossary, annotated bibliography, index. 212pp. CUP 76

SCERRATO, UMBERTO. **ISLAM**, c$19.95. A monumental pictorial investigation of Islamic civilization illustrated with 106 color photographs, maps, drawings, and charts. Also includes an anthology of Islamic texts and a history of Islamic civilization. An excellent survey for the general reader. 9½x12½", index. 192pp. G&D 76

SCHACHT, JOSEPH and C.E. BOSWORTH, eds. **THE LEGACY OF ISLAM**, c$18.75. *The Legacy of Islam takes Islam in the sense of a civilization, not merely a religion. . . . Thus in addition to chapters on Islamic theology, philosophy, and mysticism, and on Islamic religious law and constitutional theory, it contains others—and they are the majority—on aspects of Islamic political, economic, and cultural history, on Islamic art and architecture, and on Islamic medicine, science and music. Although it was the responsibility of the editor to assemble a harmonious team of contributors, no rigid uniformity of opinion, or agreement with the opinion of the editor, have been imposed, and each author is responsible for his or her contribution exclusively. The same persons and the same subjects are occasionally discussed in more than one chapter; this follows from the fact that they are of importance to more than one aspect of the Legacy of Islam.*—from the introduction. The contributors are all experts in their fields. Notes, bibliography, index. 550pp. Oxf 74

SCHIMMEL, ANNEMARIE. **MYSTICAL DIMENSIONS OF ISLAM**, c$20.10. Dr. Schimmel is professor of Indo-Muslim Culture at Harvard University and is very well known for her translations. Here she gives us an excellent balanced historical treatment of Sufism from its beginnings through the nineteenth century. After exploring the origins of the mystical movement in the meditations of orthodox Muslims on the Qur'an and the Prophetic tradition, the author then discusses the development of its different stages. Particular emphasis is placed on spiritual education and on Sufi psychology and Sufi orders. Professor Schimmel examines mystical poetry in Arabic, Persian, Turkish, Sindhi, Panjabi, and Pashto and provides selected translations. She also demonstrates how Sufi ideals permeated the whole fabric of Muslim life, providing the average Muslim—villager or intellectual—with the virtues of perfect trust in God and the loving surrender to God's will. This book reads very well and, while the scholarship is impeccable, we also get the feeling that the author has more than an academic knowledge of her subject. This is the best overall account of Sufism that we have seen and we recommend it highly. The bibliography is quite extensive, notes accompany the text, and there are indices of names, places, and subjects. 526pp. UNC 75

SCHUON, FRITHJOF. **DIMENSIONS OF ISLAM**, c$7.90. In this, the author's second book on Islam, he turns to some of the lesser known but nonetheless universal aspects of Islamic metaphysics and spirituality as embodied in the Qur'an, the Hadith (sayings of the Prophet) and in various traditional Sufi texts. In expounding his subjects Schuon refers to other religious traditions and makes known doctrines which, being rooted in the very nature of things, are both perennial and universal. An excellent work, addressed both to the Islamic scholar and to the general reader, and written especially for Westerners. Many notes, 167pp. A&U 69

_____. **ISLAM AND THE PERENNIAL PHILOSOPHY**, $9.75. Here Schuon considers the relationships and diversities between all true religions and their metaphysical unity. He also discusses the connections between Shi'ism and Sunnism within Islam and reflects on the dilemma of evil and the quranic promise for the afterlife. Index, 228pp. WIF 76

_____. **UNDERSTANDING ISLAM**, $1.45. Schuon's purpose is to explain the basics of the Islamic belief. In achieving this aim, he considers four essentials: the nature of the Muslim perspective, the doctrine about and function of the Qur'an, the role of the Prophet, and Sufism. An excellent introductory volume, highly recommended. Many notes, 159pp. Pen 61

SEMAAN, KHALIL. **ASH-SHAFII'S RISALAH**, $1.50. Ash-Shafi'i lived in the eight century. Al-Risalah was the first book written on Islamic jurisprudence and Hadith (criticism) and it is still one of the most important works on the subject. This volume presents a summary of the main points in the work, along with a short biographical study of the author. 96pp. MuA 61

SHABISTAN, MAHMUD. **THE SECRET GARDEN**, $2.25. *We know very little about the life of the author . . . but his work is important out of all comparison . . . because it is a compendium of Sufi terminology in the form of question and answer.* A fourteenth century work, arranged topically. Includes an introductory essay on Sufi thought. 81pp. Dut 74

SHAH, AMINA. **ARABIAN FAIRY TALES**, c$5.50. This is a delightful collection of some of the most beloved tales from the Arab world. Ms. Shah, the sister of Idries Shah, has travelled widely and she retells these tales from the living oral tradition, capturing well the idiom of the original. She includes twenty-eight fascinating stories about caliphs and dervishes, fairies and jinn, and one wonderful one about the wily Grand Vizier. This is the best translation of Arabian fairy tales that we know of. The text includes many wood engravings. 175pp. Mul 69

_____. **FOLK TALES OF CENTRAL ASIA**, c$5.40. Stories from the oral tradition collected by the author in her travels. Delightful tales. 148pp. Oct 70

SHAH, IDRIES

Shah has travelled throughout the Middle East and has collected a massive number of tales, aphorisms and stories. He has made contemporary renderings of them and published numerous books. He was born into an Afghan family that traced its descent back to the Prophet. He has his own school in England now. The purpose of these tales is not only to entertain, but also to provide concrete mind examples of non-linear thinking. And all are a delight to read.

SHAH, IDRIES. **THE BOOK OF THE BOOK**, c$2.45. A strange work in which the first few pages contain stories, and the rest of the book has blank pages (many of them). Perhaps there is some deep esoteric meaning that we don't understand? Oct 69

_____. **CARAVAN OF DREAMS**, $1.50. A nice selection of writings. Rumi, Mulla Nasrudin, proverbs, short fables and longer stories. 207pp. Pen 68

_____. **THE DERMIS PROBE**, $2.45. Another collection of short stories and anecdotes. 191pp. Dut 71

_____. **DESTINATION MECCA**, c$7.35. Shah's only travelguide, containing a wealth of information, including philosophical material. Many photographs. 183pp. Oct 57

_____. **THE DIFFUSION OF SUFI IDEAS IN THE WEST**, c$6.00. *Sufism is, in fact, not a mystical system, not a religion, but a body of knowledge.* It is this knowledge with its very practical consequences that this book deals with. An anthology of new writings by and about Shah. 212pp. Key 72

_____. **THE ELEPHANT IN THE DARK**, c$4.90. A discussion of the interplay between Christianity and Islam and the Sufi conception of surrender to God. The material in this volume was originally presented as a lecture series at the University of Geneva. 76pp. Oct 74

_____. **THE EXPLOITS OF THE INCREDIBLE MULLA NASRUDIN**, $1.95. The appeal of Nasrudin is as universal and timeless as the truths he illustrates. He is the main actor in this collection of teaching stories that is both an anthology of humor and a book of Sufi wisdom. Many delightful illustrations are included. 159pp. Dut 72

_____. **THE MAGIC MONASTERY**, $2.75. Differs from its predecessors in that it contains not only traditional tales but also stories especially written by Shah to complete the book as a course in non-linear thinking. 208pp. Dut 72

_____. **ORIENTAL MAGIC**, $2.95. Surveys and analyzes the many varieties of magical rites and beliefs practiced in the Orient. Covers Jewish magic, Egyptian magic, the contributions of the Arabs, magic and alchemy in India, love-magic, wonder-workers of Tibet. Many illustrations, detailed categorized annotated bibliography. 206pp. Dut 56

_____. **PLEASANTRIES OF THE INCREDIBLE MULLA NASRUDIN**, $2.25. Collection of teaching stories—outstanding both as an anthology of humor and as a book of Sufi wisdom. Includes whimsical drawings. Stories by Rumi, Jami and Attar. Our personal favorite. Highly recommended, these small tales will add pleasure to everyone's life. 220pp. Dut 71

_____. **REFLECTIONS: FABLES IN THE SUFI TRADITION**, $1.75. 146pp. Pen 68

_____. **THE SECRET LORE OF MAGIC**, $3.95. Includes the entire text of the four books of the secrets of Albertus Magnus, the Book of the Spirits, the Almadel, the Book of Power, the Clavicle and the Testament, and many other ancient Grimores. Many illustrations. 316pp. CiP 58

_____. **THE SUBTLETIES OF THE INIMITABLE MULLA NUSRIDIN**, $1.75. The newest collection of the wisdom of Nasrudin. 176pp. Dut 73

_____. **THE SUFIS**, $2.95. The most comprehensive account of Sufism available. Includes chapters on the great Sufi masters, on the dervishes, and details on the metaphysical philosophy underlying Sufi practices. Highly recommended for the reader desiring a full account of Sufism. Introduction by Robert Graves. 451pp. Dou 71

_____. **TALES OF THE DERVISHES: TEACHING STORIES OF THE SUFI MASTERS OVER THE PAST 1000 YEARS**, $2.25. On one level these tales can be read as enchanting fables or folklore. However, their true function has been as Sufi teaching stories used by dervish masters to instruct their disciples in the mysteries of Sufism. This collection contains stories from Persian, Arabic, Turkish, and other cultures. 220pp. Dut 70

_____. **THINKERS OF THE EAST: TEACHINGS OF THE DERVISHES**, $1.00. 198pp. Pen 71

_____. **WAY OF THE SUFI**, $2.45. Cross section of material to form a basic course of Sufi study. Includes extensive selections from classical authors, an essay on the study of Sufism in the West; material on the four major orders, with extensive quotations from their literature; many teaching stories; and much else. The best single primer on Sufism, we think—and probably the first Shah book to read. 288pp. Dut 70

SHAH, SIRDAR IKBAL ALI. **ISLAMIC SUFISM**, $2.50. An excellent survey, discussing various aspects of Sufism, including an extensive analysis of music in Sufism and the practices of Sufism. The author is Idries Shah's father. 299pp. Wei

_____. **ORIENTAL CARAVAN**, $3.65. An anthology of Oriental mystical thought including the following: the **Divan** of Hafiz; **Nargas** by Bhai Vir Singh; the poetry of Attar; the **Rubaiyyat** of Omar Khayyam; peasant poetry of India; selections from the Talmud, the Bible, the Qur'an; of Tagore and Rumi. Nearly all genres are represented: poetry, prose, songs, fables, epigrams and aphorisms. 331pp. Ome 73

_____. **ORIENTAL LITERATURE**, $7.20. See the Comparative Religion section.

_____. **THE SPIRIT OF THE EAST**, $5.00. See the Comparative Religion section.

SHARDA, S.R. **SUFI THOUGHT**, c$19.15. A detailed study of Panjabi Sufism which includes comparisons between this form of Sufism and Hindu mystical philosophies and a study of its impact on Panjabi literature. Notes, bibliography, index. 312pp. MuM 74

SHARIB, ZAHURUL. **KHAWAJA GHARIB NAWAZ**, c$3.75. This is a biographical study of the great saint and scholar of the Chishti Order, who lived in the twelfth century. The book also contains excerpts from some of his writings and discourses. 162pp. MuA 61

SHEIKH, SAEED. **STUDIES IN MUSLIM PHILOSOPHY**, c$3.75. The first third of this scholarly work is devoted to an exposition of the four principal philosophical movements of the early medieval period—Mu'tazilism, Ash'arism, Sufism, and the Ikhwan al-Safa. The rest of the volume devotes a chapter each to the group of thinkers who were known during the same period as the *Philosophers*, i.e., those under the influence of Greek philosophy: Al-Kindi, Abu Bakr al-Razi, Al-Farabi, Ibn Sina, Al-Ghazali, Ibn Bajjah, Ibn Tufayl, Ibn Rushd, and Ibn Khaldun. Notes, bibliography, index. 262pp. MuA 69

SHERWANI, NAWAB. **LIFE OF ABU-BAKR**, $3.00. This is a very readable story of the life and important works of the First Caliph of Islam. Most of the book details Abu Bakr's battles and conquests, as that was basically what his life was devoted to. Translated from the Urdu by S.M. Haq. Index, 200pp. MuA 47

SORDO, ENRIQUE. **MOORISH SPAIN**, c$16.90. An examination of the achievements of the Moors as seen in the principal cities of Andalucia: Cordoba, Sevilla, and Granada. He traces their political and cultural development. Most of the book is devoted to Granada, where the Moorish spirit reached its greatest heights. There is a fine text which is accompanied by a spectacular series of full page illustrations, thirty-two in color and forty-eight black and white. 8x11", bibliography, index. 223pp. Ele 63

SIENY, MAHMOUD. **QUR'ANIC ARABIC**, $1.70. This is a manual developed by the Muslim Students Association for teaching the reading of Arabic script, with particular view to reading the Qur'an. The presentation seems to be as simplified as possible and also seems well organized. A pronunciation guide is also included. 27pp. IsP

SIRAJ ED-DIN, ABU BAKR. **THE BOOK OF CERTAINTY**, $2.25. *Our aim has been to express in the language of Sufism some of the universal truths which lie at the heart of all religions. Each chapter serves as a commentary upon some verse or verses of the Qur'an. The book is also based on various sayings of the Prophet, and to a certain extent upon a quranic commentary attributed to Muhyiddin ibn 'Arabi.* 108pp. Wei 52

SMITH, M.A., tr. **READINGS FROM THE MYSTICS OF ISLAM**, c$7.00. Translations from the Arabic and Persian, together with a short account of the history and doctrines of Sufism. 144pp. Luz

STEINGASS, F. **A COMPREHENSIVE PERSIAN-ENGLISH DICTIONARY**, c$45.00. A revised, enlarged, and newly reconstructed version of Johnson and Richardson's Persian, Arabic and English dictionary. 1548pp. OrB 73

STEWART, DESMOND. **THE ALHAMBRA**, c$10.00. The Alhambra is the last and finest Muslim monument in Spain. From 711 until 1492 AD Iberia was largely in Islamic hands. For part of this long period, there was peaceful intermingling of Muslim, Christian, and Jew under tolerant caliphs, culminating in a rich cultural potpourri. Many of the discoveries and speculations of Islamic Spain occurred at a time when the rest of Europe was mired in the Dark Ages and fueled the later Christian Renaissance. It is doubtful that anywhere in the world there are buildings that so completely express the spirit of an entire civilization as does the Alhambra. Here, embraced by austere walls, the achievements and aspirations, the fears and the fantasies of Muslim Spain are embodied in a scattering of buildings that are a miracle of grace and fancy. The main feature of this history of Islamic Spain and its best known monument is more than 100 illustrations, nearly half in full color. They range from vistas and close-ups of the Alhambra itself to art and

artifacts of the period. A special section contains writings about the Alhambra from the sixteenth century to the present. The close-ups of the art and architecture are beautifully presented and give an excellent picture of the civilization. Oversize, chronology, index. 172pp. Nsw 74

STODDARD, WILLIAM. **SUFISM**, c$6.95. This volume is designed as a summary of the mystical doctrines and methods of Islam. The presentation is exceedingly brief and not as clear as we might wish. Many of the major terms are discussed and Sufism is related to the Western mystical tradition and to other Eastern religions. The appendix presents a series of short quotations. Bibliography, index. 91pp. Wei 76

STOREY, C.A. **PERSIAN LITERATURE, VOLUME I, PART I: QUR'ANIC LITERATURE; HISTORY**, c$21.00. A detailed, technical, bibliographical study, covering all the major works and individual figures. Notes, 820pp. Luz 70

SUBHAN, JOHN. **SUFISM: ITS SAINTS AND SHRINES**, c$8.50. Presents material on Islamic mysticism and its saints which has heretofore only been available in Persian and Urdu literature. It outlines the general principles of Sufism, considers the teachings which are the basis of Sufi practice, the introduction of Sufism in India, the Sufi attitude toward Hinduism, and discusses the Religious Orders. 412pp. Wei 38

TOWNSON, DUNCAN. **MUSLIM SPAIN**, $3.45. A pictorial presentation, focusing on the history and civilization. Glossary, 48pp. CUP 73

TRIMINGHAM, J. SPENCER. **THE SUFI ORDERS IN ISLAM**, $2.95. The first attempt in this century to study the orders through which the organizational aspect of the Sufi spirit was expressed within the context of Islamic society. It shows how they developed and changed, traces their relationship to the unfolding of mystical ideas, and describes their rituals and ceremonial practices. Finally, the author assesses the influence of these Sufi orders upon Islamic society in general. Supplementing the text is a very extensive bibliography including sources in the Oriental as well as European languages; also a comprehensive glossary of Arabic terms. 281pp. Oxf 71

TRITTON, A.S. **TEACH YOURSELF ARABIC**, $3.95. The script and grammar of the classic language are clearly explained in a series of carefully graded lessons, each of which contains many examples and exercises. The author has many years of experience teaching Arabic and he has developed a number of excellent techniques which he imparts to the student in this text. Index, 296pp. McK 43

VALIUDDIN, MIR. **THE ESSENTIAL FEATURES OF ISLAM**, $7.50. This is a fairly scholarly study delineating the main features of Islam as revealed in the Qur'an and presented by the Prophet in terms of their practical application. Dr. Valiuddin is the head of the Department of Philosophy at Osmania University in India and has written extensively. The present account includes many quotations from the sacred literature including the Qur'an. The approach incorporates the psychological, the mystical, and the practical. All of the major Islamic schools of thought and practice are reviewed quite thoroughly. Self-published. 573pp.

_____. **LOVE OF GOD: THE SUFI APPROACH**, $4.25. An interesting attempt to analyze and determine the nature of love as understood in a sublime sense. The text is filled with quotations, given both in English and in Persian, from the works of eminent Sufis which reflect their own experiences, sentiments, and intuitive feelings. SPC 68

WATT, W. MONTGOMERY. **THE MAJESTY THAT WAS ISLAM**, $11.10. This is a detailed study of the Islamic world between 661 and 1100 AD by a noted scholar. Watt looks at the civilization as a whole, showing the close intertwining of literature and religion with politics. The volume is clearly written; however the abundance of material is probably more than the general reader would want to know. There's also an excellent subject-organized bibliography and over fifty illustrations. Index, 276pp. S&J 74

WILLIAMS, JOHN ALDEN, ed. **THEMES OF ISLAMIC CIVILIZATION**, c$15.75. This book illustrates the thematic and archetypal ideas that moulded Muslim minds and were expressed in Islamic institutions of government, law, and culture. Each chapter demonstrates, by means of selections from works of history, law, poetry, philosophy and letters, a set of attitudes commonly found in Islam. Within each chapter the texts, arranged chronologically, represent works from early Islamic to modern times. The editor provides a running commentary on the texts—many of which have been translated here for the first time. Annotated bibliography, notes, index. 382pp. UCa 71

WILLIAMS, L.F.R., ed. **SUFI STUDIES: EAST AND WEST**, $3.95. Twenty-four world scholars offer, in tribute to Idries Shah, analyses of Sufism from the literary, scientific, religious and historical points of view. The contributors include, in addition to Persian and Arab specialists, a Chinese expert on the Middle East, a Coptic-Christian savant, a Hindu monk who has made Sufism a major study, Jewish scholars, and members of both the Sunni and Shi'a persuasions in Islam. 285pp. Dut 74

WRIGHT, W., tr. **A GRAMMAR OF THE ARABIC LANGUAGE**, $16.80. A translation from the German of Caspari, edited with numerous additions and corrections. It is considered the definitive volume and includes sections on orthography and pronunciation; on the verb, the noun, the adjective; on numerals, prepositions, adverbs and conjunctions; and reviews syntax and prosody. Two volumes bound in one. Indices, 468pp. CUP 64

JEWISH MYSTICISM

In the time of the Talmud the mystical teaching was still a mystery that one might entrust only to a *master of the arts and one versed in the whispers.* Only later did the teaching reach beyond the sphere of personal transmission. The oldest writing that has been preserved to us, the Pythagorizing *Book of Creation,* seems to have arisen between the seventh and the ninth century, and the *Zohar* stems—at least in its present form—from the end of the thirteenth; between the two lies the time of the real unfolding of the Kabbala. But for a long while yet those who occupied themselves with the Kabbala remained limited to a narrow circle, even though this circle extended from France, Spain, Italy, and Germany to Egypt and Palestine. During this whole period the teaching itself remains alien to life; it is theory in the Neoplatonic sense, vision of God, and desires nothing of the reality of human existence. It does not demand that one live it, it has no contact with action. The realm of choice that meant everything to Hasidism, the later Jewish mysticism, is not immediately alive for it. It is extra-human, touching the reality of the soul only in the contemplation of ecstasy.

Only in the late ages of this epoch did new powers manifest themselves. The expulsion of the Jews from Spain gave the Kabbala its great Messianic drive. The only energetic attempt of the Diaspora to establish in exile a culture-creating community and a homeland in spirit, had ended in ruins and despair. The old abyss again opened up, and out of it again ascended, as always, the old dream of redemption, imperative as never before since the days of the Romans. The longing burned: the absolute *must* become reality. The Kabbala could not shut its eyes to it. It called the kingdom of God on earth *the world of restoration*. It took the fervor of the people into itself.

The new era of Jewish mysticism which began around the middle of the sixteenth century and which proclaimed the ecstatic act of the individual as a coworking with God to achieve redemption, was inaugurated by Isaac Luria. In his ideas about the emanation of the world out of God and the demiurgic intermediary power he was almost entirely dependent on the older Kabbala; but in his presentation of the direct influence on God and the redeeming power of the human soul that purifies and perfects itself, he gives the old wisdom a new shape and a new consequence.

Already in the Talmud it says that the Messiah will come when all souls have entered into corporeal life. The Kabbalists of the Middle Ages believed they could tell whether the soul of a man who stood before them had descended into him from the world of the unborn or was temporarily staying with him in the midst of its wanderings. The Zohar and the later Kabbala developed the teaching that received its final form from Isaac Luria. According to this teaching, there are two forms of metempsychosis: the revolution or wandering, *gilgul,* and the superabundance or impregnation, *ibbur. Gilgul* is the entrance into a man, in the moment of his conception or birth, of a soul that is on the journey. But a man who is already endowed with a soul can also, in a certain moment of his life, receive one or more souls that unite themselves with his own if they are related to it, that is, have arisen out of the same radiation of the primordial man. The soul of a dead man joins itself with that of a living man in order to be able to complete an unfinished work that it had to leave when it died. A higher, more detached spirit descends in complete fullness of light or in individual rays to an imperfect one to dwell with him and help him to completion. Or two uncompleted souls unite in order to supplement and purify each other. If weakness and helplessness overcomes one of these souls, then the other becomes its mother, bears it in its womb and nourishes it with its own being. By all these means the souls are purified of the primal darkening and the world redeemed from the original confusion. Only when this is done, when all the journeys are completed, then only does time shatter and the Kingdom of God begin. Last of all, the soul of the Messiah descends into life. Through him the uplifting of the world to God takes place.

Luria's special contribution is that he wanted to found this world process on the action of some men. He proclaimed an unconditional conduct of life for those who dedicated themselves to redemption; in ritual immersion baths and night watches, in ecstatic contemplation and unconditional love for all, they would purify the souls in a storm and call down the Messianic kingdom.

MOSES by Gustave Doré

The tendency toward mysticism is native to the Jews from antiquity, and its expressions are not to be understood, as usually happens, as a temporary conscious reaction against the dominance of the rule of the intellect. It is a significant peculiarity of the Jew, which hardly seems to have changed in thousands of years, that with him one extreme quickly and powerfully enkindles another. Thus it happened that in the midst of an unspeakably circumscribed existence, indeed out of its very limitations, there suddenly broke forth the limitless which now governed the soul that surrendered itself to it.

If, then, the strength of Jewish mysticism arose from an original characteristic of the people that produced it, so the later destiny of this people has also left its imprint on it. The wandering and martyrdom of the Jews have again and again transposed their souls into that vibration of despair out of which, at times, the lightning flash of ecstasy breaks forth. But at the same time they have hindered them from attaining the pure expression of ecstasy. They have led them to confuse the necessary, the actually experienced, with the superfluous, the borrowed, and, through the feeling that their pain was too great for them to express what was their own, to become loquacious about the alien. Thus arose works like the *Zohar,* the *Book of Splendor.* In the midst of gross speculations, glimpses of silent depths of the soul again and again light up.

The basic feeling of which this teaching was the ideal utterance found its elemental expression almost a hundred years later in the great Messianic movement that bears the name of Sabbatai Zvi. It was an eruption of the unknown powers of the people and a revelation of the hidden reality of the folk-soul. The seemingly immediate values, life and possessions, had suddenly become flat and worthless, and the people were now inclined to abandon the latter as a superfluous instrument and to hold the former only with a light hand, as a garment that slips away from the runner and that, if it hinders him too much, he can let slip by opening his fingers, in order to hurry, naked and free, to the goal. The race, supposed to be ruled by reason, became inflamed with ardor for the message.

This movement, too, collapsed, more pitifully than any of the earlier ones. And now Messianism once again intensifies itself. The real age of mortification begins. The belief in being able to compel the upper world through mystical exercises penetrates ever more deeply into the people. . . .

These martyrs of the will are the forerunners of Hasidism, the last and highest development of Jewish mysticism. Arising about the middle of the eighteenth century, Hasidism at once continued and counteracted the Kabbala. Hasidism is the Kabbala become ethos. But the life that it teaches is not ascetisim but joy in God. The word Hasid designates a *pious man*, but it is a world-piety that is meant here. Hasidism is no pietism. It dispenses with all sentimentality and emotional display. It brings the transcendent over into the immanent and lets the transcendent rule in it and form it, as the soul forms the body. Its core is a highly realistic guidance to ecstasy as to the summit of existence. . . .

The founder of Hasidism was Israel from Mesbisz (Miedjyborz), called the *Baal-Shem-Tov*, that is, *Master of the Good Name*, a designation that unites two things, the powerful, efficacious knowledge of the name of God, as the earlier wonder-working *Baale-Shem* were described, and the possession of a *good name* in the human sense of being trusted by the people. Around him and his disciples a colorful and intimate legend wove itself. He was a simple, genuine man, inexhaustible in fervor and guiding power. . . .

God, so the Baal-Shem teaches, is in each thing as its primal essence. He can only be apprehended by the innermost strength of the soul. If this strength is liberated, then it is given to man at each place and at each time to receive the divine. Each action which is slowly dedicated in itself, though it appear ever so lowly and meaningless to those who see it from the outside, is the way to the heart of the world. In all things, even in those that appear completely dead, there dwell sparks of life that fall into the souls that are ready. What we call evil is no essence, but a lack. It is *God's exile*, the lowest rung of the good, the throne of the good. It is—in the language of the old Kabbala —the *shell* that surrounds and disguises the essence of things. . . .

If, then, the life of man is open to the absolute in every situation and in each activity, man should also live his life in devotion. Each morning is a new summons. *He arises in eagerness from his sleep, for he is sanctified and has become another man and is worthy to create, and imitates God by forming his world.* Man finds God on all ways, and all ways are full of unification. But the purest and most perfect is the way of prayer. When a man prays in the fire of his being, God Himself speaks the innermost word in his breast. This is the event; the external word is only its garment. . . . Prayer shall not take place in pain and repentance, however, but in great joy. Joy alone is true service of God.

The teachings of the Baal-Shem soon found access to the people, who were not equal to its idea yet eagerly welcomed its feeling for God. The piety of this people was inclined from of old to mystical immediacy; it received the new message as an exalted expression of itself. The proclamation of joy in God, after a thousand years of a dominance of law that was poor in joy and hostile to it, acted like a liberation. In addition, the people up till then had acknowledged above them an aristocracy of Talmud scholars, alienated from life, yet never contested. Now the people, by a single blow, were liberated from this aristocracy and established in their own value. Now it was said to them that it is not knowledge that determines the quality of a man, but the purity and devotion of his soul, that is, his nearness to God. The new teaching came like a revelation of what before then one had not dared to hope for. It was received like a revelation.

Naturally, the orthodox declared war on the new heresy and conducted it by all means—excommunication, closing of synagogues and burning of books imprisonment and public mistreatment of the leaders—not even shrinkin from denunciation to the government. Nonetheless, the outcome of the battl could not here be in doubt: religious rigidity could not withstand the religiou renewal. A more dangerous opponent to this renewal arose in the Haskala the Jewish movement of enlightenment which, in the name of knowledge, o civilization, and of Europe, came forward against *superstition*. But it too which wanted to negate the people's longing for God, would not have bee able to wrest a foot of ground from the movement which satisfied this long ing if there had not commenced in Hasidism itself a decomposition that le to the decline that has continued since then.

The first cause of this decline lay in the fact that Hasidism demanded from the people a spiritual intensity and collectedness than they did not possess It offered them fulfillment, but at a price they could not pay. It indicated a the bridge to God a purity and clarity of vision, a tension and concentratio of the spiritual life of which only a few are ever capable; yet it spoke to th many. And so there arose out of the spiritual need of the people an institutio of mediators who were called *zaddikim*, that is, righteous. The theory of th mediator who lives in both worlds and is the connecting link between them through whom prayers are born above and blessing brought below, unfolde ever more exuberantly and finally overran all other teaching. The zaddi made the Hasidic community richer in security of God, but poorer in the one thing of value—one's own seeking. To this was added the growing exter nal abuses. At first, only the really worthy, most of them disciples and dis ciples of disciples of the Baal-Shem, became zaddikim. But because the zaddi received from his community an ample livelihood in order to be able to de vote to it the whole of his service, soon lesser men crowded to the benefice and because they could offer nothing else, acquired a claim through all kind of wonder-working. In many places an imposture prevailed which repulse the purer, degraded the more definite, and attracted the most confuse crowd of people.

from **THE TALES OF RABBI NACHMAN** by Martin Buber

ABELSON, J. **IMMANENCE OF GOD IN RABBINICAL LITERATURE**, c$14.50. In a long introduction Abelson explains what is meant by the idea of the immanence of God and what the Rabbinical literature consists of and he sets the stage for his discussion. Later chapters discuss the concept and the major ideas involved in it as it appears throughout the literature. The text is accompanied by extensive notes. There is also an index of Biblical and Rabbinical literature that has been quoted in the text. 399pp. SHP 12

_____. **JEWISH MYSTICISM**, c$6.75. Subtitled *An Introduction to Jewish Mysticism*, this is a survey in which Dr. Abelson has combined his wide acquaintance with Rabbinical literature with thorough research into all sources of Jewish mystical teaching to trace the development and summarize the teachings of the Qabalah. He begins with a study of the mystical tradition as found in the Old Testament and in the teachings of the Essenes. From there he discusses the Merkabah (Chariot) mysteries. The next two chapters are devoted to the teachings of Philo and to the *Kingdom of Heaven*. The next chapters get into the heart of the Qabalistic tradition, with material on the Sepher Yetsirah, the Zohar, the Sephiroth, and the soul. Dr. Abelson expects his readers to have a general familiarity with his terminology and sources, so this does not make too good an introduction for the general reader. Bibliography, index, 190pp. SHP 13

ACHAD, FATHER. **THE ANATOMY OF THE BODY OF GOD, BEING THE SUPREME REVELATION OF COSMIC CONSCIOUSNESS**, c$10.00. A detailed attempt to help the finite mind of man comprehend the infinite, through the aid of many geometrical diagrams dealing with further design on the Tree of Life. He postulates that man is body, soul and spirit—the soul acting as the mediator between the spiritual and the material. In man are found all possibilities, both finite and infinite. Achad's books are definitely for the serious student of the esoteric sciences. 111pp. Wei 69

_____. **THE EGYPTIAN REVIVAL OR THE EVER-COMING SON IN THE LIGHT OF THE TAROT**, c$10.00. Deals with new ideas which presented themselves while Achad was writing **Q.B.L.** He discusses the symbolism of the Tarot trumps according to the reformed astrological order, presented in the appendix to **Q.B.L.** He offers a summary of the earliest traditions of man, and their effect upon the present day, the Cycle of Aquarius. 123pp. Wei 69

_____. **Q.B.L. OR BRIDE'S RECEPTION—A SHORT QUABALISTIC TREATISE ON THE TREE OF LIFE**, c$10.00. An original treatise, first in a series. Deals with the formation of the Tree of Life, correspondences in the Hebrew alphabet and the Paths, the Tarot, numbers, symbols, the macrocosm and the microcosm. Includes a long appendix dealing with the reformed astrological order. Achad's intention is to give serious students of the occult a basis of learning. There are many detailed illustrations, some in color, as well as extensive use and translation of Hebrew words. 152pp. Wei 69

SHLAG, RABBI YEHUDA. **KABBALAH—TEN LUMINOUS EMANATIONS**, c$10.95. erpretation of the Sefirot or Heavenly Attributes according to the system of Rabbi Yitak Luria, known as the Ari. Also contains Hebrew to English text of the Ari's **Tree of** *fe*. Rabbi Ashlag is noted as the author of a twenty-one volume translation-commentary the Zohar from Aramaic into Hebrew and as the founder of the Research Center for e Qabalah in Jerusalem. There is a long introduction by Dr. Philip Gruberger, the prest director of the Center. 131pp. RCK 73

AKEN, DAVID. **SIGMUND FREUD AND THE JEWISH MYSTICAL TRADITION**, .95. In a provocative study Baken, himself a well-known psychologist, argues that the ots of Freudian psychoanalysis can be found in the history of Judaism and particularly the Jewish mystical tradition. The author begins by reviewing the background of Freud's velopment of psychoanalysis. The next section delves deeply into the Jewish mystical adition, with chapters on the Qabala, the Zohar, the Sabbatai Sevi, and Hasidism. The ird part develops the Moses theme in the thought of Freud; while a fourth section dissses the devil theme as it appears in the literature and as it was understood by Freud. A al section integrates Freudian psychoanalysis with the Qabala. Index, notes, 448pp. ea 58

ARDON, FRANZ. **THE KEY TO THE TRUE QUABBALAH**, c$12.00. The theory and actice of Qabalistic Hermetics or the spiritual science of magical creation. *Having also ne through this third work conscientiously, the Qabalist will suddenly have the impreson of a miracle . . . when, as a reward for his untiring honest efforts, the true name of od, apart from many other things, will be revealed to him spontaneously.* 270pp. Rug 74

ARUK, HENRI. **TSEDEK**, $2.95. An interpretation of ancient Hebraic civilization in e light of modern science, by a noted French psychiatrist. 291pp. SwH 72

LOCH, CHAYIM. **THE GOLEM: MYSTICAL TALES FROM THE GHETTO OF RAGUE**, $2.25. The Golem stories originated in the ghettos of medieval Germany and e Golem theme has provided the inspiration for a wealth of stories, plays, novels, and ccult studies up to the present day. The Golem is a mystical servant created to serve his eople in their sufferings. This is a collection of some of the most noted tales. 244pp. ul 72

LOOM, HAROLD. **KABBALAH AND CRITICISM**, c$6.95. Bloom is a literary critic ho has written studies on Yeats, Blake, and Shelley. He begins this study with a brief eview of major Qabalistic concepts. The bulk of the book is devoted to an analysis of e great Qabalistic commentators and the *revisionary ratios* they employed. Unless the eader is quite familiar with Qabalistic literature, this book will have little meaning. 127pp. ea 75

IARTIN BUBER

UBER, MARTIN. **HASIDISM AND MODERN MAN**, $3.35. Hasidism is the popular ommunal mysticism which arose in Poland in the eighteenth century and, despite bitter ersecution at the hands of traditional Rabbinism, spread rapidly among the Jews of eastrn Europe until it included almost half of them in its ranks. The essays in this volume are oncerned with the life of the Hasidim, as Buber has expressed and interpreted it. Hasidism, s Buber portrays it, is a mysticism which hallows community and everyday life rather han withdrawing from it. *For man cannot love God in truth without loving the world.* 56pp. H&R 66

_________. **I AND THOU**, $2.45. This is Buber's most important work and has long een acclaimed a classic. This is a new translation by Walter Kaufman. Kaufman has also rovided a helpful introductory essay and notes. 185pp. Scr 70

_________. **KINGSHIP OF GOD**, $2.45. This is the most important of Buber's Old estament studies and is considered a landmark in contemporary Biblical scholarship. An xcellent translation by Richard Scheimann with many notes. 228pp. H&R 73

_________. **THE KNOWLEDGE OF MAN**, $2.50. The essays in this volume represent he culmination of Buber's philosophical study of what is peculiar to man as man. The olume is edited by Maurice Friedman and contains a long introductory essay by him. There is also, in the appendix, a dialogue between Martin Buber and Carl Rogers on the atient-therapist relationship. Index, 186pp. H&R 65

_________. **THE LEGEND OF THE BAAL-SHEM**, $2.95. *This book consists of a desriptive account and twenty stories. The descriptive account speaks of the life of the Haidim, a Jewish sect of eastern Europe which arose around the middle of the eighteenth entury and still continues to exist in our day in deteriorated form. The stories tell the life of the founder of this sect, Rabbi Israel ben Eliezer, who was called Baal-Shem, that is, the master of God's Name, and who lived from about 1700 to 1760. . . . But the life about which we shall learn here is not what one ordinarily calls the real life. I do not report the development and decline of the sect; nor do I describe its customs. I only desire to communicate the relation to God and the world that these men intended, willed, and sought to live. I also do not enumerate the dates and facts which make up the biography of the Baal-Shem. I build up his life out of his legends, which contain the dream and the longing of a people. . . . I have received it from folk-books, from note-books and pamphlets, at times also from a living mouth. . . . I have received it and told it anew. . . . I bear in me the blood and the spirit of those who created it, and out of my blood and spirit it has become new.*—from the introduction. The text includes an extensive glossary. 223pp. ScB 55

_________. **MEETINGS**, c$5.95. Autobiographical fragments, recently written. Dr. Maurice Friedman's famous Buber-bibliography is appended. 115pp. OpC 73

_________. **MOSES**, $2.45. *In this book a fascinating attempt is made to depict the historical Moses. The work is rich in brilliant comment. He has profound things to say on the flight of Moses to Midian, where he met with a life resembling that of his ancestors; on the Burning Bush, where he saw fire, but no form; on Moses before Pharaoh, as the first historical instance of prophet versus king; on the contrast between Moses summoned by God, and Balaam, made use of by Him. The style is invariably clear, precise, and dignified. This is a book to be read, re-read and treasured.*—David Daube, Regis Professor, Oxford University. Notes, index, 226pp. H&R 46

_________. **ON JUDAISM**, $2.95. Twelve essays written between 1909 and 1951, covering every aspect of the Jewish religion. 242pp. ScB 67

_________. **THE ORIGIN AND MEANING OF HASIDISM**, $3.45. This volume is the culmination of Buber's lifetime re-creation and interpretation of Hasidism. All aspects of the tradition are reviewed and the material is very clearly presented. Professor Buber's work is less concerned with defining theoretical concepts than with pointing to an image of man and a way of life. 254pp. Hor 60

_________. **TALES OF THE HASIDIM—EARLY MASTERS**, $3.45. The mystical religious enthusiasm which swept eastern Europe in the eighteenth century expresses itself in stories and epigrams by and about the masters of the movement. The religious personality of these leaders, or Zaddikim, forms and guides the lives of their Hasidim. They are both man and symbol. Later, as the personalities of the Zaddikim diverged, new and varying spiritual strains flowed from them. As the movement grew and spread, problems of inner structure arose. The later tales are therefore more concerned with problems of everyday life. This collection is the most extensive available. 355pp. ScB 47

_________. **TALES OF THE HASIDIM—LATER MASTERS**, $2.95. 352pp. ScB 48

_________. **THE TALES OF RABBI NACHMAN**, c$5.00. *Rabbi Nachman . . . is perhaps the last Jewish mystic*, says Martin Buber. *He stands at the end of an unbroken tradition whose beginning we do not know. . . . I have not translated these stories of Rabbi Nachman, but retold them in all freedom, yet out of his spirit as it is present to me.* Also includes Buber's remarks on Jewish mysticism. 214pp. PSm 56

_________. **TEN RUNGS: HASIDIC SAYINGS**, $1.75. The various ways in which men struggle to perfect themselves are the *Rungs* of Hasidic lore. *No limits are set to the ascent of man, and to each and everyone the highest stands open. Here it is only your personal choice that decides*, it is said of them. *This book contains a small selection of Hasidic sayings of this nature. They all revolve around a single question: How can we fulfill the meaning of our existence on earth: And so, dear reader, these pages are not concerned with the mysteries of heaven, but with your life and mine, in this hour and the next. These sayings were scattered through hundreds of books, in versions largely distorted in the speeches and writings of the disciples who transmitted them. I have selected, reduced to the quintessence of meaning, and arranged them according to major themes. . . .* Most of the selections are a paragraph in length. Notes, index, 126pp. ScB 47

_________. **THE WAY OF MAN**, c$4.50. A collection of six short essays which discuss the way of man according to the teachings of Hasidism and clarify some major aspects of this teaching. 41pp. Wat 50

_________. **THE WAY OF RESPONSE**, $2.95. A comprehensive anthology of Buber's writings, edited by Nahum Glatzer, topically arranged and focused around the motif of response: *Buber's man is a responding man. Response establishes him as a person. . . . Nietzsche's dictum that* in the end one experiences only oneself *is counterposed by Buber's view that it is the other through whom I become fully I: if with my whole being I enter into a relationship with him.*—from the preface. The selections are generally fairly short and are more clearly presented than much of Buber's philosophical writings. Bibliography, 223pp. ScB 66

HODES, AUBREY. **MARTIN BUBER**, $2.25. This is a fine non-technical introduction to Buber's life and teachings by a South African who maintained a close relationship with Buber for twelve years. The study is informally-written and the reader can get a good feeling for Buber's life, work, and the major influences on him. Vik 71

BUTLER, W.E. **MAGIC AND THE QABALAH**, c$5.95. A very clear presentation of the subject, designed for those of us not trained in an esoteric school. A general introduction gives as good a background to the Qabala as we have read, and specific chapters relate it to psychism, the astral plane, modern psychology, and direct experience. Later chapters deal with the Qabala and the Tree of Life in more detail, without getting totally beyond comprehension. 107pp. Wei 64

CARLEBACH, SHLOMO. **THE SHLOMO CARLEBACH SONGBOOK**, $3.95. For Hasidic Jews song became a way of worship, a means of ascent. In timeless earth-transcending melodies, in tender and intimate liltings, the soul itself found voice. Schlomo Carlebach is the most noted contemporary carrier of this tradition. This is a collection of his compositions, with the notes recorded. 95pp. Zim 70

CHALEB, RABBI. **THE SIXTH AND SEVENTH BOOKS OF MOSES**, c$6.00. These two books are translated from the Hebrew and contain many spells and mystic seals and signets. 190pp. dLC nd

COHEN, GERSON, tr. **SEPHER HA-QABBALAH: THE BOOK OF TRADITION**, c$8.50. This is a history of the social and cultural climate of Jewish Spain during the *golden age* of medieval Hebrew literature, written soon after the exile of the Jews from southern Spain in the twelfth century. Abraham Ibn Daud composed the work to prove that Rabbinic tradition constituted the fulfillment of the revelation in scripture. This edition presents the original text, a translation, commentary, analysis, and extensive introductory material. Index, 423pp. Jew 67

CORDOVERO, RABBI MOSES. **THE PALM TREE OF DEBORAH**, c$8.75. Rabbi Cordovero was one of the most profound and systematic exponents of the teachings of the Zohar and a leading figure in the circle of mystics for which sixteenth century Safed in

Palestine was renowned. This book is an ethical treatise devoted to the Qabalistic significance and application of the *Imitation of God*. Little space is devoted to an exposition of Qabalistic teachings—the reader is presumed to have a background in the Qabala before entering into this essentially ethical work. Cordovero explores his theme through Qabalistic literature, especially with reference to the Sephiroth, and through Rabbinic ethical literature. The text includes a forty-five page introduction and extensive notes by the translator, Louis Jacobs. Bibliography, 133pp. SHP 60

CROWLEY, ALEISTER. **THE QABALAH OF ALEISTER CROWLEY**, c$10.00. A new edition containing *Gematria*, *Liber 777*, and *Sepher Sephiroth* (consisting of hundreds of Hebrew words with English translation). Includes an introduction by Israel Regardie, and much additional material. 296pp. Wei 73

DENNING, MELITA and OSBORNE PHILLIPS. **THE SWORD AND THE SERPENT**, c$10.00. This is a presentation of the practical applications of the Qabala as taught in modern-day Western Mystery Schools. The first part of the book is devoted to an in-depth analysis of the five emanations. The next sections explore the paths and the channels of force and the final part of the volume details practical exercises and techniques for using the material presented. The text also includes eleven full page diagrams and twenty-three Tables of Correspondences. The emphasis is on magic rather than mystical teachings. 264pp. LIP 75

DIMONT, MAX. **JEWS, GOD AND HISTORY**, $1.75. A scholarly, fascinating account of the 4,000 year history of the Jewish people. This is universally considered the best account available. 472pp. NAL 62

DRESNER, SAMUEL. **THE ZADDIK**, $3.45. The Zaddik was an individual who had attained the highest degree of spiritual solitude and was capable of being alone with God, but who was, at the same time, at the true center of his community. He was a saint, a mystic, and a holy leader and was created by the crisis in eighteenth century Judaism that produced the Hasidic movement. This is a study of the doctrine of the Zaddik told through the medium of the writings of Rabbi Yaakov Yosef of Polnoy. Some of the original Hebrew text is reproduced in the notes. 312pp. ScB 60

DUNCAN, A.D. **THE CHRIST, PSYCHOTHERAPY AND MAGIC**, c$5.25. This volume was written by a Christian theologian. *The book is in three parts. The first consists of three essays which will seek to establish the origins from which the Qabalistic tradition has sprung. These will discuss Gnosis and Gnosticism, the Qabalah in Judaism, and the relationship between magic and mysticism. . . . The second section contains an examination of the Qabalah as it is found in the modern occult tradition. . . . The third . . . section deals with the practical applications of Qabalistic occultism; its meditational techniques and their affinities with modern psychotherapy.*—from the preface. The bulk of the book is devoted to a detailed analysis of the Paths and Duncan's presentation is as clear as any we've read (despite his odd choice for a title!) and he has drawn on some of the most notable references. Notes, index, illustrations, 228pp. A&U 69

EPSTEIN, ISIDORE. **JUDAISM**, $5.95. A history of the philosophy more than a history of the people, this book traces the rise, growth, and development of the beliefs, teachings and practices of Judaism. 349pp. Pen 50

FLEER, GEDALIAH. **RABBI NACHMAN'S FIRE**, $4.95. Subtitled *An Introduction to Breslover Chassidus*, this is the first attempt to present the many facets of the Breslover doctrine (named after Rabbi Nachman of Breslov) by a follower rather than an outsider. The first section is a detailed, yet concise, biography of Rabbi Nachman and a study of the times in which he lived. The second section is a collection of the Rabbi's thoughts in the areas of both man's relationship to man and his relationship to God. 110pp. SHP 75

FOHRER, GEORG. **HISTORY OF ISRAELITE RELIGION**, $15.75. This is the most comprehensive study of Israelite religion that we know of. Dr. Fohrer is a Professor of the Old Testament at a German university. The subject is treated chronologically to the end of the Old Testament period, and there is a full consideration of other ancient Near Eastern texts. The treatment is heavy on scholarship. Therefore the text cannot be read idly but is recommended only to the interested student. The author's discussion is combined with many quotations from relevant literature. Notes, indices, 416pp. ABI 72

FORTUNE, DION. **THE MYSTICAL QABALAH**, c$10.25. An explanation of the uses of the Qabalah made by modern students of the Mysteries, the nature of primitive religion, and the psychology of mystical experience. A thorough examination of the thirty-two Mystical Paths of the Concealed Glory, relating the soul of man with the universe. This is the most readable, clear book on the Qabala available, and we recommend it highly. See the Mysticism section for more of Dion Fortune's books. 237pp. BnL 35

FRANCK, ADOLPHE. **THE KABBALAH**, c$6.95. Explains and analyzes the doctrine of the two principal works of the Qabalah, the Sefer Yetzirah and the Zohar, and then introduces the reader to the Qabalist conception of the nature of God, of the world, and of the human soul. Other chapters deal with the authenticity and antiquity of the Qabala,

and its philosophic resemblances to other ancient schools. This is one of the few readable books about the Qabala, and is a good introduction for those unfamiliar with it or who have thus far failed to grasp a glimmering of its essence. 224pp. UnB 1843

GERSH, HARRY. **THE SACRED BOOKS OF THE JEWS**, $2.95. An excellent basic introduction to Judaism's most revered texts. Includes accurate, concise summaries of some of the more complicated material and translation of original source material. 256pp. S&D 68

GESENIUS, WILLIAM. **GESENIUS' HEBREW GRAMMAR**, c$13.25. Edited and enlarged by E. Kautzsch, revised in accordance with the 28 German edition (1909) by Aleister Crowley, with a fascimile of the Siloam inscription and a table of alphabets. 614pp. O

GEWURZ, ELIAS. **THE HIDDEN TREASURES OF THE ANCIENT QABALAH**, c$3.25. An esoteric interpretation of Qabalistic material. 43pp. YPS 18

_____. **THE MYSTERIES OF THE QABALAH**, c$3.25. Esoteric interpretation of the Qabala, including chapters on the Hebrew alphabet and its hieroglyphical significance; initiation; the soul of the Qabala. 99pp. YPS 22

GINSBURG, CHRISTIAN. **THE ESSENES; THE KABBALAH**, c$6.95. Two essays—first a short treatise on the history and doctrines of the Essenes, a Jewish monastic order that predicted the coming of Christ long before he was born. The essay on the Qabala is quite scholarly, dealing with its meaning, the Books, and various Qabalistic schools through the ages. There are a large number of quotes, as well as a glossary. 245pp. Wei 186

GLATZER, NAHUM, ed. **THE ESSENTIAL PHILO**, $3.95. Philo Judaeus of Alexandria (first century AD) is known for his sweeping attempt to create a synthesis of the two cultures in which he lived: the Biblical Jewish and the philosophical Greek. He achieved this synthesis by interpreting the Bible in the light of Hellenic (Platonic and Stoic) wisdom by presenting Biblical personalities as symbols of certain central ideas; by reducing to minimum the historic and particularistic meaning of a Biblical story in favor of universalistic and generally human relevance. This volume is a selection of Philo's basic treatises. They provide an introduction to Hellenistic Judaism, information on the background of early Christian thought, and a chapter on the intellectual history of antiquity. Bibliography, index, notes, 372pp. ScB 71

GOLDSTEIN, DAVID, tr. **THE JEWISH POETS OF SPAIN**, $1.95. An anthology of poets living in Muslim Spain between the tenth and thirteenth centuries. This was the period of the greatest flowering of Hebrew verse since Biblical times. This edition includes an introduction, biographical notes, and textual notes. Indices of first lines in English and first words in Hebrew (though the text is only in English). 218pp. Pen 71

Qabalistic square

GONZALEZ-WIPPLER, MIGENE. **A KABBALAH FOR THE MODERN WORLD**, c$7.95. This is the first scientifically-oriented presentation of the Qabalistic system. Ms. Gonzalez-Wippler integrates the developments in modern physics with ancient tradition and shows how similar the two world-conceptions are. A fascinating part of her study traces the meaning of the letters of the Hebrew alphabet. This is a very good introduction to the Qabalistic teaching. The material is clearly presented and well illustrated. The beginning student can get a feeling of what the Qabala is from this text and can decide which areas s/he would like to explore in more depth—without becoming overwhelmed by a great deal of amorphous metaphysical concepts. Bibliography, 171pp. Jul 74

GRAY, WILLIAM G. **THE LADDER OF LIGHTS**, c$7.95. The Tree of Life works in relation to consciousness just like a computer, except that it operates through the consciousness of living beings. Data is fed in, stored in associative banks, and then fed out on demand. It acts as a sort of universal exchange throughout the entire chain of consciousness sharing its scheme. The Qabala, or *received teaching*, is the outcome of experiences and developments of those who have climbed the ladder of the Tree by arranging their lives according to its pattern of perfection. The Tree provides the means of receiving inner world contacts with types of consciousness normally inaccessible to the ordinary mind. It is from and through these sources that the teaching comes. This is a step-by-step guide to the Tree. 230pp. HeL 68

THE TREE OF EVIL, c$6.95. This volume is based on the Qabalistic Tree Life. It deals with the *anti-principles* or opposites of the Tree termed *Qlippoth* (literally nslated as *harlots, shells*, or *demons*). The book consists mainly of a study of the power evil and how it came into being along with a series of methods for coping with evil ough the use of the Tree of Life and other techniques derived from the Qabala and Western mystery tradition. 119pp. Hel 74

UBERGER, PHILLIP, ed. **KABBALAH: TEN LUMINOUS EMANATIONS, VOL. 2**, 0.95. This is a very intricate treatise divided into two sections: Inner Light and Inner flection—both of which are basically commentaries on the Sephiroth taken from the tings of Rabbi Isaac Luria with a long explanatory glossary and series of questions and wers provided by Rabbi Yehuda Ashlag. The main theme is a detailed analysis of the Sephiroth in their dual aspects as line and circle. Only those students quite familiar h Qabalistic literature are advised to venture into this book. 203pp. RCK 73

LEVI, Z'EV BEN SHIMON. **ADAM AND THE KABBALISTIC TREE**, $5.00. *Adam dmon is the Universe made after a likeness to God, the allegorical figure abstracted by bbalists into the diagram called the Tree of Life. This metaphysical presentation is a mprehensive formulation of universal principles and processes. Based upon the divine ects and their relationships, the Tree describes the archetypal design on which the Uni- rse is modelled. The same template applies throughout all the lesser worlds, so that even e tiny species of mankind, indeed a single human being, is directly related to the original am by virtue of faithful replication.* This book begins with an exposition of the four rlds present in every human being. Beginning with the body, the process and laws of logy are related Qabalistically, so that the connection between the body and the psyche demonstrated. This is followed by a detailed study of the psyche's awakening of the ul and its growing consciousness of the upper Qabalistic Worlds of Creation and Emana- n. The conclusion describes the progress of man into the realm of the spirit and the essence of the divine. This is a very interesting, clearly presented exposition of the study man as seen by contemporary Qabalists, illustrated with many useful drawings of the ree. Index, 333pp. Wei 74

_____. **AN INTRODUCTION TO THE CABALA—TREE OF LIFE**, $3.95. First, alevi traces its history, and outlines the metaphysical background to the tree. He then plies the material to examples observable in everyday life. These range from the struc- re of government, the hierarchy of the church, the economic system, to the manner in hich a love affair develops, to birth-life-death. The final part is devoted to a detailed udy of man and his spiritual aims and possibilities. This exposition is in modern terms nd helps the reader gain an understanding of how to use the Tree. 196pp. Wei 72

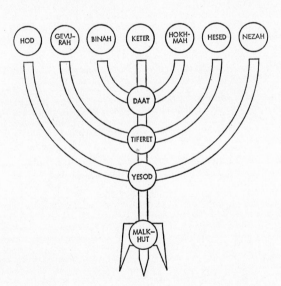

Menora. This design specified to Moses in Exodus is an earlier version of the Tree of Life.

_____. **THE WAY OF KABBALAH**, $5.00. An esoteric study which begins by ex- mining some differing ways that the Qabala has been viewed and studied through the ges. Many historical accounts are shown to be allegories of the human condition. The tter part of the book consists of a series of detailed studies of the disciplines involved in Qabalistic study. Many diagramatic trees of life illustrate the text and are used as focal oints for the exposition—showing the different stages the student passes through on the path to ultimate knowledge. An interesting presentation which attempts to make the Qabalistic teaching relevant to our age. Index, glossary, 224pp. Wei 76

HALL, MANLY P. **CABBALISTIC KEY TO THE LORD'S PRAYER**, $1.50. An esoteric interpretation of the meaning of the Lord's Prayer as it can be understood through the application of Qabalistic and Hermetic wisdom. 32pp. PRS 64

HARRISON, R.K. **TEACH YOURSELF BIBLICAL HEBREW**, $3.25. This is an extremely clear volume designed for beginners wishing to learn Biblical Hebrew. In format, it is a basic grammar—however, the emphasis is on Biblical usage and vocabulary. This volume is part of the British series **Teach Yourself Books**—a very well thought of series of manuals. 217pp. McK 55

HESCHEL, ABRAHAM. **THE SABBATH**, $2.95. This is a profound meditation on the nature and celebration of the Sabbath. Its thesis is that Judaism is a religion of time, not space, and the Sabbath symbolizes the sanctification of time, so that *the Sabbaths are our great cathedrals.* They represent a day of separation from space and the material things that fill it, a day of devotion to the eternal. Notes, 118pp. FSG 51

HOELLER, STEPHEN. **THE ROYAL ROAD**, $2.95. See the Tarot section. 119pp. TPH

JACOBS, LOUIS. **HASSIDIC PRAYER**, c$13.45. A systematic study of the methods of prayer of the Hasidic community. Rabbi Jacobs discusses such matters as contemplative and ecstatic prayer, quotes copiously from the writings of the Hasidim to illustrate his analysis, and draws parallels with the practices of other religious traditions. Index, notes, 195pp. ScB 72

JAMES, LAURA DE WITT. **WILLIAM BLAKE AND THE TREE OF LIFE**, c$2.25. See the Blake sub-section in Mysticism. ShP 56

KALISCH, ISIDOR, tr. **SEPHIR YEZIRAH—A BOOK ON CREATION**, $1.75. This met- aphysical essay is considered to be the first philosophical book that was ever written in the Hebrew language. The time of its composition and the name of its author have not been ascertained. This text includes the original Hebrew, with English translation and ex- planatory notes. 61pp. Sym 1877

KAPLAN, ARYEH, tr. **RABBI NACHMAN'S WISDOM**, c$11.25. Rabbi Nachman is one of the best-known and most often quoted of the Hasidic masters. He was a great grandson of the Baal Shem Tov. He was known for his stories and for his teachings which shed light on some of the deepest mysteries, while at the same time enhancing them with meaning for the average individual. His doctrine was one of joy, stressing that a man must find cause for happiness in everything that befalls him. This book is a translation of **Shavachay HaRan** and **Sichos HaRan**, a combined work that was first published several years after the Rabbi's death. It contains his most often quoted teachings on subjects ranging from simple everyday advice to the most esoteric Qabalistic mysteries. This book, appearing here in English translation for the first time, remains the most comprehensive volume of his teachings. Appendices present a life of Rabbi Nachman and an analysis of the text. Notes, Index, 458pp. SHP 73

KASDIN, SIMON. **THE ESOTERIC TAROT: THE KEY TO THE CABALA**, $1.95. See section on the Tarot. Wei

KNIGHT, GARETH. **EXPERIENCE OF THE INNER WORLD**, c$11.00. See the Mysti- cism section.

_____. **A PRACTICAL GUIDE TO QABALISTIC SYMBOLISM**, c$16.00. Two volumes. Compares Western occultism with yoga, analyzes the Tree of Life in full detail for each Sephirah and gives the practical applications as well as the theory of occult sym- bolism in the Western esoteric tradition. Also gives the most comprehensive analysis ever published of the twenty-two Paths of the Concealed Glory that join the Sephiroth—taking into account Hebrew trumps. A large part deals exclusively with the Tarot, tracing the history, design and the varying system of correspondences with the Tree of Life. Ends with an extensive chapter on practical methods of *working the Tree.* A very clear presentation. Recommended 541pp. Hel 65

KRAKOVSKY, LEVI. **KABBALAH: THE LIGHT OF REDEMPTION**, c$7.50. An intro- duction to the basic concepts from the Research Institute of Qabala in Jerusalem. Deals with the origin and essence of the Qabala in great detail. Recommended for those intending serious study. 267pp. RCK

_____. **THE OMNIPOTENT LIGHT REVEALED**, c$4.00. This is a review of some of the major themes of the Qabala. Rabbi Krakovsky seems out to prove that all the wis- dom of the world is contained in the Qabala and he goes a bit overboard in his hyperbole. There's not much in his presentation that cannot be found elsewhere in less dramatic form—although he does present an important point of view. Index, 106pp. Yes nd

KRAMER, SIMON. **GOD AND MAN IN THE SEFER HASSIDIM**, c$8.10. The **Sefer Hasidim** (Book of the Pious) by Rabbi Judah ben Samuel of Ratisbon is a thirteeenth cen- tury book on Jewish ethics and morals. Much has been written about this book in Hebrew, Yiddish, and German—but little of this material is available in English. The book embraces a multitude of subjects from the conduct of wo/man in relation to God and each other, worship and prayer to business regulations, table manners, and the care of animals. Dr. Kramer, President of Hebrew Theological College in Chicago, presents a full review of the material in the **Sefer Hasidim**, arranged topically. Extensive chapter notes are included. Bibliography, 285pp. Blo 66

KUSHNER, LAWRENCE. **THE BOOK OF LETTERS**, c$6.95. More than just symbols, all twenty-two letters of the Hebrew alphabet overflow with meanings of their own. Rabbi Kushner draws from ancient Judaic sources, weaving Talmudic commentary, Hasidic folk tales, and Qabalistic mysteries around the letters. Each letter is illuminated and, together with the comments, is presented in the author's original calligraphy, recalling the look and feel of ancient medieval manuscripts. For those who want to understand the Judaic spiritual heritage better this beautiful text should be very illuminating. Oversize, 64pp. H&R 75

LANGER, JIRI. **NINE GATES**, c$8.40. As a youth in Prague in the days before World War I, the author took leave of his family and went to live among the Hasidim. This book grew out of his experience and his life as a Hasid. The reader is given a vivid picture of this lifestyle and of the people: their ecstasies, austerities, feasts, and the all-pervading Rebbe, purveyor of esoteric wisdom. Just as the life of the Hasidim is filled with stories by and about the Hasidic masters, so too is this narrative interwoven with the same stories. This volume should be a delight to those readers seeking a deeper insight into the life style and meaning of the Hasidim. There's a long introduction by Langer's brother. 297pp. Cla 61

239

LEVI, ELIPHAS. **THE BOOK OF SPLENDORS**, c$7.95. Levi is a noted Hermeticist who wrote several books on the Qabala, of which this is considered the best. It has only recently been translated (although not in one place) into English. Part I provides the actual Qabalistic text, with an explanation of the resemblance between Qabalism and Freemasonry. Part II shows the connection between Qabalism, numerology and the Tarot. In an appendix, Papus supplies a summary of Levi's doctrines and teachings, with extensive information on his disciples. 191pp. Wei 73

_____. **THE GREAT SECRET**, c$11.25. This is a sequel to **The Book of Splendors**. Here Levi discusses evil and its manifestations. 188pp. TPL 75

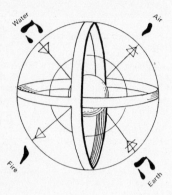

The vision of the wheels

_____. **THE MYSTERIES OF THE QABALAH**, c$10.00. This volume is a commentary on Ezekiel's **Prophecy** and the **Apocalypse of St. John**. In each case the text itself is reproduced (although not in one place) along with a survey of the esoteric meaning of the material. A profusion of drawings and emblems illustrate the text. Despite the high sounding title, this can by no means be considered a definitive study of the Qabala. In fact, the Qabala and the Tree are only referred to in passing and only in an illustrative way. A border around each page makes the book fairly hard to read and the presentation itself is scattered. 285pp. Wei 74

LEVIN, MEYER. **CLASSIC HASSIDIC TALES**, $3.95. This collection is considered to be the finest English version of the authentic Hassidic tales. The text is divided into two parts. The first relates the stories of the Baal Shem Tov and the second contains the parables of his grandson, Rabbi Nachman. The tales are well written and retain the flavor of the original. Illustrations are interspersed. Meyer Levin also supplies a forward. 357pp. Pen 75

LUZZATTO, MOSES. **GENERAL PRINCIPLES OF THE KABBALAH**, c$8.50. Rabbi Luzzatto was an eighteenth century Qabalistic scholar. His most important contribution was the detailed analysis of the *Sefirot* contained in this volume. Another work for the serious student. 232pp. Wei 70

MAHARAL. **THE BOOK OF DIVINE POWER**, $5.05. This is a collection of three essays on Torah literature which discuss the diverse aspects and levels of reality, and their interrelationships. This edition presents an unabridged selection of three of the Maharal of Prague's (Rabbi Yehuda Leove ben Bezalel) **Introductions**. The concepts of the ancient sages of Israel are expressed in contemporary terms and an illustrated appendix explains the fundamentals of classical and modern relativity which correspond to the teachings of the Torah. Index, glossary, 103pp. Fel 75

MOSES MAIMONIDES

Maimonides was unquestionably the foremost intellectual figure of medieval Judaism. Born in Cordova, Spain, forced at an early age to conceal his faith, he emigrated to Morocco and then to Palestine before settling in Egypt, where financial necessity compelled him to study medicine and where he eventually became personal physician to Saladin. Although his medical skills were renowned and his writings in this field were widely studied throughout the Western world during the following centuries, Maimonides' primary interest was theology. He devoted ten years to preparing the **Mishnah Torah** and fifteen years to **The Guide to the Perplexed**—the first written in Hebrew, the second in Arabic. These studies of Jewish law were first considered radical in their efforts to reconcile religious and scientific thought, but later became pillars of traditional Jewish faith.

FRIEDLANDER, M., tr. **THE GUIDE FOR THE PERPLEXED**, $3.50. This book is concerned mainly with finding a concord between the religion of the Old Testament and its commentaries and Aristotelian philosophy. Rather than being a philosophical treatise, it is designed to liberate wo/men from the tormenting perplexities arising from their understanding of the Bible only according to its literal meaning. This edition contains an unabridged photographic reproduction of the second revised edition of Friedlander's early twentieth century translation from the Arabic along with the translator's long introductory material discussing Maimonides' life and work and a summary of the **Guide**. The translation has aged fairly well. There is an index of scriptural passages cited. 473pp. Dov 56

GOODMAN, LENN, tr. **RAMBAM**, c$10.00. Maimonides was known by the acronym *Rambam*. In a long introduction Dr. Goodman details Maimonides' life and role in history and theology. He has also prepared new translations from the **Mishnah Torah** and **The Guide to the Perplexed**, arranging the excerpts topically to focus on Maimonides contributions. These are accompanied by commentary and analysis, clarifying the complexities of his thought and providing historical and religious background. Bibliography, index, 462pp. Vik 75

PINES, SHLOMO, tr. **THE GUIDE OF THE PERPLEXED**, $15.20/set. This is widely considered the best translation available. This edition has the additional advantage of providing extensive introductory material and notes by Professor Pines (of Hebrew University, Jerusalem) and the late Leo Strauss, a leading authority on Maimonides. A glossary and extensive indices are included in this two-volume set. 762pp. UCh 63

ROSNER, FRED, tr. **MAIMONIDES' COMMENTARY ON THE MISHNAH**, c$10.70. An English translation of the entire introduction of Moses Maimonides to his **Commentary on the Mishnah**, as well as an English version of his commentary on the first tractate of the Mishnah, tractate *Berachoth*. In his introduction Maimonides provides an historical account and description of the development of the Oral Law (**Mishnah** and **Gemara**). From there he makes a lengthy digression into the subject of prophecy. He then classifies the various types of laws contained in the **Mishnah**. There is also a dissertation on knowledge and wisdom and understanding of the purpose of the world and of all that is contained therein. Literally hundreds of footnotes accompany the text. 249pp. Fel 75

YELLIN, DAVID and ISRAEL ABRAHAMS. **MAIMONIDES: HIS LIFE AND WORKS**, c$7.95. This is a revised edition of an important work which originally appeared in 1903. The notes and bibliographic sources have been brought up to date, reflecting the scholarship of the last seventy years; supplementary notes provide material not touched upon by the original authors and elaborate upon the original notes. This is still considered one of the best biographical studies of Maimonides available. Bibliography, index, 228pp. SHP 7.

MATHERS, S.L. MACGREGOR, tr. **THE BOOK OF THE SACRED MAGIC OF ABRA MERLIN THE MAGE**, c$3.98/3.50. This is the best description of *angelic magic* that we know of. It is a translation of a fifteenth century manuscript in which the author, a Qabalist, describes a tour that he made of the world, visiting sorcerers, magicians, and Qabalists and estimating their powers and virtues. The system he presents is based mostly on Hellenistic theory of the Iamblican sort, but with Jewish increments from the Qabala, explaining the qualifications needed to become a magician, and activities which must be regularly practiced. Specific instructions are included on developing various power including clairvoyance, divining metals, healing, and much else. And a number of symbols, including various magic squares, are reproduced and explicated in the text. 316pp. Dov 1900

_____. **THE KABBALAH UNVEILED**, c$8.95. Contains translations of the following books of the Zohar: *The Book of Concealed Mystery, The Greater Holy Assembly*, and *The Lesser Holy Assembly*, with extensive notes and explanations. In a long introduction Mathers answers such questions as: what is the Qabala, who was its author, what are its general teachings, its subdivisions, why a new translation. He includes various diagrams. His is one of the most readable and comprehensive translations. 341pp. Wei 26

MECKLER, DAVID. **MIRACLE MEN**, c$5.30. A collection of tales of the Baal Shem Tov and his disciples. The stories in this collection are not found in most of the other books—in fact the Hasidic tales must number in the thousands because with the exception of a few very noted ones all the collections we know of seem to contain vastly different stories. The translation appears to be fairly good. 310pp. Blo 64

MEILSHEIM, DAVID. **THE WORLD OF ANCIENT ISRAEL**, c$3.95. See the **World of Ancient Civilizations** Series in the Ancient Civilizations section. Tud 73

MINTZ, JEROME. **LEGENDS OF THE HASIDIM**, $5.95. The Hasidim arrived in New York in great numbers in the 1940's and 1950's. Unlike the usual immigrants, they have preserved their orthodox culture and have renewed their rich oral literature of legends, parables, philosophical saying and historical accounts. Professor Mintz describes the mores and the history of the present community and analyzes the cultural content of the more than 370 tales which are included in this work. He explores the intimate relationship existing between Hasidic tale and Hasidic law, ritual, value and social structure. He discusses the role of the Rebbe, the upbringing of children, the role of women, the relationship of magic and mysticism, and the social interactions of the various groups with each other and with the outside world. The book is illustrated with many photographs and goes farther than any previous study in English in revealing the inner dynamics and spirit of the New York Hasidic community. Notes, glossary, bibliography, index. 462pp. UCh 68

MORDELL, PHINEAS. **THE ORIGIN OF LETTERS AND NUMERALS ACCORDING TO THE SEFER YETZIRAH**, $2.50. *There is no book in Jewish literature that is so difficult to understand as the Sefer Yetzirah.... After many years of study, I reached the conclusion that the Sefer Yetzirah, as the earliest Hebrew grammar, contains not only the fundamental rules of Hebrew orthography, but also an account of letters and numerals. This account it is my present purpose to set forth.* The text includes notes, diagrams, and portions of the **Sefer** in Hebrew and English translation. 71pp. Wei 14

MULLER, ERNST. **HISTORY OF JEWISH MYSTICISM**, c$4.70. *The object of this work is to give a comprehensive survey of the history of Jewish mysticism—one which shall cover the whole field and not only that part commonly known as Cabbalah. It also includes the contacts of Jewish with non-Jewish mysticism. While other works deal with various aspects of the subject in far greater detail, this work aims particularly at placing in their proper perspective the mystical spirit of the Bible itself, the mystical tendencies in the apocalyptic literature and the allegorical exegesis of the Bible and the existence of an ancient esoteric lore closely connected with the popular Agada.... The notes contain much historical and other information supplementary to the text, while the appendix fills out the picture given in the text by a selection of passages from the original works which speak for themselves.* Bibliography, index, 197pp. Yes nd

...YER, ISAAC. **QABBALAH**, c$15.00. Deals extensively with the philosophical writings of Avicebron, an eleventh century Qabalistic scholar. Avicebron was noted for the connections he made with Oriental scholarship such as the sacred Hindu texts and the **Tao Te Ching**. His translations discuss karma, meditation, esoteric and exoteric knowledg and sdom, and the Chinese Qabala. Includes many excerpts from the Qabala and the Zohar. dex, 470pp. Wei 1888

EUSNER, JACOB. **THE LIFE OF THE TORAH**, $8.00. *The Life of the Torah is a urce book intended to convey, so far as it is possible through the experience of merely ading a book, some of the meanings contained within the Jewish religious tradition. . . . hat I offer here is the chance to enter into the imaginative religious life of the pious Jew. want you to know how Jews pray—or, at least, the words they say; how they confront rah in synagogue worship and in response to its message; how they examine their souls the Days of Awe and celebrate the Sabbath and festivals of the Jewish year. I want u to know what it means for a Jew to live according to the Torah. . . . I present glimpses to the lives of some of the great rabbis.* The book is extremely well organized and the lections are uniformly excellent. Glossary, 252pp. Dic 74

_____. **THE WAY OF TORAH**, $6.65. Subtitled *An Introduction to Judaism*. Neusr presents a good textbook summary of the major features of the Jewish religion divided to the following sections: *The Mythic Structure of Classical Judaism, Torah: A Way of iving,* and *Continuity and Change in Modern Times.* The presentation is quite straightorward and quotations from important source books are included. There's also an excelnt long, topically arranged bibliography. Index, 143pp. Dic 74

EWMAN, LOUIS, tr. **THE HASIDIC ANTHOLOGY**, $5.95. A topically arranged colection of the tales, proverbs, and paradoxes by which the Hasidic masters conveyed their isdom to their disciples. Newman has translated the selections directly from the original ebrew, Yiddish, and German texts. The sayings here form a striking complement to the ore consciously *literary* compilation of Martin Buber. Newman's introduction provides guide to the history of Hasidism, its doctrines, leaders, and literature. Index, bibliography, 76pp. ScB 34

_____. **MAGGIDIM AND HASIDIM: THEIR WISDOM**, c$6.45. This is a collection f the wise sayings, aphorisms, epigrams, reflections, and comments of folk preachers, asidic religious leaders, and Rabbis. The material is garnered from a wide variety of sources nd is topically arranged in alphabetical order. Each selection is headed and the entire ook is fully indexed—all of which makes it a very handy book to use if you are seeking nformation on a particular subject or a story related to a particular idea. Newman also suplies an introduction and he has chosen his material carefully and well. 303pp. Blo 62

NOVECK, SIMON, ed. **GREAT JEWISH PERSONALITIES IN ANCIENT AND MEDI-EVAL TIMES**, $5.30. This is a nice collection of short biographical stories of Moses, David, Jeremiah, Philo, Akiba, Saadia, Halevi, Maimonides, Rashi, Abravanel, Baal Shem Tov, and Vilna Gaon. Each essay has been prepared by a well known scholar. This volume. is part of the B'nai B'rith Great Book Series. Bibliography, notes, glossary, index. 351pp. BnB 59

OESTERLEY, W.O.E. and THEODORE ROBINSON. **HEBREW RELIGION**, c$10.95. A detailed scholarly study of the origin and development of the Hebrew religion based upon modern Old Testament scholarship. This is by far the most comprehensive discussion of the subject we could imagine, tracing the religion from earliest times through the Greek period. All aspects of the religion and the resulting culture are treated fully. Indices, 448pp. SCK 37

PICK, BERNHARD. **THE CABALA**, $1.45. Of all the books we have reviewed so far on the Qabala, this one reads the easiest. That does not mean that it is the best—it's just that we have sat here for what seems like days looking into these obscure volumes and trying to figure out how to express their essences. And it's not easy because the Qabala is an exceedingly complex subject. This is a reprint of a book first published in 1903. In it Pick presents an historical review of the Qabala and studies its meaning in the light of its time and place. He begins with a survey of the name and origin and goes from there to analyses of the pre-Zohar period, the Zohar, and the post-Zohar period. This is followed by a study of Qabalistic doctrines and a mystical interpretation of the text. 115pp. OpC 74

PULLEN-BERRY, H.B. **QABALISM**, c$10.00. An interpretation which deals with the Qabala as the most ancient secret wisdom and relates it to Hermetic philosophy. 167pp. YPS 25

REGARDIE, ISRAEL. **A GARDEN OF POMEGRANATES: AN OUTLINE OF THE QABALAH**, $3.95. A presentation of the Qabala as a guidebook leading to a comprehension of both the universe and one's own self. This text is also an introduction to the magical work of the Golden Dawn and to the Tarot, and teaches the student how to classify and organize ideas, numbers and symbols. 160pp. Llp 70

_____. **THE TREE OF LIFE**, $4.50. This is an occult interpretation/explanation of the meaning of the Tree, with instructions on its use for students on the Path. A great deal of general philosophical material is also presented, much of which relates to magic. 284pp. Wei 69

RICHARDSON, ALAN. **INTRODUCTION TO THE MYSTICAL QABALAH**, $1.00. An extremely simplified review of the applications of the Qabala to magical work, with some background and explanatory material and many practical exercises. 63pp. Wei 74

SAFRAN, ALEXANDRE. **THE KABBALAH**, c$14.70. Dr. Safran is the Chief Rabbi of Geneva, Switzerland, and former Chief Rabbi of Rumania. He is a leading world Rabbinical figure and was a leader of the Jewish underground during World War II. In addition to his political activities he is regarded as a profound and original thinker. This, his most important work, is a highly scholarly attempt to show the unity and continuity of Jewish tradition and an examination of the interaction between the body of the Law and the stream of the mystical tradition of the Qabala. The approach is basically philosophical and, while the reader needs a good background, the presentation is not overly esoteric. Glossary, notes, 341pp. Fel 75

SCHACHTER, ZALMAN. **FRAGMENTS OF A FUTURE SCROLL**, $3.95. *So you meet in these pages, Reb Zalman, gourmet and master chef. You simply cannot find anybody around more determined to put it all together—a Gurdjieff number vibration with a Kabbalistic name; the I Ching with the Sefirot. What concoctions. Only somebody who is himself the possessor of a formidable appetite, open to experimentation, and innately creative can make a respectable attempt. . . . You will find a translation of a Kabbalistic prayer, a Yiddish poem, a Hassidic tale. It's good stuff, hard to come by, delightful and urgently needed. . . . Purists will complain that the reader is not given a chance to distinguish between authentic tradition and Zalman Schachter. Well organized personalities will feel that the fragments offered in these pages are uneven in quality and rather arbitrarily strung together. And there are other problems. But that's how it is with Reb Zalman, who wants to be both humanist and transcendentalist, quintessential Jew and open to the truth-sparks of every people and culture. . . . So let there be light, even if it be accompanied by a bit of chaos, inasmuch as it also results in these kinds of fragments.—from the forward by Herbert Weiner.* The book is subtitled *Hassidism for the Aquarian Age.* Bibliography, 174pp. LOG 75

Divine concentration, or Sefirothic emanation, seen ad intra

Divine radiation, or Sefirothic emanation, seen ad extra

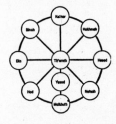
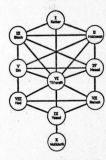

The Union of the Sefiroth in the Heart of God (Tifereth, inasmuch as it harmoizes and synthesizes all the other Sefiroth)

The Tree of the Sefiroth, representing the hierarchy from the standpoint of prototypical position and relationship

From THE UNIVERSAL MEANING OF THE KABBALAH

SCHAYA, LEO. **THE UNIVERSAL MEANING OF THE KABBALAH**, $1.95. Expounds the universal teachings of the Qabala, which relate all things to their supreme archetypes, the ten Sefiroth or principal aspects of God. This is one of the newest treatments of the subject and is highly readable. Good for those wishing an introduction, and it's the one we generally recommend. 169pp. Pen 71

SCHOLEM, GERSHOM. **KABBALAH**, c$15.00. Dr. Scholem is one of the major figures, if not the major, in modern Jewish scholarship. He has been with the Hebrew University, Jerusalem, since 1923 and is presently Professor of Mysticism and Kabbalah and also President of the Israel Academy of Sciences and Humanities. In this volume he presents a summary of his life's studies. Though the approach is academic, the presentation is not overly technical and should be understandable to most general readers. Professor Scholem begins with a study of the historical development of the Qabala and goes from there to an exploration of the basic ideas of the Qabala. This section is well organized and topically arranged. Part II, which Scholem terms *Topics*, is a lengthy exploration of nineteen major subjects, themes, and movements. Each of these discussions is self-contained and illuminating—though the technical detail at times gets overwhelming as is understandable when one considers the amount of material that is being covered. Part III presents short biographical studies of sixteen major Qabalistic personalities. The text also includes some notes and a glossary and an index. Some critics have been disappointed with this book but we feel fairly good about it. While it does not definitively cover all aspects of the subject it's hard to see how any one book can. And while it's not the most exciting book we have read, it is readable and reasonably easy to follow. 492pp. Qdr 74

_____. **MAJOR TRENDS IN JEWISH MYSTICISM**, $3.95. Scholem has done the pioneering work in the field of Jewish mysticism. This is an outline of its principal features in the form of an analysis of some of its most important phases. Stress is placed on the analysis and interpretation of mystical thought and a great deal of thought is devoted to the Qabala. Extensive notes and bibliography. 424pp. ScB 41

241

_____. THE MESSIANIC IDEA IN JUDAISM, $3.95. Scholem clarifies the Messianic concept and analyzes its transformation in the Qabala up to the paradoxical versions it assumed in the Sabbatian and Frankist movements, in which sin became a vehicle of redemption. 376pp. ScB 71

_____. ON THE KABBALAH AND ITS SYMBOLISM, $2.25. Guides the reader through the rituals and central themes in the intricate history of the Qabala. Clarifies the mystics' interpretation of the Torah and their attempts to discover the hidden meaning underlying Scripture. 204pp. ScB 69

_____. SABBATAI SEVI—THE MYSTICAL MESSIAH, $9.50. A detailed and masterful account of the Sabbatian movement from its inception to the founder's death which not only illuminates an extraordinary phenomenon in Jewish history, but is a major contribution to the general study of messianic movements and their theologies. This English translation by R.J. Werblowsky is fully illustrated and presents many new facts and enlarges and corrects the earlier Hebrew edition. 1000pp. PUP 73

SEPHARIAL. THE KABALA OF NUMBERS, $4.95. See section on Numerology. NPC 74

SIEGEL, RICHARD, ed. THE JEWISH CATALOG, $5.95. A collection of source material on every aspect of Jewish life—ideas about what to do and how to go about doing it. Both religious and cultural ideas are presented and this oversize volume is illustrated throughout. It's a neat book, and if you are into being a Jew, or interested in learning more about what it means to be Jewish you should enjoy this book. 319pp. Jew 75

SIVAN, REUVEN and EDWARD LEVENSTON. THE NEW BANTAM-MEGIDDO HEBREW AND ENGLISH DICTIONARY, $1.95. This is the most recent one-volume dictionary. The authors are noted Israeli philologists and educators. Includes 46,000 entries with a concise explanation of the essentials of Hebrew grammar. 693pp. Ban 75

STURZAKER, DOREEN and JAMES. COLOUR AND THE KABBALAH, c$9.50. An intricate study of what colors mean in connection with the Sephiroth and the Paths, and the implications that lie behind the changing colors of both Sephiroth and Paths in the several worlds of Qabalistic philosophy. Most occult teachings on color are based on the seven rays of the spectrum; an innovation introduced by the Sturzakers is the concept of twelve rays, their importance in the whole of life, manifest and unmanifest, and their interaction throughout the cosmos. This is the only Qabalistic work that discusses the meaning of color rays in their relationship to the myriad aspects of the Tree of Life. Each of the Sephiroth is discussed in a separate chapter and individual chapters are also devoted to each of the major Tarot trumps. Wei 75

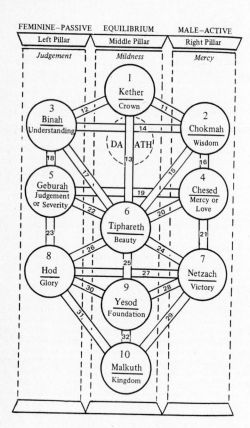

The Tree of Life and the Paths

STURZAKER, JAMES. KABBALISTIC APHORISMS, c$6.50. *The Mystical Kabbalah is a glyph or symbol system which consists of the Tree of Life and the twenty-two Major Arcana of the Tarot cards. . . . Contained within this glyph are the basic qualities that make and keep life moving. . . . This book of Kabbalistic Aphorisms has been compiled to suit the needs of all.*—from the text. The volume begins with a series of general aphorisms on the Qabala and goes from there to sections of individual aphorisms for each of the

Sephiroth. The second part of the book begins with a series of general aphorisms on the Tarot and follows with sections of individual aphorisms for each of the major arcana. Every one of the Sephiroth and major arcana sections include about fifty aphorisms so that the reader can make his/her selection depending upon the needs of the day. Many people have found these aphorisms quite useful in their daily meditations. 128pp. TPH 74

SUARES, CARLOS. THE CIPHER OF GENESIS, c$6.95. Provides a key to the code in which the Book of Genesis was written. Much that has been obscured and hidden in the traditionally accepted version now comes clear in the light of this Qabalistic study. 240pp. ShP 67

_____. THE RESURRECTION OF THE WORD, c$8.95. This volume is composed of several books, each the proclamation of a Biblical figure and at the same time each is Suares' allegorical statement of our human predicament. Suares is the scribe of this book and the characters through whom he speaks (Cain, Jonas, Judas, Jacob, Mahoyael, Ish and Adam) are the archetypes which constitute our inner and outer worlds. The central theme of the volume is Israel, seen both metaphorically and as an actual physical entity. *In this book the author now clearly defines his position in regard to the state of Israel. Israel is Jacob's name for having prevailed over Elohim.* This is a very hard book to describe. We can only say that if you have appreciated Suares' other work, you should appreciate this one. Suares says that it presents the keys of inspiration to his other books. ShP 75

_____. THE SEPHER YETSIRA, $4.95. This **Sepher** is the key work of the Qabalistic tradition and is a seed formula revealing the basic structure of energy. Suares, using the revealed cipher, breaks and explains this formula. In the process he discusses *the original astrology according to the Qabala and its zodiac* and explores what astrology reveals about the inner life. 150pp. ShP 76

THE TALMUD

*The **Talmud** is a collection of early Biblical discussions with the comments of generations of teachers who devoted their lives to a study of the Scriptures. It is an encyclopedia of law, civil and penal, human and divine. It is more, however, than a mere book of laws. It records the thoughts, rather than the events, of a thousand years of the national life of the Jewish people; all their oral traditions, carefully gathered and preserved. . . . Accepted as a standard study, it became endeared to the people who, as they were forbidden to add to or diminish from the law of Moses, would not suffer the work of their Rabbis to be tampered with in any manner. As it was originally compiled it has been transmitted to us. . . . At the first view, everything, style, method, and language, seems tangled and confused. The student, however, will soon observe two motives or currents in the work; at times harmonious, at times diverse. One displaying the logical mind, which compares, investigates, develops, and instructs; the other, imaginative and poetical. The first is called Halachah (Rule), and finds a vast field in the Levitical and ceremonial laws; the other takes possession of the ethical and historical portions of the Holy Writ. It is called Hagadah, or Legend, not so much in our present acceptance of the term, as in the wider sense of a saying without positive authority, an allegory, a parable, a tale. The **Talmud** is divided into two parts, Mishnah and Gemarah. They are continued works of successive Rabbis. . . . It was called oral or unwritten law, in contradistinction to the Pentateuch, which remained under all circumstances the immutable code, the divinely given constitution, the written law.*—H. Polano, **The Talmud**

COHEN, A. EVERYMAN'S TALMUD, $6.95. This is a comparative summary of the Talmud, beginning with a chapter explaining its history and makeup and continuing with an exploration, by subject, of its major teachings in the following order: The Doctrine of God, God and the Universe, the Doctrine of Man, Revelation, Domestic Life, Social Life, the Moral Life, the Physical Life, Folklore, Jurisprudence, the Hereafter. This is by no means an exhaustive treatment. Each of the topics could easily be expanded into a volume. However a sufficient number of extracts are offered to give the reader a good idea of Talmudic doctrine on a variety of themes without overwhelming him/her with an indigestible abundance of material. This seems to be the best one-volume summary available. Notes, index, 444pp. ScB 49

GOLDIN, JUDAH, tr. THE LIVING TALMUD, $1.50. This is a translation of **Pirke Abot** (The Wisdom of the Fathers), a collection of the sayings of the Synagogue Fathers, maxims which summarize the anguish, ecstasy, and understanding which they had experienced in their penetrating study and practice of the Law. The sages quoted here lived between the fifth century BC and the third century AD. Included in this edition too are the first English translations of many of the classical commentaries on the **Pirke Abot**, made by generations of Talmudic scholars. 247pp. NAL 55

LIPMAN, EUGENE. THE MISHNAH, $3.95. The material here has been newly translated and is designed to present significant and representative passages with a traditional commentary, and to illustrate the role of this classic text in the evolution of Jewish law and of Judaism in general. Unfortunately the material is not topically arranged so the reader interested in a particular subject has no way to locate material relevant to his/her interest (except through the index and it's hard to say how complete that is). Extensive commentary is included with each selection. 318pp. ScB 70

POLANO, H., tr. THE TALMUD, c$5.50. This is an excellent translation of some of the most important sections of the **Talmud**. The selections are from its commentaries, teachings, poetry, and legends, and all of them read uniformly well. The translator also supplies a fine introduction detailing the nature and scope of the Talmud. 383pp. Wrn 73

THE TORAH

JEWISH PUBLICATION SOCIETY, trs. THE TORAH, c$6.75. This is a new translation, which completely revises the original 1917 work. It is considered the definitive edition and includes notes and background material. The text reads well and is very nicely bound. 3+pp. Jew 62

RUNES, DAGOBERT, ed. THE WISDOM OF THE TORAH, $2.25. Presents the Torah as a book of philosophy and literature containing the following types of material: legendary tales, historical books, ritualistic books, prophetic sermons, and philosophical and poetic works. The translation is based on the King James version of the Bible. 300pp.

WEINBERG, NORBERT. THE ESSENTIAL TORAH, c$10.50. Rabbi Weinberg has written this volume to help individuals understand the words of the Torah. Each chapter is an exhaustive review of the weekly Torah selection, including a retelling in modern language of the basic story, a selection from the classical commentaries, and a synopsis of each prophetic section. This volume should be especially helpful for those attending services regularly and it can also be useful for all self-study programs. The text is quite well written. 344pp. Blo 74

Isaiah

UNTERMAN, ISAAC. THE HEBREW PROPHETS, c$8.85. Prophets among the Jews always arose whenever there was adversity in Jewish life. They represented a direct contact between God and man and the desire for justice and fairness is expressed in their writings. The prophets were the reformers and as such represent an important movement in Judaic history. This volume is composed of fairly lengthy biographical studies of the major prophets: Amos, Hosea, Isaiah, Micah, Zephaniah, Nahum, Habakkuk, Jeremiah, and Ezekiel. Two introductory sections discuss the role of the prophets and their historical sequence. Index, 211pp. Blo 70

VAUX, ROLAND de. ANCIENT ISRAEL—RELIGIOUS INSTITUTIONS, $2.95. This is a very detailed study of Israelite life in Old Testament times written primarily for the non-specialist. De Vaux is a distinguished archaeologist who has spent years researching the material he presents here. Every aspect of ancient Israel's religious institutions is covered in depth. The following are the main topics: Semitic sanctuaries, the first Israelite sanctuaries, the Temple at Jerusalem, the centralization of the cult, the priestly office, the Levites, the priesthood in Jerusalem under the Monarchy, the priesthood after the Exile, altars, the ritual of sacrifice, the history of sacrifice in Israel, the origin of Israelite ritual, the religious significance of sacrifice, the liturgical calendar, the Sabbath day, the ancient feasts, and the later feasts. Abundant Biblical references are included in the text along with several indices and a bibliography. 317pp. MGH 61

WAITE, A.E. THE HOLY KABBALAH, c$10.00. A massive study, extensively indexed, tracing Qabalistic history, literature, and philosophy down through the ages and reviewing various students of the Qabala as well as relating it to other channels of secret tradition. This is considered to be one of the best books on the Qabala—suitable for the beginning or advanced student. Many long footnotes and citations. 620pp. Stu

WEINER, HERBERT. 9½ MYSTICS: THE KABBALA TODAY, $1.95. This is a welcome attempt to present the Qabalistic teachings and the Jewish mystical tradition in an accessible way—and an attempt at which Rabbi Weiner succeeds admirably. *This book records a search for the life secrets of a mystical tradition sometimes known as the Kabbala. It describes a series of encounters wherein individuals and groups who claim intimate acquaintance with this tradition are challenged to relate their hidden wisdom to problems of our day. It also contains a good deal of historic and technical information about Jewish mysticism, but frankly, anyone interested in a purely objective, scholarly account of this latter subject will be better served by other books; this journal is on a more personal and popular level.* 342pp. McM 69

WESTCOTT, WILLIAM. THE STUDY OF THE KABALAH, c$2.95. An excellent, extremely clear introduction by a noted occultist, with explanatory diagrams. 72pp. WBI

WIESEL, ELIE. MESSENGERS OF GOD: BIBLICAL PORTRAITS AND LEGENDS, c$8.95. A moving retelling of Biblical lore. Weisel has succeeded quite well in his aim of illustrating the relevance of these ancient tales to our time and of conveying his perceptions of what the tales meant to earlier generations. Included are chapters on Adam, Cain and Abel, Isaac, Jacob, Joseph, Moses and Job. 237pp. RaH 76

_____. **SOULS ON FIRE**, $1.65. *A consummate work of art. Out of the lives and legends of Hasidic masters, out of the tales of their suffering and joy, out of the dread and darkness through which they reached for God—out of all these Elie Weisel has fashioned a work that makes these men and their times come brilliantly alive.*—Chaim Potok. 280pp. RaH 72

WORK OF THE CHARIOT. BOOK OF FORMATION (SEFER YETSIRAH), $4.00. An ancient treatise on the mystical nature of the Hebrew letters ascribed to the Patriarch Abraham. This translation is a new one, compiled from ten known texts, and includes the Sefer Yetsirah in both Ezra square Hebrew and the original Gezer. Also included: fully detailed notes; many diagrams and charts; the Shuo Kua, an ancient Chinese treatise. WkC 71

_____. **BOOK OF THE NAMES**, $12.00. A copy of the Book of Adam, explaining creation. The various scriptures give 128 names of God, a series of angelic Tree Language, and the Beards (involuting names) of the Vast Face, Small Face, and Unity. A supplement shows how to use the text for practical Qabalistic meditation. WkC 71

_____. **SIFRA DETZNIUTHA**, $2.00. A new translation of the heart of the Book of Splendor. WkC 71

_____. **TREE OF LIFE, BRANCHES I–X**, $3.00. The only English translation of the mystical teachings of Rabbi Yitzaq Luria ha'Ari, a sixteenth century Qabalist. Included are the Hebrew text and numerous diagrams illustrating the complex mystical patterns set forth in the book. WkC 70

YEHUDA, EHUD BEN and DAVID WEINSTEIN. BEN-YEHUDA'S POCKET ENGLISH-HEBREW AND HEBREW-ENGLISH DICTIONARY, $1.95. This book is considered the finest low-priced dictionary available. It is derived from the eight volume Dictionary and Thesaurus of the Hebrew Language by the author's father. Over 30,000 entries are included along with explanations of grammar and pronunciation. 678pp. S&S 61 .

ZION, RAPHAEL BEN. AN ANTHOLOGY OF JEWISH MYSTICISM, c$5.00. Presents translations of selections from the following classical texts: *The Speech of Elijah* by Tikune Zohar, *The Palm Tree of Deborah* by Rabbi Moses Cordovero, *The Portal of Unity and Faith* by Rabbi Shneur Zalman of Ladi, and *The Soul of Life* by Rabbi Hayim. Ben Zion has made no attempt to present scholarly translations. He wants to get the message of these texts across to the general reader in a readable form so that the reader can get an idea of the Jewish mystical tradition. The text includes extensive notes. 246pp. Yes nd

THE ZOHAR

The Zohar, or Book of Splendour, is a cabbalistic work written mainly in the Aramaic language. It takes the form of a commentary on the Pentateuch and is intended to reveal the hidden meaning of the biblical narrative and the divine commands. It is a complete thesaurus of Jewish mysticism, theosophy, and occult traditions. . . . The Zohar in its present form first appeared in Spain as a compilation by Moses de Leon of Avila, who claimed that the original work had been revealed to Simeon ben Jochai, a saintly Jew of the second century. . . . Whatever its origin, it is certain that The Zohar exerted a powerful influence on Jewish life in medieval ghettoes and opened up new vistas of spiritual worlds.—Ariel Bension, from *The Zohar in*

spiritual worlds.—Ariel Bension, from **The Zohar in Moslem and Christian Spain**

BENSION, ARIEL. THE ZOHAR IN MOSLEM AND CHRISTIAN SPAIN, c$15.75. We know of no better study of the Zohar (or Book of Splendor) than this book. It is well written and presents a coherent picture of the spirit and atmosphere to which the mystics of Spain's Golden Age were subjected in addition to detailing the world view of the Zohar and the major figures involved in it. Bension begins with a general survey of Jewish life in Spain; the next chapter is devoted to an exposition of the Spanish mystics, with a detailed study of their main concerns. The final two chapters in this section present an in-depth exploration of the similarities in the works of the Spanish mystics of the three faiths—Jewish, Christian and Muslim. The second, and longest, section of the book is devoted to a discussion of the Book of Splendor itself. The first chapter analyzes the Zohar itself and the story it has to tell. A final section reveals what happened to Sephardic mysticism after the Exile. Bension himself is in the direct line of descent from these original Sephardic mystics and a great deal of the information presented here derives from information that was handed down over the ages. He has also done a lot of historical research. The reader needs little or no background to be able to appreciate and understand the material presented here. Bibliography, index, 276pp. SPH 32

SCHLOEM, GERSHOM. ZOHAR, THE BOOK OF SPLENDOR: BASIC READINGS FROM THE KABBALAH, $1.95. A selection from the extensive writings which make up the vast Zohar. The historical setting of the Zohar and its literary characters are discussed in an introduction. 122pp. ScB 74

SPERLING, HARRY and MAURICE SIMON, trs. THE ZOHAR, c$42.50. This is one of the only two complete editions of the Zohar available in English—the other is considerably more expensive and contains the same translation as this edition. Five volumes, glossary, 2127pp. BnP

JUNGIAN PSYCHOLOGY

Jung's psychology is based firstly on his own experience with human beings, normal, neurotic, and psychotic. It is not a kind of psychopathology, it takes the empirical material of pathology into account, but his theories are in his own words *suggestions and attempts at the formulation of a new scientific psychology based in the first place upon immediate experience with human beings.* There is no simple formula to which this experience can be reduced; to focus on one point leads to a gain in clarity, but the network of relationships in which psychic activity consists is lost sight of. The search for precision in defining mental experience robs it of much that by nature belongs to it.

In speaking of mind and mental activity Jung has chosen the terms psyche and psychic, rather than mind and mental, since the latter are associated primarily with consciousness, whereas psyche and psychic are used to cover both consciousness and the unconscious. So-called unconscious phenomena are usually unrecognized by the one affected by them and have no connexion with the ego. If they do obtrude into consciousness—say, for instance, in the form of an emotional outburst that is out of proportion to its apparent cause—they are largely inexplicable to anyone who is unaware of the nature of unconscious motivation. *I don't know what came over me,* we say. Unconscious manifestations are not limited to the pathological, for normal people are continually acting from motives of which they are utterly unaware.

The unconscious aspect of the psyche is different from, but compensatory to the conscious. In Jung's view the conscious mind *grows out of an unconscious psyche which is older than it, and which goes on functioning together with it or even in spite of it.* Furthermore, in contrast to those who look on mind as secondary manifestation, an epiphenomenon, *a ghost in the machine,* Jung insists on the reality of the psyche—it is no less real than the physical, has its own structure, and is subject to its own laws.

Everything made by man had its beginnings in the psyche, was something he just thought of, or perhaps saw in a dream or as a vision. Our own hopes and fears may be grounded in *realities* that are recognizable to others, or they may be *purely imaginary,* but the joy or anxiety they bring is the same in either case—what we experience is real to us, if not to other people, and has its own validity, equal to, though different from, the *reality* that is generally acknowledged. Jung gives the inner or psychic process a value equal to the outer or environmental one.

Jung's conception of the psyche is of a system which is dynamic, in constant movement, and at the same time self-regulating; he calls the general psychic energy libido. The concept of libido must not be thought of as implying force as such, any more than does the concept of energy in physics; it simply a convenient way of describing the observed phenomena.

The libido flows between two opposing poles—an analogy might be drawn here with the diastole and systole of the heart, or a comparison made between the positive and negative poles of an electric circuit. Jung usually refers to the opposing poles as *the opposites.* The greater the tension between the pair of opposites the greater the energy; without opposition there is no manifest energy. Many opposites at varying levels can be enumerated; for instance, progression, the forward movement of energy, and regression, the backward consciousness and unconsciousness, extraversion and introversion, thinking and feeling, &c. The opposites have a regulating function (as Heraclitus discovered many hundred years ago), and when one extreme is reached libido passes over to its opposite. A simple example of this is to be found in the way that an attitude carried to one extreme will gradually change into something quite different: violent rage is succeeded by calm, and hatred not infrequently turns in the end to liking. To Jung the regulatory function of the opposites is inherent in human nature and essential to an understanding of psychic functioning.

Libido is natural energy, and first and foremost serves the purposes of life, but a certain amount in excess of what is needed for instinctive ends can be converted into productive work and used for cultural purposes. This direction of energy becomes initially possible by transferring it to something similar in nature to the object of instinctive interest. The transfer cannot, however, be made by a simple act of will, but is achieved in a roundabout way. After a period of gestation in the unconscious a symbol is produced which can attract the libido, and also serve as a channel diverting its natural flow. The symbol is never thought out consciously, but comes usually as a revelation of intuition, often appearing in a dream.

There is a very close association between sexuality and the tilling of the earth among primitive people, while many other great undertakings, such as hunting, fishing, making war, &c., are prepared for with dances and magical ceremonies which clearly have the aim of leading the libido over into the necessary activity. The detail with which such ceremonies are carried out shows how much is needed to divert the natural energy from its course. This transmutation of libido through symbols, says Jung, has been going on since the dawn of civilization, and is due to something very deeply rooted in human nature. In the course of time we have succeeded in detaching a certain proportion of energy from instinct and have also developed the will, but it is less powerful than we like to believe, and we still have need of the transmuting power of the symbol. Jung sometimes calls this the *transcendant function.*

Jung's view of the unconscious is more positive than that which merely sees it as the repository of everything objectionable, everything infantile—even animal—in ourselves, all that we want to forget. These things, it is true, have become unconscious, and much that emerges into consciousness is chaotic and unformed, but the unconscious is the matrix of consciousness, and in it are to be found the germs of new possibilities of life. The conscious aspect of the psyche might be compared to an island rising from the sea—we only see the part above the water, but a much vaster unknown realm spreads below, and this could be likened to the unconscious.

The island is the ego, the knowing, willing *I,* the centre of consciousness. But what belongs to consciousness, what I know about myself and the world, and can direct and control, is not fully conscious all the time. I forget, or I repress what I do not like, or what is not socially acceptable. I also have sense-perceptions of insufficient strength to reach consciousness, and I experience much that is only partly comprehended or of which I do not become fully aware. These subliminal perceptions, together with the repressed or forgotten memories, make a kind of shadow land stretching between the ego and the unconscious which could—in fact should—belong to the ego; or, to use our metaphor, it is a land which has not always been covered by the sea, can be reclaimed. Jung calls this shadow land the *personal* unconscious, ⟨di⟩stinguish it from the collective unconscious, which is how he designates ⟨the⟩ aspect of the psyche which is unconscious in the fullest sense.

⟨The⟩ personal unconscious belongs to the individual; it is formed from his re⟨pre⟩ssed infantile impulses and wishes, subliminal perceptions, and countless ⟨for⟩gotten experiences; it belongs to him alone.

⟨The⟩ memories of the personal unconscious, though not entirely under the ⟨con⟩trol of the will, can, when repression weakens (as for instance in sleep), ⟨be⟩ recalled; sometimes they return of their own accord; sometimes a chance ⟨asso⟩ciation or shock will bring them to light; sometimes they appear some⟨wh⟩at disguised in dreams and fantasies; sometimes, especially if they are ⟨cau⟩sing disturbances as in a neurosis, they need to be *dug out*.

⟨Th⟩e collective unconscious is a deeper stratum of the unconscious than the ⟨per⟩sonal unconscious; it is the unknown material from which our conscious⟨nes⟩s emerges. We can deduce its existence in part from observation of instinc⟨tiv⟩e behaviour—instincts being defined as impulses to action without con⟨scio⟩us motivation, or more precisely—since there are many unconsciously ⟨mo⟩tivated actions which are entirely personal and scarcely merit the term ⟨ins⟩tinctive—an instinctive action is inherited and unconscious and occurs ⟨uni⟩formly *and regularly*. Instincts are generally recognized; but not so the ⟨fac⟩t that, just as we are compelled to certain broad lines of action in specific ⟨cir⟩cumstances, so also we apprehend life in a way that has been determined ⟨by⟩ our history. Jung does not mean to imply by this that experience as such ⟨is⟩ inherited, but rather that the brain itself has been shaped and influenced ⟨by⟩ the remote experiences of mankind. But *Although our inheritance consists* ⟨of⟩ *physiological paths, it was neverthless mental processes in our ancestors* ⟨tha⟩*t traced these paths. If they came to consciousness again in the individual,* ⟨th⟩*ey can do so only in the form of other mental processes; and although* ⟨the⟩*se processes can become conscious only through individual experience* ⟨an⟩*d consequently appear as individual acquisitions, they are neverthless pre-* ⟨ex⟩*istent traces which are merely* filled out *by the individual experience.* ⟨Pr⟩*obably every* impressive *experience is just such a break-through into an* ⟨ol⟩*d, previously unconscious river-bed.*

⟨Th⟩is tendency, one might say this necessity, to apprehend and experience ⟨lif⟩e in a manner conditioned by the past history of mankind Jung calls arche⟨ty⟩pal, and archetypes are the *a priori, inborn forms of* intuition . . . *of per-* ⟨ce⟩*ption and apprehension. . . . Just as his instincts compel man to a specific-* ⟨all⟩*y human mode of existence, so the archetypes force his ways of perception* ⟨an⟩*d apprehension into specifically human patterns.*

⟨Ar⟩chetypes are unconscious, and can therefore only be postulated, but we ⟨be⟩come aware of them through certain typical images which recur in the ⟨p⟩syche. Jung at one time spoke of these as *primordial images* (an expression ⟨t⟩aken from Jacob Burckhardt), but later came to use the term archetype ⟨c⟩omprehensively to cover both the conscious and the unconscious aspects.

⟨W⟩e may hazard a guess that the primordial images, or archetypes, formed ⟨t⟩hemselves during the thousands of years when the human brain and human ⟨c⟩onsciousness were emerging from an animal state but their representations, ⟨i⟩.e. the archetypal images, while having a primordial quality, are modified or ⟨a⟩ltered according to the era in which they appear. Some, especially those ⟨i⟩ndicative of an important change in psychic economy, appear in an abstract ⟨o⟩r geometric form such as a square, circle, or wheel, either by themselves or ⟨c⟩ombined in a more or a less elaborate way to form a typical and particularly ⟨i⟩mportant symbol. Others present themselves as human or semi-human forms, ⟨g⟩ods and goddesses, dwarfs and giants, or they appear as real or fantastic ani⟨m⟩als and plants of which there are countless examples in mythology.

⟨T⟩he archetypes are experienced as emotions as well as images and their effect ⟨i⟩s particularly noticeable in typical and significant human situations such as ⟨b⟩irth and death, triumph over natural obstacles, transitional stages of life like ⟨a⟩dolescence, extreme danger, or awe-inspiring experience. In these circum⟨s⟩tances an archetypal image that might have been drawn in the caves of ⟨A⟩uvergne will often appear in the dreams of the most modern of men.

⟨J⟩ung holds dreams to be natural and spontaneous products of the psyche, ⟨w⟩orth taking seriously, and producing an effect of their own, even if this is neither realized nor understood. Dream language is symbolic amd makes constant use of analogics, hence its frequently obscure or apparently meaningless character.

The existence of the collective unconscious can be inferred in the normal man from the obvious traces of mythological images in his dreams—images of which he had no previous conscious knowledge. It is sometimes difficult to prove that no such knowledge ever existed, but in certain kinds of mental disorder there is an astonishing development of mythological imagery which could never be accounted for by the individual's own experience.

Jung has spent much time in studying myths, for he considers them to be fundamental expressions of human nature. When a myth is formed and expressed in words, consciousness, it is true, has shaped it, but the spirit of the myth—the creative urge it represents, the feelings it expresses and evokes, and even in large part its subject-matter—come from the collective unconscious. Myths, it is true, often seem like attempts to explain natural events, such as sunrise and sunset, or the coming of spring with all its new life and fertility, but in Jung's view they are far more than this, they are the expression of how man experiences these things. The rising of the sun then becomes the birth of the God-hero from the sea. He drives his chariot across the sky, and in the west a great mother dragon waits to devour him in the evening. In the belly of the dragon he travels the depth of the sea, and after a frightful combat with the serpent of the night he is born again in the morning. This is a mythical explanation of the physical process of the sun's rise and descent, but its emotional content makes it more than this. Primitive people do not differentiate sharply between themselves and their environment, they live in what Levy-Bruhl calls *participation mystique*, which means that what happens without also happens within, and vice versa. The myth therefore is an expression of what is happening in them as the sun rises, travels across the sky, and is lost to sight at nightfall, as well as the reflection and explanation of these events.

Because myths are a direct expression of the collective unconscious, they are found in similar forms among all peoples and in all ages, and when man loses the capacity for myth-making, he loses touch with the creative forces of his being. Religion, poetry, folk-lore, and fairy-tales, depend also on this same capacity. The central figures in all religions are archetypal in character, but as in the myth, consciousness has had a share in shaping the material. In primitive cults this is much less than in the higher and more developed religions, so that their archetypal nature is clearer. The most direct expression of the collective unconscious is to be found when the archetypes, as primordial images, appear in dreams, unusual states of mind, or psychotic fantasies. These images seem then to possess a power and energy of their own—they move and speak, they perceive and have purposes—they fascinate us and drive us to action which is entirely against our conscious intention. They inspire both creation and destruction, a work or art or an outburst of mob frenzy, for they are *the hidden treasure upon which mankind ever and anon has drawn, and from which it has raised up its gods and demons, and all those potent and mighty thoughts without which man ceases to be man.* The unconscious therefore, in Jung's view, is not merely a cellar where man dumps his rubbish, but the source of consciousness and of the creative and destructive spirit of mankind.

To attempt to define the collective unconscious is to attempt the impossible, for we can have no knowledge either of its boundaries or its true nature; all that we can do is to observe its manifestations, describe them, and try to understand them so far as is possible, and a large part of Jung's work has been devoted to this task. Of the archetypes he says, *Indeed, not even our thought can clearly grasp them, because it never invented them.* Nevertheless it has been possible to isolate various figures, which recur in dreams and fantasy series, which appear to have a typical significance for human beings, and which can be correlated with historical parallels and myths from all over the world; these Jung, after much careful research work, has described as some of the principal archetypes affecting human thought and behaviour, and has named the *persona*, the *shadow*, the *anima* and *animus*, the *old wise man*, the *earth mother*, and the *self*.

Here again we need to remember, when speaking of archetypes of the collective unconscious, that there are no watertight compartments in the mind, and that even the archetypes can have a personal aspect. The anima image, for instance, is conditioned both by the age-long experience men had of women, and the actual personal experience a man has with a woman or women.

—condensed from **AN INTRODUCTION TO JUNG'S PSYCHOLOGY** by Frieda Fordham

Mythic Sea Serpent

ADLER, GERHARD. **THE LIVING SYMBOL**, c$15.00. A detailed study of a case of neurosis and its analytical treatment, showing the basic pattern of the individuation process and the practical application of Jung's theories. Includes patients' drawings and paintings. Index, 475pp. PUP

_____. **STUDIES IN ANALYTICAL PSYCHOLOGY**, $1.95. This is a review of the main concepts of analytical psychology by one of the most eminent Jungian analysts, divided into the following sections: A Comparative Study of the Techniques of Analytical Psychology, Study of a Dream, The Ego and the Cycle of Life, Consciousness and Cure, A Psychological Approach to Religion, and C.G. Jung's Contribution to Modern Consciousness. *Not only on account of the lucidity of its exposition, but also because of its wealth of illustrative case-histories, this book fills a gap in psychological literature. It gives both the professional and the psychologically minded layman a welcome set of bearings in territory which—at any rate to begin with—most people find rather hard of access. But the examples drawn direct from life offer an equally direct approach, and this is an aid to understanding. I would like to recommend this book most cordially to the reading public.*—C.G. Jung. Index, illustrations, notes, 250pp. Put 69

ALEX, WILLIAM. **DREAMS, THE UNCONSCIOUS AND ANALYTICAL THERAPY**, $1.25. See Dreams section. RPM

BENNETT, E.A. **WHAT JUNG REALLY SAID**, $2.95. An incisive analysis of the development of Jung's work and thinking from his early experiments and meetings with Freud through the development of Jung's ideas of personality analysis and classification, the collective conscious, dreams, active imagination, alchemy, and psychotherapy. Recommended for a brief general overview of Jung's ideas. 186pp. ScB 67

BERTINE, ELEANOR. **JUNG'S CONTRIBUTION TO OUR TIMES**, c$8.00. This volume is the collected papers of Dr. Bertine, one of the first American physicians to work with Carl Jung in Zurich, and one of the first to make use of the principles of analytical psychology in her work as a practicing therapist and analyst. The papers represent forty years of professional activity in depth psychology and were written in an informal style to convey to non-professionals, in as direct a manner as possible, the personal relevance of Jungian psychology. Introduction by Dr. Edward Edinger. Notes, 288pp. JFP 67

CAMPBELL, JOSEPH, ed. **THE PORTABLE JUNG**, c$8.95/3.95. This is the most comprehensive anthology of Jung's writings available. *I have opened this anthology with papers introducing the elementary terms and themes of Jung psychology. Once acquainted with these, the reader will be prepared to range at will through* **The Collected Works**; *and my second aim, consequently, has been to provide a usable guide to that treasury of learning. For Jung was not only a medical man but a scholar in the grand style, whose researches, particularly in comparative mythology, alchemy, and the psychology of religion, have inspired and augmented the findings of an astonishing number of the leading creative scholars of our time.... My final aim, accordingly, has been to provide such a primer and handbook to Jung's writings that if a reader will proceed faithfully from the first page to the last, he will emerge not only with a substantial understanding of Analytical Psychology, but with a new realization of the relevance of the mythic lore of all peoples to his own psychological opus magnum of Individuation.*—from the introduction. The translations are all taken from **The Collected Works** and Campbell supplies an excellent introduction along with notes and a chronology. Campbell himself is a noted scholar (see Mythology section for a description of his work) and was a close friend and associate of Jung. 692pp. Vik 71

CARUS, CARL. **PSYCHE**, $7.55. The name of Carus appears often in Jung's writings when he speaks of precursors to the theory of the unconscious. This translation of Part I of **Psyche**, entitled *The Unconscious*, was made by a number of individuals and it offers the student of Jung's thought its appropriate background, the roots of which reach into Romantical medical philosophy and a traditional way of regarding the psyche before Nietzsche and Freud. This edition also includes a precis of Parts II and III by Murray Stein. An introduction by James Hillman examines the parallels between Jung and Carus. 94pp. Spr 70

CASTILLEJO, IRENE de. **KNOWING WOMAN**, $2.45. Subtitled *A Feminine Psychology*, this presents a unique approach to self-understanding for all women: *I love the book. It is*

very wise and very pertinent for women today.—Anais Nin. *A woman today lives in perpetual conflict. She cannot slay the dragon of the unconscious without severing her essential contact with it; without in fact destroying her feminine strength and becoming a mere pseudo-man. Her task is a peculiarly difficult one. She needs the focused consciousness her animus alone can give her, yet she must not forsake her woman's role of mediator to man. Through a woman, man finds his soul. She must never forget this. Through woman, not through a pseudo-man. Through man, woman finds the animus who can press the soul she has never lost. Her burning need is to trust her own diffuse awareness to know what she knows and to learn to speak of it, for until it is expressed she does not wholly know it.*—from the book. Ms. de Castillejo is a noted Jungian psychologist. 188pp. H&R 73

COX, DAVID. **THE TEACHINGS OF C.G. JUNG**, $1.95. This volume presents a very simplified synopsis of Jung's psychological thought. The first chapters of the book discuss psychology in general and review contemporary theories other than those of Jung. The next chapters (The Collective Unconscious, Psychological Types, Psychic Development, Archetypes, and the Self) elucidate the central concepts of Jungian psychology and a final chapter details the author's own experiences in Jungian analysis (as a patient, not an analyst!). This is a very basic primer, designed for those who wish some understanding of Jungian thought. Only the psychological aspects are discussed. 191pp. H&R 68

EDINGER, EDWARD. **EGO AND ARCHETYPE**, $3.95. Edinger is a psychiatrist who presently Chairman of the New York Institute of the Jung Foundation. This is a remarkably lucid synthesis of Jung's basic ideas in the form of a detailed journey through religion, legend, and folklore into the deepest regions of the psyche. Part I explores changing relations between the ego and the archetypal psyche at different stages of development. Part II explores the ways the ego can relate to symbolic imaging and describes some of the categories of experience an individual encounters. In Part III the goal of individuation and its symbolism is discussed and a remarkable series of dreams is presented. Includes 63 related plates. Recommended. 317pp. Pen 72

ERANOS YEARBOOKS

The Eranos Conferences have been conducted at Ascona, Switzerland since 1933 where some of the world's best minds could meet at a round table of ideas. During the war, the meetings continued with a group of scientists who examined the roots of the spiritual impulse that had formed the civilization that seemed to be destroying itself. The Eranos materials represent a unique contribution to the unfolding understanding of man and are a paramount historical, psychological and spiritual masterpiece of collective human intelligence and creative exploration. Each volume is c$12.50.

ERANOS YEARBOOKS. **VOL. I—SPIRIT AND NATURE**. The contributors include C.G. Jung, who regularly particulated in the Eranos Conferences, and a number of outstanding European thinkers. Topics range from the spirit in fairy tales to the history of the spirit in antiquity and include the spirit of science, the spirit of psychology, the Indian conception of psychology and the transformation of the spirit in the Renaissance. 514pp. PUP 54

_____. **VOL. II—THE MYSTERIES**. Thirteen European scholars are presented in this volume concerning the manifestations of the spiritual impulse in the varied sacred traditions of our great religions and those of antiquity. Subjects include the Orphic mysteries and the Greek spirit; the ancient mysteries in the societies of their time; their transformation and most recent echoes; the mysteries of Osiris in ancient Egypt; the pagan and Christian mysteries. 492pp. PUP 55

_____. **VOL. III—MAN AND TIME**. The contributors include Mircea Eliade, Hellmut Wilhelm, C.G. Jung, and Erich Neumann. Contents include time and eternity in Indian thought, the concept of time in the Book of Changes, the relation of time to death, time in Islamic thought and transformation of science in our age. 434pp. PUP 57

_____. **VOL. IV—SPIRITUAL DISCIPLINES**. Participants include Eliade, Martin Buber, Heinrich Zimmer and Jung. Topics discussed include significance of Indian Tantric Yoga, spiritual guidance in contemporary Taoism, psychology of ancient Mexican symbolism, contemplation in Christian mysticism, and the position of art in the psychology of our time. 527pp. PUP 60

_____. **VOL. V—MAN AND TRANSFORMATION**. Speakers included are D.T. Suziki, Paul Tillich, Jean Danielou, Zimmer, and Eliade. Topics include the birth of a new consciousness in Zen, symbols in ancient Byzantine mysticism, immortality and death and rebirth in the light of India. 433pp. PUP 64

_____. **VOL. VI—THE MYSTIC VISION**. Essays by Ernesto Buonaiuti, Wilhelm Koppers, Zimmer, and other noted scholars. 500pp. PUP 68

EVANS-WENTZ, W.Y. **TIBETAN BOOK OF THE DEAD**, $2.95. See Tibetan Buddhism section. Oxf 60

_____. **THE TIBETAN BOOK OF THE GREAT LIBERATION**, $3.95. See Tibetan Buddhism section. Oxf 54

FORDHAM, FRIEDA. **AN INTRODUCTION TO JUNG'S PSYCHOLOGY**, $2.50. Ms. Fordham is a Jungian analyst. She worked closely with Jung and his wife in the preparation of the first edition of this book. Jung himself had the following to say about the final product: *She has delivered a fair and simple account of the main aspects of my psychological work. I am indebted to her for this admirable piece of work.* We agree, and to this day the book remains the best simple introduction to Jungian psychology. The author begins with a general analysis of analytical psychology and from there devotes chapters to Jung's major themes: Psychological Types, Archetypes of the Collective Unconscious,

on and the Individuation Process, Psychotherapy, Dreams, and Psychology and Edu-
ı. A final chapter, Jung on Himself, was added after the publication of **Memories, ns, and Reflections**, and it contains a biographical study culled from that volume other material. Recommended. Notes, introduction, glossary, index, 159pp. Pen 66

DHAM, MICHAEL. **CHILDREN AS INDIVIDUALS**, c$9.00. Dr. Fordham was the ungian to apply the concept of analytical patterns to the study of child development. book is a radically revised version of his original work, **The Life of Childhood**. It is a of child maturation, expressed through comprehensive investigation of the self, and iduation, in childhood. Dr. Fordham's extensive analytical practice with children of es has provided a rich store of case material including play behavior, drawings, fan- and dreams. Notes, index, bibliography, illustrations, 223pp. JFP 69

NZ, MARIE-LOUISE von. **INTERPRETATION OF FAIRY TALES**, $7.55. *Until t the seventeenth century, it was the adult population that was interested in fairy Their allocation to the nursery is a late development, which probably has to do with ejection of the irrational, and the development of the rational, outlook—so that they to be regarded as nonsense and old wives' tales and good enough for children. Now- s we do not allow ourselves to take fairy tales seriously—except in Jungian psychology Fairy tales are the purest and simplest expression of collective unconscious psychic esses. Therefore their value for the scientific investigation of the unconscious exceeds of all other material . . . In myths or legends, or any other more elaborate mytholog- material, we get at the basic patterns of the human psyche through an overlay of cul- material. But in fairy tales there is much less specific conscious cultural material and fore they mirror the basic patterns of the psyche more clearly . . . . After working many years in this field, I have come to the conclusion that all fairy tales endeavour escribe one and the same psychic fact . . . . This unknown fact is what Jung calls the which is the psychic totality of an individual and also, paradoxically, the regulating er of the collective unconscious. Every individual and every nation has its own modes xperiencing this psychic reality. Different fairy tales give average pictures of different es of this experience. They sometimes dwell more on the beginning stages, which deal the experience of the shadow and give only a short sketch of what comes later. Other s emphasize the experience of the animus and anima and of the father and mother ges behind them . . . . Others emphasize the motif of the inaccesssible or unobtainable sure and the central experiences. There is no difference of value between these tales, ause in the archetypal world there are no gradations of value for the reason that every etype is in its essence only one aspect of the collective unconscious.*—M.L. von Franz. s is Dr. von Franz' basic volume on fairy tales. It includes a review of the literature, xamination of various theories of the fairy tale and its interpretation, a detailed study one tale, and an exploration of shadow, animus, and anima motives in the tales. Once volume is digested, the reader can move on to some of the more detailed studies. Dr. Franz writes clearly and presents an abundance of examples to back up her theories. pp. Spr 73

_______. **C.G. JUNG**, c$15.00. Each individual's life follows a pattern which, from point of view of analytical psychology, respresents the *myth* or archetypal outline of inner and outer events of one's own biography. The book, subtitled *His Myth in Our e*, refers to such a pattern in the life of Jung. Dr. von Franz, who worked closely with g for over twenty-five years, traces the development of basic Jungian concepts such as collective unconscious, the archetypes, the psychological types, active imagination, creative instinct, and the process of individuation from their origin in specific dreams g had throughout his life (and which he discusses in his autobiography) to their eventual pirical documentation in the voluminous books and papers he published over a period sixty-five years. This is neither an academic biography of Jung nor a primer of Jungian ught. Rather, it is a history of the growth and development of one man's creative wers during a lifetime of dialogue with the unconscious. Dr. von Franz is one of the nders of the C.G. Jung Institute in Zurich and this is an important, though quite tech- al, addition to the literature on Jungian psychology and its founder. Long bibliography index, 366pp. JFP 75

_______. **NUMBER AND TIME**, c$16.15. Jung's work in his later years suggested t the seemingly divergent sciences of psychology and modern physics might, in fact, approaching a unified world model in which the dualism of matter and psyche would resolved. Jung believed that the natural integers are the archetypal patterns that reg- e the unitary realm of psyche and matter, and that number serves as a special instrument man's becoming conscious of this unity. In this volume Dr. von Franz explores Jung's pothesis. Her discussion of the theory of number draws on material from Eastern stud- , ethnology, archaeology, and mythology, as well as from natural sciences and mathe- tics. The book includes explorations of the psychological aspects of mathematics, a cussion of number as a psychophysical energy pattern, and a description of mandalas. addition she develops Jung's theory of synchronicity. Written in a clear style and replete th illustrations which help make the mathematical ideas visible, **Number and Time** is a ece of original scholarship which introduces a view of how *mind* connects with *matter* the most fundamental level. Notes, bibliography, index, 342pp. NUP 74

_______. **PATTERNS OF CREATIVITY MIRRORED IN CREATION MYTHS**, .45. A psychological interpretation of twelve creation motifs presented by creation ths in the cosmogonies of peoples from North and South America, Africa, the Near ıst, and other parts of the world. In this lecture series, one of the longest and most sig- ficant of her seminars, Dr. von Franz examines the motifs of *The Two Creators; Deus ber; The First Victim; World Egg, Primordial Man, and Fire; Chains of Generations; eds of the World;* and *Creation through Meditation*. An aim of these lectures is to help e individual recognize creation themes in dreams as they relate to individual creativity. dex, 250pp. Spr 72

_______. **PROBLEMS OF THE FEMININE IN FAIRY TALES**, $7.85. A collection the edited transciptions of a series of twelve lectures exploring the feminine psychology women (and of men!) in the archetypal patterns of fairy tales from many lands. Dr. on Franz draws practical psychological counsel from these archetypes and gives us sev- al case studies showing their application. There is also a discussion of symbolic themes and images that appear in dreams and fantasies. 194pp. Spr 72

_______. **THE PROBLEM OF PUER AETERNUS**, $9.45. Puer aeternus *is the name of a god of antiquity . . . . [It] means eternal youth, but we also use it sometimes to indicate a certain type of young man who has an outstanding mother complex and who therefore behaves in certain typical ways . . . . The two most typical disturbances . . . are, as Jung points out, homosexuality and Don Juanism.*—M.L. von Franz. In this series of lectures Dr. von Franz explores this archetypal configuration in two literary works: **The Little Prince** by Antoine de Saint-Exupery and **The Kingdom without Space** by Bruno Goetz. She presents a fascinating picture of the attitudes, virtues, and neurotic traits of this type. 293pp. Spr 70

_______. **A PSYCHOLOGICAL INTERPRETATION OF THE GOLDEN ASS OF APULEIUS**, $7.55. A study of the archetypal pattern of transformation as depicted in the classical novel about Lucius, the young Roman who was turned into an ass, had many adventures, and then went through the Isis mysteries. Dr. von Franz also presents the original *Eros and Psyche* story, as a tale within a tale. She also gives us a wealth of scholarly amplification, insights, and anecdotes, and the whole account is related to basic theories of analytical psychology. The material in this volume was taken from a series of lectures Dr. von Franz gave at the Jung Institute in Zurich and a final section of the book contains questions and answers from the lectures. 188pp. Spr 70

_______. **SHADOW AND EVIL IN FAIRY TALES**, $13.60. This volume joins together two distinct lecture series, *Shadow* and *Evil*, to present these major motifs as they are depicted in fairy tales. As with all of Dr. von Franz' other books, the material is relevant to an individual's *darkness* today. A thorough index of images and motifs is also included. 284pp. Spr 74

FRANZ, MARIE-LOUISE von and JAMES HILLMAN. **LECTURES ON JUNG'S TYPOLOGY**, $6.75. A collection of two lecture series, on by Dr. von Franz, the other by James Hillman. Dr. von Franz discusses the inferior functioning of Jung's eight psychological types and gives examples of psychological pitfalls and potentials drawn from her analytical practice. Dr. Hillman's lectures differentiate feeling from other psychological acts and expose some misconceptions about feeling, the anima, and the mother-complex. 150pp. Spr71

FREY-ROHN, LILIANE. **FROM FREUD TO JUNG**, $3.95. Dr. Frey-Rohn began her own psychological career in 1936 under the supervision of Dr. Jung. As one of his closest colleagues, she collaborated with him in many of his investigations, especially in the fields of medieval astrology and synchronicity. This volume presents a comparative study of the psychology of the unconscious as seen in the work of Freud and Jung. The basic view of Jung, that the psyche is a conscious-unconscious totality seeking to realize itself, stands in sharp contrast to Frued's mechanistic view of it as the effect of prior causes. Hence Freud stresses the pathological whereas Jung looks to the creative and self-transcending aspects of man's nature. The last part of the book is devoted to an analysis of the development of Jung's ideas subsequent to the death of Freud, particularly his concept of archetypes. Notes, bibliography, index, 358pp. Del 74

FROMM, ERIC. **THE FORGOTTEN LANGUAGE: AN INTRODUCTION TO THE UNDERSTANDING OF DREAMS, FAIRY TALES, AND MYTHS**, $2.95. See section on Dreams. Grv 51

GRINNELL, ROBERT. **ALCHEMY IN A MODERN WOMAN**, $6.95. This is a *case study* in the way Jung's exposition of a young scientist's dreams in **Psychology and Alchemy** is: a *case study*. Looking through dreams and symptoms, and illuminating their meanings in the light of alchemical and Gnostic parallels, the author penetrates into the hidden collective background of a *modern woman* and investigates the archetypal movements and thoughts in the recesses of her soul. This is a very interesting study, quite unlike anything we've ever seen before. Notes and a very complete index are included. 175pp. Spr 73

HALL, CALVIN and VERNON NORDBY. **A PRIMER OF JUNGIAN PSYCHOLOGY**, $1.50. This is a well-written volume which carefully summarizes the main features of Jung's work. The primer begins with a biographical study of Jung and goes from there into analyses of the following major topics: The Structure of the Personality, The Dynamics of Personality, The Development of Personality, Psychological Types, Symbols and Dreams, and Jung's Place in Psychology. Each of the major topics is divided up into subsections and each major section is followed by a summary. The material is very well organized and takes the reader step-by-step through Jung's concepts. There's also a guide to reading Jung, with suggestions for introductory reading in various subject areas. Index, 150pp. NAL 73

HALL, MANLY P. and HENRY DRAKE. **STRUCTURE AND LAWS OF THE HUMAN PSYCHE**, $1.50. The reprint of Hall and Drake's correspondence course in which they summarized the main features of Jung's analytical psychology. 16pp. PRS 53

HANNAH, BARBARA. **STRIVING TOWARDS WHOLENESS**, c$10.00. This is a study of the psychic processes in individuals which move them to strive for wholeness of personality and integration of all their innate capacities. Since this inner drama manifests itself with special intensity in the lives of creative individuals, Ms. Hannah has taken for the heart of her work the biographies and literary productions of five major English novelists —Robert Louis Stevenson, Mary Webb, Charlotte, Emily, and Anne Bronte—and one nonliterary artist, Branwell Bronte, whose life was interrelated with that of his three sisters. Bibliography, notes, 316pp. JFP 71

HARDING, M. ESTHER. **THE 'I' AND THE 'NOT-I'**, $2.95. General essays on Jung's concept of ego development and theory of personality: the collective unconscious, anima, animus, shadow, archetypes. 254pp. PUP 65

_______. **THE PARENTAL IMAGE**, c$9.00. Using material which ranges from the creation myth of ancient Babylon to current case studies, Dr. Harding offers a penetrating study of one of mankind's eternal tasks: the individual's need to rebel, psychologically, against the tyranny of the parental image. She is primarily concerned with the injury the subjective image of the parents sustains whenever such a rebellion occurs and the processes under which this injury is healed through the techniques of analytical psychology. 256pp. JFP 65

_____. PSYCHIC ENERGY: ITS SOURCE AND ITS TRANSFORMATION, $3.95. Harding, who studied for many years with Jung, here analyzes the transformation of instinctive drives into constructive or detrimental living patterns. In a second section, she discusses the transformation of these energies in the development of higher consciousness. Based mainly on Jung's ideas but not notably derivative. Good bibliography, 517 pp. PUP 63

_____. THE WAY OF ALL WOMEN, $3.95. This has been acclaimed as one of the best books available on feminine psychology since it first appeared in 1933. This edition has been brought up-to-date in various ways by the author and new sections on old age and on friendships between men and women have been added. Other major sections discuss work, marriage, maternity, and the psychological relationships between a woman and her family and friends, both male and female. Dr. Harding is a Jungian psychologist who is best known for her work with women and families. She stressed the need of woman to work toward her own wholeness and develop the many sides of her nature and emphasized the importance of unconscious processes. Introduction by C.G. Jung. Bibliography, index, 332pp. H&R 70

_____. WOMAN'S MYSTERIES, ANCIENT AND MODERN, $3.95. A fascinating psychological interpretation of the feminine principle as portrayed in myth, story, and dreams, integrated with a discussion of the inner life of women. 272pp. H&R 71

HENDERSON, JAMES. A BRIDGE ACROSS TIME, c$8.50. Dr. Henderson examines the importance of myths and archetypes in education and in literature. He develops this theme by demonstrating that history acquires new meaning by relating these archetypes to a nation's growth, with particular emphasis on the re-interpretation of modern Germany. The author uses Jungian concepts to illustrate how insights gained by individuals have contributed to the evolution of the society's consciousness. Dr. Henderson is Senior Lecturer in History and International Affairs at the Institute of Education, London University. Bibliography, notes, 205pp. Tur 75

HENDERSON, JOSEPH and MAUD OAKES. THE WISDOM OF THE SERPENT, $1.95. A Jungian psychiatrist and an anthropologist explore the meanings and manifestations of death through ritual, religion, and myth. They feel that the knowledge that man must die is the force that drives man to create. The tribal initiation of the shaman and the archetype of the serpent exist universally in man's experience, exemplifying the death of the Self and a rebirth into a transcendant, *unknowable* life. The authors trace the images and patterns of psychic liberation through personal encounter, the cycles of nature, spiritual teachings, religious texts, myths of resurrection, poems, and epics. This is a fascinating study, extensively illustrated, with notes and an index. 314pp. McM 63

HERZOG, EDGAR. PSYCHE AND DEATH: MYTHS AND DREAMS IN ANALYTICAL PSYCHOLOGY, c$8.00. An account of the changing forms of death images as man himself has changed and developed. It reveals, also, that the images of ancient and primitive peoples reappear with startling similarity in contemporary dreams. 224pp. JFP 67

HILLMAN, JAMES. INSEARCH, $2.25. Subtitled *Psychology and Religion*, this is a plea for the separation of church and clinic in which Dr. Hillman proposes that the care of the soul be returned to pastoral counselors, arguing that clinical professionalism is beginning to do as much damage as did ignorance and moralisms about the psyche in the last century. Questioning whether an individual can have mental health at all unless it is founded on a sense of soul, he suggests that one befriend his own unconscious, confront the shadow side of his loving, and establish, through creative insearch, a living sense of soul. Dr. Hillman is Director of Studies at the C.G. Jung Institute in Zurich. 126pp. Scr 67

_____. LOOSE ENDS, $8.20. Subtitled, *Primary Papers in Archetypal Psychology*, this is a collection of twelve papers and talks, including a major Eranos Lecture *Abandoning the Child*. The other papers are divided into two categories, Themes and Theories. They include the following: Pothos: The Nostalgia of the Puer Eternus; Betrayal; Schism as Differing Visions; Three Ways of Failure and Analysis; Toward the Archetypal Model of the Masturbation Inhibition; On the Psychology of Parapsychology; Why *Archetypal* Psychology?; Plotino, Finico, and Vico as Precursors of Archetypal Psychology; Archetypal Theory: C.G. Jung; and Methodical Problems in Dream Research. There is also a checklist of the English publications by James Hillman. 212pp. Spr 75

_____. THE MYTH OF ANALYSIS, c$4.00. *Analysis will be ended when we discover what myth it is enacting, a discovery which may not come all at once but which occurs as insights reveal the relation of analysis to soul-making. For soul-making is what binds us there, fascinated: not just the diagnosis of what is wrong, not even the cure of our sickness, but the potential in analytical psychology for soul-making . . . . Part One develops this perspective and gives credit to the creative power of analysis . . . . Part Two could be subtitled The End of the Unconscious. Its focus is on the analyst as professional; its theme, psychological language. The focus of Part Three is on analytical consciousness; its theme, analysis and its goal.* This is a very detailed study, drawing heavily on mythological themes and archetypes. Index, 313pp. NUP 72

_____. RE-VISIONING PSYCHOLOGY, c$12.50. This volume focuses on the soul as the rightful concern of psychology. In an introductory section Hillman attempts to define and describe what he means by the soul. In the chapters that follow he develops the main lines of the soul-making process, nourished by the accumulated insights of the Western experience, extending from the Greeks through to the Renaissance and the Romantics to Freud and especially to Jung. In the process he draws on mythology, philosophy, history, and religion, and on the ideas of the major individual figures in the field of depth psychology: *All depth psychology has already been summed up by this fragment of Heraclitus: 'You could not discover the limits of the soul (psyche), even if you traveled*

every road to do so; such is the depth (bathum) of its meaning (logos). The text incl extensive notes and an index. 283pp. H&R 75

HOCHHEIMER, WOLFGANG. THE PSYCHOTHERAPY OF C.G. JUNG, c$8.00. Hochheimer is one of the few non-Jungians to write sympathetically about Jung. He practicing analyst and Director of the Institue for Pedagogical Psychology of the Sch of Education in Berlin. He integrates his experience as an analyst with a review of main tenets of Jungian psychology, and his discussion includes extensive quotations fr Jung's own writings. Index, bibliography, notes, 168pp. JFP 69

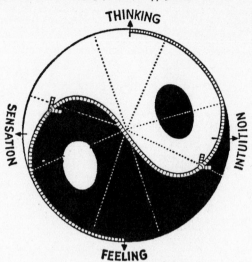

Analogy of Jungian Functions to Yin/Yang from
THE PSYCHOLOGY OF C.G. JUNG by Jolande Jacobi

JACOBI, JOLANDE. THE PSYCHOLOGY OF C.G. JUNG, $3.25. The first edition this work appeared in 1940 and it has been revised and updated eight times to adapt it Jung's most recent findings and to present the material in a clearer form. Dr. Jung wro the following in a preface to the first edition: *My endeavours in psychology have be essentially pioneer work, leaving me neither time nor opportunity to present them syste atically. Dr. Jacobi has taken this difficult task upon herself with a happy result, havi succeeded in giving an account free from the ballast of technical particulars. This cons tutes a synopsis that includes or at least touches upon all essential points, so that it is po ible for the reader . . . to orient himself readily whenever needful.* The book is well writte however it should not be considered as a general introduction to the reader who is mere interested in getting a feeling for Jung's work. The emphasis is on theoretical and practic applications and the text is both scholarly and comprehensive. Wherever possible Dr. Jaco has used Jung's own words. She has also included a series of nineteen *pictures from t unconscious* and several diagrams as well as a short biographical sketch and a plethora textual notes. The text also includes the most extensive bibliography we've seen. Inde 226pp. YUP 73

_____. THE WAY OF INDIVIDUATION, c$4.75. According to Dr. Jung, indiv duation is man's potentiality to come to fullest awareness of his psyche and thus achieve wholeness. In the light of her studies and of her own practical experience, D Jacobi contrasts the difference between the natural growing process and that deepened b methodical and analytical insight. She draws on myths and religious rituals, and on initi tion ceremonies. Particular emphasis is placed on the phases of transition between th first and second halves of life, and on the distinction between the characteristics and goa of each period. This edition includes a biographical sketch of Dr. Jacobi, notes, bibli graphy, and index. 186pp. HBJ 67

JACOBSOHN, HELMUTH, MARIE-LOUISE von FRANZ, and SIEGMUND HURWITZ TIMELESS DOCUMENTS OF THE SOUL, c$12.00. *Within the covers of this small boo are three extraordinary documents . . . . When we hear, through Professor Jacobsohn new interpretative translation, a world-weary Egyptian of four thousand years ago speak ing with his soul and wrestling with the problem of suicide, we can rediscover a connectio both to him in that time and to this theme in ourselves today. So, too, when we read th dreams of Descartes or the visionary text of the Hasidic Maggid, we hear examples of ma in dialogue with the voice of the unconscious. Although widely disparate in time and plac and content, these three papers stem from the same root. They have one experience in com mon. They tell of the inroads of the unconscious into consciousness and of the attempts o the conscious personality to come to terms with this other force in the psyche.—Jame* Hillman. Notes, index, 275pp. NUP 68

JAFFE, ANIELA. FROM THE LIFE AND WORK OF C.G. JUNG, $1.00. Dr. Jaffe wa Jung's private secretary for many years and had access to all his papers. It was to her tha he dictated Memories, Dreams, Reflections. We found the most interesting essay in thi collection to be a sensitive portrait of Jung in his last years. There's also a very good review of Jung's alchemical work. The other two essays discuss *Parapsychology: Experience and Theory* and *C.G. Jung and National Socialism*. The collection is most valuable as a highly personal account of Jung and some of his major ideas and life events. Notes, 146pp. H&R 7

_____. THE MYTH OF MEANING IN THE WORK OF C.G. JUNG, $2.25. Dr Jaffe, as editor of Memories, Dreams, Reflections, was uniquely associated with Jung. In this book she has singled out for special study one thematic complex from the profusion of ideas in his work: *What is the meaning of life and of Man?* 186pp. Pen 71

, C.G. **ANALYTICAL PSYCHOLOGY**, $1.95. Transcription of the Tavistock
...res given by Jung in 1935: *... these lectures provide an extremely clear, readable,
...at times amusing exposition of Jung's theories. In them Jung not only describes his
...s on the structure of the mind, giving lucid accounts of his psychological types, of
...ersonal and collective unconscious and of archetypes, but also explains vividly his
...iques of dream analysis and active imagination and the role played by transference
...alytic therapy.*—Charles Rycroft, **The New York Review of Books**. The lectures were
...ered to professionals and questions and answers follow each one. 240pp. RaH 68

_____. **ANSWER TO JOB**, $2.95. Jung's very personal attempt to deal with the
...tion of evil in terms of the significance of theological concepts in man's psychic life.
...of Vol. II of the Collected Works. 136pp. PUP 69

COLLECTED WORKS

definitive edition of Dr. Jung's writings, translated from the German by
..C. Hull. Each volume is 6x9" and contains bibliography and index. A
listing of the papers in each volume is available in many of the other books
...d in this section, including **Memories, Dreams, Reflections**. A 10% discount
...ffered to individuals buying the entire set (the cost would then be $226.).

_____. **VOL. 1: PSYCHIATRIC STUDIES**, c$8.50. Jung's earliest writings, includ-
...his first publication, *On the Psychology and Pathology of So-Called Occult Phenomena.*
...papers date from 1902-05. 285pp. PUP 70

_____. **VOL. 2: EXPERIMENTAL RESEARCHES**, c$17.50. Includes Jung's
...ous word-association studies in normal and abnormal psychology, two lectures on the
...ciation method given in 1909 at Clark University, and three articles on psychophysical
...arches from American and English journals in 1907 and 1908. Charts, tables, 661pp.
...' 73

_____. **VOL. 3: THE PSYCHOGENESIS OF MENTAL DISEASE**, c$9.50. Nine
...ies including *The Psychology of Dementia Praecox* and *The Content of the Psychoses.*
...book reflects the development of Jung's thinking through the years on the nature of
...tal illness. Many essays discuss schizophrenia. Jung's work in this area was important
...kground to his development of the theories of psychic energy and of the archetypes.
...pp. PUP 60

_____. **VOL. 4: FREUD AND PSYCHOANALYSIS**, c$11.00. The substance of
...g's published writings on psychoanalysis and its founder between 1906 and 1916, and
...later studies in reassessment. 388pp. PUP 70

_____. **VOL. 5: SYMBOLS OF TRANSFORMATION**, c$16.00/5.95. A complete
...sion of **Psychology of the Unconscious** (originally published 1911-13), one of Jung's
...st influential works and his first important statement of his independent position. The
...ys discuss the symbolic parallels from religion, mythology, ethnology, art and literature,
...the concept of the libido as mainly psychic energy from the unconscious expressed as
...scious symbols. Over 100 plates and line drawings illustrate the text. 597pp. PUP 67

_____. **VOL. 6: PSYCHOLOGICAL TYPES**, c$15.00. This is a new translation of
...of the most important of Jung's longer works. The volume also contains an appendix
...four shorter papers on psychological typology published between 1913 and 1935. The
...tem of personality types developed by Jung was central to his work because *it is one's
...chological type which from the outset determines and limits a person's judgment.*
...re is also a great deal of material on the spiritual activity of the psyche. 632pp. PUP 71

_____. **VOL. 7: TWO ESSAYS ON ANALYTICAL PSYCHOLOGY**, c$12.00/3.95.
...ays which state the fundamentals of Jung's psychological system: *On the Psychology
...the Unconscious* and *The Relations Between the Ego and the Unconscious* with their
...ginal versions in an appendix. Historically these essays mark the end of Jung's intimate
...ociation with Freud and sum up his attempt to integrate the psychological schools of
...ud and Adler into a comprehensive framework. 369pp. PUP

_____. **VOL. 8: THE STRUCTURE AND DYNAMICS OF THE PSYCHE**, c$15.00.
...hteen studies span some forty years and illustrate the development of Jung's ideas.
...ranged in thematic groupings and including the following important works: *On Psychic
...ergy, On the Nature of the Psyche,* and *Synchronicity.* 606pp. PUP 69

_____. **VOL. 9, PART I: THE ARCHETYPES AND THE COLLECTIVE UNCON-
...IOUS**, c$15.00. Twelve studies of the archetypes, illustrated with paintings by analytical
...ients. Three essays set the theoretical framework, six describe specific archetypes, and
...ee define the process of individuation. Includes Jung's study of Mandalas. 79 plates,
...in color, 474pp. PUP 69

_____. **VOL. 9, PART II: AION: RESEARCHES INTO THE PHENOMENOLOGY
...' THE SELF**, c$11.50. A late work, devoted to the archetype of the self and its tradi-
...nal historical equivalent, the Christ figure. Extensive references to Christian, Gnostic,
...d alchemical symbolism are included along with summations of the concepts of the
...o, the shadow, and the anima and animus. 365pp. PUP 68

_____. **VOL. 10: CIVILIZATION IN TRANSITION**, c$15.00. Essays bearing on
...e contemporary scene and on the relation of the individual to society, including papers
...tten during the twenties and thirties focusing on the upheaval in Germany, and two
...jor works of Jung's last years, *The Undiscovered Self* and *Flying Saucers.* The essays
...cuss our unconscious premises and the need for self-knowledge to avoid being over-
...me by social pressures. Illustrations, 630pp. PUP 70

_____. **VOL. 11: PSYCHOLOGY AND RELIGION, WEST AND EAST**, c$15.00.
...ght essays on Western religion (mainly Christian symbolism) and its psychological com-

ponents, including the *Answer to Job*, and six essays on Eastern religion, including forewards
to the **I Ching**, Suzuki's **Introduction to Zen Buddhism**, and other works on yoga, meditation, and Tibetan Buddhism. 712pp. PUP 69

_____. **VOL. 12: PSYCHOLOGY AND ALCHEMY**, c$15.00. See the Alchemy
section. PUP 58

_____. **VOL. 13: ALCHEMICAL STUDIES**, c$15.00. See the Alchemy section.
PUP 67

_____. **VOL. 14: MYSTERIUM CONIUNCTIONIS**, c$15.00. See the Alchemy
section. PUP 70

_____. **VOL. 15: THE SPIRIT IN MAN, ART, AND LITERATURE**, c$7.50/1.95.
In the nine essays that comprise this volume, written between 1922 and 1941, Jung's attention was directed mainly to the qualities of personality that enable the creative spirit
to introduce radical innovations into realms as diverse as medicine, Oriental studies, the
visual arts, and literature. The source of artistic creativity in archetypal structures is also
considered. The individuals discussed include Paracelsus, Freud, Picasso, Richard Wilhelm,
and James Joyce. 176pp. PUP 66

_____. **VOL. 16: THE PRACTICE OF PSYCHOTHERAPY**, c$12.50. Essays on
aspects of analytical therapy, specifically the transference, abreaction, and dream analysis
which form an excellent introduction to Jung's psychological thought. Also contains an
essay *The Realities of Practical Psychotherapy* found among Jung's posthumous papers.
Illustrations, 406pp. PUP 66

_____. **VOL. 17: THE DEVELOPMENT OF PERSONALITY**, c$7.50. Papers on
child psychology, education, and individuation, underlining the overwhelming importance
of parents and teachers in the genesis of the intellectual, feeling, and emotional disorders
of childhood. The final paper deals with marriage as an aid or obstacle to self-realization.
243pp. PUP 54

_____. **VOL. 18: THE SYMBOLIC LIFE**, c$20.00. This volume is a miscellany of
writings that Jung published after the Collected Works had been planned, minor and fugi-
tive works that he wished to assign to a special volume, and early writings that came to
light in the course of research. The volume opens with three important longer works: The
Tavistock Lectures (1935), *Symbols and the Interpretation of Dreams* (Jung's last work,
1961), and *The Symbolic Life.* These are followed by some 120 shorter works arranged on
the model of the Collected Works and including forewards, reviews, addresses, and letters.
400pp. PUP

_____. **CRITIQUE OF PSYCHOANALYSIS**, $2.95. Extracted from Vol. 4 and 18.
Includes *The Theory of Psychoanalysis, Psychoanalysis and Neurosis, Freud and Jung:
Contrasts,* and other papers critical of orthodox psychoanalysis published between 1912
and 1953. Index, 260pp. PUP

_____. **DREAMS**, $3.95. Extracts from Vol. 4, 8, 12, and 16 including *The Anal-
ysis of Dreams, On the Significance of Number Dreams, General Aspects of Dream Psychology, On the Nature of Dreams, Individual Dream Symbolism in Relation to Alchemy,* and
The Practical Use of Dream Analysis. Plates, bibliography, index, 354pp. PUP 74

_____. **FOUR ARCHETYPES: MOTHER/REBIRTH/SPIRIT/TRICKSTER**, $2.45.
Extracted from Vol. 9, Part I and including *Psychological Aspects of the Mother Arche-
type, Concerning Rebirth, The Phenomenology of the Spirit in Fairytales,* and *On the
Psychology of the Trickster-Figure.* 182pp. PUP 69

_____. **THE FREUD/JUNG LETTERS**, c$17.50/6.95. Contains the entire extant
correspondence between the founder of psychoanalysis and his chosen heir. A detailed
annotation identifies more than 400 persons, 500 publications, and the many literary and
topical allusions in the more than 350 letters. 693pp. PUP 74

_____. **C.G. JUNG LETTERS, I: 1906-50**, c$20.00. Jung's correspondence with
such notable figures as Sigmund Freud, Karl Abraham, Hermann Hesse, Mary Mellon,
Henry A. Murray, Victor White, Richard Wilhelm, Heinrich Zimmer, and others. Edited
and annotated by Gerhard Adler and Aniela Jaffe. 621pp. PUP 73

_____. **C.G. JUNG LETTERS, 2: 1951-1961**, c$20.00. A selection from Jung's
copious correspondence during the last decade of his life, characterized by profound statements on philosophy and religion and moving letters on personal and human themes.
With a full index of the two volumes. The set of Letters sells for $35. 625pp. PUP 75

_____. **MAN AND HIS SYMBOLS**, c$7.95/1.75. At the age of 83, Jung worked
out the complete plan for this book, including the sections that he wished his four closest
associates to write. He devoted the closing months of his life to editing the work and writing his own key section. Throughout the book, Jung emphasizes that man can achieve
wholeness only through a knowledge and acceptance of the unconscious—a knowledge acquired through dreams and their symbols. More than 500 illustrations complement the
text and provide a unique running commentary on Jung's thought. Most of these symbols
are omitted from the pocket edition. The large book is one of the best deals in our catalog and is highly recommended. 320pp. Dou 64

_____. **MANDALA SYMBOLISM**, $3.95. Jung's discovery of the mandala provided
the key to his entire system: *The self, I thought, was like a monad which I am, and which
is my world. The mandala represents this monad, and corresponds to the microcosmic
nature of the psyche.* This volume is taken from Vol. 9, Part I of the Collected Works and
contains two important papers on mandala symbolism, with many full color illustrations,
and a useful popular summary of the subject. 131pp. PUP 69

_____. **MEMORIES, DREAMS, REFLECTIONS**, c$15.00/2.95. *Jung's work, with* _its copious disclosures of his inner life, is perhaps as near as one can get to a literary confession—profuse in subjective materials, dreams, premonitions, projections, but relatively bare of data about more commonplace external events._—Lewis Mumford. This autobiographical account was edited and in part transcribed by Aniela Jaffe from Jung's conversation. The cloth edition is revised and all the references in it are in accordance with the Collected Works, A fascinating document, probably the best introduction to Jung. 445pp. RaH 63

_____. **MODERN MAN IN SEARCH OF A SOUL**, $2.95. A collection of lecture-essays on: dream analysis, the primitive unconscious, the relationship between psychology and religion, the spiritual problem of modern man, and an analytical account of the difference between the theories of Jung and Freud. 254pp. HBJ 33

_____. **ON THE NATURE OF THE PSYCHE**, $2.95. A difficult work which summarizes Jung's basic theoretical position. Illustrations from religion, anthropological data and symbolistic studies clarify Jung's notions of the unconscious, its relationship to consciousness, the collective unconscious and the archetypes. Essays from Vol. 8 of the Collected Works. 174pp. PUP 60

_____. **THE PSYCHOANALYTIC YEARS**, $2.95. Extracts from Vol. 2, 4, and 17. Includes _Psychoanalysis and Association Experiments, Freud's Theory of Hysteria, A Contribution to the Psychology of Rumour,_ Morton Prince _'The Mechanism and Interpretations of Dreams:' A Critical Review, On the Criticism of Psychoanalysis, Concerning Psychoanalysis, The Significance of the Father in the Destiny of the Individual,_ and _Psychic Conflicts in a Child._ Index, 174pp. PUP 74

_____. **PSYCHOLOGICAL REFLECTIONS**, $3.45. A new anthology of selections from Jung's writings between 1905-61, edited by Jolande Jacobi from over 100 works and arranged under the following headings: The Nature and Activity of the Psyche, Man in His Relation to Others, The World of Values, and On Ultimate Things. 395pp. PUP 70

_____. **PSYCHOLOGY AND EDUCATION**, $2.95. Jung repeatedly underlined the importance of parents and teachers in the genesis of the intellectual, feeling, and emotional disorders of childhood. Other aspects discussed in this volume are psychic conflicts in the child, gifted children, and the significance of the unconscious in education. Essays from Vol. 17 of the Collected Works. 158pp. PUP 54

FIRE RAINS FROM HEAVEN by Albrecht Durer

_____. **PSYCHOLOGY AND RELIGION**, $2.45. Using a wealth of material from ancient and medieval Gnostic, alchemistic, and mystical literature, Jung discusses the religious symbolism of unconscious processes and possible continuity of religious forms that have appeared and reappeared through the centuries. Many notes. 131pp. YUP 38

_____. **PSYCHOLOGY OF DEMENTIA PRAECOX**, $2.95. Extracted from Vol. 8 of the Collected Works. Includes the title essay and three later studies: _On the Psychogenesis of Schizophrenia, Recent Thoughts on Schizophrenia,_ and _Schizophrenia._ Index, 236pp. PUP 60

_____. **THE PSYCHOLOGY OF THE TRANSFERENCE**, $2.95. Jung has an authoritative account of his handling of the transference between analyst and p in the light of his conception of the archetypes and man's inner life, drawing a close pa between the modern psychotherapeutic process and the symbolical pictures in a sixt century alchemical text, the _Rosarium philosophorum._ Excerpted from Vol. 16 o Collected Works. 206pp. PUP 66

_____. **SYNCHRONICITY**, $2.45. Extracted from Vol. 8 of the Collected W and containing a parapsychological study of the meaningful coincidence of events, sensory perception, and similar phenomena. Index, 142pp. PUP 73

_____. **THE UNDISCOVERED SELF**, $2.45. _Many authors have written u books and countless papers in an attempt to make clearer Dr. Jung's gigantic insight have all failed. But with this little book . . . Dr. Jung has achieved, at the age of 83, no one else could. Any literate layman can understand it and, in so doing, will g good clear comprehension of Dr. Jung's basic concept. READ IT._—Philip Wylie. 1 LBC 58

JUNG, C G. and C. KERENYI. **ESSAYS ON A SCIENCE OF MYTHOLOGY, $** Interesting, suggestive essays by Jung and the classical scholar C. Kerenyi on the a types of the child and the Kore, or Maiden Goddess. The myth-themes join in the Myst of Eleusis where the mother-daughter goddess bears a divine child. Bibliography, 20 PUP 63

JUNG, EMMA. **ANIMUS AND ANIMA**, $3.05. 94pp. Spr 74

JUNG, EMMA and MARIE-LOUISE von FRANZ. **THE GRAIL LEGEND**, c$9.35. Jung devoted her last thirty years to an extensive study of the Grail Legend. _It was the intention of Emma Jung . . . to examine the Grail legend from a historical or lite point of view but to rely, in these respects, on the numerous and distinguished ach ments of other scholars. Rather, the material provided by the Grail stories will be co ered here from the standpoint of C.G. Jung's depth psychology. Like alchemy an curious symbolic productions, these poetic fantasy creations and their symbolism are illustrative of deepseated, unconscious religious processes that are still of the greatest nificance, for they prepare the way to, and anticipate, the religious problem of mo man._—M.L. von Franz. Dr. von Franz completed the work at the request of Dr. Jung a his wife's death. Bibliography, notes, index, 452pp. Hod 71

KERENYI, C. **ASKLEPIOS: ARCHETYPAL IMAGE OF THE PHYSICIAN'S EXISTEN** c$14.00. See Mythology section. PUP

_____. **ELEUSIS: ARCHETYPAL IMAGE OF MOTHER AND DAUGHT** c$19.50. See Mythology section. PUP

_____. **PROMETHEUS: ARCHETYPAL IMAGE OF HUMAN EXISTEN** c$16.00. See Mythology section. PUP

_____. **ZEUS AND HERA: ARCHETYPAL IMAGE OF FATHER, HUSBA AND WIFE**, c$13.50. See Mythology section. PUP

KERENYI, CARL, et al. **EVIL**, c$12.75. In the conviction that the human problems s sumed under evil from the dark background that is largely responsible for man's anxi and that it is more important today than ever before to gain deeper insights into this s ject, the C.G. Jung Institute in Zurich invited eight eminent scholars to analyze evil fr the perspective of his or her own particular discipline and interests. The contributor this volume include Carl Kerenyi, George Widengren, Victor Maag, Marie-Louise von Fra Martin Schlappner, Liliane Frey-Rohn, Karl Lowith, and Karl Schmid. Index, notes, 279 NUP 67

KLUGER, RIVKAH. **PSYCHE AND THE BIBLE**, $7.50. Three lectures on Old Testam themes. The first, and longest one, _The Idea of the Chosen People: A Contribution to Symbolism of Individuation,_ takes up a controversial Biblical concept and convincin elucidates its psychological depths. _King Saul and the Spirit of God_ examines the Book Samuel regarding Saul's madness and the relation between the spirit of God, divine pro ecy, and melancholy. _The Queen of Sheba_ presents a study of the legends concerning K Solomon and the Queen of Sheba, a mysteriously symbolic figure from the South. information presented in these lectures is based on analytical experience and Old Te ment research. Notes, 143pp. Spr 74

_____. **SATAN IN THE OLD TESTAMENT**, c$7.40. In this monograph, Riv Kluger investigates Satan from a psychological viewpoint which leads to farreaching ref tions on the nature of the God-image in the Old Testament. Satan is seen here as the i enemy, fundamental to consciousness, which arises from tension. Satan's final purpos seen as the development of self-limitation through self-opposition. This paper forme separate section of the German edition of one of Jung's books, **Symbolik des Geistes**, other parts of which are now in Vol. 9, 11, and 13 of the Collected Works. Index, no 191pp. NUP 67

LASZLO, VIOLET de, ed. **THE BASIC WRITINGS OF C.G. JUNG**, c$3.95. Selecti from Jung's work grouped into sections of the psyche, pathology and therapy, the r gious function, and human development. With an introduction by the editor on the se tions against the background of Jung's work. Very useful. 575pp. RaH 59

_____. **PSYCHE AND SYMBOL**, $2.95. A selection from Jung's writing explain the function and origin of symbols: phenomenology of the spirit in fairy tales; the p chology of the child archetype; foreward to the **I Ching**; forerunners of the idea of s chronicity; commentaries on the **Tibetan Book of the Dead** and the **Secret of the Gol Flowers**; and a few other works. 385pp. Dou 58

LAYLARD, JOHN. **A CELTIC QUEST**, $8.85. Subtitled _Sexuality and Soul in Individ_ this is a depth-psychology study of the Mabinogion legend of Culhwch and Olwen. ...cludes three sections inter-connecting Greek myth, boar culture in exotic societies, ...tions of incest and marriage, and one's personal individuation. This is a fascinating ...y of a classic ancient Welsh saga that is not well known today. Index, notes, 254pp. ...75

...ER, G.A. **ANCIENT INCUBATION AND MODERN PSYCHOTHERAPY**, c$8.00. ...ough this study we see that the illnesses of the soul and its healing do not change much ...ugh time. Therefore, as the author implies, one essential aspect of the archetypal root ...psychotherapy is provided by the attitudes and practices of ancient incubation. The ...ls of incubation, at the core of which was sleeping within a religious preserve for the ...ose of receiving healing dreams and visions, are here succinctly described so that the ...eptive reader can make the connections between the classical procedures in antiquity ...the events of modern psychotherapy .... Professor Meier brings to this work not ...is experience as a practicing medical analyst, but a passion for the past, especially ...research in Greek religion.—from the Preface by James Hillman. 172pp. NUP 67

...UMANN, ERICH. **AMOR AND PSYCHE—THE PSYCHIC DEVELOPMENT OF THE** ...MININE, c$8.50/2.95. Contains both the tale of Amor and Psyche and an interesting ...lysis of its spiritual and mythical background which suggest a fresh view of the psychic ...of women. Neumann was the one among Jung's pupils who was most creative in build- ...on Jung's work and carrying it forward in new explorations and syntheses. Notes, ...pp. PUP 56

_____. **THE ARCHETYPAL WORLD OF HENRY MOORE**, c$10.00. An applica- ...of analytical psychology to the art of Henry Moore, based on the sculptor's treatment ...the themes of mother and child and the reclining figure, both of which express the ...etypal feminine. 107 halftone illustrations, 154pp. PUP

_____. **ART AND THE CREATIVE UNCONSCIOUS**, c$10.50/3.45. Four essays: ...nard da Vinci and the Mother Archetype, Art and Time, A Note on Marc Chagall, and ...ative Man and Transformation. Discusses the nature of art in relationship to the collec- ...consciousness and to the time and place and the individual artist. 233pp. PUP 69

_____. **THE CHILD**, c$8.00/2.95. Neumann's final book, an examination of the ...cture and dynamics of the earliest development of ego and individuality. In it we pro- ...ss from the primal relationship of child and mother through to the emergence of the ...-self constellation, via a child's relationship to: 1) its own body; 2) its self; 3) the thou; ...4) being in the world. 221pp. JFP 73

SATAN TEMPTING CHRIST WITHIN A CIRCLE by Rembrandt

_____. **DEPTH PSYCHOLOGY AND A NEW ETHIC**, c$7.00/1.95. *To Neumann* ...e basic problem of modern man is the problem of evil: conventional ethics have proved ...capable of containing or transforming its destructive forces .... Awareness of evil chal- ...ages the individual: he has to learn to realise, acknowledge, and live with his own dark

side. Instead of suppressing, or repressing, the shadow and consequently projecting it out- *side, it has to be integrated. Only thus can modern man achieve fuller consciousness and a* *higher degree of integration; the ambiguity of one's own existence, the awareness of both* *positive and negative forces within the individual and the collective becomes the point of* *departure for a new ethical attitude.*—from the Foreward by Gerhard Adler. Index, notes, 158pp. H&R 69

_____. **THE GREAT MOTHER**, c$15.00/4.95. An exploration of the manifesta- tion, in myths and symbols both ancient and modern, of the primordial image of the Great Mother. *Neumann's creative intuition has enabled him to read in these records of the past* *a content and meaning that throws a beam of light on the psychological history of man- kind*....—M. Esther Harding. Includes 185pp of illustrative plates. 424pp. PUP 63

_____. **THE ORIGINS AND HISTORY OF CONSCIOUSNESS**, c$18.00/4.95. An original and creative interpretation of the relations between psychology and mythology. According to thesis, individual consciousness passes through the same archetypal stages of development that marked human consciousness as a whole. Half the book is devoted to an analysis of the mythological stages in the evolution of consciousness and the other half to the psychological stages in the development of personality. Many illustrations. 517pp. PUP 54

ODAJNYK, VOLODYMYR. **JUNG AND POLITICS**, $4.95. *Jung never wrote a treatise* *that systematically defines the implications of his psychological theories for politics. His* *views on the subject are dispersed throughout his works, although a number of books and* *essays are closely concerned with politics, either explicitly or by implication and logical* *extension. Hence, this book represents a compilation of those of Jung's ideas that have* *political and/or social implications, gleaned from his voluminous writings on various sub- jects, a comparison of those ideas with Freud's, and a consideration of just what Jung's* *ideas imply for the social and political future of humanity.*—from the Preface. Index, 205pp. H&R 76

PERRY, JOHN. **THE FAR SIDE OF MADNESS**, $2.75. Dr. Perry is a Jungian psychoan- alyst and is a lecturer at the Jung Institute in San Francisco. In this volume (and in his psychiatric work) he concentrates not on the causes or chemistry of schizophrenia, but instead on our empathetic understanding of the individual's inner processes. Perry calls his work a study of the *intrapersonal* process between the patient and the therapist and he shows that the so-called abnormal ideas and imagery of the schizophrenic actually reveal archetypal patterns common to all persons that are merely made manifest in this altered state of consciousness. Knowledge of these patterns offers the therapist a key to helping the patient to a natural reorganization of the psyche. Bibliography, notes, index, 177pp. PrH 74

_____. **THE LORD OF THE FOUR QUARTERS**, $1.50. See the Mythology sec- tion. 303pp. McM 66

POST, LAURENS van der. **JUNG AND THE STORY OF OUR TIME**, $3.95. Jung and the author had a close friendship lasting sixteen years. In this biographical study the evo- lution of Jung's creative beliefs and the impact of his personality are surveyed in depth in reconstructions of conversations that touch on examples of Jung's ideas and attitudes while exploring interests shared by the two men. In putting together this book van der Post has used many hours of interviews conducted for his now-famous BBC telelvision film, **The Story of Carl Gustav Jung**, in addition to his personal discussions and letters. *Van der* *Post is clear, downright, correct, and yet beautiful; in other words, he is a most reliable* *guide for all those who are interested in C.G. Jung without having known him well person- ally. In the future they will have to read not only Jung's* **Memories, Dreams, Reflections** *and his letters but most definitely this highly worthwhile book.*—Professor C.A. Meier, M.D., Successor to the Chair of Psychology created for and held by C.G. Jung in Zurich. 276pp. RaH 75

PRATT, JANE. **CONSCIOUSNESS AND SACRIFICE**, $1.75. An interpretation of two episodes in the Indian myth of Manu: *Manu in the Flood* and *Manu and the Sacrifice*. 70pp. Spr 67

PROGOFF, IRA. **AT A JOURNAL WORKSHOP**, c$12.50. See the Consciousness Expan- sion section. 320pp. DHL 75

_____. **DEATH AND REBIRTH OF PSYCHOLOGY**, $2.95. A synthesis and uni- fication of the central concepts in the seemingly diverse systems of Freud, Jung, Adler, and Rank, out of which emerges a new conception of the nature of man. Progoff is direc- tor of Dialogue House. 285pp. MGH 56

_____. **DEPTH PSYCHOLOGY AND MODERN MAN**, $2.95. Depth psychology considers that what a person professes to believe, or what he thinks he believes, is not as important as what he experiences. Depth psychology is concerned, therefore, not with new doctrines for modern man, but with providing ways of experience by which each per- son, according to his individual nature, can relate himself in actuality to the ultimate real- ities of life. 299pp. MGH 59

_____. **JUNG'S PSYCHOLOGY AND ITS SOCIAL MEANING**, $2.50. An intro- duction to Jung's ideas and some discussion of their significance for our thinking about the individual and society. Goes into more depth than Bennett's introduction. 313pp. Dou 53

_____. **JUNG, SYNCHRONICITY, AND HUMAN DESTINY**, $2.75. This volume, in process for twenty years, was discussed and worked on with Jung himself. It is a lucid exposition and interpretation of the profound, but complex, concept of synchronicity and provides a hypothesis to approach areas of human experiences inaccessible to our accepted categories of cause and effect thinking. Includes material on the **I Ching** and a bibliography. 176pp. Del 73

_____. THE SYMBOLIC AND THE REAL, $2.95. In this book the advanced conceptions of depth psychology are brought to bear upon the fundamental human problems of modern civilization. The result is a perspective and a program of psychological practice for individuals and groups by which the modern person can establish contact with the deepest levels of his being. 249pp. MGH 63

SERRANO, MIGUEL. EL/ELLA, c$5.00. This is an allegory of man's search for unity; it explores a mythic reality that transcends the conflicting dualities—man/woman, black/white, young/old—that divide man from nature and against himself. El/Ella is divided into three sections, which reflect the spiritual journey-quest as it has been experienced in the Himalayas, the Pyranees, and the Andes. Part One deals mainly with the rites of Tantric love. Part Two is concerned with the Cathars, an order of medieval mystics in Provence whose dualistic belief in the existence of absolute evil as well as absolute good led to their extermination as heretics in the so-called Albigensian Crusade. Part Three deals with the Andes, and, again, a secret order to which the central characters, a man and a woman, belong. 75pp. H&R 72

_____. C.G. JUNG AND HERMAN HESSE, A RECORD OF TWO FRIENDSHIPS, $1.95. Sets forth records of various conversations and correspondence between Serrano (a Chilean writer) and Jung and Hesse. Topics common to these mystical thinkers are touched on. 120pp. ScB 66

_____. THE SERPENT OF PARADISE, $2.95. See Indian Philosophy section. H&R

_____. THE ULTIMATE FLOWER, $1.95. A mystical and poetic account of a man's search for things which do not really exist but which are more real than reality. Based on a conversation with Jung on the nature of the Self. Illustrations. 102pp. HRP 69

_____. THE VISITS OF THE QUEEN OF SHEBA, $1.95. This book is an extraordinary piece of work. It is dreams within dreams, highly poetic. The poetic genius has transformed the primordial material into almost musical shapes.—C.G. Jung. 61pp. H&R72

SINGER, JUNE. BOUNDARIES OF THE SOUL: THE PRACTICE OF JUNG'S PSYCHOLOGY, $2.95. As an analyst, Dr. Singer follows Jung's lead, stressing the unconscious rather than the conscious, the mystical rather than the scientific, the creative rather than the productive, the religious rather than the profane. This is an excellent work which gives an insight into all aspects of psychotherapy. Notes and bibliography. 514pp. Dou 71

JOB SACRIFICES TO YAHWEH by William Blake

_____. THE UNHOLY BIBLE—A PSYCHOLOGICAL INTERPRETATION OF WILLIAM BLAKE, $4.75. A speculative study of William Blake's life, poetry, and art in terms of Jungian archetypes. Includes an introductory essay, a detailed commentary on The Marriage of Heaven and Hell, a shorter commentary on The Bible of Hell. Notes, bibliography, and illustrative plates. 286pp. H&R 70

SPEIGELMAN, J. MARVIN. THE TREE: TALES IN PSYCHO-MYTHOLOGY, c$9.95. See the Mythology section.

SPRING PUBLICATIONS. SPRING 1960, 1961, 1962, $15.75. SPRING originated in 1940-41 as a collection of papers originating out of the Analytical Psychology Club of New York. In 1960 it was transformed into a printed magazine and in 1970 SPRING appeared as an expanded yearbook, the only Annual of Archetypal Psychology and Jungian Thought, with emphasis on new insight and criticism, translations, and hitherto unpublished writings by and about C.G. Jung. The series is edited by James Hillman. This Omnibus Edition presents twenty-three articles including three installments of Jung's Vision Seminar, Jung on Parapsychology, two papers on the I Ching by Richard Wilhelm, Symbols by Edward Edinger, Individual and Group by Whitmont, Mystical Man by Neumann, Dream Books by Jacobi, Indian World Mother by Zimmer, and much else. 470pp. Spr 73

_____. SPRING 1973, $9.45. 295pp. Spr 73

_____. SPRING 1974, $7.35. 302pp. Spr 74

_____. SPRING 1975, $9.45. This newest volume includes Jung's psycholog commentary on Kundalini Yoga, Zimmer's The Chakras of Kundalini Yoga, Reflecti on the Horoscope of C.G. Jung, and much else. The contributions to this series are formly excellent—though often on quite obscure subjects. 304pp. Spr 75

STORR, ANTHONY. C.G. JUNG, $1.95. A critical study which focuses primarily Jung's intellectual life and on the formation of his major ideas. Dr. Storr also expl Jung's biography, in particular his association with and subsequent divergence from mund Freud. 119pp. Vik 73

ULANOV, ANN. THE FEMININE IN JUNGIAN PSYCHOLOGY AND IN CHRISTI THEOLOGY, c$16.15. I have followed a carefully planned sequence of presentation analysis, beginning with Jung's approach to the psyche, and following with a discussio what can be gathered concerning the nature of the feminine. Out of this I have drawn c clusions that seem to me to be inescapable for what we call religious experience. No index, 358pp. NUP 71

VITALE, AGOSTO, et al. FATHERS AND MOTHERS, $5.05. A collection of pap examining family matters from an archetypal angle: Agosto Vitale, Saturn: The Trans mation of the Father; Murray Stein, The Devouring Father; Vera con der Heydt, On Father in Psychotherapy, Erich Neumann, The Moon and Matriarchal Consciousness; James Hillman, The Great Mother, Her Son, Her Hero, and the Puer. 142pp. Spr

WEAVER, RIX. THE OLD WISE WOMAN: A STUDY OF ACTIVE IMAGINATIO c$8.00. Jung dealt with material arising from the method of Active Imagination in his private seminars and in Memories, Dreams, Reflections. This book offers the first opp tunity to witness the development and unfolding of the process. Accompanied by a c prehensive commentary that makes it easy for the reader to understand the nature a importance of the method. Includes a glossary and bibliography. 176pp. JFP 73

WEHR, GERHARD. PORTRAIT OF JUNG, $2.95. A profusely illustrated biogra written for the general reader and covering all aspects of Jung's life, influences, and ide Very easy reading. Bibliography, 173pp. HeH 71

WHEELWRIGHT, JOSEPH, ed. THE REALITY OF THE PSYCHE, c$12.00. A collect of the eighteen papers presented at the Third International Congress for Analytical Psych ogy. Some of the specific subjects are the following: Recurring patterns of order comm to both matter and psyche; The role of the ego as subjective observer; The symbol a diagnostic and therapeutic factor; Symbols of individuation in children; The symbol a connecting factor between the subjective and objective worlds; the unus mundus: the c world of matter and non-matter. The contributors are among the most noted Jungia Notes, illustrations, 316pp. JFP 68

_____. THE ANALYTIC PROCESS, c$12.00. A collection of papers from Fourth International Congress for Analytical Psychology, each presented in its origi language with an English translation. The papers range from a study of transformati symbols in the astrological tradition and the favorite fairy tale from childhood as a the peutic factor in analysis to the clinical phenomenon of transference and counter-transf ence and aspects of analytical child psychology. The twenty-one papers range wid through the field of Jungian psychology elucidating new aspects and developments. Not illustrations, bibliography. 326pp. JFP 71

WHITMONT, EDWARD. THE SYMBOLIC QUEST, c$9.00. An enlargement of Jun explorations, based on our ability to develop an understanding of the language of unconscious, which is a symbolic expression emerging in the form of images throu dreams, fantasies, and art forms. Examples from case material illuminate the princip discussed. 347pp. H&R 69

WICKES, FRANCES. THE INNER WORLD OF CHOICE, $3.95. This is a powerf well written volume. In 1954-55, when Dr. Wickes presented seminars on Choice a Decision at the Jung Institute in Zurich, Jung himself asked her to enlarge her mater into book form. This volume shows how the unconscious mind constantly challenges to grow, psychologically and spiritually, and to act to free ourselves from fear, apath and dependence. The author reviews all the major tenets of Jungian psychology and ill trates her narrative with case histories from her own practice. Jung's ideas of the wom in man and the man in woman are especially well presented and there is also an excelle discussion of archetypal imagery in dreams and folklore. Notes, bibliography, 336p PrH 76

_____. THE INNER WORLD OF CHILDHOOD, $1.25. See the Education a Childhood section.

WILHELM, RICHARD. THE SECRET OF THE GOLDEN FLOWER, $2.45. See secti on Chinese Philosophy. 165pp. HBJ 62

ZBINDEN, HANS, et al. CONSCIENCE, c$10.00. This book brings together seven diff ent perspectives on the phenomenon of the human conscience. The essays were origina presented as individual lectures under the auspices of the C.G. Jung Institute, Zuric Index, notes, 221pp. NUP 70

KRISHNAMURTI AND THAKAR

ne cannot talk of Krishnamurti's teaching because he does not set himself up as a teacher; one cannot talk of his philosophy because he would not call himself a philosopher. He himself says that his words are merely a mirror in which to see ourselves. Indeed, Krishnamurti's thought illumines, with however rich a variety, a great central fact: namely, that for each individual human, problems can be solved in only one way—for and by himself.

s a small child, Krishnamurti was recognized by Annie Besant and C.W. eadbeater as a *teacher*, who, like the Buddha and Christ, would show the ay out of the world's confusion. He was given an extensive education in the est and a religious organization for him to lead was established. At his installation, he dissolved the organization, saying *I maintain that Truth is a athless land and you cannot approach it by any path whatsoever, by any region, by any sect. That is my point of view and I adhere to that absolutely nd unconditionally.* In addition to the books listed below, we have a full section of records of Krishnamurti. Check the listing in the Records section.

KRISHNAMURTI, J. AT THE FEET OF THE MASTER, c$1.00. When he was a boy, rishnamurti wrote down the precepts for right living contained in this small book. It has een a source of inspiration and guidance for thousands of people. 71pp. TPH

_____. THE AWAKENING OF INTELLIGENCE, $2.65. A master work of completely new material comprehensively covers Krishnamurti's teachings since 1967. The lks and dialogues across America, Europe, and India have been taken from tapes. 15 hotographs. Avo

_____. BEGINNINGS OF LEARNING, c$10.00. Krishnamurti's newest volume, a ollection focused on his educational beliefs: *When we stop learning in our relationship, hether we are studying, playing, or whatever we are doing, and merely act from the nowledge we have accumulated, then disorder comes.* The first half consists of discusons between Krishnamurti and staff and students at Brockwood School; the second exands his talks to parents and teachers into short essays. 254pp. H&R 75

_____. BEYOND VIOLENCE, $2.25. Talks and discussions on the urgent need or change in human values. 175pp. H&R

_____. COMMENTARIES ON LIVING, $2.25/each. A series of commentaries aken from Krishnamurti's notebooks in which he touches upon many problems—our opes, fears, illusions, beliefs, and prejudices—and in the simplest language seems to pierce o their roots. Three volumes, over 250pp each. TPH 56-60

_____. EDUCATION AND THE SIGNIFICANCE OF LIFE, c$4.00. See the Education section.

_____. THE FIRST AND LAST FREEDOM, $2.95. 288pp. H&R 54

_____. THE FLIGHT OF THE EAGLE, $2.50. *I say one can live . . . only when ne knows how to be free from all the stupidities of one's life. To be free from them is nly possible in becoming aware of one's relationship, not only with human beings, but ith ideas, with nature, with everything.* One of our favorite selections. 156pp. H&R 71

_____. FREEDOM FROM THE KNOWN, $1.95. In this volume Krishnamurti hows how people can free themselves from the tyranny of the expected—no matter what heir age. And, by first changing themselves, people can then change the whole structure f society and their relationships. 124pp. H&R 69

_____. THE IMPOSSIBLE QUESTION, c$2.00. Here Krishnamurti speaks of varous aspects of living, and each of these talks is followed by a dialogue. Topics include ear and pleasure, the act of looking and truly seeing, religion, and mechanical thoughts. 90pp. H&R 73

_____. KRISHNAMURTI'S NOTEBOOK, c$10.00. For a seven month period a umber of years ago Krishnamurti kept an intimate daily record of his perceptions, observations, and states of consciousness. The record starts and ends abruptly and Krishnamurti has never revealed what prompted him to begin it since he had never kept such a notebook before and has not kept one since. Though the entries are hardly ever personal, he reader can get a better feeling for the man himself than in any other book that we know of. The wellspring of Krishnamurti's teaching is also apparent throughout. 256pp. H&R 76

_____. LIFE AHEAD, $2.50. Addressed particularly to young people. Discusses he essentials of right education. 191pp. H&R 63

_____. THE ONLY REVOLUTION, c$5.95. 175pp. H&R 70

_____. THE PENGUIN KRISHNAMURTI READER, $2.30. Another excellent ntroduction to Krishnamurti's thought, divided into three sections: *Problems of Living,*

For the Young, and *Questions and Answers.* Extracts from **The First and Last Freedom, Life Ahead** and **This Matter of Culture.** 251pp. Pen 64

_____. THE SECOND PENGUIN KRISHNAMURTI READER, $2.65. This volume incorporates **The Urgency of Change** and **The Only Revolution,** two of Krishnamurti's most popular and influential books. In it he comes to grips with the problems that beset the individual's search for happiness and discusses the difficulties of living peacefully in an increasingly hostile world. 318pp. Pen 73

_____. THINK ON THESE THINGS, $1.95. This book consistently outsells our other Krishnamurti books three or four to one. It is definitely many people's favorite collection and is as good a place to learn Krishnamurti's philosophy as any of his books. H&R 70

_____. THE URGENCY OF CHANGE, c$5.95. In these talks Krishnamurti enters into dialogue with people who often find themselves unable to cope with the world, with other people, and with themselves. He makes practical suggestions and covers a variety of specific topics including awareness, fear, relationships, conflict, morality, love and sex, perfection, suffering, belief, dreams, and much else. 154pp. H&R 70

_____. YOU ARE THE WORLD, $2.50. *In oneself lies the whole world, and if you know how to look and learn, then the door is there and the key is in your hand. Nobody on Earth can give you either that key or the door to open, except yourself.* Talks at American universities. 175pp. H&R 72

LUTYENS, MARY. KRISHNAMURTI, c$8.95. This is a personal account of the first thirty-eight years of Krishnamurti's life which traces his development from the days when as a boy in India, he was heralded by the leaders of the Theosophical Society as the vehicle for the coming messiah until, as a young man with extraordinary conviction, he was able to make a clean ideological break from the individuals and organizations that sought to confine him to a traditional messianic role. Related partly in Krishnamurti's own words, this book reveals his many doubts and difficulties, as well as his achievements. It discusses his close relationship with Annie Besant and C.W. Leadbeater and the traumas and loneliness involved in his spiritual maturation and his special position. Ms. Lutyens' mother was Krishnamurti's chief confidante in those early years, and with this book his letters to Lady Emily Lutyens and his own account of the spiritual experience which changed his life are published for the first time. Mary Lutyens has edited four collections of Krishnamurti's work. Chronology, notes, index. 337pp. FSG 75

VIMALA THAKAR

She is an Indian woman whose philosophy is little known in the U.S. Krishnamurti has contributed most to her intellectual and spiritual development and she has been closely associated with him for over fifteen years. Her philosophy is quite similar to his—though it has more heart and is less strictly intellectual. She feels that drastic psychological change is necessary and possible if mankind as a whole is to become liberated. Her books consist mainly of her talks, throughout the world, with questions and answers. She is not a guru and does not refer us to other gurus, but instead feels that we must look within and release our own essence. She has no fixed methods to attain this but says that one can live in meditation all day long, whatever one is doing. Her meditation includes observation, both of one's surroundings and oneself, without judgment, as well as living in present time. *This life seems to have no purpose; no direction whatsoever; it has not indicated any pattern yet. The only thing I can say is—it is overwhelmingly new; the freshness and the newness keep one ever alert, ever keen and ever insecure. Though the journey has come to an end I have not arrived. Perhaps there is nowhere to arrive. . . . It seems to be that life is its own purpose; life its own direction. Life is dynamic and those who live are on an eternal voyage.*

THAKAR, VIMALA. CHALLENGE TO YOUTH, $5.50. 143pp. VPT 72

_____. FRIENDLY COMMUNION, $2.25. A series of spiritual poems. 62pp. VPT

_____. MUTATION OF MIND, $4.60. 180pp. VPT 72

_____. ON AN ETERNAL VOYAGE, $3.25. An autobiographical account of her philosophy and how it evolved. Includes verbatim reports of some of her conversations with Krishnamurti. This seems to be the book to start with. 69pp. VPT 69

_____. SILENCE IN ACTION, $3.25. Talks in the U.S. 88pp. VPT 68

_____. TOWARDS TOTAL TRANSFORMATION, $2.25. 84pp. VPT 70

_____. UNIVERSITY TALKS, $1.75. 48pp. VPT 70

_____. VOYAGE INTO ONESELF, $3.75. 108pp. VPT 72

LIFE ENERGIES

Life energies are primary forms of energy which generate electricity, light, and matter, including the matter of our bodies and the matter of stars. Radionics and radiesthesia, meaning sensitivity to radiations, are techniques of using these primary energies to diagnose and treat illness. Dowsing, the detection of water, oil, and minerals, by sensitive persons using a rod or a pendulum or sometimes just their feelings, relies on energy forms common to man and minerals. Pyramid researchers believe that certain shapes focus and collect these types of energies; researchers in Kirlian electrophotography believe that changes in life energies can be seen. Ancient Indian theories explain how these energies enter through certain points on the body known as chakras. Writers like Walter Russell and Nikola Tesla, who made electricity available through the invention of the AC generator and the AC motor, describe how the primary energies of the universe can be used to produce heat, light, and other energies needed by humankind. It is by an increasing understanding of these more basic energy forms that the New Age will be shaped.

ARCHDALE, F.A. **ELEMENTARY RADIESTHESIA AND THE USE OF THE PENDULUM**, $3.00. 33pp. HeR 61

ASKEW, STELLA. **HOW TO USE THE PENDULUM**, c$3.00. This is a clear instruction manual which includes a great deal of background material explaining the process of dowsing and various examples and illustrations. Oversize, 38pp. HeR 55

BARRETT, WILLIAM and THEODORE BESTERMAN. **THE DIVINING ROD**, c$10.00. Sir William Barrett was a physicist and chemist and Theodore Besterman served for many years as Investigations Officer of the Society for Psychical Research, London. This is a recent reprint of the first major experimental and psychological study of dowsing. The authors made a thorough study of contemporary dowsers under closely controlled conditions. One of their most notable contributions is to show that the two main theories about dowsing—a straight physical explanation and a psychical one—can be fused into a unified theory solidly grounded in scientific procedure. Leslie Shepard's foreword to this edition reviews the recent literature on the subject. Extensive bibliography, notes, index. 361pp. UnB 68

BEARNE, ALASTAIR. **ENERGY, MATTER AND FORM**, $10.00. This is an overview of the whole area of paranormal phenomena and perception, especially as it interfaces with the life forces and energies of the universe. The first section discusses the use of energies and vibrations by psychics, and the second surveys more directly energies and vibrations and their effects. Many graphic examples are incorporated into Bearne's exposition. The final section (about half the book) is devoted to detailed instructions on using the techniques introduced earlier. The book is self-published and is not laid out very clearly. There's a great deal of good material, but the presentation is often hard to follow. Illustrations, 8x11", bibliography. 143pp. UTP 76

BEASLEY, VICTOR. **DIMENSIONS OF ELECTRO-VIBRATORY PHENOMENA**, $10.00. *The accounts presented in this volume are concerned with the possible influence which certain radiational or electro-vibratory forces might exert upon human behavior. The term electro-vibratory is meant to have a generic application. We might have substituted in its place the standard term, electromagnetism, but electromagnetism, as understood by science, refers only to a definite spectrum of what is probably an infinite range of vibrations occurring in nature.* It's a fine work, which, while it reads like a Ph.D. dissertation (which it is), clearly summarizes a great body of information. A scientific account illustrated with many excellent charts and drawings. Notes, bibliography. 106pp. UTP 75

BEASSE, PIERRE et al. **A NEW AND RATIONAL TREATISE OF DOWSING**, $5.00. This is a practical textbook which explains all aspects of dowsing and details how to dowse for a variety of things including subterranean springs, buried treasures, coal fields, ores, oil, and much else. Line drawings throughout illustrate the instructions. The second half of the book surveys medical dowsing and astro dowsing and again gives clear practical techniques. Many case studies are also cited and examined. A very complete work. 214pp. HeR 41

BELL, A.H., ed. **PRACTICAL DOWSING, A SYMPOSIUM**, c$6.95. Colonel Bell is founder of the British Society of Dowsers. Here he has written a comprehensive wo suitable both to those not very knowledgeable about the scope and nature of dowsing a to those who have done some study of the subject. The writers of the articles are all experts. Articles include: *Dowsing for Water, Dowsing and Archaeology, Tracing the Lo Dowsing from a Distance, The Neutralization of Harmful Rays, Spiritual and Men Healing, Hypnotic Cures and the Relief of Pain by Touch, Close-up Dowsing for Medic Purposes, Distant Healing, Medical Dowsing with Rules and Discs,* and *The Lauren Technique of Psionic Diagnosis and Treatment.* Index, 206pp. Bel 65

BLAIR, LAWRENCE. **RHYTHMS OF VISION**, c$8.95. See the Mysticism sectio

BORDERLAND SCIENCES. **THE LAKHOVSKY MULTI-WAVE OSCILLATOR**, $3. A detailed study of the material related to the MWO, with diagrammatic instructio Also includes summary studies of Mark Clement's **The Waves that Heal** (a review Lakhovsky's work), John O'Neill's **Nikola Tesla's Giant Oscillator**, and Lakhovsk **Curing Cancerous Plants with Ultra Radio Frequencies.** Oversize, 42pp. BSR nd

BOYLE, JOHN. **THE PSIONIC GENERATOR PATTERN BOOK**, $4.95. Plans and d grams for constructing a dozen psi-activating devices, including a pyramid, an *occ illuminator* that you can use like a crystal ball, the cone cluster generator that rota with the energy from your body, dowsing rods, various other kinds of generators, au meters, and much else. Oversize, 89pp. PrH 75

BROWN, JOHN. **I DISCOVER THE IMMORTAL B-CELL**, $2.00. This is a recent repri of Brown's pioneering study in which he describes the finding and development of a ne form of cell life—a catalyst that releases radiant energy to all living things which can a sorb it through water. This edition includes many illustrations and additional mater by Hilary Dorey, Joe Sloan, Riley Crabb, Henry Gallart, and Thomas David. Oversi 42pp. BSR 73

BURR, HAROLD SAXTON. **BLUEPRINT FOR IMMORTALITY**, c$5.60. A comprehe sive account of Dr. Burr's discovery that all living things are molded and controlle by electro-dynamic fields, which can be measured and mapped with standard mode voltmeters. *These fields of life, or L-fields, are the basic blueprints of all life on this pla et. . . . The Universe is an ordered system, the human organism an ordered componen In short, the universe has meaning and so have we.* Thousands of experiments by Dr. Bu and his colleagues over a period of nearly forty years have confirmed that L-fields exi in all forms of life. Dr. Burr was a member of the faculty of Yale Medical School fo forty-three years. 192pp. Spe 72

CAMERON, VERNE. **AQUAVIDEO**, $4.95. Subtitled *Locating Underground Wate through the Sensory-Eye of Verne Cameron,* this is an in depth, fully illustrated study just that. Cameron is considered a master dowser who has been recognized and acclaime by many authorities as being the most highly developed American dowser ever. The boo is not very well organized and the writing style is overly adulatory; nevertheless there more information here that in all the other books on the subject combined, including in troductory and biographical material; and chapters on locating underground wate determining water volume, reading the geological signs, quakes and earth movement, lo cating geysers and hot springs. There's also a great deal of material on the phenomenon dowsing and on Cameron's analysis of it as well as a study of dowsing devices. Index 158pp. ECa 70

_____. **MAP DOWSING**, $2.75. *Map dowsing is a term applied to the locating persons, animals, objects, and substances from a distance, either above, in or below ground or water, by means of a pointer, map, chart, photo, and dowsing instrumen* This is a detailed, explanatory pamphlet, including illustrations and background materia 40pp. ECa 71

_____. **OIL LOCATING**, $2.75. In the early 1950's, Cameron perfected th Cameron *Aurameter* (a water-compass device), followed by his gyrating *Petroleometer* He has located many highly productive underground oil and water sites and is acclaime for his subsurface oil and water theories. Here he relates his experiences and presents hi theories on how to do it. Illustrations, 39pp. ECa 71

CAVE, FRANCIS, ed. **THE ELECTRONIC REACTIONS OF ABRAMS**, $4.00. Dr. brams did pioneering work in the early twentieth century in the field of radionics. *A brams . . . takes the stand that all material things are radioactive and that if sufficiently delicate apparatus can be devised, the degree of radioactivity of all matter can be meas ured in such a way that when its radioactive characteristics are ascertained, it would be possible from this data to determine the actual substance being examined, without even seeing it*—from the foreword. Abrams developed the instruments and the conceptual framework from which all the subsequent research has stemmed. Half of this book is de voted to Dr. Cave's foreword and the other half is a reprint of Abrams' original paper. I includes many detailed examples and instructive material. Oversize, illustrations. 36pp. HeR 22

CHRAPOWICKI, MARYLA de. **SPECTRO-BIOLOGY**, $2.00. *Spectro-Biology is a system of cosmic correspondence, dealing with the fundamental principles of the bio-chemical relationship which binds human physiology to the whole of Nature and which offers a complete synthesis of all branches of science in their mutual relation to Life. . . . The object of this book is . . . to offer a method whereby we can calculate . . . what the nor mal biological factor of each individual body should be. . . . To show that health is a purely biological state and a direct result of radiation, while disease is but a relative con dition. . . . To prove that there is a changeless and universal method of diagnosis whereby* _e can not only determine the cause of disease, but which enables us to preserve a normal_ _te of health. . . ._–from the foreword. 62pp. HeR 65

OOPER-HUNT, C.L. **RADIESTHETIC ANALYSIS**, $3.00. A practical handbook by a _r_dionic practitioner covering the following topics: polarity, colors, resonant key notes, _t_rasensory perception, diagnosis, the etheric body, unconscious disturbing energies, _n_d _dis-ease_. 40pp. HeR 69

_R_ABB, RILEY, ed. **RADIONICS**, $6.50. Crabb is the director of Borderland Sciences _r_esearch Foundation. Here he gives us a detailed scientific study in three parts. Part I _o_vers the history and development of radionics, with sections on the doctors and the _q_uipment, techniques of diagnosis, colored light and disease, and amplification for treat_m_ent. Part II, entitled _Radionics Instruments and How to Make Them_, includes a modi_f_ed drown circuit, a diagnostic instrument diagram, and an atlas of diagnostic and treat_m_ent rates. Part III consists of an interview with Dr. Leonard Chapman, a radionics prac_t_ioner. Oversize, 77pp. BSR nd

_____. **THREE GREAT AQUARIAN AGE HEALERS**, $2.00. The work of three _d_octors is examined. First Crabb discusses the work of William Lang, a surgeon who died _n_ 1938, but who carries on his practice through the medium George Chapman at Arles_b_ury clinic in England. Lang (through Chapman) explains how a spirit doctor works. _n_ the second section Crabb analyzes _New Age Color Therapy_ developed by Drs. S. Pan_c_oast and George Starr White, and explains the basic Qabalistic principles on which all _u_ccessful color therapy must be established: balance and rhythm. Includes many illus_t_rations and technical drawings, including the construction of a simple, duo-rhythm _c_olor machine along the lines developed by Dr. White. Oversize, 62pp. BSR 68

_A_KIN, H.S. **HIGH-VOLTAGE PHOTOGRAPHY**, $4.95. _High voltage photography,_ _k_nown also by other names including Kirlian photography, electrophotography, and coro_n_a-discharge photography, is a technique for making photographic prints or visual obser_v_ations of electrically-conductive objects with no light source other than that produced _b_y a luminous corona-discharge at the surface of an object in a high-voltage, high-fre_q_uency electric field._ This is the most comprehensive manual we know of, intended as a _p_ractical guide for experimenters, as well as for the non-technical readers who may skip _v_er the technical material (of which there is an abundance). Construction methods and _n_struction techniques are very fully presented in both written and diagrammatic form. _O_versize, notes. 65pp. HSD 76

_A_VIS, ALBERT and WALTER RAWLS. **THE MAGNETIC EFFECT**, c$6.00. The _a_uthors present and discuss biomagnetic experiments and research that have been success_f_ully duplicated by members of the orthodox scientific community. The findings which _t_hey discuss can be applied to the treatment of such conditions as arthritis, cancer, _g_laucoma, sexual problems, and aging. Notes, 128pp. ExP 75

_____. **MAGNETISM AND ITS EFFECTS ON THE LIVING SYSTEM**, c$8.00. _T_his is a well-researched investigation into the discovery that a magnet has not one effect _n_ the living system but two effects, each supplied by one of the two forms of energy _t_hat are transmitted from each pole of any magnet, including the earth, which itself is _a_ giant magnet. The authors feel that this discovery (which they term _biomagnetics_) can _l_ter the genetics of plants, animals, and all forms of life. Here they present the fruits of _t_heir years of intensive research, illustrated with many case studies and examples as well _s_ many diagrams. Chapters include: _Understanding Magnetism, The Effects of the Two_ _P_oles on the Living System, Cancers and Tumors and Magnetism, The Bioelectric Control _f Nerve Pain, Magnetism and Gravity,_ and _The Human Biomagnetic Aura._ Notes, 139pp. _x_P 74

_____. **THE RAINBOW IN YOUR HANDS**, c$5.95. _By your very thoughts you_ _c_an offer help, good will, happiness to all around you. You can live a better life. All you _h_ave to do is have an understanding about your natural energy and direct your hands _t_oward building a more natural world. We will explain the presence and use of this energy._ _Y_ou will be the judge concerning its effectiveness. . . . The great healers and comforters _o_f history used this natural healing power._–from the introduction. 101pp. ExP 76

_D_AY, LANGSTON and GEORGE de la WARR. **MATTER IN THE MAKING**, c$7.50. _D_ay here describes the course of research and discovery at the Delawarr Laboratories in _E_ngland during the 1955-65 period. In a previous work, **New Worlds Beyond the Atom**, _t_he author explained that Mr. de la Warr and his staff had discovered new forms of radia_t_ion, hitherto unknown to science, which shed light on some of the enigmas of physics _a_nd biology, such as the origin of shapes and forms in nature, the means whereby vital _e_nergy passes to living things, and the mystery of the creation of matter out of an appar_e_nt void. The researchers found that we must work with nature, not against her, to dis_c_over in what forms the unifying force appears when it descends to the level of matter. _T_he Delawarr Laboratories have been the center for all recent radionic research and this _b_ook, written for the general public, enables us to see how the discoveries can affect our _d_aily lives. Includes chapters on the radionic box and how it works, on music and color, _a_nd on thought, light, and sound. There are also many case studies and photographs and _d_iagrams are interspersed throughout. A well written account. 161pp. Wat 66

_____. **NEW WORLDS BEYOND THE ATOM**, c$7.50. The new worlds beyond _t_he atom are found in a universe of energies more primordial than those of matter and are _s_till unexplored by mainstream science. George de la Warr's research with these energies _b_egan with increasing the growth rate of plants by using sound waves. Later he found that _a_ plant's vibrations could be detected by a machine with aerials made to the right wave _l_engths and using a person as the receiver. Carrying the idea further, he learned that he _c_ould detect and treat human diseases using the same type of machine, due to the dif_f_erent vibrational rates of different illnesses. By tuning the frequency of a patient's blood _s_pecimen he was even able to photograph diseased tissue over long distances, showing an _i_mmediate connection between life forms beyond the vibration rate of ordinary matter. _P_hotographs, 136pp. EPG 73

EEMAN, L.E. **COOPERATIVE HEALING**, $1.50. Eeman, over forty years ago, demonstrated that vitality (or human ectoplasm) flows like electricity. He showed that unhealthy spiritual, mental, emotional and physical states can be brought into a healthy, balanced state by hooking up the positive and negative areas with copper screens and wires. Excerpts from Eeeman's book **Cooperative Healing** (long out of print) are included here along with the results of research and testing being carried out by the Borderland Sciences researchers. Illustrations, oversize. 20pp. BSR nd

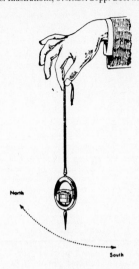

North

South

FINCH, W.J. **THE PENDULUM AND POSSESSION**, $4.00. Finch is a healer who has had years of experience in the use of the pendulum. He has gathered his findings together and organized them in this practical instruction manual. The explanations are detailed and quite precisely stated. The book covers the following areas: _What is a pendulum?, history of the pendulum, what makes a pendulum work?, everyday uses for a pendulum, how to use a pendulum, measuring people, interpretations from irregular pendulum movements, recording your data,_ and _making comparative measurements._ The last part of the book is devoted to a section on possession. 116pp. EsP 71

FLANAGAN, G. PATRICK. **BEYOND PYRAMID POWER**, $3.95. This is a discussion of tensor fields, Flanagan's new name for the energies and forces which he discussed in previous books and referred to as pyramid power. Here he relates the results of his four years of research since his initial pyramid publications. He feels that he has made great strides and he also believes that his earlier theses are no longer valid. In addition to a general discussion, Flanagan also graphically details the construction of instruments which measure the tensor fields, including pyramids, spirals, and cones, and explains how and why they capture this energy. 67pp. DeV 75

_____. **THE PYRAMID AND ITS RELATION TO BIOCOSMIC ENERGY**, $3.00. A pamphlet detailing some of Flanagan's early studies. Oversize.

_____. **PYRAMID POWER**, c$6.95. Flanagan is currently the best known person doing practical research on the pyramid. He discusses the most important aspects of his work in this volume and includes information on the history of pyramid energy studies and other studies of energy in recent years. The major portion of the book is devoted to pyramid research projects and measuring devices. He includes detailed instructions. Illustrations, notes, index. 173pp. PyP 75

GALLERT, MARK, ed. **NEW LIGHT ON THERAPEUTIC ENERGY**, c$8.40. A detailed, advanced work which presents the wisdom and experience of many pioneers in the healing arts in simplified and practical form. Theory, equipment and instructions for use in practice are all included for most of the methods presented. Includes illustrated essays by George Starr White, Wilhelm Reich, George Lakhovsky, L.E. Eeman, William Schussler and many others. Recommended for the serious student. 256pp. Cla

GEORGE, KARL. **DOWSING**, $4.95. George himself was a dowser and he feels that he has made some important advances in dowsing which he would like to pass on to others. This book consists of a biographical statement and a general history of dowsing. It also contains a detailed description of 189 of his own dowsing cases, each one briefly evaluated. The cases are topically arranged. 140pp. Geo 74

_____. **DOWSONOLOGY**, $3.30. Dowsonology is George's special healing technique. He achieves healing by positively charging dowsing rods with the positive ion structure of a healthy person. When the positively charged rods are used to treat an unhealthy person the person's ion structure is changed and his or her ailments are relieved. Practical instructions are presented in this pamphlet—although George's writing style leaves much to be desired. 20pp. Geo 74

_____. **ION SCENT**, $3.30. Further research is presented on the effects of ions on dowsing rods. 30pp. Geo 74

GRAVES, TOM. **DOWSING**, $4.65. This is a practical, easy-to-follow guide to the techniques of dowsing and their applications. Sixty illustrations, 160pp. Tur 76

HILLS, CHRISTOPHER. **NUCLEAR EVOLUTION**, $4.00. This is a strange book which contains some interesting insights of a philosophical nature. It is subtitled _A Guide to_

Cosmic Enlightenment, and it contains Hills' thoughts about the consciousness which will be necessary to bring in the new age. A discussion of colors and consciousness is also included. Hills' exposition is often hard to follow. Notes, 152pp. Cen 68

_____. **SUPERSENSONICS**, $15.00. Hills defines supersensonics as the spiritual physics of all vibrations from zero to infinity. This is an incredibly detailed—albeit scattered—account of every aspect of the subject. It is oriented toward the specialist and we recommend this book only to those who are deeply interested in this area and who have a working knowledge of physics. **Supersensonics** is divided into the following general topics: the science of radiational physics, light, and supersensonic detectors. Many illustrations illuminate the text. 8½x11", 603pp. UTP 76

HUNA RESEARCH BULLETINS. MANA, $2.00. This is the complete text of lesson/ instructions which Max Freedom Long sent to members of the Huna Research Association for the experimental use of Huna in the early days of the research. Mana was Long's name for the vital force in humans which he discovered during his research with the Kahunas in Hawaii (see the Mysticism section for more of Long's work). Oversize, 20pp. HRA 72

KERRELL, BILL and KATHY GOGGIN. THE GUIDE TO PYRAMID ENERGY, $3.95. This is one of the most popular of the recent books on pyramid energy and it is also considered one of the best. The authors have spent many years researching the subject and, while their bias is obvious, they present their results with a fair amount of objectivity. The book begins with a general examination of pyramid energy, including directions on how to prove it and use it. The second section discusses a variety of specific topics including dowsing energies and pyramids, gems, stones, and minerals, psychic healing, and the Great Pyramid. Illustrations, bibliography. 172pp. PPV 75

KORTH, LESLIE HEALING MAGNETISM, $1.25. A general study by a noted British osteopath with chapters on magnetism, contact therapy and hypnotherapy, healing magnetism in practice, magnetopathic technique, examples of hand emanations, breathing, and the odic force. Bibliography, 64pp. Wei 65

KRIPPNER, STANLEY and DANIEL RUBIN, eds. THE ENERGIES OF CONSCIOUS-NESS, c$12.95. A collection of papers from the Second Western Hemisphere Conference on Kirlian Photography, Acupuncture, and the Human Aura. Includes information on the latest findings in electrophotography, as well as some of the first American research in acupuncture and auras. The papers are all fairly technical and are extensively illustrated. Notes, 252pp. G&B 75

_____. **THE KIRLIAN AURA**, $3.95. See the Color and Aura section.

LAKHOVSKY, GEORGES. THE SECRET OF LIFE, $5.00. An important work on the subject of electricity and radiation in man and the universe. The author shows that the fundamentals of electricity can be seen in the basic functions of the human body. All living entities and even the cells of which they are comprised are rapidly pulsing electrical oscillators that project streams of radiating energy throughout their environment. The quality of the radiations differs with the nature of their source. The fascinating subject of cosmic stellar radiations is discussed with its possible consequences for humanity. 213pp. HeR 35

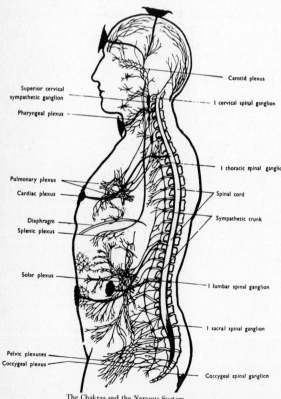

Superior cervical sympathetic ganglion
Pharyngeal plexus
Pulmonary plexus
Cardiac plexus
Diaphragm
Splenic plexus
Solar plexus
Pelvic plexuses
Coccygeal plexus

Carotid plexus
I cervical spinal ganglion
I thoracic spinal ganglion
Spinal cord
Sympathetic trunk
I lumbar spinal ganglion
I sacral spinal ganglion
Coccygeal spinal ganglion

The Chakras and the Nervous System, From Enigma to Science, by George Meek

LANE, EARL, ed. ELECTROPHOTOGRAPHY, $4.95. See the Color and Aura secti

LAYNE, MEADE. THE CAMERON AURAMETER, $4.70. This study details the c tributions of Verne Cameron to the science of dowsing for water and it describes the p formance of the instrument invented by him, the aurameter or water compass. Chap include an introduction by Layne, Cameron's own story, delineation of the human au the aurameter and *vitic* (nerve energy derived from magnet and carbon), psychic vestigations, Eeman circuits, and locating underground water. Many illustrations and tailed instructions. Oversize, 89pp. BSR 70

MANN, W. EDWARD. ORGONE, REICH AND EROS, $3.95. See the Reich secti

MEEK, GEORGE. FROM ENIGMA TO SCIENCE, c$6.95. This is a scattered study various facets of the paranormal with an emphasis on the use of body energies. Meek l quoted and cited the studies of many of the most noted researchers in this field. App dices list the major related organizations in the U.S. and Great Britain, publications, a an extensive subject indexed bibliography—all with full addresses. Illustrations (includ color Kirlian photographs), index. 199pp. Wei 73

MERMET, ABBE. PRINCIPLES AND PRACTICE OF RADIESTHESIA, $7.00. This far and away the best book on radiesthesia ever written. Abbe Mermet was both a searcher and a practitioner and he expresses his theories and techniques with extraordin clarity. We recommend this book to all who are interested in radiesthesia. Notes, ind 230pp. Wat 35

FRANZ MESMER

Mesmer (1734-1815), the architect of modern hypnotism, is one of the mo controversial and fascinating figures in medical and scientific history. has been considered both a quack and a charlatan, and also the father psychotherapy. Early in his study of medicine Mesmer suggested that t sun, moon, and planets might have a direct influence on human bodies way of a subtle fluid—and that when this force (a kind of universal energ exerts itself, the fluid expands and contracts the nervous system. Althou this theory received little attention at the time, it was the forerunner of l theory of animal magnetism through which he achieved remarkable cur of functional disorders. Mesmer's experiments today remain an inspiratio to all the researchers in the field of life energies.

BURANELLI, VINCENT. THE WIZARD FROM VIENNA, c$8.95. This is a fine b graphical study of Mesmer which emphasizes his psychiatric contributions. It is vivid written and both the times and the main characters come to life. Many quotations fro critics of Mesmer and from Mesmer's defenses and theories are included. Annotat bibliography, 256pp. CMG 75

EDEN, JEROME. ANIMAL MAGNETISM AND THE LIFE ENERGY, c$8.50. Over 2 years ago Dr. Franz Anton Mesmer announced his controversial discovery for treati disease which he called *animal magnetism*—the word *animal* in this case meaning pe taining to the soul. Mesmer was denounced by his fellow scientists and to this day l contributions are not widely appreciated. Eden reviews Mesmer's discoveries and i cludes a great deal of material from Mesmer's own writings on his principles, method and case histories. Notes, index. 221pp. ExP 74

WYCKOFF, JAMES. FRANZ ANTON MESMER, c$8.95. This biographical study Mesmer emphasizes his medical researches. Wyckoff has also written a biography of W helm Reich and a Reichean perspective is apparent in this work. Wycoff writes very w and his study is especially valuable for the light that it sheds on Mesmer's esoteric i fluences. 152pp. PrH 75

MILNER, DENNIS and EDWARD SMART. THE LOOM OF CREATION, c$14.9 Milner and Smart believe that they have discovered experimental evidence for the forc of creation described by mystics. They have spent over ten years painstakingly researc ing this thesis and they have drawn on a wide spectrum of data. In advancing their thes they begin with a review of the nature of man and his development in earlier culture This is followed by a survey of *the experiences and viewpoint of Expanded Awareness* which they discuss the human experience and the processes of creation and evolution. third section details their experiments with etheric forces and a fourth is an extensi annotated bibliography. The presentation is highly esoteric and is largely based on th philosophical speculations of Rudolf Steiner (see the Steiner section) and Guenthe Wachsmith. A great deal of fascinating material is advanced but the book is written an organized in such a way that the author's concepts elude the reader no matter how car fully s/he studies the material. This is another recent work which has potential, b which very often lacks clarity. Too bad! Profusely illustrated in color and black an white. 7½x10", index. 319pp. H&R 76

OTT, JOHN. HEALTH AND LIGHT, $1.95. Subtitled *The Effects of Natural and Artif cial Light on Man and Other Living Things*. Ott, head of the Environmental Health an Light Research Institute in Florida, is the leading researcher in this area. Here he presen some of his studies and many case histories to show the subtle effects the new light tec nology is having upon our physical and mental well-being. Bibliography, illustration references, index. 208pp. S&S 73

PYRAMID ENERGY GENERATOR / PYRAMID ENERGY PLATE COMBINATIO This set is based on Pat Flanagan's designs. The **Pyramid Energy Generator** is designe so that energy flows from the peak of each pyramid on the generator. There's also built-in magnetic field which eliminates the necessity of aligning the pyramids along north-south axis. The **Plate** works like a battery. It's made of anodized aluminum whic

ks up the energy given off by the generator. Available in three sizes: 3x5" generator
plate, $7.50; 4x5" generator and plate, $10.95; 4x5" generator and 8x10" plate,
3.95.

RAMID POWER. **PYRAMID ENERGY KIT**, $2.95. Includes three 6" base pyramids
de of heavy cardboard, an instruction booklet, and a compass.

_____. **PYRAMID ENERGY SCIENCE LAB KIT**, $9.95. Includes the book
e **Guide to Pyramid Energy**, by Kerrell and Goggin, 12" base open frame pyramid,
base heavy cardboard pyramid, brine shrimp water preparation, container of seeds,
planting trays and soil, two magnets and *magnetic dust*, and a compass. Complete
ructions are also included and each part of the pyramids is formulated with the cor-
t angles to make an exact replica of the Great Pyramid.

ICHENBACH, KARL von. **THE ODIC FORCE: LETTERS ON OD AND MAGNET-**
M, c$5.00. Von Reichenbach was a chemist, metallurgist, technologist and expert on
teorites. He discovered a mysterious force, named it *od*, published his findings in
rmany in 1845, and continued his study until his death in 1869. His findings were
gely ignored until Wilhelm Reich rediscovered this energy and named it the *orgone*.
at von Reichenbach discovered was the mysterious vital force or energy permeating
ure. It is blue in color and can be demonstrated visually by heat, and by electric
arge, in plants, and animals, including humans—but it can only be perceived by very
sitive people under careful guidance by a sympathetic scientist. This edition includes
uable supplementary material. 119pp. UnB 68

_____. **RESEARCHES ON THE VITAL FORCE**, c$10.00. Baron von Reichen-
ch (1788-1869) was one of the great scientists of the nineteenth century. He spent over
o decades experimenting with the mysterious force which he named *od*, and described
effects as manifested in sensitive persons. This is the most extensive presentation of his
earches in the areas of magnetism, electricity, heat, light, crystallization, and chemical
raction in relation to the vital force. Illustrations, 514pp. UnB 74

CHARDS, W. GUYON. **THE CHAIN OF LIFE**, c$10.95. This is an interesting study by
noted radiesthesic practitioner. Richards delves far deeper into the subject than do
st writers and his own personal experiences make illuminating reading. The account
gins with a review of how he became interested in radiesthesia and discusses Abrams'
coveries and his own experiments with the atom. A second section discusses esoteric
d occult anatomy, with special reference to the needs of radiesthesic practitioners.
e final 100pp. survey the uses of radiesthesia in a variety of specific areas including
ncer and color, and also discuss color and thought forms. A technical study, illustrated
th many tables and graphs. Index, 220pp. Spg 54

USSELL, EDWARD. **DESIGN FOR DESTINY**, $1.25. A synthesis and interpretation
the work of many scientists, providing a link between science and religion, intellect
d perception, man and his universe. Russell was especially close to Harold Burr, whose
oneering work with L-fields (the permanent electro-magnetic fields which mold the con-
antly changing material of the cells) is described in great detail. Other scientists dis-
ussed include L.L. Vasiliev, J.B. Rhine, Wilder Penfield. An important book for the lay-
erson. Well researched and annotated. 213pp. RaH

_____. **REPORT ON RADIONICS**, c$10.95. This is the most comprehensive
count of radionics available, as seen through the eyes of a reporter. He describes the
evelopments over the past half century and talks about the major practitioners, many
whom he knew or knows personally. The material is well written and includes many
se studies from both sides of the Atlantic. This is an excellent introduction for the non-
rofessional and provides a good overview for all. Illustrations, notes, bibliography.
55pp. Spe 73

USSELL, WALTER. **THE SECRET OF LIGHT**, c$15.00. A technical examination of
ght and vibration in all its manifestations. Many of Russell's own complex diagrams
lustrate the text. 302pp. USP 47

USSELL, WALTER and LAO. **ATOMIC SUICIDE?** c$10.00. After pointing out the
ealth dangers of atomic energy, including cancers and mutations, Russell presents a view
the harmonics of energy and matter. It is a vision of the patterns making up the physi-
al world: how the elements in atoms and stars evolve out of each other, how electricity,
magnetism, and light manifest in the motion of the creative energy. The processes in-
olved in continuing creation of matter give a life-affirming alternative to radioactive
uels. Many diagrams illustrate his theory. 304pp. USP 57

CHUL, BILL and ED PETTIT. **THE SECRET POWER OF PYRAMIDS**, $1.75. A good
ntroduction to effects of pyramids and pyramid shapes on plants and people, on the
istory and construction of pyramids, altered states of consciousness and pyramids,
nd the relation of ancient earth energy grids and the pyramids. Photographs and bib-
iography. 223pp. Faw 75

HEARS, C. CURTIS. **SCIENCE OF SELF-HEALING**, $4.10. This book is not so much
bout self-healing as it is about nutrition, metaphysical concepts of disease, and the use
f radiesthesia in divining disease and nutritional imbalances. Dr. Shears has written ex-
ensively on nutrition (see the Nutrition section) and this book deals with the more meta-
hysical aspects of health. He calls for more radiesthetic operators who are trained in nu-
ritional science and this combination is apparently being developed at his Nutritional
cience Research Institute of England. 55pp. NuS 75

ANSLEY, DAVID. **RADIONICS: INTERFACE WITH THE ETHER-FIELDS**, c$10.95.
his is an excellent esoteric exposition of radionics, geared toward the practitioner and
he knowledgeable layperson. The following chapter headings should give the reader a
ood feeling for the content and orientation: *An Esoteric Ether-Field Construct, The
Connective Tissue of Space, The Geometric Etheric Link, Radionic Etheric Photography,
Radionic Potentizing—Remedies from the Ether-Field, Scanning the Human Aura, The*

Spine and Radionic Therapy, Bio-Dynamic Rhythm, and *Some Esoteric Aspects of
Radionics.* Many examples taken from Tansley's practice are included within the body of
the text. 124pp. HSP 75

_____. **RADIONICS AND THE SUBTLE ANATOMY OF MAN**, $3.50. Radionics
is defined as a method of diagnosis and therapy which is primarily concerned with the
utilization of subtle force fields and energies for the purpose of investigating and com-
batting the causes of disease. Tansley relates radionics to laws and principles governing
the etheric, emotional and mental levels of existence. He includes valuable data on the
esoteric constitution of man, the etheric body, the force centers, the chakras, vitality and
prana. 95pp. HSP 72

NIKOLA TESLA

O'NEILL, JOHN. **PRODIGAL GENIUS: THE LIFE OF NIKOLA TESLA**, $3.45. O'Neill
was a personal friend of Tesla. This is the story of his life and work. 326pp. McK 44

TESLA, NICOLA. **INVENTIONS, RESEARCHES AND WRITINGS OF NICOLA TESLA**,
$10.00. This volume was put together by Thomas C. Martin, an electrical engineer, with
the approval and blessings of Tesla himself. It is basically a record of the pioneering work
done by Tesla in the field of electrical invention. It includes his lectures, miscellaneous
articles and discussions, and makes note of all his inventions up to the time of publication
(1893), particularly those bearing on polyphase motors and the effects obtained with currents of high potential and high frequency. 496pp, spiral bound offset edition. HeR 70

_____. **NIKOLA TESLA—LECTURES, PATENTS, ARTICLES**, $30.00. The
purpose of this massive volume (published by the Nikola Tesla Museum) is to acquaint
the reader with Tesla's most important works in the numerous fields of science to which
he dedicated himself. The first part contains Tesla's most important lectures in chronological order. The second part deals with Tesla's patents, selected from those registered
at the Patent Office of the U.S. These are divided into select groups, each arranged according to the order of registration. The third part, which contains a cross section of
Tesla's scientific and technical articles, is also divided into select groups. Photographs.
spiral bound, oversize. 833pp. HeR 73

TOMLINSON, H. **MEDICAL DIVINATION**, c$5.25. Discusses the author's latest tech-
niques and explores fundamental concepts concerning the relationship of radiesthesia and
cosmology. 86pp. HSP 66

TOMPKINS, PETER and CHRIS BIRD. **THE SECRET LIFE OF PLANTS**, $1.95. See the
Consciousness Expansion section.

WESTLAKE, AUBREY. **THE PATTERN OF HEALTH**, $3.95. Dr. Westlake set out to
study medicine from the standpoint of health, instead of disease. He has been studying
the supersensory healing force which, under so many names, keeps on being rediscovered
without the discoverer seeming to know that someone else has done so before. He discusses
the discoveries of Dr. Guyon Richards, Bach, Reichenbach, Wilhelm Reich and Eeman.
He also describes his own experiences in radiesthesia and homeopathy. A fascinating
book, highly recommended. 200pp. ShP 73

WETHERED, VERNON. **AN INTRODUCTION TO MEDICAL RADIESTHESIA AND
RADIONICS**, c$9.25. Written primarily for doctors, especially those interested in home-
opathy. Describes radiesthetic techniques for diagnosis and treatment affording mathematical precision and assessing the function of organs, the severity of disease and determination of treatment. 194pp. Dan

_____. **THE PRACTICE OF MEDICAL RADIESTHESIA**, c$4.00. This is the
latest work by Wethered, Vice President of the British Society of Dowsers and a well-
known researcher in this field. It shows how the practitioner can learn simple methods
of pendulum testing and includes chapters on the psychic factor in pendulum work,
energy levels in elements and people, and nuclear fall-out. It also relates radiesthesia
to homeopathic diagnosis and prescribing. 150pp. Fow 67

WHITE, GEORGE S. **THE FINER FORCES OF NATURE**, $7.00. *This hand-book,
explaining, describing, and illustrating my original method of using the* **Finer Forces
of Nature** *for diagnosing and treating all manner of unhealth, is a condensation and
revamping of voluminous literature that I have written on the subject, augmented with
new discoveries gained through many additional years of study and clinical experience.*
Includes many illustrations in two colors, and photographs. Index, 231pp. HeR 69

WILLEY, RAYMOND. **MODERN DOWSING**, $5.00. This is a comprehensive presen-
tation which begins with a general discussion of dowsing and then goes into a detailed
study of the tools of dowsing. Other chapters survey holds and movements utilizing many
types of rods. Virtually every type of rod is discussed and there's also information on
dowsing without devices and using the pendulum. Map dowsing is also surveyed in detail.
Many case studies and explicit instructions are included. The author is a trustee of the
American Society of Dowsers. This is the best overall manual to use if you want to learn
how to dowse. 196pp. EsP 76

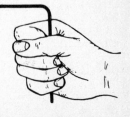

MEDITATION

There are a great many types of meditation. I shall very briefly describe the four major classes that most of them fit into.

How does the individual choose which path to follow? There are no absolute rules. Starting with the area you personally feel strongest and most secure in is often the best way. Later, after having worked seriously on this route, you may wish to change to or combine it with another. All lead to the same place eventually. All are hard. Where you are *now*, before you start, is important. The task is difficult enough without making it harder by beginning with your weakest area. Which path *feels* most natural for you as an individual? Start with this one and stay with it for the months necessary to determine if you have made a mistake or if you have chosen correctly.

One teacher of the mystic way, Rabbi Nahman of Bratislava, wrote, *God chooses one man with a shout, another with a song, another with a whisper.*

There is one additional test of a meditation program that should always be kept in mind. It generally should make you feel better when you do it than when you do not do it. After each meditation, sit for a few minutes with no particular program. Just let yourself *be* for this time (about ten to twenty percent of this time you actually spend on the meditation). Then ask yourself how you feel compared to how you felt before you started the meditation. If the work you are doing is the right kind of work for you, then most of the time the answer will be that you fell better, more *put together*, more of one piece and less fragmented. If this response does not usually occur, then do not continue with this meditation. If you persevere with the meditation program which is *right* for you, then after amonth or so you will find yourself becoming *addicted to feeling good* and will find your motivation increasing to continue this work regularly.

The Path Through the Intellect

The path of the intellect appears to many people, and to many mystics, to be a contradiction in terms. It uses the intellect to go beyond the intellect, the will, and directed thought processes to transcend themselves. . . . The basic structure of the path of the intellect is that the student first reaches an intellectual understanding of the two realities, the two ways of perceiving and relating to the world, and then, by a series of training exercises—meditations—deepens this understanding. At the same time he is strengthening his personality structure by the discipline. By the use of structure meditations forcing his mind to do what is impossible in our usual ways of perceiving and thinking he completes the process. These three parts of the intellectual path combine to force his understanding of the two ways of relating to reality to become a total organismic comprehension. In the Bhagavad-Gita, this is the first of the paths taught by Krishna to Arjuna. In the modern Eastern tradition we see it most clearly in the approach of Krishnamurti.

For many Westerners, particularly perhaps for intellectuals, this may be the path of choice. It can provide an accustomed method of working at the beginning of the path so that a sense of rightness and security is built up by the time the harder and more upsetting parts of the work are reached.

The Path Through the Emotions

The path through the emotions has probably been the most widely followed of all the mystical paths. The Christian monastic who spends years practicing his devotions, ceaselessly working at his ability to love, to feel, to accept, expand and express his *Caritas*, his caring, is on this route. So is the student of Bhakti-Yoga in the East. The Sufi poet Rumi wrote, *The astrolabe of the mysteries of God is love.* There was an insistence on the part of the Baal Shem Tov (the founder of Hasidic mysticism) on the importance of love and feeling in approaching the One. The Eastern follower of this route with the most influence on the West today is probably Meher Baba.

The path through the emotions concentrates on meditations that loosen the feelings and expand the ability to relate to others, to care and to love. Unstructured meditations are used more by the follower of this path than by

those who follow other routes. The basic theory held by meditational sch[ools] of this kind (and by nearly all others) is that the more free, untroubled[,] complete a human being is, the more he has overcome the stunting of [his] growth due to his cultural training and early experiences, the more he [will] naturally love and the better he will relate to others. Some meditatio[nal] schools concentrate on learning to love the self, some on learning to l[ove] others, some on learning to love God. Ultimately all arrive at the same pla[ce,] loving all three. From the mystic's viewpoint there is no separation betw[een] self, others, and God, and learning to fully care for one leads to fully car[ing] for all.

The Route of the Body

Until quite recently this route has been very little used in the West. Follow[ow]ing it, one learns to be aware of one's body and bodily movements and [to] heighten this awareness through practice, until, during the period of medita[tion,] this awareness completely fills the field of consciousness to the exclus[ion] of anything else. Practiced consistently it leads to the same results as do [the] other routes. The best known Eastern forms are Hatha Yoga, T'ai Chi a[nd] the Dervish dances of the Sufi mystical tradition.

A dervish told Nikos Kazantzakis, *We bless the Lord by dancing. . . . Beca[use] dancing kills the ego, and once the ego has been killed, there is no furth[er] obstacle to prevent you from joining with God.*

There is the Hasidic tale of the great Rabbi who was coming to visit a sm[all] town in Russia. It was a very great event for the Jews in the town and ea[ch] thought long and hard about what questions they would ask the wise m[an.] When he finally arrived, all were gathered in the largest available room a[nd] each was deeply concerned with the questions they had for him. The Rab[bi] came into the room and felt the great tension in it. For a time he said noth[ing] and then began to hum softly a Hasidic tune. Presently all there were hum[m]ing with him. He then began to sing the song and soon all were sing[ing] with him. Then he began to dance and soon all present were caught up in [the] dance with him. After a time all were deeply involved in the dance, all fu[lly] committed to it, all just dancing and nothing else. In this way, each one [be]came whole with himself, each healed the splits within himself which ke[pt] him from understanding. After the dance went on for a time, the Rabbi gra[d]ually slowed it to a stop, looked at the group, and said, *I trust that I ha[ve] answered all your questions.*

In the complete absorption in one's bodily integration and bodily moveme[nt] the meditator is brought slowly and gradually to doing just one thing at [a] time. This, as in the other routes, integrates and strengthens the personali[ty] organization and brings one both the readiness and the need for developing [a] new way of perceiving and responding to reality. Further, this particular pa[th] integrates the different bodily aspects with each other and with the person[al]ity in particular.

The Path of Action

The path of action consists of learning how to *be* and to perceive and relate [to] the world during the performance of a particular type of skill. This approa[ch] has been most widely used in the East. Various skills have been used: archer[y,] flower arrangement, aikido and karate (two methods of unarmed combat) [in] the Zen tradition, and rug weaving in the Sufi tradition. Singing and pray[er] have been used in the Christian tradition.

Perhaps one of the clearest statements of this path in Christianity is in *Th[e] Little Way* of Saint Theresa of Lisieux. Her way consisted of doing all t[he] small tasks of everyday life with the knowledge that each one is a part of t[he] total harmony of the universe. They were done with love and *with total co[n]centration* and the attitude that this task was the most important thing to [be] doing at that moment.

As one learns the mystic's way of being in the world during the performan[ce] of a specific skill, the long, hard practice disciplines and strengthens the pe[r] nality. The pure concentration of doing what you are doing and being aware of nothing else is again the impossible task for our everyday way of being, and so the new way is gradually forced into conscious existence. Just as the effect of doing an intellectually oriented or a bodily oriented meditation has, over a period of time, an impact on the rest of your daily perceptions and actions, so also does the effect of action-oriented meditations tend to spread out to the rest of your life. It goes without saying that you will become quite expert at the particular skill you work with, but this is not the real goal of the work. The real goal is to help you grow and develop as a total human being, not to become a better archer or karate expert. There is no particular reason to suppose that Zen-trained archers are better or worse archers than those who have spent an equivalent amount of time practicing with bow and arrow. However, the Zen-trained archers have developed their personality organizations in a way the other archers have not.

This has been a very brief discussion of the major *routes* of mystical training. Many meditations are combinations of different routes and most schools of meditation include more than one of these paths. Each person should find the combination of routes best suited to him as an individual. There is no one *best* way for all; there is a best way for each individual. Sex or age is not a factor. For example, the way of the body can be followed by individuals of any age through sensory awareness or the Alexander method. Each person must find his own best program depending on his own personality structure. You try to get a sense of how you would feel best working as you are now, not as you would like to be. A program is built with your present reality as its base. Then stay with each meditation you try for the several weeks necessary to learn how to use it. At the end of that time, if you feel better *after* you do it than you did before, continue. Otherwise, experiment further.

There is one warning sign in meditation that should always be obeyed. This is a sense that you should not be doing this particular meditation, that it is *wrong* for you. It is a clear feeling that what you are doing does not fit well with the structure of your being and is damaging or deforming it in some way. When and if (it is quite rare) you have this sense about what you are doing, stop doing it. I am not speaking about anxiety. If you feel anxious during a meditation, you will probably act as you usually do in other situations when you are anxious: some people stop whatever they're doing at the moment and reevaluate the situation; some people plunge ahead. Personally, since I do not believe in heroics in personal growth, I recommend the first course, but each person will make his own choice.

I am speaking of a definite and clear feeling that you are doing something to yourself that you should not be doing. Always obey this warning. Stop the meditation you are doing and do not resume it until at least several months have passed and you understand fully the reasons you felt that way and that these reasons no longer exist. By and large, if a meditation makes you feel that it is doing you harm, you are never going to get much out of working with it. You might just as well let it go completely and use other forms of meditation. I have never heard of anyone having this feeling when doing Breath Counting or Contemplation. However, it does happen, rarely, with other forms of this work.

In any serious meditation program there will be dry, dull periods when you just feel bored with the work. These feelings are part of your resistance. Stay with it, if you can, during these periods. Work *harder* at it. Presently it will pass (as it becomes apparent to you that this method of resisting discipline does not work) and you will find the meditation a deeper, richer experience at the end of the dry period than it was before.

Although *discipline* and *will* have become, for many people today, trigger words that they immediately respond to negatively, they are necessary in understanding meditation. One student of meditation asked me, *How do I keep bringing my mind back to the breath counting?* He looked quite surprised, for a moment, when I said, *By means of your active will.* After thinking about my answer for a moment, he was quite satisfied with it.

The Bhagavad-Gita puts it plainly: *Patiently, little by little, a man must free himself from all mental distractions, with the aid of the intelligent will.*

—condensed from **HOW TO MEDITATE** by Lawrence LeShan

ALDER, VERA. **THE FIFTH DIMENSION**, $3.50. Discusses what meditation is, and how it works: which of its techniques are most suited to ourselves; and to what results we can look forward. She sees meditation as only a part of a complete way of life which will help humanity to advance. A step by step approach is given. 220pp. Wei 40

ARYA, USHARBUDH. **SUPERCONSCIOUS MEDITATION**, $3.00. Dr. Arya is a leading disciple of Swami Rama and the founder and principal teacher of the Meditation Temple in Minneapolis. This is a detailed exposition of a traditional Indian meditation technique which is geared toward the Westerner. A great deal of background philosophy is included with the text and both basic and more advanced techniques are presented. 141pp. Him 74

BAILEY, ALICE. **LETTERS ON OCCULT MEDITATION**, c$7.00/2.75. Given to a group of students over a period of years. These letters describe the technique of occult meditation, which includes the establishment of correct alignment of the personality with the inner spiritual entity or soul and the resulting soul contact and inspiration. 375pp. Luc 22

BAKER, DOUGLAS. **MEDITATION**, $14.50. The format here is identical to that of Baker's other oversize volumes, and there is an equal amount of full-color and black-and-white illustrations. This is Volume II of his **Seven Pillars of Ancient Wisdom** series, and is an extensive treatise on meditation: its nature, types, stages in individual meditation, techniques, and effects. The material is all discussed at great length and the approach is from the esoteric tradition. The exercises are clearly presented and visualization material accompanies them. This has been a surprisingly popular series considering its price and for those who desire a more in depth relation of the esoteric nature of man, this is an ideal volume. Over 200pp. Bak 75

BAKER, M.E. PENNY. **MEDITATION—A STEP BEYOND WITH EDGAR CAYCE**, $1.25. An in depth look at meditation based entirely on what Cayce taught through his readings. The material is logically organized and contains extensive quotations from the Cayce readings. Bibliography, 166pp. Pin 73

BALLENTINE, R., ed. **THE THEORY AND PRACTICE OF MEDITATION**, $1.95. A collection of essays on meditation by a variety of Indian intellectuals associated with Swami Rama. The selections are fairly clear, although a great number of Sanskrit words are used. 97pp. Him 75

BENSON, HERBERT. **RELAXATION RESPONSE**, $1.95. *In the midst of all the blather about mind cures and faith healing and the angry refutations of both, Dr. Herbert Benson has written an unsentimental, astonishingly sensible book about stress, relaxation and how certain techniques known to religious people for eons can actually help ordinary people to better health. There is no legerdemain here, just good research, solid reasoning and good sense. This book will not end the causes of stress in anyone's life. That may be impossible. But it may help many of us to live with stress more comfortably and maybe even to life longer because we do.*—Harvey Cox, Professor, Harvard Divinity School. Bibliography, index, 158pp. Avo 75

BLOFELD, JOHN. **THE TANTRIC MYSTICISM OF TIBET**, $3.25. See the Tibetan sub-section of the Buddhism section.

BOWNESS, CHARLES. **THE PRACTICE OF MEDITATION**, $1.25. A practical guide to meditation which includes many preparatory steps and answers many often wondered questions. Very clearly written. 63pp. Wei 71

BROOKE, AVERY. **DOORWAY TO MEDITATION**, $3.95. This is a lovely, thoughtful book about praying, and being, and approaching God, and meditating. The text is hand written and is accompanied by many pictures. Rather than saying what meditation is or what meditating means, Brooke gives the reader an idea of what the meditative life is. He is saying that meditation and prayer can be found and practiced in all forms of daily life and every act can be a manifestation of the love of God. This can be a wonderful gift for someone whom you want to turn on to a more contemplative life. Oversize, 111pp. Vin 73

_____. HOW TO MEDITATE WITHOUT LEAVING THE WORLD, $3.95. Subtitled *A Step-By-Step Description of How to Learn and Teach Meditation in the Judaeo-Christian Tradition*, this is a wonderfully clear manual which teaches meditation with extensive references to the Bible. The text is not overly theological and should be an excellent tool for those who are uncomfortable with the Eastern emphasis in most meditation manuals. Oversize, 96pp. Vin 75

BRUNTON, PAUL. **THE SECRET PATH**, $1.75. See the Mysticism section. Dut 35

_____. **THE QUEST OF THE OVERSELF**, $3.50. A clearly rendered work which seeks to clarify the subject and techniques of spiritual self-understanding. Brunton outlines with precisioned skill certain activities whereby any sincere individual may penetrate deeply into regions of higher consciousness and thus gain greater insight, illumination, and spiritual fulfillment. 230pp. Wei 37

CHAUDHURI, HARIDAS. **PHILOSOPHY OF MEDITATION**, $3.25. Chaudhuri was a disciple of Sri Aurobindo and the founder of the California Institute of Asian Studies. His life's work was the integration of Eastern and Western philosophy and that is the theme of this treatise. The language is fairly academic and the reader needs a good background in mystical terminology (especially Sanskrit). The emphasis is on theoretical concepts rather than practical techniques. 88pp. CIF 65

CHINMAYANANDA. **THE ART OF MEDITATION**, $1.50. A spiritually-oriented treatise on the philosophy and practice of meditation. The book has a nice feeling to it and the instructions are very clear. 48pp. Chn 66

_____. **HASTEN SLOWLY**, $1.50. During his Himalayan retreat in 1969, Swami Chinmayananda composed these twelve fortnightly bulletins for the benefit of students and devotees in India and abroad. In these discussions, his deliberate emphasis was on the certain fundamental differences which seekers generally meet within themselves as they move ahead in their inner search. As usual, his writing is exceptionally clear and contains many quotations from the sacred texts. 78pp. Chn 74

COLEMAN, JOHN. **THE QUIET MIND**, c$5.95. Coleman was an intelligence agent stationed in Thailand. While there he came to admire the Thais and sensed that they had a healthy, serene grasp of the fundamentals of living. After his cover as a spy was exposed he set out to immerse himself in their culture in the hopes of discovering the secret of a *quiet mind*. This volume records his pilgrimages to Thailand, Burma, Sikkim, Tibet, Japan, India, and Nepal, and his experiences with many kinds of spiritual disciplines. Also included are reports of his conversations with Krishnamurti, D.T. Suzuki, and U Ba Khin. The reader can get a good feeling of the various kinds of disciplines from Coleman's narrative and the book as a whole forms an interesting dialogue. Index, 239pp. H&R 71

CONZE, EDWARD. **BUDDHIST MEDITATION**, $2.50. A translation of the most important documents. The bulk of the selections have been taken from Buddhaghosa's *Path of Purity*. An introduction discusses the meaning of Buddhist meditation, its range and principal divisions, documents, and its relation to modern psychology. Glossary, 183pp. H&R 56

COOKE, GRACE. **THE JEWEL IN THE LOTUS**, c$3.95. Grace Cooke is the medium through whom White Eagle delivers his teaching. In this volume she develops the material presented in her first book on meditation and draws on the accounts of some of her students. A section of the book is devoted to an analysis of the symbols brought to light during meditation. The book also includes teaching from White Eagle, offering a practical, deeply inspiring picture of the place of meditation in everyday life. Ms. Cooke's work is inspiring and illuminating and is especially recommended to those who prefer the Western, Christian-oriented approach. 156pp. WET 73

_____. **MEDITATION**, c$3.90. An inspirational book which sets forth in a clear and straightforward style a safe method of meditation and spiritual unfoldment which can be practiced alone or in groups. Ms. Cooke's spiritual guide is known as White Eagle and much of his practical philosophy is incorporated in this book. 167pp. WET 55

DHIRAVAMSA. **THE WAY OF NON-ATTACHMENT**, $7.80. The author is a Thai monk who teaches in England and the U.S. This book is subtitled *The Practice of Insight Meditation* and it seems to be designed to present the basic principles in a way that is accessible to the modern Western mind. All of the chapters are short and virtually no Pali terms are used. The main concepts are clearly presented and Dhiravamsa has a good way of using metaphors to make his presentation clearer. All the techniques are related to living in the modern world and integrating the practice with one's daily life. This is an excellent handbook and on the whole it is the clearest instruction manual on insight meditation we have seen—although it is no more than an introductory treatise. An appendix summarizes the principles of insight meditation. 156pp. Tur 75

DOWNING, GEORGE. **MASSAGE AND MEDITATION**, $1.65. Downing is the author of our most popular massage book, entitled, surprisingly, **The Massage Book**. This book's point of view is . . . *that massage and meditation are in key aspects very much alike. Beyond that, the two activities can be put together in ways which give new depth to both. And you yourself can begin to experience what it can be to integrate the two. You can do this easily, independently of how much previous experience you have or haven't had with either*. Both philosophy and practical instructions are included in this little volume. 85pp. RaH 74

DUMONT, THERON A. **THE POWER OF CONCENTRATION**, c$5,00. This exposition centers on the powers and riches that can be obtained by focusing and concentrating the

mind. Practical guidance is given. 183pp. YPS 18

DURCKHEIM, KARLFRIED. **HARA**, $3.95. Durckheim is a philosopher and psyc therapist. He abandons the old dualistic thinking about man in terms of body and se which is the hallmark of Western thought, and shows how man must always be taken one whole. Realization of the Self can never be a spiritual development alone, but m include the body. In Japan Durckheim discovered the teaching and tradition of *hara*, J anese for the vital center. He found that through the experience of it man can be fr from his persistent conceptual thinking, which inevitably blocks his access to being. T volume includes material on the practice of hara and texts by three Japanese masters hara. It is an unusual work, containing some fine insights. Illustrations, 208pp. Wei

_____. **THE JAPANESE CULT OF TRANQUILITY**, $2.95. See Zen Buddh section. Wei 60

EASTCOTT, MICHAEL. **THE SILENT PATH**, $3.50. Deals with what meditation is: ion; practical details; concentration; charts of the planes of consciousness; the differ kinds of meditation—e.g., reflective, receptive, creative, prayerful; and unification and services rendered by meditation. Each chapter deals with a separate aspect of meditat but the chapters are so linked that one gains a very clear picture of the goal. Highly reco mended. 166pp. Wei 69

八　　　人牛俱忘

From SILENT MUSIC by William Johnston

EBON, MARTIN, ed. **TM: HOW TO FIND PEACE OF MIND THROUGH MEDITATION** $1.50. Despite the title, this is a general collection of essays about meditation and als about other ways of inner growth. Many techniques are described by their proponen and no critical evaluation is offered by the editor. The selection is fairly good, and, whi the emphasis is on the Eastern tradition, several essays also discuss Western approache such as Silva Mind Control, biofeedback, and self-hypnosis. Two of the essays survey Ze meditation, and one, *The Psychology of Eastern Meditation*, is by C.G. Jung. Bibliography 246pp. NAL 75

GARDNER, ADELAIDE. **MEDITATION—A PRACTICAL STUDY**, $1.45. Deals wit the background, methods, progressive stages and obstacles to meditation. Includes a sec tion on group meditation and various meditational exercises. A theosophical approach 116pp. TPH 68

GOLDSMITH, JOEL S. **THE ART OF MEDITATION**, c$5.95. A regular program of dai meditations which will help a person realize his oneness with God and to find a cleare view of himself and his world. A Christian, inspirational approach. 154pp. H&R 5

GOVINDA, LAMA. **MEDITATION**, $2.50. See Tibetan Buddhism section.

HANSON, VIRGINIA, ed. **APPROACHES TO MEDITATION**, $1.75. Writers familia with meditation from different religious and philosophical backgrounds, of both East an West, contributed to this work. Among them are Lama Govinda, Chogyam Trungpa, I.K Tamai, and Simons Roof. Includes different approaches for people of varying tempera ments. A good selection 147pp. TPH 73

_____. **GIFTS OF THE LOTUS**, $1.50. A book of daily meditations taken from the sacred literature of many traditions. The sources for each meditation are given. 191pp TPH 74

HAPPOLD, F.C. **PRAYER AND MEDITATION**, $3.95. Divided into two parts—the firs is a study of the nature of prayer and its expression at all levels of spirituality in all th main religions; the second is a collection of prayers, devotions and meditations for *all sort and conditions of men*, and containing much original material in prose and verse never be fore printed. 381pp. Pen 71

HIRAI, TOMIO. **ZEN MEDITATION THERAPY**, $3.25. Hirai is a Japanese psychiatris specializing in psychophysiology. He has done extensive studies of seated Zen meditation connection with brain waves and he applies Zen to the treatment of neuroses. His work has been quite influential in Japan. This book presents a synthesis of his findings and also includes practical techniques and exercises. 103pp. Jap 75

HITTLEMAN, RICHARD. **RICHARD HITTLEMAN'S GUIDE TO YOGA MEDITATION**, $.50. The largest section deals with the essence of yoga philosophy and meditation. It includes various meditational exercises, many illustrated with photographs and diagrams. A smaller section illustrates various yoga asanas. Very clearly written. A good book for the beginning student who wants practical information. 192pp. Ban 69

HUMPHREYS, CHRISTMAS. **CONCENTRATION AND MEDITATION**, $2.25. The basic principles of mind-development presented by a leading figure in world Buddhism. The student is guided through successive levels of concentration and meditation. Physical and mental exercises, the objects of thought, and underlying philosophical ideas are described at every stage. No knowledge of Buddhist thought is necessary to understand these teachings. *The ultimate aim of this progressive course in mind-development is to bring the student to a point of spiritual attainment beyond which this or any other text would not presume to lead.* Recommended. 242pp. Pen 35

INGRAHAM, E. **MEDITATION IN THE SILENCE**, $1.00. *This little book is presented to the student as a textbook covering the principles and practices of the silence. The endeavor is to make clear the various points involved in the practice of the silence, and to render the benefits of that practice clear to every student. Inasmuch as the silence is fundamentally for the purpose of bringing man into an understanding relationship with God, it is a form of prayer.... The effectiveness of prayer does not depend on the form followed but on the spirit involved.... Let us study together the simple means by which we may commune with God and the ways by which we may most effectively appropriate the blessings that He has had for us since the beginnings of time.*—from the Foreward. 59pp. USC

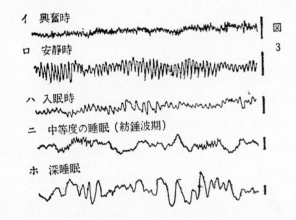

EEG graph paper showing the different brainwaves. From top to bottom: excited state (beta); restful state (alpha); drowsy state (irregular theta); moderate sleep (spindle waves and delta); deep sleep (delta).
From SILENT MUSIC by William Johnston

JOHNSTON, WILLIAM. **SILENT MUSIC**, $1.95. Johnston is an Irish Jesuit with a degree in mystical theology who has taught at Sophia University in Tokyo for the past twenty years. He is the author of a number of books which combine Zen with Christian mysticism. He regards the advances in biofeedback as a sign that science is entering into the world of contemplation and prayer and the resulting dialogue between the scientist and the mystic interests him greatly. He has subtitled this volume *The Science of Meditation*. He begins this study with a survey of the latest scientific research into altered states of consciousness, brainwaves, and biofeedback, and draws out their implications for the practice of meditation. He then outlines the ways, common to many religious traditions—Eastern and Western— by which one enters into the deeper states of consciousness. He feels that love—the most powerful energy in the cosmos—is central to all meditation. He also touches on the therapeutic value of meditation and its potential in the healing of the body and the mind, and on the *passive energy* one can get from meditation. This is an excellent presentation of the mystical potential of meditation for the betterment of humanity and a welcome and unique addition to the literature. Glossary, bibliography, index. 190pp. H&R 74

JYOTIRMAYANANDA. **MEDITATE THE TANTRIC YOGA WAY**, $3.45. Explains in detail ten different techniques of Tantric meditation that have been practiced for centuries. They include preparatory exercises or asanas which allow the meditator to sit motionless for a period of time; and breath control, pranayama, which calms the mind. The treatment of the various techniques is unique and quite complicated. It is only .recommended to those schooled in Tantra, although it is quite clearly written. Glossary. 117pp. Dut 73

KAMPF, HAROLD. **IN SEARCH OF SERENITY**, c$4.15. This is a review of meditational techniques through the ages, with an emphasis on the Christian approach. Chapters also discuss meditation and Subud and the meditational techniques of Joel Goldsmith. Kampf ends with a discussion of *How to Meditate* and a bibliography. 63pp. TPL 74

LESHAN, LAWRENCE. **HOW TO MEDITATE**, c$5.95/1.95. This is an excellent practical guide to meditation. Drawing upon the meditational practices of such disciplines as Zen, Sufism, and yoga, and on Christian and Jewish mysticism, LeShan describes specific exercises and programs ranging from breath counting and simple mantras to group movement and sensory awareness. LeShan is a practicing psychologist and a noted parapsychological researcher. Recommended as a basic primer. Notes, 210pp. Ban 74

LOUNSBERRY, G. CONSTANT. **BUDDHIST MEDITATION**, $2.45. A non-technical book which includes chapters on subjects of meditation especially suitable for Westerners. More than half of the book is a compilation of specific practices, one of which is the *Meditation of Peace*, designed especially for Westerners. Glossary and bibliography. 177pp. Ome 73

LUK, CHARLES (LU K'UAN YU). **SECRETS OF CHINESE MEDITATION**, $3.95. Lu K'uan Yu has devoted his life to presenting as many Chinese Buddhist texts as possible to the Western world. He is among the foremost scholars. He presents here long extracts from ancient and modern classics in which the emphasis is practical so that the reader can pick out and use that which most appeals to him. Ch'an, Mahayana and Taoist methods are presented. Two chapters are devoted to Taoist yoga. An excellent work for the serious seeker. Glossary, 231pp. Wei 64

MANGALO, BHIKKU. **THE PRACTICE OF RECOLLECTION**, $1.00. *The Practice of Recollection* (satipatthana) *is one of the basic practices of Buddhism. Buddhism is rightly famous amongst the family of religions for its clarity and its undogmatic approach to the question of the realisation of the Truth. It is not surprising therefore that we find right at the heart of Buddhism a stress on the need for training the mind to a greater awareness and clarity. This is done by the simple, yet eminently reasonable and practical expedient of keeping the mind focused on the present, on what is, here and now.... The practice of recollection has the ... advantage that, once one has acquired the habit, it can and indeed* should *be practised at all times and throughout the day, whatever one's occupation.* —from the Foreward. 26pp. BuS 70

MATA, ANJANEE. **MEDITATION CARDS**, $3.95. This packet of forty-nine cards is about the neatest way to get into meditation that we know of. The cards themselves have a lovely feel to them, both in terms of the handwriting and the message—and the approach should be welcome by those who have unsuccessfully tried to get into the more traditional books. It's nice when someone takes a subject that has been written about endlessly and transforms it. The material goes far beyond meditation into all kinds of exercises for expanding awareness and each individual can pick out the exercises that particularly appeal to her/him at a given moment by selecting certain cards. The instructions are excellent and they give a good idea of the spiritual background of the exercises–without being unnecessarily heavy. We are delighted with the idea and with the cards and we recommend them highly. Anj 75

MERTON, THOMAS. **MYSTICS AND ZEN MASTERS**, $3.25. Sixteen essays on the way of meditation or contemplation in both Eastern and Western religions. Merton was a Trappist monk but his interests were not confined to Christianity and Zen. This volume contains insights into all religions. Extensive notes and bibliography. 288pp. Del 61

MICHAEL, RUSS. **WHY AND HOW OF MEDITATION**, $3.95. The mechanics of occult meditation presented in a clear way. The elucidation of the physical, emotional, and mental bodies is included as well as a means of preparing them prior to the meditative state. Useful for anyone who meditates, and a practical technique for those just learning. Recommended. 165pp. Mil 75

MUKERJI, A.P. **SPIRITUAL CONSCIOUSNESS**, c$5.50. This is a fairly scattered Indian treatise on some of the more basic ways to attain spiritual consciousness. The highly moralistic text reflects the spirit of the time in which it was written and it may seem unnecessarily heavy to contemporary readers. Some good insights are presented, and exercises are included—however the material is not very clearly organized and we definitely do not suggest this as an instructional manual. 191pp. YPS 11

NARANJO, CLAUDIO and ROBERT ORNSTEIN. **ON THE PSYCHOLOGY OF MEDITATION**, $2.45. Two innovative psychologists here unite their work in an examination of both the spiritual ground of all forms of meditation and the implications for modern psychology of the manifold approaches to meditation. A very clear presentation. Recommended especially for those schooled in humanistic psychology. Many footnotes. 248pp. Vik 71

PARAMANANDA, SWAMI. **CONCENTRATION AND MEDITATION**, $2.50. Swami Paramananda, a disciple of Swami Vivekananda, was one of the first Indian teachers to come to the U.S. He founded the Boston Vedanta Center in 1909 and a monastic community in California in 1923–both of which are still active centers under the direction of his disciples. His teaching is clear and is practically-oriented, and while it represents a traditional Hindu approach, Western philosophy is well integrated. The emphasis is on the philosophy, although techniques and inspirational thoughts also abound. Short excerpts from sacred texts are interspersed throughout. 130pp. VdC 74

_____ . **SILENCE AS YOGA**, $2.50. In ancient India the yogi who sought to realize his divine self would retreat to the seclusion of the forest or to the quiet of a Himalayan cave. Today's spiritual aspirant sits down to meditate amongst the noise of modern society. In the series of lectures presented here Swami Paramananda discusses this problem and stresses that true silence is achievable if an individual can enter completely within himself so that he will not be disturbed or distracted by any external commotion. 82pp. VdC 74

PARAMPANTHI, SWAMI. **CREATIVE SELF-TRANSFORMATION THROUGH MEDITATION**, $3.95. Despite the fact that the author is an Indian, this book is very Western oriented and seems to present a good course of study for those who want to learn about meditation without a teacher. The Swami begins with a review of the benefits of meditation, and he discusses what meditation is. Then some *preliminary steps toward meditation* are presented along with a preview of meditational techniques. Once the background is given the author sets out a six week graduated program, each with a number of variations which can be creatively adapted to individual preferences and lifestyles. Some might put down this presentation as *peace of mind* meditation, but if that's what you want this book is as good as any we know of. The directions are clear and the philosophical material is fairly straightforward. 157pp. Ata 74

PURYEAR, HERBERT and MARK THURSTON. **MEDITATION AND THE MIND OF MAN**, $2.50. This is a psychologically-oriented examination of the Edgar Cayce readings on meditation. It is not intended to be a definitive text, but rather to show how the universal principles and laws can be applied. Frequent references to Lama Govinda's **Foundations of Tibetan Mysticism** and **The Secret of the Golden Flower**, an ancient Taoist text, give the reader an idea of the universal quality of the information which came through the Christ-oriented superconsciousness of Edgar Cayce. The text is divided into the following sections: Fundamental Concepts of the Nature of Man, The Nature of the Mind, Meditation, The Pattern and the Power, Ideals. A final section presents a systematic approach to meditation from the Edgar Cayce readings. This is the most detailed presentation of the Cayce material on meditation available. 107pp. ARE 75

REPS, PAUL. **TEN WAYS TO MEDITATE**, c$4.95. Ten (or twenty-two, depending on how you count them) picture poems which, in the words of Aldous Huxley, *will take one further towards the realization of the ancient self-knowledge than all the roaring or pathetic eloquence of generations of philosophers.* 57pp. Wea 69

RIEKER, HANS-ULRICH. **THE SECRET OF MEDITATION**, $3.95. *The great advantage of this book is its concreteness. One gets the feel of meditation from it, learns to know it as something which is not a strange world of its own. For everything which disturbs our lives also disturbs meditation; and everything which helps meditation also helps our tranquility and our success in daily life. Three appendices deal with Meditation in Japanese Zen Buddhism, Meditation in the Wonderland of Tibet, and . . . Meditation in Christianity. Taken all in all, this is the ideal book to put in the hands of an intelligent friend who wants to know what this Buddhism business is all about. It is also a book for all Buddhists to read and re-read.* — **The Middle Way.** This is a practical, helpful book, written by a Buddhist monk of Swiss origin. 176pp. Wei 55

RITTELMEYER, FRIEDRICH. **MEDITATION**, c$4.80. See the Steiner section.

ROOF, SIMONS. **GREATNESS OF BEING**, $7.50. An excellent guide to beginner/intermediate meditation from a point of view which encompasses all religions and philosophies. Meditation, study and service are discussed in detail; there are many chapters devoted to special exercises in the disciplines. Appendices deal with daily meditation forms and an integrated schedule of daily work. The emphasis is on meditation as a way of life leading to *greatness of being* rather than as an isolated phenomenon. The material is well presented, in a scholarly and yet eminently readable manner. Includes many quotes from other sources. Rcommended as an inspiration to all. 8½x11. 149pp. MSE 73

ROZMAN, DEBORAH. **MEDITATING WITH CHILDREN**, $5.95. This is an unusual text which outlines practical techniques for introducing meditation to children. The exercises are presented in detail and the instructional material is very clear. The text is quite spiritual and is written in language which should appeal to children. There are exercises for both individuals and groups. This is a very good book which can be used by itself and also serve as a base from which a teacher or parent can work in developing more individualized techniques. Oversize. 63pp. UTP 75

SADHU, MOUNI. **CONCENTRATION: GUIDE TO MENTAL MASTERY**, $3.00. A practical sequel to **In Days of Great Peace**. The central idea is to give the reader real knowledge of his mind and the methods of directing it as a tool of his consciousness. After some explanatory chapters, the student is introduced to the exercises. Sadhu uses an eclectic method, taking material from both Western and Eastern sources. 219pp. Wil 59

_____. **IN DAYS OF GREAT PEACE**, $2.00. The author, a disciple of Ramana Maharishi, describes how he mastered the techniques of jnana yoga and achieved the transcendent spiritual state (samadhi). This is probably the best attempt by a European to describe without technicalities what samadhi is, what meditation is about, and why Indians worship their gurus. His rare facility for describing his own mental and spiritual states enables him to pass on to the reader his knowledge and enthusiasm. The book is written around contemporary diary entries with flashbacks to an earlier life. It is an authentic autobiographical account of his life with Ramana Maharishi, an inspired Hindu yogi, and explains convincingly how such a man can teach through silence. First book in trilogy: **In Days/Concentration/Samadhi.** 212pp. Wil 52

_____. **MEDITATION**, $3.00. A continuation of material presented in **Concentration** and its companion volume, **Samadhi.** This should not be considered an introductory work. Its aim is to give the student a manual, from which he may be able to obtain reasonable theoretical knowledge of the subject, plus a systematic guide for the development of practical abilities in himself. Includes introductory exercises, beginning, inter-

mediate and advanced meditations as well as a final section on an introduction to conte[m]plation. The meditations are taken from all the world's scriptures and are well-present[ed] and easy to follow. 350pp. Wil 67

SARASWATI, SWAMI SATYANANDA. **MEDITATIONS**, c$12.00. A detailed, techni[cal] treatise which discusses the theory of meditation expounded in the Upanishads, Tantr[a] and in various yogic systems. Much of the information presented here has never been wr[it]ten down in an organized manner before. Many different techniques are offered and t[he] instructions are clear. Background information on consciousness and on psychologi[cal] and physiological processes is also given. This book should be extremely helpful to in[di]viduals with a thorough grounding in Indian philosophy. Illustrations, index, 307p[p.] BiS 75

SARAYDARIAN. **THE SCIENCE OF MEDITATION**, c$8.00. This book teaches clear[ly] the ageless techniques of true meditation in the context of mankind's entrance into a ne[w] age of the One Humanity. The practices and suggestions are calculated to lead the aspira[nt] from *the unreal to the real, from darkness into light and from death to immortality.* I[n]cluded are detailed instructions and guidelines for group meditation and meditation at t[he] full moon, with an explanation of the use of the Great Invocation. Recommended. 364p[p.] AEG 71

SAYADAW, MAHASI. **PRACTICAL INSIGHT MEDITATION**, $2.25. A further examina[tion] tion of the Satipatthana mindfulness meditation, its basic and progressive stages. An ad[vanced] vanced study into the elements of mind and an in depth investigation aimed at expandin[g] consciousness. Includes an excerpted translation and commentary on the original Mah[a] Satipatthana Sutra. 65pp. UnP 72

_____. **THE PROGRESS OF INSIGHT**, $2.50. See the Buddhism section.

SECHRIST, ELSIE. **MEDITATION—GATEWAY TO LIGHT**, $1.50. An inspirational trea[tise] tise by a woman closely associated with the Edgar Cayce work. 52pp. ARE 64

SHADDOCK, E.H. **AN EXPERIMENT IN MINDFULNESS**, $2.95. Describes Rear Admira[l] Shaddock's practice of Satipatthana, a Buddhist exercise in mindfulness, under a Burmes[e] meditational master, Mahasi Sayadaw. This is not a dry text book, but a living account o[f] the three weeks he spent at the center, the people he met, what he did and the effect i[t] had upon him. Recommended for those who get bogged down in books full of Sanskri[t] and Pali terms. 158pp. Wei 58

SHASTRI, HARI PRASAD. **MEDITATION, ITS THEORY AND PRACTICE**, $1.20. Clea[r] instructions on meditation for both the beginner and the more advanced student. Includes the psychological and spiritual principles on which meditation is based. 64pp. ShS 3[6]

SIVANANDA, SWAMI. **CONCENTRATION AND MEDITATION**, c$5.75. A very prac[ti]tical text detailing the steps to the meditative state including excellent information on the theory and practice of concentration; the preliminaries for meditation; the practice o[f] meditation; kinds of meditation; physical, mental and higher obstacles in meditation; and meditational experiences. Sivananda was one of the most noted Swamis of this century and was the guru to Swamis Satchidananda and Vishnudevananda. He writes very clearly and to the point. All his books, especially this one, are recommended. Glossary. 423pp. DLS 54

_____. **THOUGHT POWER**, $1.35. An analysis of thought power: its physics and philosophy; its laws and its dynamics; functions, values and uses; development; varieties of thoughts; methods of thought control; thought-transcendence; and thought-power and God realization. Includes philosophy and practical instruction. 152pp. DLS 63

SMITH, BRADFORD. **MEDITATION: THE INWARD ART**, $3.50. A Quaker's treatise on meditation: what it is and how to do it; the different forms of meditation—Hindu, Buddhist, and Zen; group meditation and Quaker meetings; and some meditations. 224pp. Lip 63

STONE, JUSTIN. **JOYS OF MEDITATION**, $3.50. A treatise which covers various kinds of Eastern meditation techniques. Detailed instructions are given which should be adequate for the beginner, but it's a pretty scattered volume. Illustrations, glossary. 95pp. SnB 73

STREET, NOEL and JUDY DUPREE. **HOW TO MEDITATE PERFECTLY**, $1.95. The title of this book is somewhat deceptive. Meditation is discussed throughout, however the strictly instructional material is limited to a few pages. Most of the text is devoted to a philosophical and psychological discussion of meditation, and an exploration of spiritual and psychic development. Nothing is discussed in depth, but many topics, such as the chakras, karma, and healing, are briefly reviewed. The text is Christian-oriented. 93pp. LoA 73

SUJATA. **BEGINNING TO SEE**, $2.50. A collection of epigrams about living in the world by an American who was a Buddhist monk and now runs the Stillpoint Institute: *thoughts are not necessarily connected with reality. That is why the Buddha taught us to be aware of them before we are influenced by them. . . . To be free we must be comfortable in being someone, anyone or no one at any time in any place . . . each morning, if we commit ourselves to finding the truth of every situation then miracles will come to us all day long. . . . Your pain can be the breaking of the shell which encloses your understanding.* The book is hand written and illustrated and is filled with many gems. UnP 75

SUZUKI, SHUNRYU. **ZEN MIND, BEGINNER'S MIND—INFORMAL TALKS ON ZEN MEDITATION AND PRACTICE**, c$4.95/2.95. See section on Zen Buddhism. Wea 70

SWEARER, DONALD. **SECRETS OF THE LOTUS**, $1.95. Discusses meditation within both the Satipatthana (Theravada) and Zazen (Zen) traditions, employing classical texts with explanatory commentary and contemporary exposition. A final chapter discusses the responses of university students to an experimental meditation workshop employing these techniques. Glossary. 235pp. McM 71

TARTHANG TULKU, ed. **CALM AND CLEAR**, $4.75. Translations of two Tibetan meditational texts which were done by Tarthang Tulku and his students who run a meditation center in Berkeley, California. They were especially chosen to make the depth and subtlety of Tibetan Buddhism available to the West. Both texts are short, relatively simple, practice-oriented, and emphasize a step-by-step development which begins at the most fundamental level. A long introduction and extensive commentary on the root verses help to clarify the teaching. A beautiful presentation. We recommend it highly. Dha 73

_____. **CRYSTAL MIRROR, VOL. III**, $4.75. See Tibetan Buddhism section.

TEMPLE, SEBASTIAN. **HOW TO MEDITATE**, c$6.50. An excellent practical guide to several yoga techniques of meditation, including an extensive section on kundalini. Very clear instructions. 177pp. Rad 71

THERA, NYANAPONIKA. **THE HEART OF BUDDHIST MEDITATION**, $3.95. See the Buddhism section. 223pp. Wei 62

_____. **THE POWER OF MINDFULNESS**, $2.25. See the Buddhism section. UnP

TRANSCENDENTAL MEDITATION

BLOOMFIELD, HAROLD. **TM—DISCOVERING INNER ENERGY AND OVERCOMING STRESS**, $1.95. There has been an incredible outpouring lately of books about meditation in general and Transcendental Meditation in particular. This is the most extensive *authorized* treatise on the subject and it has been very popular, even reaching the best seller list. This, like all other TM books, is not a how-to manual. Rather it is a description of the technique, its applications, and its effects from a psychological and physiological point of view. All of the authors have had extensive experience with TM and they present a scholarly study which is backed up by charts, diagrams, and references. Index, 290pp. Del 75

CAMPBELL, ANTHONY. **SEVEN STATES OF CONSCIOUSNESS**, $1.95. Subtitled *A Vision of Possibilities Suggested by the Teaching of Maharishi Mahesh Yogi*, this is a fine exploration of the common ground between science and mystical religion, illustrated by quotations from the Maharishi's writings and the literature of mysticism, as well as from scientists and humanistic psychologists such as Maslow. The author has been practicing TM since 1967 and he incorporates his personal experiences into the exposition. Bibliography, 181pp. H&R 74

_____. **TM AND THE NATURE OF ENLIGHTENMENT**, $1.95. This volume goes far beyond the usual treatises on TM and delves into an examination of the dangers inherent in the rigid separation in the West between the spiritual and material worlds and how this dichotomy can be resolved. It is a sophisticated presentation which reveals some of the complexities of the Maharishi's thought and of the TM process. Modern science and mystical thought are examined in depth and reconciled. An interesting study, originally published in Great Britain as **The Mechanics of Enlightenment**. Notes, bibliography, index, 223pp. H&R 75

DENNISTON, DENISE and P. McWILLIAMS. **THE TM BOOK**, $3.95/1.95. This account, illustrated with many simple line drawings, graphs, and tables, is designed to turn the reader on to the practice of TM. The material covered is usually in the form of questions and answers and is divided into the following areas: What TM Is Not, What TM Is, What TM Does, Learning TM (this section says you must learn it personally from a trained teacher, and does not explain how to learn it), and TM—Solution to All Problems. The book is very well thought of by the TM organization and it does seem to give a better feel for the approach and its basis than any other work we've seen. It's a good presentation as long as you don't mind books with a lot of hype. The book has been very popular. 224pp. PSS 75

EBON, MARTIN. **MAHARISHI**, $1.50. A collection of essays and articles on *his life/his times/his teachings/his impact* from a variety of sources. 159pp. NAL 62

FOREM, JACK. **TRANSCENDENTAL MEDITATION**, $3.50/1.95. This is *the* approved introduction to TM and the Science of Creative Intelligence. Forem traces the growth of Maharishi's worldwide movement, explains the principles of SCI in great detail, and reviews the scientific research on TM. He also points out the practical application of TM and SCI and draws parallels between the teachings of Maharishi and the insights of modern-day physics, education, psychology and other disciplines. Forem began practicing TM in 1967 and has been teaching it since 1970. 274pp. Dut 73

GIBSON, WILLIAM. **A SEASON IN HEAVEN**, $1.50. This is Gibson's log of the time he spent studying Transcendental Meditation with 1,000 young people and the Maharishi in Spain. Part narrative, part essay, it includes descriptions of students and the Maharishi at work—but underlying the work is Gibson's effort to track down what the mystics mean by *cosmic consciousness*. This *hunt* makes an illuminating tale and the author has succeeded in presenting as good a picture of the Maharishi and his teaching as we have read anywhere. One point of caution, this is definitely not a how-to book. 182pp. Ban 74

HEMINGWAY, PATRICIA. **THE TRANSCENDENTAL MEDITATION PRIMER**, $1.95. This is a very personal account of the author's experience in Transcendental Meditation. The technique, introductory and advanced lectures and initiation are all explored in depth. From there Ms. Hemingway reviews the benefits she and others experienced in the following areas: energy and stress, sleep, work, creativity, overcoming destructive habits, physical impact, sex and love, relating to others, and learning. A final section discusses the residence course and asanas (or postures). While the author is obviously pro-TM, she still gives a fairly objective account backed up with the latest research findings. And the personal, first-person style makes for easy reading. Notes, index, 382pp. Del 75

KANELLAKOS, DEMETRI and JEROME LUKAS. **THE PSYCHOBIOLOGY OF TRANSCENDENTAL MEDITATION**, $4.40. This is a comprehensive review of the published and unpublished scientific and popular literature up to about January, 1974 on Transcendental Meditation. Each of the studies is summarized—and in many cases extensively so. Oversize, indices, 171pp. MIU 74

KROLL, UNA. **THE HEALING POTENTIAL OF TRANSCENDENTAL MEDITATION**, $3.95. Dr. Kroll is an English physician who has written on spiritual healing and prayer and on topics related to the Christian church. Here she explores the similarities and differences between TM and Christian prayer and strongly advocates the benefits of TM. She also explores and reacts to the claims of the TM organization from the standpoint of a Christian and a medical doctor. The approach in this volume differs greatly from the other books on TM. Notes, bibliography, 176pp. Kno 74

MAHARISHI MAHESH YOGI. **MAHARISHI ON THE GITA**, $2.95. See Indian Philosophy section. Pen 67

_____. **TRANSCENDENTAL MEDITATION—SERENITY WITHOUT DRUGS**, c$10.00/3.95/1.75. Formerly titled **The Science of Being and Art of Living**. The Maharishi has attempted to disseminate a simple method of deep meditation which is systematic and productive of measurable and predictable results to the widest audience. He has dedicated his life to the goal of the spiritual regeneration of the world. This is his major work to date. It presents the ancient Vedic wisdom in understandable Western terms which guide the student to peace and increased awareness. 320pp. MIU 63, NAL 63

McWILLIAMS, PETER. **THE TM PROGRAM: A BASIC HANDBOOK**, $1.95. The bulk of the book graphically cites and analyzes the research that has been done and the rest of the book describes exercises and discusses techniques and philosophy. Pretty slim pickings—useful for those who want to read everything there is on TM. Non-critical. 128pp. Faw 76

ROBBINS, J. and DAVID FISHER. **TRANQUILITY WITHOUT PILLS (ALL ABOUT TRANSCENDENTAL MEDITATION)**, $1.75. The first major investigation of TM. It deals with what TM is, how to meditate, how TM works, people who meditate. It also includes an extensive chapter entitled *Everything You Need to Know About TM* and one on the author's personal TM experiences. 163pp. Ban 72

WHITE, JOHN. **EVERYTHING YOU WANT TO KNOW ABOUT TM INCLUDING HOW TO DO IT**, $1.95. The title speaks for itself. It is more critical than most accounts and does include instructions, of sorts. It is also fairly well written. Glossary, bibliography. 191pp. S&S 76

TRUNGPA, CHOGYAM, ed. **THE FOUNDATIONS OF MINDFULNESS**, $3.95. See the Tibetan subsection of Buddhism.

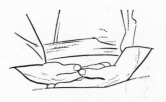

_____. **MEDITATION IN ACTION**, $2.25. Chogyam Trungpa is the former abbot of a Tibetan monastery. He is a meditation master in the Kagyupa and Nyingmapa lineages. He has established two meditation centers: Tail of the Tiger in Vermont and Karma Dzong in Boulder, Colorado. This book is a classic on the subject of meditation, recommended by teachers of all paths. It presents various aspects of meditation in a very clear manner. 74pp. ShP 69

_____. **THE MYTH OF FREEDOM AND THE WAY OF MEDITATION**, $3.95. See the Tibetan subsection of Buddhism.

WATTS, ALAN. **MEDITATION**, c$3.95/1.25. Thoughts to meditate upon plus a series of illustrations. It's a pretty gift book rather than a full treatment of the subject. Many associated topics are discussed such as incense and chanting. 63pp. CeA 74

WHITE, JOHN, ed. **WHAT IS MEDITATION**, $2.95. A good selection of essays on various methods of meditation written by experienced meditators which gives the reader a comparative approach so that s/he can experiment with different techniques and then delve more deeply into whichever one feels best. Practical techniques as well as theory are offered. Contributors include: Alan Watts, Swami Chinmayananada, Gopi Krishna, Claudio Naranjo, Robert de Ropp, Chogyam Trungpa, and Joel Goldsmith. 276pp. Dou 74

WILLIS, JANICE. **THE DIAMOND LIGHT—AN INTRODUCTION TO TIBETAN BUDDHIST MEDITATION**, $2.45. See the Tibetan subsection of Buddhism. S&S 72

WILSON, JIM. **FIRST STEPS IN MEDITATION FOR YOUNG PEOPLE**, $1.15. A collection of Christian, inspirational sayings designed to help young people realize God through personal experience. 43pp. Cla 57

WOOD, ERNEST. **CONCENTRATION**, $1.50. A practical manual by a Theosophist who has written extensively on yoga and Indian philosophy. It outlines the art of concentration and mind control as a first step leading to the deeper experience of meditation. Many exercises are included. 154pp. TPH 49

MUSIC

HALL, MANLY P. **THE THERAPEUTIC VALUE OF MUSIC**, $1.50. Transcription of a lecture on music therapy as practiced in a variety of cultures from ancient times to the present. Emphasis is placed on the Greek and Egyptian usages. 45pp. PRS 55

HEINDEL, MAX. **THE MUSICAL SCALE AND THE SCHEME OF EVOLUTION**, $1.25. 96pp. Ros 49

_____. **MYSTERIES OF THE GREAT OPERAS**, c$3.50. An esoteric analysis of **Faust, Parsifal, The Ring of the Niebelung, Tannhauser**, and **Lohengrin**. Index, 176pp. Ros 21

HELINE, CORINNE. **BEETHOVEN'S NINE SYMPHONIES AND NINE SPIRITUAL MYSTERIES**, $3.95. A unique description of the spiritual significance of Beethoven's great compositions in their relation to the nine spiritual mysteries. 77pp. NAP

_____. **COLOR AND MUSIC IN THE NEW AGE**, $2.95. See the Color and Aura section.

_____. **THE COSMIC HARP**, c$4.50. *The whole solar system is one vast musical instrument. . . . The signs of the Zodiac may be said to be the sounding board of the cosmic harp and the seven planets are the strings; they emit different sounds as they pass through the various signs and therefore, they influence mankind in a diverse manner.* —Max Heindel. This book analyzes both the signs and noted musicians born under them. 99pp. NAP 69

_____. **ESOTERIC MUSIC, BASED ON THE MUSICAL SEERSHIP OF RICHARD WAGNER**, c$4.50. An original portrayal of the music of Wagner as the expression of grand, celestial rhythms and harmonies brought to earth for human inspiration. Wagner's striking conceptions convey the depth of the human soul and reveal the drama of the ancient temple mysteries in a new way. 274pp. NAP

_____. **HEALING AND REGENERATION THROUGH MUSIC**, $1.00. A fine introduction to the philosophy behind the therapeutic and beneficial effects of music with some practical suggestions and methods for applying the techniques. 40pp. NAP 68

_____. **MUSIC—THE KEYNOTE OF HUMAN EVOLUTION**, c$4.95. A beautiful explanation of the importance of music and its role as a symbol of human evolution. All manifestations can be expressed as portions of a cosmic symphony, says the author, who with keen insight and a depth of understanding explores the history of music, its expression in various cultures and times, and its significance and potential at the dawn of a new era. 144pp. NAP 65

JEANS, JAMES. **SCIENCE AND MUSIC**, $3.35. This is an excellent physical analysis of musical sounds. The discussion begins with an explanation of the development of the human faculty of hearing. It is established that each sound can be represented by a curve. An examination of the general properties of sound curves follows. Questions on the transmission and reproduction of sound curves are answered in a discussion of tuning forks and pure tones. The various methods of producing sound, and the qualities of the sound produced, are further discussed as they relate to vibrations of strings and harmonics, and vibrations of air. Harmony and discord are also considered. In the final chapters on the concert room and hearing, the discussion focuses on the transmission of sound from its source in the eardrum and from the eardrum to the brain. A general theory of acoustics is also covered as well as acoustical analyses. Many illustrations, index. 258pp. Dov 37

KHAN, HAZRAT INAYAT. **MUSIC**, $2.95. See the Islam section.

_____. **THE MYSTICISM OF SOUND**, $2.00. *Every Sacred Scripture, every Holy Picture, every spoken word produces the impression of its identity upon the mirror of the soul, but Music stands before the soul without producing any impression whatever of either name or form of this objective world, thus preparing the soul to realize the Infinite.* This small treatise is excerpted from Khan's larger work with the same name and is divided into the following topics: the silent life, vibrations, harmony, name, form, rhythm, music, abstract sound. 94pp. HeR 23

SCOTT, CYRIL. **MUSIC: ITS SECRET INFLUENCE THROUGHOUT THE AGES**, c$5.00. A fascinating investigation into the esoteric implications of music. Scott, himself a noted composer, first discusses pure music, inspiration and invention in the sphere of Western music; and then the music of the Deva (spirit intelligences) is considered in relation to the occult constitution of man and the lives and work of various composers. An historical section traces the beginnings of music and religion and their combined effects on classical civilizations of the past. Includes a good bibliography. 208pp. Wei

SHANKAR, RAVI. **MY MUSIC—MY LIFE**, $2.95. A good basic introduction to North Indian music including information on history, theory, and instruments. Some autobiographical material is also included and a final section gives detailed instructions on how to play a sitar. Oversize, glossary. 160pp. SYS 68

STEBBING, LIONEL, ed. **MUSIC—ITS OCCULT BASIS AND HEALING VALUE**, $9.10. An excellent, comprehensive selection of writings on music in the light of Rudolf Steiner's Spiritual Science (see Steiner section) by people in diverse disciplines. 212pp. NKB 58

_____. **MUSIC THERAPY**, $7.70. This compilation is arranged according to ailments and also including a few longer articles. The contributors are almost all followers of Rudolf Steiner and his research is included. Each of the selections is only a paragraph or so long. 96pp. NKB 76

STRAVINSKY, IGOR. **POETICS OF MUSIC**, $1.95. Six lessons which provide a glimpse into the thought processes of Stravinsky's mind. Topics include the phenomenon of music, the composition of music, music typology, leading Russian musicians, and the performance of music. 149pp. HUP 42

SZEKELY, EDMUND. **LUDWIG VON BEETHOVEN**, $1.75. Szekely thinks of Beethoven as a superman, a hero, a revolutionary—or, as he states it, *a Prometheus of the modern world, suffering, creating, and eternal.* This short study is divided into the following chapters: *The Enchanted Prometheus, Hero and Revolutionary, His Musical Ancestors, His Life, His Works, The Fifth Symphony, The Ninth Symphony, The Last Days.* 23pp. Aca 73

WINSTON, SHIRLEY. **MUSIC AS THE BRIDGE**, $1.75. Selections from the Cayce readings which reveal what Cayce had to say about music in all its forms. Ms. Winston provides connective material. 68pp. ARE 72

ZUCKERKANDL, VICTOR. **THE SENSE OF MUSIC**, $3.45. This is a detailed study which could easily be used as a textbook. The material is very clearly presented and, while it is recommended only to those who are deeply interested in music, it does contain a great deal of basic information. The information is divided into the following general categories: melody, texture and structure, meter and rhythm, polyphony, harmony, and harmony and melody. Index, notes, 246pp. PUP 59

_____. **SOUND AND SYMBOL: MUSIC AND THE EXTERNAL WORLD**, $3.95. *Mr. Zuckerkandl believes that music has a special kind of reality; it is outside us, it takes place in the external world, but it is neither a physical phenomenon nor a projection of psychic states; we cannot trace what we hear in music to the properties of sound waves, nor can we call it a hallucination in which psychological responses become objectified. Music conceived in this way has important implications for metaphysical philosophy: it insists upon a broad conception of the external world, and the examples it provides of motion and time and space become as significant as those of science.* — **The Musical Quarterly**. Notes, bibliography, index. 399pp. PUP 59

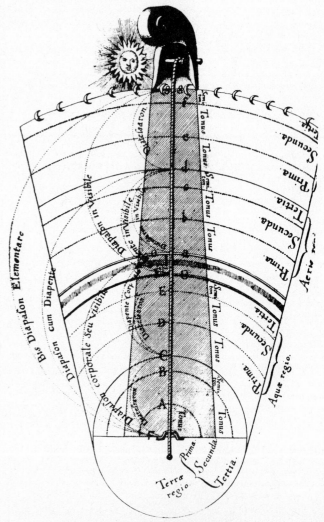

The Divine Monochord

MYSTICISM

Mysticism is the experience of an all-embracing Reality that pervades and transcends the world of phenomena in which we live our earthly lives. The mystic is one who has had this experience and whose life has been transformed by it. This transformation is made manifest by more perfect living and a heightened awareness of relationships.

The experience is one of an expanded consciousness, and it is right at the outset to consider some aspects of consciousness as they concern man. One of the most important qualities of living things is their tendency to react, or respond, to outside and interior stimuli. This response is the outer manifestation of consciousness. All living cells have their own consciousness, and in the higher animals there is an awareness of the immediate environment and an intelligent response to it. In man there is in addition a brooding self-consciousness, for he is a reflecting being. He reflects not only about the outside world but also about himself, his relationship with other men, and his future actions. Animals appear to be much more a part of their environment than does man, who is alienated from nature and is a wanderer on the path of life. He is a creature of isolation, and he fears the unknown which he can sense as the wholly other, but which he cannot understand. Man's evolution of consciousness to self-awareness is described mythologically in the story of the Fall in the Book of Genesis.

Man's conscious life is related to that aspect called mind, or psyche. Both words are confusing; indeed consciousness itself can be described only in terms of its manifestations. The word mind has been restricted to the thinking, or intellectual, function by some psychologists, and psyche literally means soul. Nevertheless, in this account these two words will be used to embrace all those aspects of consciousness which manifest themselves in volition, thought, and feeling.

The psyche is pluridimensional, as Assagioli points out in his book **Psychosynthesis** (*Pages 16-20*). The central point is the conscious self or *I*. It is also called the personal or existential self. This is the point of self-awareness, and is unfortunately not known to many. It makes its existence felt in times of crisis and decision, particularly when unpleasant choices of a moral nature have to be made, choices between doing what we know is morally wrong but expedient and doing what is morally right but contrary to the general feeling of the society in which we work. This self can also be experienced in meditation when we move beyond the identification we usually have with our body, our emotions, and our thoughts. It is then that a centre of pure self-awareness is experienced. Unfortunately most of us do not know ourselves, and are moved hither and thither by outside circumstances or inner drives and impulses. When we are in command of our bodies, emotions, and thoughts the conscious self is ruling. Its action is the will. Most of the actions that we make are not willed at all, but are really passive movements in response to outer or inner circumstances, as already noted. The will is of great importance and is to be defined as the action of the conscious self.

Surrounding the conscious self there is a field of consciousness of which we are directly aware. It comprises the incessant flow of ideas, impulses, feelings, and thoughts which we can observe and judge. Outside the field of consciousness there are psychic contents of which we are not immediately aware, and this vast realm of the psyche is rather confusingly called the unconscious. Some of its contents resemble those of the field of consciousness and are under easy recall by the memory, but many of these contents are so powerfully submerged, or repressed, that they are hidden persistently from the field of consciousness. This great realm, called the lower unconscious, is the preserve of the psychoanalyst. In it are stored the primitive urges and fundamental drives such as survival, sex, and aggressiveness, and also painful memories too unpleasant to be faced directly. They may be released during sleep when they are exteriorised, usually symbolically, as dreams.

But there is another part of the unconscious called the higher unconscious or the superconscious. It is high in that its drives are more exalted than are those of the lower unconscious. They tend towards man's realisation of his own humanity, and include humanitarian, ethical, heroic, altruistic, and aesthetic actions and ideals. It must be admitted that the superconscious is not acknowledged as such by most psychoanalysts. They would explain its highly-valued impulses merely as sublimations of the lower unconscious which can no longer be satisfied. Thus altruism is *explained* as thwarted aggression, and aesthetic appreciation attributed to unsatisfied sexual desires. But the impulses of the superconscious are spontaneous and unexpected. They break into consciousness suddenly as intuition, inspiration, creative imagining, compassion, and love (not merely personal but also universal). The scientific *breakthrough* is often due to a sudden inspiration on the part of the research worker. It is in geniuses that the superconscious shows itself most emphatically. Most of these are gifted in one particular way, and it would appear that the particular superconscious impulse (such as musical composition or mathematics) impinges on their field of consciousness. The great universal geniuses gifted in many fields (such as Leonardo da Vinci and Goethe) would appear to have their field of consciousness permanently elevated into the superconscious realms of the psyche.

Surrounding and interpenetrating the personal unconscious is what Jung calls the collective unconscious. No man is an island, for we are all in psychic communication with one another, and the collective unconscious includes the shared experience of the race extending from its primitive beginning up to the present time. It includes primitive archaic structures and also forward-looking activities of a superconscious character.

The great injunction of the Delphic oracle was, *Know thyself*. We begin to know ourselves in the moral crises that have already been mentioned. Through the painful progress of life and its many experiences unconscious depths are revealed to us. Psychoanalytic theory (if not therapy), especially the Jungian type, is very helpful in this respect. But there are times when a greater reality of self is revealed to us. It is, as it were, for a moment that the enclosed, isolated personal self, so aware of its separation, opens out to reveal something far greater than itself. It becomes luminous, extensive, all-embracing yet free. The sense of separation has changed into one of intimate communion with all other selves, and yet the identity of the self is clearer and more beautiful than ever. This is the experience of the Higher Self, also called the Spiritual Self, or the Transpersonal Self. It is the heart of mysticism, and the aim of the mystic journey is to discover the true Self and learn of its relationship with the universe and with God.

It would appear from this account that we have two selves, a personal existential self and a spiritual transpersonal one. This is true in appearance, but in reality there is only one self, the Spiritual Self, which forms the highest point of the superconscious. In everyday life its image is reflected dully in the outer personality as the existential self. But when life is lived abundantly, in the context that Jesus spoke of, the existential self becomes bright and radiant, approaching closer and closer to its source, the Spiritual Self. In mystical experience the two selves coincide, and in the highest development of mysticism, the Unitive Life, the mystic lives continually at the level of his Spiritual Self.

The Spiritual Self is called the soul in religious literature. The famous question of Mark 8: 36, *What shall it profit a man if he gain the whole world and lose his own soul?* is translated in the New English Bible thus, *What does a man gain by winning the whole world at the cost of his true self?* The soul is the essence of the person, and shines most clearly when the outer trappings of personality have been shed. This occurs partially in times of crisis and fully during mystical experience. The main qualities of the soul, which is the highest part of the mind, are abstract reasoning, intuitive understanding, and spiritual realisation. This is a direct grasp, through illumination, of the nature and destination of the journey that it undertakes to its own completion.

According to the teaching of the mystics there is a point called the *apex of the soul* or the *centre of the soul*. This is the Spirit, the highest and holiest part of the Spiritual Self. It is that aspect of Reality immanent in all created things. It is through the Spirit that we know of that which is called God in the Western theistic tradition. In the Vedanta Spirit is the Atman, which is identical with Brahman, Ultimate Reality. The Spirit is therefore both within the individual psyche (or mind) and outside it. It is through the shared Spirit that mystical unity is realised.

—from AN **APPROACH TO MYSTICISM** by Martin Israel

"Hear without terror that in the forest are hidden a deer and an unicorn.
In the body there is soul and spirit."

ACHAD, FRATER. ANCIENT MYSTICAL WHITE BROTHERHOOD, $4.00. *This book is prepared with a sacred reverence to the Great Spiritual Teachers who have preceded us in life on earth and whose endless task is to point to the base of reference for mankind, to which he must become oriented.... The chapters of this book represent a record of such guidance which has come to certain individuals who were sincerely seeking it, not for self alone, but to share that knowledge.* 174pp. CSA 74

_____. **MELCHIZEDEK TRUTH PRINCIPLES**, $4.50. See Inspiration section.

ALDER, VERA STANLEY. THE FIFTH DIMENSION, $3.50. See Meditation section.

_____. **THE FINDING OF THE THIRD EYE**, $3.50. One of the best overall introductions to the field of the esoteric sciences. The author employs her rare gift of accurate summarizing and couples it with vision and an inclusive grasp of today's problems. A practical application of the Ageless Wisdom teachings to enrich our lives both individually and collectively is outlined by a survey of breathing, color, diet, astrology, numbers and sound plus essential information concerning the inner Path. 187pp. Wei 38

_____. **THE INITIATION OF THE WORLD**, $3.75. As a short, comprehensive sketch of that body of teachings called the Ageless Wisdom or Perennial Philosophy, this book is easily one of the best. Includes excellent chapters on reincarnation, evolution, initiation, the Hierarchy, Shamballa, and the passage of the Secret Wisdom down the ages. Closes with a comparison of those teachings with the recent discoveries of modern science. 251pp. Wei 39

_____. **THE SECRET OF THE ATOMIC AGE**, $3.50. In this book the subject of man's transmutation is considered and his emergence from the chrysalis of matter into the illimitable regions of his own being. The enlightening discussion revolves around the problem of releasing the atomic energy which comprises the essential human being. This is a process of liberation and the achievement of true freedom which is the evolutionary transformation of man into the status of immortal divinity. 191pp. Wei 58

_____. **WHEN HUMANITY COMES OF AGE**, $3.50. The human race hovers on the verge of extraordinary possibilities and achievement. We are coming out of our adolescence and entering adult maturity. With this as her theme, the author outlines man's history by revealing the inner secrets which conditioned it. She gives us practical suggestions and information that can lead to a more fulfilled life while aiding in the dissolution of much that today holds the human family in bondage to an obsolete past. 233pp. Wei 56

_____. **WISDOM IN PRACTICE**, $3.00. Using reasonable methods and logical processes the author shows the imperative requirement that will lead the family of man out of the present period of conflict. This requirement is simply the fulfillment of the law of love. Wisdom and love are one and the same thing. They are divine energies and states of consciousness available to all men and women. With convincing psychological clarity we are led to the essence of spiritual discovery by self analysis and honest observation. 177pp. Wei 70

ANGEBERT, JEAN-MICHEL. THE OCCULT AND THE THIRD REICH, $3.95. Rather than being merely another book on occultism and Hitler's Third Reich, this is an excellent survey of the ancient mystery tradition in Western Europe. The volume begins with an account of the search for the Grail and a clear explanation of the meaning of the Grail and the neo-pagan crusade against the Grail. This is followed by a review of the Aryan myth of the beginnings and a study of the development of gnosis (or supreme knowledge) in the Zoroastrian and Manichean schools and an analysis of Christianity and gnosis. Another chapter reviews the centers of initiation and secret esoteric orders. A final section shows how all the previously discussed material led directly to the rise of Hitler. It

begins with a full discussion of Nietzsche and *superman*, followed by an interpretative analysis of Wagner. After this there's a review of the secret origins of Nazism and the Hitlerian cosmogony. Final sections relate some of the esoteric events during Hitler's hegemony. This is a fascinating serious study, with extensive textual notations. Jean-Michel Angebert is the joint signature of Michel Bertrand and Jean Angelini, two French scholars who have extensively researched the role of mystic cults in European history. Lewis Sumberg, the translator, holds his doctorate in French medieval history and literature from the University of Paris. Index, bibliography. 325pp. MGH 74

ANRIAS, DAVID. THROUGH THE EYES OF THE MASTERS, c$5.95. An intriguing book that contains sketched portraits of ten masters of the wisdom with a message from each of them concerning different aspects of modern life and the spiritual path. 87pp. Wei 32

ARGUELLES, JOSE. THE TRANSFORMATIVE VISION, $6.95. **The Transformative Vision** combines history and myth, psychology and art, to provide a major new assessment of the role of creativity in human behavior. Man's psyche—the primary intuitive being—is seen in conflict with his techne—the side that creates order. When these two sides of man's nature are in harmony, the author explains, aesthetic activity flourishes. Dr. Arguelles traces the history of human expression from the Renaissance to the present, arguing that modern history is characterized by an increasing repression of man's psychic self by the technical side of his nature. Notes, index, bibliography. 368pp. ShP 75

AZRAEL. FIRST BOOK OF AZRAEL, $4.00. This series was received as channeled messages from the Great White Brotherhood or Spiritual Hierarchy of our planet. They contain teachings concerning the deeper life with practical instruction. A blend of head and heart for the sincere aspirant. 189pp. DeV 65

BACHEMAN, WILLIAM. THE STEINERBOOKS DICTIONARY OF THE PSYCHIC, MYSTIC AND OCCULT, $2.25. The newest of the metaphysical dictionaries, and also the most concise. The definitions are clear and the cross-references ample. Illustrations. 235+pp. Mul 73

BAKER, DOUGLAS. ANTHROPOGENY, $12.00. An esoteric history of man's origins, divided into sections on man, time, and fossils, cosmogenesis, the coming of man, and the early root races. The format is the same as Baker's other big books and as usual there is an abundance of illustrations, both color and black-and-white, and some fold-out charts. Bak 75

_____. **ESOTERIC PSYCHOLOGY**, $17.00. A detailed, albeit scattered, analysis of esoteric psychology based on the seven rays divided into the following sections: the need for an esoteric psychology, the seven rays—their nature, origin, and function, rays of aspect, rays of attribute, and ray analysis. The format is the same as Baker's other big books and many color illustrations are included. Index, 168pp. Bak 75

_____. **THE JEWEL IN THE LOTUS**, $12.50. Vol. 1 of **The Seven Pillars of Ancient Wisdom**, a series of 8x12" illustrated accounts. Dr. Baker's books are a bit hard to describe. The illustrations are generally in full color and deal with all aspects of esoteric psychology including information on the chakras, the rays, color, sound, and magnetism. The material on the seven rays is as extensive as any we've seen and the illustrations make the text more comprehensible. Baker seems to come out of the Theosophical/Arcane tradition (although we're not sure of this) and he is a physician, so a knowledge of occult anatomy is incorporated into the text. About 250pp. Bak 74

_____. **THE OPENING OF THE THIRD EYE**, $5.50. Baker begins with a survey of the references to the third eye throughout history and *the nature of the material out of which the third eye is fashioned*. This is followed by a discussion of *the equipment that fashions it*, and a detailed presentation of the techniques for opening the third eye. Many line drawings and a few color plates illustrate the text. 128pp. Bak nd

BLAIR, LAWRENCE. RHYTHMS OF VISION, c$8.95. This is an important new book which falls outside a restricted category and encompasses many disciplines. Dr. Blair is basically discussing energies in all forms of life and the correspondences between man and the natural world. He analyzes many of the phenomena generally classified under the rubric of the *occult* and shows how similar the ancient teachings are to the discoveries of scientists over the ages. Perhaps the most illuminating section of the book is Blair's extensive discussion of number and form, much of which is based on Rudolf Steiner and his disciples. There are also many beautiful illustrations. While Blair has done a fine job of researching and compiling a great deal of material, his presentation is scattered and not nearly as clearly written as we would like. 244pp. ScB 76

WILLIAM BLAKE

William Blake was born in London in 1757. He was a visionary from birth. Blake never attended school. He began drawing as a child, and apprenticed to an engraver at a young age. This training was to stand him in good stead. When no one else would publish his books, he made them himself. In fact, all of his books except one were what he called *Illuminated Printing*: hand drawn, engraved, and then colored by Blake and his wife. The art and the lettering form a whole and often the letters flow into and become part of the illustration—this combined with Blake's deliberately archaic language sometimes makes his exact words unclear. But perhaps this, too, is part of the style.

Blake's basic purpose in all his work was the discovery and recording of new truths about the human soul. These truths are often couched in a language and style which even the most serious student is hard put to understand. So at the reader *had* to put aside all previous conceptions, Blake invented his own mythology, his own style. He was not content to be read mindlessly, enjoyed easily—he wanted to force his reader to think along with him. Blake heartily embraced the idea that the ancients concealed the Divine Mysteries under symbols: *What is Grand is necessarily obscure to Weak men. That which can be made Explicit to the Idiot is not worth my care.* Blake's thought was *to open the immortal Eyes of Man inwards, into the Worlds of Thought.*

He believed a thought to be wholly true only the first time it is said. Blake's readers must dig, participate actively; thus Blake deliberately wrote unclearly, scattering clues throughout his writings. Even his simplest and clearest statements have vast implications behind them. He was so far ahead of his time that we are just beginning to understand and appreciate him. Many of his once strange theories are now commonplace to psychologists.

Blake is a monumental figure, whose unique combination of art and literature is his timeless contribution to our understanding of the human psyche.

Recording available; for description see Blake in Records section.

Portrait of Blake by John Linnell

BLAKE, WILLIAM. **BOOK OF JOB**, $4.95. See the Bibles section.

_____. **THE BOOK OF THEL**, c$10.00. A full color reproduction, along with a fully annotated text and an extensive introduction offering a new interpretation of the poem. 96pp. Oversize.

_____. **THE MARRIAGE OF HEAVEN AND HELL**, $10.00. This is considered by many to be Blake's most important philosophical work. The twenty-seven plates have been very carefully reproduced in color and Sir Geoffrey Keynes, doyen of Blake scholars, has written the introduction and a commentary on each of the plates. Also included are enlargements in color of the interlinear drawings. This is the first time that this work has been made available in the form in which Blake intended it to be read. *Through freely using satire and paradox, Blake gives in this book some of the most explicit statements of his mental attitudes. . . . Blake gave the qualities, Good and Evil, meanings opposite to their usual acceptation. . . . Angels and Devils change places, Good is Evil. Heaven is Hell.* Oxf 75

BLUNT, ANTHONY. **THE ART OF WILLIAM BLAKE**, $5.95. This is a general introduction to Blake's art, including summaries of his major doctrines and separate studies of each of his major works. A series of well over one hundred plates follows the text. The re-

productions are fairly good. The text is as simplified as anyone can make Blake's obstruse work and many quotations from the actual writings are included. Oversize, index, bibliography. 122pp. H&R 59

BRONOWSKI, J., ed. **WILLIAM BLAKE**, $1.95. This is a good selection of many of Blake's major poems and parts of his longer works as well as some of his letters. Both the early lyric poems and the later prophetic works are included. Introduction, index, 251pp. Pen 58

DAMON, S. FOSTER, ed. **BLAKE'S GRAVE: A PROPHETIC BOOK**, c$8.00. Blake's illustrations for Robert Blair's **The Grave**, arranged as Blake directed. With notes and a commentary by S. Foster Damon, the editor. Oversize, 45pp.

DIGBY, GEORGE. **SYMBOL AND IMAGE IN WILLIAM BLAKE**, c$16.15. *The right understanding of Blake's symbols and images is essential, for they are the language by means of which the intuitive imagination expresses itself, and for Blake this was a live language, not a dead one.*—from the introduction. 77 plates are illustrated and discussed at length. Chapter I is an elucidation of Blake's symbols and ideas presented in the form of a commentary on *The Gates of Paradise*, a pictorial treatise on the life of man. Chapter II is a study of the basis of visionary art, discussed with reference both to analytical psychology and Eastern religion. Notes, bibliography, index. 163+pp. Oxf 57

ERDMAN, DAVID, ed. **THE ILLUMINATED BLAKE**, $7.95. The wedding of poetry and painting in Blake's illuminated works was the result of his desire that readers be *spectators* as well. This oversize volume presents for the first time an edition of the entire illuminated canon, each plate selected for clarity of detail from among Blake's several original etched and painted copies, and each accompanied by descriptive and interpretative commentary by Erdman. All but the largest plates are reproduced in their original sizes. The commentary is uniformly excellent and this volume is probably the best single one for those interested in his imagery. Unfortunately all the plates are black-and-white with the exception of the cover—although color reproductions would make the cost of the volume prohibitive. Introduction, index, notes. 415pp. Dou 74

_____. **THE SELECTED POETRY OF BLAKE**, $2.50. An excellent selection of Blake's poems, taken from all periods of his life and from both major and minor works. Erdman is one of the finest current Blake scholars. Introduction, 332pp. NAL 76

ESSICK, ROBERT and JENIJOY LABELLE, eds. **NIGHT THOUGHTS OR, THE COMPLAINT AND THE CONSOLATION**, $4.00. A reproduction in its entirety of the four sections of Edward Young's poem **Night Thoughts**, illustrated with forty-three designs by the young William Blake. Blake's images of angels, spirits, poets, sensuous women, Life, Death, Reason, Truth, and others reveal Blake's artistic vision in its early stages. The editors contribute extensive commentary on the plates. Dov 75

JAMES, LAURA. **WILLIAM BLAKE AND THE TREE OF LIFE**, c$2.25. This is a highly esoteric interpretation of one of Blake's most deftly hidden doctrines: the doctrine of *the False Tongue beneath Beulah*. The volume quotes extensively from Blake's writings and interprets them in the light of Qabalistic teachings. Several illustrations are also included. The combination of Blake and the Qabala—both of which we have a hard time understanding—makes it a bit difficult to judge this volume. However, if you are into either subject this text should provide you with some interesting insights. 126pp. ShP 56

KAZIN, ALFRED, ed. **THE PORTABLE BLAKE**, $4.95. This is an excellent selection of Blake's work including selections from **Poetical Sketches**; the complete texts of **Songs of Innocence** and **Songs of Experience**; verses and fragments of poems from the years 1793–1810; selections from his letters; **The Prophetic Books** (this is the longest section); selections on art, money, and the age; some of his last works, including **The Book of Job** (with its illustrations); and selections from Crabb Robinson's **Reminiscences**. Kazin also provides a 55pp. introduction. Index, 713pp. Vik 68

KEYNES, GEOFFREY, ed. **BLAKE: COMPLETE WRITINGS**, $10.70. This is the definitive edition of Blake's writings. The writings are printed in chronological sequence, with a section of Blake's letters at the end, followed by notes. This edition includes substantive corrections and additions, lines are numbered, and Blake's designs are reproduced where they are essential to an understanding of the text. Sir Geoffrey prepared the first edition of Blake in three illustrated volumes in 1925. 944pp. Oxf 74

PALEY, MORTON. **ENERGY AND THE IMAGINATION**, c$15.00. *This book proposes to study the thought of William Blake as it developed from the works of his early maturity through his great culminating statement, **Jerusalem**. I have tried to see Blake in his time, and as having a deliberately chosen relationship to certain intellectual and literary traditions of the past. The principal aim is not the tracing of specific sources, but the provision of a background against which the unique figure of Blake stands more clearly outlined. . . . I have focused on two concepts, Energy and the Imagination, and have tried to show how these were defined in the several phases of Blake's thought.*—from the preface. Notes, index. 282pp. Oxf 70

PLOWMAN, MAX, ed. **BLAKE'S POEMS AND PROPHECIES**, $2.95. Includes the full texts of the following works: **Songs of Innocence** and **Songs of Experience**, **The Book of Thel**, **The Marriage of Heaven and Hell**, **Visions of the Daughters of Albion**, **Milton**, **Jerusalem**, and **The Gates of Paradise**. This volume also contains most of the works that remain in manuscript, including **The Last Judgment**, **The Everlasting Gospel**, and nearly forty other poems. **The Poetical Sketches** are also presented. The editor supplies notes, an introduction, a few illustrations, and a bibliography. 475pp. Dut 27

RAINE, KATHLEEN. **WILLIAM BLAKE**, $5.25. This is without question the finest *popularly priced* edition of Blake's art available. Ms. Raine is a well known Blake scholar and her fine text is supported by 156 plates, many in color. The reproduction is excellent. Index, 216pp. Pra 70

America: A Prophecy by William Blake, 1793. Orc in the fires of energy. For Blake, "War is energy enslav'd."

SINGER, JUNE. THE UNHOLY BIBLE, $4.75. This is a speculative study of Blake's life, poetry, and art in terms of Jungian archetypes. Black-and-white reproductions of the plates from **The Marriage of Heaven and Hell** are included and a large part of the text is devoted to an analysis of this poem. The other major section of the text is devoted to analyses of the later prophetic writings. Dr. Singer is a Jungian analyst. Notes, bibliography, index. 286pp. H&R 70

WOLF-GUMPOLD, KAETHE. WILLIAM BLAKE, c$4.95. *Three elements in Blake cohere and form a unity: his life, his poetry and his art. The understanding of one is often to be sought in the other, or both the others. Their unity is so close because all three stem from the same source, Blake's absolute loyalty to his spiritual vision. It is with these three inseparable elements that the present volume deals. There can be no better, indeed no other approach to Blake's genius.*—from the introduction by A.C. Harwood. Ms. Wolf-Gumpold is an Anthroposophist and she interprets Blake in the light of Rudolf Steiner's Spiritual Science. Twenty-three color plates and a great number of quotations from Blake's work accompany the interpretative text. Notes, bibliography, index. 164pp. RSP 69

BRANTL, GEORGE, ed. THE RELIGIOUS EXPERIENCE, c$17.40. *I have attempted to include representative writings from theory, personal narrative and fiction. . . . I have attempted to include complete stories where possible rather than parts of novels.* The four books which this mammoth tome is divided into constitute four modes or stages of religious experience. Book I: *The Image and the Idol* presents the way of immanence in which God is found inward to nature and identified somehow with the finite and with what man finds of value in this world. Book II: *Beyond the Gods* describes the way of transcendence in which the infinity of God is asserted in such a way that God is wholly other than the finite and is completely incommensurable with finite values. Book III: *In Place of God* discusses the atheistic and agnostic positions as alternatives to the theistic mode of religious experience. Book IV: *A Gift of Presence* questions the possibility of a new way of experience in which transcendence and immanence come together in such a way as to avoid the problems inherent in their separation. The editor has chosen his selections from a very wide range and he provides introductions to each selection. Boxed, two volumes, 1162pp. Brz 64

BRENNAN, J.H. ASTRAL DOORWAYS, c$6.50. A clear, absorbing presentation of concentration and visualization exercises which must be perfected before the reader attempts an astral journey. These are followed by the four main *Doorways* through which one arrives on the astral plane, namely: the five Tattva Symbols, the Tarot, the Qabala, the I Ching. Brennan devotes a chapter to the use of hypnosis, either alone, or in conjunction with one of the other *Doorways*. Ways of heightening the astral experience are also discussed. Many illustrations. 115pp. Wei 71

_____. **THE OCCULT REICH**, $1.50. This is the least scholarly of the books on this subject and it is the easiest to read. No notes or references back up the material and it's hard to say how accurate the portrayal is. A great deal of related material is included. 184pp. NAL 74

BROMAGE, BERNARD. IN TUNE WITH YOUR DESTINY, $1.00. A guidebook for daily living, with chapters on the meaning of life, how to outgrow self-pity, the awareness of being alive, and similar topics. 63pp. Wei 69

BROOKE, AVERY, ed. ROOTS OF SPRING, $4.95. An inspiring pictorial anthology about the creations of the earth and man's life on earth. The selections are very well chosen and the drawings add to the overall feeling. Oversize, 96pp. Vin 75

BRUNTON, PAUL. HERMIT IN THE HIMALAYAS, $3.50. Dr. Brunton was a British journalist who developed an interest in comparative religion, mysticism and philosophy. He travelled extensively in the Orient, living among yogis, mystics and holy men. His accounts are among the most enlightening and readable available. This volume is a blend of narrative, travel, and profound spiritual experience. Illuminating hints on yoga and the mystical practices of the East are conveyed to the reader against the backdrop of scenic descriptions and personal thoughts. 188pp. Wei 37

_____. **THE HIDDEN TEACHINGS BEYOND YOGA**, $4.00. *I have to put up with the fact that this new book is so different in character and tone from those which have preceded it that the general reader is going to have a difficult time should he plunge into it with the lightheartedness with which he may have plunged into the others. Its pages made hard writing for me and must make harder reading for others. It needs sustained and concentrated attention, demands keen thinking, and propounds tough problems. . . I deliberately emphasized the insufficiencies of ordinary mysticism, the defects of ordinary yogis and the mistakes commonly made by meditators.* 365pp. Wei 41

_____. **THE INNER REALITY**, $3.50. This work has been selected and expanded from addresses privately given before small audiences on four continents. Absolute clearness of exposition was sought rather than elaborate treatment of theme. Topics include what is God, a sane religion, practical help in yoga, psycho-spiritual self analysis, the Scripture of the yogis, errors of the spiritual seeker, the Gospel according to John, and the mystery of Jesus. 244pp. Wei 39

_____. **A MESSAGE FROM ARUNACHALA**, $3.00. Arunachala Hill, in South India, has a high status in Hindu sacred tradition. Ramana Maharshi, with whom Dr. Brunton studied, dwelt at the base of Arunachala. This volume is an application of the main teaching of Maharshi, the doctrine *Know Thyself*, and it is applied to various problems of modern life. 144pp. Wei 36

_____. **THE QUEST OF THE OVERSELF**, $3.50. See Meditation section.

_____. **A SEARCH IN SECRET EGYPT**, $3.50. See Ancient Egypt section.

_____. **A SEARCH IN SECRET INDIA**, $3.50. See Indian Philosophy section.

_____. **THE SECRET PATH**, $1.75. Brunton's first book, a practical spiritual handbook. *He presents a system of practice and meditation that should open new vistas of livingness for those who would glory in the consciousness of the immortal spiritual essence or Over-Self. Each of us who practices this secret inner way can become a disseminator of true light, can change himself and thus become fit to change others.*—Alice Bailey 128pp. Dut 35

_____. **THE SPIRITUAL CRISIS OF MAN**, $3.50. A detailed look at the plight of mankind today, and recommendations for transcending the materialism and intellectualism of our age. 224pp. Wei 52

_____. **THE WISDOM OF THE OVERSELF**, $3.75. Emphasizes the spiritual value and significance of sleep and dreams, the development of intuition, the universality of mind and the infinity of time and space as well as helpful information concerning meditation. 276pp. Wei 43

BUCKE, RICHARD. COSMIC CONSCIOUSNESS, c$2.98. A classic study in the evolution of the human mind, first published in 1901. In reviewing the mental and spiritual activity of the human race, Dr. Bucke discovers that at intervals certain individuals have appeared who are gifted with the power of transcendental realization or illumination. He devotes a chapter to the life and work of each of these individuals and provides excellent interpretative material. Recommended. 326pp. Cau 1900

BURNET, JOHN. EARLY GREEK PHILOSOPHERS, c$13.50. This is a detailed scholarly study with chapters on the Milesian School, science and religion, Herakleitos of Ephesos, Parmedies of Elea, Empedokles of Akragas, Anaxagoras of Klazomenai, the Pythagoreans, the younger Eleatics, Leukippos of Miletos. Index, 375pp. ACB 30

CASSIER, ERNST, PAUL KRISTELLER and JOHN RANDALL, eds. THE RENAISSANCE PHILOSOPHY OF MAN, $1.95. A review of three major currents of thought dominant in the earlier Italian Renaissance: classical humanism (Petrarch and Valla), Platonism (Ficino and Pico) and Aristotelianism (Pomponazzi). A short work of the Spanish Vives is included to exhibit the diffusion of the ideas of the humanists and Platonism outside Italy. In general the original texts are presented, in translation, with commentary, notes and introductory material. 405pp. UCh 48

CAVENDISH, RICHARD, ed. THE ENCYCLOPEDIA OF THE UNEXPLAINED, c$17.95. This is a unique reference book on all aspects of the esoteric sciences and parapsychology. The articles are written by experts in the area and are often in depth accounts giving background that is not readily available anywhere else. They are alphabetically arranged and cross-referenced and well illustrated. An index of people and book titles cites those too obscure to be covered by the extensive cross-referencing and a bibliography lists over 500 titles. At first glance this appears to be another flashy book on the *occult*—but this first impression is proved wrong. This is a useful addition to all serious collections of books in the area. Oversize, 304pp. MGH 74

CERMINARA, GINA. INSIGHTS FOR THE AGE OF AQUARIUS, $2.95. An excellent and illuminating examination of the problems of mankind's various religions from the perspective of a new scientific discipline called General Semantics. With keen aptitude the author separates dogma from the universal essence of religious experience and provides us with more precise knowledge and a means of reconciling and eliminating the schisms in human belief. 304pp. TPH 73

CANEY, EARLYN. **REMEMBERING**, c$8.95. This is a very personal autobiography detailing the author's search for spiritual awareness and of her experiences on the path. Ms. Chaney and her husband Robert were the founders of Astara and they remain the guiding forces in that organization. 382pp. NAP 74

CANEY, SHELDON. **MEN WHO HAVE WALKED WITH GOD**, $3.45. A sequence of finely developed biographical and interpretative studies of individual mystics from Lao Tse and the Buddha through Plato and Plotinus and Jacob Boehme to Brother Lawrence and William Blake. An excellent work for the general reader. Recommended. 403pp. Del 45

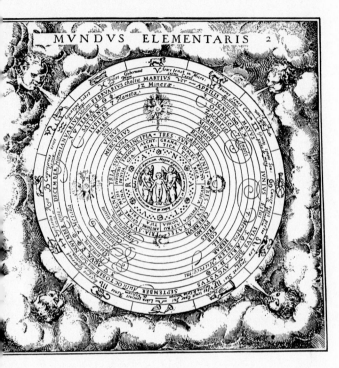

CROW, W.B. **THE ARCANA OF SYMBOLISM**, c$5.00. Includes symbology from classical mythology, the Old and New Testament, the Qabala, the Tarot, the Koran, the elements, the planets, and the zodiac. 96pp. Wei 70

DANTE. **THE INFERNO**, $1.50. Dante Alighieri is one of the greatest poets of all time. The **Inferno** presents a visionary journey through the nine circles of Hell, where anguished men and women expiate earthly sins of lust and greed, malice and betrayal, in varying degrees of torment. It may seem odd that we list this classic at all—and perhaps even odder that we classify it under Mysticism. And yet it is a classic account of the way of an individual soul from sin to purgatory and of the truths Dante revealed in the Middle Ages still pertain to today's confused world. This is an excellent poetic translation into modern English by John Ciardi, with notes, introduction, and background material. 288pp. NAL 54

_____. **DANTE'S INFERNO**, $6.95. This is a fine reproduction of the nineteenth century edition of the **Inferno** illustrated by Gustave Dore. The translator, Henry F. Cary, provides extensive footnotes. 8½x11", 183pp. TWC 76

_____. **THE PARADISO**, $1.50. Having passed through Hell and Purgatory, Dante is led through the upper sphere wherein lie the sublime truths of divine will and purpose. This is the most mystical of the three books, and the symbols of medieval Christianity mingle with those of classical antiquity; the boundaries of science, religion, and art are dissolved by a passionate unity of vision. 388pp. NAL 70

_____. **THE PURGATORIO**, $1.50. In this volume (the second) Dante describes his journey to the renunciation of sin. It is the journey upward toward God, and from the top of Purgatory Dante rises up to enter the presence of God with a soul that has been purified. In Purgatory individuals cleanse themselves from the *seven deadly sins* and rejoice as they purify themselves to receive divine love. 380pp. NAL 61

DAVIDSON, GUSTAV. **A DICTIONARY OF ANGELS, INCLUDING THE FALLEN ANGELS**, $4.95. A work of remarkable scholarship, the fruit of some fifteen years of research in Talmudic, gnostic, Qabalistic, apocalyptic, patristic, and legendary texts, among works of art and the range of literature. *Delightful reading and a unique reference work.*—Isaac Bashevis Singer. The sources for each entry are given and the bibliography is 24pp., double columns. Profusely illustrated. 386pp. McM

DAVIS, ROY EUGENE. **DARSHAN—THE VISION OF LIGHT**, $3.95. This is the revealing account of Davis' spiritual life. Many incidents and events of Yogananada's life are reported as well as the intimate revelations of the author's deep inner life. 204pp. CSA 71

_____. **THE PATH OF SOUL LIBERATION**, $1.95. See the Vedanta sub-section of Indian Philosophy.

_____. **SECRETS OF INNER POWER**, $2.95. 191pp. CSA 64

_____. **STUDIES IN TRUTH**, $3.00. A number of observations containing practical suggestions and insightful messages for the daily search for self-realization. 165pp. CSA

_____. **THIS IS REALITY**, $3.95. See Patanjali sub-section of Indian Philosophy.

_____. **TIME, SPACE AND CIRCUMSTANCE**, $2.95. In this volume Davis summarizes and restates his teaching in a number of important areas including health and healing, meditation, the extension of awareness, and higher vision. As is true with all of Davis books, the material is oriented toward self-transformative techniques for the individual. 140pp. Fel 73

DAY, HARVEY. **OCCULT ILLUSTRATED DICTIONARY**, c$8.50. This is a very complete dictionary, with clearly written entries. Unfortunately the book is not available in paperback and is fairly expensive considering its size. The volume is totally cross-referenced and the entries are very up-to-date. 156pp. Oxf 76

DILLARD, ANNIE. **PILGRIM AT TINKER CREEK**, $1.95. This is a mystical journey into the world of nature which has been immensely popular, has won a Pulitzer Prize, and has been compared by many with Thoreau's **Walden.** *One day I was walking along Tinker Creek thinking of nothing at all and I saw the tree with the lights in it. I saw the backyard cedar where the mourning doves roost charged and transfigured, each cell buzzing with flame. I stood on the grass with the lights in it, grass that was wholly fire, utterly focused and utterly dreamed. It was less like seeing than like being for the first time seen, knocked breathless by a powerful glance. . . . I had been my whole life a bell, and never knew it until at that moment I was lifted and struck.* 279pp. Ban 74

DOYLE, ARTHUR CONAN. **THE COMING OF THE FAIRIES**, $3.95. We all know about the author through his master detective Sherlock Holmes, yet few realize that Sir Arthur was an enthusiastic occultist who lectured throughout Europe and in America on higher metaphysical and psychic subjects. He was quite knowledgeable in the hidden side of nature as exemplified in this series of articles and letters by Doyle and others. Controversial photographs are included of fairies and nymphs. 196pp. Wei 21

DRURY, NEVILLE. **THE PATH OF THE CHAMELEON**, c$8.75. A profusely illustrated volume which traces the sacred esoteric tradition underlying all the great religions as well as the Western magical tradition. It explains the ways in which man seeks, in a very real sense, to become a god, to be spiritually reborn, and describes the journey of the soul. 162pp. Spe 73

DRURY, NEVILLE and STEPHEN SKINNER. **THE SEARCH FOR ABRAXUS**, c$8.40. This work ties together various methods for attaining a recognition of reality deriving almost exclusively from the Western esoteric tradition. It describes various schools of thought, occult and psychic practices, and their practitioners. Much consideration is given to the Qabala, the root springs of much of Western thought. Also discussed are magic, witchcraft, sorcery, astral conditions and the growth of human consciousness which is today so evident and which is finding expression in the search for a meaningful philosophy and valid explanations for life's mysteries. 148pp. Spe 72

DURCKHEIM, KARLFRIED von. **THE WAY OF TRANSFORMATION: DAILY LIFE AS SPIRITUAL EXERCISE**, $5.20. A wonderful jewel whose aim is to show that daily life, especially its routine, can be used for growth and can itself be lived as a spiritual exercise: *Every moment is the best of all opportunities*, runs an old Buddhist saying. Highly recommended. 104pp. A&U 71

EEMAN, L.E. **THE TECHNIQUE OF CONSCIOUS EVOLUTION**, c$6.15. The argument of this book—supported by Eeman's own experience and philosophical understanding—is that evolution can reach its maximum development only through the conscious and deliberate use of creative power by the individual. He describes practical techniques to release and redirect potential energy. This is a revised, enlarged version of the author's **Self and Superman**. 212pp. Dan 56

EMERSON, RALPH WALDO. **THE PORTABLE EMERSON**, $4.25. Presents a good cross section of his work, including essays from his three books (**Programs, The Ways of Life**, and **People**), and selections from his poems, journals, and letters. The volume is edited by Mark van Doren, who supplies notes throughout and an introduction. 664pp. Vik 46

EPICTETUS

Epictetus was born in Greece in the first century AD. He spent a considerable part of his life in Rome, first as a slave, and then as a teacher of the Stoic philosophy of which he is perhaps the best exponent.

BONFORTE, JOHN. **EPICTETUS**, c$6.00. This is an attempt to present Epictetus' **Discourses** in a form easily accessible to the modern reader. The author has taken them, as translated by Higginson, and reframed them into a series of dialogues in contemporary English, on contemporary themes. 178pp. PhL 74

EPICTETUS. **THE ENCHIRIDION**, $1.05. This is a brief summary of the basic ideas of Stoic philosophy and an introduction to the techniques required to transform Stoic philosophy into a way of life. It has been studied and widely quoted by philosophers down the ages. Introduction, bibliography. 39pp. BoM 48

_____. **MORAL DISCOURSES, ENCHIRIDION, AND FRAGMENTS**, c$6.75. This edition of Epictetus' work is the most comprehensive available and was translated by Elizabeth Carter well over 200 years ago. W.H.D. Rouse has edited this edition and supplied additional notes. Ms. Carter provides an excellent introduction which reviews Epictetus' teaching and Stoic philosophy. Glossary, notes. 384pp. Dut 10

EYRE, MARGERY. **THE SEEKER AND THE FINDING**, c$8.10. *A woman's search for inner truth* is the subtitle. *The lessons in this book are a record of the experiences through which I passed in my efforts to become more aware of God, and His will for my life on earth. By them the varying aspects of my need were met; and it is because I realize that so many other people seek as I did, with needs similar to my own, that I want to share the great joys that have become mine.* Index, 144pp. TPL 74

FAUSSET, HUGH. **THE LOST DIMENSION**, $1.55. A profound interpretation of the spiritual quest and the search for God within. Fausset has written a number of books on ancient Indian philosophy and this viewpoint is apparent in this volume. 80pp. Wat 66

FINDHORN

CADDY, EILEEN. **THE SPIRIT OF FINDHORN**, c$6.95. Eileen shares some of the uplifting messages that have inspired and guided the Findhorn community over the years and the faith that translated those visions into gardens, buildings, and a community. A biographical study by one of the members of the community is also included. The messages themselves are in the form of poetry and are illustrated with line drawings. 139pp. H&R 76

DIVINA. **THE LIVING SILENCE**, $2.50. Divina is also known as Dorothy MacLean and she is best known as a resident of the Findhorn community. *The contents of this book are messages I received by the still small voice within, generally during the quiet of the early morning. They come with an awareness of meaning and feeling which I then put into words. They have been edited slightly and arranged in their present style.* The messages are presented in the form of short poems. 104pp. FiP 71

________. **WISDOMS**, $2.00. *These messages were received from the inner divinity at various quiet moments in 1971. They have been left in their original order and form, in the knowledge that they can be as helpful to others as they were to me.* The messages are in prose. 60pp. FiP 72

EDWARDS, ALEXIS. **GUIDELINES**, $3.25. A collection of messages, poetry, and songs received in daily meditation, and emerging from and expressing his experiences at that time. Illustrated with abstract photographs and line drawings. 92pp. FiP nd

ELIXIR. **GOD SPOKE TO ME**, $3.95. The Findhorn community was founded and developed in obedience to the voice of God within, through daily messages received by Elixir in times of silent meditation. This volume presents selections from the guidance she received in the period between 1969–71. 119pp. FiP 73

FINDHORN COMMUNITY. **THE FINDHORN GARDEN**, c$10.00/5.95. Since its founding fourteen years ago, the Findhorn community, situated in Scotland on a sandy peninsula jutting into the North Sea, has been visited and written about by many. The only other book is Paul Hawken's **The Magic of Findhorn**. This is the first time that this amazing story has been written and photographed by the community itself. The history and development of the site from a trailer park (or caravan park as the British call it) sitting on sand and gravel into a garden flourishing with over 128 varieties of vegetables, fruits, and herbs; the transformation of this tiny group into one of the most enduring *new age* communities; and the philosophy which sustains the community are told in the words of the community's founders and present-day members. The community has demonstrated that it is love which makes plants as well as people grow and it is the same love that exudes throughout the book. Over 150 beautiful photographs illustrate the text. *One radiant energy pervades and gives rise to all life. While it may speak to us through plants, nature spirits or the human beings with whom we share life on this planet, all are reflections of the deeper reality behind and within them. Myth has become reality in the Findhorn garden, not to present us with a new form of spiritualism, but to offer us a new vision of life, a vision of unity. Essentially, the devas and nature spirits are aspects of our own selves, guiding us toward our true identity, the divine reality within. The story of the garden is the celebration of this divine life in its myriad forms. May the joy we experience in participating in this celebration deepen our commitment to revealing the total beauty of ourselves and of life around us.* Oversize, 180pp. H&R 75

FINDHORN FOUNDATION. **LINKS WITH SPACE**, $1.00. Spiritual communications from the Lord Maitreya and two other *beings* on the purpose and meaning of UFO's. Introduction by David Spangler. 24pp. FiP

HAWKEN, PAUL. **THE MAGIC OF FINDHORN**, c$8.95/2.25. *There have been stories about Findhorn where people talk to plants with amazing results; stories of vegetable and flower gardens animated by angelic forms; forty-pound cabbages, eight-foot delphiniums, and roses blooming in the snow; people heard talking to plants and angels in a casual and informal way; a land where nothing is impossible and legends are reborn. . . . What I found seems larger than a forty-pound cabbage. Fairies and elves seem tame stuff compared with what one experiences there. Findhorn may be a manifestation of light and power which could transform our planet within a lifetime, or it could be an illusory bubble on the troubled waters of the world civilization that will burst leaving no traces. . . . I can appreciate that much of what you read will seem implausible and incredible. I do not ask you to believe this account, for it is only written through one man's eyes.* A well written, fascinating descriptive account. 216pp. Ban 74

SPANGLER, DAVID. **FESTIVALS IN THE NEW AGE**, $3.25. Festivals have played an important part in the life of all people in all ages. In this book Spangler explores the meaning of the four seasonal festivals which have been celebrated since ancient times: Christmas, spring equinox, Midsummer, and Michaelmas. He feels that celebrating these festivals can be a means of psychologically and spiritually unifying man and his environment and the purpose of this book, as he sees it, is to help individuals participate in these holy days. The book itself is beautifully produced, with multicolored pages. 92pp. FiP 75

________. **LAWS OF MANIFESTATION**, $2.50. By applying the laws of manifestation (the principles of attracting to oneself, through love, whatever materials, energy or help are needed to promote wholeness or further growth), Findhorn has expanded fr[om] one small caravan on a sand dune into a large community. This book was written by Spa[ng]ler at a time when the community was seeking a greater understanding of the nature [of] manifestation and it is a lucid statement of the principles involved. 92pp. FiP

FORTUNE, DION. **APPLIED MAGIC**, c$4.50. A selection of previously unpublished w[rit]ings in which the practical application of magical and occult techniques is stressed. To[pics] include the group mind, the psychology of ritual, the circuit of force, three kinds of re[al]ity, non-humans, a magical body and the occult field today. There is also an excelle[nt] long, esoteric glossary. 110pp. Wei 62

________. **ASPECTS OF OCCULTISM**, c$4.50. Nine essays, each illuminating a d[if]ferent aspect of occultism. Topics include: teachings concerning the aura and the ast[ral] plane, Christianity and reincarnation, the sacred centers, God and the gods, and some hel[ps] to meditation. As usual, Dion Fortune has presented her material very well. All of h[er] books are highly recommended. 87pp. Wei 62

________ **THE COSMIC DOCTRINE**, c$7.95. The many facets of life on earth [as] well as on higher planes are touched upon with some consideration of the great laws a[nd] principles which govern evolution and all forms of planetary expression. An informativ[e] well written outline of the fundamental precepts of the esoteric sciences and the livi[ng] body of knowledge which is the fountain of human philosophy, inspiration and wisdo[m]. 157pp. Hel 66

________. **THE ESOTERIC PHILOSOPHY OF LOVE AND MARRIAGE**, c$3.50. A[n] unusual book which demonstrates that the higher aspects of sex are essential to the d[e]velopment of the perfect man, and which warns of the dangers which may atttend ign[o]rant handling of unseen forces. To the esotericist, sex in its sevenfold scope is a source [of] energy rather than a temptation. Dion Fortune explains the teachings of esoteric doctrin[e] relating to sex. Wei 67

________. **THE MYSTICAL QABALAH**, c$10.25. See the Jewish Mysticism sectio[n].

________. **PRACTICAL OCCULTISM IN DAILY LIFE**, c$2.95. Helpful suggestio[ns] for applying principles of occult science. Emphasis is laid upon the importance of at[ti]tude, character, keen judgment and concentration. Advice is given on remembering pa[st] incarnations, working out karma, and the uses and limitations of divination. 66pp. Wei 3[?]

________. **PSYCHIC SELF DEFENSE**, c$6.00. Complete first hand descriptions [of] psychic attacks, and practical instructions in methods of diagnosis, detection, and defens[e]. A very detailed account of every aspect, and the only book available on the subject. 210p[p]. Wei 30

________. **SANE OCCULTISM**, $3.50. Deals with the many pitfalls of occultism, d[e]scribing both the dangers and the safeguards. Topics include the *left-hand path*, astrolog[y], past lives, prophecy and divination, group karma, Eastern methods and Western bodie[s], secrecy in occult fraternities. 192pp. Wei 67

________. **THROUGH THE GATES OF DEATH**, $2.50. See Reincarnation sectior[n].

________. **THE TRAINING AND WORK OF AN INITIATE**, c$5.95. The Wester[n] esoteric systems derive from three main sources: Qabalistic, Egyptian, and Greek. Fro[m] these roots an unbroken tradition of initiation has been handed down from adept to neo[]phyte. The complete system is discussed here. This volume is a complementary work t[o] **The Esoteric Orders and Their Work**. 126pp. Wei 30

FORTUNE, DION et al. **THE NEW DIMENSIONS RED BOOK**, c$6.00. A collection o[f] essays on the practical aspects of the Western mystery tradition. Contents include: Dio[n] Fortune, *The Myth of the Table Round*; W.E. Butler, *Psychic and Occult Contacts*; Garet[h] Knight, *A Guide to Experiments in Astral Magic*; Israel Regardie, *Magic in East and West*; William Gray, *The Four Magical Instruments*. 106pp. Hel 68

FRANKLYN, JULIAN, ed. **DICTIONARY OF THE OCCULT** c$2.98. Thousands of in[]dividual entries are keyed to long detailed articles on major aspects of occultism and ar[e] readily identified by reference to a numbered paragraph in the appropriate article. Thus instead of a piecemeal definition, the reader can trace entries to their proper context, providing a thorough background and some related material. The articles have been writte[n] by experts and bibliographical material is given. First published in 1935. 301pp. Caa 7[3]

GASKELL, G.A. **DICTIONARY OF ALL SCRIPTURES AND MYTHS**, c$15.00. Th[e] most definitive study of the origin, nature and meaning of the sacred language of the scrip[]tures and myths connected to the various religions of the world. Over 5,000 entries includ[]ing numerous quotations from authoritative sources. Completely cross-referenced. 844pp Jul 60

GRAY, W.G. **THE ROLLRIGHT RITUAL**, c$8.50. *The famous Stone Circle of the* Roll[]rights *in Oxfordshire . . . is well known to folklorists. . . . This account . . . is the outcome of many years of personal contact with the Stones themselves on* Inner *levels of investigation. . . . In a normal and natural way, the Stones spoke through their own symbology of what they stood for in the past, and how this infallibly indicates the future we could expect if we are willing to follow the Pattern they laid out so long ago. Since the enquirer in this case was a working magical ritualist, the Stones revealed their ancient ritual structure translated into timeless terms of truth with the most startling spiritual significance and an intense impact of authenticity.* 166pp. Hel 75

GUENON, RENE. **THE REIGN OF QUANTITY AND THE SIGNS OF THE TIMES**, $2.65. This is an attack on the scientific orientation of the modern world. Guenon looks back to an ancient wisdom, once common to both East and West, but now almost entirely lost. Contemporary civilization itself—with its industrial societies and illusory notions of ress—is his target. In particular, he shows that today's sciences and social sciences are [dom]inated by a quantitative approach; that they neglect the idea of quality. To this *reign [of q]uantity* he opposes the sacred metaphysics of the ancients, which he sees as rooted in [th]e truth. Notes, index. 363pp. Pen 53

_____. SYMBOLISM OF THE CROSS, c$10.50. The cross, which is the particular [them]e of this study, is a universal traditional symbol which is far from being confined to [Chri]stianity, central though it may be to that religion. This is a scholarly study which re[late]s the symbolism of the cross in all the world's religions. Notes, 148pp. Luz 58

[GU]THRIE, W.K.C. A HISTORY OF GREEK PHILOSOPHY, VOL. I: THE EARLIER [PRE]SOCRATICS AND THE PYTHAGOREANS, c$21.00. Beginning with the infancy of [Wes]tern philosophy in Ionia in the sixth century BC, Professor Guthrie discusses in turn [the] doctrines of Thales, Anaximander and Anaximenes, and shows how Pythagoras and [his] followers then took the subject in a new direction, from the subject of matter to the [stu]dy of form. He treats separately the related doctrine of Alcmaeon and the work of the [phil]osopher-poet Xenophanes; and the volume concludes with a study of the thought of [Her]aclitus. This is without question the most modern comprehensive account of ancient [Gree]k philosophy. The text is well written and should be approachable to the general [rea]der as well as a valuable tool for the serious scholar. Notes, index, bibliography. 554pp. [HP] 71

[HA]ICH, ELIZABETH. INITIATION, $5.00. See the Ancient Egypt section.

[MA]NLY PALMER HALL

[Ma]nly Hall's work in comparative religion and philosophy is highly recom[me]nded. His books are always clear. He established the Philosophical Research [So]ciety (3910 Los Feliz Blvd., Los Angeles, California 90027) in 1934 as a [cen]ter for the integration of religion, philosophy, and psychology into one [sy]stem of instruction. In his lectures there and in his writings he always em[ph]asizes the practical aspects of philosophy and religion as they apply to [dai]ly living. He restates for modern man those spiritual and ethical doctrines [wh]ich have given to humanity its noblest ideals and most adequate codes of [liv]ing. Lectures are ongoing at the Society, they publish a quarterly journal, [an]d they have one of the best libraries anywhere. Hall's books are an excel[le]nt place to start the study of metaphysics.

[Pr]ints of three mystical paintings designed by Manly Hall, in color, 9x13, [ar]e available: *Opening of the Third Eye*, a symbolic head of Minerva, showing [th]e interior of the brain in a state of spiritual exaltation; *Synthetic Emblem[at]ic Cross*, signifying the unification of all religious and philosophical doc[tr]ines; and *The Seven Spinal Chakras*, according to yogic doctrine. Each is [$1].50.

[H]ALL, MANLY P. THE ADEPTS IN THE EASTERN ESOTERIC TRADITION, PART [I:] THE LIGHT OF THE VEDAS, $3.00. This series deals with those individuals seeking [to] ascend, through disciplines of spiritual development, toward conscious knowledge of [th]e hierarchy. The Adept tradition descended to the modern world through the migra[ti]ons of the Aryan people, hence it is fitting that the first part of this work is devoted to [th]e religious mysteries of Hinduism. 111pp. PRS 52

_____. THE ADEPTS IN THE EASTERN ESOTERIC TRADITION, PART II: [T]HE ARHATS OF BUDDHISM, $3.00. 112pp. PRS 53

_____. THE ADEPTS IN THE EASTERN ESOTERIC TRADITION, PART III: [T]HE SAGES OF CHINA, $3.00. 113pp. PRS 57

_____. THE ADEPTS IN THE EASTERN ESOTERIC TRADITION, PART IV: [T]HE MYSTICS OF ISLAM, $3.00. See the Islam section.

_____. THE ADEPTS IN THE WESTERN ESOTERIC TRADITION: ORDERS [O]F THE UNIVERSAL REFORMATION, $3.00. This section is devoted to the secret [s]ocieties of the sixteenth and seventeenth centuries and their leading figures. 102pp. PRS 49

_____. ADVENTURES IN UNDERSTANDING, c$6.50. The verbatim notes of [ei]ght recent lectures dealing with the practical problems of modern living. 218pp. PRS 69

_____. AMERICA'S ASSIGNMENT WITH DESTINY, c$5.75. The story of the [u]nfolding of the esoteric tradition in the Western Hemisphere. The work begins with the [ri]tes and mysteries of the Mayas and Aztecs; parallels are drawn between the miracles of [t]he North American Indian priests and those of the fakirs of India; an account is given [o]f the Incas and their possible contact with Asia; and finally the settlement in the U.S. is [d]iscussed at great length. A much more interesting account than Hall's **Secret Destiny of America**. 119pp. PRS 51

_____. CODEX ROSAE CRUCIS, c$15.00. See Rosicrucian section.

_____. COLLECTED WRITINGS, VOL. I, c$6.50. Five early works, written in the [1]920's and personally selected by Mr. Hall because they represent many of the basic ideas [up]on which his philosophy of life has been built. 332pp. PRS 58

_____. COLLECTED WRITINGS, VOL. II, c$6.50. This volume, unfolding a basic [t]heme, presents eight sages and seekers of the modern (sixteenth to twentieth century) [w]orld: Nostradamus, Francis Bacon, Johann Comenius, Jacob Boehme, Comte de St. Ger-

main, William Blake, Thomas Taylor, and Gandhi. Illustrations, 316pp. PRS 59

_____. COLLECTED WRITINGS, VOL. III, c$6.50. Includes the following essays and poems: *Atlantis, An Interpretation; The Sacred Magic of The Qabala; The Riddle of the Rosicrucians; Universal Reformation of Trajano Bocalini; Zodiackos: The Circle of Holy Animals;* and *An Essay on the Fundamental Principles of Operative Occultism.* 303pp. PRS 62

_____. DIONYSIAN ARTIFICERS, c$5.50. See Rosicrucian section.

_____. AN ESSAY ON THE FUNDAMENTAL PRINCIPLES OF OPERATIVE OCCULTISM, $1.50. This essay was written to accompany the three well-known paintings designed by Mr. Hall and described in the introduction to this sub-section. The relation is not direct—this is really a step-by-step to development along the path. 53pp. PRS 62

_____. FIRST PRINCIPLES OF PHILOSOPHY, $6.75. An informal study of philosophy, *an attempt to rescue the wisdom of the ancients from scholasticism's ponderosity,* covering metaphysics, logic, ethics, psychology, aesthetics, and theurgy. 199pp. PRS 42

_____. FREEMASONRY OF THE ANCIENT EGYPTIANS, c$6.95. See Ancient Egypt section.

_____. GREAT BOOKS ON RELIGION AND ESOTERIC PHILOSOPHY, $2.00. Most of the books in this listing are long out of print. However, Mr. Hall's description of the topics and his introductory material on building a library are often fascinating. 85pp. PRS 66

_____. THE GURU, c$5.50. A story of the holy or mystic life in India, as told by a disciple reminiscing upon many years of association with his Hindu teacher. 142pp. PRS 58

_____. HEALING: THE DIVINE ART, c$8.00. See the Healing section.

_____. THE INNER LIVES OF MINERALS, PLANTS AND ANIMALS, $1.50. Transcription of a lecture on the title theme. 31pp. PRS 73

_____. INITIATION OF PLATO, $1.50. PRS

_____. INVISIBLE RECORDS OF THOUGHT AND ACTION, $1.75. Two essays bound in one volume. The title selection discusses the theory and practice of psychometry and the other essay is entitled *The Use and Abuse of the Natural Psychic Powers Within Us and Around Us.* 62pp. PRS 69

_____. IS EACH INDIVIDUAL BORN WITH A PURPOSE? $1.50. Reprinted from lecture notes. 32pp. PRS 60

_____. JOURNEY IN TRUTH, c$6.50. Vol. I of Hall's survey of *Idealistic Philosophy,* this volume traces the great thinkers of the classical world from Orpheus to St. Augustine and includes sections on Pythagoras, Plato, Socrates, Diogenes, Aristotle and Plotinus. 270pp. PRS 45

_____. LECTURES ON ANCIENT PHILOSOPHY, c$6.50. Although complete in itself, this volume is designed to complement **Secret Teachings.** It includes two series of lectures on symbolism and the ancient mysteries and is an effort to clarify the subject of classical pagan metaphysics. 513pp. PRS 29

_____. LOST KEYS OF FREEMASONRY, c$3.75. See the Rosicrucian section.

_____. MAN: GRAND SYMBOL OF THE MYSTERIES, c$10.00. See the Healing section.

_____. MEDICINE OF THE SUN AND MOON, $1.50. See the Oriental Medicine section.

_____. MYSTERY OF THE HOLY SPIRIT, $1.50. A treatise on the Holy Spirit in Western and Eastern religious philosophy. 32pp. PRS 74

_____. THE MYSTERIES OF HUMAN BIRTH, $1.50. PRS

_____. THE MYSTICAL CHRIST, c$7.00. See the Christianity section.

_____. THE OCCULT ANATOMY OF MAN, $1.50. 36pp. PRS 57

_____. OLD TESTAMENT WISDOM, c$7.50. See the Bibles section.

_____. PATHWAYS OF PHILOSOPHY, c$6.50. An enlightening journey tracing the passage of Platonic wisdom from the days of the Grecian Golden Era through the centuries until modern time. The influence of this philosophy is shown in the lives and words of such great men as Diogenes, Paracelsus, Francis Bacon, Boehme, and Emerson. Vol. II of Hall's survey of *Idealistic Philosophy.* 253pp. PRS 47

_____. THE PHOENIX, c$12.50. An illustrated review of occultism and philosophy covering the following topics: Blavatsky; Meditation, Concentration and Retrospection; Comte de St. Germain; Cycle of Transmigration; the Great Pyramid; and the Ladder of Souls (mystery of the descent of the spiritual man into the body). 9x14", 91 magnificent illustrations. 175pp. PRS

_____. REINCARNATION: THE CYCLE OF NECESSITY, $7.00. See the Reincarnation section.

_____. **RESEARCH ON REINCARNATION**, $1.75. See the Reincarnation section.

_____. **SEARCH FOR REALITY: TEN LECTURES ON PERSONAL GROWTH**, c$9.00. PRS

_____. **SECRET DESTINY OF AMERICA**, c$6.50. Mr. Hall has gathered fragments of a little known history which indicates that the seeds of democracy were planted here 1000 years before the beginning of the Christian era. He traces these ideas through the birth of the American state. 200pp. PRS 42

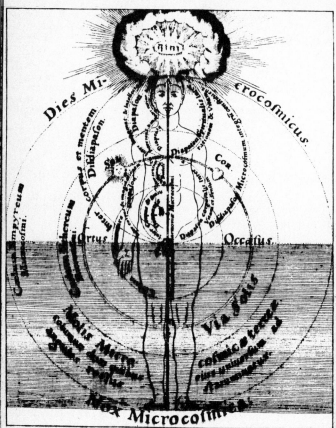

—From *Collectio Operum.*

The harmonic intervals of the human body

_____. **SECRET TEACHINGS OF ALL AGES**, c$20.00. An encyclopedic outline of Masonic, Hermetic, Qabalistic and Rosicrucian symbolic philosophy—a comprehensive survey and interpretation of the esoteric teachings concealed within the rituals, allegories, and mysteries of all ages. This is Hall's major work and we recommend this fascinating compilation highly. The illustrations alone are worth the price of the book and the text can be studied for years. Every aspect of the occult sciences is covered in depth and even in the areas where we have the most knowledge, Hall's presentation is invariably enlightening. Profusely illustrated, 9x14. An ideal gift for all on the path. 254pp. **Secret Teachings** has just been republished in its original size and format (12x18½"), including 54 color plates and over 200 black-and-white ones, $85.00. The supply on this printing is limited and there's no telling when it will be reprinted again. PRS 62

_____. **SELF-UNFOLDMENT BY DISCIPLINES OF REALIZATION**, c$6.50. The theme of this book is that illumination is as natural as life itself. Its purpose is to develop awareness and thoughtfulness so that it becomes part of you. Hall outlines in detail various practical exercises and discusses the theory behind them. 221pp. PRS 42

_____. **STUDIES IN CHARACTER ANALYSIS**, $2.50. See Divination section.

_____. **SURVEY COURSE IN PHILOSOPHY**, $3.50. This is a twelve lesson course based upon the introduction to **Secret Teachings**, with a series of questions following each lesson. Bound in a loose-leaf notebook. Each lesson is about 7pp. PRS 60

_____. **THERAPEUTIC VALUE OF MUSIC**, $1.50. See the Music section.

_____. **TWELVE WORLD TEACHERS**, c$6.50. A summary of the lives and teachings of the following prophets whose inspiration led others to a more enlightened way of thinking: Akhenaten, Hermes, Orpheus, Zoroaster, Buddha, Confucius, Lao Tzu, Plato, Jesus, Muhammad, Padmasambhava, and Quetzalcoatl. Recommended. 254pp. PRS 37

_____. **WOMAN: THE MOTHER OF ALL LIVING**, $1.50. A lecture reviewing the role and status of woman throughout the ages. 33pp. PRS 55

_____. **WORDS TO THE WISE**, c$6.50. A collection of essays based on the author's extensive experience as a teacher which explains metaphysics and gives practical instruction to the neophyte. 169pp. PRS 63

HAMMARSKJOLD, DAG. MARKINGS, $3.25. A remarkable record of the spiritual of Hammarskjold, a noted public official and former Secretary General of the United tions. He described the manuscript as a *sort of white book concerning my negotiat with myself and with God.* 222pp. Fab 64

HANSON, VIRGINIA, ed. THE SILENT ENCOUNTER, $2.75. This is a collection o says on the mystical experience by writers from varying backgrounds and experien Some of the essays were originally published as part of a special set of issues of **The Ar ican Theosophist**. The coverage is quite comprehensive and most of the selections are go 240pp. TPH 74

HAPPOLD, F.C. MYSTICISM, $3.95. An excellent work in two parts: a study, desig as an introduction to the anthology and covering all of the topics in the anthology; an excellent anthology covering all aspects of Eastern thought, the Christian mystics cluding many of the lesser known ones), and the Sufis. Each selection is accompanied introductory paragraphs on the text. Highly recommended. 407pp. Pen 63

HECKETHORN, C.W. THE SECRET SOCIETIES OF ALL AGES AND COUNTRI c$15.00/set. A definitive account of secret societies: their reasons for being, initiati and ceremonies, codes and customs, rise and fall. Traces their evolution, uncovering prising similarities between some of the most distant in time and space. First writter 1875 and completely revised in 1897 after twenty-three years of additional research, th two volumes have no peer. Includes a complete list of the authorities cited. Definitely light reading. 716pp. UnB 65

HEINDEL, MAX. ETHERIC VISION AND WHAT IT REVEALS, $1.50. *The materia this booklet is a reprint (with some revisions and additions) of monthly lessons sent by The Rosicrucian Fellowship to its members, and is a summary of studies and researc conducted by students in the Esoteric Section of the Fellowship.* It presents material o available elsewhere in Besant and Leadbeater's **Occult Chemistry** and includes material the chemical ether, the life ether, the light ether, and the reflecting ether. The presentat is extremely clear and the material is very helpful for the student seeking a full picture the cosmos. 110pp. Ros 65

_____. **NATURE SPIRITS AND NATURE FORCES**, $.75. This is a compilat of material from many of Heindel's books divided into the following chapters: *The Eth and Laws of Nature, Heaven World Activity and Nature Force, The Mission of Christ a the Festival of the Fairies, Forces of Different Periods, The Earth Spirit* and *The Cons tion of the Earth and Volcanic Eruptions.* 43pp. Ros 37

_____. **OCCULT PRINCIPLES OF HEALTH AND HEALING**, $4.00. See Healing section.

HELINE, CORINNE. MAGIC GARDENS, c$4.95. *Every flower bears a starry impri declared Paracelsus. From the Zodiac came the veritable secrets of God. The Star Ang are transmitters, and flowers become symbols of their communicators. The closer c communion with the angels, the deeper will be our understanding of the mysteries of t plant kingdom and the greater our realization of the spiritual ministry of the world flowers.* 122pp. NAP 44

_____. **STAR GATES**, c$4.95. In terms of the Christian mysteries, the author o lines the inner spiritual significance of the seasons and the ministry and activity of the a gelic kingdom during these times. 198pp. NAP

_____. **THE TWELVE LABORS OF HERCULES**, $1.50. The twelve labors s forth in perfect sequence the twelve steps in the passage of the Sun through the Zodia and represent at the same time the way of attainment for the aspirant. This study also ce relates the labors of Hercules with the life of the Biblical Samson. 69pp. NAP 44

HELINE, THEODORE. AMERICA'S DESTINY, $1.00. *According to the prophetic pr mise of the Great Seal it is the destiny of the U.S. to bring forth a New Order of the Age* This booklet discusses the symbolism of the Seal and the esoteric background of th country. 50pp. NAP 37

_____. **THE ARCHETYPE UNVEILED**, $1.00. An illustrated study of the sou patterns formed by the creative word. 24pp. NAP 65

The obverse and reverse of the Great Seal of the United States of America demonstrate the mystic significance of the number thirteen, which appears frequently in the Seal.

HIERONIMUS, ROBERT. THE TWO GREAT SEALS OF AMERICA, $2.50. This is a de tailed history and interpretation, including many illustrations and quotations from sourc material. Bibliography, 50pp. Svt 73

OWE, GRAHAM and L. LeMESURICK. **THE OPEN WAY: A STUDY IN ACCEPTANCE,** $5.25. *The teaching of this book is that we should be willing to let Life be our teacher, and let it teach us exactly as it does and what it wills. All other teachers are only fit to serve if they can teach us the way of willing and active obedience to the Law, which is the truth of our experience. Now. To the all-important question:* What is the Way of Life? *The answer is* Walk on! 220pp. Wat 58

HUXLEY, FRANCIS. **THE WAY OF THE SACRED,** $2.25. This is an exploration of the rites and symbols, beliefs and tabus which have come to be considered sacred. Through the sacred, man tries to achieve communion with the divine, and also with his/her own physical nature. S/he sets apart, physically or ritually, things that overwhelm him/her. In particular, Huxley explores the symbolism of the sacred, because it is only in symbolic terms that the sacred can be approached. He presents 307 illustrations, 32 in full color, which show some of the objects that men have singled out in their search for the sacred and some of the ways men and women have represented, in art, the world that is apart, sacred and divine. The text is geared toward the general reader, however, some knowledge of mythology would be helpful in understanding the references. Index, 320pp. Del 74

ISRAEL, MARTIN. **AN APPROACH TO MYSTICISM,** $1.25. This is a clearly written general survey of mysticism in both the East and the West, with the emphasis on the Christian tradition. The reader can get as good a feeling of the mystical experience from this volume as from any other that we know of. It is divided into the following sections: *Mysticism, Some Psychological Considerations; The Mystical Experience; Mysticism and Religion, The Face of God; Mysticism and Religion, God and the World; Mysticism in Wordly Living; The Fruits of Mysticism;* and *Survival and Immortality.* The material here was originally presented as a series of lectures. Bibliography, 49pp. ChF 68

_________. **AN APPROACH TO SPIRITUALITY,** $1.25. Another collection of lectures, this time more oriented toward the Christian experience. The following are the main topics: *Spirituality in the World; Revelation through Relationships; The Vision of God; The Place of Discipline; Prayer and Meditation; The Dark Night of the Soul;* and *The Spiritual Life.* 49pp. ChF 71

_________. **THE POWER OF THE SPIRIT IN EVERYDAY LIVING,** $.95. Transcription of three Christian-oriented lectures: *The Importance of Prayer and Meditation; Problems of Relationships–Oneself;* and *Problems of Relationships–Other People.* 32pp. ChFnd

JAMES, WILLIAM. **THE VARIETIES OF RELIGIOUS EXPERIENCE,** $1.50. A classic of philosophical, religious and scientific thought: *The problem I have set myself is a hard one: . . to make the hearer or reader believe, what I myself invincibly do believe, that, although all the special manifestations of religion may have been absurd (I mean its creeds and theories), yet the life of it as a whole is mankind's most important function.* 416pp. McM 61

JASPERS, KARL. **ANAXIMANDER, HERACLITUS, PARAMENIDES, PLOTINUS, LAO-TZU, NAGARJUNA,** $3.25. A collection of biographical and critical essays on each of these great men, taken from Jaspers' magnum opus, **The Great Philosophers**, and edited by Hannah Arendt. Ample quotations from the philosophical works of the individuals are included within the body of the text and each figure is seen as a person rather than as merely a bundle of abstract ideas. The individual accounts are very well organized. Index, bibliography. 138pp. HBJ 66

_________. **SPINOZA,** $2.75. A detailed study of Spinoza's (1632–77) life and work, taken from Jaspers' **The Great Philosophers**, topically arranged and including many quotations from Spinoza's own writings. The book is well organized–often too well organized in the Germanic tradition so that the text does not flow. A tremendous amount of material is crammed into these pages. Bibliography, 120pp. HBJ 66

JONES, GLADYS. **THE GREEK LOVE MYSTERIES,** c$6.95. Subtitled *An Occult Study of the Problems and Sicknesses of Love.* This volume does not read very well and Ms. Jones does not seem to have anything very striking to say on the subject. She also includes a profusion of some pretty poor poetry. The teaching, such as it is, is based on the ancient teaching as transmitted to Ms. Jones by her spirit guide. 219pp. NAP 75

JONES, MARC E. **OCCULT PHILOSOPHY,** c$13.50. A rather difficult work in which this noted astrologer discusses established esoteric doctrines concerning transmutation, adepts, karma and reincarnation. Much of the book is devoted to an exposition of his theory that all existence and experience are organized according to a Pythagorean basis of number, a Platonic structure of operational concepts, and an Aristotelian organization. Includes an extensive glossary of both Eastern and Western terminology. 436pp. Sab 48

KIENINGER, RICHARD. **OBSERVATIONS I, II, III,** $1.95/each. Collections of essays on every conceivable theme by the man who wrote **The Ultimate Frontier**. Each is about 90pp. Stl

KNIGHT, GARETH. **EXPERIENCE OF THE INNER WORLDS,** c$11.00. The material in this volume was designed for a course in Christian Qabalistic magic. The first half of the book presents a general review of the Western mystery tradition, drawing on Biblical sources, the traditions of the ancient Near East, Arthurian and Grail legends, and alchemy. The second half presents practical teachings on various aspects of Western occultism, including material derived from the Qabala and the work of Agrippa, Dee, Bruno, Campanella, the Rosicrucians, Kircher, Fludd, and others. There's also a personal record of the occult work conducted by Knight over the last ten years. Practical exercises are given at the end of each chapter. Knight's work is very well thought of. He integrates his material well and his practical teaching is quite easy to follow. Illustrations, bibliography. 254pp. Hel 75

_________. **OCCULT EXERCISES AND PRACTICES,** c$3.00. A beginner's guide to practical occultism, giving basic practical exercises in developing clairvoyance, clairaudience, astral projection, attracting opportunities, recovering memories of past incarnations, projecting etheric force, breathing, relaxation, meditation, magical visualization, spiritual exercises and prayer. Includes bibliography. 68pp. Wei

KOLLERSTROM, OSCAR. **THE ACTUAL AND THE REAL,** c$7.85. Kollerstrom is a practicing psychoanalyst, trained by Georg Groddeck. This is a very personal work in which the author attempts to discuss spiritual questions in language acceptable to a psychologist. It is subtitled *A Way of Thinking About Reality* and this is the main thrust of the volume. Included are chapters on death and reincarnation as well as a complete summary of Groddeck's philosophy. Bibliography, 206pp. Tur 74

KUESHANA, EKLAL. **THE ULTIMATE FRONTIER,** $1.90. A very popular account of the ancient Brotherhoods and their profound, worldwide influence during the past 6,000 years. The whys, whence and whither of human existence are explored and many mysteries are elucidated in layman's terms. 224pp. Stl 63

LANDAU, RON. **GOD IS MY ADVENTURE,** $1.20. Landau was a spiritual seeker who was very serious about his quest. He got to know the individuals he discusses in this volume quite well in many instances and he recounts many first-hand conversations. This is a fascinating account which gives personal glimpses into many spiritual leaders. Landau seems to be the closest and most sympathetic toward Rudolf Steiner and Krishnamurti and the most critical of Gurdjieff. Other individuals discussed at length include Count Keyserling, Stefan George, Meher Baba, George Jeffreys, Dr. Frank Buchman, and P.D. Ouspensky. This book was a best seller in the 1930's. Index, 255pp. A&U 35

LONG, MAX FREEDOM. **GROWING INTO LIGHT,** c$4.50. Readings, exercises, and affirmations to help the individual working alone to put the Huna principles to work in his own life. 177pp. Dev 55

_________. **THE HUNA CODE IN RELIGIONS,** c$7.50. A wonderful new light on religions traced back 4,000 years to ancient Egypt then identified in the Old Testament, and later in the Gospels; carried to India and even China, then, finally, on to Polynesia, where the word-symbol code language was preserved with care for almost twenty centuries. Long reports on the amazing things uncovered by applying the code to the secret teachings hidden in the Gospels, yoga and Buddhism. Includes an extensive dictionary of the Hawaiian language. 367pp. Dev 65

_________. **INTRODUCTION TO HUNA,** $2.00. This recently reissued volume was the first work which Long published on his researches. It summarizes the material that he presented more fully in his later works and is especially thorough in its discussion of the Huna system. 79pp. EsP 45

_________. **PSYCHOMETRIC ANALYSIS,** c$4.50. Discusses psychometric analysis of human character and mentality especially as revealed through an instrument called the Biometer. The research was done under the auspices of the Huna Research Society. 118pp Dev 59

_________. **THE SECRET SCIENCE AT WORK,** c$6.50. Describes the work of the Huna Research Associates in proving the validity of the Huna principles and the practical use of them today as well as much new information on allied lines. 343pp. Dev 53

_________. **THE SECRET SCIENCE BEHIND MIRACLES,** c$6.50. This is the basic book on Huna. In it Long tells about the authentic miracles performed by the Kahunas of Hawaii: instant healing, changing the future for the better, control of winds and weather. From a long study of the language used by the Kahunas, Long discovered in the roots of significant words, clues to the secret knowledge held by the miracle workers. They understood and used a system of psychology undreamed of by our modern psychologists. They knew and used three kinds of vital-mental forces, including that which is responsible for hypno-suggestive phenomena. They generated these forces with ease, working with three levels of consciousness. To manipulate these forces they made use of three kinds of invisible substance of which we know almost nothing, although one form of it has often been seen partly solidified in seance rooms as *ectoplasm*. Their knowledge explains many of the mysteries of psychic phenomena. A fascinating account, highly recommended. 408pp. Dev 48

_________. **SELF-SUGGESTION,** c$4.50. See the Hypnotism section.

M. **DAYSPRING OF YOUTH,** c$8.50. A record of instruction received during different states of Yoga practice, revealed in order that others, by similar practice, may develop and unfold their inner powers. *At the beginning and end of each age there is a pouring forth of hierarchal cosmic streams of energy, and as they intermittently enter the earth's atmosphere and unite we find in this radiation that instruction best fitted for the time.* Wei 33

MAETERLINCK, MAURICE. **THE GREAT SECRET,** c$5.95. The author, who received the Nobel Prize for Literature, studies the one secret doctrine of the meaning of life as it originated in India, and was carried to Egypt, Persia, Chaldea, Greece, the Gnostics and Neoplatonists, the Qabala, the alchemists, the modern occultists, and psychical research. This doctrine was always the same, but it remained the possession of the initiates, while the masses worshipped religions which had little or no resemblance to the secret doctrine. Maeterlinck sets forth this secret here. 277pp. UnB 69

MENDL, R.W.S. **REVELATION IN SHAKESPEARE,** $4.40. This is an authoritative study of the supernatural, spiritual and religious elements in Shakespeare's works. Hitherto these aspects have been only partially discussed, usually in relation to specific plays. Here Mendl presents a comprehensive analysis which quotes amply from the plays. Index, 223pp. D&B 64

MICHAEL, RUSS. **DIVINE PSYCHOLOGY,** $3.95. A clearly written, introductory work on the subject of the new esoteric psychology with brief explanations of such subjects as meditation, the etheric body, sex, the nature of human personality, and other topics. 142pp. Tar 72

_____. **THE SCIENCE OF OCCULTISM**, $3.95. A comprehensive, introductory account by this student of the Arcane School with material on numbers, man's bodies, meditation, the rays, adepts, reincarnation, initiation, scientific basis for the soul, thought, and much else. Very clearly written. 140pp. Tar 71

_____. **THE WHITE BROTHERHOOD**, $3.95. This is an inspirational summary of the teachings of the Brotherhood, including information on the steps along the way from aspirant on up. We are not overly impressed with Michael's books. He uses a lot of words and gives himself a lot of praise but he does not seem to be saying anything very special or very well. 113pp. Mil 75

MOORE, JOHN, ed. **MAKE BELIEVE**, $4.65. A collection of topical meditations in poetic form, written by the editor, we assume, since no other credits are given. Here are parts of a few of them: *Learning, or knowledge about a thing/ induces the mistaken belief and assumption/ that the name and properties of the thing are what it is.* And: *This principle is essential to understanding the One Philosophy;/ you cannot change any thing;/ but how it is seen can change/ and that in itself brings about the change in things.* And: *All Things in the sensorily perceived world are past;/ for how can any thing take attention if it is not already there?/ Any thing sensed in the moment now must already be created/ otherwise it could not be there to be witnessed,/ and, being already there, it is in the past.* 150pp. Tur 73

NASR, SEYYED. **MAN AND NATURE**, c$4.00. Transcription of a series of four lectures on the title theme. *The thesis presented in this book is simply this: that although science is legitimate in itself, the role and function of science and its application have become illegitimate and even dangerous because of the lack of a higher form of knowledge into which science could be integrated and the destruction of the sacred and spiritual value of nature. To remedy this situation the metaphysical knowledge pertaining to nature must be revived and the sacred quality of nature given back to it once again.* Nasr is best known for his writings on Sufism. Index, 153pp. A&U 68

OPHIEL. **THE ART AND PRACTICE OF THE OCCULT**, $3.00. Ophiel calls this his basic book on the foundations of occult knowledge. Magical rituals and meditations are revealed and the reader is taught how to become a gnostic, or *one who knows*. With this deeper knowledge comes power over nature. 170pp. Wei 67

OTTO, RUDOLF. **MYSTICISM: EAST AND WEST**, $2.45. A scholarly analysis/comparison of the classic types of Occidental mysticism, as interpreted by the medieval German mystic Meister Eckhart, with the Oriental system as interpreted by Shankara. Conformities in the doctrine of salvation, way of knowledge, soul, creation, and religion are examined as well as the many differences, notably those concerned with ethical conduct. 282pp. McM 32

PAUWELS, LOUIS and JACQUES BERGIER. **IMPOSSIBLE POSSIBILITIES**, $1.25. A venture into the realms of human potential and the possible future of humanity when new scientific discoveries unveil the secrets of the universe. An intriguing collection of data and facts. 253pp. Avo 68

_____. **MORNING OF THE MAGICIANS**, $1.50. A probe into many aspects of our recent history and our complex civilization with esoteric explanations for such diverse events as Hitler's leap to power and atomic energy development. It touches a vast range of scientific, social, historical and occult topics and yet retains a lightness that other books on such subjects lack. Avo 60

PERCIVAL, HAROLD. **THINKING AND DESTINY**, $9.25. *The book explains the purpose of life. That purpose is not merely to find happiness . . . neither is it to save one's soul. The real purpose of life . . . is this: that each one of us will be progressively conscious in ever higher degrees in being conscious . . . of nature, and in and through and beyond nature. By nature is meant all that one can ever be made conscious of through the sense.* This is a detailed exploration of all aspects of being in the world. 1014pp. WdF 46

PHILLIPS, DOROTHY, ELIZABETH HOWES and LUCILLE NIXON, eds. **THE CHOICE IS ALWAYS OURS**, $1.95. This is a very wide-ranging anthology of short pieces about the spiritual path from religious and psychological sources. The selections are arranged into eleven major topical groups and they are quite well chosen, covering virtually every topic that we can think of. An incredibly large number of different writers are included. All in all this is a good anthology, with some pieces of course better than others, but with a generally high standard. There's something for everyone here. The material is fully indexed. Bibliography, 492pp. TPH 75

PLATO

PLATO. **THE COLLECTED DIALOGUES**, c$14.70. Edith Hamilton and Huntington Cairns, the editors, set out to choose the contents of this collection from the work of the best British and American translators of the last hundred years. Hamilton also contributed prefatory notes to each essay; and Cairns, an introductory essay on Plato's philosophy and writings. 1769pp. PUP 63

_____. **COMPLETE TEXTS OF GREAT DIALOGUES OF PLATO**, $2.95. A modern translation by W.H.D. Rouse of Ion, Meno, Euthydemus, Symposium (The Banquet), The Republic, Crito, and Phaedo. 607pp. NAL 56

SHRINE OF WISDOM. **THE HUMAN SOUL IN THE MYTHS OF PLATO**, c$2.65. Plato incorporated many myths in his dialogues, and in this volume the Shrine of Wisdom has selected and arranged those relating to the nature of the human soul, together with explanatory passages. It reveals many of the problems which perplex modern man: What are we? Why are we here? What is our purpose? How may we achieve it? An enlightening study. 68pp. ShW 36

PLOTINUS (204—70)

Plotinus holds a very important place in the history of thought—important in philosophy, more important in theology and in the development of mysticism.

Heir to the great philosophies of the ancient world, those of Plato, Aristotle, and the Stoics, he borrowed from all of them the insights which he needed, but without surrendering at any point the dominant influence of Platonism. Eclectic in appearance but powerfully unified by the strength of a single pervading impulse, his system has, by various channels often obscure and often indirect, come to be and remained one of the guiding forces in the thought of the West. . . . He is the last great philosopher of antiquity, and yet in more than one respect, and notably in the stress which he places on the autonomy of spirit, he is a precursor of modern times.

He is in the West the founder of that speculative mysticism which expresses in intellectual or rather supra-intellectual and negative categories the stages and states of union with the Absolute. It is a mysticism wholly philosophical, transposed into a new key which is specifically Plotinian; and it differs very greatly from the mysticism of St. Paul or St. John with which through the centuries it runs parallel or combines, often unconsciously, though at times also it is in conflict with the Gospel mysticism.—from the introduction to MacKenna's translation.

MACKENNA, STEPHEN. **PLOTINUS: THE ENNEADS**, c$25.00. This is universally acknowledged as the definitive translation. It originally appeared in five volumes between 1917 and 1930. This is the fourth edition, revised by B.S. Page—with the five volumes in one. Professor Paul Henry supplies an excellent long introduction which discusses Plotinus' thought and compares it with philosophers both before and after him. We recommend **The Enneads** highly to all readers who wish to immerse themselves in and gain an understanding both of classical mysticism and of mystical philosophy in general. The text reads amazingly well and does not seem dated at all. This is truly timeless literature. All of Plotinus' writing is presented here. Bibliography, notes. 708pp. Fab 69

RIST, J.M. **PLOTINUS: THE ROAD TO REALITY**, c$16.50. This is a very good study of Plotinus' philosophy, beginning with a biographical sketch (taken basically from Porphyry's **Life**, with extensive critical commentary) and including a discussion of some of Plotinus' major concepts: The One, The Logos, Beauty, The Descent of the Soul, Free Will, Happiness, The Self and Others, and Faith. Rist concludes with a discussion of Neoplatonic faith. Notes, bibliography, index. 280pp. CUP 67

TAYLOR, THOMAS, tr. **PLOTINUS ON THE BEAUTIFUL AND ON INTELLIGIBLE BEAUTY**, $2.55. Taylor is best known for his excellent translations of Porphyry and Plato. *Plotinus on the Beautiful* is translated by the editors of the Shrine of Wisdom and *On Intelligible Beauty* by Taylor. 32pp. ShW 32

PLYM, DON and THEA. **A MACRO-PHILOSOPHY FOR THE AQUARIAN AGE**, $2.00. *It is the purpose of this book to present the larger macrocosmic view or philosophy of life in which the real causes and, thus, the real solutions of all human problems can be seen and considered. . . . An old way of life . . . is dying: But a new age is being born. . . . This book is designed to aid man in his adaptations to this new age by presenting the foundation for world peace and unity—macro philosophy.* 158pp. MDC 70

_____. **2150—A MACRO LOVE STORY**, $2.00. A visionary novel about the future of mankind, told from the viewpoint of a young man living in the uncertain world of 1970 who visits the world of 2150 during his sleep-dream state. The tone of the book is hopeful as it glances into the near future when humanity develops a new dimension of para-psychological awareness and evolves into a magnificent race possessing god-like attributes. 168pp. MDC 71

PONCE, CHARLES. **THE GAME OF WIZARDS**, $2.50. This is a disappointing book which could be quite informative, but which just misses being so. Ponce sets out to show that the esoteric sciences reflect the symbolic structure of the subconscious mind. In his discussion he reviews alchemy, the I Ching, the Qabala, the Tarot, and astrology at some length. Many of the classic writers are quoted, their main theories analyzed and references to contemporary research on altered states of consciousness are scattered throughout the text. A separate chapter is devoted to each of the esoteric sciences and the presentation is sometimes quite good. The book is probably worth reading if you want a general overview of the subjects discussed and don't want to read a book about each one, but it could be better. We prefer Ralph Metzner's **Maps of Consciousness**, though this book stresses the *occult* more. Illustrations, 240pp. Pen 75

PYTHAGORAS

D'OLIVET, FABRE, tr. **GOLDEN VERSES OF PYTHAGORAS**, $3.95. This edition includes the Greek text of the verses along with a French translation and then this translation is again translated into English and each verse is discussed in detail. These verses are an excellent expression of the ancient mystery teachings and d'Olivet himself was an initiate who understood the deepest meanings of these teachings. 172pp. Wei 1813

OLIVER, GEORGE. **THE PYTHAGOREAN TRIANGLE**, c$8.95. Oliver was a nineteenth century freemason. This is a photographic reprint of his study of the Pythagorean numbers and their relations to freemasonry. 253pp. Wiz 1875

PHILLIP, J.A. **PYTHAGORAS AND THE EARLY PYTHAGOREANISM**, c$13.45. Pythagoras and his followers are cast by historians in four important roles: they are reputed to ve originated the mathematical disciplines, harmonics, and, in a large measure, astro-my; they are said to have propounded theories of the nature of our universe to which, differing ways, Parmenides, Empedocles, Anaxagoras, and Democritus reacted; they e reputed to have made the alliance between religion and philosophy that made philo-phy in the ancient world a way of life; and their thought exerted a major influence on ato, particularly on his mathematical theories. This volume is a survey of these assertions y a noted scholar. The exposition is topically organized. Notes, bibliography, index. 22pp. UTo 66

OWE, N. **COMMENTARIES OF HIEROCLES ON THE GOLDEN VERSES OF PYTH-GORAS**, $2.45. Translation of an important fifth century commentary. Included also e translations of the verses themselves. Each verse is followed by commentary. 132pp. PH 71

HRINE OF WISDOM EDITORS, trs. **THE GOLDEN VERSES OF THE PYTHAGOR-ANS**, c$4.00. This is the most recent translation of the verses. The aim of the translation to make the practical teaching expounded in the verses accessible to contemporary man. translation of the entire text is followed by translations of the stanzas. with a commen-ry following each. 32pp. ShW nd

TANLEY, THOMAS. **PYTHAGORAS**, c$12.00. A photographic reprint of Stanley's sev-nteenth century study of the Pythagorean philosophy and the doctrines attributed to ythagoras and his followers. 9x13", double column. 93pp. PRS 70

AVENSCROFT, TREVOR. **THE SPEAR OF DESTINY**, $1.95. A fascinating account f the occult aspects of Hitler's rise to power, based largely on reports of Dr. Walter Stein, ho had intimate knowledge of Hitler's occult activities and became a confidential advis-r to Churchill after his escape from Germany. The text ranges beyond the direct history nto discussion of the grail legend, Rudolf Steiner, **The Secret Doctrine**, the origin of the ryan race in Atlantis, etc. None of the material is documented. 362pp. Ban 73

EDGROVE, H. STANLEY. **MAGIC AND MYSTICISM: STUDIES IN BYGONE BE-IEFS**, $2.95. A scholarly study, with chapters on medieval thought; Pythagoras and his hilosophy; medicine and magic; superstitions concerning birds; ceremonial magic; talis-ans; architectural symbolism; and the phallic element in alchemical doctrine. Illustra-ons, 205pp. CiP

REGARDIE, ISRAEL. **THE ROMANCE OF METAPHYSICS**, c$7.95. Regardie wrote his book in 1942 in an attempt to establish certain points of relationship between the arious metaphysical philosophies and modern psychology. He presents a comprehensive iscussion of Christian Science, New Thought (I.N.T.A. and Neville), Unity, and more nodern approaches to enlightenment. 288pp. ArP 46

_____. **THE MIDDLE PILLAR**, $3.95. Subtitled *A Co-Relation of the Principles f Analytical Psychology and th Elementary Techniques of Magic.* 162pp. LlP 70

NICHOLAS ROERICH (1874—1947)

Roerich was one of the greatest mystics of the twentieth century. He was Russian and for many years taught in Russia. After the Revolution he came to the United States and established a number of institutions. His aim was to bring humanity together through education and culture. He was a poet and painted many mystital works, some of which are on exhibition today at the Nicholas Roerich Museum in New York City. He traveled throughout the world and spent a great deal of time in the East and his philosophy is heavily Eastern oriented. He called his system *Agni Yoga.* Agni yoga is the yoga of fire. Fire symbolizes life, knowledge, feeling and action. In terms of conscious-ness, this is the yoga which deals with intuition, immediate inner perception, direct insight, instant understanding. *All preceding Yogas, given from the highest sources, took as their basis, a prescribed quality of life. And now, at the advent of the age of Maitreya is needed a Yoga comprising the entire life; all embracing, evading nought. . . . You may suggest to me a name for the Yoga of life, but the most precise name will be Agni Yoga. It is precisely the element of fire which gives to this Yoga of self sacrifice its name. While in other Yogas the dangers were diminished through exercise, in the Yoga of fire the perils are increased. Because fire as an all-binding element manifests itself everywhere and thereby admits realization of the subtlest energies. . . . This is the most unifying Yoga, exacting its obligation to construct the entire life in conformation to a discipline externally imperceptible. If this unreplace-able discipline will not be regarded as chains but will turn to the joy of re-sponsibility, we can consider the first Gates open. When the cooperation with the far-off worlds is realized, then will the second Gates unbar. And when the foundation of evolution will be understood, the bolts will fall from the third Gates. And finally, when the supremacy of the densified astral body is real-ized, then the locks of the fourth Gates unbolt. Parallel with this ascent the central fires of knowledge are kindled and amidst the lightning of subtlest energies, unfold this straight knowledge.—**Agni Yoga.***

AGNI YOGA SOCIETY. **AGNI YOGA**, c$10.00. AgY 54

_____. **AUM: SIGNS OF AGNI YOGA**, c$10.00. AgY 36

_____. **BROTHERHOOD**, c$10.00. AgY 37

_____. **COMMUNITY**, c$10.00. AgY 26

_____. **FIERY WORLD, VOL. I**, c$10.00. AgY 33

_____. **FIERY WORLD, VOL. III**, c$10.00. AgY 35

_____. **HEART**, c$10.00. AgY 32

_____. **LEAVES OF MORYA'S GARDEN, I: THE CALL; II: THE ILLUMINA-TION**, c$10.00/each. AgY 52

_____. **INFINITY, VOL. I AND II**, c$10.00/each. AgY 57

PAELIAN, GARABED. **NICHOLAS ROERICH**, c$6.00. Dr. Paelian wrote his doctoral thesis on the teachings of Roerich, and this material forms the basis of this book. The book discusses the sources of Roerich's inspiration, his life work, and his contribution to mod-ern education. Extensive quotations from Roerich's writings accompany the text. Bibliog-raphy, 110pp. AeG 74

ROERICH, NICHOLAS. **FLAME IN CHALICE**, c$5.40. A collection of poems: *In the poetry of Roerich . . . there is a fullness and expansion of consciousness, a vibration of light and color, a sense of prophecy and ongoing, of search, discovery and fulfilment that is as much part of his singing word as of the colors and contours of his brush.—*from the intro-duction. 106pp. AgY 29

_____. **THE INVINCIBLE** c$10.00. A wide ranging collection of essays discussing the ancient teachings, fairy tales, general philosophy, and much else. 395pp. AgY 74

ROOF, SIMONS. **ABOUT THE AQUARIAN AGE**, $3.95. The books by Simons Roof re-state the ancient esoteric teachings in a fresh manner that is pertinent and applicable to this time period. As the title suggests, this book discusses the coming of the Aquarian Age and the Aquarian outlook. Other chapters review evolution, reincarnation and karma, the kingdoms of life, Aquarian psychology and Aquarian values, and much else. 61pp. MSE 71

_____. **THE AQUARIAN DISCIPLES**, $3.95. Sets forth the goal and purpose of the Aquarian disciples in our age—the emphasis being on a fresh outlook, a greater sense of group consciousness, and an identity with both humanity and nature. 50pp. MSE 70

RUDHYAR, DANE. **OCCULT PREPARATIONS FOR THE NEW AGE**, $3.25. See the Astrology section.

RUSSELL, GEORGE W. (AE) **THE CANDLE OF VISION**, $2.25. This book is generally considered one of the most important records of the mystic life ever written. *Rarely and more rarely does any artist or poet interest himself in the processes of his mental and spirit-ual life. . . . Only readers who can recall some experiences similar to those described by AE will find themselves able to accept the work for what it is—a statement of uncommon fact; and only those who have developed their intuition to some degree will be able to ap-preciate the spirit of truth in which* **The Candle of Vision** *is written.—*A.R. Orage. Russell was an Irish mystic who was a key figure in the great Irish literary renaissance and was great-ly influenced by the ideas of the theosophical movement. This volume includes chapters on dreams, meditation, imagination, intuition, and much else. Introduction, 186pp. TPH 65

SADHU, MOUNI. **WAYS TO SELF REALIZATON**, $2.00. Observations concerning the inner life, its practices and external demonstration; some intimate recollections of the author's experiences with Ramana Maharshi, the modern Indian saint; and helpful insights on such subjects as eternity, the fourth dimension, marriage, and occult experiences. See the Meditation section for more of Mouni Sadhu's books. 242pp. Wil 62

SALINGER, J.D. **FRANNY AND ZOOEY**, $1.50. Salinger's books all deal, in one way or another, with the spiritual crisis confronting modern man. He explores this problem primarily through the Glass family, all of whom are intelligent and sensitive enough to suffer greatly from modern life. This book deals with a crisis in Franny, youngest member of the family, who is troubled by the injunction to *pray without ceasing* which she has read in **The Way of the Pilgrim**. Her older brother Zooey helps to resolve this crisis by out-lining her responsibilities to her profession as an actress, and to a world of people in which each of us is a Christ. The story is beautifully told with both pathos and humor. It is Sal-inger's most popular work, and quite possibly his best. 202pp. Ban 55

_____. **NINE STORIES**, $1.50. The stories in this book were written before any of Salinger's novels. Each is a little gem, carefully constructed and as enigmatic and thought provoking as the Zen koan which introduces the collection. The opening story, *A Perfect Day for Bananafish*, tells the story of Seymour Glass' suicide in Miami Beach at the age of 31. Seymour is to become the central figure of the Glass family as Salinger further devel-ops his theme of spiritual crisis. The final story, *Teddy*, is a concise and beautiful explica-tion of Advaita Vedanta. 198pp. Ban 53

_____. **RAISE HIGH THE ROOF BEAM, CARPENTERS**, $1.50. Seymour is the most important figure in the Glass family. His brother Buddy, a writer who narrates both parts of this book, calls him *a ringding enlightened man, a God-knower*. For his brothers and sisters, understanding Seymour's suicide becomes the key solving the puzzle of the world. In the first part of the book, Buddy describes Seymour's wedding day, and the sec-ond part is *a thesaurus of undetached prefatory remarks about him*. 213pp. Ban 63

H. SARAYDARIAN

H. Saraydarian was born in Asia Minor. Since his childhood he has tried to understand the mystery called man. He visited monasteries, ancient temples and mystery schools in order to find the answers to his burning questions.

He lived with Sufis, dervishes, Christian mystics and with teachers of occult lore. He is a student of the Arcane School who has started his own institution, the Aquarian Educational Group (30188 Mulholland Highway, Agoura, California 91301). His teachings are similar to those presented by Alice Bailey but the language is free from her complicated verbal obstacles. All serious students will find his work of immense practical value.

SARAYDARIAN, H. **COSMOS IN MAN**, c$10.00/$8.00. New Age concepts of the cosmos and its relation with man. Chapters on: Super-human and monadic evolution, the Aura and the etheric body, the cosmic rays, and advanced meditation techniques. Special meditations on: the Plan, the art of healing, communication with the Master. Teachings on: visualization, karma, sources of spiritual energy, and much else. This is the newest of his practical manuals. 278pp. AEG 73

_____. **THE GREAT INVOCATION**, $1.00. A section reprinted from **Science of Becoming Oneself**. AEG nd

_____. **THE HIDDEN GLORY OF THE INNER MAN**, c$6.00. A revised edition of **The Magnet of Life**, Saraydarian's first attempt at a comprehensive explanation of the nature of the human soul and its expression through the personality. The explanations and teachings are clear and precise as far as the vocabulary and the material permits. The text includes quotations from many sources including Agni yoga and theosophy. 105pp. AEG 75

_____. **THE SCIENCE OF BECOMING ONESELF**, c$8.00. An immensely practical, enlightening work which clearly explains many difficult esoteric concepts and presents numerous exercises which lead the reader step-by-step into an expanded consciousness. Includes many diagrams, clarifying the more difficult material. The terminology used is well defined in the text. Highly recommended for all serious students desiring a discipline. 319pp. AEG 69

_____. **THE SCIENCE OF MEDITATION**, c$8.00. See the Meditation section.

SCHARFSTEIN, BEN-AMI. **MYSTICAL EXPERIENCE**, $2.50. This is a fairly academic analysis of the mystical experience which begins with a review of the rationale for and defenses of mysticism and goes from there to an analysis of various mystical techniques. A final chapter is devoted to an exploration of *The Eleven Quintessences of the Mystical State*. This is a very readable book and in terms of Professor Scharfstein's aims as we see them, it is quite a successful one. One cannot expect to get a glimpse of the mystical experience from a book which discusses mystical experience in general—but with this qualification in mind, the general reader and the psychologist can get a good overview of the subject from this volume. Notes, index. 195pp. Pen 73

SCHUON, FRITHJOF. **LOGIC AND TRANSCENDENCE**, $6.65. Huston Smith had this to say about Schuon: *The man is a living wonder; intellectually a propos religion, equally in depth and breadth, the paragon of our time. I know of no living thinker who begins to rival him.* Schuon's philosophical writing is excellent; however, it is recommended only to those who are well versed in comparative religion and mystical philosophy. Many of his references are fairly obscure. This is a collection of chapters on a variety of subjects, each one independent of the others. He writes very clearly and quotes from source material. Many foreign words are used within the body of the text, although they are usually defined in the notes. 273pp. H&R 75

_____. **SPIRITUAL PERSPECTIVES AND HUMAN FACTS**, c$6.15. A philosophical examination of the ways in which a knowledge of unity admist multiplicity and the necessary diversity that extends from unity, can awaken and illumine the human mind and lead to deeper understanding. The differing *spiritual contours* of the Christian, Jewish, Islamic, Hindu and Far Eastern worlds are shown as a result of necessary differences in their perspective and symbolism. 213pp. Prn 69

SCOTT, CYRIL. **THE INITIATE: SOME IMPRESSIONS OF A GREAT SOUL**, c$7.95. A fascinating investigation into the esoteric implications of music. Scott, himself a noted composer, first discusses pure music, inspiration and invention in the sphere of Western music; and then the music of the Deva (spirit intelligences) is considered in relation to the occult constitution of man and the lives and work of various composers. A historical section traces the beginnings of music and religion and their combined effects on classical civilizations of the past. Includes a good bibliography. 208pp. Wei 20

_____. **THE INITIATES IN THE DARK CYCLE**, c$5.50. This is the second sequel to **The Initiate**, continuing the teaching and the personal impressions. 232pp. Wei 32

_____. **THE INITIATE IN THE NEW WORLD**, c$5.95. Sequel to **The Initiate**, offering further glimpses of the master interwoven with excerpts from his discourses. 302pp. Wei 35

SEPHARIAL. **A MANUAL OF OCCULTISM**, $4.00. Written by a well known occultist and astrologer, this book provides fundamental information on many aspects of the secret sciences including sections on astrology, palmistry, divination, numerology, talismans, Tarot and dreams. 356pp. Wei

SHIRLEY, RALPH. **OCCULTISTS AND MYSTICS OF ALL AGES**, $2.95. First published in 1920, this scholarly volume examines the lives and teachings of Apollonius, Plotinus, Michael Scot, Paracelsus, Swedenborg, Cagliostro, and Anna Kingsford. 224pp. CiP 72

SHRINE OF WISDOM. **IDEAL PHILOSOPHY**, $1.25. *What is Ideal Philosophy? In brief, it is that which enables the sincere thinker progressively to approach and understand the nature and purpose of the universe, including himself and his fellow man.* This is a very clear presentation of this philosophy, with chapters on purpose, ideas, morality, science,

religion, and philosophy. 123pp. ShW 65

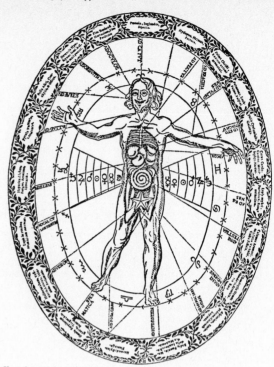

Chart showing the relationship between the human body and the exterior universe

SHUMAKER, WAYNE. **THE OCCULT SCIENCES IN THE RENAISSANCE—A STUDY IN INTELLECTUAL PATTERNS**, c$15.00. This scholarly study offers a summary and analysis of five esoteric *scientific* systems: astrology, natural or white magic, witchcraft, alchemy, and the meditative philosophy associated with Hermes Trismegistus. To many Renaissance men, these systems were considered sources of truth about the meaning and order of human life. The author's primary aim is to enlarge the modern comprehension of these systems. The text is well illustrated and there are many source notes and a comprehensive bibliography. 290pp. UCP 72

SINCLAIR, JOHN. **THE OTHER UNIVERSE**, $4.40. This volume discusses the ancient teachings in the light of the approaches of modern day esoteric groups. Sinclair is an English actor who has explored many of the paths and seems to be most influenced by the Arcane School and the teachings that have been channelled through Alice Bailey. The account is fairly scattered; however, some interesting ideas are presented, especially in the discussion of the possibility of self-initiated action by groups of individuals working through organons (*instruments of group consciousness*). Bibliography, 128pp. Rid 73

SPALDING, BAIRD. **LIFE AND TEACHINGS OF THE MASTERS OF THE FAR EAST**, c$4.00/each. These five volumes present the teaching Spalding received in his journeys (on the astral plane?) to India. No one was ever sure whether the masters he spoke about were still in their bodies or not. Many went with him on his *tours* to India, but no one reported seeing his masters. Whatever their source, the teachings presented in these volumes are clear and oriented toward illuminating Western man. Some of our customers consider them to be among the best collections of teachings available. Dev 55

SPENCE, LEWIS. **AN ENCYCLOPEDIA OF OCCULTISM**, $5.95. A compendium of information on occult science, mysticism, individuals, and general metaphysics. First published in 1920, this volume is still considered the most comprehensive available—although the entries are not often as juicy with gossip as Cavendish's. The listings give bibliographical references and the text includes a number of plates. This oversize book is an important reference work for all libraries. 440pp. CiP 60

STACE, WALTER, ed. **THE TEACHINGS OF THE MYSTICS**, $1.95. A superb compendium of mystical writings and teachings, including Hindu and Upanishadic teachings, Sri Aurobindo, Zen and Buddhist selections, Lao Tzu, Plotinus, numerous Christian and Islamic mystics, the Zohar and contemporary mystical experiences. Stace provides an excellent introduction, interpretative commentaries, and explanations. 240pp. NAL 60

STARCKE, WALTER. **THE GOSPEL OF RELATIVITY**, $3.95. *This book was written during the 1970's, not long before the end of the world. It was written by one of those who had a great struggle of his own trying to face the crisis.... I submit this book because it is valuable to see how the truths which eventually led to the freedom of mankind were voiced at this time.... I was one of the young who survived. this book was written by one of my teachers, and I am grateful because, although he was barely on the edge of understanding, he helped me to find out who I am.* A well illustrated, interesting essay/novel. 111pp. H&R 73

_____. **THIS DOUBLE THREAD**, $2.50. Starcke's first book, explaining what is wrong with our society and why—and what we can do to make our lives more meaningful and satisfactory. 146pp. H&R 67

_____. THE ULTIMATE REVOLUTION, $2.50. Starcke's personal formulas and philosophy for finding a more meaningful, harmonious, and satisfying life. 155pp. H&R 69

RONG, MARY, ed. LETTERS OF THE SCATTERED BROTHERHOOD, c$4.95. A collection of mystical messages of inspiration. Fragmentary quotations are interspersed through the text which bear witness to the likeness of spiritual experience throughout the ages. 190pp. H&R 48

TAYLOR, THOMAS. THOMAS TAYLOR THE PLATONIST— SELECTED WRITINGS, $24.25. Taylor (1758–1835) prepared the first full English translation of Plato and Aristotle. He is also noted for his translations of and commentaries on Plotinus, Porphyry, and Iamblichus. This edition is edited by Kathleen Raine and G.M. Harper, both of whom supply introductory essays. Illustrations. 549pp. PUP 69

THOREAU, HENRY. THE ILLUSTRATED WALDEN, $3.95. This is a complete rendering of the text accompanied by a beautiful selection of photographs by Herbert Gleason and a historical introduction by J. Lyndon Shanley. Walden is universally considered one of the most sensitive portraits of the natural world ever written. Index, 387pp. PUP 73

THOULESS, ROBERT. AN INTRODUCTION TO THE PSYCHOLOGY OF RELIGION, $3.75. A detailed academic study which applies the science of psychology to problems of religion and explores such questions as: Why do people believe? Why are their beliefs often held with irrational strength? How are changes in belief produced? How are religious belief systems related to mental health? Much of the material is based on statistical surveys and both Eastern and Western religions are considered. Index, 160pp. CUP 71

THREE INITIATES. THE KYBALION, c$5.50. See the Ancient Egypt section.

UNDERHILL, EVELYN. MYSTICISM, $3.75. Divided into two sections: the first, called *The Mystic Fact*, explains the relation of mysticism to vitalism, psychology, etc., and the second, *The Mystic Way*, describes the awakening, purification and training of the self in its ascent on the path which leads to *the blessedness of Unitive life*. An appendix contains a historical sketch of European mysticism and the most complete topical bibliography we've seen. Her most important work. 519pp. Dut 61

_____. PRACTICAL MYSTICISM, $2.25. Introduces the methods and practice of mysticism to those who have no prior knowledge of the subject. What mysticism is and what it has to offer the average person, how it helps to solve problems, how it increases efficiency, and how it can harmonize with the duties and ideals of an active life. 169pp. Dut 15

VAN DUSEN, WILSON. THE PRESENCE OF OTHER WORLDS: THE FINDINGS OF EMMANUEL SWEDENBORG, $1.75. *I had pursued all the principal writers in psychoanalysis and psychotherapy. Only Carl Jung even approached the stature of Swedenborg. Swedenborg knew personally . . . that Self which Jung knew only by speculation on its symbolic manifestations. . . . My purpose is simple, to bring Swedenborg within the reach of many. There are a number of keys to aid this grasp. It is necessary to understand the age and circumstances in which he worked. He lived at the dawn of science in the eighteenth century. He had mastered all the sciences of his day. Though the strange rightness of his later psychological-spiritual findings would later get him labeled as either a great mystic or a madman, he never changed fundamentally from the scientist who simply wanted to understand and describe the whole existence. When he finished all the known outer world he started to work on the mind. . . . Swedenborg was looking for God within. . . . As he became a more appropriate instrument through . . . changes, the Hand of the Divine became more apparent. Finally . . . he was introduced into heaven and hell. Perhaps many down through time had had glimpses of the worlds beyond this one, but Swedenborg was to have direct and relatively constant access for many years.*—from the introduction. This is an excellent study of Swedenborg and VanDusen seems to have achieved his aim of making this great mystic accessible to the general reader. He also gives us an annotated guide to Swedenborg's writings. Notes, 255pp. H&R 74

VASTO, LANZA del. MAKE STRAIGHT THE WAY OF THE LORD, c$7.95. Lanza del Vasto is the acknowledged leader of the nonviolent movement in France. A disciple of Gandhi, who bestowed upon him the name of Shantidas (Servant of Peace), he founded the Community of the Ark in France as a nonsectarian working order of individuals who put nonviolent principles into practice in their daily lives. This volume contains the essence of his teachings in selections from ten of his books. In the first part he speaks of stillness, attention, singing, and love. In the second he deals with basic concepts such as knowledge, energy, creation. And the final part is concerned with social realities such as wealth and poverty, labor, war, and peace. 254pp. RaH 74

WAITE, A.E. AZOTH OR THE STAR IN THE EAST, c$10.00. Azoth *was written at a time when Waite was immersed in the mysteries of alchemy and its texts, of which he came to have an unrivaled knowledge. . . . He realized that mysticism consisted of both transcendental science and transcendental religion, and that the alchemy of transformation was both physical and spiritual.*—from the introduction by L. Shepard. In this book he surveys the entire field in great detail. 239pp. UnB 73

_____. LAMPS OF WESTERN MYSTICISM, $2.45. In the light of the author's conviction that this is the most opportune moment in history to discover higher levels of consciousness and unveil the deeper aspects of man's being, this work relates the mystical journeys of a number of prominent figures of Western civilization. 330pp. Mul 73

_____. THE OCCULT SCIENCES, $6.00. According to Waite, this volume embraces *in a compressed and digested form, the whole scope of occult knowledge, expressed in the language of a learner.* Topics include magical practices, alchemy, divination, astrology, Qabala, mystics, Rosicrucians, Freemasons, mesmerism, spiritualism, and theosophy. 292pp. HeR 72

WHITMAN, WALT. LEAVES OF GRASS, c$5.95. This is a beautifully produced, unabridged edition, with an illustration at the beginning of each chapter. 781pp. RaH 50

WILSON, COLIN. THE OCCULT, $3.95. In the first part Wilson stresses the connection between creativity and psychic sensitivity, the tapping of the subconscious mind for the forces that are normally inaccessible to consciousness. The second part is a history of mages and adepts, set in their historical background. The third part concerns witchcraft, vampirism, the history of spiritualism, etc. The last chapter takes up the metaphysical questions that arise out of occultism, and concludes with the nature of man's latent powers. We learned a great deal from reading this book—in fact, much more than we really wanted to know. Includes a good bibliography. 601pp. RaH 71

A SYLPH from sketch by Howard Wookey. The sylphs were volatile, changeable entities, passing to and fro with the rapidity of lightning. They work through the gases and ethers of the earth and are kindly disposed toward human beings. They are nearly always represented as winged, sometimes as tiny cherubs and at other times as delicate fairies.

From sketch by Howard Wookey.

WILLIAM BUTLER YEATS (1865-1939)

No one can fully comprehend the poetry of Yeats without taking account of his deep and lifelong preoccupation with occultism and mysticism. In one of his letters he wrote: *The mystical life is the centre of all that I do and all that I think and all that I write.*

As a young man Yeats became involved in theosophy. After a few years he was initiated into the Hermetic Order of the Golden Dawn and he learned about the Qabala, astrology, and Rosicrucianism—all of which were to play a major part in his poetry. He was also part of the Irish literary renaissance and the mystical ideas of the Celts were restated in many of his poems.

BACHEHAN, H.R. W. B. YEATS AND OCCULTISM , c$7.95. This is the only systematic treatise available which analyzes the impact that Western and Eastern occultism had upon Yeats' creative work. The text reads like a scholarly paper and is accompanied by a profusion of notes. Many quotations from Yeats' work are included. Illustrations, notes, bibliography. 296pp. Wei 74

RAINE, KATHLEEN. DEATH-IN-LIFE AND LIFE-IN-DEATH, $7.00. A detailed analysis of two of Yeats' poems. Ms. Raine, a noted Blake scholar, defines Yeats' philosophy of the continuation and growth of the soul as revealed in *Cuchulain Comforted* and *News for the Delphic Oracle*. She also shows Yeats' debt to his predecessors, especially Blake and Plotinus, and reveals the deep faith that Yeats had in those principles which shaped his life and art. The text is illustrated by plates from Blake and others. Notes, 63pp. Dol 74

ROSENTHAL, M.L. ed. SELECTED POEMS AND TWO PLAYS OF WILLIAM BUTLER YEATS, $2.95. A selection of 195 poems representing the essential poetic achievement of Yeats, covering the years 1889 through 1939, printed from the most reliable texts and in the sequence set by Yeats himself. The two plays are *Calvary* and *Purgatory*. The editor provides notes, a glossary, and an introduction which surveys Yeats' development, his life and thought, his techniques, and his use of symbolism. Index, 275pp. McM 62

YEATS, WILLIAM BUTLER. THE AUTOBIOGRAPHY OF WILLIAM BUTLER YEATS, $2.95. A very intense personal account ranging over fifty-eight years, from Yeats' earliest memories to his winning of the Nobel Prize. All who are moved by his poetry should be fascinated by this account. Yeats' prose style is excellent. Index, 404pp. McM 65

_____. THE COLLECTED POEMS OF W.B. YEATS, c$9.95. The definitive edition, with Yeats' final revisions. Index, 480pp. McM 56

_____. A VISION, $2.95. A system of supernaturally revealed images, acquired through Mrs. Yeats' efforts at automatic writing, gave Yeats both a method by which he was able to categorize humanity and a method for dealing with history. Eventually Yeats found in these communications the metaphors for poetry he sought. A Vision is essential to any understanding of many of his most notable poems. It also contains some of the most penetrating and beautiful prose that Yeats ever wrote. 305pp. McM 37

ZAEHNER, R.C. MYSTICISM: SACRED AND PROFANE, $3.95. A scholarly, not very exciting analysis of various types of praeternatural experience ranging from the sensations produced by such drugs as mescaline to the mystical states described by the Christian and Muslim mystics and the various schools of mystical thought in India. 256pp. Oxf 57

MYTHOLOGY

The comparative study of the mythologies of the world compels us to view the cultural history of mankind as a unit; for we find that such themes as the firetheft, deluge, land of the dead, virgin birth, and resurrected hero have a worldwide distribution—appearing everywhere in new combinations while remaining, like the elements of a kaleidoscope, only a few and always the same. Furthermore, whereas in tales told for entertainment such mythical themes are taken lightly—in a spirit, obviously, of play—they appear also in religious context, where they are accepted not only as factually true but even as revelations of the verities to which the whole culture is a living witness and from which it derives both its spiritual authority and its temporal power. No human society has yet been found in which such mythological motifs have not been rehearsed in liturgies; interpreted by seers, poets, theologians, or philosophers; presented in art; magnified in song; and ecstatically experienced in life-empowering visions. Indeed, the chronicle of our species, from its earliest page, has been not simply an account of the progress of man the tool-maker, but—more tragically—a history of the pouring of blazing visions into the minds of seers and the efforts of earthly communities to incarnate unearthly covenants. Every people has received its own seal and sign of supernatural designation, communicated to its heroes and daily proved in the lives and experience of its folk. And though many who bow with closed eyes in the sanctuaries of their own tradition rationally scrutinize and disqualify the sacraments of others, an honest comparison immediately reveals that all have been built from one fund of mythological motifs—variously selected, organized, interpreted, and ritualized, according to local need, but revered by every people on earth.

A fascinating psychological, as well as historical, problem is thus presented. Man, apparently, cannot maintain himself in the universe without belief in some arrangement of the general inheritance of myth. In fact, the fullness of his life would even seem to stand in a direct ratio to the depth and range not of his rational thought but of his local mythology. Whence the force of these unsubstantial themes, by which they are empowered to galvanize populations, creating of them civilizations, each with a beauty and self-compelling destiny of its own? And why should it be that whenever men have looked for something solid on which to found their lives, they have chosen not the facts in which the world abounds, but the myths of an immemorial imagination—preferring even to make life a hell for themselves and their neighbors, in the name of some violent god, to accepting gracefully the bounty the world affords?

Are the modern civilizations to remain spiritually locked from each other in their local notions of the sense of the general tradition; or can we not now break through to some more profoundly based point and counterpoint of human understanding? For it is a fact that the myths of our several cultures work upon us, whether consciously or unconsciously, as energy-releasing, life-motivating and -directing agents; so that even though our rational minds may be in agreement, the myths by which we are living—or by which our fathers live—can be driving us, at that very moment, diametrically apart.

—from **The Masks of God: Primitive Mythology** by Joseph Campbell

ASTON, W.G. **NIHONGI,** $5.25. See the Zen sub-section of Buddhism.

BACHOFEN, J.J. **MYTH, RELIGION AND MOTHER RIGHT,** $3.45. *This selection fro the works of Bachofen offers chapters on symbols and myths. The central part is the vestigation of the religious and juridical character of Matriarchy in the Ancient World– theme that is inseparably linked with the name of Bachofen. His thought that the progre from the maternal to the parental conception of man forms the most important turni point in the history of the relations between the sexes is still echoing in anthropolog* This edition is translated by Ralph Manheim and includes 57pp of introductory mater by George Boas and Joseph Campbell. Notes, glossary, bibliography, index. 366pp. PUP

BEOWULF, $1.95. **Beowulf** (probably composed in the eighth century AD) is our on native English heroic epic. It was written by an anonymous Christian poet addressing Christian audience, but in the figure of Beowulf, the Scandinavian warrior, and his stru gles against monsters, the life and outlook of the pagan age come alive. The poem is subtle blending of themes—such as the conflict of good and evil—and an examination heroism. This is a prose translation by David Wright, with an introduction, notes, and glossary. 122pp. Pen 57

BLACKER, CARMEN and MICHAEL LOEWE, eds. **ANCIENT COSMOLOGIES,** c$21.5 See the Ancient Civilizations section.

BULFINCH, THOMAS. **BULFINCH'S MYTHOLOGY,** c$5.95. Bulfinch's versions of th ancient myths are by far the best known and most widely read of any modern version. This complete edition includes *The Age of Fable, The Age of Chivalry,* and *Legends Charlemagne.* Introduction, indices. 778pp. RaH nd

CAMPBELL, JOSEPH. **THE FLIGHT OF THE WILD GANDER,** $3.55. An enlightenin collection of six essays: *The Fairy Tale, Bios and Myths, Primitive Man as Metaphysician Mythogensis, The Symbol without Meaning,* and *The Secularization of the Sacred.* I them Professor Campbell discusses the origin and meaning of myths from many angle and discusses a number of myths in depth. We have found the collection very useful for better understanding of mythic expression and of myths in general. Illustrations, notes index. 248pp. Reg 51

_____. **HERO WITH 1000 FACES,** $3.95. Despite their infinite variety of setting incident, and costume, the myths of the world offer only a limited number of response to the riddle of life. Campbell presents the composite hero here. Apollo, the Buddha, an numerous other protagonists of folklore and religion enact simultaneously the variou phases of their common story. The relationship of their timeless symbols to those redis covered in dreams by contemporary depth psychology is a starting point for interpreta tion. This is then compared with the words of spiritual leaders such as Jesus, Lao Tzu, an Muhammad. From behind a thousand faces the single hero emerges, archetype of all myth and of man's eternal struggle for identity. 416pp. PUP

_____. **THE MASKS OF GOD, VOL. I: PRIMITIVE MYTHOLOGY,** c$8.95/3.75 The primitive roots of the mythology of the world are examined in the light of the most recent discoveries in archaeology, anthropology, and psychology. *I consider this, as his other books, of outstanding importance and scholarship, clarity and depth.... Anyone truly interested in the science of man ... will find these books a wealth of data, penetrat ingly analysed and written.*—Erich Fromm. Each volume includes extensive reference notes. 504pp. Vik 59

The Eye of Horus

_____. **THE MASKS OF GOD, VOL. II: ORIENTAL MYTHOLOGY,** c$8.95/ $3.95. An exploration of Eastern mythology as it developed into the distinctive religion of Egypt, India, China and Japan. 561pp. Vik 62

_____. **THE MASKS OF GOD, VOL. III: OCCIDENTAL MYTHOLOGY,** c$8.95/ $3.95. A systematic and fascinating comparison of the themes that underlie the art, wor ship, and literature of the Western world. 564pp. Vik 64

_____. **THE MASKS OF GOD, VOL. IV: CREATIVE MYTHOLOGY,** c$12.50/ $4.95. The whole inner story of modern culture, spanning our entire philosophical, spirit ual, and artistic history since the Dark Ages, and treating modern man's unique position as the creator of his own mythology. 730pp. Vik 68

Early Sumerian Eye Goddess figurines, 3500–3000 BC

_____. **THE MYTHIC IMAGE**, c$45.00. Dr. Campbell has spent his life studying mythology of the world's high civilizations and is considered the most noted expert in field. He has produced many definitive volumes, and this mammoth tome, in addition ing a summation of his life's work, is the last volume of the Bollingen Series to be d and it sums up and enlarges on much of the work that the series has done in explor- the innumerable facets of symbology that are revealed through religion, mythology, hology, and the arts. Here Campbell presents nearly 450 color and black-and-white il- ations of mythic art from Mesopotamian, Egyptian, Indian, Chinese, European, and ec culture covering five millennia. Starting with the relation of dreams to myth, Camp- distinguishes two orders of myths: that of the relatively simple, nonliterate folk tra- n and that of the infinitely more complex literate civilizations that culminated in the l of the world's great religions, Buddhism, Christianity, and Islam. He traces the devel- ent of the mythologies and, with text and pictures, demonstrates the important dif- nces between Oriental and Occidental interpretations of dreams and myth. Ideas of e-time, cosmology, the sacrificed god, and transformation and transmutation are pre- d through narrative and image. An extraordinarily beautiful volume. Index, notes, size. 563pp. PUP 74

_____. **MYTHS TO LIVE BY**, $1.95. In this book, the foremost American author- on world myth untangles popularly confused notions about myth and demonstrates particular myths continue to reflect human needs. Based on a series of talks, he relates hs to Zen, to schizophrenia and the inward journey of LSD, to the moon walk and outward journey, to the confrontation of East and West in religion, etc. 291pp. Ban 72

_____. **MYTHS, DREAMS, AND RELIGION**, $2.75. A transcription of eleven re- d lectures delivered under the auspices of the Society for the Arts, Religion and Con- porary Culture on one topic, _Myth and Dream._ Five of these speakers were theolo- s, three psychiatrists, two orientalists, and one a student of comparative mythology. pp. Dut 70

LUM, PADRAIC. **THE CHILDREN OF ODIN: THE BOOK OF NORTHERN MYTHS**, .95. See the Children's Books section.

_____. **MYTHS OF THE WORLD**, $3.50. Well written renditions of the most im- rtant myths from the following traditions: Egyptian, Babylonian, Persian, Jewish post- ristian period, Greek, Roman, Graeco-Roman, Celtic, Finnish, Icelandic, Indian, Chi- se, Japanese, Polynesian, Peruvian, Central American and Mexican, and Zuni. Many of myths presented here are not readily available elsewhere and this is an excellent cross- tion of a great many traditions. Introduction, index. 357pp. G&D 30

OMARASWAMY, ANANDA and SISTER NIVEDITA. **MYTHS OF THE HINDUS ND BUDDHISTS**, $3.95. See the Indian Philosophy section.

OURLANDER, HAROLD. **A TREASURY OF AFRICAN FOLKLORE**, c$14.95. _In his es, myths, epics and legends, the African bridges back to the morning of his creation, erts the worth and weaknesses of the human species, ponders on courage, life and death, d reflects the learning of centuries about the character of man._ Courlander is a specialist African and Afro-American life and traditions and here he presents a definitive account the oral literature, traditions, myths, legends, and epics of Africa. He's a good story- er, too. Illustrations, bibliography, index. 636pp. Crn 75

AVIDSON, H.R. ELLIS. **GODS AND MYTHS OF NORTHERN EUROPE**, $2.50. This he only popular treatment of Northern European mythology that we know of. It is the rk of a scholar who specializes in Norse and Germanic mythology. All the important ds and goddesses are discussed. In addition to a retelling of many of the stories, there is air amount of interpretative material. The myths are topically arranged and the retellings d well. Glossary, index. 250pp. Pen 64

DOWSON, JOHN. **A CLASSICAL DICTIONARY OF INDIAN MYTHOLOGY**, c$10.00. See the Indian Philosophy section.

DUMEZIL, GEORGES. **GODS OF THE ANCIENT NORTHMEN**, c$13.45. An English translation of some of the most important and representative of Dumezil's writings in the field of Germanic mythology. Dumezil is without question the premier scholar in the field of Indo-European mythology and culture and his work, while not widely known, has been highly influential. Excellent introductory material is included along with many notes. The work is edited and translated by Einar Haugen. Index, 195pp. UCP 73

MIRCEA ELIADE

Mircea Eliade and Joseph Campbell stand at the forefront of the study of mythology in the twentieth century. While Campbell's emphasis is on the psychological meaning of myths, in the Jungian sense, Eliade stresses the basic religious nature of all myths and his writings are considerably more academic than Campbell's. Many more of Eliade's works are described in the Compar- ative Religion section. _On the one hand, Eliade entertains the notion of the ambivalence of the sacred, which is an ongoing recognition of the practical reality (concreteness) of an object, that has become a sacred symbol. . . . On the other hand, Eliade understands the existential function of myth as an art form, which is both an act of creative thought and an effort to make a world out of often chaotic natural reality. Yet Eliade's distinctive approach as his- torian of religion is best understood when we notice the pervasive attention that he gives to the element of religious experience in both myth and ritual as symbolic realities. He thus calls our attention to something in the life of primitive peoples that is critically important beyond the anthropological confirmation that they are indeed human beings with the art of common sense and a remarkable inclination toward myth-making. Eliade, in sum, in- sists that behind and beyond the linguistic structure and pragmatic function of myths lies the conception, gestation, and birth of myth out of the depths of genuine religious experience._ —from the introduction to Beane and Doty's **Reader.**

BEANE, WENDELL and WILLIAM DOTY, eds. **MYTHS, RITES, SYMBOLS: A MIR- CEA ELIADE READER**, $3.95/each. _I should like to express my deep gratitude to the editors of this volume. . . . They have gone to a great deal of trouble in excerpting selec- tions from various publications that have spanned the last forty years, and I believe that they have been enormously successful in choosing passages that effectively and honestly present my central ideas on the interpretation of religious ideology, behavior, and insti- tutions. . . . I am delighted with their choice of texts, and their careful editing has made them uniformly accessible for the use of the nonspecialist._—Mircea Eliade. Both of the volumes include the same introductory material. Volume I is divided into the following major sections: _The Structure of Myths, The Greatness and Decadence of Myths, Cos- mogenic Myth and Sacred History, Sacred Time and Myths, Varieties of Sacred Time, Intercommunication, Ritual Performance, Mythic Archetype, The Sacred and the Pro- fane, Entering the Cosmos and Society, Forming and Recreating, Reflecting and Main- taining the Sacred._ Volume II covers the following material: _Prestige and Power of the Sacred Specialist, The Shaman as Specialist Par Excellence, Women's Mysteries, Men's Mysteries, Classical and Christian Mysteries, Mysticism: Yoga and the Mystic Light, The Nature and Function of Religious Symbolism, World-Patterning Symbols, Symbols for Transitions in Life, Symbols Concerning Paradise._ Notes, 493pp. H&R 76

The falcon of Horus astride an oryx, an analogy to the triumph of truth and justice over evil

ELIADE, MIRCEA. **MYTH AND REALITY**, $2.45. An important work on the nature and significance of myths—ranging from the ancient Egyptians and classical Greeks to the works of Picasso and James Joyce. Aimed at the general reader. Notes, bibliography, index. 212pp. H&R 63

_____. **THE MYTH OF THE ETERNAL RETURN**, $2.95. This is an essay on mankind's experience of history and its interpretation, beginning with a study of the trad- itional or mythological view, and concluding with a comparative estimate of modern approaches. *I consider it the most significant of my books; and when I am asked in what order they should be read, I always recommend beginning with* **The Myth of the Eternal Return.** Excellent bibliography and many notes. 195pp. PUP 54

_____. **MYTHS, DREAMS, AND MYSTERIES,** $3.25. The central theme of this book is the meeting and confrontation of the two types of mentality which might be called the traditional and the modern; the first being characteristic of man in archaic and Oriental societies, the second of man in modern societies of the Western type. This is a detailed analysis of each, and of their encounter. Includes reference notes. 254pp. H&R 57

_____. **RITES AND SYMBOLS OF INITIATION: THE MYSTERIES OF BIRTH AND REBIRTH,** $2.95. Here Eliade takes one particular subject, the almost universal pre- velance in human culture of some force of initiatory rite and custom, and treats it in a way that is at once scholarly and interpretative. This book is not merely a collection of data, but also a profound attempt to discern the underlying meaning and purpose of ini- tiation. Includes many source notes. 181pp. H&R 58

_____. **SHAMANISM,** $4.95. A brilliant treatise on the characterization and pecu- liarities of shamanism, and including a definition of this phenomenon of man's religious fervor. The book contains a compilation and description of shamanistic rituals, practices, and techniques in a variety of different cultures. Excellent bibliography and notes, index. 622pp. PUP 64

_____. **THE TWO AND THE ONE,** $2.75. A scholarly comparison of religious ex- periences and beliefs which synthesizes psychology, anthropology, and religion. 223pp. H&R 62

EVANS, BERGER. **DICTIONARY OF MYTHOLOGY,** $1.50. A fairly comprehensive dictionary, emphasizing the myths of Greece and Rome and also covering Norse mythol- ogy, the Arthurian legends, and the most often encountered figures from Egyptian and Babylonian mythology. The material is alphabetically arranged and the entries are fairly short. Cross-references, index. 333pp. Del 70

FELDMANN, SUSAN, ed. **AFRICAN MYTHS AND TALES,** $1.25. A collection of stor- ies and myths from a number of African cultures and traditions. All the tales are quite short. Introduction, bibliography. 318pp. Del 63

FRANZ, MARIE-LOUISE von. **PATTERNS OF CREATIVITY MIRRORED IN CREA- TION MYTHS,** $9.45. See the Jungian Psychology section.

_____. **A PSYCHOLOGICAL INTERPRETATION OF THE GOLDEN ASS OF APULEIUS,** $7.55. See the Jungian Psychology section.

JAMES FRAZER

FRAZER, JAMES. **FOLKLORE IN THE OLD TESTAMENT,** $5.95. Frazer has compiled all the sections of **The Golden Bough** which are concerned solely with the stories and cus- toms of the Old Testament and presented them in this volume. He also includes counter- parts of these stories from a variety of other cultures which show the universality of the psychic experience which evoked these tales. For example, there are stories of a great flood from at least twenty different cultures, none of which were likely to have had anything at all to do with the ancient Hebrews. The volume is topically organized and contains an amazing amount of different myths and stories. The book was put together sometime in the last century and was out of print for quite a long time. Includes a very complete index. 523pp. Har 75

_____. **THE GOLDEN BOUGH,** c$7.95/4.95. A momumental survey of ancient man which shows that, contrary to the popular thought, he was enmeshed in a nightmare of magic, taboos, and superstititions. This work describes ancient man's primitive methods of worship, sex practices, magic, strange (to us) rituals and festivals. The tone of this vol- ume is very much that of *the white man's burden*—but it is a greatly respected classic. This edition was abridged by Frazer himself and is considered the authorized version. A com- plete thirteen volume edition of this classic is available for $200.00. 864pp. McM 22

GASTER, THEODOR. **THE NEW GOLDEN BOUGH,** $2.25. A modernized, readable abridgement. We prefer this version—while it is not as authoritative as Frazer's own, it is a work of impeccable scholarship and it is written in a lively style. If you are deeply inter- ested in Frazer's work, it would probably be helpful to have both versions, since they do contain somewhat different selections. Introduction, notes, index. 859pp. NAL 59

FREUND, PHILIP. **MYTHS OF CREATION,** $2.95. *I became curious about the creation myths of other religions and races, the tales of how the world began.... I was fascinated*

by the myths because of their poetic quality.... *What held my interest... was the* *that I might learn something fundamental and permanent about the mind of man—at* *myself—by contemplating mythology, and especially man's always daring stories of* *beginning. What follows is a voyage of exploration.... In these stories we can see* *man reasoned when he looked at the world and first tried to explain it to himself. Le* *examine his answers, his earliest and latest attempts at understanding his universe, not o* *in primitive myth but in recent science.* Index, 244pp. TrA 64

GALAHAD BOOKS. **ENCYCLOPEDIA OF WORLD MYTHOLOGY,** c$9.98. A bea fully produced anonymously written volume, 8½x12", with hundreds of color plates. text is divided into the following sections: common mythological themes, compara mythology, Egypt and the Middle East, ancient Greece, ancient Rome, Northern and C tral Europe, the Celtic realms, the mythology of animals, and the mythology of pla The account is simply written and each section is sub-divided. Each of the important g and goddesses is discussed individually. This would be a fine introduction to world m ology for children—although the print is small. Index, A&W 75

THE GILGAMESH EPIC

The origins of this ancient Sumerian epic extend back to the third milleni BC, 1500 years before Homer. It was miraculously preserved on clay tab which were deciphered in the last century. It tells of the adventures of King of Uruk in his fruitless search for immortality and of his friendship w Enkidu, a wild man from the hills. The epic also includes a legend of the Flo which agrees in many details with the Biblical story of Noah.

Gilgamesh (?), Bull, and Bird, from decorated stone ritual vase. Sumerian, early third millenium BC

HEIDEL, ALEXANDER, tr. **GILGAMESH EPIC AND OLD TESTAMENT PARALLEL** $3.75. A translation and interpretation of the Gilgamesh Epic and related Babylonian a Assyrian documents. Heidel compares them with corresponding portions of the Old Te ament in order to determine the inherent historical relationship of Hebrew and Mesop tamian ideas. Many explanatory notes, 269pp. UCh 46

MASON, HERBERT, tr. **GILGAMESH,** $1.25. A verse narrative which makes the age-o story come alive. Some background material is also included which discusses Sumeri mythology as well as aspects of the epic itself. 126pp. NAL 70

SANDARS, N.K., tr. **THE EPIC OF GILGAMESH,** $1.95. A straightforward prose ve sion, along with an excellent long introduction and a glossary. 127pp. Pen 72

GRAVES, ROBERT, tr. **THE GOLDEN ASS,** $2.95. A modern translation of the sto of Lucius Apuleius, a young man who encountered many strange adventures, includi offending a priestess of the White Goddess and suffering for his offense the indignity being turned into an ass. How Apuleius supported his misfortune and how he contrived last to appease the Goddess and resume his human form make up the body of the tale. troduction, 315pp. FSG 51

_____. **THE GREEK MYTHS,** $5.20/set. A masterwork of two volumes whi covers the creation myths, the legends of the birth and lives of the great Olympians, t Theseus, Oedipus, and Heracles cycles, the Argonaut voyage, the tale of Troy, and mu else—two hundred selections in all! All the scattered elements of each myth have been a sembled and many variants are recorded. Full references to the classical sources and co ious indices make the volumes invaluable to the scholar. A full commentary on each my explains and interprets the classical version in the light of today's archaeological and a thropological knowledge. Graves' versions are not as much fun to read as Edith Hamilton or Bulfinch's, but the books are excellent works of scholarship and are immensely helpf to those seeking a deeper understanding of the myths. Maps, 784pp. Pen 55

_____. **THE WHITE GODDESS,** $4.95. *[T]his remains a very difficult book, well as a very queer one, to be avoided by anyone with a distracted, tired or rigidly scie tific mind.... My thesis is that the language of poetic myth anciently current in the Me iterranean and Northern Europe was a magical language bound up with popular religio ceremonies in honor of the Moon-goddess, or Muse, some of them dating from the O Stone Age, and that this remains the language of true poetry. The language is called myt* and is based on a few simple magical formulas, kept close secrets for thousands of yea by her initiates. 511pp. FSG 48

EEN, ROGER. **MYTHS OF THE NORSEMEN**, $1.50. A wonderful, illustrated retell-
of all the surviving myths, molded into one continous narrative. This is labeled a child-
s book, and it makes fascinating reading for all. It's certainly the most interesting ver-
n terms of sheer readability, that we know of. Illustrations by Brian Wildsmith.
pp. Pen 60

GORY, LADY. **A BOOK OF SAINTS AND WONDERS**, c$11.35. This is a beauti-
presented, simply written collection of Gaelic myths and tales, based on *The Old
ings and the Memory of the People of Ireland*. It is divided into six books, one each
allotted to the lives of Saints Brigit, Columcille, Patrick and Brendan the Navigator
is supposed to have been to America long before the Vikings or Columbus). The other
are more mythical, one dealing with the fabulous voyage of Maeldune, and the other
led *Great Wonders of the Old Time*. Illustrations, foreward. 116pp. Oxf 06

_____. **VISIONS AND BELIEFS IN THE WEST OF IRELAND**, c$15.15. This is
y Gregory's masterwork of Irish and Gaelic folklore. She spent many years researching
material among the peasantry of Ireland. Most of the tales are quoted in the first per-
and the recollections are quite vivid. Lady Gregory herself provides a connective nar-
n along with a great deal of background material. Introduction, 365pp. Oxf 20

MAL, PIERRE, ed. **LAROUSSE WORLD MYTHOLOGY**, c$12.98. A mammoth vol-
in which twenty-three authors survey the myths of the world's major civilizations,
yzing the form and function of myth, its variations and evolution, and examining
rrent themes. The essays are often in depth studies of one particular area and should
o way be considered general presentation of the gods and goddesses of each area.
re's much more meat to the selections than that. The reader can dip into sections as
wishes and get a good idea of a major feature or features of each of the civilizations
ussed. As the title suggests, the area covered is world-wide, ranging from Egypt, India,
the ancient Near East through Greece, Rome, and Northern Europe, to the New World,
ca, and Oceania. Profusely illustrated. 9x12", index, bibliography. 560pp. Ham 65

The god of walls and moats and the god of the place

CKIN, J., et al. **ASIATIC MYTHOLOGY**, c$6.98. This is a definitive exploration, with
h section written by a leading scholar, covering the mythology of: Persia, the Kafirs,
ddhism in India, Brahmanic India, Lamaism, Indo-China and Java, Buddhism in Central
ia, Modern China, and Japan. Each section recounts the myths and explains the accom-
nying art. The history and evolution of the various religions, sects, and mythologies are
lined and the mythological personages are identified. The text is 8½x12" and is illus-
ted with 354 black-and-white pictures and 16 full color ones. This specially priced vol-
e is an incredibly good bargain. Index, 456pp. Crn nd

LL, MANLY. **DIONYSIAN ARTIFICERS**, c$5.50. This is a reprint of a rare Masonic
onograph, **Dionysian Artificers** by Hippolyto Da Costa, with extensive notes by Manly
ll. Over half the book is devoted to Mr. Hall's detailed interpretation of *The Myth of
onysius*. Both texts discuss how the laws of nature and the moral rules deduced from
em were explained in allegories, which we call myths, and were impressed on the mem-
y of the mystery ceremonies. Hall interprets the central myth of the Dionysian myster-
and explains the secret metaphysical doctrines of this cult. 105pp. PRS 36

MILTON, EDITH. **MYTHOLOGY**, c$7.95/1.50. This is our personal favorite retelling
the classic myths. Ms. Hamilton writes extremely well and she has drawn her compos-
version of the myths from a number of classical sources. The book is well organized
all the important myths are included, along with many lesser known ones. Recom-
ended. Fully indexed, 335pp. NAL 40

HAMLYN MYTHOLOGY BOOKS

These volumes are authoritative and beautifully present the myths and legends, revealing a people's traditional beliefs and customs including: deities
and heroes, supernatural figures and mystics, religious rites, rituals and symbolism, etc. Illustrated throughout with 24 pages of color pictures and over
100 black-and-white photographs of painting, sculpture, pottery, artifacts.
Each 140 to 160pp, 8½x11", c$4.95. An excellent value for the price. Ham

    Burland, Cottie – **NORTH AMERICAN INDIAN MYTHOLOGY**, 65
    Christie, Anthony – **CHINESE MYTHOLOGY**
    Davidson, H.E. – **SCANDINAVIAN MYTHOLOGY**, 69
    Every, George – **CHRISTIAN MYTHOLOGY**, 70
    Gray, John – **NEAR EASTERN MYTHOLOGY**, 69
    Hinnels, John – **PERSIAN MYTHOLOGY**, 73
    Ions, Veronica – **EGYPTIAN MYTHOLOGY**, 65
    _____. **INDIAN MYTHOLOGY**, 67
    Maccana, Proinsias – **CELTIC MYTHOLOGY**
    Nicholson, Irene – **MEXICAN AND CENTRAL AMERICAN MYTHOLOGY**
    Osborne, Harold – **SOUTH AMERICAN MYTHOLOGY**, 68
    Parrinder, Geoffrey – **AFRICAN MYTHOLOGY**, 69
    Perowne, Stewart – **ROMAN MYTHOLOGY**, 69
    Piggott, Juliet – **JAPANESE MYTHOLOGY**, 69
    Pinsent, John – **GREEK MYTHOLOGY**, 69
    Poignant, Roslyn – **OCEANIC MYTHOLOGY**, 67

HATTO, A.T. **THE NIBELUNGENLIED**, $2.95. Composed nearly eight hundred years
ago by an unnamed poet, **The Nibelungelied** is the principal literary expression of the Ger-
manic heroic legends. This great epic poem of murder and revenge recounts with strength
and directness the progress of Siegfried's love for Kriemhild, the wedding of Gunther and
Brunhild, the quarrel between the two queens, Hagen's treacherous murder of Siegfried,
and Kriemhild's eventual revenge. This is the material that Wagner used in his **Ring Cycle.**
This is an excellent prose translation, including over 100pp of introductory and background
material. Glossary, 403pp. Pen 69

HEIDEL, ALEXANDER. **THE BABYLONIAN GENESIS**, $2.45. A complete translation
of all the published cuneiform tablets of the various Babylonian creation stories from both
the Semitic Babylonian and the Sumerian material. Each account is preceded by a brief
introduction on the age and provenance of the tablets and the aim and purpose of the
story. Also included is a translation and discussion of two Babylonian creation stories
written in Greek. The final chapter presents a detailed examination of the Babylonian
creation accounts in their relation to Old Testament literature. Notes, illustrations. 166pp.
UCh 51

HENDERSON, JOSEPH and MAUD OAKES. **THE WISDOM OF THE SERPENT**, $1.95.
See the Jungian Psychology section.

HOMER

FITZGERALD, ROBERT, tr. **THE ILIAD**, $2.95. The Greeks considered the **Iliad** their
greatest literary achievement, and no epic poem in any language has ever rivaled it. Out of
a single episode in the tale of Troy—Achilles' withdrawal from the fighting and his return
to kill the Trojan hero Hector—Homer created a timeless, dramatic tragedy. His characters
are heroic but their passions and problems are human and universal, and he presents them
with compassion, understanding, and humor against the harsh background of war. This is
a poetic rendition that has been highly acclaimed. Fitzgerald has attempted to recreate
the original action in blank verse, as conceived by Homer himself. 595pp. Dou 74

_____. **THE ODYSSEY**, $2.95. Homer's **Odyssey** is a great epic poem about the
adventures of Odysseus during his return from the Trojan War and the drama of his home-
coming. The **Odyssey** often reads like a novel and many of Odysseus' adventures have become legendary. This is a translation into blank verse. *Fitzgerald's new* **Odyssey** *deserves
to be singled out for what it is—a masterpiece. At last we have an* **Odyssey** *worthy of the
original. What Fitzgerald brings back is, first of all, that crucial and elusive quality of
freshness qnd delight so conspicuously absent from other translations.*—**The Nation.** Fitzgerald also includes background information. 507pp. Dou 61

RIEU, E.V., tr. **THE ILIAD**, $2.25. A very well composed rendition, accompanied
by introductory material and a glossary. 491pp. Pen 50

_____. **THE ODYSSEY**, $1.95. A sensitive prose translation, with a good intro-
duction. 365pp. Pen 46

HOOKE, S.H. **MIDDLE EASTERN MYTHOLOGY**, $1.95. An account, based on primary
sources, of the mythology of the following people: Sumerians, Babylonians, Egyptians,
Ugarites, Hittites, Canaanites, and Hebrews. In addition Professor Hooke discusses the nature and function of myth very fully and devotes a chapter to mythological elements in
the New Testament. Notes, index. 199pp. Pen 63

IONS, VERONICA. **THE WORLD'S MYTHOLOGY**, c$10.98. A beautifully produced
general survey which covers the following areas: the Near East, Egypt, Persia, India, Greece,
Rome, Celtic Britain and Gaul, Scandinavia, China, Japan, the Americas, the South Pacific
and Australia, and Africa. 366 stunning color plates are the main feature of the volume.
Many are full page. These are beautifully reproduced and make the book extremely valuable to those who are interested in mythological art. The written text is adequate. Bibliography, index, 8x11". 350pp. Ham 74

JACKSON, KENNETH H., tr. **A CELTIC MISCELLANY**, $3.50. An anthology of poetry
and prose. Includes passages on Celtic magic, religion, love, nature, and various adventure

stories, as well as various kinds of poetry and a glossary. 343pp. Pen 51

JONES, GWYN and THOMAS, trs. THE MABINOGION, $2.50. A good translation of eleven stories from the Welsh **Mabinogion**: the four branches of the Mabinogi, *Pwyll, Branwen, Manawydan,* and *Math*; four independent native tales, *The Dream of Macsen, Wledig, Lludd and Llefelys, Culhwch and Olwen* (the earliest Arthurian tale in Welsh), and *The Dream of Rhonabwy,* a romantic looking-back to the heroic age of Britain; and three romances, *The Lady of the Fountain, Peredur,* and *Gereint Son of Erbin* (later Arthurian stories with abundant evidence of Norman influences). The translations are fairly dry and they are well regarded in terms of scholarship. Introduction, notes. 327pp. Dut 74

JUNG, C.J. and C. KERENYI. ESSAYS ON A SCIENCE OF MYTHOLOGY, $2.95. See the Jungian Psychology section. 200pp. PUP 49

KERENYI, C. ASKLEPIOS, c$14.00. An investigation of the archetypal significance of the *Divine Physician* in the course of an exploration of the sacred sites of his cult. 58 plates, notes, bibliography, index, oversize. 178pp. PUP 59

_____. DIONYSOS: ARCHETYPAL IMAGE OF INDESTRUCTIBLE LIFE, c$27.50. An historical account of the religion of Dionysus from its origins in the Minoan culture down to its transition to a cosmopolitan religion in the late Roman Empire. Notes, bibliography, index, 146 plates. PUP 75

_____. ELEUSIS: ARCHETYPAL IMAGE OF MOTHER AND DAUGHTER, $6.95. A complete examination of the Eleusian mysteries that draws upon archaeology, history, art, and literature and considers their relation to Greek mythology and human nature. 65 plates, notes, bibliography, index. 290pp. ScB 67

_____. THE GODS OF THE GREEKS, $7.50. Drawing on a wealth of sources, from Hesios to Pausanias and from the Orphic Hymns to Proclus, Professor Kerenyi provides a clear and scholarly exposition of all the most important Greek myths. The narrative is lively and highly readable and is complemented by an appendix detailing the references to all the original texts and illustrations taken from vase paintings. An exhaustive study which is more psychologically oriented (in the Jungian sense) than other retellings of the Greek myths. Introduction, indices. 304pp. T&H 51

_____. PROMETHEUS: ARCHETYPAL IMAGE OF HUMAN EXISTENCE, c$16.00. An examination of the myth of Prometheus and its meaning for the Greeks, combined with a study of mythmaking as an archetypal function of mankind. Eighteen plates, notes, bibliography, index. 178pp. PUP 63

_____. ZEUS AND HERA: ARCHETYPAL IMAGE OF FATHER, HUSBAND, AND WIFE, c$13.50. A study of the relationship between the gods and the mortals who worshipped them. The origins of the Greek religion are discussed and Homer's role in decisively shaping the mythological tradition is emphasized. Notes, illustrations, bibliography, index. 229pp. PUP 75

KINSELLA, THOMAS, tr. THE TAIN, $8.00. A translation of the **Tain Bo Cuailnge**, center-piece of the eighth century Ulster cycle of heroic tales and Ireland's nearest approach to a great epic. This translation is based on the partial texts in two medieval manuscripts and includes a group of related stories which prepare for the action of the **Tain**. 31 brush drawings and 3 maps, as well as detailed notes. 283pp. Oxf 69

KIRK, G.S. THE NATURE OF GREEK MYTHS, c$15.00. Kirk is a renowned classical scholar and is presently Professor of Greek Elect at Cambridge University. This is a distinguished discussion and interpretation of both the fundamental characteristics and meaning of the Greek myths. Professor Kirk recounts some of the most important myths and carefully considers both the development and function of Greek mythology, from its original beginnings as the oral tradition of a structured society to its ultimate role as a key element of philosophy. His presentation relies heavily on contemporary scholarship and he gives us a detailed review of the five major modern theories of myth. He also reviews the historical background of the Greek myths. Notes, bibliography. 331pp. OvP 75

KRAMER, SAMUEL, ed. MYTHOLOGIES OF THE ANCIENT WORLD, $1.95. Using the most up-to-date translations of primary material, ten leading scholars survey ancient mythologies. Included in this volume are the following: *Mythology in Ancient Egypt*—

Rudolf Anthes; *Mythology of Sumer and Akkad*—Samuel Kramer; *Hittite Mytholo[gy]* Hans Guterbock; *Canaanite Mythology*—Cyrus Gordon; *Mythology of Ancient Gre[ece]* Michael Jameson; *Mythology of India*—W. Norman Brown; *Mythology of Ancient I[ran]* M.J. Dresden; *Myths of Ancient China*—Derk Bodde; *Japanese Mythology*—E. Dale S[aun]ders; and *Mythology of Ancient Mexico*—Miguel Leon-Portilla. Many quotations from primary myths are included in the selections and the essays are uniformly informative quite well written. Notes, bibliography, index. 480pp. Dou 61

_____. SUMERIAN MYTHOLOGY, $2.95. *No people has contributed mor[e to] the culture of mankind than the Sumerians, and yet it has been only in recent years [that] our knowledge of them has become at all accurate or extensive. [This book is] our [first] authoritative sketch of the great myths of the Sumerians, their myths of origins, of [crea-] tion, the nether world, and the deluge. The book is profusely illustrated with particu[larly] fine photographs.*—Theophile Meek. Notes, index. 135pp. UPa 44

LAROUSSE. NEW LAROUSSE ENCYCLOPEDIA OF MYTHOLOGY, c$9.98. It is [con-] fusing that there are two Larousse oversize books on mythology. Both seem to be ex[cel-] lent surveys and while much of the same material is covered here as in the edition ed[ited] by Professor Grimal, all of the selections are completely different. Again, the volum[e is] divided into a number of essays by individual scholars, this time covering the follow[ing] cultures: prehistoric, Egyptian, Assyro-Babylonian, Phoenician, Greek, Roman, Ce[ltic] Teutonic, Slavonic, Finno-Ugric, Persian, Indian, Chinese, Japanese, American, Ocea[nic] and African. Nearly 600 illustrations (many in color) accompany the text. We canno[t re-] commend one of these Larousse volumes over the other—both are equally excellen[t, so] take your pick—but do pick one if you are interested in a pictorial survey with a fin[e ac-] companying text. 8x11½", index. 521pp. Ham 68

LARSEN, STEPHEN. THE SHAMAN'S DOORWAY, c$10.00. Subtitled *Opening [the] Mythic Imagination to Contemporary Consciousness,* this is a fascinating exploratio[n of] the myths that are relevant to today's world and an illuminating examination of the t[ech-] niques of consciousness that we can best use to relate to them. Larsen states his indeb[ted-] ness to Joseph Campbell in the preface, and Campbell's influence can be felt through[out] the book. The mythic examples are drawn from contemporary society and related to [the] more ancient traditions and theories. This is a very successful study which we highly commend to all who are interested in a deeper understanding of the cosmos and man['s re-] lationship to it. Illustrations, notes. 256pp. H&R 76

LAYLARD, JOHN. A CELTIC QUEST, $8.85. A depth-psychology study of the Mab[ino-] gion legend of Culhwch and Olwen which retells the main tales, with extensive comm[en-] tary. Glossary, index. 254pp. Spr 75

LEACH, MARIA, ed. FUNK AND WAGNALLS STANDARD DICTIONARY OF FO[LK] MYTHOLOGY AND LEGEND, c$17.95. This is without doubt the finest work of [its] type that we know of. The over eight thousand entries are essays in themselves. This [is a] revised one volume edition of the original work, complete and uncut. The entries are [uni-] formly excellent and while the Western tradition is emphasized the coverage of East[ern] mythology and religion is quite complete. We recommend this volume to everyone wh[o is] studying mythology and religion in any depth. The entries read well and are extremely [in-] formative, having been prepared by noted scholars. The volume is fully indexed. 1251[pp.] Cro 72

LEEMING, DAVID. MYTHOLOGY, c$10.00. This is a topically arranged pictorial sur[vey] of mythology divided into the following general areas: *Primitive Fears, Universal Und[er-] standings; Man, Myth, and History; The Psychological Perspective; The Hero with a Th[ou-] sand Faces; The Mythmakers;* and *Mythology Today.* 184 beautiful illustrations are [in-] cluded, one third of them in color. A final section presents excerpts from a variety [of] creation myths. Bibliography, index, 8x10". 192pp. Nsw 76

MAC CULLOCH, J.A. THE CELTIC AND SCANDINAVIAN RELIGIONS, c$13.45. [An] excellent overview discussing the people, their worship, their mythic heroes and myt[ho-] logical writings, their religious ideas, and their cosmology. Very clearly written and w[ell] organized. Indices, 180pp. Gre 48

MAGNUSSON, MAGNUS and HERMANN PALSSON, trs. LAXDAELA SAGA, $2.95. [A] thirteenth century Icelandic saga which is best known for its tragic love triangle. The I[ce-] landic ideas of property and of courtly chivalry are clearly presented and it has been [the] most popular of all the medieval sagas over the centuries. The translators also provid[e a] 42pp introduction, a long glossary, maps, and a chronology. 267pp. Pen 69

_____. NJAL'S SAGA, $2.95. A late thirteenth century Icelandic prose saga bas[ed] on historical events in Iceland in the tenth century. It describes a fifty-year blood fe[ud] from its violent beginnings to its tragic end in a spare, simple style. It is generally cons[id-] ered the mightiest of all the Icelandic prose sagas. Long introduction and glossary, chr[on-] ology, maps. 378pp. Pen 60

_____. THE VINLAND SAGAS: THE NORSE DISCOVERIES OF AMERIC[A,] $1.95. Two medieval Icelandic sagas translated in this volume tell of the discovery [of] America by Norsemen five centuries before Columbus. The sagas describe how Erik [the] Red founded an Icelandic colony in Greenland and how his son, Leif the Lucky, la[ter] sailed south to explore and, if possible, exploit the chance discovery by one of his men [of] an unknown land which is today believed to be North America. 124pp. Pen 65

MARKALE, J. WOMEN OF THE CELTS, c$17.95. See the Ancient Britain sub-section [of] Ancient Civilizations.

MARRIOTT, ALICE and CAROL RACHLIN. PLAINS INDIAN MYTHOLOGY, c$7.[95.] A fine retelling of both the great myths (stories of creation and of the gods) and the min[or] myths (tales which teach manners, behavior, and ethics, and explain common phenomen[a.] Also includes stories of the eighteenth and nineteenth centuries and stories from conte[m-] porary times. Bibliography, 197pp. Cro 75

EAD, G.R.S. ORPHEUS, c$7.55. A scholarly, expansive treatise. Orpheus, we are told, not an historical individual but was *the living symbol that marked the birth of theology d science and art in Greece.* The author explores the mythology and tradition that are a rt of the vast body of mystery wisdom of which Orpheus, in whatever culture he may e found, is the eternal exponent. Excellent, detailed bibliography, 207pp. Wat 1896

IDDLETON, JOHN, ed. MYTH AND COSMOS, $8.00. A well organized collection of adings in mythology and symbolism. Included are essays on the *Creator Spirit* and on arious beliefs in intermediaries between the spiritual power and wo/men including deities, riests, prophets, shamans, and others. The selections cover a wide variety of cultures and, hile the scholarship is uniformly excellent, they are not overly technical. This is a volume the *Texas Press Sourcebooks in Anthropology.* Notes, bibliography, index, 368pp. Tx 67

ORFORD, MARK and ROBERT LENARDON. CLASSICAL MYTHOLOGY, $9.35. *hat makes this excellent primer on classical mythology particularly attractive for under-raduate teaching is the balanced blend of source material in translation, of judicious com-ents on major trends in ancient religion, and of the highly desirable emphasis, documented y pertinent illustrations and quotations, on the reception of classical myths in European rt and literature.*—Alfred Henrichs, University of California, Berkeley. A very well organ-zed, comprehensive presentation. Bibliography, index. 498pp. McK 71

URRAY, HENRY, ed. MYTH AND MYTHMAKING, $3.95. A collection of essays by oseph Campbell, Clyde Kluckhohn, Mircea Eliade, Harry Levin, Andrew Lytle, Robert ee Wolff, Philip Rieff, Jerome Bruner, Marshall McLuhan, Henry Murray, and others ong with selections from the writings of Mark Schorer, Georges Sorel, and Thomas Mann. oth traditional and modern perspectives on myth are provided, as well as a variety of elevant issues: definition, historical and thematic examples, and political and artistic ap-lications. 375pp. Bea 59

EUMANN, ERICH. THE GREAT MOTHER, c$15.00/4.95. See the Jungian Psychology ection.

IVEDITA, SISTER. CRADLE TALES OF HINDUISM, $1.95. See the Indian Philosophy ection.

O'FLAHERTY, WENDY. HINDU MYTHS, $2.95. See the Indian Philosophy section.

PERRY, JOHN. THE LORD OF THE FOUR QUARTERS, $1.50. A Jungian psychiatrist traces the archetypes of the royal sacred father/king through the myths of the Nile, the ancient Near East, Indo-European ancient cultures, ancient China, and the ancient Amer-icas. The volume is well organized and includes a profusion of quotations from primary myths and of illustrations. A fascinating study, though often fairly dry. Many notes and an excellent topically-organized long bibiliography are also included along with an exten-sive introduction. Index, 272pp. McM 66

RADIN, PAUL. THE TRICKSTER: A STUDY IN AMERICAN INDIAN MYTHOLOGY, $2.95. The myth of the Trickster—ambiguous creator and destroyer, cheater and cheated, subhuman and superhuman—is one of the earliest and most universal expressions of man-kind. Nowhere does it survive in more starkly archaic form than in the episodes of the Winnebago Trickster Cycle, recorded here in full. Anthropological and psychological anal-yses by Radin, Kerenyi, and Jung reveal the Trickster as filling a two-fold role: on the one hand he is *an archetypal psychic structure that harks back to an absolutely undifferentiated human consciousness, corresponding to a psyche that has hardly left the animal level*; and on the other hand, his myth is a present-day outlet for the most unabashed and lib-erating satire on the onerous obligations of social order, religion, and ritual. 236pp. ScB 56

ROHEIM, GEZA. THE ETERNAL ONES OF THE DREAM, $4.95. A psychoanalytic in-terpretation of Australian myth and ritual. All the major myths are discussed and analyzed at length. The analysis is Freudian rather than Jungian in tone and this is clearly a schol-arly work. The following are some of the major topics: the meaning of totemic myth, the dual heroes, the origin of circumcision, the phallic ritual, the concentric circle and the fer-tility rite, destruction and restitution, the rainbow serpent, wandering ancestors, and the totem sacrament. A great deal of background information is also included. Notes, index. 283pp. IUP 45

_____. THE GATES OF THE DREAM, $5.95. *This monumental work, alas, the author's swan song, crowns her life's work.... While the story suggests dream theory, the bulk of the volume is devoted to the application of the dream theory to anthropology and to the psychoanalytic interpretation of myth and folklore. In this respect it will serve as a sourcebook of the first order.... It is crammed to capacity with anthropologic mat-erial, showing an almost fabulous erudition and encyclopedic knowledge of the mytholo-gies of all times and all parts of the earth, reminiscent of James Frazer and W. Wundt.—* **American Journal of Psychotherapy.** Notes, index. 562pp. IUP 52

_____. THE PANIC OF THE GODS, $2.00. Four essays: *Primitive High Gods; nimism and Religions; Aphrodite, or the Woman with a Penis* and *The Panic of the Gods.* he material is based mainly on Roheim's experiences with Australian and Melanesian na-ives. The volume is edited by Werner Muensterberger, who also supplies an introduction. otes, glossary. 250pp. H&R 72

_____. THE RIDDLE OF THE SPHINX, $3.95. An in depth study of Central Australian primitives which focuses on the totemic mythology and rituals of the tribes of this area and on their demon beliefs, fairy tales, and magic. There is a detailed psychoan-alytic interpretation of the rites and customs. An introduction by Werner Muensterberger and Christopher Nichols discusses Roheim and psychoanalytic anthropology. Notes, index. 312pp. H&R 74

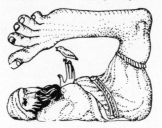

Monopod, a one-footed African race. When they tire of hopping in the heat of the day they lie on their backs with their leg extended above to pro-tect them from the burning Ethiopian sun.

Moloch is a fiery and bloodthirsty idol with a vast furnace burning in his belly.

SEDGWICK, PAULITA. MYTHOLOGICAL CREATURES, c$6.95. See the Children's Books section.

SPENCE, LEWIS. MYTHS AND LEGENDS OF THE NORTH AMERICAN INDIANS, $5.50. See the American Indian Religion section.

SPIEGELMAN, J. MARVIN. THE TREE—TALES IN PSYCHO-MYTHOLOGY, c$9.95. *Psychomythology stands for a...union in fact and imagination,...a marriage of psych-ological knowledge with the type of fantasy that reaches the universal, archetypal, myth-ological level....Rather than concerning itself with the motivations of an individual, psycho-mythology relates to the collective psyche and its drama. Paradoxically, the per-turbations of the modern man, occupied with his struggle for individuation, is both the source and core of it....Psycho-mythology is a literature in which an individual's fan-tasy transcends the personal level, reaching the unconscious. In addition, the work is consciously connected with either available religious or mythical material and is clearly intended as a work of art.*—from the introduction. This is a fine collection of stories in this genre. 471pp. PhH 74

SQUIRE, CHARLES. CELTIC MYTH AND LEGEND, $4.95. This is one of the most comprehensive studies of Celtic mythology, legend, and poetry ever produced. It has been out of print for many years and has only recently been reprinted. Both the ancient Gaelic and British Celts are represented and all the chief characters of Celtic mythology are repre-sented. The stories are well written and commentary is interspersed. Included are tales about the Gaelic gods and the giants they battled, the heroes of the **Mabinogion,** and the British epics down through King Arthur and his knights. Bibliography, index. 453pp. NPC 75

STEINER, RUDOLF. ANCIENT MYTHS—THEIR MEANING AND CONNECTION WITH EVOLUTION, c$5.75. See the Steiner section.

STURLUSON, SNORRI. THE PROSE EDDA, $2.25. A twelfth or thirteenth century col-collection and arrangement of the pagan deities, myths, and legends of the past—with many quotations from the **Poetic Edda.** Though Sturluson himself was a Christian he had a strong interest in the past and wanted to present as complete an account of it as was pos-sible. UCa 54

TRIPP, EDWARD. CROWELL'S HANDBOOK OF CLASSICAL MYTHOLOGY, c$11.95/ $5.95. This is a comprehensive, alphabetically arranged handbook of Greek and Roman mythology. The myths are retold as completely as possible in one place, so the narrative does not have to be pieced together out of several entries. All significant versions of each myth are given and the accounts are drawn almost exclusively from original sources, all of which are fully cited. The entries include not only characters and events, but nearly all the places mentioned in the myths, the constellations named for mythological personages, and brief descriptions of the principal classical works. Plentiful cross-references are also provided. There's also a pronouncing key and several maps. The paperback edition is known as the **Meridian Handbook.** 646pp. Cro 70

WATTS, ALAN. THE TWO HANDS OF GOD, $1.50. A fascinating exploration and ex-position of the myths of polarity, those crucial symbolic relationships such as light and darkness, good and evil, which illustrate the inner unity of opposites. These mythological themes, centering on the idea that explicit opposition conceals implicit unity, are illustrated by a treasury of stories and myths from Chinese, Indian, Egyptian, Iranian, and early Christ-ian sources. 23 plates, notes, bibliography, index. 256pp. McM 69

ZIMMER, HEINRICH. THE KING AND THE CORPSE: TALES OF THE SOUL'S CON-QUEST OF EVIL, $3.45. A group of popular stories from East and West, linked to one another by their common concern for the problem of man's eternal conflict with the forces of evil. Zimmer's commentary discloses the meanings within each apparently unrelated symbol and suggests the philosophical wholeness of this assortment of myth. Beginning with a tale from the Arabian Nights, the theme unfolds through legends from Irish pagan-ism, medieval Christianity, the Arthurian cycle, and early Hinduism. 338pp. PUP 48

_____. MYTHS AND SYMBOLS IN INDIAN ART AND CIVILIZATION, $3.95. See the Indian Philosophy section.

NATURAL CHILDBIRTH

The books that we discuss are all attempts to show how a woman can heal her physical body and spirit while undergoing the experience of pregnancy. As Norbert Glas puts it: *She is forced to provide, in her body, the place where her child is to live for nine months. In the beginning of pregnancy it is as if there were all the time a slight physical conflict between the developing embryo, and the mother, who up to the moment of conception, has lived as an individual being in her own body. Thus the body as well as the soul has to come to the right degree of selflessness in order to make way for the child. The latter to a certain extent dislodges the being of the mother from her body. At first the mother feels this interference with her organism a great deal, and suffers from it. But as soon as she becomes used to it, which happens after the first three months, she can gain much in a spiritual way. She has more connection now with the heavenly forces than before pregnancy, because her mind has become slightly detached from her body. So she has the possibility of soul-experiences of a higher order than in her life apart from pregnancy. She should try to listen more and more to what speaks to her inwardly. In this way she comes to a closer connection with the child, and realizes how far away it still is in the supersensible world. . . . The soul and spirit of the woman are to a certain extent displaced from her physical body, and she becomes thereby more connected with the heavens; the child, on the other hand, is descending from the spiritual world and gradually shaping its earthly body. The mother thus gains, during her pregnancy, a growing relationship to, and a closer understanding for the realms from which her child is coming down. This is the true reason for the great change that can be observed in the pregnant woman; she can become wiser and gain in knowledge. She should recognize how she is lifted up from the ordinary course of life, and is thereby given the possibility of devoting herself to the new task.*

—from **Conception, Birth and Early Childhood** by Norbert Glas.

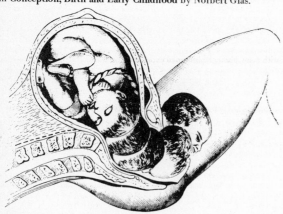

ARMS, SUZANNE. IMMACULATE DECEPTION, $6.95. *This is a book about childbirth in America. It is neither a medical textbook, nor a political treatise, nor a whole birth catalog. Rather, it is a statement that grew out of my need to understand and explain my own birth experience. It is my contribution to anyone interested in the American way of birth.* This is an excellent comprehensive collection of essays on many topics related to women and childbirth in America. It is illustrated with many photographs and also quotes extensively from the experiences of individual women. Oversize, bibliography. 317pp. HMC 75

_____. **A SEASON TO BE BORN**, $2.95. Eloquent photographs and a simple personal text create an emotional experience for the reader as s/he watches the Arms' move through pregnancy and the birth and celebration of their daughter. 112pp. H&R 73

BEAN, CONSTANCE. METHODS OF CHILDBIRTH, $1.95. *I cannot praise this book highly enough . . . a trailblazing contribution toward enlightening women everywhere. Bean covers what everyone else leaves out. . . . It also drives home the message that The woman educated for childbirth keeps her adult role. For those who wish the latest medical and statistical reasons why such a role is best for mother and baby, this is the book to turn to.—Ms Magazine.* Includes chapters on childbirth and childbirth education, methods of preparation, labor and delivery, drugs and anesthesia, father, mother, and baby, breast feeding, and the childbirth education class. Notes, bibliography, glossary. 235pp. Dou 74

BING, ELISABETH. MOVING THROUGH PREGNANCY, $1.95. A series of exercises which can be incorporated into the everyday schedule of a pregnant woman. Clear photographs of each exercise are included. The exercises themselves have been developed by Ms. Bing in her classes and have been tested extensively. 175pp. Ban 75

_____. **SIX PRACTICAL LESSONS FOR AN EASIER CHILDBIRTH**, $1.5
This is one of the best of the Lamaze instruction manuals. It is written by one of the founders of the American Society for Psychoprophylaxis in Obstetrics and one of the best-known pioneers in introducing the Lamaze method to America. The book is easy follow, packed with information, and cheap. Even if you have a good Lamaze class, you find the book useful for review. 128pp. Ban 73

BRADLEY, ROBERT. HUSBAND-COACHED CHILDBIRTH, c$7.95. Since 194 Dr. Bradley has been practicing and promoting the principles of true natural childbirth including the concept of an active role for the husband as the *labor coach.* Here he giv practical pointers on what happens during the various months of pregnancy and duri labor and actual birth, psychological hints for living with a pregnant woman, and how the man can help with exercises and diet and give the woman support during cris periods. 224pp. H&R 74

BRADY, MARGARET. HAVING A BABY EASILY, c$4.70. This is a recent reprint of very comprehensive 1944 English manual. The material is very British and covers are not referred to in other books. She includes the following main chapters: *Diet, Sunshin Fresh Air, Sleep, Elimination, Avoiding Morning Sickness, Physical Training, Spiritu Outlook, The Confinement, Breast Feeding, Weaning,* and *Routine and Management the New Born Baby.* Glossary, index. 234pp. HFA 68

BRICKLIN, ALICE. MOTHER LOVE, $4.95. Subtitled *The Book of Natural Chi Rearing*, this is a lovely volume covering the following main topics: *Baby Closeness Birth, Baby-Led Nursing and Nutrition, Baby and the Family.* The account is person and the approach positive. Oversize, annotated bibliography, notes, index. 110pp. RuP 7

BROOK, DANAE. NATUREBIRTH: YOU, YOUR BODY, AND YOUR BABY, $3.9 This is a comprehensive, beautifully produced volume which discusses all aspects natural childbirth. The first section is a thorough review of the realities of childbirth t day which raises important and provocative questions. The second section is a practic guide to pregnancy and labor which includes new techniques for preparation for natur birth, information on the effects of drugs, a section on the ailments common to pregna cy—with a discussion of midwifery and herbal and homeopathic remedies, and a serie of exercises. Illustrations, bibliography. 304pp. RaH 76

BURNETT, C.W.F. THE ANATOMY AND PHYSIOLOGY OF OBSTETRICS, $4.4 This is a short textbook for students and midwives. All the important information included and the discussion is not as overwhelmingly detailed as the other textbook The material is clearly presented and excellent line drawings accompany the text. Inde 215pp. Fab 69

CLYNE, DOUGLAS. A CONCISE TEXTBOOK FOR MIDWIVES, $12.00. A con prehensive discussion of virtually every aspect of midwifery. The book has been used a text for student midwives in England for many years and this fourth edition has bee carefully revised. While not as complete as Myles' **Textbook**, the presentation is e ceedingly clear and there are line drawings throughout. Index, 448pp. Fab 75

CRISP, TONY. YOGA AND CHILDBIRTH, c$7.80. Despite its intriguing title th is basically just another book on childbirth with very little about yogic exercises ar almost no pictures. The emphasis is on methods of relaxation through breathing ar physical movement. There are also a number of hints on what to do about proble areas that might arise. Index, 128pp. TPL 75

DICK-READ, GRANTLY. CHILDBIRTH WITHOUT FEAR, $1.75. This is a classic wo on natural childbirth based on the author's conclusions after many years of study and o servation as an obstetrician. Described in detail are the development of the child fro conception to birth, the anatomy and physiology of mother and child during pregnanc and delivery, the reasons for fear and the resulting painful labor when the mother has n been prepared for childbirth, and the proper place of anesthetics in natural childbirt Also includes a short section of simple exercises (terribly illustrated). Index, 384pp. H&R 5

EIGER, MARVIN and SALLY OLDS. THE COMPLETE BOOK OF BREASTFEEDING $1.50. Dr. Eiger is one of New York's leading pediatricians and Ms. Olds is a medic writer who nursed her own three children. Their presentation is the most comprehensi one available, with clearly written material on all aspects of the subject. Recommende Includes many photographs, a long bibliography, and an index. 208pp. Ban 72

VY, DONNA and ROGER. PREPARATION FOR CHILDBIRTH, $1.75. The Lamaze
ethod prepares a woman emotionally, intellectually, psychologically, and physically
r childbirth. It includes body-building exercises, stretching exercises, neuro-muscular
ntrol (relaxation), and breathing techniques—complete with diagrams and photographs
tlining each sequence from labor through delivery. The material is well written and the
ader can get a feeling of the childbirth experience from the presentation. Recommend-
. Bibliography, index. 224pp. NAL 70

_____. **PREPARATION FOR BREAST FEEDING**, $2.95. A very full exploration
breastfeeding, with information on the physiology involved. Psychological and physical
oblems the mother and baby may encounter are also discussed and suggestions made.
otographs and line drawings illustrate the exposition. Very clearly written. Index, bib-
ography. 125pp. Dou 75

LAS, NORBERT. CONCEPTION, BIRTH AND EARLY CHILDHOOD, $2.50. A sensi-
ve, intuitive account of the soul entering into a new physical vehicle and the effects the
nception process has on the mother, based on Rudolf Steiner's Spiritual Science and
n Dr. Glas' own experience. As the title suggests there are chapters on conception,
egnancy, and birth—all oriented around the spiritual development of mother and
ild. The major part of the book is devoted to an analysis of the newborn's coming into
e world and developing his/her senses, will, feeling, and ego. We highly recommend this
olume to all who want to understand the deeper meaning and potentiality of the birth
rocess. 152pp. API 72

ARTMAN, RHONDDA. EXERCISES FOR TRUE NATURAL CHILDBIRTH, c$9.95.
s. Hartmann is a registered nurse and has been active in the American Academy of Hus-
and-Coached Childbirth and the La Leche League. She has taught the exercises illus-
ated here since she had the first of her five children. The approach is practical, with
asy to follow instructions arranged under *how*, *where*, and *when*. The photographs do
ot seem to be terribly helpful—they are not detailed enough and there are too few of
hem. The exercises are arranged in sequence so that you will have your body and muscles
eady by full-term pregnancy. It's not a great book—but there is so little available on the
ubject that anything is welcome, and the written instructions are good. Index, 139pp.
&R 75

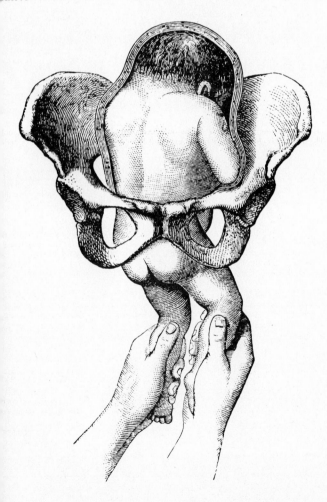

HAZELL, LESTER. COMMONSENSE CHILDBIRTH, $1.95. *Commonsense Childbirth
is one of the most important and valuable books ever written on the art and science of
having a baby. It is not written by a male obstetrician, but by a mother who, because of
her unhappy obstetrical experience with her first child, determined to discover for herself
whether childbirth could not be a happy and rewarding experience. What she discovered
is set out in her wonderful book for all prospective parents, as well as obstetricians, to
read.*—Ashley Montagu. Index, 281pp. Ber 76

HODSON, GEOFFREY. THE MIRACLE OF BIRTH, $1.75. Hodson, probably the most
intuitive theosophist of this century, presents his clairvoyant study of the formation and
development of the emotional, mental, and physical bodies of a being during the prenatal
period. The material is based on his observation of one individual. 64pp. TPH 29

KIPPLEY, SHEILA. BREAST FEEDING AND NATURAL CHILD SPACING, $1.95. A
dry survey backed up with case studies and reviews of the recent research. Every aspect is
well covered. Index, 216pp. Pen 74

KITZINGER, SHEILA. THE EXPERIENCE OF CHILDBIRTH, $2.95. This is an excel-
lent book, designed by Ms. Kitzinger as a complete manual of physical and emotional
preparation for the expectant mother. The physiology of pregnancy, the development of
the fetus, and the successive stages of labor are described in detail. Moving on from the
pioneer work of Grantly Dick-Read and later psychoprophylactic techniques, Ms. Kitzinger's research and teaching focus particularly on the psychological aspects of childbearing, on the preparation of both wife and husband not only for birth but for parent-
hood and marital adjustment, and on the woman's changing relationship with her own
mother. This revised edition includes a full discussion of the touch-relaxation method
which she has developed, and she has also added many personal accounts of labor recorded by some of her pupils. Recommended. Index, 280pp. Pen 72

_____. **GIVING BIRTH**, $2.65. A collection of first-hand accounts of women's
(and their husbands') experiences during the birth experience: *I believe that this is one of
the most important things about preparation for childbirth—that it should not simply
superimpose a series of techniques, conditioned responses to stimuli, on the laboring
woman, but that it can be a truly creative act, in which she spontaneously expresses herself and the sort of person she is.* Glossary, 222pp. SBL 61

LAMAZE, FERDNAND. PAINLESS CHILDBIRTH: THE LAMAZE METHOD, $1.75.
Lamaze is a French physician who developed the most widely used method of natural
childbirth. Much of this book is devoted to a theoretical presentation of the physiology
of childbirth along with transcriptions of lectures on various related areas. This is a
reference book rather than a work designed to turn a woman on to the idea of natural
childbirth. Illustrations, index. 191pp. S&S 70

LA LECHE LEAGUE. WOMANLY ART OF BREASTFEEDING, $4.00. The La Leche
League has been one of the primary groups in the natural childbirth movement and they
have been the foremost exponents of breastfeeding: *Breastfeeding gives the baby back to
the mother. Her baby securely in her arms, she finds her motherly response, like her milk,
is never measured, but ample.* This book, written by seven of the founders, was designed
as the La Leche League manual, developed originally for mothers too far away from a
group to attend meetings. The following topics are discussed: *why breastfeeding?, plan-
ning for baby, nutritional know-how for nursing mothers, some common worries and old
wives' tales, your baby arrives, how to mother the newly-born child, special circumstances
and the father's role.* Bibliography, index. 166pp. LLL 63

LANG, RAVEN. BIRTH BOOK, $6.00. This is one of the best home birth books, com-
plete with many photographs, varied experiences, and an interesting history of childbirth.
Some of the information is practical, including various home remedies, a bibliography,
and equipment needed for home delivery. Some is a little less conventional, such as the
recipe for placenta stew. Oversize. GeP 72

LEBOYER, FREDERICK. BIRTH WITHOUT VIOLENCE, c$7.95. This is an important
new book that asks us, for the first time, to focus our attention on the infant just born—
to examine and radically change what is being done in hospitals all over the world to the
new human being who has just emerged, after hours of unavoidable tumult and pain,
from the once-peaceful womb. The man who makes this plea is Frederick Leboyer, whose
revolutionary techniques for easing the birth trauma are stirring great interest. He has
himself delivered more than 10,000 babies. Of these, the last 1,000 have been brought
into the world in the new way that he fully and clearly describes here. Leboyer shows us
exactly what we can do to replace the ugly mask of terror that we have until now taken
for granted in the newborn with the peaceful, rapt expression that is apparent in the
photographs of babies delivered without violence. Oversize, many photographs. 115pp.
RaH 75

_____. **LOVING HANDS**, c$7.95. This is a beautiful book which shows us how,
in the weeks and months following a baby's birth, we can use the flowing rhythms of the
traditional Indian art of baby massage to communicate our love and strength to infants in
a primal language of touch and sensation. The actual techniques of this massage, and the
embracing vision that animates them, are seen through the person of a radiant young
Indian mother, whom Dr. Leboyer met with, observed, and photographed with her babies
in India. 9¾x11", 139pp. RaH 76

LINDEN, WILHELM zur. A CHILD IS BORN, $3.95. What do we really mean when we
say: *A child is born?* Dr. zur Linden is concerned with a total answer to the question. Indeed he holds that it is impossible to answer any single aspect of it without facing them
all. He regards the child as a threefold being of body, soul, and spirit and feels that the
organism in the womb is already being prepared by the child himself as a vehicle for the
expression of his soul and spirit. It must be nurtured and nourished as such a vehicle
both before and after birth. Dr. zur Linden details physical treatment and environment
based on Rudolf Steiner's Spiritual Science. Many practical suggestions on nutrition and
childcare during pregnancy, birth, and early childhood are given. Index. API

LOVELL, PHILLIP M. PREGNANCY AND CHILD CARE THE NATURAL WAY,
$5.50. A hip but somewhat scattered manual for natural childcare and pregnancy. Many
potential problem areas are discussed and advice on proper care is given. The material is
oriented toward the philosophy we believe in but the tone is often a bit heavy. 252pp.
NuB 72

MARZOLLO, JEAN, ed. 9 MONTHS, 1 DAY, 1 YEAR, $4.95. *9 Months, 1 Day, 1 Year
is one of the few books that deal with the whole period of pregnancy, birth, and that first*

special year as a new parent. It's a book of feelings, facts, and opinions that you can talk back to, laugh with, and share as part of your own experience. I particularly like the fact that it concentrates on both parents and not on just mothers. When you are about to become a parent or have just become one, you're at your most vulnerable. This book provides support, cheer, and companionship without the condescending and patronizing tone often found in doctors' books. The book is written by a number of mothers and is well organized. Appendices contain sources of infant paraphernalia and an excellent annotated bibliography. All in all this is an enjoyable and useful book. Oversize, index. 191pp. H&R 75

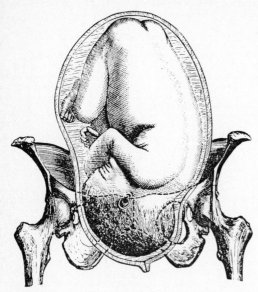

MAY, INA. **SPIRITUAL MIDWIFERY**, $5.95. *This is a spiritual book, and at the same time it is a revolutionary book. It is spiritual because it is concerned with the sacrament of birth—the passage of a new soul into this plane of existence. . . . This book is revolutionary because it is our basic belief that the sacrament of birth belongs to the people and that it should not be usurped by a profit-oriented hospital system. . . . We live in a self-sufficient farming community in Tennessee. . . . We deliver our own babies by natural childbirth, and some other people's, too. Among us we have delivered over 350 babies at the time of this writing.* The book is divided into the following sections: *Amazing Birthing Tales, You and Your Baby, Instructions for Midwives.* A profusion of photographs and drawings accompanies the text. Index, 378pp. BPC 75

MEDVIN, JEANNINE. **PRENATAL YOGA**, $2.50. In answer to numerous requests, here finally is an excellent yogic manual for the expectant mother. The format is oversize and the postures are well described and illustrated. There are also many related line drawings and excellent general philosophical material. The explanations are very complete. 55pp. FPC 75

MILINAIRE, CATERINE. **BIRTH**, $5.95. This is our most popular general book on natural childbirth. The information is plentiful and the enthusiasm, catching. Some of the chapters cover prenatal care, mother's body care, birth choices, birth experiences, fathers, newborn infant care, and birth customs around the world. The text is oversize with a lot of illustrations and photographs. There's a bit of visual chaos but when you get beyond that there's a great deal of useful information. A good gift book for the mother-to-be (or even a good present for yourself!). 356pp. Crn 74

MITCHELL, INGRID. **GIVING BIRTH TOGETHER**, c$8.95. This is the first English translation of the leading German manual on natural childbirth. The author is one of the leaders in the movement in Europe. She has organized her presentation into six graded lessons which are designed to aid the mother-to-be in developing the capacity to be awake, aware, and in optimal control of her body during labor and childbirth. Photographs and line drawings illustrate the exercises and some of the physiology and there is a series of color photographs of an actual birth. Many case histories are included. All in all, this is an excellent work which complements the currently available works on the Lamaze method. Bibliography, 139pp. Sea 75

MYLES. **TEXTBOOK FOR MIDWIVES**, $17.65. This is the most comprehensive treatment of midwifery we can imagine. This new edition, the eighth, has been thoroughly revised and updated to ensure adequate presentation of modern thought and practice. It is also profusely illustrated with technical and more general material. The material is British but it can be applied to the American situation without any difficulty. 848pp. Lon 74

NILSSON, LENNART. **HOW WAS I BORN?** c$5.95. A collection of incredible photographs which give an artistic as well as accurate and realistic picture of a human being's physical development from the moment of conception until birth. Here, step by step, you can follow the stages of fetal development: when the different organs are formed, when the heart begins to beat, when the arms and legs begin to move, etc. In this way the new life, which takes shape hidden from the world, becomes vivid and more easily perceived as a new and independent individual. Oversize, with many full color photographs. Index, 160pp. Del 66

NOBLE, ELIZABETH. **ESSENTIAL EXERCISES FOR THE CHILDBEARING YEAR**, $4.95. Ms. Noble is an Australian physical therapist specializing in obstetrics and gynecol-

ogy. Her exercise program stresses an understanding of the biomechanics of the entire maternity cycle and the rationale for, and against, certain exercises. She shows how to recognize weakness and dysfunction and offers therapeutic exercises for conditions arising from the burdens of pregnancy on the average woman. Postpartum restoration is also discussed. Line drawings illustrate the text and illustrated, one page summaries of prenatal, postpartum, and Caesarean exercises provide handy references. Oversize, 192pp. HMC 76

PRYOR, KAREN. **NURSING YOUR BABY**, $1.95. This is a scholarly advocacy of breastfeeding, complete with pictures and household hints. In Part I Ms. Pryor discusses the nursing relationship, how breasts function, the composition of milk, the mother instinct, doctors, milk banks, the La Leche League, and attitudes toward breastfeeding. Part II contains practical information: brassieres, diet, putting the baby to breast for the first time, leaking, night feeding, vitamins, weaning. Extensive bibliography, index. 289pp. S&S 63

RAPHAEL, DANA. **THE TENDER GIFT: BREASTFEEDING**, $3.45. This book differs from other books on breastfeeding in two ways. First, a great deal of space is devoted to a comprehensive survey of breastfeeding, past and present, in many cultures, and even among animal groups. Second, the instructional material on breastfeeding is mainly devoted to suggested nursing techniques, based upon the author's extensive research and her own experience. This volume is highly recommended by the La Leche League. Glossary, notes, bibliography, index. 200pp. ScB 73

ROSEN, MORTIMER. **IN THE BEGINNING**, $3.95. A non-technical study of the development of intelligence and the nervous system during the months between conception and birth. Illustrations, index. 143pp. NAL 75

SOUSA, MARION. **CHILDBIRTH AT HOME**, c$7.95. This is the most comprehensive unified manual on childbirth at home yet produced. The author provides practical information on how to prepare for the home birth. Recommended prenatal nutrition, exercises, and classes are discussed along with descriptions of equipment and bedding. Ms. Sousa also tells how to recruit experienced medical supervision in the case of an emergency. Notes, bibliography, index. 221pp. PrH 76

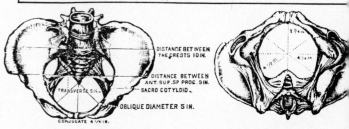

TANZER, DEBORAH and JEAN BLOCK. **WHY NATURAL CHILDBIRTH?** $3.95. To find out if natural childbirth is a better way to have children, Dr. Tanzer conducted a pioneering study of the psychological impact of childbirth. Through a series of tests and interviews, she studied two groups of women: one using conventional medication and a conventional approach, the other using the techniques of natural childbirth. She reports the results of her study here. The many cases cited overwhelmingly show the psychological benefits of the natural approach. Notes, index. 312pp. ScB 72

URBANOWSKI, FERRIS. **YOGA FOR NEW PARENTS**, $6.95. A personal portrayal of the author's experience of birth and the aftermath. The photographs of Ms. Urbanowski while pregnant do not show her exercising, which is a pity. The exercises are all demonstrated in a non-pregnant state. The photographs are not terribly clear, but the accompanying instructions are quite complete. The many photographs all have captions representing the author's philosophy. Oversize, bibliography. 126pp. H&R 7?

WARD, CHARLOTTE and FRED. **THE HOME BIRTH BOOK**, $6.95. A beautifully illustrated book which explores the home birth alternative in all its dimensions: personal, medical, psychological, sociological, and historical. A sensitive essay by Ms. Ward accompanied by excellent photographs by her husband describes the actual home birth experience of the Ward family. Two doctors discuss the questions most frequently asked by couples considering home birth. Psychologists point out the advantages of home birth for the child and the child's family. There's also a sociological survey and interviews with typical home birth families. Oversize, 149pp. InS 76

WEINER, J. and J. GLICK. **A MOTHERHOOD BOOK**, $1.95. A first-person narrative of two young mothers and their experiences and thoughts about giving birth and the months afterward. Topics include: *Motherhood as a Possibility, Pregnancy, Giving Birth and Coming Down, Motherhood as a Physical Reality, Motherhood as a Psychic Reality.* The book is vividly written and should be illuminating and helpful to all mothers-to-be. Annotated bibliography, index. 131pp. McM 74

WHITE, GREGORY. **EMERGENCY CHILDBIRTH: A MANUAL**, $4.50. This is an excellent manual on emergency childbirth. All the essentials are succinctly covered under the following main topics: pregnancy and labor; delivery of the baby; unusual deliveries; hemorrhage; special care required by some babies; and pregnancy, labor or delivery which is complicated by illness or accidental injuries. An especially useful section contains condensed instructions for emergency use, arranged for quick reference. This book is very well regarded and it has been very hard to get, so we are glad to make it more generally available. 63pp. PTF 58

WRIGHT, ERNA. **THE NEW CHILDBIRTH**, $1.95. Ms. Wright is an authority on the Lamaze birth technique. Here she deals thoroughly with Lamaze preparation and birth. The explanations and diagrams are complete, and the chapter on *the necessary father* is excellent. Index, 205pp. S&S 67

NUMEROLOGY

Numerology is the science of numbers or vibrations and was one of the sciences practiced by men of great wisdom in ages long past. They realized that everything is made up of vibrations. They knew that this universal law applied to people as well as to things and that it could be used to determine a great deal about individuals. It is in fact part of what makes us individuals. Each number has its own vibratory influence and therefore its own characteristics. Through a few simple rules and formulas we can begin to see how these influences come into play in our lives and have a definite influence over us.

Numerology has in common with [astrology and palmistry] the belief that a person comes into a life at a certain time and with a certain name, not as a matter of chance but as a matter of choice, and that from these things much can be told about the person and his life. Even if you cannot agree with the idea that your birth name and birth date are not a matter of chance, there is no reason to argue with the theory that they have a definite effect upon your life, and upon this fact numerology is based. You may be surprised to find out just how much your numbers can tell about you and your life. . . . This information is based upon calculations made from the numbers derived from the birth date and from the letters of the name given at birth. Not only can much be told from one's name at birth, but also from nicknames and name changes made throughout life.

Part of the beauty of numerology is that you do not have to study long and hard before you can begin to put what you have learned to use. You can quickly learn a few basic facts and formulas that will immediately help you to begin to understand yourself and others better. From there, you can go on to learn more and more up to any point you wish.

—from **It's All in Your Numbers** by Kathleen Roquemore

ANDERSON, MARY. **THE SECRET POWER OF NUMBERS**, $1.00. An introductory survey, with sections on the meaning of numbers, words and numbers, meaning of the birthday, divining with numbers. 64pp. Wei 72

BUTLER, CHRISTOPHER. **NUMBER SYMBOLISM**, c$7.00. This book traces the history of numerological allegory from its beginnings in Greece and its appearance in early Biblical exegesis, to its effect upon the syncretic philosophical and scientific thought of the Renaissance. According to Butler the numerological tradition had three main elements—a cosmological science of creation according to numbers, a belief that the numbers of the Bible had an allegorical significance, and a symbolic arithmetic connected with magic, the occult, and astrology. This study is a far cry from the usual books on numerology and all who are interested in a deep understanding of the meaning of numbers should find it a welcome addition to the literature. Notes, index, bibliography. 198pp. RKP 70

CAMPBELL, FLORENCE. **YOUR DAYS ARE NUMBERED**, $4.245. This has been considered *the* basic numerology text. Every aspect of the subject is clearly discussed and the book is well organized. Recommended as a good beginners' manual. 246pp. Gat nd

CHEIRO. **BOOK OF NUMBERS**, $1.50. Cheiro clearly demonstrates how the science of numbers may be applied to your own life and affairs. He gives the numerical value of birth dates, names, etc., and he shows how to calculate from these figures the most propitious times for important decisions and transactions. Cheiro was mainly noted for his palmistry books, but all of his work is well regarded. 188pp. Arc 64

COATES, AUSTIN. **NUMEROLOGY**, c$10.50. This volume presents a very sophisticated system developed by the author, based on forty years of experience and personal observation. Coates is a British foreign service officer and has spent most of his adult life in the East. He feels that his system is in accord with the **I Ching** and with Buddhist principles. The text is graphically illustrated and the author presents his system very clearly. Many case studies illustrate the volume. Index, 127pp. Mll 74

GOODMAN, MORRIS. **MODERN NUMEROLOGY**, $2.00. A very simplified text which covers all the basic material. The exposition bears a strong resemblance to sun sign astrology books. 157pp. Wil 45

HELINE, CORINNE. **SACRED SCIENCE OF NUMBERS**, $3.50. A series of lecture lessons dealing with the sacred science of numbers, especially the significance of numbers one through thirteen. For more information on Corinne Heline see her listings in the Mysticism and Christianity sections. For those interested in the spiritual significance of numbers this is probably the best work. NAP

HITCHCOCK, HELYN. **HELPING YOURSELF WITH NUMBERS**, $2.45. This is a highly informative volume, especially for those who are interested in the self-help approach. The author is a theosophist and a member of Astara (a metaphysical organization), so she includes spiritual values in her exposition. The instructions are easy to follow and a great deal of material is introduced. 238pp. PrH 72

KOZMINSKY, ISIDORE. **NUMBERS—THEIR MEANING AND MAGIC**, $2.00. The first half describes the symbols and meanings of numbers; the second half discusses the numer-

ical values of letters, the Qabala of Pythagoras, prophesying, and colors, metals and gems which harmonize with numbers. 100pp. Wei

LAURIE, JOHN. **THE SCIENCE OF NUMEROLOGY THROUGH THE LAW OF VIBRATION**, $3.00. A study of the spiritual values of the numbers as they relate to the soul's development. Included are chapters on cycles and marriage. Some interesting ideas are presented, but Laurie does not write well and his exposition is scattered. 75pp. HeR 59

MENNINGER, KARL. **NUMBER WORDS AND NUMBER SYMBOLS**, c$24.20. This is a wide ranging scholarly work which recounts the development of numbers in cultures throughout history and in all parts of the world. Menninger presents many examples of how both the numbers and the numerals, in the course of their evolution, have come to reflect the cultural style, the linguistic patterns, and the conceptual outlook of both their makers and users. In addition to the more academic uses of numbers, the author also discusses the mystical, numerological, and religious significance of numbers. Anyone with a deep interest in numbers will find this a fascinating survey. It is profusely illustrated with photographs and line drawings and the writing style is not technical. Index, 480pp. MIT 69

MOORE, GERUN. **NUMBERS WILL TELL**, $1.95. Those who are deeply interested in numerology feel that this is one of the best books available. Moore himself is a well known numerologist and his presentation here is exceedingly clear. His system is based on Pythagoras and on Cheiro and like them he uses the Chaldean alphabet. Every conceivable aspect of daily life in which numbers play a part is discussed and step-by-step directions are given for choosing numbers that would be more favorable. 178pp. G&D 73

OJHA, ASHUTOSH. **NUMEROLOGY FOR ALL**, $2.00. A complete presentation of the Indian science of numbers. A great deal of space is devoted to astrological correspondences. 188pp. HPB 73

OMARR, SYDNEY. **THOUGHT DIAL**, $2.00. Omarr devised the *thought dial* as a means of probing into an individual's subconscious. The technique, as he outlines it here, is simple and is based on a special number symbolism. The system resembles horary astrology in part and it can also be used to answer any number of pending questions. The system itself is hard to describe, and we don't totally understand it. But if you are interested the book appears to give fairly complete instructions along with a great number of case studies. 172pp. Wil 58

ROQUEMORE, KATHLEEN. **IT'S ALL IN YOUR NUMBERS**, c$10.95. This is the most comprehensive book on numerology that we have seen. It is well written and organized and covers many areas in depth that are either not dealt with in other books or are just briefly touched on. First she presents information on the basic characteristics of numbers, how to interpret them, and how to calculate what your numbers are. From there she goes on to discuss what numerology has to say about the self (inner and outer), the life cycles, and much else. The author takes a very spiritual approach in her presentation and integrates numerology with the other esoteric sciences. This book should help the interested reader immensely to gain insight into what numbers mean in every aspect of life. Recommended. Index, 31pp. H&R 75

SEPHARIAL. **THE KABALA OF NUMBERS**, $4.95. This is a classic study on the esoteric significance of numbers. Sepharial studied the systems of the ancients and discovered that for them the laws governing the whole of nature and the underlying spiritual world are traceable only in terms of numbers. This is a fascinating, comprehensive study and is indispensable for the serious student of metaphysics. Includes diagrams, tables, examples, practical instruction, and historical material. 388pp. NPC

_____. **THE NUMBERS BOOK**, c$3.20. An introductory study for the general student, clearly written, with both practical and interpretative material. Topics include the mysticism of numbers, names and numbers, numbers and characters, and divination by numbers. 128pp. Fou 57

STEBBING, LIONEL. **THE SECRETS OF NUMBERS**, $2.05. A serious spiritual study of numbers based on the Pythagorean system and more directly on Rudolf Steiner's spiritual science. It includes a survey of the essence and meaning of the numbers one to twelve as well as the significance in human life of the eighteen years, seven months cycle and the thirty-three year rhythm cycle discovered by Rudolf Steiner. Bibliography, 76pp. NKB 63

VALLA, MARY. **THE POWER OF NUMBERS**, $3.95. A compilation of lessons in numerology as taught by the author. Her analysis of a number in each of its five positions derived from the birth date and name has been based on notes taken during thirty years of private counseling and research. The discussion is quite different from the other books we've seen and includes the general vibrations of the number, the soul path, destiny, mental image, and other aspects. An interesting philosophical/spiritual work. 214pp. DeV 71

VAUGHN, RICHARD. **NUMBERS AS SYMBOLS OF SELF DISCOVERY**, c$8.95. This is a detailed text, designed as an aid to self-understanding. The first section explains the numerological meaning of your name. It is divided into three basic sections: character, personality, and motivation—and each number is analyzed in detail. The second part analyzes fate, or the general pattern of one's life in accordance with one's number. The third section evaluates the eighty-one character patterns, with examples of famous personalities. A final section gives the number patterns of over 1000 famous personalities. 450pp. LIP 73

WESTCOTT, W. WYNN. **NUMBERS: THEIR OCCULT POWER AND MYSTIC VIRTUES**, c$3.70. A scholarly, yet readable overview of numerology through the ages. Includes excellent material on Pythagoras and Pythagorean views of numbers and the Qabalistic view of numbers. The majority of the book details the properties of numbers according to the Bible, the Talmud, the Pythagoreans, the Romans, Chaldeans, Egyptians, Hindus, medieval musicians, Hermetic musicians and Rosicrucians. Also presents a selected bibliography. 127pp. All 1890

NUTRITION

Nutrition has a nice scientific sound. There is, nevertheless, an incredible range of opinion. On one side is Dr. Frederick Stare of Harvard University, who believes that sugary cereals and nitrate-laden hot dogs (and other products of the giant food industry) are good for you. This food industry is considerably larger than the military-industrial complex; its power to influence public opinion through Harvard University, the FDA, the AMA, and many other establishment organizations is great. On the other side are the exponents of extreme dietary theories, often drawing on a very limited knowledge of physiology and a highly selective look at scientific studies.

We have tried to select books which, on the whole, appear to be scientifically sound. Virtually all of them would be condemned by Frederick Stare and those who see the world his way. These are the voices that say that Americans are the best-fed people in the world, and that if we select from the basic four types of food we will be well nourished. Merely to dip into a few of these books shows us how wrong that cheerful optimism is. This is an area, unlike homeopathy, for instance, where all of us can apply what we learn to our own lives to good effect.

ADAMS, RUTH and FRANK MURRAY. **THE GOOD SEEDS, THE RICH GRAINS, THE HARDY NUTS,** $1.50. Written by a pair of prolific (and good) authors on nutritional subjects, this book first gives an up-to-date review of the evidence against refined carbohydrates that comprise half the average American diet, then goes on to discuss the many natural alternatives, their value and use. Short bibliography, tables, index. 250pp. Lar 73

AIROLA, PAAVO. **ARE YOU CONFUSED?** $3.95. Dr. Airola is our favorite naturopathic writer. Trained in Europe, he brings a wide background to all his books. In this one he examines the pros and cons of many issues still debated by nutritionists: high versus low protein diet, whether to take supplements, the value of milk, how to fast, distilled versus mineralized water, and much more. An excellent first reader on nutrition which will save you much confusion later. Recommended. Index, 222pp. HPP 71

BIELER, HENRY. **FOOD IS YOUR BEST MEDICINE,** $1.95. In more than fifty years of practice, Dr. Bieler has had great experience with nutritional therapy. He believes disease is caused by toxemia which results in cellular impairment, that most use of drugs is harmful, and therefore that food is your best medicine. All readers might not go all the way with Dr. Bieler, but there is a lot to learn here about human physiology. The book has been very popular; unfortunately the print in the paperback edition is small and hard to read. Index, 236pp. RaH 65

BIRCHER-BENNER, M. **CHILDREN'S DIET,** $2.05. First published in 1935, this book sets out many of Dr. Bircher-Benner's ideas as applied to children. After discussing the deterioration of our civilized diet, he considers the relationship of diet and disease, discusses the particular problems of childhood, and then gives his recommendations as to what should and should not be given to children. He places great importance on raw foods but doesn't rely on these exclusively. These ideas have been more popular in Europe than here. We find much of value in them. 66pp. Dan 64

_____. **EATING YOUR WAY TO HEALTH,** $1.95. This is primarily a cookbook with introductory material about the diet utilized over many years at the Bircher-Benner Clinic in Switzerland. It avoids stimulants, meat or alcohol. To many, Dr. Bircher-Benner is best known as the inventor of *muesli*, that delicious cereal of grains, fruits and nuts. He believes that the high quality of food energy obtained from the freshest possible food as near as possible to its living state is of vital importance. Index, 341pp. Pen 61

_____. **SALT-FREE NUTRITION,** $2.75. Written by the staff of the Bircher-Benner Clinic, this is one of fifteen guides to diet for particular purposes. A fifteen page discussion of salt metabolism and conditions requiring a salt free diet is followed by extensive diet suggestions and recipes. 132pp. Nas 67

BURTIS, C.E. **THE FOUNTAIN OF YOUTH,** $1.45. Subtitled *Longer Life Through Natural Foods*, this book, though old, is still a good round-up of a lot of the essential material and scientific data. The chapter on synthetic versus natural food is particularly useful in discussing differences revealed by chromatographs and prismic examinations. Small print. Footnotes, 254pp. Arc 64

CHEN, PHILIP. **SOYBEANS FOR HEALTH AND LONGER LIFE,** $1.25. This work goes beyond the usual book extolling the virtues of one food or another. Invaluable to any homesteader wishing to make the most of this remarkable food, it has directions for growing and storing soybeans, and making milk, curd and sauce. Many recipes. Bibliography, index. 178pp. Kea 73

CLARK, LINDA. **BE SLIM AND HEALTHY,** $1.50. Linda Clark is a prolific nutrition writer with a large following. This little book contains a wealth of good nutritional advice from the viewpoint of one who wants to reduce or stay slim. An important feature is her *Stop and Go Carbohydrate Computer*. This simplifies low carbohydrate dieting. You merely look up each item, keep your intake to sixty grams, favoring the nutritional ones marked *go* and avoiding those marked *stop*. 161pp. Kea 72

_____. **GO STOP CARBOHYDRATE COMPUTER,** $.95. A convenient pocket edition of the tables found in **Be Slim and Healthy.** 46pp. Kea 73

_____. **KNOW YOUR NUTRITION,** $3.50. This is the most comprehensive of the recent Linda Clark books, adapted from her nutrition course that ran in **Let's Live.** It deals primarily with the various vitamins and minerals, their effects, how and why to take them, etc. Ms. Clark writes in a popular, easy-to-read manner which is generally well balanced. She does, however, frequently quote other popular writers such as Adelle Davis rather than original sources. Index, 250pp. Kea 73

_____. **LIGHT ON YOUR HEALTH PROBLEMS,** $1.25. Questions and answers topically arranged, from her column in **Let's Live** magazine. 127pp. Kea 72

_____. **STAY YOUNG LONGER,** c$1.25.

COLIMORE, BENJAMIN and SARAH. **NUTRITION AND YOUR BODY,** $3.95. Most nutrition books repeat the same information about what vitamins and minerals do and why they are important. That's all in here. But the refreshing thing about this book is that it gives a very good and clear presentation of the anatomy and physiology involved, so that if you are not technically trained you'll get a better understanding of what it's all about by reading this book than most others. Illustrated with photographs and line drawings that help to explain the text. Also contains various food tables, technical references and bibliography. Recommended. Index, 220pp. NAP 74

DAVIS, ADELLE. **LET'S EAT RIGHT TO KEEP FIT,** $1.95. The late Adelle Davis is so well known as to require no introduction here. This is her basic book, which contains a great deal of useful information but is somewhat scattered and difficult to comprehend. It should not be read as a first book on nutrition—many people have unfortunately been put off from learning the basics of good nutrition after getting bogged down half way through this book. Includes tables of food composition, and an excellent index. 334pp. NAL 70

_____. **LET'S HAVE HEALTHY CHILDREN,** $1.95. Extensively revised from the original edition, this was the last of the Davis books to come out in paperback. (It's a good practice to read the most recent editions of the Davis books, since she changed her views on a number of topics as new studies came to her attention.) This book should be read by all mothers-to-be and re-read as the children grow. It has advice on prenatal nutrition, how to have an easier delivery, and care and feeding of the child, as well as tables of food composition and an excellent index. 381pp. NAL 72

DAY, HARVEY. **THE BREATH OF LIFE,** c$4.50. An unusual book covering the physiology of breathing, effects of bad air, yogic breathing methods, the importance of skin and the effects of sunshine and bathing. The author, who was raised in India, has combined some very esoteric ideas and findings with more conventional scientific views. Bibliography, 126pp. TPL 65

ELWOOD, CATHERINE. **FEEL LIKE A MILLION,** $1.75. We have long viewed this as one of the best beginning books on nutrition. The first section explains the various nutrients, the second section discusses health problems and their relation to nutrition and the final section covers various foods and the fundamentals of good diet. There is an excellent chapter on the food value of sprouts and how to make them. Ms. Elwood is a trained nutritionist who also has the facility to write simply. Tables, bibliography, index. 366pp. S&S 56

BANIK, ALLEN. **YOUR WATER AND YOUR HEALTH**, $1.25. Dr. Banik is the foremost advocate of distilled water for health. He reviews the arguments that soft water associated with heart disease, suggesting the problem is not lack of minerals but other pollutants that soft water dissolves out of pipes. If you want to get a home still, this is the book for you. Bibliography, 126pp. Kea 74

CALDWELL, GLADYS and PHILIP ZANFAGNA. **FLUORIDATION AND TRUTH DECAY**, $3.50. *Fifteen years of total involvement in viewing the American fluoridation scene has convinced me that fluoridation is the most disastrous and costly consumer fraud of this polluted century. . . . The purpose of this book is to tell you the truth about fluoridation, and in doing so we take you behind the scenes to show you that the fertilizer factories are unable to control or dispose of their deadly fluoride, to show you the tank truck labeled DANGER CORROSIVE ACID unloading its fluoride garbage into the nation's drinking water under the guise of a public health program, and to reveal how dangerous fluoridation is to your health.*—from the introduction. This is a very well documented study. 301pp. Top 74

CLARK, LINDA. **ARE YOU RADIOACTIVE?** $1.25. Discusses radioactivity from x-rays, luminous dials, food irradiation, microwave ovens, fluorescent lights, color TV, microwave towers and nuclear plants, its effects on our bodies, and what foods or remedies can be taken to mitigate these effects. Bibliography, 128pp. Pyr 74

GARRISON, OMAR. **THE DICTOCRAT'S ATTACK ON HEALTH FOODS AND VITAMINS**, $.95. Don't read this book if you don't want to be outraged or if you wish to reserve your faith in the goodness and disinterest of the federal officials who protect us from *nutritional nonsense*. It documents the fact that many official acts have been motivated by economic, political and personal considerations rather than by concern for consumer protection, discusses the vendettas against Carlton Fredericks, Adelle Davis, Rachel Carson and others, and shows the connections between the U.S. agencies, big food) business, and big universities. 340pp. Arc 70

HALL, ROSS. **FOOD FOR NOUGHT—THE DECLINE IN NUTRITION**, $3.95. A biochemist attacks the increased use of chemicals to produce larger crops, fatter livestock, tenderer texture and better flavor—not because the chemicals are dangerous in themselves (although they often are) but because they destroy basic nutritional values. A well documented technical survey, geared toward awakening the general public. Glossary, notes, index. 324pp. RaH 76

HIGHTOWER, JIM. **EAT YOUR HEART OUT**, c$8.95. This is an important book which reveals how the food we buy in the supermarkets is controlled in price and quality by huge conglomerates who bleed the helpless consumer dry while reaping exorbitant profits for themselves. This book documents just how high the costs are, and why they are getting higher. It is subtitled *How Food Profiteers Victimize the Consumer*, and Hightower presents a good case backing up his claims. It's a technical study, but one that is well worth reading. Extensive notes, index. 294pp. Crn 75

HUNTER, BEATRICE. **CONSUMER BEWARE**, $3.95. Fifteen years ago, Beatrice Trum Hunter received an award from the Friends of Nature for her work in educating the public to the dangers of pesticides. She is the Rachel Carson of today. This book says it all and as well as anybody has said it. With a wealth of detail about the machinations of industry and the FDA, this book tells you just what you can expect to find in your supermarket foods. If this doesn't drive you to your local natural foods store, we don't know what will. Well documented, with fifty pages of references. Recommended. Index, 431pp. Ban 71

_____. **FOOD ADDITIVES AND YOUR HEALTH**, $1.25. Which food additives are dangerous, which are not? This slim book (not as comprehensive as Jacobson's) provides some of the answers. Slip it in your purse when you go to the supermarket and start reading labels. Bibliography, index. 116pp. Kea 72

_____. **THE MIRAGE OF SAFETY**, c$9.95. Subtitled *Food Additives and Federal Policy*, Ms. Hunter's latest book describes how safety tests for food additives are conducted and why present methods are inadequate. Physicians are reporting adverse effects of specific additives on their patients and new startling information about the hazards of additives is being revealed in various basic research projects. All these are documented by Ms. Hunter along with suggestions about what can be done at the policy level and at the personal level. Bibliography, index. 192pp. Scr 75

JACOBSON, MICHAEL. **EATER'S DIGEST**, $2.50. This is the best collection of data on food additives we have seen. Reasoned, balanced, and scientifically based, Dr. Jacobson's book tells us what to be wary of and what is OK. Over a hundred additives, good and bad, are carefully discussed in terms of usage, history, and relevant experimental data. Another very useful section gives many of the FDA's food standards which state what foods may or must contain that is not listed on labels. Read the standards for bread and ice cream and you'll never feel the same about them again. Appendices include a list of additives that have been banned, much of the GRAS (generally recognized as safe) list, chemical formulas and an excellent glossary of terms. Bibliography, index. 260pp. Dou 72

LERZA, CATHERINE and MICHAEL JACOBSON, eds. **FOOD FOR PEOPLE, NOT FOR PROFIT**, $1.95. Prepared for Food Day, 1975, this is the most complete, up-to-date fact book with everything you want to know about the food crisis and then some. Contains fifty-four articles, organized around food production, costs, nutrition, world food, food and the poor, and the government and the food industry. If you have to write a speech or an article, or simply want to be a well-informed citizen about the food problem from all angles, this is your book. Also contains a chapter on action ideas for the activist, and a number of useful appendices including excellent references and other sources of further information and action. Recommended. 466pp. RaH 75

MARINE, GENE and JUDITH VAN ALLEN. **FOOD POLLUTION: THE VIOLATION OF OUR INNER ECOLOGY**, $2.95. Written by two reporters who claim not to be food freaks, this book runs through all the usual information about what the greedy manufacturers are doing to our food and what the government isn't doing about it. An interesting, well documented narrative. As they say in the preface, *If you know what this book tells you, and choose white bread and poison-riddled food, you are an adult making a free choice. If you eat it because you don't know any better, or cannot afford better, you are a victim.* Index, 385pp. HRW 72

NULL, GARY. **BODY POLLUTION**, c$2.45. Another book on additives and other substances we put into our bodies, polluting our vital systems and destroying our health. Includes an alternative program of natural nutrition. Gary Null is a young health food store owner, health food magazine publisher, and, with his staff of research assistants, a prolific writer. His books are readable compilations of material in the general literature, sometimes, however, showing evidence of hasty putting together without a consistent point of view. Index, 214pp. Arc 73

ROBBINS, WILLIAM. **AMERICAN FOOD SCANDAL**, $3.50. *William Robbins carefully documents and forcefully presents the facts about agribusiness giants and huge food companies—they are not more efficient at farming and processing; they're more efficient at farming us, the taxpayers and consumers.*—Former Senator Fred Harris. Index, 280pp. Mor 74

SCHROEDER, HENRY. **THE POISONS AROUND US**, c$10.00. Mankind has, throughout time, seen fit to dig up metals from deposits in the earth and scatter them over the face of the globe. That some of them are toxic has worried him little in the past. But now he is slowly becoming concerned. In this book one of the world's foremost authorities on the relations of metals to human health discusses metals and other elements as pollutants and as substances beneficial to life. He places the industrial metals and elements to which man is exposed today in their proper perspective, and explains which are toxic, which are necessary, and which are inert. His findings are based on experimental evidence amassed in studies and the book is written in nontechnical language. Notes, bibliography, index. 146pp. IUP 74

TAUB, HAROLD. **KEEPING HEALTHY IN A POLLUTED WORLD**, $2.95. Taub is a former executive editor of **Prevention**. In this book he not only tells us about all the dangers of our polluted environment, but goes on to prescribe practical measures by which we can defend ourselves. These include nutritional programs, intelligent use of vitamin supplements, special exercises, and other simple modifications of our way of life that can increase our chances of survival. Bibliography, index. 246pp. Pen 74

VERRETT, JACQUELINE and JEAN CARPER. **EATING MAY BE HAZARDOUS TO YOUR HEALTH**, $2.95. *This is a soberly gripping book by a courageous Food and Drug Administration scientist and a lucid consumer writer. The story they tell about the silent violence in your food—how it got there and the FDA's abysmal lack of courage to make the food companies obey the law—makes you want to do something about it. As* **Eating May Be Hazardous to your Health** *points out, you can help do it as a tough and active citizen. The choice is clear: if consumers don't control their government, the food industry will.*—Ralph Nader. Dr. Verrett is the scientist who first blew the whistle on cyclamates. Since she has been a biochemical researcher within the FDA for over fifteen years, this book is more of an inside expose than most of this genre. Index, 256pp. S&S 74

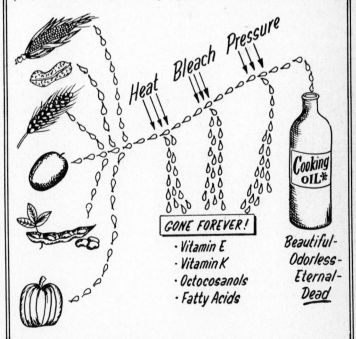

Heat Bleach Pressure

Cooking OIL*

GONE FOREVER!
· Vitamin E
· Vitamin K
· Octocosanols
· Fatty Acids

Beautiful-
Odorless-
Eternal-
Dead

WINTER, RUTH. **BEWARE OF THE FOOD YOU EAT**, $1.25. This is a revised edition of **Poisons in Your Food**. It examines raw foods and their processing, meats, packaged foods, water supply, vending machines, restaurants, fertilizers, pesticides, additives, sanitary practices, new foods, and ingredients introduced without inspection. There is a useful chapter teaching the reader how to read food freshness codes. Extensive documentation. Index, 280pp. NAL 71

FREDERICKS, CARLTON and HERBERT BAILEY. FOOD FACTS AND FALLACIES, $1.45. Carlton Fredericks, with a Ph.D. in Public Health Education, has taught nutrition at NYU and several other universities in addition to teaching over the radio for many years. We find his views eminently sound; anti-establishment of course, but also critical of the health food stores where criticism is needed (and it often is). This book covers a wide range of subjects: supplements, fluoridation, various diseases, aging, mental illness, sex and diet, weight, the FDA and AMA, etc. Tables, index. 380pp. Arc 65

FREDERICKS, CARLTON. **LOOK YOUNGER, FEEL HEALTHIER**, $2.95. This is Dr. Fredericks' most comprehensive book. He covers gynecological problems, low blood sugar, diabetes, weight control (including sample diets), nutrition for pregnant women, megavitamin therapy, aging, additives, supplements, nutrition for babies, and much more. There is a good chapter on how to shop in a health food store. Individual vitamins and minerals are discussed. A hypoglycemic diet is provided. All in all, a very readable, sometimes mind-boggling book which should increase your alienation from the system but at the same time give you a plethora of good scientific facts with which to defend yourself and your health. Recommended. Index, 310pp. G&D 72

_____. **PSYCHO-NUTRITION**, c$7.95. Another book on megavitamin, ortho-molecular therapy. Fredericks is not only one of the best-known and most knowledgeable nutritionists, but also the recently-elected President of the International Academy of Preventive Medicine. He discusses hypoglycemia, schizophrenia, autism, allergies—the whole range of problems reflecting biochemical abnormalities which can frequently be cured nutritionally. Many case histories and research findings are cited. Because Dr. Fredericks is an authority, not just a popular writer, this is a good book to give someone with a personal need to be turned on to this new therapy which is still damned by much of the medical and psychiatric orthodoxy. Appendix: *Where to Seek Help*, index, 224pp. G&D 76

FRYER, LEE and DICK SIMMONS. WHOLE FOODS FOR YOU, $4.95. A simple, often amusing, guide to supermarket shopping, concentrating upon products available national-ly rather than health foods. The authors examine meat, fruit, dairy products, frozen foods, cereals, etc., telling you what you should be getting, what you probably are get-ting, and what to do about it. There's a lesson in how to read bread labels, charts showing price comparisons in relation to nutrition, and many little tidbits, nicely packaged to get the facts to persons who may have trouble wading through weightier nutritional tomes. Lee Fryer has been associated for many years with efforts to rationalize organic food production with modern technology so as to make it more widely available and cheap. 218pp. MCh 74

GRANT, DORIS. RECIPE FOR SURVIVAL, $3.95. Doris Grant is a popular writer in England on health topics. By exploring subjects such as environmental contaminants of air, water and food, Ms. Grant demonstrates how modern man's mode of life is related to modern diseases, and how we can help ourselves to reduce the damage. Particularly interesting data on bread. While written for an English audience, most of the information translates well to our society. 224pp. Kea 73

GREGORY, DICK. **DICK GREGORY'S NATURAL DIET FOR FOLKS WHO EAT: COOKIN' WITH MOTHER NATURE**, $1.75. *An introduction to natural foods written with an eye to good health and an ear for the witty line. Even for those not ready to replace sirloin with soy bean (economic considerations notwithstanding), Gregory's discourse on the typical mistreatment of the digestive tract should be informative—it certainly is amusing. There are sections on Gregory's various fasts (with how-to hints for the interested), suggested diets for putting on and taking off weight, and even a discus-sion of natural food substitutes (fruit and vegetable juices) for your favorite alcoholic concoction. Good fun and a good guide for those who feel they are what they eat.—* **New York Times.** A popular book. Bibliography, index. 171pp. H&R 73

HARRIS, BEN CHARLES. KITCHEN MEDICINES, $.95. *The more one studies the therapeutic values of our everyday Nature-all foods, the more will he understand that these foods become the healing agent of most, if not all, organic ailments. Proper selec-tion and balance of organically grown vegetables and fruits, plus proper eating and hygienic habits, become the required fraction of prevention of such disorders. From all-spice to wheat, this book collects a wealth of data, both scientific and traditional, about the medicinal value of the common foods we eat.* Interesting reading as well as a useful reference work. Bibliography, index by disease or symptom. 174pp. S&S 61

HAUSCHKA, RUDOLF. NUTRITION, $10.50. Dr. Hauschka, a follower of Rudolf Steiner, bases this book on many years' research at the Clinical-Therapeutic Institute in Arlsheim, Switzerland. It is a serious, important and difficult book, of interest to those who wish to explore the effects of cosmic forces on nutrition. It represents a scientific

study of the proposition that matter is merely a solidification of a spiritual process a that, where life is involved, the mechanical and chemical laws covering the mineral ki dom are insufficient to explain what happens. Not recommended for general read but if you are into bio-dynamic gardening or anthroposophy, you will find a great deal ponder here, going far beyond other nutritional texts. Bibliography, index. 212 Wat 51

HAUSER, GAYLORD. DICTIONARY OF FOODS, $1.95. Brief descriptions of nu tional values and uses of common (and some uncommon) foods. Lists of acid and alkali forming foods, table of how long various foods stay in the stomach. Index, 135pp. Lus

HOLMES, FENWICKE. PSYCHO-DIETETICS, $4.00. *My dietetic method is based on overall knowledge of physics, chemistry, physiology, religion, and psychology, but also bears reference to mental science as now practiced in advanced schools of me physics around the world.* A mixture of natural hygiene and a spiritual and inspiratior point of view. 121pp. DeV 73

HUNTER, BEATRICE. FACT BOOK ON FERMENTED FOODS AND BEVERAGE $1.25. This is another uniquely valuable little book for the homesteader's or do-it-yo self library. Fermentation is an effective method of preservation of many foods, it i creases digestibility, and adds zest to the diet. Ms. Hunter has looked far and wide to te us about a great variety of fermented foods from many corners of the world and—bett yet—how to make many of them ourselves. Bibliography, index. 116pp. Kea 73

_____. **THE NATURAL FOODS PRIMER**, $2.50. Subtitled *Help for the Bew dered Beginner*, it might be a good one to slip to a loved one whom you are trying to tu on to good food. Tells what to look for, how to shop, how to prepare natural foods, wh equipment you need, and how to adjust your favorite recipes. Includes a long glossa and description of the basic natural foods. Index, 156pp. S&S 72

HUNTER, BEATRICE, et al. YOUR NATURAL HEALTH SAMPLER, $1.25. An ir pulse book, with a bit of Hunter, Linda Clark, Carlson Wade, etc., with no theme exce its subtitle: *The Best of Today's Writings on Health, Nutrition, Diet and Beauty.* 132p Kea 73

JACOBSON, MICHAEL. NUTRITION SCOREBOARD, $2.50. Michael Jacobson, Ph.D. in microbiology, is Co-director of the Center for Science in the Public Interest Washington, D.C. He has been an indefatigable campaigner for a greater sense of r sponsibility on the part of the big food industry in avoiding dangerous additives an providing more nutritious food. The book discusses all the important nutrients and the provides a unique rating of many common foods. The rating formula gives positive cred to protein, unsaturated fat, starch and naturally-occurring sugars, five vitamins, tw minerals, trace elements and fiber. A food loses points for saturated fat, a fat conter above 20%, and added sugar and corn syrup. Orange juice ranks 62; soda pop is −9: granola and milk are 45; chuckles candy is −98. A very useful compendium. 102pp. CFS 7

JENSEN, BERNARD. HEALTH MAGIC THROUGH CHLOROPHYLL, $4.45. Bernar Jensen has been a well-known and well-regarded naturopath and nutritionist for som forty-five years. This book, though somewhat scattered, contains a wealth of materia about the use of chlorophyll and greens in the diet for health and for healing. Dr. Jense calls this book one of his *Magic Survival Kits*, (the other two are still to come). Throug out it are useful tips on food in relation to survival should our society seriously brea down. Index, 154pp. Jen 73

KADANS, JOSEPH. ENCYCLOPEDIA OF FRUITS, VEGETABLES, NUTS, AN SEEDS FOR HEALTHFUL LIVING, $2.95. Kadans, a Ph.D. and N.D., is President o Bernadean University, an organization which gives correspondence courses in naturop athy. This book is in three parts: I, a brief discussion of various nutrients and metaboli factors; II, a detailed listing of the various foods giving nutritive values, reported healt benefits, and preparation and use; and III, a useful *Symptomatic Locator Index*, whic lists all the foods under symptom headings. Lots of good information but marred by poo printing—page 41 is from another book by the same publisher! 215pp. PrH 73

KEYES, KEN. LOVING YOUR BODY, $3.50. Ken Keyes is known to many of our cus tomers as the author of the **Handbook to Higher Consciousness**, our all-time best seller This book, originally published as **How to Live Longer-Stronger-Slimmer** in 1966, co bines Keyes' easy way of writing with the usual good advice on how to eat an optima diet, plus two special features: an excellent food table which includes Keyes' own *Vita min-Mineral Index*, giving a rating of food value per one hundred calories for hundred of foods; and a nutrition analysis form that you can fill out for yourself. 238pp. LLC 74

KINDERLEHRER, JANE. HOW TO FEEL YOUNGER LONGER, c$8.95. The author i senior editor of **Prevention** magazine. It's the best thing we've seen for older people, dis cussing the nutritional aspects of the ailments and diseases of the aging. Chapters on feet teeth, digestion, menopause, arthritis, heart, back, sleep, how to handle hospital visits an more. Written in a sprightly, upbeat style. We particularly enjoyed the chapter on diges tion, which points out the evils of antacids and the virtues of HCL, another case where most people do exactly the wrong thing to solve their problem. Index, 220pp. Rod 74

LAMB, LAWRENCE E. METABOLICS, c$9.95. 264 pp. H&R 74

MC GRATH, WILLIAM. BIO-NUTRONICS, $1.50. Good general advice on health and nutrition by a naturopathic doctor. His *Ten Commandments* of bio-nutronics include *Feast on the Bread of Life*, i.e., by loving; *Avoid Eating the Bread of Affliction*, i.e. stress; eat fresh, organic foods as close to the original state as possible; avoid highly pro cessed, chemicalized, de-vitalized foods; eat 75% live carbohydrates, 20% protein and 5% unsaturated fat; eat more light-filled foods, etc. Index, 216pp. NAL 72

MELLOR, CONSTANCE. HANDBOOK OF HEALTH, $1.10. This is a nicely writter book which concentrates on good health and how to maintain it. Ms. Mellor begins with discussion of our daily needs and she surveys the types of foods we should eat, the balance we should aim at, and what kind of supplementation is needed. Each of the vitamins and minerals is discussed and many good tips are related. Other major topics include the *six wonder foods* (brewer's yeast, wheat germ, millet seed, yogurt, honey, and molasses), juices, fasting, and vegetarianism. Food tables and information on herbal remedies are also included in an appendix. 125pp. HSP 66

MILTON, R.F. **BASIC NUTRITION AND CELL NUTRITION**, $1.50. This slim volume goes into more details about cells, how they operate and their needs, enzymes, etc., than most. It simplifies with the aid of diagrams and should be quite helpful to someone who wants to go beyond knowing what to eat to understand better why. 70pp. Prv 70

NATURAL BEAUTY

CASTLETON, VIRGINIA. **THE HANDBOOK OF NATURAL BEAUTY**, c$9.95. A comprehensive volume which features hundreds of ways to make homemade cosmetic preparations and also explains which type of individual needs each preparation. Ms. Castleton also offers a variety of tips and suggestions and explains exercise routines. An appendix contains a table of *Basic Beauty Foods and What They Do For You*. Index, 305pp. Rod 75

CLARK, LINDA. **FACE IMPROVEMENT THROUGH EXERCISE AND NUTRITION**, $1.75. Illustrated with full page drawings, Ms. Clark's book presents a systematic approach to eye area problems, double chins, foreheads, etc. Includes cosmetics, diet, exercises, and even the art of serenity. 124pp. Kea 73

_____. **SECRETS OF HEALTH AND BEAUTY**, $1.25. This is the most popular book on natural beauty. Ms. Clark is a prolific writer and an indefatigable researcher. In this volume she explains the importance of a proper diet and use of supplements for glowing health and gives cosmetic recipes. She also discusses exercise and surveys some of the most common beauty problems. Index, 255pp. Pyr 69

CRENSHAW, MARY ANN. **THE NATURAL WAY TO SUPER BEAUTY**, $1.75. Ms. Crenshaw is not a nutritionist, but a **New York Times** fashion and beauty reporter. The book is based on her own personal experiences plus a lot of research. This is the book that launched the lecithin-cider vinegar-B-6-kelp craze that helped to fatten the vitamin manufacturers, whatever it did for the consumer. (A number of our nutrition buffs have read this book and reported that it does have a lot of valuable information in it.) Very extensive food nutrition tables but in very small type. Index, 432pp. Del 75

MESSEGUE, MAURICE. **WAY TO NATURAL HEALTH AND BEAUTY**, c$6.95. Described as the world's most famous natural healer, M. Messegue describes here how, using only vegetables, fruits and herbs, one can prepare many treatments for ailments, health and beauty. Lots of good practical advice and a few recipes as well. Index, 254pp. McM 74

NULL, GARY. **THE NATURAL ORGANIC BEAUTY BOOK**, $1.25. Nutritional advice on hair, skin, yoga, etc. Bibliography, index, 220pp. Del 72

PREVENTION MAGAZINE, ed. **NATURAL WAY TO HEALTHY SKIN**, $2.95. Based on articles in **Prevention** over the years, this book discusses a wide of variety of skin conditions (burns, shingles, acne, athlete's foot, warts, etc.) as well as the functions of skin, how to maintain it in a healthy condition, and cosmetic advice. Index, 202pp. Rod 72

RUTLEDGE, DEBORAH. **NATURAL BEAUTY SECRETS**, $1.25. How to put egg on your face and do all sorts of natural things like grandmother did. Nowadays the cosmetics manufacturers are putting together very similar preparations at outrageous prices. This book is simple and straightforward and has sold over 200,000 copies. Index, 152pp. Ber 66

STEINHART, LAURENCE. **EDGAR CAYCE'S SECRETS OF BEAUTY THROUGH HEALTH**, $1.50. Because of Edgar Cayce's excellent track record in diagnosis and prescription, whatever he said about health and beauty is worth listening to. This book collects all the relevant readings: care of the skin, eyes, teeth, and hair; food and exercise; physiotherapy; elimination. The last part of the book goes beyond most health and beauty books, delving into reincarnation, recycling the mental body, vibratory influences, dreams and rejuvenation. Steinhart has done a good job of integrating the readings with other relevant information and putting it all together in easily readable fashion. 216pp. Ber 74

THOMAS, VIRGINIA. **MY SECRETS OF NATURAL BEAUTY**, $2.95. Organic beauty treatments, facial and figure exercises and formulas for money-saving lotions and cosmetics you can make at home yourself, from the beauty editor of **Prevention**. 148pp. Kea 72

WINTER, RUTH. **A CONSUMER'S DICTIONARY OF COSMETIC INGREDIENTS**, $3.95. Recently promulgated regulations will soon require that all of the ingredients of cosmetics be listed in descending order of amount contained. This can be of great help to persons who have found themselves allergic to various cosmetics without knowing what it was in them that caused the problem. To most of us, a list of ingredients will be fairly meaningless for—far more than food ingredients—they are chemicals we have never heard of. Hence the need for this dictionary with hundreds of definitions and indications of possible toxicity. 236pp. Crn 74

NITTLER, ALAN. **A NEW BREED OF DOCTOR**, $1.50. Dr. Nittler was an ordinary doctor who got interested in nutritional rather than drug therapy, and was expelled from the medical societies as a result. This book tells his personal story as well as giving much sound advice. It is directed, in part, to other doctors, in the hope that it will encourage them to take part in the medical revolution that is now beginning. Some parts of the book are therefore quite technical, though most can be read by the layperson. If you are interested in going to a nutritional doctor, this book is good advance preparation. Index, 202pp. Pyr 74

NULL, GARY. **COMPLETE QUESTION AND ANSWER BOOK OF GENERAL NUTRITION**, $1.25. 236pp. Del 72

_____. **FOOD COMBINING HANDBOOK**, $1.25. This says more about food combining than any other book we know of. It explains in great detail the digestive system, the function of enzymes, the various foods and the effects of different combinations on digestion; it has a chapter on ulcers and one on fasting. If digestion is your problem, you should find a great deal in here which will be of help. Bibliography, 140pp. Pyr 73

NULL, GARY and STEVE. **THE COMPLETE HANDBOOK OF NUTRITION**, $1.50. This is probably the most useful, and certainly the most comprehensive, of the Gary Null books. It is one of the better general nutrition texts including, in addition to the usual information on vitamins, minerals, etc., treatment of food combining, acid-alkaline balance, fruit and juices, fasting, herbs, beauty hints, poison in foods, etc. Good value. Bibliography, index. 413pp. Del 72

NUTRITION SEARCH, INC. **NUTRITION ALMANAC**, $4.95. This is not a book to sit down and read. It is, however, the best single source book on nutrition available, the product of team research over several years. It can be used to help the reader work out a total plan for personal nutrition, or it can answer questions about food, nutrition and health. The first and largest section discusses over forty vitamins and minerals in terms of description, absorption and storage, dosage and toxicity, deficiency effects and symptoms, beneficial effect on ailments, human tests, and animal tests. This is followed by a section on synergistic effects, providing an easy-to-follow guide for understanding which nutrients are compatible or antagonistic. Next is a brief section on available forms of nutritive supplements and their relative effectiveness. Then a long discussion of various diseases and ailments, in layperson's language, is accompanied by a list of nutrients (and quantities) that have been found to be beneficial. Next is a discussion of various foods and their values, including a list of rich sources of nutrients. A table of food composition gives the complete nutrient analysis of over 600 foods. Other tables include essential amino acid contents of foods and a nutrient allowance chart. There is an extensive bibliography, a good glossary and index. Highly recommended. 8x10", 263pp. McH 75

ORGANIC GARDENING AND STAFF. **ORGANICALLY GROWN FOODS**, $2.95. 98pp. Rod 73

PAGE, MELVIN and H. LEON ABRAMS, JR. **YOUR BODY IS YOUR BEST DOCTOR!** $1.25. Dr. Page, a dentist, has been one of the pioneers in nutritional studies for more than forty years. This book, co-authored by an anthropologist, reports many of his findings. The theme is that our bodies contain a built-in blueprint for good health but most of us spend our lives trying to tear it up. Page shows how to cooperate with it, in terms of what to eat and what not to eat. Good discussion of body chemistry, functions of glands, etc. Extensive discussion of degenerative diseases and effects of sugar, milk, coffee, etc. Good bibliography, 236pp. Kea 72

PASSWATER, RICHARD. **SUPERNUTRITION**, $1.95. Relying on extensive research in medical and scientific literature, the author, a biochemist, demonstrates that nutritional deficiencies exist in almost everyone's diet and that these deficiencies maintain the current high incidence rates of heart disease, cancer, and mental and emotional disturbances. He presents the evidence showing that low cholesterol diets have not decreased heart disease and shows that such diets are, in fact, detrimental to health. In the concluding chapter he presents a program of megavitamin therapy easily tailored to anyone's specific needs and makes the challenge that such a program can reduce the incidence of heart disease by 60%, cancer by 30%, cure most cases of schizophrenia, and save over a million lives a year. All in all, an excellent book. Charts, tables. 256pp. S&S 75

PELSTRING, LINDA and JO ANN HAUCK. **FOOD TO IMPROVE YOUR HEALTH**, $1.50. This is a reference book in two parts: I, an alphabetical listing indicating the vitamin and mineral content of hundreds of foods from abalone to zucchini, along with a discussion of how these elements work for or against your body; II, a listing of common health problems with information about nutritional deficiencies that cause them and what to eat to help make up those deficiencies. Bibliography, 221pp. Pin 74

PFEIFFER, CARL. **MENTAL AND ELEMENTAL NUTRIENTS**, c$9.95. See the Healing section.

RODALE, J.I. AND STAFF. **COMPLETE BOOK OF FOOD AND NUTRITION**, c$11.95. This vast, somewhat outdated book presents an encyclopedic picture of the health values (and dangers) of many different foods, food components, chemicals, etc. Its limitation is that it is drawn from articles in **Prevention** magazine; its coverage therefore is somewhat more opportunistic than logical. Nevertheless, we believe it is an important reference work. Index, 1054pp. Rod 61

_____. **THE HEALTH SEEKER**, c$10.95. Like the previous book, this one reprints material on a variety of disease and health problems ranging from accidents and acne to water softeners and x-rays. Lots of good material here but it must be kept in mind that the original articles represented particular points of view and were not written in an encyclopedic fashion. Good index, 928pp. Rod 62

RODALE PRESS, eds. **NUTS AND SEEDS—THE NATURAL SNACK**, $2.95. Following an introductory discussion of the value of seeds as food, this book reprints a number of articles on different seeds and their health value, follows with a section on growing nuts and seeds (comprehensive as to varieties, but not sufficiently detailed to be a good farmer's guide), and finally presents a few snack recipes. Index, 173pp. Rod 73

RODALE, ROBERT. **THE BEST HEALTH IDEAS I KNOW**, $1.50. Robert Rodale, the current editor of **Prevention** and **Organic Gardening and Farming**, here reprints a number of his recent articles covering topics such as the use of folk medicine, cutting down on meat, the importance of zinc, and tomorrow's health trends. Index, 192pp. Avo 74

SHELTON, HERBERT. **FOOD COMBINING MADE EASY**, $1.50. Dr. Shelton is one of the leading lights of the American Natural Hygiene Society, composed of people who favor eating the right foods, mostly raw, fasting, and generally avoiding or eliminating toxicity in the body as the key to health. This small book summarizes his views on food combining, explaining the digestive process and how wrong combinations can play hob with that process. There's a lot to this, though we admit our own weaknesses for food keeps us from following these principles very often. Includes suggested menus. 71pp. Shl 51

_____. **HEALTH FOR THE MILLIONS**, $1.45. This is a good introduction to the whole natural hygiene story: how our bodies utilize food, what to eat and what not to eat, cooking, food combining, how to eat, physical activity, keeping the body clean, etc. The hygienic way involves moderation and self-discipline—something that few of us are very good at. But it holds up for us a standard against which to measure our shortcomings. 314pp. ANH 68

SOBEL, DAVID and FAITH HORNBACHER. **TO YOUR HEALTH**, $4.95. *The initial idea for this book came from a headache. The headache said, in its own insufferable way, There are many simple, practical things you could do to take care of yourself, why don't you do them?* The text is handwritten and illustrated and includes a wide variety of practical techniques and exercises on the following topics: eyes and seeing, feet, hair, skin and bath, tooth care, good eating, breathing, relaxation, body movement, the great laughter cure, body rhythms, creating healthy environments, body-mind, inner work. Also includes a good, topically arranged annotated bibliography. 191pp. Vik 74

STEINER, RUDOLF. **PROBLEMS OF NUTRITION**, $.95. A brief lecture on the spiritual, esoteric effects of consuming meat, alcohol, coffee, milk, etc. *If by eating meat a person is relieved of too large a portion of his inner activities, then activities will develop inwardly that would otherwise be expressed externally. His soul will become more externally oriented, more susceptible to, and bound up with, the external world. When a person takes his nourishment from the realm of plants, however, he becomes more independent and more inclined to develop inwardly. He will become master over his whole being. The more he is inclined to vegetarianism, the more he accepts a vegetarian diet, the more he will be able also to let his inner forces predominate.* 22pp. API 69

TURCHETTI, RICHARD. **NEW AGE NUTRITION**, c$7.95. Beginning with a brief review of our basic needs (vitamins, minerals, protein, etc.), this book goes on to devote chapters to environmental stress, orthomolecular medicine, drugs, food contamination, pregnancy and diet. The drug chapter gives a very good summary of the dangers and nutritional treatment of various forms of drug abuse, ranked in the following order of danger: glue sniffing, amphetamines, alcohol, cigarettes, barbiturates, heroin, hallucinogens, marijuana. The authors draw on many good sources, but unfortunately complete references are not provided. Index, 153pp. Reg 74

VEGETARIANISM

ALTMAN, NATHANIEL. **EATING FOR LIFE**, $2.45. This is the best single book on vegetarianism that we have seen. It draws on material from many sources, particularly those that are objective and scientific and have no vested interest in vegetarianism. It looks at the subject from the standpoint of morality, anatomy and physiology, health and nutrition, the world food shortage and ecology. It includes a good summary of the main principles of nutrition, recipes and food value charts. Well documented. Bibliography, index. 142pp. TPH 73

BARKAS, JANET. **THE VEGETABLE PASSION**, c$8.95. Only incidentally a nutrition book, this is primarily a social history of vegetarianism, full of anecdotes and gossip about famous vegetarians; for example, what Hitler had for breakfast. Well researched and full of details, fascinating and otherwise. Illustrations, bibliography, index. 224pp. Scr 75

HUR, ROBIN. **FOOD REFORM: OUR DESPERATE NEED**, c$10.95. This is a far out and controversial book; it is also a very thoroughly researched book. The author spent some three years doing nutritional (book) research and he has 600 footnotes and many more references. Where does he come out? He advocates the SGA diet: sprouts, greens and algae—up to two pounds per day of greens, a similar amount of sprouts, and a very small amount of seaweed. Mr. Hur's arguments for this diet are both nutritional and ecological. This is not an easy book to read and is not suggested for someone just getting into the subject. But if you are ready to go deep and test your ideas against a lot of relevant research, you'll find a great deal in this book to mull over. 264pp. Hei 75

LAPPE, FRANCES. **DIET FOR A SMALL PLANET**, $5.95/$1.95. See the Cookbooks section.

NULL, GARY. **PROTEIN FOR VEGETARIANS**, $1.50. Goes beyond the title to deal generally with how vegetarians (and others, for that matter) can assure an adequate diet.

THE FOOD PROTEIN CONTINUUM

From Frances Lappe's
Diet For A Small Planet

Includes extensive food value tables, including a table of the contents of many foods in terms of the twelve principal amino acids. Bibliography, 189pp. Pyr 75

SZEKELY, EDMOND BORDEAUX. **SCIENTIFIC VEGETARIANISM**, $1.75. *It is plain scientific fact that the two greatest dangers in our food consumption today, from the standpoint of the world's greatest killer, heart disease, are animal fats and refined carbohydrates. A vegetarian diet, followed scientifically (that is, to include all the basic requirements of proteins, vitamins, minerals, enzymes, and the right kind of fats and carbohydrates), will inevitably prolong life, strengthen vitality and increase resistance to disease.*—from the preface. Deals with theory, types of food to eat and not to eat, ecological considerations, and effects of thoughts on the body. 47pp. Aca 74

VITAMINS AND MINERALS

ADAMS, RUTH. **THE COMPLETE HOME GUIDE TO ALL THE VITAMINS**, $1.95. This is a basic book about vitamins and what they are, with a brief rundown of each of the major ones. Tables, index. 253pp. Lar 72

ADAMS, RUTH and FRANK MURRAY. **MINERALS**, $1.65. A very interesting, detailed account of the minerals and trace elements—both those important to health and those which pose a threat. A great deal of attention is paid to the problems of pollution. A good account of the fluoridation controversy with many detailed studies for those looking for ammunition is included. Index, 290pp. Lar 74

BAILEY, HERBERT. **VITAMIN E**, $1.65. This was one of the first books to awaken the public to the importance of vitamin E, in the face of the suppressions and distortions of the medical establishment. Written by a veteran medical writer, it provides extensive research details and references. 203pp. Arc 64

_____. **THE VITAMIN PIONEERS**, $.95. This is a fascinating account of the key discoveries of various vitamins and their importance to our health. It details the great resistance of the FDA and much of the medical profession to many usages which are generally accepted today and some which still are not, thus giving us a good background from which to judge many of the criticisms we still hear from the establishment. Bailey is a long-time medical reporter. For many, this will prove an easier way to begin learning about vitamins than books packed with technical details. 239pp. Pyr 70

CYAN, ERWIN di. **VITAMIN E AND AGING**, $1.25. Among the various theories of aging, two—the oxidation and free radical theories—suggest an important role for vitamin E. Free radicals are portions of chemical compounds in the body which break off, are highly reactive, and enter into connections with unsaturated fatty acids, causing them to oxidize rapidly. Vitamin E is an anti-oxidant and it helps to neutralize the effects of free adicals. This book, conservatively written, includes material from the International Conference on Vitamin E and its Role in Cellular Metabolism, held in 1971. Glossary, bibliography, index. 176pp. Pyr 72

_____. VITAMINS IN YOUR LIFE, $2.95. This is an excellent survey of vitamins and minerals and their importance to our health. The author, who has been a drug consultant for over thirty years, writes essentially from the health establishment point of view, but he is not unsympathetic to the heretical views of Pauling on vitamin C, Hoffer and Osmond on niacin, etc. Each vitamin is discussed with respect to use, deficiency effects and sources. Toxicity levels and use of supplements are also covered. The treatment of trace elements is quite thorough. Recommended. Bibliography, index. 223pp. S&S 74

PREVENTION MAGAZINE, ed. VITAMIN A, $2.95. Recent studies have shed new light on the many ways vitamin A is important to our health. At the same time, deficiencies seem to be more widespread than with virtually any other vitamin among North Americans of all income groups. This reflects both bad nutritional habits and the effects of pesticides and pollutants. This book tells the story in a clear and readable way. Index, 130pp. Rod 72

RODALE, J.I. AND STAFF. THE COMPLETE BOOK OF MINERALS FOR HEALTH, c$13.95. This is the most recent of the Rodale Press' encyclopedic compilations of articles about various subjects. It is divided into six books: I. *The Macronutrients*, II. *Trace Minerals*, III. *Harmful Elements*, IV. *Mineral Deficiency Diseases*, V. *Foods and their Minerals*, and VI. *Vitamin and Mineral Interactions*. Not a book to read through, but good to dip into or to look up a wider variety of information about various minerals than you are likely to find anyplace else. Index, 786pp. Rod 72

_____. THE COMPLETE BOOK OF VITAMINS, c$13.95. This classic has a great deal of interesting material but it is overpriced and outdated. Much of it is reprinted from **Prevention** magazine, without re-editing and all the references are at least ten years old. Nevertheless it provides a lot of general information, including useful documentation for supporters of natural vitamins and large doses. Good index, 688pp. Rod 66

ROSENBERG, HAROLD and A.N. FELDZAMEN. THE DOCTOR'S BOOK OF VITAMIN THERAPY, $2.45. This is our favorite of the vitamin books. Dr. Rosenberg is one of that rare breed of nutritionally well educated M.D.'s and is past president of the International Academy of Preventive Medicine. Dr. Feldzamen (Ph.D.) is former editorial director of the Encyclopedia Britannica Education Corporation. This up-to-date book covers all the vitamin issues as well as providing the basic information. It makes a strong case for vitamin supplementation in our society. Its most useful feature is a series of tables by age, sex, and weight, giving recommendations for optimum levels of vitamin intake: on the order of 1000–1500 mg. of vitamin C, 200–600 IU of vitamin E, and 200–1000 mg. of vitamin B-3. There is also an excellent critique of the Government's Recommended Daily Allowances of Vitamins which we found convincing. Unfortunately the book lacks footnotes and an index. Highly recommended. 350pp. Ber 74

SCHROEDER, HENRY. THE TRACE ELEMENTS AND MAN, c$7.95. This is not a popular nutrition book but a serious, heavy (and fascinating) book by a distinguished scientist, Professor of Physiology Emeritus, Dartmouth Medical School. Dr. Schroeder believes that when animals—including man—became terrestrial, they brought with them the need for those trace elements that occur naturally in sea water. Other elements locked into the earth's crust are poisonous to man and have recently been released into the environment by industrial man. Good reading for those who ask *why?* Index, 171pp. DAC 73

SHUTE, WILFRED. VITAMIN E BOOK, c$8.95. This is Dr. Shute's latest update on the use of vitamin E for heart patients, and also its use in the treatment of burns, diabetes, skin ailments and circulatory diseases. He reviews various methods of treatment (proposed, widely used, and rejected), discusses the ineffectiveness of many current drugs, and demonstrates why many treatments now in common use are not only valueless but essentially dangerous. Notes, bibliography, index. 225pp. Kea 75

_____. VITAMIN E FOR AILING AND HEALTHY HEARTS, $1.65. The Shute brothers are the two doctors who—via 30,000 patients and forty years—did more than anyone else to prove the value of vitamin E for the heart. This is a fairly technical book, best for professionals or persons with heart problems who want to be able to talk effectively with their doctors. While primarily concerned with heart disease, the book does review research reports on E's use in treating many other diseases as well. Bibliography,

index. 208pp. Pyr 69

STONE, IRWIN. THE HEALING FACTOR: VITAMIN C AGAINST DISEASE, $1.95. This is the definitive book on vitamin C. Stone, a noted biochemist, has been researching ascorbic acid for some forty years; it was he who turned Linus Pauling on to its virtues in large doses. Man is virtually alone among animals in not producing his own vitamin C. If he did so in similar amounts to other animals relative to body size, we would each utilize two to four grams a day, rising to fifteen grams while under stress. By treating ascorbic acid as a minimum daily requirement instead of the crucial enzyme it really is, we are living in a state of sub-clinical scurvy, symptoms of which have been attributed to other ailments. Glossary and extensive references. 258pp. G&D 72

SZEKELY, EDMOND BORDEAUX. THE BOOK OF MINERALS, $1.50. Similar to his vitamin book, this is a brief guide to the role of each mineral in our basic biological functions, our requirements for each, mineral deficiency symptoms, best natural sources in order of importance, and a list of symptoms with minerals to take for each. For quick reference it's hard to beat. 38pp. Aca 71

_____. THE BOOK OF VITAMINS, $1.95. This is a neat little summary, in outline form, of a lot of useful information. It begins with lists of vitamin deficiency symptoms in the various systems of the human body, then goes on to deal with each vitamin, listing role, positive biological functions, deficiency symptoms and best natural sources. An easy-to-use quick reference. 38pp. Aca 71

VITA CHART. VITAMINS AND MINERALS CHART, $3.00. This 11x14" plastic chart (see illustration) is the neatest summary of vitamin and mineral information we've seen. Printed in color on both sides, it is not a substitute for a book about the vitamins but is an excellent memory jogger for those of us who have read many of the books and still can't keep all the details in mind. We particularly like the information on dosage—both the government's RDA and suggested supplementary ranges, complemented by specific information on the amounts contained in standard quantities of principal sources. VCh 76

WADE, CARLSON. MAGIC MINERALS. $1.95. Following a review of the minerals, Wade devotes chapters to their relationship to various aspects of health. Useful information, though we don't care for his vivid writing: *How to Make your Blood Stream a River of Eternal Youth, How Three Magic Mineral Sources Can Give You Added Mineral Power*, etc. 229pp. Arc 72

_____. VITAMINS AND OTHER FOOD SUPPLEMENTS, $1.25. A useful brief guide for the newcomer to the shelves of a health food store. Explains the use of vitamins, minerals and items such as lecithin, wheat germ and yoghurt. Very pro health food stores. 119pp. Kea 72

WEBSTER, JAMES. VITAMIN C, $1.25. A good, straightforward review of the research, expressed in terms comprehensible to the layperson. 158pp. ASC 71

WADE, CARLSON. FACT BOOK ON FATS, OILS AND CHOLESTEROL, $1.50. *This book will offer you the vital facts about fats and cholesterol and how a slight adjustment can add years to your lifeline of health. You will learn the difference between saturated and unsaturated fats and what they mean for your heart and artery health. You will learn how to plan a low fat diet that has all the delicious taste of a high fat diet. You will also be given the latest doctor-approved fat-controlled diet plans to help you cooperate with your own doctor for your individual case. You will discover how you can use natural foods to help control and even wash the cholesterol in your system.*—from the introduction. 125pp. Kea 73

_____. HELPING YOUR HEALTH WITH ENZYMES, $1.95. Discusses how enzymes help build resistance against disease, help us recover from illness and tiredness, help relieve aches and pains, subdue skin irritations, affect weight, etc. Also deals with fasting, food combining, raw foods, proper breathing, and acid-alkaline balance. Index, 224pp. Arc 66

_____. MIRACLE PROTEIN: SECRET OF NATURAL CELL-TISSUE REJUVENATION, c$8.95. PrH 75

_____. NATURAL HORMONES, $2.45. The idea of this book is to eat foods and to take mineral baths, fasts and exercises which stimulate the glands that produce hormones. The foods include grapes, beans and peas, rose hips, herbs, seeds, sprouts, apple cider vinegar, carob meal, honey, millet and fresh juices. Wade also discusses the various glands, what they do and how they may be helped. Index, 236pp. PrH 72

WILLIAMS, ROGER. NUTRITION AGAINST DISEASE, $1.95. Dr. Williams is perhaps responsible for more original work in the field of vitamin research than any living scientist. He was the first man to identify pantothenic acid; he also did pioneer work on folic acid and gave it its name. He is past president of the American Chemical Society and has received many awards and honorary degrees. His basic thesis is that the nutritional micro-environment of our body cells is crucially important to our health and that deficiencies in this environment constitute a major cause of disease. He has found that our inherited needs for various nutritive factors vary tremendously. This book discusses the general theory, then applies it to birth defects, heart disease, obesity, dental disease, arthritis, old age, mental disease, alcoholism and cancer. The work is supported by some 1100 medical and scientific citations. Recommended. Index, 370pp. Ban 71

_____. NUTRITION IN A NUTSHELL, $1.95. In this small book, Dr. Williams undertakes to set forth in simple language some of the basic facts of nutrition, such as what nourishing food contains, where nutrition starts, what a vitamin is and what it does. It is written from a biochemical point of view, is scientifically sound, and can be helpful in giving us the kind of information that will permit us to sort out the sound nutritional ideas from those that proceed from an excess of zeal and a lack of hard evidence. Index, 171pp. Dou 62

OCCULT ANATOMY

ASIMOV, ISAAC. THE HUMAN BODY, $1.50. This is a well written, informative study which explains the structure and operation of the human body utilizing both anatomy and physiology. As usual Asimov makes his subject understandable and exciting to the layperson. Illustrations, index. 320pp. NAL 63

_____. **THE HUMAN BRAIN**, $1.25. This is a companion volume to Asimov's **The Human Body**. Asimov explores the physical structure of the cerebral hemisphere and the functioning of the hormones, pancreas, thyroid, adrenal cortex, gonads, nerves, nervous system, cerebrum, brain stem and spinal cord, senses, ears, eyes, reflexes, and mind—all of which are controlled by the brain. The text is well illustrated with line drawings and the material is explained with the clarity for which Asimov is noted. Index, 357pp. NAL 63

BAKER, DOUGLAS. ESOTERIC ANATOMY, $16.00. Dr. Baker is an English physician who is well versed in the esoteric sciences. Many of his observations seem to be derived from theosophy. This study is more interesting than many of his books because it draws heavily on his own experiences and observations. Each part of the human anatomy is explored and graphically illustrated and the esoteric organs are discussed as fully as the exoteric ones. The illustrations are often in color and many of the line drawings are clear and presented in a scientific manner. On the whole the book is less scattered than many of Baker's books. 8x11½", very fully indexed. 247pp. Bak 76

CROUCH, JAMES. INTRODUCTION TO HUMAN ANATOMY, $6.95. A well organized, comprehensive, and extensively illustrated laboratory manual which is designed for premedical students. The illustrations are large and very clearly drawn and, while it is designed to be used for dissection, it should be helpful to anyone who wants to learn the details of human anatomy. Extensive descriptive material accompanies the plates. There's also a section of questions. Glossary, 8½x11", index. 269pp. MPC 73

DUMONT, THERON. THE SOLAR PLEXUS OR ABDOMINAL BRAIN, $1.00. Dumont believes that the solar plexus is one of man's four brains (the others being the cerebrum, the cerebellum, and the medulla oblongata) and it rules man's emotional center and regulates his vitality and health. In this small book he examines the solar plexus, explains its role, and details a series of exercises for awakening the solar plexus. 64pp. YPS nd

GRAY, HENRY. GRAY'S ANATOMY, $7.95. This is the first paperback edition of the classic 1901 edition of Gray's Anatomy. It is a very comprehensive, dryly written study of every part of the human body, and it includes over 600 line drawings. For a reason that we cannot fathom, this has become an underground best seller. It's certainly not bedtime reading—but for anyone interested in human anatomy it is a must either by itself or as a supplement to more approachable volumes. A weighty tome, fully indexed, 1257pp. RuP 74

HALL, MANLY P. MAN: GRAND SYMBOL OF THE MYSTERIES, c$10.00. A new edition of Hall's fascinating essays on occult anatomy, profusely illustrated with woodcuts and line drawings. Includes chapters on the *macrocosm and the microcosm, the story of the cell, the brain and the release of the soul, the heart, the seat of life, the spinal column and the world tree (the tree of life), kundalini, the pineal gland, sight,* and much else. Hall relates his material to the ancient mystery teachings and as usual incorporates a great deal of fascinating philosophy. For more on Hall see the Mysticism section. Oversize, extensive index. 254pp. PRS 72

_____. **THE OCCULT ANATOMY OF MAN**, $1.50. An interesting treatise based on the ancient mystery teachings. 36pp. PRS 57

HEINDEL, MAX. THE VITAL BODY, $2.50. An esoteric treatise based on Rosicrucian philosophy. Heindel defines the vital body as follows: *The vital body is made of ether and pervades the visible body as ether permeates all other forms, except that human beings specialize a greater amount of the universal ether than other forms. That ethereal body is our instrument for specializing the vital energy of the Sun.* 198pp. Ros 50

KAPP, M.W. GLANDS: OUR INVISIBLE GUARDIANS, c$5.75. This is an excellent esoteric analysis of the glands based on Rosicrucian philosophy and on the ancient mystery teachings. Each of the glands is discussed at length. Index, 97pp. Amo 58

LEADBEATER, C.W. THE CHAKRAS, c$4.75/$3.45. According to Hindu teachings, there are subtle psychic sense organs in man's body which channel psychic energies and vital force, and are related to the glandular and nervous systems. They are also said to serve as a link between physical, psychic, and super-physical states of consciousness. These centers are called chakras, a Sanskrit term meaning wheels or discs. Leadbeater's book was first published in 1927, and has become a classic in its field. It is handsomely illustrated with ten color plates and many drawings. The material is comprehensive and very clearly illuminated. Highly recommended. 132pp. TPH

NILSSON, LENNART. BEHOLD MAN, c$25.00. Nilsson is a Swedish photographer who has been working on close-ups of the life of living things since the early 1950's, progressing from insects to small sea animals and finally to human beings. Many of his photo-graphs were published in **Life** magazine. **Behold Man** takes the reader on a remarkab[le] odyssey inside the human body. In 350 photographs, most of them in color, the extr[a]ordinary complexity and variety of the body is presented in a way that has never befo[re] been seen. Employing newly designed optical devices, powerful electron microscope[s] and specially calibrated instruments capable of magnifying minute tissues to thousands [of] times larger than life size, Nilsson opens up the unseen landscape of our bodies and th[e] processes that sustain them. His pictures reveal the secrets of how our senses work, ho[w] the body communicates with itself, and how such crucial cycles as respiration, digestio[n] and reproduction are carried out. His camera investigates every region of the body, fro[m] the structure of a single cell to the most delicately balanced interaction of bodily fun[c]tions. Supported by a clear, straightforward text, many line drawings and extensi[ve] captions, **Behold Man** invites every reader to share its beautiful and mysterious discoverie[s] about the human body and how it works. Oversize, index. 254pp. LBC 73

PEARCE, EVELYN. ANATOMY AND PHYSIOLOGY FOR NURSES, $5.45. This [is] far and away the best anatomy book for both the layperson and the professional tha[t] we know of. Each part of the body is discussed and illustrated and even the smalle[st] areas can be readily viewed. The material is well organized and the explanations ar[e] clear and to the point. Excellent line drawings. Glossary, fully indexed. 411pp. Fab 7[?]

RAYNER, CLAIRE, ET AL. ATLAS OF THE BODY AND MIND, c$25.00. This is [a] stunning book which takes the reader on a voyage through the workings of the huma[n] body, emphasizing the elaborate interactions of the mind and body. The thorough text[—] supported by over 400 color paintings, photographs, and cutaway drawings—plus an ex[-] tensive glossary and complete index, make this an invaluable resource. The text is divide[d] into the following major sections: *evolution of man, framework of the body, energy fo[r] the machine, control systems, the senses, the brain, the intellect, defenses of the body[,] reproduction, span of life,* and *the future.* An amazing book which can be studied ove[r] a lifetime. 10¾x14½", 208pp. RMN 76

RENDEL, PETER. INTRODUCTION TO THE CHAKRAS, $1.00. This is a well writte[n] concise study. The first six chapters explain the occult anatomy of man. The magneti[c] polarities and energy fields are discussed as they relate to the flow of vitality and th[e] seven chakras. Special emphasis is placed on the brow and the crown chakras. The nex[t] chapters deal with the application of these principles in practice through yoga and sel[f] training. A final chapter traces the relationship between astrology and the chakras. Ren[-] del emphasizes recognition of the principles involved and the energies which constitut[e] the system, and the control and use of these energies. Includes illustrations throughou[t.] Highly recommended as a basic primer for all interested in energy. 64pp. Wei 74

ROSICRUCIAN FELLOWSHIP. THE MYSTERY OF THE DUCTLESS GLANDS, $1.25[.] An examination of the structure, function, and spiritual significance of the seven ductless glands. The spiritual function of the glands is based on information given by Max Heindel and the physiological structure and function is based on a textbook on the ductless glands written by Dr. Louis Berman. 85pp. Ros 40

SCIENCE OF LIFE BOOKS. GLANDS AND YOUR HEALTH, $1.25. A simplified treatise which discusses each one of the glands and explains the vital role played by the glands in the human organism. Includes information on weight control, hormone chemistry, feeding the glands, brain function, and the effect of the endocrine and sex glands on personality. 64pp. SLB 75

TODD, MABEL. THE THINKING BODY, $8.00. This is an interesting book which combines anatomical line drawings with excellent explanatory material. Ms. Todd orients her study toward an understanding of the fundamental facts underlying the principles of body dynamics. *The basic principles on which the theories are built are discussed at length and these are used to illustrate the final action and control of the body activity, and the influence of unconscious sensations on body control and body action is stressed.* —from the foreword. Bibliography, index. 342pp. DaH 37

The world tree in the human body.

OCCULT NOVELS

ASHE, GEOFFREY. THE FINGER AND THE MOON, c$6.95. This is a strange novel which originiated in a study of myth and magic—extending the insights of Carl Jung and Robert Graves and evaluating the ideas of modern magicians. It takes place in England and focuses on the *mysteries of Britain*. Ashe himself is a well known archaeologist, specializing in the early history of Britain and in the Arthurian legends. This is his first and only novel. 251pp. DyC 73

COLLINS, MABEL. THE IDYLL OF THE WHITE LOTUS, c$2.95. *The ensuing pages contain a story which has been told in all ages and among every people. It is the tragedy of the soul. Attracted by Desire, the ruling element in the lower nature of Man, it stoops to sin; brought to itself by suffering, it turns for help to the redeeming Spirit within; and in the final sacrifice achieves its apotheosis and sheds a blessing on mankind.* 152pp. TPH 13

CORELLI, MARIA. ARDATH, $2.00. Maria Corelli's books are among the most popular mystical, visionary novels ever written. Long out of print, most of the books are now available. Amh nd

_____. BARABBAS, $3.00. Subtitled *A Dream of the World's Tragedy*. 317pp. Amh nd

_____. FREE OPINIONS, FREELY EXPRESSED, $5.00. Ms. Corelli's thoughts on *Certain Phases of Modern Social Life and Conduct*. 353pp. HeR 05

_____. THE LIFE EVERLASTING, c$4.95. This love story is one of Ms. Corelli's most popular books. 439pp. Bor

_____. THE MURDER OF DELICIA, $3.50. 274pp. HeR 1896

_____. A ROMANCE OF TWO WORLDS, $2.75. This is considered Ms. Corelli's masterpiece, written when she was twenty-two and depicting her spiritual and psychic experiences. 324pp. Mul 73

_____. A SONG OF MIRIAM AND OTHER STORIES, $4.00. 236pp. HeR nd

_____. SOUL OF LILITH, $2.00. Amh nd

_____. THE STRANGE VISITATION, $2.50. 188pp. HeR nd

_____. TEMPORAL PROSE, $3.00 258pp. Amh nd

_____. THE YOUNG DIANA, $5.00. Subtitled *An Experiment of the Future*. 381pp. HeR 18

FORTUNE, DION. AVALON OF THE HEART, c$5.00. A plea for the resanctification of holy places such as Avalon, a former island which is now part of the low-lying terrain of Somerset. Avalon may once have been an Atlantean colony; it is the land of Arthur, Merlin, and Morgan LeFay; and a center where ancient pagan and Christian practices met. Dion Fortune urges all seekers to study their native tradition and to again make pilgrimages to the holy sites. 110pp. Wei

_____. THE DEMON LOVER, c$6.00. A novel of a man's spiritual quest for ultimate truth and inner knowledge and of his journey through death and evil to a new life, hope and redemption. 286pp. Wei 57

_____. THE GOAT FOOT GOD, c$6.50. The fifteenth and twentieth centuries meet in this compelling fictional work. A widower buys a former monastery, now a farm, determined to evoke Pan, the goat foot god. Instead he becomes possessed by the spirit of a former prior from the monastery, who was killed when he was found practicing pagan rituals. 383pp. AqP 36

GRANT, JOAN. EYES OF HORUS, $1.75. See the Ancient Egypt sub-section of Ancient Civilizations.

_____. FAR MEMORY, $1.95. Joan Grant became aware as a child of her uncanny gift of *far memory*—the ability to recall in detail previous incarnations, both male and female, in other centuries and in other lands. Her books, published as historical novels, have been praised for their extraordinary vividness and rich detail, and are in fact Ms. Grant's memories of her earlier lives. This is her autobiography, focusing on her early years. 285pp. Crg 56

_____. LIFE AS CAROLA, $1.50. The story of Carola's life in sixteenth century Italy as the illegitimate child of an Italian nobleman. 271pp. Avo 39

_____. LORD OF THE HORIZON, $1.95. See the Ancient Egypt sub-section of Ancient Civilizations.

_____. RETURN TO ELYSIUM, $1.50. Lucina lived in Greece, then went to Rome and founded a mystic cult. Not content with this she died and finally discovered an existence that transcended death. 303pp. Avo 47

_____. SO MOSES WAS BORN, $1.75. See the Ancient Egypt sub-section of Ancient Civilizations.

HESSE, HERMANN. DEMIAN, $1.50. This is a moving portrait of a young man's growing awareness of his own identity and of his powers. It is one of Hesse's most popular works and is the one that is usually read first. 147pp. Ban 25

_____. THE GLASS BEAD GAME, $4.35. A translation of Hesse's final work (also known as **Magister Ludi**). It is a difficult philosophical work. *The Glass Bead Game is an act of mental synthesis through which the spiritual values of all ages are perceived as simultaneously present and vitally alive. The Game itself is the focal point and raison d'etre of an entire province, a utopian society devoted wholly and exclusively to affairs of the mind and imagination.* Introduction, 570pp. HRW 69

_____. NARCISSUS AND GOLDMUND, $2.45. A beautifully written tale of a young boy's spiritual development and his relationship with another young man who be-comes his mentor and guide. 312pp. Ban 30

_____. STEPPENWOLF, $2.95. *It seems to be that of all my books* **Steppenwolf** *is the one that was more often and more violently misunderstood than any other. . . . The Treatise and all those spots in the book dealing with matters of the spirit, of the arts and the immortal men oppose the Steppenwolf's world of suffering with a positive, serene, superpersonal and timeless world of faith. This book . . . tells of griefs and needs; still it is not a book of a man despairing, but of a man believing.*—Hermann Hesse. 252pp. RaH 29

LYTTON, EDWARD. VRIL: THE POWER OF THE COMING RACE, $2.25. An Englishman of the last century gives his view of the future of mankind when men have released and controlled some of their vast inner powers. It is a vision of caution and warning to a civilization that would develop a material paradise and neglect its spiritual responsibility. 248pp.

RAMPA, T. LOBSANG. AS IT WAS! $1.95. In his newest book, Rampa retells his life story, beginning with the predictions made at his birth based on an astrological reading. 191pp. Crg 76

_____. BEYOND THE TENTH, $1.95. Rampa's occult novels are the most popular ones we know. People always seem to buy a few of them at a time and are soon back for others. Rampa, an Englishman, contends that a Tibetan lama is writing of his life through him, and had in fact fully occupied his body following a slight concussive accident. In this, his tenth book, he gives advice and teachings on the care of man's physical and spiritual form, and in the process answers many questions often asked by his readers. 158pp. Crg 69

_____. CANDLELIGHT, $1.95. Most of the letters Rampa receives are full of questions about all aspects of metaphysics: pendulums, dowsing, how to levitate, how to teleport, etc. Here he answers many of these questions and discusses many other topics ranging from God and good and evil to acupuncture and the press. 174pp. Crg 73

_____. THE CAVE OF THE ANCIENTS, $1.50. The sequel to **The Third Eye**, this is the story of Rampa's life in remote Himalayan lamaseries where he learned some of the ancient wisdom: the meaning of life and death; the secrets of hypnotism, telepathy and clairvoyance, the relationship between the mind and the brain. 223pp. RaH 63

_____. CHAPTERS OF LIFE, $1.25. Detailed predictions and comments on the events taking place in the astral world. 223pp. Crg 67

_____. DOCTOR FROM LHASA, $1.95. A detailed autobiography of the Tibetan lama who speaks through Rampa. 200pp. Crg 59

_____. FEEDING THE FLAME, $1.95. *It is said It is better to light a candle than to curse the darkness. In my first ten books I have tried to light a candle, or possibly two. In this, the eleventh book, I am trying to Feed the Flame.* More answers to questions on a wide variety of topics. 190pp. Crg 71

_____. THE HERMIT, $1.95. A young monk receives the wisdom of the ages from an old blind hermit. 159pp. Crg 71

_____. MY VISIT TO VENUS, $2.95. A narrative of Rampa's voyage to Venus. 42pp. Sau 66

_____. THE RAMPA STORY, $.95. Rampa presents the teachings given to him by the Tibetan, emphasizing the ramifications of the human personality and ego and the realities of reincarnation. 216pp. Ban 60

_____. THE SAFFRON ROBE, $.95. The story of Rampa's youth in the lamaseries of Tibet and a presentation of the teachings of Buddhism. 198pp. Ban 66

_____. THE THIRD EYE, $1.50. Rampa's first book, in which he describes his spiritual training and the painful physical operation whereby his third eye was opened. 219pp. RaH 56

_____. THE THIRTEENTH CANDLE, $1.95. Rampa's thirteenth book, emphasizing healing and life after death. Includes a selection of *wise sayings* taken from all his books. 173pp. Crg 72

_____. TWILIGHT, $1.75. Rampa here answers some of the many questions he has received on a variety of subjects including UFO's, astral travel, the aura, marriage and divorce, the law of karma, hypnotism, and much else. 204pp. Crg 75

_____. WISDOM OF THE ANCIENTS, $1.95. Most of this book consists of a dictionary of the occult, following which are supplements on breathing, stones, foodstuffs, and exercises. 158pp. Crg 65

_____. YOU FOREVER, $1.95. Presents a special course of instruction in psychic development and metaphysics. Crg 65

WAITE, ARTHUR. THE QUEST OF THE GOLDEN STAIRS, $2.95. An allegory of the exploration and discovery of an individual's innermost being. Set in a mystical *other world*, it tells of the quest of a noble prince in search of fame and fortune. Fairies and magic abound throughout the narrative. 176pp. NPC 27

ORIENTAL MEDICINE

One of the remarkable events of the past decade has been the conditional acceptance by organized medicine of acupuncture. That it works is obvious, but why it works is a mystery to Western science. Thus we have here one of the most interesting and strong bridges between Western orthodoxy and the alternate reality that is the basis for many of the books throughout this catalog.

In the late 1800's, Michael Faraday said: *. . . all matter or any substance— dense, liquid or gaseous—owes whatever power it may possess to the type of electrical charge or vibration given off by that substance.* Our bodies are electrical generators. They have their positive and negative poles. The heart represents the negative; the brain, right side, represents the positive. They need to be in balance. Acupuncture or acupressure are ways of contacting the electrical centers in the body, influencing the flow of energy, and bringing about balance. These techniques are not unique to China but are found among traditional healing methods of the ancient Egyptians, Eskimos, Bantu and some Brazilian Indians, to name a few.

The popularity of acupuncture has led to an unprecedented outpouring of new books on this and related subjects, a development for which we can all be thankful. Some of these are technical for professionals; others are practical for do-it-yourself laypeople. We have tried to indicate which is which. In this section we deal with therapeutic massage. For sensual massage and other body therapies, see the Body Movement section.

ACADEMY OF TRADITIONAL CHINESE MEDICINE. **AN OUTLINE OF CHINESE ACUPUNCTURE**, c$12.50. *The aim of compiling this book is to provide source material for study by medical personnel in China and other countries, and to popularize the science of acupuncture and moxibustion. After studying this book one should have a preliminary understanding of the development of acupuncture and moxibustion in China, together with their basic theory and application in clinical treatment. In the selection of material for this book, every effort has been made that it be concise, practical, and easily understood.* The book was published in mainland China and is an extremely detailed study which should be of great interest to all practitioners. 133 plates, including two 20x13" full views of the human body; many are in color. 10½x7½", index. 319pp. FLP 75

ACUPUNCTURE RESEARCH INSTITUTE. **ACUPUNCTURE MADE EASY**, $6.95. *This is a little classic produced by experienced teachers of this modernized ancient art, intended as a textbook for use by the up to one million bare-foot doctors. I warmly recommend it even for any western beginning student. . . .—Won Kwan-Pak, the Hong*

Kong acupuncturist who gave the translators the original book. Includes a good general introduction, a section detailing the most commonly used acupuncture points (including the Chinese characters for the point, transliteration, location, indication, and technique— along with a detailed drawing) and a section on ailments treatable with acupuncture, sub-divided by ailments. Indices to points and ailments. 97pp. ChB 75

AUSTIN, MARY. **TEXTBOOK OF ACUPUNCTURE THERAPY**, c$15.00. The author is a practicing acupuncturist in the U.S. Her topics include an explanation of the bipolar energy of the body and the ways it can be balanced, anatomical descriptions and illustrations showing the exact location of acupuncture points, the nature of the five elements and how the needle is used correctly in therapy, a discussion of the daily and seasonal effects upon acupuncture therapy, the techniques of needle, massage and Moxa therapy. A comprehensive textbook. ASI 72

BEAN, ROY. **HELPING YOUR HEALTH WITH POINTED PRESSURE THERAPY**, c$7.95. Dr. Bean is a naturopath who has used the techniques he outlines here for twenty years in his private practice. The book is organized according to specific ailments and the methods for relieving the discomfort are fully discussed. Unfortunately the discussion is not accompanied by illustrations, however general instructions on Dr. Bean's technique are offered at the beginning of the book. Index, 204pp. PrH 75

BERGSON, ANIKA and VLADIMER TUCHACK. **ZONE THERAPY**, $1.25. A fully illustrated step-by-step guide to applied pressure therapy, arranged according to ailments. Each of the discussions is brief, but the directions seem to be clear. While this is by no means a definitive volume, it can serve as an introduction. 149pp. Pin 74

BLATE, MICHAEL. **THE G-JO HANDBOOK**, $6.95. *G-Jo . . . is roughly translated from the Chinese as meaning* first aid. *However, the techniques described in the following pages are substantially different from the splinting, bandaging, and such, one often considers when thinking of Western-style first aid. The G-Jo techniques primarily rely upon finger-tip stimulation of tiny pressure points. . . . This handbook details a number of ancient, oriental techniques that may . . . supplement and add to the effectiveness of standard, Western first aid methods. This traditional, Eastern way of first aid is not limited to emergency situations. The same techniques may be effective in relieving pain or various symptomatic disorders.—from the introduction.* The material is organized by ailments which are cross-referenced to the appropriate point and the points are illustrated. There's also some instructional material. Bibliography, 223pp. Flk 76

BRESSLER, HARRY. **ZONE THERAPY**, $4.50. Zone therapy relieves pain and distress in the body by giving pressure on certain parts of the body to bring relief, by reflex action, to other parts of the body. This is a discussion of the history of the therapy and extensive instructions for treatment of various ailments. 73pp. HeR 55

CADRE. **ACUPUNCTURE MANIKIN**, $90.00. The official teaching model used in China today. Soft, plastic body, hand painted meridians, and varnished mahogany stand, 20" tall. Available either with English numbering system or Chinese calligraphy (specify which you want). Includes an explanatory booklet of acupuncture points. (A 10" tall display model is available for $30—Chinese calligraphy, no booklet). Cad

_____. **ACUPUNCTURE WALL CHART**, $5.00. Includes meridian points, extra points, points used for anesthesia, three full length views of the body, plus seven detailed inserts including one showing ear points. 23x35". Cad

_____. **ATLAS OF THE EAR**, $16.00. A spiral-bound atlas containing four illustrations, 12x12", three in color, on heavy card stock. Shows the front and back of the ear with individual views of acupuncture points, nerves, veins, and arteries, and the paths of the six ear meridians. Cad

_____. **FOUR CHARTS**, $7.00. A comprehensive package of four full color anatomy charts, each 14x30", English reference atlas, and pamphlet on acupuncture anesthesia—drawn in the old Chinese style and suitable for framing. Includes explanatory material. Cad

_____. **LIFE SIZED EAR MODELS**, $13.00/pair. Plastic, showing the ear points and stylized morphology. Cad

_____. **TEXOPRINT CHARTS**, $25.00. A set of three 24x37½" wall charts on cleanable, wrinkle resistant Texoprint. The numbering system has been especially prepared by the AJCM committee on nomenclature. Cad

CARTER, MILDRED. **HELPING YOURSELF WITH FOOT REFLEXOLOGY**, $2.95. The various organs, nerves, and glands in your body are connected with certain *reflex areas* on the bottoms of your feet, such as the soles and toes. This book shows how it is possible, through massaging these reflex areas in certain simple ways known as *reflexology*, to bring relief from pains and diseases. Illustrated with many pictures and charts. Mildred Carter is a professional reflexologist who has been in practice over fourteen years. She studied under Eunice Inhgam. 190pp. PrH 75

_____. **HAND REFLEXOLOGY: KEY TO PERFECT HEALTH**. c$8.95. Ms. Carter is a well-known professional reflexologist, whose book on foot reflexology is the most popular one on the subject. This is the only book on hand reflexology and it is as well organized and clearly illustrated as the author's previous text. She begins with general techniques and then goes on to detail techniques for specific ailments. Index, 257pp. PrH 75

CERNEY, J.V. **ACUPUNCTURE WITHOUT NEEDLES**, $2.95. A text on acupressure geared toward its use in the cure of various common ailments. Includes a general explana-

ry section as well as detailed chapters on home treatments and treatment of ailments in e head, neck, chest, back and spine, sex organs, legs and feet, and gastro-intestinal and dominal tract. Fully illustrated and geared toward the layperson. Index, 299pp. S&S

IAN, PEDRO. **ACUPUNCTURE, ELECTRO-ACUPUNCTURE, ANAESTHESIA,** .95. What is acupuncture and what are the new discoveries? Chan offers much informa- n from his experience and research that helps to answer these questions. Copiously ustrated with pictures from China. 44pp. ChB 72

_____. **ANIMAL CHART**, $8.50. Shows pertinent acupuncture points in anatomi- lly correct locations for the horse, cow, pig, chicken, and duck. Also illustrates several pes of needles used for animal acupuncture. Full colors, 20x29". ChB

_____. **BODY CHART**, $12.00, flat/$6.50, folded. Bilingual, Chinese and English Dr. Mann's number code). Originally designed by the Chinese Medical College of Peking. hows the positions of acupuncture meridians and points in relation to the human body d internal organs. The courses of the meridians are indicated with different colors r patterns. Three views: anterior, posterior, and lateral. ChB

_____. **EAR ACUPUNCTURE CHART**, $8.50. Shows ear points and prescriptions n the eighty-three diseases where ear acupuncture has proved to be beneficial. Also de- cribed are all points and combinations used in acupuncture anesthesia. It also shows leographic diagrams (front and back) of the auricle for ear acupuncture. Translated from number of authoritative Chinese sources. Three colors, 20x29". ChB

_____. **EAR POINT CHART**, $10.00, flat/$5.00, folded. Bilingual, Chinese and nglish. Two main views: one full anterior showing over 100 auricular points; another hirty-eight points are shown on the back of the ear. Also includes a preliminary presenta- on of therapeutic functions of some major ear points, compiled by the Zoological Re- earch Institute of the Chinese Academy of Sciences. Full color, 20x29". ChB

_____. **ELECTRO-ACUPUNCTURE**, $8.50. _Electro-acupuncture therapy is a new_ _concept in the healing sciences integrating conventional acupuncture with modern tech-_ _nology. Its uniqueness is a therapeutic apparatus which transmits electrical currents of_ _different characteristics through acupuncture needles to human subjects, in order to give_ _symptomatic relief and therapeutic results._ Subtitled _Its Clinical Applications in Therapy,_ this is a compilation of Chinese translations and references, well organized and including ntroductory and instructional material and detailed chapters on the treatment of various ailments. Extensive illustrations of the points and of the equipment. Notes, 103pp. ChB 74

_____. **FINGER ACUPRESSURE (NEW EDITION)**, $2.50/$1.50. Chan, using his own experience as well as that of other professionals, has picked out the most effec- tive acupuncture points to treat certain common disorders by utilizing the finger tech- nique (known generally as shiatsu). Here he presents the treatment for about eighty common disorders. Following each disorder is the name of the point and a description of the location as well as a drawing of the anatomical location with relation to the skeletal structure, and a photograph illustrating the treatment. With simple instructions. 67pp. The $1.50 version is not revised. ChB

_____. **HAND ACUPUNCTURE CHART**, $8.50. Shows all new points of the hand in relation to the surface and anatomical location. Each point is clearly defined and indicated for many specific symptoms. Included also is a series of diagrams showing needling techniques in hand acupuncture. Three colors, 20x29". ChB

_____. **WONDERS OF CHINESE ACUPUNCTURE**, $4.50. _This monograph by_ _Pedro Chan has encompassed traditional Chinese medicine for those who desire a short_ _but concise explanation and correlation of Chinese and Western medicine.... There is a_ _good correlation between the two types of medical practice and the application of an in-_ _tegrated medical approach to patient treatment._—Howard Morse, M.D., Chairman, De- partment of Anesthesia, White Memorial Medical Center. Many illustrations. 133pp. ChB 73

CHAN'S BOOKS. **ACUPUNCTURE DIRECTORY**, $2.50. Lists of acupuncture literature, treatment centers, organizations, and suppliers. 35pp. ChB 74

CLAUSEN, TORBEN. ed. **PRACTICAL ACUPUNCTURE**, $7.95. _The main purpose of_ _translating this book has been to provide some insight into fundamental aspects of acu-_ _puncture as practiced today by millions of health workers in China. Therefore, a short_ _popular and contemporary handbook was selected (more than 2.5 million copies sold_ _in China up to 1970)._ As stated in the preface to the Chinese edition, the present text is written with the intention of making basic techniques of acupuncture available to people with a minimum of medical training. This is by no means an easy introduction. It is designed for practical use and is fully illustrated. Includes two introductory sections— _How to locate acupuncture points_ and _The techniques of acupuncture and moxibustion_— along with a detailed analysis of the position of the individual points. The terminology used corresponds to the classification system proposed by Felix Mann on the basis of Soulier de Morant's now classical system. This is considered the best overall work avail- able for the beginning practitioner. Notes, 160pp. FAD 73

DIMOND, E. GREY. **MORE THAN HERBS AND ACUPUNCTURE**, c$7.95. In 1971 Dr. Dimond, a cardiologist, made the first of three trips to the People's Republic, playing a key role in developing the original medical exchanges between the U.S. and China. He was specifically interested in learning about the medical education, acupuncture anesthesia, herbal medicine, and medical care. This is a very readable account of his experiences in China and of his observations of the Chinese medical system. 223pp. Nor 75

DUKE, MARC. **ACUPUNCTURE**, $1.50. One of the newest books in this field. A de- tailed introduction for the general reader as well as the serious student which details the current work being done all over the world plus the technique and philosophy. Well illus- trated. Indexed, with an extensive bibliography. 201pp. Pyr 72

EWART, CHARLES. **THE HEALING NEEDLES**, $1.25. Charles Ewart was a patient of Dr. Louis Moss, one of England's pioneering acupuncturists. Here he gives us the story of Moss' battle to gain recognition for acupuncture in England including many detailed case histories of patients with widely varying ailments. 137pp. Kea 73

FITZGERALD, WILLIAM and EDWIN BOWERS. **ZONE THERAPY**, $5.50. This is ac- tually three books in one. It includes George S. White's **Zone Therapy**. Fitzgerald was the pioneer in the field and this is the basic source book, not as readable as some of the later manuals, but important nonetheless. HeR 72

GEOGRAPHIC HEALTH STUDIES PROGRAM. **A BAREFOOT DOCTOR'S MANUAL**, $12.25. This is an amazing book which was originally put together in 1970 by the Institute of Traditional Chinese Medicine. The manual lists and describes 197 common and preva- lent diseases, some 522 herbs (with 338 illustrations), and offers several hundred tested and tried remedies based on effectiveness, popular use, ease of preparation, and economy. The manual was prepared for use by the rural _barefoot doctors_ and has been translated under the auspices of the U.S. Department of Health, Education, and Welfare. We recom- mend the manual highly to all who are interested in healing and particularly in Chinese medicine. Oversize, 974pp. GPO 74

GRAZIANO, JOSEPH. **FOOTSTEPS TO BETTER HEALTH**, $4.00. This is an over- priced book for the amount of material it contains. However, it is the only book on pressure point therapy that is illustrated with large photographs of the feet with the ap- propriate point for each ailment marked. 32pp. Grz 73

HALL, MANLY P. **THE MEDICINE OF THE SUN AND MOON**, $1.50. A well written philosophical treatise on the principles behind the Chinese concept of healing. See the Mysticism section for more on Hall. 32pp. PRS 72

HASHIMOTO, M. **JAPANESE ACUPUNCTURE**, $1.75. Dr. Hashimoto runs a success- ful acupuncture clinic in Tokyo. This book embodies her system of pulse diagnosis and her philosophy of healing. Includes a glossary. 80pp. Liv 68

HOUSTON, F.M. **THE HEALING BENEFITS OF ACUPRESSURE**, $4.95. This is a very clearly illustrated guide to the practice of acupressure. Each of the acupoints is shown in a large drawing of the part of the body in which it is found along with an analysis of the parts of the body the point affects. There's also a detailed analysis of how to manipulate the point. The material is arranged according to the parts of the body in which the points are found. In addition there's introductory instructional material, a long glossary, and an extensive index. An excellent instructional manual for the begin- ning practitioner. Oversize, 96pp. Kea 74

HUANG, HELENA. **EAR ACUPUNCTURE**, c$14.50. This is a translation of a medical book written and published in the People's Republic of China. It was compiled and edited after more than ten years of experience in the development and practice of the technique by a team of acupuncturists. Ear acupuncture involves the treatment of disease through the application of acupuncture techniques to the external ear. The technique seems to be effective in treating a large variety of common diseases. This work also de- scribes the inter-relationship between the ear and internal organs of the body in the theory of traditional Chinese medicine, and much related material. Includes twelve full page plates and numerous charts detailing the points used in treating common diseases. An excellent reference work for the practitioner and serious researcher. Indexed, 149pp. Rod 72

HUARD, PIERRE and MING WONG. **CHINESE MEDICINE**, $2.45. An historical text by two French doctors, both of whom are leading authorities on Oriental medicine. Ex- tensively illustrated. Contents include the evolution of Chinese medicine, Western medi- cine in modern China, and traditional medicine in modern China. 237pp. MGH 68

INGHAM, E.D. **STORIES THE FEET CAN TELL**, $4.45. Ms. Ingham was the first important reflexologist. She worked with patients and physicians for many years and her work is the basis of all that is done today. This is her first book. Many case studies are cited and there is extensive instructional material. Introductory chapters explain the method and the rest of the text deals with specific ailments. Includes a reflexology chart. 109+pp. Ing 38

_____. **STORIES THE FEET HAVE TOLD**, $4.45. This is the second book. It presents a detailed account of the Ingham Reflex Method of Compression Massage. The material is along the same line as the earlier work, but this book incorporates more ad- vanced techniques and later findings. Includes a reflexology chart. 110pp. Ign 51

IRWIN, YUKIKO and JAMES WAGENVOORD. **SHIATZU**, $5.95. Ms. Irwin has prac- ticed shiatsu for over twenty-five years and was trained in Japan. Her book is one of the few pressure point manuals which is written by a Western practitioner. Her discussion is geared to the Westerner and to Western ailments. She begins with a discussion of shiatsu techniques and goes from there to a survey of shiatsu as a remedy for the following dis- orders: insomnia, headache, stiff neck and sore shoulders, lower back pain, constipation and diarrhea, and tennis elbow. The book is illustrated throughout with line drawings and the step-by-step instructions are exceedingly clear. 6x9", 239pp. Lip 76

JAIN, K.K. **AMAZING STORY OF HEALTH CARE IN NEW CHINA**, c$7.95. Dr. Jain is a Canadian neurosurgeon who visited China in 1971. He recorded what he saw and learned and presents an overview of all aspects of medical care in China today. Acupuncture is just one of the many methods of Chinese medicine that he evaluates. Other topics include herbs, folk medicine, and China's medical traditions. Observations and impressions of the Chinese lifestyle and the future of Chinese medicine are also included along with many photographs. Index, 184pp. Rod 73

LANGRE, JACQUES de. **ACUPUNCTURE, DO-IN AND SHIATSU ATLAS**, $4.25. All acupuncture meridians are shown in relation to surface anatomy and skeletal configuration. Thirty-six of the major treatment points are specifically indicated. Printed in three colors, 23x35". Hap

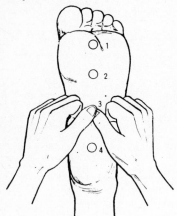

_____. **FIRST BOOK OF DO-IN**, $1.50. A therapeutic and restorative technique of self-massage written in both French and English. Contains over sixty photographs which show every step of the technique, making it easy to follow. A glossary contains all common health problems and internal-external natural remedies. The material is not very well organized and is often hard to follow. 30pp. Hap

_____. **SECOND BOOK OF DO-IN**, $7.50. The material that de Langre introduced in the first book has been greatly expanded here. The emphasis is on practical exercises and techniques, all of which are well explained and illustrated with photographs and line drawings. The techniques range from yogic-type exercises to various forms of self-massage utilizing acupressure points. A great deal of background philosophy is also presented incorporating Oriental ideas with Western ones. A very popular, self-learning instructional manual. Oversize, 150pp. Hap 74

LAVIER, J. **POINTS OF CHINESE ACUPUNCTURE**, c$5.00. A detailed technical text translated, indexed, and edited by Dr. Philip Chancellor. It is divided into four parts: *General Topography of the Meridians, Regional Topography of the Points of Acupuncture, Bio-energy,* and *Synthesis of Symptomatic Treatment.* Each of the numbered points is illustrated and named. 115pp. HSP 74

LAWSON-WOOD, DENIS and JOYCE. **ACUPUNCTURE HANDBOOK**, c$7.00. A textbook for students and practitioners which presents a Westernized form of the science. Correspondences are indicated which link the therapeutic effect of each acupuncture point to a specific homeopathic remedy. A preface describes the discoveries of Professor Kim Bong Han of North Korea. Includes photographs of the meridian points. 141pp. HSP 64

_____. **FIVE ELEMENTS OF ACUPUNCTURE AND CHINESE MASSAGE**, $4.80. An approach which stresses foreseeing and preventing disease rather than suppressing symptoms. The terms used are readily understandable to the general reader. HSP 65

_____. **THE INCREDIBLE HEALING NEEDLES**, $1.25. This is a good general layperson's introduction to acupuncture, with material on the individual meridians, yin and yang, diagnosis, and Oriental theories on health. A well written exposition, with many clear diagrams. 63pp. Wei 74

_____. **MULTILINGUAL ATLAS OF ACUPUNCTURE**, c$20.30. Seventeen color plates (19¼x18") of anatomical drawings of the major acupuncture points as they are located on the body. Explanatory text in English, French, German, Russian, Spanish, and Swedish. The drawings are large and the points clearly illustrated. HSP 67

LEONG, LUCILLE. **ACUPUNCTURE, A LAYMAN'S VIEW**, $1.50. This is an overview of acupuncture by a woman who has academically studied the literature and has had a close relationship with a number of acupuncturists. Included are chapters on the philosophy of acupuncture, acupuncture in practice, why it works, and case studies of acupuncture treatments. There are also many illustrations and photographs and a glossary. Bibliography, 139pp. NAL 74

LIU, DA. **TAOIST HEALTH EXERCISE BOOK**, $3.95. This is more than a mere illustration of the exercises. Da Liu has attempted to explain the philosophy behind the exercises and how this philosophy relates to Western men and women. Included are tai chi ch'uan movements, breathing exercises, explanations of the acupuncture meridians, and material on curative herbs. Nicely illustrated. 135pp. QFx 74

LIU, ZHAOYUAN. **ACUPUNCTURE CHARTS**, c$22.75. This is the finest set of charts that we know of. All the information is drawn from and all the drawings are based upon Chinese medical books and charts published by the People's Republic. Four color charts are included: three showing all 361 points of the fourteen principal meridians, the 117 *strange* points, 110 newly discovered points, and one chart showing ear and hand acupuncture areas. Each point is referenced by the abbreviations and numbers commonly adopted in the West, and the Chinese name of each point is given along with its transliteration, as is the equivalent point number. The charts fold out of a bound book and measure 26x14". They are also available in a larger size as wall charts for $25.00. CCC 75

LOH, WEI PING. **ACUPUNCTURE-ANESTHESIA TEXTBOOK**, $5.95. A technical manual incorporating the latest research. Every aspect of the subject is discussed and the text is illustrated with charts and line drawings. For practitioners only. CMP 74

LU, HENRY. **THE CHINESE VERSIONS OF MODERN ACUPUNCTURE**, c$40.00. This is the most comprehensive presentation of the theoretical foundations and basic techniques of acupuncture published in the English language. Dr. Lu, in translating materials prepared by the Shanghai Institute of Acupuncture and Moxibustion, brings together the texts currently used for the training of acupuncturists throughout China. 328pp. AOH

MC GAREY, WILLIAM. **ACUPUNCTURE AND BODY ENERGIES**, c$6.95. Dr. McGarey has been Director of the Medical Research Division of the Edgar Cayce Foundation since 1965 and has been instrumental in activating research programs designed to evaluate concepts in the Cayce readings as they pertain to physiology and therapy. Since 1970 he has been the Director of the A.R.E. Clinic in Arizona, a medical group actively engaged in various research projects designed to explore the material in the Cayce readings at a clinical and laboratory level. *This book . . . will deal with my ideas of how acupuncture fits into the Western scheme of things; how these various laws and concepts of acupuncture appear to the Western doctor who is philosophically inclined; and . . . what might be expected as one learns about this ancient art of healing the body and puts it to the test.* McGarey spent over two years studying and practicing acupuncture before beginning this book. Notes, illustrations, index. 146pp. Gab 74

MANAKA, YOSHIO. **QUICK AND EASY CHINESE MASSAGE**, c$2.50. This pocket-sized book is the clearest presentation of the material we've seen. The first four chapters cover the basic principles, the next eight demonstrate specific practices, and the other sixteen discuss treatments for various physical problems. Clear photographs illustrate each remedy. Highly recommended. Jap 73

MANAKA, YOSHIO and IAN URQUHART. **THE LAYMAN'S GUIDE TO ACUPUNCTURE**, c$7.95/$3.95. In addition to presenting a concise but thorough introduction to the concepts underlying acupuncture, the authors discuss diagnosis, uses of different kinds of needles, treatment procedures, treatment of children, moxibustion, and pressure massage, and finally some empirical experiments now going on. The text is amplified by a wealth of illustrations, including both traditional woodcuts and up-to-date photographs and drawings. This is the best work on acupuncture for the layperson that we have seen. 143pp. Wth 72

MANN, FELIX, ed. **ACUPUNCTURE—THE ANCIENT CHINESE ART OF HEALING**, revised, $1.95. Mann, a leading British acupuncturist, here describes the basic principles and laws, according to the theories of traditional Chinese medicine. There are chapters on yin and yang, the five elements, the theories of pulse diagnosis, the laws of acupuncture, *qi*–the energy of life. This second edition contains about 50% new material and has been almost entirely rewritten. Sixty-eight drawings, 232pp. RaH 71

_____. **ATLAS OF ACUPUNCTURE**, c$13.50. This is considered to be the definitive acupuncture atlas. Includes front, rear, and side views, giving the points and meridians in relation to surface anatomy. Done in book form on heavy paper with the illustrations continuing from page to page without a break. 7½x14". HeG 66

_____. **THE MERIDIANS OF ACUPUNCTURE**, c$7.55. The course, function and symptomatology of the fifty-nine meridians, which constitute the basis of classical Chinese acupuncture, are portrayed in detail. In addition the traditional Chinese physiology and pathology of the twelve main groups of internal organs are described and correlated with Western scientific medicine wherever possible. Fifty-three full page drawings. 174pp. HeG

_____. **THE TREATMENT OF DISEASE BY ACUPUNCTURE**, c$9.75. In Part I, *Function of Acupuncture Points*, each point is listed separately and a full account of the symptoms and diseases that may be influenced by stimulating a specific point is given, following the classical Chinese pattern. In Part II, *The Treatment of Disease*, the majority of diseases amenable to acupuncture are tabulated with the corresponding acupuncture points used for treatment. The first part of this section is based entirely on Chinese sources, while the second describes the experiences of Mann and other European doctors. HeG

MATSUMOTO, TERUO. **ACUPUNCTURE FOR PHYSICIANS**, $19.60. This is a very technical survey with extensive illustrations and photographs of the clinical practice of acupuncture. Also includes many case studies and a description of research going on now and proposed research. The language and approach make this book suitable only for practitioners. Index, notes, extensive bibliography. 203pp. Tho 74

MEDICINE AND HEALTH PUBLISHING COMPANY. **AN EXPLANATORY BOOK OF THE NEWEST ILLUSTRATIONS OF ACUPUNCTURE POINTS**, $5.50. A detailed study which analyzes the points illustrated in Cadre's **Newest Illustrations of Acupuncture Points**. Includes the transliterated name, location, main treatment, needling methods for the meridian points in each of the parts of the body discussed. Over 640 new points are discussed. Fully indexed by the parts of the body and the transliterated name and Chinese characters. Oversize, 100pp. Cad 73

MOSS, LEWIS. **ACUPUNCTURE AND YOU**, c$1.98. A British M.D.'s report of his successful use of acupuncture and its application in the Western world. BoS 64

AKATANI, YOSHIO. **A GUIDE FOR APPLICATION OF RYODORAKU AUTONO-MOUS NERVE REGULATORY THERAPY**, $5.00. A technical study, fully illustrated with photographs, drawings, and tables. 25pp. ChB 72

AMIKOSHI, TOKUJIRO. **SHIATSU: JAPANESE FINGER PRESSURE THERAPY**, 3.95. When a part of the human body is in pain, the instinct is to touch it. When the eyes are tired, the instinct is to rub them. The word *shiatsu*, composed of the elements *shi* (fingers) and *atsu* (pressure) means a method of treating illness with digital compression. Pressure points are well illustrated and easy to follow. One of the important features of shiatsu treatment is that you can do it anywhere and by yourself. Three minutes of proper shiatsu massage when you are tired will have you feeling like a new person. 8½x11". 82pp. Jap 69

_____. **SHIATSU THERAPY**, $4.95. A companion volume to Namikoshi's earlier work, **Shiatsu**, this book is divided into two parts: *The Theory of Shiatsu Therapy* and *Shiatsu Techniques*. The section on techniques is the major part of the book. First Namikoshi gives instructions on general techniques; then he goes from there to give details on giving a shiatsu treatment to each part of the body. All of the instructions are illustrated and the material is well organized and clearly presented. This seems to be the most practical of all the books we've seen on shiatsu. Recommended. Oversize, 89pp.

NEWLAND, ANTHONY and WEI LOH. **ACUPUNCTURE-ANESTHESIA: ITS SCIENTIFIC BASIS AND APPLICATION**, $8.40. This is a fuller exploration of the subject than Dr. Loh's earlier book. As the title suggests, professional applications are stressed and all the necessary instrumentation is discussed. Much of the book is devoted to surgical applications for a large number of ailments and there are also discussions of acupuncture-analgesia in dental practice. The whole book is clearly written and is illustrated throughout with photographs and line drawings. For practitioners only. 128pp. CMP 75

NOGIER. **TREATISE OF AURICULAR THERAPY**, c$44.50. A classic of the French School. Cad 72

OHASHI, WATARU. **DO-IT-YOURSELF SHIATSU**, $5.95. This is a self-help acupuncture manual directed at Westerners by a man who has been teaching and practicing shiatsu in the U.S. for a number of years. The book is well illustrated with photographs and line drawings of the points and of actual shiatsu practice and all the instructional material is clear and easy to follow. Each part of the body is discussed in its own chapter and the book begins with introductory explanations of Ohashi's techniques. There's also a section on treatments for common ailments. Recommended. Oversize, 144pp. Dut 76

PORKERT, MANFRED. **THE THEORETICAL FOUNDATIONS OF CHINESE MEDICINE**, c$20.00. A systematic account of the system of correspondences that underlies all of Chinese medicine. The book is based directly and exclusively on Chinese sources, including recent Chinese secondary literature. Illustrations, bibliography, index. 384pp. MIT 74

SERIZAWA, KATSUSUKE. **MASSAGE: THE ORIENTAL METHOD**, $3.95. With the help of photographs and diagrams, the author explains how to get relief from headaches, body pain, and stiffness through the use of Japanese massage, a unique method which combines Western massage, shiatsu, and Chinese *amma* (which stimulates nerves). Lots of photographs and drawings explain exactly where and how to rub, tickle, punch, kick and bat the body into divine bliss! 8½x11", 78pp. Jap

_____. **TSUBO: VITAL POINTS FOR ORIENTAL THERAPY**, c$18.00. According to the medical philosophy of the East, the human body is operated and controlled by means of two groups of organs. As long as these organs operate harmoniously, the body remains healthy. Disturbances in any of them mean illness. A system of energy circulation provides the power by means of which the organs can operate in harmony. This larger system is broken down into fourteen smaller systems, called meridians, extending throughout the whole body. Along them are points where the flow of energy to the organs tends to stagnate. These points, called the tsubo, are the basic subject of this book. At the tsubo, actual physiological changes occur, revealing internal disorders and malfunctions in one or more of the organs. The tsubo are more than indicators of trouble; they are the places where therapy can be expected to produce maximum effect. Serizawa, the leading authority on tsubo research, explains how to locate the tsubo and how to apply acupuncture, massage, shiatsu, and moxa therapy to them. His text is clear and straightforward enough for the layperson while being detailed and informative enough for the professional. Hundreds of excellent charts and diagrams make the locations of the tsubo and the practical aspects of treatment easy to understand. 7x10", index. 256pp. Jap 76

SILVERSTEIN, M.E., I LOK CHANG and NATHANIEL MACON, trs. **ACUPUNCTURE AND MOXIBUSTION**, $2.95. This is the actual handbook used by the barefoot doctors in the People's Republic of China. This handbook for medical practice includes all the basics the Chinese practitioners need to know. It lists dozens of common illnesses and tells precisely how to treat them, illustrating the acupuncture points with clear diagrams and discussing the theory behind the practices. 118pp. ScB 75

THIE, JOHN. **TOUCH FOR HEALTH**, $8.95. Subtitled *a practical guide to natural health using acupuncture touch and massage to improve postural balance and reduce physical and mental pain and tension*, this is an unusual compendium of techniques. Dr. Thie, a chiropractor, developed most of them himself and he has used them extensively with his patients and students. Well illustrated with photographs and an explanatory text. Arranged by parts of the body and fully indexed by ailment and part of the body. 11½x11", 108pp. DeV 73

VEITH, ILLSA. **THE YELLOW EMPEROR'S CLASSIC OF INTERNAL MEDICINE**, c$9.50/$3.95. Written in the form of a dialogue in which the emperor seeks information from his minister on all questions of health and the art of healing, **The Yellow Emperor's**

Classic has become a landmark in the history of Chinese civilization. It is the oldest known document of Chinese medicine. In her translation and introductory study, Dr. Veith has succeeded in giving an excellent picture of early Chinese medicine. Many illustrations and references. An essential work for anyone studying Oriental medicine. 253pp. UCP 49

WALLNOFER, HEINRICH and A. VON ROTTAUSCHER. **CHINESE FOLK MEDICINE AND ACUPUNCTURE**, $1.25. Deals less with acupuncture and more with traditional Chinese folk medicine than any other book on this list. The ingredients, recipes and remedies are printed just as they have been handed down from one generation to another. Contains sections on fundamentals of Chinese medicine, its evolution, Chinese anatomy and physiology, Chinese pathology, treatment methods, as well as medicinal herbs, drugs, and love medicines. Well illustrated. 180pp. NAL 65

WEXU, MARIO. **THE EAR GATEWAY TO BALANCING THE BODY: A MODERN GUIDE TO EAR ACUPUNCTURE**, c$24.50. A comprehensive textbook of ear acupuncture, the first written by a Western acupuncturist. Dr. Wexu combines his extensive personal clinical experience with traditional and modern Chinese and Western sources. Anatomical descriptions and detailed charts clearly illustrate how to locate and work with over 300 ear points, both alone and in combination with body points. Case histories illustrate the applications for specific ailments. 191pp. ASI 75

WORSLEY. **IS ACUPUNCTURE FOR YOU**, $2.50. This is the finest general introduction to acupuncture yet published for the layperson and patient. It is presented in question and answer format. Beginning with *What is Acupuncture?* and *How does it work?*, Dr. Worsley then discusses the techniques with needles, moxa, etc., treatable illnesses, consultation and diagnosis, duration and effects of treatment. 81pp. H&R 73

WU WEI-PING. **CHINESE ACUPUNCTURE**, c$7.50. Essentially a textbook for practitioners who wish to follow the classical Chinese tradition. Dr. Wu is the sixteenth generation in his family of acupuncturists. He is the President of the Chinese Acupuncture Society and head of the School of Acupuncture in Tai-Pei, Taiwan. He wrote this book to be used as a text for his students. 181pp. HSP 62

YAU, P.S., tr. **SCALP NEEDLING THERAPY**, c$7.50. Acupuncture on the scalp is a new technique worked out by a young Chinese physician. It has proved effective in a variety of cases. This is a translation of a text on the technique and it includes general instructions as well as specific applications. Illustrations, 65pp. M&H 75

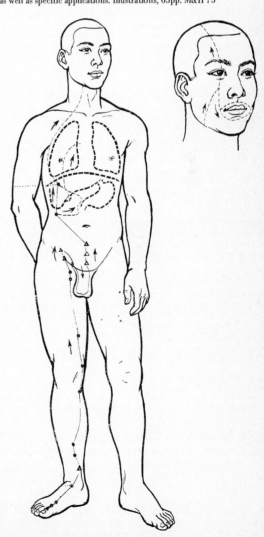

PALMISTRY

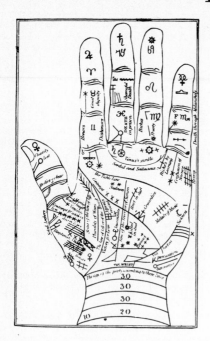

ABAYAKOON, CYRUS. **ASTRO-PALMISTRY: SIGNS AND SEALS OF THE HAND**, c$20.00. This is a neat new book which inclues a great deal of information not readily available elsewhere. The author supplies a profusion of well-marked line drawings of sample hands. Astrological correspondences are noted and the explanatory information is very complete. Abayakoon gets carried away at times with his symbols, but all in all this is a fine presentation which would be helpful to both beginning and advanced students. 8½x11", 190pp. ASI 75

ANANDA, S.K. **RAHU AND KETU IN PALMISTRY**, c$1.00. 48pp. Ast 73

ANDERSON, MARY. **PALMISTRY—YOUR DESTINY IN YOUR HANDS**, $1.00. 64pp. Wei 73

BASHIR, MIR. **YOUR PAST, YOUR PRESENT AND YOUR FUTURE THROUGH THE ART OF HAND ANALYSIS**, c$8.95. This is the most comprehensive recent study of the art and science of palm reading. Bashir is a Pakistani, now living in London, and is widely regarded as one of the most noted contemporary palmists: *The human hand is a map of life. It reveals the potential of an individual, indicates events which have happened or will happen in his life and provides an accurate assessment of both his psychological and physiological make-up. . . . Hand analysis is a science; it is also an art. It is a systematic body of knowledge with fundamental laws which must be clearly understood; its real value lies in the proper application of these laws, in the ability of the palmisty to balance what are perhaps contradictory markings before coming to a final judgement on the character and destiny of the individual.*—from the introduction. Every aspect of analysis is very clearly and well covered and there are many line drawings and a section of palm prints. Recommended. Index, 269pp. Dou 73

BENHAM, W.G. **THE LAWS OF SCIENTIFIC HAND READING**, c$15.00. This is an essential work for the serious student, containing prints and photographs of many interesting hands. The section on chirognomy is more valuable than the section on cheiromancy, which appears to be based more on reasoning than on systematic observation. 650pp. Haw 46

BROEKMAN, MARCEL. **THE COMPLETE ENCYCLOPEDIA OF PRACTICAL PALMISTRY**, $2.95. This is the most modern manual available. It is well organized, profusely illustrated, and quite comprehensive. It is divided into four sections: lines and markings dealing with events; lines that indicate character and potential; the location of answers to specific questions such as love, marriage and success; and case histories. Broekman's approach is that our hands seem to reflect our inner self, telling us our strengths and weaknesses. Recommended as a good introductory text. 187pp. PrH 72

CHEIRO. **LANGUAGE OF THE HAND—THE CLASSIC OF PALMISTRY**, $.95. This is by far the most comprehensive of all the inexpensive manuals. 224pp. Arc 64

_____. **PALMISTRY FOR ALL**, $.95. A profusely illustrated introductory account which explains precisely how to interpret the meaning of the lines of the hands as well as the significance of the shape of the hand, thumb, and fingers. 143pp. Arc 69

FRITH, HENRY **PALMISTRY SECRETS REVEALED**, $2.00. This is a good general work, describing the meanings of the most commonly found marks and lines on the hand, and what each line means in relation to other factors. Frith is one of Britain's foremost palmists. Easy reading for those who simply want to get an idea of what palmistry is all about. 127pp. Wil 52

GETTINGS, FRED. **THE BOOK OF PALMISTRY**, c$4.98. This is far and away the be introductory study that we know of. Gettings has selected over 200 palm prints, photographs, and line drawings of hands to illustrate his exposition, and about one hundred a in color. A number of beautiful old plates are also included. All the basic information o the shape of the hand and the lines is clearly presented and the exposition is illustrate with case studies. 8½x11", 143pp. Tri 74

_____. **THE HAND AND THE HOROSCOPE**, c$5.98. Gettings has written book on both palmistry and astrology. His expertise is clearly in the area of palmistry and h introductory book is the best we know of. Here he integrates palmistry with astrology an shows how insights and information from one discipline help to unlock the meanings o another. He presents a system for cross-referencing and relating the two and his accoun is fully illustrated with diagrams and over 275 illustrations, twenty-five in color. Include are palm prints, photographs, and line drawings. All the material is clearly explained an the orientation is practical, Glossary, 8½x11", 203pp. Tri 73

_____. **PALMISTRY MADE EASY**, $2.00. Covers palmistry in a very general way including specific case histories, many palm prints and an annotated bibliography of th most important palmistry books. 156pp. Wil 66

JAQUIN, NOEL. **PRACTICAL PALMISTRY**, c$2.98. Jaquin was a very well known Bri tish palmist who emphasized psychological understanding in his work, and developed number of pioneering theories. His books contain useful insights for the practicing palm ist and other disciplines are incorporated into his exposition. This book develops Jaquin' thesis that *the human hand reveals with detailed exactitude the psychological composi tion of the individual.* Many case studies are included and the illustrations are in the form of palm prints. Index, 173pp. TSC 64

_____. **SECRETS OF HAND READING**, c$2.65. Another of Jaquin's analyses o personality type and mental makeup through palmistry. The presentation is illustrated with line drawings and a number of interesting ideas are included. Case studies, index 184pp. TSC 69

MORGAN, JEAN-MICHEL. **PALMISTRY**, c$4.98. An introductory study, illustrated with a large number of line drawings and color and black-and-white photographs. It's pretty book and the instructional material seems adequate. Oversize, 107pp. Ari 7?

OJHA, ASHUTOSH. **PALMISTRY FOR ALL**, $2.00. A very complete presentation o the Indian system of palm reading. Illustrated with small line drawings. 236pp. HPB 7?

PSYCHOS. **THE COMPLETE GUIDE TO PALMISTRY**, $.95. A general manual, with ex tensive interpretative material, but poor illustrations. 158pp. Arc 59

ST. GERMAIN, COMTE de. **THE PRACTICE OF PALMISTRY**, c$8.95/$4.95. A simple but very comprehensive book on the study of palms written in an encyclopedic fashion Recommended for the beginning student as well as the advanced palmist. Profusely illus trated with over 1,000 drawings, this book is a detailed, practical manual with a wealth of information. 416pp. NPC nd

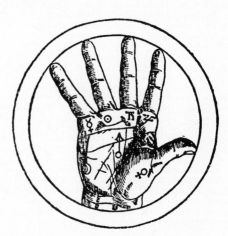

SEN, K.C. **HAST SAMUDRIKA SHASTRA: THE INDIAN SCIENCE OF HAND READING**, c$7.65. Mr. Sen is an Indian who has devoted his life to the study of palmistry. He brings together all the important theories here rather than presenting his own. The illustrations are not very good, but the interpretations are extensive and clearly presented. This text delves into areas not covered by our other books. 256pp. TSC nd

STEINBACH, MARTEN. **MEDICAL PALMISTRY**, $1.50. A complete survey of medical palmistry with many diagrams and clear descriptive material. A final chapter discusses common ailments and the related signs to look for. 192pp. NAL &5

PARAPSYCHOLOGY

er since the emergence of experimental science, some of the finest minds man have developed astute arguments against the existence of what are lled paranormal phenomena. The medieval Western world had its Knowdge of Divine Truth from the Bible, and its knowledge of secular truth in e encyclopedias inherited from the classical Greeks, especially Aristotle. nd no further questions needed to be propounded.

took enormous courage for anyone to question those unquestionable thorities. As an example, Aristotle had stated a fact which any thinking erson immediately will realize is true: A heavy stone, dropped from a height, ill hit the earth sooner than a light stone. How foolish it must have seemed an intelligent man living in Pisa in the 1590s to watch someone actually imb to the top of the local tower and drop two stones, one heavy and one ght, just to see for himself which one would land first. Galileo did exactly hat, of course, and discovered that both stones landed at precisely the same noment. This was one of the first pragmatic experiments to yield measurble, quantitative data. But Galileo was guilty of still greater heresy, as were Copernicus and Kepler. These men did not accept the evidence their eyes learly gave them: that the sun moves around the earth from east to west. They refused to accept the obvious, and the better to study heavenly bodies, hey went so far as to employ telescopes. After many laborious measurements, hey arrived at the preposterous conclusion that contrary to what was selfevident, the earth in fact revolved around the sun. With a swoop of the elescope (through which many eminent men refused to look), the earth was thrust from the center of the universe to become an insignificant planet moving, like all the other planets, in an orbit around the sun.

Could Aristotle be wrong?

Could the Bible contain untruths?

Anathema. Martydrom.

No matter. These early men of science had turned the key in the lock, and others burst open the door to practical explorations of the world in which they lived. Alchemy, that bizarre search to transmute base metals into gold, gave way to chemistry, which eventually not only transmuted lead into gold (although uneconomically), but transformed chemicals into clothing, vitamins, and electrical power. And along every step of the way, men of unquestioned genius would scoff at each other's ideas. When Kepler, for instance, suggested that the tides of the ocean might be due to the influence of the moon, Galileo dismissed the idea as an *occult fancy*.

And throughout, the established Divine Truth continued to wield its powerful influence on men's minds. Even that profligate genius Isaac Newton, who defined the law of gravity and invented a new mathematics, the calculus, to help his studies—even Newton believed that the world was created by God in 4004 BC and that He kept the Universe in order by correcting from time to time the slightly irregular movement of some planets.

Darwin and Pasteur and Einstein and Jeans and a host of scientists, year after year, with discovery upon discovery, made it less and less necessary to believe that Divine Truth ruled the world. In fact, it became untenable to accept Biblical *facts*. Geologists made it perfectly clear that the earth could not have been created in seven days: rather the earth seems originally to have been a blob of incandescence which was tossed from the sun billions of years ago and took aeons to cool, develop vapors, condense into liquids, and eventually form the planet as we know it today. From its pinnacle as Divine Revelation, the Bible fell to the status of an allegory, ennobling in its sentiments perhaps (although how bloody and violent at times). It is permissible, surely, to interpret Adam and Eve as a parable of good and evil and possibly unbridled passion. But God did not create man from a handful of dust, nor woman from man's rib. We are reasonably sure that man evolved from his simian forbears, who evolved from their forbears, all the way back to the first creatures that emerged from water to make their homes on dry land.

No need to believe in Divine Miracles, either. Let the Bible tell of how

Jesus walked on water, fed multitudes with a few fishes and loaves, healed the lepers and the blind and the crippled with a touch of his hand. We have created our own miracles, and they are far more impressive. We can levitate gigantic machines as far as the moon or Mars. We can feed multitudes with artificially manufactured foods, freezing the surplus for supply in years to come. Pasteur, Semmelwiess, Fleming, Salk, and many other men—not God— have delivered us from the scourges of plague and pox, cholera and scurvy and syphilis and a host of other diseases. For physical disease, physical remedy. No need to invoke a magic ritual like the *laying on of hands* or *spiritual healing*.

Of course there still exist primitive societies with witch doctors, medicine men, shamans, and curanderos creating their special magic brews and rituals through which they claim miraculously to heal the sick, speak in tongues, prophesy, and destroy their enemies by sticking pins in dolls. Primitive men know no better.

But modern men do. Why regress to the cult of the occult? We live in a glorious age: Is it not a far better thing to study man as he is today, to understand better his behavior in this complex word in which we live? Why revive prescientific notions and superstitions about prophetic dreams, magic healing, and the like?

Such are the arguments with which parapsychology is persistently plagued.

By the end of the nineteenth century the kings of the scientific world, our physicists, believed that the basic laws of the universe (gravity, thermodynamics, electricity, etc.) had been deciphered. To be sure, there remained a few trivial irregularities to be untangled, but they believed that in the foreseeable future the science of physics could close forever its magnificent Bible of eternal, verifiable truths.

But an odd thing happened. In trying to tidy up those *trivial irregularities*, vast new mysteries emerged, beautifully encapsulated in this paragraph from Nobel-prize-winner Albert Szent-Gyorgy:

At the turn of this century, four important discoveries were made which marked the beginning of a new period in man's history. X-rays (1895), the electron (1895), radioactivity (1896), and the quantum (1900) were discovered, these discoveries being followed soon by relativity (1905). None of these were, or could be, revealed by our senses. They meant that surrounding man there was a world of which he had no inkling before, about which his senses could give him no information.

Suddenly the material universe of the physicist had begun to dissolve into smaller and smaller *bits* that could no longer justifiably be called matter. It was one thing for Galileo to drop stones that he could see, measure, and weigh. But physicists found themselves in a universe where not even their most sensitive instruments could detect the myriad, invisible essences unleashed by the smashing of the atom and christened positrons, neutrinos, mesons, etc. Like the genie let out of its bottle, these essences produced new mysteries for which there were no quick and tidy solutions.

Is it possible that there exist still other undiscovered energies? Are there biological energies in animals and man about which we still know nothing? Only after man invented radar and sonar did we discover that the bat and the dolphin had been equipped with those sophisticated communication devices all along. Man, after thousands of years, harnessed electricity, but the eel had been using it skillfully for thousands of years before man. Only sixty-odd years ago, when Hans Berger announced that electrical currents could be detected emerging from the heads of men, he was considered as funny as Pasteur had been when he announced that invisible bugs in milk carry disease.

Are there energies radiating from people, which might be channels of communication? Perhaps those radiations, as scientists are beginning to find, exist in the very cell itself. Have they always been there, or have they developed recently? Darwin's evolution, after all, brought us to the species of man, but Darwin did not state that evolution, like Harry Truman's buck, stops here. Are we evolving into another state of being?

In the recorded history of the world, several *trivial irregularities* have been regularly described in the realm of human behavior. Certain people were considered to have the ability to detect water, or oil, beneath the ground. Others reportedly were able to detect the thoughts or happenings of people miles away. Some persons, it was claimed, could predict the outcome of a future event. Others were supposed to be able to move objects just by thinking about them.

These are all rare occurrences, obviously. And perhaps they are trivial. But it was the *trivial irregularities* of planetary orbits that led to the discovery of unknown but existing planets. Thus, possibly those as yet inexplicable (unproven?) irregularities of human behavior may prove to have considerable significance in the study of man.

Let us keep in mind that *nothing* is dogma. Your explanations about inexplicable phenomena may be as valid as anyone's. The main point is that certain phenomena which according to classical science were impossible are now being regarded by some scientists as, perhaps, probable.

—from **The Probability of the Impossible,** by Dr. Thelma Moss.

ABBOT, A.E., ed. **CLAIRVOYANCE,** $2.00. A short presentation on supersensible consciousness quoting mainly anthroposophical writers. 61pp. Eme 63

ABHEDANANDA, SWAMI. **LIFE BEYOND DEATH,** c$3.75. This is a critical study of spiritualism and especially of the spiritualist phenomena that were so popular in the nineteenth century. Swami Abhedananda presents the Vedantic point of view (see the Indian philosophy section) and discusses life after death, rebirth of the soul, spirit communication, mediumship, and much else. It's an interesting presentation which serves as a good counterpoint to most spiritualist literature. 240pp. RVM 44

AGEE, DORIS. **EDGAR CAYCE ON ESP,** $1.25. See the Edgar Cayce section.

ASHBY, ROBERT H. **THE GUIDE BOOK FOR THE STUDY OF PSYCHICAL RESEARCH,** $3.50. An essential source book for the serious student. Includes an excellent essay on the nature of psychical research; extensive annotated bibliographies for both the beginning and advanced student as well as many additional listings; a chapter detailing procedures for sitting with a medium; a section enumerating the resources in England and the U.S. available to the student; biographical sketches of important figures in the movement; and an excellent glossary. 190pp. Wei 72

BARBANELL, MAURICE. **SPIRITUALISM TODAY,** c$6.50. After almost forty years of research and inquiry, Barbanell is acknowledged to be one of the best-informed authorities on spiritualism as we know it today. He edits **Psychic News,** a weekly newspaper and **Two Worlds,** a monthly magazine. This is a survey of many of the leading spiritualists today, replete with case studies. Illustrations, index. 174pp. Jnk 69

_____. **THIS IS SPIRITUALISM,** c$6.95. This is an earlier survey of spiritualism, discussing all aspects of the subject. Photographs. Spi 59

BRADLEY, DOROTHY and ROBERT. **PSYCHIC PHENOMENA,** $.95. An M.D. who is also a hypnotist examines case histories of floating objects, power of prayer on plants, and patterns of living. 224pp. War 69

BROWN, BETH. **ESP WITH PLANTS AND ANIMALS,** $1.00. A brief popularized account of some of the recent experiments. 150pp. S&S 71

BROWNING, NORMA. **PETER HURKOS: I HAVE MANY LIVES,** c$6.95. Hurkos' biography, produced through a series of tape-recorded interviews with Ms. Browning. Hurkos reveals how he received his psychic gift after an accident in which he fell four stories from a ladder and lapsed into a deep coma. To all outward appearances he lay unconscious and near death for four days. In fact, he regained consciousness almost immediately in another world before a jury of nine men—each one the spirit of a learned historical figure. Hurkos was sent back to life, but with new gifts and knowledge. This volume explores Hurkos' experience and subsequent developments in his life. 223pp. Dou 76

_____. **THE PSYCHIC WORLD OF PETER HURKOS,** $1.25. The author is a reporter with a reputation for exposing frauds. Although she began her research into Hurkos with many doubts she finished by being completely convinced of his great psychic powers. The text includes detailed descriptions of the police cases such as the Tate murders and the Boston Strangler on which he has been an official consultant. 237pp. NAL 70

BUTLER, W.E. **HOW TO DEVELOP CLAIRVOYANCE,** $1.25. A very practical outline—highly recommended as such. 64pp. Wei 68

_____. **HOW TO DEVELOP PSYCHOMETRY,** $1.00. Psychometry is the power to measure and interpret the *soul of things,* picking up the hidden vibrations and impres-

sions which have been recorded upon material objects. Includes a good amount of background material as well as practical suggestions. Highly recommended. 63pp. Wei 7

_____. **AN INTRODUCTION TO TELEPATHY,** $1.25. The newest of Butle short practical treatises. 64pp. Wei 75

CARRINGTON, HEREWARD. **YOUR PSYCHIC POWERS AND HOW TO DEVELO THEM,** c$1.98. Carrington was a noted psychic researcher and he has presented an e cellent detailed instruction manual, based on first-hand research and study over decade Because of its wide scope it is also a complete conspectus of the whole range of psych phenomena—psychometry, seeing the aura, telepathy, clairvoyance, automatic writin spiritual healing, trance mediumship, materialization, astral projection and many oth areas of parapsychology. This fine work has been out of print for many years and on recently reissued. Recommended as a good introduction to the field. 358pp. Cau 7

CHANEY, ROBERT. **ADVENTURES IN ESP,** $3.95. A very simply written practic guide covering the following material: the art of ESP, clairvoyance, psychometry, i tuition, visualization, vocalization, and vitalization. A positive, self-help approach taken. Illustrated throughout. 137pp. Ata 65

COLTON, ANN REE. **ETHICAL ESP,** c$8.95. A clairvoyant discusses lower and highe ESP, the root races and their psychic powers, zodiacal powers and the glands, and relate topics within the context of the responsible use of ESP. 367pp. APC 71

COOKE, GRACE. **THE NEW MEDIUMSHIP,** c$2.75. A comprehensive presentation by noted English medium. 91pp. WET 65

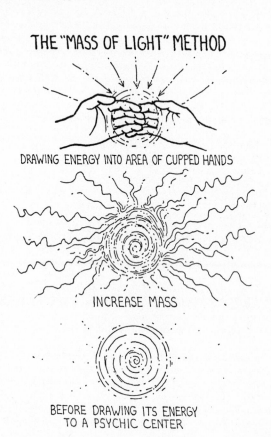

THE "MASS OF LIGHT" METHOD

DRAWING ENERGY INTO AREA OF CUPPED HANDS

INCREASE MASS

BEFORE DRAWING ITS ENERGY TO A PSYCHIC CENTER

CRAWFORD, DR. QUANTZ. **METHODS OF PSYCHIC DEVELOPMENT,** $2.95. *This book gives you the absolute basics of psychic development—the philosophy you must know to understand the phenomena involved, exercises that prepare you and then open your psychic centers, and then the techniques for controlling and using these new powers. The exercises are all simple. . . .—from the introduction. Perhaps the exercises are too simple. We recommend extensive spiritual development before attempting to harness these powers—and caution and moderation at all times. 102pp. LIP 73

CROOKALL, ROBERT. **INTERPRETATION OF COSMIC AND MYSTICAL EXPERIENCES,** c$6.70. In the first part, experiences of at-one-ment with inanimate and animate objects are described. The second part relates the at-one-ment experiences communicated by the dead. 175pp. Cla 69

_____. **THE NEXT WORLD AND THE NEXT,** c$5.75. Crookall, a noted psychic investigator, holds that enough evidence is now available to conclude that survival of bodily death and occasional communication with mortals thereafter are virtual certainties. He presents both a careful survey of various communications and an analysis of the statements given in the communications. 152pp. TPH 66

_____. **THE SUPREME ADVENTURE**, c$8.00. A meticulous, exhaustive compila-
on which analyzes the personal testimonies of death and survival taken from a great
ariety of sources. 267pp. Cla 61

ROOKES, SIR WILLIAM. **CROOKES AND THE SPIRIT WORLD**, c$10.00. In the
ineteenth century Sir William Crookes ran a series of experiments with D.D. Home,
ho was able to move tables and other objects by direct mind action, and with Florence
ook, who produced visual materializations, in order to understand psi phenomena in
erms of universal laws. This historically interesting collection of papers describes the
xperiments. 250pp. Tap 72

UMMINS, GERALDINE. **SWAN ON A BLACK SEA: A STUDY IN AUTOMATIC
RITING, THE CUMMINS-WILLETT SCRIPTS**, c$6.50. The value and quality of these
ripts has been assessed quite differently by various parapsychologists, but they are clear-
 among the most important mediumistic materials published. The introduction is per-
eptive and valuable. 168pp. RKP 65

URTIS, ROBERT. **ON ESP**, c$5.95. This is a simply written survey of parapsychology
eared toward older children and covering the following topics: what ESP is, mental
elepathy, clairvoyance and precognition, psychokinesis, travels in dreams, faith healing,
nd modern brain research. Glossary, index. 86pp. PrH 75

EAN, DOUGLAS, et al. **EXECUTIVE ESP**, c$7.95. An electrochemist, a professor of
ndustrial engineering, and the authors of **Psychic Discoveries Behind the Iron Curtain**
escribe how decisions based on hunches and gut feeling resemble precognition and
elepathic phenomena in parapsychology, how these abilities can be trained, and
ow psi can be effectively used in business. A good overview of recent psi research and its
ractical applications. Bibliography and references. 290pp. PrH 74

EAN, STANLEY, ed. **PSYCHIATRY AND MYSTICISM**, c$15.00. This is an excellent
anthology of writings based on a series of three panel-symposia on psychic phenomena
held at the 1972, 1973, and 1974 annual meetings of the American Psychiatric Association. The book is divided into four sections, the first of which is a compilation of papers
on metapsychiatry, mysticism, parapsychology, psi phenomena, telepathy and precognition. The second section deals with the energy fields of man, electromagnetism, Kirlian
photography, meditation, and biofeedback. Section III includes papers on positive and
negative aspects and public health implications of psychic healing and shamanism. The
final section considers transcendental and transpersonal experiences (with and without
drugs) of nonpsychotics compared to the sensory capacity of psychotics. Illustrations,
notes, index. 447pp. NeH 75

DELACOUR, JEAN-BAPTISTE. **GLIMPSES OF THE BEYOND**, $1.25. Based on ac-
counts of people who have been clinically dead and brought back to life, this book contains descriptions which relate to out-of-body experiences currently being studied by
parapsychologists. 216pp. Del 73

DOYLE, ARTHUR CONAN. **THE HISTORY OF SPIRITUALISM**, c$5.98. *My one aim
in life is that this great truth, the return and communion of the dead, shall be brought
home to a material world which needs it so badly.* As one of Conan Doyle's biographers
explains, *besides Conan Doyle the deeply involved observer of his own time, there was
another Conan Doyle, whom one is tempted to call a mystic....Let us rather call him
a sage.* This is the Conan Doyle who produced this work, *to give man the strongest of all
reasons to believe in spiritual immortality of the soul, to break down the barrier of death,
to found the grand religion of the future.* This is a facsimile of the 1924 edition, recently
reprinted. Index, 346pp. Avn 26

EDMUNDS, H. TUDOR. **PSYCHISM AND THE UNCONSCIOUS MIND**, $2.75. Collec-
ted articles from the **Science Group Journal** of the English Theosophical Research Centre.
Very interesting studies on etheric vision and radiation, psychic perceptivity, psychometry,
telepathy, auras, radiesthesia, human consciousness. Recommended. 254+pp. TPH 68

EDMUNDS, SIMEON. **ESP EXTRASENSORY PERCEPTION**, $2.00. A review of much
of the research in the field, written for the layperson by a well-known psychic. Each
chapter is followed by references. 204pp. Wil 65

EDWARDS, HARRY. **THE MEDIUMSHIP OF JACK WEBER**, c$3.20. From 1938 to
1940 Jack Weber held a number of seances to demonstrate his ability in producing ecto-
plasmic structures, table levitation, and materializing objects. Illustrated with thirty-six
photographs. 119pp. Hea 62

FODOR, NANCY. **ENCYCLOPEDIA OF PSYCHIC SCIENCE**, $6.95. A vast, comprehen-
sive survey covering the entire field up to 1933, its date of publication. Hundreds of articles and biographies. Every conceivable subject is covered, often in great detail, and each
entry is cross referenced. It's an altogether fascinating work, the only one of its kind,
which provides, in effect, a whole library on the subjects concerned. We recommend it
highly. 416pp. CiP 66

GARRETT, EILEEN

Ms. Garrett is widely considered one of the finest mediums of this century.
In addition to her psychic abilities she is highly respected for her experiments with psychic phenomena and her cooperation with the scientific
community.

ANGOFF, ALLAN. **EILEEN GARRETT AND THE WORLD BEYOND THE SENSES**,
c$6.95. A biography by a friend and associate of twenty-five years describing Eileen

Garrett's first awakenings of precognitive abilities, the early unhappiness caused by those
talents and the eventual application of her trance mediumship to scientific studies.
241pp. MoR 74

GARRETT, EILEEN. **AWARENESS**, c$5.00. An excellent presentation of Ms. Garrett's
concept of the universal nature of human consciousness and the laws relating to this
consciousness in action. Topics include sleep and dreams, hypnosis and suggestion, dis-
sociation and awareness, the breath and color, the way inward, perception and communication, and death and survival. 308pp. GtP 43

_____. **MANY VOICES**, c$7.95. Ms. Garrett's autobiography, from her early
years in Ireland where she first made contact with the *little people* through her parapsychology experiments. It is a very frank account. Index, 254pp. Put 68

_____. **TELEPATHY—IN SEARCH OF A LOST FACULTY**, c$4.00. A clear, sub-
jective explanation of telepathy, probing its origins, its manifestations, and its functions.
Bibliography, 210pp.

GARRETT PUBLICATIONS. **BIOGRAPHICAL DICTIONARY OF PARAPSYCHOLO-
GY**, c$12.00. A comprehensive international study. 371pp. GtP 64

URI GELLER

EBON, MARTIN, ed. **THE AMAZING URI GELLER**, $1.50. A collection of essays from
a variety of sources. Illustrations, 168pp. NAL 75

GELLER, URI. **MY STORY**, $1.95. The autobiography of the well-known Israeli psychic
who can bend metal, repair broken watches, propel objects across a room or make them
dematerialize by direct mind action. Recounts his experiences of growing up with ESP
and his recent, now famous, experiments at the University of London and Stanford Research Institute. Good descriptions of contemporary psi research in which the basic concepts of science are being questioned. Photographs of Uri, leading psi researchers, and of
metal bending experiments. 282pp. War 75

PANATI, CHARLES, ed. **THE GELLER PAPERS**, c$10.00. Panati is a science editor at
Newsweek as well as a physicist. He has talked with a number of the scientists who have
worked with Geller and has collected here their major technical papers and reports. He
has also contributed a lengthy introduction explaining the rationale behind the various
experiments and setting forth the credentials of the researchers. The book contains all
the charts, diagrams, and photographic evidence originally included in the papers themselves and a closing chapter discusses the significance of the scientific work so far done
with Geller and speculates on where it may someday lead. 327pp. HMC 76

PUHARICH, ANDRIJA. **URI**, $1.95. This is a detailed account of *the Mystery of Uri
Geller* by the man who brought him to America. Uri's psychic powers and background
are discussed in detail. A major part of the book is devoted to a highly controversial
account of Uri and Puharich's extended contact with extra-terrestrials whom they felt
were responsible for and were controlling Uri's psychic powers. Puharich is a medical
doctor who has studied some of the most noteworthy examples of paranormal activities
to have occurred in recent times. 285pp. Ban 74

RANDI, JAMES. **THE MAGIC OF URI GELLER**, $1.75. The Amazing Randi is a well-
known stage magician. In this volume he sets out to expose Uri Geller by explaining *the
real magic behind his psychic feats.* Glossary, bibliography. 308pp. RaH 75

GIBSON, WALTER and LITZKA. **THE COMPLETE ILLUSTRATED BOOK OF THE
PSYCHIC SCIENCES**, $1.50. Surface treatments of every conceivable form of mystic
science and divination including extensive discussions of astrology, palmistry, graphology,
the Tarot, telepathy, colors, dreams. Good for those who wish a taste of what it's all
about. 439pp. S&S 66

_____. **THE MYSTIC AND OCCULT ARTS**, $2.95. Practical instructions in
developing the following: clairvoyance, psychometry, crystal gazing, receiving messages
psychically, precognition, telepathy, radiesthesia, astral projection. Very complete instructions. 224pp. PrH 69

GUIRDHAM, ARTHUR. **A FOOT IN BOTH WORLDS**, $7.85. A doctor's autobiography
of psychic experience which shows clearly the consistent purpose of the psychic entities
which have intervened in his life. The story shows the systematic way Guirdham was prepared by his experiences. 244pp. Spe 73

HAMMOND, DAVID. **THE SEARCH FOR PSYCHIC POWER**, $1.50. This is a good sur-
vey of some of the newest individuals and developments in the field of psi. The articles
were originally printed in **Psychic Magazine** and each one covers the topic quite well.
The individuals discussed include Uri Geller (who can bend metal with his mind), Pat
Price (who can receive and transmit psychic energy from within a shielded room designed
to prevent the passage of any known wave), Ingo Swann (who can affect an underground
instrument in a similarly shielded room), and scientists like Harold Puthoff, Russell Targ,
Milan Ryzl, and Victor Adamenko. Other topics include Transcendental Meditation, biofeedback, and mind control. Hammond's thesis is that these individuals and developments
are part of *a giant leap forward in man's evolution*, and this account is an attempt at a
study of parapsychological research in this light. Notes, bibliography. 291pp. Ban 75

HANSEL, C.E.M. **ESP, A SCIENTIFIC EVALUATION**, $2.45. A good history of the
statistical approach to psi research in which extensive tabulations of card guesses and dice
throws are made in order to verify the factual nature of telepathy, clairvoyance, and psychokinesis. References and bibliography. 263pp. Scr 66

HAPGOOD, CHARLES. **VOICES OF SPIRIT THROUGH THE PSYCHIC EXPERIENCE OF ELWOOD BABBITT**, c$8.95. Babbitt is a trance medium who purports to have the spirits of famous persons such as Mark Twain, Einstein, and Wordsworth speaking through him. He is known for his *life readings*, in which he looks back through an individual's past and previous lives and offers advice based on clairvoyant knowledge. Professor Hapgood has been studying Babbitt and his work for over eight years. In this book he offers full-length transcripts of the communications which have come through Babbitt and interprets his spiritual teachings. He also relates the phenomenon of trance mediums to recent research in parapsychology. Glossary, index. 338pp. Del 75

HARDY, ALISTER, ROBERT HARVIE and ARTHUR KOESTLER. **THE CHALLENGE OF CHANCE**, $2.95. A marine biologist from Oxford and a psychologist from London University report on experiments in the telepathic transmission of line drawings and pictures to two hundred subjects. Additional comments by Arthur Koestler. 309pp. RaH 73

HAYNES, RENEE. **THE HIDDEN SPRINGS—AN ENQUIRY INTO ESP**, $2.95. A newly revised edition of this comprehensive, very clearly written volume. Good bibliography. Recommended as a good introduction to the field. LBC 61

HERON, LAURENCE. **ESP IN THE BIBLE**, c$5.95. A member of the Spiritual Frontiers Fellowship, writing from the standpoint of Protestant scholarship, Heron covers the telepathy of King David in the death of Absalom, the precognition of John Calvin, and illumination experienced by Moses and Paul. He believes that the Bible is an historical record of psychic events from the call of Abraham in the Bronze Age to the visions of a seer in the Book of Revelation during the era of Imperial Rome. Recommended. References, 212pp. Dou 74

HEYWOOD, ROSALIND. **BEYOND THE REACH OF SENSE**, $3.45. A general survey which discusses the events that led to the formation of the British Society for Psychical Research, survival after death, and mediumship. 252pp. Dut 74

HOME, DANIEL. **INCIDENTS IN MY LIFE**, c$7.95. The autobiography of a sensational nineteenth century psychic medium who not only produced the conventional spirit messages but also the tangible presence of spirits themselves. He also could perform many miracles similar to those of Indian fakirs such as floating in the air, handling red-hot coals and elongating his body. 287+pp. UnB 1863

HUDSON, THOMSON. **THE LAW OF PSYCHIC PHENOMENA**, $2.95. This book is regarded as the greatest classic in the field, first published in 1892. The author correlated all psychic phenomena and for the first time placed all mental and spiritual therapy on a scientific basis. In addition, he studied the soul of man precisely as the physical sciences are studied, namely by observation and a systematic classification of facts. We recommend it highly to all serious seekers. 409pp. Wei 1892

HUSON, PAUL. **HOW TO TEST AND DEVELOP YOUR ESP**, c$8.95. Offers ESP training procedures and tells of ways of using ESP in daily life. Includes a concise review of college courses on psi, a glossary of parapsychology terms, a guide to technical journals, a bibliography, and index. 215pp. S&D 75

JACOBSON, NILS. **LIFE WITHOUT DEATH?** $1.75. Dr. Jacobson is a Swedish psychiatrist who has done considerable research in the field of parapsychology. His book has two purposes: to introduce the reader to the full range of *paranormal* phenomena, clairvoyance, psychometry, telepathy, precognition, psychokinesis, etc.; and to show how research in all these areas bears upon the question of survival after death. Each phenomenon is illustrated with case histories and a description of relevant ongoing research throughout the world. This is an excellent comprehensive account and we recommend it highly. The text is fully indexed and includes a glossary, and an extensive section of bibliography and notes. 283pp. Del 71

JOHNSON, RAYNOR. **THE IMPRISONED SPLENDOUR**, $2.95. One of the most widely read syntheses of science, psychical research, philosophy, and religion yet produced. Dr. Johnson has the advantage of a first-rate mind, thorough scientific training, many years of teaching, broad and deep interests in psychical research and mysticism, and an al-

most unique ability to pull disparate strands of data and approaches together into a si, nificant whole. Highly recommended. Bibliography, 424pp. TPH 53

_____. **NURSLINGS OF IMMORTALITY**, $3.00. A philosophical view of psi whether clairvoyance can be described as x-ray vision or whether it is really precognitio, what psi means to our understanding of the physical world—and on the nature of Go, creation, man, evil and the *next life* by a physicist and Master of Queen's College, Unive sity of Melbourne. 279pp. H&R 57

_____. **PSYCHICAL RESEARCH**, $1.75. A clear, readable, and thorough intro duction. The explanations are illustrated with some well chosen examples from the anna, of psychical research; the problems inherent in the discipline are discussed; and guideline, as to the evaluation of evidence are given. Bibliography, 176pp. Cro 55

KARDEC, ALLAN. **THE BOOK OF MEDIUMS**, c$7.50. If there exists an encyclopedi, on the subject of spiritualism and mediumship, this is it. The entire field is approached wit, a practical and scientific attitude by one who was intimately knowledgeable on the subject. This and the **Law of Psychic Phenomena** are the most noted nineteenth century texts. 456pp. Wei 70

_____. **THE SPIRITS BOOK**, c$7.50. A very complete, clear exposition of the principles of spiritualist doctrine on the immortality of the soul; the nature of spirits an, their relations with men; the moral law; the present life, the future life, and the destiny o the human race—according to the teaching of spirits of high degree, transmitted throug, various mediums and collected and set in order by Kardec at the end of the nineteenth, century. 424pp.

KNIGHT, DAVID, ed. **THE ESP READER**, c$2.98. A collection of articles on the grea, mediums, messages from the ouija board, incarnation and reincarnation, and survival afte, death from William James, F.W.H. Myers, J.B. Rhine, Edgar Cayce, Jeane Dixon, Arthur Ford, D.D. Home and others. 432pp. Cst 69

KOESTLER, ARTHUR. **THE ROOTS OF COINCIDENCE**, $1.95. Brings together in an, intriguing and persuasive way the various strands of psychical research, mysticism, biolo, gy, physics, and philosophy. This is one of the most impressive syntheses of parapsychol, ogy's discoveries and purview with those of physics yet to appear. Essential reading for the scientifically oriented student. References, bibliography. 159pp. RaH 72

KRIPPNER, STANLEY. **SONG OF THE SIREN**, c$12.50. Krippner is one of the most noted writers and researchers in the field of parapsychology. He has been involved in this study for most of his adult life and in this account he charts that involvement over the last twenty years in an informal manner. This is a survey of the developments in parapsychology during that period as seen through the life and adventures of one man. Many of the main individuals, experiments, and findings are reviewed in an informal way. Krippner attended conferences and traveled in the U.S.S.R. and Czechoslovakia and he reports on his experiences. His most extensive experience was at the Maimonides Dream Lab—and this is also discussed. An interesting non-technical account. Notes, index. 328pp. H&R 75

LEADBEATER, C.W. **CLAIRVOYANCE**, c$3.00. A highly developed clairvoyant discusses the theoretical/philosophical basis of clairvoyance. A very clear account which has been very popular since first published in 1899. 226pp. TPH 1899

LE SHAN, LAWRENCE. **THE MEDIUM, THE MYSTIC AND THE PHYSICIST**, $1.95. Dr. LeShan, a researcher on the paranormal and psychic healing, examines the Clairvoyant Reality (as he terms it) from three supposedly separate viewpoints—those of the medium, the mystic and the physicist—and finds each view startlingly similar. An important book. Notes, bibliography. 284pp. RaH 66

MC CONNELL, R.A. **ESP CURRICULUM GUIDE: A SCIENTIST EXAMINES THE REALITY OF ESP**, $1.95. The author, actively engaged in ESP research, hopes to provide a means by which interested persons can teach a relevant and exciting presentation of this field. He outlines the most important books and gives exact procedures for classroom or home experiments. Scientifically oriented, but suitable for the general reader. 128pp. S&S 70

MC CREERY, CHARLES. **PSYCHICAL PHENOMENA AND THE PHYSICAL WORLD**, $1.25. McCreery is the Research Officer at the Institute of Psychophysical Research, Oxford, England. This is an illuminating examination of such events as lucid dreams, out-of-the-body experiences, apparitions, materializations, and psychokinesis as well as a probing exploration of the philosophical implications of these phenomena. Includes a number of case studies. 179pp. RaH 73

_____. **SCIENCE, PHILOSOPHY AND ESP**, c$7.85. An introduction to psychical research for the general reader dealing with telepathy and psychokinesis. References, 199pp. HHL 72

MAETERLINCK, MAURICE. **THE UNKNOWN GUEST**, c$7.95. The *guest* in the title is the faculty in man that connects him with paranormal phenomena which in this case are premonitions, haunted houses, and the Elberfeld Horses that could apparently communicate with men and perform arithmetic calculations. 340pp. UnB 15

MANNING, MATTHEW. **THE LINK**, $1.95. Matthew Manning is a young Englishman who mentally bends metal by causing a change in its molecular structure; produces automatic drawings in the style of Picasso, Durer and other artists; and psychokinetically propels objects across rooms. Dr. George Owen of the New Horizons Research Foundation in Toronto believes Manning to be the most gifted psychic in the Western world. Dr. Brian Josephson, Nobel prize recipient in physics, 1973, has stated that the phenomena produced by Matthew Manning will have important implications for physics. This is Matthew's own story. Photographs, 200pp. HRW 75

ARRYAT, FLORENCE. **THERE IS NO DEATH**, c$2.98. Written over eighty years ago y a woman who attended the seances of Florence Cook, the medium investigated by r William Crookes, the book recounts the author's personal experiences with the leading ensitives in nineteenth century English spiritualism. 248pp. Cau 73

MEEK, GEORGE. **FROM ENIGMA TO SCIENCE**, c$6.95. The author has devoted everal years to traveling over much of the globe making a study of the paranormal and as made an effort to focus the findings of psychical research, parapsychology, physics, stronomy, psychiatry, biochemistry, medicine, physiology, and occult literature on an xplanation of man's psi ability. This is a scattered account which contains some useful nd interesting material. Photographs, 199pp. Wei 73

MERRY, ELEANOR. **SPIRITUAL KNOWLEDGE**, c$4.75. A sensitive and insightful uide to the understanding of parapsychological phenomena written from an anthropo-ophical viewpoint. 115pp. NKB 35

MITCHELL, EDGAR. **PSYCHIC EXPLORATION**, c$17.50. A monumental work divided nto twenty-nine chapters on every area of psychic research—each written especially for his book by a noted scientist. Most of the articles are fairly technical and are accompanied by notes. Glossary, index. 708pp. Put 74

MONTGOMERY, RUTH. **A SEARCH FOR TRUTH**, $1.25. Ms. Montgomery tells how Senator Everett Dirksen found healing power in a Bible verse, how William Faulkner's widow discovered a feminine spirit sharing their antebellum estate, and of her own con-acts with the psychic world. 237pp. Ban 68

_____. **A WORLD BEYOND**, $1.50. *Arthur Ford's own account of life in the next stages of existence beyond the portal that man calls death*, transmitted through his friend, Ruth Montgomery. 176pp. Faw 71

MOON, MARGARET and MAURINE. **WEDGE: THE EXTRAORDINARY COMMUNI-CATIONS OF AN EARTHBOUND SPIRIT**, $3.95. Jude Wedge recalls life in the seven-teenth century from the spirit world through a ouija board connected to an electric type-writer. He tells of his loves, worries, and hopes in the rustic idiom of his time. 113pp. LIP 75

MOSS, THELMA. **THE PROBABILITY OF THE IMPOSSIBLE**, $4.50. Written by one of the leading researchers in Kirlian electrophotography, the book presents a parapsycholo-gist at work in her laboratory and in the field. She explores the assumptions of parapsy-chologists and shows how the scientific psychical researcher attempts to recreate, capture, and analyze the elusive phenomena of the paranormal. She leads the reader along a con-tinuum from everyday experiences through events that only happen rarely and under special circumstances on to the seemingly impossible experiences of both well-known and little-heralded psychics. She convincingly presents arguments for a psychic world as real as the material one. Several Kirlian photographs. Recommended. References, 394pp. NAL 74

MUHL, ANITA. **AUTOMATIC WRITING**, c$4.50. Dr. Muhl is a psychiatrist who has ap-plied the method of automatic handwriting to an understanding of her patients' psychic processes over a period of more than thirty years. In this volume she presents the results of her experiences emphasizing the psychological meaning of the experiments. Many case studies are included. Bibliography, 193pp. GtP 63

MURPHY, GARDNER. **CHALLENGE OF PSYCHICAL RESEARCH**, $3.95. A well-known psychologist's collection of scientific research on telepathy, clairvoyance, precog-nition, and psychokinesis. Contrary to the climate of disbelief to which such phenomena have been subjected by many of his fellow psychologists, they are treated respectfully and seriously by Dr. Murphy. 303pp. H&R 70

MURPHY, JOSEPH. **PSYCHIC PERCEPTION: THE MAGIC OF EXTRASENSORY POWER**, $2.95. An inspirational text which instructs the reader on the practical applica-tions of ESP in every conceivable field. 242pp. PrH 71

OPHIEL. **THE ART AND PRACTICE OF CLAIRVOYANCE**, $3.50. Everyone has clair-voyant powers; this book tells how to use and develop them further. Ophiel teaches the basis of clairvoyance, use of the tree of life and the basic elements in directing your clair-voyance to work through mental images and their associations. 137pp. Wei 69

OSBORNE, ARTHUR. **THE EXPANSION OF AWARENESS**, $1.95. A profound study of Osborne's quest for the meaning of life and his investigation of extrasensory percep-tion, the implications of telepathy, and the possibility of survival and rebirth. These ques-tions lead to a discussion of the purpose of existence, the validity of mystical experience, and the achieving of deeper awareness and enlightenment. An excellent account which in-cludes one of the most complete bibliographies we've seen. 272pp. TPH 61

_____. **THE FUTURE IS NOW**, $2.50. A complete treatment of precognition, in-cluding a review of scientific studies and of the existing explanations. 250pp. TPH 61

_____. **THE MEANING OF PERSONAL EXISTENCE IN THE LIGHT OF PARA-NORMAL PHENOMENA, REINCARNATION AND MYSTICAL EXPERIENCE**, c$3.95. A discussion of the implications of supernormal phenomena such as clairvoyance, clair-audience, precognition and telepathy with an investigation of the possibility of reincar-nation and mystical experience. Well researched and highly informative. 214pp. TPH 66

OSTRANDER, SHEILA and LYNN SCHROEDER. **THE ESP PAPERS**, $1.95. Trans-lations by East European and Soviet scientists of papers never before published in the West. Subjects include: autosuggestion, possession, stigmata, pain control, reincarnation, hypnosis, clairvoyance, speed learning, and much else. Notes, index. 236pp. Ban 76

_____. **PSYCHIC DISCOVERIES BEHIND THE IRON CURTAIN**, $1.50. The authors traveled to the Soviet Union in 1967 to attend a conference on ESP. This is the story of what they read, saw, and heard. Includes material on mental telepathy, hypnotism, faith healing, precognition, psychokinesis, auras around plants and animals, brain control, astrological birth control, levitation, sightless vision, dowsing, acupuncture, prophecy, psychotronics—the list goes on and on. The treatment in each case is quite thorough. Many references. 448pp. Ban 70

OWEN, A.R.G. **PSYCHIC MYSTERIES OF THE NORTH**, c$8.95. The Director of the New Horizons Research Foundation of Toronto has written this book primarily to make known a number of discoveries in psychic research that have been made in Canada. These discoveries are handled chronologically from the spirit communications of the native Canadian Indians, through the poltergeist phenomena of the early settlers to the psychokinesis experiments of Jan Merta. Notes, index. 243pp. H&R 75

PANATI, CHARLES. **SUPERSENSES**, $3.50. A clearly presented survey of current scientific research on psi abilities covering dream telepathy, hypnosis and psi, healing, clairvoyance, precognition, and PK. The author is a science writer for **Newsweek** and has worked in radiation and laser physics. A good introductory book to psi. Notes, index. 274pp. Dou 74

PANCHADASI, SWAMI. **CLAIRVOYANCE AND OCCULT POWERS**, c$5.50. A com-plete set of occult lessons, first prepared in 1916 by an associate of Yogi Ramacharaka. 319pp. YPS 16

PARKER, ADRIAN. **STATES OF MIND: ESP AND ALTERED STATES OF CON-SCIOUSNESS**, c$9.95. A technical study, incorporating the latest research and covering the following topics: ESP and consciousness, hypnosis and ESP, trance mediumship, dream states and ESP, out-of-the-body experiences and lucid dreams, pathological states, psychedelic states, meditation, mysticism, alpha states, and post-mortem ASC. Glossary, notes, bibliography, indices. 198pp. Tap 75

PATTERSON, DORIS. **THE UNFETTERED MIND**, $2.00. Subtitled *Varieties of ESP in the Edgar Cayce Readings.* 77pp. ARE 68

PEARCE-HIGGINS, J.D. and WHITBY, G.S., eds. **LIFE, DEATH, AND PSYCHICAL RE-SEARCH**, $6.85. A collection of essays written on behalf of the Churches' Fellowship for Psychical and Spiritual Studies, divided into sections on the nature and scope of psychical phenomena and the Bible and psychic phenomena. Bibliography, 272pp. Rid 73

PLAYFAIR, GUY. **THE FLYING COW**, c$8.40. In Brazil, if you were driving along and saw a flying cow and later told someone about it, s/he would probably ask you what color it was. Paranormal phenomena have wide acceptance in what the author calls the world's most psychic nation. This is the first book to survey the wide variety of paranor-mal events—psychic surgery, poltergeists, materializations—taking place in Brazil. Photo-graphs, references. 320pp. Sou 75

PUHARICH, ANDRIJA. **BEYOND TELEPATHY**, $2.95. First published in 1962, this is still one of the very best books available on the subject. It presents a coherent theory of psychical research, and discusses its relation to such phenomena as ESP, astral projection, yoga, and shamanism. A very scientific, well annotated collection of studies. Recom-mended. 340pp. Dou 62

RANDALL, JOHN. **PARAPSYCHOLOGY AND THE NATURE OF LIFE**, c$8.95. A dry, technical study. Randall is a biologist and here he focuses on the relation (or lack thereof) between parapsychological findings and biology and the natural world. The book traces the rise of the mechanist-reductionist theory of life from the time of Darwin to the present day and points out the psi phenomena which do not appear to be explicable in terms of that limited theory. Notes, index. 266pp. H&R 75

RAUDIVE, KONSTANTIN. **BREAKTHROUGH—AN AMAZING EXPERIENCE IN ELECTRONIC COMMUNICATIONS WITH THE DEAD**, c$10.00. The documented result of six years of scientific research. In some way, and for reasons not yet fully understood, voices of dead persons linked by affection or interest appear during play-backs of tape recordings on which no such voices were audible at the time of the original recording. The phenomena have been verified by scientists in numerous fields. 391pp. Tap 71

REYES, BENITO. **SCIENTIFIC EVIDENCE OF THE EXISTENCE OF THE SOUL**, $2.45. A very well documented theosophical text, including many case studies and an extensive bibliography. 251pp. TPH 70

RHINE, J.B. **EXTRA-SENSORY PERCEPTION**, $3.75. Subtitled *A Critical Survey of the Research in Extra-Sensory Perception*, this is perhaps the most comprehensive presen-tation of the statistical approach to ESP investigation as developed in the Duke University laboratories under Dr. Rhine. It details the mathematical and experimental methods, criticism and evidence, and the nature of ESP. It has twenty-one technical appendices, many tables, extensive notes, index. 463pp. BrP 40

RHINE, J.B. and ROBERT BRIER, eds. **PARAPSYCHOLOGY TODAY**, c$2.49. A col-lection of writings by various noted researchers. 273pp. Cst 68

RHINE, LOUISA. **ESP IN LIFE AND LAB**, $1.50. This is the second of Dr. Rhine's valuable collections of spontaneous cases taken from over 10,000 which she has gathered. The author analyzes about eighty instances after categorizing them. She is known as a common sense authority who weighs cases within the context of their specific occur-rence as well as within that of their bearing on major issues in psychical research. 275pp. McM 67

_____. **MIND OVER MATTER: PSYCHOKINESIS**, $1.95. Reports the studies from 1934 to the present, from experiments with cards and coins to such new targets as one-celled creatures and plants. Also included are various speculative paranormal occurrences. A serious and comprehensive report by one of the world's leading parapsychologists. 390pp. McM 70

_____. PSI—WHAT IS IT?, $1.95. *At last there is a book about psi that is completely scientific yet thoroughly entertaining. I can think of no better way to introduce people to para-psychology than to have them read* PSI: What is it?—Stanley Krippner. Notes, index. 247pp. H&R 75

ROGO, D. SCOTT. PARAPSYCHOLOGY: A CENTURY OF INQUIRY, $1.75. This comprehensive book traces the early turn-of-the-century attempts to bring scientific methods and critical observation to the study of psi phenomena in the work of such men as Cesare Lombroso and Sir Oliver Lodge. Rogo gives detailed accounts of breakthroughs such as Rhine's laboratory work with ESP and psychokinesis. He also covers current work on out-of-body experience, psychedelics, alpha training, and the possibilities of animal psi research. 319pp. Del 75

SABIN, KATHERINE. ESP AND DREAM ANALYSIS, c$6.95. The author demonstrates how to recognize and interpret the ESP content of dreams, make use of popular dream books for the interpretation of dreams, and train the subconscious to present ESP content of dreams. 205pp. Reg 74

SHAY, J.M. HOW TO DEVELOP ESP, $2.00. A detailed, highly simplified instruction manual in the form of subsequent lessons which covers virtually every aspect of parasensory awareness. 53pp. WAO 74

SHERMAN, HAROLD. HOW TO MAKE ESP WORK FOR YOU, $1.50. 280pp. Faw 64

_____. YOUR MYSTERIOUS POWERS OF ESP, $1.25. Sherman reviews the evidence for paranormal phenomena, presents many case studies, and discusses various aspects of the topic. 239pp. NAL 69

SINCLAIR, UPTON. MENTAL RADIO, $1.95. This volume inspired the modern scientific investigation of extrasensory phenomena. It is the account of the experiments performed by Sinclair's wife, Mary Craig Kennedy. It explains step-by-step the methods she used for spontaneous concentration and relaxation which opened her up to receiving telepathic messages and seeing pictures on hidden cards. 285pp. McM 30

SMITH, SUSY. HOW TO DEVELOP YOUR ESP, $1.25. A popularized account by a noted journalist. 286pp. Pin 72

_____. THE POWER OF THE MIND, c$7.95. A journalistic exploration of a variety of unexplained phenomena including spirit photography, Kirlian photography, healing, PK, and much else. All the newest research is incorporated in the account. Index, 294pp. Chi 75

STEARN, JESS. ADVENTURES INTO THE PSYCHIC, $1.25. A well-written, popular treatment, includes many cases. 240pp. NAL 69

STEIGER, BRAD. ESP—YOUR SIXTH SENSE, $.75. A well written account of a wide range of psychic events. It traces the roots of psi research from spiritualism, looks at psi occurrences in psychiatry, discusses Soviet research, and tells of many important out-of-laboratory experiences. A good introduction. 190pp. ASC 66

SWANN, INGO. TO KISS EARTH GOOD-BYE, c$10.00. Ingo Swann has written an extraordinarily good book on the nature of consciousness, his first encounters with psychic experiences, the history of psychic research, what it is like to be a subject in remote sensing experiments, and how he affected a sensitive magnetic device through several types of shielding. Highly recommended for those interested in contemporary psi research. Bibliography, index. 217pp. Haw 75

TALAMONTI, LEO. FORBIDDEN UNIVERSE, c$8.95. Presents evidence that the conscious mind is only a small part of the total spiritual world—the realm of dreams being just as important for instance—and includes fascinating case histories supporting the theme from many different countries and times. Many illustrations. S&D 74

TART, CHARLES. LEARNING TO USE EXTRASENSORY PERCEPTION, $3.95. This is a serious, important book which argues that the usual ways of testing for ESP are inadvertently designed to extinguish rather than to strengthen ability. Tart and his students, using a basic learning theory approach (which he discusses in detail), found a considerable level of ESP ability, and they also demonstrated that some subjects can learn to improve their abilities. Notes, bibliography, index. 184pp. UCh 76

TAYLOR, JOHN. SUPER MINDS, c$10.95. Dr. Taylor has specialized in elementary particle physics, cosmology, and brain research, and is generally concerned with promoting a wider understanding of the new frontiers of science. This is a fairly technical study, although the numerous photographs and the good layout make it approachable to general readers. The major part of the book is devoted to an analysis of the *Geller effect*—named after Uri Geller, who can bend metal objects by rubbing them or concentrating on them. Dr. Taylor believes that this phenomenon is due to the electromagnetic force field, and he details why this is so. He also speculates on methods of investigating other aspects of ESP and concludes with an absorbing account of his experiments with Uri Geller. The book has received a good press and for those interested in the subject it is an excellent addition to the available literature. Oversize, bibliography, index. 183pp. Vik 75

TENHAEFF, W.H.C. TELEPATHY AND CLAIRVOYANCE, c$16.80. A scholarly study in which Dr. Tenhaeff describes the mechanisms of memory and amnesia and then relates these mental functions to those apparently involved in telepathy, proscopy (future memory), possession and reincarnation. The author was among the first to undertake systematic psycho-diagnostic research into the personality structures of people with psi abilities. There are descriptions and photographs of his investigation of telepathic relationships between kindergarten children and their teachers. Notes, index. 161pp. Tho 65

THOULESS, ROBERT H. FROM ANECDOTE TO EXPERIMENT IN PSYCHICAL RESEARCH, c$10.00. A series of sketches of points of interest within the field by a noted psychologist. Includes much material not touched upon in other books. Recommended for the serious scholar. Many references. 193pp. RKP 72

ULLMAN, MONTAGUE, and STANLEY KRIPPNER. DREAM TELEPATHY—SCIENTIFIC EXPERIMENTS INTO THE SUPERNATURAL, $2.95. The first book to present and analyze the results of scientifically controlled experiments in telepathic dreaming. The authors head the Dream Laboratory of New York's Maimonides Medical Center. They conducted experiments over a ten year period to determine if a person acting as an *agent* could transfer his thoughts to the mind of a sleeping *subject*, thereby altering or influencing the subject's dreams. The results are recorded here in great detail, along with much other interesting material. 300pp. Pen 73

UPHOFF, WALTER and MARY JO. NEW PSYCHIC FRONTIERS, c$10.50. Written as an aid to discussion group leaders, students, and instructors, this book reviews the full range of psychic phenomena—telepathy, guides, ghosts, direct voice. It has a thirty page directory of groups world-wide doing research on these topics. References, index. 278pp. Smy 75

VAN OVER, RAYMOND. PSYCHOLOGY AND EXTRASENSORY PERCEPTION, $1.95. A collection of essays by major psychologists including William James, Carl Jung, Sigmund Freud, J.B. Rhine, Gardner Murphy. Glossary, bibliography. 416pp. NAL 72

VISHITA, SWAMI BHAKTA. GENUINE MEDIUMSHIP: THE INVISIBLE POWERS, c$5.50. A very complete account of every aspect of the subject, including many practical suggestions on how to develop various mediumistic powers. Written by an associate of Yogi Ramacharaka. 277pp. YPS 19

_____. SEERSHIP, c$5.50. A comprehensive collection of very practical lessons. 384pp. YPS nd

WEDECK, HARRY and WADE BASKIN. DICTIONARY OF SPIRITUALISM, c$1.00. An encyclopedic work on personalities, phenomena, and theories. 376pp. PhL 71

WICKLAND, CARL. THIRTY YEARS AMONG THE DEAD, $4.95. Wickland was a medical doctor who communicated with departed spirits for over thirty years, with his wife as the medium. He recorded the spirit communication verbatim and presents a large body of it in this volume. This is a classic work, long unavailable in unabridged form and only recently reprinted. NPC 24

WILSON, COLIN. STRANGE POWERS, $1.95. While writing The Occult, Wilson became fascinated by the powers of some of the people he interviewed. In this book he tells about three such people: a dowser who can leave his body, a retired nurse through whom spirits write messages about the future, a man whose reincarnation has been documented. 146pp. RaH 73

WORRALL, AMBROSE and OLGA. EXPLORE YOUR PSYCHIC WORLD, c$6.95. The Worralls are two of the most noted healers of this century. Here they give practical suggestions on how to develop one's psychic abilities. 144pp. H&R 70

PROPHECY

ASSOCIATION OF THE LIGHT MORNING. SEASON OF CHANGES, WAYS OF RESPONSE, $3.95. A psychic interpretation of the coming changes in, on, and about the earth and the corresponding transformations within man. The prophecies and teachings recorded here were received by a psychic in Virginia Beach, Virginia over the period of about a year. The earth changes prophesied are of a radical nature and they are discussed in detail. The second half of the book is a discussion of how men and women might best respond to these changes and transform themselves. Notes, 290pp. Her 74

CHEETHAM, ERIKA, tr. THE PROPHECIES OF NOSTRADAMUS, $3.95. The most recent complete edition, with an introduction to Nostradamus' life, a translation of the text and a commentary which brings the prophecies up to date and offers a guide to future trends. 432pp. Put 74

THE LUSSON TWINS. THE BEGINNING OR THE END, c$5.95. Prophecies since Biblical times (and especially recent ones like Nostradamus and Edgar Cayce) have pointed out that the last quarter of the twentieth century will be a critical one for the human race. The predictions have been of famine, revolution, earthquakes, tidal waves, and nuclear holocaust. This book presents a series of detailed predictions including the following ones: a complete map and timetable for land changes in the next twenty-five years, the shape of economic, sociological, theological, political, and topographical transformations to come, plans for a survival community and a city of the future, and new directions in science and medicine. Don 75

PRIEDITIS, ARTHUR. THE FATE OF THE NATIONS, c$12.95. The author restates many of the most noted political prophecies from the sixteenth century to the present and analyzes both their veracity and the meaning of the predictions. Many views of the future are cited. A comprehensive study which is rather badly organized. Bibliography, 428pp. LIP 74

ROBERTS, HENRY, tr. THE COMPLETE PROPHECIES OF NOSTRADAMUS, c$6.95. This is the only unabridged edition of the predictions of the world's most noted prophet. Included are the original French text, an English translation, and the translator's interpretation of each prophecy. Roberts relates the visions to actual and future world events. Those looking for clear cut predictions will not find them in Nostradamus' writings (nor in the writings of most any prophet). The messages are often couched in obscure and ambiguous language. 350pp. Nos 69

STEIGER, BRAD. REVELATION, $3.95. A presentation of actual warnings, predictions, and messages from a wide spectrum of contemporary prophets including clergymen, scientists, and psychics. Steiger also evaluates the predictions and discusses where the revelations come from. Index, 316pp. PrH 73

VAUGHAN, ALAN. PATTERNS OF PROPHECY, $1.50. This is the most scientific study of prophecy that we know of. Vaughan himself is a prophet as well as a writer and researcher. He believes that each individual has an inner or psychic blueprint, much like the physical RNA-DNA blueprint, and that prophets have the ability to recognize and read these blueprints. In this volume he synthesizes the concepts of synchronicity and coincidence, archetypal roles, prophetic dreams, and psi fields to formulate a plausible explanation for prophecy. In the process Vaughn recounts his experiences in the development of his own prophetic abilities and scrutinizes the prophecies of others. Notes, index. 266pp. Del 73

WHITNEY, EDWARD. THE COMING GREAT GOLDEN AGE OF ESOTERICISM, c$6.95. Whitney is an American surgeon who has spent over sixty years in a quest to find out *What's it all about?* He studied and practiced all the Western religions, including Christ-

ian Science and New Thought; he absorbed what he could from the various *occult* schools, and from the Eastern teachings; finally he was introduced to esotericism as taught in the Arcane School, the *I Am*, the Summit Lighthouse, and other groups. This book is a synthesis of these years of investigation, study, and application. The emphasis is on what he learned from esotericism, and the chapter-end references are mainly to esoteric publications. 281pp. Dor 69

WOLDBEN, A. AFTER NOSTRADAMUS, $2.95. Traces the course of prophecy down the ages, mostly from documents which have hitherto been almost unknown. Sources include the Vedas, the Great Pyramid, La Salette, Garabandal, St. Damiano, and Nostradamus. The text is topically arranged, and this adds to its interest since a theme can be followed and considered in depth. 186pp. Fon 72

A drawing of Nostradamus

RECORDS

AFRICA: WITCHCRAFT AND RITUAL MUSIC, $3.96. This album presents a variety of East African music including healing rituals, tribal initiations, traditional folk songs, wedding songs, and funeral songs. The music ranges from simple beating on drums and bells to melodious songs with a reggae sound played on a six-string harp. Other instruments include flutes, horns, mouth harps, and rattles. Descriptive notes. WEA

BONNY, HELEN and LOUIS SAVARY. CREATIVE LISTENING SERIES: VOLUMES I AND II and OPENING THE BIBLE, VOLUME I, $6.30/each. These recordings were developed for children by Helen Bonny, author of **Music and your Mind**, and Louis Savary, co-author of **Passages: A Guide for Pilgrims of the Mind** (see the Consciousness Expansion section). Each album contains six *music-and-imagination experiences*. The listening experience begins with a narration that outlines an image or story. This is followed by several minutes of music. The purpose of the music is to stimulate the mind of the child and suggest further imagery. The music is taken from a wide range of sources. Volume I has a variety of themes such as mother nature, zoo, safari, and undersea journey. The theme of Volume II is travel to different parts of the world. **Opening the Bible**, Volume I uses stories from the Old Testament for its listening experiences. The concept of these albums is interesting, but the musical selections are not very exciting or thought provoking. Instructions and descriptive notes. ICM

BURCHETTE, WILBURN. MUSIC OF THE GODHEAD, $6.98. Subtitled *For Supernatural Meditation*, this album consists of eight compositions, each with a meditative

theme. Wilburn Burchette's albums are very popular. The music is electronic and the liner notes advise that it be played loudly. BBP

_____. **PSYCHIC MEDITATION MUSIC**, $6.98. More electronic meditation music. BBP

_____. **WILBURN BURCHETTE OPENS THE SEVEN GATES OF TRANSCENDENTAL CONSCIOUSNESS**, $6.75. Electronic guitar music. Included is a full color booklet of instructions and art work. ODI

COPTIC MUSIC, $6.98. The Copts are Egyptian Christians. Their services are all vocal and choral, with no instrumentation. The Coptic ceremonies sound similar to the liturgical music of the West. Extensive notes, translation, transliteration, and the services in the original Coptic are included. FkR

ETHIOPIA: THE FALASHA AND THE ADJURAN TRIBE, $8.95. Side One is the complete ceremony of *Shabbot Shalom* (Friday Night Ceremony) of the Falasha—one of the last traditionally Hebraic tribes of Ethiopia. The chanting is done in Geez, an early language of Ethiopia, with occasional Hebrew words interspersed. The voices are rough and often strained. Side Two has songs of the Adjuran tribe, a semi-nomadic people. The songs have a leader chanting a line that is answered by a group often accompanied by clapping, shouts, grunts, and groans. Descriptive notes. FkR

FIESTAS OF PERU, $3.96. Examples of festival music featuring both instrumentals and vocals. Some selections are tuneful and lively with a Latin flair; others are seemingly without rhythm or melody. Instruments include harp, guitar, violin, accordion, flutes, and drums. Descriptive notes. WEA

GOLDEN RAIN, $3.96. Side One has examples of the Balinese orchestral style of music known as *Gamelan*, which emphasizes complex rhythms played on gongs, cymbals, drums flutes, and xylophones. Side Two is a recording of the famous *Balinese Monkey Chant*, a strange primitve sounding ceremony performed by 200 men. It reenacts a part of the *Ramayana* epic. Descriptive notes. WEA

HEALING SONGS OF THE AMERICAN INDIANS, $8.95. Taken from original recordings made in the early 1900's. This music is very similar to American Indian music as it has been portrayed in films. Very extensive descriptive notes. FkR

HORN, PAUL. INSIDE, $5.98. An improvisational performance recorded under the dome of the Taj Mahal. The only instrument used is the flute, with an occasional vocal accompaniment. The acoustics of the dome provide some striking echo effects. A beautiful and popular album. CRS

————. INSIDE II, $5.98. Side One combines sounds of nature with improvisational flute. Side Two includes several Bach chorales, the Kyrie—a fifteenth century mass—and more improvisations, all played on various types of flutes. CRS

THE JASMINE ISLE, $3.96. Orchestral music from Java, much more sedate than the music of neighboring Bali. Javanese music features unusual rhythms, but simple melodies. Several types of xylophones, gongs, and drums are used. Descriptive notes. WEA

KINGDOM OF THE SUN, $3.96. Subtitled *Peru's Inca Heritage*, this album features traditional songs of the Andean Indians, both vocal and instrumental. The songs have nice melodies but the rhythms are often ragged and disconcerting. Instruments include harps, violins, guitars, accordions, flutes, and drums. Descriptive notes. WEA

LITURGICAL MUSIC FROM THE RUSSIAN CATHEDRAL, $3.96. Choral music of the Russian Orthodox Church, sung without instrumental support. The harmonies and melodies are simple with rhythms similar to Gregorian chant. Descriptive notes. WEA

MUSIC FROM THE CHAPEL OF CHARLES V, $3.96. Primarily choral pieces, though some organ music is included, from the period during the sixteenth century when Charles V was elected Holy Roman Emperor. The images are similar to Gregorian chant, despite the presence of an organ and female voices. Descriptive notes. WEA

MUSIC FROM THE MORNING OF THE WORLD, $3.96. Examples of the Balinese orchestral style, *Gamelan*. Descriptive notes. WEA

MUSTAPHA TETTEY ADDY, $5.95. A master drummer of Ghana plays songs of Africa on several types of drums and bells, occasionally singing as he plays. The quality of the recording is good. A nice album for those who are in to drums. Descriptive notes. Lyr

RELIGIOUS MUSIC OF ASIA, $8.95. A sampler of the musical traditions of the major religions of the Near East, India, and East Asia. The thirteen pieces include an Islamic call to prayer, a Hindu wedding chant, a Chinese Buddhist priest chanting, and a selection from a Zen monastery morning service. A good (though very general) introduction to music of this part of the world. Descriptive notes are interesting and informative. FkR

SZEKELY, EDMUND BORDEAUX. SYMPHONY OF ANCIENT MEXICO, $5.55. The liner notes say, *Composition and rendition from Precolumbian sources and instruments by Edmond S. Bordeaux and Norma Jean Nilsson*. The instruments sound like those found in a modern orchestra, and passages of the symphony give the impression of being electronically manipulated. There are also several passages with voices. Overall, the recording is pleasant to listen to. Aca

A TREASURY OF GREGORIAN CHANTS, $6.99. A four record set. The chants are performed by monks from several monasteries. A good recording. Out

---

CHINESE AND JAPANESE MUSIC

CHINESE INSTRUMENTS

cheng—a zither with thirteen to sixteen silk strings.

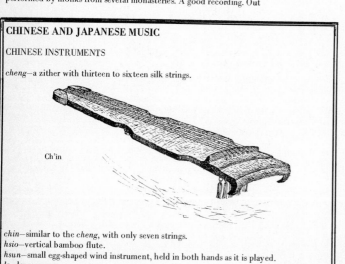

Ch'in

chin—similar to the *cheng*, with only seven strings.
hsio—vertical bamboo flute.
hsun—small egg-shaped wind instrument, held in both hands as it is played.
lo—large gongs.

---

nan-hu—a two string violin with a long neck.
pa—cymbals.

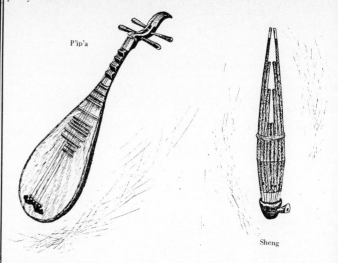

P'ip'a

Sheng

pipa—a pear-shaped lute.
sheng—a gourd with thirteen to seventeen bamboo pipes set in it, each with its own reed.
ta-pan—castinets.

A BELL RINGING IN THE EMPTY SKY, $3.96. A short album (less than thirty minutes) of two classic Japanese songs played on the *shakuhachi*. Very beautiful music Descriptive notes. WEA

BUDDHIST CHANTS, $11.95. A two record set containing two albums also sold and reviewed individually: **Japanese Temple Music** and **Zen, Goeika and Shomyo Chants**. An eleven page pamphlet of descriptive notes is included. Lyr

BUDDHIST DRUMS, BELLS AND CHANTS, $5.95. Selections from services of the temples of Kyoto, Japan featuring solos on a drum, large temple bells, and chanting and singing by both men and women. Not for the casual listener. Brief descriptive notes. Lyr

THE CHENG, $5.95. Solos on the *cheng* by two masters of the Northern and Southern traditions of ancient China. The music is light and pleasant. Descriptive notes. Lyr

CHINA'S INSTRUMENTAL HERITAGE, $5.95. Eleven folk songs covering periods from the fourteenth century to the present. The music has a light and airy quality, the melodies are simple, and the sounds of the instruments are delicate and pleasing. Instruments include the *cheng*, *hsiao*, *sheng*, *hsun*, and *nan-hu*. Descriptive notes. Lyr

CHINESE BUDDHIST MUSIC, $5.95. Examples of rituals, chants, prayers, and hymns, accompanied by bells, gongs, and other percussion instruments. Again, not an album for the casual listener. Lyr

CHINESE CLASSICAL MUSIC, $5.95. Selections featuring several classical instruments in solo performances. The instruments are the *nan-hu*, *pipa*, *ching*, and *hsio*. The music is beautiful, but the recording is very poor. Short descriptive notes. Lyr

CHINESE DRUMS AND GONG, $5.95. In addition to the drums and gongs, this album features flutes, the *cheng*, *pipa*, and *sheng*. The drums and gongs are not emphasized as much in the songs as the title would indicate. Like much of the Chinese classical music the selections have a delicate quality. Brief descriptive notes. Lyr

CHINESE TAOIST MUSIC, $5.95. Chanting by Taoist priests, usually accompanied by bells, gongs, and drums. Percussion instruments are used to set tempo and give emphasis to the chants, though there is often a randomness to their use similar to the chants of Tibet. The chants have a nasal sound with little discernible melody. Descriptive notes. Lyr

CLASSICAL CHINESE MUSIC, $8.60. An album of very pretty music, featuring the following classical Chinese instruments: the *chin*, *cheng*, *hsiao*, and *pipa*. Extensive descriptive notes. A monaural recording. Pol

EXOTIC MUSIC OF ANCIENT CHINA, $5.95. Songs played on two of China's oldest instruments, the *pipa* and the *chin*. Side One is devoted to the *pipa* and the music typically involves very rapid complex plucking, with simple melodies. The songs on Side Two, played on the *chin*, are slower and the *chin's* richer sounds are more thoughtful. Descriptive notes. Lyr

JAPANESE BUDDHIST RITUAL, $8.95. Included are morning prayers chanted by a priest accompanied on a gong and drum, typical hymns sung by a congregation, and very brief examples of various gongs used in temple services. The chanting is rapid and repetitious. The hymns are slow and melancholy, and the voices have a nasal quality. Extensive notes on Buddhism, brief notes on the recording. FkR

JAPANESE MASTERPIECES FOR THE SHAKUHACHI, $5.95. Music played on the *shakuhachi* by masters from Japan. Descriptive notes. Lyr

JAPANESE TEMPLE MUSIC, $5.95. Examples of Zen Buddhist chanting. Included are sutra chanting of the Jodo sect, a Zen priest doing solo chants, and the morning services of the Shoken sect. The chants are slow and monotonous and are often accompanied by gongs, clappers, and conch shells. Brief descriptive notes. Lyr

MUSIC FROM KOREA, VOLUME I: THE KAYAKEUM, $5.95. This album features the *kayakeum*, an ancient Korean instrument related to the Chinese *cheng*. It has several long strings passing over curved bridges and it emits a wide range of tones. It is accompanied by an hourglass shaped drum called the *changko*. The music is delicate and precise, and sounds like classical Chinese music. Descriptive notes. UWa

SHIGIN, $8.95. Shigin is an art form developed in Japan in the mid 1800's. It is a crossing of Chinese poetry (*shi*) with the Japanese samurai spirit which results in very forceful, intense recitations requiring … *complete involvement and considerable energy*. Each piece is sung by a single person occasionally accompanied by gongs, *shakuhachi*, and wire string *koto*. Very extensive notes. FkR

UNESCO COLLECTION: MUSICAL SOURCES OF JAPAN, $7.65. A recording of a ceremony of the Shingon sect that involves hymns, both individual and group chanting, and gongs, bells, conches, and even wooden staffs struck against pillars. The quality of the recording is very good. Brief descriptive notes. PPI

THE WAY OF EIHEIJI, $13.98. A two record set featuring examples from many different Zen Buddhist ceremonies and rituals of the *Eiheiji* (Temple of Great Peace). This is a well regarded collection among serious scholars. Very extensive descriptive notes. FkR

ZEN, GOEIKA AND SHOMYO CHANTS, $5.95. Three forms of Japanese Buddhist chants: the Zen chants are rapid and unemotional, *goeika* is the chanting of short poems by groups of men or women, and the *shomyo* sound very similar to Gregorian chants. Brief descriptive notes. Lyr

CHANTING AND SINGING

AN ALBUM OF ORIGINAL MUSIC, $5.00. A collection of mellow songs in the folk tradition performed by a trio of musicians. Rai

CARLEBACH, SCHLOMO. SING MY HEART, $6.00. *Carlebach pours out his deep-rooted faith, his wholehearted affirmation of belief, in soul-summoning melodies of his own composition. In interchanging intermingling moods he captures the gladness, the sadness, the warmth and the wonder, the frenzy, the fire of Chassidic life–as he himself has experienced it.*–The Jewish Chronicle, London. On this album Schlomo sings twelve songs of his own composition and is accompanied by a choir and orchestra. The text of the songs is included, in Hebrew with an English translation, in the linear notes. Zim

_____. **SONGS OF MY SOUL**, $6.00. Twelve more Hebrew songs composed and sung by Schlomo, with the accompaniment of a choir and orchestra. Zim

COMING HOHM, $5.00. A collection of songs by Rosemary Haddad, a devotee of Lee Lozowick–founder of the Hohm Community in New Jersey. The Hohm Choir and a band consisting of guitars, bass guitar, flute, sax, and drums provides backup. MOM

GARUDA, $5.95. A spiritual blending of jazz, rock, and Eastern musical traditions by The Collective Star. Side One features songs recorded in a studio. Side Two presents two songs recorded live at a performance in Boston. Rai

KRIYANANDA, SWAMI. O GOD BEAUTIFUL, $5.95. Swami Kriyananda and members of Ananda Cooperative Village sing chants composed by their guru Paramahansa Yogananda. The chants are in English, have simple tunes, and are easy to follow. AnP

_____. **SONGS OF THE SOUL**, $5.95. Traditional songs in Hindi, Bengali, and Sanskrit, and modern songs in English are sung by Swami Kriyananda and members of the Ananda Cooperative Village, accompanied on sitar and tabla (drums). Kriyananda's voice is pleasant to listen to. AnP

MUKTANANDA, SWAMI. GURU GITA, $4.98. Baba Muktananda chants the *Guru Gita*, a Sanskrit prayer. Muktananda does not have the most melodious voice and listening to it takes intense concentration. Not a pretty or joyous sound. SYD

MUSIC OF THE MANTRIC WAVE: VOLUME II, $5.95. The Collective Star's first album. Sources and inspiration for the music include Sri Aurobindo, Sri Chinmoy, Pir Vilayat Khan, American Indians, and others. Rai

THE ONENESS SPACE, $5.95. Songs with a folk orientation, by a group of students of Ken Keyes called the Love Band. The inspiration for these songs, as reflected in the lyrics, is the **Handbook to Higher Consciousness**. Lyrics included. LLC

SAI BABA CHANTS THE BAJANS, $5.00. On a record recorded on a holy festival day in India, Sai Baba chants devotional songs (*bajans*) with 15,000 devotees. Included is a twenty minute address by Sai Baba. SAI

SUFI CHOIR. CRYING FOR JOY, $5.00. An album by the Sufi Choir including *Garden of Allah*, *Jesus Was A Shepherd*, *Krishna Song*, *Cryin' For Joy*, and *Twenty-fourth Psalm*. Not as well regarded as **The Sufi Choir** album. Lyrics included. Rai

_____. **THE SUFI CHOIR**, $4.95. One of our favorite albums. Students of Samuel Lewis and Pir Vilayat Khan sing and play modern arrangements of music based on a variety of sources. Some of the songs are *Bismillah*, from the Qur'an, *Shema*, a prayer of the Jewish tradition, *The Twenty-third Psalm*, and *Rumi Blues*, based on verses by the twelfth century mystic poet. Comments on the songs and lyrics are included. Rai

SUFI SONG AND DANCE, $5.95. A collection of songs and dances featuring the Sufi Choir and members of the San Francisco Sufi Community. A twenty-two page booklet containing the words, music, and dance instructions is included. Rai

SWAHA. $6.95. An album featuring Bhagavan Das, Amazing Grace, and others, doing a variety of spiritual and devotional music. Some of the music is improvisational, some is traditional. Selections were recorded in a studio and live. There is a mixture of traditional and modern instruments (even an electric sitar) and the mixture is reflected in the music. Brief notes about the songs and some photographs are included. Rai

TEMPLE MUSIC AND CHANTS, $5.00. Chants by Swami Rama and his students, accompanied by bells, drums, and sitar. An explanation of each chant is provided. In some cases it is possible to chant with the album, though some selections are complex and difficult to follow without printed words. Him

WINDS OF BIRTH, $5.95. Spiritual folk/rock by a group of musicians and singers from Findhorn led by David Spangler and called The New Troubadours. Very pleasant and melodious songs. Our most popular record of songs. Rai

YOGANANDA. CHANTS AND PRAYERS, $5.00. A recording of the voice of Paramahansa Yogananda singing devotional chants in English and Bengali. SRF

_____. **I WILL BE THINE ALWAYS**, $5.00. This album and the two following feature selections from Yogananda's book **Cosmic Chants**. On this album the chants are sung by a choir of nuns from the Self-Realization Order. SRR

_____. **IN THE LAND BEYOND MY DREAMS**, $5.00. Organ renditions of twelve of Yogananda's chants. SRF

_____. **WHEN THY SONG FLOWS THROUGH ME**, $5.00. Monks of the Self-Realization Order sing chants by Yogananda. SRF

INDIAN MUSIC

INDIAN INSTRUMENTS

dhol—a two-headed barrel drum struck with both light and heavy sticks.
dukra—a pair of drums.
kural—bamboo flute.
mashak—Indian bagpipes.
mridangam—barrel drum.
nagara—kettle drum.
rabab—see *sarod*.
santour—see Islamic Instruments.

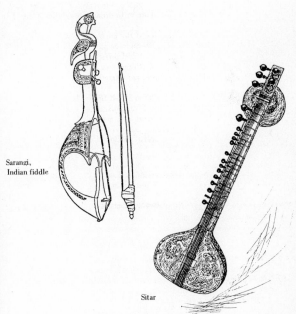

Sarangi, Indian fiddle

Sitar

sarangi—a lute with both melodic and sympathetic strings, played with a bow.
sarod—a short lute with four melodic and many sympathetic strings over a metal finger board.
saz-i-kashmir—stringed instrument similar to a lute.
sitar—a large stringed instrument, similar to a lute, with both melodic and sympathetic strings.
shahnai—double reed folk oboe.
tabi—finger cymbals.
tabla—small hand drum.
tambura—similar in shape to a *sitar*, with only four strings and used only as accompaniment for singers.
tumbaknari—drum.

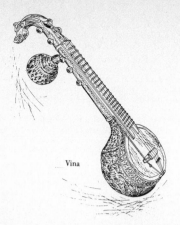

Vina

vina—a forerunner of the *sitar*, it does not have any sympathetic strings.

CLASSICAL MUSIC OF INDIA: INSTRUMENTAL, $7.65. Examples of Northern Indian instrumental music. Instruments used are the *shahnai, sarangi, tabla, sitar, sarod,* flute, and an Indian adaptation of the Western guitar. A good recording. Descriptive notes. Gra

DHYANAM/MEDITATION, $3.96. South Indian vocal music accompanied by violin, *tambura,* and *mridangam.* The performance is described as *elaborate improvisation.* The voice has a pinched nasal quality. Descriptive notes. WEA

FOUR VEDAS, $25.00. Subtitled *The Oral Tradition of Hymns, Chants, Sacrificial and Magical Formulas,* this two record set includes examples from various Vedic traditions still practiced in India. Featured on the first record are typical examples from some of the more isolated traditions, and rare pieces from the main traditions. The second record is devoted to the main portions of the Nambudiris of Kerala, a small, almost inaccessible tradition from Southwest India. Only three of the selections were recorded in a studio, and many were done on a small tape recorder—so the quality often leaves much to be desired. Very detailed and extensive descriptive notes. FkR

KALPANA IMPROVISATIONS, $3.96. Four selections, three of which are instrumental, while the fourth is an Indian Kathak dance. The dancer, telling a story through mime, chants a rhythm in nonsense syllables, then stamps the same rhythm with ankle bells. Instruments used on the record are the *sarod* and *tabla.* The album is pleasant to listen to, the rhythms draw you into the music, and the *sarod* has a light flowing sound to it. WEA

KASHMIR, $3.96. Subtitled *Traditional Songs and Dances,* this is a good introduction to the music of this province. Most of the music is vocal with no solos except in the religious music. A favorite musical form is the *chakki* in which the lead singer sings a verse that is then picked up by the group. The songs have strong rhythms and at times are very melodic. All songs are accompanied by a variety of instruments including the *santour, saz-i-kashmir, sitar, shahnai, sarangi, rabab,* and various percussion instruments. WEA

KHAN, USTAD ALI AKBAR. RAGA: MIYAN KI TODI, RAGA: ZILLA-KAFI, $7.65. An album containing improvisations on two classical Indian *ragas* (melodic patterns) by India's leading master of the *sarod.* Other instruments include *tabla,* and *tambura.* Very brief descriptive notes. Gra

MUSIC FROM THE SHRINES OF AJMER AND MUNDRA, $5.95. Selections of the type of music played in courtyards and public areas. Because this music is meant to be played indoors it is supposed to have less of the subtlety and gradual development typical of Indian music, though to our Western ears it still sounds complex. Percussion instruments and, the *mashak* are prominent. Other instruments include the *nagara, tabla,* and *shahnai.* Lyr

PALLAVI—SOUTH INDIAN FLUTE MUSIC, $3.96. This album features the *kural* accompanied by violin, *mridangam,* and *tambura.* The music has the complex melodies and rhythms typical of Indian music. A pleasant listening experience, especially for those who enjoy the flute. WEA

RELIGIOUS MUSIC OF INDIA, $8.95. A sampling of music and chants from different areas and periods. A record for the serious student, the descriptive notes have very technical musical discussions of each piece, translations and transliterations of the songs, and a brief description of their place in Indian religious life. A musical score for each song is included. FkR

SARANGI, THE VOICE OF A HUNDRED COLORS, $3.96. Three instrumental pieces, from the Northern Indian Hindusthani tradition made familiar to Western audiences by Ravi Shankar. Instruments used in addition to the *surangi* are the *tabla* and *tambura.* The album has a subdued mellow sound and is very pleasant background music. WEA

SHANKAR, RAVI. RAVI SHANKAR, $7.60. Three *ragas* interpreted by one of India's most famous *sitar* players. *Tabla* accompaniment. Descriptive notes. Gra

THE SOUNDS OF YOGA-VEDANTA. $6.98. Subtitled *A Documentary of Life in an Indian Ashram,* this recording tries to convey to the listener the sounds of a typical day at the Sivananda Ashram. Included on the first side are portions of temple services, yoga classes, and lectures by Swami Sivananda. Side Two is selections from the evening *satsang.* There is little solid information about life in the ashram; rather the album attempts to convey the feelings and impressions generated there. This album is more for the serious

student than the casual listener. FkR

UNESCO COLLECTION: MUSICAL ATLAS OF BENGAL, $7.65. Traditional folk music sung and played on drums, flutes, cymbals, and lutes. The songs have a close relationship to traditional Indian music, with its quick complex rhythms and high nasal sound of the voices. Descriptive notes. Quality of the recording on all the UNESCO albums is excellent, and we recommend them highly. PPI

UNESCO COLLECTION: MUSICAL ATLAS OF INDIA, $7.65. Traditional songs played on the *shahnai* and flute. PPI

UNESCO COLLECTION: MUSICAL SOURCES OF INDIA, $7.65/each. Three albums of North Indian music are available: **Vocal Music, Instrumental Music—Sitar, Flute, Sarangi,** and **Instrumental Music—Vina, Vichitra Vina, Sarod, Shahnai.** In **Vocal Music** each side is devoted to the development of a single traditional style of singing in which the voice is often used as an instrument, sometimes wailing mournfully, sometimes clucking or making unusual noises. The songs are accompanied by traditional instruments. The two instrumental albums each feature the instruments listed in their titles, as well as the *tabla* and *tambura.* Though the rhythms and melodies are strange to Western ears, the music is pleasant and graceful. All three albums have descriptive notes. PPI

YOGA MUSIC OF INDIA, $6.98. A collection of devotional chants, in the Vedantic tradition, accompanied by drums and *vina.* Transliteration of the chants and their general meaning are provided so that the listener may chant with the recording. Due to the complexity of the chants and the quality of the recording, chanting with the album would seem to be very difficult. FkR

ISLAMIC MUSIC

ISLAMIC INSTRUMENTS

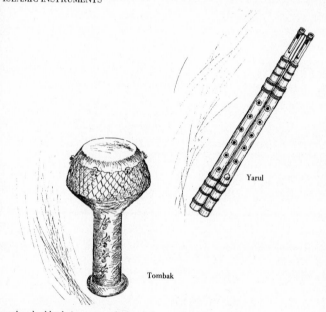

Yarul

Tombak

argul—a double clarinet; two cylindrical pipes, each with a single reed.
busoq—a long-necked lute with six strings grouped into three pairs.
dombach—a goblet-shaped wooden hand drum, also called a *zarb.*
gasba—bamboo flute.
ghaita—a short double-reed oboe.
kamadja—a four string version of the violin played upright on the knee—also known as the *kamanchen.*
lira—recorder.
nai—a bamboo flute about two feet long, one of the oldest Arab instruments.

Oud

oud—lute.

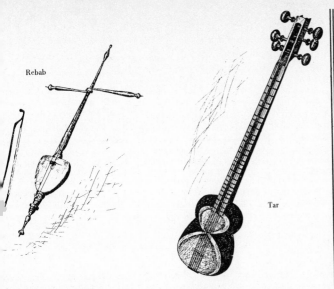

Rebab

Tar

rebab—a two string violin.

santour—a dulcimer with seventy-two strings played with light wooden mallets.

tabl—a general term for drums, both cylindrical and kettle-shaped.

tabla—wooden marching drum.

tar—a six string lute with a long neck.

zarb—see *dombach*.

ARAB MUSIC, $5.95/each. These two volumes feature Egyptian folk music. Vocal selections, all on Side One of Volume I, are lively songs sung by women and accompanied by such instruments as the *oud, rebab, argul* and *tabl*. The instrumentals, which comprise the rest of the albums, are performed on the *oud, nai,* and *tabl*. The pieces are melodic and make for pleasant listening. Lyr

ISLAMIC LITURGY, $6.98. Subtitled *Song and Dance at a Meeting of Dervishes,* and including verses from the Qur'an, prayers, and praise to Muhammad. There are no instruments and the songs often sound like prayer chants. Descriptive notes give translations and transliterations of songs and a brief description of the accompanying dances and movements. This album is only for the person seriously interested in Sufi ceremonies. FkR

MOROCCAN SUFI MUSIC, $5.95. Sufis have traditionally relied on music to attain a state of religious ecstasy. This is a selection of the music of several Sufi orders and is a good introduction to traditional Sufi music. Instruments include the *ghaita, tabla, gasba,* and *lira*. Lyr

MUSIC OF IRAN, $5.95/each. These three albums cover the twelve *dastgahs* of the Persian musical system. As with most Persian music, short poems are sometimes sung with the pieces. This is a scholarly series by Iran's foremost *santour* player. Lyr

THE OUD, $5.95. This is a very beautiful album, entirely instrumental with solos and pieces played with a small ensemble (clarinet, flute, bass, and percussion). The selections come from several Middle Eastern countries. Lyr

A PERSIAN HERITAGE—CLASSICAL MUSIC OF IRAN, $3.96. *Partly composed, partly improvised, the classical music of Persia is preponderantly instrumental. . . . The words of both composed and improvised singing are usually taken from the classics of Persian literature and from the poetry of Sufism. . . . The improvisations, which form the central portions of performances, are based on a model—the radif—which a student must memorize painstakingly before he may improvise upon it in his own personal style. Most of the radif has no meter and follows a speech-like rhythm, but it also contains metrical pieces which normally have a drum accompaniment. There are twelve modes or dastgahs (similar to the Indian raga) which form the basis for the radif.* This album features a combination of composed and improvised music, primarily instrumental, performed on four classical Persian instruments: *santour, tar, kamanchen,* and *zarb*. WEA

PERSIAN LOVE SONGS AND MYSTIC CHANTS, $5.95. A woman, Shusha, sings sixteen Persian songs both a capella and with flute and fingerdrum accompaniment. She has a rich voice and the songs range from lively to melancholy. English translations of the songs are provided. Lyr

THE PERSIAN SANTUR—MUSIC OF IRAN, $3.96. Four pieces—three include the singing of Persian poetry, the fourth is instrumental. Accompanying the *santour* are a violin and a *dombach*. WEA

SUFI CEREMONY: RIFA' CEREMONY, $6.98. Recording of an actual celebration of the Rifa'iyya Sufi order in South Africa. Participants in the ritual celebration achieve a trance state which makes them oblivious to pain and able to perform remarkable feats. The album is unclear, as if recorded from a distance. Descriptive notes. FkR

THE TAR, $5.95/each. Classical and contemporary pieces with occasional accompaniment by the *dombach* and *zarb*. Volume I is instrumental, Volume II includes several vocal pieces derived from the Sufi tradition. The music and chants have a gentle melancholy feeling. Lyr

UNESCO COLLECTION: ARABIAN MUSICAL SOURCES—ARABIAN MUSIC: MAQAM, $7.65. Examples of improvisational music built around the *maqam*—a tonal structure with a musical role similar to the Persian *dastgah* or Indian *raga*. The album has both vocal and instrumental selections, with each piece featuring a single instrument. Instruments used are the *nai, busoq, kamadja,* and *rebab*. This album, like all the albums in the **UNESCO Collection of Musical Sources**, is of excellent quality. PPI

UNESCO COLLECTION: ISLAMIC MUSICAL SOURCES—ISLAMIC RITUAL FROM YUGOSLAVIA, $7.65. Selections from an Islamic ceremony as celebrated by a Yugoslavian dervish brotherhood. Group chanting accompanied by various percussion instruments is the basis of the service. Descriptive notes. PPI

MEDITATION AND YOGA

CHRISTENING FOR LISTENING, $5.95. Meditation music played on various electronic instruments. Mild and unobtrusive. Rai

HITTLEMAN, RICHARD. YOGA FOR LIFE, FIRST AND SECOND ALBUM, $8.75/each. A somewhat commercial presentation of a yoga program developed by Richard Hittleman, one of the best known popularizers of yoga in the U.S. today. He has a long running television series on yoga and has written many books (see the Yoga section). Each album is a two record set. The first set includes a short introduction, suggestions on how best to work with the albums, and the beginning postures. The second set consists of instructions in more advanced postures. The instructions are clear and easy to follow. A book of photographs illustrating the postures is included with each album. YFH

_____. **YOGA MEDITATION**, $5.95. A short introduction to meditation followed by seven simple meditations. These include meditation with the breath, the ear, the voice, and deep relaxation. YFH

HUXLEY, LAURA. RECIPES FOR LIVING AND LOVING, $7.60. Laura Huxley (see the Consciousness Expansion section) guides the listener through two meditation experiences. Side One is entitled *Your Favorite Flower*; Side Two is called *Rainbow Walk*. Ash

KRIYANANDA, SWAMI. MEDITATIONS, $5.95. The listener is guided through two fifteen to twenty minute meditations. The instructions are clear and the music played on *sitar* and *tambura* is very conducive to relaxation and meditation. AnP

_____. **YOGA FOR SELF AWARENESS**, $9.95. A two record set. After a short introduction, a series of breathing exercises is presented. Yoga postures follow and take up the bulk of the albums. A short meditation is next. The last side of the records consists of meditational chants. The instructions are easily followed by the listener and the background music is gentle and soothing. AnP

MAY THE LOVE, THE LIGHT, THE POWER, $5.00. A beautiful album of harp music by Joel Andrews. A mellow accompaniment for meditation. Grp

MEDITATION, $4.00. An album by Eknath Easwaran, founder of the Blue Mountain Center of Meditation in Berkeley. Side One, entitled *The Three Stages of Meditation,* discusses what takes place during meditation. Side Two provides instructions in meditation. Easwaran quotes from the Sufi Rumi, the seventeenth century mystic Thomas Traherwe, Jesus, and retells various Hindu tales. BMC

RADHA, SWAMI SIVANANDA. MANTRAS, $7.65. *Songs of Yoga,* sung and played on the harmonium by Swami Sivananda Radha, a female disciple of Swami Sivananda. The *mantras* have simple melodies and appear easy to learn. A pamphlet is included that gives the meaning and the background of each *mantra*. Ash

_____. **RELAXATION**, $7.65. A course in relaxation based upon the yogic posture called *savasan* or posture of the corpse. *The purpose of this record is to give you the basic principles of the technique so that once you have mastered them, you will be able to practice it on your own. . . . [This technique] tries to stimulate you to: physically relax your body, mentally rest your mind and surrender, spiritually expand your consciousness.* Side One stresses healing; Side Two stresses creativity. Ash

SZEKELY, EDMOND BORDEAUX. JOURNEY THROUGH A THOUSAND MEDITATIONS, $11.20. A two record set that includes music inspired by a wide variety of religions and ages of man. The music is primarily electronic. A five page meditation that parallels the albums is included. Aca

SPOKEN RECORDINGS

BHAGAVAD GITA, $3.00. Eknath Easwaran reads the Sanskrit text and his own English translation. A commentary is also included. BMC

THE BHAGAVADA-GITA, $6.98. Readings of the **Gita** in English by Swami Nikhilananda and in Sanskrit by Dr. T.M.P. Mahadevan. Readings from the **Ramayana** and **Brahma's Hymns** in Sanskrit by Dr. S.R. Ranganathan are also included. Descriptive notes have both English and Sanskrit texts. FkR

BHAGAVAD GITA: THE SONG OF GOD, $6.98. A reading by Zia Mohyeddin of the translation by Christopher Isherwood and Swami Prabhavananda. Christopher Isherwood also reads his own introduction. Cae

IS MEDITATION ON GOD COMPATIBLE WITH MODERN LIFE? $7.95. A two record set features Sri Daya Mata, president of the Self-Realization Fellowship, speaking informally on the life and teachings of Paramahamsa Yogananda. SRF

JOHN, BUBBA FREE. **THE GORILLA SERMON**, $5.98. Subtitled, . . . *and Other Talks by Bubba Free John on the Radical Nature of Spiritual Life*, this two record set includes *. . . discourses on various aspects of the spiritual process, from such topics as the Master-disciple relationship, to mystical experience, and death.* (See the listings for Franklin Jones in the Indian Philosophy section.) DHP

KRISHNAMURTI, J. **THE LIGHT IN ONESELF**, $5.95. A talk given at Congress Centrum, Amsterdam, May 1968. (See the Krishnamurti section.) Kri

_____. **MIND IN MEDITATION**, $5.95. A talk given at Bangalore, India, January 1968. Kri

_____. **THOUGHT BREEDS FEAR**, $5.95. A talk given at Wimbledon Town Hall, London, March 1969. Kri

LITTLE FLOWERS OF SAINT FRANCIS, $6.95. *The selections on this album span the career of the Saint from his conversion of Bernard, who became the first of his friars, to his death. Included are the famous sermon to the birds, his conversion of the wolf . . . his stigmatization . . . and two selections from the life of Friar Juniper.* A good recording, read well. (See the Saint Francis subsection of Christianity.) Cae

MODERN CHINESE: A BASIC COURSE, $12.50. A three record set with a 249 page manual prepared by the faculty of Peking University. Thirty lessons in modern Chinese adapted especially for Americans. Includes instructions for writing characters. Dov

THE PERSIAN EPIC, $6.98. This is a Persian recitation of the epic poem **Shah Nameh** (The Book of Kings) by Abol Mansur Fedovci (see the Ancient Near East section for a description of the epic). Liner notes include the Persian text, and a selected English translation and commentary. FkR

POEMS OF SAINT JOHN OF THE CROSS, $6.98. Thirteen poems read very effectively, in English. Detailed descriptive notes include comments on the poems and the poems themselves in both Spanish and English. FkR

THE POETRY OF WILLIAM BLAKE, $6.98. *Here on this record, we can but hint at the vast expanses over which the extraordinary spirit of William Blake ranged. We have tried to represent as much of his various poetic writings, from the first* **Poetical Sketches**, *which appeared in 1738, the* **Songs of Innocence**, *from 1789, and the contrasting* **Songs of Experience**, *1794; and on the second side, the later books.* A high quality recording read by four people. Short descriptive notes. SpA

THE PSYCHEDELIC EXPERIENCE, $6.98. Readings from Timothy Leary's and Ralph Metzner's book, **The Psychedelic Experience: A Manual Based on the Tibetan Book of the Dead** (see the description in the Consciousness Expansion section). The passages were selected to serve as a guide during the *Going Out* (Side One) and the *Coming Back* (Side Two) phases of a psychedelic session. Detailed descriptive notes focus on the use of the **Tibetan Book of the Dead** and other sacred books as guides to altered states of consciousness. FkR

RAJNEESH, BHAGWAN. **BHAGWAN RAJNEESH**, $6.99. Side One consists of excerpts from a question and answer session. Side Two is entirely meditation music, played on electronic instruments. It is slow and flows smoothly. RaF

RAM DASS. **HERE WE ALL ARE**, $7.65. *These records, originally recorded on tape at a gathering at the University of British Columbia, concern a series of experiences which led me from the role of a Harvard University professor and psychologist (Richard Alpert) through my work in psychedelics and association with Timothy Leary and then on to India where I met my guru and became Ram Dass. The lecture, in addition to the more anecdotal history, included reflections on the system of yoga . . . I was being initiated into, as well as a consideration of this yoga for us in the West.* Three record set recorded in the summer of 1969. RRP

THE RUBAIYAT OF OMAR KHAYYAM, $6.98. This unique record presents two translations of **The Rubaiyat**. The first is a traditional translation, done in 1859 by Edward Fitzgerald. It follows the original structure of the poem, four-line stanzas with three rhyming and one unrhyming line. The second translation is by Robert Graves. His version (which he reads on the album) was prepared in blank verse in an effort to remain truer to the Persian. In addition to changes in structure, the content of the two translations is substantially different. According to the album jacket, much controversy has surrounded the newer Graves translation. SpA

SATCHIDANANDA, SWAMI. **SWAMI SATCHIDANANDA**, $5.00. A two record set. Three sides consist of Swami Satchidananda speaking on a variety of subjects including integral yoga, loving and giving, detachment, and what a guru is. A fourth side is devoted to chants. Rai

TIBETAN MUSIC

TIBETAN INSTRUMENTS

dabs—large shallow drum.
daman—kettle drum.
damaru—a small hourglass-shaped drum played by rapidly twisting it so that the ends of a knotted cord tied to its middle strike the heads.
damyan—a long-necked fretless lute.
dung-chen—a large trumpet, from five to twelve feet long.
dung-kar—conch shell trumpet.
gyaling—shawm.

kang-dung—short trumpet.
nga-bom—large double membrane frame drum, usually perched on a handle.
nga-chung—smaller version of the *nga-bom*.
radong—large horn, up to six feet long.
rolmo—hand cymbals.

CHO-GA, TANTRIC MUSIC OF TIBET, $5.95. An anthology of Buddhist chants and ritual music. Three chants are heard in their entirety, the rest are excerpts. Several short instrumental pieces are included, and the chants are occasionally accompanied by drums and bells. Most of the chants are interesting and make for easy listening. Instruments include the *dung-chen, gyaling, rolmo, nga-bom,* and *damaru.* The quality of the recording is good. Short descriptive notes. Lng

FESTIVALS OF THE HIMALAYAS, $3.96. Examples of the local festival music from the area between Kasmir and Tibet. The chanting is more melodic than the chanting of Tibet and Kasmir though the influence of these areas is clear. Instruments used are oboes, flutes, *gyaling*, drums, and cymbals. Descriptive notes. WEA

PADMASAMBAVA CHOPA, $5.95. This is an edited version of the four hour *chopa* (ritual) held in the Himalayan regions of Tibet. The purpose of the ritual is to dispel undesirable states of being. Chanting and instrumental sections alternate throughout the ceremony. The tone of the entire ritual is dark and melancholy and it is understandable that this ritual has often been associated with the black magic aspects of this region. Drums, bells, and horn instruments (*dung-chen* and *dung-kar*) are used. Descriptive notes. Lyr

SONGS AND DANCES OF NEPAL, $8.95. Twenty-two popular and traditional folk songs recorded during an American Himalayan expedition. The songs are sung unaccompanied or with drums, bells, and *damyan.* They are often tuneless and sound like prayer chants. The recordings were done on location in tents, homes, and in the open fields. FkR

SONGS AND MUSIC OF TIBET, $8.95. A selection of songs, instrumentals, and chants. The chants are a deep monotone. The vocal selections, many with bells and drums, often sound similar to the music associated with the American Plains Indians. Other selections have an Oriental quality. Instruments include flute, *gyaling* and *dung-kar.* FkR

THE SONGS OF MILAREPA, $5.95. These religious songs (five of the **100,000 Songs of Milarepa**) sound more like chants, occasionally accompanied by various percussion instruments. The voices are often hard to understand, due to the poor quality of the recording. Short descriptive notes. Lyr

TIBETAN BUDDHISM: TANTRAS OF GYUTO MAHAKALA, $3.96. Excerpts from a tantric rite of the Gelug tradition, one of the four main traditions of Tibetan Buddhism. This particular rite is the *mahakala (Great Black Lord of Transcending Awareness) sadhana.* The rite consists primarily of chanting accompanied by cymbals and drums with an occasional instrumental interlude featuring a pair of *radong.* The chanting is slow, sustained gutteral tones, with cymbals and drums seemingly used at random. Descriptive notes. WEA

TIBETAN BUDDHIST RITES—VOLUMES ONE, TWO, AND THREE, $5.95/each. These three recordings provide a wide variety of examples of Tibetan religious and folk music. The selections are usually short, with an average of fifteen per album, and include instrumentals, songs, and chants from various rituals, dances, and processionals. Most of the music sounds very unusual, with slow deep monotone, and loud, quick, rhythmless interludes that startle the listener. Instruments include the *gyaling, dung-kar, kang-dung, dung-chen, nga-bom, nga-chung, rolmo,* and *damaru.* The descriptive notes are non-technical and interesting. Lyr

TIBETAN FOLK AND MINSTREL MUSIC, $5.95. The first side of this album is devoted to occupational songs of nomads and peasants from many areas of Tibet. The songs are sung in a high tense quasi-falsetto tone, often accompanied by a flute or recorder. The second side consists of pieces played by village bands. The instruments included are the *gyaling, glingbu, damyan,* and *dabs,* with an occasional vocal performance. There are twenty-six selections on the album, most quite short. General descriptive notes. Lyr

TIBETAN MYSTIC SONG, $5.95. Examples of songs, developed by wandering mystics, which combine Indian religious doctrine and the folk imagery and traditions of Tibet. The songs are sung unaccompanied and sound like liturgical chants. Descriptive notes, including translations of the songs. Lyr

TIBETAN RITUAL MUSIC, $5.95. Religious music of Tibet involves both chanting and instrumental playing. *The chanting, executed with exceedingly deep and constricted voice, embraces the repetition of canonical texts and the invocation of the gods. The instrumental music provides interludes between the chanted portions of the service.* The chanting is usually gutteral, and sometimes sounds like Gregorian chant. The music is seemingly without melody or rhythm. This album has five selections and the instruments include the *gyaling, dung-kar, kang-dung, dung-chen,* and various percussion instruments. Lyr

TIBETAN SONGS OF THE GODS AND DEMONS: RITUAL AND THEATRICAL MUSIC OF TIBET, $5.95. A collection of ritual and theatrical music that includes chants that are more like liturgical prayers than the deep gutteral sounds associated with Tibet, and songs that have an Oriental feeling about them. Instruments include the *gyaling, dung-kar,* and various percussion instruments. Detailed descriptive notes. Lyr

UNESCO COLLECTION: MUSICAL SOURCES OF TIBET—TIBETAN RITUAL, $7.65. A complete Tibetan ritual that includes all the characteristics of Tibetan religious services: disembodied gutteral chanting, group chanting, sudden loud discordant noises, bells, gongs, and drums. The quality of the recording is excellent. Descriptive notes. PPI

WILHELM REICH

[R]eich was a giant of our time, a scholar and scientist of formidable intellect; [bu]t Reich was also an individual of boundless humanity. He is best known [for] his major works on the function of the orgasm, the psychology of the [m]asses, and the sexual revolution, of which he is considered by many to be [th]e father. Reich's unpopular political leanings, his break with Freud, his or[ga]sm theory, his cancer research, and his discovery of orgone energy involved [hi]m in controversy for most of his professional life. Bioenergetics (see Lowen [an]d Keleman in the Humanistic Psychology section) is one practical applica[ti]on today of work pioneered by Reich.

[Ti]me will doubtless show, however, that his most significant discoveries were [in] connection with orgone, or life energy. The story of these discoveries is [fa]scinating indeed, and a great deal of research today—mostly on the outer [fri]nges of orthodoxy—is building on the base he laid. When Reich attempted [to] use his orgone accumulators to treat cancer, he was pounced upon by the [F]DA. In 1956 he was tried in court and sentenced to two years in jail, and [w]hile there he died. In a shameful episode, reminiscent of Hitler or the Inqui[si]tion, his equipment was destroyed and most of his publications were burned [b]y the U.S. government.

[B]AKER, ELSWORTH. **MAN IN THE TRAP**, $1.95. Baker, a specialist in medical orgo[no]my who has practiced for twenty years (eleven of which were spent in close associa[ti]on with Reich) presents a fascinating, in-depth examination of the Reichan theory of [c]haracter. Dr. Baker describes varying character types in terms of specific blockings of [s]exual energy at different stages of emotional development. Drawing upon many illumin[at]ing case studies, he carefully details methods of treating these various blocks and pre[v]enting neurotic development. Notes, index. 384pp. Avo 67

[B]OADELLA, DAVID. **WILHELM REICH—THE EVOLUTION OF HIS WORK**, $3.95. [B]ased on a thorough examination of all the primary sources, including hitherto untrans[la]ted German writings and articles that have appeared only in relatively inaccessible jour[n]als, Boadella surveys the development of Reich's thought from his early psychoanalytic [w]ritings, which established him as a major revolutionary thinker, to his later innovative [an]d controversial theories. Supplementing the main text are articles by a number of Reich's [c]lose associates. Boadella is the editor of the Reichan journal **Energy and Character: The [J]ournal of Bio-energetic Research**. Notes, bibliography, index. 400pp. Reg 73

[C]HESSER, EUSTACE. **SALVATION THROUGH SEX**, $1.95. A good critical but friendly [r]esume of Reich's life and work by an English psychiatrist. Relates Reich's ideas to more [r]ecent research and social development but includes little on the orgone period. It has [b]een described accurately as a *layman's guide to Reich that defines, in clear and non-tech[n]ical terms, the essence and meaning of his thought*. Bibliography, 172pp. Pop 72

[E]DEN, JEROME. **ORGONE ENERGY**, c$6.00. In his famous *Oranur Experiment*, Reich [f]ound that the interaction of atomic energy and orgone energy as antithetical forces pro[d]uced and contaminated a deadly form of orgone energy called oranur or DOR. Eden be[li]eves that our atmosphere is becoming increasingly contaminated with oranur and, if [a]llowed to proliferate, this will constitute the most serious threat to planetary life. 156pp. [E]xP 72

[G]REENFIELD, JEROME. **WILHELM REICH VS. U.S.A.**, c$10.00. A detailed explora[ti]on of Reich's trial and time in jail as well as a summary of the U.S. government's case [a]gainst him. Nor 74

[M]ANN, W. EDWARD. **ORGONE, REICH AND EROS**, $3.95. A fascinating study in [w]hich Mann describes Reich's theory of orgone energy and its applications and shows [h]ow they relate to current energy theories as well as to the Hindu-yogic concepts of prana [a]nd the vital force theory behind acupuncture. Mann discusses the whole range of exper[i]mentation in the area of biological rhythms, the effects of weather on health and beha-

vior, psychic healing, and the results of his own work with orgone energy accumulators as healing devices. This work offers a rich exploration of the frontiers of the scientific and spiritual imagination. Often it's difficult reading; however, we recommend it highly to all seriously interested in the subject. Excellent bibliography, 382pp. SrS 73

RAKNES, OLA. **WILHELM REICH AND ORGONOMY**, $1.45. Raknes was a close collaborator of Reich's until his death. This is an autoritative introduction to orgonomy—the science of life energy. Discusses the liberation of sexual energy, the nature of the orgasm, and the bearing of life energy on religion, education, medicine and psychology. Presents a good inside look at the later orgone experiments. 183pp. Pen 70

REICH, PETER. **THE BOOK OF DREAMS**, $1.50. This book, by Reich's son, moves in a series of images, like a movie, between past and present, dream and reality. As the images interweave, layer after layer of defenses and fears and uncertainties are stripped away until Peter is finally able to see both himself and his father with clear eyes and an open heart. 191pp. Faw 73

REICH, WILHELM. **THE CANCER BIOPATHY**, $4.95. In his controversial theories, reprinted here for the first time, Reich defines cancer not as a tumor—the tumor is merely a late manifestation of the disease—but as a systemic disease due to chronic thwarting of natural sexual functioning. The material here was originally published as Vol. II of **The Discovery of the Orgone**, Vol. I being **The Function of the Orgasm**. Illustrations, photographs, index. 458pp. FSG 73

_____. **CHARACTER ANALYSIS**, $4.95. First published in 1933, this has been the most influential of Reich's works in analytic circles. It is concerned with the way in which character responses are embedded in the body—the body armor which represents feelings. S&S 45

_____. **EARLY WRITINGS, VOL. I**, $4.95. Included here are an important early work, *The Impulsive Character*, and a number of his other papers, all of which are an integral part of the development that led to the discovery of orgone energy. Notes, introduction. 341pp. FSG 75

_____. **ETHER, GOD AND DEVIL—COSMIC SUPERIMPOSITION**, $3.45. In the first of these books printed together, Reich describes the process of functional thinking and reveals how the inner logic of this objective thought technique led him to the discovery of cosmic orgone energy. In **Cosmic Superimposition** he shows how man is rooted in nature. The superimposition of two orgone-energy systems which is demonstrable in the genital embrace is revealed as a common functioning principle that exists in all of nature. Illustrated, 308pp. FSG 49

_____. **THE FUNCTION OF THE ORGASM**, $3.95/$1.95. Possibly Reich's most important work, this is an intellectual autobiography of sorts, summarizing his medical and scientific work over a period of twenty years. Illustrated, 400pp. S&S 73

_____. **THE IMPULSIVE CHARACTER AND OTHER WRITINGS**, $3.95. A selection of the full texts of some of Reich's early writings. The following works are included: *The Impulsive Character*, *Biophysical Papers*, *The Basic Antithesis of Vegetative Life Functions*, *The Orgasm as an Electrophysical Discharge*, and *Experimental Investigation of the Electrical Function of Sexuality and Anxiety*. The selections are a bit less analytical than those in the other work on Reich's early writings. 211pp. NAL 74

_____. **INVASION OF COMPULSORY SEX-MORALITY**, $3.45. Growing out of his involvement with the question of the origin of sexual suppression, this attempt to explain historically the problem of sexual disturbances draws upon the ethnological works of Morgan, Engels and, in particular, Malinowski, whose studies of the Trobriand Islanders confirmed Reich's clinical discoveries. 215pp. FSG 71

_____. **LISTEN LITTLE MAN**, $2.95. Tells of the inner storms and conflicts of Reich, who watched over decades, first naively, then with amazement, and finally with horror, what the *Little Man* does to himself—how he suffers and rebels, how he esteems his enemies and murders his friends; how, whenever he gains power as a representative of the people, he misuses it. More apt today than when it was written in 1945. Illustrated by William Steig. 126pp. FSG 74

_____. **THE MASS PSYCHOLOGY OF FASCISM**, $3.95. Views fascism as the expression of the irrational character structure of the average human being whose primary biological needs and impulses have been suppressed for thousands of years. The social function of this suppression and the crucial role played in it by the authoritarian family and the church are carefully analyzed. 423pp. S&S 70

_____. **THE MURDER OF CHRIST**, $2.75. Explores the meaning of Christ's life and reveals the universal scourge that caused his death—the *emotional plague of mankind*. Here is the blunt truth about people's ways of being, acting, and emotional reacting—by which they murder the living in whatever form it may appear. 228pp. FSG 53

_____. **REICH SPEAKS OF FREUD**, $4.95. Discusses the personally tragic but scientifically vital implication of his relationship with Freud. Based on a tape-recorded interview conducted by a representative of the Freud Archives. Illustrations, 290pp. FSG 67

_____. **SELECTED WRITINGS: AN INTRODUCTION TO ORGONOMY**, $4.95. This anthology is not intended to replace any of Reich's works, but rather to serve as an introduction to them. Includes the *Oranur Experiment* and *Cosmic Orgone Engineering*.

Bibliography, 560pp. FSG 51

_____. THE SEXUAL REVOLUTION, $2.95/$1.95. Reich here criticizes prevailing sexual conditions and demonstrates by way of individual examples the conflicts of marriage, the revolution in family life, and the problems of infantile and adolescent sexuality. Includes a detailed study of the sexual revolution that occurred briefly in Russia after its revolution. 273pp. S&S 62

RYCROFT, CHARLES. WILHELM REICH, $1.65. A critical analysis of Reich's wo... excluding his later orgone work, which describes his life as *tormented, persecuted, a... futile.* 115pp. Vik 69

WYCKOFF, JAMES. WILHELM REICH: LIFE FORCE EXPLORER, $.95. This is ... and away the finest short biographical study of Reich available. Wyckoff understan... Reich's theories and he is sympathetic. Bibliography, 144pp. Faw 73

REINCARNATION AND KARMA

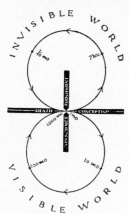

ABHEDANANDA, SWAMI. DOCTRINE OF KARMA—A STUDY IN ITS PHILOSOPHY AND PRACTICE, c$2.50. Discusses the law of causation and how individuals can transcend it through yoga. A clear work by a noted philosopher-monk of the Ramakrishna order. 137pp. RVM 44

_____. REINCARNATION, c$2.00. Lucid, illuminating discussions on reincarnation, transmigration, evolution, and the law of karma. 99pp. RVM 00

ATKINSON, WILLIAM. REINCARNATION AND THE LAW OF KARMA, c$5.50. Begins with a philosophical discussion of the concept of reincarnation and then traces the concept through all the great civilizations—explaining the reincarnational beliefs of each one. Other topics include *Between and Beyond Incarnations, The Justice of Reincarnation, The Argument for Reincarnation, The Proofs of Reincarnation, The Arguments Against Reincarnation,* and *The Law of Karma.* Later in his life Atkinson was known as Yogi Ramacharaka. An excellent work. 249pp. YPS 08

AUROBINDO, SRI. THE PROBLEM OF REBIRTH, c$3.50. A very complete philosophical treatment of reincarnation and karma by one of the greatest philosophers of twentieth century India. 189pp. SAA 52

BANERJEE, H.N. and WILL OURSLER. LIVES UNLIMITED, c$5.95. Consists mainly of narratives based on case histories gathered by Professor Banerjee of the Parapsychology Department, University of Rajhesthan in Jaipur India. He spent over fifteen years collecting them all over the world. The stories are used to demonstrate that people do remember previous lives and to illustrate the different approaches to reincarnation taken by Buddhists, Hindus, Tibetans and Western believers as well as the varieties and categories of reincarnation and the future possibilities of scientific study. Glossary and notes. Dou 74

BENNETT, COLIN. PRACTICAL TIME TRAVEL, $1.00. Clear, practical instructions for various methods of travelling back to past lives. Also contains related material of a more philosophical nature which makes interesting reading. 64pp. Wei 71

BERNSTEIN, MOREY. THE SEARCH FOR BRIDEY MURPHY, $1.75. This is the true story of a Colorado housewife's recollections under hypnosis of a previous existence in eighteenth century Ireland. When the case first became known almost twenty years ago it was an instant sensation and it remains the best documented case of its type to this date. 352pp. Avo 56

BESANT, ANNIE. DEATH AND AFTER, $1.95. A short exegesis on the state of man's being and his abodes after physical death. A person's desires, character and stage in evolution will determine the nature of his after death experiences as he absorbs the essence of his earthly experience in preparation for rebirth. 100pp. TPH 1893

_____. KARMA, c$1.50. Karma is the law of cause and effect that makes each one of us responsible for our thoughts, words and actions and determines that we always *reap what we sow.* Here is a scientific explanation of that law in the light of its ability to liberate humanity from suffering when properly appreciated and realistically applied. 83pp. TPH 1895

_____. REINCARNATION, c$1.75. Is the ancient tradition regarding the progressive birth of the human soul in numerous physical bodies an actual fact or just a fantasy? This small manual is designed to furnish the public with a simple explanation of the theosophical teachings. 95pp. TPH 1892

_____. A STUDY IN KARMA, c$1.50. 75pp. TPH 12

BRENNAN, J.H. FIVE KEYS TO PAST LIVES, $1.00. Practical, clearly presented tec... niques. 63pp. Wei 71

CERMINARA, GINA. MANY LIVES, MANY LOVES, $1.50. An exploration of develo... ments in the field of reincarnation and parapsychology. 170pp. NAL 63

_____. MANY MANSIONS, $1.50. Cases and interpretative material taken fro... Edgar Cayce's readings. One of the most popular books on reincarnation. 240pp. NAL ...

_____. THE WORLD WITHIN, $1.25. Deals with the implications of reincarr... tion, stressing the hope and promise it holds out to man. NAL 57

CHALLONER, H.K. THE WHEEL OF REBIRTH, $3.50. This is perhaps the most fas... nating of all the works on this subject, for it is a vivid portrayal of a whole series of inc... nated lives by the one who lived them. The author projected her consciousness, with gu... ance, into the past to recall these experiences. The thread of events controlled by the la... of cause and effect is made clearly visible, and the story itself makes for enjoyable readir... 285pp. TPH 69

COLLIN, RODNEY. THE THEORY OF ETERNAL LIFE, c$5.95. See the Gurdjie... section.

COOKE, GRACE. THE ILLUMINED ONES, c$4.50. Ms. Cooke, guided by White Eag... has thought back into two past lives—in ancient Egypt and in South America. The liv... are narrated in detail and spiritual guidance is unfolded. We don't like this work as mu... as Wheel of Rebirth. 160pp. WET 66

FINDLAY, ARTHUR. ON THE EDGE OF THE ETHERIC, $1.75. A record of commu... cation the author received from friends long dead which attempts to scientifically expla... life after death. A fascinating document which has been reprinted over fifty times sin... its initial impression in 1931. 159pp. Crg 31

GLASKIN, G.M. WINDOWS OF THE MIND, c$7.95. Glaskin discovered that memori... of other incarnations exist in our brains and by using a combination of massage and me... tal exercises these memories can be brought into consciousness. He and his friends ha... amazing experiences with the technique, many of which are recounted here along with... description of the process. 267pp. Del 74

GOLDSMITH, JOEL. THE THUNDER OF SILENCE, c$5.95. An inspirational Christia... text on karmic law and living the good life. 192pp. H&R 61

GRAHAM, DAVID. THE PRACTICAL SIDE OF REINCARNATION, c$7.95. This is ... straightforward presentation which surveys all aspects of reincarnation and focuses o... case studies and on the practical benefits which can be obtained from investigating yo... past lives. The book is well written and we found it vastly more interesting and inform... tive than most books of its type. One section of the book discusses a series of case hi... tories of groups of people who simultaneously recall a shared existence in the pas... In addition, Graham discusses psychiatrists and other therapists who are successfull... using *reincarnational therapy* with their clients. Index, 210pp. PrH 76

GUIRDHAM, ARTHUR. THE CATHERS AND REINCARNATION, c$5.90. A factu... record of a woman's memories of her incarnation in the thirteenth century. Guirdham ... a psychiatrist who has carefully traced many of her memories and proven them to be acc... rate. A fascinating account of life in the Middle Ages as well as an interesting psycholo... ical study. 204pp. Spe 70

_____. WE ARE ONE ANOTHER, c$10.35. This book describes how a group o... people who had lived together in the thirteenth century reassembled in the twentieth in ... small area in western England. The book records constant, sometimes day to day, contac... with the next world. Guirdham is careful to always verify the evidence provided by th... four spirit guides. Again, the Cathers play a role in the book. 227pp. Spe 74

HALL, MANLY P. ASTROLOGY AND REINCARNATION, $1.00. PRS 36

_____. FROM DEATH TO REBIRTH, $4.00. A clear, excellent work in thre... parts. The first discusses separation from the physical body at the time of death, the sec... ond examines various beliefs about life apart from the physical body, and the third ex... plains the procedures by which a reincarnating entity returns to the physical world. Bot... Eastern and Western teachings are included. PRS 72

_____. PAST LIVES AND PRESENT PROBLEMS AND HOW TO PREPAR... FOR A FORTUNATE REBIRTH, $1.75. Transcripts of two lectures. PRS 64

_____. REINCARNATION: THE CYCLE OF NECESSITY, c$7.00. A classi... treatment of various aspects of the doctrine of rebirth. There are extensive references to...

314

nd quotations from traditional sources as well as the most extensive bibliography we have seen on the subject. Many of the topics are not touched upon at such great length in the rest of the literature. Manly Hall is one of the most noted American philosophers of our day. Highly recommended. 217pp. PRS 39

_____. RESEARCH ON REINCARNATION, $1.75. A philosophical compilation. 46pp. PRS 64

HALL, MANLY P. and HENRY L. DRAKE. **THE PHILOSOPHY AND PSYCHOLOGY OF REINCARNATION**, $1.50. 16pp. PRS 54

HANSON, VIRGINIA, ed. **KARMA**, $2.50. A collection of essays on all aspects of karma by a variety of theosophical authors. 140pp. TPH 74

HEAD, JOSEPH and S.L. CRANSTON, eds. **REINCARNATION: AN EAST-WEST AN-THOLOGY**, $2.25. An encyclopedic compilation of philosophers, theologians, scientists and other thinkers of every period of Western culture, including a section on reincarnation in all the world's religions. The impressive quality of the volume illustrates the continuing concern with reincarnation through the ages. 325pp. TPH 61

_____. REINCARNATION IN WORLD THOUGHT, c$4.98. A later and more complete work by the authors. It incorporates only the most significant passages from the previous work and begins with four introductory essays by distinguished educators. Includes quotations from philosophers who did not believe in the theory of rebirth. A massive anthology, better organized than their first effort. 443pp. Cau 67

HODSON, GEOFFREY. **REINCARNATION, FACT OR FALLACY**, $1.00. An excellent presentation of the doctrine of reincarnation or law of rebirth as a plausible and at times necessary fact of human existence. Hodson examines prevalent criticisms and investigates reincarnation in the light of Christianity and the Bible. 84pp. TPH 67

_____. THROUGH THE GATEWAY OF DEATH, c$1.25. An explanatory work concerning the transition which we call death and the various laws and factors which govern this important event. Reveals the nature of existence in higher dimensions of divine substance and explores some theosophical beliefs about the nature of man in both his mortal and immortal aspects. 67pp. TPH 53

HOLZER, HANS. **THE REINCARNATION PRIMER**, $1.75. A series of topically arranged case histories which have been investigated and verified by the author. 272pp. H&R 74

HOWE, QUINCY. **REINCARNATION FOR THE CHRISTIAN**, c$4.95. A historical and theological presentation. Good scholarship and geared to the general reader. Annotated bibliography, 112pp. Wes 74

HUMPHREYS, CHRISTMAS. **KARMA AND REBIRTH**, c$3.50. A presentation by this noted Buddhist scholar which incorporates teachings from the scriptures of the Hindus and Buddhists and theosophical writings. Humphreys writes very clearly. 110pp. Mur 43

JONES, GLADYS. **REINCARNATION, SEX AND LOVE**, c$5.95. An application of ancient beliefs to the problems of today. Includes a large number of the author's poems. 185pp. NAP 71

KAPLEAU, PHILIP. **THE WHEEL OF DEATH**, $2.25. See Zen sub-section of Buddhism.

LANGLEY, NOEL. **EDGAR CAYCE ON REINCARNATION**, $1.25. Cases selected from the readings. 286pp. War 67

LEADBEATER, C.W. **THE LIFE AFTER DEATH—AND HOW THEOSOPHY UNVEILS IT**, c$2.00. 73pp. TPH 12

LEEK, SYBIL. **REINCARNATION: THE SECOND CHANCE**, $1.50. A survey of reincarnational beliefs in a variety of cultures, East and West, along with information on what karma is and a series of case studies. 212pp. Ban 74

LEWIS, H. SPENCER. **MANSIONS OF THE SOUL—THE COSMIC CONCEPTION**, c$6.65. A very complete presentation of the Rosicrucian Order's reincarnational beliefs. 332pp. Amo 30

MONTGOMERY, RUTH. **COMPANIONS ALONG THE WAY**, $1.75. See the Christianity section.

_____. HERE AND HEREAFTER, $1.50. A popularized account consisting basically of case histories. 175pp. Faw 68

MOORE, MARCIA and MARK DOUGLAS. **REINCARNATION: KEY TO IMMORTALITY**, c$10.00. This is an excellent collection of case histories (often of noted people), with interpretative material and the overall theme that the soul does incarnate and grow from life to life. Includes many quotations and material on what the conception of reincarnation means in our lives and *how to die correctly*. The case histories are arranged topically and make fascinating reading and the book as a whole makes a convincing argument for reincarnation. The authors are noted astrologers. Includes an extensive bibliography. 394pp. ArB 68

NIKHILANANDA, SWAMI. **MAN IN SEARCH OF IMMORTALITY: TESTIMONIALS FROM THE HINDU SCRIPTURES**, c$4.95. See the Indian Philosophy section.

PARAMANANDA, SWAMI. **REINCARNATION AND IMMORTALITY**, c$2.50. Swami Paramananda integrates Vedantic philosophy with Christianity and he writes in an inspiring manner. He discusses karma as well as reincarnation in this volume. 102pp. VdC 61

PELT, GERTRUDE van. **THE DOCTRINE OF KARMA**, $1.75. A theosophical manual, with quotations from a number of the major theosophical books. 58pp. PoL 74

PERKINS, JAMES. **THROUGH DEATH TO REBIRTH**, $1.95. A theosophical presentation of the stages the soul passes through between the cycles of death and rebirth. The material is presented in the form of a series of short essays covering a great variety of topics. 124pp. TPH 61

PRYSE, JAMES. **REINCARNATION IN THE NEW TESTAMENT**, $2.00. See the Bible section.

RAMA, SWAMI. **FREEDOM FROM KARMA**, $2.50. Swami Rama and his teachings have been popular recently in the U.S., especially in the Midwest. He expresses his views on karma and daily right action here. Him 73

RAMACHARAKA, YOGI. **THE LIFE BEYOND DEATH**, c$5.50. A clear, comprehensive presentation of *the other side*. Includes a discussion of the planes of life; the soul's slumber and awakening; astral plane and its geography; astral religious experiences; astral communication, companionship and occupation; and beyond reincarnation. 192pp. YPS 09

RUTTER, OWEN. **THE SCALES OF KARMA**, $2.95. Includes material from the world's religions as well as a general exposition of the subject. 207pp. Wei 30

RYALL, EDWARD. **BORN TWICE**, c$7.95. The author chronicles his *other life*, when he was a farmer in seventeenth century England. A wealth of detail is presented. Introduction by Ian Stevenson. 214pp. H&R 74

SHARMA, I.C. **CAYCE, KARMA, AND REINCARNATION**, $3.95. Dr. Sharma is an Indian philosophy professor. Here he clarifies many of Cayce's ideas by developing parallels with Hindu thought. 177pp. H&R 75

SHERMAN, HAROLD. **YOU LIVE AFTER DEATH**, $1.25. A well written, inspirational presentation of the soul, the spirit body, the afterlife, our link with the infinite, preparing for death and for future lives, and much else. Sherman is a very popular writer in this field and his books are well thought of. 205pp. Faw 49

STEARN, JESS. **THE SEARCH FOR A SOUL: TAYLOR CALDWELL'S PSYCHIC LIVES**, $1.75. A popular account of one woman's memories, obtained through hypnosis, of her past lives. A fascinating narrative. 321pp. Faw 72

STEINER, RUDOLF. **REINCARNATION AND IMMORTALITY**, $1.95. Transcripts of five related lectures. A very clear, scholarly presentation by this master philosopher-scientist. 204pp. Mul 70

STEVENSON, IAN. **TWENTY CASES SUGGESTIVE OF REINCARNATION**, c$20.00. This is the most noted collection of case studies ever published. Stevenson is a psychiatrist who carefully researched the material presented here for a number of years. He first presents the cases and then a general discussion of the material. All sources are fully documented. Recommended for the serious student. 362pp. UPV 74

STORY, FRANCIS. **REBIRTH AS DOCTRINE AND EXPERIENCE**, c$8.40. Story was a Buddhist scholar who devoted over twenty years to investigations of cases of rebirth. His analyses were systematic and he always integrated his deep knowledge of Buddhism with his case studies. He died before completing even preliminary work on this book. It was compiled by his associate, the Ven. Nyanaponika, from fieldnotes and essays. While it is at best an uncompleted work, it remains one of the most important contributions to understanding of the rebirth phenomenon that is available today. Introduction by Ian Stevenson. Index, 292pp. BPS 75

VIVEKANANDA, SWAMI. **KARMA YOGA**, $.95. An excellent treatise on all aspects of the subject from the point of view of Hindu philosophy. Recommended. 131pp. AdA

WACHSMUTH, GUENTHER. **REINCARNATION**, c$10.00. See the Steiner section.

WEISS, JESS E. **THE VESTIBULE**, $1.25. Presents the experiences of a number of people who have died and managed to transmit their experiences in the Beyond. 128pp. S&S 72

WOODWARD, MARY ANN. **EDGAR CAYCE'S STORY OF KARMA**, $1.50. During his lifetime, Cayce gave more than 14,000 readings, one-third of which were devoted to metaphysical areas and revolved around the central theme of reincarnation. From these discourses Ms. Woodward has selected those most related to his theory of karma and has arranged the readings topically, with commentary interspersed. 283pp. Ber 72

WRIGHT, LEOLINE. **REINCARNATION**, $2.25. A theosophical manual, with quotations from some of the most important books. 113pp. TPH 75

REVEALED TEACHINGS

Anyone who moves aside from the ordinary course of life to an interest in actual spiritual development steps into bewilderment. Unless he watches himself warily he is likely to take quite innocently what the occultists call The Left Hand Path. There are tens and dozens of systems from which he can choose. Teachers of them swarm. They come in robe and turban; or in the ordinary garments of western civilization. They are mysterious, and remote, and occult and ritualistic: or they deal in plain words, plainly used. They call themselves religions; or sciences; or philosophies. They are all quite certain of themselves; and generally where they differ, they are mutually exclusive. Their followers are ordinarily enthusiasts. Furthermore, these systems all sound reasonable and logical; and, catch him right, they are capable of our seeker's belief and fanatic adherence. At least for a while.

Some of them are based on truth and reality and so are good. They differ one from the other only in the externals that make them adaptable to different types of people. But a lot of them are based on half truths. Some may be valuable enough in their native soil, but cannot bear transplanting. Some are baldly fake systems to catch suckers. Some are clever imitations of the real thing. Some are downright perversions. How is a man to determine? The difficulty is to find out what the catch is. Much of it seems, in some degree, to work. There are results. Are the results good? Are they good for *us*?

Beginning with the simplest concept of the lot: how about *holding the thought* for the purpose of *manifesting* what one desires? Can that be done? A great number of worthy folk believe in it. Some very sincere people devote themselves to teaching it. Compared to some of the more elaborate systems, this is a moderately simple magic. Nevertheless, if one examines without prejudice its structure, it seems based on laws that ought logically to work. Testimony is offered that is difficult to dismiss as coincidence.

There is evidently, said Gaelic as to this, *somewhat of a puzzle in your minds concerning the law of acquisition; the drawing to yourself of that which is outside yourself for your own use. A thing is for your own use if it passes through your manipulation, whether its object is a satisfaction of a personal desire, or is supposed to subserve a purpose. The underlying principle that clarifies the logic of the situation can be very simply stated. Nothing can be acquired without the price for it being paid.*

There are no free and gratuitous acquisitions. If a thing is acquired apparently without payment by the one demanding it, be certain the payment is made by somebody, or some group force, and the price deferred is charged against that one's credit.

The simplest method for acquiring material possession for any purpose whatever is through the economic law that each clearly understands. The payment is made in the token you call money, which represents a well-understood and defined need of effort, service or exchange. If you desire an object, you know exactly its price; and furthermore you know what payment of that price means to you in those terms. So you may evaluate exactly its desirability as balanced against its price.

Material possession may also be acquired by the invocation of more subtle laws than those of economics. The acquisition is certain to one who thoroughly understands this law, and can inject into it enough dynamics for its operation. But the material object does not come into possession from a storehouse of gratuities. There must be expended for it a price. That price is not a fixed unit, as is the money token of the lesser economic law. It is a variable, depending on what coin you possess, and what coin you owe. There is also a dependence on your purpose of investment, and its singleness. Each alloy of lesser purpose alters the coinage and as accurately as does one operating under economic law the amount and kind of payment. As for the other who invokes law blindly, he is a foolish man who takes from the shelves careless and unknowing of price, of kind of payment, of time of payment, or rate of interest.

That, in brief, is the danger of the invocation by rote of laws not understood, except in effects. Nothing comes into your hands but you are charged with

its price. Know that you must pay before you strike the bargain. Know from whom, if anybody, you are borrowing your credit, and what repayment will be demanded of you. Aside from higher considerations, it is a grave foolishness to take, on such blind credit, that which may at least be worked for if not obtained, by a comprehended law.

Another danger in the invocation of half understood occult laws, is that one thereby affiliates himself psychically with a group whose individual constituents are unknown to him. If the affiliation is active, it implies a certain degree of responsibility—a certain degree, mind you—of each for the others. It is always well to pause before undertaking blind liabilities. That is the reason why we consider it generally undesirable to teach miscellaneous and unchosen groups. Spiritual matters are rarely, after the first simplicities, susceptible to mass dissemination. A teacher should be responsible for and very sure of what he teaches, of course; but he should not forget that in the gathering together of those whom he would instruct he has also a responsiblity, in that he is exposing them, more or less uninsulated, one to the other. The usual protection is a ritualism that soon hardens to the crumbling point of disintegration; or a formalism which beats in rebound from the surface of the mind.

This has always been recognized by the genuine teachers of the world. Those Masters who have addressed the multitude of mankind have told but a few and simple things. When it has become desirable to teach higher matters, it has always been to the few chosen. So in general distrust the one who would instruct you together with the multitude in the higher things of spirit. He offers you but the outward shells that have contained, but contain no longer; or, if the things he offers have power, that power may be misused, and yours will be part of the responsibility to work it out.

Now I must not be misunderstood. The prophet vivifying the spirit of the multitude is a real and living and constructive force. The seer who opens to vision the flash of a vista performs a necessary spiritual vivification. But whatever he tells the multitude—if you examine it when the glory of irradiation has cooled—is but an old simplicity which men have known. Nor do I decry those gatherings in the temples of understood worship which have as their end, not knowledge or power, but communion with the source. The formalisms and rituals of such gatherings, if they be not the lip service of rote, are simply the opening hands to the door.

With these discriminations I leave this imperfect warning to your consideration. The Master said, if there be two or three gathered together in my name. He spoke not of a multitude.

I might add a wee word. He who addresses the multitude in occult knowledge, himself stands in grave danger of entering the darker path, unless he well understands. For in the powers he passes on he must himself follow or resolve the ultimate use to which they may be put. I do not say he will be responsible in the full sense, as is the misuser; but he has endorsed the note.

How about books conveying such knowledge? Are they harmful? one of us asked.

If you ignorantly put the practices you see in books into use: yes. If read for information for a rounded knowledge: no. Specific directions for the acquisition of specific powers we of the Wisdom do not knowledgedly place in books. If innocently disclosed, it is through ignorance or half-knowledge. I speak now of formulae for power. I do not speak of formulae for purely spiritual growth. There is a great distinction. If formulae are given for self-defense, etc., they are an antidote to uncountenanced disclosure.

The evocation of powers or forces is a purely natural thing, just as you evoke the power of steam by building your fire, containing your water, and compressing your vapor into the proper channels. Any fool can make steam if he knows but a simple procedure, purely mechanically. Any fool can evoke any natural force provided he knows the more or less complex circumstances necessary to call it into being. The power is always the same. The effect of the power depends upon the machine through which it works. If one de-

elops a steam pressure of, say, five hundred pounds, he may usefully employ in a machine adapted to that pressure; whereas in a frailer structure adapted one hundred pounds only, he would meet with disaster.

ow there are, to abandon the figure, certain degrees of power that are generated according to the strength of the machine. It is as though, when you ad built a mechanism capable of withstanding and using a hundred pounds f steam, the hundred pounds would be automatically generated and supplied exact force and quantity by the mere fact of the machine's existence. And hen you had constructed a machine of five hundred pounds capacity, the ressure would also automatically and without intervention on your part ccompany the mechanism. It is actually thus with the powers of the human ntity. The machine in this case being the stable and eternal character or soul r spiritual body or degree of development or evolution to which he has atained, and the so called psychic and other powers are the steam pressure hat automatically accompanies the machine.

Now conceive that by a short cut, as you call it, your possessor of the hunred pound machine should by artifice, and not by automatic means, raise is pressure to a hundred and fifty pounds, instead of building up the machne to that capacity and so acquiring it in the usual course. Without doubt he machine would run in an accelerated manner until something broke. In a road and general way this is the difficulty with any forcing of added capacity; is building an additional fire to raise the pressure. The attention is directed o the wrong end of the problem. Instead of saying, if I develop the capacity he powers will be supplied, one says, If I develop the powers I can do more vith the old machine.

The measure of capacity in the human machine is character, the soul capacity, he degree of evolution, the eternal body, whatever you will; and that, like he human body, is a complex thing. By lifting a heavy weight in mechanical nanners you may develop enormous muscles; but if, at the same time, a coresponding nervous vitality is not also developed, the result is not a stronger nan but a weaker man.

To change the figure, it is possible by the application of water and artificial orcing methods to grow enormous and fairly in a very short season, but it is not possible to grow sturdily without the stiffening and stabilizing ingredient f time. There is no known system which, in a finite world conditioned by space and time can successfully rid itself of this one ingredient. For there is n extricable fibre of all finite things, and sooner or later its lack makes itself known by absence of stability. Many systems are incomplete; they do not contain all the ingredients—only those which mechanically bring about the fair and watery fruit without the substance.

There are apparent exceptions. You have often seen a wee rain fall upon the seeded earth, and the sun has shone, and once more the earth is dry and brown. And in the days later it has rained again, and like magic in a few hours the grasses have sprung from the hard surface. The regular and orderly process of nature had been going on in due course, until the seed was developed to the very point of germination. Had not the second rain come so soon, naught would have happened until by the slower moisture already accumulated the shoots had come more slowly forth. The second rain did not force the process, did not bring a development by a short cut, but merely furnished a favorable condition for the earlier unfolding of what was actually already complete. In this manner it may happen that conscious exercises, consciously performed, in a very few cases might bring a result; but it would be a result already achieved.

You build your machine by building yourself. You build yourself by the exercise of decision, moment to moment. You get the materials for decision from what you have received. You received in proportion to your receptivity. Receptivity is a part of the pressure that comes with the machine. Build your machine. Let force, power, the ability to make rabbits come out of hats, take care of itself. When you have a rabbit machine, rabbits will be plentiful.

There are certain consciousnesses and always have been on your plane who are in reality advanced beyond the necessity for its particular conditions, but who, for reasons of service, or as one who enters a condition in order to better understand it, do dwell upon your planet. These are the true adepts, and are generally unknown, except for some especial and individual purpose.

They are above the necessity of personal contact in order to do their work. They possess methods of reaching those capable of receiving what they have to offer, which transcend in certainty the ordinary methods of human intercourse. As usually described, merely incidental and accompanying insignificances are portrayed as the living reality. They are advanced consciousnesses furnished with attributes which naturally and inevitably accrue to that growth. They are not men who have by practice and study acquired extraneous powers as one collects jewels.

In order to gain the advancement in consciousness to which the so-called adept has grown, certain phases of growth must be reached, lived out, and passed through. This is true throughout all nature. Before the human infant can be born, it must review its own biological history. Before it gains the elements of moral consciousnee, it must in brief pass through its own history of their acquisition, through fear, through hunger, through the simple passions, until the moral nature has become subtle.

Now symbolize these things. Say that in place of passing through the inner experiences of growth, you illustrate each of these states by a physical symbol. Can you not see that the visitor from another planet, to whom our processes were unfamiliar, might take the symbol for a literal fact, and report to his fellows on his return that, to reach the beginning of a moral nature, the human young must perform certain ceremonies of casting out fear, etc.?

In exactly the same way the symbolism which was intended to shadow forth in illustrative form the perfectly normal steps in development and growth which lead to that higher consciousness you call the adept, have been taken in their literal meaning.

The artificial stimulation of powers, beyond that which is natural to the state of development, merely accentuates and makes more vivid those traits of character which the individual already possesses. His better parts work for good more easily, his selfish parts are more selfish, his evil propensities are made more potent. There is no change in the proportionate ensemble. There is furthermore grave danger of a disunited personality, and for this reason:

In even a fairly harmoniously constituted human entity the lowest possibilities are not so very much lower than the highest possibilities, and as the top rises so does the lower level, so that always there is in the constituent make up of that man a certain compactness. But if with the same characteristics and without intrinsic change therein, the good is intensified and thrown higher, so to speak, and the selfishness and evil are intensified and thrown lower, so to speak—as of diverging lines—then, you can see, that the compactness is in danger of becoming scattered and lost. That is another of the dangers of forced growth.

I would like to change the figure. It is important.

Conceive of the human entity as a sphere composed of atoms of a certain size, these atoms representing all the diverse psychic characteristics of which mankind is composed. Now in the natural growth of this sphere, in expansion, the atoms also increase in size, so that always the surface of the sphere remains, through the always intimate juxtaposition of these increasing atoms, unbroken.

But conceive the sphere enlarged in its circumference of power by artificial methods rather than natural growth. The atoms of which it is composed have not enlarged in correspondence. Hos could they, since there is no growth, only an extension of the radii of power? And since this is so, they are no longer in juxtaposition on the surface, and your entity is open to whatever winds of destruction may be astir.

There are several classes of very definite results to be obtained from any of these practices.

First of all there are those who strive for the purely mechanical acquisition of certain wonderful-seeming but actually trivial powers. Those, if pursued for themselves, are at worst dangerous, and at best unbalancing, as we have seen.

Another class, a grade above the last, is actually and earnestly striving toward an ideal such as is depicted in the popular conception of the adept. These people are in no danger except that of losing a balance that they must later supply. In essence their only mistake is in striving to become something and using certain means solely with that end in view, instead of realizing that in any growth that is sure and solid, each means, no matter how small and trivial, is for the period of its employment the end itself, and must be so approached and so considered.

Then of course there is the third class which realizes this point, the members of which are developing in the only possible way, and who in real truth supply to the particular religion or sect or cult of philosophy or what-not, its only real life. All the rest are merely the showy but parasitic growth; and were the cult actually dependent on them alone, it could not endure.

A discussion followed concerning retirement from the ordinary trivialities of ordinary life, in order to concentrate more effectively on spiritual growth; in other words, adjusting the lesser things in life to the greater.

It is not by conscious taking of thought, and withdrawing from life for the purpose of pursuing spirituality like an elusive and rather solitary fox, that one attains—unless the withdrawal seems, not a question, but the most natural thing in the world. It is not at that point that the necessary effort which is the price of all growth must be applied. The effort must always be to expand, to reach out, to gain more contacts, to live everyday life with a leaven of sympathy, and to walk on the highest plane of which one is capable. If these things are done naturally and simply and eagerly and with a will, spirituality, as you call it, will flood in, bringing with it all its gifts of intuition, of spiritual wisdom, of cosmic contact. But that is a thing which must be left to the care of itself. All the other is yours to do, and to its doing you bring all that you can of that which comes to you on the flood.

For that you will find you need no years of solitude, no hours of meditation; but in the ideal perfection of the process, the flash of time between the raising and lowering of the eyelid will be quite sufficient to your enrichment.

'Is there any truth in the people who are always running down the intellect and its cultivation?' it was asked.

The intellect is the focus point of consciousness, most favorable in earth life to the development of any entity. The main difficulty is that people tend to build a lightproof and completely impermeable wall around the intellect, to the exclusion of all other preparation of those fields in which one will shortly roam. There is a due and balanced proportion in all things. A focus point, but its very nature as a focus, is of paramount importance for the immediate need, but is of decidedly secondary importance as compared with the whole field.

The reason that the intellect is cried down and the intuitional faculties are exalted is that in ordinary life the reverse is ordinarily true. All education is directed towards the intellectual at the expense of the intuitional. Thus a precept which is in general true is overemphasized by those who have not a full comprehension of truth.

Seek ye first the Kingdom of Heaven, and all things shall be added unto you. This text, like all the richly figurative Oriental texts of that day, is a generalization based on indirections, and like most of those texts has been wrenched from a figurative to a literal meaning. The most unfitted men conceived they were obeying the text and seeking the Kingdom of Heaven by going into monasteries. As a matter of fact, that kind of life was the very last way men of that particular type could seek the Kingdom of Heaven.

The text merely means, lead the best life of which you are capable in the station to which you are called; and it has not been wrenched from that meaning by two thousand years of contrary interpretation.

The different systems of development are adapted to different people. The mistake, and the deadly mistake, is in going out consciously and intellectually and selecting one of them. It will select you. When you consciously review these formulitic systems and pick out one for predetermined experiment, without an inner urge of the sub-currents toward it, the result is invariably bad. That is where your intellect comes into its own. Obtain an intellectual

understanding of everything you can, but without consciously determine selection. If there is in what you thus intellectually encounter a whole or fragment, fitted for your unfoldment from the unconscious to the consciou of what you already possess or are developing into, be assured that withou volition on your part it will do its work.

The primary object in your physical world of any development whateve whether of a person, a living thing, or the very rock of the fields, is not t produce a definite result by means of a process, but to enable an added po tion of ultimate reality to clothe or manifest itself in physical form. Yo may take a man, and without demanding effort on his part beyond the mech anical performance of certain specified exercises, cause him to come int possession of the power to perform very definite, very wonderful and ver startling things. By so doing you apparently cause things to happen of fa reaching effect. As an actuality you have done nothing more than brin about a rearrangement of the affected elements; abnormally, and in such fashion that although the apparent effects are of great magnitude, the fina effects are almost nothing—because in the balance of nature a readjustmen into what would have been the result of the original form will inevitabl take place.

This is because no reality, no portion of reality, has been precipitated, mani fested, clothed by, and so made an entity of the physical world, by this pro cess. The only way this can be done is by a definite, normal and ordinar effort of the free will, acting seriatim, without gap, in the course of its regula progress of development. Any effect, no matter how large, of the forme method, as respects both the individual who performs it and the portion o the universe by which he is intimately surrounded, is illusory and fleeting Any effect, no matter how minute, that is a product of directed effort, i permanent, both in building up the one who evokes it and in adding to th sum total of universal progress. The one is of no substance; the other is a solid as the foundation of the cosmos itself.

Precipitation on the physical plane must come from those endowed with the physical faculties. It must be a living human being—living in your sense—who performs. No others but the great creative intelligences are able by the check ing quality of their ideas actually to create on the physical plane. If we would effect an actual manifestation or clothing of any portion of reality in your sphere, we must not only work through the intermediation of one of your selves, but we must do it indirectly, so to speak, by arousing you to make your own effort. We can direct you straight away to do a certain thing, sim ply by telling you to do it; and you will do it and will apparently gain to a certain effect. But in the result will be no iota of the substance of reality, nor permanence; and in the inevitable readjustments it will be as if it never had been. Of what avail then to lead you on by direct advice?—One blows down the wind! What you want, what the flow of progress wants, what we want, is rather the single grain of sand than the oceans of drifting fog.

And I must repeat that the only mechanism we know to place this clothed reality in your world is the carnate human will. And for exactly the same reason as that which underlies the insubstantiality of these occult practices— that is why you are not more helped by us.

—from the **GAELIC MANUSCRIPTS** by Stuart Edward White

tablish through the centuries. This truth postulates one—and only one—basic reality, a fundamental something from which everything stems. In **Our Unseen Guest** this long sought reality is isolated as consciousness—*the highest expression known to man of a single common denominator.* This book was widely read and was very influential. The material in Stewart Edward White's books and the Seth books by Jane Roberts continue this excellent teaching. 320pp. Bor 20

COOLEY, ANNE, ed. GUIDANCE FROM SILVER BIRCH, c$4.75. An anthology of the communications of Silver Birch, a famous spirit-guide. The material is topically arranged and the language is very clear. 120pp. Spi 66

MATHES, J.H. and LENORA HUETT. THE AMNESIA FACTOR, $4.95. Lenora Huett is a gifted medium, J.H. Mathes an airline pilot and UFO investigator who, through her, contacted his two *guides*. About two-thirds of the book consists of Mathes' experiences and ideas and questions; the rest is the answers of the guides. Mathes had a prior interest in **The Urantia Book** and the various Seth books, and quite a bit of the discussion relates to the kind of cosmological ideas found in these books. Indeed there is some specific information given by the guides about Seth. The title refers to the idea that when we come into this plane of existence we are given amnesia about our larger selves so that we will play the game and gain the most experience we can while on earth. Bibliography, glossary, index. 169pp. CeA 75

MONTGOMERY, RUTH. A WORLD BEFORE, c$7.95. Arthur Ford and Ms. Montgomery's other spirit guides have dictated the story of creation and the lost worlds of Atlantis and Lemuria to her via automatic writing. This is a detailed presentation of much of the information she received. CMG 76

MOSES, W. STAINTON. MORE SPIRIT TEACHINGS, c$4.50. A sequel to **Spirit Teachings**. 124pp. Spi 52

—————. **SPIRIT TEACHINGS**, c$6.95. Reverend Moses is regarded as the man who gave spiritualism its bible. He was one of the most remarkable mediums of the nineteenth century. This book, which came through him by automatic writing, is regarded as spiritualism's greatest classic. It contains the religious, philosophical and ethical implications of spiritualism, as viewed by the spirit world. The production of this book took over seven years. 291pp. Spi 49

NADA-YOLANDA. ANGELS AND MAN, c$6.00. *The relationships and the responsibilities between the angelic and the man kingdoms are of great importance, yet are not understood by Earthman. Instead of divine truths, man here has been plied with man-made conceptions, descriptions, definitions and fallacies through writings and paintings. The purpose of this book is to present a true revelation of this subject.... The eleven discourses are the actual words of the seven archangels as channeled vocally through Nada-Yolanda.... The glossary contains explanations of 145 possibly unfamiliar terms.* 138pp. MAM 74

—————. **EVOLUTION OF MAN—SPIRITUAL, MENTAL, PHYSICAL**, c$6.00. Presents material designed to help man understand his past experience with the earth and the solar system and to see what lies ahead. Topics include the Biblical record, the fall of man, sonship with God, man's bodies, environmental relationships, free will, soul, good and evil, devolution and re-evolution. Glossary, 160pp. MAM

—————. **HOW TO DO ALL THINGS—YOUR USE OF DIVINE POWER**, c$5.00. Mark Age's metaphysical textbook explaining methods whereby one can achieve more spiritual understanding, by reliance upon the inherent divine power and infinite spiritual resources to be found within each individual. MAM

—————. **MARK AGE PERIOD AND PROGRAMS**, c$10.00. This is the first Mark Age book, containing excerpts of the channeled communications. It provides a comprehensive coverage of the hierarchical plan and program as presented through Mark Age concerning the nature, powers, history and development of man and the plan to begin a new level of spiritual evolution. This is the basic text and includes a comprehensive glossary. 350pp. MAM 70

—————. **VISITORS FROM OTHER PLANETS**, c$10.00. See the UFO section.

NEWBROUGH, JOHN. THE OAHSPE BIBLE, c$12.50. This book was supposedly transmitted to Newbrough by archangelic beings. The text concerns the 24,000 year history of the earth as well as the occurrences in the spiritual world during the same period. It is written in Biblical style English and includes photographic reprints of portraits of evolved spiritual beings. There is also an index-glossary. Oversize, 921pp. Amh 1892

OMANANDA, SWAMI. THE BOY AND THE BROTHERS, c$6.10. The story of the relationship between the author and an illiterate Cockney from the London slums with a gift for healing and prophesy, who was used by the *Brothers* as a vehicle. This is the first book in the series. *The Boy*, while in a trance state, gave teachings which seemed to imply knowledge that he could not have acquired in any normal manner. These teachings were accepted as authoritative by many who heard them. 316pp. Spe 59

—————. **TOWARDS THE MYSTERIES**, c$5.90. A more developed presentation of the Brothers' teachings, given over a period of twenty years and now edited by the Swami. *The thoughts contained in the teachings are as deep as and as high as those in the* **Upanishads** *and the* **Bhagavadgita**, writes Dr. B.L. Atreya, Head of the Department of Indian Philosophy and Religion at Banaras University. 360pp. Spe 68

ROBERTS, JANE. ADVENTURES IN CONSCIOUSNESS, c$7.95. *Aspect psychology ... accepts as normal the existence of precognitive dreams, out-of-body experiences, revelatory information, alterations of consciousness, peak experiences, trance mediumship, and other psychological and psychic events...I utilize different levels of awareness to examine the nature of the psyche and its reality ...I've also examined my own trance*

Jane Roberts by Robert Butts

material, and from my side of consciousness scrutinized Seth's reality as it appears in my experience, and in his behavior and writings. This is the fullest exploration Jane has made of her work with Seth and how this work has altered her psychological thought. Index, 296pp. PrH 75

—————. **THE COMING OF SETH**, $1.95. Originally titled **How to Develop Your ESP Power**, this was Jane's first attempt to write out her experiences with psi phenomena. It includes her early work with the ouiji board (the mechanism through which Seth originally contacted her) and some of her other early experiments. Of interest mainly to Seth aficionados. Jane herself says that *All the books that Seth and I later wrote emerged from these pages.* Bibliography, 252pp. S&S 66

—————. **DIALOGUES OF THE SOUL AND MORTAL SELF IN TIME**, c$6.95. This is a collection of the poetry that came to Jane while she was in a state of altered consciousness, what she termed *peak experiences.* The poetry is very personal—she says it is her soul talking—and quite philosophical. Many drawings by her husband, Robert Butts, illustrate the text. An introduction, *Poetry and Transcendent Experience*, discusses the production of the poems and the poems themselves. 142pp. PrH 75

—————. **THE EDUCATION OF OVERSOUL SEVEN**, c$6.95. *With* **The Education of Oversoul Seven**, *Jane Roberts brings us a great bright sad funny dream set before waking in ink and paper. We have a strange feeling, as Seven learns that it is us learning too—that it is us flickering back and forth across centuries discovering who we've been all along, as though we've somehow done this before, and forgotten. In the adventures of Seven and in the dream of this book it's almost as if, for a long happy moment, we can remember.—Richard Bach.* 226pp. PrH 73

—————. **THE NATURE OF PERSONAL REALITY**, c$7.95/$4.95. *Seth's main idea is that we create our personal reality through our conscious beliefs about ourselves, others, and the world. Following this is the concept that the point of power is in the present, not in the past of this life or any other. He stresses the individual's capacity for conscious action, and provides excellent exercises designed to show each person how to apply these theories to any life situation*—from the introduction by Jane Roberts. This is the second book Seth has written by himself, and, as you can see from the quotation above, he brings many of the theoretical concepts presented in **Seth Speaks** down to the practical level for use by the reader. As usual, he speaks clearly and to the point. We recommend this book highly. 523pp. PrH 75

—————. **THE SETH MATERIAL**, c$7.95/$3.95/$1.95. This is a result of the combined work of medium Jane Roberts and her cooperation with an out-of-body teacher named Seth. The philosophy presented is profound and very easily understandable. It was selected as the best of a continuous presentation of material upon dreams, health, reincarnation, astral projection and man's subconscious and his relation with his creator. Included are pictures of the author during her sessions and discussion of efforts to establish that Seth was indeed a separate entity and not part of Roberts' subconscious. One of the best introductions to the entire field that we know of. 304pp. PrH 70

—————. **SETH SPEAKS**, c$7.95/$4.95/$1.95. In this century there have been many presentations of ultimate truth through revelation. This we believe is the best. It was dictated by Seth in the form of a book over a period of two years and required virtually no editing. If you are just getting into this field and want to hear the case for Seth, read **Seth Material** first. If you are ready to get into the real teaching, start here. Topics include reincarnation, how thoughts form matter, the soul and the nature of its consciousness, the death experiences and after death experiences, the multidimensional God, probable systems, men and gods, alternate presents and multiple focus, the meaning of religion, and much else. Highly recommended. 505pp. PrH 72

SMITH, SUSY. THE BOOK OF JAMES, $1.25. Susy Smith started out as an agnostic, but, after reading **The Unobstructed Universe** in 1955, she got interested in parapsychology, worked under Dr. Rhine at Duke, and has since become an indefatigable researcher and author in this field. In 1967 she produced this manuscript which she is convinced is automatic writing coming through her from a discarnate entity she believes to be William James. On the whole, James is concerned to make the case for life after death, in terms familiar to those who have read much of this genre. He ventures little into broader metaphysical or cosmological questions. One interesting area is his denial of reincarnation. He contends that sometimes a soul will possess the body of a baby and have a second lifetime but it is very confusing to the soul and twice is enough. He argues that most of the well-known proofs of reincarnation are actually cases of possession. Bibliography, 186pp. Ber 74

SOLOMON, PAUL. **EXCERPTS FROM THE PAUL SOLOMON TAPES,** c$5.95. Virginia Beach, last home of Edgar Cayce, seems to spawn similar types of psychic activity. Paul Solomon (not his real name) appeared on the psychic scene in 1972 and now has his own Fellowship of the Inner Light and gives readings on healings, past lives, predictions, etc. This book covers selections on Atlantis and Lemuria, diet and health, sex, healing, spiritual growth, world prophecy, etc. Solomon sounds a lot like Edgar Cayce in these selections, including his convoluted style which makes for difficult reading. The book **Season of Changes,** is also believed to be by Paul Solomon. 149pp. Her 74

STANFORD, RAY. **CREATION,** $2.00. A study of the origins of man and his pre-history as explained through the unconscious mind of Ray Stanford. 36pp. AUM 66

_____. **FATIMA PROPHECY,** c$7.95. Apparitions of the *Mother of Jesus* have have been recorded throughout history. The message of modern Marian apparitions seems to have become focused on certain urgent matters, both spiritual and humanistic. The purpose of this book is to present accurate accounts of the more impressive, recent apparitions and offer an interpretation of their message and meaning. Most of the text was given in the form of psychic readings through Stanford's unconscious mind. Includes a glossary and photographs of some of the apparitions. 194pp. AUM 72

_____. **SPEAK, SHINING STRANGER,** c$8.95. An extensive selection of readings given through Ray Stanford, one of the most noted present day mediums and the main force behind the Association for the Understanding of Man, P.O. Box 5310, Austin, Texas 78763. The readings discuss healing, meditation, marriage and death, the nature and proper function of psychic communications, and much else. Stanford provides an introduction. 252pp. AUM 75

STEIGER, BRAD, ed. **WORDS FROM THE SOURCE,** c$6.95. Over the years Louis has delivered readings on a great variety of subjects while in a trance state. The readings come from an entity which calls itself the Source. Steiger has selected the most significant parts of this trance material and has arranged it topically. The information presented contains a wealth of insights and every conceivable area is covered at some length. The Source relates his material very clearly and he can best be compared to Seth in terms of his information and his style. Index, 168pp. PrH 75

STORM, STELLA, ed. **PHILOSOPHY OF SILVER BIRCH,** c$6.00. A comprehensive study of Silver Birch's philosophy, topically arranged. 158pp. Spi 69

URANTIA

BEDELL, CLYDE. **CONCORDEX OF THE URANTIA BOOK,** c$12.00. This volume should be immensely helpful to all those seriously studying the **Urantia Book.** 439pp. Bed 74

SADLER, WILLIAM. **APPENDICES TO A STUDY OF THE MASTER UNIVERSE,** c$20.15. These **Appendices** expand on the information presented in Sadler's earlier work. 372pp. SSF 75

_____. **A STUDY OF THE MASTER UNIVERSE,** c$10.00. This is a development of some of the key concepts in the **Urantia Book** based on years of study and contemplation of the material. 150pp. SSF 68

URANTIA FOUNDATION. **URANTIA,** c$20.00. A massive *received teaching* which details the story of the universe, the story of our galaxy, the history of Urantia (the Earth) and the life and teachings of Jesus (*the Son of God and the Son of Man*). This is the most comprehensive account of the cosmos and the cosmic plan imaginable. We know some people (a few) who've read **Urantia** several times and say that it contains the wisdom of the ages. Perhaps it does. If you have a lot of time for concentrated study, read it and find out. 2097pp. UrB 55

WHITE, RUTH and MARY SWAINSON. **GILDAS COMMUNICATES.** c$7.00. Gildas is an inner guide who communicates through an English woman. This is a book of his teachings concerning the new age. 222pp. Spe 71

_____. **SEVEN INNER JOURNEYS,** c$8.50. This is an account of the emergence of Gildas in Ruth White's consciousness, including information on the training and psychological/spiritual purification that she has gone through in order to become a clearer channel. 216pp. Spe 74

WHITE, STEWART. **THE BETTY BOOK.** c$5.50. *This book is the record, condensed, of the excursions of Betty, a psychic intimately known to me and of absolute integrity, into the world of other-consciousness—and of communications received by her from forces which I have ventured to call the invisibles. These excursions, made in a condition of trance or otherwise, began in the year 1919 and have continued ever since. They are recorded in the following pages with no idea of adding to the existing literature of automatic writing and kindred phenomena; but in the belief that, as embodying a workable philosophy of life, they may be of aid to seekers after spiritual life.*—S.E. White. 302pp. Dut 30

_____. **THE GAELIC MANUSCRIPTS,** $9.40. The material in this volume was collected by White just before his death and the manuscript was privately printed. White himself seems to have been the channel through which the material was given. The book needs editing, but the basic material is often quite enlightening and it is more sophisticated than most *received communications.* Many advanced ideas are presented and the whole work seems designed to resolve long standing questions such as man's relation to the cosmos, the meaning of conflict and of pleasure and pain, the purpose of existence, the pitfalls on the spiritual path, and much else. Oversize, spiral bound. 154pp. PaP 74

_____. **THE UNOBSTRUCTED UNIVERSE,** $2.95. The communication presented here was channeled to White by his wife Betty six months or so after her death. We feel that it presents the best report on what it's like *on the other side* that we know of. The presentation is straightforward and is not embellished. Forty actual conversations are reproduced, along with White's running commentary. This is truly a classic and we recommend it highly to all those who seek a deeper understanding of the ultimate meaning of it all. White's work was a forerunner of the material that Seth presents and those who find Seth enlightening will also appreciate Betty's teaching. Betty's transmission is especially clear since she had the experience of both receiving and transmitting communication. 320pp. Dut 40

WHITE EAGLE. **THE GENTLE BROTHER,** c$2.00. White Eagle is a member of the White Brotherhood—a group which has been transmitting from century to century the inner truths which have been revealed to man. He has been speaking through the mediumship of Grace Cooke for nearly fifty years. His presentations are always clear and to the point and his writings are very popular—especially in England—and are inspirationally oriented. This book is a collection of short extracts to be used for daily guidance in living the spiritual life. 69pp. WET 68

_____. **GOLDEN HARVEST,** c$2.00. Guidance for the aspirant as s/he treads the spiritual path, and passes through the tests along the way. 62pp. WET 58

_____. **MORNING LIGHT—ON THE SPIRITUAL PATHS,** c$2.00. This book was one of the first that White Eagle transmitted. It sets forth the reason for life on earth and tells how man descended from higher realms into the confined life of incarnation on earth to obtain various experiences and to achieve, in the end, enlightenment. 62pp. WET 57

_____. **THE PATH OF THE SOUL,** c$3.00. The great initiations of every soul on its journey toward perfection, as exemplified in the life of Jesus. WET

_____. **THE QUIET MIND,** c$2.00. A small pocket book of White Eagle's sayings. 100pp. WET 72

_____. **SPIRITUAL UNFOLDMENT I,** c$3.50. White Eagle's practical advice and guidance on how to develop psychic and spiritual gifts, including healing. Index, 143pp. WET 61

_____. **SPIRITUAL UNFOLDMENT II,** c$3.50. Discourses on the nature and work of man's unseen companions in the fairy and angelic kingdoms, and how man can train himself to see and cooperate with them. Index, 109pp. WET 69

_____. **SUNRISE,** c$2.00. Discourse on how man, while on earth, can build a bridge between the two worlds so that death cannot separate him from those he loves. 62pp. WET 58

_____. **WISDOM FROM WHITE EAGLE,** c$3.00. Talks to students, with practical advice on spiritual matters, meditation, and life in the world today. Index, 99pp. WET 67

ROSICRUCIANISM AND FREEMASONRY

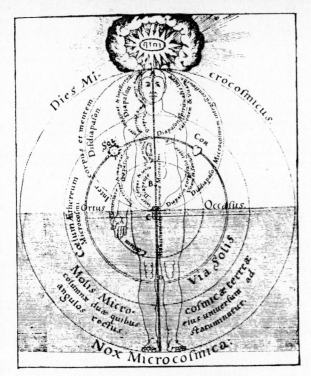

The Day and Night of the Microcosm, Robert Fludd

ALLEN, PAUL. **A CHRISTIAN ROSENKREUTZ ANTHOLOGY**, c$30.25/$15.00. See the Alchemy section.

BAILEY, FOSTER. **THE SPIRIT OF MASONRY**, $1.75. See the Theosophy section.

BUCK, J.D. **SYMBOLISM OR MYSTIC MASONRY**, c$4.00. An excellent condensed presentation of the esoteric elements of Freemasonry, emphasizing the hermetic tradition. 164pp. WBI 25

CASTELLS, F. de P. **ARITHMETIC OF FREEMASONRY**, c$2.70. *Arithmetic is one of the Seven Liberal Arts and Sciences on which the Craft has been founded; it has been a potent factor in the development of the human mind, and may help us to understand some of the principles which underlie our Masonic Ritual.* This is an interesting interpretative study, emphasizing the numbers 3, 5, 7 and their multiples and including material on the Qabala. 83pp. Lew 69

_____. **THE GENUINE SECRETS IN FREEMASONRY: PRIOR TO AD 1717**, c$8.40. A speculative, esoteric study whose thesis is that Freemasonry is Qabalism in another garb. The detailed text shows how each item of the Masonic ceremonial has been derived from the Qabala. The author has done a tremendous amount of research and has written many books—of which this is the culmination. His scholarship seems to be excellent, and while his thesis is controversial, he makes a good case for it. The reader does not have to know much about the Qabala to follow the presentation. Index, 327pp. Lew 71

_____. **ORIGIN OF THE MASONIC DEGREES**, c$7.55. This is a detailed, esoteric study which emphasizes the role of the Qabalists and Rosicrucians in the formation of the rituals and ceremonies. Index, 450pp. Lew 28

COIL, HENRY. **COIL'S MASONIC ENCYCLOPEDIA**, c$22.50. This is the newest comprehensive Masonic encyclopedia available. Coil is a life-long Mason and he spent many years compiling the material. A great deal of historical material is included and many of the individual entries read like essays. This is considered the definitive work. 731pp. Mac 61

_____. **A COMPREHENSIVE VIEW OF FREEMASONRY**, c$6.00. This is an excellent study which discusses all aspects of Freemasonry and covers its development throughout the world from the earliest times to the present. Bibliography, index. 258pp. Mac 73

_____. **FREEMASONRY THROUGH SIX CENTURIES**, c$25.00/set. This two volume set is a definitive historical study. Bibliography, index. 721pp. Mac 68

COOPER-OAKLEY, ISABEL. **THE COUNT OF SAINT-GERMAIN**, $2.50. This is regarded as perhaps the most important source book on the life and work of the Comte. The author travelled widely in search of the original material presented here. Personal diaries and private records as well as the so-called Mitchell papers are among the previously untapped sources. Cooper-Oakley provides deep insight into the history of eighteenth century Masonry, the work of the Rosicrucians and alchemists, and the life and work of Christian Rosenkreutz. Good bibliography. 248pp. Mul 70

DENCE, A.F. **AN INTERPRETATION OF CRAFT FREEMASONRY**, c$2.05. An exposition of the true meaning of the first, second, and third degree initiatory rituals. Vividly written. 42pp. Lew nd

DUNCAN, MALCOLM. **DUNCAN'S RITUAL OF FREEMASONRY**, $3.95. *The purpose of this work is not so much to gratify the curiosity of the uninitiated as to furnish a guide for the neophytes of the Order, by means of which their progress from grade to grade may be facilitated. Every statement in the book is authentic. . . .—from the preface.* 281pp. McK 76

GARVER, WILL. **BROTHER OF THE THIRD DEGREE**, c$8.50. A portrayal of a young man's struggle to attain ranking as an initiate of the third degree in a mystery school of occultism. It is replete with detailed descriptions of Masonic work and practices viewed from an esoteric angle. 377pp. Bor 1894

HALL, MANLY P. **CODEX ROSAE CRUCIS**, c$15.00. *After reading the recent histories of the Order, I feel that Rosicrucianism needs a restatement. As no other apologist has appeared, I have ventured this present treatise to clarify the subject from the injustices heaped upon it by friends, foes, and impartial historians.* This is the definitive work, very extensively illustrated in color and black and white reproductions of old plates. Half the book is devoted to an exact reproduction of the D.O.M.A. manuscript, with a complete English translation and a chapter on Hall's opinions concerning the symbols. A magnificent, illuminating work, highly recommended. 10x14", 113pp. See the Mysticism section for more of Hall's fine work. PRS 38

_____. **DIONYSIAN ARTIFICERS**, c$5.50. See the Mythology section.

_____. **LOST KEYS OF FREEMASONRY**, c$3.75. A concise exploration of all aspects of Masonry: *The true Masonic Lodge is a Mystery School, a place where candidates are taken out of the follies and foibles of the world and instructed in the mysteries of life, relationships, and the identity of that germ of spiritual essence within, which is, in truth, the Son of God, beloved of his father.—from the introduction.* 100pp. Mac 23

_____. **THE MOST HOLY TRINOSOPHIA OF THE COMTE de ST. GERMAINE**, c$10.00. St. Germain prepared this work for the instruction of his own disciples in the Qabalistic, hermetic, and alchemical mysteries. This unique work is now for the first time translated and published from the original manuscript. The great Illuminist, Rosicrucian and Freemason who termed himself the Comte de St. Germain is without question one of the most baffling personalities of modern history. His activities are traceable for the more than 100 years between 1710-1822. When once asked about himself, he replied that his father was the Secret Doctrine, and his mother the Mysteries. Includes a photostatic facsimile of the original manuscript and notes and commentaries. 220pp. PRS 62

HAYWOOD, H.L. **THE NEWLY MADE MASON**, c$5.00. *A short, clear and interesting reading giving a summary of what every Initiate would like to know about Masonry.* Includes history, philosophy, and information on the day-to-day workings of the orders. 220pp. Mac 48

MAX HEINDEL

Max Heindel was the founder of the Rosicrucian Fellowship, headquartered at Mount Ecclesia, Oceanside, California. There is a dispute between this Fellowhip and AMORC (to be mentioned later) over who the true Rosicrucians are. Heindel said that he was *an authorized messenger of the Elder Brothers of the Rose Cross, who are working to disseminate throughout the Western World the deeper Spiritual meanings which are both concealed and revealed within the Christian religion.* They are also very involved in astrology and produce the only American ephemerides and other tools.

HEINDEL, MAX. **ANCIENT AND MODERN INITIATION**, $2.50. A discussion of the general plan of initiation for humanity as outlined in the mystery teachings of all ages from Atlantean times to the Christian era. 148pp. Ros 31

_____. **FREEMASONRY AND CATHOLICISM**, $2.50. Subtitled *An exposition of the cosmic facts underlying these two great institutions as determined by occult investigation.* 110pp. Ros 19

_____. **GLEANINGS OF A MYSTIC**, c$3.50. An aggregate of writings on the mystical path by one who made practical in his life the basic precepts of spiritual living. Includes helpful information and suggestions concerning marriage, the coming Christ, and the new age. 196pp. Ros 22

_____. **MYSTERIES OF THE GREAT OPERAS**, $3.50. See the Music section.

_____. **OCCULT PRINCIPLES OF HEALTH AND HEALING**, $4.00. See the Healing section.

_____. **THE ROSICRUCIAN CHRISTIANITY LECTURES**, $4.50. The lectures presented here were first delivered by Heindel during November of 1908. They represent the direct teaching of the Elder brothers of the Rosicrucian Order which he received in 1907-8. Topics include: the riddle of life and death, spiritual sight and spiritual worlds, sleep, dreams, trance, life and activity in heaven, astrology, the angels as factors in heaven, the mystery of the Holy Grail, and much else of interest to seekers on the path. 374pp. Ros 39

_____. **THE ROSICRUCIAN COSMO-CONCEPTION**, c$4.50/$3.50. Heindel's most important work, giving a complete outline of the Western wisdom teachings. It contains a comprehensive outline of the evolutionary processes of man and the universe, correlating science with religion. Part I is a treatise on the visible and invisible world, and the method of evolution, rebirth and the law of cause and effect: Part II takes up the scheme of evolution in general and the evolution of the solar system and the Earth in particular. Part III discusses Christ and his mission, future development of man, initiation, and esoteric training. The paperback edition contains only a topical index; the cloth one has an alphabetical index also. 702pp. Ros 09

_____. **THE ROSICRUCIAN MYSTERIES**, c$3.00. A survey of some of the Rosicrucian doctrines and conceptions concerning the nature of man and his relationship to the universe. Discusses some of life's problems with their solutions and gives a view of life and death. 155pp. Ros 11

_____. **THE ROSICRUCIAN PHILOSOPHY IN QUESTIONS AND ANSWERS, VOLUMES I, II**, c$5.00/each. The questions contained in these two volumes were answered by Heindel in his magazine, **Rays from the Rose Cross**, 1913-19. The answers are often quite detailed and sometimes include illustrations. Fully indexed, 1017pp. Ros 47

_____. **TEACHINGS OF AN INITIATE**, $3.00. Touches upon a wide variety of subjects, including the World War in the light of spiritual misunderstanding, the esoteric significance of Easter and the scientific method of spiritual unfoldment. 203pp. Ros 27

HELINE, CORINNE. **MYSTIC MASONRY AND THE BIBLE**, $3.75. 173pp. NAP 63

HORNE, ALEX. **KING SOLOMON'S TEMPLE**, c$8.95. A detailed speculative study based both on academic research and on extracts from Masonic rituals and legends. Index, 352pp. Wil 72

LAWRENCE, JOHN. **THE KEYSTONE**, c$5.75. An analysis of some of the most important historical events and Masonic symbols as they are seen by the Masons. This is a collection of essays; the author is an English Mason and has written extensively on Masonry. The following are some of the selections: *The Keystone, The Triangle, The Columns of Wisdom, Strength and Beauty, The Discipline of the Craft, Religion and Freemasonry, Babylon, The Queen of Sheba.* 335pp. Lew 25

LEADBEATER, C.W. **THE HIDDEN LIFE IN FREEMASONRY**, $8.00. An exploration of the esoteric side of Masonry written to give the brethren a fuller understanding of the mysteries of the craft. All aspects of Masonry are discussed. Illustrations, index, 382pp. HeR 26

Rosicrucian Design from Robert Fludd's: "Summum Bonum"

H. SPENCER LEWIS

Lewis was the founder of AMORC (the Ancient Mystical Order of Rosicrucians) in San Jose, California. This is the most popular of the present-day Rosicrucian groups. They do extensive advertising and have a large, devoted following. The AMORC books form a very practical teaching for the spiritual aspirant.

LEWIS, H. SPENCER. **ESSAYS OF A MODERN MYSTIC**, c$6.65. Amo

_____. **MENTAL POISONING**, c$5.75. Amo

_____. **ROSICRUCIAN PRINCIPLES FOR THE HOME AND BUSINES** c$6.60. Amo 29

_____. **ROSICRUCIAN QUESTIONS AND ANSWERS**, c$5.75. Based on th teachings of AMORC, the questions answer a broad gamut of philosophical inquiry. Al included is a history of the Rosicrucian order. 329pp. Amo

_____. **SELF MASTERY AND FATE WITH THE CYCLES OF FATE**, c$6.6 See the Biorhythm section.

_____. **A THOUSAND YEARS OF YESTERDAYS**, c$5.75. An explanation the manner in which a soul undergoes the process of reincarnation, written in story for with the mystic principles woven into the content. 75pp. Amo

LYTTON, EDWARD BULWER. **ZANONI: A ROSICRUCIAN TALE**, $2.45. A dramat occult novel involving important historical and political Rosicrucian figures set against th backdrop of explosive France in the days of its revolution. It is the story of the strugg between the head and the heart and that conflict's only possible resolution, the baptis of spiritual initiation. 405pp. Mul 71

MACKEY, ALBERT G. **MACKEY'S REVISED ENCYCLOPEDIA OF FREEMASONR** c$25.00/set. This three volume set is considered the best over-all work available. Mac

_____. **MACKEY'S SYMBOLISM OF FREEMASONRY**, c$4.00. A detaile exposition of the legends, myths, and symbols which illustrate and explain the scien and philosophy of Freemasonry. This is an excellent study by one of Freemasonry's mo noted writers. Don't be fooled by the publication date; this book was written long ag Notes, glossary, index. 364pp. Pow 75

MAGUS INCOGNITO. **THE SECRET DOCTRINE OF THE ROSICRUCIANS**, c$4.50. very comprehensive account of the beliefs of the Rosicrucians, including information the soul of the world, the universal androgyne, the planes of consciousness, the sevenfo soul of man, the soul's progress, the aura and auric principles, and the seven cosmic pri ciples. 256pp. YPS nd

NEWTON, JOHN. **RELIGION OF MASONRY**, c$3.75. This is generally considered th best presentation of the subject ever written. Notes, annotated bibliography. 160pp. Mac

OLIVER, GEORGE. **THE PYTHAGOREAN TRIANGLE**, c$8.95. See the Pythagora subsection of Mysticism.

PERCIVAL, HAROLD. **MASONRY AND ITS SYMBOLS**, $3.00. *This valuable litt book should be in the possession of every sincere Mason who desires more LIGHT on an a truer understanding of the symbols of Masonry, of the ceremonies in which he take part, and of their deep esoteric significance.* —Harold Percival. 73pp. WdF 52

STEINER, RUDOLF. **ROSICRUCIANISM AND MODERN INITIATION**, c$4.50. Tran scriptions of lectures. See Steiner section for more on his philosophy. 96pp. API 5

_____. **THEOSOPHY OF THE ROSICRUCIAN**, c$4.95. Transcriptions of le tures. 168pp. RSP 54

STEINMETZ, GEORGE. **FREEMASONRY—ITS HIDDEN MEANING**, c$5.75. A spiri ual interpretation of the esoteric work of the Masonic lodge. The lectures and symbols o the first three degrees are carefully and systematically analyzed and true Masonic philos ophy is reviewed. 218pp. Mac 48

_____. **THE LOST WORLD—ITS HIDDEN MEANING**, c$3.50. A correlation o the allegory and symbolism of the ancient mystery teachings and the Bible with that o Freemasonry. Bibliography, index. 262pp. Mac 53

WAITE, ARTHUR EDWARD. **THE BROTHERHOOD OF THE ROSY CROSS**, c$10.0C Waite was not a member of this order, but in his philosophy he identified himself closel with the ancient beliefs espoused by the Rosicrucians. This is a very complete account o the origins of Rosicrucianism, its original doctrines and their unfolding and changing, it relationship to Freemasonry, and much else. Includes biographical material on the mo noted Rosicrucians, including a full chapter on Robert Fludd. This text includes extensiv source and explanatory notes. A massive effort. Waite tends to be a bit ponderous a times since he includes all the research he can garner—but is generally well respected 654pp. UnB 73

_____. **A NEW ENCYCLOPEDIA OF FREEMASONRY**, c$35.00/set. A compre hensive view of the history, literature and myths concerning Freemasonry with explana tions of Masonic ritual and symbolism. Two volumes, many references, notes. 950pp UnB 70

_____. **THE REAL HISTORY OF THE ROSICRUCIANS**, $6.00. Another o Waite's in depth studies. In addition to the strictly historical and interpretative materia Waite provides individual chapters on some of the most important Rosicrucian figures an translations of some important documents. Oversize, 311pp. HcR 1887

WARD, A.H. **MASONIC SYMBOLISM**, c$2.00. A series of short papers originally pre pared for delivery at lodge meetings. The symbolism connected with the first thre degrees is discussed at length and there is also material on *the lost word.* 110pp. TPH 2.

ZAIN, C.C. **ANCIENT MASONRY**, $5.95. See the Astrology section.

SACRED ART

RANO, LUISA. **THE MEDIEVAL HEALTH HANDBOOK**, c$20.00. The illuminated anuscripts known as **Tacuinum Sanitatis** were handbooks of the late 1300's and early 400's which illustrated and explained the effects of foods, flowers, winds, waters, seasons, and even human emotions upon a person's health. This boxed book contains reproductions from five of the most important **Tacuina**, along with a descriptive text. 291 lates, 48 in color. Oversize, 156pp. Brz 76

RGUELLES, JOSE and MIRIAM. **MANDALA**, $6.95. The mandala as a symbol of the holeness of the total experience of reality is a basic form—an expression of many of an's highest ideals, whether expressed in religious, philosophical or scientific terms. It as appeared throughout man's history, serving as a universal and essential symbol of integration, harmony and transformation. This profusely illustrated beautiful volume presents he philosophical, religious, psychological and artistic basis of the mandala. Highly recommended. Extensive bibliography, 140pp. ShP 72

ARYAN, K.C. and SUBHASHINI. **HANUMAN IN ART AND MYTHOLOGY**, c$60.00. Hanuman is known as the perfect servant. He played a large role in the **Ramayana** and is oday worshiped by followers from many traditions. He was proficient in all the shastras: ine arts, science, philosophy. All the facets of his many-sided personality have been brought out in this volume. Hanuman has inspired not only Indian artists and artisans but also those of Nepal, Burma, Indonesia, Thailand, Bali, Java, and many other areas. Certain yantras and mantras associated with Hanuman have also been included in this volume along with over 200 plates, some in color. A chapter on mythology and folklore relates various episodes from Hanuman's life. 10x10", 80pp. RPr 75

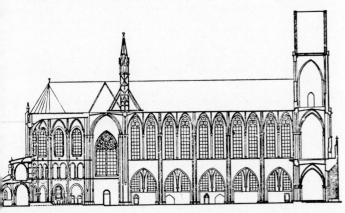

Magdeburg Cathedral

AUBERT, MARCEL. **THE ART OF THE HIGH GOTHIC ERA**, c$6.95. The soaring lines of the great Gothic cathedrals bear living witness to the piety of the Middle Ages. This book traces the Gothic style between 1220 and 1350. All the major cathedrals are discussed in terms of the architecture, sculpture, and paintings. The text is illustrated with 55 color plates, 24 black-and-white illustrations, and 65 drawings. The reproductions are excellent and each plate is fully commented on. Chronology, bibliography, index. 227pp. Crn 65

AYNES, CLEMENT. **THE PICTORIAL LANGUAGE OF HIERONYMUS BOSCH**, c$12.90. In recent years there has been a willingness to recognize in the paintings of Bosch a spiritual content and message rather than a mere phantasmagoria of sexual and satanic ideas. This volume, written by an anthroposophist, reveals the secrets of Rosicrucian philosophy and spiritual teachings hidden in Bosch's mysterious works. Reproductions (in color and black-and-white) of Bosch's major and minor works are included, with detailed commentary, and his most noted works are broken down and their various parts analyzed. A fascinating study. 9½x12½", bibliography, index. 124pp. NKB 75

BAIN, GEORGE. **CELTIC ART**, $4.00. The construction principles of Celtic arts were rediscovered in the middle of this century by Bain. Until then the intricate knots, interlacements and spirals used in illuminating Celtic literature and in decorating craftwork and jewelry seemed almost impossible. In this pioneering work he shows how simple principles, no more difficult than those used in needlepoint, were used to create some of the finest artistic works ever seen. Step-by-step procedures carefully introduce the rules and methods of Celtic knot work and the well known designs from the great manuscripts and stone work. Altogether over 225 different patterns are presented, with modification suggestions, 110 artifacts, and a great number of letters. Explanatory material accompanies the illustrations. Oversize, 159pp. Dov 51

BAYLEY, HAROLD. **THE LOST LANGUAGE OF SYMBOLISM**, c$16.25. Bayley surveys the results of his lifetime study of the origin of letters, words, names, fairytales, folklore, and mythologies. The information the author presents is not in a readily accessible format, unfortunately, but the approach is unusual and reflects the inner meaning of the symbols. The book includes 1418 line drawings and is fully indexed. Esoteric information is emphasized. 411pp. BnL 12

BINYON, LAURENCE, J.V.S. WILKINSON and BASIL GRAY. **PERSIAN MINIATURE PAINTING**, $6.00. Three experts examine and discuss the collection of Persian miniatures assembled for the Exhibition of Persian Art in London in 1931. 225 of the pictures are reproduced here, together with the authors' presentation of background, descriptions,

analyses, and evaluations, not only of the paintings shown but of Persian art as a whole. All periods and schools are represented. This is both a definitive treatise and a magnificent introduction to the subject. Nine color plates, introduction, appendices, bibliography, indices. 226pp. Dov 33

BLUNT, WILFRID. **SPLENDORS OF ISLAM**, c$10.95. See the Islam section.

BOURGOIN, J. **ARABIC GEOMETRICAL PATTERN AND DESIGN**, $4.00. By forbidding the representation of the human figure, the Muslim religion pushed Islamic art along a path much different than that of traditional European art. Islam translates artistic impulse into elaborate geometric patterns and linear design which became perfected over the centuries. This book contains 190 examples which exhibit the wide range of this geometrical art. 8x10-3/4", 211pp. Dov 1879

BRIESSEN, FRITZ van. **THE WAY OF THE BRUSH**, c$25.00. **The Way of the Brush** *is an exceedingly handsome, lavishly illustrated book that is important because it opens the door on a whole new (to the western mind) world of art, the painting techniques and the symbolism of China and Japan. It is the most readable, the most authoritative, and the most comprehensive explanation of its kind to be published in many years. Indeed, it deservedly may be called unique.*—Chicago Sunday Tribune. The text is topically arranged and the presentation is exceedingly thoughtful. 284 finely reproduced illustrations, many in color, accompany the text. A fine work which we recommend heartily. 7½x10¾", appendices, glossary, bibliography, index. 329pp. Tut 62

BROOKS, ROBERT and VISHNU WAKANKAR. **STONE AGE PAINTING IN INDIA**, c$15.00. In the sandstone caves of Central India are found a greater number and variety of Stone Age paintings than in any other region of the world. Indian Stone Age art has remained largely unexplored. This is the first book length discussion and it is profusely illustrated with sixty-seven color plates and sixty-five duotones. The reproductions are excellent and the text matches the quality of the paintings. 128pp. YUP 76

BURCKHARDT, TITUS. **ART OF ISLAM: LANGUAGE AND MEANING**, c$25.00. See the Islam section.

_____. **SACRED ART EAST AND WEST**, c$8.60. A work of wide scope, covering Hindu, Christian, Islamic, Buddhist and Far Eastern art—conveying the distinctive characteristic of each, while at the same time emphasizing their unity of principle. Every sacred art is deeply rooted in the religion in which it originates, and it plays an indispensible part in preserving the character and continuity of the sacred civilization connected with that religion. See the Islam section for more of Burckhardt's work. Everything he has written is highly recommended. Profusely illustrated. 160pp. Prn 67

CARROLL, DAVID. **THE TAJ MAHAL**, c$11.95. The Taj Mahal is the artistic jewel of the Mogul Empire in India. It stands today as an exquisitely wrought memorial both to the love match that gave it life and the artisans who created it. Its exterior and interior surfaces are entirely covered with inlaid designs executed in some thirty-five varieties of semiprecious stone; its portals are framed by intricate calligraphic inscriptions; and its formal gardens are a triumph of the landscape architect's craft. About 120 illustrations—nearly half in color—supplement this history of the Mogul dynasty. Notes, bibliography, index. 11½x9", Nsw 72

CIRLOT, J.E. **A DICTIONARY OF SYMBOLS**, c$4.98. This is considered the definitive work on symbology. It is an invaluable tool for all who seek to understand esoteric literature, especially graphically represented traditions such as alchemy and the Tarot. The dictionary is also illuminating in dream analysis. It is arranged alphabetically by subject and the individual analyses are often in-depth essays on the topic, complete with relevant quotations and cross-references. Many illustrations are also included. The individual entries range from esoteric topics such as the chakras and the elements to mythological characters and themes. An excellent tool for all students and readers. Index, 454pp. PhL 62. A slightly revised edition containing some additional material is available for c$15.00.

COOK, ROGER. **TREE OF LIFE**, $5.95. The Tree of Life, appearing in an infinite variety of forms in the symbolism of the great world religions, mythology, and folklore, is a universal symbol for the inner directions of the cosmic process and its goal: the unity of mankind and the world. Revealing the living presence of a transcendent power which mankind has traditionally both feared and adored, the Tree embodies in its seasonal transformations the perpetual renewal of the cosmos from a sacred source at the center of the world. The Tree of Life appears as a perennial focus of man's inner world in both the Judeo-Christian and Muslim traditions. This oversize book traces the Tree throughout these traditions with 165 illustrations (31 in full color), all descriptively analyzed, and excellent introductory material. Part of Avon's *Art and Cosmos* series. 128pp. Avo 74

COOMARASWAMY, ANANDA. **THE ARTS AND CRAFTS OF INDIA AND CEYLON**, $2.95. The life of Ananda Coomaraswamy was dedicated to interpreting the East to the West. In this book he surveys two thousand years of creation in the Indian subcontinent and shows that the arts and crafts reflect many different ways of life and complex ways of vision. 225 illustrations are included and Hindu, Buddhist, and Mogul art are all discussed. Index, 272pp. FSG 13

_____. **CHRISTIAN AND ORIENTAL PHILOSOPHY OF ART**, $2.25. A collection of nine essays covering a variety of themes. The book was originally entitled **Why Exhibit Works of Art?** Bibliography, 146pp. Dov 43

_____. **THE ORIGIN OF THE BUDDHA IMAGE**, c$19.15. A detailed study and analysis which attempts to show that the Buddha image originated out of pre-existing Indian forms. The text is extensively annotated and is illustrated with 73 different images of the Buddha. 8½x11", 42pp. MuM 72

_____. THE TRANSFORMATION OF NATURE IN ART, $3.00. This is a deeply philosophical work on Asiatic art principles. Coomaraswamy begins with an examination of Indian and Chinese treatises on aesthetic theory and art manuals. He follows this with a review of the medieval European aesthetic in terms of the fourteenth century mystic Meister Eckhart. Further chapters investigate, through Indian texts, the psychology of the Indian viewer of art as well as the origin and use of images in India. Glossaries, bibliography, notes. 255pp. Dov 34

EL-SAID, ISSAM and AYSE PARMAN. GEOMETRICAL CONCEPTS IN ISLAMIC ART, c$19.50. See the Islam section.

ENCISO, JORGE. DESIGNS FROM PRE-COLUMBIAN MEXICO, $2.00. A sourcebook of 300 clearly reproduced designs, each of which was found on a small round clay object. Each plate is captioned. 116pp. Dov 71

_____. DESIGN MOTIFS OF ANCIENT MEXICO, $2.50. A collection of 766 vigorous designs, divided into the following section: geometric motifs, natural forms and flora, the human body, and artificial forms. Very clear, black reproductions. 166pp. Dov 47

GOETZ, HERMANN. THE ART OF INDIA, c$6.95. This handsome book traces Indian art—including architecture, painting, sculpture, and handicrafts—from its origin in the late Stone Age to the most recent developments. This is an excellent work which should appeal to specialists and general readers alike. Accompanying the text are over 60 hand-tipped color plates and several maps. There's also a bibliography, a glossary, and a chronology. The author has spent his lifetime studying Indian art. Index, 283pp. Crn 59

GORDON, ANTOINETTE. TIBETAN RELIGIOUS ART, c$16.00. See the Tibetan sub-section of Buddhism.

HALL, JAMES. DICTIONARY OF SUBJECTS AND SYMBOLS IN ART, c$12.50. This is a fine work which complements Cirlot's excellent volume. The emphasis here is on Biblical and classical themes on which European art is based. Mythological themes are also covered in detail. Esoteric symbology is not touched upon in any depth. All of the entries are quite clear and cover the material well. Illustrations, bibliography, cross-references. 345pp. H&R 74

HEER, FRIEDRICH. THE FIRES OF FAITH, c$10.00. See the Christianity section.

HILLIER, J.R. JAPANESE DRAWINGS, $5.95. Japanese drawings are usually impromptu, unelaborated pieces drawn freely from nature. The Japanese masters executed their drawings for the sheer joy of exhibiting brushwork—they drew flower, bird, landscape, and nature scenes without any illustrative intent other than to provide an occasion for aesthetic design. In their drawings the viewer can enjoy the interplay of the strong, circumscribing line contrasted against the flat silhouettes of the wash. This collection of Japanese drawings from the seventeenth to the nineteenth century presents a wide selection of outstanding works. Ninety plates are included, more than half in color. An introduction discusses Japanese drawings. 8½x9¾", notes on artists, bibliography. 139pp. LBC 65

JAMES, DAVID. ISLAMIC ART: AN INTRODUCTION, c$3.98. David James is the curator of Islamic art at the Chester Beatty Library in Dublin. This is the best introductory survey that we know of. It is clearly written, comprehensive, and includes 60 color plates and 61 photographs and line drawings. The entire Islamic world is surveyed. 8½x11½", glossary, index. 96pp. Ham 74

KANDINSKY, WASSILY. CONCERNING THE SPIRITUAL IN ART, $6.00. This is one of the only books on this subject and it is an illuminating work that also contains a great deal of information on colors. Illustrated, oversize. 92pp. Wit 47

KOCH, RUDOLF. THE BOOK OF SIGNS, $1.50. A collection of primitive and medieval symbols are redrawn by the author, with a hand-drawn text discussing their meaning. 104pp. Dov 30

KURTH, WILLI. THE COMPLETE WOODCUTS OF ALBRECHT DURER, $6.00. Durer was a master in various mediums, but it was in woodcut design that his creative genius reached its highest expression. This book is a collection of all his extant woodcuts, 346 in all. Although sacred objects predominate, many other motifs are treated. The plates are arranged in chronological order permitting the reader to view the development of Durer's art. An introduction and textual notes on the plates are also included. 8½x12¼", 285pp. Dov 27

LEHNER, ERNEST. SYMBOLS, SIGNS AND SIGNETS, $4.00. This is an excellent collection of non-copyright art which will be invaluable to anyone doing layout work. We use this book extensively in all the material we produce. The book is divided into thirteen sections: Symbolical Gods and Deities, Astronomy and Astrology, Alchemy, Magic and Mystic, Church and Religion, Heraldry, Monsters and Imaginary Figures, Japanese Crests, Marks and Signets, Watermarks, Printer's Marks. All the symbols have full explanatory notes. Oversize, bibliography. 221pp. Dov 50

LINGS, MARTIN. THE QURANIC ART OF CALLIGRAPHY AND ILLUMINATION, c$25.00. See the Islam section.

LLOYD, SETON. THE ART OF THE ANCIENT NEAR EAST, $4.50. Long before the beginnings of written history, the Near East gave birth to works of monumental sculpture and painting. By the time Athens was bursting into flower as a center of Western culture, Egypt, Mesopotamia, and their neighbors could look back on nearly twenty-five centuries

of continous artistic development. This volume has 249 plates, many in color, and a great deal of commentary. Index, 302pp. Pra 61

MACFARQUHAR, RODERICK. THE FORBIDDEN CITY: CHINA'S ANCIENT CAPITAL, c$11.95. A history of Peking which reproduces through 150 illustrations (one third in color) the art and architecture of the splendid imperial city. Many photographs and maps also illuminate the volume and the text discusses the history of the forbidden city from its founding in the eighth century to the present time. One section presents literary descriptions of the city. A beautifully produced book. Oversize, bibliography, index. 172pp. Nsw 72

MATSUSHITA, TAKAAKI. INK PAINTING, $7.95. A good study, enhanced by 170 black-and-white and color illustrations, of the most vital form of Japanese painting. Oversize, glossary, bibliography, index. 124pp. Wea 74

MICHELL, JOHN. THE EARTH SPIRIT: ITS WAYS, SHRINES AND MYSTERIES, $5.95. See the Ancient Civilizations section.

MOOKERJEE, AJIT. YOGA ART, c$39.50. Yoga art (also known as tantric art) is formed of a number of mystical configurations that seek to clarify the viewer's perceptions and to unite him or her with the cosmic forces. The images are largely abstract and geometric and are based on a complicated system of colors, numbers, and proportions. Mookerjee is the world's foremost expert on this type of art and he contributes an authoritative text which describes the philosophical underpinnings of the art and provides an invaluable explanation of the symbolic systems that underlie the art. Richly illustrated, the book includes 76 color and 58 black-and-white reproductions of meditative drawings, sculpture, pages from illuminated manuscripts, mandals, and yantras. All have a purity of conception and design. An exceedingly beautiful book. 10x11½", 208pp. NYG 75

MURRAY, PETER and LINDA. THE ART OF THE RENAISSANCE, $6.95. This is a widely respected general survey which discusses both the period and the individual artists and artistic movements. Architecture, sculpture, painting, book illustration, and all aspects of the arts of design are reviewed. 250 illustrations (some in color) illuminate the text. Index, 286pp. Pra 63

MUSTERBERG, HUGO. SCULPTURE OF THE ORIENT, $3.50. Dr. Musterberg, a noted authority on Oriental art, has selected the best pieces from many collections. He covers the whole range of Oriental sculpture from the twentieth century BC to the eighteenth century AD, and from every tradition. There are Shinto, Buddhist, Hindu, Jainist and other religious sculptures as well as secular pieces from a wide variety of periods and locations—over 150 in all. 8½x11", 160pp. Dov 72

NARAZAKI, MUNESHIGE. HOKUSAI, $8.95. Hokusai was the most prolific of the ukiyo-e (pictures of the floating world) masters. He is noted for the special relationship between figure and landscape in his work—a perfect fusion in which neither element dominates nor is dominated. He also gives his figures a remarkable sense of life through the use of color and light. This volume reproduces the entire Thirty-six Views of Mt. Fuji (his most noted work), the ten prints he added to the series, and ten pages of details from the most famous of the prints in the series—all in full color. An account of his life and work is also included along with analyses of several of the prints. 7x20", 96pp. Kod 68

NAYLOR, MARIA, ed. AUTHENTIC INDIAN DESIGN, $5.00. A collection of 2500 designs that come from all over the U.S. and date from prehistoric times to the end of the nineteenth century. All the reproductions are clear. Introduction, 8x11". 242pp. Dov 75

NEUMANN, ERICH. ART AND THE CREATIVE UNCONSCIOUS, $3.45. See the Jungian Psychology section.

NORELLI-BACHELET, PATRIZIA. SYMBOLS AND THE QUESTION OF UNITY, c$7.25. Every breakthrough, every Age that introduces a new element in evolution, must also bring with it a new understanding of symbols, because the way in which man reveals himself and his higher states of consciousness in symbols tells us what the stage of evolution is and the achievements of any given Age. Symbols are the language whereby man expresses his experience of God, and whereby the Supreme reveals the part and image of Himself that man is in the process of expressing. These articles were prepared originally for publication in the journal of the Sri Aurobindo Ashram. They are mainly concerned with astrological and astronomical symbols and with mythology and sacred numbers. 157pp. Ser 74

NORDENFALK, CARL. CELTIC PAINTING, $9.95. In the seventh and eighth centuries a series of illuminated manuscripts emerged from monasteries and island workshops. These include such famous manuscripts as The Book of Kells, The Lindisfarne Gospels, and The Book of Durrow, with their intricate designs as well as their extravagantly elongated and knotted representations of hounds, birds, snakes, lizards, and mythical monsters. The artists who labored on these manuscripts refused to attempt naturalistic representation, so that they could be as free with the figures in a picture as if they were calligraphic designs. This is a beautifully produced volume which includes forty-eight plates in four colors plus gold as well as many other illustrations and an excellent text. 8x11", 128pp. Brz 76

PAL, PRATAPADITYA. THE ART OF TIBET, c$16.50. See the Tibetan sub-section of Buddhism.

_____. NEPAL: WHERE THE GODS ARE YOUNG, c$19.95. See the Tibetan sub-section of Buddhism.

PURCE, JILL. THE MYSTIC SPIRAL, $4.95. The spiral is the natural form of growth, and has become, in every culture and every age, man's symbol of the progress of the soul toward eternal life. As the inward-winding labyrinth, it constitutes the hero's journey to he still center where the secret of life is found. As the spherical vortex, spiraling through its own center, it combines the inward and outward directions of movement. In this engrossing book, Jill Purce traces its significance. as one of mankind's central symbols from the double spirals of Stone Age art and the interlocking spirals of the yin/yang symbol to the whorls of Celtic crosses and the Islamic arabesque. The excellent introductory text illuminates many difficult alchemical and cosmological concepts and the illustrations, drawn from many traditions, can be studied and appreciated endlessly by those seeking an understanding of the mysteries of the cosmos. It can be looked at merely as a beautiful coffee table book or as a collection of some of the most inspiring drawings and paintings we've seen. It's one of our favorite books and we recommend it highly. Part of Avon's *Art and Cosmos* series. 174 illustrations, 32 in full color. Oversize, 128pp. Avo 74

RAINE, KATHLEEN. **WILLIAM BLAKE**, $5.25. See the Blake sub-section of Mysticism.

RAWSON, PHILIP. **THE ART OF SOUTHEAST ASIA**, $5.95. The countries of Southeast Asia are situated between two great civilizations—the Indian and the Chinese. From earliest times, they have, in their art, blended indigenous forms with those of their powerful neighbors, creating styles that are uniquely their own. This is the first authoritative study of their art in English and Rawson includes works of art in every category—from large architectural complexes to tiny bronzes. In addition, he gives the reader a great deal of information about the history, traditions, social organization, and religious beliefs of the societies of the area. He also synthesizes and clarifies the origins and evolution of artistic styles and the historical setting. Glossary, bibliography, index, 251 illustrations (some in color). 288pp. Pra 67

_____. **THE ART OF TANTRA**, c$17.50. See the Tantra section.

_____. **TANTRA: INDIAN CULT OF ECSTASY**, $4.95. See the Tantra section.

RAWSON, PHILIP and LASLO LEGEZA. **ṬAO: THE EASTERN PHILOSOPHY OF TIME AND CHANGE**, $4.95. See the Chinese Philosophy section.

ROBINSON, B.W. **PERSIAN DRAWINGS**, $5.95. This book details the art of illuminated miniatures, which reached its peak in the medieval depictions of the adventures of the mythical hero, Rustam. In most cases Persian drawings and paintings illustrate some literary text. They are, in other words, pictures with a story, outstanding for splendid colors (real gold, true ultramarine, unmixed vermilion), subtly organized narrative elements, a wealth of detail, and a perfected draftsmanship. 100 plates—most in color—from the fourteenth through the nineteenth century are included in the volume and the text examines the various schools and styles of Persian drawing. Bibliography, 8½x9". 142pp. LBC 65

ROLA, STANISLAS de. **THE SECRET ART OF ALCHEMY**, $4.95. See the Alchemy section.

ROWLAND, BENJAMIN. **THE ART OF CENTRAL ASIA**, c$6.95. A superbly illustrated explanation and critique of the ancient art forms of a variety of countries. Spanning the period from the death of Alexander the Great to the end of the classical, Mazdean, and Buddhist civilizations in Central Asia in the seventh century when Islamic hordes wreaked destruction upon their cultures, this book is a vivid chronicle of the artistic heritage of the whole area. 91 illustrations, 56 in color. Bibliography, chronology, index. 232pp. Crn 74

ROWLEY, GEORGE. **PRINCIPLES OF CHINESE PAINTING**, $4.95. A series of essays written around the themes of subject matter and its interpretation and style. To explain what makes a painting Chinese, Professor Rowley penetrates into the Chinese way of looking at life, and he has produced a profound, illuminating document. This is a fine book which should be invaluable to students who seek to deepen their understanding of the principles of Chinese art. An excellent feature of the text is the author's examination of a number of individual works. 47 plates, 8½x11", index. 132pp. PUP 59

雪舟初

Rats drawn by the boy, Sesshu, come to life, Hokusai

SAWA, TAKAAKI. **ART IN JAPANESE ESOTERIC BUDDHISM**, c$12.50. See the Zen sub-section of Buddhism.

SHARKEY, JOHN. **CELTIC MYSTERIES**, $5.95. See the Ancient Britain sub-section of Ancient Civilizations.

SINGH, MADANJEET. **HIMALAYAN ART**, $3.95. A handsome book which explains both the history of the mountain kingdoms and the complicated mythology reflected in their sacred art. 168 plates are included—almost half in color. An excellent introductory work. Bibliography, 287pp. McM 68

SIREN, OSVALD. **THE CHINESE ON THE ART OF PAINTING**, $3.95. An authoritative handbook which gives the history and philosophy of Chinese art as it unfolded in the stated intentions and reflections of the artists themselves. Siren presents the writings of Chinese painter-critics from the fourth through the nineteenth century. He also examines their aesthetic aims and ideals in relation to various schools of Chinese religion and philosophy. The selections are arranged according to the historical sequence of dynasties. Notes, index. 259pp. ScB 63

SMITH, BRADLEY. **JAPAN: A HISTORY IN ART**, c$12.95. This uniquely beautiful book presents the history of Japan through twenty centuries—as seen, remembered, and recorded by her artists. It captures and clarifies the Japanese vision of life in its richness, delicacy, and complexity of pattern. Each of the 288 plates is faithfully reproduced in color. Each was chosen not only for its extraordinary beauty, but as a storytelling panel in a vast, dramatic, historical panorama that encompasses the rise and fall of dynasties, the sweep of religious and political movements, the flowering of the arts, and the minutiae of daily life. This is an amazing book and it is one of the best bargains that we know of. 9x13", bibliography, 295pp. Dou 64

SZE, MAI-MAI. **THE WAY OF CHINESE PAINTING**, $2.95. See the Chinese Philosophy section.

TARTHANG TULKU. **SACRED ART OF TIBET**, $5.45. See the Tibetan sub-section of Buddhism.

TIBETAN THANKA PORTFOLIO, $25.00. See the Tibetan sub-section of Buddhism.

TRUNGPA, CHOGYAM. **VISUAL DHARMA: THE BUDDHIST ART OF TIBET**, $7.95. See the Tibetan sub-section of Buddhism.

TSUDA, NORITAKE. **HANDBOOK OF JAPANESE ART**, $5.50. This book *offers the Westerner a comprehensive view of Japanese art through Japanese eyes. . . . It surveys the full range of achievement in painting, sculpture, architecture, ceramics, lacquerware, woodblock printmaking, metalwork, textiles, garden making, and other artistic fields.* —from the foreward. The approach is chronological, and the art of each historical period is introduced by the categories in which it found its most significant expression during that period. Extensively illustrated, bibliography, index. 526pp. Tut 76

WATTS, ALAN. **EROTIC SPIRITUALITY**, $3.95. See the Indian Philosophy section.

WEITZMANN, KURT. **LATE ANTIQUE—EARLY CHRISTIAN PAINTING**, $9.95. Reproductions and discussions of a number of illuminated manuscripts from this period including such famous works as **The Cotton Genesis, The Vienna Genesis,** and **The Rossano Gospels.** Forty-eight plates in four colors plus gold and many additional illustrations. 8x11", 128pp. Brz 76

WELCH, STUART. **PERSIAN PAINTING**, $9.95. Of all the sacred art books in this section, this is our favorite. The sixteenth century saw a flowering of classical miniature painting in Persia and the pages reproduced in this volume represent the most unusual and dazzling miniatures in these manuscripts. Within settings exquisitely portrayed, a world of great luxury and delicacy unfolds on every folio as palaces open onto fountains and gardens, lovers and warriors sigh or are vanquished—all realized in shimmering, jewel-like paintings. Forty-eight miniatures are reproduced here in full color and the text traces the historical development that accompanied the art and clarifies the fine points of each mixture. 8x11", 127pp. Brz 75

WILLIAMS, C.A.S. **OUTLINES OF CHINESE SYMBOLISM AND ART MOTIVES**, c$12.50. See the Chinese Philosophy section.

WOSIEN, MARIA-GABRIELLE. **SACRED DANCE**, $4.95. Creation is movement, and the sacred dance arises from the need to identify with the eternal round of the creative forces in the cosmos. Dancing intensifies awareness, so that the dancer begins to understand how the universe is made up of infinite patterns of motion around a still center. A primordial element of religious tradition all over the world, the dance was a vital part of early Christian worship, and survives in the whirling, orbiting movements of the dervishes of Turkey. In images ranging from Botticelli's dancing angels to the dance patterns of the South Seas, this book evokes one of man's oldest and profoundest impulses—to act out the movements of the powers he senses within himself and within the world. An illuminating introductory text is followed by 142 illustrations, 30 in full color—all described at length. Part of Avon's excellent *Art and Cosmos* series. Avo 74

WRAY, ELIZABETH, et al. **TEN LIVES OF THE BUDDHA**, c$15.00. See the Jataka Tales sub-section of Buddhism.

YOSHIKAWA, ITSUJI. **MAJOR THEMES IN JAPANESE ART**, c$12.50. Both an introduction to Japanese art and an overview of its rich history, this volume serves two major purposes: to survey the development of Japanese art from its primitive beginnings to the nineteenth century, and to interpret significant aspects of its splendid and often unique achievements. Every representative trend, style, and school is covered by the text and the 175 illustrations (42 in color). 7½x9½", 166pp. Wea 76

ZIGROSSER, CARL. **MEDICINE AND THE ARTIST**, $5.00. Many of the greatest artists have been attracted to medical scenes. This volume reproduces 137 extraordinary works of art from the fifteenth century to the present in which some aspect of medicine or health is the subject. In addition to the prints there is an illuminating commentary on each. 8x11", index. 190pp. Dov 59

SACRED GEOMETRY

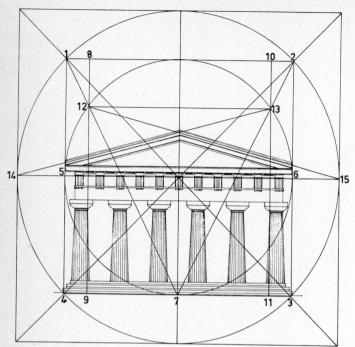

Temple of Poseidon, from Brunes, The Secrets of Ancient Geometry

Geometry in ancient times was simply the culture-creating tool with which most things were made, and . . . the importance of this particular tool to the unfolding of culture itself was vital. The system has its roots in the very beginning of time, further back in Man's history even than the ancient Egyptian dynasties, and the existence and application of the system can be shown over an incalculable length of time right up until the Middle Ages, when it finally died out still swathed in a mantle of secrecy and silence.

The system was attributed immeasurable significance as late as the period of speculation in Greece 2,500 years before our own time, and one can read of it in Plato's eighth book, in which he describes the explanation by Timaeus the philosopher on the universe and its composition.

This chapter describes in detail portions of the old geometric system, geometry being employed as a picture of the universe and the power of the deity, not as we use geometry today as an explanatory symbol between the speaker and the subject with the geometric pictures and vice versa, uniting these as one. The text is so cunningly composed that a thorough knowledge of the system is required in order to appreciate the full significance of the subject matter. This attempt to conceal was, of course, intentional, as both Timaeus' speech and Plato's subsequent written report were meant for the initiated and therefore to be comprehensible only to them.

The actual system and its formation have been secret from the beginning, a secret kept within certain, clearly defined circles. The holders of this knowledge, of course, made extensive use of the system and its principles in solving a number of practical and well-known projects, but merely making use of the system is not quite the same as making it public.

Ancient geometry . . . was employed over a tremendous area, and we are able to follow its path from Egypt and her neighbouring countries out across Europe, and its effects can be noted in both Near and Far East. . . .

In those ancient times the accepted procedure was for Temple brethren from one country to seek out temples in another country or region in order to receive information and teaching there.

Once such a brother had spent some time—perhaps many years—in a foreign temple he would journey back to his mother temple with his treasures: the knowledge and learning he had attained.

This was the manner in which secret knowledge was transferred from one temple to another and from one country to another.

A part of the mysticism which was in this manner handed from temple to temple was ancient geometry, and this knowledge (remaining in the hands of the same groups of initiated brethren) slowly, gradually spread over wider and wider areas. And bearing in mind the many strongholds, the numerous temples within which its principles were practised, one can understand how the system has survived the decline of certain nations and the birth of others.

Seldom were the secrets of the temples entrusted to print. Communication was by word of mouth. But before a Temple brother received any teaching from the inner circle he had to pledge solemnly never to reveal the secrets to any outside party.

Over an endless period of time these secrets remained intact and it was not until a century before the real period of geometric reflection began in Greece that a murmur of the geometric terminology escaped from the inner Temple circle, when Pythagoras returned to his homeland after many years in Egyptian temples and started up a school in which he offered, among other studies, the teaching of a new geometric theory to non-initiated Greek students.

He never revealed or taught the geometry which he had learned from the Egyptian masters since he remained true to his promises not to do so, but his new teachings were on associated lines and this was sufficient to set the ball rolling.

The price of Pythagoras's crime of apparently having profaned the secret knowledge of the Temple was high: at the age of eighty he was forced to flee his country, leaving his material wealth and school to his enemies.

But in fact Pythagoras had not revealed any of the mysteries; these were still sacred, and two distinct geometric schools of thought now existed in Greece.

One was the ancient, traditional form of geometry whose outlines were still guarded by the temples as a part of their mystic knowledge, and this was the system of which Pythagoras and his contemporaries had full details.

The second arose from the teachings of Pythagoras in his school, where he instructed non-initiated in associated theories as a preliminary to abstract geometric thinking.

These theories were not actually secret, but from this training sprang groups of scholars who tried independently to solve the riddles of ancient geometry, without success.

Through the Temple society the old system had a close contact with the creative intelligentsia who were generally recruited from the temples, and it was therefore the ancient system which was employed in any practical problems facing the temple brethren or their cronies.

The new geometric line of thinking was the rebel released to the public, and this was the system openly discussed by all and sundry outside temple society.

There were experiments, arguments, discussions, assumptions; in short, the new thoughts were transformed into a new and developing science.

Temple society had no comment to make on the new schools of thought. For one thing, it felt a certain superiority in this direction, and for another there could be no question of joining in the discussions since this would have been impossible without revealing the Temple's own system. This would have been tantamount to a breach of promise.

Moreover, there was no need for a revision of thought in the temples for two thousand years were to go by before the emergent system definitely won over the ancient, traditional form. And the Middle Ages were well under way before the ancient system died out entirely, presumably with the passing of the last monastic brothers to have a knowledge of it.

Dome of the Rock, Jerusalem

Right from the earliest days the erection of churches and monasteries has been the prerogative of the Temple and, later, the Church. When, well through the Middle Ages, this last privilege was taken from them the remains of the ancient geometrical knowledge was passed on to various guilds of craftsmen, and of the knowledge which had at one time been the bloom of all wisdom only the sad remains were left in the form of the craftsmen's guiding rules.

In those periods of importance enjoyed by the system it was handed on by word of mouth, never put in writing. But if it should occasionally happen that mention was made of it in writing, the text was composed of esoteric terms and the phrasing of these was such that knowledge of the system itself was essential if the reader was to understand what the text was all about. Only the initiated could make sense from such a text, while for others it remained more or less unintelligible nonsense, and this is why students of ancient writing have been unable to trace any useful references to the old geometric system.

In this way ancient geometry ruled supreme up until about 100 years after the Pythagoras era. From this point onwards a new school of geometric thought developed, differing from the old although having its roots there.

The ancient system of geometry is actually a related form to the one we know today, but the differences are yet so numerous and profound that it is impossible to substitute the one system for the other. Any attempt in this direction could be compared with using a measuring stick with an unknown graduation. The result finally obtained cannot be transformed straight into a form with which we are familiar.

For a complete comprehension of the old system it is therefore essential that one spends the necessary time to study and reflect upon it and the thoughts which form its foundation. Any omission in this respect and a short cut to the analysis of certain buildings produces nothing but a scanty appraisal of the logic of the system's application. For although one employs—inevitably—one's knowledge of geometric principles, it is not sufficient in this instance.

Ancient geometry is not a difficult subject. It arose among people who possessed virtually no knowledge of figures, and was based on the logical consideration of primitive drawings, each drawing containing in itself the answer to the immediate problem.

A square can be divided into four smaller squares by entering a cross. That is something everyone can understand, and this is the kind of observation of which the entire system is composed.

Once a person has picked up this knowledge and appreciated the line of thinking which has prompted it, he is able to follow the system and its application from one region to another and from one period in time to another.

Naturally experiences of this nature had to take on some written form otherwise they would be forgotten, and this form of expression was a number of geometric symbols which in their construction and development illustrate the particular geometrical aspect which they characterise.

This habit of expressing an idea of a situation by means of a single symbol is a natural course of action, and we see the same type of thing used today in chemistry, mathematics, physics and many other spheres.

This procedure has furthermore the advantage that it maintains the already mentioned principle of secrecy. To the knowledgeable the symbol contained a distinct significance, while any person ignorant of the secret saw merely an undecipherable mystic sign which remained so unless he subsequently received information about its content.

[If] ancient geometry and its symbols are traced from their origin, one can go from temple to temple, from church to church, fitting them into the system known in ancient literature as the harmony of harmonies.

A study of education before the 15th century shows that it was mainly confined to Church circles, i.e. that the Church ran the existing schools and a higher education inevitably involved an even more intimate association with the Church and its domain.

The further back we look into time, the more pronounced this tendency becomes and in the very earliest days it was only possible—outside the Temple—to receive training as a craftsman or a warrior. The art of reading and writing could only be achieved within the Temple walls and a man had to be accepted into the respective temple order as a brother before he could share in this knowledge. The mere ability to read and write placed a man in the same class as a wise sage, and not unnaturally this group of learned brethren was tiny in proportion to a country's population.

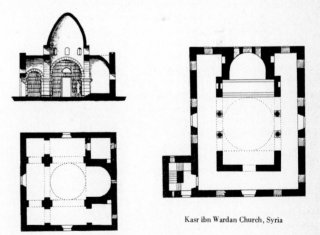

Kasr ibn Wardan Church, Syria

The roots of all monastic orders twine stubbornly back through time, to the Egyptian era which was roughly 8,000 years ago, and one can well understand the colossal build-up of tradition behind the Temple. In their respective countries or regions the temples were independent of each other and yet linked in a form of brotherhood in which knowledge and age had priority.

Egypt possessed both these qualifications and her temples consequently provided the main source of inspiration for counterparts elsewhere. History tells us that around 3000 B. C. it was a common thing to undertake a journey to the Egyptian temples with the aim of gathering wisdom and knowledge.

Literature carries reports of men who having gained their immediate fame sought the teachings of Egypt, but it was not exclusively to men of noteworthy ability that this education was offered. The normal set-up was for a man who had spent a specific number of years in his mother temple to be urged by the temple hierarchy to travel to other temples with the object of learning from them. And in those days—as is often the case today—it was men with the finest qualifications or the best connections who won their way to the main source, namely the Egyptian temples.

If we regard the ancient writers on this basis, we find two main groups.

One was the initiated temple brethren who had been in the earliest times the only existing writers.

We cannot expect to find in any of their written remains the slightest open reference to any concrete point in the mysteries of knowledge of the Temple since their pledge bound both mouth and pen all the way to the grave, and if they had entrusted any scrap of information to writing which might remotely be associated with the forbidden subjects, it would be composed in such a way as to make it unintelligible to anyone but their fellow brethren—and therefore would not be understood by the translators of later years.

Their pledge of silence, however, did not prevent them penning thoughts on other subjects. There was no shortage of subject matter in advancing societies, but Temple wisdom was taboo.

Gradually, as civilisation progressed, the art of reading and writing became an accomplishment achieved by expanding groups of the population and thus writers began appearing outside the Temple walls.

Nor from this group of writers can we expect any information regarding the temples and their secrets, for the simple reason that they had no information to reveal. Certainly their talk was perhaps more open and less restricted than the Temple group's, and they were willing to discuss eagerly the Temple secrets, but their talk was based on conjecture and half truths. They were not bound by any promises but it did not really matter since they had no actual information to dispense.

Later observers would find it very difficult to differentiate between the writer who, sworn to silence, avoids certain subjects known to him and about which he must neither speak nor write, and the writer who pens screeds and screeds on something of which he has no genuine knowledge.

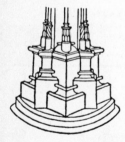 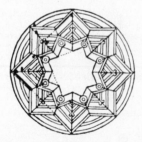

Elevation and Plan of Gothic Canopy Supports

Later observers might well interpret circumstances incorrectly, concluding that the one who never writes of life in the Temple knows nothing of it, whereas he who does write about it must be doing so from a knowledge of the Temple. And in fact the opposite is probably true.

The result would be that the information with which research students of later years worked would be wrong in many vital respects, and consequently many of the tracks which they followed would lead nowhere, end blindly. There would be no cohesion among the various loose bricks with which the student worked.

From this standpoint I think one must treat with a certain amount of caution much of the surviving literature stemming from before 1400 A. D. as well as later comment and translations. All the information contained therein ought not be accepted on face value as fact, even though it does have its roots so far distant from our own period.

Then the question arises: Is there no way of penetrating in some small man-

ner this veritable wall of silence in order to gain a foothold on the other side from which to proceed further?

Have these Temple societies left nothing in their wake which one could use, independent of ancient literature, in one's reflections and the progress from there?

Yes, they have indeed and the evidence in convincing, but in order to be able to decipher these traces one must hold the key to their significance. And these keys lie hidden in the secrets of ancient geometry.

Evidence and remains of Temple society can be found almost all over the world in the form of temple structures dedicated to the glorification of high idols or ideologies, and these buildings followed a distinct plan of construction in their measurements and dimensions—based on the geometric system which is no longer with us.

This age-old system of geometry begins at such an early stage that it is one of the first series of experiences Man collected, together with speculation on time itself—a period of time which coincided with the epoch of Temple mystics.

The basis of this speculation is a study of the Sun and Moon, both of which of course leave the image of a circle in the mind.

This circle, combined with the figure seven, and a concept I have termed *The Sacred Cut*, are some of the ingredients of this ancient geometric system.

The old temples enjoyed a dominating sense of power which was based on the knowledge and learning which they kept secret. All knowledge and experience was assembled over thousands of years in the Temple, and by permitting educated groups to share to a greater or lesser extent in this pool of knowledge the Temple brethren wielded—through these groups—infinite power.

—from **THE SECRETS OF ANCIENT GEOMETRY** by Tons Brunes

ADAMS, HENRY. MONT-SAINT-MICHEL AND CHARTRES, $1.95. This classic work grew out of the visits of Adams to northern France and it reflects the profound impression that the great cathedrals of that region had on him. Its subtitle is *A Study of Thirteenth Century Unity*, and the broad scope of the book, together with Adams' insight into the period, makes it one of the finest expressions of the spirit of the Middle Ages ever written. In addition, the book is an examination of the faith that brought the cathedrals into being. Index, 455pp. Dou 13

ASTEN, H. KELLER von. ENCOUNTERS WITH THE INFINITE, c$17.40. This is a very hard-to-describe book which integrates geometric concepts with the anthroposophical philosophy developed by Rudolf Steiner and expanded by his followers. The text consists of a number of multicolored line drawings and a detailed interpretative text discussing form and linear symbolism. 9x10", 364pp. KeV 71

BARAVALLE, HERMANN von. GEOMETRIC DRAWING AND THE WALDORF SCHOOL PLAN, $2.25. See the Waldorf Education sub-section of Steiner.

BRUNES, TONS. THE SECRETS OF ANCIENT GEOMETRY AND ITS USES, c$55.50/ set. This is an amazing set of books which graphically demonstrates Brunes' theory that the construction of the great buildings from ancient times through the Middle Ages was based on an ancient, mystical form of geometry developed in the temple at an early date and verbally transmitted among the brethren under vows of secrecy. Through an abundance of measured drawings of building from the Great Pyramid to Cologne Cathedral and an excellent interpretative text Brunes reconstructs this geometry and reveals its sec-

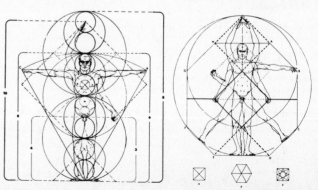

The Harmonics of Sacred Geometry Applied to Man (from Blair, Rhythms of Vision)

rets. This is a monumental work which has been acclaimed throughout the world. While it certainly will not apeal to most people we cannot recommend it highly enough to those who are seriously interested in the ancient mystery teachings. It is one expensive set that is well worth the price. It is beautifully produced and the material is not obtainable anywhere else. 381 illustrations, including a number of fold-outs, oversize, two volumes. 583pp. Rho 67

CAMP. L. SPRAGUE de. **THE ANCIENT ENGINEERS**, $1.95. See the Ancient Civilizations section.

The Labyrinth of Chartres

CHARPENTIER, LOUIS. **THE MYSTERIES OF CHARTRES CATHEDRAL**, $1.75. *M. Charpentier says in effect that Chartres and other medieval cathedrals, like the great monuments of Egypt and Greece, were the manifestation of a secret communicated to mankind by occult or mystical means. This, he claims, required the services of a man equipped to receive a dedication in occult language; a man competent to translate this message into numbers and a master craftsman who knew what he was about and could express such numbers or relationships in curves, verticals and volumes. Moreover, the secret of true gothic was communicated to man with a view to a fuller realization of his own quality. A fascinating, profusely illustrated study.* 190pp. Avo 66

CRITCHLOW, KEITH. **ORDER IN SPACE**, $8.95. A design source book which can be used as a practical tool by the architect, designer, or scientist who has to deal with such problems of space. Oversize, many illustrations. 120pp. Vik 65

FULLER, BUCKMINSTER. **SYNERGETICS**, c$25.00. This massive volume is a distillation of Fuller's lifetime study. Here Fuller introduces the tetrahedral model as a new frame of reference to simplify understanding of the physical universe. His models are energetic relationships between events, not things. As usual with Fuller's work, the presentation is highly complex and demands careful study. Many illustrations of geometric models are included. Bibliography, 906pp. McM 75

GOVINDA, LAMA. **PSYCHO-COSMIC SYMBOLISM OF THE BUDDHIST STUPA**, $4.95. See the Buddhism section.

HAWKINS, GERALD. **BEYOND STONEHENGE**, c$12.95. See the Ancient Civilizations section.

_____. **STONEHENGE DECODED**, $2.45. See the Ancient Britain sub-section of Ancient Civilizations.

HORNE, ALEX. **KING SOLOMON'S TEMPLE IN THE MASONIC TRADITION**, $5.00. See the Rosicrucians and Freemasons section.

KENAWELL, WILLIAM. **THE QUEST AT GLASTONBURY**, c$8.50. A biographical study of Frederick Bond, the man who dedicated his life to unearthing (literally and figuratively) the truth concerning England's ancient Glastonbury Abbey. Bond's observations about the Abbey are also included in the text along with photographs and line drawings. Notes, bibliography. 318pp. GtP 65

LETHABY, WILLIAM. **ARCHITECTURE: MYSTICISM AND MYTH**, c$10.00. This book was a milestone in the linking of mysticism and transcendental experience to the design process. The author examined folk customs, myths, and tales of many ancient civilizations in presenting his view of architecture as not just a battle of styles, nor exclusively a matter of function, but rather an expression of secret meanings that lie deeply embedded in the human psyche and are linked to ancient and universal symbolism. It's a fascinating study which has not been equaled to this day. Introduction, illustration, bibliography. 304pp. Brz 1882

MACAULY, DAVID. **CATHEDRAL**, c$7.95. The Gothic cathedral is one of man's most magnificent expressions as well as one of his grandest architectural achievements. This richly illustrated book shows the intricate step-by-step process of a cathedral's growth. The plan is agreed on; the site is chosen; each craftsman's contribution is presented; his tools and materials are described. The details of the construction are graphically explained, the black-and-white pen studies and architectural diagrams are beautifully drawn, and the brief narrative is illuminating. This is a prize-winning, noted book—designed for young adults, but suitable for all. 9½x12", glossary. 80pp. HMC 73

_____. **PYRAMID**, c$7.95. See Ancient Egypt sub-section of Ancient Civilizations.

MICHELL, JOHN. **CITY OF REVELATION**, c$1.49. See the Ancient Civilizations section.

PLUMMER, GORDON. **THE MATHEMATICS OF THE COSMIC MIND**, c$12.50. This work is an unusual approach to a profound study of the universe and man. Taking as a basis the vast system of theosophy as outlined in Blavatsky's **Secret Doctrine**, and applying the complexities of mathematical symbolism, Plummer leads the student toward his own discovery of some of the deeper realities of existence and of consciousness. The book represents the culmination of the author's life long study. His concepts are embodied in diagrams and color plates. 217pp. TPH 66

SIMSON, OTTO von. **THE GOTHIC CATHEDRAL**, $3.95. *The value of the Gothic Cathedral lies in its approach to two essential problems. . . . The first one is concerned with the appreciation of Gothic architecture. . . . It was symbolical in its conception . . . ; mystical in its aim, and calculated in its principles. . . . Von Simson shows that in Gothic architecture history creates its own symbols, whether political, economic, intellectual, or artistic, all of them following an independent but convergent spiritual pattern.* – **Yale Review**. Notes, bibliography, index. 283pp. PUP 56

TAYLOR, THOMAS. **THE THEORETIC ARITHMETIC OF THE PYTHAGOREANS**, c$12.50. For those with the mental equipment suitable for the utilization of the science of numbers as a means to knowledge and wisdom, this will serve as a major contribution. Pythagoras held that arithmetic and the numerical sciences were an approach to the divine and a way of communion with the gods. Also contained are the essentials of that taught by such men as Iamblichus, Boeticus and Nichomachus. 248pp. Wei

TOMPKINS, PETER. **SECRETS OF THE GREAT PYRAMID**, c$17.50. See the Ancient Egypt sub-section of Ancient Civilizations.

VANDENBROECK, ANDRE. **PHILOSOPHICAL GEOMETRY**, $7.00. This is a detailed analysis of geometric forms and concepts, heavily illustrated. 8½x11", 166pp. Sad 72

WATSON, PERCY. **BUILDING THE MEDIEVAL CATHEDRALS**, $2.45. A pictorial study, illustrated with photographs and detailed line drawings. The text is quite simplified and covers the following general topics: *where they built and why, the Norman cathedral, the workers and their task, the Gothic cathedrals,* and *cathedrals since the Middle Ages.* 48pp. CUP 76

WENNINGER, MAGNUS. **POLYHEDRON MODELS**, $4.95. The author describes how to make models of all the known uniform polyhedra and some of the stellated forms. The book is fully illustrated and the instructions are clearly presented. Oversize, notes. 211pp. CUP 71

WINSTON, RICHARD and CLARA. **NOTRE-DAME DE PARIS**, c$11.95. Notre Dame is a fine example of the Gothic cathedral and it has stood at the very center of French history since its construction. This beautiful photographic study reproduces a great deal of the important art inside and studies the architecture in detail. An interpretative text reviews the cathedral's history and some of the important events that happened in and around it. The architecture itself is analyzed in depth and the photographs are absolutely magnificent. There's also a section of excerpts from writings inspired by the grandeur of the cathedral. Notes, bibliography, chronology, plus short analyses of the other French Gothic cathedrals. Oversize, index. 172pp. Nsw 71

Nautilus Shell

RUDOLF STEINER

Rudolf Steiner (1891–1925), founder of anthroposophy, was concerned to describe the path of spiritual development most suited to the modern scientific age, a path emphasizing clarity, objectivity, and inner freedom; this path proceeds from the normal human powers of thinking, feeling, and willing to the higher modes of consciousness which he termed Imagination, Inspiration, and Intuition. Thus the anthroposophical path of knowledge calls upon the whole man, challenging him to harmoniously balance the scientific (thinking), artistic (feeling), and practical (willing) aspects of his nature. In his last years Steiner developed with special intensity the subject of karma and reincarnation (the latter in a new and Christian form), which he considered vital for the modern age.

Anthroposophy, though rooted in perceptions of the spiritual world, has a very profound significance for very practical spheres of human life and action. Notable among the areas already influenced by the work of Rudolf Steiner are education, agriculture, nutrition, medicine, history, economics, social order, religion, and various arts, including the new art of eurhythmy which expresses in movement the inner forces comprising the inherent essence of speech and music. The theory of learning in Steiner schools is founded on a progression of child development in which there is a gradual awakening of the child's intellectual consciousness—from learning by doing and by imitating, then understanding feelingly, and finally in the high school years, understanding conceptually. Steiner himself wrote very little. Most of his work was devoted to lecturing. And most of the books that follow are in reality transcripts of his lectures. We have found that the best introduction to his thought is **Knowledge of Higher Worlds**. Other basic books include **The Philosophy of Freedom, Theosophy, Occult Science** and **Christianity as a Mystical Fact**. All of these are described below. Since there is such a profusion of titles and our space is limited we have opted for listing many of them and reviewing only a few since the title can suffice.

ABBOT, A.E. **CLAIRVOYANCE**, $1.25. 61pp. EME 63

ASTEN, H. KELLER von. **ENCOUNTERS WITH THE INFINITE**, $17.40. See the Sacred Geometry section.

BITTLESTON, ADAM and JOHN DAVY. **THE GOLDEN BLADE**. This is an annual publication put together by the Anthroposophical Society in Great Britain. The quality of the articles is uniformly excellent and, in addition to essays about current developments in anthroposophy, each issue contains translations of a few previously unpublished Steiner lectures. Book reviews are also included. Each issue is about 100pp. The following are now available: 1973, $2.75; 1974, $3.00; 1975, $3.50; 1976, $3.50.

CARLGREN, FRANS. **RUDOLF STEINER**, $2.75. This is a beautifully produced biographical study of Steiner. The reader can get a good feeling of all aspects of Steiner's life and work from this short, well-organized volume and it is as good an introduction to Steiner as any we can think of. Many photographs are included. 81pp. PAV 72

CHU, PAUL. **LIFE BEFORE BIRTH, LIFE ON EARTH, LIFE AFTER DEATH**, $2.95. A topical condensed discussion of the following material, by an anthroposophist: the mysteries of the being of man, the works of Rudolf Steiner, man's supersensible members after death, creation, Jesus and the Christ Being, the mission of the Hebrew people, Lucifer and Ahriman, sleep, reincarnation and karma. This is an interesting, clear digest. 194pp. API 72

DAVY, JOHN, ed. **WORK ARISING FROM THE LIFE OF RUDOLF STEINER**, $7.50. A collection of articles published to mark the fiftieth anniversary of the death of Rudolf Steiner. Includes essays on art and architecture, education, medicine, agriculture, sociology, and religion—all of which give a clear impression of how Steiner's suggestions for working in these various fields have been put into practice and borne fruit in the world. There are additional essays on Steiner himself, the essentials of his thinking, and the society he founded. Illustrations, 240pp. RSP 75

EASTON, STEWART. **MAN AND WORLD IN THE LIGHT OF ANTHROPOSOPHY**, $6.95. A comprehensive introduction to Steiner's work and thought written by a man who has been active in the Anthroposophical Society for over forty years. The first part of the book discusses anthroposophy as a body of knowledge; the second, the role of anthroposophy in practical life, includes chapters on education, science, and the arts. Notes, index. 536pp. API 75

FREEMAN, ARNOLD. **RUDOLPH STEINER'S MESSAGE TO MANKIND**, $1.25. A topically organized short summary of Steiner's main ideas. 47pp. NKB 63

FRIELING, RUDOLF. **THE ESSENCE OF CHRISTIANITY**, $.85. See the Christianity section.

FYFE, AGNES. **MOON AND PLANT**, $6.75. An analysis of the capillary-dynamolysis studies of the formative or etheric forces in plants suggested by Rudolf Steiner and re-

searched by some of his followers. The theoretical basis of the technique is discussed, experiments are cited, and practical instruction is offered. Many photographs illustrate the results of some studies. 30pp. SCR 75

GLAS, NORBERT. **THE FULFILLMENT OF OLD AGE**, c$5.50. In this profound book Dr. Glas *tells how all of us, young or old, may grow older gracefully and continue to live a fruitful life right up to the end. The secret he reveals may be summed up in the words acceptance and metamorphosis: inward acceptance of the truth that we are no longer young, and that this truth has practical consequences, and the transformation of our declining sense faculties into their spiritual counterparts.*—**The Golden Blade**, 1973. 131pp. API 70

GOETHE, JOHANN. **AUTOBIOGRAPHY OF JOHANN WOLFGANG VON GOETHE**, $10.25/set. Goethe was Steiner's spiritual mentor and and Goethe's philosophy and scientific approach to the study of the natural world is reflected in Steiner's work. Therefore Goethe's autobiography provides important background information for an understanding of Steiner's philosophy. Two volumes, 869pp. UCh 74

_____. **THE METAMORPHOSIS OF PLANTS**, $2.45. A new edition of Goethe's major work on plants, with an introduction by Steiner. 155pp. Bio 74

_____. **THEORY OF COLORS**, $5.95. See the Color and Aura section.

GROHMAN, GERBERT. **THE PLANT**, $11.00. The observations in this volume are based on the principle of metamorphosis first described by Goethe. Grohmann's book ranges from detailed description of single plants to a relation of the plant kingdom to the whole earth—to insect and bird, to climate and altitude, as well as to man. A hundred plates and diagrams illustrate the exposition. 209pp. RSP 74

HARTMANN, GEORG. **THE GOETHEANUM GLASS WINDOWS**, $5.40. This is a beautiful book which reproduces the windows in full color and discusses their symbolism. Many black-and-white drawings are also included. Bibliography, 75pp. PAV 72

HARWOOD, A.C., ed. **THE FAITHFUL THINKER: CENTENARY ESSAYS ON THE WORK AND THOUGHT OF RUDOLF STEINER**, c$3.35. This volume of essays, timed to coincide with the centenary of Steiner's birth, contains articles on his concept of mind and time, on his outlook on psychology, on his philosophy of evolution and of history, and his Christian beliefs, as well as on education, curative education, and agriculture. His work in the fields of mathematics, physics, and color is also studied. Photographs, 251pp. Hod 61

HEIDENREICH, ALFRED. **THE RISEN CHRIST AND THE ETHERIC CHRIST**, $1.75. Transcription of a series of lectures which discuss *the Being of Christ as it is shown in the writings of the New Testament* and refer often to Steiner's thoughts on the Christ. 47pp. RSP 69

KONIG, KARL. **THE HUMAN SOUL**, $2.50. A spiritual study which incorporates psychological understanding. 118pp. API 73

KYBER, MANFRED. **THE THREE CANDLES OF LITTLE VERONICA**, $4.50. A beautifully illustrated story of a child's soul in this world and the other; physically set in the lonely northern countryside along the Baltic coast of Germany before the age of motor transport. 192pp. Wal 72

LIEVEGOED, BERNHARD. **TOWARDS THE TWENTY-FIRST CENTURY: DOING THE GOOD**, $3.25. Transcription of a series of talks before a group of young people. Their theme is the dangers young people face in the world today and the way to meet them. 82pp. SBC 72

LUND, KNUD. **UNDERSTANDING OUR FELLOW MEN**, $4.65. A Danish psychologist discusses the role of the sour temperaments in a correct judgment of character, how to train one's observation to this end, and how to understand life in the light of the temperaments. 164pp. NKB 58

MACBETH, NORMAN. **DARWIN RETRIED**, $2.45. A carefully documented repudiation of classical Darwinism and its supporters which maintains that errors have been discovered in the reasoning behind the theory about which the public has not been informed. Mr. Macbeth suggests the necessity of a fresh start in the study of the evolutionary mechanism. 172pp. Del 71

MAYER, GLADYS. **BEHIND THE VEILS OF DEATH AND SLEEP**, $1.50. A new approach to the subject of life after death based on Steiner's spiritual science. 44pp. NKB

MERRY, ELEANOR. **ASCENT OF MAN**, c$11.00. See the Ancient Civilizations section.

_____. **EASTER—THE LEGENDS AND THE FACTS**, c$3.90. A profound discussion of the spiritual foundations of Easter, based on the ancient mystery teaching and reviewing related material in the old Celtic legends of the Holy Grail and the story of Parsifal, and in Goethe's **Faust**. A moving presentation which makes the true meaning of this holy day come alive. Index, 153pp. NKB 67

_____. **SPIRITUAL KNOWLEDGE**, c$4.25. An overview of a variety of subjects including the relation of the living to the dead, life after death, the truth about spiritualism, mediumship, automatic writing, and astral projection, how to distinguish between the genuine and the spurious in occult science, and much else. Index, notes. 115pp.

_____. THE YEAR AND ITS FESTIVALS, c$1.95. A beautifully written spiritual discussion. 94pp. RSP 52

PELIKAN, WILHELM. THE SECRETS OF METALS, $2.95. A fascinating book containing chapters on lead, tin, iron, gold, copper, zinc, aluminum, etc., and the cosmic aspect of the metallic nature. 179pp. API 73

PFEIFFER, EHRENFRIED. SENSITIVE CRYSTALLIZATION PROCESSES, $10.00. A demonstration and discussion of the formative forces in the blood based on Pfeiffer's extensive research. Seventy-eight photographs are included, and each plate is extensively analyzed. Notes, bibliography. 59pp. API 36

POPPELBAUM, H. A NEW ZOOLOGY, $11.95. A deep study of the formative forces in animals based on Steiner's spiritual science and on the writings of Guenter Wachsmith. Many illustrations. 192pp. PAV 61

RAFFE, MARJORIE, C. HARWOOD and M. LUNDGREN. EURHYTHMY AND THE IMPULSE OF DANCE, $2.50. This booklet contains reproductions of the complete series of thirty-five drawings for eurhythmy arising from the collaboration of Rudolf Steiner and Edith Marion. They are preceded not simply by an introduction to eurhythmy, but by a study of the search for renewal of the arts of movement and dance. 63pp. RSP 74

RAPHAEL, ALICE. GOETHE AND THE PHILOSOPHER'S STONE, c$8.50. A study of the symbolical patterns in *The Parable* and the second part of **Faust**. Notes, index. 273pp. GtP 65

RITTELMEYER, FRIEDRICH. MEDITATION, c$4.80. Dr. Rittelmeyer was a leading figure in the Lutheran Church in Germany at the beginning of this century. He became a close associate of Rudolf Steiner. *Meditation is a word of such wide meaning that it only loosely applies to the content of this book. Its particular purpose is to demonstrate how certain pictures and sayings from St. John's Gospel can be so thought and imagined that they come alive in the heart, uniting it with the being of Christ through His words and His deeds. Christ experienced, rather than Christ believed in or known of, is the aim. Practical advice on the meditative life is included by the way. . . . Everyone will find demonstrated how truly practical it is to look for Christian exercises in meditation within the text of the Gospels themselves.*—from the foreward. 248pp. CCP 36

SAVITCH, MARIE. MARIE STEINER-VON SIVERS, c$6.45. A biographical study of the wife of Rudolf Steiner. 238pp. RSP 67

SCHINDLER, MARIA. EUROPE, A COSMIC PICTURE, c$15.75. Looked at from an earthly standpoint, the countries of Europe appear to be separate and segregated—but Maria Schindler takes the cosmic perspective that Europe is a whole, a zodiac incarnate, and that the various peoples of Europe are the bearers of the twelvefold divine creative impulses of the zodiac. Initially the book focuses on the spiritual mission of Europe which is connected with the evolution of Christianity. Ms. Schindler feels that the theme of Europe's destiny is the quest for the Holy Grail. Passing from country to country, the book gives a lucid account of the birth of each nation and its subsequent historical development. 52 beautiful plates are included. 12x13", index. 240pp. NKB 75

SCHURE, EDOUARD. FROM SPHINX TO CHRIST: AN OCCULT HISTORY, $2.50. Rudolf Steiner considered Schure to be *one of the best guides for finding the path to the spirit in our day,* stating that the ideas expressed in his writings *can awaken within every human being a premonition of the solution of the riddles of existence.* We found his work rather white-Western-Christian supremacist. This is a comprehensive presentation beginning with planetary evolution and Atlantis. 284pp. Mul 70

_____. THE GREAT INITIATES, $6.95. A collection of essays which discuss some of the great masters throughout history and their teachings and deeds. Mul 76

SCHWENK, THEODOR. SENSITIVE CHAOS, c$14.95. A pictorial study of the creation of flowing forms in water and air which draws on Steiner's teaching and presents the true spiritual nature of water. Oversize, 216pp. ScB 76

SHEARS, C. CURTIS. NUTRITIONAL SCIENCE AND HEALTH EDUCATION, $7.95. See the Nutrition section.

SHEPARD, A.P. THE SCIENTIST OF THE INVISIBLE, c$9.25. An excellent introduction to the life and work of Steiner. It gives a clear description of the man, his times, his teachings and work in many fields. Highly recommended. 221pp. Hod 54

STEBBING, LIONEL. MUSIC: ITS OCCULT BASIS AND HEALING VALUE, $9.10. See the Music section.

_____. MUSIC THERAPY, $7.70. See the Music section.

STEINER, RUDOLF. AGRICULTURE, $5.50. A new edition of these long out-of-print lectures. Fascinating material for all gardeners, including color illustrations and practical advice. 175pp. Bio 74

_____. ANCIENT MYTHS: THEIR MEANING AND CONNECTION WITH EVOLUTION, c$5.75. 121pp. SBC 71

_____. ANTHROPOSOPHICAL LEADING THOUGHTS, c$7.50. This volume contains paragraphs written by Steiner for members of the Anthroposophical Society, dealing with anthroposophy as a path of knowledge. **Leading Thoughts** and **Letters** (see below) were formerly available as a volume entitled **The Michael Mystery.** 220pp. RSP 73

_____. ART IN THE LIGHT OF THE MYSTERY, WISDOM, c$4.95. 169pp. RSP 70

_____. AWAKENING TO COMMUNITY, c$6.50. In these lectures Steiner speaks of ways in which anthroposophical groups can become true communities through their members awakening ever more consciously to the soul-spiritual element in their fellows. 178pp. API 75

_____. A BACKGROUND TO THE GOSPEL OF ST. MARK, c$4.95. 220pp. RSP 68

_____. BETWEEN DEATH AND REBIRTH, c$11.50. The main concern of these lecture is with life after death, after the *Kamaloka* period. *They disclose some of those factors in a person's life on earth which will influence his experiences during this period as well as those in the spiritual world which will affect his future earth-life. They also make clear the great significance for the spiritual progress of our connection with the earth and speak of the influence the living may have on the souls of the dead.*—from the introduction. 188pp. RSP 75

_____. THE BHAGAVAD GITA AND THE EPISTLES OF PAUL, $2.75. 102pp. API 71

_____. BUILDING STONES FOR AN UNDERSTANDING OF THE MYSTERY OF GOLGOTHA, c$6.95. *The Mystery of Golgotha must be regarded as the central point in human evolution. From the Fall until the Mystery of Golgotha man experienced a progressive decline of his spiritual forces. The forces of corruption had increasingly invaded his soul and threatened to make man an automaton of the spirit. And from the Mystery of Golgotha until the end of the Earth cycle all that was lost before the Mystery of Golgotha will gradually be retrieved once more.* It seems that the material in this volume would require very intensive as well as patient effort to begin to grasp the importance of what Steiner would probably consider the greatest mystery. 239pp. RSP 72

_____. THE CALENDAR OF THE SOUL, c$3.95. A meditative verse for each week of the year, beginning at Easter, following the progress of the soul's living response to the seasons. 120pp. API 74

_____. CHRIST AND THE HUMAN SOUL, c$2.75. 78pp. RSP 72

_____. CHRIST IN THE TWENTIETH CENTURY, $.95. 20pp. API 71

_____. CHRISTIANITY AS A MYSTICAL FACT, $2.95. A revised edition of this important and basic book. Here Steiner describes the character of the ancient mystery teachings and then uses it to illumine mythology, the Greek sages, Plato and the neo-Platonists, the Gospels (especially the story of the raising of Lazarus), and post-Christian writings like those of Augustine. He also looks to the future and discusses the significance for the modern age of the ever-renewing *Christ Impulse.* 195pp. RSP 47

_____. THE CONCEPTS OF ORIGINAL SIN AND GRACE, $.95. 32pp. RSP 73

_____. COSMIC MEMORY: ATLANTIS AND LEMURIA, $2.50. See the Ancient Civilizations section.

_____. THE COURSE OF MY LIFE: AN AUTOBIOGRAPHY, $4.50. *Not* recommended as an introduction to Steiner. 384pp. API 51

_____. THE CASE FOR ANTHROPOSOPHY, $1.95. *Is the spiritual science of Rudolf Steiner a reliable and badly needed method of knowledge? What right has it to call itself a science at all?* These are among the questions answered in this volume. 93pp. RSP 70

_____. THE DEAD ARE WITH US, $.95. 32pp. RSP 73

_____. THE DRIVING FORCE OF SPIRITUAL POWERS IN WORLD HISTORY, $2.50. 95pp. SBC 72

_____. EARTHLY DEATH AND COSMIC LIFE, c$4.95. Lectures in this volume were given at a time during the first world war when many souls were passing through the gate of death. *The desire for knowledge that will help to realise true links between the Living and the Dead is no less intense to-day, nor is the need of an approach in keeping with that healthy and vigilant consciousness which is proper to the modern age any less great.*—from the introduction. 160pp. RSP 64

_____. EASTER FESTIVAL IN RELATION TO THE MYSTERIES, $1.95. 78pp. RSP 68

_____. EGYPTIAN MYTHS AND MYSTERIES, $2.95. See the Ancient Egypt sub-section of Ancient Civilizations.

_____. ELEVEN EUROPEAN MYSTICS, $2.50. Steiner relates how eleven men who lived during the period bridging Middle Ages to Renaissance resolved within themselves the conflict between their spiritual perceptions and the emerging scientific world then coming to birth. 251pp. SPu 71

_____. ETHERISATION OF BLOOD, $1.25. API 35

_____. THE EVOLUTION OF CONSCIOUSNESS, c$5.95. 198pp. RSP 66

_____. FACING KARMA, $.95. 20pp. API 75

_____. THE FOUR SEASONS AND THE ARCHANGELS, c$4.50. 90pp. RSP 68

_____. **FRIEDRICH NIETZSCHE: FIGHTER FOR FREEDOM**, $4.50. Four fairly long lectures covering Nietzsche's character, path of development, philosophy, personality, and psychotherapy. 222pp. SPu 60

_____. **FROM JESUS TO CHRIST**, c$5.50. See the Christianity section.

_____. **FROM SYMPTOM TO REALITY IN MODERN HISTORY**, c$11.95. In these nine lectures Steiner surveys some of the great developments in European consciousness and outlook since the fifteenth century that have gradually formed the Europe of the twentieth century. 246pp. API 75

_____. **THE GOSPELS.** Steiner has a great deal to say about the gospels. Each writer is examined as a person and a spiritual force in history. Steiner also touches on what each conveys on material and metaphysical levels about Christ and the Christ being and how each gospel relates to writings before and after it. The following books on the gospels are available: **The Gospel of St. John**, c$5.50; **Lectures on the Gospel of St. Luke**, $4.95; **The Gospel of St. Mark**, c$4.95; and **The Gospel of St. Matthew**, c$5.50.

_____. **THE GUARDIAN OF THE THRESHOLD**, $2.95. A play subtitled *Soul Events in Dramatic Scenes*. 128pp. SBC 73

_____. **GUIDANCE IN ESOTERIC TRAINING**, $4.95. The three booooklets **From the Contents of the Esoteric School** are now available in one volume, containing practical advice and specific meditations for those concerned with inner self development. 109pp. RSP 72

_____. **HUMAN AND COSMIC THOUGHT**, c$2.95. Among the information covered is the relation of the seven planets to the twelve zodiac signs and the significance of sun, moon and Earth. Steiner discusses *man's place within the spiritual cosmos from the standpoint of spiritual astrology*. 72pp. RSP 61

_____. **INITIATION AND ITS RESULTS**, $3.00. 180pp. HeR nd

_____. **THE INNER ASPECT OF THE SOCIAL QUESTION**, $1.95. These lectures seek to give an understanding of the spiritual background of the social situation and indicate the moral prerequisites essential to any form of reorganization. 70pp. RSP 74

_____. **INNER DEVELOPMENT OF MAN**, $.75. 22pp. API 70

_____. **INVESTIGATIONS IN OCCULTISM**, $4.50. 206pp. HeR 29

_____. **KARMIC RELATIONSHIPS.** Steiner gave eighty-two lectures on karma in 1924 and this cycle represents his most advanced thinking on the subject. The most important of these lectures are transcribed in the volumes in this series. Each is about 200pp. I, c$5.75; II, c$7.50; VI, c$4.75; VI, c$5.50; VII, c$5.50.

_____. **KNOWLEDGE OF HIGHER WORLDS AND ITS ATTAINMENT**, c$4.95/$3.50. Steiner's famous work outlining certain spiritual practices designed as a normal and healthy path of training. It presents in detail the means whereby everyone can develop a new knowledge of the higher worlds of soul and spirit. 272pp. API 47

_____. **THE LAST ADDRESS**, c$2.90. 23pp. RSP 67

_____. **A LECTURE ON EURYTHMY**, $1.25. An introduction which Steiner gave in 1923 to the then new art of movement called eurhythmy. He deals mainly with the interpretation of speech but *always regarded it as essential that in a performance there should be the interpretation of speech as well as of music.*—from the introduction. 36pp. RSP 67

_____. **LIFE BETWEEN DEATH AND REBIRTH**, $3.95. A collection of sixteen lectures which can be taken as complementary to those contained in **Between Death and Rebirth**. 308pp. API 68

_____. **LINKS BETWEEN THE LIVING AND THE DEAD**, $1.25. 64pp. RSP 73

_____. **LORD'S PRAYER**, $.95. 26pp. API 70

_____. **LOVE AND ITS MEANING IN THE WORLD**, $.95. 27pp. RSP 72

_____. **MACROCOSM AND MICROCOSM**, c$4.95. 209pp. RSP 68

_____. **MAN AS A BEING OF SENSE AND PERCEPTION**, $2.20. 53pp. RSP 58

_____. **MAN AS A PICTURE OF THE LIVING SPIRIT**, $.95. 32pp. RSP 72

_____. **MAN AS A SYMPHONY OF THE CREATIVE WORLD**, c$5.95. A series of lectures on the kingdoms of nature and their relationship to man. 222pp. RSP 70

_____. **MAN—HIEROGLYPH OF THE UNIVERSE**, c$5.95. Sixteen lectures which discuss man's search for concrete, realistic knowledge of his whole being and of the position he occupies in the universe. 220pp. RSP 72

_____. **MAN IN THE LIGHT OF OCCULTISM**, c$4.75. *In this cycle of lectures we propose to consider man in his spiritual nature from three standpoints. . . . I refer to the standpoints of occultism, theosophy, and philosophy.* 214pp. RSP 45

_____. **MAN IN THE PAST, PRESENT AND FUTURE**, $1.95. 78pp. RSP 66

_____. **MAN'S BEING, HIS DESTINY AND WORLD EVOLUTION**, c$5.95. Steiner relates man's being to the extensive spaces of the cosmos in his discussion of the

period between falling asleep and waking and the path pursued by man between death and a new birth. 114pp. API 52

_____. **METHODS OF SPIRITUAL RESEARCH**, $1.75. 128pp. RSP 71

_____. **THE MISSION OF FOLK-SOULS**, c$5.95. Eleven lectures which study national characteristics from the viewpoint of the psychic and spiritual elements that underlie them. 189pp. RSP 70

_____. **MYSTERIES OF THE EAST AND OF CHRISTIANITY**, $2.25. A discussion of the nature of the mysteries, the void, the Zarathustrian initiation, the music of the spheres, the inner relationship between the Egyptian mysteries and the grail, and much else. 79pp. RSP 70

_____. **MYSTERY KNOWLEDGE AND MYSTERY CENTERS**, c$4.95. These lectures were given immediately before the refounding of the Anthroposophical Society when Steiner wished to see the esoteric life developed more strongly. In the lecture series Steiner speaks of man's soul and of the ancient mystery teachings and what modern man can learn from these teachings. The teachings reviewed include the Ephesian, the Hibernian, the Eleusinian, and those of the Samothracian Kabiri. 207pp. RSP 73

_____. **MYSTIC SEALS AND COLUMNS**, $7.50. HeR nd

_____. **THE OCCULT MOVEMENT IN THE NINETEENTH CENTURY**, c$6.50. 190pp. RSP 73

_____. **OCCULT MYSTERIES OF ANTIQUITY AND CHRIST**, $2.50. 243pp. SPu 61

_____. **OCCULT READING AND OCCULT HEARING**, $2.95. *The physical world is no more than a written page before us. If we only stare at it, we can observe it without being able to read it at all. Neither do we know anything of the world if we look at it only with the faculty of physical perception, for then we do not decipher, we do not really penetrate into the world. We must read then world, learn its meanings.*—Rudolf Steiner. 80pp. RSP 75

_____. **THE OCCULT SIGNIFICANCE OF THE BHAGAVAD GITA**, c$5.50. 142pp. API 68

_____. **THE OCCULT SIGNIFICANCE OF THE BLOOD**, $.95. 32pp. RSP 67

_____. **OCCULT SIGNS AND SYMBOLS**, $1.95. 74pp. API 72

_____. **AN OUTLINE OF OCCULT SCIENCE**, c$7.50/$4.50. No single book can be said to contain the whole of anthroposophy, but this book comes the closest. It sets out in systematic fashion the fundamental facts concerning the nature and constitution of man, his history, and the history of the universe. 388pp. API 72

_____. **OVERCOMING NERVOUSNESS**, $.95. 19pp. API 69

_____. **PATHS TO KNOWLEDGE OF HIGHER WORLDS**, $1.20. 36pp. SBC 47

_____. **THE PHILOSOPHY OF FREEDOM**, c$4.95/$2.50. The central statement of Steiner's philosophy of liberation based on the mode of higher thinking. He emphasizes that an illumined use of the faculty of mind can be the means to spiritual attainment and is the factor that will lead to true inner and outer freedom. 234pp. RSP 64

_____. **THE PORTAL OF INITIATION**, $2.95. 160pp. SBC 73

_____. **PRACTICAL TRAINING IN THOUGHT**, $.95. 25pp. API 66

_____. **PROBLEMS OF NUTRITION**, $.95. See the Nutrition section.

_____. **REINCARNATION AND IMMORTALITY**, $1.95. See the Reincarnation and Karma section.

_____. **RESULTS OF SPIRITUAL INVESTIGATION**, $1.75. 121pp. Mul 71

_____. **THE RIDDLES OF PHILOSOPHY**, $6.95. 479pp. API 73

_____. **ROSICRUCIAN AND MODERN INITIATION**, c$3.95. 95pp. RSP 65

_____. **SIGNS AND SYMBOLS OF THE CHRISTMAS MYSTERIES**, c$3.50. 62pp. API 69

_____. **THE SOCIAL FUTURE**, $2.50. These lectures are designed to show that the threefold social order can bring about a healthy social organism that will overcome the polarizing tendencies of modern life and make the economy the servant of society rather than its master. 151pp. RSP 68

_____. **THE SOUL'S AWAKENING**, $2.95. 149pp. SBC 73

_____. **THE SOUL'S PROBATION**, $2.95. 128pp. SBC 73

_____. **SPIRITUAL GUIDANCE OF MAN**, $1.95. 85pp. SPI 50

_____. **THE SPIRITUAL HIERARCHIES**, c$5.50. 140pp. SPI 70

_____. **SPIRITUAL SCIENCE AND MEDICINE**, $6.95. See the Healing section.

_____. STAGES OF HIGHER KNOWLEDGE, $2.50. A further study of the information discussed in **Knowledge of Higher Worlds**, concerned with the three stages of imagination, inspiration, and intuition. 72pp. API 67

_____. STRUCTURE OF THE LORD'S PRAYER, $.95. API 71

_____. SUPERSENSIBLE INFLUENCES IN THE HISTORY OF MANKIND, $2.95. 83pp. RSP 56

_____. SUPERSENSIBLE IN MAN AND THE WORLD, $3.95. 92pp. SPu 64

_____. SUPERSENSIBLE MAN, c$3.95. 102pp. RSP 61

_____. THEOSOPHY—AN INTRODUCTION TO SUPERSENSIBLE KNOWLEDGE, c$5.75/$2.95. As Steiner puts it, *The purpose of this book is to give a description of some of the regions of the supersensible world. The reader who is only willing to admit the existence of the sensible world will look upon this description as merely an unreal product of the imagination. Whoever looks for paths that lead beyond this world of the senses, however, will soon learn to understand that human life only gains worth and significance through insight into another world.* This is one of the best introductions to Steiner's thought. 195pp. API 71

_____. THEOSOPHY OF THE ROSICRUCIANS, c$4.95. 168pp. RSP 66

_____. THREEFOLD SOCIAL ORDER, $1.95. A description of the optimum social order and the means by which it can be achieved. 82pp. API 66

_____. THREE STREAMS IN THE EVOLUTION OF MANKIND, c$4.50. 124pp. RSP 65

_____. TRUE AND FALSE PATHS IN SPIRITUAL INVESTIGATION, c$5.95. 222pp. RSP 69

_____. THE TRUE NATURE OF THE SECOND COMING, $1.75. 81pp. RSP 61

_____. VERSES AND MEDITATION, c$5.95. 254pp. RSP 61

_____. WAKING OF HUMAN SOUL AND THE FORMING OF DESTINY, $1.75. 25pp. SBC 70

_____. THE WISDOM OF MAN, OF THE SOUL, AND OF THE SPIRIT, c$7.50. 204pp. API 71

_____. WONDERS OF THE WORLD, ORDEALS OF THE SOUL, REVELATIONS OF THE SPIRIT, c$5.50. 190pp. RSP 63

_____. THE WORK OF THE ANGELS IN MAN'S ASTRAL BODY, $1.25. 40pp. RSP 60

_____. WORLD ECONOMY, $3.25. 188pp. RSP 49

_____. THE WRONG AND RIGHT USE OF ESOTERIC KNOWLEDGE, $1.95. 72pp. RSP 31

STEINER, RUDOLF and ITA WEGMAN. FUNDAMENTALS OF THERAPY, c$3.50. 159pp. RSP 25

UNGER, GEORGE. FLYING SAUCERS: PHYSICAL AND SPIRITUAL ASPECTS, $1.60. 42pp. NKB 58

WACHSMUTH, G. THE EVOLUTION OF MANKIND, $10.20. See the Ancient Civilizations section.

_____. REINCARNATION, c$10.60. See the Reincarnation and Karma section.

WALDORF EDUCATION

Rudolf Steiner had repeatedly spoken of the need for a deeper understanding of man himself and of his relationship to the world. When he called together the teachers who were to carry responsibility for the first [Waldorf] school, he gave them a new conception of the growing child and its needs. He shows how during the first seven years the little child is building its own bodily form. At birth it was given the body prepared for it by its parents and gradually this has to be replaced out of its own living forces. It is damaging to the child's health if at this stage it is approached intellectually. It needs its growth powers to build a sturdy frame. It has to explore its surroundings by finding out what its body can do, by balancing, running, and climbing. It has to acquire skills in doing up buttons and tying shoe laces. It is learning how to relate itself to the world of space, and when attempts are made to stimulate its intellect the child's forces of growth are disturbed. . . . We have one great help in educating children under seven, and that is their power of imitation. . . . It is all important that those who look after little ones be worthy of imitation. . . . The different stages of the child's growth are marked by physiological changes. . . . Thus through the different stages of childhood and youth pupils are enabled to unfold their own capacities. From healthy imitation in the first years they develop

strength of will. Through joy in what they learn under the guidance of a loved teacher, their feelings are enriched and give life to their thinking. During their adolescence they discover the creative quality of thought. Then they can face life with confidence in their own powers.—from Eileen Hutchins' *The Normal Child* in Davy's **Work Arising.**

BARAVALLE, HERMANN von. ASTRONOMY, AN INTRODUCTION, $3.50. 41pp. S&G 74

_____. GEOMETRIC DRAWING AND THE WALDORF SCHOOL PLAN, $2.25. 58pp. S&G 67

_____. INTRODUCTION TO PHYSICS IN THE WALDORF SCHOOLS, $2.25. 44pp. S&G 67

_____. PERSPECTIVE DRAWING, $2.25. 50pp. S&G 68

_____. TEACHING OF ARITHMETIC AND THE WALDORF SCHOOL PLAN, $3.00. 90pp. S&G 67

EDMUNDS, FRANCIS. RUDOLF STEINER'S GIFT TO EDUCATION—THE WALDORF SCHOOLS, $3.95. Edmunds has spent much of his adult life teaching in Waldorf schools and lecturing on education and the Waldorf school movement. In this book he gives a clear idea of what is meant by education based on the principles of Rudolf Steiner, both in idea and practice. Many classroom stories enliven the exposition. 144pp. RSP 75

GERBERT, HILDEGARD. EDUCATION THROUGH ART, $3.95. 77pp. SBC nd

GLAS, NORBERT. CONCEPTION, BIRTH AND EARLY CHILDHOOD, $2.50. See the Natural Childbirth section.

GLAS, WERNER. SPEECH EDUCATION IN THE PRIMARY GRADES OF WALDORF SCHOOL, $3.50. 103pp. Sun 74

GRUNELIUS, ELIZABETH. EARLY CHILDHOOD EDUCATION AND WALDORF SCHOOL PLAN, $2.00. 47pp. S&G 66

HARWOOD, A.C. THE RECOVERY OF MAN IN CHILDHOOD, $6.70. Harwood has devoted a lifetime to the spread of Steiner's thought, not only in the field of education but also in its general application to life. He has lectured extensively on Waldorf education throughout the world and has been extremely involved in developing Steiner schools in the U.S. and Germany. He is also chairman of the Anthroposophical Society in Great Britain. This study of Waldorf education is universally considered the best overall presentation of the philosophical underpinnings of the system. It is very clearly written and we recommend it highly. Index, 211pp. Hod 58

_____. THE WAY OF A CHILD, $2.50. *This little book is entirely based on the study of Rudolf Steiner's books and lectures on childhood and education, and many years of experience as a teacher in a school founded to carry out his ideas.*—from the foreword. 144pp. RSP 40

KONIG, KARL. THE FIRST THREE YEARS OF THE CHILD, c$5.50. Discusses in detail the three gifts that the child carries with him from the time of his birth—the ability to walk upright, to speak, and to think. 130pp. API 69

_____. THE HANDICAPPED CHILD, $.50. 19pp. NKB 54

LINDEN, WILHELM zur. A CHILD IS BORN, $3.95. See the Natural Childbirth section.

MC ALLEN, AUDREY. THE EXTRA LESSON, $5.50. Exercises in movement, drawing, and painting for helping children in difficulties with writing, reading, and arithmetic. 76pp. RSB 74

METAXA, GEORGE. MUSIC FOR CHILDREN'S EURYTHMY AND DANCE, $3.00. 26pp. S&G nd

NIEDERHAUSER, HANS and MARGARET FROHLICH. FORM DRAWING, $4.50. Form drawing is the term used for the exercises practiced in Waldorf Schools which help train the dexterity of the children's hands in writing letters and numbers. This training goes gradually much further than writing; by learning to look at the relationships between all parts of one's drawing and also at the relation between one's drawing and the page as a whole, one develops a sense for composition and a foundation is laid for what later on will be the study of geometry. This is a practical guide which includes many exercises and examples. Oversize, 57pp. SGB 74

STEINER, RUDOLF. CURATIVE EDUCATION, c$7.50. Transcription of a course of lectures for doctors and curative teachers which discusses a great variety of physical and mental disturbances and outlines suggestions for the treatment of a disturbed child. 222pp. RSP 62

_____. DISCUSSIONS WITH TEACHERS, c$4.50. 166pp. RSP 67

_____. EDUCATION AS AN ART, $1.95. Transcription of three lectures by Steiner and three articles by other authors. 126pp. Mul 70

_____. EDUCATION AS A SOCIAL PROBLEM, c$5.50. This is one of Steiner's most basic writings on Waldorf education. 128pp. RSP 69

_____. **THE KINGDOM OF CHILDHOOD**, $3.50. In these lectures Steiner shows how essential it is for a teacher to work upon himself, not merely to use his natural gifts but to transform them, to seek for unsuspected power in himself; never to become a pedant, but to make ample use of humor and keep his teaching and himself lively and imaginative. And above all, Steiner insists on the grave importance of doing everything in the light of the earthly world. 162pp. API 64

_____. **A MODERN ART OF EDUCATION**, $3.50. Formerly titled *Education and Modern Spiritual Life*, this series of twelve lectures discusses walking, speaking, thinking, emancipation of the will, and practical insights. 232pp. RSP 28

_____. **THE STUDY OF MAN**, $4.95. These lectures were given as a preparation for their task to teachers of the original Waldorf School. They not only detail Steiner's educational views, but reveal his fundamental views on the psychology of man. 193pp. API

_____. **THE YOUNGER GENERATION**, $3.95. Subtitled *Educational and Spiritual Impulses for Life in the Twentieth Century.* 179pp. API 73

WILKINSON, ROY. **THE DEVELOPMENT OF LANGUAGE**, $1.20. Wilkinson's books are geared toward use in the classroom and at home and are generally considered excellent manuals. 21pp. WLK 73

_____. **LEARNING TO WRITE AND READ**, $1.20. 17pp. WLK 73

_____. **MAN AND ANIMAL**, $2.60. 22pp. WLK 75

_____. **PLANT STUDY–GEOLOGY**, $2.60. 34pp. WLK 75

_____. **QUESTIONS ANSWERED ON THE RUDOLPH STEINER EDUCATION**, $2.25. SBC nd

_____. **SOCIAL ASPECTS**, $1.25. 16pp. WLK 73

_____. **STUDIES IN PRACTICAL ACTIVITIES**, $2.60. 26pp. WLK 75

_____. **TEACHING HISTORY I: INDIA AND PERSIA**, $1.40. 27pp. WLK 73

_____. **TEACHING HISTORY II: EGYPT, CHALDEA, BABYLONIA**, $1.40. 33pp. WLK 74

_____. **TEACHING HISTORY III: GREECE AND ROME**, $2.60. 37pp. WLK 74

_____. **THE TEMPERAMENTS**, $1.55. 25pp. WLK 73

WETZL, JOSEPH. **THE BRIDGE OVER THE RIVER**, $2.95. Subtitled *Communications from the Life after Death of a young artist who died in World War I.* 99pp. API 74

WINKLER, FRANZ. **FOR FREEDOM DESTINED**, c$6.95. Subtitled *Mysteries of Man's Evolution in the Mythology of Wagner's Ring Operas and Parsifal.* 174pp. WaI 74

_____. **MAN: BRIDGE BETWEEN TWO WORLDS**, $4.50. Notes, bibliography, index. 268pp. WaI 60

ZEYLMANS VAN EMMICHOVEN, F.W. **THE FOUNDATION STONE**, c$2.75. 118pp. RSP 63

EDMUND SZEKELY

Born in one of the oldest, most eminent of European families, Szekely has made it his life's task to present ancient wisdom and philosophy of many varied cultures and traditions in a form uniquely compatible with modern understanding. Holding degrees from a number of prominent European universities, he is a learned philologist in Sanskrit, Aramaic, Greek and Latin and in ten modern languages.

In addition to his fifty or so published booklets on scientific subjects, he has written approximately thirty-eight volumes on philosophy, archaeology, medicine, psychology, and related subjects in a variety of foreign languages. He has devoted himself to the discovery and dissemination of materials that are conducive to the immediate evolution of man and society. In 1962, he established a center in southern California for the furtherance of spiritual growth and dedicated to the pursuit of man's higher possibilities through education, meditation, and spiritual living.

_____. **THE BOOK OF HERBS**, $2.25. See the Herbs section.

_____. **THE BOOK OF MINERALS**, $1.95. Aca 71

_____. **THE BOOK OF SURVIVAL**, $3.75. 2000 years ago the Essenes used the methods outlined here to create a flowering oasis at the Dead Sea. Aca

_____. **THE BOOK OF VITAMINS**, $1.75. See the Nutrition section.

_____. **COSMOS, MAN AND SOCIETY**, $4.50. Eleven lectures dealing with the subject of meaningful living in the twentieth century. This is his most comprehensive work on the subject, only recently reprinted. 134pp. Aca 73

_____. **COSMOTHERAPY OF THE ESSENES**, $2.80. *This book outlines the methods and techniques by which we may contact the Cosmic Ocean of Life and experience within ourselves the powers which keep the universe in equilibrium and eternal evolution.*—from the introduction. 64pp. Aca 75

The Jaguar God Hit by Spanish Spear (Codex Vaticanus)

Tezcatlipoca Hit by Spanish Spear (Codex Borgia)

ASHUR, the Assyrian God of War

SZEKELY, EDMUND BORDEAUX. **ARCHEOSOPHY: A NEW SCIENCE**, $2.50. Archeosophy is an application of philosophy to archaeology, through the medium of ancient symbols and pictographs. Illustrated, 31pp. Aca 73

_____. **THE ART OF ASHA–JOURNEY TO THE COSMIC OCEAN**, $9.50. A comprehensive study of the Sumerian and ancient Persian origins of the Essene traditions, and also of the esoteric key to the most ancient form of chess: an all-encompassing synthesis of art, music, science, philosophy, and the basis of the most ancient system of psychoanalysis. This is a magnificent art edition in a large album format with over 100 illustrations. 146pp. MiM 66

_____. **DEATH OF THE NEW WORLD**, $4.80. A narrative, taken from 200 original native drawings and pre-Columbian codices, which tells the story of the idyllic life in an Aztec paradise, the signs and portents of the coming disaster, the Conquest itself, and the story of the destruction of the native world. Many illustrations. 47pp. Aca 73

_____. THE DIALECTICAL METHOD OF THINKING, $1.75. Presents the thirty-four methodical principles of the great thinkers and scientists which can be the guide to the solution of all problems. Aca nd

_____. THE ESSENE BOOK OF CREATION, $3.80. More ancient than the Biblical Genesis, the Essene book of creation profoundly reveals man's purpose in life and the three paths to truth: the path of nature, the path of knowledge, and the path of intuition. Large album, profusely illustrated. 69pp. Aca 75

_____. THE ESSENE CODE OF LIFE, $2.50. Presents the way of life followed by the Essene brotherhoods at the Dead Sea and Lake Mareotis. Szekely derived his information from an original Aramaic document found in the eighteenth century by a Frenchman which records the discourses between the Roman historian Josephus Flavius and Banus, an Essene master. 42pp. Aca 75

_____. THE ESSENE GOSPEL OF PEACE, $1.00. See the Fasting section.

_____. THE ESSENE JESUS, $3.80. A re-evaluation based on the Dead Sea Scrolls. Includes the Essene interpretation of the Sermon on the Mount and an analysis of the meaning of Christmas. Large album edition, illustrated with the etchings of Doré. 71pp.

_____. THE ESSENES, BY JOSEPHUS AND HIS CONTEMPORARIES, $1.50. Life in the brotherhood of the first century Essenes is described in considerable detail by noted historians and writers of the period—Josephus Flavius, Philo, Plinius and others. Aca 70

_____. THE ESSENE SCIENCE OF LIFE, $2.80. A companion to the **Gospel of Peace**, this book presents the health system of the Essenes in detail. 54pp. Aca 70

_____. THE ESSENE TEACHINGS OF ZARATHUSTRA, $1.50. Zarathustra, the great Persian sage, profoundly inspired the Essene traditions. This volume includes ancient legends and authentic texts from the Zend Avesta. Aca 74

_____. THE ESSENE WAY, $8.50. A profusely illustrated oversize volume containing Dr. Szekely's lectures at the Creative Essene Workshop and Seminar held in 1975. Includes practical instructions. Aca 76

_____. THE ESSENES AND THE VATICAN, $4.80. A detailed account of the history of this text subtitled *The Discovery of the Essene Gospel of Peace*. Aca 76

_____. THE EVOLUTION OF HUMAN THOUGHT, $1.50. The basic ideas and teachings of eighty-seven great philosophers and thirty-eight schools of philosophy from 1000 BC to the present. 32pp. Aca 71

_____. FATHER, GIVE US ANOTHER CHANCE, $5.80. A study of the decline of our civilization and the rebirth of a new culture. This volume explains how to create the *Creative, Self-Sufficient Health Homestead*. 63pp. Aca 69

_____. THE FIERY CHARIOTS, $4.80. A presentation of the Essene brotherhood at the Dead Sea in Roman times on political intrigues, the audacity of the zealots, the decadence of the rulers, and the Brothers of Light who brought peace to the age. 96pp. Aca 71

_____. LA FILOSOFIA DEL MEXICO ANTIGUO, c$15.00. A comprehensive, two volume presentation—written in Spanish and illustrated with hundreds of photographs.

_____. FROM ENOCH TO THE DEAD SEA SCROLLS, $3.80. This volume distills the essence of Szekely's books on the Essenes. The recent Dead Sea Scrolls further corroborate his original texts. All the beauty of the Essene knowledge is contained here: the Essene communions, the sevenfold peace, the mystical Tree of Life, and how we can learn to apply the Essene teachings in our daily lives. Includes translated excerpts from the Dead Sea Scrolls. 93pp. Aca 75

_____. THE GAME OF GODS, $1.50. An archaeological reconstruction of the world picture of ancient America.

_____. HEALING WATERS, $3.00. Guidebook to fifty European water cures. 57pp. Aca 73

_____. HOW THE GREAT PAN DIED: THE ORIGIN OF CHRISTIANITY, $7.50. A controversial and thorough study of the origins of Christianity, representing forty years of research. Large album format. 127pp. Aca 68

_____. JOURNEY THROUGH ONE THOUSAND MEDITATIONS: A SYNTHESIS OF NATURE AND EIGHT THOUSAND YEARS OF WISDOM, $8.50. An encyclopedia of the greatest teachings of history. Many illustrations, oversized and unbound. Aca

_____. THE LIVING BUDDHA, $5.80. A comparative study of the teachings of the Buddha and of yoga. Includes a lucid explanation of the state of consciousness which the Buddha termed nirvana, the Buddha's teaching about the cause of suffering and the path of self-perfection, and a discussion of the purpose and necessity of understanding the essence of the teaching of Patanjali. A large album, profusely illustrated. 71pp. Aca

_____. LOST SCROLLS OF THE ESSENE BROTHERHOOD, $4.50. Book III of the **Essene Gospel of Peace**, presenting translations of the following ancient texts: *The Sevenfold Vow, The Essene Worship,* and *Texts from the Lost Essene Scrolls.* An appendix illustrates original fragments of the scrolls in Hebrew and Aramaic. Beautifully illustrated throughout. 148pp. Aca 74

_____. LUDWIG VON BEETHOVEN, $1.75. See the Music section.

_____. MAN IN THE COSMIC OCEAN, $1.75. Presents a key to understanding the origin, structure, and function of the universe. This volume is more esoteric than Szekely's other works. 52pp. Aca 70

_____, SCIENTIFIC VEGETARIANISM, $1.75. See the Nutrition section.

Illustrations from: The Soul of Ancient Mexico

_____. THE SOUL OF ANCIENT MEXICO, $7.50. A monumental work, presenting a complete philosophical reconstruction of the world picture of the Toltec-Aztec civilizations, and the key to understanding the spiritual significance of their rituals—including the Toltec Ball Game. Large album, illustrated with hundreds of photographs. 135pp. Aca 68

_____. TALKS, VOL. I: THE LIVING JESUS AND THE MEANING OF CHRISTMAS, $1.95. Aca

_____. TALKS, VOL. II: WILL POWER, THE FUTURE OF HUMANITY, AND SLEEP, A SOURCE OF HARMONY, $1.95. 36pp. Aca 72

_____. TOWARD THE CONQUEST OF THE INNER COSMOS, $5.80. A journey through different paths penetrating the innermost reality of our spiritual experience. A study of unorthodox approaches in Oriental wisdom, Western art and mystic poetry. Large album, profusely illustrated. 63pp. Aca 69

_____. TREASURY OF RAW FOODS, $1.95. See the Fasting section.

_____. UNKNOWN BOOKS OF THE ESSENES, $4.60. Book II of the **Essene Gospel of Peace**, presenting translations of the following ancient texts: *The Vision of Enoch, From the Essene Book of Moses, Communions with the Angels of the Earthly Mother, Communions with the Angels of the Heavenly Father, The Sevenfold Peace from the Essene Book of Jesus, Fragments Identical with the Dead Sea Scrolls, From the Essene Book of the Teacher of Righteousness, From the Essene Gospel of John,* and *From the Essene Book of Revelations.* Beautifully illustrated. 128pp. Aca 75

_____. THE ZEND AVESTA OF ZARATHUSTRA, $4.80. See the Ancient Near East sub-section of Ancient Civilizations.

TANTRA

Tantra is an Indian cult; but since it has evolved continuously from the remotest antiquity it is not limited to any of the particular Indian religions which arrived later on the historical scene. Groups of Hindus, Buddhists and Jains share Tantrik ideas and do Tantrik things; but there are symbols in the vast natural caverns of palaeolithic Europe (c. 20,000 BC) which can be accurately matched with symbols still used today by Tantrikas. Hundreds of generations have devoted themselves to developing and refining Tantra, so that it now conveys with extraordinary purity the most essential patterns of human symbolic expression.

It would be wrong to call Tantra a religion; that term has too many misleading overtones nowadays for far too many people. Tantra is not a *way of thought*, either. Thought, in the sense of ordinary logical and very useful reasoning, Tantra sees as one of the chief causes for people gradually becoming disillusioned and miserable in what they believe to be their world. So Tantra works with action. Above all, Tantra is not something to be read about in books, although in fact there are numerous Sanskrit books known as Tantras. The earliest, a Buddhist one, probably goes back to the sixth century AD. The most recent are nineteenth century. But what these texts consist of are prescriptions for action, including mental action, which are the whole purpose of the texts. If you don't do what your Tantra describes, then you will never get the point.

The Tantrik pictures were also meant ultimately to be used, not just looked at. They are undeniably impressive; but that is not all. They are made expressly to stimulate a special kind of mental activity, and to evoke psychosomatic forces. Used in rituals which include yoga, offerings, meditation and sexual intercourse, they can change a person completely, providing him with a new basis for his life. At first, all these procedures need to be carried through in the most basic fact; for only in this way can they displace the banal everyday reality which presses so forcibly on people's lives. Later, when a Tantrika reaches a high level of achievement after many long years of effort and assimilation, the pictures may be visualized and carried out subjectively, without any risk of their collapsing into fantasy. For Tantra has no dealings with fantasy. What it describes and maps is a world of realities, a world which can only be visited by following the maps. It is there to be found; but someone who has not visited it can have no idea of what it is like. For there is no way of examining it from the outside. It is what we are—

although we don't usually realize the fact—and we can never step out of it to take an analytical view.

Tantra, in fact, plunges one back into the roots of one's own identity, not just by discussing social roles and interpersonal communication, and not by offering the kind of clear-cut or comforting answers given by the dogmatic theology of straight religions. Tantra says *If you do these things which Tantrikas have discovered, you will find yourself in a position to experience what the truth is about yourself and your world, as directly as you can experience the street*. Needless to say, to do those things, to get into the position from which you can experience the truth, involves a total change of personality. This takes every kind of effort—physical, sexual, mental, moral; and most are just the kinds of effort that nothing in Western education or tradition prepares one for. Tantra calls on energies in the human body and its world which most people usually dissipate in their ultimately pointless exertions and *recreations*. But, most important of all, Tantra positively cultivates and bases itself on what most people dismiss as the pleasures of life. It does *not* say solemnly *You must abstain from all enjoyment, mortify your flesh, and obey the commands of a jealous Father-God*. Instead, it says *Raise your enjoyment to its highest power, and then use it as a spiritual rocket-fuel*. This, of course, seems a dangerous revolutionary doctrine to the orthodox in any religion. And to the orthodox the Tantrika is a scandal.

—from **Tantra: The Indian Cult of Ecstasy** by Philip Rawson

ARTS COUNCIL OF GREAT BRITAIN. **CATALOG OF TANTRA EXHIBITION,** c$10.20. This is the catalogue of the first major exhibition of tantric art to be held anywhere. The exhibit was organized by Philip Rawson and was held in London in 1971. Much of the art comes from the collection of Ajit Mookerjee. 360 plates are included; seventeen are large color plates, but most, unfortunately, are reproduced in a small size. The presentation of the plates is well organized and a large amount of excellent explanatory material accompanies them. Rawson contributes an illuminating introductory survey. The text itself is oriented toward the serious student of tantric art and should in no manner be considered introductory. 8x12", bibliography. 151pp. Luz 72

BHARATI, AGEHANANDA. **THE TANTRIC TRADITION,** $4.50. An important academic work which critically analyzes the literary, linguistic, ideological, and anthropological aspects of tantra. Professor Bharati documents his exposition with freshly translated passages from Indian and Tibetan texts. He gives special emphasis to mantra, initiation, the male-female polarity, and to the history and development of tantra in India and Tibet. *Professor Bharati's survey of Tantrism is an outstanding achievement. For the first time Tantrism has been dealt with in relation to the total intellectual climate.*—Herbert Guenther. This edition includes notes and a 33pp annotated bibliography. Index, 348pp. Wei 65

BLOFELD, JOHN. **TANTRIC MYSTICISM OF TIBET: A PRACTICAL GUIDE TO THE THEORY, PURPOSE, AND TECHNIQUES OF TANTRIC MEDITATION,** $3.25. See the Tibetan subsection of Buddhism.

CHAKRAVARTI, CHINTAHARAN. **TANTRAS: STUDIES ON THEIR RELIGION AND LITERATURE,** c$14.40. This is a detailed study of a little-explored area of Indian thought covering the following topics: *The Tantras—What They Stand For, Antiquity of Tantricism, The Age and Authorship of the Tantras, Place of the Tantras among the other Sastras, Ideals of Tantra Rites, How and Where the Tantras Originated, Tantra Schools, Literature of the Tantras, Tantric Authors and their Works, Tantric Form of Worship and Tantric Dieties, Kali Worship in Bengal, Cult of Durga and Durga Worship in Bengal*, and a description of the text *Paramanandamatasamgraha*. Extensive textual notes in both Sanskrit and English are included. Index, 129pp. PPu 63

DASGUPTA, SHASHI. **AN INTRODUCTION TO TANTRIC BUDDHISM,** $3.95. This is a recent reprint of a pioneering work on tantric Buddhism. Almost all of the material presented is taken from unpublished manuscripts. The book was not well received when it was originally published and its flaws are apparent to the knowledgeable reader—however it does present some important material and introduces some controversial ideas. This edition is a reprint of the original one and is not at all well printed. That, combined with the author's scattered writing style, makes the book hard to read. Extensive notes, indices. 211pp. ShP 50

GUENTHER, HERBERT. **THE TANTRIC VIEW OF LIFE,** c$8.50. Guenther, a well-known Tibetologist, here offers a major contribution towards the understanding of tantric Buddhism. The meaning of tantra is clearly defined and the philosophy of tantra is presented in depth. Various aspects are elucidated through original translations from important tantric texts and commentaries from Tibetan. The book concludes with a valuable discussion of the role of aesthetics and art and is illustrated with Tibetan thankas and Indian sculpture. Notes, 168pp. ShP 72

GUENTHER, HERBERT and CHOGYAM TRUNGPA. **THE DAWN OF TANTRA,** $3.50. *In* **The Dawn of Tantra** *the reader meets a Tibetan and Westerner whose grasp of*

Buddhist tantra is real and unquestionable.... Dr. Guenther and Chogyam Trungpa met in Berkeley, California, in 1972, where together they gave a public seminar on Buddhist tantra. **The Dawn of Tantra** *is the edited record of that seminar including part of the general discussion. Two other talks by Guenther and Trungpa are also included.* Illustrations, 92pp. ShP 75

GUPTA, SANJUKTA, tr. **LAKSMI TANTRA,** c$45.00. A translation of an important text which elucidates the Pancaratra system. Pancaratra is the oldest surviving Vishnuite sect. Detailed notes, illustrations, index. 434pp. Bri 72

JYOTIRMAYANANDA, SWAMI. **MEDITATE THE TANTRIC YOGA WAY,** $3.45. See the Meditation section.

PANDIT, M.P. **GEMS FROM THE TANTRAS: FIRST SERIES,** c$2.50. Pandit has been closely associated with Sri Aurobindo and the Mother. This volume is drawn from the **Kularnava** tantra, a presentation of practical teachings for seekers on the path. Topically arranged, including the Sanskrit text, English translation, and commentary. 106pp. Gan 70

_____. **GEMS FROM THE TANTRAS: SECOND SERIES,** c$2.50. Selections from various tantras emphasizing the consciousness aspect of the *Eternal Reality (Sat-Chit-Ananda)* and its special significance for the spiritual growth of man. Same format as the first series. 114pp. Gan 69

_____. **KULARNAVA TANTRA,** c$4.00. The **Kularnava** is one of the most frequently cited texts in tantric literature. The text presents all the fundamentals of the tantric school and its underlying philosophy and ethical and social implications. This edition includes an introduction by Arthur Avalon and a detailed, topically organized study by Pandit which summarizes the text itself. 128pp. Gan 73

_____. **KUNDALINI YOGA,** c$2.75. A brief, simple study of Woodroffe's **The Serpent Power,** summarizing the main principles of tantra yoga. 78pp. Gan nd

_____. **LIGHTS ON THE TANTRA,** c$2.50. A topically arranged discussion of the doctrines and practices of the tantras and their contribution to the spiritual and religious culture of India—in the light of Sri Aurobindo's thought. Includes extensive notes. 107pp. Gan 57

RAJNEESH, BHAGWAN SHREE. **THE BOOK OF THE SECRETS,** c$10.00. A well edited collection of eight discourses on an ancient scripture on tantra attributed to Lord Shiva and known as **Vigyana Bhairava Tantra.** In this scripture Shiva gives 112 meditation techniques, based on tantric principles, and here Rajneesh explains these methods. The style is spontaneous and Rajneesh incorporates material from many disciplines. Rajneesh is one of the most respected contemporary Indian masters and his appeal is especially great among the intellectuals. He is a former university professor and he has learned well how to organize and present difficult concepts in a lively, clear manner. 402pp. H&R 74

RAWSON, PHILIP. **THE ART OF TANTRA,** c$17.50. Rawson is the author of a number of books of Asian art and was the organizer of the recent exhibition of tantric art held in London under the auspices of the Arts Council of Great Britain. He writes this book as an interpreter, explaining with the aid of many illustrations of classic examples of tantric art, how tantra invites its followers to a personal meditative and visual exploration of self and the world. An exquisite book; we recommend it highly for those who wish to a detailed study. 176 plates, twenty-five in color. 7½x10", extensive notes, bibliography, glossary. 216pp. NYG 73

_____. **TANTRA: THE INDIAN CULT OF ECSTASY,** $4.95. This is Rawson's second book on the subject, the better introduction for the general reader. While a large part of his first book is devoted to extensive analysis of various elements of tantra, this book has 190 illustrations, thirty-two in full color, and a good general introduction. Its aim is to turn as many people as possible on to the symbolic imagery of tantra and

thereby to an understanding of the underlying philosophy. Highly recommended as both a beautiful coffee table book and an illuminating text for the seeker. 8x12", 128pp. Avo 74

RIVIERE, J. MARQUES. **TANTRIK YOGA,** $2.95. The information presented in this comprehensive instruction manual is adapted from the original Sanskrit texts. It discusses the esoteric anatomy of the human body, the chakras and the kundalini, and presents methods of breath control, asanas (postures), mental and meditational exercises. Riviere also discusses Chinese, Japanese and Tibetan techniques for the benefit of students who wish to know how they accord with the Hindu practices he presents. Glossary, 126pp. Wei 34

SNELLGROVE, D.L. **THE HEVAJRA TANTRA,** c$36.65/set. This two volume set includes an introduction discussing tantric development and the contents of the **Hevajra Tantra** and follows with a complete translation and full explanatory notes based on the earliest commentaries. The second volume contains the Sanskrit and Tibetan texts of the **Tantra** and the Sanskrit text of one of the early commentaries, the **Yogaratnamala,** glossary, Sanskrit-English vocabulary, index. 363pp. Oxf 59

TSUDA, SHINICHI. **THE SAMVARODAYA-TANTRA: SELECTED CHAPTERS,** c$34.50. This edition includes the transliterated Sanskrit and Tibetan texts, an English translation, and commentary. In all, nineteen chapters have been selected. Tibetan-Sanskrit and Sanskrit-Tibetan glossaries (both with English translation) are also included. Many notes, 408pp. Hok 74

WAYMAN, ALEX. **THE BUDDHIST TANTRAS,** c$12.50. See Tibetan Buddhist section.

WOODROFFE, JOHN. **GARLAND OF LETTERS,** c$6.25. Sir John Woodroffe was a justice of the high court of India at Calcutta during the last part of the nineteenth century. Under the pseudonym Arthur Avalon, he devoted himself to making tantra known to the Western world as well as to the educated Hindus who learned about tantra only from his translations. Sir John was thus writing for two Puritan audiences, to whom he was trying to justify the sexual elements in tantra—and his work must be read in light of this. In any case, it remains the most substantial body of tantric scholarship extant and is still very well considered. The reader should be warned that Woodroffe uses a great number of Sanskrit terms in his exposition without defining them—so a basic knowledge of Sanskrit or a good glossary is essential. This volume is a comprehensive treatise on the power, meaning and uses of mantras. Gan 74

_____, tr. **HYMNS TO THE GODDESS/HYMNS TO KALI,** c$6.25. Two separate works. **Hymns to the Goddess** is a translation of twenty-nine hymns to the *Divine Mother of the Universe* from Sanskrit scriptures, by Shankara. **Hymns to Kali** is a translation of the **Karpuradi-Stotra,** twenty-two verses to Kali, the *Divine Mother* attributed to Shiva—with the commentary of Vimalananda-Swami. 335pp. Gan 73

_____. **INTRODUCTION TO TANTRA SASTRA,** c$3.00. Forms an introduction to the *Great Liberation* and a key to understanding tantric concepts. Gan nd

_____, tr. **ISOPANISAD/WAVE OF BLISS/THE GREATNESS OF SIVA,** c$4.00. **Isopanisad:** Isha Upanishad with tantric commentary by Satyananda; **Wave of Bliss:** a hymn in praise of Shakti, dealing with the kundalini, chakras, and tantric mantras; **The Greatness of Siva:** an ancient hymn attributed to Pushpadanta, with commentary. 180pp. Gan

_____. **THE PRINCIPLES OF TANTRA,** c$17.50/set. A translation of **The Tantra Tattva,** which lucidly explains the basis of the religious philosophy of tantra. Woodroffe provides extensive commentary. This is one of the most important tantric commentaries. Two volumes, 954pp. Gan 70

_____. **THE SERPENT POWER,** $5.00. A translation of two important works on tantric yoga: **Sat-Chakra-Nirupana** and **Padhuka-Panchaka,** including descriptions of the spiritual centers of consciousness and awakening of the kundalini. This is the most extensive discussion of kundalini available, as well as Woodroffe's most popular and probably his most important translation. Dov 19

_____. **TANTRA OF THE GREAT LIBERATION,** $3.95. Translation of **The Mahanirvana Tantra,** which is essentially a series of conversations between the God Shiva and his consort-energy, Shakti. Shiva gives instructions for meditation exercises and mental projections, yogic exercises, mantras for concentration and mind training, ceremonies of Shaktic worship, physiological information on the system of chakras, and the role of tantrism in life. Sir John has supplied extensive footnotes to explain the cryptic text, as well as a 130 page introduction explaining the anatomy of the chakras, various forms of tantra and mandalas, and the Siddhis. 405pp. Dov 13

_____, tr. **TANTRARAJA TANTRA/KAMA-KALA-VILASA,** $5.00. **Tantraraja Tantra** is an analytical resume of the *King among the Tantras*; **Kama-Kil-Vilasa** is the translation of an early text on Shakti tantra by Punyananda. Transliterated Sanskrit text with commentary by Natananda and Woodroffe. 246pp. Gan 71

TAROT

In view of what is known of the Tarot cards it seems likely that they were devised to represent grades or stages in a system of initiation. In some ways Tarot imagery resembles that of alchemy, which, as C.G. Jung has shown, was for its more perceptive devotees a system of Hermetic training leading to spiritual enlightenment.

Western alchemy probably evolved in Egypt, in the Hellenistic civilisation of Alexandria, which was also an early stronghold of Gnosticism. If this is so, then the alchemical treatises and the Tarot cards are both examples of the secret language of symbolism which initiates of all ages have devised to instruct their disciples and confound the profane.

Each of the twenty-two major trumps describes a stage in the journey of life which is crucial in some way. Only by solving the riddle which each card in turn presents can the way ahead be opened up and the development of the personality taken further.

The Spanish Tarot

According to Jung, the individuation process encompasses the whole of life, but falls naturally into two halves. The first half is concerned with the individual's relationship to the world outside himself; it is directed towards the development of the conscious mind and the stabilisation of the ego.

The second half reverses this process and confronts the ego with the depths of its own psyche, seeking to establish links with the inner self, the true centre of consciousness.

The two phases oppose one another, yet are complementary. The first half of life can be thought of as solar in nature, as it is outward-turning, active, positive, expansive. The second half is lunar in nature, being introspective, meditative, and passive in its relationship to the physical universe.

If we examine the twenty-two Tarot trumps with this in mind, we find that they fall naturally into two groups, with The Wheel of Fortune significantly at the mid-point.

The turning-point between one half of life and the other is of critical importance; at the high-point of physical existence one is suddenly confronted with the inevitability of death. As Jung himself has said: *At the stroke of noon the descent begins. And the descent means the reversal of all the ideals and values that were cherished in the morning.*

The cards dealing with the first half of the life-cycle commence with the un-numbered card, The Fool, and end with The Wheel of Fortune.

The Fool can be seen as the newly born child entering the world, pure, innocent, and unaware of itself as a separate entity; it is still enveloped in the folds of the unconscious.

The second card, The Magician, symbolises the dawning of self-awareness and the emergence of the individual ego. Man is shown wielding the magical weapons of consciousness, with which he will conquer the world.

The next four cards, The High Priestess, The Empress, The Emperor, and The High Priest, allude to the four powers that the infant ego is subject to: male and female, material and spiritual. These cards might also be said to refer to the channels through which the individual relates to his surroundings; the four Jungian *functions*: Intuition, Feeling, Sensation, and Thought.

Card VI, The Lovers, indicates the first decisive choice in life, the rejection in adolescence of one's family in favour of a mate. With this card the individual becomes responsible for his actions, and thus for his destiny.

Next we see The Chariot, signifying the need for successful adaptation to the laws of society, and the construction of a safe *vehicle*, or persona, in which to proceed through the world.

Justice coincides with the onset of physical maturity, and indicates that until now the individual's development has been one-sided, the conscious aspect having been developed at the expense of the unconscious. The time has come when the balance must be redressed if psychic stagnation is to be avoided. Justice is the voice of conscience.

The Hermit describes the process of self-examination which will follow if the promptings of conscience are heeded. The broad highway travelled by the Charioteer has come to an end, and a new and narrower path must now be found.

Then we arrive at the Wheel of Fortune, the mid-point of life, the stage at which the peak is passed and the descent begins.

In the next card, the Hermit has successfully reorientated himself by realising that his apparently insurmountable difficulties are common to all mankind. The insight that his sufferings are not peculiar to him alone gives him the detachment necessary to subdue the fears within, as the woman in the card Fortitude is seen overcoming the lion. Only by a fearless confrontation can the primeval forces of the unconscious be disarmed.

The Hanged Man symbolises the reversal of values and aims which should take place during the second half of life. Courage is needed to renounce the past in favour of an uncertain future. But the sacrifice must be made for psychic progress to continue.

The next card, Death, is sometimes entitled Transformation, as it points to a transformation of consciousness which must now take place. The ego must be transcended; the death of the old self must be sought in order that the energy locked within it might be released and directed towards the maturation of the higher self.

Temperance reveals that the sacrifice of the demands of the ego has resulted in a renewal of contact with the powers of life. The greatest challenge of the quest, the descent into the underworld in search of that which was lost, has ended in victory; consciousness is in communion with the unconscious, and the imbalance shown earlier by Justice is being redressed.

The Devil indicates that the dangers of the journey are not yet over, however. The forces of the unconscious have been released, and the seeker must either submit to the mindless powers of instinct, or else absorb and transmute them into a higher and positive form.

The reverse side of The Devil, Satan or the demiurge, is the glorious angel Lucifer, the light-bringer. The next card, The Tower, graphically describes the gift of Lucifer. His light is the fire of enlightenment which descends like a flash of lightning, destroying everything in its path which is not compatible with its own nature. It is the surge of power which is felt when the psychological blocks between the lower and higher selves are removed, and the light of God irradiates the personality.

The Star is a symbol of higher consciousness, the Evening Star which will act as a guide during the darkness which must follow the blinding brilliance of the divine lightning-bolt.

The Moon symbolises the final great trial which must be gone through, the dark night of the soul which follows the withdrawal of the inward light, and everything is seen as illusion. The text here is one of faith.

Swiss Tarot Cards

The Sun represents the reconciliation of the opposites, the coming together of the mortal and immortal selves. This card is analogous to the marriage of the royal brother and sister in alchemy. The night is past and a new day is dawning.

Judgement shows the rebirth of the integrated self, therefore figures are seen rising from the dead on the Day of Judgement.

The World is a mandala, the androgynous figure dancing within an encircling wreath being a symbol of psychic wholeness which expresses in its symmetry the complete order and fulfillment of the mature psyche.

It can also be seen as a representation of a child in the womb, in which case it leads naturally on to the card at the beginning of the sequence, the Fool, the newborn child commencing its journey through life. This would accord well with the Gnostic doctrines regarding reincarnation and the succession of lives leading on to higher and still higher attainment.

If the major arcana of the Tarot pack illustrates twenty-two important stages in the path of life, then each card can be interpreted at several levels. It can point to important principles and forces operating in the world; it can unveil significant processes in the expansion of mystical consciousness; it can indicate the emergence of as yet unevolved aspects of personality, and when reversed, it can warn of physical or psychic pitfalls which may be encountered.

The Tarot speaks in the language of symbols, the language of the unconscious, and when approached in the right manner it may open doors into the hidden reaches of the soul.

The mysterious beauty of the cards provides a stimulus that awakens one's intuitive faculties, leading on to an understanding which lies outside the scope of the intellect. As the mind explores the Tarot images, it uncovers meanings and significances which cannot be fully defined or brought completely into the light of reason.

The Tarot links the world of man with the world of the spirit, binding together all levels of reality and opening inner doors which were hitherto closed. A large part of the enduring value of these cards lies in the fact that their imagery cannot be fitted into any hard and fast dogma; they can never be

fully comprehended and therefore offer new and original insights to everyone who studies them.

The cards are vehicles for the powers of life, the archetypal contents of the unconscious. Thoughtful meditation on their enigmatic designs can lead to a stirring of the creative forces of the psyche, and inward illumination which not only expands the confines of the conscious mind but also serves to activate the hidden faculties of the unconscious.

—from **The Tarot** by Alfred Douglas.

————————◆————————

BLAKELEY, JOHN. **THE MYSTICAL TOWER OF THE TAROT**, $15.10. This is an unusual, highly esoteric interpretation of the Tarot. Its most interesting feature is a translation of a Sufi allegory which bears a striking resemblance to the pictorial representation of the path as presented in the major arcana. There's also an excellent presentation of the inner meaning of the cards and a good study of the origins of the Tarot. Throughout the book both the ancient mystery teachings and the wisdom of the East are cited and their relationship with the Tarot is fully explored. Also included are color plates of two major arcana decks along with a number of other color plates. Notes, bibliography, index. 207pp. Wat 74

BUTLER, BILL. **DICTIONARY OF THE TAROT**, c$7.95. This is a handy summary of the meanings of the cards in nineteen of the most commonly used Tarot decks. The comparison between the different interpretations can be useful to the student who seeks to find his/her own meaning rather than merely relying on one commentator. Both the major and minor arcana are discussed card by card, and there are also sections on the history of the Tarot, methods of divination, a long glossary defining both the terms used and the esoteric symbology. Both the design and the interpretation for each card and for each kind of deck are summarized separately. A useful compendium for all students of the Tarot. Bibliography, 254pp. ScB 75

Visconti Sforza Tarocchi Deck

CALVINO, ITALO. **TAROTS**, c$100.00. This is an exquisitely produced volume, 9x14", hand-lettered on beautiful blue handmade paper. The Visconti-Sforza cards are reproduced full size in color. These cards are without question the most beautiful ancient cards still extant. The background is mainly in gold leaf and the individual figures are movingly portrayed. Calvino presents an allegory of the journey through the Tarot entitled *The Castle of Crossed Destinies*, and there is also a critical examination of the cards along with background notes and a survey of the origin of Tarot cards. Limited edition, boxed. 161pp. Ric 75

CASE, PAUL FOSTER. **THE BOOK OF TOKENS**, c$6.25. Comprised of meditations on the occult meaning of the twenty-two Hebrew letters, illustrated by the twenty-two major Tarot keys. 200pp. BuA 34

B.O.T.A. Tarot Deck

_____. **HIGHLIGHTS OF THE TAROT**, $1.75. An excellent introduction to the esoteric significance of the Tarot. Includes a brief analysis of each of the twenty-two major arcana cards, a history of the Tarot, coloring instructions for the B.O.T.A. deck, and other background material. Very clearly presented material for the beginning student. Coloring instructions for the minor arcana are available for $1.25. 64pp. BuA 31

_____. **THE TAROT: A KEY TO THE WISDOM OF THE AGES**, c$4.50. A fine, in depth analysis of each of the twenty-two major arcana cards. The presentation is designed to stimulate the reader's intuitive understanding of each card's symbolism. Case presents each card as a meditational key to self growth and awareness. The whole is related to the Qabala, the Hebrew alphabet, numbers, color, and sound. There are separate chapters on methods of study, the esoteric meaning of numbers, and Tarot divination. If you've read the Case booklet and like his approach (as we do!) then move on to this material. We feel that this is the most enlightening overall book and recommend it highly. 214pp. Mac 47

CAVENDISH, RICHARD. **THE TAROT**, c$19.95. Despite its coffee-table format, this is an excellent serious study of the Tarot, with explanatory diagrams and tables, illustrated with 176 color and black and white plates. Cavendish presents what is known about the Tarot, its history, its uses and significance. He describes the earliest known packs and their development through changes in religious and political thought. Tracing the history of the arcane meanings attributed to the Tarot from the eighteenth century to the present, he gives a concise but comprehensive account of the divergent interpretations of the Tarot, providing a card-by-card analysis of them in relation to the Qabala, the letters of the Hebrew alphabet, symbolic animals, the elements, planets and signs of the zodiac, human qualities, and other key ideas. He also describes the use of the Tarot in magic and meditation, and provides explicit instructions on laying out and reading the cards. Many of the cards illustrated are not generally available and seeing the varying symbology helps the student gain an intuitive feeling for the meaning of the cards. If it were not for the price we would recommend this book highly. Even at the price, it is a good book to have. 8½x11", bibliography, index. 191pp. H&R 75

CIRLOT, J.E. **A DICTIONARY OF SYMBOLS**, c$4.98. See the Sacred Art section.

CROWLEY, ALEISTER. **THE BOOK OF THOTH**, c$12.95/$5.95. An attempt to translate the mysteries of the Qabalah and the Tarot into pictorial form. Describes the theory of Tarot including its Egyptian origins and relationship to the Qabalah, the meaning of major and lesser arcana cards. Includes lavishly illustrated, intensely colored pictorial interpretations of each of the cards. Oversize, 287pp. Wei 44

CURTISS, HARRIETTE and F. HOMER. **THE KEY OF DESTINY**, $5.00. This is a fine esoteric presentation of the Tarot, covering the eleventh to the twenty-second card. An advanced student seeking to deepen his understanding would be inspired by the material presented here. The numerological significance is examined in depth as is the Hebrew letter corresponding to each of the arcana. Christian and mythological references are also incorporated. Illustrations, index. 328pp. WII 23

_____. **THE KEY TO THE UNIVERSE**, $5.50. This is the first volume of the Curtiss' set, covering the arcana from one to ten. There is also material on the origin of numerical systems and on symbology. As in the other work three chapters are devoted to each arcana—one on the number, another on the corresponding Hebrew letter, and a third discussing the specific symbology of the card. Illustrations, index. 392pp. WII 17

DOANE, DORIS CHASE and KING KEYES. **HOW TO READ TAROT CARDS**, $2.95. A comprehensive how-to manual based on the Egyptian Tarot. Ms. Doane is a noted astrologer and was an associate of Zain and the Church of Light for many years. She presents fourteen sample Tarot readings, explaining the technique at great length. Other sections present key phrases for each of the seventy-eight cards and astrological symbolism. There is also background material and a section on how to use the cards. 207pp. Cro 67

DOUGLAS, ALFRED. **THE TAROT**, $1.95. We feel that this is the best overall introduction to the origin, meaning and uses of the Tarot. Long sections are devoted to the symbolism of the Tarot as it has developed over the ages and to the meaning of each of the major and minor arcana cards in the light of modern Jungian psychology and archetypes. Material on consulting the Tarot is also presented and there are sections on *Meditation and the Tarot* and *The Esoteric Tarot*. Fully indexed, with a good bibliography. A very well written and organized book and the one we usually recommend to our customers. 249pp. Vik 72

Crowley Thoth Deck

GARDNER, RICHARD. **EVOLUTION THROUGH THE TAROT**, c$4.40. A presentation of the major arcana in terms of their explanation of the meaning and purpose of human existence. Some of the exposition is based on related teachings of Jesus and parallels are made with the Gospels. A chapter is devoted to each of the trumps. Illustrations, bibliography. 112pp. Rig 70

_____. **TAROT SPEAKS**, c$7.50. Gardner is a psychic and here he uses his psychic abilities and lets each of the major arcana cards speak through him and tell the reader its message. Illustrations, 105pp. Rig 71

GETTINGS, FRED. **THE BOOK OF TAROT**, c$3.98. This is a very good general study. Gettings begins with a general introduction and then goes on to an in depth analysis of the major arcana cards. Each of the cards is illustrated in color and many of the cards are shown in several different versions. Gettings seems to prefer the Marseilles deck and so this is the one most often illustrated, but samples of the Rider-Waite and the Crowley deck are also included. Related material (including some alchemical woodcuts) is also presented. There's also some material on the minor arcana, consulting the Tarot, and the historical background of the Tarot, as well as a bibliography. A beautifully prepared, well written volume—recommended both as a coffee table book and as an illuminating volume. Oversize, 144pp. Ham 73

GRAVES, F. **WINDOWS OF THE TAROT**, $3.95. A brief presentation of the symbolism of each of the seventy-eight cards of the Aquarian Tarot deck, along with an explanation of their divinatory meanings. Also includes background material, astrological correspondences, and directions for laying out spreads. 95pp. M&M 73

GRAY, EDEN. **THE COMPLETE GUIDE TO THE TAROT**, $1.50. Eden Gray's books are the most popular introductory books on the Tarot. This is her most comprehensive

Rider-Waite Tarot Deck

one. Each of her books is illustrated with all seventy-eight cards of the Waite-Rider deck, accompanied by an analysis of the symbolism of the card and its divinatory meaning. Three techniques for reading the cards are detailed at length, and additional instructional material is provided. A third of the book outlines the Qabala, astrology, and numerology—systems of thought that illuminate the Tarot. There's also a glossary and a bibliography. This is the best of the books specifically keyed to the Waite-Rider deck, though the emphasis is on divination rather than self-understanding. 248pp. Ban 70

_____. **MASTERING THE TAROT**, $1.50. This is the newest of Gray's Tarot books, incorporating more of her personal philosophy and tips than the others. The only reading that is outlined is the Keltic spread—and this is given at great length, accompanied by sample readings. There are interesting sections on other methods of divination using the cards and a glossary. Again, each card is analyzed in detail. 221pp. NAL 71

HARGRAVE, CATHERINE. **A HISTORY OF PLAYING CARDS**, $5.00. The most thorough history available of cards from the fourteenth to the twentieth century. More

Tarot of Marseilles

than 1400 cards of all styles are illustrated and discussed. 462pp. Dov 30

HELINE, CARINNE. **TAROT AND THE BIBLE**, c$5.95. See the Bible section.

HOELLER, STEPHAN. **THE ROYAL ROAD**, $2.95. A handbook of Qabalistic meditations on the major arcana, expressing the quintessence of what Hoeller conceives to be the principal spiritual experiences embodied in each of the twenty-two paths. The meditations are connected to the twenty-two paths connecting the ten sephiroth on the Tree of Life. The approach is psychological and the reader is well prepared for the journey he is to undertake by the ample background material the author supplies. A very useful work for those who seek to understand the Qabala and the Tarot and their interrelations. Illustrations, 130pp. TPH 75

HOLY ORDER OF MANS. **JEWELS OF THE WISE**, $3.50. Just as the **Keystone of Tarot Symbolism** is quite similar to Case's **Highlights**, this volume closely resembles Case's **The Tarot**, although the presentation is more Christian oriented. Each of the twenty-two cards of the major arcana is analyzed in depth and the exposition includes information on the corresponding color, number, letter of the Hebrew alphabet, and astrological sign and quality. Even though the similarity to Case is great, some additional valuable insights can be found here. Illustrations, 198pp. HOM 74

_____. **KEYSTONE OF TAROT SYMBOLS**, $2.00. The Holy Order of MANS is a non-sectarian teaching order of minister-priests who have dedicated their lives to teaching and living the universal law of creation in accordance with the teachings of Jesus Christ. Their teachings are derived from the ancient Christian mysteries. The twenty-two major arcana are discussed and a Hebrew letter is assigned to each. The exposition includes coloring instructions and meditational phrases. An interesting esoteric interpretation in light of the thirty-two Paths of Wisdom. 108pp. HOM 71

Aquarian Tarot

HOTEMA, HILTON. **THE LAND OF LIGHT**, $4.00. *Includes an interpretation of the Tarot based on the ancient philosophy which symbolized the Cosmic Phenomena that was presented to the Neophyte in the Sacred Drama of Initiation, and included the strangest mysteries of existence, such as Reincarnation, Resurrection, and Eternal Life.* 157pp. HeR nd

KAHN, YITZHAC. **TAROT AND THE GAME OF FATE**, c$3.50. An interpretation of the Tarot that makes it applicable to real experience—as a poetic and magic symbology. Like a set of poems, the interpretation is direct and comprehensible. A second section of the book contains illustrated explanations of card patterns, and a system for discovering a corresponding card of the major arcana for any planetary position in an astrological chart. MBS

KAPLAN, STUART. **TAROT CLASSIC**, $2.95. A good introductory book, keyed to the Tarot Classic. Describes the current interest in the Tarot, the ancient origin of the cards and the earliest known European references to Tarot, the oldest packs still in existence, the development of the Tarot, the divinatory meanings of each of the major arcana and minor arcana cards, and sample card spreads and methods of divination. Includes illustrations of almost all the extant decks. The annotated bibliography is by far the most extensive we've seen. 243pp. G&D 72

KASDIN, SIMON. **THE ESOTERIC TAROT: THE KEY TO THE CABALA**, $1.95. An intensive discussion of the twenty-two major arcana cards using unusual symbols with specific reference to the Hebrew alphabet and Sepher Yitzerah. The illustrations do not resemble any deck we've seen. 96pp. Wei 73

KNIGHT, GARETH. **A PRACTICAL GUIDE TO QABALISTIC SYMBOLISM**, c$16.00/ set. See the Jewish Mysticism section.

KOPP, SHELLEY. **THE HANGED MAN**, c$7.95. See the Humanistic Psychology section.

LAURENCE, THEODOR. **HOW THE TAROT SPEAKS TO MODERN MAN**, c$1.00. An enlightening presentation of the twenty-two major arcana cards. Each card is analyzed in four separate sections: the physical plane, the psychological plane, the spiritual plane, and the philosophical plane—and each time the discussion brings out new symbolism in the cards. There is also a brief introductory section and an unclear bit on the spreads. 216pp. Bel 72

_____. **THE SEXUAL KEY TO THE TAROT**, $1.25. An analysis of each card in terms of its sexual imagery. Keyed to the Rider-Waite deck. 128pp. NAL 71

LIND. FRANK. **HOW TO UNDERSTAND THE TAROT**, $1.25. A description of the major arcana cards, emphasizing their mythological properties, with some reference to the lesser arcana cards and methods of divination. 63pp. Wei 69

LONG, MAX. **TAROT CARD SYMBOLOGY**, $6.00. Long is well known for his pioneering studies of the psychological system of the Kahuna priests of Hawaii (see the Mysticism section). He believes that the Kahunas had a hand in inventing the Tarot and that they built into the cards a secret set of symbols aimed at preserving the knowledge they had developed. Long used the cards extensively in his personal life and he felt that he had found the key to understanding the symbolism of the cards. This volume presents a series of articles that Long wrote on the meaning of the cards. 83pp. HRA 72

MANSER, ANN and CECIL NORTH. **PAGES OF SHUSTAH**, $7.95. A contemporary reinterpretation of the Tarot cards. The cards and the accompanying deck (available separately for $5.50) present four broad levels of interpretation—the material, the emotional, the mental, and the spiritual. There are seventy Pages divided into five suits of fourteen Pages each. *This is a brief description of the...Pages...with a method of laying the Pages out for meditation or prognostication. Each Page is endowed with a deeply subjective meaning. When They are spread and studied as directed Their forecasting of events to come will prove startlingly accurate. Used as a means of concentration and meditation the Pages will reveal the secrets of arcane wisdom hidden within the personality of each individual who studies them. Each of the cards is illustrated in the book.* 140pp. PSh 74

MAXWELL, JOSEPH. **THE TAROT**, c$7.85. Maxwell was a serious student of the hermetic teachings who lived from 1858-1938 and was influential in the occult-spiritual revival of those times. He was a lawyer by profession and his writing style reflects his legalistic bent. This volume is a resume of Maxwell's experience and wisdom. Included is a study of the major arcana and a survey of the minor, with a comprehensive view of their esoteric symbolism and both their astrological and numerological significances, as well as the color symbolism. A general discussion of the Tarot is also included. 223pp. Spe 75

MAYANANDA. **THE TAROT FOR TODAY**, c$6.75. Subtitled *Being notes relative to the twenty-two paths of the Tree of Life and the Tarot Trumps together with a new way of approach to this Ancient Symbol, more suited to the present Aquarian Age and entitled The Horus Arrangement.* Describes the origin of the cards, descriptions of each of the major arcana, symbolism, tradition and Qabalistic applications. 255pp. Zeu 63

NORDIC, ROLLA. **TAROT SHOWS THE PATH**, $3.00. A personal, inspiring interpretation of the symbolism of the major arcana directed at students on the path. The orientation is somewhat Christian. Illustrations, 127pp. EsP 60

PAPUS. **THE TAROT OF THE BOHEMIANS: ABSOLUTE KEY TO OCCULT SCIENCE,** c$6.50/$3.00. Papus was the pseudonym of a learned French physician. He contributed significantly to the occultism of the Tarot and the assimilation of the twenty-two trump cards to the twenty-two letters of the Hebrew alphabet. He was a Mason and a Rosicrucian. This is a very complex work for the serious student, describing his Tarot codices and presenting his diagrams and summarizing his personal thesis. This is the deepest of all the Tarot books and also the most fascinating. There is a long introduction by A.E. Waite as well as Papus' excellent introductory material. Topics include the esotericism of numbers, the sacred word YOD-HE-VAU-HE, extensive material on the symbolism of the Tarot in relation to the Qabala and the Hebrew alphabet, and on divination and the application of the Tarot. Keyed to the French and Marseilles decks. 380pp. Wil nd

ROBERTS, RICHARD. **TAROT AND YOU**, $3.95. Explains the Tarot as a symbolic system of self-knowledge, self-integration and self-transformation using a *free association* method. It gives transcripts of actual taped Tarot readings using the beautiful Aquarian deck. The evocative picture on each card releases a unique meaning for each reader. Includes an introduction and eight spreads. Keyed to the Aquarian deck. 296pp. M&M 71

SADHU, MAUNI. **THE TAROT**, $3.00. An excellent series of 101 lessons which describe the twenty-two major arcana cards from the standpoints of symbolism, hermetism, numerology, relationship to the Hebrew alphabet and astrological relationships. This is a very practical exposition for the serious student, well illustrated. 494pp. Wil 62

SHARPE, ROSALIND and JOHN COOKE, eds. **THE WORD OF ONE: AQUARIUS TAROT NOTES**, $6.95. A series of teachings revealed through the ouija board to the same group of five people to whom the **New Tarot for the Aquarian Age** was revealed. The material is keyed to these cards and the session transcriptions presented here are verbatim. 414pp. Tar 75

STURZAKER, DOREEN and JAMES. **COLOUR AND THE KABBALAH**, c$9.50. The authors present an intricate study of what colors mean in connection with the ten

Holy Order of MANS Tarot

Tarot Classic

ephiroth, the twenty-two paths, and the twenty-two major Tarot trumps, as this relates
to the several worlds of Qabalistic philosophy. Most occult teacings on color are based on
the seven rays of the spectrum; an innovation-introduced by the Sturzakers is the concept
of twelve rays, their importance in the whole of life, manifest and unmanifest, and their
interaction throughout the cosmos. This is the only Qabalistic work which discusses the
meaning of the color rays in their relationship to the myriad aspects of the Tree of Life.
The presentation is very esoteric, but good for those who wish to delve deeper into the
rays and how both the color rays and the Qabala relate to the Tarot trumps. 287pp. Wei 75

STURZAKER, JAMES. **KABBALISTIC APHORISMS**, c$6.50. See the Jewish Mysticism
section.

THIERENS, A.E. **ASTROLOGY AND THE TAROT**, $2.95. Despite the title, the bulk
of this volume is devoted to the Tarot, with only occasional references to astrological
correspondences. This is one of the only books that delves into the esoteric meaning of
the individual minor arcana cards. The suits and the major arcana cards are also esoterically analyzed. 159pp. NPC 75

USSHER, ARLAND. **THE TWENTY-TWO KEYS OF THE TAROT**, c$7.00. The inner
meaning of the major arcana cards comes to life in Ussher's narrative. Each of the cards is
discussed separately and they are all interrelated. Many mythological, Hebraic and Ger-
manic references are included in the exposition. We get a clearer picture of the meaning
of each card from this short work than from any other of similar length that we can think
of. The illustrations are from the Marseilles deck. Introduction, 54pp. Duf 70

WAITE, A.E. **THE PICTORIAL KEY TO THE TAROT**, c$2.98/$2.25. This is the grand-
daddy of all other modern Tarot books and Waite is the man who designed the most popular deck. A good, long introduction discusses the symbolism and antiquities of the cards.
Each card is briefly analyzed and there is a study of methods of divination and a description of several spreads as well as an annotated bibliography. The $2.98 edition is over-
size and contains color reproductions of each of the cards. 344pp. Wei 10

WARNER, REBECCA. **TAROT**, $4.95. This is the only beginning book keyed specifically
to the Marseilles deck. The symbolic meanings of both the major and minor arcana are
briefly analyzed. Short sections are included on the Tarot and numerology and the Tarot
and astrology and there are also directions on reading the cards. Oversize, bibliography.
87pp. SMP 74

WESTCOTT, W., tr. **THE MAGICAL RITUAL OF THE SANCTUM REGNUM**, c$7.50.
Esoteric interpretations of the major trumps, as seen by Eliphas Levi. 113pp. Wei 1896

The Egyptian Tarot

ZAIN, C.C. **THE SACRED TAROT**, $5.95. Thirteen comprehensive lessons on the Tarot
for the serious occultist. Includes information on the chronology of the Tarot, reading
the Tarot, its scope and use, and a section on the Sacred Tarot as a doctrine of Qabalism.
Illustrated with many charts and reproductions of the author's Egyptian Tarot. See Astrology section for more on Zain and his lessons. 416pp. ChL 36

TAROT DECKS

AQUARIAN TAROT, $6.00. This is an unusual interpretation of a medieval deck, il-
lustrated by David Palladini. The colors are muted pastels: pinks, lavender, blues. The
symbolic figures are not as evocative as in some of the other decks. Seventy-eight cards;
the minor arcana cards also have pictures on them.

B.O.T.A. MAJOR TAROT KEYS, $5.75. 4x7" oversize cards, uncolored. This is our
favorite deck. The designs on the cards are often similar to the Waite-Rider deck, but
there are substantial differences in the symbolism. The idea behind an uncolored deck is
that as you color in each card you concentrate on every aspect of the card and its symbolism becomes a part of your being. As you color the cards in you also add your vibrations to them and they become more responsive to you. The cards bear an Arabic number
in the lower left and a Hebrew letter in the lower right corner. Case's **Highlights of the
Tarot** has coloring instructions.

B.O.T.A. TAROT DECK, $5.00. Small cards, including the fifty-six cards of the minor
arcana. We found that it was hard to color in some parts of the large cards, so we definitely don't recommend this small deck for coloring. The minor arcana is illustrated by
designs rather than by pictures.

CROWLEY THOTH DECK. $10.00. This is a variation of the Egyptian deck, designed by
Aleister Crowley. The colors and designs are quite macabre. Some feel that they are the
most hauntingly beautiful cards that they have seen—others recoil from them. Oversize.
These cards are a complete departure from the usual Tarot designs.

THE EGYPTIAN TAROT, $4.95. Full deck, black and white and suitable for coloring.
The cards are rich in Egyptian symbolism—all of which is fully explored in Zain's books.
The designs are a complete departure from traditional Tarot symbols.

THE ENGLISH DECK, $7.80. The original copy of this deck is in the British Museum, so
its authenticity as a traditional deck is not questioned. The figures themselves are crudely
drawn, and the traditional symbology is apparent. The cards are on heavy stock and are
brightly colored.

GRAND ETTEILLA EGYPTIAN GYPSIES TAROT, $6.50. This deck is the real Egyp-
tian and Qabalistic Tarot as interpreted in the seventeenth century by the famous French
diviner, M. Alliette, based upon the theories of Compte de Gebelin. The Fool, instead of
appearing as the first card, is placed as the last card. The designs represent a departure
from the standard symbolic pictures. The designs on the cards are mostly full length
figures and the titles are double-ended and vary to take into account reverse meanings.
117pp explanatory booklet.

**GRAND TAROT BEL-
LINE**, $23.10. These
seventy-eight cards of the
Grand Format were cre-
ated by the Magus Ed-
mond in the nineteenth
century and used by him
in readings for Napoleon
III. Later revised and
published by the Magus
Belline, each card is a
work of art. The cards
are for professionals and
are printed on fine quality card stock, and var-
nished for long life. The
card titles and instruc-
tion booklet are in
French only. This is
the finest deck we have
seen, 6x3", in a velvet-
lined box.

Grand Tarot Belline

HOLY ORDER OF MANS. **TAROT TWENTY-TWO KEYS**, $3.00. Black and white designs. The Holy Order of MANS' book has explicit coloring instructions. The cards are similar in design to the B.O.T.A. deck—including the correspondent Hebrew alphabet. 4x7", major arcana.

THE NEW TAROT FOR THE AQUARIAN AGE, $7.95. A new deck whose symbols were given via the ouija board. The cards were dictated in exact detail, even to color and the placement of symbols. They were revealed at sessions that were not undertaken for the purpose of obtaining Tarot symbols. The board said that the reason for their dictation at this time was both to rescue the cards from their plight as fortune-telling devices and to herald the coming of a new age. We don't care for the imagery, though it is quite evocative. Ralph Metzner speaks quite highly of the deck and feels that the images seem to have a direct electrical-emotional *charge*. Includes the Royal Maze (a guide to the game of destiny) and three instruction booklets totaling well over 200pp.

New Tarot for the Aquarian Age

SPANISH TAROT, $5.50. Brightly colored classical designs, based on an original deck from 1738 which can be found in a Spanish museum. Good reproductions. The card names are in Spanish and the instruction booklet is bilingual.

Spanish Tarot

SWISS TAROT CARDS, $4.75. A small, full color seventy-eight card deck—based on classical designs.

RIDER-WAITE TAROT DECK, $5.00. The famous seventy-eight card deck designed by Pamela Coleman Smith under the direction of Arthur E. Waite. The outstanding feature of this deck is that all of the cards are presented in emblematic designs readily suitable for divination in contrast to the rigid forms of swords, batons, cups, and coins previously used in Tarot decks. This is far and away the most popular and the most commonly used deck. In color. A miniature version of these cards is available for $3.35.

TAROT ARTISTA, $6.00. Full deck, in four colors. This Tarot deck is a combination of many Tarots. The major arcana cards give variations on the symbolic vocabulary (in French). Each card has its own significance and meaning. French instruction booklet.

Royal Fez Morrocan Tarot Deck

Tarot Artista

THE ROYAL FEZ MOROCCAN TAROT DECK, $5.50. A very traditional deck, with simple, classical illustrations and a delicate feeling. Seventy-eight cards, instruction booklet.

TAROT CLASSIC, $5.50. The eighteenth century Tarot Classic deck is based upon original woodcuts by Claude Burdel. This deck is based on his designs, with slight modifications such as the printing of the names of the cards in English. Full deck, in color, with instruction booklet.

TAROT OF MARSEILLES, $6.00. This is one of the most ancient French decks available. Its illustrations relate the symbolic laws of the universe in a very clear manner. 48pp instruction booklet, full deck in color.

VISCONTI SFORZA TAROCCHI DECK, $25.20. This is far and away the most beautiful and the most evocative of the classical decks. It is an excellent reproduction of the original deck from 1430. The background of the cards is gold foil and the images are exquisitely presented. All serious students of the Tarot should own this deck. Seventy-eight cards, instruction booklet, 4x7".

WAITE DECK, $6.00. The same symbols as the Rider-Waite deck—but the colors are a good deal more intense in this version.

THEOSOPHY

ASHISH, SRI MADHAVA. **MAN, SON OF MAN**, c$5.50. A companion volume to **Man, the Measure of All Things** by Ashish and Krishna Prem, taking the form of a commentary on the **Stanzas of Dzyan**, outlining the processes of human evolution which have culminated in man as he is today. This is a deep book, designed to invoke a thoughtful response in the reader. The **Stanzas** were first presented to the modern world in Blavatsky's **Secret Doctrine** and are otherwise unknown to orthodox scholarship. The selections are topically organized and form an excellent presentation of the theosophical cosmology. Index, 355pp. TPH 70

ALICE BAILEY

The works of Alice Bailey form an important contribution to spiritual literature. Of the twenty-five volumes appearing in her name, eighteen of them are actually the result of collaboration with a Tibetan sage, Djwal Khul, sometimes called D.K. or the Tibetan Master.

These eighteen books represent thirty years of cooperative effort. D.K. would transmit the contents to Alice Bailey telepathically. Alice Bailey was not a medium in the usual sense, but was rather an alert and active participant.

Many believe that the profound teachings made available through this work are the most advanced presentation of divine revelation given to humanity as well as the most extensive survey of the *Ageless Wisdom Teaching*.

The books cover a wide area of information, with emphasis on the new *science of soul contact* and the practical demonstration of spiritual principles in the daily life. The aim of the teachings is to lay a foundation for the demonstration of esoteric truths and spiritual realities and provide the knowledge necessary to carry humanity into the New Age, once the information has been assimilated and properly utilized.

The authors make no claim or pretense of authority but simply ask that the information and teaching be accepted or rejected on the merits of its own usefulness and the individual intuitive process.

Alice Bailey was also instrumental in the formation of various organizations. These include the Arcane School, created in 1923 as a training school for discipleship. It is a correspondence school which provides sequential courses of study and meditation based on esotericism as the science of service and as a way of life.

ARCANA WORKSHOP. **FOR FULL MOON WORKERS**, $1.25. *This is an unfinished how to manual. It is unfinished because we are always discovering more about the science of invocation and evocation with which full moon work is concerned. This how to manual represents the discoveries, experiments and experiences of an eighteen year effort by a trained meditating group. And it is offered with the hope that it will help in the forming of full moon meditation groups all over the world.* 16pp. ArW nd

_____. **FULL MOON MAGIC**, $.75. See the Astrology section.

_____. **FULL MOON MEDITATONS**, $1.00. See the Astrology section.

_____. **THE FULL MOON STORY**, $2.25. This is the basic full moon study divided into the following sections: purpose of full moon observance, new world religion, necessity for groups (inner and outer), and the immediate task. 65pp. ArW nd

BAILEY, ALICE. **THE CONSCIOUSNESS OF THE ATOM**, c$5.75/$2.00. Lectures discussing evolution as it progressively affects the atomic substance of all forms, subjective and objective. 163pp. LPC 61

_____. **THE DESTINY OF THE NATIONS**, c$5.50/$1.75. A presentation of the rudiments of national psychology through an appreciation of the astrological and seven ray rulerships and influences upon the nations. 161pp. LPC 49

_____. **DISCIPLESHIP IN THE NEW AGE, VOL. I**, c$12.50/$5.50. A series of personal instructions given to a small group of chelas (disciples) over a period of fifteen years, with related teaching on a number of subjects. 847pp. LPC 72

_____. **DISCIPLESHIP IN THE NEW AGE, VOL. II**, c$12.50/$5.25. Includes information about the dynamics of meditation at the time of the full moon in order to facilitate spiritual contact and the registering of divine impressions via the link from soul-mind-brain. 818pp. LPC 55

_____. **EDUCATION IN THE NEW AGE**, c$5.75/$2.00. This book lays a foundation and presents a framework for the philosophy, techniques, and goals of true education as it will be understood in the new *era of the One Humanity* that is dawning upon the horizon of our troubled times. Education is the technique of conscious evolution and the building of the bridge of consciousness that links the human personality with the divine soul. 153pp. LPC

_____. **EXTERNALISATION OF THE HIERARCHY**, c$12.50/$5.00. An absorbing series of pamphlets, letters and instructions to disciples during the war and immediately afterward. 744pp. LPC 57

_____. **FROM BETHLEHEM TO CALVARY**, c$8.50/$2.75. Follows the path of Christ through six stages of initiations: birth, baptism, transfiguration, crucifixion, resurrection, and ascension. 292pp. LPC 65

_____. **FROM INTELLECT TO INTUITION**, c$6.50/$2.25. Development of the intellect is shown as a means to an end and one step on the way to a fully awakened and active mental body. 275pp. LPC 60

_____. **GLAMOUR: A WORLD PROBLEM**, c$7.25/$2.25. 290pp. LPC 50

_____. **INITIATION, HUMAN AND SOLAR**, c$6.25/$2.50. Recommended as a good introduction to the books, as it lays the groundwork for much of the material later presented. Includes the rules for aspirants and an explanation and description of the *occult hierarchy* of the planet. LPC 51

_____. **LABOURS OF HERCULES**, $1.75. An esoteric interpretation of the zodiacal signs as viewed through the myths of Hercules. Each of the signs is discussed at length. 111pp. LPC 74

_____. **LETTERS ON OCCULT MEDITATION**, c$7.50/$3.00. See the Meditation section.

_____. **THE LIGHT OF THE SOUL**, c$9.00/$3.75. A restatement of Patanjali's **Yoga Sutras**—the classic work on Raja yoga. 458pp. LPC 55

_____. **PROBLEMS OF HUMANITY**, $1.75. Discusses problems such as the following: continuing cleavages in consciousness; psychological evaluations and reactions to world conditions; national, religious, class, or racial prejudice; conditions of literacy, disease and poverty. 181pp. LPC 64

_____. **THE REAPPEARANCE OF THE CHRIST**, c$6.00/$2.25. A joyous message concerning imminent revelations and the emergence of the *spiritual hierarchy* of our planet, led by the Christ, in the immediate future once humanity has prepared itself. Includes information outlining the *New World Religion*, the *Science of Invocation* and the meaning and application of the *Great Invocation*. 191pp. LPC 48

_____. **THE SOUL AND ITS MECHANICS**, c$5.75/2.25. Presents the method by which the soul and the personality vehicles interact and function together. 165pp. LPC 65

_____. **THE SOUL THE QUALITY OF LIFE**, c$9.00. A third compilation, again topically organized. LPC 74

_____. **TELEPATHY AND THE ETHERIC VEHICLE**, c$6.00/$2.50. Includes practical instruction. 219pp. LPC 50

_____. **A TREATISE ON COSMIC FIRE**, c$17.00/$7.75. Deals with the underlying structure of occult teaching for the present era, with vast cosmic processes reproduced through all areas of life from universe to atom. The most timeless, profound, and least understood of all Bailey's books. 1367pp. LPC

_____. **A TREATISE ON THE SEVEN RAYS: ESOTERIC PSYCHOLOGY, VOL. I**, c$8.50/$3.75. The sequence of books under the overall title of **A Treatise on the Seven Rays** is based on the fact, the nature, and the quality of the seven basic streams of energy pervading our solar system, our planet, and all that moves within its orbit. The psychology volumes are concerned first with basic energy patterns and structures, and second, with the soul and personality of man and with the working out of the plan for humanity. 460pp. LPC 36

_____. **A TREATISE ON THE SEVEN RAYS: ESOTERIC PSYCHOLOGY, VOL. II**, c$11.00/$6.25. 818pp. LPC 42

_____. **A TREATISE ON THE SEVEN RAYS: ESOTERIC ASTROLOGY**, c$14.00/$5.00. LPC 51

_____. **A TREATISE ON THE SEVEN RAYS: ESOTERIC HEALING, VOL. IV**, c$10.50/$5.75. Information on the energy factors, karmic and ray influences, the psychology and astrology of the soul, and the laws and rules fundamental to the practice of esoteric healing. 771pp. LPC 53

_____. **A TREATISE ON THE SEVEN RAYS: THE RAYS AND THE INITIATIONS, VOL. V**, c$10.50/$5.25. The first part of this volume details rules for groups and the second part is concerned with the nine major expansions and consciousness through which the initiate becomes progressively liberated from various forms of our planetary life, ultimately proceeding upon his chosen path. 820pp. LPC 60

_____. **A TREATISE ON WHITE MAGIC**, c$10.50/$4.00. Gives the rules for magical creation and the science of the control of the emotional body and the elevation of human consciousness into the fifth kingdom of nature or the kingdom of souls. Also contains extensive practical hints on day-to-day living. 705pp. LPC 51

_____. **THE UNFINISHED AUTOBIOGRAPHY**, c$7.50/$3.25. 304pp. LPC 51

BAILEY, FOSTER. **CHANGING ESOTERIC VALUES**, $1.50. Foster Bailey was Alice Bailey's husband and was active in her work. This is an edited and enlarged version of four lectures he gave in 1954. The material covered shows esotericism to be a practical science of service, *responsible for the well-being of the human race in conformity with the Divine Plan.* 80pp. LPC 54

_____. **RUNNING GOD'S PLAN**, $2.00. Practical essays on a variety of topics applicable to the present day. 188pp. LPC 72

_____. **THE SPIRIT OF MASONRY**, $1.75. Contains five in a series of instructions D.K. intended to give to a group of Masons through the agency of Alice Bailey. The instructions were never completed and Foster was asked to publish them along with some articles on the Masons. 143pp. LPC

BANKS, NATALIE. **THE GOLDEN THREAD**, $1.25. A concise summation of the passage of the *Ageless Wisdom Teachings* throughout the ages, periods, and epochs of our earth's history from the ancient past to modern times. 95pp. LPC 63

A STUDENT. **PONDER ON THIS**, $4.25. *Scattered through all my writings over the years is a mass of information which needs collating and bringing together, as a basis for the instruction of disciples.* The present compilation is an attempt in this direction. A South African student (or students) has topically arranged hundreds of extracts from the Tibetan's teaching in alphabetical order. The hope is that this selection will bring D.K.'s teaching to the attention of a wider circle of students. A massive, greatly needed effort. 431pp. LPC 74

_____. **SERVING HUMANITY**, c$9.00. An excellent continuation of the compilations commenced in **Ponder**. There is some intentional overlapping as some of the quotations previously used help to round out the present volume. *It is only through constant reiteration that men learn, and these things must be said again and again.* The selections seem to go into far greater depth in this volume. 513pp. LPC 72

BARBORKA, GEOFFREY. **THE MAHATMAS AND THEIR LETTERS**, c$8.95. This is an in depth study of the letters that A.P. Sinnett received from the Mahatmas. A few of the letters are examined at length and a great deal of material is devoted to assaying the authenticity of the letters and discussing how they were received. Various proofs and testimonials are offered. Index, 427pp. TPH 73

_____. **THE PEOPLING OF THE EARTH**, c$10.00. This is an exploration of the origins of man based on the section of **The Secret Doctrine** devoted to anthropogenesis. Taking as the basis for his exposition the mysterious stanzas from the **Book of Dzyan** as translated by H.P. Blavatsky, Barborka traces the origin and evolution of man. The reader needs to be familiar with theosophical vocabulary and literature in order to follow the account. The author provides a very complete index. 247pp. TPH 75

BARKER, A. TREVOR, ed. **MAHATMA LETTERS TO A.P. SINNETT**, $5.95. These letters were written between the years 1880 and 1884 to A.P. Sinnett, an English civil servant in India, by two Mahatmas of Tibet whom H.P. Blavatsky had acknowledged as her teachers and the inspirers of her **Isis Unveiled** and **The Secret Doctrine**. These letters discuss the cosmology and the life and development of the human race as well as far reaching concepts of religious and scientific thought. Very important material for all readers interested in theosophy. 430pp. TUP

BENJAMINE, HARRY. **EVERYONE'S GUIDE TO THEOSOPHY**, c$4.50. A topically organized overview of the main features of theosophy. The information is clearly presented and all the important concepts are included. The book is well thought of by the Theosophical Society. 149pp. TPH 69

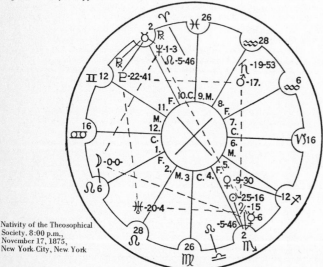

Nativity of the Theosophical Society. 8:00 p.m., November 17, 1875, New York City, New York

ANNIE BESANT

Annie Besant was Blavatsky's chosen vehicle to head the Theosophical Society

following the latter's death. In her early years with the Society Ms. Besant carried on a great number of clairvoyant experiments with her close associate C.W. Leadbeater. Later she turned her full attentions to administration and it was she, more than anyone else, who built up the Society. In addition to her organizational skills she began a series of excellent educational institutions in India, many of which are still ongoing today, over seventy-five years later. She also published innumerable short books (many of which were transcriptions of lectures) and a few major ones. Most are out of print; we are listing all the ones that are presently available. She wrote and talked clearly and succinctly.

BESANT, ANNIE. **THE ANCIENT WISDOM**, c$3.75. This was written to serve as a basic introduction to the *Ageless Wisdom*. 362pp.

_____. **THE BIRTH AND EVOLUTION OF THE SOUL**, c$1.50. Two lectures on the title theme. 51pp. TPH 1895

_____. **DAILY MEDITATIONS ON THE PATH AND ITS QUALIFICATIONS** c$1.25. TPH 22

_____. **DEATH AND AFTER**, c$1.75. See the Reincarnation and Karma section.

_____. **DHARMA**, $1.00. Transcriptions of three lectures on differences, evolution, and right and wrong. 72pp. TPH 18

_____, ed. **DOCTRINE OF THE HEART**, c$1.50. A series of extracts from letters received by the author from her Indian friends. *They are not given as being of any authority, but merely as containing thoughts that some of us have found helpful, and that we wish to share with others.* Ms. Besant has also contributed an introduction. 107pp. TPH 1899

_____. **ESOTERIC CHRISTIANITY**, c$3.25/$1.95. See the Christianity section.

_____. **INITIATION—THE PERFECTING OF MAN**, $3.00. Transcriptions of the following lectures: *The Man of the World, His First Steps; Seeking the Master; Finding the Master; The Christ-Life; The Christ Triumphant, and the Work of the Hierarchy; Why We Believe in the Coming of a World Teacher.* 149pp. HeR 23

_____. **AN INTRODUCTION TO YOGA**, c$2.25. See the Patanjali sub-section of Indian Philosophy.

_____. **KARMA**, c$1.50. See the Reincarnation and Karma section.

_____. **LAWS OF THE HIGHER LIFE**, c$1.50. Transcriptions of three lectures: *The Larger Consciousness, The Law of Duty,* and *The Law of Sacrifice.* 68pp. TPH 12

_____. **MAN AND HIS BODIES**, c$2.75. Describes man's occult constitution of his personality as an aggregate of bodies or vehicles through which his immortal self or soul manifests and expresses itself. This includes his physical, etheric, astral, and mind bodies. 117pp. TPH 12

_____. **MAN: WHENCE, HOW AND WHITHER**, c$6.50. See the Ancient Civilizations section.

_____. **THE MASTERS**, c$1.50. An exploration of the masters *as facts and ideals:* who they are, where they live, their work, and how students can find them. There's also a section on *the perfect man* and the initiatory stages toward perfection. 54pp. TPH 12

_____. **THE PATH OF DISCIPLESHIP**, c$3.75. A beautifully written work that reveals the depth of the author's mystical perception and understanding of the sacred path within oneself. Includes qualifications for discipleship, the life of the disciple and the future progress of humanity. 153pp. TPH 10

_____. **REINCARNATION**, c$1.75. See the Reincarnation and Karma section.

_____. **RIDDLE OF LIFE**, c$1.50. A survey of basic theosophical teachings on a variety of subjects central to our understanding of the universe and man's place in it. Included are chapters on man's bodies, on the law of re-birth, and much else. 69pp. TPH 11

_____. **THE SEVEN PRINCIPLES OF MAN**, c$1.50. Describes in simple language the theosophical concept of man as a divine being clothed in different garments or sheaths through which he is able to function at different levels of existence. 103pp. TPH 31

_____. **SOME PROBLEMS OF LIFE**, c$1.50. A discussion of various topics related to the title theme. 139pp. TPH 19

_____. **A STUDY IN CONSCIOUSNESS**, c$3.50. This is one of Annie Besant's major works. As the title suggests, it is a study of consciousness in all its aspects. The book begins with a study of monads and their development and goes from there to an exploration of memory, will, desire, and emotion. As with all of the author's books, the reader needs to be well versed in theosophy in order to comprehend the exposition. Index, 382pp. TPH 04

_____. **A STUDY IN KARMA**, c$1.00. See the Reincarnation and Karma section.

_____. **TALKS WITH A CLASS**, $2.25. A series of short essays on a great variety of subjects. A great deal of material is covered. 206pp. TPH 22

_____. **THOUGHT POWER**, $1.45. An excellent manuscript detailing the activities of the mind and the laws and principles that govern its functioning. Well written and concise, this work will assist the serious student in understanding himself and enable him to develop his mental capabilities. Includes a description of the esoteric constitution of man to place the intellect in its correct perspective. 121pp. TPH 66

BESANT, ANNIE and C.W. LEADBEATER. **OCCULT CHEMISTRY**, $3.50. This is without question one of the most important of the Besant/Leadbeater works. It contains an illustrated report of their clairvoyant observations of the chemical elements and the constituent units of the cosmos. Leadbeater was an especially gifted clairvoyant and this is a fascinating presentation of an area that is still relatively unexplored to this day. 121pp. HeR 19

_____. **TALKS ON THE PATH OF OCCULTISM, VOL. I**, c$6.25. A detailed commentary on **At the Feet of the Master**, the inspiring small book attributed to Krishnamurti and some say written by C.W. Leadbeater. Index, 474pp. TPH 26

_____. **TALKS ON THE PATH OF OCCULTISM, VOL. II**, c$4.95. An in depth commentary on Blavatsky's **The Voice of Silence**. Index, 425pp. TPH 26

_____. **THOUGHT FORMS**, $3.95. See the Color and Aura section.

NETHERCOT, A.H. **THE FIRST FIVE LIVES OF ANNIE BESANT**, c$15.45. A meticulously written biography of Annie Besant which traces Besant's lives in England through her conversion to theosophy and her first departure for India. The author titles these lives as follows: *The Christian Wife, The Atheist Mother, the Martyr of Science, The Socialist Labor Agitator,* and *The Chela of the Mahatmas.* Notes, index. 422pp. UCh 60

_____. **THE LAST FIVE LIVES OF ANNIE BESANT**, c$15.45. Ms. Besant's last lives: *The Indian Educator, Propagandist and Mystic; President of the Indian National Congress; The Deserted Leader,* and *Life in Death.*Included in this volume are the stories of her role in the campaign for Indian Home Rule and her relationship with Krishnamurti—the young boy whom she educated to be the new Messiah and who finally repudiated the doctrines she and her associates inculcated in him. This is a fascinating tale for all those who are interested in theosophy. Notes, illustrations, index. 483pp. UCh 63

H.P. BLAVATSKY

Mme. Blavatsky, or H.P.B., as she is known to theosophists, is a mysterious figure who first came to public notice in the 1870's in the U.S. She was reputed to have spent about forty years traveling and meeting with the masters of wisdom in the East and especially in Tibet. She remained in contact with these masters throughout the rest of her life. The reality of this contact was one of the most controversial aspects of her controversial life. She joined forces with Colonel Olcott in the late 1870's and together they founded the Theosophical Society. They traveled to India a few years later and settled there for a period of time. India became the headquarters of the Society and many facets of Indian philosophy were incorporated into theosophical teachings. Some say, and with a fair amount of justice, that it was the Theosophical Society as much as anything else that reintroduced the ancient traditions to establishment Indian society. H.P.B.'s two major works—**Isis Unveiled** and **The Secret Doctrine**—remain the basic works and still sell well to this day.

BARBORKA, GEOFFREY. **H.P. BLAVATSKY, TIBET AND TULKU**, c$9.00. Barborka begins this study with a disclaimer stating that it is *not* a biography in the usual sense of the term because so little is known of Blavatsky's life and motivations that a biographical study would be impossible. A short biographical sketch is presented in the first chapter, followed by brief surveys of Tibetan religion, language, and religious leaders and a hypothetical analysis of Blavatsky's time in Tibet and her connections with the Tibetans who became her teachers. The bulk of the volume is devoted to an analysis of the ways that Blavatsky did her writing and her role as a Tulku and its meaning. Many quotations from her writings are included in the text along with a profusion of Eastern terminology. This is definitely not an introductory study. Notes, bibliography, index. 487pp. TPH 66

BARKER, A. TREVOR, ed. **THE LETTERS OF H.P. BLAVATSKY TO A.P. SINNETT**, c$10.00. A collection of revealing letters between H.P.B. and one of her closest associates. The historical references cannot always be taken at face value—the letters were written long after many of the events occurred and Blavatsky herself admits that her memory is not very exact. In any event this compilation should be fascinating reading for all students deeply interested in theosophy and they form one of the only primary sources on the founder of the Theosophical Society that has come down to us. Most of the biographical material on Blavatsky has come from these letters. Notes, index. 409pp. ThU 25

BESANT, ANNIE. **H.P. BLAVATSKY AND THE MASTERS OF THE WISDOM**, $2.05. A short study which purports to trace H.P.B.'s contacts with the Masters and to refute the attacks made on her character and veracity. 60pp. TPH 07

BLAVATSKY, H.P. **AN ABRIDGMENT OF THE SECRET DOCTRINE**, $2.25. 260pp. TPH 66

_____. **COLLECTED WRITINGS VOL. I–XI**, c$10.00/each. This massive compendium contains every word ever written by H.P.B. with the exception of **Isis Unveiled** and **The Secret Doctrine**. TPH

_____. **DYNAMICS OF THE PSYCHIC WORLD**, $1.95. This is a compilation from Blavatsky's writings. Topics include natural law and psychic phenomena, thought power, spiritual progress, and soul dynamics. 132pp. TPH 72

_____. **FROM CAVES AND JUNGLES OF HINDUSTAN**, c$12.50. Volume XI of the **Collected Writings**. This book was a major work and it contains H.P.B.'s impressions of India, the Indian people, and Indian religious philosophy. It can be read both as a travelogue and as a serious study of the author's impressions of a foreign and, at that time, little known civilization. Notes, index. 759pp. TPH 75

_____. **INDEX TO THE SECRET DOCTRINE**, c$5.00. 172pp. ThC 39

_____. **ISIS UNVEILED**, c$15.00/$10.50 (two volumes); c$12.00 (one volume). This book, totalling more than 1300 pages in two volumes, was H.P.B.'s first. It unites an historical review of religious and scientific ideas with the spirit of the quest for truth. Many chapters are devoted to study and explorations of manifestations of the occult from antiquity to the nineteenth century. The philosophies and sciences of the ancients are examined, not as objects of scholarly research, but in the spirit of a genuine renaissance. Of special interest to the West is an investigation of the origins of Christianity, including extensive study of the teachings of the Gnostic sects of the first centuries, and an explanation of the mysteries of Jesus. Much is said of the lore of initiates, and throughout will be found the theme of occult knowledge and its adept teachers. The first truly scientific account of the vast subject of magic is offered in this great work, which is subtitled *A Master Key to the Mysteries of Ancient and Modern Science and Theology.* **Isis** is an exposition of the materialism of modern science and the obscurantism of modern religion. 1403pp. ThU 1877

_____. **KEY TO THEOSOPHY**, c$5.00/3.50. Subtitled *A clear exposition, in the form of question and answer, of the ethics, science, and philosophy for the study of which the Theosophical Society has been founded.* Includes an excellent glossary and index. 426pp. ThU 1889

_____. **THE SECRET DOCTRINE**, c$12.50/9.00 (two volumes); c$12.00 (one volume); c$30.00 (six volume authorized edition). Completed in 1888, eleven years after **Isis**. The systematic character of this work is revealed by the subjects treated at length in its pages: *Cosmogenesis, Cosmic Evolution, Anthropogenesis, The Evolution of Symbolism, The Archaic Symbolism of the World Religions, Science and the Secret Doctrine Contrasted.* Its subtitle is *The Synthesis of Science, Religion, and Philosophy.* It differs from **Isis** in that it deliberately unfolds a specific teaching about the nature of things. Half of its 1500 pages are devoted to explanations of this teaching as found in an ancient scripture wholly unknown to the modern world. It is shown that the *Wisdom Religion* has been the inspiration of every great religion and religious teacher, and that one archaic doctrine underlies all the traditional beliefs of both East and West. The remaining portions of the volumes contain discussion and criticism of scientific conceptions. In the introduction H.P.B. wrote: **The Secret Doctrine** *is not a treatise, or a series of vague theories, but contains all that can be given out to the world in this century.* It is therefore the basic source of all theosophical teachings in this cycle. 1505pp. ThU 1888

_____. **SECRET INSTRUCTIONS TO PROBATORS OF AN ESOTERIC SCHOOL**, $11.75. A reproduction of an extremely rare document. Many colored illustrations. 122pp. HeR 69

_____. **STUDIES IN OCCULTISM**, $2.50. Ten years after the publication of **Isis Unveiled**, foreseeing the rapid and potentially hazardous development in the twentieth century of man's latent powers, the author, in a series of articles now collected here, warned against the misuse of knowledge, lest the *psychic outrun the spiritual.* 212pp. ThU 1891

_____. **THEOSOPHICAL GLOSSARY**, c$6.00. Gives information on the principal Sanskrit, Pahlavi, Tibetan, Pali, Chaldean, Persian, Scandinavian, Hebrew, Greek, Latin, Qabalistic and Gnostic words, and occult terms generally used in theosophical literature. 389pp. ThC 1892

_____. **THE VOICE OF THE SILENCE**, c$3.00/$1.95. Rendition into English of selected passages from **The Book of the Golden Precepts**. It is a manual of devotion of unsurpassing beauty which speaks to the heart and mind of aspiring souls. 110pp. TUP 28

HANSON, VIRGINIA, ed. **H.P. BLAVATSKY AND THE SECRET DOCTRINE**, $2.25. A collection of essays which originally appeared in a special issue of **The American Theosophist** which was devoted to a study of H.P.B.'s contributions to the intellectual, moral, and spiritual atmosphere of her world and to her magnum opus. 227pp. TPH 71

JINARAJADASA, C., ed. **H.P.B. SPEAKS, VOL. I**, c$1.95. Selections from letters written by H.P.B. from 1875 on, her diary for 1878, and some extracts from her scrapbook. 248pp. TPH 50

_____. **H.P.B. SPEAKS, VOL. II**, c$2.25. A continuation of the material presented in the first volume. 181pp. TPH 51

MURPHET, HOWARD. **WHEN DAYLIGHT COMES**, $3.50. A well written biographical study which we found fascinating. All of the scandal and the achievements are fully revealed and the survey is as impartial as one could expect an in-house document to be. This is as good a first book to read on theosophy as any we know of. Notes, bibliography, index. 292pp. TPH 75

NEFF, MARY, ed. **PERSONAL MEMOIRS OF H.P. BLAVATSKY**, $2.25. A compilation from H.P.B.'s letters, personal journal entries, and other records. Index, 322pp. TPH 37

OLCOTT, HENRY STEEL. **INSIDE THE OCCULT: THE TRUE STORY OF MADAME H.P. BLAVATSKY**, $3.95. This is a recently reprinted and retitled edition of **Old Diary**

Leaves. Col. Olcott was H.P.B.'s closest associate and confidant for many years and in this volume, compiled we presume from his diaries, he details the early experiences of the Theosophical Society in New York before the trip to India. Many of his personal insights about H.P.B. and their mutual work are revealed. Index, 491pp. RuP 75

H.P. Blavatsky. Sketch by an unknown artist, probably around 1877

PURUCKER, GOTTFRIED de. **H.P. BLAVATSKY: THE MYSTERY**, $4.95. The chapters of this book first appeared serially in **The Theosophical Path** (the house organ of Katherine Tingley's branch of the Society) in the 1930's. More than a simple biography of Blavatsky, the book presents an analysis of the basic theosophical teachings as expounded in Blavatsky's writings and oral teachings. The exposition is topically arranged and clearly written. 242pp. PoL 74

RYAN, CHARLES J. **H.P. BLAVATSKY AND THE THEOSOPHICAL MOVEMENT**, $4.95. A newly revised edition of one of the first major studies of the title theme. Much of the volume is devoted to biography, however the emphasis is on the achievements of the Society rather than on anecdotes. There is also an analysis of H.P.B.'s major literary works. Two final chapters carry the Society and the movement up to the present time. Bibliography, index. 367pp. ThU 37

CHALLONER, H.K. and ROLAND NORTHOVER. **OUT OF CHAOS**, c$6.00. An enlightening guide through the pitfalls of modern society. The authors have studied all the great religions and philosophies and they offer a distillation of the teaching here. Topics discussed include not only religion but also politics, economics, and education. Includes a topically arranged list of recommended books. 216pp. TPH 67

COLLINS, MABEL. **LIGHT ON THE PATH AND THROUGH THE GATES OF GOLD**, $1.95. Written down by Mabel Collins, this theosophical classic centers its series of *occult rules* on the ancient yet ever modern theme of self knowledge and self mastery. Bound together with **Through the Gates of Gold**, this volume offers a view of those foundation principles comprising the spiritual core of all religions. Recommended. **Light on the Path** is also available in a small leatherette edition for $1.75. 114pp. ThU 1888

CONGER, MARGARET. **COMBINED CHRONOLOGY**, $2.00. Designed to be used with **The Mahatma Letters to A.P. Sinnett** and **The Letters of H.P. Blavatsky to A.P. Sinnett**. 52pp. ThU 73

EDGE, HENRY. **THE ASTRAL LIGHT**, $1.75. A theosophical manual which begins with a study of what astral light is and goes on to discuss the astral light and karma and the astral light and evolution. There are also sections on the denizens of the astral light and the social influence of astral light. A very complete presentation of the subject. 57pp. PoL 75

_____. **EVOLUTION**, $2.00. A volume in the publisher's series of theosophical manuals which briefly explores the title theme. 71pp. PoL 75

GARDNER, EDWARD. **FAIRIES**, c$5.75. A record of clairvoyant observations of brownies, elves, gnomes, mannikins, sea spirits, fairies, sylphs and angels. Includes the famous Coltingley photographs purporting to be of actual fairies, as well as extensive interpretative material. 53pp. TPH 45

_____. **THE PLAY OF CONSCIOUSNESS**, c$2.00. A fine introduction to the subject of occult philosophy and the explanations of esoteric science re the nature and relationship of man and god, life and light, instinct and intuition, will and mind, cause and effect and the significance, purpose and meaning of the human center of consciousness. 100pp. TPH 39

_____. **THE WEB OF THE UNIVERSE**, c$3.00. A good basic outline and explanation of the broad doctrines of the *Ageless Wisdom Teaching* concerning our universe, man and consciousness, and the scheme of the solar system. 103pp. TPH 36

GROVES, C.R. and CORONA TREW, eds. **MAN'S EXPANDING HORIZON**, $1.00. A publication from the Science Group of the London Theosophical Research Centre which discusses evolution and man's role in the universe. 64pp. TPH nd

GEOFFREY HODSON

Next to Annie Besant and C.W. Leadbeater, Hodson is about the best known twentieth century theosophist. He is especially noted for his clairvoyant studies of devas and fairies.

He writes eloquently and gets into areas that none of the other theosophists cover. Early in his career Hodson conducted the famous London Psychical Research Society's investigation of Mme. Blavatsky as a fraud and deeply hurt the Theosophical Society. He obviously later changed his mind and became a devoted theosophist and was also active in the Liberal Catholic Church.

HODSON, GEOFFREY. **ANGELS AND THE NEW RACE**, $.75.

_____. **BROTHERHOOD OF ANGELS AND OF MEN**, c$4.25. This is the first of a five volume set of writings dictated to Hodson by one of the *Members of the Angelic Hosts*. Here he explores the idea of collaboration between angels and gives some guidance on how to conduct this collaboration. This is an inspiring collection of messages divided into chapters on patience, peace, education, joy, vision, thoroughness, unity, and methods of invocation. 65pp. TPH 27

_____. **THE CALL TO THE HEIGHTS**, $3.50. *This book is conceived, written, and published as an offering to those who are experiencing an inward longing for spiritual light and truth, and who are seeking a way of living through which these experiences may find intelligent and useful expression.* It is written in the form of a number of short essays on a variety of areas related to spiritiual development. Glossary, index. 219pp. TPH 76

_____. **FAIRIES AT WORK AND AT PLAY**, c$5.25. Hodson is a highly developed clairvoyant who has observed, according to E.L. Gardner, *a vast variety of etheric and astral forms, large and small, working together in organised co-operation on what we must call the life side of Nature, stimulating growth, bringing colour to the flowers, brooding over beautiful spots, playing in waves and waterfalls, dancing in the wind and the sunlight— in fact, another order of evolution running parallel to and blended with our own.* This is a detailed account of his observations. 126pp. TPH 25

_____. **THE KINGDOM OF THE GODS**, c$13.50. An extraordinary book dealing with the angelic or deva evolution which parallels human evolution and is concerned in part with the assistance of the evolution of nature and with the building, growing and destroying processes of all forms. They form a hierarchical scale of existence from nature, spirits, sprites and fairies on up to the grand archangels. The book is filled with beautiful paintings done from clairvoyant perception of the angelic hosts and deva spirits and it contains description of their activities and functions. 245pp. TPH 52

_____. **MAN THE TRIUNE GOD**, $2.25. *This book is the fourth of a series of volumes containing teachings given to the author by a member of the Angelic Hosts. In this work the angel teacher seeks to portray the splendour of the human path of evolution. He describes the transcendent powers of the God in man, dwells upon the glories of those realms of consciousness in which the divine in man has its spiritual home.* 65pp. TPH 32

_____. **MAN'S SUPERSENSORY AND SPIRITUAL POWERS**, c$2.25. The author delves into many areas of spiritual research and training. He covers a large territory of the *Secret Wisdom* in a clear, concise manner. The fundamental doctrine upon which the statements and teaching are based is that man is essentially divine and is in the process of becoming a god. 194pp. TPH 69

_____. **MIRACLE OF BIRTH**, $1.75. See the Natural Childbirth section.

_____. **OCCULT POWERS IN NATURE AND MAN**, c$2.50. Transcriptions of a series of lectures. The first presents a survey of the material covered in the subsequent lectures. *With unusual clarity there is developed a theosophical conception of the unfolding Cosmos. . . . The remaining chapters outline a synthesis of theosophical ideas about the nature of man and his relationship with his origins.* 169pp. TPH 55

_____. **THE PATHWAY TO PERFECTION**, $2.25. An excellent book dealing with the rudiments of theosophy. Contains a fine chapter that descriptively explains the seven ray types of disciplines. 77pp. TPH 54

_____. **REINCARNATION: FACT OR FALLACY?** $1.00. See the Reincarnation and Karma section.

_____. THE SOUL'S AWAKENING, c$3.00. The author penetrates into the world of dawning soul consciousness and reveals with clarity some of the aspects of spiritual evolution. Slightly more than half the book is given to answering questions on a wide range of metaphysical and occult subjects. 93pp. TPH 63

_____. THE SUPREME SPLENDOUR, $2.25. The newest of Hodson's books, this is a study of the universal creative processes, of God, of man *as a Creator In-the-Becoming*, and of the archangelic intelligences who presented the material to him and who are his teachers. 111pp. TPH 69

_____. THROUGH THE GATEWAY OF DEATH, c$1.25. See the Reincarnation and Karma section.

_____. VITAL QUESTIONS ANSWERED, c$1.75. The following general topics are covered in this volume: individual and racial evolution, successive lives on earth, super-physical beings and states of consciousness, adeptship and the adepts, the spiritual life, the sacred language of allegory and symbol, theosophical answers to human problems, man's supersensory powers, and health and disease. Also included is a listing of theosophical literature arranged in the order in which it should be read to obtain a progressive knowledge of theosophy. 209pp. TPH 59

HOPKINS, JOHN. THE MEASURE OF THE UNIVERSE, $4.25. This volume builds on the material presented in *The Seed of Wisdom*. It is *concerned with humanity as a whole and with the relationship between humanity and those higher centres of consciousness within the body of our planet, and with even higher centres within our solar system and the universe*. The following are the main topics: man—the microcosm, man and the macrocosm, purpose and perfection, the hierarchy of souls, esoteric astrology, the measure of the universe, evolutionary forces. Glossary, 151pp. Com 76

_____. THE SEED OF WISDOM, $4.00. The purpose of this volume is to serve as an introduction to the teaching expounded by Alice Bailey. All the basic material and topics are reviewed and restated here and Hopkins presents his material a great deal more clearly than does his mentor. The following are the main topics: the constitution of man, the etheric body, energy centers and the endocrine glands, the soul and the doctrine of rebirth, evolution, the world of energies, the seven rays, meditation. 120pp. Com 72

JINARAJADASA, C., ed. LETTERS FROM THE MASTERS OF THE WISDOM, c$2.50. Topically arranged letters to individual theosophists from *the Elder Brothers who were the true Founders of the Theosophical Society* written between 1870—1900. Index, 186pp. TPH 19

JOHNSON, RAYNOR. THE IMPRISONED SPLENDOUR, $2.95. See the Parapsychology section.

JUDGE, WILLIAM. PRACTICAL OCCULTISM, c$3.75. Judge was the founder of the Theosophical Society in the U.S. This is a selection of his letters from 1882—91 when he was beginning to actively present to America a *Western Occultism* considered by him to be the foundation upon which civilization is built. 307pp. ThU 51

C.W. LEADBEATER

Leadbeater was a controversial figure who worked closely with Annie Besant and who was the Theosophical Society's chief clairvoyant for a long period. It was he who continued the contacts with the Masters and he devoted much of his time to training the initiates in the ancient wisdom. He writes clearly and directly and, next to those of H.P.B., his books are the most popular and generally considered the most authoritative theosophical manuals.

LEADBEATER, C.W. THE ASTRAL PLANE, c$2.75. See the Astral Projection section.

_____. THE CHAKRAS, $3.45. See the Occult Anatomy section.

_____. CLAIRVOYANCE, c$3.00. See the Parapsychology section.

_____. THE DEVACHANIC PLANE, c$2.25. A theosophical manual which describes Leadbeater's clairvoyant investigation of that higher level of existence called Devachan in Eastern philosophy where bliss is said to be experienced before a new incarnation begins. This is the area commonly thought of as *heaven*. 147pp. TPH 1896

_____. THE HIDDEN LIFE IN FREEMASONRY, $8.00. See the Rosicrucians and Freemasons section.

_____. THE HIDDEN SIDE OF THINGS, c$8.50. An in depth investigation divided into the following major topics: *How We Are Influenced*—by planets, by the sun, by natural surroundings, by nature spirits, by centers of magnetism, by ceremonies, by sounds, by public opinion, by occasional events, by unseen beings; *How We Influence Ourselves*—by our habits, by physical environment, by mental conditions, by our amusements; *How We Influence Others*—by what we are, by what we think, by what we do, by collective thought, by our relation to children, by our relation to lower kingdoms. Leadbeater also includes a long chapter discussing *Our Attitude Toward These Influences*. Index, 619pp. TPH 13

_____. HOW THEOSOPHY CAME TO ME, c$3.25. A short biographical study. 136pp. TPH 30

_____. THE INNER LIFE, c$10.50/set. There is a tradition that comes from the ancient mystery schools that those who wish to train themselves may tread a path of discipleship and spiritual growth, and that they can be helped on their way by teachers who have trod the path before them. In this two volume work Leadbeater speaks of this path and writes of the inner life of the aspirant. 749pp. TPH 10

_____. INVISIBLE HELPERS, c$3.75. *There is an ancient tradition that in times of human crisis help may come from an unseen source, that invisible servers are working to assist people in need, both in this world and in the next*. In this volume Leadbeater describes several such cases. Index, 238pp. TPH 1896

_____. THE LIFE AFTER DEATH, $2.25. See the Reincarnation and Karma section.

_____. MAN, VISIBLE AND INVISIBLE, $4.50. See the Color and Aura section.

_____. THE MASTERS AND THE PATH, c$8.95. This is generally considered Leadbeater's major work. Drawing on his personal clairvoyant experiences and the experiences of others he writes about the personalities of the Masters, their homes, their work, their nature and their powers. He also describes the various stages of the path the aspirant has to tread to get into contact with the Masters, from probation to acceptance as their disciples, and beyond to higher levels. 332pp. TPH 25

_____. THE MONAD, c$2.75. A series of essays on higher consciousness. TPH 20

_____. THE PERFUME OF EGYPT, c$2.75. A collection of stories, all of them said to be true. 265pp. TPH

_____. THE SCIENCE OF THE SACRAMENTS, c$12.95. A clairvoyant study of the occult forces at work during the Holy Eucharist and other sacraments and services of the Liberal Catholic Church. This volume is one of the most important studies available of the esoteric sacraments and is generally considered the definitive work on Liberal Catholicism. Notes, index. 657pp. TPH 20

_____. A TEXTBOOK OF THEOSOPHY, c$3.45. An excellent introduction to the basic concepts of theosophy including information on the nature of the universe, the constitution of man, the meaning of death and the purpose of existence. 163pp. TPH 12

LESLIE-SMITH, L.H., ed. THE UNIVERSAL FLAME, c$5.00. This book was published in honor of the centenary of the Theosophical Society. *The articles, contributed by members of the Theosophical Movement in a number of countries, deal with basic principles of the Wisdom Religion. . . . The book seeks to present in terms that are easily comprehensible the fundamental nature of the deep and stimulating ideas of this philosophy, known throughout the modern world as Theosophy—Wisdom of, and about, God.* 263pp. TPH 75

LINTON, GOERGE and VIRGINIA HANSON, eds. READERS GUIDE TO THE MAHATMA LETTERS TO A.P. SINNETT, c$4.95. 316pp. TPH 72

LYTYENS, MARY. KRISHNAMURTI, c$8.95. See the Krishnamurti section.

MEAD, G.R.S. THE DOCTRINE OF THE SUBTLE BODY, $1.45. The idea that the physical body of man is but the outer expression of an invisible, more dynamic embodiment of the soul is a very ancient one, and has persisted through many traditions. This work examines the *doctrine of the Subtle Body* as it has appeared in Western philosophical thought and early Christian teaching. 109pp. TPH 19

_____. THE WORLD MYSTERY: FOUR COMPARATIVE STUDIES IN GENERAL THEOSOPHY, $4.00. A highly esoteric presentation consisting of the following essays: *The World-Soul, The Soul-Vestures, The Web of Destiny*, and *True Self-Reliance*. Only a dedicated theosophist could obtain much value from these selections. Index, 200pp. HeR 07

"The Lamasery" in New York

MURPHET, HOWARD. HAMMER ON THE MOUNTAIN, c$7.95. A scholarly biography of Henry Steel Olcott, one of the principal founders of the Theosophical Society and the companion of Mme. Blavatsky in her travels. Includes 30 photographs, index. 339pp. TPH 72

OSBORN, ARTHUR. **THE COSMIC WOMB**, $2.25. A detailed investigation which considers such fundamental questions as the nature of God and ultimate reality and the relationship of the individual to the infinite. In addition Osborn includes material on survival and immortality, a discussion of the mind-brain relationship, accounts of mystical and psychic experiences, and a section on God and evil and on the essentials of the spiritual life. Osborn's other books are listed in the Parapsychology section. Bibliography, index. 235pp. TPH 69

PERKINS, JAMES. **A GEOMETRY OF SPACE CONSCIOUSNESS**, c$4.75. An abstract exploration of man's physical and mental place in the cosmos. Illustrations, 153pp. TPH 64

PLUMMER, GORDON. **THE MATHEMATICS OF THE COSMIC MIND**, c$12.50. See the Sacred Geometry section.

POWELL, ARTHUR. **THE ASTRAL BODY AND OTHER ASTRAL PHENOMENA**, c$7.95/$2.75. See the Astral Projection section.

_____. **THE CAUSAL BODY**, c$9.00. The causal body is the most subtle sheath or body which encloses man's higher ego. In it is contained the residues and cumulative essence of the entire gamut of the soul's experience while in human form through innumerable incarnations. A wealth of information is contained herein, derived from the diligent inquiry of numerous theosophically inclined individuals. 334pp. TPH 27

_____. **THE ETHERIC DOUBLE**, $2.45. See the Astral Projection section.

_____. **THE MENTAL BODY**, c$10.75. The third of the author's treatments on important aspects of esoteric science based on well known theosophical literature. Discusses phenomena of the mental plane such as thought transference and explains such mental activities as concentration and meditation. Index, 316pp. TPH

_____. **THE SOLAR SYSTEM**, c$9.50. An occult description of the life and evolution of our solar system with its planetary chains and hierarchy of spiritual lives. Index, 356pp. TPH 30

PREM, SRI KRISHNA and SRI MADHAUA ASHISH. **MAN, THE MEASURE OF ALL THINGS**, c$5.50. In this study of the symbols of cosmic origins, the authors have traced the story of the emergence of human consciousness from its divine source, seen as a symbolic, though nonetheless true, account in terms of the evolution of the concrete universe. The book throws a new light upon the **Stanzas of Dzyan**, that little known collection of verses on which Blavatsky based her monumental **Secret Doctrine**. **Dzyan** is analyzed stanza by stanza. 360pp. TPH 69

PRESTON, E.W. **THE STORY OF CREATION**, c$1.50. According to **The Secret Doctrine**. 109pp. TPH 47

PURUCKER, G. de. **THE ESOTERIC TRADITION**, $9.00/set. A massive two volume evaluation and explication of the ancient mystery teachings. Every aspect of the subject is discussed at great length. Dr. de Purucker was head of the Theosophical Society from 1929 to his death in 1942. There's a 70pp index. 1180pp. ThU 40

_____. **FOUNTAIN—SOURCE OF OCCULTISM**, $8.50. Subtitled *A modern presentation of the ancient universal wisdom based on* **The Secret Doctrine** *by H.P. Blavatsky*. Index, 749pp. ThU 74

_____. **FUNDAMENTALS OF THE ESOTERIC PHILOSOPHY**, $3.50. Opening with an elucidation of the three fundamental postulates on which **The Secret Doctrine** is based, the author continues his commentary on key passages selected from this masterwork. In the process he presents a comprehensive outline of the cosmic principles on which theosophy is based. This is a good introductory study. Index, 555pp. ThU 32

_____. **MAN IN EVOLUTION**, $3.00. A scientific and philosophical rendering of some conceptions of the teachings about the continual growth in human consciousness. Bibliography, index. ThU 41

_____. **OCCULT GLOSSARY**, $2.50. This compilation of Sanskrit, Tibetan and occult terms has immense value for the student of theosophical writings who is burdened by the difficult terminology. 193pp. ThU 33

_____. **STUDIES IN OCCULT PHILOSOPHY**, $4.50. This book is largely an elucidation of meaningful passages in **The Mahatma Letters** and **The Secret Doctrine**. It gives both the mechanics and the philosophy behind the birth and evolution of man and the earth; the processes of life, death and rebirth; and other universal concepts. Index, 744pp. ThU 45

ROSS, LYDIA. **CYCLES: IN UNIVERSE AND MAN**, $2.00. An overview of the title theme—one of the publisher's series of theosophical manuals. 85pp. PoL 75

ROSS, LYDIA and CHARLES RYAN. **THEOSOPHIA—AN INTRODUCTION**, $1.75. This is about the best introductory survey of theosophy that we know of. All the main tenets are concisely and clearly reviewed. The format is questions and answers. 57pp. PoL 74

SINNETT, A.P. **ESOTERIC BUDDHISM**, c$7.95. *For untold thousands of years the system outlined here-in has been entrusted to those who were willing to pass through a lifetime of probation, to prove themselves worthy of being entrusted with nature's most subtle and profound secrets, the penalty for indiscretion being personal disaster.* An excellent introduction to the study of Eastern hermetica and to theosophical beliefs on the secret doctrine, by the man who received the Mahatma letters. 241pp. Wiz 1883

_____. **THE OCCULT WORLD**, c$5.00. Written by the president of the London Lodge of the Theosophical Society, this provocative work relates many incidents concerning Mme. Blavatsky. Much of the internal life of the esoteric movement of late nineteenth century is revealed and is of interest today since modern metaphysics has its roots in those days. 181pp. TPH 69

Leading English and American theosophists in 1891: (Clockwise from top) Bertram Keightley, Mrs. Cooper-Oakley, Walter Old, William Q. Judge, G.R.S. Mead, Mme. Wachmeister, and Colonel Olcott

TAIMNI, I.K. **MAN, GOD, AND THE UNIVERSE**, $3.45. A thoughtful investigation of the theosophical cosmology by one of the leading contemporary theosophical writers. Many diagrams and charts illuminate the exposition. The presentation is well written. Glossary, bibliography, index. 482pp. TPH 69

_____. **SCIENCE AND OCCULTISM**, c$7.95. In addition to his theosophical activities Taimni was a professor of chemistry at an Indian university for many years. So he is eminently qualified to discuss science and occultism. He presents an in depth, conceptual investigation which is illustrated with several diagrams. 317pp. TPH 74

_____. **SELF-CULTURE IN THE LIGHT OF OCCULTISM**, $2.25. A fairly obtuse work which discusses ultimate reality, consciousness, and self discovery. 314pp. TPH 45

VAN DER LEEUW, J.J. **THE CONQUEST OF ILLUSION**, $1.95. A clear exposition of the nature of illusion and the need to pierce its veil and find the reality that exists at every moment of time. 234pp. TPH 28

_____. **THE FIRE OF CREATION**, $2.95. An exploration of the Holy Ghost. The author was a priest in the Liberal Catholic Church. 234pp. TPH 28

WOOD, ERNEST. **INTUITION OF THE WILL**, c$2.25. An examination of the stages an initiate passes through according to the theosophical tradition. 144pp. TPH 26

_____. **THE SEVEN RAYS**, c$3.00. It was in Blavatsky's **Secret Doctrine** that the modern world was first presented with the phrase *the seven rays*. It went along with a statement that all things and beings in the world—all forms of mind and matter—arose from combinations of seven fundamental impulses. This is a detailed presentation of the rays including a study of the source of the rays; an analysis of the characteristics of each ray; an essay on the use and danger of knowledge of the rays; and a short Sanskrit glossary. 205pp. TPH 25

_____. **A STUDY OF PLEASURE AND PAIN**, c$3.00. The theme of this book is that pain is functional in the advancement and enrichment of life in nature and in man, and is therefore to be received with understanding. How pain arises and how it ceases, and the different kinds of pain are fully discussed and case studies are cited. 97pp. TPH 62

WRIGHT, LEOLINE L. **MAN AND HIS SEVEN PRINCIPLES**, $1.75. Another in Point Loma's series of theosophical manuals. 53pp. PoL 75

UFO'S AND UNEXPLAINED PHENOMENA

Some 40 UFOs of two types were seen over Basle on August 7, 1566

ADAMSKI, GEORGE. **BEHIND THE FLYING SAUCER MYSTERY**, $.95. *The purpose of this book is to share with my . . . friends . . . knowledge gained through personal experiences during the years since* **Inside the Flying Saucers** *was published.* Adamski has probably had more contacts with people in UFO's than any other person writing on the subject. Here he details his most memorable experiences. 159pp. War 67

_____. **INSIDE THE FLYING SAUCERS**, $1.25. A first person narrative of the author's encounter with people from other planets who reveal to him their concepts of the universal order. 192pp. War 67

ARNOLD, KENNETH and RAY PALMER. **THE COMING OF THE SAUCERS**, $3.00. This is a documentary report of the *Tacoma Incident* (sighting) and its aftermath by two of the participants. 192pp. Amh 52

BERGIER, JACQUES. **EXTRATERRESTRIAL INTERVENTION**, $1.25. Written by Bergier and the editors of INFO, this book provides documentation of many of the assertions of those who claim that extraterrestrial visitation is not theory but fact. Ranging widely over the world and through the scientific disciplines the authors discuss four areas of extraterrestrial activity: actual, but no longer existing civilizations, contemporary or historical cases of visitation, evidence based on animals that do not fit into accepted scientific categories, and actual cases of intervention in everyday lives. 164pp. NAL 74

_____. **SECRET DOORS OF THE EARTH**, c$7.95. Another of Bergier's interpretations of *improbable facts*, all concerned with the mysteries of the earth: secret passageways to other worlds within the visible earth, secret societies formed by extraordinary beings who are as old as the planet, centers of energy created by these secret societies which communicate with extraterrestrial intelligences, and much else. 159pp. Reg 75

BERLITZ, CHARLES. **THE BERMUDA TRIANGLE**, $1.95. Berlitz, a noted researcher, has put together the definitive work to date on the Bermuda Triangle, reviewing many of the bizarre disappearances connected with it and proposing intriguing theories of the strange forces that may be at work here. See the Ancient Civilizations section for more of Berlitz' books. Illustrations, bibliography. 203pp. Avo 74

BERNARD, RAYMOND. **THE HOLLOW EARTH**, $1.50. Bernard presents the theory that the earth is not a solid globe at all, but has openings at the two poles which lead to a vast subterranean civilization more advanced than the ones on the external crust. Bernard supports his theory with research into the North Pole expeditions of Cook and Perry and Admiral Byrd. 191pp. Del nd

BLUM, RALPH and JUDY. **BEYOND EARTH: MAN'S CONTACT WITH UFO'S**, $1.75. A well-regarded general account of recent UFO sightings by trained observers. The incidents are detailed and the follow-up research is discussed. 32pp of illustrations, bibliography, index. 248pp. Ban 74

BOWEN, CHARLES, ed. **THE HUMANOIDS**, $3.95. A collection of articles by noted scientists and astronomers such as Aime Michel, Jacques Vallee, Dr. W. Buhler, and Gordon Creighton which fully document landings and contacts (over 300 of them) between beings from outer space and people on the earth. Many previously unpublished reports are presented and some of the most spectacular cases are evaluated. 256pp. Reg 69

BUCKLE, EILEEN. **THE SCORITON MYSTERY**, c$6.55. The *Scoriton* case is one of the most noted and puzzling in UFO annals. This is a full investigation of the incidents involved and the investigation by Ms. Buckle and Norman Oliver—both seasoned, serious UFO investigators. Both the original incidents and subsequent telepathic communications from *Space People* are discussed and evaluated. 303pp. Spe 67

CLARK, JEROME and LOREN COLEMAN. **THE UNIDENTIFIED**, $1.50. This is an extensive general review which traces UFO sightings back to medieval times. The authors discuss the cases and present their hypothesis from the perspective of the latest UFO findings. In the process they look at stories of fairies, religious visions, *paraufological* experience, and early aircraft contacts. Many of the most noted cases are cited and first hand reports are included. The bibliography is the most extensive we've seen. Index, 272pp. War 75

EBON, MARTIN, ed. **THE RIDDLE OF THE BERMUDA TRIANGLE**, $1.50. A collection of interpretative articles and first person accounts of some of the mysterious happenings in the area known as the Bermuda Triangle. 207pp. NAL 75

EMENEGGER, ROBERT. **UFO'S—PAST, PRESENT AND FUTURE**, $1.50. Emenegger was a skeptic until he saw the documents that form the basis of this book. Once exposed to these facts his feelings changed and he has attempted to add credibility to the subject through this carefully researched book. He has documented all his sources and often quotes directly from the U.S. Government case histories. The material is presented in an easy-to-read fashion and is illustrated throughout. 180pp. RaH 74

FLAMMONDE, PARIS. **UFO'S EXIST!** c$12.95. This is billed as the definitive history and analysis of the UFO phenomenon, beginning with the earliest records and continuing to the present age—and it does seem to be comprehensive. Flammonde has compiled a wealth of historical data, eyewitness testimony, and scientific opinion. Extensive quotations and summaries of ancient writings are included along with an excellent survey of modern sources and incidents. Notes, bibliography, index. 406pp. Put 76

FOWLER, RAYMOND. **UFO'S—INTERPLANETARY VISITORS**, c$8.50. This is the newest compendium of UFO sightings available. Fowler, chairman of the New England branch of the National Investigations Committee on Aerial Phenomena, the largest civilian organization in the U.S., has been able to type the UFO's as to shape, size, color. He also discusses the implications of the UFO's and poses questions as to the nature of the beings on the ships. Notes, index. 365pp. ExP 74

FRY, DANIEL. **THE WHITE SANDS INCIDENT**, c$3.95. Dr. Fry is a scientist, researcher and electronics engineer. This is an account of his encounter with a flying saucer, his ride in it, and a verbatim record of his conversations with the pilot. 120pp. DeV66

FULLER, JOHN. **INCIDENT AT EXETER**, $1.25. A detailed account of this noted UFO sighting, witnessed by five people, including two officers of the local police department. 221pp. Ber 65

_____. **THE INTERRUPTED JOURNEY**, $1.25. This is the story of the time Betty and Barney Hill spent aboard an alien spacecraft, being questioned and subjected to physical examinations by metallic gray humanoids. The encounter has been well documented by two of the most noted UFO resarch organizations. Under hypnosis, the Hills discussed and recorded the event and much of the material here is taken from these tapes. Illustrations, 350pp. Ber 66

GARDNER, MARSHALL. **A JOURNEY TO THE EARTH'S INTERIOR**, $6.00.A very thorough exploration of possible life in the interior of the earth, illustrated and citing all the important research and theories up to the date of publication. HeR 20

HOBANA, ION and JULIEN WEVERBERGH. **UFO'S FROM BEHIND THE IRON CURTAIN**, $1.95. This is a very complete account by two European investigators which is full of good scholarship and material unavailable in any other source. The various sightings are discussed in detail and first-person accounts are included along with many

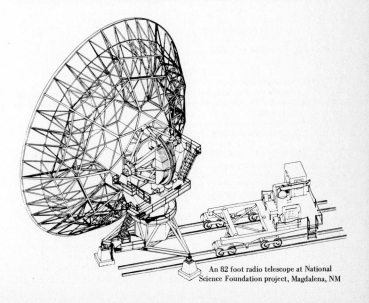

An 82 foot radio telescope at National Science Foundation project, Magdalena, NM

351

photographs and line drawings. Includes an excellent annotated bibliography and a complete listing of references and sources for the illustrations. 407pp. Ban 74

HYNEK, J. ALLEN. **THE UFO EXPERIENCE—A SCIENTIFIC INQUIRY**, $1.95. This is considered the best general book on UFO's—recommended to both scientists and general readers. Dr. Hynek is a noted astronomer and has been scientific consultant to the U.S. Air Force on the matter of UFO's for many years. He wrote this volume to answer the questions of anyone who is curious about the UFO phenomenon as a whole, who would like to have it appraised and to appraise it himself. Illustrations, index. 309pp. RaH 72

HYNEK, J. ALLEN and JACQUES VALLEE. **THE EDGE OF REALITY**, $5.95. Two of the U.S.'s most eminent researchers have collaborated on this report of what serious scientists now believe about UFO's. From the outset, Hynek and Vallee make their position clear: UFO's represent an unknown but real phenomenon. In this book they examine some specimen UFO reports—including those allegedly involving humanoids—and describe the patterns that have been perceived. They also establish a framework for the study of the UFO phenomenon. Index, 316pp. Reg 75

JACOBS, DAVID. **THE UFO CONTROVERSY IN AMERICA**, $1.95. This is an authoritative, fully documented study. Using previously inaccessible Air Force documents, personal interviews, private correspondence, and a wealth of wide-ranging published and unpublished materials, Professor Jacobs has written a definitive history of UFO's from the first wave of sightings in 1896-7 to the present. *Dr. Jacobs' most admirable work has put the UFO controversy into scholarly perspective. It is indispensible reading for any who seek an informed view of the tortuous history of the UFO phenomenon.*—J. Allen Hynek. Extensive chapter notes, bibliography, index. 378pp. NAL 75

KEEL, JOHN. **THE EIGHTH TOWER**, c$8.95. This volume, subtitled *The Cosmic Force Behind All Religious, Occult and UFO Phenomena*, is a strange amalgam of case histories from a variety of sources—most of which are directly or indirectly related to UFO's. Notes, illustrations. 218pp. Dut 75

_____. **OUR HAUNTED PLANET**, $.95. An account of innumerable instances in man's recent history that indicate contact with an *ultra-terrestrial* source of information. This contact may be physical, psychic or otherwise and is certainly often inexplicable by conventional means. The author sees these occurrences as a part of an extensive overhaul of the planet and an evolutionary mutation of humanity into collective *cosmic consciousness* 177pp. Faw 71

_____. **THE MOTHMAN PROPHECIES**, $1.50. In December, 1967, a 700 foot bridge spanning the Ohio River in West Virginia suddenly collapsed, sweeping scores of people into the water and killing thirty-eight. In the months before the disaster, the area had been haunted by strange monsters and apparitions, and mysterious lights had traveled over the area on a regular schedule. Keel, a noted UFO investigator, spent a year investigating the many bizarre events and he here gives his findings, especially as they relate to the so-called Mothman, a primeval monster with blazing red eyes and a pair of bat-like wings. 269pp. NAL 75

KEYHOE, DONALD. **ALIENS FROM SPACE**, $1.50. Major Keyhoe is a graduate of the U.S. Naval Academy and the Naval Aviation Training Station. He has written many noted books and articles on UFO's. This book is his newest, a very detailed documented account. His objective is to make all of the evidence available to the public, and his reportage is objective and is well considered by the experts. Indexed, 322pp. NAL 74

_____. **FLYING SAUCERS FROM OUTER SPACE**, $1.75. A well organized, thoroughly documented review of recent UFO cases. The details of each case are outlined and the evidence is cited and evaluated. Most of the incidents reported took place in the U.S. and much of the documentation comes from U.S. Air Force files. Notes, index. 256pp. Tdm 69

KLASS, PHILIP. **UFO'S EXPLAINED**, $2.45. Klass, senior avionics editor for **Aviation Week and Space Technology** magazine, has been called the *Sherlock Holmes of UFOlogy* because of his scientific, painstaking approach that has enabled him to provide new insights into UFO cases that other investigators have pronounced totally inexplicable except as extraterrestrial spaceships. In this, his third book, he carefully analyzes the full spectrum of the UFO questions and provides well substantiated answers. The cases include some of the best-known ones. Klass developes ten *UFOlogical Principles* which will better enable readers to understand UFO reports. Illustrations, notes, index. 369pp. RaH 74

KRASPEDON, DION. **MY CONTACT WITH FLYING SAUCERS**, c$5.25. This is considered the most outstanding book on flying saucer contact to have been published since Adamski. It recounts in detail actual conversations and gives factual descriptions of how flying saucers actually fly and are motivated, and how they overcome the forces of gravity. It also shows how these principles could be used by scientists. A serious, scholarly study. Illustrations, 205pp. Spe 59

KUSCHE, LAWRENCE. **THE BERMUDA TRIANGLE MYSTERY—SOLVED**, $1.95. Despite the pretentious title, this does seem to be the fullest investigation of the enigma of the Bermuda Triangle available. Many of the most noted happenings are described and analyzed and what factual backing there is is cited. Kusche also reviews the major theories and advances his own. Bibliography, notes, index. 313pp. War 75

LESLIE, DESMOND and GEORGE ADAMSKI. **FLYING SAUCERS HAVE LANDED**, c$8.80. A well documented account which includes first person reports of actual meetings with people from other planets and includes photographs of UFO sightings. Bibliography, 232pp. Spe 70

LORENZEN, CORAL and JIM. **ENCOUNTERS WITH UFO OCCUPANTS**, $1.95. A detailed analysis of some of the most important recent UFO encounters by two of the chief members of the Aerial Phenomena Research Organization. The case studies are detailed and sources are noted. There's also an attempt at evaluation. This seems to be a more serious study than most of the ilk. Bibliography, index. 440pp. Ber 76

LUNAN, DUNCAN. **INTERSTELLAR CONTACT**, c$9.95. In 1973, Lunan, an eminent Scottish scientist, deciphered the mysterious radio signals that had puzzled scientists ever since they were first received in the 1920's. He identified them as a series of star maps apparently transmitted by a spaceprobe circling the earth. The messages pointed to an origin in the constellation Bootes 13,000 years ago—from a planet long considered uninhabitable. This discovery has since been supported by the January 1974 account that Russian scientists have been detecting similar signals. In this volume Lunan analyzes the meaning of these communications, and in addition he reconstructs old myths, old maps, and other early man-made records with an eye toward historical proof of contacts with other intelligences. The text is supported by notes and line drawings. 334pp. Reg 74

MC CAMPBELL, JAMES. **UFOLOGY**, $4.95. McCampbell is a scientist/engineer who has done pioneering research. Here he brings his research in the following areas together: certified UFO's, the vehicles, composition and luminosity, sounds, electrical interference, physiological effects, flight and propulsion, pilots and passengers, and activities on Earth. **UFOLOGY** *is a pioneering attempt to come to grips with the physical nature of the UFO phenomenon. It points the way clearly to a scientific approach to the problem which can surely be applauded by physical scientists. The author combines logical and systematic marshalling of facts with provocative speculation to reveal an implied treasure chest of knowledge which could prove of monumental benefit to mankind.*—Dr. J. Allen Hynek. 153pp. CeA 73

MACVEY, JOHN. **WHISPERS FROM SPACE**, c$8.95. Macvey is an internationally renowned expert on astronomy and astronautics. In this clearly written, well researched account he assesses the possibility that our universe is populated with intelligent beings—some of whom may belong to a culture which is vastly more technologically advanced and socially sophisticated than our own. Beginning with a discussion of the origin of the galaxies, planets, and earthly life, he considers the entire prospect of inter-stellar communications and travel, expertly translating complex astrophysical concepts into language comprehensible to the general reader. Extensive illustrations and explanatory diagrams. 250pp. McM 73

MC WANE, GLENN and DAVID GRAHAM. **THE NEW UFO SIGHTINGS**, $1.25. A journalistic analysis of some of the most noted 1973 and 1974 sightings, with photographs. 173pp. War 74

MICHEL, AIME. **FLYING SAUCERS AND THE STRAIGHT LINE MYSTERY**, c$6.95. Michel is a French mathematician and engineer. Almost by accident he noticed that the sightings of a single day, even though they might occur far apart, fall clearly and precisely along straight lines. Making further tests, he found that these straight lines form highly characteristic patterns—webs and networks that unmistakably suggest a systematic aerial exploration. Michel carefully builds his thesis that some kind of outside intelligence must govern the movements of these UFO's in all their manifestations. This is a very careful scientific study which nonetheless should prove fascinating to those who are interested in the UFO phenomenon. Many case studies are included along with detailed notes and illustrations. Index, 285pp. Plp 58

_____. **THE TRUTH ABOUT FLYING SAUCERS**, $1.25. It's hard to say something different about yet another UFO book—especially since it is an area in which we are not very interested. This one, however, looks a good deal more interesting than most. It seems to be well written and the cases studied are from all over the world and seem to be different than the oft-cited ones. Michel is a good writer and a good investigator and his explanations and theories are from very reputable sources and are very clearly presented. Index, 270pp. Pyr 56

NADA, YOLANDA. **VISITORS FROM OTHER PLANETS**, c$10.00. This book presents, in biographical form, many of the thousands of interdimensional communications and the experiences of Yolanda, primary Mark Age channel or prophet. For more on Mark Age, see their books discussed in the Revealed Teachings section. **Visitors** explains the nature and purpose of our visitors, using their own words, explanations and suggestions. A very detailed account. Index, 334pp. MAM 74

REHN, K. GOSTA. **UFO'S—HERE AND NOW!** c$9.95. Rehn is a Swedish lawyer and Sweden's most active UFO investigator. Here he summarizes the results of the recent international investigations and presents his own observations. Eye-witness accounts from all over the world are reviewed and analyzed and photographs of the vehicles are included. Also included are hitherto unpublished discussions of the UFO's method of propulsion and a new theory explaining the physical and psychological effects of UFO radiation. Bibliography, 198pp. AbS 74

RYAN, PETER and LUDEK PESEK. **UFO'S AND OTHER WORLDS**, $1.75. A brief survey of UFO sightings and theories, accompanied by many artistic drawings. Part of Penguin's Explorer series for junior high school students. Index, 48pp. Pen 75

SAGAN, CARL, ed. **COMMUNICATION WITH EXTRATERRESTRIAL INTELLIGENCE**, $6.95. The proceedings of an international conference on communication with extraterrestrial intelligence held in Soviet Armenia in 1971. The book includes verbatim transcripts of prepared talks and free discussions, carefully worded resolutions, excerpts from relevant articles, and several brief position papers. The material is quite technical and several of the selections are diagrammatically illustrated. Glossary, index. 440pp. MIT 73

_____. **THE COSMIC CONNECTION**, $1.75. This is the first book by Sagan written for the general reader. In non-technical language he describes the possibilities of extraterrestrial life, tells how we can go about finding them, and and discusses the impact of this search and its discoveries on our lives. An important work, well illustrated. Index, 274pp. Del 73

_____. OTHER WORLDS, $1.95. This is an interesting collection of photographs, drawings, cartoons, quotations, and short essays on a vast array of cosmic phenomena. 160pp. Ban 75

SAGAN, CARL and THORTON PAGE, eds. UFO'S: A SCIENTIFIC DEBATE, $3.95. Fifteen distinguished scientists, from such disparate fields as astronomy, physics, meteorology, psychiatry, psychology, and sociology discuss all aspects of UFO's. They present photographs and detailed descriptions of sightings, analyze the reports of witnesses and data from equipment such as radar, and propose (or reject) hypotheses to explain the sightings. They devote special attention to the credibility of witnesses, natural phenomena that have been identified as UFO's, the unexplained cases, the connection between the UFO phenomenon and the news media, psychological factors affecting popular belief in UFO's, and the possibility that intelligent life elsewhere in the universe is trying to contact Earth. Index, 310pp. Nor 72

SALISBURY, FRANK. THE UTAH UFO DISPLAY, c$7.95. Dr. Salisbury's book is built around the carefully documented and hitherto unreported accounts of a variety of individuals who, over a period of time, have witnessed a most spectacular display of UFO's in the Uintah Basin area in Utah, and who have systematically recorded them. These sightings run into the hundreds. Only the very best and most thoroughly investigated are included here in the form of interviews, after which the author, a scientist, examines the possibilities, the various pros and cons involved, and then sums up his thoughts on these particular sightings and on sightings in general. 299pp. DAC 74

SANDERSON, IVAN. INVESTIGATING THE UNEXPLAINED, c$8.95. A compendium of unexplained mysteries of the natural world. Sanderson was a biologist and his case studies include unusual animals and other *live* things; *cooked* things; *human* things, under which category he discusses the zodiac, electricity, and airplanes; and *inhuman* things. Plates, notes and photographs. 339pp. PrH 72

_____. INVISIBLE RESIDENTS, $.95. Subtitled *A Disquisition upon Certain Matters Maritime, and the Possibility of Intelligent Life under the Waters of this Earth.* Sanderson was a scientist who did a great deal of pioneering research. Here he presents the evidence he has accumulated after analyzing centuries of reports of strange marine happenings. All of his citations are well documented and his whole case is very well presented. Notes, index. 248pp. Avo 70

_____. UNINVITED VISITORS, c$6.95. A biologist looks at the possible implications of how extraterrestrials survive, where they come from, and why they come—with a special appendix of the Jessup case and a bibliography. 245pp. Reg 67

SHKLOVSKI, I.S. and CARL SAGAN. INTELLIGENT LIFE IN THE UNIVERSE, $3.75. The product of a unique international collaboration between a world famous Russian astronomer and an Assistant Professor of Astronomy at Harvard, this book covers the origins of the universe, the evolution of stars and planets, the beginnings of life on Earth, and the development of intelligence and technical civilizations among galactic communities. It is the outstanding summary of the present state of scientific knowledge and philosophical interest in these areas. Not easy reading but worth the struggle. Profusely illustrated. 509pp. Del 66

SPENCER, JOHN WALLACE. NO EARTHLY EXPLANATION, $1.75. This is a not overly sensationalized account of the UFO phenomenon: its history, the major citings, possibilities of extraterrestrial origin of life on earth, present-day extraterrestrial communications, and much else. Spencer attempts an objective presentation and it does seem fairly adequate as a mass-market account. We're not sure what his credentials are, though. Includes photographs and drawings. 178pp. Ban 74

STEIGER, BRAD. MYSTERIES OF TIME AND SPACE, $1.75. Steiger explores the underlying patterns of mysteries which challenge our most basic concepts of history, geology, and physics. He examines cases never before written about and cites eyewitness accounts (including his own). Steiger is the author of over forty books on a wide variety of topics. Photographs, bibliography, index. 232pp. Del 74

STEIGER, BRAD and JOHN WHITE, eds. OTHER WORLDS, OTHER UNIVERSES, c$7.95. A collection of essays weaving science, religion, philosophy, archaeology, and even folklore into a new perception of the universe. The main topics are the following: *The Search for Extraterrestrial Life, The Prehistory of Earth, A Look at UFO's, The Astral Plane and Beyond, Return to Godhead;* the contributors include Jacques Vallee, Rudolf Steiner, Arthur Ford, Timothy Leary, Oliver Reiser, Yogi Ramacharaka, Ivan Sanderson, and David Spangler. The editors supply a long introduction to each section, tying it all together and presenting the necessary background. Bibliography, 262pp. Dou 75

STONELEY, JACK and A.T. LAWTON. CETI, $1.50. Stoneley is a journalist and Lawton an authority on advanced electronics. Together they have collected an intriguing array of material on communication with extraterrestrial intelligence. Included are reports on how scientists plan to communicate across space and descriptions of the means of communication already being used. Diagrams, notes, index, bibliography. 254pp. War 76

STRINGER, E.T. THE SECRET OF THE GODS, c$14.90. An outline of Tellurianism, which seeks to explain the mysteries of life. It presents a fresh view of the world, derived from evidence provided by the techniques of occultism and mysticism, throws new light on UFO's and ancient civilizations, and provides rational explanations of astrology, psychic phenomena and radiesthesia. The author is a professional British scientist and geographer. 256pp. Spe 74

TEMPLE, ROBERT. THE SIRIUS MYSTERY, c$10.95. This is a well documented, often mind boggling book which advances the thesis that the existence of civilization on the earth is a result of contact from inhabitants of a planet in the system of the star Sirius prior to 3000 BC. There are traditions in present-day Africa that the origins of civilization

come from Sirius and these traditions are traced back by Temple to the ancient Mediterranean civilizations of Egypt and Sumer. The author also shows that not only did these civilizations possess great learning and wealth but they possessed knowledge dependent on nuclear physics and astrophysics—which they claimed was taught to them by visitors from Sirius! Temple is a scholar with impeccable credentials and he presents a mass of objective data which amply supports his thesis. We recommend this book heartily to all those interested in ancient civilizations and extraterrestrial visitations. Notes, bibliography, index. 301pp. SMP 76

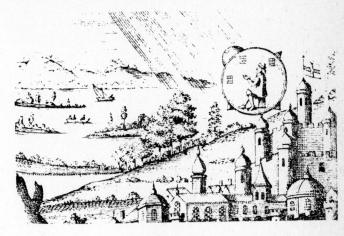

An early rendition of a UFO

TOMAS, ANDREW. ON THE SHORES OF ENDLESS WORLDS, c$7.30. The story of the origin of life on this planet and some of the discoveries of modern science are woven into an entrancing tale, full of speculation and folklore. A well written account that seems a bit less scattered and a great deal more serious than most of the countless books on this topic. Includes illustrations, bibliography, and index. 230pp. Sou 74

TRENCH, BRINSLEY LE POER. MYSTERIOUS VISITORS, c$6.95. Trench is the chairman of Contact, the world's largest UFO-watching organization. He has written many books on the subject (see the Ancient Civilization section for some of his other titles). Here he presents a possible solution to the UFO enigma. He delves into the origin of UFO's: are they from other planets in our own galaxy or could they be from space-time continuums or invisible universes intersecting our own? He offers some new explanations for the riddles of the ages, and gives the reader a glimpse of future contacts. One of the most fascinating sections offers a new, extraterrestrial explanation of the mysteries of Western religions. A very readable, well documented account. Notes, index. 192pp.

_____. SECRET OF THE AGES, $1.95. Trench examines various theories about the point of origin of UFO's and presents a strong case for his theory that UFO's originate from inside the earth. He postulates that visitors from outer space came to this planet eons ago. They became the god-kings of Atlantis, erected huge edifices around the world. They also constructed gigantic tunnel systems in which to take refuge from both the unstable seismic conditions prevailing in that era and attack from other extraterrestrials. When Atlantis was submerged, many of the Atlanteans took refuge in the tunnel systems, and according to Trench, their descendents are still there inside the earth today, complete with the old Atlantean space craft and a very advanced technology. Trench also discusses evidence which indicates that the earth is hollow, with entrances in both the polar regions. Extensive notes, index. 192pp. Ban 74

VALLEE, JACQUES. ANATOMY OF A PHENOMENON—UNIDENTIFIED OBJECTS IN SPACE: A SCIENTIFIC APPRAISAL, $1.50. A detailed discussion of the sightings between 1947 and 1964, a period of great activity. Vallee also discusses present methods used to examine the phenomenon, and proposes a scientific system of classification. Illustrations. RaH 74

_____. THE INVISIBLE COLLEGE, c$8.95. *In this book I propose to examine the hypothesis that UFO's may constitute a control system; that they are not necessarily caused by extraterrestrial visitors, nor the result of misidentifications and hoaxes on the part of deluded witnesses. If the hypothesis is true, then what the witnesses have seen were manifestations of a process not unlike that of a thermostat in a house. The thermostat is a mechanism that stabilizes the relationship between our body temperature requirements and the changing weather outside. Similarly, UFO's may serve to stabilize the relationship between man's consciousness needs and the evolving complexities of the world which he must understand. This book will explore this phenomenon. . . . In this book I will not confine myself to the examination of the physical reality, but will frankly step from this into the experiential and even to the mythical.—from the introduction.* Many case studies are included and the account is well organized. Illustrations, bibliography, index. Dut 75

_____. PASSPORT TO MAGONIA, $4.95. Vallee is an expert in computer technology and sometime NASA consultatnt. He is also one of the most respected UFO investigators working today. Here he discusses and explores many of the most interesting reports of communication with extraterrestrials and turns his attention to the fact that throughout history, in all parts of the world, there is a consistent folk tradition dealing

8

with visitation—from heaven, hell, Elfland, Magonia, or wherever. Such incidents, experiences, and patterns provide the background material upon which Vallee bases this exhaustive study of the phenomenon of visitation, from the very earliest days to the present. In addition, this book contains a comprehensive catalog detailing all pertinent facts of some 900 sightings in the past hundred years. Index, 372pp. Reg 69

VALLEE, JACQUES and JANINE. **CHALLENGE TO SCIENCE: THE UFO ENIGMA**, $1.95. A formidable presentation by noted researchers of evidence for the global nature of UFO phenomena—with computerized classification of data, charts, graphs, photographs, and an extensive bibliography. 268pp. RaH 66

VESCO, RENATO. **INTERCEPT UFO**, $1.95. A well researched study which reviews the official government coverup and documents a variety of sightings. Many case studies are included. Vesco also makes predictions about future landings and presents his own interpretation of the U.S. government's policy on UFO's. Notes, photographs. 338pp. Pin 71

WILSON, CLIFFORD. **UFO'S AND THEIR MISSION IMPOSSIBLE**, $1.50. Dr. Wilson's public involvement with UFO's began with a series of radio and television appearances rebutting van Daniken's claims. Since then he has surveyed the literature and here presents his summary of the salient features of the major books and the major theories. Notes, bibliography. 235pp. NAL 74

WINER, RICHARD. **THE DEVIL'S TRIANGLE**, $1.50. An interesting account which reviews and evaluates some of the best known historical cases of disappearances in the Bermuda Triangle and presents Winer's own observations based on his on-site investigations. Bibliography, index. 158pp. Ban 75

WOMEN

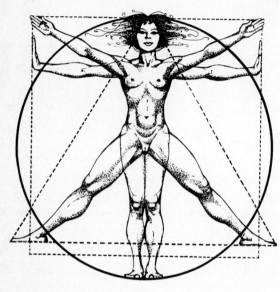

BARBACH, LONNIE. **FOR YOURSELF: THE FULFILLMENT OF FEMALE SEXUALITY**, $3.95. This is a psychologically oriented study of the development of sexuality in women, sympathetically written and illustrated with many case studies. Bibliography, index. 236pp. Dou 75

BOSTON WOMEN'S HEALTH BOOK COLLECTIVE. **OUR BODIES OURSELVES**, $4.95. An extensively revised edition of this landmark book which presents women's views on their bodies and their health. Much of it naturally is concerned with sexuality: its anatomy and physiology, lovemaking, relationships, lesbians, rape and self-defense, VD, birth control, abortion, childbearing, menopause. The book is detailed, explicit, well illustrated, and filled with anecdotes by women as antidotes to the usual descriptions of women's sexuality written by men. There is a brief chapter on nutrition and a long one on health care. Although not everyone will agree with the feminist view which sometimes comes across heavily, every woman (or man, for that matter) will find a lot of value in this book. Recommended. Bibliography, 276pp. S&S 76

CASTILLEJO, IRENE de. **KNOWING WOMAN**, $2.45. See Jungian Psychology section.

DODSON, BETTY. **LIBERATING MASTURBATION**, $3.50. Subtitled *A meditation on Self Love Dedicated to Women*, this pamphlet is divided into the following chapters: *The Romanticized Image of Sex, Sharing Masturbation, Going Public, Consciousness Raising, Becoming Cunt Positive, Bodysex Workshops*, and *Masturbation as Meditation*. Many case studies and individual reports are included and many pages are devoted to graphic line drawings of women's sex organs. 60pp. BsD 74

GREER, GERMAINE. **THE FEMALE EUNUCH**, $1.95. This is one of the most significant of the recent rash of books on women. It is a serious and yet highly readable study which topically discusses the roles that women are involved in and how they came to play the roles. Virtually every aspect of female life in our contemporary society is portrayed and analyzed and positive recommendations are made. Appropriate quotations are interspersed throughout the exposition. Notes, 380pp. Ban 70

GRINNELL, ROBERT. **ALCHEMY IN A MODERN WOMAN**, $6.95. See the Jungian Psychology section.

HALL, MANLY P. **WOMAN: MOTHER OF ALL LIVING**, $1.50. A discourse on the role of women and the worship of women in various cultures throughout history. 33pp. PRS 55

HARDING, ESTHER. **THE WAY OF ALL WOMEN**, $3.95. See the Jungian Psychology section.

_____. **WOMAN'S MYSTERIES: ANCIENT AND MODERN**, $3.95. See the Jungian Psychology section.

HORNER, I.B. **WOMEN UNDER PRIMITIVE BUDDHISM**, c$15.20. See the Buddhism section.

JONGEWARD, DOROTHY AND DRU SCOTT, eds. **AFFIRMATIVE ACTION FOR WOMEN**, $5.95. A practical guide edited by the president of the Transactional Analysis Management Institute which includes information about the current status of women and presents strategies for positive change. 343pp. AdW 75

_____. **WOMEN AS WINNERS**, $4.95. A collection of exercises, case histories, and techniques for personal change based on transactional analysis and on Gestalt therapy. Notes, index. 318pp. AdW 76

LACEY, LOUISE. **LUNACEPTION**, $1.75. This is an unusual story of the author's search for a new approach to contraception and the discoveries that search led to. After investigating all the generally used techniques she came upon the technique of *lunaception*, which could be used to determine when she would ovulate and also enabled her to synchronize her body cycle with the phases of the moon and thus make a connection between herself and the universe. She tells how it helps her predict, for a given day, her mood, her energy level, and even her self-image—and she supplies charts and the other information needed to try the technique. We've never heard of it before, and we would not recommend relying on it without further scientific testing, but it sounds like an interesting idea. Notes, bibliography, index. 167pp. War 75

MANDER, ANICA and ANNE RUSH. **FEMINISM AS THERAPY**, $2.45. The authors are active in the feminist movement in Berkeley, California. Here they discuss their work and the work of others in women's consciousness raising. They also explore the use of the concepts of feminism as the philosophical base for a new theory and practice of psychology. A personal account. 129pp. RaH 74

PHELAN, NANCY and MICHAEL VOLIN. **YOGA FOR WOMEN**, $1.50. See the Yoga section.

RAMAKRISHNA-VEDANTA CENTRE. **WOMEN SAINTS OF EAST AND WEST**, $4.95. See the Comparative Religion section.

ROSENBLUM, ART, ed. **THE NATURAL BIRTH CONTROL BOOK**, $3.00. A review and discussion of a variety of natural techniques including mind control conception, astrological birth control, the ovulation method, lunaception. All the necessary tables are included. Annotated bibliography, 156pp. ARF 76

RUSH, ANNE KENT. **GETTING CLEAR**, c$10.00/$5.95. An excellent collection of body therapies, verbal therapies, and awareness techniques in use in the Bay Area in California. *This book is written to be experienced and not just read. You can use it by picking sections and subjects interesting to you and trying out some of the exercises. Any of them done over a period of time will become more useful; but even done once, each will have immediate results. . . . I am writing for women because I am a woman and can tell you what tools have been useful to me.* Topically arranged, illustrated. Highly recommended for all. 289pp. RaH 73

ULANOV, ANN. **THE FEMININE IN JUNGIAN PSYCHOLOGY AND IN CHRISTIAN THEOLOGY**, c$16.15. See the Jungian Psychology section.

WASHBOURN, PENELOPE. **BECOMING WOMAN**, c$8.95. An examination of ten potential crisis points in a woman's life, such as the onset of menstruation, leaving home, marriage, and parenthood. Ms. Washbourn sees these occasions when the issue of personal identity is raised as fundamentally spiritual crises. She defines a negative reaction as the violation of a woman's essential identity and a positive one as a discovery of self-trust, renewal, and new identity. Varying reactions for each stage are fully described and there is an examination of how women of other cultures have dealt with these situations. Bibliography, index. 192pp. H&R 76

WHITEHOUSE, GEOFFREY. **EVERYWOMAN'S GUIDE TO NATURAL HEALTH**, $4.70. See the Healing section.

YOGA

ACHARYA, PUNDIT. **BREATH, SLEEP, THE HEART, AND LIFE**, $3.95. This is a compilation of four books by Pundit Acharya, originally published in the 1950's: **You Haven't Slept, This Precious Heart, Internal Respiration,** and **Breath is Life**. This presentation is a combination of practical exercises, Acharya's philosophy of life, and examples and analogies showing the human condition. 189pp. DHP 75

ALEXANDROU, EVANGELOS. **CHRISTIAN YOGA AND YOU**, $4.95. A typical hatha yoga manual, showing basic asanas, with directions. The photographs are large and the postures are well executed. The text is bilingual, Spanish and English. Oversize, spiral bound. 90pp. Chs 75

BEHANAN, KOVOOR. **YOGA, A SCIENTIFIC EVALUATION**, $3.00. This is a scientific, but non-technical study of the physiological and philosophical aspects of yoga, written under the auspices of the Institute of Human Relations, Yale University. Dr. Behanan clearly explains and evaluates fundamental concepts of Hindu thought and relates these ideas to familiar Western philosophical conceptions. This is the best book of its type available. Glossary, 281pp. Dov 37

BERNARD, THEOS. **HATHA YOGA**, $3.50. A good philosophical discussion of various aspects of yoga: asanas, purification, pranayama (breathing), mudras (gestures), and samadhi. The text is extensively annotated and is accompanied by photographs of many of the asanas (postures) and a bibliography. 104pp. Wei nd

BRENA, STEVEN, M.D. **YOGA AND MEDICINE**, $2.45. This book contends that the average human has far too little control over his own mental and physical health. With this in mind, Dr. Brena, an American physician, reviews both the medical and the yogic concepts of anatomy, physiology, nutrition, respiration, sexual activity, pathology and pain. In each case he makes a comparative analysis, stressing the many similarities as well as the fundamental differences. Notes and illustrations. 179pp. Pen 72

CARR, RACHEL. **BE A FROG, A BIRD, OR A TREE**, c$5.95. Subtitled *Creative Yoga Exercises for Children*, this is a delightful addition to the proliferating books on yoga. The thirty exercises presented here are different from traditional yogic poses. Ms. Carr has made use of every child's most creative tool—his or her imagination—in developing the techniques. The child pretends to be a jumping frog, a shooting arrow, a sturdy tree growing in the forest, and much else. The instructions for each exercise are written in the form of children's verse, the model pictured is a child, and the print is large enough for the child to read it him/herself. There's also a section of background notes for parents or teachers. Oversize, 96pp. Dou 73

_____. **YOGA FOR ALL AGES**, $3.95. Rachel Carr has devised a six stage yoga course which she feels should enable everyone to enjoy the benefits of yoga with less than thirty minutes of practice a day. Progressing from simple movements to the more complex in stages, these exercises aim at physical conditioning, easing of tensions, and the promotion of physical, mental, and emotional well-being. Very clear instructions, well illustrated with photographs. Oversize, index. 160pp. S&S 72

_____. **THE YOGA WAY TO RELEASE TENSION**, $1.95. Subtitled *Rachel Carr's Techniques for Relaxation and Mind Control*, this is a combination of a variety of exercises, illustrated with line drawings. Included is information on breathing and muscles and how they work along with exercises for different parts of the body and exercises to increase stamina and muscular action. 147pp. H&R 74

CHRISTENSEN, ALICE and DAVID RANKIN. **EASY DOES IT—YOGA FOR PEOPLE OVER SIXTY**, $3.50. This is an excellent manual, based on the authors' extensive work with older people. An elderly woman is the model for the illustrations and they are presented in a step-by-step format. There's also a fair amount of background and introductory material as well as a series of cautions and hints. Included also are breathing instructions and meditation instruction. A six week daily routine is also presented. 8½x11", spiral bound. 56pp. Sar 76

_____. **THE LIGHT OF YOGA BEGINNER'S MANUAL**, $2.95. This oversize manual is specially designed to visually illustrate and clearly explain yoga for beginners. The spiral binding allows the manual to remain flat on the floor, and the student therefore can easily refer to it while doing the exercises. Each pose is illustrated with drawings step-by-step and the presentation is the clearest we have seen. The descriptive and philosophical material is also good. Highly recommended as an instruction book. 61pp. S&S

DECHANET, J.M. **YOGA IN 10 LESSONS**, $1.95. An introductory book for those who do not wish to be overburdened with yogic theory and simply desire instruction in the postures. Each lesson begins with a section on the necessary theory and is followed with clear instructions for the exercises. Fifty-two exercises are described, along with information on the therapeutic effects and the attendant dangers, if any. 174pp. S&S nd

DEVI, INDRA. **FOREVER YOUNG, FOREVER HEALTHY**, $1.50. *This book is not intended as a treatise, but as a practical guide to a better, healthier and longer life. It will tell you how to breathe correctly; how and what to eat; how to relax and exercise your body and mind....*—Indra Devi. Ms. Devi spent twelve years in India studying and has taught the techniques all over the U.S. to many prominent personalities. Topics include breathing, relaxation, correct posture, fasting, insomnia, headaches, arthritis, asthma, and much else. Her books are very well written and clear, with many anecdotes and illustrations of the postures. Recommended as a good general introduction to the the practicalities. Bibliography, 171pp. Arc 53

_____. **RENEW YOUR LIFE THROUGH YOGA**, $1.50. A good presentation of yogic and non-yogic relaxation techniques. Includes philosophical material on tension, a long discussion of the art of relaxation with practical suggestions; the science of breathing; yoga postures illustrated for relieving tensions and inducing relaxation; a section on the essence of yoga, and an excellent discussion of nutrition and diet. 256pp. War

_____. **YOGA FOR AMERICANS**, $1.50. A complete, six week course in hatha yoga with diets, recipes, exercises, and special guides for overweight, arthritis and asthmatics. Profusely illustrated. NAL

DISKIN, EVE. **YOGA FOR CHILDREN**, $4.95. A graded, illustrated guide. The book is attractively designed and the instructional material is clear. In addition, there is a series of hints for parents and teachers. We like Rachel Carr's book better, but this volume contains more exercises, and different ones than Carr's. Oversize, index. 206pp. War 76

GARDE, DR. R.K. **PRINCIPLES AND PRACTICE OF YOGA THERAPY**, c$4.45. Dr. Garde is an Indian physician. In this book he clearly shows which diseases can be helped by yoga asanas in conjunction with the help of other yoga adjuncts such as correct breathing. He also includes information on homeopathy and the cell salts, massage, music, the correct diet, and even prayers. This is a very detailed, illustrated account. Excellent glossary. 132pp. Tar nd

GOSWAMI, SHYAM SUNDAR. **HATHA-YOGA**, c$12.00. Special features in this book: (1) both the dynamic and static aspects of each exercise have been explained as well as correct techniques in breathing, (2) exercise plans containing the right combinations to suit different ages, sex, conditions of health, etc., (3) breath control exercises explained in a clear and practical manner. The expositions of the exercises are the most detailed we've ever seen. The tone of the book is oriented toward the health aspects of yoga rather than the philosophy. Includes several exercise plans and diets. It is subtitled *An Advanced Method*, and indeed it is. 221pp. Fow nd

HITTLEMAN, RICHARD. **BE YOUNG WITH YOGA**, $1.50. Hittleman is quite probably the most prolific writer on yoga in America today. He has had frequent television instruction programs and he is very well known. His emphasis is on yoga as a form of exercise, rather than on the spiritual benefits, although he does get into the philosophy somewhat. He presents his material clearly and writes well. Many thousands have used his books as their introduction to yogic practices and exercises. We also stock several of his instructional records—see the Records section for descriptions. This book presents a seven week program of exercises along with a series of exercises for specific ailments. The instructions are very complete and a variety of special hints are also offered. Photographs illustrate the text. Index, 239pp. War 62

_____. **GUIDE TO YOGA MEDITATION**, $1.50. See the Meditation section.

_____. **INTRODUCTION TO YOGA**, $1.75. A general presentation, with some basic postures and philosophy along with diet suggestions. 192pp. Ban 69

_____. **WEIGHT CONTROL THROUGH YOGA**, $1.25. 208pp. Ban 71

_____. **YOGA FOR HEALTH**, $2.35/each. These three books present a very simplified series of yogic postures, with instructions and background material. The postures are illustrated with line drawings and various hints are included. **Book Three** presents information on the principles of nutrition along with sample menus and recipes. Oversize, about 40pp each. YFH 62

_____. **YOGA PHILOSOPHY AND MEDITATION**, $2.35. Here Hittleman attempts to distill the essence of Indian philosophy, especially as it relates to yoga. He does an all right job of it and does manage to cover, albeit briefly, all the essentials. 37pp. YFH 64

_____. **YOGA 28 DAY EXERCISE PLAN**, c$4.95/$1.95. Presents a detailed four week exercise plan. Very good materal for a self-teaching program. Also some philosophy.

The $4.95 edition has much larger pictures and text. Recommended as the best step-by-step, day-by-day instruction book. 320pp. WPC 69

HUTCHINSON, RONALD. **YOGA**, $7.98. This is an oversized book, with over 100 illustrations (thirty-two in full color) detailing the philosophy behind yogic practice, discussing meditation and pranayama, and illustrating and explaining many asanas. The material is beautifully presented and designed to turn people on to yoga who are totally unfamiliar with it. Bibliography, index. 126pp. Ham 74

IIJIMA, KANJITSU. **BUDDHIST YOGA**, $6.95. See the Buddhism section.

IYENGAR, B.K.S. **LIGHT ON YOGA**, c$9.95/$4.95. *Probably the most complete Hatha Yoga book*—**Whole Earth Catalog**. 600 pictures and an incredible amount of detailed descriptive text as well as philosophy. The purpose is to describe as simply as possible the asanas (postures) and pranayama (breathing exercises) in the light of our own era, its knowledge and its requirements. Includes detailed primary, intermediate, and advanced asana courses, a table that correlates asanas with the plates that illustrate them, and a detailed glossary. Inyegar's school of yoga is probably the best known in India today and his techniques have been very influential with yoga teachers throughout the world. Highly recommended. 342pp. ScB 65

JOHN, BUBBA FREE. **CONSCIOUS EXERCISE AND THE TRANSCENDENTAL SUN**, $1.95. A compilation from some of Bubba's oral and written instructions. There's some philosophy, but basically the book is a collection of exercises. Included is the famous **Surya Namaskar** (or welcome of the sun). The illustrations are poorly drawn and the reader would find it hard to learn from them. 83pp. DHP 74

KRIYANANDA, SWAMI. **YOGA POSTURES FOR SELF-AWARENESS**, $2.95. Swami Kriyananda was a direct disciple of Yogananda. He is the founder of Ananda Cooperative Village in California. Stress is placed in this book on the usefulness of yoga postures for spiritual development and for achieving a harmony of mind and soul as well as body. Many postures are illustrated and discussed and there is additional background material. 85pp. AnP 67

KUVALAYANANDA, SWAMI. **POPULAR YOGA ASANAS**, c$7.95. This definitive work explains the yamas, nyamas (mental exercises) and the asanas (physical exercises) from the view of yoga-sastra. Yamas, freely translated, mean inoffensiveness, truthfulness, and continence. Nyamas represent purification, contentment, mortification, study, and complete self-surrender to the Lord. Yoga-sastra holds that the influence of the mind on the body is most important, although asanas have a very definite place in the book. This is an excellent serious study—recommended as the next step after some of the introductory yoga books. Over 80 illustrations, detailed glossary, and many notes. 213pp. Tut 31

_____. **PRANAYAMA**, c$5.00. A comprehensive, practical text which outlines eight varieties of pranayama advocated by noted hatha yoga teachers through the ages and four varieties taught by Patanjali. The pertinent texts are summarized and many translations are included. Step-by-step instructions for each exercise are also given. Some illustrations, though they are not very good. Glossary, 168pp. PPr 66

LYSEBETH, ANDRE von. **YOGA SELF TAUGHT**, $2.95. This is the most detailed, comprehensive yoga book we've seen. The photographs show all the intermediate stages of each asana and there is excellent background material for each one including information on the technique, variants, duration, the order in which a series of asanas should follow each other, the method of breathing, how and where to concentrate the mind, the effects of the exercise, and so on. The philosophical chapters are also excellent, and even here much of the material is practical. The whole book is well organized and illustrated and we recommend it highly for both the beginning student and the more advanced one (advanced variations of the postures are also given). 264pp. H&R 68

MAJUMDAR, S.K. **INTRODUCTION TO YOGA**, c$7.50. *In the following pages, I have tried to give the substance of yoga, its principles and practices, as they have come down to us from an immemorial past....It is my wish to present yoga as a living tradition, not as a system of fixed formulas, to be found in books or schools. Yoga is not a special religion or a particular philosophical doctrine. It is the wisdom of life. It is experience.* This is an excellent book, with a long section on principles and perspective; an illustrated practical section; a good chapter on meditation; a selection of quotations from 5000 years of yogic literature; and a glossary. Recommended as an excellent overall introduction. 318pp. UnB nd

MEDVIN, JEANNINE. **PRENATAL YOGA**, $3.50. See the Natural Childbirth section.

MISHRA, RAMMURTI. **FUNDAMENTALS OF YOGA**, $2.50. This is an excellent beginning text on yogic philosophy. Dr. Mishra is an endocrinologist who also teaches at the California Institute of Asian Studies and other colleges. This was originally written to serve as a text for his classes. The material presented is quite comprehensive and geared toward practical application. Topics include various detailed exercise techniques; the chakras and the kundalini; opening the third eye; breathing; and much else. The reader should be warned that the text is replete with Sanskrit vocabulary—there is a glossary-index which helps, but the reading is still slow going though the expositions are clear. Graphic illustrations. 217pp. Dou 59

MOORE, MARCIA and MARK DOUGLAS. **DIET, SEX AND YOGA**, c$6.95. *This book discusses attitudes about the body and presents ways of gaining increased physical control by means of diet, exercise, deep breathing, relaxation, and creative visualization....Essentially, we are talking not only about diet, sex, and yoga, but about your life and what you can do about it.* This is a very clearly written account, fully indexed. 283pp. ArB 66

_____. **YOGA: SCIENCE OF THE SELF**, c$6.95. This is quite a successful attempt at a Westernization of yogic philosophy. Few Sanskrit terms are used, and even

these are defined in the glossary. The philosophical material is clearly written and good. Topics include a general discussion of yoga as an ancient wisdom, emphasizing the hatha and raja displines; a long section on yoga and psychic development, psychoanalysis, and philosophy; and a presentation of esoteric yoga. There is a section of asanas, but the pictures are inadequate. Good bibliography. 288pp. ArB 67

OKI, MASAHIRO. **PRACTICAL YOGA: A PICTORIAL APPROACH**, $3.95. A Zen Buddhist approach to yoga. The first section covers the nature of yoga, health, nourishment, fasting, sex. The latter half gives practical instructions and over 400 step-by-step photographic analyses of yoga poses, corrective exercises, and emotion and breath control. A large, easy to follow book for both the novice and the regular practioner. 80pp. Jap 71

_____. **YOGA THERAPY**, $5.95. See the Healing section.

PHELAN AND VOLIN. **YOGA FOR WOMEN**, $1.50. Provides a good overview. Presents the philosophy and the practice, with some illustrations—but not enough to learn in any depth. 155pp. H&R 63

RAMA, SWAMI. **JOINTS AND GLANDS EXERCISES**, $1.75. A series of exercises, illustrated with line drawings. 46pp. Him 74

SATCHIDANANDA, SWAMI. **INTEGRAL YOGA HATHA**, $5.95. A pictorial guide to hatha yoga asanas—includes bodily postures, methods for deep relaxation, breath control, cleansing processes and systems of mental concentration. This clearly designed guide can be used individually in the home or in conjunction with yoga classes. The pictures are quite large and the technical instruction comprehensive, but often only the final position is pictured, not the intermediate steps. This is our most popular hatha yoga book and is generally very well regarded. Recommended. 189pp. HRW 70

SIVANANDA, SWAMI. **YOGIC HOME EXERCISES**, $1.50. This is a more detailed presentation of asanas, including the same type of information as in **Yoga Practice**, as well as many pages of theoretical material. Drawings illustrate the text. 101pp. TSC 65

_____. **YOGA PRACTICE**, c$2.40. This book presents a regime of yogic exercises developed especially for Western man. Sivananda describes the method of doing each asana, and explains its effect on the body, the physical defects it can remedy, and includes an illustration of each asana. Includes additional practical advice. 64pp. TSC nd

SLATER, WALLACE. **HATHA YOGA**, $1.25. Presents a very simplified basic course of hatha yoga postures, including meditation and mind control exercises, and advice on personal hygiene and diet. 65pp. TPH nd

STEARN, JESS. **YOGA, YOUTH, AND REINCARNATION**, $1.50. This is a personal, anecdotal account of Stearn's initiation into yogic practices as a student of Marcia Moore. In the process he discourses on astrology, reincarnation, and diet and health. The appendix details yoga warm-ups, routines, and breathing; this material is illustrated. Glossary. 344pp. Ban 65

URBANOWSKI, FERRIS. **YOGA FOR NEW PARENTS**, $6.95. See the Natural Childbirth section.

VISHNUDEVANANDA, SWAMI. **COMPLETE ILLUSTRATED BOOK OF YOGA**, c$5.95/$1.95. All the essential knowledge of the mental science of yoga is contained in this handbook: asanas, breathing exercises, concentration, meditation, diet, and philosophy. Swami Vishnudevananda, teacher of hatha and raja yoga, explains and instructs in clear and direct language the means to the conquest of old age, disease and death through the development and understanding of timeless yogic wisdom. This is one of our most popular yoga books, and we recommend it highly. The $5.95 edition is an especially good value; it has excellent large photographs. 415pp. S&S 60

VITHALDAS, YOGI. **THE YOGA SYSTEM OF HEALTH AND RELIEF FROM TENSION**, c$1.98. An excellent presentation of the therapeutic aspects of yoga as taught by the author in his school in New York. Includes diets and mental and physical exercises. 124pp. Crn 57

YESUDIAN, SELVARAJAN. **YOGA WEEK BY WEEK**, c$6.95. A presentation of fifty-two weeks of exercises which provides a carefully graded, step-by-step course in yoga. The line drawings illustrating the postures could not be worse and the explanations are adequate, but hardly more. Much of the material is discussed at greater length in **Yoga and Health**, so this volume can only be seen as a complement to the earlier one and cannot stand by itself. Inspiring quotations and line drawings of nature scenes are interspersed. 243pp. H&R 75

YESUDIAN, SELVARAJAN and ELISABETH HAICH. **YOGA AND HEALTH**, $1.50. Explains the achievement of physical and mental well-being by means of yoga. From a general discussion of principles the authors move on to practical hatha yoga, and in this section describe carefully the three essential factors to be combined: control of consciousness, breath control, and physical postures. The text is well illustrated and the exposition is excellent. This is the best work of this type that we've seen. 184pp. H&R 53

MANLY P. HALL ON BOOKS

We have many requests for that perfect book which tells everything about a certain subject—the book that has breadth, depth, and combines the highest scholarship with deep spiritual understanding, and presents it all in simple words. Sad to say, these greatly desired volumes do not have actual existence. There is no book that tells all about everything, nor is there any author so completely adequate that everything he says can be accepted without question. This means that it is nearly always necessary to compare a number of works dealing with the same general area in order to gain adequate perspective in the field. For example, I am frequently asked what is the best book on Buddhism, or what is the most accurate translation of the Bible; or again, what is the most reliable life of Christ. It would seem that such questions should not present any special difficulties, but in practice, they are impossible to answer in a meaningful way. Each of us responds in a different degree to the contents of a printed page. Some prefer to receive their inspiration from highly mystical writing; others require a more prosaic, factual style. The text that seems to meet the needs of one person leaves another hopelessly confused. That wonderful book that answers everything for everybody will not be found. It has not been written because man himself is incapable of reconciling all conflicts of opinion within his own nature. Truth has been diffused, and fragments have come to be scattered through the works of countless scholars, sages and saints. They must be gathered up, these pearls of wisdom, as they were scattered, one by one.

In older days, the library was the most important room in the house. In contemporary living, it is likely to be two or three shelves alongside of a real or simulated fireplace. The modern collector does not wish to be burdened with a vast weight of literature. It is expensive to move from one place to another, a major consideration with apartment dwellers. What little shelf space there is, must often be divided according to the different interests of the members of the family. Even if a small bookcase is introduced, it is essential that accumulations of books shall be held to a realistic minimum. The broader the interests of the student, the more he must sacrifice penetration to coverage. It is probably best, therefore, that he uses the facilities of his public library as much as possible, reserving his private space for volumes difficult to secure in public sources. . . .

It would be nice to believe that a good working library could be built up with a carefully selected group of books numbering not over a hundred volumes. This can probably be accomplished, but only through a gradual process of careful selection. Books at first included may later be rejected because the material is presented more authoritatively in a more comprehensive volume. This brings up another point. In recent years, there has been a great deal of cribbing from old authorities. Many modern writers are merely paraphrasing the ancients, or quoting or misquoting standard texts that are rather too dry to invite general reading. My experience has been that if we are sufficiently interested in any subject to study it at all, we should be willing to read the texts of its original and principal exponents. If we think Plato is worth reading, we should read Plato, and not a score of smaller popular digests, extracts, opinions, criticisms, or essays bearing upon this great Greek thinker. By going back to the original authors, we can save ourselves a great deal of confusion. In the last twenty years, the tendency generally has been to disparage the great spiritual and cultural leaders of the past. Their works have been assailed by immature minds, their characters have been slandered, and their writings have been translated by highly prejudiced authorities. This can all avoided if we cling to what may be termed authoritative texts.

Most readers are working on a voluntary basis. They are taking time from other activities to study a little in quest of self enlightenment or spiritual consolation. This means that no reader should drown in his books. Do not read until your mind is worn out and you are past comprehension. Do not attack the subject as though you must master it in a few hours or even a few weeks. Many who know how to read words, do not know how to read meaning. Philosophy is no field for scanning, nor does it help much to study beyond a point of endurance. Old Dr. Elliott, the editor of the famous **Harvard Classics**, recommended not over an hour a day—but let it be a good hour, undisturbed by other conditions. Let the attention be quietly pointed to the theme. Let each sentence be read slowly and pondered in relation to context. If the sub-

ject enters unexpected areas, look up the meanings of unusual words, and familiarize yourself with other authors suddenly introduced, or personages and events that may be used to point out a moral or clinch an argument.

Take plenty of time to explore the author's general perspective. What is he trying to tell us? What cause is he defending? What fallacy is he attacking? In the use of weapons, is he fair and just, or is he allowing skill alone to give him advantage over perhaps others wiser than himself? Is he charitable, patient, and obviously sympathethic with the vital concerns of mankind? It is good to become familiar with the author as a person and a scholar, but remember that no author is so great that he has a right to your unquestioned allegiance. On the other hand, no author is so poor that he may not have something that will help you. In any case, you will gain inward growth, because the book is a mirror held to your own face, and you will get out of it what there is in you. Some books are better mirrors than others, of course. Some draw forth one side of our natures, some another, but the power of the book is its power to release your own thought, not to impose its thoughts upon you. As you read, be mindful of the words of Lord Bacon, *Read not to accept, nor to deny, nor to agree, nor to criticize or condemn, but to weigh and consider.*

All honest and honorable books give us an understanding of human nature, human hearts, human minds. They are valuable and good. In times of emergency, stress, or pain, a great book is a good friend. Those who never develop an appreciation for good books, are failing to provide for those later years of living when restrictions of vitality and health may make it impossible to carry on the numerous activities that once took their time. We may all be faced with years in which we will have to depend upon our inner lives for richness of experience. These can be very good years, but if we have never found the friendship of books, if we have never found the kinship of thought, if we have never reached across the intervals that unite or divide minds and consciousness, we are in danger of long and lonely years. So each person should learn to love good books, and should use them with care and thoughtfulness, not taking his philosophy out of books, but finding in them the release of his own dreams, the enrichment of his own purposes. Books deserve a dignified place in our plan of life, and persons who use their moderate means for the enrichment of culture, will spend more wisely than those who are content to spend for creature comforts.

There has been discussion concerning the relative merits of reading as distinguished from and contrasted to actual attendance at lectures and cultural programs. I am still inclined to feel that there is more to be gained, in many instances, by reading than by listening, especially where the qualifications of a speaker are uncertain. We have a tendency to be over-influenced by the spoken word. We appreciate this fact in politics, but are inclined to overlook it in education. We can be disarmed by oratory. The glib speaker may hold us spellbound, but add very little to our real knowledge. Often, also, we are required to make decisions too rapidly because of the continuing flow of ideas over which we have no control. In some areas, verbal instruction can be a useful supplement, but I doubt if it is ever an adequate substitute for the slow, quiet, plodding method of laboring with the written records of man's achievements. It is also true that home study will facilitate the advancement of scholastic programs. If a person long out of school wishes to continue his education, he can prepare himself in advance by reading carefully and wisely in selected fields. Not only will he be better equipped so far as knowledge is concerned, but he will have established good study habits, which will save much time and energy. . . .

A good point to bear in mind in gathering references is to try, wherever possible, to secure indexed editions. Some reprints and paperbacks omit indexes, and abridgments and condensations usually suffer from this fault. A massive volume without an index is extremely unwieldy, entailing considerable waste of time and energy. Even if it costs a little more to have a well-indexed copy, it is well worth the difference.

In buying new books, most readers promptly throw away the dust jacket. If you are a serious student, pause for a moment and examine the jacket. It may well be the only source of information concerning the author or editor of a book, his qualifications, his motives, and the point of view which he expects to develop. There is also a possibility that the back flap or outside of the jacket will include a list of other books by the same author, or related books by prominent authorities. In books of popular price, the dust jacket is often in color, and may include an illustration. In some instances, a plate in color on the dust jacket is reproduced in black and white only within the text, or is missing entirely. While dust jackets are not attractive on shelves, and quickly become torn and disfigured, important ones can be filed away for future reference. It is unwise, however, to paste fragments of the dust jacket onto the inside covers of the book itself.

It is not usually necessary to index a small library, but some collectors like to keep a card file or a loose leaf notebook listing their volumes. One advantage of this process is that if a book is loaned, the name of the borrower can be recorded on the index card, and removed when the book is returned. Many a book is lost simply because the lender cannot remember who borrowed it. File cards also permit annotations about matter of special interest discovered in books. I have noticed that even in volumes reasonably indexed, many choice items have been overlooked in the listings. For some reason, this is consistently true with references bearing upon metaphysical or mystical matters. A rather reputable author whose book was well indexed, made three references to astrology, but these were ignored by the indexer, who evidently believed he was doing his author a kindness. . . .

The world of religious and philosophical thought is a vast region not quickly to be explored. It cannot be assumed that anyone can accomplish much by simply diving in without some kind of organized plan. As most readers are of mature years, they already have partly awakened interests which they wish to improve. They want to add to their knowledge of some subject that already concerns them, or for which they have evidenced an affinity. Sometimes this interest has arisen from the personal problems of living; perhaps the individual has been challenged and needs deeper insight to sustain himself through an emergency. A good many have belonged to organizations, and have begun to ask themselves whether the organization was as sincere and genuine as it claimed to be. It seemed that only some discreet investigation could answer such a question.

—from **GREAT BOOKS ON RELIGION AND ESOTERIC PHILOSOPHY** by Manly P. Hall

AFTERWORD

We hope you have found reading this guide both useful and enjoyable. We'd like to hear from you with any comments you have, pro or con. We'd also like to see you if you come to Washington.

Yes! is more than just a bookshop. We provide food for spirit, mind and body, as we also have a natural food store and a lovely self-service vegetarian restaurant. We occupy three old buildings in Georgetown with a delightful patio in the middle with a fountain and plants and birds.

The bookshop is very open, with carpeting, lots of seats, plants, and classical music. You can browse and read and when you get hungry, step into the garden for a meal or a snack.

Yes! is a business which exists to provide goods and services to the public, honestly, efficiently and profitably. Yes! is also a spiritual place. The extent to which this is true is a function of the collective input of the forty-five people who work here and the people who come here, as well as the aspirations of the principal owners, managers, and long-time staff. A two-way flow is involved: we put our energy into Yes!'s development, and being at Yes! has a strong impact on our development.

Why do we call ourselves Yes!? We say Yes! to life. If we have any unifying concept, it is that of living in harmony with nature, our own as well as that around us. Along with this is the belief that our purpose in this world is to work on our own development and evolution, and through that the development and evolution of humankind in general. We recognize that there are many paths, and if they are trod by committed seekers they all ultimately lead to the same place. Some people on the Yes! staff are followers of particular spiritual disciplines. Others are not. We get along by not trying to convert others to our own path, but by remaining open to others, whatever path they are on, and wherever on it they are. We try to create at Yes! a warm, loving atmosphere which will welcome people of all ages, races, and cultures.

We hope we will have the opportunity one day to welcome you to Yes!

ACKNOWLEDGMENTS

I would like to thank the people who helped me put this book together:

Blenda Femenias and Becky Siebens who did the typesetting on our IBM selectric electronic composer; Ramesh Bishop and Virginia Hedden who did the layout and other art work; Lee Lewis and Brian Lindquist who did most of the proofreading; Wayne Hagood and Barbara McCormick who prepared the author index by computer; and Ralph Raphael who did the record reviews. Thanks also to all the customers and friends who have helped me with their ideas and advice and have taught me much of what I know about this field.

And special thanks to my husband Ollie who helped with all aspects of the production, wrote many of the nutrition reviews, and whose patience, love, and understanding helped me through this often seemingly endless task.

In addition, I wish to thank the authors and publishers of the following books from which I have taken excerpts and condensed material to use as introductions to sections. The acknowledgments follow the order that the selections appear in **Books for Inner Development**.

Alchemy by Titus Burckhardt, English translation copyright 1967 by Vincent Stuart and John M. Watkins, Ltd, and published by Viking Penguin, Inc.

The View over Atlantis by John Michell, copyright 1972 by the author and published by Sphere Books, Ltd.

Maps of Consciousness by Ralph Metzner, copyright 1971 by the author and published by Macmillan Publishing Co., Inc.

The Tao of Physics by Fritjof Capra, copyright 1975 by the author and published by Shambhala Publications.

The Laughing Man Magazine, Volume I, Number 1, copyright 1976 by The Laughing Man Institute for Traditional and Esoteric Studies.

Chinese Mystics edited by Raymond Van Over, copyright 1973 by the editor and published by Harper and Row.

Yoga and Psychotherapy by Swami Rama, Rudolph Ballentine, and Swami Ajaya, copyright 1976 by the Himalayan International Institute of Yoga Science and Philosophy of USA and published by them.

The Uses of Enchantment by Bruno Bettelheim, copyright 1976 by the author and published by Alfred A. Knopf (Random House).

Gurdjieff: Making a New World by J.G. Bennett, copyright 1973 by the author and published by Harper and Row.

The Theory of Celestial Influences by Rodney Collin, copyright 1954 by the author and published by Samuel Weiser, Inc.

Introduction to Islamic Civilisation edited by R.M. Savory, copright 1976 by Cambridge University Press and published by them.

The Tales of Rabbi Nachman by Martin Buber, copyright 1956 by the author and published by Horizon Press.

An Introduction to Jung's Psychology by Frieda Fordham, copyright 1966 by the author and published by Viking Penguin, Inc.

How to Meditate by Lawrence LeShan, copyright 1974 by the author and published by Bantam Books, Inc.

An Approach to Mysticism by Dr. Martin Israel, published in 1968 under the joint auspices of the Mysticism Committee of the Churches' Fellowship for Psychical and Spiritual Studies, and the College of Psychic Studies.

The Masks of God: Primitive Mythology by Joseph Campbell, copyright 1969 by the author and published by Viking Penguin, Inc.

The Probability of the Impossible by Dr. Thelma Moss, copyright 1974 by the author and published by the New American Library.

The Gaelic Manuscripts by Stewart Edward White, published by Panthean Press.

The Secrets of Ancient Geometry by Tons Brunes, copyright 1967 by the author and published by Rhodos.

The Tarot by Alfred Douglas, copyright 1972 by the author and published by Viking Penguin, Inc.

Great Books on Religion and Esoteric Philosophy by Manly P. Hall, copyright 1966 by The Philosophical Research Society, Inc., and published by them.

HOW TO OBTAIN THESE BOOKS

If you wish to read any of these books and they are not in your local library, show the reviews to your librarian and ask her or him to order them for you. In this way you will help to awaken your librarian to the importance of these books and help to make them more widely available to others.

The same thing goes for bookstores. Try to get the books at the store where you bought this **Guide**. If they don't have them in stock, ask if they will special order them for you. We have provided the publishers' addresses for the benefit of other bookstores who wish to order these books. Or check your yellow pages for a local store that might stock these kinds of books.

If you cannot obtain them locally, you can buy them from us. That's the business we are in, and we normally have all these books in stock. We do a large mail-order business all over the world and we get the books out the same day the order comes in. So if you wish to get the books from us, read the following ordering information carefully:

ORDERING INFORMATION

All sales are final. We can accept no returns unless the book is defective in some way. We have tried to say enough in the reviews to give you good guidance on the books. However, if you would like some additional information about a book before you buy it, write and ask us.

Our prices are net. We sell at retail only. If you are interested in buying at wholesale, contact the publishers of the books. We offer a 5% discount on orders over $50.00 and 10% for ten or more copies of the same book.

Book prices are continuing to rise as books are reprinted. If an increase is substantial, we'll notify you before filling the order. If it's slight, we'll send you the book and let you pay the balance later. If the price has dropped or we can substitute a paperback, we'll do so, and send you a credit slip. We will automatically supply the paperback edition whenever possible, unless you specifically request hardcovers. If you wish hardcovers on books not so shown in the **Guide**, query us and we'll tell you if we can special order them for you.

If we are temporarily out of stock on a title, we will back order it and send it to you as soon as it is available. If the book is out of print we will let you know and send you a credit slip.

Domestic orders, please send us a check or money order payable to Yes! Inc.; D.C. residents please add 5% sales tax. We do not take credit cards or sell on credit; however we can keep money on account for you and you can draw on it as you order. Overseas orders, please send us a bank check or money order, payable in U.S. dollars. We cannot accept personal checks from foreign banks (including Canada). We send our books by surface mail. If you wish your order sent airmail, send us an amount for postage equal to the cost of the book. We will refund any unused money or bill you for the balance.

When you order books we will do our best to serve you quickly and efficiently. If we make any mistakes, please let us know. We will not be satisfied until you are.

POSTAGE AND HANDLING CHARGES

DOMESTIC

Books and records are sent special fourth class mail or UPS. We automatically insure at our expense all orders over $30.00.

Our charge for domestic postage and handling is $.50 for the first book and $.30 for each additional book. Alternatively, if it will save you money, you may figure 7% of the total order with a minimum of $1.00.

Other items are sent by third class mail or UPS. Shipping charges on them are as follows: Biorhythm calculators, 85 cents; pyramids, $1.10; pendulums, 60 cents; tarot decks, 85 cents; posters, 60 cents for one or two; aura goggles, $1.10.

INTERNATIONAL

We cannot insure international parcels and we cannot take responsibility for their safe arrival. We recommend that they be sent registered. Registration costs $2.10 for each $22.00 worth of books, except to Canada where up to $140 worth of books can be registered for $2.10.

Our charge for international postage and handling is $.55 for the first book and $.35 for each additional book. Alternatively, if it will save you money, you may figure 8% of the total order with a minimum of $1.25. Registration fees are additional.

Charges for non-book items are the same as domestic above.

SUPPLEMENTS

We plan to issue periodic supplements to this **Guide** which will provide reviews of new books and indicate price changes, paperback editions, and books which have gone out of print. They will be arranged according to the same subject headings used in the **Guide**.

These supplements will be sent free automatically to our mail order customers.

Others, such as libraries or bookstores, who wish to obtain this information may do so at a cost of $2.00 per year (a minimum of three supplements). If you wish to subscribe to this service, please fill out and send in the coupon below.

Yes! Bookshop
1035 31st Street NW
Washington, DC 20007

Enclosed is _____$2.00 for one year, _____$4.00 for two years, of issues of supplements to **Books for Inner Development**.

Name _____

Address _____

City _____ State _____ Zip _____

ORDER FORM

For office use only	GUIDE page no.	Author	Title	Price	For office use only
			You owe us		
			We owe you		
			TOTAL PRICE		
			POSTAGE & HANDLING 50 cents 1st book, 30 cents each additional		
			AMOUNT ENCLOSED		

Name: _____

Address: _____

_____ Zip: _____

Is this a new address? If so, old zip: _____

date received _____ check no. _____ checked by _____ picked by _____

packed by _____ date shipped _____ via _____ no. _____

YES! BOOKSHOP, 1035 31st STREET N.W., WASHINGTON, D.C. 20007

ORDER FORM

For office use only	GUIDE page no.	Author	Title	Price	For office use only	
			You owe us			
			We owe you			
			TOTAL PRICE			
			POSTAGE & HANDLING 50 cents 1st book, 30 cents each additional			
			AMOUNT ENCLOSED			

Name: _____

Address: _____

_____ Zip: _____

Is this a new address? If so, old zip: _____

date received_____ check no._____ checked by_____ picked by_____

packed by_____ date shipped_____ via _____ no._____

PUBLISHERS' CODES AND ADDRESSES

A&U   George Allen and Unwin Ltd, Park Lane, Hemel Hempstead, Hertfordshire, England
Aar   Aardvark Publishers, Inc, 247 Central Park West, New York, NY 10024
AAs   The Astrological Association, 8 Stuart Close, Great Wakering, Essex, England
Abi   Abingdon Press, 201 Eighth Ave South, Nashville, TN 37202
AbP   IDHHB, Inc, PO Box 1556, Crestline, CA 92325
Abr   Harry N Abrams, Inc, 110 E 59th St, New York, NY 10022
ABS   Aramic Bible Society, PO Box 6406, St Petersburg Beach, FL 33736
AbS   Abelard-Schuman, Ltd, 450 Edgeware Rd, London W2, England
ACa   Astronomical Calendar, Dpt of Physics, Furman University, Greenville, SC 29613
Aca   Academy Books, 3085 Reynard Way, San Diego, CA 92103
ACB   Adam & Charles Black; 4,5 & 6 Soho Square, London W1V 6AD, England
ACS   Astro Computing Services, Neil Michelsen, Box 199, Pelham, NY 10803
AdA   Advaita Ashrama, 5 Dehi Entally Rd, Calcutta 14, India
Ada   H Eugene Adams, 6550 Wetherole St, Forest Hills, NY 11374
AdW   Addison-Wesley, Jacob Way, Reading, MA 01867
AEG   Aquarian Educational Group, 30188 Mulholland Hwy, Agoura, CA 91301
Aeo   Aeon Books, Coreki Corp, 8044 Van Nuys Blvd, Panorama City, CA 91402
AFA   American Federation of Astrologers, PO Box 22040, Tempe, AZ 85282
AgY   Agni Yoga Society, 319 W 107th St, New York, NY 10025
AHI   Arnold-Heinemann India, AB/9 Safdarjang Enclave, New Delhi 16, India
All   Allied Publishers Ltd, 15 Graham Rd, Ballard Estate, Bombay 400001, India
Alt   Altai Press, Inc, Triad Reprints, PO Box 569, Cooper Sta, New York, NY 10003
AMa   Ananda Marga Publications, 27160 Moody Rd, Los Altos, Hills, CA 94022
Amb   K H Ambjornson, 443 Melrose Ave, San Francisco, CA 94127
Amh   Amherst Press, Amherst, WI 54406
AmM   American Media, PO Box 1365, Thousand Oaks, CA 91360
Amo   AMORC, Rosicrucian Park, San Jose, CA 95114
ANH   Natural Hygiene Press, 1920 Irving Park Rd, Chicago, IL 60613
Anh   Anhinga Press, PO Box 13501, Gainesville, FL 32604
Anj   Anjanee Mata, Box 454, Laytonville, CA 95454
AnP   Ananda Publications, Alleghany Star Route, Nevada Cita, CA 95959
ANW   Astrology Center of the Northwest, 522 NE 165th, Seattle, WA 98155
AOH   Academy of Oriental Heritage, Office 308, Ford Bldg, 193 E Hastings St, Vancouver, V6A 1N7 BC, Canada
AOP   And/Or Press, 3431 Rincon Annex, San Francisco, CA 94119
APH   Asia Publishing House, 420 Lexington Ave, New York, NY 10017
API   Anthroposophic Press, Inc, 258 Hungry Hollow Rd, Spring Valley, NY 10977
APM   Academy of Parapsychology and Medicine, 314 Second St, Los Altos, CA 94022
APP   Astro-Philosophical Publishing Co, Denver, CO
AqP   Aquarian Press, 91 St Martin's Ln, London WC 2, England
ArB   Arcane Books, US Route 1-A, York Harbor, ME 03911
Arc   ARCO, 219 Park Ave South, New York, NY 10003
ARE   ARE Press, PO Box 595, Virginia Beach, VA 23451
ARF   Aquarian Research Foundation, 5620 Morton St, Philadelphia, PA 19144
ArP   Aries Press, 32 W Randolph St, Chicago, IL 60601
ARS   Atma Ram & Sons, Kashmere Gate, Delhi-6, India
ArW   Arcana Workshops, 407 N Maple Dr, No. 214, Beverley Hills, CA 90210
AsA   Astro-Analytics, Shirley M Winter, 1030 W Service Ave, West Covina, CA 91790
AsB   Astrological Bureau, 5 Old Quaker Hill Rd, Monroe, NY 10950
ASC   Award Sales Corp, c/o NAL, PO Box 800, Bergenfield, NJ 07621
Ash   Ashram Records, N 2918 Stout, Spokane, WA 99206
ASI   ASI Publishers Inc, 127 Madison Ave, New York, NY 10016
Asi   The Asia Society, 112 E 64th St, New York, NY 10021
AsP   Association Press, 291 Broadway, New York, NY 10007
Ata   Astara, 21 S Mariposa Ave, Los Angeles, CA 90004
Ath   Atheneum, c/o Book Warehouse, Inc, Vreeland Ave, Totowa, NJ 07512
Atp   Anthropological Publications, Oosterhout NB, The Netherlands
AtU   Atlantis University, Box 69990, Los Angeles, CA 90069
Aty   C R Anthony & Co, 300 Park Ave, New York, NY 10010
AUB   American University of Beirut, Beirut, Lebanon
AuE   Aura Electronics, Westhavenkade 97, Vlaardingen, Netherlands
AUM   Association for the Understanding of Man, PO Drawer 5310, Austin, TX 78763
Avo   Avon Books, 250 W 55th St, New York, NY 10019
Awa   The Awakener, PO Box 1081, Berkeley, CA 94701

B&J   Barrie & Jenkins, 24 Highbury Crescent, London N5 1RX, England
BaB   Basic Books, 10 E 53rd St, New York, NY 10022
Bak   Douglas Baker, *Little Elephant*, High Road, Essendon, Hertfordshire, England
Ban   Bantam Books, 666 Fifth Ave, New York, NY 10019
BaP   Barre Publishers, South St, Barre, MA 01005
BBC   British Broadcasting Corp, 35 Marylebone High St, London W1M4AA, England
BBP   Burchette Brothers Productions, PO Box 1363, Spring Valley, CA 92077
BBU   Bhavan's Book University, Chowpatty, Bombay 7, India
BDP   Birth Day Publishing Co, San Diego, CA
Bea   Beacon Press, 25 Beacon St, Boston, MA 02108
Bed   Clyde Bedell, Santa Barbara, CA
Beg   Beguine Library, Berkeley, CA 94701
Beh   Behavioral Publications, 72 Fifth Ave, New York, NY 10011
Bel   G Bell & Sons, Ltd, 6 Portugal St, London WC2A 2HL, England
Ber   Berkley Books, 390 Murray Hill Pkwy, East Rutherford, NJ 07073
BES   Barron's Educational Series, Inc, 113 Crossways Park Dr, Woodbury, NY 11797
BGr   Bernice Grebner, 231 Montclair Ave, Peoria Heights, IL 61614
Bih   Bihar School of Yoga, Monghyr, Bihar, India
Bje   S Banerjee, P 469, CIT Keyatala, Calcutta 29, India
Bkh   Y Beroukhim & Sons, Tehran, Iran

Bla   Blackie & Sons, Ltd, Bishopbriggs, Glasgow G64 2Nz, Scotland
BlB   Bellerophon Books 133 Steuart St, San Francisco, CA 94105
BlE   Blaine Etheridge Books, 13977 Penrod St, Detroit, MI 48223
Blo   Bloch Publishing Co, 915 Broadway, New York, NY 10010
BMC   Blue Mountain Center of Meditation, Box 381, Berkeley, CA 94701
BnB   B'nai B'rith Adult Jewish Education, 1640 Rhode Island Ave, Washington, DC 20036
BnL   Ernest Benn, Ltd, Sovereign Way, Tonbridge, Kent, England
BnP   Rebecca Bennet Publications, 5409 18th Ave, Brooklyn, NY 11204
BoM   Bobbs Merrill, 4300 W 62nd St, Indianapolis, IN 46208
Bor   Borden Publishing Co, 1855 W Main St, Alhambra, CA 91801
BPC   Book Publishing Co, Route 1, Box 197 A, Summertown, TN 38784
BPS   Buddhist Publication Society, Box 61, Kandy, Sri Lanka
BPT   Baha'i Publishing Trust, 415 Linden Ave, Wilmette, IL 60091
BPu   Buddhist Publications, Institute for Buddhist Psychology and Central Asian Studies, Zurich, Switzerland
BrH   British Homoeopathic Association, 27a Devonshire St, London W1N 1RJ, England
Bri   E J Brill, Oude Rihn 33a-35, Leiden, Netherlands
BrP   Branden Press, 221 Columbus Ave, Boston, MA 02116
Brz   George Braziller, Inc, 1 Park Ave, New York, NY 10016
BsD   Bodysex Designs, Box 1933 GPO, New York, NY 10001
BSR   Borderland Sciences Research Foundation, PO Box 548, Vista, CA 92083
Btk   Bhatkal Books International, 35-C Tardeo Rd, Bombay 34, India
BuA   Builders of the Adytum, PO Box 42278, Dept 0, Los Angeles, CA 90042
BUC   Buddha's Universal Church, 720 Washington St, San Francisco, CA
BuS   Buddhist Society, 58 Eccleston Square, London SW1V, 1PH, England
BVB   Bharatiya Vidya Bhavan, Bombay, India

C&B   Caler & Boyars, Ltd, 18 Brewer St, London W1, England
C&W   40 William IV St, London WC2N 4DE, England
CaD   Carolyn Dodson, PO Box 1233, Louisville, KY 40201
Cad   Cadre, 124 28th Ave, San Mateo, CA 94403
Cae   Caedmon Records, 505 Eighth Ave, New York, NY 10018
Can   Cancer Book House, 2043 N Berendo St, Los Angeles, CA 90027
Cap   Capra Press, 631 State St, Santa Barbara, CA 93101
Cas   Bruno Cassirer, Ltd, 31 Portland Rd, Oxford OX2 7E2, England
Cau   Causeway Books, 95 Madison Ave, New York, NY 10016
CBC   Cosmobiology Center, 539 S Grant St, Denver, CO 80209
CCC   China Cultural Corp, PO Box 3724, Hong Kong
CCL   Cambridge Circle, Ltd, 463 Vande Hei Rd, Green Bay, WI 54301
CCl   Christian Classics, 205 Willis St, Westminister, MD 21157
CCP   Christian Community Press, 34 Glenilla Rd, London NW 3, England
CeA   Celestial Arts, 231 Adrian Rd, Millbrae, CA 94030
CeC   Celestial Communications, 110 York St, Brooklyn, NY 11201
Cer   Alfons Cers, Box 08347, Milwaukee, WI 53208
Ces   Cesara Publications, Huntington Castle, Clonegal, Enniscorthy, Eire
CFS   Center for Science in the Public Interest, 1779 Church St, NW, Washington, DC 20036
ChB   Chan's Books, 2930 W Valley Blvd, Alhambra, CA 91803
ChF   Churches' Fellowship for Psychical and Spiritual Studies, St Mary Abchurch, Abchurch Ln, London EC4N 7BA, England
Chi   Chilton Book Co, 150 Parish Dr, Wayne, NJ 07470
ChL   Church of Light, Box 76862, Sanford Sta, Los Angeles, CA 90076
Chn   Chinmaya Books, USA, PO Box 2753, Napa, CA 94558
ChP   Chalru Publications, Box 744, Pasadena, CA 91102
Chr   Chronicle Books, 870 Market St, No 508, San Francisco, CA 94102
Chs   Christananda Publishing Co, 977 Ashbury St, San Jose, CA 95126
CIF   Cultural Integration Fellowship, 3494 21st St, San Francisco, CA 94110
CiL   City Lights, 1562 Grant Ave, San Francisco, CA 94133
CiP   Citadel Press, 120 Enterprise Ave, Secaucus, NJ, 07094
Cir   Circle Books, 2728 Elmwood, Ann Arbor, MI 48104
Cla   James Clarke & Co, Ltd, 7 All Saints Passage, Cambridge CB2 3LS, England
CMG   Coward, McCann & Geoghegan, Inc, 200 Madison Ave, New York, NY 10016
CMP   Century Medical Publications, PO Box 706, La Porte, IN 46350
CMT   Central Chimaya Mission Trust, Band Box House, 254D, Dr Annie Besant Rd, Prabhadevi, Bombay 400-025, India
Cno   Canon Press, 1014 Washington Bldg, Washington, DC 20005
CNP   Clarkson N Potter, Inc, 419 Park Ave South, New York, NY 10016
CoI   Constellation International, 51 Madison Ave, New York, NY
Col   Columbia University Press, 562 W 113th St, New York, NY 10025
Com   Compton Russell, Ltd, The Old Brewery, Tisbury, Salisbury, Wiltshire, England
Cop   R C Copriviza, 71 Oakwood St, San Francisco, CA
Cor   Cornell University Press, 124 Roberts Place, Ithaca, NY 14850
Cos   Cosmic Researchers, PO Box 1119, Atascadero, CA 93422
CPT   Chinmaya Publications Trust, 175 Rasappa Chetty St, Madras 3, India
CRC   CRCS Publications, Professional Mall Bldg, 231 E St, Suite 8, Davis CA 95616
Cre   Gordon Cremonesi Publishers, New River House, 34 Seymour Rd, London N8 OBE, England
Crg   Corgi Books, Transworld Publishers, Ltd, Cavendish House, 57-59 Uxbridge Rd, Ealing, London W 5, England
Cro   Thomas Crowell Co, Conklin Book Center, Inc, Baker Dr, Conklin, NY 13748
Crn   Crown Publishers, 1 Park Ave South, New York, NY 10016
CRS   Columbia Record Sales Service Center, Lamb's & Woodbury Rd, Pitman, NJ 08071
CSA   CSA Press, Lakemont, GA 30552
Csm   Cosmo Publications, 24-B, Ansari Rd, Daryaganj, Delhi 110006, India

CSP   Coombe Springs Press, Sherborne House, Sherborn near Cheltenham, Gloucestershire GL 54 3D2, England

CSq   Cooper Square Publishers, Inc, 59 Fourth Ave, New York, NY 10003

CSS   Chowkhamba Sanskrit Series, Chowkhamba, PO Box 8, Varanasi 1, India

Cst   Castle Books, 110 Enterprise Ave, Secaucus, NJ 07094

Ctr   Centaur Press, Ltd, Fontwell, Sussex, England

CUP   Cambridge University Press, 510 North Ave, New York, NY 10022

CuP   Cunningham Press, 3063 W Main St, Alhambra, CA 91801

Cur   Curzon Press, 88 Gray's Inn Rd, London WC1, England

CWL   Ch'eng Wei-shih Lun Publication Committee, 3 Fontana Gdns, Causeway Hill, Hong Kong

CWP   Ch'eng W'en Publishing Co, Box 22605, Taipei, Taiwan

DAC   Devin-Adair Co, Inc, 1 Park Ave, Old Greenwich, CT 06870

DaH   Dance Horizons, 1801 E 26th St, Brooklyn, NY 11229

Dan   C W Daniel, 60 Muswell Rd, London N10, England

Dar   Darr Publications, 2527 Broadway, Toledo, OH 43609

Dav   T Patrick Davis, 227 E High Point St, Peoria, IL 61614

Day   Daystar Press, PO Box 1261, Ibadan, Nigeria

Del   Dell, c/o Montville Warehousing Co, Change Bridge Rd, Pine Brook, NJ 07058

DeV   DeVorss & Co, PO Box 550, Marina Del Rey, CA 90291

Dha   Dharma Publishing, 5856 Doyle St, Emeryville, CA 94608

DHL   Dialogue House Library, 45 W Tenth St, New York, NY 10011

DHP   Dawn Horse Press, Persimmon, Star Route 2, Middletown, CA 95461

Dia   Dial/Delacourte, 1 Dag Hammarskjold Plaza, New York, NY 10017

Dic   Dickenson Publishing Co, Belmont, CA 94002

Diw   Diwan Press, Fields Book Store, 1419 Polk St, San Francisco, CA 94109

DLS   Divine Life Society, PO Shivanandanagar, Dt Tehri-Garhwal, UP, Himalyas, India

DMd   Dodd, Mead, 79 Madison Ave, New York, NY 10016

Dol   Dolmen Press, 8 Herbert Pl, Dublin 2, Ireland

Dom   Domel Enterprises, PO Box 3829, Albuquerque, NM 87110

Don   Donning Co, Inc, 205 34th St, Suite 107, Virginia Beach, VA 23451

Dor   Dorrance & Co, Inc, 1617 J F Kennedy Blvd, Philadelphia, Pa 19103

Dou   Doubleday & Co, 501 Franklin Ave, Garden City, NY 11530

Dov   Dover Publications, 180 Varick St, New York, NY 10014

DPC   Dorene Publishing Co, Inc, 2809 Main St, Dallas, TX 75226

DRC   Digicomp Research Corp, Ithaca, NY 14850

DTP   Doubletree Press, Inc, PO Box 1321, Walla Walla, WA 99362

Duf   Dufour Editions, Inc, Chester Springs, PA 19425

Dut   Dutton & Co, 201 Park Ave South, New York, NY 10003

DyC   John Day Co, 257 Park Ave South, New York, NY 10010

EbV   Ebertin Verlag, D 7080 Aalen/Wurtt, Federal Republic of Germany

ECa   El Cariso Publishers, PO Box 176, Elsinore, CA 92330

EdE   Ediciones Euroamericanos, Perugino 35-1, Mexico 19, D F, Mexico

EEP   Este Es Press, Norlin Library, University of Colorado, Boulder, CO 80302

Eer   Wm B Eerdmans Publishing Co, 255 Jefferson Ave SE, Grand Rapids, MI 49502

Ehr   Ehret Publishing Co, Beaumont, CA

Ele   Elek Books, 54-58 Caledonian Rd, London, N1 9RN, England

Eme   Emerson Press, 28 Dean St, London NW2, England

EMV   Editores Mexicanos Unidos, SA, L Gonzales Abregon 5-B, Apartado 45-671, Mexico 1, DF

EPG   E P Group, Bradford Road, East Ardsley, Wakefield, Yorkshire, WF3 2JN, England

EPI   Elmi Publication Institute, Nasser Khosrow Ave, Teheran, Iran

Erb   Erbonia Books, Inc, PO Box 396, New Paltz, NY 12561

EsH   Essence of Health Publishing Co, PO Box 2821, Durban, South Africa

EsP   Esoteric Publications, PO Box 1529, Sedona, AZ 86336

Esp   Espiritu, Houston Center for Human Potential, 1214 Miramar, Houston, TX 77006

EUP   Edinburgh University Press, 22 George Square, Edinburgh, Scotland

EvC   M Evans & Co, Inc, 216 E 49th St, New York, NY 10017

EWC   East-West Cultural Center, 2865 W Ninth St, Los Angeles, CA 90006

EWP   East West Publications Fonds BV, PO Box 7616, The Hague, The Netherlands

ExP   Exposition Press, 900 S Oyster Bay Rd, Hicksville, NY 11801

Fab   Faber Books, 3 Queen Square, London WCiN 3AU, England

Faw   Fawcett Publishers, Fawcett Bldg, Fawcett Pl, Greenwich, CT 06830

Fel   Frederick Fell Publishers, Inc, 386 Park Ave South, New York, NY 10016

Fid   Fides Publishers, Inc, PO Box F, Notre Dame, Indiana 46556

FiP   Findhorn Publications, The Park, Findhorn Bay, Forres, Moray, Scotland

FkR   Folkways Records, 701 Seventh Ave, New York, NY 10036

Fld   Philipp Feldheim, 96 E Broadway, New York, NY 10002

Flk   Falkynor Books, Davis, FL

FLP   Foreign Language Press, Peking, China

FlP   Fleet Press Corp, 160 Fifth Ave, New York, NY 10010

FoI   Formur Inc, 4200 LaClede Ave, St Louis MO 63108

Fon   Fontana Books, PO Box 4, Godalming, Surrey, GU7 1JY, England

Fos   FOSSU, PO Box 93, Redondo Beach, CA 90277

Fou   W Foulsham & Co, Yeovil Rd, Slough, SL1 4JH, England

Fow   L N Fowler & Co, 1201/1203 High Rd, Chadwell Heath, Romford, Essex, England

Foy   W & G Foyle, Ltd, 119-125 Charing Cross Rd, London, WC 2, England

FPC   Freestone Publishing Co, PO Box 357, Albion, CA 95410

Fre   W H Freeman & Co, 660 Market St, San Francisco, CA 94104

FSF   Four Seasons Foundation, Bolinas, CA

FSG   Farrar, Straus & Giroux, 19 Union Square West, New York, NY 10003

FVT   Friends of Vimala Thakar, PO Box 41, Berkeley, CA 94701

Fwn   Frewin & Co, Ltd, Volombo, Sri Lanka

G&B   Gordon & Breach, 440 Park Ave South, New York, NY 10016

G&D   Grosset & Dunlap, Inc, 51 Madison Ave, New York, NY 10010

GaB   Galahad Books, 95 Madison Ave, New York, NY 10016

Gab   Gabriel Press, 4018 N 40th St, Phoenix, AZ 85018

Gan   Ganesh & Co (Madras) Private Ltd, Madras 17, India

GaP   Garnstone Press, 59 Brompton Rd, London SW 3 1DS, England

Gar   Garden Way Publishing Co, Charlotte, VT 05445

Gat   The Gateway, Ferndale, PA 18921

GBF   Guru Bawa Fellowship, 5820 Overbrook Ave, Philadelphia, PA 19131

Gdn   Richard Gardner, 10 Sudeley St, Brighton Bn1 2HE, England

GeB   Geo Books, Western Book Service, PO Box 3975, San Francisco, CA 94119

Geo   Mrs. Karl George, 1405 Valley Dr, Laurel, MT 59044

GeP   Genesis Press, Cupertino, CA

GeW   Gemini World, PO Box 565, Dayton, OH 45402

Gir   Maurice Girodias Associates, Inc, 220 Park Ave South, New York, NY 10003

Glo   Globe Bookshop, PO Box 69218, Los Angeles, CA 90069

GlP   Glide Publications, 330 Ellis St, San Francisco, CA 94102

Gol   Golden Press, 1220 Mound Ave, Racine, WI 53404

GOP   Great Ocean Publishers, 738 S 22nd St, Arlington, VA 22202

GPO   US Government Printing Office, Asst Public Printer, Superintendent of Documents, Washington, DC 20402

Gra   Gramaphone Co, Ltd, EMI House, 20 Manchester Square, London, W1, England

Gre   Greenwood Press, 51 Riverside Ave, Westport, CT 05880

Grp   The Group, Inc, 507 Brentwood Ave, Daytona Beach, FL 32017

Grv   Grove Press, Inc, 53 E 11th St, New York, NY 10003

Grz   Joseph Graziano, 2207 W Clarendon Ave, Phoenix, AZ 85015

GSR   Golden Seal Research Headquarters, PO Box 27821, Hollywood, CA 90027

GtP   Garrett Publishing, 200 Park Ave South, New York, NY 10003

HFA   Health for All Publishing Co, Gateway House, Bedford Park, Croydon, CR9 2AT, Surrey, England

HFC   Hodges, Figgis & Co, Ltd, 20 St Stephens Green, Dublin 2, Ireland

HHL   Hamish Hamilton, Ltd, 90 Great Russell St, London CC 1B 3PT

Hia   Hiawatha Publishing Co, Derry, Iowa 50220

Hic   Isabel M Hickey, 35 Maple St, Watertown, MA 02172

Hie   Hieratic Publishing Co, PO Box 133, Medford, MA 02155

Him   Himalayan Institute, 1505 Greenwood Rd, Glenview, IL 60025

Hip   Hippocrene Books, 171 Madison Ave, New York, NY 10016

HMC   Houghton Mifflin Co, Wayside Rd, Burlington, MA 01803

Hod   Hodder & Stoughton, Mill Rd, Dunton Green, Sevenoaks, Kent, England

HOH   HOHM, PO Box 75, Tabor, NJ 07078

Hoi   Hoikusha Publishing Co, Ltd, 20, 1-chrome, Uchikyuhoji-machi, Higashi-ku, Osaka, 540 Japan

Hok   Hokuseido Press, 3-12 Kanda Nishikicho, Chiyoda-ku, Tokyo, Japan

Hol   A J Holman Co, E Washington Square, Philadelphia PA 19105

HOM   Holy Order of MANS, 20 Steiner St, San Francisco, CA 94117

HoP   Homeopathic Publishing Co, Bradford Holsworthy, Devon EX 22 7 AP, England

Hor   Horizon Press, 156 Fifth Ave, New York, NY 10010

HPB   Hind Pocket Books, Ltd, G T Road, Delhi 110032, India

HPG   Hutchinson Publishing Group, 3 Fitzboy Square, London W1P 6JD, England

HPP   Health Plus Publishers, PO Box 22001, Phoenix, AZ 85028

HRA   Huna Research Associates, 126 Camellia Dr, Cape Giradeau, MO 63701

HRW   Holt, Rinehart & Winston, 383 Madison Ave, New York, NY 10017

HSD   H S Dakin, 3456 Jackson St, San Francsisco, CA 94118

HSP   Health Science Press, Rustington, Sussex, England

H&R   Harper & Row, Scranton, PA 18512

HaI   Harold Institute, PO Box 11024, Winston-Salem, NC

Ham   Hamlyn Publishing Group, Ltd, Hamlyn House, The Centre, Feltham, Middlesex, England

Hap   Happiness Press, 160 Wycliff Way, Magalia, CA 95954

Har   Hart Publishing Co, Inc, 15 W Fourth St, New York, NY 10012

Has   Haskell House Publishers Ltd, 280 Lafayette St, New York, NY 10012

Haw   Hawthorne Books, Inc, 260 Madison Ave, New York, NY 10016

HBJ   Harcourt Brace Jovanovich, 757 Third Ave, New York, NY 10017

HCI   HC Publishers, Inc, 220 Fifth Ave, New York NY 10001

HDI   Human Dimensions Institute, 4380 Main St, Buffalo, NY 14226

Hea   The Healer Publishing Co, Burrows Lea Shire, Guilford Surrey, England

HeG   Heineman Group—Windmill Press, Kingswood, Tadworth, Surrey, Kent 206 TG, England

HeH   Herder & Herder, Inc, 232 Madison Ave, New York, NY 10016

Hei   Heidelberg Publishers, 3707 Kerbey Lane, Austin, TX 78731

Hel   Helios Book Service, 8, The Square, Toddington near Cheltenham, Gloucestershire, GL54 5DL, England

Hem   Hemisphere Press, 263 Ninth Ave, New York, NY

HeP   Hemkunt Press, 1—E/15 Patel Rd, New Delhi—8, India

HeR   Health Research, 70 Lafayette St, Mokelume Hill, CA 95245

Her   Heritage Store, PO Box 444-B, Virginia Beach, VA 23458

HeS   Health Science, Box 15000, Santa Ana, CA 92705

HeY   Healing Yourself, 402 15th Ave East, Seattle, WA 98112

Hug   Dorothy Hughes, 1833 Queen Anne Ave North, Seattle, WA 98109

Hum   Humata Publishers, BOS 56, CH-3000, Bern 6, Switzerland

HUP   Harvard University Press, 79 Garden St, Cambridge, MA 02138

HuP   Humanities Press, 171 First Ave, Atlantic Highlands, NJ 07716

IAS   Institute for Astrological Studies, 60 St Claire Ave West, Suite 8, Toronto, M4V 1M7, Canada

IBC   Indian Book Co, 36 C Connaught Pl, New Delhi, India 110001

ICA   Intercultural Assoc, Box 277, Thompson, CT 06277

ICS   Institute of Carmelite Studies, 2131 Lincoln Rd, NE, Washington, DC 20002

IET   Indian Book House Educational Trust, 12 Hassa Mahal, Dalamal Park, 223, Cuffe Parade, Bombay 400005, India

IHC   International Health Council, 15328 Edolyn Ave, Cleveland, Ohio 44111

IIC   Institute of Islamic Culture, 2 Club Rd, Lahore, Pakistan

Ikh   Ikhwan Press, Tucson, AZ

ImP   Images Press, 1750 Arch St, Berkeley, CA 94709
Ind   Indepedent News, 75 Rockefeller Plz, New York, NY 10019
Ing   Eunice D Ingham, PO Box 948, Rochester, NY 14603
INS   InScape Corp Publishers, 1621 K St, NW, Suite 5107, Washington, DC 20006
Int   International University Press, 315 Fifth Ave, New York, NY 10016
IPB   Islamic Publications Bureau, PO Box 3881, Lagos, Nigeria
IPG   Independent Publishers Group, c/o David White, Inc, 60 E 55th St, NY, NY 10022
IPS   Istituto Poligrafico Dello Stato, Libreria Dello Stato, Piazza G Verdi, 10, Rome, Italy
IPy   Institute of Pyramidology, 31 Station Rd, Herpenden, Hertfordshire, England
Isl   Islamic Center, 2551 Massachusetts Ave, Washington, DC
IsP   Islamic Publications, 3702 W 11th Ave, Gary, IN 46404
IUP   Indiana University Press, 10th & Morton Sts, Bloomington, IN 47401
IWP   Illuminated Way Press, PO Box 82388, San Diego, CA 92138

Jac   Ivy Jacobson, 6374 Encinita Ave, Temple City, CA 91780
Jal   Jalmar Press, Inc, 391 Munroe St, Sacramento, CA 95825
Jap   Japan Publications Trading Co, Inc, 200 Clearbrook Rd, Elmsford, NY 10523
Jay   Jaymac Co, 12 Bryce Ct, Belmont, CA 94002
Jen   Jensen's Nutritional & Health Products, PO Box 8, Solana Beach, CA 92075
Jew   Jewish Publication Society, 1528 Walnut St, Suite 800, Philadelphia, PA 19102
JFP   CG Jung Foundation for Analytical Psychology, 815 2nd Ave, NY, NY 10017
JPA   P&A A Jersey, 140 46th St, Pittsburgh, PA 15201
JPH   Jaico Publishing House, 44,45 Ezra St, Calcutta, India
JRC   Johnson Reprint Co, 111 Fifth Ave, New York, NY 10003
JTL   Japan Times Ltd, 5-4 Shibaura 4-chome, Minato-ku, Tokyo, Japan
Jul   Julian Press, Inc, 150 Fifth Ave, New York, NY 10011

Kau   Wm Kaufmann, Inc, 1 First St, Los Altos, CA 94022
Kay   Kayhan Press, Tehran, Iran
KBS   Kokusai Bunka Shinkokai, 1-1-18, Shirokane-dai, Minato-ku, Tokyo, Japan
Kea   Keats Publishing Co, PO Box 876, New Canaan, CT 06840
KeV   Verlag Walter Keller, CH-4143, Dornach, Leitmenweg 5, Switzerland
Key   Keysign Press, 1720 15th St, Boulder, CO 80302
Kly   Kalyani Publishers, Ludhiana, Delhi, India
Kno   John Knox Press, 340 Ponce de Leon Ave, NE, Atlanta, GA 30308
Kod   Kodansha International/USA, Ltd, 599 College Ave, Palo Alto, CA 94306
Kri   Krishnamurti Foundation of America, 111 S Signal St, PO Box 216, Ojai, CA 93023

LaF   Lama Foundation, Box 444, San Cristobal, NM 87564
Lan   Lang Publishing Co, Ltd, Aylesbury, Bucks, England
Lar   Larchmont Books, 25 W 45th St, New York, NY 10036
LBC   Little Brown, & Co, 34 Beacon St, Boston, MA 02106
Lew   A Lewis (Masonic Publishers) Ltd, Ian Allan Group, Terminal House, Sitepperton TW 17 8AF, England
Lip   J B Lippincott Co, E Washington Square, Philadelphia, PA 19105
Lit   Litton Educational Publishers, 300 Pike St, Cincinnati, Ohio 45202
LjP   Little John Publishing Co, Box 123 C, Isabella, MO 65676
LLC   Living Love Center, 1730 La Loma Ave, Berkeley, CA 94709
LLL   La Leche League, 9616 Minneapolis Ave, Franklin Park, IL 60131
LLP   Llewellyn Publications, PO Box 3383, St Paul, MN 55165
LnB   Links Books, 33 W 60 St, New York, NY 10023
Lng   Dorje Ling, PO Box 1410, San Rafael, CA 94902
LoA   Lotus Ashram, Inc, 128 NE 82nd Ter, Miami, FL 33138
Lod   Lodestar, Box 31003, San Francisco, CA 94131
LOG   Leaves of Grass Press, Germantown, PA 19144
Lon   Longman, Inc, 72 Fifth Ave, New York, NY 10011
Lor   Lorigan Enterprises, Chicago, IL
LPC   Lucis Publishing Co, 866 United Nations Plz, Suite 566, New York, NY 10017
LRP   Lamplighters Roadway Press, 44 Fairview Plaza, Los Gatos, CA 95030
LtA   Littlefield Adams, 8 Adams Dr, Totowa, NJ 07512
LuH   Lund Humphries, 12 Bedford Square, London WC1, England
Lus   Lust Enterprises, Inc, 490 Easy St, PO Box 777, Simi CA 93065
Luz   Luzac & Co, PO Box 157, 46 Great Russell St, London WC1B 3PE, England
Lyr   Lyrichord Discs, Inc, 141 Perry St, New York, NY 10014

M&H   Medicine & Health Publishing Co, 17 Gough St G/F, Hong Kong
M&M   Morgan & Morgan Publishers, 145 Palisade St, Dobbs Ferry, NY 10522
MaB   Manor Books, c/o Curtis Circulation Co, 841 Chestnut St, Philadelphia, PA 19105
Mac   Macoy Publishing Co, PO Box 9825, Lakeside Branch, Richmond, VA 23228
MAM   Mark Age Metacenter, 327 NE 20th Ter, Miami, FL 33137
MAm   Media America, 12 E Market St, Bethlehem, PA 18018
MAP   Middle Atlantic Press, Box 312, Somerset, NJ 08873
Mas   Mason's Bookshop, 789 Lexington Ave, New York, NY 10021
Mat   Matagiri, Mt Tremper, NY 12457
May   Mayflower Books, 4 Upper James St, London W1R 4BP, England
MBI   Meher Baba Information, Box 1101, Berkeley, CA 94701
MBS   Magus Book Shop, Box 9353, Berkeley, CA 94704
MCh   Mason Charter, 384 5th Ave, New York, NY 10018
McK   David McKay Co, 750 Third Ave, New York, NY 10017
McM   MacMillan Co, 866 Third Ave, New York, NY 10022
MCP   Mel Cobb's Paperworkshop, 1539½ Westwood Blvd, Los Angeles, CA 90024
MDC   Motivation Development Centre, 115 Harvard SE, Albuquerque, NM 87106
Meh   Meher Era Publications, Avatar Meher Baba Poona Center, 441/1 Somwar Peth, Poona 11, India
Mer   Merco, 620 Wyandotte East, Windsor, Ontarrio, Canada N9A 3J2
Mey   Norman Mayer, 115 Dover Rd, Wellesley, MA 02181
MGH   McGraw-Hill Book Co, Princeton Road, Highstown, NJ 08520
Mil   Millennium Publishing Co, 3333 Connecticut Ave, NW, Washington, DC 20008
MiM   Mille Meditations, Tierra Del Sol, CA
MiP   Miu Press, 1015 Gayley, Los Angeles, CA 90024

MIT   MIT Press, 28 Carleton St, Cambridge, MA 02142
MIU   Maharishi International University, 1015 Gayley Ave, Los Angeles, CA 90024
Mll   Frederick Muller, Ltd, Victoria Works, Edgeware Rd, London NW2 6LE, England
MNM   Museum of New Mexico Press, PO Box 2087, Santa Fe, NM 87501
Mnr   Minerva, S A, Geneva, Switzerland
MNT   Montana Books, 1716 N 45th St, Seattle, WA 98103
MoB   Motilal Banarsidass, Bungalow Rd, Jawaharnagar, Delhi-7, India
Moh   Mohan Enterprises, PO Box 8334, Rochester, NY 14618
MOM   Mind of Man Book Dist, PO Box 75, Tubor, NJ 07078
Mor   Wm Morrow & Co, Wilmore Warehouse, 6 Henderson Dr, West Caldwell, NJ 07006
Mou   Mouton Publishers, Herderstraat 5, The Hague, Netherlands
MPC   Mayfield Publishing Co, 285 Hamilton Ave, Palo Alto, CA 94301
MRG   Metaphysical Research Group, Archers Ct, The Ridge, Hastings, Sussex, England
MSE   Mountain School for Esoteric Studies, 300 Kenruck St, Newton, MA 02158
MTI   Merry Thoughts, Inc, 2, Bedford Hills, New York, 10507
MuA   Muhammad Ashraf, Kashmiri Bazar, Lahore, Pakistan
Mud   Mudra, 2940 Seventh St, Berkeley, CA 94710
Muk   K L Mukhopadhyay, Calcutta, India
Mul   Multimedia , 100 S Western Hwy, Blauvelt, NY 10913
MuM   Munshiram Manoharlal, PO Box 5715, 54 Rani Jhansi Rd, New Delhi, India
Mur   John Murray, 50 Albemarle St, London, England W 1

NAF   New Age Foods, 1122 Pearl St, Boulder, CO 80302
Nag   Nagel Publishers, Geneva, Switzerland
NAL   New American Library, PO Box 120, Bergenfield, NJ 07621
NAP   New Age Press, 4636 Vineta Ave, La Canada, CA 91011
Nas   Nash Publishing Co, Los Angeles, CA
Nat   Naturegraph Publishers, 8339 W Dry Creek Rd, Healdsburg, CA 95448
NDP   New Directions Publishing Corp, 333 Sixth Ave, New York, NY 10014
NeH   Nelson-Hall, 325 W Jackson Blvd, Chicago, IL 60606
NHP   New Horizons Press, Box 1758, Chico, CA 95926
Nit   Nitty Gritty Productions, PO Box 457, Concord, CA 94522
NKB   New Knowledge Books, PO Box 9, Horsham, Sussex, RH12 2LB, England
NoP   Norwalk Press, PO Box 13266, Phoenix, AZ 85002
Nor   W W Norton & Co, Inc, 500 Fifth Ave, New York, NY 10036
Nos   Nostradamus, Inc, 5 Millbrook Ct, Great Neck, NY 11021
Noy   Noyes Press, Mill Road at Grad Ave, Park Ridge, NJ 07656
NPC   Newcastle Publishing Co, PO Box 7589, Van Nuys, CA, 91409
Nsw   Newsweek Books, 444 Madison Ave, New York, NY 10022
NUP   Northwestern University Press, 1735 Benson, Evanston, Il 60201
NuS   Nutritional Science Research Institute, Mulberry Tree Hall, Brookthorpe, Gloucester, England, GL4 OUU
NWC   National War College, Taipei, Taiwan
NYG   NY Graphic, Greenwich, CT 06830
NYT   Quadrangle/New York Times Book Co, 10 E 53rd St, New York, NY 10022
NYU   New York University Press, Washington Square, New York, NY 10003

Oce   Ocean Books, Ltd, 17 Shaftesbury Ave, London W1, England
Oco   Octopus Books, 59 Grosvenor St, London W1, England
Oct   Octagon Press, 14 Baker St, London W1M 1Da, England
ODI   Other Dimensions, Inc, 104½ Washington St, Decorah, IA 52101
OHa   J Phillip O'Hara, 20 E Huron, Chicago, IL 60611
OKT   Order of the Knights Templars of Aquarius, La Maison de Leoville, St. Ouen, Channel Island
OLL   Orient Longman's Ltd, 3/5 Asaf Ali Rd, New Delhi-1, India
OmA   Omega Associates, 11920 S Harvard Ave, Chicago, IL 60628
Oma   Omangod Press, PO Box 142, Stouton MA 02072
Ome   Omen Press, PO Box 12457, Tucson, AZ 85711
OMF   George Ohsawa Macrobiotic Foundation, 1471 10th Ave, San Francisco, CA 94122
One   101 Productions, 834 Mission St, San Francisco, CA 94103
OpC   Open Court, Box 599, La Salle, IL 61301
OrB   Oriental Books Reprint Corp, 54 Ram Jhansi Rd, New Delhi, India 110055
OrC   Orbimetrix Co, PO Box 2252, Canoga Park, CA 91306
OrI   Orientalia, Inc, 61 Fourth Ave, New York, NY 10003
OrP   Oriental Publishers, 1488 Pataudi House, Daryagnj, Delhi 6, India
OvP   Overlook Press, Lewis Hollow Rd, Woodstock, NY 12498
Owe   Peter Owen, 12 Kendrick Mews, Kendrick Pl, London SW 7, England
Oxf   Oxford University Press, 16-00 Pollitt Dr, Fair Lawn, NJ 07410

P&M   P&M Enterprises, 4947 Oakland Dr, Lyndhurst, OH 44124
Pal   Paladin, Frogmore, St Albans, Hertfordshire, AL22NF, England
Pan   Panther Books, Ltd, Frogmore, St Albans, Hertfordshire AL22NF, England
PaP   Panthean Press, Box 1122, Litchfield, CT 06759
PaR   Para Research, 964 Washington St, Gloucester, MA 01930
PAs   Professional Astrologers, Inc, PO Box 2616, Hollywood, CA 90028
Pau   Paulist Press, 400 Sette Dr, Paramus, NJ 07652
PAV   Philosophisch-Anthroposophischer Verlag, am Goetheanum, 4143 Dornach/Sol, Switzerland
PBD   Popular Book Depot, Lamington Rd, Bombay 7, India
PBR   Paragon Book Reprint Corp, 14 E 38th St, New York, NY 10016
Pea   Peach Publishing Co, 1123¾ N Sweetzer Ave, W Hollywood, CA 90069
Pen   Viking Penguin, Inc, 625 Madison Ave, New York, NY 10022
PhH   Phoenix House, 7453 Melrose Ave, Los Angeles, CA 90046
PhL   Philosophical Library, 15 E 40th St, New York, NY 10016
Pin   Pinnacle Books, 275 Madison Ave, New York, NY 10016
PjP   Panjandrum Press, 99 Sanchez St, San Francisco, CA 94114
Plp   S G Phillips, 305 W 86th St, New York, NY 10024
PMP   Parents Magazine Press, 52 Vanderbilt Ave, New York, NY 10017
PnB   Pan Books, Ltd, 33 Tothill St, London SW1, England
PoL   Point Loma Publications, PO Box 9966, San Diego, CA 92109
Pol   Polydor Records, 17-19 Stratford Pl, London W1N, England

PoP	The Potted Plant, 226 Hamilton Ave, Palo Alto, CA 94301
Pop	Popular Library, 600 Third Ave, New York, NY 10016
Pow	Charles T Powner Co, PO Box 796, Chicago, IL
PPC	Pakistan Philosophical Congress, 873-875/C, Block 2, PECHS, Karachi-29, Pakistan
PPI	Philips Phonogram, Inc, One IBM Plz, Chicago, IL 60611
PPL	Pagurian Press, Ltd, 10 Whitney Ave, Toronto 5, Canada
PPr	Popular Prakasham, 35C Tardeo Rd, Bombay 34 WB, India
PPu	Punthi Pustak, 34 Mohan Bagan Lane, Calcutta 4, India
Pra	Praeger Publishers, PO Box 1323, Springfield, MA 01101
PrH	Prentice-Hall, Inc, Englewood Cliffs, NJ 07632
Prm	Promontory Press, 95 Madison Ave, New York, NY 10016
Prn	Perennial Books, Ltd, Pates Manor, Bedfont, Middlesex, England
Pro	Proactive Press, Box 296, Berkeley, CA 94701
PrP	Prophecy Pressworks, Bolinas, CA 94924
PRS	Philosophical Research Society, Inc, 3341 Griffith Pk Blvd, Los Angeles, CA 90027
Prv	Provoker Press, Lakeshore Rd, St Catherines, Ontario, Canada
PSh	Pages of Shustah, 415 S 12th St, Omaha, NE 68102
PSI	PSI Rhythms, 2382 S Dixie Ave, Dayton, OH 45409
PSm	Peter Smith, 6 Lexington Ave, Magnolia, MA 01930
PsP	Psychic Press, 23 Great Queen St, London WC2 5BB, England
PSS	Price/Stern/Sloan, 410 N La Cienega Blvd, Los Angeles, CA 90048
PSU	Pennsylvania State University, 215 Wagner Bldg, University Park, PA 16802
PTF	Police Training Foundation, 3412 Ruby St, Franklin Park, IL 60131
PuD	Publications Division, Ministry of Information and Broadcasting, Government of India, New Delhi, India
PUP	Princeton University Press, Princeton, NJ 08540
Put	G P Putnam's Sons, 390 Murray Hill Pkwy, East Rutherford, NJ 07073
Pyr	Pyramid Publications , 9 Garden St, Moonachie, NJ 07074
Pyt	Pythagorean Publications, 38 Kermoor Ave, Sharples, Bolton, Lancs, England
QFx	Quick Fox, Inc, 33 W 60th St, New York, NY 10023
QPr	Quicksilver Productions, c/o Jim Maynard, Box 702, Ashland, OR 97520
QSp	Quick Specs, PO Box 55, Blackwood Terrace, NJ 08096
Qua	Quarto Productions, 323 Castro St, San Francisco, CA 94114
Qur	Bernard Quaritch, 5-8 Lower St John, Golden Square, London W1R 4AU, England
Rad	Radial Press, 7404 S Mason Ave, Chicago, IL 60638
RaF	Rajneesh Foundation, Shree Rajneesh Ashram, 17 Koregaon Park, Pune–1, India
RaH	Random House, 457 Hahn Rd, Westminister, MD 21157
Rai	Rainbow Bridge, PO Box 40208, San Francisco, CA 94140
RaP	Ranney Publications, PO Box 270, Mountain Center, CA
RaS	Radhasoami Satsang Beas, India
RCK	Research Center of Kabbalah, 200 Park Ave, Suite 303 East, New York, NY 10017
RdB	Redwing Book Co, 303 Newbury St, Boston, MA 02215
Reg	Henry Regnery Co, 180 N Michigan Ave, Chicago, IL 60601
ReP	Regnery Press, Ltd, 43 New Oxford St, London WC1, England
Rey	Ronald Rey, Route 1, Box 900, Haines City, FL 33844
RHI	Rams Head, Inc, 353 Sacramento St, San Francisco, CA 94111
Rho	Rhodos, Strandgade 36, Copenhagen K, Denmark
Ric	Franco Maria Ricci Publisher, Parma, Italy
Rid	Rider & Co, 3 Fitzroy Square, London W1, England
Rig	Rigel Press, 21 Cloncurry St, London SW6, England
Rin	C Ringer & Co, 23 Lallbazar St, Calcutta 1, India
RKP	Routledge & Kegan, Broadway House, Reading Rd, Henley-on-Thames, Oxon RG9 1EN, England
RMN	Rand McNally, PO Box 7600, Chicago, IL 60680
Rod	Rodale Press, 33 E Minor St, Emmaus, PA 18049
Ros	Rosicrucian Fellowship, Oceanside, CA 92054
RPP	Real People Press, Box F, Moab, Utah 84532
RPr	Rekha Prakashan, 16 Daryaganj, Delhi 110006, India
RRP	Rada Record Pressings, Ltd, 7802 Express St, Barnaby 2, BC, Canada
RSB	Rudolf Steiner Bookshop, 35 Park Rd, London NW1 6XT, England
Rsn	George Rosen, Inc, 6700 White Stone Rd, Baltimore, MD 21207
RSP	Rudolf Steiner Press, 35 Park Rd, London NW1 6XT, England
RTP	Rama Tirtha Pratisthan, 14 Marwari Gali, Lucknow, UP, India
Rud	Tana Rudhyar, PO Box 174, Escondido, CA 92025
Rug	Dieter Ruggeberg Booksellers & Publishers, Postfach 13 07 29, D-56 Wuppertal 1, West Germany
RUP	Rutgers University Press, 30 College Ave, New Brunswick, NJ 08901
RuP	Running Press, 38 S 19th St, Philadelphia, PA 19103
RuS	Ruhani Satsang, Sawan Ashram, Delhi-7, India
RVC	Ramakrishna-Vivekananda Center, 17 E 94th St, New York, NY 10028
RVM	Ramakrishna Vedanta Math, 19-B Raja Rajkrishna St, Calcutta, India
S&B	Science & Behavior Books, PO Box A J, Cupertino, CA, 95014
S&D	Stein & Day, Inc, Scarborough House, Briarcliff Manor, NY 10510
S&J	Sidgwick & Jackson, Ltd, 1 Tavistock Chambers, Bloomsbury Way, London WCiA 2SG, England
S&S	Simon & Schuster, 1 W 39th St, New York, NY 10018
SAA	Sri Aurobindo Ashram Trust, Pondicherry, India
SAB	Sino-American Buddhist Assoc, 1731 15th St, San Francisco, CA 94103
Sab	Sabian Publishing Co, Stanwood, WA 98292
Sad	Sadhana Press, Box 35, South Otselic, NY 13155
Sag	Sagar Publications, 18 Indian Oil Bhawan, New Janpath Market, New Delhi, India
Sak	Frances Sakoian, 1 Monadnock Rd, Arlington, MA 02174
SAI	SAI Foundation, 7911 Willoughby Ave, Los Angeles, CA 90046
SAP	Solar Age Press, Box 53022, New Orleans, LA 70160
Sar	Saraswati Studio, 12429 Cedar Rd, Cleveland Heights, OH 44106
Sau	Saucerian Press, Inc, Box 2228, Clarksburg, WV 26301
SBC	Steiner Book Centre, 151 Carisbrooke Crescent, N Vancouver, BC, V7N2S2, Canada
SBL	Sphere Books, Ltd, 30/32 Gray's Inn Road, London WCiX 8JL
ScB	Schocken Books, 200 Madison Ave, New York, NY 10016
Sch	Scherman, 68/6 Kidwai Nagar, Extension-1, Kanpur, India
SCK	Society for Promoting Christian Knowledge, Holy Trinity Church, Marylebone Road, London NW1 4DU, England
SCl	Sierra Club, Sun Box, 1050 Mills Tower, San Francisco, CA 94104
SCR	Society for Cancer Research, Arlesheim, Switzerland
Scr	Charles Scribner's Sons, Vreeland Ave, Totowa, NJ 07512
Sea	Seabury Press, 815 Second Ave, New York, NY 10017
SeD	Sett Dey & Co, 40A Strand Rd, PO Box 563, Calcutta 700001, India
See	Seed Center, 162 University Ave, Palo Alto, CA 94301
Ser	Servire Book Dispatch, 53 W Ham Lane, Stratford, London E15 4PH, England
SGA	Shree Gurudev Ashram, Ganeshpuri, India
SGB	St George Book Service PO Box 225, Spring Valley, NY 10977
Sha	Sharvic Publishing Co, Salt Lake City, UT
Shl	Dr Shelton, PO Box 1277, San Antonio, TX 78206
SHP	Sepher-Hermon Press, Inc, 175 Fifth Ave, New York, NY 10010
ShP	Shambhala Publications, 2045 Francisco St, Berkeley, CA 94709
Shr	Sheriar Press, Inc, PO Box 1023, North Myrtle Beach, SC 29582
SHS	Spiritual Healing Sanctuary, Burrows Lea, Shere, Guildford, Surrey, England
ShS	Shanti Sadan, 29 Chepstow Villas, London W11, England
ShW	Shrine of Wisdom, Fintry, Brook, Godalming, Surrey, England
SIU	Southern Illinois University Press, PO Box 3697, Carbondale, IL 62901
SJU	St John's University Press, Grand Central & Utopia Pkwys, Jamaica, NY 11432
Ski	Charles Skilton Publishing Group, 90 The Broadway, London SW19, England
SLB	Science of Life Books, 4-12 Tattersal Ln, Melbourne, Victoria 3000, Australia
SLS	Spoken Language Services, PO Box 783, Ithaca, NY 14850
SMP	St Martin's Press, 175 Madison Ave, New York, NY 10010
Smy	Colin Smythe, Ltd, 6 Station Rd, Gerrards Cross, Bucks, England
SnB	Sun Books, PO Box 4383, Albuquerque, NM 87106
Snd	Sandollar Press, 1930 De La Vina, Santa Barbara, CA
SNY	State University of New York Press, 99 Washington Ave, Albany, NY 12210
Sol	Solunar Research Publications, PO Box 1073, Station A, Bay City, MI 48706
Som	Somaiya Publications Pvt, Ltd, 172 Naigaum Cross Rd, Bombay 14, India
Sou	Souvenir Press, Ltd, 95 Mortimer St, London W1N 8HP, England
SpA	Spoken Arts, Inc, New Rochelle, NY 10801
SPC	Sufi Publishing Co, 53 W Ham Lane, London E15 4PH, England
SpC	Spiritual Community, PO Box 1080, San Rafael, CA 94902
Spe	Neville Spearman, Ltd, 112 Whitfield St, London W1, England
Spi	Spiritualist Press, 23 Great Queen St, London WC2, England
Spr	Spring Publishers, Postfach 190, 8024 Zurich, Switzerland
SRa	Sri Rama Foundation, Inc, Davis CA
SRe	Sufism Reoriented, 1300 Boulevard Way, Walnut Creek, CA 94595
SRF	Self Realization Fellowship, 3880 San Rafael Ave, Los Angeles, CA 90065
SRM	Sri Ramakrishna Math, Mylapore, Madras, India
Srm	Starmast Publications, PO Box 704, Berkeley, CA 94701
SRT	Sri Ramanasramam Tiruvaunamalai, S India
SSA	Shree Shree Anandamayee Sangha, Bhadaini, Varanasi, India
SSB	Sat Sandesh Books, Sant Bani Ashram, Franklin, NH 03235
SSF	Second Society Foundation, 333 N Michigan Ave, Suite 701, Chicago, IL 60601
SSk	South Sky Book Co, 107-115 Hennessy Rd, Hong Kong
SSS	Sri Sathya Sai Publication & Education Foundation, Brindavan Whitefield, Bangalore, India
Sta	Claude Stark, Inc, PO Box 431, West Dennis, MA 02670
Stk	Stackpole, Cameron & Kelker Sts, Harrisonburg, PA 17105
Stl	The Stelle Group, PO Box 5900, Chicago, IL 60680
Str	Sterling Publishing Co, 419 Park Ave South, New York, NY 10016
Stu	Lyle Stuart, 120 Enterprise Ave, Secaucus NJ 07094
Suf	Sufi Order, 23 Rue de la Tuileries, Suresnes 92/Paris, France
sun	Sunbridge College Press, Inc, 41 S Cannon Dr, Wilmington, DE 48214
SUP	Stanford University Press, Stanford, CA 94305
Svt	Savitria Press, AUM, Inc, 2405 Ruscombe Ln, Baltimore, MD 21209
Swa	Swallow Press, Inc, 811 W Junior Ter, Chicago, IL 60613
SwH	Swan House, PO Box 170, Brooklyn, NY 11223
SYD	SYDA, Box 11071, Oakland, CA 94611
Sym	Symbols & Signs. PO Box 4536, North Hollywood, CA 91607
T&H	Thames & Hudson, 30 Bloomsbury St, London WC1B 3QP, England
Tap	Taplinger Publishing Co, Inc, 200 Park Ave South, New York, NY 10003
Tar	Tarnhelm Press, Lakemont, GA 30552
Tay	Maxine Taylor, 4 Independence Place, NW, Atlanta, GA 30318
TCP	Two Continents Press, 30 E 42nd St, New York, NY 10017
Tdm	Tandem, 14 Gloucester Rd, London SW 7, England
ThC	Theosophy Co, 245 W 33rd St, Los Angeles, CA 90007
Tho	Charles Thomas, Publishers, 301-327 E Lawrence Ave, Springfield, IL 62703
ThU	Theosophical University Press, PO Box Bin C, Pasadena, CA 91109
TIA	TIA Publications, PO Box 45558, Los Angeles, CA 90045
Tnt	Alec Tiranti Ltd, 72 Charlotte St, London W1, England
Tok	Tokuma Shoten Publishing Co, Ltd, 10-1 Shimbashi 4-chome, Minato-ku Tokyo 105, Japan
Tom	Tomorrow Publications, Ltd, Denison House 296 Vauxhall Bridge Rd, London SW1, England
Top	Top-Ecol Press, 3025 Highridge Rd, La Crescenta, CA 91214
TPH	Theosophical Publishing House, PO Box 270, Wheaton IL 60187
TPL	Thorsons Publishers Ltd, Denington Estate, Wellingborough, Northants NN8 2RQ, England
TrA	Transatlantic Arts, North Village Green, Levittown, NY 11756
Tri	Triune Books, London, England
TrS	Traditional Studies Press, Box 984 Adelaide St PO, Toronto, Canada M5C 2K4
Top	Top-Ecol Press, 3025 Highridge Rd, La Crescenta, CA 91214
TPH	Theoso

TSC	Taraporevala Sons & Co, 210 Dr Dadabhai Naorji Rd, Bombay, India
Tud	Tudor Publishing Co, 31 W 46th St, New York, NY 10036
Tur	Turnstone Books, 37 Upper Addison Gdns, London W14 8AJ, England
Tus	Tusum Ling, Route 1, Box 299, Burton, WA 98013
Tut	Charles E Tuttle Co, Inc, Rutland, VT 05701
UAP	University of Alabama Press, Drawer 2877, University, AL 35486
UCh	University of Chicago Press, 11030 S Langley Ave, Chicago, IL 60628
UCP	University of California Press, 2223 Fulton St, Berkeley, CA 94720
UHa	University of Hawaii, East-West Center Press, Honolulu, HI 96822
UMP	University of Michigan Press, 615 E University, Ann Arbor, MI 48106
UnB	University Books, Inc, New Hyde Park, NY
UNC	University of North Carolina Press, Chapel Hill, NC 27514
UND	University of Notre Dame Press, Notre Dame, IN 46556
Ung	Frederick Ungar Publishing Co, 250 Park Ave South, New York, NY 10003
UNM	University of New Mexico Press, Albuquerque, NM 87131
UnP	Unity Press, PO Box 1037, Santa Cruz, CA 95061
UOK	University of Oklahoma Press, 1005 Asp Ave, Norman, OK 73069
UPD	Universal Publishing & Distributing Corp, 235 E 45th St, New York, NY 10017
UPV	University Press of Virginia, PO Box 3608, Charlottesville, VA 22903
Ura	Uranus Publishing Co, 5050 Calatrana Dr, Woodland Hills, CA 91364
UrB	Urantia Brotherhood, 533 Diversey Pkwy, Chicago, IL 60614
UrP	Uranian Publications, PO Box 114, Franksville, WI 53126
USC	Unity School of Christianity, Unity Village, MO 64063
USG	US Games System, Inc, 468 Park Ave South, New York, NY 10016
USP	University of Science & Philosophy, Swannanoa, Waynesboro, VA 22980
UTo	University of Toronto Press, 33 E Tupper St, Buffalo, NY 14203
UTP	University of the Trees Press, Box 644, Boulder Creek, CA 95006
UTx	University of Texas Press, Box 7819, Austin, TX 78712
UWa	University of Washington Press, Seattle, WA 98105
Val	Valhalla Paperbacks, Ltd, 1331 21st St, NW, Washington, DC 20036
VCh	Vita Chart, PO Box 478, Riverdale Sta, Bronx, NY 10471
VdC	Vedanta Centre, 130 Beechwood St, Cohasset, MA
VdP	Vedanta Press, 1946 Vedanta Pl, Hollywood, CA 90068
Vik	Viking Penguin, Inc, 625 Madison Ave, New York, NY 10022
VNR	Van Nostrand Reinhold Co, 300 Pike St, Cincinnati, OH 45202
VPH	Vikas Publishing House, Ltd, 5 Daryaganj, Ansari Rd, Delhi 6, India
VPI	Viking Penguin, Inc, 625 Madison Ave, New York, NY 10022
VPT	Vimal Prakashan Trust, Ahmedabad 6, India
Vul	Vulcan Books, 12722 Lake City Way, Seattle, WA 98125
VVR	Vishveshvaranand Vedic Research Institute, PO Sadhu Ashram, Hoshiarpur, India
Wad	Wadsworth Publishing Co, Inc, Belmont, CA 94002
Wal	Waldorf Institute/Adelphi University, Garden City, NY 11530
Wal	Walker & Co, 720 Fifth Ave, New York, NY 10019
WAO	We Are One, PO Box 1130, Plattsburgh, NY 12901
WAP	Neale Watson Academic Publications, 156 Fifth Ave, New York, NY 10010
War	Warner Paperback Library, 75 Rockefeller Plz, New York, NY 10019
Wat	Watkins, 45 Lower Belgrave St, London SW1W OLT, England
WdF	The Word Foundation, PO Box 769, Forest Hills, NY 11375
WEA	WEA Distributing Co, Philadelphia Branch, 106 Gaither Dr, Mt Laurel, NJ 08057
Wea	Weatherhill, 149 Madison Ave, New York, NY 10016
Wei	Samuel Weiser, Inc, 625 Broadway, New York, NY 10012
Wes	Westminster Press, Witherspoon Bldg, Rm 1133, Philadelphia, PA 19107
WET	White Eagle Publishing Trust, Liss, Hampshire, England
WHP	Winged Heart Press, Sufi House, 6 Parkwood Rd, Wimbledon, London SW19, England
WIF	World of Islam Festival Publishing Co, Ltd, 85 Cromwell Road, London SW7 5BW, England
Wil	Wilshire Book Co, 12015 Sherman Rd, North Hollywood, CA 91605
Win	Wingbow Press, Berkeley, CA
Wit	Wittenborn & Co, 1018 Madison Ave, New York, NY 10021
Wiz	Wizards Bookshelf, Box 66, Savage, MN 55378
WkC	Work of the Chariot, PO Box 2226, Hollywood, CA 90028
WLK	Mr R Wilkinson, Foresters Cottage, Highgate, Forest Row, Sussex, England
Wll	Willing Publishing Co, PO Box 51, San Gabriel, CA
WoP	Woodbridge Press, PO Box 6189, Santa Barbara, CA 93111
WPC	Workman Publishing Co, Inc, 231 E 51st St, New York, NY 10022
Wrn	Frederick Warne, 101 Fifth Ave, New York, NY 10003
WrW	Writers Workshop, 162/92 Lake Gdns, Calcutta 45, India
WSU	Washington State University Press, Pullman, WA 99163
Wte	H C White Publications, PO Box 8014, Riverside, CA 92505
Wts	Franklin Watts, 845 Third Ave, New York, NY 10022
WUP	Wesleyan University Press, 331 E Main St, Middletown, CN 06457
WWW	World Without War Council, 1730 Grove St, Berkeley, CA 94709
Wyd	Peter H Wyden/Publisher, 750 Third Ave, New York, NY 10017
Yes	Yesod Publishers, 75 Prospect Park West, Brooklyn, NY 11215
YFH	Yoga for Health, PO Box 475, Carmel, CA 93921
YPH	YMCA Publishing House, 5 Russell St, Calcutta, India
YPS	Yogi Publication Society, PO Box 148, Des Plains, IL 60016
YUP	Yale University Press, 92 A Yale St, New Haven, CN 06520
ZCe	Zen Center, 300 Page St, San Francisco, CA 94102
Zen	Zen Center of Los Angeles, Inc, 927 S Normandie Ave, Los Angeles, CA 90006
Zeu	Zeus Press, 171 Strand, London, WC2, England
Zim	Zimrani Records, Inc, 305 W 79th St, New York, NY 10024

377